INDEX TO

TENNESSEE WILLS & ADMINISTRATIONS

1779 - 1861

by

Byron & Barbara Sistler

Nashville, Tennessee

1990

Tennessee Wills and Administrations 1779-1861

Copyright © 1990
Byron and Barbara Sistler

Originally published by:
Byron Sistler & Associates, Inc.
Nashville, Tennessee
1990

Reprinted
Janaway Publishing, Inc.
2006, 2010

Janaway Publishing, Inc.
732 Kelsey Ct.
Santa Maria, California 93454
(805) 925-1038
www.janawaygenealogy.com

ISBN 978-1-59641-064-0

Made in the United States of America

KEY TO COUNTY SYMBOLS

The symbol is followed by name of county and then the earliest year estate records can be found. If an asterisk (*) follows the county name, this means only wills appear in this volume.

A	Anderson 1830	L	Lauderdale 1837
Be	Benton 1837	La	Lawrence 1829
Bo	Blount* 1795	Le	Lewis 1842
Br	Bradley* 1859	Li	Lincoln 1810
C	Campbell 1806	Ma	Madison 1821
Ca	Cannon 1836	Ms	Marshall* 1835
Cr	Carroll* 1822	Mu	Maury 1807
Ct	Carter 1794	Mc	McMinn 1820
Ce	Cheatham 1856	Me	Meigs 1836
Cl	Claiborne 1839	Mo	Monroe 1833
Cf	Coffee* 1836	Mt	Montgomery 1795
D	Davidson 1784	O	Obion 1833
Dk	Dekalb 1838	R	Rhea 1825
Di	Dickson 1804	Ro	Roane 1801
Dy	Dyer* 1853	Rb	Robertson 1796
F	Fayette 1836	Ru	Rutherford 1804
Fr	Franklin* 1808	Se	Sevier* 1849
G	Gibson 1825	Sh	Shelby* 1830
Gi	Giles* 1814	Sm	Smith 1803
Gr	Grainger 1796	St	Stewart 1812
Ge	Greene 1783	Su	Sullivan* 1838
Gu	Grundy 1838	Sn	Sumner* 1788
Hr	Hardeman 1824	T	Tipton 1824
Hd	Hardin 1836	V	Van Buren 1840
Hw	Hawkins* 1797	W	Warren 1827
Hy	Haywood 1826	Wa	Washington* 1779
Hn	Henry 1822	Wy	Wayne 1848
Hu	Humphreys 1837	We	Weakley 1828
Je	Jefferson 1792	Wh	White 1810
Jo	Johnson 1836	Wi	Williamson 1800
K	Knox 1792	Wl	Wilson 1802

INTRODUCTION

This work is an attempt to name all wills and most administrations found in the 62 Tennessee counties where such records, through 1861, have survived. Each entry is as follows:

Name of deceased; year of the probate, or of first mention of the estate; where the original record can be found; county symbol (see key to county symbols).

Identification of where the record can be found is represented by the following symbols:

abl	Administrators bonds & letters
Alpha	No page #s--in alphabetical order
as	Administrators settlements
db	Deed book
eb	Estate book
gs	Guardian settlements
ib	Inventory book
lr	Loose records
lw	Loose wills
mr	Miscellaneous records
rb	Record book
wb	Will book
#	Page # is from a published book--see bibliography

This symbol is followed by the letter or number of the record book, and then the page number. If the book has pagination errors we have placed an asterisk (*) after the page number to indicate this is the second page of that number in the book. Where no symbol as above is shown we have used the microfilm roll number in place of a symbol. If the deceased was black we used a capital B in parentheses.

With few exceptions the names in the index were taken from microfilmed copies of the original county records. This microfilm is available at the Tennessee State Library & Archives in Nashville.

Examples from page 1 of this volume:

Aaron, John 1808 wb-1-294 (Rb)--Record is from Robertson Co, will book 1, p. 294

Abernathy, James E. 1848 lr (Gi)--Record is from Giles Co. loose wills, 1848. (The Giles Co. entries, by the way, are from a published book. See bibliography).

Acuff, Martha 1850 33-3-275 (Gr)--This is from Grainger Co. Roll 33, book 3, p. 275.

Adams, John Q. 1863 wb-#1 (Mc)--Record taken from will book abstracted in published McMinn Co. will book, p. 1

Occasionally we found a county record book which was lacking numbers on one or more pages. In such cases, to help identify where in that book the record could be found, we would show the number of the last numbered page, followed by a + to indicate the reader should examine the page(s) after that one to find the record.

In general we attempted to insert notation regarding an estate only once, when it first appeared in the records. Exceptions were (1) if there was an actual will, the page number is shown even if there was a previous entry for that estate; (2) if a later insertion had been found with a more complete name--full name instead of initials, etc.--or a substantially different spelling of what seemed to be the same name; (3) if ten years of more had elapsed since last entry for that name.

Guardian proceedings and settlements are found sprinkled throughout many of the original books. While these contain much data of genealogical value, we omitted these references as not within the scope of this particular work.

We are fairly confident of the accuracy of the entries as we did not rely on secondary sources except where we were satisfied as to the reliability of the compiler. The one exception is the Shelby County Wills, microfilmed copies of which we were not permitted to buy from the Shelby County authorities, and the State Library has likewise been deprived of them. So for these we used the WPA books, copies of which were kindly lent us by Dr. James Johnson, head of the Local History and Travel Department of the Memphis Public Library.

It should be remembered, incidentally, that wills and other estate records are not always found in the county where the deceased had lived.

Byron Sistler
Barbara Sistler

Nashville, TN
August 1990

- A -

Aaron, John 1808 wb-1-294 (Rb)
Abbott, David 1857 wb-f-32 (G)
Abbott, Jane G. 1845 wb-1-121 (Sh)
Abbott, John 1828 wb-2-617 (Je)
Abbott, O. H. P. (Dr.) 1851 wb-#175 (Wl)
Abbott, S. M. 1859 wb-f-340 (G)
Abel, George 1829 wb-1-145 (Hy)
Abel, T. L. 1846 wb-d-303 (Hd)
Abell, James A. 1846 wb-d-225 (Hd)
Abell, James H. 1839 wb-b-153 (Hd)
Abell, John L. 1846 wb-d-241 (Hd)
Abels, Alex 1836 wb-d-23 (St)
Abernatha, Benjamin 1855 wb-b-370 (We)
Abernathy, Burwell 1836 lr (Gi)
Abernathy, Ephraim P. 1843 wb-b-40 (We)
Abernathy, James 1837 lr (Gi)
Abernathy, James E. 1848 lr (Gi)
Abernathy, James Rolla 1845 lr (Gi)
Abernathy, John Y. 1846 lr (Gi)
Abernathy, Laban 1833 wb-10-183 (D)
Abernathy, Liles E. 1843 lr (Gi)
Abernathy, Littleton F. 1856 wb-b-397 (We)
Abernathy, Mary 1855 rb-17-360 (Ru)
Abernathy, Richard 1852 lr (Gi)
Abernathy, Robert 1823 wb-A-354 (Li)
Abernathy, Thomas 1841 wb-1-65 (Sh)
Abernathy, William D. 1848 lr (Gi)
Abington, John T. 1857 wb-j-275 (O)
Abington, William B. 1857 wb-j-273 (O)
Able, Cain 1852 wb-1-18 (R)
Able, John 1840 wb-a-423 (R)
Abston, Joshua 1812 wb-4-197 (D)
Ace?, H. L. 1853 wb-g-497 (Hn)
Achey, D. 1855 rb-o-2 (Mt)
Achey, Jacob 1836 rb-g-445 (Mt)
Acklen, James Vance 1844 wb-1-220 (Fr)
Acklin, Christopher 1852 wb-11-284 (K)
Acklin, Joseph 1841 wb-1-193 (Fr)
Acklin, Mary A. 1860 wb-1-396 (Fr)
Aclin, Christopher 1856 wb-e-44 (Hy)
Acord, Barbary 1840 wb-c-153 (Ro)
Acord, Cornelius 1840 wb-c-153 (Ro)
Acord, Jonas 1851 wb-15-153 (D)
Acre, Edward C. 1845 wb-f-276 (St)
Acre, Henly 1825 wb-b-31 (St)
Acre, John J. 1832 wb-c-185 (St)
Acree, Edward C. 1847 wb-f-435 (St)
Acree, John B.? 1834 wb-c-341 (St)
Acree, John R. 1843 wb-f-1 (St)

Acree, Polly 1846 wb-f-333 (St)
Acuff, Carter 1817 wb-A-190 (Li)
Acuff, Martha 1850 33-3-275 (Gr)
Acuff, Richard 1836 wb-1-214 (Gr)
Acuff, Richard 1856 wb-3-387 (Gr)
Acuff, William 1817 wb-A-160 (Li)
Acuff, William 1818 wb-A-206 (Li)
Acuff, William 1840 wb-5-84 (Gr)
Adair, Charles 1817 wb-A-199 (Li)
Adair, David 1821 wb-3-245 (K)
Adair, J. B. 1858 gs-1-184 (F)
Adair, James (Sr.) 1823 wb-#20 (Wa)
Adair, James 1802 wb-1-99 (K)
Adair, James 1851 wb-c-451 (Wh)
Adair, John 1827 wb-4-228 (K)
Adam, Nancy P. 1854 wb-b-333 (We)
Adam, Robert 1819 rb-c-184 (Mt)
Adam, William 1832 rb-8-470 (Ru)
Adams, Abryham 1812 wb-A-24 (Li)
Adams, Alfred W. 1853 wb-a-430 (F)
Adams, Allen 1839 lr (Sn)
Adams, Allen 1839 wb-3-0 (Sm)
Adams, Andrew E. 1803 wb-2-331 (D)
Adams, Benjamin 1806 wb-3-134 (D)
Adams, Benjamin 1817 rb-b-404 (Mt)
Adams, Britan 1834 wb-1-132 (Hy)
Adams, Caroline 1840 rb-i-5 (Mt)
Adams, Catharine 1842 rb-i-392 (Mt)
Adams, David 1813 wb-1-7 (Fr)
Adams, David 1830 wb-9-368 (D)
Adams, David 1831 rb-f-304 (Mt)
Adams, David 1853 wb-11-382 (K)
Adams, Edwin H. 1829 rb-e-510 (Mt)
Adams, Eleanor (Mrs) 1858 rb-o-585 (Mt)
Adams, Elener 1856 rb-o-20 (Mt)
Adams, Elizabeth 1854 wb-e-480 (Ro)
Adams, G. W. 1849 wb-#164 (Wl)
Adams, George 1861 wb-17-260 (Rb)
Adams, George W. 1841 wb-e-217 (Hn)
Adams, Giles 1850 wb-e-194 (Ro)
Adams, Hiram 1854 wb-5-153 (Ma)
Adams, Howell, esq. 1814 wb-a-16 (Di)
Adams, Jacob 1833 wb-5-267 (Wi)
Adams, James 1819 rb-c-73 (Mt)
Adams, James 1839 rb-h-216 (Mt)
Adams, James 1859 wb-#130 (Wl)
Adams, James 1859 wb-13-66 (Wi)
Adams, John 1795 wb-1-27 (Je)
Adams, John 1796? wb-#24 (Wa)
Adams, John 1821 rb-c-455 (Mt)
Adams, John 1857 wb-#126 (Wl)

Adams, John 1860 wb-a-362 (Cr)
Adams, John B. 1853 wb-h-174 (Hu)
Adams, John Q. 1863 wb-#1 (Mc)
Adams, Joseph H. 1839 wb-a-39 (L)
Adams, Martha 1854 wb-16-310 (D)
Adams, Martin 1834 wb-1-121 (Fr)
Adams, Martin 1844 wb-a-57 (Ms)
Adams, Mary Ann 1853 wb-15-547 (D)
Adams, Nathan 1840 wb-10-456 (Rb)
Adams, Nathan 1840 wb-10-458 (Rb)
Adams, Nathan 1851 wb-b-301 (We)
Adams, P. B. 1857 wb-1-152 (Be)
Adams, Phillip 1860 wb-h-405 (Hn)
Adams, R. H. 1832 rb-f-447 (Mt)
Adams, Reaves 1810 wb-a-28 (Di)
Adams, Rebecca 1843 wb-e-585 (Hu)
Adams, Reubecca 1845 wb-b-115 (We)
Adams, Revis 1855 wb-h-436 (Hu)
Adams, Richard 1827 rb-e-177 (Mt)
Adams, Richard H. 1837 rb-g-497 (Mt)
Adams, Richard K. 1818 wb-7-289 (D)
Adams, Robert 1820 wb-A-300 (Li)
Adams, Robert W. 1861 wb-f-487 (Ro)
Adams, Samuel 1841 wb-b-313 (Hd)
Adams, Samuel 1854 wb-a-269 (Di)
Adams, Sarah 1839 wb-10-273 (Rb)
Adams, Silvester 1839 wb-e-226 (Hu)
Adams, Sumner 1842 wb-a-108 (Cr)
Adams, Thomas 1799 wb-2-160 (D)
Adams, Thomas 1823 wb-3-630 (Wi)
Adams, Thomas 1829 rb-e-484 (Mt)
Adams, Thomas E. 1854 ib-H-134 (F)
Adams, Thomas P. 1859 as-c-140 (Ms)
Adams, Wiley 1841 wb-7-487 (Wi)
Adams, William (Sr.) 1855 wb-#116 (Wl)
Adams, William 1793 wb-1-6 (K)
Adams, William 1808 wb-3-197 (D)
Adams, William 1831 wb-#93 (Wl)
Adams, William 1842 Ir (Sn)
Adams, William 1848 wb-14-173 (D)
Adams, William 1855 wb-16-94 (Rb)
Adams, William C. 1854 wb-n-219 (Mt)
Adams, William H. 1836 wb-1-302 (Hy)
Adams, William L. 1859 39-2-284 (Dk)
Adams, William W. 1858 wb-b-53 (Ms)
Adams, William sr. 1828 wb-6-247 (Rb)
Adams, Williamson 1822 wb-8-107 (D)
Adams, Willie 1843 wb-8-128 (Wi)
Adams, Wilson 1831 wb-#92 (Wl)
Adams, Wm. C. 1857 wb-h-687 (Hu)
Adamson, Elijah 1826 wb-#65 (Wl)

Adamson, Jesse 1825 wb-#60 (Wl)
Adamson, John 1806 wb-1-0 (Sm)
Adamson, John 1810 wb-0-89 (K)
Adamson, Joseph 1855 39-2-49 (Dk)
Adamson, Joseph 1857 39-2-222 (Dk)
Adamson, Joseph B. 1835 wb-a-51 (Cr)
Adamson, Lucinda 1856 39-2-171 (Dk)
Adamson, Sarah Ann 1851 r39-1-189 (Dk)
Adamson, Simon 1812 wb-2-53 (Je)
Adamson, Susan 1856 39-2-167 (Dk)
Adamson, Susannah 1827 wb-#68 (Wl)
Adamson, Thomas 1816 wb-2-33 (Je)
Adamson, Wells 1838 wb-a-3 (Dk)
Adamson, William 1811 wb-#10 (Wl)
Adamson, William 1826 wb-#64 (Wl)
Adcock, Benjamin 1848 r39-1-77 (Dk)
Adcock, Benjamin 1851 r39-1-187 (Dk)
Adcock, David 1851 r39-1-187 (Dk)
Adcock, George W. 1854 as-c-290 (Di)
Adcock, Henderson 1842 wb-a-154 (Di)
Adcock, Henry 1826 wb-5-432 (Rb)
Adcock, Isaac 1852 r39-1-237 (Dk)
Adcock, James 1848 r39-1-99 (Dk)
Adcock, John 1822 rb-5-237 (Ru)
Adcock, John 1848 wb-b-254 (Mu)
Adcock, Joseph 1851 wb-15-19 (Rb)
Adcock, William 1858 wb-13-57 (K)
Addkins, Elijah 1847 wb-1B-40 (A)
Aden, Albert B. 1858 wb-1-261 (Be)
Aden, Bennett 1858 wb-12-482 (Wi)
Aden, Ira 1842 mr-2-22 (Be)
Aden, Ira H. 1845 mr-2-131 (Be)
Adkerson, A. G. 1856 rb-18-131 (Ru)
Adkerson, James 1854 rb-16-706 (Ru)
Adkerson, James E. 1854 rb-17-191 (Ru)
Adkin, Joseph 1843 wb-8-169 (K)
Adkins, Amos 1818 wb-2-408 (Wi)
Adkins, Drury 1858 as-c-492 (Di)
Adkins, Elijah 1830 wb-#206 (Mu)
Adkins, Elijah 1850 db-O1-58 (A)
Adkins, Elijah P. 1829 wb-#176 (Mu)
Adkins, Henry 1860 wb-a-289 (T)
Adkins, Jane 1858 wb-f-137 (Mu)
Adkins, John 1816 wb-#25 (Mu)
Adkins, Joseph 1830 wb-4-405 (K)
Adkins, Morris 1852 ib-1-237 (Cl)
Adkins, William 1807 wb-#41 (Mu)
Adkins, William 1817 wb-#34 (Mu)
Adkinson, A. G. 1858 rb-19-464 (Ru)
Adkinson, Eliza 1857 rb-18-557 (Ru)
Adkinson, William 1855 rb-17-548 (Ru)

Adkisson, Sarah 1855 wb-h-361 (Hu)
Adkisson, William J. 1857 wb-17-259 (D)
Afflack, John 1844 wb-#143 (Wl)
Agee, Asa 1853 wb-a-238 (Dk)
Agers, Kinchen 1857 wb-e-68 (Hy)
Ahart, Elizabeth 1840 wb-c-175 (Ro)
Aiken, Elizabeth 1848 wb-#44 (Wa)
Aiken, Richard 1854 ib-H-201 (F)
Aikin, James 1813 wb-#6 (Mu)
Aikin, Samuel 1844 wb-8-146 (Wi)
Aikin, William B. 1849 148-1-272 (Ge)
Aikman, Thomas H. 1850 wb-1-220 (Bo)
Aikman, William 1805 wb-1-184 (K)
Ailesworth, George 1842 wb-c-66 (Wh)
Ailor, George 1848 rb-14-217 (Ru)
Ailor, James 1852 wb-11-299 (K)
Ailor, Jourden 1848 rb-14-465 (Ru)
Ailsworth, George 1817 wb-a-65 (Wh)
Ailsworth, Susannah 1852 wb-d-87 (Wh)
Ainn (correct), George 1855 wb-g-695 (Hn)
Akers, Benjamin F. 1855 mr-2-606 (Be)
Akers, Isaac 1840 wb-e-95 (Hn)
Akers, Jessee 1848 wb-d-111 (G)
Akers, Mary J. 1847 wb-d-78 (G)
Akers, Peter 1834 wb-x-267 (Mu)
Akers, William 1860 wb-1-375 (Be)
Akin, Ezekiel 1850 rb-4-57 (Mu)
Akin, Harrison 1814 wb-#18 (Wl)
Akin, James (Jr.) 1822 wb-#165 (Mu)
Akin, James 1824 wb-#80 (Mu)
Akin, John 1846 6-1-1 (Le)
Akin, Joseph B. 1860 wb-f-389 (G)
Akin, William 1825 wb-#133 (Mu)
Akin, William H. 1853 wb-1-31 (Dy)
Akins, Samuel W. 1834 wb-x-134 (Mu)
Akins, Samuel W. 1854 wb-f-49 (Mu)
Alan, John 1821 wb-a-143 (Wh)
Albert, Elizabeth 1836 wb-1-182 (Gr)
Albertson, Arthur 1839 wb-1-155 (Li)
Albertson, Elizabeth 1841 wb-1-180 (Li)
Albright, Anna 1853 wb-10-548 (Wi)
Albright, John 1827 rb-e-133 (Mt)
Albright, Joseph 1840 wb-e-355 (Hu)
Alby, Andius 1859 wb-e-277 (Wh)
Alcock, Jane 1820 rb-c-389 (Mt)
Alder, Barnabas 1860 iv-C-2 (C)
Alderson, Anne 1851 rb-4-244 (Mu)
Alderson, B. D. 1849 wb-b-467 (Mu)
Alderson, B. D. 1849 wb-f-76 (Mu)
Alderson, Curtis 1816 wb-3-208 (St)
Alderson, James 1815 wb-#20 (Mu)

Alderson, James C. 1811 wb-1-158 (Sn)
Alderson, James C. 1811 wb-a-41 (Ro)
Alderson, James C. 1815 wb-#13 (Mu)
Alderson, James C. 1824? wb-#75 (Mu)
Alderson, James M. 1856 wb-4-79 (Je)
Alderson, Jane 1836 wb-x-315* (Mu)
Alderson, John 1819 wb-#44 (Mu)
Alderson, John B. 1850 wb-4-81 (Mu)
Alderson, John G. 1828 wb-#184 (Mu)
Alderson, John S. 1826 wb-#149 (Mu)
Alderson, John S. 1839 wb-y-441 (Mu)
Alderson, Josiah 1824? wb-#130 (Mu)
Alderson, Sarah 1854 wb-f-34 (Mu)
Alderson, Taswell S. 1842 wb-z-404 (Mu)
Alderson, Thomas 1858 wb-17-442 (D)
Alderson, William 1830 lr (Sn)
Alderson, William 1838 wb-y-172 (Mu)
Alderson, William B. 1843 wb-z-503 (Mu)
Aldredge, William W. 1851 wb-1B-200 (A)
Aldridge, Abnes 1828 wb-1-23 (Li)
Aldridge, Aron 1821 wb-#44 (Mu)
Aldridge, Joel 1854 wb-3-184 (Gr)
Aldrige, Clement 1832 wb-c-199 (St)
Alexander, A. O. 1852 ib-1-203 (Ca)
Alexander, Abner 1857 wb-A-124 (Ca)
Alexander, Andrew 1823 wb-A-328 (Li)
Alexander, Andrew M. 1815 wb-#16 (Wl)
Alexander, Benjamin F. 1855 wb-f-82 (Mu)
Alexander, Benjamin G. 1843 wb-3-212 (Hy)
Alexander, Charles P. 1848 ib-1-28 (Ca)
Alexander, Clarissa 1849 wb-d-184 (G)
Alexander, Daniel 1857 rb-19-79 (Ru)
Alexander, David B. 1842 5-2-299 (Cl)
Alexander, Deborah 1827 wb-1-8 (Hw)
Alexander, Dinah 1858 wb-7-15 (Ma)
Alexander, Ebenezer 1857 wb-12-372 (K)
Alexander, Elam 1824 wb-#164 (Mu)
Alexander, Elexis 1816 rb-3-189 (Ru)
Alexander, Elizabeth 1850 wb-g-387 (Hu)
Alexander, Elizabeth C. 1855 wb-f-83 (Mu)
Alexander, Elliazor 1808 wb-#37 (Mu)
Alexander, Ezekial 1813 wb-#9 (Mu)
Alexander, Ezekiel 1835 wb-#112 (Wl)
Alexander, G. H. 1849 wb-g-226 (Hu)
Alexander, George 1837 wb-#118 (Wl)
Alexander, George 1847 148-1-219 (Ge)
Alexander, George 1847 wb-#156 (Wl)
Alexander, George 1850 wb-2-71# (Ge)
Alexander, George 1856 wb-2-154 (Li)
Alexander, Grandison 1842 wb-3-528 (Ma)
Alexander, Henry 1806 wb-3-118 (D)

Alexander, Isaac 1855 39-2-84 (Dk)
Alexander, J. D. 1859 wb-h-373 (Hn)
Alexander, J. H. 1856 wb-6-426 (Ma)
Alexander, James 1829 wb-1-45 (W)
Alexander, James 1851 wb-g-542 (Hu)
Alexander, James H. 1852 wb-2-257 (La)
Alexander, James J. 1841 wb-7-285* (K)
Alexander, James M. 1857 wb-f-128 (Mu)
Alexander, Jane 1832 wb-#237 (Mu)
Alexander, Jesse 1846 wb-1-124 (Sh)
Alexander, John 1829 rb-8-10 (Ru)
Alexander, John 1851 wb-4-171 (Mu)
Alexander, John M. 1826 wb-#142 (Mu)
Alexander, John S. 1826 wb-#150 (Mu)
Alexander, Joseph 1847 wb-g-214 (Hn)
Alexander, Josiah 1839 wb-b-290 (G)
Alexander, Josiah A. 1840 lr (Sn)
Alexander, Josiah M. 1862 wb-f-439 (G)
Alexander, Lawson 1838 wb-b-380 (Ro)
Alexander, Lawson 1855 wb-e-539 (Ro)
Alexander, Levi 1831 rb-8-235 (Ru)
Alexander, M. B. 1853 wb-2-150 (Sh)
Alexander, Martha 1845 wb-2-124 (W)
Alexander, Martha 1853 ib-1-255 (Ca)
Alexander, Mary 1832 wb-2-40# (Ge)
Alexander, Mary 1846 wb-5-34 (Ma)
Alexander, Mathew 1843 wb-f-162* (Hn)
Alexander, Matthew 1823 lr (Sn)
Alexander, Miles 1842 wb-f-87 (Hn)
Alexander, Minty 1840 wb-1-174 (Li)
Alexander, Mires 1835 wb-d-125 (Hn)
Alexander, Moses 1822 wb-#44 (Mu)
Alexander, Nathan 1823 wb-1-1# (Ge)
Alexander, Obediah 1831 wb-#223 (Mu)
Alexander, Paris 1848 wb-5-53 (Ma)
Alexander, Polly 1813 wb-#31 (Mu)
Alexander, Polly 1845? wb-#147 (Wl)
Alexander, Pritchett 1860 rb-20-466 (Ru)
Alexander, R. P. 1841 wb-e-179 (Hn)
Alexander, Randolph 1855 wb-g-650 (Hn)
Alexander, Rankin 1853 wb-5-39 (Hr)
Alexander, Richard 1856 wb-7-0 (Sm)
Alexander, Robert 1821 wb-#38 (Wl)
Alexander, Robert 1841 wb-e-210 (Hn)
Alexander, Robert P. 1841 wb-e-214 (Hn)
Alexander, Susan 1848 wb-9-111 (Wi)
Alexander, Susanna 1841 lr (Sn)
Alexander, Thomas 1855 wb-11-511 (Wi)
Alexander, Thomas 1855 wb-16-536 (D)
Alexander, Thomas sr. 1861 149-1-229 (Ge)
Alexander, William 1818 rb-4-187 (Ru)

Alexander, William 1828 wb-2-27# (Ge)
Alexander, William 1830 lr (Sn)
Alexander, William 1831 wb-1-66 (W)
Alexander, William 1839 wb-a-49 (Ms)
Alexander, William 1839 wb-e-71 (Hn)
Alexander, William H. R. 1854 wb-g-620 (Hn)
Alexander, William R. 1846 wb-b-200 (We)
Alexander, William R. 1849 rb-15-187 (Ru)
Alexander, William S. 1823 wb-1-23 (Ma)
Alexander, William W. 1836? wb-1-268 (Hy)
Alexander, William W. 1839 wb-2-7 (Hy)
Alexander, Zenos H. 1856 wb-c-72 (L)
Aley, Jones 1846 wb-#1 (Mc)
Alford, George W. 1835 wb-10-401 (D)
Alford, J. M. 1848 wb-d-374 (Hd)
Alford, J. W. 1859 wb-4-328 (La)
Alford, James L. 1851 wb-g-502 (Hu)
Alford, Jesse A. 1851 wb-b-132 (L)
Alford, John 1838 wb-11-189 (D)
Alford, John 1847 wb-d-389 (Hd)
Alford, John N. 1847 wb-d-381 (Hd)
Alford, Nancy 1851 wb-g-446 (Hu)
Alford, Nancy E. 1853 wb-h-130 (Hu)
Alford, Richard B. 1853 wb-h-171 (Hu)
Alford, Robert 1837 wb-e-43 (Hu)
Alford, William 1835 wb-b-62 (G)
Alford, William M. 1847 wb-1-432 (La)
Alford, Willie 1853 wb-#112 (Wl)
Alford, _____ 1847 wb-d-365 (Hd)
Algia, John F. 1858 wb-1-85 (Dy)
Alison, Andrew 1829 wb-1-11 (La)
Allbright, Caroline 1847 wb-f-119 (O)
Allbright, Harvy 1849 wb-1-369 (Li)
Allbright, John 1841 wb-1-194 (Li)
Allcorn, James 1834 wb-#104 (Wl)
Allcorn, John 1807 wb-#6 (Wl)
Allcorn, John 1829 wb-#81 (Wl)
Allcorn, Prudence 1854 wb-16-414 (D)
Alldredge, W. W. 1847 wb-1B-9 (A)
Alldridge, Nathan 1828 wb-4-325 (K)
Alldridge, Nathan 1840 wb-7-105 (K)
Alldridge, William 1821 wb-3-304 (K)
Allen, A. W. (Mrs.) 1858 rb-o-541 (Mt)
Allen, A. W. 1858 rb-o-567 (Mt)
Allen, Aletha H. 1859 wb-4-293 (La)
Allen, Alethia B. 1854 wb-16-453 (D)
Allen, Alexander 1845 wb-1-123 (Sh)
Allen, Alexander M. 1837 rb-g-620 (Mt)
Allen, Amanda 1842 wb-3-549 (Ma)
Allen, Andrew J. 1839 wb-b-173 (O)
Allen, Archibald 1814 wb-A-218 (Li)

Allen, B. C. 1850 mr-2-364 (Be)
Allen, Benjamin 1846 wb-13-412 (D)
Allen, Burton 1851 wb-a-190 (Cr)
Allen, Carter 1847 wb-14-97 (D)
Allen, Charles 1848 wb-9-37 (Wi)
Allen, Charles M. 1848 wb-9-62 (Wi)
Allen, Christopher 1843 wb-c-127 (G)
Allen, Daniel 1861 149-1-240 (Ge)
Allen, David 1839 wb-1-482 (Hy)
Allen, Dempsey 1835 wb-a-24 (O)
Allen, Dempsey 1836 wb-a-115 (O)
Allen, Dixon 1835 wb-10-487 (D)
Allen, Dixon 1851 wb-15-27 (D)
Allen, Drury 1850 rb-l-630 (Mt)
Allen, Eli 1860 rb-20-686 (Ru)
Allen, Elizabeth 1834 wb-#13 (Mo)
Allen, Elizabeth 1836 wb-a-114 (O)
Allen, Elizabeth 1851 wb-#1 (Mc)
Allen, Elizabeth 1858 gs-1-65 (F)
Allen, Elizabeth 1859 wb-3e-87 (Sh)
Allen, Ezekiel 1838 wb-a-2 (Dk)
Allen, F. N. 1853 wb-11-8 (Wi)
Allen, George 1822 wb-#43 (Wl)
Allen, George 1836 wb-b-227 (Wh)
Allen, George 1837 wb-#117 (Wl)
Allen, George 1847 rb-k-486 (Mt)
Allen, George 1855 as-b-178 (Ms)
Allen, George S. 1853 wb-16-204 (D)
Allen, Gideon 1856 as-b-239 (Ms)
Allen, Grant 1841 wb-3-0 (Sm)
Allen, Hamblin 1846 wb-a-274 (F)
Allen, Hannah 1833 wb-3-0 (Sm)
Allen, Henry 1841 wb-12-153* (D)
Allen, Henry 1849 wb-g-336 (Hn)
Allen, Hugh 1797 wb-1-60 (K)
Allen, Isaac 1848 wb-14-234 (D)
Allen, J. F. 1854 ib-h-1 (F)
Allen, James 1798 wb-1-254 (Je)
Allen, James 1830 wb-#206 (Mu)
Allen, James 1830 wb-b-105 (Hn)
Allen, James 1840 wb-7-300 (Wi)
Allen, James 1845 rb-j-456 (Mt)
Allen, James 1846 wb-b-183 (We)
Allen, James 1855 ib-h-284 (F)
Allen, James 1857 wb-1-153 (Be)
Allen, James C. 1849 wb-1-259 (Mc)
Allen, James jr. 1847 wb-b-239 (We)
Allen, James sr. 1847 wb-b-240 (We)
Allen, Jane 1830 wb-9-461 (D)
Allen, Jeremiah 1823 wb-8-252 (D)
Allen, Jeremiah 1825 wb-8-419 (D)

Allen, Jeremiah 1837 wb-1-122 (La)
Allen, Jesse 1858 wb-b-31 (Dk)
Allen, Jessse 1861 wb-3e-187 (Sh)
Allen, John 1808 as-1-208 (Ge)
Allen, John 1815 wb-1-0 (Sm)
Allen, John 1816 wb-4-429 (D)
Allen, John 1828 rb-e-300 (Mt)
Allen, John 1835 wb-6-55 (Wi)
Allen, John 1847 wb-#1 (Mc)
Allen, John 1848 r39-1-63 (Dk)
Allen, John 1850 wb-14-472 (D)
Allen, John H. 1860 wb-13-173 (Wi)
Allen, John J. 1827 rb-e-57 (Mt)
Allen, John L. 1855 ib-h-464 (F)
Allen, John T. 1836 lw (Ct)
Allen, John W. 1852 wb-10-404 (Wi)
Allen, Johnathan 1830 wb-#1 (Mc)
Allen, Joseph 1847 wb-2-66# (Ge)
Allen, Joseph W. 1817 wb-1-0 (Sm)
Allen, Judith 1813 wb-a-222 (St)
Allen, Judith 1854 ib-h-16 (F)
Allen, Judith F. 1855 ib-h-422 (F)
Allen, Lawson 1861 wb-13-455 (Wi)
Allen, Mark 1828 wb-1-17 (W)
Allen, Mary 1845 wb-#148 (Wl)
Allen, Mathew 1837 wb-11-27 (D)
Allen, Morris S. 1849 wb-2-60 (Sh)
Allen, Moses 1844 wb-#141 (Wl)
Allen, Moses 1846 wb-a-70 (Dk)
Allen, Myrick 1846 as-a-132 (Ms)
Allen, Nancy 1851 wb-7-0 (Sm)
Allen, Nancy 1858 wb-f-186 (G)
Allen, Nancy T. 1845 wb-8-326 (Wi)
Allen, Orman 1803 wb-1-88 (Sn)
Allen, Ralph 1835 wb-1-375 (Hr)
Allen, Richard 1835 wb-2-192 (Sn)
Allen, Richard 1839 abl-1-116 (T)
Allen, Richard 1845 rb-j-378 (Mt)
Allen, Richard 1850 wb-14-472 (D)
Allen, Robert 1811 wb-2-33# (Ge)
Allen, Robert 1815 wb-4-338 (D)
Allen, Robert 1815 wb-4-353 (D)
Allen, Robert 1844 wb-7-0 (Sm)
Allen, Robert C. 1842 wb-#137 (Wl)
Allen, S. A. 1842 wb-f-32 (Hn)
Allen, Samuel 1827 wb-a-10 (Cr)
Allen, Samuel 1845 wb-8-292 (Wi)
Allen, Samuel 1851 wb-2-74# (Ge)
Allen, Samuel 1852 r39-1-236 (Dk)
Allen, Samuel A. 1841 wb-e-249 (Hn)
Allen, Samuel B. 1844 wb-A-36 (Ca)

Allen, Samuel H. 1832 wb-2-0 (Sm)
Allen, Sarah 1848 wb-1-3 (Bo)
Allen, Sarah Jane 1848 wb-9-185 (Wi)
Allen, Sophronia 1848 wb-9-112 (Wi)
Allen, Susan 1855 wb-6-205 (Ma)
Allen, Theophilus N. 1853 wb-10-458 (Wi)
Allen, Thomas 1848 wb-2-17 (Sh)
Allen, Thomas 1855 wb-6-140 (Ma)
Allen, Thomas 1858 wb-b-49 (F)
Allen, Thomas J. 1842 wb-12-324* (D)
Allen, Valentine 1840 rb-i-2 (Mt)
Allen, Valentine 1857 rb-o-509 (Mt)
Allen, W. H. 1853 wb-g-503 (Hn)
Allen, W. H. 1859 wb-3e-111 (Sh)
Allen, W. W. 1859 wb-h-370 (Hn)
Allen, Walter C. 1848 wb-2-21 (Sh)
Allen, Walter jr. 1856 wb-3-353 (Gr)
Allen, William 1831 wb-9-519 (D)
Allen, William 1842 wb-12-154 (Rb)
Allen, William 1845 wb-a-95 (Ms)
Allen, William 1849 wb-#164 (Wl)
Allen, William 1852 wb-10-258 (Wi)
Allen, William 1852 wb-5-182 (Je)
Allen, William 1852 wb-a-174 (T)
Allen, William B. 1856 39-2-151 (Dk)
Allen, William C. 1857 wb-e-79 (Hy)
Allen, William E. 1833 wb-#102 (Wl)
Allen, William H. 1841 wb-a-31 (Dk)
Allen, William H. 1850 wb-g-375 (Hn)
Allen, William S. 1844 wb-8-172 (Wi)
Allen, William T. 1837 wb-d-97 (St)
Allen, William W. 1849 wb-9-232 (Wi)
Allen, Willie 1831 wb-1-6 (Sh)
Allensworth, Priscilla E. 1861 rb-p-612 (Mt)
Allerton, Samuel 1829 wb-b-62* (Hn)
Alley, Elizabeth 1861 wb-18-431 (D)
Alley, Herbert 1839 wb-10-194 (Rb)
Alley, Herbert 1839 wb-10-262 (Rb)
Alley, James 1825 wb-5-46 (Rb)
Alley, Miles 1818 rb-c-83 (Mt)
Alley, Miles 1824 wb-4-104 (Rb)
Alley, Nancy 1831 wb-7-435 (Rb)
Alley, Samuel 1836 rb-g-480 (Mt)
Alley, Samuel sr. 1838 rb-h-41 (Mt)
Alley, Samuel, sr. 1836 wb-2-212 (Sn)
Allford, Jane 1843 wb-13-3 (D)
Allgood, William 1840 wb-#132 (Wl)
Allinspacker, George 1852 wb-2-114 (Sh)
Allison, Adam 1845 wb-d-145 (Hd)
Allison, Adam B. 1842 wb-b-442 (Hd)
Allison, Andrew 1841 wb-b-373 (G)

Allison, Andrew 1861 wb-18-467 (D)
Allison, Daniel M. 1841 wb-c-10 (Wh)
Allison, David 1799 wb-0-25 (K)
Allison, Elizabeth 1838 wb-e-63 (Hu)
Allison, Hanah 1859 wb-1-319 (Be)
Allison, Henry 1841 wb-c-12 (G)
Allison, Hugh 1836 wb-10-548 (D)
Allison, Hugh H. 1842 wb-c-68 (G)
Allison, Isaiah 1857 wb-#123 (Wl)
Allison, Jacob 1857 wb-2-171 (Li)
Allison, James 1795 wb-#5 (Wa)
Allison, James 1821 Wb-3-243 (Wi)
Allison, James 1841 rb-i-212 (Mt)
Allison, James 1841 wb-a-54 (Ms)
Allison, James 1849 rb-15-9 (Ru)
Allison, Jane 1818? wb-#36 (Wa)
Allison, John 1853 wb-3-128 (W)
Allison, John sr. 1855 wb-3-240 (W)
Allison, Joseph 1828 wb-3-0 (Sm)
Allison, Nancy 1849 rb-15-1 (Ru)
Allison, Polly 1821 wb-3-224 (K)
Allison, Richard Harrison 1838 wb-11-172 (D)
Allison, Robert 1792 wb-#4 (Wa)
Allison, Robert 1812 wb-#13 (Wa)
Allison, Robert 1819 wb-#16 (Wa)
Allison, Robert 1857 wb-f-105 (G)
Allison, Robert 1861 lr (Gi)
Allison, Robert 1861 wb-#64 (Wa)
Allison, Robert S. 1851 wb-g-523 (Hu)
Allison, Robert V. 1835 wb-b-59 (G)
Allison, Samuel 1848 wb-1-47 (Jo)
Allison, Samuel P. 1858 wb-12-542 (Wi)
Allison, Thomas 1847 wb-1-138 (Sh)
Allison, Uriah 1829 wb-b-41 (Ro)
Allison, William 1834 wb-5-399 (Wi)
Allison, William 1845 wb-d-318 (Hd)
Allison, William 1861 wb-13-451 (Wi)
Allman, Aaron 1840 wb-e-142 (Hn)
Allman, J. E. 1856 wb-h-177 (St)
Allman, James 1858 rb-o-659 (Mt)
Allman, John E. 1856 wb-h-205 (St)
Allman, Thomas 1837 wb-d-104 (St)
Allman, Thomas 1837 wb-d-106 (St)
Allmond, Hezekiah 1853 wb-f-22 (Mu)
Allspaugh, Henry 1852 wb-1-72 (Jo)
Allsup, David 1842 lr (Sn)
Allsup, Robert R. 1836 wb-1-130 (Li)
Allsup, William 1856 wb-h-263 (St)
Ally, James 1818 rb-c-39 (Mt)
Ally, James 1838 wb-10-70 (Rb)
Almond, Aaron 1842 wb-f-101* (Hn)

Almond, Elizabeth 1835 wb-6-76 (Wi)
Almond, John V. 1833 wb-10-205 (D)
Almond, William W. 1834 wb-c-331 (St)
Alor, George 1848 rb-14-336 (Ru)
Alor, Jordan 1848 rb-14-423 (Ru)
Alor, Joseph 1848 rb-14-423 (Ru)
Alphin, Ivie 1854 wb-e-200 (G)
Alsap, Elizabeth 1827 wb-#72 (Wl)
Alsbrook, Isham 1841 wb-e-160 (St)
Alsbrook, Martha 1852 wb-xx-91 (St)
Alsbrook, Willie 1831 wb-7-365 (Rb)
Alsbrooks, John 1841 wb-e-130 (St)
Alsobrook, Micajah 1857 wb-c-121 (L)
Alsop, Jesse 1848 wb-4-332 (Hr)
Alston, Alexander S. J. 1836 wb-a-44 (T)
Alston, Edley 1850 wb-9-381 (Wi)
Alston, James 1834 wb-5-365 (Wi)
Alston, James 1849 wb-5-70 (Ma)
Alston, James 1857 wb-12-356 (Wi)
Alston, John 1837 wb-6-300 (Wi)
Alston, Joseph J. 1834 wb-a-30 (T)
Alston, Mary H. 1850 wb-a-143 (T)
Alston, Nancy 1855 ib-h-416 (F)
Alston, Samuel W. 1857 wb-a-270 (T)
Alston, Thomas 1830 wb-#206 (Mu)
Alston, Thomas P. 1861 wb-d-124 (L)
Alston, William 1838 wb-2-375 (Ma)
Alsup, Burrel 1837 mr-1-26 (Be)
Alsup, David 1815 wb-3-66 (St)
Alsup, John & Elizabeth 1829 wb-#79 (Wl)
Alsup, John 1816 wb-#23 (Wl)
Alsup, John 1828 wb-#74 (Wl)
Alsup, Martha 1857 rb-o-429 (Mt)
Alsup, Richard 1840 wb-#133 (Wl)
Alsup, Samuel 1855 wb-1-21 (Be)
Alsup, Samuel 1857 wb-#123 (Wl)
Alsup, Susan 1830 wb-#85 (Wl)
Alsup, Susannah 1821 wb-#37 (Wl)
Alsup, Thomas 1827 wb-1-59 (Hr)
Alsup, Thomas 1829 wb-1-125 (Hr)
Alsup, William 1819 wb-#35 (Wl)
Alsup, William 1840 wb-#131 (Wl)
Alsup, William F. M. 1859 wb-#130 (Wl)
Altmeyer, Christian 1861 wb-f-210 (Mu)
Altom, John 1851 ib-1-126 (Wy)
Altom, Margaret 1852 ib-1-173 (Wy)
Altom, R. W. 1849 wb-g-322 (Hn)
Altom, William 1857 wb-1-18 (Hw)
Altum, J. C. 1858 wb-1C-406 (A)
Altum, Spencer 1855 wb-1C-260 (A)
Altum, William 1846 wb-1-409 (La)

Alvenson, Elijah 1857 wb-e-144 (Wh)
Alvis, Charles D. 1862 wb-1-26 (Hw)
Alvis, Martha 1816 wb-1-243 (Sn)
Alvis, Zachariah 1862 wb-f-434 (G)
Alvison, J. C. 1855 wb-12-168 (K)
Alwell, Thomas 1856 rb-o-224 (Mt)
Ament, Henry 1851 wb-15-75 (D)
Ames, John 1836 wb-1-146 (Gr)
Ames, John G. 1816 wb-#22 (Wl)
Ames, Thomas (Sr.) 1826 wb-#62 (Wl)
Ames, Thomas 1825 wb-#61 (Wl)
Amions, Wm..H. 1851 wb-a-397 (F)
Amis, Haynes 1847 wb-1-13 (Hw)
Amis, John 1853 wb-4-615 (Mu)
Amis, John 1859 lr (Gi)
Amis, Lucy 1818 wb-1-6 (Hw)
Amis, Thomas 1797 wb-1-1 (Hw)
Amis, William 1809 wb-1-3 (Hw)
Ammen, Peter 1859 wb-3e-111 (Sh)
Ammons, Josiah 1844 wb-3-192 (Hr)
Amonett, James 1854 wb-2-167 (Sh)
Amonett, James H. 1846 wb-7-0 (Sm)
Amonett, Synthia 1857 wb-8-33 (Sm)
Amons, ____ (Mr.) 1823 wb-A-357 (Li)
Amos, Elizabeth 1856 wb-f-25 (Ro)
Amos, James 1854 wb-15-507 (Rb)
Amos, William 1856 wb-f-25 (Ro)
Amyx, Isaac 1849 wb-1-15 (Hw)
Anders, Charlotte 1841 wb-a-71 (L)
Anderson (B), Garland 1850 rb-l-615 (Mt)
Anderson, A. 1811 wb-#10 (Wl)
Anderson, Aaron 1855 wb-1-16 (Hw)
Anderson, Abraham 1816 wb-2-199 (Wi)
Anderson, Absolem A. 1859 wb-5-96 (Hr)
Anderson, Agnes 1847 wb-f-468 (St)
Anderson, Alexander 1804 wb-1-82 (Sn)
Anderson, And. 1844 wb-7-0 (Sm)
Anderson, Ann 1839 wb-y-363 (Mu)
Anderson, Ann 1839 wb-y-378 (Mu)
Anderson, Ann 1846 wb-9-268 (K)
Anderson, Ann C. 1859 gs-1-324 (F)
Anderson, B. B. 1848 wb-4-276 (Hr)
Anderson, C. C. 1836 wb-a-141 (O)
Anderson, C. C. 1859 wb-3e-112 (Sh)
Anderson, Caleb 1842 wb-c-23 (G)
Anderson, Charles 1825 lw (Ct)
Anderson, Churchwell C. 1837 wb-a-148 (O)
Anderson, Cornelius 1839 wb-d-346 (St)
Anderson, Daniel 1819 rb-c-74 (Mt)
Anderson, David 1822 wb-1-7 (Hw)
Anderson, David 1858 wb-h-506 (St)

Anderson, David O. 1840 wb-1-191 (Fr)
Anderson, Elijah 1816 rb-b-323 (Mt)
Anderson, Elizabeth 1800 wb-1-1# (Ge)
Anderson, Elizabeth 1817 wb-2-335 (K)
Anderson, Elizabeth 1847 wb-14-115 (D)
Anderson, Elizabeth 1847 wb-8-612 (Wi)
Anderson, Elizabeth 1859 wb-i-41 (St)
Anderson, Frances 1854 wb-b-252 (L)
Anderson, Francis 1830 wb-2-0 (Sm)
Anderson, Francis 1838 wb-#121 (Wl)
Anderson, Francis F. 1825? wb-#165 (Mu)
Anderson, Francis T. 1827 wb-#157 (Mu)
Anderson, Gabriel 1813 wb-#13 (Wl)
Anderson, Gabriel 1850 wb-5-76 (Ma)
Anderson, Gabriel 1853 wb-2-141 (Sh)
Anderson, Garland 1850 wb-m-20 (Mt)
Anderson, Geo. W. jr. 1851 rb-15-587 (Ru)
Anderson, George 1844 wb-a-112 (F)
Anderson, George 1853 rb-16-538 (Ru)
Anderson, George 1854 wb-16-437 (D)
Anderson, George A. 1859 wb-18-313 (D)
Anderson, George W. 1848 rb-14-390 (Ru)
Anderson, Harrod J. 1861 wb-e-165 (Hy)
Anderson, Henry C. 1852 rb-16-241 (Ru)
Anderson, Hiram 1842 lr (Gi)
Anderson, Isaac 1844 wb-#2 (Mc)
Anderson, Isaac 1847 wb-2-226 (W)
Anderson, Isaac 1855 wb-h-361 (Hu)
Anderson, Isaac 1856 wb-1-2 (Bo)
Anderson, Isabella 1851 wb-a-274 (Ms)
Anderson, Jabos? 1835 wb-b-197 (Wh)
Anderson, Jackson 1837 rb-9-458 (Ru)
Anderson, Jacob 1834 wb-5-292 (K)
Anderson, Jacob 1848 wb-c-333 (Wh)
Anderson, Jacob 1852 as-c-143 (Di)
Anderson, James 1797 wb-0-18 (K)
Anderson, James 1817 wb-2-292 (K)
Anderson, James 1831 wb-#90 (Wl)
Anderson, James 1836 wb-2-134 (Ma)
Anderson, James 1837 wb-6-167 (K)
Anderson, James 1844 wb-8-265 (K)
Anderson, James 1846 wb-2-220 (W)
Anderson, James 1848 wb-g-32 (St)
Anderson, James 1853 wb-n-68 (Mt)
Anderson, James 1855 149-1-21 (Ge)
Anderson, James 1856 wb-3-437 (W)
Anderson, James 1860 wb-13-284 (K)
Anderson, James 1860 wb-e-377 (Wh)
Anderson, James C. 1852 wb-2-129 (Sh)
Anderson, James C. 1857 wb-12-460 (Wi)
Anderson, James F. 1848 wb-g-56 (St)

Anderson, James L. 1852 wb-d-93 (Wh)
Anderson, James M. 1844 wb-1-1 (Bo)
Anderson, James jr. 1858 wb-e-211 (Wh)
Anderson, Jane 1821 wb-#49 (Wl)
Anderson, Jane 1837 wb-e-26 (Hu)
Anderson, Jane 1846 wb-13-473 (D)
Anderson, Jasper 1837 wb-11-74 (D)
Anderson, Jefferson 1856 wb-6-243 (Ma)
Anderson, Jno. 1848 wb-a-333 (F)
Anderson, Joel 1850 wb-9-372 (Wi)
Anderson, Joel A. 1854 ib-H-163 (F)
Anderson, John 1801 wb-1-67 (Sn)
Anderson, John 1817 lw (Ct)
Anderson, John 1817 wb-1-0 (Sm)
Anderson, John 1818 wb-7-288 (D)
Anderson, John 1831 wb-b-33 (Wh)
Anderson, John 1836 wb-1-218 (W)
Anderson, John 1837 wb-11-21 (D)
Anderson, John 1837 wb-2-225 (Ma)
Anderson, John 1847 148-1-183 (Ge)
Anderson, John 1856 wb-3e-19 (Sh)
Anderson, John 1860 wb-1-376 (Be)
Anderson, John C. 1850 wb-m-78 (Mt)
Anderson, John D. 1834 lw (Ct)
Anderson, John S. 1836 wb-2-139 (Ma)
Anderson, John W. 1858 wb-#126 (Wl)
Anderson, Jonathan 1849 wb-1-14 (Hw)
Anderson, Joseph 1839 wb-6-421 (K)
Anderson, Joseph M. 1849 wb-c-357 (Wh)
Anderson, Lutilda 1860 wb-17-60 (Rb)
Anderson, Mansfield 1858 rb-19-156 (Ru)
Anderson, Mansfield G. 1860 rb-20-389 (Ru)
Anderson, Mansfield Y. 1859 rb-20-106 (Ru)
Anderson, Mathew 1829 wb-b-51 (Hn)
Anderson, Matthias 1827 wb-a-249 (Wh)
Anderson, N. S. 1851 wb-14-661 (D)
Anderson, Nancy 1817 wb-1-0 (Sm)
Anderson, Nancy C. 1851 wb-a-402 (F)
Anderson, Nathan 1855 wb-d-219 (Wh)
Anderson, Nathaniel 1816 lr (Sn)
Anderson, Patrick 1819 wb-#33 (Wl)
Anderson, Pauldin 1831 wb-#91 (Wl)
Anderson, Peter 1824 wb-1-54 (Fr)
Anderson, Pleasant C. 1855 wb-d-273 (Wh)
Anderson, Pleasant C. 1855 wb-d-283 (Wh)
Anderson, Rebecca 1843 wb-8-191 (K)
Anderson, Rebecca 1859 149-1-146 (Ge)
Anderson, Richard 1838 wb-1-49 (Sh)
Anderson, Richard 1848 wb-4-388 (Hr)
Anderson, Richard 1858 wb-f-144 (Mu)
Anderson, Richard B. 1844 wb-d-274 (O)

Anderson, Robert 1832 wb-1-257 (Hr)
Anderson, Robert 1848 wb-c-272 (Wh)
Anderson, Robert H. 1853 wb-d-198 (Wh)
Anderson, Robert W. 1852 wb-10-356 (Wi)
Anderson, Robert W. 1853 wb-d-156 (Wh)
Anderson, Samuel 1855 wb-g-706 (Hn)
Anderson, Samuel 1859 rb-20-184 (Ru)
Anderson, Samuel 1860 rb-20-476 (Ru)
Anderson, Samuel W. 1845 rb-k-26 (Mt)
Anderson, Samuel W. D. H. 1853 wb-h-May (O)
Anderson, Stanford 1841 wb-a-64 (F)
Anderson, Stanford 1856 ib-h-540 (F)
Anderson, Thomas 1841 wb-7-267 (K)
Anderson, Thomas 1856 wb-j-179 (O)
Anderson, Thomas J. 1855 wb-16-538 (D)
Anderson, Thornberry 1824 rb-d-369 (Mt)
Anderson, Thornsbury 1824 rb-d-375 (Mt)
Anderson, Timothy 1817 rb-b-398 (Mt)
Anderson, W. M. 1849 wb-4-433 (Hr)
Anderson, W. P. 1850 wb-4-563 (Hr)
Anderson, William 1825 lr (Gi)
Anderson, William 1828 wb-#78 (Wl)
Anderson, William 1829 wb-c-15 (St)
Anderson, William 1830 wb-b-17 (Wh)
Anderson, William 1831 wb-5-42 (K)
Anderson, William 1833 wb-5-42* (K)
Anderson, William 1834 wb-x-210 (Mu)
Anderson, William 1840 rb-10-622 (Ru)
Anderson, William 1847 wb-5-39 (Ma)
Anderson, William 1851 wb-15-17 (D)
Anderson, William 1857 wb-16-462 (Rb)
Anderson, William 1857 wb-b-48 (Ms)
Anderson, William 1859 wb-i-57 (St)
Anderson, William B. 1827? wb-#164 (Mu)
Anderson, William C. 1848 wb-9-163 (Wi)
Anderson, William E. 1833 wb-5-281 (Wi)
Anderson, William E. 1857 wb-j-240 (O)
Anderson, William J. 1854 wb-a-474 (F)
Anderson, William J. 1854 wb-xx-313 (St)
Anderson, William M. 1840 wb-2-145 (Hr)
Anderson, William P. jr. 1828 wb-9-272 (D)
Anderson, William W. 1859 wb-7-0 (Sm)
Andes, Frederick 1830 wb-#29 (Wa)
Andes, John 1857 wb-f-122 (Ro)
Andes, William 1857 wb-#58 (Wa)
Andress, Alpheus A. 1857 wb-4-67 (Je)
Andrew, Samuel 1829 wb-b-40 (Ro)
Andrew, Samuel 1840 wb-c-98 (Ro)
Andrew, Thomas 1823 wb-1-25 (Ma)
Andrews, Alexander 1837 wb-d-129 (St)
Andrews, Anderson 1857 wb-h-423 (St)

Andrews, Baker 1836 rb-g-416 (Mt)
Andrews, Benjamin 1828 as-a-181 (Di)
Andrews, Benjamin 1832 as-a-221 (Di)
Andrews, Benjamin 1847 rb-k-481 (Mt)
Andrews, Brockenbrough 1853 wb-11-42 (Wi)
Andrews, Brockenbrough B. 1854
   wb-11-103 (Wi)
Andrews, C. W. 1837 wb-9-345 (Rb)
Andrews, Caroline 1849 wb-9-319 (Wi)
Andrews, D. B. 1861 wb-d-129 (L)
Andrews, David 1857 wb-h-413 (St)
Andrews, E. M. 1831 wb-1-205 (Hr)
Andrews, E. W. 1832 wb-1-235 (Hr)
Andrews, Edmund 1845 wb-b-110 (We)
Andrews, Edward 1831 wb-1-196 (Hr)
Andrews, Ephraim 1809 wb-1-45 (Wi)
Andrews, Ephraim 1831 wb-1-192 (Hr)
Andrews, Ephraim 1837 wb-6-364 (Wi)
Andrews, Ephraim B. 1847 wb-8-614 (Wi)
Andrews, Etheldred 1813 wb-2-109 (Rb)
Andrews, George 1842 wb-7-547 (Wi)
Andrews, Gray 1854 wb-#114 (Wl)
Andrews, Gray 1856 wb-h-477 (Hu)
Andrews, James (or John?) 1850 wb-9-470 (Wi)
Andrews, James 1814 rb-2-304 (Ru)
Andrews, James 1850 wb-9-584 (Wi)
Andrews, James M. 1839 wb-7-51 (Wi)
Andrews, John (esq.) 1808 rb-2-40 (Ru)
Andrews, John 1812 rb-2-188 (Ru)
Andrews, John 1813 rb-2-271 (Ru)
Andrews, John 1831 wb-#227 (Mu)
Andrews, John 1842 wb-7-534 (Wi)
Andrews, John 1842 wb-7-547 (Wi)
Andrews, John 1856 wb-1C-297 (A)
Andrews, Jones 1844 wb-8-135 (Wi)
Andrews, Littleberry 1845 wb-a2-210 (Mu)
Andrews, Mark 1821 wb-3-211 (Wi)
Andrews, Mark 1831 wb-5-40 (Wi)
Andrews, Mark 1852 wb-d-86 (Wh)
Andrews, Mark L. 1851 wb-10-132 (Wi)
Andrews, R. L. 1839 wb-7-33 (Wi)
Andrews, Richard L. 1839 wb-7-91 (Wi)
Andrews, Samuel 1857 wb-7-0 (Sm)
Andrews, Samuel M. 1860 wb-13-174 (Wi)
Andrews, Stith H. 1856 wb-12-50 (Wi)
Andrews, Thomas 1852 wb-10-168 (Wi)
Andrews, Thomas P. 1854 wb-e-220 (G)
Andrews, Wilbon 1849 wb-#164 (Wl)
Andrews, William 1829 wb-4-459 (Wi)
Andrews, William 1854 wb-15-592 (Rb)
Andrews, William 1857 wb-16-373 (Rb)

Andrews, William B. 1825 wb-#151 (Mu)
Andrews, Winnefred 1827 wb-4-243 (Wi)
Anglin, Caleb 1856 rb-o-257 (Mt)
Anglin, John 1828 wb-a-130 (Di)
Anglin, John 1844 as-b-207 (Di)
Anglin, John 1857 as-c-466 (Di)
Anker, S. 1860 wb-e-137 (Hy)
Answorth, James 1850 wb-#172 (Wl)
Antheney, Milan 1817? wb-#39 (Mu)
Anthony, Frances 1836 rb-9-363 (Ru)
Anthony, Hannah 1857 mr (Gi)
Anthony, James G. 1860 wb-d-66 (L)
Anthony, John 1824 wb-4-7 (K)
Anthony, John 1825 rb-6-122 (Ru)
Anthony, John 1836 rb-9-374 (Ru)
Anthony, John 1836 wb-1-89 (La)
Anthony, John D. 1839 wb-6-413 (K)
Anthony, Joseph 1842 wb-d-10 (Ro)
Anthony, Josiah 1854 wb-3-194 (Sn)
Anthony, Philip sr. 1860 wb-18-218 (D)
Anthony, Sarah 1853 wb-10-499 (Wi)
Anthony, William 1847 wb-9-1 (Wi)
Anthony, William B. 1827 rb-e-251 (Mt)
Anthony, Zephenia H. B. 1846 rb-13-690 (Ru)
Antwine, William sr. 1853 wb-1-32 (Dy)
Apperson, Albert 1838 rb-h-173 (Mt)
Apperson, Albert A. 1838 rb-h-151 (Mt)
Apperson, Jacob 1822 rb-d-23 (Mt)
Apperson, Jacob 1831 rb-f-177 (Mt)
Apperson, Jacob 1832 rb-f-328 (Mt)
Apperson, William R. 1842 rb-i-429 (Mt)
Apple, George 1851 wb-15-183 (D)
Applebury, Richard 1857 wb-3e-56 (Sh)
Appleby, William 1808 wb-1-37 (Wi)
Applegate, H. A. 1856 wb-j-81 (O)
Applegate, Henry A. 1858 wb-k-260 (O)
Applegate, James M. 1839 wb-b-176 (O)
Appleton, James 1833 wb-1-44 (La)
Appleton, James 1840 wb-12-70* (D)
Appleton, James 1848 wb-2-30 (La)
Appleton, John 1813 wb-2-65 (Rb)
Applewhite, Charlotte 1838 wb-7-5 (Wi)
Applewhite, Harry 1836 wb-a-168 (O)
Applewhite, Henry 1848 wb-g-34 (O)
Applewhite, Jane 1839 wb-b-102 (O)
Applewhite, Rebeccah 1835 rb-g-181 (Mt)
Arbuckle, James 1849 wb-d-166 (G)
Arbuckle, Joseph 1821 rb-5-135 (Ru)
Arbuckle, Joseph 1832 rb-8-463 (Ru)
Arbuthnot, Fanny 1839 wb-2-263 (Sn)
Archer, George 1819 wb-A-278 (Li)

Archer, Jacob 1808? lr (Sn)
Archer, James 1862 iv-C-169 (C)
Archer, Josiah 1842 wb-#140 (Wl)
Archer, Ruth 1841 wb-a-76 (F)
Archer, Thompson 1833 wb-x-50 (Mu)
Archey, D. A. 1856 rb-o-33 (Mt)
Argo, David 1848 wb-2-269 (W)
Arledge, Clement 1851 wb-1-288 (Fr)
Armfield, Jacob 1815 rb-b-280 (Mt)
Armitage, John 1851 148-1-376 (Ge)
Armour, David 1852 wb-2-118 (Sh)
Armour, John T. 1858 wb-b-50 (F)
Armour, Mary 1856 wb-3e-34 (Sh)
Armour, S. H. 1836 wb-d-245 (Hn)
Armour, Solomon H. 1833 wb-c-150 (Hn)
Armstead, Jesse 1852 wb-5-118 (Ma)
Armstead, Martin 1859 rb-p-182 (Mt)
Armstead, Robert 1853 wb-n-164 (Mt)
Armstead, Robert 1853 wb-n-170 (Mt)
Armstead, Robert sr. 1859 rb-p-112 (Mt)
Armsted, John 1834 wb-3-0 (Sm)
Armstrong, Aaron 1860 wb-13-368 (K)
Armstrong, Abner 1855 wb-16-487 (D)
Armstrong, Alexander 1842 148-1-30 (Ge)
Armstrong, Alexander 1853 148-1-467 (Ge)
Armstrong, Andrew 1846 wb-#2 (Mc)
Armstrong, Cary 1854 wb-#3 (Mc)
Armstrong, Drury Paine 1856 wb-12-287 (K)
Armstrong, Elias J. 1855 wb-f-71 (Mu)
Armstrong, Elizabeth 1835 wb-5-364 (K)
Armstrong, Francis 1854 wb-15-589 (Rb)
Armstrong, Francis W. 1843 wb-12-447* (D)
Armstrong, George A. 1854 as-b-158 (Ms)
Armstrong, James 1813 wb-2-63 (K)
Armstrong, James 1834 wb-5-427 (Wi)
Armstrong, James 1836 wb-1-211 (Hy)
Armstrong, James 1837 wb-y-108 (Mu)
Armstrong, Jane 1849 wb-a-155 (Cr)
Armstrong, John 1812 wb-2-36 (K)
Armstrong, John 1813 wb-1-4 (Hw)
Armstrong, John 1830 wb-1-61 (Hy)
Armstrong, John 1847 wb-1-331 (Li)
Armstrong, John 1853 wb-#3 (Mc)
Armstrong, John 1857 as-c-67 (Ms)
Armstrong, John B. 1836 wb-3-0 (Sm)
Armstrong, John C. 1851 wb-15-138 (D)
Armstrong, Joseph W. 1816 wb-1-0 (Sm)
Armstrong, Josiah 1857 wb-12-449 (K)
Armstrong, Knox 1842 wb-A-26 (Ca)
Armstrong, Knox 1850 wb-d-253 (G)
Armstrong, Lanclet 1829 wb-1-7 (La)

Armstrong, Martin W. B. 1827 wb-9-112 (D)
Armstrong, Mary 1846 wb-8-452 (Wi)
Armstrong, Mathew 1851 lr (Sn)
Armstrong, Moses 1857 wb-12-444 (K)
Armstrong, Nancy 1836 wb-1-207 (Gr)
Armstrong, Priscilla 1856 wb-#3 (Mc)
Armstrong, Robert 1796 wb-0-15 (K)
Armstrong, Robert 1849 wb-10-140 (K)
Armstrong, Robert 1851 wb-15-57 (D)
Armstrong, Robert 1859 wb-13-97 (K)
Armstrong, Samuel 1806 wb-1-90 (Sn)
Armstrong, Samuel 1832 rb-8-468 (Ru)
Armstrong, Samuel M. 1827 wb-#3 (Mc)
Armstrong, Seth 1859 wb-1-19 (Hw)
Armstrong, Thomas 1843 wb-#3 (Mc)
Armstrong, Thomas 1855 wb-a-277 (Di)
Armstrong, Thomas 1858 wb-17-485 (D)
Armstrong, William 1810 wb-1-3 (Hw)
Armstrong, William 1817 wb-1-6 (Hw)
Armstrong, William 1850 wb-1-237 (Bo)
Armstrong, William 1856 wb-#3 (Mc)
Armstrong; William 1860 wb-1-23 (Hw)
Armstrong, William Sr. 1850 wb-#4 (Mc)
Armstrong, William T. 1858 wb-2-433* (Me)
Armstrong, William T. 1858 wb-3-1 (Me)
Armstrong, William sr. 1835 wb-1-8 (Hw)
Armstrong, William sr. 1846 wb-8-453 (Wi)
Arne, William 1840 wb-2-173 (Hr)
Arnelle, Davaid R. 1852 wb-f-14 (Mu)
Arnet?, Samuel 1836 wb-d-219 (Hn)
Arnett, A. J. 1859 wb-h-351 (Hn)
Arnett, Sam A. 1837 wb-d-165* (Hn)
Arnett, Samuel 1848 wb-g-236 (Hn)
Arnett, Samuel S. 1835 wb-d-147 (Hn)
Arnett, William 1820 wb-1-41 (Fr)
Arnold, Aaron 1850 wb-g-395 (Hu)
Arnold, Asa 1836 rb-9-373 (Ru)
Arnold, Caleb 1851 wb-b-200 (L)
Arnold, Daniel 1842 wb-11-264 (Rb)
Arnold, Elenor 1860 rb-20-422 (Ru)
Arnold, Elijah 1859 wb-17-1 (Rb)
Arnold, Harold 1816 wb-#21 (Wl)
Arnold, Henry 1818? wb-#31 (Wl)
Arnold, Hopson 1823 wb-#63 (Mu)
Arnold, J. H. 1826 wb-#165 (Mu)
Arnold, J. W. 1858 wb-f-158 (G)
Arnold, James 1808 rb-2-58 (Ru)
Arnold, Jno. 1834 wb-1-484 (Ma)
Arnold, John 1824 lw (Ct)
Arnold, John 1824 rb-6-6 (Ru)
Arnold, John 1825? as-a-146 (Di)

Arnold, John 1837 rb-10-58 (Ru)
Arnold, John H. 1828 wb-#172 (Mu)
Arnold, John K. 1860 wb-1-21 (Hw)
Arnold, John W. 1839 rb-10-540 (Ru)
Arnold, John W. 1840 rb-10-481 (Ru)
Arnold, Lee 1838 wb-b-227 (G)
Arnold, Martha 1850 wb-10-430 (K)
Arnold, Michael 1823 wb-a-188 (Ro)
Arnold, Nancy sr. 1859 wb-f-244 (G)
Arnold, Nathan 1859 wb-f-259 (G)
Arnold, Thomas 1820 wb-#37 (Wl)
Arnold, Thomas 1825? as-a-147 (Di)
Arnold, Wilie 1860 wb-1-350 (Be)
Arnold, William (Capt) 1857 rb-19-180 (Ru)
Arnold, William 1814 rb-2-291 (Ru)
Arnold, William 1849 wb-#177 (Wl)
Arnold, William 1857 rb-19-43 (Ru)
Arnold, Wyatt 1850 mr-2-156 (Be)
Arnold, Zachariah 1834 wb-1-102 (Li)
Arnold?, William 1856 wb-e-437 (G)
Arnott, William M. 1860 wb-1-21 (Hw)
Arnwine, Albartis 1857 wb-#4 (Mc)
Arnwine, John 1858 wb-#4 (Mc)
Aron, William 1857 wb-h-317 (St)
Arrendell, Richard 1857 wb-1-117 (Jo)
Arrington, Edward 1836 wb-b-132 (G)
Arrington, Henry 1857 wb-#128 (Wl)
Arrington, Miles B. 1853 wb-15-539 (D)
Arrington, Onner 1852 wb-xx-74 (St)
Arthur, Ann 1852 wb-15-461 (D)
Arthur, Benjamin 1840 as-a-60 (Ms)
Arun, William 1840 wb-2-169 (Hr)
Ash, Hugh B. 1858 wb-#5 (Mc)
Ash, James R. 1858 wb-#5 (Mc)
Ash, Robert 1858 wb-#5 (Mc)
Ashborn, A. S. 1837 abl-1-17 (T)
Ashby, Alexander 1841 wb-1-176 (Li)
Ashby, Peter 1858 wb-2-210 (Li)
Asher, John 1855 wb-1-98 (Jo)
Asher, William E. 1859 wb-#61 (Wa)
Asherst, John 1834 wb-1A-73 (A)
Ashley, Joshua 1828 wb-1-26 (W)
Ashley, Nathaniel 1828 wb-9-162 (D)
Ashley, Noah 1832 wb-b-186 (Ro)
Ashley, William 1856 wb-7-0 (Sm)
Ashley, William H. 1856 wb-h-487 (Hu)
Ashley, Willie H. 1855 wb-h-457 (Hu)
Ashlin, Dicey 1847 wb-8-604 (Wi)
Ashlin, William 1821 Wb-3-272 (Wi)
Ashly, Wiley 1860 wb-#5 (Mc)
Ashman, Lewis 1821 rb-5-157 (Ru)

Ashmore, Hezekiah 1829 wb-3-57 (Je)
Ashworth, C. W. 1840 wb-#133 (Wl)
Ashworth, Jasper R. (Sr.) 1853 wb-#115 (Wl)
Ashworth, John 1840? wb-b-205 (Hd)
Ashworth, John C. 1841 wb-b-282 (Hd)
Ashworth, Joseph 1838 wb-b-190 (Hd)
Askew, Bryant 1845 wb-a2-289 (Mu)
Askew, Drew A. 1853 mr-2-525 (Be)
Askew, Elen 1857 wb-1-125 (Be)
Askew, Elisha 1840 wb-d-401 (St)
Askew, John 1817 wb-#39 (Mu)
Askew, John F. 1856 wb-1-46 (Be)
Askew, Josiah 1835 wb-c-408 (St)
Askew, Lemuel 1846 wb-f-286 (St)
Askew, Martha 1857 wb-1-125 (Be)
Askew, Mary 1849 wb-g-117 (St)
Askew, Sarah 1845 wb-f-261 (St)
Askew, Winburn 1860 wb-i-259 (St)
Askew, Winburn H. 1859 wb-i-88 (St)
Askey, John 1841 wb-2-279 (Sn)
Askins, Catherine 1836 wb-#110 (Wl)
Asply, John 1835 wb-2-185 (Sn)
Aston, Alexander 1853 wb-#108 (Wl)
Aston, Daniel 1831 wb-#91 (Wl)
Aston, Daniel T. 1854 ib-H-195 (F)
Atchey, D. A. 1855 wb-n-607 (Mt)
Atchison, John G. 1844 wb-c-186 (G)
Atchley, Joseph 1829 wb-a-67 (R)
Atchley, McCampbell 1852 wb-#5 (Mc)
Atchley, Thomas 1857 wb-1-24 (Se)
Ater, George 1841 wb-b-339 (Hd)
Atherly, Johnathan 1808 wb-3-198 (D)
Athey, Thomas J. 1829 wb-9-343 (D)
Atkerson, Selah 1817 wb-7-125 (D)
Atkin, Joseph 1824 wb-4-141 (Rb)
Atkins, Abie 1859 wb-b-73 (F)
Atkins, Asa 1830 wb-b-75 (Hn)
Atkins, Celia 1849 wb-g-118 (St)
Atkins, Charles W. 1841 wb-7-161 (K)
Atkins, Henry 1849 wb-g-328 (Hn)
Atkins, J. F. 1859 wb-4-231 (La)
Atkins, James 1825 wb-4-286 (Rb)
Atkins, John 1813 wb-2-8 (Wi)
Atkins, John 1845 wb-g-35 (Hn)
Atkins, Margaret 1860 rb-p-427 (Mt)
Atkins, Meredith 1852 wb-3-22 (Gr)
Atkins, Milbrey 1850 wb-g-390 (Hn)
Atkins, Moris 1849 5-3-273 (Cl)
Atkins, Nathan 1840 wb-5-55 (Gr)
Atkins, R. S. 1847 wb-g-227 (Hn)
Atkins, Richard 1847 wb-g-224 (Hn)

Atkins, Thomas S. 1817 wb-2-278 (Wi)
Atkins, Winneford 1848 wb-g-298 (Hn)
Atkins, Winston 1833 wb-1-14 (Gr)
Atkinson, Edward 1822 wb-#5 (Mc)
Atkinson, Edward 1856 rb-18-187 (Ru)
Atkinson, Elizabeth 1855 wb-12-1 (Wi)
Atkinson, J. L. 1837 wb-#116 (Wl)
Atkinson, James 1854 rb-16-704 (Ru)
Atkinson, John 1814 Wb-2-57 (Wi)
Atkinson, John 1837 wb-6-324 (Wi)
Atkinson, John 1840 wb-#5 (Mc)
Atkinson, Joseph 1830 wb-#109 (Wl)
Atkinson, Joshua 1802 wb-#1 (Wl)
Atkinson, Joshua 1846 rb-k-229 (Mt)
Atkinson, Martha 1831 wb-#94 (Wl)
Atkinson, Martha J. 1832 wb-#96 (Wl)
Atkinson, R. D. 1848 wb-4-300 (Hr)
Atkinson, Richard D. 1845 wb-4-2 (Hr)
Atkinson, Ruthy J. 1860 wb-13-179 (Wi)
Atkinson, Sarah 1858 rb-19-427 (Ru)
Atkinson, William 1826 wb-#6 (Mc)
Atkinson, William 1831 wb-#225 (Mu)
Atkinson, William D. 1845 wb-3-303 (Hr)
Atkinson, Wm. 1853 rb-16-711 (Ru)
Atkison, Celia 1816 wb-7-100 (D)
Atkisson, Miles W. 1860 wb-18-132 (D)
Atnip, Benjamin 1840 wb-a-16 (Dk)
Atnip, Jamima 1851 r39-1-207 (Dk)
Ator, S. A. 1846 wb-d-262 (Hd)
Ator, Sarah 1844 wb-d-131 (Hd)
Ators, S. Anderson 1844 wb-d-121 (Hd)
Attkisson, Ruth 1829 wb-4-459 (Wi)
Attwood, Joseph P. 1839 wb-2-102 (Hr)
Atwell, Thomas 1857 rb-o-440 (Mt)
Atwood, Edwin 1822 wb-#43 (Wl)
Atwood, Edwin Y. 1846 wb-7-0 (Sm)
Atwood, Elender 1826 rb-6-225 (Ru)
Atwood, Harvey 1852 wb-h-Oct (O)
Atwood, Joseph P. 1836 wb-2-182 (Ma)
Atwood, Thomas 1843 wb-1-220 (Li)
Atwood, Thompson 1835 wb-3-0 (Sm)
Audres, John 1820 rb-5-31 (Ru)
Auld, Colin 1841 wb-3-342 (Ma)
Ault, Conrod 1852 wb-1-21 (R)
Ault, Michael 1827 wb-4-229 (K)
Ausmus, Frances 1859 ib-2-550 (Cl)
Ausmus, Hiram 1859 ib-2-547 (Cl)
Aust, Frederick 1812 wb-#12 (Wl)
Austell, William 1849 wb-4-22 (Je)
Austin, Abraham J. 1852 wb-a-251 (Di)
Austin, Charles sr. 1842 wb-3-0 (Sm)

Austin, Drewry 1831 wb-1-71 (Li)
Austin, Edwin 1847 wb-14-101 (D)
Austin, Henry 1842 lr (Sn)
Austin, James 1840 lr (Gi)
Austin, John 1840 wb-12-14 (D)
Austin, John 1840 wb-12-75* (D)
Austin, John 1845 mr (Gi)
Austin, John 1846 wb-1-278 (Li)
Austin, John 1858 wb-e-267 (Wh)
Austin, John sr. 1860 wb-e-323 (Wh)
Austin, Patrick 1850 wb-14-550 (D)
Austin, Polly 1833 wb-5-306 (Wi)
Austin, Raleigh 1832 wb-5-159 (Wi)
Austin, Sarah Emily 1851 wb-14-608 (D)
Austin, W. J. 1853 as-c-255 (Di)
Autry, Elijah 1858 wb-a-333 (Cr)
Autry, Rederick 1855 wb-#6 (Mc)
Avant, Abner 1822 wb-1-0 (Sm)
Avant, Abram 1824 wb-2-0 (Sm)
Avant, Thomas 1839 wb-2-97 (Hr)
Averett, Henry W. 1857 rb-o-492 (Mt)
Averett, Nancy 1836 rb-g-331 (Mt)
Averett, Samuel 1849 wb-#167 (Wl)
Averitt, Washington 1853 wb-n-143 (Mt)
Averrett, Martha 1857 lr (Sn)
Averson, Joseph 1854 lr (Sn)
Avery, Alexander 1846 wb-d-16 (G)
Avery, Allen 1821 wb-#38 (Wl)
Avery, John 1847 wb-14-41 (D)
Avery, John W. 1841 wb-#135 (Wl)
Avery, Peter 1816 wb-a-92 (Ro)
Avett, Thomas 1849 wb-a-355 (F)
Awalt, Michael 1835 wb-1-141 (Fr)
Aycock, R. G. 1858 wb-f-228 (G)
Aydelotte, Arthur 1814 wb-#18 (Mu)
Aydolett, John 1806 wb-#4 (Wl)
Ayers, Joseph 1845 wb-a2-271 (Mu)
Ayers, Zaccheus 1812 wb-a-50 (Ro)
Ayre, Samuel W. 1861 wb-3e-167 (Sh)
Ayres, Alfred M. 1840 wb-#133 (Wl)
Ayres, D. B. 1829 wb-4-380 (K)
Ayres, David 1835 wb-5-376 (K)
Ayres, David B. 1825 wb-4-45 (K)
Ayres, David B. 1827 wb-#6 (Mc)
Ayres, Elizabeth H. 1861 wb-7-88 (Ma)
Ayres, Jonathan 1821 wb-3-300 (K)
Ayres, Joseph 1805 wb-1-166 (K)
Ayres, Polly 1827 wb-4-242 (K)
Ayres, Susan 1849 wb-14-145 (Rb)

- B -

Babb, Archibald 1851 wb-2-73# (Ge)
Babb, Burwell 1847 wb-13-119 (Rb)
Babb, Burwell 1847 wb-13-69 (Rb)
Babb, Er 1854 wb-2-78# (Ge)
Babb, Henry B. 1842 wb-f-115 (Hn)
Babb, Hiram 1858 wb-f-191 (Ro)
Babb, James 1847 wb-b*-13 (O)
Babb, Jesse 1835 wb-9-114 (Rb)
Babb, John P. 1842 wb-f-20 (Hn)
Babb, Phillip 1843 wb-2-60# (Ge)
Babb, Phillip sr. 1843 wb-2-34# (Ge)
Babb, Seth 1836 wb-2-47# (Ge)
Babb, Thomas 1840 wb-#132 (Wl)
Baber, Alexander 1840 wb-b-346 (G)
Baber, Peter 1858 wb-16-676 (Rb)
Baber, William 1838 wb-#123 (Wl)
Bacchus, William 1842 wb-#151 (Wl)
Bachelor, William 1861 wb-i-301 (St)
Bachelor, William B. 1861 wb-i-324 (St)
Bachman, Jonathan 1861 wb-1-11 (Su)
Bachman, Nathan 1859 wb-1-116 (Su)
Backary, Elizabeth 1840 rb-10-509 (Ru)
Backus, George 1832 wb-9-577 (D)
Bacon, Allen S. sr. 1848 wb-e-113 (Ro)
Bacon, Charles 1821 wb-#19 (Wa)
Bacon, Isaac 1826 wb-#24 (Wa)
Bacon, James 1853 wb-5-215 (Je)
Bacon, John 1857 wb-#59 (Wa)
Bacon, John 1858 wb-#59 (Wa)
Bacon, Jonathan 1859 wb-#63 (Wa)
Bacon, Michael 1804 wb-1-33 (Hw)
Badget, Jesse 1845 wb-#149 (Wl)
Badgett, Benton 1824 wb-#90 (Mu)
Badgett, James 1842 wb-7-304 (K)
Badgett, James M. 1852 wb-11-285 (K)
Badgett, James sr. 1835 wb-5-356 (K)
Badgett, John 1816 wb-1-233 (Sn)
Badgett, Mary 1845 wb-9-96 (K)
Badgett, Robert Don 1834 wb-5-318 (K)
Badgett, Samuel 1830 wb-1-8 (Bo)
Badlett, Isaac 1815 wb-#18 (Wl)
Baggatt, John 1857 rb-o-354 (Mt)
Baggerly, David 1819 wb-2-261 (Li)
Baggerly, Rebecca 1857 wb-2-195 (Li)
Baggett, Eli 1851 wb-14-446 (Rb)
Baggett, Granberry 1845 wb-12-484 (Rb)
Baggett, Henry 1815 rb-b-283 (Mt)
Baggett, Jesse J. 1834 wb-8-387 (Rb)
Baggett, John 1815 rb-b-281 (Mt)

Baggett, John 1848 mr-2-270 (Be)
Baggett, William 1851 wb-14-416 (Rb)
Baggett, William G. 1851 wb-14-437 (Rb)
Bagley, Daniel 1828 wb-a-14 (Cr)
Bagley, Elisha 1858 wb-2-244 (Li)
Bagley, Henry C. 1852 as-b-74 (Ms)
Bagley, Robert W. 1848 as-a-165 (Ms)
Bagley, Sarah 1853 as-b-118 (Ms)
Bagley, William H. A. 1844 wb-a-128 (Cr)
Bagwell, Drury 1841 rb-i-202 (Mt)
Bagwell, G. P. 1847 rb-k-545 (Mt)
Bagwell, John W. 1846 rb-k-302 (Mt)
Bagwell, Julia 1843 rb-j-39 (Mt)
Bagwell, Lunsford 1825 wb-a-207 (Wh)
Bagwell, Nicholas E. 1835 rb-g-184 (Mt)
Bagwell, Pleasant 1846 rb-k-332 (Mt)
Bagwell, Samuel 1825 rb-d-428 (Mt)
Bagwell, Thomas 1838 wb-c-10 (Ro)
Bagwell, W. J. 1859 wb-i-138 (St)
Bailes, James 1853 wb-#6 (Mc)
Bailey, Allen 1838 wb-d-275 (St)
Bailey, Andrew 1829 wb-#6 (Mc)
Bailey, Benjamin 1785 rb-c-357 (Mt)
Bailey, Gabrial F. 1845 wb-12-291 (Rb)
Bailey, Gala 1846 rb-k-215 (Mt)
Bailey, George C. 1853 wb-xx-262 (St)
Bailey, Henry 1816 rb-b-309 (Mt)
Bailey, Henry 1834 wb-5-440 (Wi)
Bailey, Henry 1834 wb-c-333 (St)
Bailey, Henry 1857 wb-a-255 (T)
Bailey, Henry L. 1848 rb-l-1 (Mt)
Bailey, Hiram 1850 wb-m-125 (Mt)
Bailey, Ishmael 1855 wb-6-80 (Ma)
Bailey, Jacob 1844 rb-j-83 (Mt)
Bailey, Jesse 1857 rb-o-287 (Mt)
Bailey, Jessee 1857 rb-o-290 (Mt)
Bailey, Johmael 1855 wb-6-1 (Ma)
Bailey, John 1836 wb-1-460 (Hr)
Bailey, John 1842 wb-11-143 (Rb)
Bailey, John 1853 wb-e-95 (G)
Bailey, John C. 1860 wb-f-334 (Ro)
Bailey, John H. 1839 wb-7-204 (Wi)
Bailey, John T. 1844 wb-12-153 (Rb)
Bailey, John W. 1834 wb-1-49 (La)
Bailey, Lucinda 1851 wb-m-386 (Mt)
Bailey, Margaret 1805 as-1-130 (Ge)
Bailey, Nancy 1829 wb-#7 (Mc)
Bailey, Nancy 1848 wb-14-23 (Rb)
Bailey, Peleg 1855 wb-6-150 (Ma)
Bailey, Richard T. 1836 wb-1-497 (Hr)
Bailey, Richd. J. 1842 wb-2-402 (Hr)

Bailey, Robert 1830 wb-9-424 (D)
Bailey, Robert 1860 wb-i-261 (St)
Bailey, Robert A. 1846 wb-a-288 (F)
Bailey, Sterling A. 1815 wb-4-378 (D)
Bailey, Thomas sr. 1830 wb-2-41# (Ge)
Bailey, Thos. J. 1849 wb-a-366 (F)
Bailey, Vincent 1858 ib-1-559 (Ca)
Bailey, Washington 1850 wb-#175 (WI)
Bailey, Washington L. 1849 wb-#170 (WI)
Bailey, William 1821 wb-1-0 (Sm)
Bailey, William 1824 wb-1-0 (Sm)
Bailey, William S. 1828 rb-e-252 (Mt)
Bailey, Wm. 1850 wb-d-233 (G)
Bailey, Wm. 1855 wb-n-522 (Mt)
Bailiff, Thomas 1852 wb-a-226 (Dk)
Bailiff, Thomas 1854 wb-7-0 (Sm)
Baily, C. J. 1838 wb-1-158 (La)
Baily, Henry 1835 wb-6-66 (Wi)
Baily, Henson 1828 wb-4-337 (K)
Baily, Pollie 1858 rb-o-702 (Mt)
Baily, R. T. 1837 wb-1-514 (Hr)
Baily, Robert 1818 wb-a-114 (Ro)
Baily, William 1815 wb-3-99 (St)
Baily, William 1836 wb-#111 (WI)
Baily, William sr. 1828 wb-1-42 (Hw)
Baily, Zachariah 1844 rb-j-214 (Mt)
Bain, Andrew 1861 39-2-408 (Dk)
Bain, Britian 1840 mr-1-313 (Be)
Bain, R. L. 1857 ib-1-420 (Ca)
Bain, William 1841 wb-b-347 (Hd)
Bain, William 1860 39-2-358 (Dk)
Bain, _____ 1841 wb-b-358 (Hd)
Baine, Daniel 1820 rb-c-354 (Mt)
Baine, Samuel R. 1859 wb-#7 (Mc)
Bains, W. C. 1850 6-2-51 (Le)
Baird, Adam 1826 rb-6-210 (Ru)
Baird, Alexr. 1841 wb-b-403 (G)
Baird, Ann Jemima 1859 wb-#130 (WI)
Baird, Charles G. 1861 wb-f-418 (G)
Baird, Daniel G. 1856 wb-16-290 (Rb)
Baird, James 1860 wb-#133 (WI)
Baird, James H. 1849 wb-#168 (WI)
Baird, John 1825 wb-8-407 (D)
Baird, John 1832 wb-#245 (Mu)
Baird, John 1851 wb-d-350 (G)
Baird, John A. 1854 39-2-45 (Dk)
Baird, John W. 1819 wb-7-327 (D)
Baird, Lemuel M. 1851 rb-16-116 (Ru)
Baird, Reuben 1849 wb-7-0 (Sm)
Baird, Samuel 1815 wb-1-0 (Sm)
Baird, Sheldon 1862 wb-#135 (WI)

Baird, Thomas 1856 wb-16-255 (Rb)
Baird, Thomas J. 1842 wb-#136 (Wl)
Baird, W. D. 1860 rb-20-699 (Ru)
Baird, William 1816 wb-#24 (Wl)
Baird, William 1840 wb-#136 (Wl)
Baird, William 1853 wb-#108 (Wl)
Baird, William D. 1843 rb-12-345 (Ru)
Baird, William D. 1859 rb-20-203 (Ru)
Baits, Anthony 1845 wb-1-267 (Li)
Baker, Alexander 1847 wb-#7 (Mc)
Baker, Andrew 1842 A-468-1 (Le)
Baker, Andrew J. 1840 wb-#7 (Mc)
Baker, Ann 1854 wb-e-213 (G)
Baker, Bartholomew 1853 wb-e-71 (G)
Baker, Charles 1796 wb-2-47 (D)
Baker, Christopher 1854 wb-11-472 (K)
Baker, Cynthia G. 1838 rb-10-194 (Ru)
Baker, Daniel 1860 wb-1-143 (Jo)
Baker, David 1834 eb-1-309 (C)
Baker, E. R. 1834 as-a-247 (Di)
Baker, Edmond 1853 6-2-122 (Le)
Baker, Elizabeth 1819 wb-#37 (Wl)
Baker, Elizabeth M. H. H. 1855? wb-#7 (Mc)
Baker, Esther 1861 wb-13-466 (K)
Baker, Francis B. 1844 wd-13-24 (D)
Baker, George 1826 eb-1-163 (C)
Baker, George 1847 wb-1B-18 (A)
Baker, George W. 1852 wb-#7 (Mc)
Baker, Hannah 1826 wb-1-2# (Ge)
Baker, Henry 1802 wb-1-106 (K)
Baker, Hiram 1842 wb-12-310* (D)
Baker, Hiram 1842 wb-12-320* (D)
Baker, Isaac 1818 wb-1-2# (Ge)
Baker, Isaac 1839 wb-1-19 (Me)
Baker, Isaac 1854 lr (Sn)
Baker, J. B. 1859 as-c-198 (Ms)
Baker, J. K. 1851 wb-15-206 (D)
Baker, Jacob 1853 wb-#24 (Mo)
Baker, James 1801 wb-1-58 (Je)
Baker, James 1829 wb-a-16 (Cr)
Baker, James F. 1848 wb-g-90 (Hu)
Baker, James W. 1847 lr (Sn)
Baker, Jane 1840 as-a-462 (Di)
Baker, John 1814 wb-2-58 (Je)
Baker, John 1819 wb-#35 (Wl)
Baker, John 1825 wb-8-456 (D)
Baker, John 1830 rb-f-38 (Mt)
Baker, John 1842 wb-12-275* (D)
Baker, John 1844 wb-#144 (Wl)
Baker, John 1846 wb-7-0 (Sm)
Baker, John 1848 wb-d-137 (G)

Baker, John 1860 wb-13-297 (K)
Baker, John E. 1845 rb-j-356 (Mt)
Baker, John sr. 1827 rb-e-140 (Mt)
Baker, Judy 1854 wb-16-405 (D)
Baker, L. A. (Mrs.) 1859 gs-1-222 (F)
Baker, Martin 1836 wb-d-187 (Hn)
Baker, Mary 1842 as-b-69 (Di)
Baker, Mary 1852 wb-5-133 (Je)
Baker, Mary 1854 wb-5-355 (Je)
Baker, Meshack 1823 wb-#45 (Wl)
Baker, Michael 1812 wb-a-55 (Ro)
Baker, Moses W. 1856 wb-12-278 (K)
Baker, Nancy (Mrs.) 1833 rb-f-477 (Mt)
Baker, Nancy 1831 rb-f-257 (Mt)
Baker, Nancy 1831 rb-f-303 (Mt)
Baker, Nathan 1824 rb-6-59 (Ru)
Baker, Nathaniel 1826 wb-#8 (Mc)
Baker, Nicholas 1792 wb-1-246 (D)
Baker, Richard T. 1859 wb-e-269 (Wh)
Baker, Richard T. 1859 wb-e-276 (Wh)
Baker, Richmond 1842 as-b-101 (Di)
Baker, Samuel 1842 wb-c-91 (G)
Baker, Samuel 1845 wb-e-41 (O)
Baker, Samuel A. 1846 wb-f-83 (O)
Baker, Sarah H. 1853 wb-#109 (Wl)
Baker, Thomas 1851 wb-11-110 (K)
Baker, Thomas 1854 ib-2-79 (Cl)
Baker, W. B. 1855 ib-h-398 (F)
Baker, William 1804 wb-1-142 (K)
Baker, William 1807 rb-2-30 (Ru)
Baker, William 1815 rb-b-258 (Mt)
Baker, William 1825 wb-#8 (Mc)
Baker, William 1833 wb-#103 (Wl)
Baker, Williamson 1823 wb-8-274 (D)
Baker, Wm. 1841 as-a-494 (Di)
Baker, Zach. 1803 wb-2-333 (D)
Baker, Zacheus 1813 wb-4-206 (D)
Balance, Sarah 1826 wb-4-110 (Wi)
Balch, Alfred 1853 wb-16-182 (D)
Balch, Amanda 1838 wb-1-41 (Sh)
Balch, Hezekiah 1809 wb-2-33# (Ge)
Balch, John 1847 wb-4-56 (Je)
Balch, John K. 1837 wb-1-34 (Sh)
Balden, Lenas 1809 wb-4-56 (D)
Balderidge, Andrew W. 1855 wb-b-361 (We)
Balderson, Joseph 1852 wb-b-188 (L)
Baldrey, John S. 1840 wb-10-451 (Rb)
Baldridge, Isabella 1850 wb-4-119 (Mu)
Baldridge, James L. 1861 wb-f-417 (G)
Baldridge, John 1819 wb-2-283 (Je)
Baldridge, John 1826 wb-#138 (Mu)

Baldridge, John L. 1834 wb-10-280 (D)
Baldridge, John L. 1834 wb-10-305 (D)
Baldridge, Margaret 1835 wb-x-251* (Mu)
Baldridge, Susan 1860 lr (Sn)
Baldridge, William R. 1851 rb-4-284 (Mu)
Baldry, William 1854 wb-15-447 (Rb)
Baldwin, Ezekiel 1834 wb-b-238 (Ro)
Baldwin, Francis J. 1846 wb-d-208 (Ro)
Baldwin, Hutor? 1801 wb-1-247 (Je)
Baldwin, Jesse 1838 wb-c-7 (Ro)
Baldwin, John 1853 wb-15-396 (Rb)
Baldwin, Moses 1835 wb-1-425 (Hr)
Baldwin, Nancy 1847 wb-e-38 (Ro)
Baldwin, Nicholas 1840 wb-1-53 (Hw)
Baldwin, Thomas K. 1856 wb-1-66 (Hw)
Baldwin, Thomas S. 1853 wb-e-390 (Ro)
Baldwin, William 1845 wb-1-60 (Hw)
Baldwin, William 1851 wb-2-97 (Me)
Balentine, Lemuel 1829 rb-7-176 (Ru)
Balentine, William R. 1837 wb-10-66 (Rb)
Bales, John 1830 wb-3-108 (Je)
Baley, Charles 1852 wb-h-Feb (O)
Baley, David 1830 wb-b-77 (Ro)
Baley, John R. 1847 wb-b-214 (We)
Baley, William 1835 rb-9-201 (Ru)
Ball, Abner 1818 wb-1-267 (Sn)
Ball, Elisha 1861 wb-13-450 (K)
Ball, James 1821 lr (Sn)
Ball, James 1829 wb-#177 (Mu)
Ball, Lewis 1832 wb-2-41# (Ge)
Ball, Moses 1831 wb-1-44 (Hw)
Ball, Spencer 1847 wb-5-36 (Ma)
Ball, Susanna 1847 wb-g-221 (Hn)
Ball, Tanda 1826? wb-#151 (Mu)
Ball, Thomas 1828 wb-#26 (Wa)
Ball, Wesley 1860 wb-1-74 (Hw)
Ball, William C. 1847 wb-#153 (Wl)
Ball, Wilson 1836 wb-x-389 (Mu)
Ballance, Abraham 1825 wb-4-31 (Wi)
Ballard, Alexander sr. 1839 wb-1-52 (Hw)
Ballard, Benjamin P. 1847 wb-5-46 (Ma)
Ballard, H. G. 1859 gs-1-261 (F)
Ballard, H. G. 1859 gs-1-317 (F)
Ballard, Isaac 1849 mr-2-345 (Be)
Ballard, James 1821 wb-1-0 (Sm)
Ballard, John 1861 rb-p-554 (Mt)
Ballard, John M. 1852 wb-h-78 (Hu)
Ballard, Thomas 1813 wb-1-340 (Wi)
Ballard, Washington 1860 wb-f-375 (Ro)
Ballard, Wiley 1854 rb-17-162 (Ru)
Ballard, William 1852 wb-e-363 (Ro)

Ballenger, James 1837 wb-#37 (Wa)
Ballentine, David 1838 wb-b-209 (G)
Ballentine, David 1850 rb-l-548 (Mt)
Ballew, Abraham J. 1851 wb-#8 (Mc)
Ballew, Hester 1819 wb-1-0 (Sm)
Ballew, William 1850 wb-#8 (Mc)
Ballew, William P. 1843 wb-12-460* (D)
Ballinger, Jacob & Mary 1850 wb-#9 (Mc)
Ballinger, James ca. 1800 wb-1-51 (Je)
Ballinger, Moses 1814 wb-2-76 (Je)
Ballinger, Moses 1828 wb-3-139 (Je)
Ballinger, Peter 1840 wb-3-0 (Sm)
Ballon, John B. 1859 rb-20-48 (Ru)
Ballow, Ann F. 1854 wb-11-160 (Wi)
Ballow, Battenby 1828 wb-9-180 (D)
Ballow, Eli P. 1852 mr-2-462 (Be)
Ballow, James 1853 wb-10-593 (Wi)
Ballow, Thomas 1813 wb-2-25 (Wi)
Ballowe, Sarah 1859 wb-1-294 (Be)
Balthrip, Edward 1851 wb-g-441 (Hu)
Balthrop, E. S. 1853 wb-h-107 (Hu)
Balthrop, Edward S. 1847 as-b-336 (Di)
Balthrop, Frank 1858 wb-a-70 (Ce)
Balthrop, Henry F. 1855 wb-16-580 (D)
Balthrop, Mary 1843 wb-a-158 (Di)
Balthrop, Susanah 1840 wb-e-357 (Hu)
Balthrop, Wiley 1858 as-c-540 (Di)
Balthrop, William 1839 as-a-435 (Di)
Baltimore, William 1859 ib-1-568 (Ca)
Baly, Margaret 1805 wb-1-2# (Ge)
Bame, Alexander 1859 39-2-315 (Dk)
Bancroft, John 1852 wb-#59 (Wa)
Bandy, R. C. 1861 wb-18-469 (D)
Bandy, Richard 1815 wb-#21 (Wl)
Bandy, Wilshire 1853 wb-15-481 (D)
Bane, Alexander 1856 39-2-170 (Dk)
Bane, Peter 1851 r39-1-187 (Dk)
Banes, Henry 1857 wb-1-145 (Be)
Banister, Marshall 1845 wb-13-152 (D)
Banks, Elijah 1860 wb-8-66 (Sm)
Banks, Elijah S. 1860 wb-f-396 (G)
Banks, James M. 1835 wb-6-70 (Wi)
Banks, James M. 1850 wb-9-425 (Wi)
Banks, Joseph P. 1833 wb-3-0 (Sm)
Banks, Karenhappoch 1821 wb-1-0 (Sm)
Banks, M. C. 1855 wb-15-713 (Rb)
Banks, Richard 1814 wb-1-0 (Sm)
Banks, Samuel M. 1861 wb-18-612 (D)
Banks, Simon 1840 wb-1-306 (W)
Banks, Solomon 1846 wb-1-224 (Fr)
Banks, Thomas 1827 wb-3-0 (Sm)

Banks, Thomas 1828 wb-3-0 (Sm)
Banks, William jr. 1823 wb-1-0 (Sm)
Bannan, Owen 1850 wb-2-80 (Sh)
Bannat, John 1801 wb-1-3# (Ge)
Banner, Henry 1829 wb-#34 (Wa)
Bannet?, Rachel 1820 wb-1-1# (Ge)
Banton, Lewis 1824 rb-6-30 (Ru)
Banzer, George 1851 wb-15-73 (D)
Barbee, A. C. 1854 wb-n-492 (Mt)
Barbee, Ann 1853 wb-#110 (Wl)
Barbee, Augustus 1846 rb-k-306 (Mt)
Barbee, George 1834 wb-8-458 (Rb)
Barbee, James C. 1837 wb-1-558 (Hr)
Barbee, James C. 1845 wb-c-213 (G)
Barbee, John 1830 wb-#88 (Wl)
Barbee, John 1855 wb-#116 (Wl)
Barbee, John 1856 rb-o-176 (Mt)
Barbee, Thomas 1834 wb-#107 (Wl)
Barbee, William 1833 wb-#103 (Wl)
Barbee, Young P. 1852 wb-g-429 (Hn)
Barber, John 1834 rb-9-144 (Ru)
Barber, John 1855 wb-n-641 (Mt)
Barber, Joseph 1851 wb-#177 (Wl)
Barber, Thaddius W. 1838 wb-b-3 (O)
Barckly, Felix 1809 wb-1-293 (K)
Barclift, Samuel 1848 wd-14-226 (D)
Barcroft, Jonathan 1849 wb-#45 (Wa)
Bard, William 1826 wb-#64 (Wl)
Bardine, Jefferson 1852 wb-#179 (Wl)
Bare, A. B. J. 1852 wb-5-50 (Je)
Bare, George 1861 wb-1-255 (Su)
Bare, Henry 1831 wb-3-168 (Je)
Barens, George 1857 39-2-183 (Dk)
Barfield, James 1843 wb-a-165 (L)
Barfield, Nancy 1830 wb-4-497 (Wi)
Barfield, Stephen 1818 wb-2-378 (Wi)
Barford, Thomas 1814 wb-a-219 (St)
Barger, John 1859 wb-1-7 (Su)
Barham, Elizabeth 1847 wb-14-33 (D)
Barham, Newsom 1840 wb-12-43* (D)
Barham, Sowel 1856 wb-a-267 (Cr)
Barham, Thomas 1860 wb-a-346 (Cr)
Barham, William P. 1850 wb-9-379 (Wi)
Barifoot, Thomas 1817 wb-3-234 (St)
Baringer, John 1821 wb-1-0 (Sm)
Barkely, F. L. 1860 wb-f-367 (G)
Barker, Alexander M. 1830 rb-f-21 (Mt)
Barker, Ambrose 1816 wb-A-144 (Li)
Barker, Edward S. 1840 rb-i-31 (Mt)
Barker, George 1841 wb-z-233 (Mu)
Barker, George W. 1860 wb-13-227 (Wi)

Barker, Gilbert 1852 lr (Sn)
Barker, Gustin H. 1850 mr-2-393 (Be)
Barker, Howell W. 1838 mr-1-255 (Be)
Barker, J. R. 1853 wb-15-387 (Rb)
Barker, James 1853 wb-e-68 (G)
Barker, John E. 1813 wb-1-0 (Sm)
Barker, Laban 1848 ib-1-1 (Wy)
Barker, Martha 1848 ib-1-1 (Wy)
Barker, Mary 1852 wb-5-71 (Je)
Barker, Milly 1847 wb-1-310 (Li)
Barker, Nancy 1850 rb-4-57 (Mu)
Barker, Samuel 1844 wb-d-259 (O)
Barker, Samuel 1858 wb-1-226 (Be)
Barker, Thomas 1827 wb-#72 (Wl)
Barker, William 1853 wb-e-118 (G)
Barker, William H. 1838 wb-11-404 (D)
Barkesdale, Nathaniel 1831 rb-8-329 (Ru)
Barkesdale, Thomas W. 1857 rb-o-487 (Mt)
Barket, A. (Dr.) 1816 wb-A-407 (Li)
Barkin, James R. 1853 wb-15-363 (Rb)
Barkley, Daniel 1854 wb-#53 (Wa)
Barkley, Henry P. 1854 wb-#54 (Wa)
Barkley, James 1837 wb-A-6 (Ca)
Barkley, John 1806 wb-3-72 (D)
Barkley, John 1831 wb-3-0 (Sm)
Barkley, John 1850 rb-15-416 (Ru)
Barkley, Sarah 1846 wb-#43 (Wa)
Barkley, Thomas 1847 wb-9-407 (K)
Barkly, Elizabeth 1852 wb-5-30 (Hr)
Barksdale, John R. 1854 wb-a-219 (Cr)
Barksdale, N. G. 1856 wb-#27 (Mo)
Barksdale, Nathan & Johnathan 1855
    wb-#9 (Mc)
Barksdale, Nathaniel 1831 rb-8-254 (Ru)
Barksdale, Randolph 1844 rb-12-590 (Ru)
Barksdale, Thomas 1830 wb-3-0 (Sm)
Barksdale, William 1834 rb-9-212 (Ru)
Barlow, Henson 1829 wb-3-41 (Je)
Barlow, Howard 1839 rb-10-307 (Ru)
Barmore, William 1850 wb-b-103 (L)
Barnard, Elisha 1836 wb-2-209 (Sn)
Barnard, Jacob 1835 wb-3-187 (Sn)
Barnard, Jesse W. 1842 wb-a-85 (F)
Barnard, John 1832 wb-1-129 (Gr)
Barnard, John 1843 5-2-305 (Cl)
Barnard, Robert 1843 5-2-335 (Cl)
Barnard, William J. 1845 wb-d-150 (Ro)
Barnes, Asa A. 1858 wb-h-265 (Hn)
Barnes, Barnett 1839 wb-d-314 (St)
Barnes, Benjamin 1859 wb-18-92 (D)
Barnes, Britton 1848 wb-14-60 (Rb)

Barnes, Charles 1845 mr-2-170 (Be)
Barnes, Davis W. 1859 wb-1-312 (Be)
Barnes, Dorcas 1858 wb-i-7 (St)
Barnes, George 1852 wb-10-419 (Wi)
Barnes, George 1859 wb-b-43 (Dk)
Barnes, George A. 1858 rb-19-403 (Ru)
Barnes, Henry 1814 wb-1-189 (Sn)
Barnes, Henry 1832 wb-10-34 (D)
Barnes, Henry 1848 wb-14-249 (D)
Barnes, Hilliard 1844 wb-f-206 (St)
Barnes, J. W. O. 1856 wb-b-18 (Ms)
Barnes, James 1812 wb-2-19 (Je)
Barnes, James 1820 wb-2-295 (Je)
Barnes, James 1825 wb-1-0 (Sm)
Barnes, James 1832 wb-c-183 (St)
Barnes, James 1841 wb-12-245* (D)
Barnes, James 1861 rb-20-756 (Ru)
Barnes, James W. 1829 wb-#182 (Mu)
Barnes, James sr. 1842 wb-e-226 (St)
Barnes, Jesse 1845 wb-13-243 (D)
Barnes, Jesse 1845 wb-13-295 (D)
Barnes, John 1824 wb-#89 (Mu)
Barnes, John 1851 wb-g-362 (St)
Barnes, John 1854 wb-3-228 (W)
Barnes, John M. 1852 wb-15-277 (D)
Barnes, Joseph 1790 wb-1-28 (Sn)
Barnes, Joseph 1811 wb-#12 (Wa)
Barnes, Joseph 1839 rb-h-291 (Mt)
Barnes, Lewis 1857 lr (Sn)
Barnes, Malachi 1846 lr (Sn)
Barnes, Mary 1844 rb-j-124 (Mt)
Barnes, Mary 1844 wb-f-153 (St)
Barnes, Mathew 1811 rb-a-497 (Mt)
Barnes, Nancy 1858 wb-12-603 (Wi)
Barnes, Nathaniel 1816 wb-2-220 (Wi)
Barnes, Pipkin 1841 wb-z-266 (Mu)
Barnes, Reps 1821 rb-c-463 (Mt)
Barnes, S. F. 1860 wb-b-93 (Ms)
Barnes, Samuel 1816 wb-A-145 (Li)
Barnes, Sarah 1861 39-2-400 (Dk)
Barnes, Seth 1836 wb-x-383 (Mu)
Barnes, Susanna 1815 Wb-2-175 (Wi)
Barnes, Thomas 1851 wb-c-452 (Wh)
Barnes, Thomas H. 1840 rb-h-406 (Mt)
Barnes, V. B. 1860 rb-20-597 (Ru)
Barnes, W. O. 1858 as-c-118 (Ms)
Barnes, Wilkerson 1854 wb-f-53 (Mu)
Barnes, William 1840 wb-e-14 (St)
Barnes, William 1850 wb-4-96 (Mu)
Barnes, William 1853 wb-f-27 (Mu)
Barnes, William 1853 wb-xx-246 (St)

Barnes, William C. 1848 A-468-80 (Le)
Barnes, Wright 1836 wb-2-210 (Sn)
Barnet, Jarret 1822 rb-5-251 (Ru)
Barnet, John 1852 wb-4-517 (Mu)
Barnet, Joseph 1855 39-1-350 (Dk)
Barnett, Ann 1840 wb-3-226 (Ma)
Barnett, Carter 1842 wb-d-20 (Ro)
Barnett, David 1842 wb-#9 (Mc)
Barnett, E. E. 1857 wb-12-478 (Wi)
Barnett, Elizabeth 1839 wb-d-353 (St)
Barnett, George W. 1839 mr-1-55 (Be)
Barnett, Henry 1825 wb-8-444 (D)
Barnett, Hugh 1855 wb-6-183 (Ma)
Barnett, James P. 1827 wb-4-202 (Wi)
Barnett, Jesse F. 1855 wb-h-120 (St)
Barnett, John 1832 wb-a-145 (R)
Barnett, John 1836 wb-#115 (Wl)
Barnett, John 1836 wb-1-225 (W)
Barnett, John 1837 wb-e-24 (Hu)
Barnett, John 1841 wb-3-321 (Ma)
Barnett, John 1844 wb-4-279 (Ma)
Barnett, John 1855 wb-1-66 (Hw)
Barnett, Michael 1852 wb-5-57 (Je)
Barnett, Robert 1818 wb-#28 (Wl)
Barnett, Robert 1821 wb-3-292 (K)
Barnett, S. M. 1858 wb-1-225 (Be)
Barnett, William 1827 wb-1-42 (Hr)
Barnett, William 1827 wb-a-41 (R)
Barnett, William 1839 wb-a-420 (R)
Barnett, William 1846 wb-#9 (Mc)
Barnett, William 1849 wb-7-0 (Sm)
Barnett, William R. 1849 A-468-126 (Le)
Barnhart, Conrad 1828 wb-2-27# (Ge)
Barnhart, Conrad 1856 149-1-49 (Ge)
Barnhill, John 1848 5-3-319 (Cl)
Barns, Benjamin 1809 wb-4-75 (D)
Barns, Benjamin 1846 wb-b-208 (We)
Barns, Elbert D. 1851 as-b-60 (Ms)
Barns, Elizabeth 1834 lr (Sn)
Barns, Jesse 1846 mr-2-217 (Be)
Barns, John 1832 wb-x-412 (Ma)
Barns, Jonathan 1829 wb-#173 (Mu)
Barns, Moses sr. 1801 wb-1-56 (Je)
Barns, Repp 1827 rb-e-79 (Mt)
Barns, Sarah 1848 wb-b-271 (Mu)
Barns, Valuntine 1860 rb-20-466 (Ru)
Barns, William C. 1853 6-2-115 (Le)
Barns, William C. 1854 6-2-120 (Le)
Barnsfield, James 1821 wb-#38 (Wl)
Barnwell, John 1847 5-3-206 (Cl)
Barnwell, John 1855 ib-2-219 (Cl)

Barr, Alexander 1845 wb-g-47 (Hn)
Barr, Caleb 1823 wb-1-55 (Fr)
Barr, Elizabeth 1838 wb-2-244 (Sn)
Barr, Francis M. 1852 mr-2-441 (Be)
Barr, Hugh 1831 lr (Sn)
Barr, Hugh W. 1845 wb-g-52 (Hn)
Barr, Isaac 1804 rb-2-7 (Ru)
Barr, James 1855 lr (Sn)
Barr, James N. 1840 wb-b-8 (We)
Barr, Patrick 1838 wb-2-228 (Sn)
Barr, Peter 1829 wb-1-40 (Hw)
Barr, Sarah Ann 1858 lr (Sn)
Barr, William 1842 lr (Sn)
Barr, William G. 1845 wb-#148 (Wl)
Barr, William M. 1837 wb-#118 (Wl)
Barrat, Joseph 1855 wb-e-361 (G)
Barratt, Randolph 1857 rb-19-26 (Ru)
Barratt, William 1849 wb-g-166 (St)
Barratt, Wyley 1860 wb-i-253 (St)
Barrens, Alexander 1821 wb-1-2# (Ge)
Barret, Elizabeth 1847 rb-k-613 (Mt)
Barret, Franklin 1860 wb-4-372 (La)
Barret, Joseph 1856 39-2-284 (Dk)
Barret, Sampson 1845 rb-j-449 (Mt)
Barrett, Hugh 1860 wb-1-69 (Hw)
Barrett, James 1855 39-2-48 (Dk)
Barrett, John O. 1858 gs-1-40 (F)
Barrett, Joseph H. 1855 ib-1-368 (Ca)
Barrett, Randol 1854 rb-17-185 (Ru)
Barrett, Thomas 1838 wb-1-50 (Hw)
Barrett, Ward sr. 1854 wb-A-90 (Ca)
Barrett, William N. 1860 wb-1-70 (Hw)
Barrett, Wilson 1860 wb-f-356 (G)
Barringer, Daniel 1814 wb-2-65 (Je)
Barron, John 1838 eb-1-387 (C)
Barron, Joseph 1793 wb-#5 (Wa)
Barron, Joseph 1816 wb-1-222 (Sn)
Barron, Walker 1829 wb-#28 (Wa)
Barrons, Elizabeth 1847 wb-14-33 (D)
Barrons, John A. 1839 wb-b-347 (Wh)
Barrott, Charlotte 1823 lr (Sn)
Barrow, Ann E. 1831 wb-9-556 (D)
Barrow, Matthew 1856 wb-17-53 (D)
Barrow, Micajah 1806 wb-3-78 (D)
Barrow, Ruffin 1800 lr (Sn)
Barrow, Willie 1825 wb-8-483 (D)
Barrow?, John 1859 wb-f-303 (G)
Barry, A. G. 1861 wb-17-261 (Rb)
Barry, David 1850 lr (Sn)
Barry, James L. 1856 rb-18-189 (Ru)
Barry, M. A. 1855 wb-#117 (Wl)

Barry, Redmond D. 1821 lr (Sn)
Barry, Richard 1839 wb-11-584 (D)
Barry, Seth 1838 wb-y-170 (Mu)
Barry, W. F. 1859 wb-3e-99 (Sh)
Barry, William 1820 wb-1-0 (Sm)
Bartee, William B. 1838 wb-d-206 (St)
Barthe (Boothe?), Charles S. 1826
    wb-1-151 (Ma)
Barthe, Charles 1828 wb-1-177 (Ma)
Bartholomew, Margaret 1851 wb-#180 (Wl)
Bartholomew, Thomas 1851 wb-#175 (Wl)
Bartin, Bradly 1856 rb-o-168 (Mt)
Bartless, Elizabeth C. 1851 wb-2-108 (Sh)
Bartlet, Isaac 1847 5-3-274 (Cl)
Bartlet, James 1845 5-3-58 (Cl)
Bartlet, John 1847 5-3-270 (Cl)
Bartlet, John 1850? ib-1-216 (Cl)
Bartlet, Nicholas 1814 wb-2-97 (K)
Bartlett, Elijah 1815 wb-a-37 (Wh)
Bartlett, Frances 1835 wb-#109 (Wl)
Bartlett, George 1848 wb-9-193 (Wi)
Bartlett, Isaac 1815 wb-#27 (Wl)
Bartlett, James 1815 wb-a-39 (Wh)
Bartlett, Nathan 1837 wb-b-270 (Wh)
Bartlett, Thomas 1825 wb-5-76 (Rb)
Bartlett, Winnay 1852 wb-d-85 (Wh)
Bartlett?, Joshua 1828 wb-a-335 (Wh)
Barton, Aquila 1837 wb-2-253 (Ma)
Barton, Benjamin 1808 wb-1-0 (Sm)
Barton, Benjamin 1825 wb-2-0 (Sm)
Barton, David 1815 rb-3-47 (Ru)
Barton, David 1833 rb-9-22 (Ru)
Barton, David 1837 wb-3-462 (Je)
Barton, Deubart? 1817 rb-4-27 (Ru)
Barton, Elizabeth 1860 rb-20-699 (Ru)
Barton, Howard 1841 rb-11-144 (Ru)
Barton, Isaac 1831 wb-3-165 (Je)
Barton, Isaac H. 1844 rb-12-431 (Ru)
Barton, J. B. 1859 wb-h-339 (Hn)
Barton, James 1823 wb-#47 (Wl)
Barton, Jesse 1839 rb-10-441 (Ru)
Barton, John 1855 wb-n-583 (Mt)
Barton, John 1859 iv-C-46 (C)
Barton, Joseph 1847 wb-g-230 (Hn)
Barton, Joseph sr. 1848 wb-g-240 (Hn)
Barton, Joshua 1858 wb-A-134 (Ca)
Barton, Keziah 1846 wb-5-418 (Gr)
Barton, Peter 1834 wb-1-117 (Hy)
Barton, Rutha 1859 rb-20-35 (Ru)
Barton, Samuel 1812 wb-#33 (Wl)
Barton, Samuel 1825 wb-#60 (Wl)

Barton, Samuel 1861 wb-3e-169 (Sh)
Barton, Stephen 1827 wb-#65 (Wl)
Barton, Swinfield 1854 rb-17-159 (Ru)
Barton, Swinfield 1857 rb-18-367 (Ru)
Barton, Tamzor 1839 wb-3-0 (Sm)
Barton, Thomas 1817 rb-4-47 (Ru)
Barton, Thomas 1833 rb-9-17 (Ru)
Barton, Thomas 1840 wb-b-306 (G)
Barton, William 1820 rb-c-364 (Mt)
Barton, William 1820 wb-a-136 (Wh)
Barton, William 1825 rb-d-465 (Mt)
Barton, William jr. 1818 rb-b-512 (Mt)
Basey, James T. 1840 wb-b-221 (Hd)
Basey, Sims M. 1844 wb-13-61 (D)
Basford, James 1826 rb-d-522 (Mt)
Basford, Thomas A. 1860 wb-a-160 (Ce)
Basham, Drury 1838 wb-1-177 (La)
Basham, Jonathan 1819 eb-1-88 (C)
Bashart, Jacob sr. 1854 wb-g-623 (Hn)
Bashaw, Benjamin 1837 wb-11-80 (D)
Bashers, James 1853 6-2-103 (Le)
Basinger, George 1847 wb-d-75 (G)
Basinger, John 1853 wb-e-37 (G)
Basinger, Michael 1846 wb-2-77# (Ge)
Baskerville, Richard 1838 wb-2-242 (Sn)
Basket, John 1838 wb-c-27 (Ro)
Basket, Richard 1815 wb-#14 (Wa)
Basket, William 1839 wb-2-65# (Ge)
Baskett, Jane 1840 wb-c-91 (Ro)
Baskett, Wilson 1850 wb-e-215 (Ro)
Baskin, Moses 1842 abl-1-244 (T)
Bason, Isaac 1841 wb-a-74 (F)
Bass, Amzi 1862 wb-#137 (Wl)
Bass, Cader 1859 wb-#128 (Wl)
Bass, Cato 1858 wb-#128 (Wl)
Bass, George M. 1832 wb-1-347 (Ma)
Bass, George W. 1845 wb-c-166 (Wh)
Bass, Heartuele 1826 rb-7-83 (Ru)
Bass, Henry S. 1838 wb-2-300 (Ma)
Bass, James 1853 as-b-113 (Ms)
Bass, James sr. 1826 rb-6-219 (Ru)
Bass, Jethro 1853 wb-xx-181 (St)
Bass, John B. 1852 wb-#180 (Wl)
Bass, Kinchen P. 1818 wb-2-374 (Wi)
Bass, Kintchen T. 1852 wb-a-413 (F)
Bass, Maclin 1837 wb-1-285 (Hy)
Bass, Nancy T. 1843 wb-c-126 (G)
Bass, Peter 1831 wb-9-465 (D)
Bass, Rachel 1852 r39-1-262 (Dk)
Bass, Sarah 1829 rb-8-125 (Ru)
Bass, Sion 1847 wb-#154 (Wl)

Bass, Solomon 1807 wb-#5 (Wl)
Bass, Susan 1825 wb-#60 (Wl)
Bass, Theophilus 1826 wb-#64 (Wl)
Bass, Uriah? 1829 rb-8-102 (Ru)
Bass, Wyatt 1842 wb-c-16* (G)
Bassett, Burwell W. 1842 wb-1-56 (Hw)
Bassett, Nathaniel 1832 wb-1-46 (Hw)
Bassford, John 1848 wb-14-74 (Rb)
Bassham, A. B. 1855 wb-3-283 (La)
Bassham, Richard 1854 wb-3-205 (La)
Bassham, Richard 1856 wb-3-377 (La)
Bassham, Samuel H. 1850 wb-2-142 (La)
Basswell, William 1840 wb-#9 (Mc)
Baster, John 1815 wb-#19 (Wl)
Basye, Isaac 1814 wb-4-302 (D)
Batchelor, John 1861 wb-e-161 (Hy)
Bateman, Enoch 1846 wb-8-401 (Wi)
Bateman, Evan 1842 wb-7-566 (Wi)
Bateman, Henry 1851 wb-15-9 (D)
Bateman, Henry W. 1856 wb-12-187 (Wi)
Bateman, Isaac 1833 wb-5-269 (Wi)
Bateman, Isaac Newton 1848 wb-14-276 (D)
Bateman, Jonathan 1818 wb-2-377 (Wi)
Bateman, Parker 1815 Wb-2-167 (Wi)
Bateman, William 1843 wb-8-1 (Wi)
Bates, Alexander 1840 wb-1-300 (W)
Bates, Allen 1842 wb-1-430 (W)
Bates, Benjamin 1826 wb-2-0 (Sm)
Bates, Harrison 1852 wb-xx-75 (St)
Bates, Isaac 1855 wb-7-0 (Sm)
Bates, John 1842 wb-#142 (Wl)
Bates, Mary Ann 1846 wb-1-140 (Sh)
Bates, Matthew 1813 wb-1-0 (Sm)
Bates, Nathan 1834 wb-1-70 (Gr)
Bates, William 1844 wb-#9 (Mc)
Bates, William 1848 ib-1-1 (Ca)
Batey, Christopher T. 1849 rb-15-49 (Ru)
Batey, Easter 1857 39-2-183 (Dk)
Batey, James 1835 rb-9-213 (Ru)
Batey, James 1855 39-2-86 (Dk)
Batey, James 1856 rb-18-156 (Ru)
Batey, James M. 1856 rb-18-163 (Ru)
Batey, W. D. 1858 rb-19-382 (Ru)
Batey, William 1835 rb-9-239 (Ru)
Batey, William D. 1858 rb-19-436 (Ru)
Batey, William F. 1850 rb-15-492 (Ru)
Batin, Money 1835 rb-9-213 (Ru)
Batson, Alexander 1857 rb-o-368 (Mt)
Batson, Elizabeth 1859 rb-p-152 (Mt)
Batson, Francis 1831 rb-f-153 (Mt)
Batson, Richard 1856 wb-h-489 (Hu)

Batson, Richard 1856 wb-h-490 (Hu)
Batson, Thomas 1831 rb-f-201 (Mt)
Batson, Thos. H. 1861 rb-p-650 (Mt)
Batt, Henry? Bruce? 1840 wb-a-55 (F)
Batte, Gardner 1834 lr (Gi)
Batte, Viola 1840 rb-10-479 (Ru)
Batte, William 1845 wb-a-269 (F)
Batten, Nancy 1838 rb-10-141 (Ru)
Battle, Isaac 1816 wb-7-53 (D)
Battle, Mary 1857 ib-1-471 (Wy)
Battle, William M. 1851 wb-14-659 (D)
Batton, Henry 1839 rb-10-249 (Ru)
Batton, John B. 1859 rb-19-568 (Ru)
Batton, Ransom 1853 as-b-116 (Ms)
Batts, Benjamin 1842 wb-11-341 (Rb)
Batts, Benjamin B. 1842 wb-11-376 (Rb)
Batts, Jeremiah 1854 wb-15-599 (Rb)
Batts, Olive 1844 wb-12-118 (Rb)
Batts, Olive 1844 wb-12-158 (Rb)
Baty, Ann 1854 rb-17-210 (Ru)
Baty, D. W. 1859 rb-20-4 (Ru)
Baty, Rowlen 1817 rb-4-70 (Ru)
Baty, Thos. H. 1857 wb-b-37 (Ms)
Bauchem, Henderson 1856 wb-g-725 (Hn)
Baucom, Bennett 1832 wb-a-35 (Cr)
Baugass, John 1847 wb-b-153 (Mu)
Baugh, Daniel 1857 wb-12-407 (Wi)
Baugh, James 1843 wb-8-68 (Wi)
Baugh, Joel 1856 ib-h-539 (F)
Baugh, Martin 1842 lr (Gi)
Baugh, Philip W. 1860 wb-13-337 (Wi)
Baugh, William 1800 wb-2-165 (D)
Baugh, William 1825 wb-2-29 (Ma)
Baugh, Wyatt W. 1860 wb-13-172 (Wi)
Baugus, Briant 1835 wb-1-24 (Sh)
Bauhman, Jno. C. 1809 wb-4-36 (D)
Baulch, James H. 1855 wb-3-251 (La)
Baulch, James W. 1852 wb-3-64 (La)
Bauton, Lewis 1826 rb-6-267 (Ru)
Bawcum, Henderson 1854 wb-g-558 (Hn)
Baxter, David 1828 rb-7-195 (Ru)
Baxter, Hail 1857 149-1-72 (Ge)
Baxter, James 1844 148-1-94 (Ge)
Baxter, James P. 1859 wb-2-288 (Li)
Baxter, Jeremiah 1833 wb-x-80 (Mu)
Baxter, John 1838 wb-#123 (Wl)
Baxter, John 1838 wb-b-66 (O)
Baxter, Katharine 1842 wb-2-58# (Ge)
Baxter, Katherine 1844 wb-a-96 (Ms)
Baxter, Margaret E. 1856 wb-6-223 (Ma)
Baxter, Mary 1840 wb-b-16 (We)

Baxter, Robert 1850 rb-l-635 (Mt)
Baxter, Robert 1851 wb-m-403 (Mt)
Baxter, Robert sr. 1850 wb-m-34 (Mt)
Baxter, Robt. 1860 wb-17-124 (Rb)
Baxter, Ruth 1831 wb-2-40# (Ge)
Baxter, Samuel 1838 wb-b-63 (O)
Baxter, Theodore 1861 rb-p-646 (Mt)
Baxter, William 1844 wb-3-458 (Hy)
Bay, John 1828 wb-#86 (Wl)
Bayler, Joel 1838 wb-1-45 (Hw)
Bayles, John 1857 wb-2-95# (Ge)
Bayles, Reuben 1827 wb-#25 (Wa)
Bayles, Samuel 1825 wb-#21 (Wa)
Bayless, Burrell 1827 rb-e-174 (Mt)
Bayless, Burrell 1828 rb-e-201 (Mt)
Bayless, Isaac B. 1850 wb-10-484 (K)
Bayless, John 1810 rb-a-381 (Mt)
Bayless, John 1824 wb-4-26 (K)
Bayless, John 1836 rb-g-416 (Mt)
Bayless, John 1858 wb-13-58 (K)
Bayless, Joseph P. 1840 rb-h-390 (Mt)
Bayless, Robert 1840 rb-h-389 (Mt)
Bayless, Sarah 1853 wb-#10 (Mo)
Bayley, Henry 1847 wb-a-263 (Ms)
Bayley, Walter 1790 wb-#3 (Wa)
Baylis, Joel 1857 wb-h-433 (St)
Baylis, John 1823 wb-#19 (Wa)
Bayliss, Arabella T. 1837 wb-d-110 (St)
Bayliss, Brittain 1835 wb-c-393 (St)
Bayliss, Cullen 1836 wb-c-494 (St)
Bayliss, Patience 1859 rb-p-183 (Mt)
Bayliss, Sally 1835 wb-c-466 (St)
Bayliss, Thomas 1846 wb-f-391 (St)
Bayliss, William 1828 wb-b-240 (St)
Bayliss, Willie 1838 wb-1-164 (We)
Bayne, Catharine 1825 lr (Sn)
Bays, Andrew 1833 wb-#104 (Wl)
Bayse, L. M. 1840 wb-12-138* (D)
Baysinger, Levi 1860 wb-k-368 (O)
Baysinger, Michael 1860 wb-#9 (Mc)
Beach, Elijah 1828 wb-1A-13 (A)
Beach, James 1851 wb-15-62 (D)
Beacham, Isaac 1827 wb-b-8 (Hn)
Beachboard, Levi 1852 wb-1-247 (Su)
Beakley, John 1845 A-468-16 (Le)
Beakley, William 1798 wb-1-48 (Sn)
Beal, Livingston C. 1851 rb-4-271 (Mu)
Beale, James W. 1849 wb-9-161 (Wi)
Beale, Richard 1859 wb-13-163 (Wi)
Beall, Philip 1814 wb-2-129 (K)
Beall, Samuel J. 1839 wb-6-496 (K)

Beals, Jacob 1834 wb-2-43# (Ge)
Beals, Jacob 1852 148-1-407 (Ge)
Beals, John 1851 148-1-349 (Ge)
Beals, Rachel 1841 wb-2-56# (Ge)
Beals, Rebecca 1849 148-1-292 (Ge)
Beals, Samuel 1848 wb-2-68# (Ge)
Beals, Solomon 1849 148-1-293 (Ge)
Beals, Solomon 1852 wb-2-75# (Ge)
Beals, Solomon sr. 1833 wb-2-42# (Ge)
Beals, William 1836 wb-2-47# (Ge)
Bean, Absa. 1835 wb-b-82 (G)
Bean, Benjamin 1846 wb-d-14 (G)
Bean, Conner 1859 wb-1-383 (Fr)
Bean, Daniel M. 1818 wb-7-270 (D)
Bean, Jacob 1856 wb-12-276 (K)
Bean, Jesse 1852 wb-1-15 (R)
Bean, Mordecai 1853 wb-1-63 (Hw)
Bean, William 1782 wb-#1 (Wa)
Beanland, Edward 1815 wb-#13 (Mu)
Beanland, Edward W. 1829 wb-#185 (Mu)
Beard, Adam 1825 wb-a-90 (Hn)
Beard, Bird N. 1858 wb-13-9 (Wi)
Beard, David 1815 wb-1-205 (Sn)
Beard, David 1855 wb-#116 (Wl)
Beard, Elijah 1848 as-a-153 (Ms)
Beard, James 1847 wb-d-320 (Hd)
Beard, John 1826 wb-4-113 (Wi)
Beard, John 1850 wb-1-303 (Su)
Beard, John C. 1822 wb-A-288 (Li)
Beard, Lewis 1836 wb-a-77 (T)
Beard, Lewis 1841 wb-2-243 (Hy)
Beard, Mary 1853 wb-11-82 (Wi)
Beard, Robert 1831 wb-#32 (Wa)
Beard, William 1830 wb-#87 (Wl)
Bearden, Ann 1856 wb-12-266 (K)
Bearden, H. 1857 wb-a-34 (Ce)
Bearden, Haywood 1858 wb-a-42 (Ce)
Bearden, M. D. 1854 wb-12-25 (K)
Bearden, Richard 1845 wb-9-112 (K)
Bearden, Richard 1846 wb-9-162 (K)
Beardin, John 1837 wb-2-221 (Sn)
Beardin, John 1850 wb-2-84 (Sh)
Beasley, Archer 1839 wb-1-383 (Li)
Beasley, Burton 1817 lr (Gi)
Beasley, Charles 1816 wb-7-17 (D)
Beasley, E. E. (Mrs) 1854 rb-16-783 (Ru)
Beasley, Eliza E. 1853 rb-16-648 (Ru)
Beasley, Elizabeth G. 1840 wb-e-127 (Hn)
Beasley, Emsley 1838 wb-10-154 (Rb)
Beasley, Emsley 1839 wb-10-269 (Rb)
Beasley, Henry 1858 wb-7-0 (Sm)

Beasley, Isham 1855 wb-7-0 (Sm)
Beasley, James 1843 rb-i-506 (Mt)
Beasley, John 1848 wb-7-0 (Sm)
Beasley, John J. 1860 wb-#9 (Mc)
Beasley, John P. 1848 wb-9-202 (Wi)
Beasley, John W. 1850 rb-15-561 (Ru)
Beasley, Philip 1819 wb-3-102 (Wi)
Beasley, Robert E. 1814 Wb-2-76 (Wi)
Beasley, Stephen 1829 lr (Sn)
Beasley, Thomas 1828 rb-7-313 (Ru)
Beasley, William 1834 wb-x-292 (Mu)
Beasley, William 1861 wb-i-291 (St)
Beasley, William C. 1857 wb-h-162 (Hn)
Beasley, William D. 1837 wb-y-18 (Mu)
Beasley, Zachariah 1840 wb-7-249 (Wi)
Beasly, Eliza E. 1856 rb-18-22 (Ru)
Beasly, Esau 1845 wb-a2-245 (Mu)
Beasly, Merrel 1854 wb-a-451 (F)
Beasly, Thomas 1838 rb-10-112 (Ru)
Beaton, —— 1814 wb-a-246 (St)
Beaton, Christopher 1845 mr-2-141 (Be)
Beatty, Henry 1846 wb-8-513 (Wi)
Beatty, J. 1859 6-2-143 (Le)
Beaty, Arthur 1811 wb-1-216 (Bo)
Beaty, David 1817 wb-7-142 (D)
Beaty, Esther 1857 39-2-188 (Dk)
Beaty, John 1849 wb-1-362 (Li)
Beaty, John 1852 wb-f-14 (Mu)
Beaty, Robert 1822 wb-1-5 (Bo)
Beaty, Rowlin 1826 rb-6-222 (Ru)
Beaty, Thomas H. 1859 as-c-210 (Ms)
Beaty, William 1815 wb-4-365 (D)
Beaty, Wm. D. 1860 rb-20-640 (Ru)
Beaty, Wm. F. 1851 rb-16-69 (Ru)
Beauchamp, John W. 1846 wb-#150 (Wl)
Beaumont, F. S. 1861 rb-p-646 (Mt)
Beaven, E. L. 1852 wb-m-501 (Mt)
Beaver, Michael 1847 wb-a-318 (F)
Beaver, William sr. 1816 wb-A-129 (Li)
Beavers, David C. 1849 rb-15-18 (Ru)
Beavers, Elizabeth 1816 wb-A-141 (Li)
Beavers, Spencer 1849 lr (Gi)
Beazley, John 1845 wb-13-181 (D)
Beazley, Sally 1847 wb-14-23 (D)
Beck, Ebenezer 1841 as-a-56 (Ms)
Beck, Edward 1850 wb-m-16 (Mt)
Beck, Henry 1850 wb-1-377 (Li)
Beck, Jesse 1858 wb-h-264 (Hn)
Beck, John 1808 wb-3-206 (D)
Beck, John 1814 wb-4-288 (D)
Beck, John E. 1818 wb-7-271 (D)

Beck, Patsy 1835 rb-g-99 (Mt)
Beck, Wm. J. 1855 as-c-388 (Di)
Beckley, Henry S. 1851 wb-b-291 (We)
Becknal, Micajah 1806 as-1-150 (Ge)
Beckner, Jos. D. 1858 wb-1-71 (Hw)
Beckton, George W. 1853 rb-16-467 (Ru)
Beckum, Phillis 1826 wb-3-0 (Sm)
Beckwith, James 1860 39-2-339 (Dk)
Becton, John H. 1853 wb-2-143 (Sh)
Becton, John Slade 1803 wb-2-307 (D)
Becum, Simon 1827 wb-#160 (Mu)
Becum, Stephen 1837 wb-y-70 (Mu)
Becun, David 1839 wb-y-639 (Mu)
Beddo, Abbert W. 1854 wb-1-69 (R)
Bedford, Benjamin 1824? as-A-86 (Di)
Bedford, John H. 1850 wb-7-0 (Sm)
Bedford, Mary 1852 wb-h-Apr (O)
Bedford, Mary E. 1854 wb-i-152 (O)
Bedford, Mary M. 1849 wb-g-126 (O)
Bedford, Robert 1813 rb-3-111 (Ru)
Bedford, Robert 1860 rb-20-692 (Ru)
Bedford, Seth 1844 wb-d-278 (O)
Bedford, Thomas 1805 rb-1-23 (Ru)
Bedsaul, George 1856 wb-f-76 (Ro)
Bedwell, A. 1847 wb-g-225 (Hn)
Bedwell, Elisha 1819 wb-a-131 (Wh)
Beech, Elizabeth B. 1841 wb-7-475 (Wi)
Beech, James B. 1846 wb-8-396 (Wi)
Beech, John B. 1830 wb-4-542 (Wi)
Beech, Lodowick B. 1841 wb-7-466 (Wi)
Beech, Lodwick B. 1850 wb-9-353 (Wi)
Beech, Peter S. 1856 wb-12-77 (Wi)
Beech, Sarah 1859 wb-13-84 (Wi)
Beeil?, John 1840 wb-1-55 (Hw)
Beelar, Ann 1842 wb-5-179 (Gr)
Beelar, David 1837 wb-1-230 (Gr)
Beelar, William 1840 wb-5-67 (Gr)
Beeler, Daniel 1843 wb-1-245 (La)
Beeler, Daniel 1855 wb-3-257 (La)
Beeler, John 1842 wb-#10 (Mc)
Beeler, John 1861 wb-4-29 (La)
Beeler, John H. 1852 wb-2-263 (La)
Beeler, Joseph 1846 wb-2-104 (Gr)
Beeler, Joseph 1846 wb-5-433 (Gr)
Beeler, Peter 1836 5-2-58 (Cl)
Beeler, Polly 1847 wb-2-125 (Gr)
Beeler, Provy 1857 wb-1-144 (Be)
Beeler, Provy 1857 wb-1-145 (Be)
Beeler, Woolery 1855 wb-3-203 (Gr)
Beesley, John 1819 rb-4-185 (Ru)
Beesley, Major P. 1847 rb-14-80 (Ru)

Beesley, Thomas 1828 rb-7-153 (Ru)
Beesley, William 1846 rb-13-711 (Ru)
Beeton, Asa 1809 wb-4-66 (D)
Beeton, Dorcas 1809 wb-4-66 (D)
Beeton, G. W. 1855 rb-17-428 (Ru)
Beeton, George 1809 wb-4-66 (D)
Beets, Daniel 1849 wb-1B-117 (A)
Beets, John 1849? wb-1B-161 (A)
Beevers, Abraham 1845 rb-13-411 (Ru)
Belcher, Littleberry 1835 wb-#111 (Wl)
Belden, Charles 1846 wb-9-172 (K)
Belew, Samuel 1842 wb-c-19 (G)
Belew, Thomas 1816 wb-2-206 (Wi)
Bell, A. L. 1837 wb-#120 (Wl)
Bell, Amzi 1837 wb-#120 (Wl)
Bell, Andrew 1833 wb-1-16 (Sh)
Bell, B. L. 1860 wb-13-273 (K)
Bell, Bayard T. (Dr.) 1852 wb-15-170 (Rb)
Bell, Bayard T. 1835 rb-g-231 (Mt)
Bell, Bayard T. 1840 rb-h-441 (Mt)
Bell, Benjamin 1827 wb-b-209 (St)
Bell, Benjamin 1848 wb-14-238 (D)
Bell, Blackstone L. 1860 wb-13-307 (K)
Bell, Celea 1846 wb-#159 (Wl)
Bell, Chalres 1845 lr (Sn)
Bell, Clement L. 1834 wb-10-383 (D)
Bell, Daniel 1816 wb-7-10 (D)
Bell, David 1805 rb-a-258 (Mt)
Bell, David 1837 wb-6-164 (K)
Bell, Dorson 1857 wb-h-121 (Hn)
Bell, Elijah 1857 wb-h-647 (Hu)
Bell, Elisha 1834 wb-#106 (Wl)
Bell, Evaline 1861 wb-18-582 (D)
Bell, Ewing 1849 wb-7-0 (Sm)
Bell, George 1818 wb-#29 (Wl)
Bell, George 1822 wb-8-127 (D)
Bell, George 1830 wb-9-364 (D)
Bell, George 1839 wb-1-12 (Bo)
Bell, George 1843 mr-2-40 (Be)
Bell, George 1844 wb-7-0 (Sm)
Bell, Henry 1816 wb-7-99 (D)
Bell, Hezekiah 1849 wb-#168 (Wl)
Bell, Hugh F. 1832 wb-10-12 (D)
Bell, Hugh F. 1850 wb-14-342 (Rb)
Bell, Hugh R. 1849 wb-7-0 (Sm)
Bell, J. 1852 wb-f-4? (Mu)
Bell, J. L. 1860 wb-a-151 (Ce)
Bell, J. William 1836 wb-1-28 (Sh)
Bell, Jacob 1859 wb-a-136 (Ce)
Bell, Jacob 1861 wb-a-206 (Ce)
Bell, Jain 1823 wb-8-251 (D)

Bell, James 1823 wb-#50 (Wl)
Bell, James 1826 wb-#183 (Mu)
Bell, James 1828 rb-7-93 (Ru)
Bell, James 1835 wb-9-56 (Rb)
Bell, James 1837 wb-6-93 (K)
Bell, James 1841 wb-#151 (Wl)
Bell, James 1845 A-468-30 (Le)
Bell, James 1848 wb-d-120 (G)
Bell, James 1851 rb-15-618 (Ru)
Bell, James 1851 wb-14-473 (Rb)
Bell, James 1854 wb-g-559 (Hn)
Bell, James 1856 wb-#57 (Wa)
Bell, James C. 1814 wb-2-36# (Ge)
Bell, James G. 1857 wb-f-71 (G)
Bell, James Smith 1861 wb-13-481 (K)
Bell, James W. 1858 rb-19-435 (Ru)
Bell, Jane 1861 lr (Gi)
Bell, Jessee E. 1844 wb-c-159 (G)
Bell, John 1797 wb-2-73 (D)
Bell, John 1816 wb-1-2# (Ge)
Bell, John 1821 wb-3-267 (Rb)
Bell, John 1834 wb-#105 (Wl)
Bell, John 1836 wb-2-168 (Ma)
Bell, John 1838 wb-d-258 (St)
Bell, John 1845 wb-g-84 (Hn)
Bell, John 1846 wb-a-143 (Cr)
Bell, John 1849 wb-g-252 (O)
Bell, John 1852 wb-4-582 (Mu)
Bell, John 1854 rb-17-187 (Ru)
Bell, John 1855 wb-16-465 (D)
Bell, John G. 1849 wb-#164 (Wl)
Bell, John P. 1846 as-b-339 (Di)
Bell, Joseph 1837 wb-6-142 (K)
Bell, Joseph 1853 rb-16-664 (Ru)
Bell, Joseph C. 1850 rb-15-438 (Ru)
Bell, Joseph M. 1858 wb-17-441 (D)
Bell, Joseph W. 1860 rb-20-643 (Ru)
Bell, L. M. 1861 wb-18-466 (D)
Bell, Lemuel 1825 wb-b-24 (St)
Bell, Lucy 1837 wb-9-397 (Rb)
Bell, Martha 1854 wb-g-558 (Hn)
Bell, Mary 1829 wb-#81 (Wl)
Bell, Mary 1859 wb-#17 (Mo)
Bell, Mary Ann 1847 wb-a-178 (Di)
Bell, Middleton 1814 wb-#17 (Wl)
Bell, Montgomery 1855 wb-16-589 (D)
Bell, Nathaniel 1848 wb-9-174 (Wi)
Bell, R. W. 1855 wb-16-51 (Rb)
Bell, Rebecah 1816 wb-4-476 (D)
Bell, Rebecca 1816 wb-7-79 (D)
Bell, Rebecca K. 1843 wb-4-99 (Ma)

Bell, Regard? T. 1855 wb-n-574 (Mt)
Bell, Reuben H. 1830 wb-1-4 (Sh)
Bell, Robert 1816 wb-4-447 (D)
Bell, Robert 1816 wb-7-77 (D)
Bell, Robert 1835 wb-a-272 (R)
Bell, Robert D. 1849 wb-#169 (Wl)
Bell, Rosanna 1860 wb-a-369 (Cr)
Bell, Rowland 1848 wb-#166 (Wl)
Bell, Samuel 1821 wb-7-492 (D)
Bell, Samuel 1824 wb-3-339 (St)
Bell, Samuel 1837 wb-11-82 (D)
Bell, Samuel 1840 wb-3-546 (Je)
Bell, Samuel 1843 wb-8-116 (K)
Bell, Samuel Claibean 1852 wb-a-275 (Ms)
Bell, Samuel K. 1834 wb-#104 (Wl)
Bell, Sarah 1852 lr (Sn)
Bell, Sarah E. 1860 rb-20-637 (Ru)
Bell, Shade 1846 as-b-341 (Di)
Bell, Shadrick 1846 wb-a-169 (Di)
Bell, Sterling 1824? wb-#165 (Mu)
Bell, Tabitha 1859 wb-17-624 (D)
Bell, Thomas 1792 wb-#4 (Wa)
Bell, Thomas 1839 wb-12-34* (D)
Bell, Thomas 1848 wb-#46 (Wa)
Bell, Thomas D. 1850 wb-a-208 (Di)
Bell, W. R. 1858 wb-16-566 (Rb)
Bell, Walker 1858 wb-e-100 (Hy)
Bell, Walter 1842 as-b-82 (Di)
Bell, William 1813 wb-2-67 (K)
Bell, William 1815 wb-2-151 (K)
Bell, William 1828 wb-#186 (Mu)
Bell, William 1829 wb-#187 (Mu)
Bell, William 1836 wb-2-131 (Ma)
Bell, William 1836 wb-a-8 (F)
Bell, William 1843 wb-f-166 (Hn)
Bell, William 1849 lr (Sn)
Bell, William 1853 wb-a-210 (Cr)
Bell, William R. 1816 wb-2-218 (Wi)
Bell, William R. 1828 wb-9-189 (D)
Bell, William jr. 1803 wb-1-8 (Wi)
Bell, Zachariah P. 1824 rb-6-73 (Ru)
Bellah, Moses 1828 rb-7-117 (Ru)
Bellah, Moses 1828 rb-7-295 (Ru)
Bellah, Samuel 1832 rb-8-497 (Ru)
Bellamy, John 1860 rb-p-493 (Mt)
Bellar, Walter 1812 wb-1-0 (Sm)
Bellows, M. R. 1858 wb-#10 (Mc)
Belote, Brown 1860 gs-1-596 (F)
Belote, Henry 1827 lr (Sn)
Belote, Jeremiah 1822 lr (Sn)
Belote, John 1826 lr (Sn)

Belote, Martha J. 1857 lr (Sn)
Belotte, George W. 1854 wb-5-45 (Hr)
Belshaw, Richard 1829 wb-3-0 (Sm)
Belt, Benjamin 1837 rb-10-539 (Ru)
Benbrook, John 1830 wb-4-541 (Wi)
Bender, Daniel 1833 lr (Sn)
Benderman, John A. 1844 wb-a2-119 (Mu)
Benner, Ed R. 1859 wb-#128 (Wl)
Bennet, Joseph 1816 wb-#22 (Wl)
Bennet, Nancy 1831 wb-c-92 (St)
Bennet, William 1828 wb-b-287 (St)
Bennett, Benjamin 1859 39-2-322 (Dk)
Bennett, Catharine 1831 lr (Sn)
Bennett, Elizabeth 1845 wb-9-109 (K)
Bennett, Fletcher 1860 wb-k-361 (O)
Bennett, George 1823 wb-3-601 (Wi)
Bennett, George W. 1861 wb-13-418 (Wi)
Bennett, Henry 1824 wb-8-389 (D)
Bennett, Henry 1842 wb-a-35 (Dk)
Bennett, John 1808 ib-1-225 (Ge)
Bennett, John 1852 mr-2-477 (Be)
Bennett, John 1854 wb-#113 (Wl)
Bennett, John C. 1842 wb-#137 (Wl)
Bennett, Joseph W. 1859 wb-13-118 (Wi)
Bennett, Mason 1816 rb-b-330 (Mt)
Bennett, Nicholas 1839 wb-b-347 (Wh)
Bennett, Peter 1822 wb-3-378 (K)
Bennett, Polly 1846 wb-1-125 (Sh)
Bennett, V. M. 1859 wb-k-137 (O)
Bennett, Walter 1814 Wb-2-79 (Wi)
Bennett, William 1823 lr (Sn)
Bennett, William 1859 39-2-311 (Dk)
Bennett, William F. 1829 wb-#81 (Wl)
Bennett, William J. 1842 wb-c-67 (Wh)
Bennett, William L. 1841 wb-7-485 (Wi)
Benoit, Earnest 1832 wb-9-601 (D)
Benson, Early 1861 lr (Gi)
Benson, Eli 1842 wb-a-93 (Ms)
Benson, Isaac C. 1854 wb-16-327 (D)
Benson, John 1815 Wb-2-130 (Wi)
Benson, Robert 1845 wb-12-422 (Rb)
Benson, W. C. 1846 wb-13-61 (Rb)
Benson, William 1831 wb-7-492 (Rb)
Benson, William B. 1837 rb-10-59 (Ru)
Benson, Wm. W. 1835 rb-9-212 (Ru)
Benthal, Daniel 1816 wb-#24 (Wl)
Benthal, Daniel 1822 lr (Sn)
Benthal, Daniel 1855 wb-6-132 (Ma)
Benthal, James 1836 wb-#115 (Wl)
Benthall, Daniel 1797 wb-1-39 (Sn)
Benthall, Daniel 1816 wb-#23 (Wl)

Benthall, David 1831 wb-#90 (Wl)
Benthall, Enos 1816 lr (Sn)
Benthel, William 1850 wb-2-111 (La)
Bentley, James 1829 lr (Sn)
Bentley, Jeremiah 1857 lr (Sn)
Bentley, John A. 1857 wb-c-130 (L)
Bentley, Lee M. 1856 wb-4-440 (La)
Bentley, M. A. (Dr.) 1854 wb-1-6 (Gu)
Bentley, Melton L. 1860 wb-4-386 (La)
Bentley, William 1857 lr (Sn)
Bently, Baalam H. 1842 as-a-63 (Ms)
Bently, Jeremiah 1841 wb-1-219 (La)
Benton, Benjamin 1823 wb-2-0 (Sm)
Benton, Epaphroditus 1829 wb-7-43 (Rb)
Benton, Jessee 1812 Wb-2-91 (Wi)
Benton, John 1814 Wb-2-107 (Wi)
Benton, Lavina 1860 wb-17-264 (Rb)
Benton, Margaret 1860 wb-17-264 (Rb)
Benton, Mary 1844 wb-12-180 (Rb)
Benton, Mary 1860 wb-17-59 (Rb)
Benton, Nancy 1807 wb-1-28 (Wi)
Benton, Sherwood 1859 wb-16-756 (Rb)
Benton, Tide? L. 1857 wb-2-350 (Me)
Berge, Nathaniel 1844 rb-13-15 (Ru)
Berger, Jane 1850 ib-1-117 (Ca)
Berkett, David M. 1856 wb-1-79 (Be)
Berkley, Rufus K. 1855 wb-16-486 (D)
Berkley, William E. 1854 wb-g-627 (Hn)
Bernard, William S. 1837 wb-10-137 (Rb)
Berry, Adam H. 1835 wb-10-527 (D)
Berry, Alfred H. 1853 wb-2-49 (Li)
Berry, Augustine 1842 wb-f-88 (Hn)
Berry, Daniel 1852 wb-15-362 (D)
Berry, Edwin 1828 rb-e-272 (Mt)
Berry, Enoch 1848 wb-A-63 (Ca)
Berry, George 1829 wb-1-6 (Bo)
Berry, Harris 1846 wb-g-160 (Hn)
Berry, Isaac 1837 wb-9-375 (Rb)
Berry, James 1814 Wb-2-105 (Wi)
Berry, James 1814 rb-3-107 (Ru)
Berry, James 1826 rb-6-193 (Ru)
Berry, James 1854 rb-17-116 (Ru)
Berry, James L. 1857 rb-18-407 (Ru)
Berry, John 1841 wb-#136 (Wl)
Berry, John 1856 wb-a-9 (Ce)
Berry, Keziah 1802 wb-2-258 (D)
Berry, Leanard L. T. 1838 wb-6-470 (Wi)
Berry, Lewis 1824? as-A-72 (Di)
Berry, Mack 1819 wb-#32 (Wl)
Berry, Mark 1827 wb-#68 (Wl)
Berry, Martha (Mrs.) 1857 wb-b-415 (We)

Berry, Martha 1805 wb-1-169 (K)
Berry, Martha 1814 wb-4-319 (D)
Berry, Mary 1860 wb-18-192 (D)
Berry, Samuel 1831 wb-b-108 (Ro)
Berry, Sanford 1836 wb-0-5 (Cf)
Berry, Thomas 1805 wb-1-255 (Bo)
Berry, Thomas 1844 wb-8-205 (Wi)
Berry, Thomas S. 1836 wb-6-158 (Wi)
Berry, W. W. 1835 wb-1-387 (Hr)
Berry, William 1789 wb-1-122 (D)
Berry, William 1810 wb-1-222 (Wi)
Berry, William 1823 wb-1-39 (Hw)
Berry, William W. 1835 wb-1-366 (Hr)
Berryhill, Andrew J. 1827 wb-#152 (Mu)
Berryhill, Samuel 1847 wb-b-230 (We)
Berryhill, Thomas J. 1827 wb-#152 (Mu)
Berryhill, Wm. M. 1837 wb-11-77 (D)
Bertick, Tabitha 1847 wb-g-297 (Hn)
Beshaw, Benjamin 1835 wb-10-530 (D)
Beskide, William 1826 wb-#135 (Mu)
Bess, John 1851 wb-14-648 (D)
Best, John 1834 wb-1-21 (Sh)
Best, John 1851 wb-15-191 (D)
Best, L. F. 1856 wb-c-30 (L)
Bethel, John 1849 33-3-141 (Gr)
Bethell, Isaac C. 1861 rb-21-93 (Ru)
Bethell, Samuel 1806 wb-1-0 (Sm)
Bethell, W. G. 1860 wb-k-312 (O)
Bethshares, William 1849 rb-15-47 (Ru)
Bethshares, William H. 1847 rb-14-78 (Ru)
Bethshares, William S. 1847 rb-14-95 (Ru)
Bethshears, Thomas 1859 rb-19-570 (Ru)
Bettes, William 1852 wb-#178 (Wl)
Bettes, Wyett 1828 wb-#72 (Wl)
Bettis, Sarah 1860 wb-3e-147 (Sh)
Bettis, Tilman 1854 wb-2-156 (Sh)
Betts, Caty 1838 wb-11-121 (D)
Betts, Jonathan 1837 wb-2-249 (Ma)
Betts, Peninnah 1856 wb-6-230 (Ma)
Betts, Selden 1849 wb-5-71 (Ma)
Betts, Thomas 1845 wb-13-244 (D)
Betts, William 1835 wb-2-65 (Ma)
Betts, Zacheriah 1823 wb-8-218 (D)
Betty, Henry 1849 wb-9-243 (Wi)
Betty, Isaac 1821 wb-1-0 (Sm)
Betty, Isaac 1831 wb-2-0 (Sm)
Betty, J. 1833 wb-2-0 (Sm)
Betty, John 1816 wb-1-0 (Sm)
Betty, John 1828 wb-2-0 (Sm)
Betty, William H. 1833 wb-5-220 (Wi)
Bevens, Thomas 1804 wb-#2 (Wl)

Bevil, Allan 1834 rb-f-571 (Mt)
Bevil, Elisha 1833 wb-c-80 (Hn)
Bevil, Mann? 1832 rb-f-395 (Mt)
Bevil, Martin 1836 wb-d-239 (Hn)
Bevil, Mary 1834 rb-f-571 (Mt)
Bevill, Daniel 1846 wb-5-23 (Ma)
Bevill, Henry R. 1841 wb-2-266 (Hr)
Beville, Ann G. 1841 wb-2-217 (Hr)
Bevils, Robert 1815 rb-b-76 (Mt)
Bevins, David 1848 wb-d-110 (G)
Bewley, Calvin F. 1848 33-3-37 (Gr)
Bibb, Benjamin 1826 wb-9-57 (D)
Bibb, Cary 1809 wb-4-28 (D)
Bibb, Jacob 1844 wb-a-162 (Di)
Bibb, James 1809 wb-4-73 (D)
Bibb, James 1816 wb-7-67 (D)
Bibb, Minor 1844 as-0-311 (Di)
Bibb, Robert F. 1850 wb-a-207 (Di)
Bibb, Thomas H. 1834 wb-1-448 (Ma)
Bibby, William 1842 wb-12-292* (D)
Bibby, William 1842 wb-12-312* (D)
Bible, Ann E. 1842 148-1-28 (Ge)
Bible, Chrisley 1807 as-1-173 (Ge)
Bible, Christian 1807 as-1-162 (Ge)
Bible, Christian 1832 wb-2-41# (Ge)
Bible, Christopher 1809 ib-1-255 (Ge)
Bible, Henry M. 1837 wb-#1 (Mo)
Bible, Jacob 1850 wb-2-71# (Ge)
Bible, John 1850 wb-2-72# (Ge)
Bible, Lewis 1845 148-1-139 (Ge)
Bible, Phillip 1837 wb-2-53# (Ge)
Bible, Thomas F. 1842 ib-2-84 (Ge)
Bible, Thomas J. 1861 149-1-231 (Ge)
Bickers, H. E. 1861 wb-7-87 (Hr)
Bickervell, Elizabeth 1850 wb-2-69 (Sh)
Biddle, Charles 1839 wb-1-354 (Gr)
Biddle, John 1856 wb-#57 (Wa)
Biddle, Thomas 1826? wb-#25 (Wa)
Bidwell, Archibald 1847 wb-g-260 (Hn)
Bidwell, Charles 1848 wb-14-109 (Rb)
Bidwell, Charles 1849 wb-14-243 (Rb)
Bidwell, J. W. 1852 wb-15-200 (Rb)
Bidwell, Martha 1855 wb-15-789 (Rb)
Biebers, Henry B. 1858 wb-5-87 (Hr)
Biffle, Elizabeth 1855 ib-1-348 (Wy)
Biffle, Jacob 1845 A-468-18 (Le)
Biffle, John 1850 ib-1-49 (Wy)
Biffle, Mary W. 1850 ib-1-49 (Wy)
Biffle, Nathan 1853 ib-1-249 (Wy)
Biffle, Ursula 1857 ib-1-469 (Wy)
Biffle, Voluntine 1855 ib-1-334 (Wy)

Bigbee, Madison H. 1839 wb-10-1 (Rb)
Bigelow, Elijah 1830 wb-1-222 (Ma)
Bigelow, Luther 1832 wb-10-30 (D)
Bigers, J. M. 1861 as-c-250 (Ms)
Biggar, Joseph 1833 wb-5-268 (Wi)
Biggar, Katharine 1852 wb-10-168 (Wi)
Biggar, Robert 1820 wb-3-178 (Wi)
Biggar, Thomas 1828 wb-4-356 (Wi)
Biggars, Martha 1824 wb-3-703 (Wi)
Bigger, Mariah 1858 wb-b-71 (Ms)
Bigger, Robert 1837 rb-g-633 (Mt)
Bigger, Robert 1855 wb-a-375 (Ms)
Biggers, Eleanor 1812 wb-A-19 (Li)
Biggers, Sarah 1812 wb-A-12 (Li)
Biggers, Sarah 1823 wb-A-340 (Li)
Biggle, John G. 1836 wb-x-390 (Mu)
Biggs, Andrew 1844 wb-12-226 (Rb)
Biggs, Benjamin 1846 wb-1-139 (Sh)
Biggs, E. J. 1857 wb-16-379 (Rb)
Biggs, Elijah 1842 wb-11-180 (Rb)
Biggs, James 1859 wb-3e-120 (Sh)
Biggs, James W. 1823 wb-a-20 (Hn)
Biggs, Joel 1845 wb-f-246 (St)
Biggs, Joel 1855 wb-h-86 (St)
Biggs, John 1837 wb-d-119 (St)
Biggs, Joseph 1849 lr (Sn)
Biggs, Luke 1858 wb-f-220 (G)
Biggs, Reuben P. 1825 wb-8-486 (D)
Biggs, Sarah 1851 wb-15-19 (Rb)
Biggs, _____ 1850 wb-2-75 (Sh)
Bigham, Andrew 1834 wb-#10 (Mc)
Bigham, James 1829 wb-#186 (Mu)
Bigham, James 1831 wb-7-309 (Rb)
Bigham, Sarah 1846 wb-a-156 (Ms)
Bigham, William 1842 wb-a-65 (Ms)
Bilbo, William 1821 wb-1-0 (Sm)
Bilbro, William 1852 wb-#178 (Wl)
Biles (Boiles?), Obediah 1850 rb-15-439 (Ru)
Biles, Charles 1839 wb-e-44 (Hn)
Biles, Jane 1849 wb-#164 (Wl)
Biles, John 1822 rb-5-197 (Ru)
Biles, John W. 1854 wb-g-559 (Hn)
Biles, Joseph C. 1844 wb-2-35 (W)
Biles, Joseph C. 1844 wb-2-37 (W)
Biles, Lucretia Tennessee 1855 wb-g-656 (Hn)
Biles, Michael 1840 wb-e-108 (Hn)
Biles, Michael 1840 wb-e-121 (Hn)
Biles, T. J. 1854 wb-g-623 (Hn)
Biles, Thomas 1822 wb-#42 (Wl)
?iles, Thomas 1846 wb-#152 (Wl)
L ies, William D. 1837 wb-a-258 (O)

Bill, Isaac N. 1854 wb-f-48 (Mu)
Bill, Joseph W. 1858 rb-19-402 (Ru)
Bill, Willson 1839 wb-y-461 (Mu)
Billew, Rebeccah 1803 wb-2-335 (D)
Billings, Benjamin H. 1833 wb-#102 (Wl)
Billings, David 1855 wb-#118 (Wl)
Billings, Henry 1838 wb-a (T)
Billings, John 1818 wb-a-101 (Wh)
Billings, Peter 1848 r39-1-58 (Dk)
Billingsley, James B. 1840 wb-#173 (Wl)
Billingsley, John 1849 wb-#173 (Wl)
Billington, Ezekiel 1850 as-b-12 (Ms)
Billow, James 1856 wb-12-94 (Wi)
Billow, Rachel 1839 wb-#128 (Wl)
Bills, Daniel 1839 wb-a-31 (Ms)
Bills, Garsham 1847 as-a-142 (Ms)
Bills, Isaac 1824 wb-#145 (Mu)
Bills, Isaac N. 1839 wb-y-416 (Mu)
Bills, Isaac N. 1856 wb-5-65 (Hr)
Bills, J. H. 1836 wb-x-377 (Mu)
Bills, J. N. 1835 wb-x-259* (Mu)
Bills, Lilias 1850 wb-b-598 (Mu)
Bills, Placebo Milton 1829 wb-#184 (Mu)
Bills, Sandy K. 1855 wb-a-374 (Ms)
Bingaman, Newton H. 1853 as-b-137 (Ms)
Bingham, A. 1844 wb-#139 (Wl)
Bingham, Anna Jane 1859 wb-h-371 (Hn)
Bingham, James 1828? wb-#172 (Mu)
Bingham, James 1841 wb-z-261 (Mu)
Bingham, James M. 1860 wb-i-245 (St)
Bingham, John A. 1845 wb-#157 (Wl)
Bingham, Martain 1831 wb-c-90 (St)
Bingham, Martin 1851 wb-g-341 (St)
Bingham, R. S. 1845 wb-f-264* (Hn)
Bingham, Thomas 1854 wb-11-317 (Wi)
Bingham, William 1835 wb-x-279* (Mu)
Bingham, William 1843 rb-12-387 (Ru)
Binghqm, Franklin M. 1839 wb-7-28 (Wi)
Binkley, A. H. 1861 wb-a-221 (Ce)
Binkley, Daniel 1825 wb-8-460 (D)
Binkley, David 1860 wb-17-24 (Rb)
Binkley, Frederick 1858 wb-17-473 (D)
Binkley, Henry 1845 wb-12-549 (Rb)
Binkley, Jacob 1845 wb-12-517 (Rb)
Binkley, Jacob 1846 wb-13-28 (Rb)
Binkley, John 1843 wb-13-2 (D)
Binkley, John H. 1849 wb-14-417 (D)
Binkley, Joseph 1840 wb-12-59* (D)
Binkley, Peter 1811 wb-1-397 (Rb)
Binkley, Robert F. 1860 wb-18-296 (D)
Binkley, Sarah 1857 wb-16-430 (Rb)

Binton, Richard 1810 wb-1-0 (Sm)
Binum, Tapley 1839 as-a-445 (Di)
Binum, William 1830 wb-#215 (Mu)
Birchett, James sr. 1816 wb-1-0 (Sm)
Bird, Dabny D. 1856 wb-g-772 (Hn)
Bird, Drewry 1854 wb-h-36 (St)
Bird, Edward 1839 wb-1-465 (Hy)
Bird, Genny 1847 rb-k-460 (Mt)
Bird, Henry D. 1837 wb-d-148 (St)
Bird, J. K. 1859 wb-k-75 (O)
Bird, Jerry 1846 rb-k-231 (Mt)
Bird, John 1825 rb-d-522 (Mt)
Bird, John sr. 1845 148-1-120 (Ge)
Bird, Richard 1808 wb-3-193 (D)
Bird, Richard 1814 wb-A-51 (Li)
Bird, Richard Taylor 1852 wb-a-173 (T)
Birdsong, Henry 1847 lr (Gi)
Birdsong, Miles 1826 wb-1-24 (Hr)
Birdsong, William L. 1854 wb-5-45 (Hr)
Birdwell, Benjamin 1856 wb-1-594 (Su)
Birdwell, George 1816 wb-7-108 (D)
Birdwell, Isaac S. 1852 mr-2-446 (Be)
Birdwell, Joseph 1801 wb-1-83 (K)
Birmingham, Henry 1856 as-b-251 (Ms)
Birmingham, John 1840 as-a-23 (Ms)
Birmingham, William 1848 wb-1-339 (Li)
Birmingham, William 1861 wb-k-391 (O)
Birthright, Lemuel 1832 rb-8-423 (Ru)
Birthright, R. E. 1859 wb-k-52 (O)
Birthright, Samuel 1832 rb-9-10 (Ru)
Birthright, Williamson J. 1845 wb-b-114 (We)
Bishop, Benjamin 1807 wb-3-160 (D)
Bishop, David 1830 wb-1-60 (W)
Bishop, Edmund 1858 wb-7-13 (Ma)
Bishop, Jacob 1822 wb-3-377 (K)
Bishop, Jones 1823 wb-1-0 (Sm)
Bishop, Joseph 1852 wb-xx-113 (St)
Bishop, Joseph sr. 1846 5-3-111 (Cl)
Bishop, Stephen 1840 wb-7-1 (K)
Bishop, Stephen 1853 wb-11-334 (K)
Bishop, Thomas 1842 wb-#11 (Mc)
Bishop, W. F. 1846 wb-1-402 (La)
Bishop, William A. 1857 wb-4-117 (La)
Biskirk, Wiliam H. 1860 wb-c-331 (L)
Bissel, C. A. 1846 vb-g-116 (Hu)
Biswell, John G. 18.. wb-x-369 (Mu)
Bittick, Samuel F. 18.. wb-10-484 (Wi)
Bittle, George 1860 wb-..-347 (D)
Bittleman, John 1819 wb-#90 (Mu)
Bivens, Alfred W. 1858 ib-2-99 (Wy)
Bivens, Anderson 1857 wb-h-629 (Hu)

Bivins, Alexander 1847 mr-2-244 (Be)
Bivins, Fielder 1844 rb-13-36 (Ru)
Bivins, James 1859 rb-20-128 (Ru)
Bivins, Jesse A. 1854 rb-17-322 (Ru)
Bivins, Stephen 1858 ib-2-61 (Wy)
Bizzell, James 1855 wb-11-512 (Wi)
Black, Andrew 1839 wb-b-330 (Wh)
Black, Catharine 1855 wb-15-721 (Rb)
Black, Elender 1860 wb-2-91# (Ge)
Black, Elizabeth 1851 wb-e-315 (Ro)
Black, Elizabeth Folkes 1853 wb-7-0 (Sm)
Black, George 1840 wb-3-204 (Ma)
Black, George B. 1840 wb-3-211 (Ma)
Black, Hirum 1815 wb-2-183 (Rb)
Black, James 1800 wb-1-74 (K)
Black, James 1849 wb-b-550 (Mu)
Black, James A. 1835 rb-9-250 (Ru)
Black, James A. 1855 wb-3-248 (W)
Black, John 1827 eb-1-178 (C)
Black, John 1839 wb-3-32 (Ma)
Black, John 1844 wb-1-170 (Bo)
Black, John 1846 wb-13-469 (D)
Black, John 1855 lr (Gi)
Black, John B. 1854 ib-H-190 (F)
Black, John D. 1856 ib-h-478 (F)
Black, Lucy A. (Miss) 1851 rb-16-97 (Ru)
Black, Lucy A. 1851 rb-15-567 (Ru)
Black, Mary 1816 rb-3-210 (Ru)
Black, Mary 1860 wb-17-62 (Rb)
Black, Peter 1856 rb-o-22 (Mt)
Black, Ro 1847 wb-4-144 (Hr)
Black, Robert 1821 wb-1-0 (Sm)
Black, Robert 1841 rb-i-148 (Mt)
Black, Robert 1845 wb-3-225 (Hr)
Black, Robert 1847 lr (Gi)
Black, Robert 1851 wb-2-196 (La)
Black, Robert 1852 wb-h-Jul (O)
Black, Saml. 1835 rb-g-214 (Mt)
Black, Saml. P. 1837 rb-10-56 (Ru)
Black, Samuel 1838 rb-10-99 (Ru)
Black, Sanford 1846 wb-#150 (Wl)
Black, Thomas 1816 rb-3-203 (Ru)
Black, Thomas G. 1823 wb-#46 (Mu)
Black, William 1815 wb-2-179 (Rb)
Black, William 1829 wb-2-31# (Ge)
Black, William 1836 wb-6-88 (Wi)
Black, William 1843 wb-12-439* (D)
Blackamon, Jno. 1787 wb-1-54 (D)
Blackamore, John 1803 wb-2-325 (D)
Blackard, Thos. 1856 wb-6-327 (Ma)
Blackard, W. R. 1836 wb-1-237 (Hy)

Blackard, Washington R. 1837 wb-1-349 (Hy)
Blackard, William 1820 lr (Sn)
Blackbraun, Shuble G. 1839 wb-y-486 (Mu)
Blackburn, A. (Rev.) 1859 wb-13-232 (K)
Blackburn, Ambrose 1820 wb-#67 (Mu)
Blackburn, Andrew 1837 wb-4-96 (Je)
Blackburn, Andrew 1859 wb-13-206 (K)
Blackburn, Andrew D. 1856 wb-12-242 (Wi)
Blackburn, Archibald 1823 wb-#20 (Wa)
Blackburn, Benjamin 1791 wb-#3 (Wa)
Blackburn, Dianna 1830 wb-3-112 (Je)
Blackburn, Edward 1847 wb-b-89 (Mu)
Blackburn, Edward 1853 wb-5-314 (Je)
Blackburn, Francis 1835 wb-x-247* (Mu)
Blackburn, G. W. 1840 wb-#128 (Wl)
Blackburn, George 1839 wb-#125 (Wl)
Blackburn, James 1834 wb-1-113 (Li)
Blackburn, John 1805 wb-1-299 (Je)
Blackburn, John 1854 wb-e-247 (G)
Blackburn, Samuel 1835 wb-#11 (Mc)
Blackburn, Shuble Y. 1838 wb-y-126 (Mu)
Blackburn, Sterling 1848 33-3-62 (Gr)
Blackburn, Thomas 1845 wb-1-171 (Bo)
Blackburn, William 1795 wb-1-38 (K)
Blackburn, William C. 1826 wb-#64 (Wl)
Blackburn, William H. 1826 wb-#62 (Wl)
Blackburn, William J. J. 1853 wb-5-198 (Je)
Blackfarr, William 1812 wb-4-177 (D)
Blackley, Charles 1816 wb-2-270 (K)
Blackman, A. J. 1858 rb-19-437 (Ru)
Blackman, Admiral J. 1847 wb-f-127+ (O)
Blackman, Ann C. 1849 wb-b-478 (Mu)
Blackman, Bennet 1833 wb-x-84 (Mu)
Blackman, Charles H. 1861 wb-18-453 (D)
Blackman, Edmond 1816 wb-4-438 (D)
Blackman, James A. 1858 rb-19-480 (Ru)
Blackman, John 1844 wb-a2-146 (Mu)
Blackman, Lazarus 1852 rb-16-322 (Ru)
Blackman, Ollen M. 1840 rb-11-50 (Ru)
Blackman, Polly 1827 rb-6-317 (Ru)
Blackmon, Edmond 1816 wb-7-20 (D)
Blackmore, William M. 1853 lr (Sn)
Blacks?, Anna 1857 wb-3-362 (W)
Blackshare, Jesse 1803 Wb-1-116 (Wi)
Blackshor, Thomas N. 1861 wb-k-468 (O)
Blackston, Mary M. 1856 wb-#12 (Mo)
Blackwell, ⸱ ⸱⸳ 1842 wb-7-350* (K)
Blackwell, Arms⸱⸱ ᵈ 1847 wb-#19 (Mo)
Blackwell, David 183⸱. ⸱b-1-52 (Hw)
Blackwell, David 1842 rb-c-284 (Ro)
Blackwell, George 1840 wb-c-230 (Ro)

Blackwell, George W. 1840 wb-c-123 (Ro)
Blackwell, James G. 1852 as-b-54 (Ms)
Blackwell, John 1860 wb-3e-132 (Sh)
Blackwell, John sr. 1849 wb-a-193 (Ms)
Blackwell, Stephen J. 1839 wb-a-30 (L)
Blackwell, Thomas 1858 wb-12-493 (Wi)
Blackwell, Thomas C. 1856 mr (Gi)
Blackwell, Thos. 1853 as-b-134 (Ms)
Blackwell, William 1826 wb-b-25 (Ro)
Blackwell, William 1860 wb-3-42 (Me)
Blackwood, Ann 1816 wb-A-121 (Li)
Blackwood, James 1850 rb-15-448 (Ru)
Blackwood, James sr. 1852 rb-16-344 (Ru)
Blackwood, John 1789 wb-1-3# (Ge)
Blackwood, John 1856 ib-1-464 (Wy)
Blackwood, John 1856 ib-2-3 (Wy)
Blackwood, William P. 1849 wb-b-493 (Mu)
Blagg, William 1826 wb-2-489 (Je)
Blain, Adaline A. 1854 ib-h-38 (F)
Blain, Alexander 1855 ib-h-318 (F)
Blain, James 1855 wb-12-155 (K)
Blain, John 1816 wb-7-17 (D)
Blain, John 1830 wb-9-450 (D)
Blain, Robert 1855 wb-12-96 (K)
Blain, Robert sr. 1855 wb-12-130 (K)
Blair, A. M. 1849 wb#19 (Gu)
Blair, Abigail 1861 wb-5-116 (Hr)
Blair, Alexander 1839 wb-1-363 (Gr)
Blair, Andrew 1829 wb-#177 (Mu)
Blair, Andrew 1829 wb-#187 (Mu)
Blair, Dorcas 1860 wb-3e-134 (Sh)
Blair, George D. 1861 wb-3e-186 (Sh)
Blair, George W. 1853 wb-f-18 (Mu)
Blair, James 1827 wb-b-31 (Ro)
Blair, James 1828 wb-#11 (Mc)
Blair, James 1840 wb-5-71 (Gr)
Blair, James H. 1860 rb-p-406 (Mt)
Blair, James R. 1845 wb-1-274 (Li)
Blair, John (Sr.) 1818 wb-#15 (Wa)
Blair, John 1803 wb-#9 (Wa)
Blair, John 1819 wb-#17 (Wa)
Blair, John 1828 rb-e-370 (Mt)
Blair, John 1845 wb-4-299 (Ma)
Blair, John 1849? wb-1-220 (Bo)
Blair, John 1855 wb-6-71 (Ma)
Blair, John 1858 wb-f-144 (Ro)
Blair, John C. 1845 wb-13-246 (D)
Blair, John H. 1850 wb-m-99 (Mt)
Blair, John M. 1848 rb-l-137 (Mt)
Blair, Martha 1855 wb-6-72 (Ma)
Blair, Richey 1856 rb-17-609 (Ru)

Blair, Robert 1802 wb-#8 (Wa)
Blair, Smith 1833 wb-#103 (Wl)
Blair, Susan (Mrs) 1848 rb-l-166 (Mt)
Blair, Susan 1848 rb-l-129 (Mt)
Blair, Taylor H. 1844 wb-a2-101 (Mu)
Blair, Thomas 1845 wb-1-266 (Li)
Blair, Thomas 1847 wb-0-70 (Cf)
Blair, Thomas B. 1836 rb-g-441 (Mt)
Blair, Thomas B. 1848 rb-l-130 (Mt)
Blair, Thos. W. 1854 wb-f-37 (Mu)
Blair, William 1833 wb-1-88 (Li)
Blair, William 1841 wb-1-191 (Li)
Blair, William 1843 wb-d-49 (Ro)
Blair, William 1854 wb-A-93 (Ca)
Blair, William 1856 wb-a-262 (Cr)
Blair, William 1857 wb-17-292 (D)
Blair, William K. 1853 wb-15-510 (D)
Blair, Wily 1854 wb-e-499 (Ro)
Blake, Elizabeth 1843 wb-1-228 (Li)
Blake, James 1848 wb-g-301 (Hn)
Blake, John 1828 wb-1-13 (Li)
Blake, William 1831 wb-1-187 (Hr)
Blake, William F. 1858 wb-2-252 (Li)
Blakeley, Jannet 1829 wb-#184 (Mu)
Blakely, James H. 1830 rb-8-66 (Ru)
Blakely, Lydia 1836 wb-a-315 (R)
Blakely, Nancy 1832 wb-a-224 (G)
Blakely, Robert 1828? wb-#27 (Wa)
Blakely, Sarah 1850 wb-b-626 (Mu)
Blakeman, Hannah 1851 33-3-414 (Gr)
Blakemore, Daniel 1860 wb-b-101 (Ms)
Blakemore, Elizabeth 1856 wb-e-394 (G)
Blakemore, Elizabeth 1856 wb-e-442 (G)
Blakemore, George M. 1847 rb-k-418 (Mt)
Blakemore, George N. 1848 rb-l-109 (Mt)
Blakemore, James B. 1847 wb-d-32 (G)
Blakemore, Margrett W. 1854 wb-e-150 (G)
Blakemore, Olley A. 1843 wb-c-101 (G)
Blakemore, Olly 1824 wb-a-67 (G)
Blakemore, Thomas 1832 lr (Sn)
Blakemore, Wiley B. 1854 wb-e-191 (G)
Blakemore, William 1818 rb-4-145 (Ru)
Blakemore, William 1824 wb-a-70 (G)
Blakeney, Harriet 1822 -t- - -93 (Mt)
Blakeney, James 1823 rb-d-155 (Mt)
Blakeney, Thomas 1822 rb-d-38 (Mt)
Blakeney, Thomas 1841 rb-i-88 (Mt)
Blakeny (B), Harriet 1823 rb-d-89 (Mt)
Blakney, Thomas 1840 rb-h-455 (Mt)
Blalock, Charles 1842 wb-#138 (Wl)
Blalock, Charles 1853 wb-#109 (Wl)

Blalock, Elbert 1856 wb-2-320 (Mc)
Bland, Arthur 1816 wb-2-215 (Wi)
Bland, John 1856 wb-e-52 (Hy)
Bland, Naoma 1851 wb-14-607 (D)
Bland, Naomy 1851 wb-14-601 (D)
Bland, Oseola 1861 wb-b-100 (F)
Bland, Oseola 1861 wb-b-98 (F)
Bland, Samuel 1833 wb-10-265 (D)
Bland, William 1812 wb-A-22 (Li)
Blank, George 1824 wb-a-73 (Hn)
Blank, George W. 1825 wb-a-79 (Hn)
Blankenship, Allen 1853 wb-e-100 (G)
Blankenship, Daniel 1840 wb-#132 (Wl)
Blankenship, David 1858 wb-f-218 (G)
Blankenship, Gad 1847 wb-13-178 (Rb)
Blankenship, Hezekiah 1816 wb-1-0 (Sm)
Blankenship, John N. 1834 wb-8-457 (Rb)
Blankenship, John W. 1843 wb-c-94 (G)
Blankenship, Laban 1855 wb-e-340 (G)
Blanks, Amy 1856 wb-3-283 (W)
Blanks, Ingram 1825 rb-6-174 (Ru)
Blanks, John 1848 wb-2-282 (W)
Blanks, William 1806 rb-a-372 (Mt)
Blanton, C. L. 1856 wb-1-346 (Fr)
Blanton, Celia 1853 rb-16-465 (Ru)
Blanton, Henry 1849 wb-g-156 (St)
Blanton, Henry 1859 wb-i-110 (St)
Blanton, James 1861 wb-i-333 (St)
Blanton, Joel 1811 wb-#10 (Wl)
Blanton, Joel 1841 wb-a-30 (Dk)
Blanton, John 1836 wb-x-306* (Mu)
Blanton, John D. 1835 wb-x-294* (Mu)
Blanton, John F. 1833 rb-9-64 (Ru)
Blanton, John W. 1860 wb-h-388 (Hn)
Blanton, Nelson 1820 rb-5-63 (Ru)
Blanton, Richard 1803 rb-a-156 (Mt)
Blanton, Richard 1847 wb-f-440 (St)
Blanton, Richard 1858 wb-0-160 (Cf)
Blanton, Scilly 1854 rb-17-245 (Ru)
Blanton, Smith 1852 wb-0-114 (Cf)
Blanton, Thomas 1846 rb-13-606 (Ru)
Bleakley, Charles 1828 wb-4-305 (K)
Bledsoe, Abraham 1815 lr (Sn)
Bledsoe, Anthony 1788 lr (Sn)
Bledsoe, Anthony T. 1851 wb-2-94 (Sh)
Bledsoe, Benjamin sr. 1806 wb-1-190 (K)
Bledsoe, George Ann 1849 wb-14-431 (D)
Bledsoe, Haywood 1839 wb-a-82 (Cr)
Bledsoe, Isaac 1787 lr (Sn)
Bledsoe, Isaac M. 1845 wb-c-217 (G)
Bledsoe, Jesse 1840 wb-12-66* (D)

Bledsoe, John 1856 wb-a-2 (Ce)
Bledsoe, Lewis 1849 wb-1-355 (Li)
Bledsoe, Major 1857 wb-f-88 (G)
Bledsoe, P. T. 1860 as-c-576 (Di)
Bledsoe, Robert W. 1831 lr (Sn)
Bledsoe, Thomas 1794 wb-1-26 (Sn)
Bledsoe, W. G. 1859 wb-f-329 (G)
Bledsoe, William 1829 wb-1-42 (Li)
Bledsoe, Willis 1847 wb-14-42 (D)
Blevens, Sarah 1818 wb-1-86 (Ct)
Blevins, David 1831 wb-a-90 (R)
Blevins, Horder 1860 wb-3-60 (Me)
Blevins, Hugh T. 1837 wb-1-4 (Me)
Blevins, James 1849 wb-1-293 (Me)
Blevins, John T. 1858 wb-2-385 (Me)
Blevins, Leander 1850 wb-1-61 (Jo)
Blevins, William 1841 wb-2-57# (Ge)
Blevins, William R. 1854 wb-1-103 (Jo)
Blevins, William R. 1855 wb-1-100 (Jo)
Bley, Philip 1818 wb-7-272 (D)
Blocker, Eliza 1855 wb-3e-9 (Sh)
Blockley, G. 1836? as-a-314 (Di)
Blockley, Gustavus 1838 as-a-402 (Di)
Blood, Thomas Y. 1851 wb-2-104 (Sh)
Bloodworth, Avi 1803 lr (Sn)
Bloodworth, Jesse 1854 wb-b-250 (L)
Bloodworth, Sumner 1842 wb-#138 (Wl)
Bloodworth, Webb 1859 wb-#128 (Wl)
Bloodworth, William 1850 mr-2-356 (Be)
Bloomer, Daniel 1838 wb-1-49 (Hw)
Blount, Drewry B. 1859 wb-i-58 (St)
Blount, Jacob 1809 wb-1-284 (K)
Blount, John 1835 wb-1-375* (Hr)
Blount, John 1859 gs-1-504 (F)
Blount, John Gray 1833 wb-1-406 (Ma)
Blount, John Gray 1833 wb-1-72 (Hy)
Blount, John Gray 1833 wb-b*-4 (O)
Blount, John Gray 1845 wb-5-62 (Ma)
Blount, Reading 1831 wb-9-501 (D)
Blount, Redding 1840 wb-b-269 (Hd)
Blount, Thomas 1812 wb-1-9 (Sh)
Blount, Thomas 1812 wb-a-22 (T)
Blount, Thomas 1812 wb-b*-6 (O)
Blount, Thomas 1815 --- · ˙˙'˙ (D)
Blount, Thomas 1832 wb-1-240 (Hr)
Blount, Thomas 1832 wb-9-588 (D)
Blount, Willie 1836 rb-g-264 (Mt)
Blue, James D. 1854 wb-2-160 (Sh)
Blue, N. W. 1835 wb-2-24 (Ma)
Blunt, John 1853 wb-5-44 (Hr)
Blunt, Nealey (Mrs) 1854 wb-h-71 (St)

Blurton, Bryant 1815 wb-#18 (Wl)
Blythe, A. J. 1860 wb-h-406 (Hn)
Blythe, Andrew 1830 lr (Sn)
Blythe, Elizabeth 1861 wb-13-469 (Wi)
Blythe, Jacob 1844 wb-1-323 (La)
Blythe, Jacob 1850 wb-2-136 (La)
Blythe, Jacob jr. 1846 wb-1-391 (La)
Blythe, James 1799 wb-1-53 (Sn)
Blythe, James 1829 wb-4-381 (Wi)
Blythe, James 1856 wb-6-272 (Ma)
Blythe, John 1834 wb-5-384 (Wi)
Blythe, Richard 1828 lr (Sn)
Blythe, Thomas sr. 1823 wb-A-315 (Li)
Blythe, William 1825 wb-4-13 (Wi)
Boales, William 1858 wb-e-88 (Hy)
Boardman, Margaret M. 1860 rb-p-314 (Mt)
Boardman, William Z. 1856 wb-17-56 (D)
Boatman, Henry 1843 wb-5-266 (Gr)
Boaz, Thomas 1834 wb-10-284 (D)
Boaz, William 1852 wb-f-10 (Mu)
Bobbet, Stephen 1833 wb-8-174 (Rb)
Bobbett, Drury 1844 wb-12-120 (Rb)
Bobbett, James 1846 wb-c-331 (G)
Bobbett, James 1857 wb-f-64 (G)
Bobbett, Lucy 1857 wb-f-73 (G)
Bobbett, Stephen 1831 wb-5-47 (Wi)
Bobbitt, Arthur 1856 wb-6-352 (Ma)
Bobbitt, Mary 1853 wb-e-108 (G)
Bobet, James 1846 wb-c-327 (G)
Bobett, James 1814 wb-1-0 (Sm)
Bobo, Chaney 1844 wb-12-197 (Rb)
Bobo, Hiram 1830 rb-f-114 (Mt)
Bobo, Hiram 1831 rb-f-186 (Mt)
Bobo, Love C. 1842 rb-i-225 (Mt)
Boddie, Elijah 1851 lr (Sn)
Boddie, Willis H. 1841 wb-z-238 (Mu)
Bodin, Margaret 1855 wb-#117 (Wl)
Bodine, J. M. 1837 wb-11-59 (D)
Bodine, John 1814 wb-#14 (Wl)
Bodine, John M. 1838 wb-11-480 (D)
Bodine, Wesley 1859 wb-1-50 (Se)
Bodine, Western 1841 wb-#135 (Wl)
Bodkin, William S. 1844 wb-c-198 (G)
Bodoin, Penelope 1847 wb-#155 (Wl)
Boen, Abraham 1852 148-1-420 (Ge)
Boen, Eldridge 1852 wb-g-564 (Hu)
Bogard, Ader 1834 wb-c-334 (St)
Bogard, Charles 1836 wb-d-1 (St)
Bogard, Hiram T. 1854 wb-h-34 (St)
Bogard, Jacob 1820 wb-#93 (Mu)
Bogard, Joseph C. 1855 wb-h-145 (St)

Bogard, ___ 1820 wb-#45 (Mu)
Bogart, Jeremiah 1837 wb-#33 (Wa)
Bogart, Samuel 1833 wb-1-83 (Ct)
Boggs, John 1848 wb-10-84 (K)
Boggus, William R. 1847 6-2-9 (Le)
Bogle, Andrew 1813 wb-1-215 (Bo)
Bogle, Elisabeth 1843 wb-1-169 (Bo)
Bogle, George 1855 wb-A-102 (Ca)
Bogle, George B. 1859 wb-A-147 (Ca)
Bogle, J. H. 1857 ib-1-439 (Ca)
Bogle, Joseph 1792 wb-0-1 (K)
Bogle, Joseph 1814 wb-#15 (Wl)
Bogle, Joseph 1849 wb-1-9 (Bo)
Bogle, Joseph 1857 ib-1-421 (Ca)
Bogle, Joseph H. 1856 iv-1-583 (Ca)
Bogle, Lucinda 1854 ib-1-317 (Ca)
Bogle, Samuel 1807 wb-#4 (Wl)
Bogle, Samuel 1846 wb-1-4 (Bo)
Bogle, Thomas 1815 wb-#17 (Wl)
Bogle, Thomas 1826 wb-#62 (Wl)
Bogle, William G. 1861 wb-13-468 (K)
Bogus, Peter 1841 wb-e-407 (Hu)
Bohanan, William 1844 wb-c-150 (Wh)
Bohannon, Henry 1810 wb-a-8 (Wh)
Bohannon, Hiram 1844 wb-f-290 (Hn)
Bohannon, Lewis 1853 wb-d-134 (Wh)
Bohannon, William 1816 wb-a-57 (Wh)
Bohanon, Thomas 1841 wb-c-16 (Wh)
Boisseau, William H. 1856 wb-16-255 (Rb)
Boisseaux, W. H. 1856 wb-16-229 (Rb)
Bolding, John 1838 wb-#12 (Mc)
Boles, David 1829 wb-2-29# (Ge)
Boles, Thomas 1848 wb-g-102 (Hu)
Boles, William 1848 wb-4-95 (Je)
Boley, Ephram 1846 wb-d-19 (G)
Bolin, Andrew 1832 lw (Ct)
Bolin, John 1839 wb-1-54 (Hw)
Bolin, John 1853 wb-1-43 (R)
Boling, Edmond sr. 1834 wb-2-44# (Ge)
Boling, Enoch 1815 wb-a-71 (Ro)
Boling, Joseph 1834 wb-1-131 (Hy)
Bolles, Nancy 1845 wb-13-64 (Ru)
Bolli, Christopher Edward 1854 wb-12-38 (K)
Bolling, Harriet E. 1858 wb-12-468 (K)
Bolotes, Henry A. 1850 wb-2-70 (Sh)
Bolton, Asa 1851 rb-15-567 (Ru)
Bolton, Charles 1847 wb-1-143 (Sh)
Bolton, Charles 1847 wb-7-0 (Sm)
Bolton, Geraldus 1846 wb-#150 (Wl)
Bolton, James B. 1840 wb-3-209 (Ma)
Bolton, Joel 1804 wb-#2 (Wl)

Bolton, Joel 1849 wb-#168 (Wl)
Bolton, Valentine 1854 wb-#54 (Wa)
Bolton, William 1840 wb-c-356 (Hu)
Bomar, John W. 1854 wb-g-562 (Hn)
Bomar, Reuben 1857 wb-h-166 (Hn)
Bomar, W. W. 1837 wb-1-560 (Hr)
Bomar, William 1841 wb-e-310 (Hn)
Bomar, Wm. J. 1857 as-c-427 (Di)
Bomer, E. H. 1860 wb-5-103 (Hr)
Bomer, Nancy 1851 wb-g-416 (Hn)
Bomer, Pauline 1851 wb-g-413 (Hn)
Bomer, Spencer 1841 wb-e-297 (Hn)
Bomer, W. W. 1855 39-2-49 (Dk)
Bond, Benjamin 1840 wb-e-222 (Hn)
Bond, Charles A. 1856 wb-6-196 (Ma)
Bond, Elizabeth M. 1855 wb-11-433 (Wi)
Bond, Emily K. 1849 ib-1-77 (Ca)
Bond, George H. 1856 wb-6-230 (Ma)
Bond, Isabella M. E. 1855 wb-11-486 (Wi)
Bond, James 1851 wb-10-1 (Wi)
Bond, James 1852 wb-#180 (Wl)
Bond, James B. 1851 wb-10-28 (Wi)
Bond, James M. 1854 wb-11-404 (Wi)
Bond, Jesse B. 1861 39-2-415 (Dk)
Bond, John 1795 wb-0-11 (K)
Bond, John 1816 wb-#23 (Wl)
Bond, John 1829 wb-c-36 (St)
Bond, John 1851 wb-#175 (Wl)
Bond, John B. 1848 wb-9-169 (Wi)
Bond, John H. 1854 wb-11-97 (Wi)
Bond, Joseph 1848 wb-g-271 (Hn)
Bond, Lewis 1842 wb-#139 (Wl)
Bond, Lewis 1851 wb-5-93 (Ma)
Bond, Margarett L. 1852 wb-10-169 (Wi)
Bond, Morris L. 1825 wb-3-768 (Wi)
Bond, Nancy M. 1861 wb-13-439 (Wi)
Bond, Page 1859 wb-f-181 (Mu)
Bond, Peter 1829 wb-#12 (Mc)
Bond, Robert & Frances 1859 wb-#128 (Wl)
Bond, Sarah C. 1857 wb-12-422 (Wi)
Bond, Solomon 1853 rb-16-464 (Ru)
Bond, Thomas 1843 wb-3-679 (Ma)
Bond, Thomas B. 1848 wb-9-112 (Wi)
Bond, Thomas J. 1848 wb-9-111 (Wi)
Bond, Thos. 1856 wb-16-230 (Rb)
Bond, William 1816 wb-#23 (Wl)
Bond, William 1820 wb-3-119 (Wi)
Bond, William 1829 wb-4-457 (Wi)
Bond, William 1835 wb-#109 (Wl)
Bond, William 1845 wb-#159 (Wl)
Bond, William 1846 wb#18 (Gu)

Bond, William 1850 wb-9-469 (Wi)
Bond, William 1856 wb-3e-19 (Sh)
Bond, William 1856 wb-e-463 (G)
Bond, William W. 1856 wb-12-63 (Wi)
Bonds, Daniel B. 1861 rb-21-49 (Ru)
Bonds, Emily K. 1849 ib-1-82 (Ca)
Bonds, John 1833 wb-10-94 (D)
Bondurant, Benjamin 1845 wb-b-118 (We)
Bondurant, Edward 1821 wb-8-29 (D)
Bondurant, Hillary H. 1838 wb-1-189 (We)
Bondurant, Jacob M. 1859 wb-18-85 (D)
Bondurant, James E. 1859 wb-b-439 (We)
Bone, Abner 1853 as-c-263 (Di)
Bone, Abner W. 1833 wb-#99 (Wl)
Bone, Adnah 1847 wb-#156 (Wl)
Bone, Amos M. 1850 rb-15-235 (Ru)
Bone, Hugh Y. 1853 wb-e-79 (G)
Bone, John 1827 wb-#67 (Wl)
Bone, John 1838 wb-#123 (Wl)
Bone, Robert 1829 wb-#82 (Wl)
Bone, Ruth 1844 wb-d-144 (O)
Bone, Squire 1843 wb-d-37 (O)
Bone, Thomas 1833 wb-#101 (Wl)
Bone, William 1825 wb-#57 (Wl)
Bone, William L. 1849 rb-15-162 (Ru)
Boner, A. L. 1854 wb-5-153 (Ma)
Bonham, Isaac S. (Rev.) 1852 148-1-397 (Ge)
Bonham, James S. 1853 wb-1C-47 (A)
Bonner, Ezekiel 1845 wb-#12 (Mc)
Bonner, James 1857 wb-2-202 (Li)
Bonner, James 1860 wb-#13 (Mc)
Bonner, John 1842 wb-#140 (Wl)
Bonner, John H. 1845 wb-2-77 (W)
Bonner, Thomas 1835 wb-1-571 (Ma)
Bonner, Thomas L. 1834 wb-#105 (Wl)
Bonner, William 1846 wb-a-119 (T)
Bonnor, Elizabeth 1847 wb-2-243 (W)
Bonnor, John 1847 wb-2-230 (W)
Bonsel, Simeon 1844 wb-d-233 (O)
Bonum?, John 1835 wb-#144 (Wl)
Booher, Christian 1844 wb-1-31 (Su)
Booher, William 1850 wb-1-188
Booker, Albert 1856 wb-f-107 (Mu)
Booker, Ann 1843 wb-11-501 (Rb)
Booker, Henry L. 1841 wb-z-154 (Mu)
Booker, James G. 1846 wb-a2-511 (Mu)
Booker, John 1814 wb-2-124 (K)
Booker, John 1831 wb-5-59 (K)
Booker, John 1858 wb-a-276 (T)
Booker, Magdelane 1831 wb-5-60 (K)
Booker, Merett H. 1839 wb-y-425 (Mu)

Booker, Peter R. 1839 wb-y-447 (Mu)
Booker, Peter R. 1849 wb-b-436 (Mu)
Booker, Richard 1827 rb-7-105 (Ru)
Booker, Richardson 1827 rb-7-287 (Ru)
Booker, Samuel 1858 wb-1-237 (Be)
Booker, Shields 1829 wb-6-409 (Rb)
Booker, Shields 1845 wb-12-528 (Rb)
Bookout, Jesse 1847 wb-#13 (Mc)
Bookout, Jessee 1836 wb-b-27 (Hd)
Bookout, Marmaduke 1830 wb-1A-48 (A)
Books, B. G. 1855 wb-6-30 (Ma)
Boon, Allen D. 1857 wb-6-441 (Ma)
Boon, Amelia 1849 wb-9-286 (Wi)
Boon, Daniel 1843 wb-4-77 (Ma)
Boon, Elizabeth 1818 wb-3-155 (Rb)
Boon, Elizabeth 1843 wb-#13 (Mc)
Boon, Israel 1839 wb-#13 (Mc)
Boon, John 1834 rb-g-63 (Mt)
Boon, John 1843 wb-4-100 (Ma)
Boon, John 1843 wb-a-104 (F)
Boon, Josiah G. 1844 wb-c-188 (G)
Boon, Matthias 1835 wb-2-31 (Ma)
Boon, Miles 1838 wb-1-575 (Hr)
Boon, Nathan 1814 wb-3-2 (St)
Boon, Richard 1823 wb-4-2 (Rb)
Boon, Robert G. 1838 abl-1-50 (T)
Boon, Simeon 1847 rb-14-64 (Ru)
Boon, Sion 1836 wb-b-123 (G)
Boon?, Jessee 1829 wb-#13 (Mc)
Boone, Danel 1856 wb-3-401 (La)
Boone, Daniel W. 1858 wb-4-214 (La)
Boone, Richard J. 1829 wb-1-43 (Hy)
Boone, Simeon W. 1847 rb-14-94 (Ru)
Booth, Abijah 1832 wb-1-208 (Hr)
Booth, Ailsey 1856 wb-5-417 (Je)
Booth, Edwin E. 1825 wb-4-60 (K)
Booth, Elijah 1834 wb-1-353 (Hr)
Booth, George C. 1844 rb-12-587 (Ru)
Booth, Henry 1833 lr (Sn)
Booth, Henry sr. 1813 wb-4-238 (D)
Booth, John 1827 wb-b-15 (Hn)
Booth, Joseph 1805 wb-#9 (Wa)
Booth, Mark 1858 rb-o-713 (Mt)
Booth, Peter 1826 wb-9-62 (D)
Booth, Polly 1835 wb-b-75 (G)
Booth, Stephen 1832? wb-1-67 (Hy)
Booth, William 1855 ib-h-420 (F)
Boothe, Abel W. 1837 wb-#116 (Wl)
Boothe, David 1807 wb-#6 (Wl)
Boothe, Lucy 1848 wb-4-368 (Hr)
Boothe, Pleasant 1856 rb-o-128 (Mt)

Boram, James 1843 wb-a-102 (T)
Boram, John 1840 wb-c-99 (Ro)
Boram, John 1847 wb-a-129 (T)
Bordeaux, John W. 1846 wb-a-301 (F)
Boren, Absolem 1816 wb-#14 (Wa)
Boren, Chance (Chana?) 1834 wb-#40 (Wa)
Boren, James 1796 wb-#6 (Wa)
Boren, Jane 1847 wb-#47 (Wa)
Boren, Jeremiah 1857 wb-16-533 (Rb)
Boren, John 1800 wb-2-166 (D)
Boren, John 1814 lr (Sn)
Boren, John 1834 wb-1-418 (Ma)
Boren, John 1835 wb-9-12 (Rb)
Boren, John 1841 wb-11-98 (Rb)
Boren, Leonard 1849 wb-14-151 (Rb)
Boren, Lydia 1831 wb-7-296 (Rb)
Boring, Amon 1839 rb-10-310 (Ru)
Boring, Joshua 1849 wb-1-221 (Bo)
Boring, Martha L. 1854 rb-17-324 (Ru)
Boring, Nancy 1841 rb-11-318 (Ru)
Borkley, John 1849 wb-1-271 (Fr)
Borlieu, Nathan 1846 rb-k-258 (Mt)
Boro, Vincent 1858 wb-3e-84 (Sh)
Borren, N. B. 1851 as-b-23 (Ms)
Borrow, Sarah 1852 wb-e-13 (G)
Borum, John 1846 wb-#160 (Wl)
Borum, Mary 1851 wb-2-103 (Sh)
Borum, Mary Jane 1855 wb-c-42 (L)
Bosher, Leonard 1843 wb-1-84 (Sh)
Boshers, Henry 1856 ib-1-414 (Wy)
Bosley, Beal 1860 wb-18-327 (D)
Bosley, John 1844 wb-13-74 (D)
Bosley, Lyddy Ann 1856 wb-3e-15 (Sh)
Bosley, Philip 1816 wb-a-89 (Ro)
Bosley, Rebeccah 1788 wb-1-51 (D)
Boss, Jethro 1850 wb-g-311 (St)
Boss, Jethro 1850 wb-g-315 (St)
Bost, John 1841 wb-1-380 (W)
Bost, William 1852 wb#20 (Gu)
Bost, William H. 1855 wb#24 (Gu)
Bostelle, John 1823 rb-d-238 (Mt)
Bostick, Absalom 1848 wb-b-283 (Mu)
Bostick, Don F. 1839 wb-12-7* (D)
Bostick, Hanoah 1837 wb-6-347 (Wi)
Bostick, Harden P. 1861 wb-18-529 (D)
Bostick, John 1850 wb-9-354 (Wi)
Bostick, John 1857 wb-3e-41 (Sh)
Bostick, John jr. 1855 wb-11-446 (Wi)
Bostick, John sr. 1850 wb-9-449 (Wi)
Bostick, Littleberry R. 1838 wb-d-209* (Hn)
Bostick, M. M. 1859 rb-19-624 (Ru)

Bostick, Manoah 1837 wb-6-374 (Wi)
Bostick, Moses 1818 wb-1-0 (Sm)
Bostick, R. W. H. 1853 wb-11-41 (Wi)
Bostick, Richard W. H. 1854 wb-11-93 (Wi)
Bostick, William 1836 wb-1-154 (Fr)
Bostwick, Thomas 1839 wb-2-46 (Hr)
Boswell, George G. 1853 wb-xx-304 (St)
Boswell, George W. F. 1849 wb-a-156 (Cr)
Boswell, K. G. 1852 wb-2-279 (La)
Boswell, Walter 1844 wb-f-167 (St)
Boswell, William 1855 wb-3-340 (La)
Boswell, William 1856 wb-3-374 (La)
Bosworth, William 1859 wb-18-61 (D)
Botkin, Hugh 1801 wb-0-31 (K)
Bottel, Henry 1835 wb-#35 (Wa)
Botter, William 1836 wb-1A-141 (A)
Bottles, Henry 1825 wb-#33 (Wa)
Bottoms, Thomas 1858 wb-3-53 (Me)
Botts, Aaron 1857 wb-b-27 (Dk)
Botts, Jane T. 1842 wb-12-310* (D)
Boughter, Samuel 1854 wb-xx-312 (St)
Boulden, Benjamin 1860 wb-a-325 (V)
Bouldin, Polly 1853 wb-3-159 (W)
Boulding, Thomas 1824 wb-4-226 (Rb)
Boulton, Hansford A. 1861 wb-f-424 (G)
Boulton, John 1858 iv-C-58 (C)
Boulton, Lent 1832 wb-3-0 (Sm)
Bounds, Francis sr. 1859 wb-13-243 (K)
Bounds, Jesse 1804 wb-1-146 (K)
Bounds, Thomas 1834 wb-b-137 (Wh)
Bourdeaux, John W. 1846 wb-a-293 (F)
Bourne, Ambrose F. 1840 wb-10-452 (Rb)
Bourne, Charity Elizabeth 1839 wb-10-271 (Rb)
Bournes, Benjamin F. 1857 rb-o-373 (Mt)
Boutell, John 1824 rb-d-309 (Mt)
Boutelle, John jr. 1828 rb-e-278 (Mt)
Bove, Daniel 1841 wb-3-441 (Ma)
Bove, George 1849 wb-4-433 (Hr)
Bowden, Allen Blanton 1855 wb-3-328 (La)
Bowden, Elias 1843 wb-f-161 (Hn)
Bowden, Elias W. 1849 wb-g-341 (Hn)
Bowden, Elias sr. 1854 wb-g-557 (Hn)
Bowden, F. W. 1848 wb-0-86 (Cf)
Bowden, James M. 1849 wb-a-208 (Ms)
Bowden, Thomas 1848 wb-g-278 (Hn)
Bowden, William 1842 wb-0-31 (Cf)
Bowdry, Joshua 1854 wb-3-203 (La)
Bowen, Abner 1828 wb-1-7 (Sh)
Bowen, Allen 1858 as-c-549 (Di)
Bowen, Benjamin 1826 wb-#131 (Mu)
Bowen, Charity E. 1838 wb-10-220 (Rb)

Bowen, David A. 1842 wb-7-394 (K)
Bowen, George T. 1829 wb-9-279 (D)
Bowen, Jeremiah 1822 wb-1-0 (Sm)
Bowen, John 1838 wb-1-44 (Sh)
Bowen, John H. 1822 lr (Sn)
Bowen, John H. 1827 wb-2-0 (Sm)
Bowen, John M. 1849 wb-10-214 (K)
Bowen, Jordan A. 1835 as-a-266 (Di)
Bowen, Lucy T. 1845 wb-12-313 (Rb)
Bowen, Mary 1820 lr (Sn)
Bowen, Rease 1844 as-b-210 (Di)
Bowen, Reece 1810 wb-1-322 (K)
Bowen, Thomas 1804 wb-2-354 (D)
Bowen, William 1832 wb-1-10 (Bo)
Bowen, William G. jr. 1845 wb-b-84 (We)
Bowen, William H. 1812 wb-a-138 (St)
Bower, Daniel 1857 wb-3-356 (Gr)
Bower, Peter 1798 wb-1-253 (Bo)
Bower, Richard 1841 wb-c-238 (Ro)
Bower, William 1855 wb-e-553 (Ro)
Bower, William sr. 1855 wb-e-537 (Ro)
Bowerman, John 1857 wb-#14 (Mc)
Bowerman, Peter 1835 wb-1-5 (Bo)
Bowers, Andrew 1850 wb-2-346 (Gr)
Bowers, Andrew 1861 rb-p-580 (Mt)
Bowers, Cloe 1835 wb-1-399 (Hr)
Bowers, David 1856 wb-e-407 (G)
Bowers, Elizabeth 1848 148-1-261 (Ge)
Bowers, Elizabeth Ann 1805 wb-3-116 (D)
Bowers, George 1854 ib-H-98 (F)
Bowers, Gideon A. 1854 wb-5-503 (Je)
Bowers, Giles 1819 wb-#30 (Wl)
Bowers, Henry 1818 wb-#15 (Wa)
Bowers, James 1789 wb-1-1# (Ge)
Bowers, James 1844 wb-d-115 (Ro)
Bowers, James 1860 rb-p-513 (Mt)
Bowers, Jesse 1823 wb-#49 (Wl)
Bowers, Joel 1855 149-1-3 (Ge)
Bowers, John 1803 wb-2-306 (D)
Bowers, John 1806 as-1-146 (Ge)
Bowers, John 1849 wb-1-258 (Fr)
Bowers, John 1856 149-1-38 (Ge)
Bowers, John 1858 wb-16-609 (Rb)
Bowers, John sr. 1849 wb-2-70# (Ge)
Bowers, Jonas 1853 as-2-268 (Ge)
Bowers, Leonard 1840 lw (Ct)
Bowers, Mary A. 1846 wb-b-190 (We)
Bowers, Moses 1859 wb-2-90# (Ge)
Bowers, Nancy 1815 wb-#16 (Wl)
Bowers, Nancy H. 1846 wb-b-189 (We)
Bowers, P. Y. 1858 wb-f-202 (G)

Bowers, Phillip 1854 wb-2-78# (Ge)
Bowers, Rebecca 1849 lw (Ct)
Bowers, Sarah 1841 wb-2-192 (Hr)
Bowers, W. 1847 rb-k-678 (Mt)
Bowers, W. 1850 wb-4-589 (Hr)
Bowers, William 1840 wb-2-140 (Hr)
Bowers, William P. 1823 wb-8-247 (D)
Bowers, William P. 1841 wb-12-225* (D)
Bowers, William P. 1852 wb-15-225 (D)
Bowers, Wm. 1847 rb-k-482 (Mt)
Bowle, John 1821 wb-8-31 (D)
Bowles, David 1851 148-1-373 (Ge)
Bowles, Rewben 1844 rb-j-264 (Mt)
Bowles, Thomas E. 1841 rb-i-193 (Mt)
Bowles, Thomas E. 1845 rb-j-393 (Mt)
Bowles, William P. 1851 wb-2-186 (La)
Bowlin, Michael 1834 wb-1-126 (Fr)
Bowling, Elizabeth E. 1835 wb-1-144 (Fr)
Bowling, Gabriella C. 1853 wb-n-199 (Mt)
Bowling, J. P. 1859 rb-p-225 (Mt)
Bowling, Sidney 1830 wb-#14 (Mc)
Bowling, W. W. 1851 wb-m-332 (Mt)
Bowling, W. W. 1851 wb-m-378 (Mt)
Bowling, Wm. 1851 wb-m-319 (Mt)
Bowls, John 1842 5-2-254 (Cl)
Bowman, Andrew H. 1845 148-1-135 (Ge)
Bowman, Benjamin 1833 wb-b-122 (Wh)
Bowman, Bursheba 1861 wb-f-439 (Ro)
Bowman, Cornelius 1847 148-1-184 (Ge)
Bowman, Daniel 1833 wb-#33 (Wa)
Bowman, Daniel 1844 rb-12-431 (Ru)
Bowman, Daniel 1861 rb-21-149 (Ru)
Bowman, David 1839 rb-10-368 (Ru)
Bowman, Eleanor 1841 148-1-26 (Ge)
Bowman, Elizabeth 1847 wb-#45 (Wa)
Bowman, Harvey 1859 wb-13-152* (K)
Bowman, Harvey 1859 wb-13-233 (K)
Bowman, Iredale 1851 wb-d-1 (Wh)
Bowman, Iredale 1851 wb-d-5 (Wh)
Bowman, Jacob 1847 wb-1-62 (Hw)
Bowman, James F. 1855 rb-17-413 (Ru)
Bowman, James T. 1855 rb-17-468 (Ru)
Bowman, John (Rev.) 1851 148-1-357 (Ge)
Bowman, John 1810 ib-1-306 (Ge)
Bowman, John 1810 wb-1-3# (Ge)
Bowman, John 1827 rb-7-343 (Ru)
Bowman, John 1841 148-1-25 (Ge)
Bowman, John 1841 wb-c-232 (Ro)
Bowman, John 1843 wb-#40 (Wa)
Bowman, John 1847 wb-2-67# (Ge)
Bowman, Joseph 1818 rb-4-181 (Ru)

Bowman, Joseph 1831 rb-8-362 (Ru)
Bowman, Joseph 1850 wb-#49 (Wa)
Bowman, Levi 1814 wb-a-24 (Wh)
Bowman, Robert 1817 wb-1-0 (Sm)
Bowman, Ruben sr. 1841 wb-e-190 (Hn)
Bowman, Saml. (Maj.) 1838 rb-10-153 (Ru)
Bowman, Saml. 1855 rb-17-516 (Ru)
Bowman, Samuel 1843 wb-8-176 (K)
Bowman, Samuel 1846 wb-#42 (Wa)
Bowman, Samuel D. 1843 wb-12-412* (D)
Bowman, Samuel D. 1843 wb-12-432* (D)
Bowman, Samuel sr. 1838 rb-10-102 (Ru)
Bowman, Samuel sr. 1847 wb-9-360 (K)
Bowman, Sherwood 1829 wb-1A-5 (A)
Bowman, Sperling sr. 1841 148-1-9 (Ge)
Bowmen, William 1839 wb-e-87 (Hn)
Bowser, Martha 1846 wb-#43 (Wa)
Bowyer, John 1820 wb-7-452 (D)
Bowyer, Peter G. 1823 wb-8-167 (D)
Box, Abraham 1856 wb-h-582 (Hu)
Box, Edward 1852 wb-h-Jun (O)
Box, Edward C. 1852 wb-h-Jul (O)
Box, John W. 1848 wb-g-90 (Hu)
Box, Joseph 1860 wb-k-359 (O)
Box, Larkin 1857 wb-f-127 (Mu)
Box, Lindley 1852 wb-h-77 (Hu)
Box, Michael 1832 wb-a-133 (R)
Box, Robert 1821 wb-1-47 (Fr)
Box, Samuel 1836 wb-3-409 (Je)
Boxley, George 1832 wb-a-157 (R)
Boyan, Joseph H. 1840 wb-a-45 (F)
Boyce, Meshack 1849 lr (Gi)
Boyce, Rebecca C. 1857 wb-6-428 (Ma)
Boyd, Aaron 1858 wb-b-67 (Ms)
Boyd, Addison 1831 wb-1-311 (Ma)
Boyd, America A. 1827 wb-4-228 (Wi)
Boyd, Andrew 1825 wb-8-409 (D)
Boyd, Andrew 1829 wb-#186 (Mu)
Boyd, Armstead 1815 wb-2-151 (Wi)
Boyd, Armstead W. 1853 wb-15-274 (Rb)
Boyd, Catharine 1840 wb-7-72 (K)
Boyd, Catherine 1859 wb-13-118 (K)
Boyd, Charles H. 1854 wb-a-458 (F)
Boyd, David 1835 wb-9-67 (Rb)
Boyd, David H. 1851 wb-d-345 (G)
Boyd, Edward 1851 wb-g-397 (St)
Boyd, Eliza 1845 wb-f-282 (Hn)
Boyd, Elizabeth 1853 wb-16-130 (D)
Boyd, Elizabeth 1861 wb-19-24 (D)
Boyd, Elizabeth J. 1856 wb-17-64 (D)
Boyd, Fathy 1846 wb-#159 (Wl)

Boyd, Francis 1857 wb-#14 (Mc)
Boyd, George 1835 rb-g-98 (Mt)
Boyd, George C. 1847 rb-k-561 (Mt)
Boyd, George G. 1841 wb-7-465 (Wi)
Boyd, George W. 1830 wb-9-412 (D)
Boyd, George sr. 1830 wb-c-56 (St)
Boyd, Harrison 1818 wb-2-378 (Wi)
Boyd, Henry 1839 wb-#38 (Wa)
Boyd, Henry 1848 33-3-35 (Gr)
Boyd, Isabella 1838 wb-d-250 (St)
Boyd, James 1821 Wb-3-248 (Wi)
Boyd, James 1826 wb-#131 (Mu)
Boyd, James 1828 wb-9-215 (D)
Boyd, James 1841 wb-2-223 (Hy)
Boyd, James W. 1847 wb-8-593 (Wi)
Boyd, Jeter L. 1854 ib-1-303 (Wy)
Boyd, Joel 1828 rb-7-187 (Ru)
Boyd, John 1802 wb-1-100 (K)
Boyd, John 1838 wb-11-275 (D)
Boyd, John 1838 wb-11-426 (D)
Boyd, John 1841 lr (Sn)
Boyd, John 1846 wb-9-265 (K)
Boyd, John 1846 wb-g-134 (Hn)
Boyd, John 1853 wb-16-72 (D)
Boyd, John 1853 wb-xx-173 (St)
Boyd, John R. 1819 wb-3-103 (Wi)
Boyd, Joseph B. 1846 wb-13-378 (D)
Boyd, Laird B. 1842 wb-z-465 (Mu)
Boyd, Lamira 1838 wb-11-429 (D)
Boyd, Martha 1843 wb-8-40 (Wi)
Boyd, Mary 1845 wb-8-246 (Wi)
Boyd, Mary J. 1857 wb-17-228 (D)
Boyd, Michael 1849 wb-e-175 (Ro)
Boyd, Milton B. 1856 wb-6-205 (Ma)
Boyd, Nancy 1832 wb-5-139 (K)
Boyd, Nancy 1859 wb-17-610 (D)
Boyd, P. W. 1862 wb-i-357 (St)
Boyd, Paralee R. 1860 wb-b-450 (We)
Boyd, Penelope 1855 wb-a-238 (Cr)
Boyd, R. 1851 wb-14-674 (D)
Boyd, R. P. 1839 wb-11-537 (D)
Boyd, Racheal 1837 wb-11-43 (D)
Boyd, Rebecca 1857 as-c-27 (Ms)
Boyd, Richard 1825 wb-8-494 (D)
Boyd, Richard S. 1841 wb-2-238 (Hr)
Boyd, Robert 1793 wb-1-300 (D)
Boyd, Robert 1810 wb-a-2 (Wh)
Boyd, Robert 1823 wb-a-184 (Wh)
Boyd, Robert 1840 wb-a-1 (V)
Boyd, Robert 1853 wb-16-55 (D)
Boyd, Rutha A. M. 1852 wb-2-130 (Sh)

Boyd, Samuel 1859 wb-0-164 (Cf)
Boyd, Samuel B. 1855 wb-12-107 (K)
Boyd, Susan 1845 wb-c-265 (G)
Boyd, Washington L. 1860 wb-13-168 (Wi)
Boyd, Whitmell H. 1830 wb-9-390 (D)
Boyd, William 1805 wb-1-270 (Bo)
Boyd, William 1825 wb-1-13 (Bo)
Boyd, William 1826 wb-4-122 (K)
Boyd, William 1834 wb-1-109 (Hy)
Boyd, William 1840 wb-7-65 (K)
Boyd, William 1844 148-1-93 (Ge)
Boyd, William 1844 wb-#143 (Wl)
Boyd, William G. 1841 wb-7-464 (Wi)
Boyd, William H. 1848 wb-#156 (Wl)
Boyd, William J. 1829 wb-4-366 (Wi)
Boydston, Elizabeth 1861 wb-d-132 (L)
Boyed, R. S. 1847 wb-4-217 (Hr)
Boyers, Joseph 1847 5-3-288 (Cl)
Boyers, Joseph 1852 ib-2-39 (Cl)
Boyet, Parthena 1858 as-c-89 (Ms)
Boyett, Bethena 1853 wb-a-315 (Ms)
Boyett, Elijah 1844 wb-e-4 (O)
Boyett, Thomas H. 1860 wb-k-212 (O)
Boykin, Ely 1855 wb-6-26 (Ma)
Boykin, Mary 1860 wb-7-75 (Ma)
Boykin, Robert 1816 lr (Sn)
Boylan, Alexander 1854 ib-h-90 (F)
Boyle, George 1851 148-1-375 (Ge)
Boyle, James 1831 lr (Sn)
Boyle, Mathew H. 1847 wb-1-232 (Bo)
Boyle, William 1812 lr (Sn)
Boyles, Barnabas sr. 1831 wb-1-73 (Li)
Boyles, Robert 1828 lr (Sn)
Bozarth, James 1845 wb-a-61 (Dk)
Bozarth, Levi 1856 wb-b-15 (Dk)
Bozarth, Sarah 1859 39-2-282 (Dk)
Bozarth, Sarah 1860 39-2-336 (Dk)
Boze, Elizabeth 1859 wb-8-27 (Sm)
Bozoth, Levi 1840 wb-a-20 (Dk)
Brabson, John 1849 wb-1-4 (Se)
Brabson, John M. 1848 wb-#46 (Wa)
Brack, D. 1846 wb-g-152 (Hn)
Brack, Durham 1841 wb-e-272 (Hn)
Brackin, Andrew J. 1852 wb-3-435 (W)
Brackin, Elizabeth 1821 lr (Sn)
Brackin, William 1833 lr (Sn)
Bradberry, Ann E. 1845 rb-j-321 (Mt)
Bradbury, George 1843 wb-z-471 (Mu)
Bradbury, William 1842 wb-1-8 (Bo)
Braden, Alexander 1832 wb-1-335 (Ma)
Braden, Andrew 1847 wb-1B-3 (A)

Braden, Charles 1840 wb-#129 (Wl)
Braden, Dorothy 1847 wb-1B-3 (A)
Braden, Henry 1852 ib-1-250 (Cl)
Braden, Isaac 1857 wb-c-117 (L)
Braden, Joseph 1857 mr (Gi)
Braden, Samuel 1824 wb-#49 (Wl)
Braden, William 1826 wb-1-58 (Ma)
Bradford, Allery 1826 wb-b-89 (St)
Bradford, Booker 1833 wb-3-0 (Sm)
Bradford, David 1824 wb-3-289 (St)
Bradford, David 1825 wb-4-294 (Rb)
Bradford, David 1832 wb-2-0 (Sm)
Bradford, David A. 1857 wb-c-131 (L)
Bradford, Davis 1818 wb-1-0 (Sm)
Bradford, Eli M. 1838 rb-10-201 (Ru)
Bradford, Elizabeth 1838 wb-11-291 (D)
Bradford, Elizabeth 1841 wb-12-120* (D)
Bradford, Harris 1836 wb-b-122 (G)
Bradford, Helyard 1838 wb-1-354 (Hy)
Bradford, Henry 1828 wb-b-234 (St)
Bradford, Hillery 1825 wb-b-35 (St)
Bradford, J. F. 1860 wb-1-340 (Be)
Bradford, James 1813 wb-1-0 (Sm)
Bradford, James 1814 wb-1-0 (Sm)
Bradford, James 1849 rb-15-6 (Ru)
Bradford, James 1852 wb-5-63 (Je)
Bradford, James 1860 wb-1-324 (Be)
Bradford, James C. 1853 wb-b-198 (L)
Bradford, James F. 1852 wb-#14 (Mc)
Bradford, John 1827 wb-9-122 (D)
Bradford, John 1837 wb-11-284 (D)
Bradford, Joseph 1859 wb-1-383 (Fr)
Bradford, L. A. 1813 wb-1-176 (Sn)
Bradford, Mary Jane 1835 wb-10-515 (D)
Bradford, Mary M. 1842 wb-12-301* (D)
Bradford, Mary M. 1842 wb-12-318* (D)
Bradford, N. B. 1833 wb-3-233 (Je)
Bradford, Nancy B. 1848 wb-d-108 (G)
Bradford, Napolean B. 1833 wb-3-264 (Je)
Bradford, Robert 1815 wb-#16 (Wl)
Bradford, Robert 1840 wb-12-84* (D)
Bradford, Susan C. 1857 wb-16-355 (Rb)
Bradford, Thomas 1861 39-2-452 (Dk)
Bradford, Thomas B. 1834 wb-c-208 (Hn)
Bradford, Thomas G. 1849 wb-c-375 (Wh)
Bradford, William 1831 lr (Sn)
Bradford, William W. 1833 wb-c-300 (St)
Bradford, William W. 1844 wb-f-128 (St)
Bradley, Aaron 1815 wb-A-89 (Li)
Bradley, Albert 1839 wb-#127 (Wl)
Bradley, Anthony 1845 wb-#158 (Wl)

Bradley, Charles 1855 wb-g-649 (Hn)
Bradley, David 1832 wb-#93 (Wl)
Bradley, Ed. S. 1858 wb-7-0 (Sm)
Bradley, Edward 1830 wb-3-0 (Sm)
Bradley, Everett 1856 wb-#121 (Wl)
Bradley, George 1852 wb-#179 (Wl)
Bradley, George sr. 1815 wb-1-0 (Sm)
Bradley, Hetty 1859 rb-19-528 (Ru)
Bradley, James 1806 wb-1-0 (Sm)
Bradley, James 1830 wb-3-0 (Sm)
Bradley, James 1859 wb-1-130 (Jo)
Bradley, James H. 1861 wb-13-421 (Wi)
Bradley, John 1809 wb-#8 (Wl)
Bradley, John 1821 lr (Sn)
Bradley, John 1837 wb-#118 (Wl)
Bradley, John 1840 wb-7-104 (K)
Bradley, John 1853 rb-16-565 (Ru)
Bradley, John Jr. 1815 wb-#22 (Wl)
Bradley, Jonas 1852 wb-#180 (Wl)
Bradley, Joseph 1839 wb-10-301 (Rb)
Bradley, Leland J. 1861 wb-13-457 (Wi)
Bradley, Nancy 1845 wb-a2-314 (Mu)
Bradley, Nancy 1858 ib-2-100 (Wy)
Bradley, Nancy 1860 wb-e-318 (Wh)
Bradley, Orville 1845 wb-1-61 (Hw)
Bradley, Richard 1827 lr (Sn)
Bradley, Richard 1852 wb-2-260 (La)
Bradley, Sally 1851 wb-c-448 (Wh)
Bradley, Sally 1857 wb-e-166 (Wh)
Bradley, Sally jr. 1857 wb-e-146 (Wh)
Bradley, Stephen S. 1853 wb-10-610 (Wi)
Bradley, Thomas 1811 wb-#9 (Wl)
Bradley, Thomas 1822 wb-#42 (Wl)
Bradley, Thomas 1849 wb-9-288 (Wi)
Bradley, Virginia A. C. 1852
    wb-15-63 (Rb)
Bradley, William 1815 wb-2-195 (K)
Bradley, William 1835 wb-#15 (Mc)
Bradley, William 1844 wb-8-305 (K)
Bradley, William 1845 wb-1-57 (Hw)
Bradley, William 1858 wb-h-454 (St)
Bradly, Alfred G. 1831 wb-b-52 (Wh)
Bradly, Jonathan 1839 wb-#35 (Wa)
Bradon, Edward 1847 wb-5-499 (Gr)
Bradon, John sr. 1840 5-2-180 (Cl)
Bradshaw, Ann W. 1860 wb-a-293 (T)
Bradshaw, Benjamin 1832 wb-4-46 (Je)
Bradshaw, Charles 1828 wb-1-1 (We)
Bradshaw, David 1848 wb-b-289 (We)
Bradshaw, Elias 1826 wb-#165 (Mu)
Bradshaw, J. A. 1856 wb-e-430 (G)

Bradshaw, James C. 1851 wb-#169 (Wl)
Bradshaw, Joel sr. 1824 wb-a-187 (Wh)
Bradshaw, John 1843 wb-a-100 (T)
Bradshaw, John C. 1833 wb-10-213 (D)
Bradshaw, Joseph 1851 wb-14-661 (D)
Bradshaw, Mary 1848 wb-#156 (Wl)
Bradshaw, Thomas 1841 wb-#134 (Wl)
Bradshaw, William 1814 wb-#20 (Mu)
Bradshaw, William 1826 wb-#141 (Mu)
Bradshaw, William P. 1846 A-468-63 (Le)
Brady, Jemina 1847 wb-b-224 (We)
Brady, John 1800 wb-0-27 (K)
Brady, John 1814 wb-0-123 (K)
Brady, Susan C. 1859 rb-20-152 (Ru)
Brady, William J. 1830 rb-8-405 (Ru)
Brady, Wm. 1851 rb-16-504 (Ru)
Brag, Henry 1828 wb-b-263 (St)
Bragg, Dasher 1858 ib-1-558 (Ca)
Bragg, David 1844 wb-1-223 (Su)
Bragg, Edward 1859 wb-A-152 (Ca)
Bragg, John 1833 wb-3-236 (Je)
Bragg, John 1857 wb-h-104 (Hn)
Bragg, Moore 1816 wb-2-212 (Wi)
Bragg, Nicholas 1854 wb-5-356 (Je)
Bragg, Thomas 1836 rb-9-296 (Ru)
Braime, James 1847 rb-k-643 (Mt)
Brakebill, Katharine 1851 wb-11-2 (K)
Brakefield, John W. 1860 wb-1-395 (Fr)
Brakefield, Lucy 1848 wb-1-247 (Fr)
Brakefield, William 1840 wb-10-541 (Rb)
Braley, John 1839 wb-a-77 (Cr)
Bram, Elizabeth 1845 wb-7-0 (Sm)
Bramblet, Larkin 1852 wb-e-7 (G)
Brame, Charles B. 1859 wb-b-79 (F)
Brame?, William S. 1836 wb-a-3 (F)
Bramhall, Thomas 1827 wb-1-40 (Hw)
Bramlett, Lunsford 1853 lr (Gi)
Bran, Joseph T. 1852 wb-2-127 (Me)
Branan, William 1849 wb-2-42 (Sh)
Branch, B. 1855 ib-h-426 (F)
Branch, Benj. 1859 gs-1-518 (F)
Branch, Benjamin 1819 wb-7-352 (D)
Branch, Benjamin C. 1848 wb-g-26 (O)
Branch, Bryant M. 1839 wb-b-287 (G)
Branch, James 1846 wb-a2-348 (Mu)
Branch, James sr. 1844 wb-a2-75 (Mu)
Branch, Jessee B. 1861 wb-a-392 (Cr)
Branch, John N. 1852 wb-2-121 (Sh)
Branch, Joseph 1827 wb-4-253 (Wi)
Branch, Joseph 1834 wb-5-371 (Wi)
Branch, Levi 1832 wb-1-339 (Ma)

Branch, Nancy 1845 wb-13-304 (D)
Branch, Nancy L. 1841 wb-z-292 (Mu)
Branch, Nancy Lucinda 1841 wb-z-530 (Mu)
Branch, Richard H. 1858 gs-1-150 (F)
Branch, Robert 1821 wb-#39 (Wl)
Branch, Robert C. 1838 wb-#121 (Wl)
Branch, Robert C. C. 1839 wb-#128 (Wl)
Branch, Thomas 1831 wb-#93 (Wl)
Branch, Thrusirilus M. 1840 wb-z-62 (Mu)
Branch, W. E. 1859 gs-1-340 (F)
Branckler, Daniel 1846 wb-8-379 (Wi)
Brand, Barnet 1842 wb-b°-15 (O)
Brand, Joseph 1797 wb-0-21 (K)
Branden, Jonathan 1848 wb-a-152 (Cr)
Brandon, Cornelius 1853 ib-1-249 (Ca)
Brandon, Cornelius 1853 ib-1-256 (Ca)
Brandon, George 1825 wb-b-18 (St)
Brandon, George 1844 rb-12-555 (Ru)
Brandon, John 1830 wb-#15 (Mc)
Brandon, John 1836 wb-2-46# (Ge)
Brandon, John 1846 148-1-147 (Ge)
Brandon, John E. 1852 ib-1-248 (Ca)
Brandon, Josiah 1842 wb-1-213 (Li)
Brandon, Lemuel 1860 wb-2-312 (Li)
Brandon, Nancy 1860 wb-A-157 (Ca)
Brandon, Richard 1834 lr (Gi)
Brandon, Thomas 1786 wb-1-1# (Ge)
Brandon, Thomas 1789 wb-1-1# (Ge)
Brandon, Thomas 1846 wb-2-64# (Ge)
Brandon, William 1855 149-1-19 (Ge)
Brandon, William 1857 wb-h-374 (St)
Branham, Benjamin 1822 wb-a-173 (Ro)
Brank, R. H. 1827 wb-#160 (Mu)
Brank, Robert H. 1829 wb-#185 (Mu)
Branly, Charles J. 1830 wb-1-40 (Hy)
Brannan, Robert 1858 wb-1-367 (Fr)
Branner, Michael 1832 wb-4-37 (Je)
Branner, Turner 1859 wb-13-198 (K)
Brannon, James 1816 wb-7-52 (D)
Bransford, John 1831 wb-3-0 (Sm)
Bransford, John 1838 wb-11-422 (D)
Bransford, L. M. 1857 wb-17-182 (D)
Bransford, Murray L. 1856 wb-17-149 (D)
Bransford, Richard R. 1850 wb-7-0 (Sm)
Bransford, Samuel W. 1848 wb-14-258 (D)
Branson, Dan 1830 wb-3-77 (Je)
Branson, Daniel 1829 wb-3-393 (Je)
Branson, Eli 1855 wb-e-533 (Ro)
Brantley, Charles 1803 rb-a-180 (Mt)
Brantley, Eliza J. 1858 rb-o-672 (Mt)
Brantley, Hannah M. 1852 wb-10-190 (Wi)

Brantley, Hugh 1856 rb-o-62 (Mt)
Brantley, J. M. (Mrs.) 1852 wb-10-206 (Wi)
Brantley, James 1810 rb-a-344 (Mt)
Brantley, James 1845 rb-j-344 (Mt)
Brantley, John 1841 wb-2-284 (Hr)
Brantley, John 1841 wb-2-294 (Hr)
Brantley, Lewis 1856 rb-o-68 (Mt)
Brantley, Lucy 1850 wb-m-151 (Mt)
Brantley, Naomi 1854 wb-n-372 (Mt)
Brantley, Phillip 1843 wb-3-100 (Hr)
Brantley, Sarah A. 1851 as-b-6 (Ms)
Brantley, Thomas 1814 rb-b-177 (Mt)
Brantley, Thomas 1814 rb-b-180 (Mt)
Brantley, William 1841 rb-i-104 (Mt)
Brantley, William 1856 wb-16-229 (Rb)
Brantly, Abraham 1850 wb-m-106 (Mt)
Brantly, Benjamin C. 1849 as-a-190 (Ms)
Brantly, Mary 1851 rb-4-247 (Mu)
Brantly, Neander 1854 wb-n-341 (Mt)
Brantly, Neona 1856 rb-o-186 (Mt)
Branum, David P. 1853 wb-1-7 (Bo)
Branum, Turner 1860 wb-13-251 (K)
Brasel, William 1826 lr (Sn)
Brasfield, Caleb 1847 wb-b-211 (We)
Brasfield, Catharine 1848 wb-b-263 (We)
Brashear, Jesse 1822 rb-5-253 (Ru)
Brashears, Margaret 1856 wb-f-49 (Ro)
Brashears, Robert 1857 wb-f-119 (Ro)
Brasher, Henry 1829 wb-1-4 (La)
Brasher, Jesse 1847 wb-1-420 (La)
Brasher, John 1852 wb-3-95 (La)
Brasher, John 1854 wb-#114 (Wl)
Brasher, Robert S. 1816 wb-a-74 (Ro)
Brasher, William 1836 wb-a-120 (Di)
Brashers, Robert 1852 wb-3-81 (La)
Brasier, Man 1836? as-a-310 (Di)
Brassell, Pharely 1852 wb-7-0 (Sm)
Brassfield, Willie 1828 wb-a-105 (G)
Braswell, Elizabeth 1856 wb-3e-30 (Sh)
Braswell, Samuel 1852 wb-15-169 (Rb)
Bratcher, Allen 1836 wb-1-219 (W)
Bratcher, Canady 1835 wb-1-79 (W)
Bratcher, Charles 1833 eb-1-303 (C)
Bratcher, John 1821 eb-1-113 (C)
Bratcher, Moses J. 1859 gs-1-336 (F)
Brattenboucher, John Jacob 1836 wb-b-37 (Hd)
Bratton, G. A. 1839 wb-2-65 (Hy)
Bratton, Henry 1824 wb-1-0 (Sm)
Bratton, Hugh W. 1838 wb-b-261 (G)
Bratton, James 1815 wb-1-0 (Sm)
Bratton, James E. 1854 39-1-346 (Dk)

Bratton, John 1833 wb-1-125 (Fr)
Bratton, John W. 1835 wb-b-80 (G)
Bratton, Thomas 1856 39-2-156 (Dk)
Brawley, Thomas 1827 wb-#162 (Mu)
Brawly (Braley), Hugh Press? 1811
    rb-2-165 (Ru)
Brawly, William 1840 wb-y-638 (Mu)
Braxton (B), William 1839 5-2-57 (Cl)
Bray, Henry 1827 wb-1-33 (Hw)
Bray, Iredell D. 1855 wb-2-105 (Li)
Bray, Jane 1851 wb-1B-265 (A)
Bray, John 1860 wb-1-409 (Fr)
Brazeale, David R. 1848 wb-e-112 (Ro)
Brazeale, Henry 1856 wb-f-1 (Ro)
Brazeale, James 1854 wb-e-498 (Ro)
Brazier, Jacob 1859 wb-16-812 (Rb)
Breadenbucker, John J. 1836 wb-b-1 (Hd)
Breathett, Edward 1838 wb-11-430 (D)
Breathitt, Edward 1837 wb-11-170 (D)
Breazeale, Benjamin Franklin 1850
    wb-e-208 (Ro)
Breazeale, John 1814 wb-a-63 (Ro)
Breazeale, Willis 1860 wb-f-386 (Ro)
Breckenridge, Alexander 1823 wb-#57 (Mu)
Breckenridge, Hannah C. 1851 wb-2-197 (La)
Breckinridge, Alexander (Sr.) 1813 wb-#9 (Mu)
Bredin, Charles 1840 wb-#128 (Wl)
Breeden, James 1815 wb-1-34 (Hw)
Breeden, James 1853 as-b-101 (Ms)
Breeden, John 1854 wb-n-228 (Mt)
Breeden, John 1859 wb-1-55 (Se)
Breeden, Mark 1832 wb-3-191 (Je)
Bredin, A. M. 1859 wb-1-388 (Fr)
Breedlove, Thomas 1831 wb-#92 (Wl)
Breedlove, Thomas C. 1826 wb-#63 (Wl)
Breedwell, George 1858 wb-#28 (Mo)
Breedwell, Washington 1858 wb-#13 (Mo)
Breniche, Lucas 1858 wb-3e-76 (Sh)
Brenin, William 1836 rb-g-274 (Mt)
Brent, Elizabeth 1849 wb-14-430 (D)
Brent, Hugh 1825 wb-8-430 (D)
Brents, Thomas 1842 as-a-72 (Ms)
Bressie, John 1832 lr (Sn)
Brett, Bartholomew 1861 wb-#134 (Wl)
Brevard, Benjamin 1840 wb-e-348 (Hu)
Brevard, Dave? Maria 1838 wb-a-27 (F)
Brevard, John 1827 wb-3-0 (Sm)
Brewer, Benjamin 1833 wb-1-396 (Ma)
Brewer, Benjamin 1836 wb-2-99 (Ma)
Brewer, Benjamin 1847 mr-2-256 (Be)
Brewer, Benjamin 1850 ib-1-118 (Ca)

Brewer, Daniel 1843 mr-2-60 (Be)
Brewer, Elisha 1823 wb-8-280 (D)
Brewer, Enoch 1855 ib-1-346 (Wy)
Brewer, G. W. 1852 ib-1-176 (Wy)
Brewer, George W. 1852 ib-1-185 (Wy)
Brewer, Henry 1842 wb-#138 (Wl)
Brewer, Henry 1853 ib-1-221 (Wy)
Brewer, Henry J. 1858 ib-2-87 (Wy)
Brewer, James 1853 wb-15-276 (Rb)
Brewer, Jesse 1850 ib-1-117 (Ca)
Brewer, Jo B. 1850 ib-1-145 (Ca)
Brewer, John 1844 wb-a-165 (Di)
Brewer, John 1850 wb-g-375 (Hn)
Brewer, John A. 1856 wb-16-326 (Rb)
Brewer, John A. 1857 wb-16-354 (Rb)
Brewer, Jones 1853 wb-15-315 (Rb)
Brewer, Lewis 1857 wb-#15 (Mc)
Brewer, Martha 1853 rb-16-466 (Ru)
Brewer, Nicholas 1851 mr-2-404 (Be)
Brewer, Russel 1858 wb-3-442 (W)
Brewer, Sally 1857 wb-16-535 (Rb)
Brewer, Sylvanus 1839 5-2-91 (Cl)
Brewer, W. 1849 wb-4-500 (Hr)
Brewer, William 1817 wb-A-161 (Li)
Brewer, William 1837 wb-1-247 (W)
Brewer, William 1847 wb-4-190 (Hr)
Brewer, William 1848 wb-2-297 (W)
Brewer, William 1849 ib-1-30 (Wy)
Brewer, Wineford 1837 wb-2-259 (Ma)
Brian, Joseph H. 1846 wb-d-210 (Hd)
Briant, John 1856 wb-e-404 (G)
Briant, John F. 1852 wb-4-599 (Mu)
Briant, John G. 1860 wb-#16 (Mc)
Briant, Rebecca 1826 wb-#62 (Wl)
Briant, William F. 1840 wb-#16 (Mc)
Brice, Con 1859 wb-3e-139 (Sh)
Brice, John 1827 wb-9-80 (D)
Brice, William 1828 wb-1-8 (Sh)
Bricker, Michael 1806 wb-#10 (Wa)
Brickle, James 1841 wb-7-435 (Wi)
Brickle, Jeremiah 1837 rb-g-513 (Mt)
Brider, Tobias 1847 wb-a-320 (F)
Bridge, Barnes 1818 wb-#90 (Mu)
Bridgeforth, David 1840 lr (Gi)
Bridgeforth, Samuel 1851 rb-4-271 (Mu)
Bridges, Baynes 1818 wb-#78 (Mu)
Bridges, David 1859 wb-#128 (Wl)
Bridges, Drury 1812 wb-#24 (Mu)
Bridges, Drury 1812 wb-#4 (Mu)
Bridges, Elizabeth 1841 wb-#148 (Wl)
Bridges, Ephraim 1837 wb-b-379 (Ro)

Bridges, H. D. 1850 wb-4-589 (Hr)
Bridges, Helen E. 1853 wb-#16 (Mc)
Bridges, Joseph 1849 wb-7-0 (Sm)
Bridges, Morris D. 1847 wb-4-251 (Hr)
Bridges, Moses 1848 wb-1-251 (Fr)
Bridges, Ruben 1861 wb-1-378 (Be)
Bridges, Thomas 1858 wb-7-0 (Sm)
Bridges, William 1806 wb-1-155 (Wi)
Bridgewater, Margarett 1844 wb-12-121 (Rb)
Bridgewater, William H. 1854 ib-h-222 (F)
Bridgman, William 1840 eb-1-432 (C)
Bridwell, Aden 1837 wb-1-9 (Me)
Bridwell, Elias 1826 wb-a-12 (R)
Brien, Emily J. 1860 wb-18-193 (D)
Brien, Susanna 1845 wb-9-110 (K)
Brien, William 1835 rb-g-211 (Mt)
Brient, George W. 1851 wb-e-303 (Ro)
Brient, John O. 1825 wb-#58 (Wl)
Brigance, John 1798 wb-1-47 (Sn)
Brigance, John 1816 lr (Sn)
Briggs, Amos 1859 wb-17-576 (D)
Briggs, Elizabeth M. 1849 rb-l-333 (Mt)
Briggs, George W. 1855 39-2-51 (Dk)
Briggs, Henry 1856 wb-16-142 (Rb)
Briggs, James 1831 wb-#224 (Mu)
Briggs, Samuel 1809 wb-1-0 (Sm)
Briggs, Samuel 1831 wb-#234 (Mu)
Briggs, Sarah (Mrs) 1854 rb-17-266 (Ru)
Briggs, Sarah 1853 rb-16-594 (Ru)
Briggs, Sterling 1858 wb-12-584 (Wi)
Brigham, David 1830 wb-c-68 (St)
Brigham, Indimson 1827 wb-b-192 (St)
Brigham, James 1815 rb-b-77 (Mt)
Brigham, James H. 1841 wb-e-430 (Hu)
Brigham, James H. 1852 wb-xx-4 (St)
Brigham, James M. 1857 wb-h-350 (St)
Brigham, Jane 1860 wb-i-251 (St)
Brigham, John 1838 wb-e-73 (Hu)
Brigham, John 1841 wb-e-385 (Hu)
Brigham, John 1852 wb-h-76 (Hu)
Brigham, Mary 1856 wb-h-284 (St)
Brigham, Mary 1857 wb-h-443 (St)
Brigham, Robert M. 1853 wb-xx-242 (St)
Brigham, Robert W. 1852 wb-xx-98 (St)
Brigham, Thomas 1849 wb-g-169 (St)
Brigham, William 1849 wb-g-185 (St)
Bright, James 1822 wb-1-0 (Sm)
Bright, Jervis 1846 wb-#153 (Wl)
Bright, John 1836 wb-6-44 (K)
Bright, John H. 1850 wb-#7 (Mo)
Bright, Michael 1858 149-1-126 (Ge)

Bright, Michael 1859 wb-2-90# (Ge)
Bright, Michael sr. 1842 wb-2-59# (Ge)
Bright, Thomas 1855 wb-3-270 (W)
Bright, William 1851 wb-3-87 (W)
Bright, William sr. 1853 wb-2-71 (Li)
Brightwell, John C. 1850 wb-d-260 (G)
Briles, Sarah 1855 wb-16-572 (D)
Briles, Sarah Ann 1844 wd-13-18 (D)
Briley, Samuel 1824 lr (Sn)
Brim, Daniel 1830 wb-9-460 (D)
Brim, John 1848 wb-9-129 (Wi)
Brim, Joseph 1819 wb-1-0 (Sm)
Brim, Raliegh 1846 wb-d-226 (Hd)
Brim, William 1845 wb-d-171 (Hd)
Brinkley, Alexander 1823 wb-8-202 (D)
Brinkley, Eli 1857 wb-17-255 (D)
Brinkley, Henry 1853 wb-a-436 (F)
Brinkley, James 1855 wb-16-512 (D)
Brinkley, Mark A. 1849 wb-#170 (Wl)
Brinkley, Samuel 1816 wb-#23 (Wl)
Brinkly, Alexander 1825 wb-8-410 (D)
Brinley, Stephen 1843 wb-#16 (Mc)
Brinson, Drury D. 1834 wb-c-382 (St)
Brinson, Jesse 1817 wb-#25 (Wl)
Brisby, John 1852 wb-4-381 (Mu)
Briscoe, George 1836 wb-x-350 (Mu)
Brister, James 1833 wb-1-74 (W)
Bristow, Benjamin 1808 wb-1-262 (Rb)
Bristow, John 1848 rb-k-801 (Mt)
Bristow, John 1848 rb-l-15 (Mt)
Brit, Mary 1859 wb-#16 (Mc)
Britain, Jno. S. 1860 wb-18-405 (D)
Brite, Jeptha 1846 wb-b-188 (We)
Briton, James M. 1815 wb-2-112 (Je)
Britt, Holland 1856 wb-a-268 (Cr)
Britt, John 1823 wb-1-2# (Ge)
Britt, Malinda 1847 wb-#161 (Wl)
Britt, Rowland 1816 wb-2-254 (K)
Britt, Zedakiah 1856 rb-o-216 (Mt)
Britt, Zedekiah 1859 rb-p-264 (Mt)
Brittain, Cullen 1830 wb-b-129 (Hn)
Brittain, Dorothy 1853 as-b-141 (Ms)
Brittain, Henry 1839 wb-3-95 (Ma)
Brittain, James W. 1856 wb-b-21 (Ms)
Brittain, John 1859 rb-20-193 (Ru)
Brittain, Joseph 1855 wb-e-538 (Ro)
Brittain, Levi 1851 ib-1-225 (Cl)
Brittain, Polly 1824 wb-1-0 (Sm)
Brittain, Robert 1839 wb-c-71 (Ro)
Brittain, William 1847 wb-e-34 (Ro)
Brittan, Richard 1814 wb-1-0 (Sm)

Britten, John 1804 as-1-82 (Ge)
Britten, Samuel 1840 wb-3-0 (Sm)
Britton, Abraham 1813 wb-1-0 (Sm)
Britton, Abraham 1818 wb-#28 (Wl)
Britton, Henry C. 1841 wb-3-471 (Ma)
Britton, John H. 1848 wb-#166 (Wl)
Britton, Margarett 1819 wb-1-0 (Sm)
Britton, William 1853 wb-1-37 (R)
Britton, William H. 1840 wb-a-474 (R)
Britton, William T. 1852 wb-m-460 (Mt)
Britton, William sr. 1843 148-1-62 (Ge)
Brittonham, Polly 1849 wb-d-181 (G)
Brizendine, John 1850 lr (Sn)
Brizendine, John B. 1856 lr (Sn)
Brizendine, Leroy 1839 wb-2-252 (Sn)
Brizendine, Thomas 1837 wb-d-142* (Hn)
Brizendine, Thomas D. 1839 wb-e-45 (Hn)
Broach, George 1843 wb-f-155 (Hn)
Broach, S. S. 1854 wb-g-642 (Hn)
Broadaway, Benjamin 1850 ib-1-113 (Wy)
Brock, Elbert 1853 wb-#16 (Mc)
Brock, Isaac 1855 wb-#17 (Mc)
Brock, James 1817 eb-1-65 (C)
Brock, James 1858 wb-a-270 (V)
Brock, Micajah 1854 wb-e-443 (Ro)
Brock, Obediah 1860 wb-13-334 (K)
Brock, Samuel 1838 wb-b-321 (Wh)
Brock, Sherod 1815 eb-1-50 (C)
Brockett, M. W. 1850 wb-g-272 (O)
Brockett, William 1821 wb-1-0 (Sm)
Brockler, Daniel 1845 wb-8-365 (Wi)
Brockwell, Martin W. 1852 wb-h-Sep (O)
Brockwell, Thomas N. 1854 ib-h-256 (F)
Brodie, John 1830 rb-f-140 (Mt)
Brogan, John 1852 wb-#178 (Wl)
Brogan, R. G. 1847 wb-#153 (Wl)
Brogan, Reason G. 1849 wb-#164 (Wl)
Brogden, Willis 1841 wb-e-301 (Hn)
Brogden, Wily 1841 wb-e-302 (Hn)
Brogdon, Willie sr. 1836 wb-d-250 (Hn)
Broiles, Alfred 1831 rb-8-297 (Ru)
Broiles, Elizabeth 1850 rb-15-300 (Ru)
Broils, Elijah 1852 rb-16-221 (Ru)
Broils, Matthias 1818 rb-4-113 (Ru)
Broils, Matthias 1842 rb-12-176 (Ru)
Bromaker, F. 1838 wb-11-288 (D)
Bromley (Brumley), John 1850 ib-1-89 (Wy)
Bronson, Jesse A. 1837 wb-d-58 (St)
Bronson, Solomon 1849 wb-10-121 (K)
Brook, Elizabeth 1856 ib-h-505 (F)
Brook, Elizabeth 1857 ib-2-43 (Wy)

Brook, William 1846 wb-b-131 (We)
Brooks, Abner sr. 1854 wb-f-50 (Mu)
Brooks, Amanda 1849 wb-9-296 (Wi)
Brooks, Armstead 1839 5-2-83 (Cl)
Brooks, Artha 1806 wb-#13 (Wl)
Brooks, Arthur 1820 wb-A-307 (Li)
Brooks, B. 1845 wb-d-206 (Hd)
Brooks, Benjamin 1823 wb-1-29 (Ma)
Brooks, Bennett 1845 wb-d-194 (Hd)
Brooks, Browder 1846 wb-d-216 (Hd)
Brooks, Christopher 1832 wb-5-135 (Wi)
Brooks, Christopher 1854 wb-16-394 (D)
Brooks, Ebenezer 1799 wb-1-29 (Hw)
Brooks, Elijah 1827 wb-4-213 (Wi)
Brooks, Elijah G. 1849 wb-9-302 (Wi)
Brooks, Elizabeth 1852 wb-f-13 (Mu)
Brooks, G. P. 1840 5-2-172 (Cl)
Brooks, George 1836 wb-6-279 (Wi)
Brooks, George 1853 ib-1-264 (Cl)
Brooks, George A. 1849 wb-9-248 (Wi)
Brooks, George Magdalen K. 1841
    wb-7-457 (Wi)
Brooks, Hannah 1841 wb-7-466 (Wi)
Brooks, Henry 1853 wb-7-0 (Sm)
Brooks, Hezekiah 1836 wb-x-416 (Mu)
Brooks, Hezekiah 1838? 5-2-1 (Cl)
Brooks, Isaac 1829 wb-#189 (Mu)
Brooks, James 1827 wb-4-155 (Wi)
Brooks, James 1848 wb-14-68 (Rb)
Brooks, James 1852 wb-2-124 (Sh)
Brooks, James 1855 ib-h-323 (F)
Brooks, Jesse 1834 wb-d-63 (Hn)
Brooks, John 1830 lr (Gi)
Brooks, John 1842 wb-7-585 (Wi)
Brooks, John 1844 wb-8-316 (K)
Brooks, John 1845 wb-g-25 (Hn)
Brooks, John sr. 1831 wb-9-472 (D)
Brooks, Joseph 1834 wb-1-23 (Sh)
Brooks, Keziah 1841 wb-z-124 (Mu)
Brooks, Leonard 1845 wb-1-136 (Me)
Brooks, Liles 1799 wb-#7 (Wa)
Brooks, M. G. 1848 as-a-165 (Ms)
Brooks, Mariah L. 1850 wb-a-380 (F)
Brooks, Mathew 1806 wb-#13 (Wl)
Brooks, Matthew 1812 wb-4-182 (D)
Brooks, Moses 1830 wb-5-22* (K)
Brooks, Moses T. 1861 wb-18-605 (D)
Brooks, Priscilla 1845 wb-8-355 (Wi)
Brooks, Robert 1816 wb-2-231 (K)
Brooks, Robert 1821 wb-1-51 (Fr)
Brooks, Robert 1840 as-a-38 (Ms)

Brooks, Samuel 1824 wb-#76 (Mu)
Brooks, Samuel 1851 wb-4-151 (Mu)
Brooks, Samuel T. 1814? wb-#29 (Mu)
Brooks, Sarah 1836 wb-2-169 (Ma)
Brooks, Stephen 1833 wb-x-79 (Mu)
Brooks, Stephen 1850 wb-2-81# (Ge)
Brooks, Thomas 1853 ib-1-225 (Wy)
Brooks, Thomas F. 1846 wb-e-297 (O)
Brooks, W. C. 1859 wb-h-327 (Hn)
Brooks, Wilks 1849 wb-2-45 (Sh)
Brooks, William 1836 wb-d-200 (Hn)
Brooks, William 1850 wb-g-352 (Hn)
Brooks, William B. 1836 wb-a-42 (T)
Brooks, William D. 1854 wb-1-64 (Hw)
Brookshire, Fairley 1824 wb-8-294 (D)
Brookshire, James 1813 rb-2-228 (Ru)
Broom, Brittain 1815 rb-b-278 (Mt)
Broom, Francis E. 1844 wb-a-233 (F)
Broom, Henry D. 1852 wb-a-415 (F)
Broom, Jessee H. 1844 wb-a-226 (F)
Broom, John 1860 wb-b-84 (F)
Broom, Jonathan 1814 wb-#90 (Mu)
Broom, Mary 1814? wb-#30 (Mu)
Broom, Melus 1846 wb-#17 (Mc)
Broom, Miles 1816 wb-1-0 (Sm)
Broom, P. P. 1855 ib-h-294 (F)
Broom, Thomas 1852 wb-a-419 (F)
Broomfield, Elisha 1841 wb-7-468 (Wi)
Brothers, Frances 1856 rb-18-122 (Ru)
Brothers, Francis 1845 rb-13-218 (Ru)
Brothers, John 1825 rb-6-110 (Ru)
Brothers, John 1847 rb-14-181 (Ru)
Brothers, John F. 1847 rb-14-65 (Ru)
Brothers, Thomas 1850 rb-15-440 (Ru)
Brotherton, James 1851 wb-2-72# (Ge)
Brotherton, Jane 1852 wb-2-76# (Ge)
Brotherton, William 1838 wb-2-49# (Ge)
Brotherton, William 1856 149-1-40 (Ge)
Broughton, Partheny A. O. 1854 mr-2-541 (Be)
Brow, George 1857 wb-#123 (Wl)
Browder, Darius 1848 wb-e-88 (Ro)
Browder, Fredrick 1815 wb-2-158 (Wi)
Browder, James 1849 wb-1-259 (Me)
Browder, John 1818 wb-a-110 (Ro)
Browder, Rhoda 1838 wb-6-456 (Wi)
Brown, A. 1850 wb-g-305 (Hu)
Brown, A. Brooks 1860 wb-#17 (Mc)
Brown, A. C. 1841 wb-12-26 (D)
Brown, A. Y. 1849 as-b-414 (Di)
Brown, Aaron 1828 lr (Gi)
Brown, Aaron V. 1860 wb-18-134 (D)

Brown, Alexander 1814 rb-b-193 (Mt)
Brown, Alexander 1853 wb-2-78# (Ge)
Brown, Alford 1848 as-c-39 (Di)
Brown, Amos 1852 wb-5-181 (Je)
Brown, Andrew 1833 wb-1-120 (Fr)
Brown, Andrew 1861 rb-p-528 (Mt)
Brown, Ann 1820 wb-1-0 (Sm)
Brown, Bedford 1821 wb-#42 (Wl)
Brown, Bedford 1826 wb-8-521 (D)
Brown, Benedict W. 1837 wb-x-474 (Mu)
Brown, Benedict W. 1837 wb-y-17 (Mu)
Brown, Benjamin 1828 lw (Ct)
Brown, Benjamin 1836 wb-6-116 (Wi)
Brown, Benjamin 1854 wb-h-212 (Hu)
Brown, Bernard 1843 lr (Sn)
Brown, Catharine 1855 wb-f-62 (Mu)
Brown, Charles 1816 wb-2-230 (Wi)
Brown, Charles 1824 wb-#146 (Mu)
Brown, Charles 1830 wb-1-224 (Ma)
Brown, Charles V. 1838 wb-y-154 (Mu)
Brown, Chas. 1848 wb-4-335 (Hr)
Brown, Clabourn 1835 wb-d-124 (Hn)
Brown, Coleman 1838 wb-b-301 (Wh)
Brown, Cyntha C. 1846 wb-5-460 (Gr)
Brown, Dance 1860 lr (Sn)
Brown, Daniel 1828 wb-#183 (Mu)
Brown, Daniel 1829 wb-9-348 (D)
Brown, Daniel 1836 wb-1-133 (W)
Brown, Daniel 1836 wb-a-89 (O)
Brown, Daniel 1852 wb-2-44 (Li)
Brown, Darious G. 1843 wb-1-569 (W)
Brown, Darius Q. 1840 wb-1-310 (W)
Brown, David 1839 wb-b-103 (O)
Brown, David 1845 148-1-136 (Ge)
Brown, David sr. 1843 wb-2-59# (Ge)
Brown, Davis 1837 lr (Gi)
Brown, Dorcas 1861 wb-1-412 (Fr)
Brown, Duncan 1847 lr (Gi)
Brown, Duncan 1861 wb-f-213 (Mu)
Brown, Easther W. 1858 wb-b-65 (F)
Brown, Eldridge 1852 wb-h-213 (Hu)
Brown, Elijah 1814 wb-1-204 (Bo)
Brown, Elijah 1861 wb-a-304 (T)
Brown, Elizabeth 1827 wb-#171 (Mu)
Brown, Elizabeth 1833 wb-#99 (Wl)
Brown, Elizabeth 1837 wb-1-39 (Sh)
Brown, Elizabeth 1848 wb-b-303 (Mu)
Brown, Elizabeth 1855 lr (Gi)
Brown, Ephraim 1841 wb-7-366 (Wi)
Brown, Ezekiel 1817 wb-7-168 (D)
Brown, George 1851 wb-14-609 (D)

Brown, Gilbert A. 1848 wb-2-291 (W)
Brown, Grief F. 1851 wb-b-552 (Mu)
Brown, Henry 1839 wb-1-271 (W)
Brown, Henry 1852 wb-10-212 (Wi)
Brown, Henry W. 1853 wb-1-77 (Jo)
Brown, Henry sr. 1842 wb-c-276 (Ro)
Brown, Honor 1837 wb-a-55 (T)
Brown, Hu 1838 wb-6-274 (K)
Brown, Hugh 1789 wb-1-28 (Hw)
Brown, Hugh 1792 wb-0-40 (K)
Brown, Hugh 1851 rb-4-199 (Mu)
Brown, Hugh 1851 wb-11-79 (K)
Brown, Hugh M. 1852 mr-2-484 (Be)
Brown, Isaac C. 1839 rb-10-271 (Ru)
Brown, J. 1854 wb-12-33 (K)
Brown, J. A. 1850 wb-2-82 (Sh)
Brown, J. P. 1859 wb-17-604 (D)
Brown, J. P. W. 1851 wb-15-142 (D)
Brown, J. W. 1847 rb-k-521 (Mt)
Brown, J. Z. W. 1851 wb-15-11 (D)
Brown, Jacob 1831 wb-#34 (Wa)
Brown, Jacob 1841 wb-#38 (Wa)
Brown, James 1795 wb-2-34 (D)
Brown, James 1813 wb-1-0 (Sm)
Brown, James 1819 wb-1-310 (Ma)
Brown, James 1826 lr (Sn)
Brown, James 1827 wb-#163 (Mu)
Brown, James 1829 wb-1-162 (Ma)
Brown, James 1829 wb-1-40 (Li)
Brown, James 1832 wb-3-0 (Sm)
Brown, James 1834 rb-f-541 (Mt)
Brown, James 1839 wb-b-324 (Wh)
Brown, James 1842 148-1-40 (Ge)
Brown, James 1843 wb-3-0 (Sm)
Brown, James 1847 wb-a-161 (Ms)
Brown, James 1848 rb-l-96 (Mt)
Brown, James 1855 wb-#26 (Mo)
Brown, James 1857 wb-2-85# (Ge)
Brown, James 1859 wb-1-128 (Jo)
Brown, James H. 1828 wb-#187 (Mu)
Brown, James N. 1829 wb-#192 (Mu)
Brown, James P. 1848 wb-b-175 (Mu)
Brown, James P. 1852 wb-10-415 (Wi)
Brown, James R. 1855 wb#23 (Gu)
Brown, Jane 1845 wb-f-261 (St)
Brown, Jane B. 1847 wb-14-18 (D)
Brown, Jehu 1852 wb-4-383 (Mu)
Brown, Jeremiah 1838 rb-h-170 (Mt)
Brown, Jesse 1814 wb-#17 (Mu)
Brown, Jesse 1827 wb-#72 (Wl)
Brown, Jesse 1842 wb-12-258* (D)

Brown, Jethro 1818 wb-#45 (Mu)
Brown, Joel 1836 wb-2-209 (Sn)
Brown, Joel E. 1845 wb-1-263 (Li)
Brown, Joel M. 1849 rb-l-474 (Mt)
Brown, John (the elder) 1846 wb-a2-453 (Mu)
Brown, John 1795 wb-2-28 (D)
Brown, John 1796 wb-1-46 (K)
Brown, John 1812 wb-#8 (Mu)
Brown, John 1821 wb-3-228 (K)
Brown, John 1830? wb-#29 (Wa)
Brown, John 1833 wb-1-46 (Gr)
Brown, John 1833 wb-d-5 (Hn)
Brown, John 1834 wb-#18 (Mc)
Brown, John 1835 wb-x-284* (Mu)
Brown, John 1836 wb-#113 (Wl)
Brown, John 1836 wb-10-645 (D)
Brown, John 1838 rb-h-77 (Mt)
Brown, John 1839 wb-A-13 (Ca)
Brown, John 1845 wb-2-60 (W)
Brown, John 1848 wb-c-136 (Ro)
Brown, John 1849 wb-10-228 (K)
Brown, John 1849 wb-a-212 (Di)
Brown, John 1851 rb-15-600 (Ru)
Brown, John 1858 wb-f-150 (Mu)
Brown, John 1860 wb-13-267 (K)
Brown, John B. 1834 wb-1-446 (Ma)
Brown, John D. 1843 wb-12-467* (D)
Brown, John E. 1846 wb-8-481 (Wi)
Brown, John F. 1830 wb-1-223 (Ma)
Brown, John L. 1842 wb-12-258* (D)
Brown, John L. 1845 wb-1-120 (Sh)
Brown, John M. 1847 6-2-24 (Le)
Brown, John P. W. 1852 wb-15-223 (D)
Brown, John R. 1853 wb-h-93 (Hu)
Brown, John Sr. 1851 as-c-132 (Di)
Brown, John W. 1837 rb-h-21 (Mt)
Brown, John W. 1849? wb-#48 (Wa)
Brown, John sr. 1849 rb-15-4 (Ru)
Brown, Jonathan 1829 wb-#18 (Mc)
Brown, Joseph 1814 Wb-2-96 (Wi)
Brown, Joseph 1843 wb-8-192 (K)
Brown, Joseph A. 1858 wb-12-557 (Wi)
Brown, Joshua 1842 wb-7-314 (K)
Brown, Joshua D. 1852 wb-2-32 (Li)
Brown, Josiah G. 1861 wb-18-469 (D)
Brown, Lent 1851 rb-16-136 (Ru)
Brown, Leonard 1833 lr (Sn)
Brown, Leroy 1844 wb-3-103 (Hr)
Brown, Littleton 1815 Wb-2-145 (Wi)
Brown, Lockey 1825 rb-d-479 (Mt)
Brown, Lucy 1860 as-c-223 (Ms)

Brown, Luther 1851 33-3-396 (Gr)
Brown, M. S. 1852 wb-1-70 (Jo)
Brown, Mahala 1850 wb-10-337 (K)
Brown, Martha 1855 lr (Gi)
Brown, Martha 1861 wb-18-569 (D)
Brown, Mary 1838 wb-b-230 (G)
Brown, Mary 1845 wb-a2-193 (Mu)
Brown, Mary 1848 rb-k-702 (Mt)
Brown, Mary Ann 1853 wb-#9 (Mo)
Brown, Matt 1809 lr (Sn)
Brown, Matthew 1839 abl-1-115 (T)
Brown, Matthew 1839 wb-#124 (Wl)
Brown, Maunce 1846 wb-7-0 (Sm)
Brown, Melzer 1860 gs-1-614 (F)
Brown, Michael 1826? wb-#25 (Wa)
Brown, Morgan 1840 wb-12-74* (D)
Brown, Morgan W. 1853 wb-16-167 (D)
Brown, Moses 1838 wb-11-209 (D)
Brown, Moses 1838 wb-11-261 (D)
Brown, N. T. P. 1851 wb-15-3 (D)
Brown, Nancy 1847 wb-8-535 (Wi)
Brown, Nancy C. 1854 wb-e-505 (Ro)
Brown, Nathaniel 1814 Wb-2-99 (Wi)
Brown, Nathaniel 1836 wb-6-109 (Wi)
Brown, Nimrod 1836 wb-2-205 (Sn)
Brown, O. T. 1859 wb-k-142 (O)
Brown, P. P. 1854 ib-h-70 (F)
Brown, Pearson 1822 wb-1-0 (Sm)
Brown, Perthine 1854 wb-g-559 (Hn)
Brown, Peter 1842 148-1-33 (Ge)
Brown, Peter 1858 149-1-103 (Ge)
Brown, Philip J. 1849 rb-15-118 (Ru)
Brown, Polly 1848 rb-k-734 (Mt)
Brown, Pryor L. 1854 wb-12-2 (K)
Brown, R. L. 1856 wb-2-151 (Li)
Brown, Richard 1825 lr (Sn)
Brown, Robert 1840 wb-e-267 (Hu)
Brown, Robert 1849 lr (Sn)
Brown, Robert 1849 wb-3-15 (W)
Brown, Robert 1854 ib-h-215 (F)
Brown, Robert 1855 rb-17-495 (Ru)
Brown, Robert A. 1857 wb-b-45 (F)
Brown, Robert C. 1842 wb-3-491 (Ma)
Brown, Robert H. 1841 as-a-493 (Di)
Brown, Robert M. 1861 wb-k-439 (O)
Brown, Robert T. 1838 wb-2-287 (Ma)
Brown, Robert T. 1851 lr (Sn)
Brown, Rosser 1820 as-A-74 (Di)
Brown, Ruffin 1838 wb-2-269 (Ma)
Brown, Ruffin 1838 wb-6-515 (Wi)
Brown, Russell 1858 wb#38 (Gu)

Brown, S. R. D. 1858 wb-f-161 (G)
Brown, Samuel 1818 wb-e-9 (Hy)
Brown, Samuel 1826 wb-1-2# (Ge)
Brown, Samuel 1836 wb-1-122 (Gr)
Brown, Samuel 1840 wb-#131 (Wl)
Brown, Samuel 1848 wb-9-181 (Wi)
Brown, Samuel 1852 wb-d-90 (Wh)
Brown, Samuel 1857 wb-4-149 (La)
Brown, Samuel 1858 wb-2-255 (Li)
Brown, Samuel D. 1853 wb-16-100 (D)
Brown, Sarah 1836 wb-1-1 (Me)
Brown, Sarah 1852 lr (Gi)
Brown, Sarah 1860 wb-#18 (Mc)
Brown, Silviah 1834 rb-g-159 (Mt)
Brown, Silvy 1852 wb-m-538 (Mt)
Brown, Skelton 1821 lr (Sn)
Brown, Spencer H. 1837 wb-6-295 (Wi)
Brown, Sterling 1850 as-b-34 (Ms)
Brown, Sterling M. 1847 wb-a-162* (Ms)
Brown, Susan 1833 wb-5-294 (Wi)
Brown, Susan 1845 wb-8-283 (Wi)
Brown, Susannah 1841 wb-7-374 (Wi)
Brown, T. D.. 1855 wb-i-243 (O)
Brown, Theoderick C. 1842 wb-7-511 (Wi)
Brown, Thomas 1793 wb-1-282 (D)
Brown, Thomas 1829 wb-#179 (Mu)
Brown, Thomas 1829 wb-#28 (Wa)
Brown, Thomas 1836 lr (Gi)
Brown, Thomas 1837 wb-1-534 (Hr)
Brown, Thomas 1839 wb-2-53# (Ge)
Brown, Thomas 1848 wb-e-117 (Ro)
Brown, Thomas 1849 wb-1-392* (W)
Brown, Thomas 1849 wb-3-18 (W)
Brown, Thomas 1854 ib-h-24 (F)
Brown, Thomas 1859 wb-e-213 (Wh)
Brown, Thomas 1859 wb-e-273 (Wh)
Brown, Thomas 1860 rb-20-590 (Ru)
Brown, Thomas 1861 wb-#23 (Mo)
Brown, Thomas C. 1840 wb-7-286 (Wi)
Brown, Thomas Parsons 1821 wb-1-1# (Ge)
Brown, Thomas S. 1818 wb-7-282 (D)
Brown, Thos. A. 1842 wb-0-29 (Cf)
Brown, Valentine 1840 wb-3-0 (Sm)
Brown, W. A. 1849 wb-g-148 (O)
Brown, W. C. 1844 wb-3-153 (Hr)
Brown, Walter 1814 wb-3-13 (St)
Brown, Wesley C. 1837 wb-1-555 (Hr)
Brown, William (Capt.) 1824 wb-A-385 (Li)
Brown, William 1800 lr (Sn)
Brown, William 1804 wb-1-85 (Sn)
Brown, William 1807 wb-1-233 (K)

Brown, William 1818 wb-3-51 (K)
Brown, William 1827 rb-6-290 (Ru)
Brown, William 1835 wb-2-51# (Ge)
Brown, William 1836 wb-b-220 (Wh)
Brown, William 1837 wb-1-229 (W)
Brown, William 1840 wb-7-321 (Wi)
Brown, William 1842 wb-c-72 (G)
Brown, William 1853 148-1-456 (Ge)
Brown, William 1853 wb-e-424 (Ro)
Brown, William 1856 wb-12-219 (Wi)
Brown, William C. 1846 wb-2-180 (W)
Brown, William D. 1859 wb-17-578 (D)
Brown, William F. 1829 wb-#182 (Mu)
Brown, William F. 1843 rb-12-297 (Ru)
Brown, William F. 1861 wb-f-419 (Ro)
Brown, William H. 1828 wb-4-282 (Wi)
Brown, William H. 1828 wb-9-153 (D)
Brown, William H. 1860 wb-b-91 (Ms)
Brown, William L. 1830 wb-9-406 (D)
Brown, William L. 1846 wb-d-214 (Ro)
Brown, William M. 1847 wb-8-595 (Wi)
Brown, William P. 1841 wb-12-151* (D)
Brown, William R. 1846 wb-#151 (Wl)
Brown, William R. 1855 lr (Gi)
Brown, Wm. M. 1855 wb-n-688 (Mt)
Brown, Wm.? E. 1847 wb-b-135 (Mu)
Brown, Zenas M. 1839 lr (Gi)
Brownin, Benjamin F. 1847 wb-a-74 (Dk)
Browning, Elias 1809 rb-2-80 (Ru)
Browning, Elizabeth 1853 wb-h-185 (Hu)
Browning, George 1817 wb-3-246 (Rb)
Browning, Jacob 1857 wb-h-712 (Hu)
Browning, James 1831 wb-#93 (Wl)
Browning, Marshal 1841 wb-b-402 (G)
Browning, Mary 1852 wb-d-401 (G)
Browning, Nimrod 1860 wb-17-144 (Rb)
Browning, Robert 1850 wb-g-415 (Hu)
Browning, Roger 1825 wb-2-29# (Ge)
Brownlee, James 1827 wb-4-262 (Wi)
Brownlow, George 1855 lr (Gi)
Brownlow, James 1856 lr (Gi)
Broyle, Adam 1816 wb-2-38# (Ge)
Broyle, Lewis 1804 as-1-75 (Ge)
Broyles, Abraham 1823 wb-a-187 (Wh)
Broyles, Adam 1782 wb-#1 (Wa)
Broyles, Ephraim 1851 wb-2-73# (Ge)
Broyles, Ephraim B. 1856 149-1-30 (Ge)
Broyles, Jacob 1798 wb-1-1# (Ge)
Broyles, James M. 1842 wb-#3 (Mo)
Broyles, John 1848 wb-2-69# (Ge)
Broyles, Lewis 1804 wb-1-3# (Ge)

Broyles, Ruben 1846 wb-c-245 (Wh)
Broyless, James (Sr.) 1839 wb-#37 (Wa)
Bruce, Amos 1853 mr-2-500 (Be)
Bruce, Arnold 1817 wb-A-179 (Li)
Bruce, James 1818 wb-1-0 (Sm)
Bruce, James 1845 mr-2-120 (Be)
Bruce, Jeremiah 1834 wb-3-310 (Je)
Bruce, Joel 1829 wb-1-36 (Li)
Bruce, John P. 1855 as-b-185 (Ms)
Bruce, Thomas 1850 ib-1-215 (Cl)
Bruce, W. F. 1859 wb-1-288 (Be)
Bruce, W. K. 1861 rb-p-597 (Mt)
Bruce, William Wallace 1845 wb-1-106 (Sh)
Bruce, Wm. H. 1861 rb-p-637 (Mt)
Brucheen, John J. 1856 as-b-212 (Ms)
Brumbelow, Lewis 1850 wb-14-340 (Rb)
Brumberlow, William 1853 wb-15-315 (Rb)
Brumfield, Nancy 1828 rb-e-379 (Mt)
Brumfield, Obediah 1825 rb-d-499 (Mt)
Brumfield, Obediah 1829 rb-e-431 (Mt)
Brummett, William 1840 wb-1A-278 (A)
Bruner, Jacob 1847 wb-2-67# (Ge)
Brunson, Asahel 1815 rb-b-277 (Mt)
Brunson, Asahel 1828 rb-e-205 (Mt)
Brunson, Asahel 1828 rb-e-358 (Mt)
Brunson, Daniel sr. 1829 wb-c-13 (St)
Brunson, Isaac 1825 wb-b-26 (St)
Brunson, Joshua 1838 lr (Gi)
Brunson, Penelope 1832 rb-f-337 (Mt)
Brunts, Elizabeth 1857 ib-1-421 (Ca)
Bruster, William 1853 wb-d-157 (Wh)
Bruthinton, Henry 1829 wb-1-43 (Hw)
Bruton, Samuel 1843 wb-d-71 (Hd)
Bruton, Thomas P. 1846 wb-5-35 (Ma)
Bryan, A. K. 1856 wb-16-199 (Rb)
Bryan, Asa 1830 wb-7-64 (Rb)
Bryan, Asa 1839 rb-h-248 (Mt)
Bryan, Asa 1841 wb-11-23 (Rb)
Bryan, Asa M. 1847 rb-k-513 (Mt)
Bryan, Asa N. 1836 rb-g-334 (Mt)
Bryan, Daniel 1837 wb-#115 (Wl)
Bryan, Dennis 1837 rb-h-20 (Mt)
Bryan, Edmond 1818 wb-3-13 (Rb)
Bryan, Elizabeth 1838 wb-2-50# (Ge)
Bryan, F. P. 1860 wb-#18 (Mc)
Bryan, Hardy 1825 rb-d-427 (Mt)
Bryan, Hardy S. 1835 wb-9-37 (Rb)
Bryan, Hardy W. 1856 wb-17-146 (D)
Bryan, Henry 1853 wb-15-514 (D)
Bryan, Henry H. 1835 rb-g-222 (Mt)
Bryan, Henry M. 1851 wb-15-139 (D)

Bryan, J. B. 1846 wb-#149 (Wl)
Bryan, J. T. 1853 wb-2-176 (Me)
Bryan, James 1846 wb-a2-520 (Mu)
Bryan, James 1853 rb-16-709 (Ru)
Bryan, James H. 1844 wb-12-169 (Rb)
Bryan, Jeremiah 1834 wb-1-103 (Li)
Bryan, John 1829 wb-1-159 (Ma)
Bryan, John 1841 wb-b-425 (Wh)
Bryan, John 1845 wb-5-405 (Gr)
Bryan, John M. 1857 wb-17-397 (D)
Bryan, John O. 1823 wb-#56 (Wl)
Bryan, John W. 1844 wb-12-226* (Rb)
Bryan, John jr. 1822 wb-a-174 (Wh)
Bryan, Joseph 1838 wb-1-327 (Gr)
Bryan, Joseph T. 1859 wb-3-26 (Me)
Bryan, Margaret 1841 wb-12-222* (D)
Bryan, Mary 1858 wb-17-451 (D)
Bryan, Nancy 1859 wb-4-24 (Gr)
Bryan, Needham 1830 wb-1-165 (Hr)
Bryan, Nelson 1836 wb-#115 (Wl)
Bryan, R. H. 1858 rb-o-703 (Mt)
Bryan, Richard 1855 wb-#117 (Wl)
Bryan, Robert 1829 wb-1-97 (Ma)
Bryan, Sally Ann 1856 wb-3e-16 (Sh)
Bryan, Samuel 1832 wb-9-575 (D)
Bryan, Samuel 1847 wb-b-107 (Mu)
Bryan, Stephen G. 1838 wb-2-320 (Ma)
Bryan, William 1831 rb-g-290 (Mt)
Bryan, William 1857 wb-2-217 (Li)
Bryan, William 1858 wb-2-238 (Li)
Bryan, William B. 1839 wb-#19 (Mc)
Bryan, William M. 1851 wb-c-447 (Wh)
Bryan, William M. sr. 1855 wb-d-273 (Wh)
Bryan, Wm. 1837 wb-1-514 (Hr)
Bryant, Asa N. 1846 rb-k-266 (Mt)
Bryant, David 1850 wb-d-251 (G)
Bryant, Edward 1845 wb-a2-292 (Mu)
Bryant, Elisha 1841 wb-b-320 (Hd)
Bryant, George W. 1845 wb-d-158 (Ro)
Bryant, Hardy 1825 rb-d-418 (Mt)
Bryant, James 1798 wb-2-128 (D)
Bryant, James 1838 wb-11-326 (D)
Bryant, James H. 1856 rb-17-686 (Ru)
Bryant, James S. 1855 wb-c-1 (L)
Bryant, Jane 1857 wb-a-262 (V)
Bryant, John 1848 wb-g-93 (Hu)
Bryant, John 1857 wb-17-302 (D)
Bryant, John C. 1851 as-b-61 (Ms)
Bryant, Joseph 1836 wb-1-151 (Gr)
Bryant, Josiah 1848 wb-d-391 (Hd)
Bryant, Josiah H. 1847 wb-d-388 (Hd)

Bryant, Morgan 1817 wb-a-71 (Wh)
Bryant, Rebecca 1825 wb-#57 (Wl)
Bryant, Richard A. 1833 wb-#19 (Mc)
Bryant, S. B. R. 1860 wb-18-281 (D)
Bryant, Samuel 1821 wb-#37 (Wl)
Bryant, Samuel 1860 wb-1-76 (Hw)
Bryant, Sarah 1857 wb-17-385 (D)
Bryant, Sherrod 1854 wb-16-431 (D)
Bryant, Sherwood 1855 wb-16-583 (D)
Bryant, William 1848 ib-1-42 (Ca)
Bryant, William G. 1840 wb-b-280 (O)
Bryant, Wm. T. 1861 wb-b-113 (Ms)
Bryarly, Tate 1852 wb-m-618 (Mt)
Bryson, Daniel 1815 wb-#17 (Wl)
Bryson, James 1852 wb-f-5* (Mu)
Bryson, James M. 1847 wb-b-99 (Mu)
Bryson, Samuel 1834 wb-#108 (Wl)
Bryson, William 1824 wb-#52 (Wl)
Bucchanan, Samuel 1793 wb-1-293 (D)
Buce, T. J. 1860 wb-4-381 (La)
Buce, Thos. J. 1860 wb-4-402 (La)
Buchamp, Winy 1841 wb-e-188 (Hn)
Buchanan, Amanda H. M. 1855 wb-2-123 (Li)
Buchanan, Andrew 1813 wb-A-33 (Li)
Buchanan, Andrew 1832 wb-#32 (Wa)
Buchanan, Archibald 1823 wb-A-347 (Li)
Buchanan, Archibald 1851 wb-14-675 (D)
Buchanan, Charles B. 1836 rb-9-325 (Ru)
Buchanan, David 1844 wb-1-244 (Li)
Buchanan, David S. 1853 wb-2-78 (Li)
Buchanan, Eleanor 1858 wb-12-609 (Wi)
Buchanan, Franklin 1851 wb-2-199 (La)
Buchanan, Harvey 1861 wb-#64 (Wa)
Buchanan, James 1840 wb-y-689 (Mu)
Buchanan, James 1851 wb-15-13 (D)
Buchanan, James A. 1850 wb-1-400 (Li)
Buchanan, Jno. 1787 wb-1-69 (D)
Buchanan, John 1814 wb-#14 (Wl)
Buchanan, John 1824 wb-#76 (Mu)
Buchanan, John 1833 wb-10-133 (D)
Buchanan, John 1849 wb-9-287 (Wi)
Buchanan, John 1856 wb-2-139 (Li)
Buchanan, John 1859 wb-2-284 (Li)
Buchanan, John K. 1861 wb-19-26 (D)
Buchanan, John W. 1857 wb-2-188 (Li)
Buchanan, John no date lr (Gi)
Buchanan, Margaret 1829 wb-#188 (Mu)
Buchanan, Mary Jane 1849 wb-1-361 (Li)
Buchanan, Patrick 1823 wb-#60 (Mu)
Buchanan, Patrick 1824 wb-#68 (Mu)
Buchanan, Pryor 1853 wb-2-47 (Li)

Buchanan, Robert 1818 wb-A-207 (Li)
Buchanan, Robert 1845 wb-1-294 (Li)
Buchanan, S. G. 1853 wb-3-142 (La)
Buchanan, Samuel 1838 wb-1-149 (Li)
Buchanan, Samuel 1852 wb-2-25 (Li)
Buchanan, Sarah 1828 wb-b-35 (Ro)
Buchanan, Sarah H. 1860 wb-7-65 (Ma)
Buchanan, Susan 1860 lr (Gi)
Buchanan, Thomas 1855 wb-6-112 (Ma)
Buchanan, Thomas N. 1860 wb-k-258 (O)
Buchanan, W. S. 1854 wb-e-239 (G)
Buchanan, William 1835 wb-1-58 (La)
Buchannan, John 1834 wb-5-394 (Wi)
Buchannan, John H. 1858 wb-f-193 (G)
Buchannen, Lemuel 1848 wb-g-132 (Hu)
Buchanon, Alexander 1838 wb-11-113 (D)
Buchanon, Alexander 1838 wb-11-155 (D)
Buchanon, Archibald 1806 wb-3-120 (D)
Buchanon, James 1841 wb-12-152* (D)
Buchanon, John 1820 wb-3-198 (Wi)
Buchanon, John S. 1851 wb-d-322 (G)
Buchanon, Robert 1829 wb-9-332 (D)
Buchanon, Robert 1841 wb-12-212* (D)
Buchanon, Samuel 1817 wb-7-133 (D)
Buck, Abraham 1836 wb-#8 (Mo)
Buck, Cornelius 1838 wb-1-369 (Hy)
Buck, Humphrey 1842 wb-3-60 (Hy)
Buck, John L. 1840 rb-i-1 (Mt)
Buck, John L. 1850 rb-l-585 (Mt)
Buck, Mary 1854 wb-11-364 (Wi)
Buck, Mary W. 1855 wb-11-434 (Wi)
Buck, Peter C. 1861 rb-p-624 (Mt)
Buck, Peter S. 1861 wb-13-388 (Wi)
Buckanan, John 1837 wb-a-338 (O)
Buckanan, Samuel 1813 wb-4-241 (D)
Buckey, J. J. 1840 wb-7-26 (K)
Buckey, John 1838 wb-6-269 (K)
Buckey, John J. 1850 wb-10-403 (K)
Buckhanan, John 1848 wb-9-204 (Wi)
Buckhannon, Polley 1837 wb-d-146* (Hn)
Buckhannon, William 1828 wb-1-130 (Ma)
Buckhart, Nancy Jane 1849 wb-10-122 (K)
Buckingham, James 1831 wb-5-14 (Wi)
Buckley, David 1853? wb-#110 (Wl)
Buckley, Elizabeth 1854 wb-7-0 (Sm)
Buckley, J. C. 1846 r39-1-17 (Dk)
Buckley, James 1836 wb-1-154 (We)
Buckley, James W. 1857 wb-h-144 (Hn)
Buckley, Thomas M. 1848 rb-k-703 (Mt)
Buckley, Washington H. 1858 wb-j-354 (O)
Buckley, William C. 1854 wb-j-10 (O)

Buckner, Alfred V. 1855 wb-f-69 (Mu)
Buckner, Anthony H. 1852 wb-4-441 (Mu)
Buckner, Elisha 1846 wb-1-385 (La)
Buckner, Nancy E. 1858 wb-#20 (Mc)
Buckner, Ricey 1843 wb-z-514 (Mu)
Buckner, William 1811 rb-2-113 (Ru)
Buckner, William 1835 wb-x-289 (Mu)
Bucy, John 1859 wb-a-141 (Ce)
Bucy, Lucy 1841 wb-b-25 (We)
Bufford, William 1844 wb-f-178 (St)
Buford, Charles 1851 lr (Gi)
Buford, Edward 1828 wb-4-332 (Wi)
Buford, Edward 1842 wb-7-573 (Wi)
Buford, Emily R. 1841 wb-7-361 (Wi)
Buford, James 1811 wb-1-255 (Wi)
Buford, John R. 1839 wb-a-42 (F)
Buford, John R. 1851 wb-9-663 (Wi)
Buford, Mary W. 1857 wb-12-366 (Wi)
Buford, Mary W. 1858 wb-12-529 (Wi)
Buford, Robert 1852 wb-10-431 (Wi)
Buford, Robert J. 1856 wb-12-130 (Wi)
Buford, Spencer 1845 wb-8-301 (Wi)
Buford, Thomas 1860 lr (Gi)
Bugg, Allen 1828 wb-4-279 (Wi)
Bugg, Allen 1836 wb-6-125 (Wi)
Bugg, Anselem D. 1849 lr (Sn)
Bugg, Benjamin 1811 rb-2-146 (Ru)
Bugg, Benjamin 1813 wb-1-318 (Wi)
Bugg, Benjamin 1847 rb-14-171 (Ru)
Bugg, Ephraim M. W. 1846 wb-8-371 (Wi)
Bugg, John 1821 wb-a-29 (Di)
Bugg, John 1844 lr (Gi)
Bugg, Mary H. 1861 wb-b-97 (F)
Bugg, Samuel 1816 wb-1-218 (Sn)
Bugg, Walter L. 1844 lr (Sn)
Buie, Cornelius 1838 wb-b-103 (Hd)
Buie, Daniel 1837 wb-11-107 (D)
Buie, David 1829 wb-9-281 (D)
Buie, David 1839 wb-11-579 (D)
Buie, William 1833 wb-1-47 (La)
Bull, Balaam 1839 rb-h-335 (Mt)
Bull, Claibourn 1854 wb-3-215 (Gr)
Bull, Elisha 1861 wb-13-479 (K)
Bull, George 1836 wb-1-222 (Gr)
Bull, George 1836 wb-1-223 (Gr)
Bull, Jeremiah 1815 rb-b-210 (Mt)
Bull, John 1856 rb-o-221 (Mt)
Bull, Randal 1818 rb-a-469 (Mt)
Bull, Vincent 1839 wb-5-31 (Gr)
Bullard, B. P. 1858? ib-2-545 (Cl)
Bullard, Christopher B. 1844 5-3-2 (Cl)

Bullard, Elizabeth 1855 wb-#117 (Wl)
Bullard, G. W. 1845 wb-#158 (Wl)
Bullard, George B. 1854 ib-2-189 (Cl)
Bullard, George H. 1843? wb-#142 (Wl)
Bullard, John 1780 wb-#2 (Wa)
Bullard, John 1837 wb-A-5 (Ca)
Bullard, John 1851 ib-1-234 (Cl)
Bullard, R. N. 1835 rb-g-285 (Mt)
Bullard, Reben N. 1836 rb-g-271 (Mt)
Bullard, Reuben N. 1838 rb-h-152 (Mt)
Bullard, Rueben 1835 rb-g-212 (Mt)
Bullard, William 1852 ib-1-243 (Cl)
Bulling, Joseph 1859 wb-3-542 (Gr)
Bullington, Robert 1853 wb-#20 (Mc)
Bullington, Robert 1857 wb-f-25 (G)
Bullion, William 1843 as-b-163 (Di)
Bulloch, John 1854 wb-f-57 (Mu)
Bullock, Anna 1843 wb-c-95 (Wh)
Bullock, Charles 1815 wb-4-382 (D)
Bullock, Giles B. 1833 wb-1-399 (Ma)
Bullock, Henry G. 1859 gs-1-312 (F)
Bullock, John 1850 A-468-136 (Le)
Bullock, John 1850 A-468-140 (Le)
Bullock, Joshua 1857 wb-b-406 (We)
Bullock, L. 1859 as-c-151 (Ms)
Bullock, Nathan 1853 wb-a-292 (Ms)
Bullock, Robt. 1857 gs-1-30 (F)
Bullock, Sarah 1859 as-c-209 (Ms)
Bullock, William 1808 wb-1-43 (Wi)
Bullock, Wm. 1857 as-c-66 (Ms)
Bullon, James P. 1859 wb-3-600 (Gr)
Bulls, Barnaby 1822 wb-3-321 (Wi)
Bullus, Joseph M. 1826 lr (Sn)
Bumpass, A. 1849 wb-g-324 (Hn)
Bumpass, Ann E. 1844 rb-12-430 (Ru)
Bumpass, Augustine 1851 wb-g-395 (Hn)
Bumpass, Elizabeth 1846 rb-k-144 (Mt)
Bumpass, Garret 1845 wb-#148 (Wl)
Bumpass, Garrott 1816 wb-#23 (Wl)
Bumpass, Gemima 1851 wb-m-76 (Mt)
Bumpass, James 1830 wb-1-22 (La)
Bumpass, John 1835 rb-g-251 (Mt)
Bumpass, John 1850 rb-l-590 (Mt)
Bumpass, John G. 1855 wb-16-461 (D)
Bumpass, Lucy Ann 1842 rb-i-323 (Mt)
Bumpass, Mary 1820 wb-#35 (Wl)
Bumpass, Mary 1846 wb-#159 (Wl)
Bumpass, Nancy 1837 rb-h-12 (Mt)
Bumpass, Nancy 1858 rb-o-723 (Mt)
Bumpass, R. W. 1858 rb-19-491 (Ru)
Bumpass, Robert 1836 wb-#114 (Wl)

Bumpass, Robert 1845 rb-13-153 (Ru)
Bumpass, Robert H. 1837 wb-#118 (Wl)
Bumpass, Robert W. 1858 rb-19-517 (Ru)
Bumpass, Samuel 1831 rb-f-255 (Mt)
Bumpass, Samuel 1831 rb-f-299 (Mt)
Bumpass, Samuel 1836 rb-g-465 (Mt)
Bumpass, Samuel 1850 wb-m-4 (Mt)
Bumpass, Samuel T. 1832 rb-f-314 (Mt)
Bumpass, William 1805 wb-#2 (Wl)
Bunch, F. M. (Dr.) 1859 wb-h-430 (Hn)
Bunch, Joseph 1858 wb-#20 (Mc)
Bunch, Laford 1858 wb-1C-450 (A)
Bunch, Nancy 1840 wb-#20 (Mc)
Bunch, Paul 1840 wb-#20 (Mc)
Bunch, Samuel 1849 33-3-170 (Gr)
Bunch, Thomas 1840 wb-#3 (Mo)
Bunch, Thomas 1842 wb-e-316 (Hn)
Bunch, William 1857 wb-3-403 (Gr)
Bundrant, Claburn 1860 wb-5-62 (La)
Bundrant, Claiborn 1858 wb-4-209 (La)
Bundren, Green 1854 wb-3-221 (Gr)
Bundren, Philip 1838 5-2-46 (Cl)
Bundy, Henry 1834 wb-#106 (Wl)
Bundy, Samuel 1832 wb-3-0 (Sm)
Bundy, William 1839 wb-3-0 (Sm)
Bunn, James M. 1858 wb-c-264 (L)
Bunnell, James C. 1853 wb-n-88 (Mt)
Buntain, William 1829 wb-#80 (Wl)
Buntin, Elsa 1857 wb-b-43 (F)
Bunting, Daniel 1846 wb-5-16 (Ma)
Bunting, David 1846 rb-k-303 (Mt)
Bunting, David 1858 rb-o-549 (Mt)
Bunting, James A. 1811 rb-b-3 (Mt)
Bunting, S. A. 1850 wb-4-625 (Hr)
Bunting, Samuel A. 1846 wb-4-70 (Hr)
Buntle, Rebecca 1845 wb-f-276* (Hn)
Bunton, Daniel 1826 wb-b-101 (St)
Bunton, John 1803 lr (Sn)
Bunton, William 1839 wb-1-7 (Jo)
Bunton, William 1857 wb-b-420 (We)
Buram, Peter 1857 wb-e-131 (Wh)
Burch, Burnard M. 1849 lr (Gi)
Burch, Elizabeth 1829 wb-4-392 (Wi)
Burch, Jno. M. 1853 ib-2-48 (Cl)
Burch, John 1827 wb-4-195 (Wi)
Burch, John 1844 5-3-6 (Cl)
Burch, Thomas 1830 wb-#21 (Mc)
Burch, William 1828 wb-#21 (Mc)
Burch, William 1855 wb-16-95 (Rb)
Burcham, Henry 1856 wb-h-163 (St)
Burcham, Levi 1825 wb-b-9 (St)

Burchell, John 1856 wb-1-68 (Hw)
Burchett, Burwell 1845 5-3-59 (Cl)
Burchett, Pamelea C. 1848 wb-#165 (Wl)
Burchett, William 1856 wb-16-228 (Rb)
Burchfield, William 1851 ib-1-234 (Cl)
Burd, William 1851 wb-11-36 (K)
Burden, Manson 1852 wb-h-May (O)
Burdine, Nathaniel 1823 wb-1-0 (Sm)
Burem, Henry 1816 wb-1-36 (Hw)
Burem, Henry 1822 wb-1-38 (Hw)
Burford, Daniel H. 1817 wb-1-0 (Sm)
Burford, David 1841 wb-c-97 (O)
Burford, Jonathan 1849 wb-a-357 (F)
Burford, Patsey 1826 wb-b-94 (St)
Burford, Phillimon 1815 wb-1-0 (Sm)
Burford, Sally 1817 wb-1-0 (Sm)
Burford, Zadock H. 1860 wb-3c-148 (Sh)
Burgain, John 1806 rb-a-89 (Mt)
Burgan, Abner 1846 wb-d-7 (G)
Burge, Alfred A. 184; rb-12-564 (Ru)
Burge, Henry A. 1826 wb-4-144 (Wi)
Burge, Mary 1837 wb-6-331 (Wi)
Burge, Nathaniel J. 1844 rb-12-564 (Ru)
Burge, Thomas C. 1861 wb-18-505 (D)
Burge, Wesley 1853 lr (Gi)
Burger, Jane 1850 ib-1-121 (Ca)
Burger, John 1826 wb-#22 (Mc)
Burges, Abigail 1852 33-3-423 (Gr)
Burges, William H. 1855 wb-6-31 (Ma)
Burgess, Alsa 1853 wb-xx-178 (St)
Burgess, Edward 1840 rb-11-81 (Ru)
Burgess, Elias 1842 wb-b-404 (Hd)
Burgess, J. T. 1858 gs-1-167 (F)
Burgess, James 1830 wb-4-493 (Wi)
Burgess, James A. 1858 wb-b-63 (F)
Burgess, John 1815 wb-3-94 (St)
Burgess, John 1826? as-A-122 (Di)
Burgess, Julious 1856 wb-e-81 (Wh)
Burgess, Priscilla 1859 wb-17-580 (D)
Burgess, Rhoda 1855 wb-12-9 (Wi)
Burgess, Thomas 1829 wb-1-48 (W)
Burgess, Thomas 1849 ib-1-35 (Wy)
Burgess, William 1854 wb-11-363 (Wi)
Burgess, William jr. 1859 wb-3-536 (Gr)
Burgham, R. S. 1845 wb-f-309 (Hn)
Burgner, Peter 1824 wb-1-3# (Ge)
Burgner, Peter jr. 1828 wb-2-27# (Ge)
Burk, Isaac N. 1848 wb-e-109 (Ro)
Burk, John 1857 wb-12-409 (Wi)
Burk, John 1858 wb-f-145 (Ro)
Burk, John 1860 wb-A-158 (Ca)

Burk, Phebe 1857 wb-f-116 (Ro)
Burk, Polly 1819 wb-a-120 (Ro)
Burk, Robert A. 1862 wb-f-473 (Ro)
Burk, William Pinckney 1854 wb-#22 (Mc)
Burke, Anson 1841 wb-7-407 (Wi)
Burke, Arnold 1841 wb-a-67 (L)
Burke, Barney 1855 wb-6-70 (Ma)
Burke, Carter 1849 wb-14-425 (D)
Burke, Robert 1839 wb-c-55 (Ro)
Burke, William 1859 wb-13-207 (Wi)
Burket, George 1840 wb-5-93 (Gr)
Burket, Henry 1854 39-2-3 (Dk)
Burket, Mary 1857 wb-3-413 (Gr)
Burket, William 1825 wb-#146 (Mu)
Burkett, Robert 1826 wb-#138 (Mu)
Burkey, Christian 1829 wb-2-29# (Ge)
Burkey, Christian 1849 148-1-285 (Ge)
Burkhart, Nancy J. 1852 wb-11-288 (K)
Burkitt, Burgess 1844 wb-1-305 (La)
Burkley, Rufus K. 1860 wb-18-232 (D)
Burks, Charles 1815 wb-A-73 (Li)
Burks, John 1818 wb-1-0 (Sm)
Burks, Robert L. 1848 rb-14-424 (Ru)
Burks, Rowland 1848 r39-1-56 (Dk)
Burlason, David 1832 rb-8-499 (Ru)
Burleigh, Elizabeth 1860 wb-18-400 (D)
Burlerson, Ursula 1835 rb-9-226 (Ru)
Burleson, Aaron 1782 wb-#1 (Wa)
Burleson, Aaron 1828 wb-1-80 (Hr)
Burlison, Delila 1850 wb-3-45 (W)
Burlison, Isaac 1846 wb-#6 (Mo)
Burlison, Moses 1828 wb-1-22 (W)
Burner, Solomon 1793 wb-1-5 (K)
Burnes, James 1827 wb-1-1 (Li)
Burnes, Richard 1857 wb-h-307 (St)
Burnes, Samuel 1853 wb-3-133 (La)
Burnet, John O. 1854 ib-H-151 (F)
Burnet, Stephen 1814 wb-2-161 (Rb)
Burnett, A. 1848 ib-1-49 (Ca)
Burnett, Absalom 1827 wb-4-249 (K)
Burnett, Anderson 1848 ib-1-27 (Ca)
Burnett, Berry 1842 wb-7-360 (K)
Burnett, Brooking 1836 rb-9-311 (Ru)
Burnett, Daniel H. 1839 wb-1-487 (Hy)
Burnett, E. H. 1859 wb-18-90 (D)
Burnett, Edmond 1806 rb-2-10 (Ru)
Burnett, Henry 1817 wb-7-213 (D)
Burnett, Henry 1827 wb-9-116 (D)
Burnett, Henry 1838 rb-10-183 (Ru)
Burnett, Howel 1832 wb-5-115 (K)
Burnett, James 1815 wb-1-0 (Sm)

Burnett, James 1840 wb-c-191 (Ro)
Burnett, James 1851 rb-15-617 (Ru)
Burnett, Jeremiah 1821 wb-3-270 (K)
Burnett, Jeremiah 1840 wb-12-23* (D)
Burnett, John 1856 wb-16-115 (Rb)
Burnett, Joseph 1849 wb-9-314 (Wi)
Burnett, Leonard 1852 wb-15-312 (D)
Burnett, Martha 1831 rb-8-320 (Ru)
Burnett, Mathew 1831 rb-8-192 (Ru)
Burnett, Nancy 1837 rb-9-416 (Ru)
Burnett, Peter 1854 wb-16-438 (D)
Burnett, Polly 1806 wb-3-127 (D)
Burnett, Rebecah 1806 wb-3-127 (D)
Burnett, Reuben 1835 rb-9-227 (Ru)
Burnett, S. H. 1852 wb-15-378 (D)
Burnett, Sabry 1816 wb-1-0 (Sm)
Burnett, Sally 1806 wb-3-127 (D)
Burnett, Samuel H. 1854 wb-16-374 (D)
Burnett, Sarah 1858 rb-19-403 (Ru)
Burnett, Thomas 1822 wb-1-0 (Sm)
Burnett, Tolefor 1822 wb-3-363 (Wi)
Burnett, William 1839 wb-2-12 (Hy)
Burnett, William 1845 rb-13-225 (Ru)
Burnett, William H. 1857 wb-h-163 (Hn)
Burnett, Williamson 1833 wb-3-0 (Sm)
Burnett, Williamson 1854 wb-7-0 (Sm)
Burney, David 1852 wb-m-429 (Mt)
Burney, Dicie 1858 rb-o-717 (Mt)
Burney, John 1819 wb-3-10 (Rb)
Burney, John 1819 wb-3-35 (Rb)
Burney, John F. 1852 wb-d-379 (G)
Burney, W. L. 1858 rb-o-745 (Mt)
Burney, William 1857 wb-16-379 (Rb)
Burney, William J. 1861 wb-7-93 (Ma)
Burnham, Mary 1853 wb-10-530 (Wi)
Burnham, Newton E. 1826 wb-9-28 (D)
Burnley, Moses 1830 lr (Sn)
Burns, Allen T. 1835 wb-1-161 (Hy)
Burns, Eliza 1858 wb-#22 (Mc)
Burns, George 1812 wb-#5 (Mu)
Burns, Henry 1820 wb-A-369 (Li)
Burns, Jacob J. 1852 ib-1-181 (Wy)
Burns, James 1816 wb-#25 (Mu)
Burns, James 1826 wb-#137 (Mu)
Burns, James 1841 wb-7-242 (K)
Burns, James 1850 wb-2-101 (La)
Burns, Laurence 1811 wb-#36 (Mu)
Burns, Lucy 1858 wb-h-472 (St)
Burns, Marinia 1836 wb-a-10 (F)
Burns, Miles 1836 wb-1-500 (Hr)
Burns, Robert 1840 wb-2-81 (Hy)

Burns, Tarrance 1815 rb-3-31 (Ru)
Burnsides, George L. 1836 eb-1-335 (C)
Burnsides, Thomas 1807 wb-3-175 (D)
Burnthriger, Roda 1846 5-3-162 (Cl)
Burress, David 1805 rb-a-273 (Mt)
Burress, George H. 1829 rb-e-493 (Mt)
Burress, George H. 1829 rb-e-511 (Mt)
Burris, Isabella 1827 wb-#26 (Wa)
Burris, Jacob 1832 wb-3-0 (Sm)
Burris, Michael 1817 wb-1-0 (Sm)
Burriss, William 1840 eb-1-420 (C)
Burrough, Aaron 1842 wb-2-405 (Hr)
Burroughs, E. S. (Mrs.) 1849 wb-4-480 (Hr)
Burroughs, Eliza S. 1851 wb-5-14 (Hr)
Burrow, Freeman 1855 ib-h-277 (F)
Burrow, John 1855 ib-h-298 (F)
Burrow, Phillip 1829 wb-a-18 (Cr)
Burrows, Anthony 1822 wb-1-49 (Fr)
Burrows, Banks M. 1852 wb-a-171 (Cr)
Burrows, Charles 1816 wb-7-6 (D)
Burrows, David 1860 wb-1-75 (Gu)
Burrows, Elizabeth 1860 wb#7 (Gu)
Burrows, Samuel 1851 wb#20 (Gu)
Burrows, Thomas 1855 wb-1-12 (Gu)
Burrus, Fayett 1854 rb-17-313 (Ru)
Burrus, Joseph 1821 rb-5-100 (Ru)
Burrus, Joseph 1834 rb-9-151 (Ru)
Burrus, Lafayett 1856 rb-18-241 (Ru)
Burrus, Lucy 1825 rb-6-104 (Ru)
Burrus, S. 1835 rb-9-253 (Ru)
Burrus, Thomas 1842 wb-3-542 (Ma)
Burrus, W. C. J. 1859 rb-20-183 (Ru)
Burrus, W. J. 1859 rb-20-81 (Ru)
Burt, W. S. 1854 ib-h-10 (F)
Burt, William 1849 wb-1-260 (Fr)
Burt, William H. 1856 rb-17-617 (Ru)
Burtch, Richard 1822 wb-2-354 (Je)
Burtis, John 1855 ib-h-424 (F)
Burton, Albert G. 1840 wb-3-0 (Sm)
Burton, Ann 1845 wb-13-194 (D)
Burton, C. P. 1857 wb-17-380 (D)
Burton, Edmund 1852 wb-#178 (Wl)
Burton, Eleanor 1851 wb-2-87 (Sh)
Burton, Elizabeth 1835 wb-#122 (Wl)
Burton, George H. 1846 wb-14-2 (D)
Burton, Hardy M. 1853 rb-16-433 (Ru)
Burton, Henry H. 1853 r39-1-314 (Dk)
Burton, John 1852 wb-5-120 (Ma)
Burton, John H. 1851 wb-g-354 (St)
Burton, John H. 1860 wb-b-106 (F)
Burton, July (Julia) 1854 39-2-4 (Dk)

Burton, Maus? 1852 wb-h-Feb (O)
Burton, Nancy 1824 wb-#52 (Wl)
Burton, Perlina 1843 wb-1-223 (Li)
Burton, Peter 1834 wb-1-174 (Hy)
Burton, R. M. 1844 wb-#146 (Wl)
Burton, Rebecca 1862 wb-1-74 (Hw)
Burton, Robert M. (Col.) 1843? wb-#142 (Wl)
Burton, Robert M. 1842 wb-#141 (Wl)
Burton, Ruth 1857 rb-18-389 (Ru)
Burton, Samuel C. 1843 wb-12-390* (D)
Burton, Susan F. 1849 wb-#163 (Wl)
Burton, William 1857 wb-7-11 (Ma)
Burts, Nancy L. 1854 wb-3-196 (Gr)
Burum, Peter 1857 wb-e-106 (Wh)
Burus, Mary M. 1851 wb-1-77 (Hw)
Busbee, Alfred 1846 wb-g-133 (Hn)
Busby, Elijah 1858 wb-b-427 (We)
Busby, James 1816 lr (Sn)
Busby, Robert 1851 wb-g-346 (St)
Busby, Sarah 1856 lr (Sn)
Busby, Stephen 1861 wb-4-435 (La)
Busby, William 1830 lr (Sn)
Busey, Benjamin 1822 wb-a-5 (Cr)
Bush, Abner H. H. 1823 wb-#65 (Mu)
Bush, Ann 1854 lr (Sn)
Bush, Carter 1847 wb-14-33 (D)
Bush, E. M. 1849 mr-2-352 (Be)
Bush, Elijah M. 1851 mr-2-422 (Be)
Bush, Elkanah 1848 lr (Sn)
Bush, H. B. 1859 ib-1-566 (Ca)
Bush, Harvy B. 1859 iv-1-577 (Ca)
Bush, James H. 1856 wb-1-101 (Be)
Bush, Malcijah 1839 mr-1-280 (Be)
Bush, William 1821 wb-1-0 (Sm)
Bush, Zenas 1829 rb-f-64 (Mt)
Bushart, A. M. 1851 wb-g-428 (Hn)
Bushart, Jacob sr. 1852 wb-g-432 (Hn)
Bussell, Benjamin L. 1859 wb-1-72 (Hw)
Bussell, John E. 1846 wb-c-222 (Wh)
Bussell, John E. 1846 wb-c-227 (Wh)
Bussell, Rhodom 1859 wb-e-212 (Wh)
Buster, Isabella 1839 wb-2-52# (Ge)
Buster, William 1827 wb-a-25 (R)
Buster, William 1839 wb-a-375 (R)
Butcher, Isaac B. 1841 wb-5-171 (Gr)
Butcher, Richard 1841 wb-A-23 (Ca)
Butler, A. W. 1854 wb-16-359 (D)
Butler, Aaron 1834 mr (Gi)
Butler, Aaron 1848 wb-3-107 (Sn)
Butler, Ann 1828 rb-7-306 (Ru)
Butler, Christopher 1858 wb-f-159 (G)

Butler, David 1841 wb-3-376 (Ma)
Butler, E. C.. 1854 wb-16-328 (D)
Butler, Edward (Capt.) 1803 wb-1-123 (Rb)
Butler, Edward 1854 wb-16-294 (D)
Butler, Eleanor Ryan 1838 wb-#146 (Wl)
Butler, Elias 1821 rb-5-114 (Ru)
Butler, Elias 1838 wb-a-66 (Cr)
Butler, Elias 1849 wb-g-130 (O)
Butler, Francis 1856 wb-f-95 (Mu)
Butler, Henry 1858 wb-1-45 (Se)
Butler, Henry R. 1835 wb-16-135 (A)
Butler, Isaac 1830 rb-8-9 (Ru)
Butler, J. M. 1860 wb-3-64 (Me)
Butler, Jacob 1839 wb-1A-243 (A)
Butler, Jacob M. 1850 wb-2-1 (Me)
Butler, James 1859 wb-i-89 (St)
Butler, James H. 1857 wb-h-323 (St)
Butler, Jesse 1854? wb-#26 (Mo)
Butler, John 1838 lr (Gi)
Butler, John 1855 wb-e-359 (G)
Butler, John R. 1855 wb-16-594 (D)
Butler, Keziah 1854 wb-1C-134 (A)
Butler, Leonard 1856 wb-3e-18 (Sh)
Butler, Martha 1849? wb-1B-142 (A)
Butler, Micha 1856 wb-16-616 (D)
Butler, Phebe 1840 wb-a-84 (Cr)
Butler, Polly 1857 wb-12-406 (Wi)
Butler, Richard 1820 wb-#90 (Mu)
Butler, Samuel 1828 wb-1-15 (Li)
Butler, Thomas 1835 wb-1A-110 (A)
Butler, Thomas 1839 wb-0-33 (Cf)
Butler, Thomas 1844 wb-a-111 (T)
Butler, Thomas 1846 wb-8-379 (Wi)
Butler, Thomas Ryan 1812 wb-1-430 (Rb)
Butler, William 1833 wb-1-356 (Ma)
Butler, William 1833 wb-1-458 (Ma)
Butler, William 1858 39-2-259 (Dk)
Butler, William D. 1860 39-2-390 (Dk)
Butler, William G. 1853 wb-e-393 (Ro)
Butler, Wm. R. 1850 wb-1B-189 (A)
Butler, Wm. R. 1853 wb-1B-324 (A)
Butram, John 1841 wb-1-49 (Me)
Butt, John 1836 wb-#114 (Wl)
Butt, Samuel 1851 wb-14-589 (D)
Butt, William 1800 wb-1-77 (K)
Butterworth, Benjamin 1861 lr (Sn)
Butterworth, Bluford 1854 wb-a-248 (Dk)
Buttlar, Jacob 1839 wb-1A-235 (A)
Buttlar, Thomas 1835 wb-1A-148 (A)
Buttlar, Wm. 1836 wb-1A-156 (A)
Buttler, William 1838 rb-10-77 (Ru)

Buttram, Jacob 1855 wb-#22 (Mc)
Buttram, James 1838 wb-#23 (Mc)
Buttram, Larkin 1858 wb-#23 (Mc)
Buttrey, John 1857 wb-12-443 (Wi)
Butts, Benj. 1833 rb-9-29 (Ru)
Butts, Benjamin C. 1834 rb-9-121 (Ru)
Butts, Francis 1851 rb-16-108 (Ru)
Butts, Sarah 1858 wb-12-547 (Wi)
Butts, Willie 1832 wb-3-0 (Sm)
Buyers, William 1844 wb-a2-1 (Mu)
Byars, A. W. 1846 wb-2-181 (W)
Byars, Alexander 1846 wb-b-205 (We)
Byars, John 1852 wb-g-480 (Hn)
Byars, John L. 1857 wb-3-337 (W)
Byars, N. B. 1860 wb-h-444 (Hn)
Byars, Nicholas 1847 wb-g-214 (Hn)
Byars, Nicolas 1845 wb-f-317 (Hn)
Byars, William 1858 wb-h-245 (Hn)
Byass, John 1845 wb-f-281* (Hn)
Byers, Elizabeth C. 1859 wb-13-67 (Wi)
Byers, Herald 1846 r39-1-20 (Dk)
Byers, Isaac 1847 wb-b-129 (Mu)
Byers, Isabella E. 1841 wb-7-434 (Wi)
Byers, James 1858 wb-12-587 (Wi)
Byers, Joseph 1837 wb-1-542 (Hr)
Byers, Susannah 1858 wb-17-519 (D)
Byers, William 1837 wb-6-368 (Wi)
Byers, William 1837 wb-7-25 (Wi)
Byers, William 1851 wb-10-117 (Wi)
Byers, William 1851 wb-10-31 (Wi)
Byford, Jane 1859 39-2-290 (Dk)
Byler, Abraham 1846 rb-13-463 (Ru)
Byler, Delpha 1858 wb-c-230 (L)
Byler, William L. 1838 wb-a-21 (L)
Bynum, Elenor 1854 ib-1-307 (Wy)
Bynum, John W. 1849 wb-b-381 (Mu)
Bynum, Mark 1823 wb-#60 (Mu)
Bynum, N. M. 1837 wb-y-74 (Mu)
Bynum, Tapley 1841 as-b-27 (Di)
Bynum, Thomas 1848 wb-b-254 (We)
Bynum, William 1820 wb-#70 (Mu)
Bynum, William 1820? wb-#44 (Mu)
Byram, Benjamin 1849 wb-1-265 (Fr)
Byram, Elizabeth 1848 wb-1-254 (Fr)
Byram, Henry 1854 wb-1-325 (Fr)
Byram, Lemuel 1855 wb-15-774 (Rb)
Byram, Noah 1853 wb-15-394 (Rb)
Byram, Simon 1857 lr (Sn)
Byram, Widen E. 1850 lr (Sn)
Byrd, Baylor 1830 wb-4-544 (Wi)
Byrd, James 1845 wb-f-275 (St)

Byrd, Jesse 1848 wb-e-65 (Ro)
Byrd, Jesse 1861 wb-a-316 (T)
Byrd, John 1815 rb-b-304 (Mt)
Byrd, John 1828 rb-e-255 (Mt)
Byrd, John W. 1842 wb-c-294 (O)
Byrd, Joseph 1858 wb-f-201 (Ro)
Byrd, Lucy 1849 wb-g-203 (O)
Byrd, Richard 1803 wb-1-31 (Hw)
Byrd, Shadrach 1814 wb-a-220 (St)
Byrd, Thomas 1805 wb-1-142 (Rb)
Byrd, William 1809 wb-1-310 (Rb)
Byrd, William 1840 wb-b-233 (Hd)
Byres, David P. 1845 wb-13-177 (D)
Byrn, Absolum K. 1821 wb-#37 (Wl)
Byrn, Frances 1860 wb-d-58 (L)
Byrn, James 1825 wb-8-450 (D)
Byrn, James 1845 wb-#166 (Wl)
Byrn, James R. D. 1823 wb-#44 (Wl)
Byrn, John 1854 lr (Sn)
Byrn, Joseph 1856 lr (Sn)
Byrn, Mary 1822 wb-#44 (Wl)
Byrn, Nancy 1859 as-c-563 (Di)
Byrn, R. D. 1861 wb-d-108 (L)
Byrn, Rezin S. 1855 wb-c-85 (L)
Byrn, Thomas 1825 wb-1-46 (Ma)
Byrn, William P. 1829 wb-9-306 (D)
Byrne, John 1848 wb-13-220 (Rb)
Byrne, Laura 1841 as-b-9 (Di)
Byrnes, T. B. 1856 wb-16-660 (Rb)
Byrns, James 1850 wb-14-293 (Rb)
Byrns, Thomas 1856 wb-16-328 (Rb)
Byrum, William A. 1850 A-468-151 (Le)
Byrus, Harrel 1846 r39-1-66 (Dk)
Bysor, Mary 1851 wb-14-589 (D)
Bysor, Peter 1832 wb-9-611 (D)
Byzor, John 1821 lr (Sn)

- C -

Cabbage, Adam 1844 wb-5-304 (Gr)
Cabbage, John 1852 wb-3-41 (Gr)
Cable, Benjamin 1851 wb-1-65 (Jo)
Cable, Coonrod 1858 wb-1-119 (Jo)
Cable, Jesse H. 1854 wb-a-469 (F)
Cabler, B. G. 1854 wb-16-357 (D)
Cabler, Fredrick 1841 wb-12-260* (D)
Cadawallader, Edward 1855 wb-3e-3 (Sh)
Cage, Alfred 1850 rb-l-623 (Mt)
Cage, Clinton (col) 1861 wb-3e-174 (Sh)
Cage, Clinton 1861 lr (Sn)
Cage, Edward 1859 rb-p-143 (Mt)

Cage, James 1836 wb-#112 (Wl)
Cage, Jesse 1846 lr (Sn)
Cage, John (Capt.) 1827 wb-#72 (Wl)
Cage, John 1828 wb-#77 (Wl)
Cage, Mary 1851 wb-#23 (Mc)
Cage, Reuben 1853 lr (Sn)
Cage, Thankful 1828 wb-#73 (Wl)
Cage, William 1810 wb-1-139 (Sn)
Cage, William G. 1848 wb-14-281 (D)
Cage, William G. 1849 wb-14-415 (D)
Cage, Wilson 1847 lr (Sn)
Cagle, Charles 1823 wb-8-209 (D)
Cagle, Charles 1842 wb-1-511 (W)
Cagle, John 1826 wb-5-374 (Rb)
Cagle, John 1854 wb-3-172 (W)
Cagle, Sally 1857 wb-3-357 (W)
Cagle, Susan 1853 wb-3-146 (W)
Cagley, Jacob 1849 wb-1-196 (Bo)
Cahal, Ann C. 1856 wb-17-110 (D)
Cahal, Terry H. 1852 wb-15-253 (D)
Cahoon, Charles 1823 wb-3-634 (Wi)
Cahoon, Isom 1840 wb-b-11 (We)
Cahorn, William 1834 rb-f-557 (Mt)
Cail, Parker 1859 wb-f-328 (G)
Cain, E. G. 1841 rb-i-125 (Mt)
Cain, Elisha G. 1843 rb-i-487 (Mt)
Cain, George I. 1837 rb-10-9 (Ru)
Cain, George J. 1834 rb-9-209 (Ru)
Cain, George J. 1853 rb-16-674 (Ru)
Cain, George L. 1853 rb-16-710 (Ru)
Cain, James 1843 wb-11-433 (Rb)
Cain, Jessee 1859 ib-2-553 (Cl)
Cain, John 1841 wb-1-361 (W)
Cain, Leonard 1843 wb-1-85 (Su)
Cain, Martha M. 1853 rb-16-675 (Ru)
Cain, Martha Mary 1842 rb-12-145 (Ru)
Cain, Peter 1814 wb-A-49 (Li)
Cain, Thomas 1851 33-3-395 (Gr)
Calcote, James L. 1860 wb-18-139 (D)
Caldwell (B), Maxwell 1854 wb-xx-395 (St)
Caldwell, Abram 1855 wb-a-281 (Di)
Caldwell, Alexander 1830 wb-5-8 (K)
Caldwell, Alexander 1855 148-1-518 (Ge)
Caldwell, Amos 1852 wb-f-8 (Mu)
Caldwell, Andrew B. 1847 wb-8-534 (Wi)
Caldwell, Benoni 1837 wb-1-108 (Hw)
Caldwell, David 1816 wb-1-198 (Bo)
Caldwell, David 1835 rb-g-256 (Mt)
Caldwell, David 1855 wb-5-490 (Je)
Caldwell, David 1855 wb-g-661 (Hn)
Caldwell, Elizabeth 1853 wb-1-28 (R)

Caldwell, English 1849 ib-1-136 (Cl)
Caldwell, Ephraim B. 1846 wb-f-14 (O)
Caldwell, Esther 1856 wb-g-711 (Hn)
Caldwell, G. B. 1860 wb#7 (Gu)
Caldwell, H. N. 1846 wb-13-448 (D)
Caldwell, Isaac 1853 wb-h-Apr (O)
Caldwell, Isaac W. 1853 wb-h-Mar (O)
Caldwell, J. C. 1855 wb-j-56 (O)
Caldwell, James 1812 wb-1-87 (Hw)
Caldwell, James 1841 wb-3-381 (Ma)
Caldwell, James 1844 wb-b-61 (We)
Caldwell, James W. 1845 wb-13-173 (D)
Caldwell, James sr. 1844 lr (Gi)
Caldwell, John 1836 rb-g-337 (Mt)
Caldwell, John 1854 wb-#10 (Mo)
Caldwell, John C. 1857 wb-j-286 (O)
Caldwell, John H. 1845 wb-a2-252 (Mu)
Caldwell, John Jr. 1843 rb-i-549 (Mt)
Caldwell, John P. 1825 wb-a-2 (T)
Caldwell, John T. 1860 wb-k-250 (O)
Caldwell, John sr. 1825 rb-d-487 (Mt)
Caldwell, Joseph 1832 wb-9-583 (D)
Caldwell, Joseph 1855 wb-b-354 (We)
Caldwell, Joseph P. 1853 wb-#23 (Mc)
Caldwell, Preston 1861 wb-h-494 (Hn)
Caldwell, Rachael E. 1850 wb-9-376 (Wi)
Caldwell, Robert 1825 rb-d-414 (Mt)
Caldwell, Robert 1855 wb-c-15 (L)
Caldwell, Samuel 1841 wb-2-57# (Ge)
Caldwell, Samuel sr. 1841 rb-i-136 (Mt)
Caldwell, St. Clair F. 1856 wb-f-89 (Mu)
Caldwell, Thomas 1845 wb-1-259 (Bo)
Caldwell, Thomas 1853 wb-1-124 (Hw)
Caldwell, Thos. G. 1810 wb-1-226 (Wi)
Caldwell, Varner 1841 wb-e-229 (Hn)
Caldwell, William 1815 wb-1-0 (Sm)
Caldwell, William 1834 wb-1-352 (Hr)
Caldwell, William 1858 wb-c-243 (L)
Caldwell, William H. 1854 wb-f-53 (Mu)
Caldwell, William M. 1856 wb-j-231 (O)
Caldwell, Willis 1849 wb-g-33 (O)
Calgy, Hugh 1854 lr (Sn)
Calhoon, Hugh 1831 wb-#90 (Wl)
Calhoon, John 1830 wb-#86 (Wl)
Calhoon, Wiliam 1857 wb-3-397 (W)
Calhoon, William 1835 rb-g-286 (Mt)
Calhoon, William 1838 rb-h-65 (Mt)
Calhoon, William 1841 abl-1-229 (T)
Calhoun, A. M. 1840 wb-#129 (Wl)
Calhoun, Anderson A. 1852 wb-h-Nov (O)
Calhoun, Andrew 1837 wb-a-218 (O)

Calhoun, George 1842 rb-12-257 (Ru)
Calhoun, J. Westley 1860 wb-k-216 (O)
Calhoun, Robert W. 1841 wb-7-375 (Wi)
Calhoun, Samuel 1825 wb-#57 (Wl)
Calhoun, Samuel 1839 wb-#126 (Wl)
Calhoun, Samuel 1839 wb-#127 (Wl)
Calhoun, Stephen S. 1861 wb-k-384 (O)
Calhoun, Thomas 1855 wb-#116 (Wl)
Calhoun, Warren W. 1861 wb-k-475 (O)
Calhoun, William 1838 wb-#24 (Mc)
Calhoun, William 1840 wb-b-240 (O)
Calhoun, William W. 1856 wb-#118 (Wl)
Calhoun, Wilson W. 1839 wb-7-30 (Wi)
Call, H. A. 1852 wb-m-553 (Mt)
Call, Joseph 1847 wb-14-98 (d)
Callaghan, Maria 1845 wb-13-228 (D)
Callahan, J. (Mrs.) 1847 wb-14-72 (D)
Callahan, John Nelson 1841 wb-#24 (Mc)
Callahan, Philip 1851 wb-15-58 (D)
Callaway, Joseph 1831 wb-#2 (Mo)
Callaway, Joseph 1845 wb-9-86 (K)
Callaway, Thomas 1819 wb-3-75 (K)
Callaway, Thomas 1833 wb-5-199 (K)
Callendar, Thomas 1852 wb-15-281 (D)
Callicott, William Y. 1835 abl-3-0 (Sm)
Callicutt, John 1848 wb-g-273 (Hn)
Callie, William 1826 wb-3-0 (Sm)
Callihan, Edward 1819 wb-#70 (Mu)
Callis, Nancy M. 1854 wb-#114 (Wl)
Callis, Richard 1827 wb-#70 (Wl)
Callis, Thomas 1837 wb-#121 (Wl)
Callis, Wilkins 1859 wb-f-302 (G)
Callison, John 1855 wb-3-299 (Gr)
Callison, Samuel 1854 wb-3-192 (Gr)
Calloway, Grace S. 1853 wb-#24 (Mc)
Calloway, John R. 1858 wb-12-469 (K)
Calloway, Joseph W. 1845 wb-9-39 (K)
Calloway, Richard 1849 wb-1-269 (Fr)
Calloway, Shadrich 1842 wb-7-346 (K)
Calloway, Thomas 1844 wb-8-245 (K)
Calloway, Thomas F. 1844 wb-8-283 (K)
Calmes, Marcus 1841 abl-1-233 (T)
Calohan, Benjamin 1824? wb-#127 (Mu)
Caltharp, William 1837 wb-11-92? (D)
Calton, John F. 1858 as-c-106 (Ms)
Calvert, Mary 1842 lr (Gi)
Calvert, Willis 1851 wb-14-563 (D)
Calvett, John 1816 rb-3-130 (Ru)
Cambell, John E. 1856 as-b-233 (Ms)
Camer, K. P. 1856 wb-3-282 (W)
Cameron, Archibald 1832 wb-#24 (Mc)

Cameron, Daniel 1855 wb-16-557 (D)
Cameron, Duncan 1810 wb-1-343 (Je)
Cameron, Ewen 1846 wb-8-415 (Wi)
Cameron, Ewen 1853 wb-11-27 (Wi)
Cameron, Hugh 1796 wb-1-4# (Ge)
Cameron, Samuel 1846 wb-1-262 (Bo)
Camn, William 1806 wb-1-194 (Je)
Camp, Armstead 1851 wb-15-83 (D)
Camp, George 1835 wb-10-539 (D)
Camp, George 1836 mr-1-328 (Be)
Camp, George 1849 mr-2-336 (Be)
Camp, George A. 1848 wb-14-235 (D)
Camp, Henry C. 1854 mr-2-593 (Be)
Camp, James 1816 wb-7-12 (D)
Camp, James 1836 wb-10-619 (D)
Camp, James M. 1856 wb-1-51 (Be)
Camp, James T. 1838 wb-11-481 (D)
Camp, John 1845 wb-#24 (Mc)
Camp, Martha 1823 wb-8-270 (D)
Camp, Mary 1857 wb-1-354 (Fr)
Camp, Miles A. 1839 wb-b-353 (Wh)
Camp, Peter G. 1858 wb-3e-73 (Sh)
Camp, Sarah 1831 lr (Sn)
Camp, Sterling 1851 wb-#25 (Mc)
Campbell, Adam 1840 abl-1-203 (T)
Campbell, Alexander 1816 wb-2-273 (K)
Campbell, Alexander 1828 wb-9-215 (D)
Campbell, Alexander 1847 wb-1-428 (La)
Campbell, Alexander 1852 wb-3-78 (La)
Campbell, Alexr. A. 1846 wb-5-31 (Ma)
Campbell, Andrew 1818 wb-2-414 (Wi)
Campbell, Andrew 1831 wb-5-53 (Wi)
Campbell, Andrew C. 1850 wb-10-422 (K)
Campbell, Andrew J. 1852 rb-4-283 (Mu)
Campbell, Archibald 1802 wb-0-38 (K)
Campbell, Archibald A. 1844 wb-a2-73 (Mu)
Campbell, Barnet 1858 ib-2-518 (Cl)
Campbell, Betsey 1860 wb-17-56 (Rb)
Campbell, Col. David 1835 wb-#106 (Wl)
Campbell, Collin 1832 wb-1-85 (Li)
Campbell, Collin M. 1860 wb-f-193 (Mu)
Campbell, Daniel 1841 wb-e-204 (Hn)
Campbell, Daniel 1851 wb-d-18 (Wh)
Campbell, Daniel sr. 1849 wb-c-355 (Wh)
Campbell, David 1813 wb-2-48 (K)
Campbell, David 1830 wb-#98 (Wl)
Campbell, E. M. 1830 wb-#215 (Mu)
Campbell, Edith 1815 wb-#19 (Wl)
Campbell, Edley 1839 wb-10-314 (Rb)
Campbell, Edward 1826 wb-4-84 (Wi)
Campbell, Edward 1857 wb-f-50 (G)

Campbell, Elizabeth 1826 rb-e-3 (Mt)
Campbell, Francis 1856 wb-16-617 (D)
Campbell, Francis 1856 wb-17-65 (D)
Campbell, Francis W. 1844 wb-4-204 (Ma)
Campbell, Galaway 1859 wb-#25 (Mc)
Campbell, George 1837 wb-3-472 (Je)
Campbell, George 1856? ib-2-303 (Cl)
Campbell, George S. 1829 wb-1-110 (Hr)
Campbell, George W. 1848 wd-14-209 (D)
Campbell, Hugh 1790? wb-#23 (Wa)
Campbell, Hugh 1835 wb-#38 (Wa)
Campbell, Hugh 1839 wb-y-665 (Mu)
Campbell, Isabel 1857 wb-4-6 (Gr)
Campbell, Isabella 1852 wb-3-79 (La)
Campbell, J. A. 1849 wb-#172 (Wl)
Campbell, J. M. L. 1847 wb-a2-535 (Mu)
Campbell, James 1816 wb-#21 (Mu)
Campbell, James 1823 wb-8-266 (D)
Campbell, James 1826 wb-2-545 (Je)
Campbell, James 1827? wb-#166 (Mu)
Campbell, James 1837 wb-6-167 (K)
Campbell, James 1841 wb-1-178 (Li)
Campbell, James 1842 wb-#137 (Wl)
Campbell, James 1846 wb-a-106 (Ms)
Campbell, James 1849 ib-1-135 (Cl)
Campbell, James 1849 wb-14-433 (D)
Campbell, James G. 1838 wb-11-174 (D)
Campbell, James M. 1857 wb-16-553 (Rb)
Campbell, Jane 1831 wb-3-153 (Je)
Campbell, Jane 1838 wb-1-299 (Gr)
Campbell, Jane B. 1825 wb-4-3 (Wi)
Campbell, Jeremiah 1843 lw (Ct)
Campbell, John 1797 wb-2-59 (D)
Campbell, John 1801 wb-1-172 (Je)
Campbell, John 1808 wb-1-178 (Wi)
Campbell, John 1813 rb-b-99 (Mt)
Campbell, John 1816 wb-#21 (Mu)
Campbell, John 1838? 5-2-71 (Cl)
Campbell, John 1839 wb-#26 (Mc)
Campbell, John 1845 wb-5-358 (Gr)
Campbell, John 1846 wb-4-100 (Hr)
Campbell, John 1850 wb-b-629 (Mu)
Campbell, John D. 1841 wb-2-417 (Hy)
Campbell, John M. 1822 wb-3-361 (K)
Campbell, John P. 1848 wb-4-246 (Hr)
Campbell, John no date wb-#26 (Mc)
Campbell, Jonathan A. 1816 wb-#23 (Wl)
Campbell, Joseph 1812 wb-1-5 (Fr)
Campbell, Joseph 1835 wb-9-117 (Rb)
Campbell, Manning 1837 wb-3-0 (Sm)
Campbell, Martha 1856 wb-f-93 (Mu)

Campbell, Mary M. 1842 wb-2-522 (Hy)
Campbell, Mathew 1854 wb-#26 (Mc)
Campbell, Michael 1830 wb-9-394 (D)
Campbell, Michael 1845 wb-13-154 (D)
Campbell, Nancy 1845 wb-a2-246 (Mu)
Campbell, Nancy 1851 as-b-30 (Ms)
Campbell, Neil 1833 wb-c-13 (Hn)
Campbell, Owen 1816 wb-2-321 (Rb)
Campbell, Owen F. 1831 wb-7-466 (Rb)
Campbell, Patrick 1812 wb-2-1 (K)
Campbell, Philip 1838 wb-11-506 (D)
Campbell, Richard 1804 wb-1-136 (K)
Campbell, Robert 1806 wb-1-218 (K)
Campbell, Robert 1809 wb-2-32# (Ge)
Campbell, Robert 1848 wb-b-182 (Mu)
Campbell, Robert 1855 wb-e-322 (G)
Campbell, Robert 1858 wb-f-181 (Ro)
Campbell, Robert 1858 wb-f-187 (G)
Campbell, Samuel 1846 rb-13-709 (Ru)
Campbell, Samuel 1852 wb-15-172 (Rb)
Campbell, Samuel A. 1853 wb-15-403 (Rb)
Campbell, Sarah 1823 wb-#52 (Mu)
Campbell, Sarah B. 1854 wb-16-344 (D)
Campbell, Sidney 1861 wb-f-413 (G)
Campbell, Susannah 1850 wb-#48 (Wa)
Campbell, Thomas 1828 wb-9-220 (D)
Campbell, Thomas 1854 wb-16-251 (D)
Campbell, Thomas J. 1838 wb-#26 (Mc)
Campbell, Tilman 1857 wb-16-553 (Rb)
Campbell, Washington 1851 wb-15-30 (D)
Campbell, Washington G. 1852 wb-15-344 (D)
Campbell, Widow 1813 wb-#12 (Wl)
Campbell, William 1808 wb-#6 (Wl)
Campbell, William 1817 wb-A-163 (Li)
Campbell, William 1823 wb-A-353 (Li)
Campbell, William 1828 wb-4-289 (K)
Campbell, William 1835 wb-a-35 (T)
Campbell, William 1843 wb-11-532 (Rb)
Campbell, William 1855 wb-c-135 (L)
Campbell, William 1855 wb-c-5 (L)
Campbell, William 1858 wb-f-137 (Ro)
Campbell, William 1859 wb-A-153 (Ca)
Campbell, William 1860 wb-18-241 (D)
Campbell, William J. 1843 wb-3-373 (Hy)
Campis, L. D. 1860 wb-1-374 (Be)
Camplenor, William 1822 wb-#43 (Wl)
Camron, John 1805 wb-1-178 (K)
Camron, Polly S. 1835 wb-6-79 (Wi)
Can____, William 1830 wb-#26 (Mc)
Canaday, David 1848 wb-d-115 (G)
Canady, Patrick 1855 wb-e-374 (G)

Canaway, Timothy 1824 wb-1-0 (Sm)
Candler, John 1848 r39-1-64 (Dk)
Candler, John T. 1848 r39-1-88 (Dk)
Candler, Martha 1851 wb-a-105 (Dk)
Cane, James 1814 wb-a-212 (St)
Cane, Jesse 1814 wb-a-213 (St)
Canedy, George 1854 wb-e-212 (G)
Canier?, Robert 1859 wb-1-314 (Be)
Cannady, Isaac 1847 wb-d-42 (G)
Cannady, James 1831 wb-3-155 (Je)
Cannel, William 1815 wb-2-233 (Rb)
Cannon, A. G. 1852 as-c-164 (Di)
Cannon, A. W. 1827 wb-1-61 (Ma)
Cannon, Abraham W. 1829 wb-1-194 (Ma)
Cannon, Abram 1832 rb-9-7 (Ru)
Cannon, Anthony 1850 as-c-59 (Di)
Cannon, David K. 1843 wb-a-84 (Ms)
Cannon, Dennis 1843 wb-e-602 (Hu)
Cannon, Dennis 1853 wb-h-106 (Hu)
Cannon, Horatio 1832 wb-#112 (Wl)
Cannon, Howard 1848 lr (Gi)
Cannon, James 1809 wb-#7 (Wl)
Cannon, James R. 1843 rb-12-383 (Ru)
Cannon, Jane C. 1826? wb-#62 (Wl)
Cannon, John 1807 wb-1-237 (K)
Cannon, John 1831 wb-1-12 (Sh)
Cannon, John 1848 wb-g-20 (Hu)
Cannon, John 1852 wb-#52 (Wa)
Cannon, John M. 1839 rb-10-355 (Ru)
Cannon, John M. 1839 rb-10-360 (Ru)
Cannon, Joseph 1857 rb-19-65 (Ru)
Cannon, Joseph F. 1841 rb-12-53 (Ru)
Cannon, Letitia 1832 wb-5-154 (Wi)
Cannon, Martha 1855 wb-h-435 (Hu)
Cannon, Mary E. 1859 wb-f-290 (G)
Cannon, Minos 1829 wb-4-434 (Wi)
Cannon, Nancy 1830 wb-b-79 (Ro)
Cannon, Newton 1841 wb-12-236* (D)
Cannon, Robert 1855 wb-e-515 (Ro)
Cannon, Theophilus A. 1836 rb-9-291 (Ru)
Cannon, Theopholus 1838 rb-10-148 (Ru)
Cannon, William (Sr.) 1859 wb-#61 (Wa)
Canon, Jemima 1849 rb-15-216 (Ru)
Canon, Jemima A. 1849 rb-15-141 (Ru)
Cansler, Nathaniel H. 1830 wb-#26 (Mc)
Cansler, William Sr. 1838 wb-#27 (Mc)
Cantrell, Aaron 1835 wb-b-176 (Wh)
Cantrell, Benjamin 1846 r39-1-4 (Dk)
Cantrell, David 1859 wb-#27 (Mc)
Cantrell, Gabriel 1849 wb-#27 (Mc)
Cantrell, Hannah 1848 r39-1-91 (Dk)

Cantrell, Isaac 1843 wb-1-521 (W)
Cantrell, J. M. 1861 39-2-453 (Dk)
Cantrell, James 1840 wb-1-350 (W)
Cantrell, James 1859 39-2-283 (Dk)
Cantrell, James sr. 1859 39-2-305 (Dk)
Cantrell, John 1826 wb-a-64 (G)
Cantrell, John 1841 wb-c-12 (Wh)
Cantrell, John 1849 r39-1-120 (Dk)
Cantrell, Juliet A. D. 1840 wb-12-45* (D)
Cantrell, Juliet A. D. 1852 wb-15-449 (D)
Cantrell, L. E. 1860 wb-#27 (Mc)
Cantrell, Stephen 1827 lr (Sn)
Cantrell, Tillman 1848 r39-1-72 (Dk)
Cantrell, William J. 1848 r39-1-48 (Dk)
Caperton, Mary B. 1851 wb-5-12 (Hr)
Caperton, Susan 1856 wb-12-100 (Wi)
Caperton, Thompson 1855 wb-12-9 (Wi)
Caple, Branson D. 1839 wb-1-165 (Li)
Caplenor, Samuel 1850 wb-#174 (Wl)
Caples, Russle 1852 wb-#178 (Wl)
Capley, David 1860 wb-d-51 (L)
Caplinger, Andrew 1860 wb-d-62 (L)
Caplinger, John 1819 wb-#30 (Wl)
Caplinger, Leonard 1818 wb-#28 (Wl)
Caplinger, Samuel 1858 wb-h-199 (Hn)
Capps, Benjamin 1832 wb-10-57 (D)
Capps, Ewen 1856 wb-16-209 (Rb)
Capps, Gideon 1859 wb-f-315 (Ro)
Capps, James N. 1853 wb-e-58 (G)
Capps, James R. 1850 wb-d-275 (G)
Capps, John 1851 33-3-336 (Gr)
Capps, John 1854 mr-2-566 (Be)
Capps, John 1858 wb-17-501 (D)
Capps, Polly 1853 wb-10-594 (Wi)
Capps, William 1834 lr (Sn)
Capps, William 1851 wb-b-305 (We)
Caps, Henry 1836 wb-b-103 (G)
Caps, Hillory 1843 mr-2-48 (Be)
Caps, William 1840 5-2-178 (Cl)
Caradine, James M. 1844 wb-4-253 (Ma)
Carathe, Walter 1853 wb-b-227 (L)
Caraway, Bryant 1858 wb-f-195 (G)
Caraway, Henry 1845 wb-4-3 (Hr)
Caraway, Moses 1852 wb-#179 (Wl)
Caraway, Thomas 1835 rb-g-107 (Mt)
Carback, Elisha 1844 wb-5-304 (Gr)
Carden, Joseph W. 1824 wb-1-99 (Hw)
Carden, Larkin 1866 wb-#14 (Mo)
Carden, Leonard 1854 wb-#11 (Mo)
Carden, Reuben 1852 wb-0-115 (Cf)
Carder, Asa 1856 39-2-126 (Dk)

Carder, David 1856 39-2-156 (Dk)
Carder, John 1809 ib-1-274 (Ge)
Carder, John 1809 wb-1-5# (Ge)
Cardle, Eliz. 1846 wb-8-358 (Wi)
Cardwell, Analiza Jane 1841 wb-e-248 (Hn)
Cardwell, Findel L. 1835 wb-d-144 (Hn)
Cardwell, Francis 1845 wb-2-123 (W)
Cardwell, Frederick M. M. 1849 wb-2-62 (Sh)
Cardwell, John G. 1843 wb-3-0 (Sm)
Cardwell, Norflet L. 1841 wb-e-248 (Hn)
Cardwell, Perrin 1855 wb-12-88 (K)
Cardwell, Richard 1818 wb-3-15 (K)
Cardwell, T. L. 1834 wb-c-130 (Hn)
Careney, Tho. L. 1830 wb-7-238 (Rb)
Carey, Daniel 1820 wb-1-95 (Hw)
Carey, Dennis 1842 wb-7-299 (K)
Carey, James B. 1849 wb-10-124 (K)
Carey, Joseph H. 1849 wb-10-105 (K)
Carey, Mary M. 1857 wb-f-102 (G)
Carey, William A. 1860 wb-13-297 (K)
Carey, William M. 1860 wb-13-316 (K)
Carithers, Jane 1852 wb-h-Sep (O)
Carl, Jacob 1845 wb-8-302 (Wi)
Carl, Jacob 1857 wb-12-396 (Wi)
Carl, Jacob B. 1854 wb-11-90 (Wi)
Carlile, Robert 1809 wb-1-199 (Wi)
Carlin, James 1813 wb-#13 (Wl)
Carlin, Patsy 1846 wb-#165 (Wl)
Carlin, Spence 1833 wb-#102 (Wl)
Carlisle, Rosannah 1803 as-1-4 (Ge)
Carlton, Benajah 1850 rb-15-455 (Ru)
Carlton, Blake 1856 rb-18-158 (Ru)
Carlton, Frederick 1853 wb-1-4 (Su)
Carly, William 1842 wb-2-383 (Hr)
Carlyle, Sarah 1854 wb-n-343 (Mt)
Carmack, Aquilla 1819 wb-7-356 (D)
Carmack, Cornelius 1818 wb-1-93 (Hw)
Carmack, Daniel 1859 wb-17-618 (D)
Carmack, George M. 1851 wb-15-118 (D)
Carmack, John 1833 wb-c-119 (Hn)
Carmack, Joseph 1799 wb-1-34 (Rb)
Carmack, Margaret 1857 wb-2-178 (Li)
Carmack, William 1861 wb-1-136 (Hw)
Carmacks, Aquilla 1816 wb-4-458 (D)
Carman, Caleb 1841 wb-4-52 (Je)
Carman, Elijah 1840 wb-3-0 (Sm)
Carmichael, Alexander 1820 rb-5-59 (Ru)
Carmichael, Archibald 1859 wb-13-165 (Wi)
Carmichael, Archibald 1861 wb-1-134 (Hw)
Carmichael, Daniel 1848 wb-1-118 (Hw)
Carmichael, David 1857 wb-#58 (Wa)

Carmichael, Hugh 1838 wb-6-247 (K)
Carmichael, James 1816 wb-2-140 (Je)
Carmichael, James 1857 wb-3-379 (Gr)
Carmichael, James 1857 wb-4-3 (Gr)
Carmichael, John 1840 wb-c-164 (Ro)
Carmichael, Samuel W. 1856 wb-#26 (Mo)
Carmicle, John 1799 wb-#7 (Wa)
Carmon, John 1840 wb-3-551 (Je)
Carmon, William 1833 wb-3-0 (Sm)
Carnahan, Andrew 1839 rb-10-358 (Ru)
Carnahan, Andrew 1853 rb-16-413 (Ru)
Carnahan, Sarah 1859 rb-20-204 (Ru)
Carnel, Richard 1856 wb-2-131 (Li)
Carnell, Delphia 1853 wb-b-212 (L)
Carnell, James C. 1855 wb-c-11 (L)
Carnes, D. B. 1844 wb-3-176 (Hr)
Carnes, David B. 1842 wb-2-362 (Hr)
Carnes, David B. 1849 wb-4-505 (Hr)
Carnes, Edmond 1798 wb-2-131 (D)
Carnes, John 1812 rb-b-119 (Mt)
Carnes, Wm. S. 1846 wb-4-65 (Hr)
Carney, Elijah 1852 wb-15-311 (D)
Carney, Francis G. 1846 lr (Sn)
Carney, James 1839 rb-h-208 (Mt)
Carney, James M. 1834 rb-g-70 (Mt)
Carney, James W. 1835 rb-g-160 (Mt)
Carney, James W. 1837 rb-g-602 (Mt)
Carney, James Wright 1825 rb-d-466 (Mt)
Carney, Joseph 1841 wb-0-17 (Cf)
Carney, Mary 1839 wb-2-259 (Sn)
Carney, Mary 1857 wb-0-148 (Cf)
Carney, Rhoda 1846 wb-#28 (Mc)
Carney, Richard (Genl.) 1832 rb-f-416 (Mt)
Carney, Richard 1831 rb-f-219 (Mt)
Carney, Richard 1834 rb-g-41 (Mt)
Carney, Robartes 1818 rb-4-180 (Ru)
Carney, Sally 1819 rb-c-210 (Mt)
Carney, Sally W. 1842 rb-i-228 (Mt)
Carney, Samuel 1849 wb-#168 (Wl)
Carney, Shelton 1841 lr (Sn)
Carney, Stephen W. jr. 1860 rb-p-478 (Mt)
Carney, Thomas 1849 rb-l-331 (Mt)
Carney, Thomas L. 1831 rb-f-220 (Mt)
Carney, Thomas L. 1849 rb-l-476 (Mt)
Carney, Vincent 1844 wd-13-45 (D)
Carney, William L. 1830 wb-a-74 (R)
Carns, John 1824 rb-d-374 (Mt)
Carns, John B. 1840 mr-2-6 (Be)
Carny, William 1856 rb-o-211 (Mt)
Caroden, Andrew 1836 wb-2-131 (Ma)
Carodene, George 1838 wb-2-349 (Ma)

Carodene, John 1838 wb-2-350 (Má)
Carothers, Edward E. 1842 wb-z-329 (Mu)
Carothers, James 1811 wb-1-143 (Sn)
Carothers, James D. 1840 wb-7-328 (Wi)
Carothers, James L. 1860 wb-13-233 (Wi)
Carothers, Jane 1814 lr (Sn)
Carothers, Martha S. 1856 wb-12-284 (Wi)
Carothers, Peggy 1814 lr (Sn)
Carothers, Samuel 1818 wb-A-216 (Li)
Carothers, Sarah 1819 lr (Sn)
Carothers, William 1814 lr (Sn)
Carow, Henry 1860 wb-18-318 (D)
Carpenter, Eliza 1849 ib-1-136 (Cl)
Carpenter, G. M. 1855 wb-b-7 (F)
Carpenter, Hensley 1846 lr (Gi)
Carpenter, James M. 1853 ib-2-66 (Cl)
Carpenter, John 1853 wb-a-312 (Ms)
Carpenter, Johnathan 1845 wb-a-250 (F)
Carpenter, Louisa 1848 ib-1-70 (Cl)
Carpenter, Mary 1855 ib-h-393 (F)
Carpenter, Wiley 1854 wb-g-645 (Hn)
Carpenter, Yelberton 1848 wb-1-119 (Hw)
Carper, Mary 1826 wb-2-538 (Je)
Carper, McCoy 1851 wb-14-616 (D)
Carper, Sampson 1861 wb-5-113 (Hr)
Carr, Alexander 1815 wb-a-38 (Wh)
Carr, Ann 1827 wb-#64 (Wl)
Carr, Arthur 1829 wb-7-75 (Rb)
Carr, David 1849 as-a-200 (Ms)
Carr, Dickison 1802 wb-1-98 (Rb)
Carr, Elizabeth 1841 as-a-49 (Ms)
Carr, James 1820 wb-#95 (Mu)
Carr, James 1831 lr (Sn)
Carr, James 1837 rb-g-491 (Mt)
Carr, James 1839 rb-h-247 (Mt)
Carr, James K. 1857 ib-2-348 (Cl)
Carr, Jemima 1858 wb-#124 (Wl)
Carr, Jesse 1805 as-1-106 (Ge)
Carr, John (Sr.) 1818 wb-#16 (Wa)
Carr, John 1816 wb-2-330 (Rb)
Carr, John 1841 wb-1-66 (Sh)
Carr, John 1848? ib-1-79 (Cl)
Carr, John 1859 lr (Sn)
Carr, John B. 1853 wb-a-261 (Di)
Carr, King 1833 lr (Sn)
Carr, Margaret 1848 wb-9-427 (K)
Carr, Martha Ann (Mrs.) 1839 wb-1-53 (Sh)
Carr, Mary A. 1857 wb-16-432 (Rb)
Carr, Rebecca 1857 wb-A-118 (Ca)
Carr, Richard 1843 wb-#40 (Wa)
Carr, Susan 1849 as-a-200 (Ms)

Carr, Thomas 1821 wb-#39 (Wl)
Carr, Thomas D. 1832 wb-1-13 (Sh)
Carr, Walter 1824 wb-#51 (Wl)
Carr, William 1815 wb-#12 (Mu)
Carr, William 1857 wb-3e-46 (Sh)
Carr, William 1857 wb-A-117 (Ca)
Carr, William C. 1835 wb-2-195 (Sn)
Carraway, Henry 1847 wb-4-212 (Hr)
Carraway, Richard 1836 wb-1-483 (Hr)
Carrell, John 1833 wb-1-75 (Ct)
Carrell, Matthew L. 1848 wb-2-35 (La)
Carrell, Stephen 1846 wb-1-384 (La)
Carrick, John A. 1814 wb-2-128 (K)
Carrick, Samuel 1809 wb-1-301 (K)
Carrick, Seth L. 1851 wb-d-1 (Wh)
Carrigan, Samuel 1840 wb-2-56 (Hy)
Carriger, Katharine 1849 wb-1-376 (Li)
Carriger, Margaret 1854 lw (Ct)
Carrington, John J. 1840 wb-3-123 (Ma)
Carrington, Wilie 1838 wb-11-474 (D)
Carrington, William 1835 wb-10-419 (D)
Carrol, George W. 1859 wb-f-314 (G)
Carrol, Jesse 1820 wb-3-124 (Wi)
Carroll, Arthur 1855 wb-j-60 (O)
Carroll, Daniel 1859 wb-16-785 (Rb)
Carroll, Elizabeth 1845 wb-a-252 (F)
Carroll, John 1846 wb-g-155 (Hn)
Carroll, John 1852 wb-m-610 (Mt)
Carroll, Josiah 1822 wb-#43 (Wl)
Carroll, Morton 1841 wb-1A-303 (A)
Carroll, Samuel 1843 wb-a-109 (F)
Carroll, William 1835 wb-b-195 (Wh)
Carroll, William 1846 rb-k-105 (Mt)
Carroll, William 1857 wb-b-409 (We)
Carrothers, Ezekiel 1794 wb-2-7 (D)
Carrs, John Hudson 1849 wb-2-59 (Sh)
Carruth (Carouth), James 1828 wb-#28 (Mc)
Carruth, Alexander C. 1833 wb-#100 (Wl)
Carruth, James 1804 wb-1-139 (K)
Carruth, James 1831 wb-#91 (Wl)
Carruth, Samuel 1838 wb-#122 (Wl)
Carruthers, Robert (Sr.) 1828 wb-#169 (Mu)
Carsey, Sarah A. 1851 wb-10-63 (Wi)
Carsey, Thomas P. 1836 wb-6-227 (Wi)
Carsey, William P. 1847 wb-8-610 (Wi)
Carson, Andrew W. 1862 wb-h-559 (Hn)
Carson, Charles S. 1815 wb-4-347 (D)
Carson, James 1834 wb-#105 (Wl)
Carson, James 1845 wb-8-253 (Wi)
Carson, James 1856 wb-#121 (Wl)
Carson, John 1803 wb-1-268 (Je)

Carson, John 1803 wb-4-43 (Je)
Carson, John 1826 wb-4-94 (Wi)
Carson, John 1852 wb-5-48 (Je)
Carson, Joseph 1834 wb-5-343 (Wi)
Carson, Joseph 1834 wb-5-375 (Wi)
Carson, Martha A. 1852 wb-10-269 (Wi)
Carson, Moses W. 1852 wb-#51 (Wa)
Carson, N. D. 1850 wb-14-493 (D)
Carson, Norfleet P. 1857 wb-h-155 (Hn)
Carson, Obediah 1842 wb-3-108 (Hy)
Carson, Robert 1843 wb-1-530 (W)
Carson, Robert 1848 ib-1-51 (Ca)
Carson, Robert 1855 wb-11-509 (Wi)
Carson, Samuel 1815 Wb-2-172 (Wi)
Carson, Samuel 1850 wb-5-72 (Je)
Carson, Thomas 1854 wb-2-78# (Ge)
Carson, William 1787 wb-1-4# (Ge)
Carson, William 1790 wb-#3 (Wa)
Carson, William 1800 wb-1-244 (Je)
Carson, William 1804 wb-#9 (Wa)
Carson, William 1819 wb-#17 (Wa)
Carson, William 1826 wb-#28 (Mc)
Carson, William 1851 wb-10-137 (Wi)
Carson, William A. 1850 wb-2-71# (Ge)
Carson, Willis 1815 Wb-2-176 (Wi)
Carter, Abraham 1842 148-1-37 (Ge)
Carter, Abram 1832 wb-2-42# (Ge)
Carter, Alfred M. 1850 wb-1-130 (Ct)
Carter, Amos 1838 wb-#28 (Mc)
Carter, Amos 1857 wb-12-334 (K)
Carter, Anderson 1846 148-1-175 (Ge)
Carter, Benjamin 1860 lr (Gi)
Carter, Benjamin 1861 wb-2-93# (Ge)
Carter, Bernard 1853 wb-#108 (Wl)
Carter, Betsy 1848 wb-e-64 (Ro)
Carter, Burrell 1823 rb-5-314 (Ru)
Carter, Charles 1830 wb-b-143 (Wh)
Carter, Charles A. 1862 wb-#135 (Wl)
Carter, Charles Sr. 1841 wb-#29 (Mc)
Carter, Charles sr. 1830 wb-b-10 (Wh)
Carter, Christopher C. 1824 wb-8-377 (D)
Carter, Daniel 1829 wb-2-30# (Ge)
Carter, Daniel 1844 wb-8-175 (Wi)
Carter, David 1848 ib-1-18 (Wy)
Carter, Elisha 1837 wb-2-48# (Ge)
Carter, Elizabeth 1840? wb-1-87 (Ct)
Carter, Elizabeth 1841 wb-1-93 (Ct)
Carter, Elizabeth 1848 wb-2-69# (Ge)
Carter, Elizabeth 1852 wb-e-318 (Ro)
Carter, Ellis 1848 148-1-243 (Ge)
Carter, Enoch 1856 wb-5-418 (Je)

Carter, Ephraim 1824 wb-3-348 (St)
Carter, Ezekiel 1832 wb-2-145# (Ge)
Carter, Ezekiel 1841 wb-c-42 (O)
Carter, Ezekiel 1853 wb-2-77# (Ge)
Carter, Ezekiel jr. 1856 149-1-35 (Ge)
Carter, Ezekiel sr. 1853 wb-2-77# (Ge)
Carter, Francis 1852 wb-15-314 (D)
Carter, G. J. 1861 wb-#29 (Mc)
Carter, Hamilton J. 1855 wb-1-129 (Hw)
Carter, Isaac 1823 wb-3-607 (Wi)
Carter, James 1826 rb-6-184 (Ru)
Carter, James 1830 wb-b-85 (Hn)
Carter, James B. 1861 wb-5-121 (Hr)
Carter, James C. 1857 149-1-88 (Ge)
Carter, James D. V. 1855 ib-h-398 (F)
Carter, James E. 1854 wb-b-332 (We)
Carter, James F. 1859 wb-13-146 (Wi)
Carter, Jane 1844 wb-#4 (Mo)
Carter, Jesse 1847 wb-4-232 (Hr)
Carter, Jesse 1850 wb-#29 (Mc)
Carter, John 1815 wb-1-0 (Sm)
Carter, John 1821 rb-5-153 (Ru)
Carter, John 1822 wb-8-76 (D)
Carter, John 1824 rb-6-3 (Ru)
Carter, John 1832 wb-a-33 (Cr)
Carter, John 1833 wb-2-42# (Ge)
Carter, John 1842 rb-i-373 (Mt)
Carter, John 1847 wb-2-66# (Ge)
Carter, John B. 1844 wb-d-248 (O)
Carter, John M. 1848 lr (Sn)
Carter, Joseph 1820 wb-a-127 (Ro)
Carter, Joseph 1836 wb-b-285 (Ro)
Carter, Joseph sr. 1839 wb-2-256 (Sn)
Carter, Josiah 1851 ib-1-225 (Cl)
Carter, Kinchen 1837 wb-#120 (Wl)
Carter, Kinchen 1853 wb-5-134 (Ma)
Carter, Lamos M. 1793 wb-1-7 (K)
Carter, Leroy C. 1837 wb-#29 (Mc)
Carter, Levi 1809 wb-2-33# (Ge)
Carter, Levi 1845 wb-g-29 (Hn)
Carter, Levy 1809 wb-1-5# (Ge)
Carter, Lewis 1856 wb-#26 (Mo)
Carter, Lewis 1860 wb-17-60 (Rb)
Carter, Lucinda B. 1860 wb-k-168 (O)
Carter, Martha 1857 wb-2-86# (Ge)
Carter, Martin 1850 wb-e-247 (Ro)
Carter, Mary M. 1861 wb-18-611 (D)
Carter, Mashac 1858 wb-2-100# (Ge)
Carter, Mathew W. 1862 wb-2-359 (Li)
Carter, Melton 1846 148-1-174 (Ge)
Carter, Merry 1856 lr (Gi)

Carter, Milton 1852 wb-f-4? (Mu)
Carter, Nathaniel G. 1845 wb-#150 (Wl)
Carter, Newton 1848 wb-9-159 (Wi)
Carter, Rachel 1859 wb-17-580 (D)
Carter, Rady 1859 rb-20-153 (Ru)
Carter, Randolph 1837 wb-#29 (Mc)
Carter, Rhoda 1859 rb-20-277 (Ru)
Carter, Richard 1815 Wb-2-146 (Wi)
Carter, Richard D. 1841 wb-b-391 (G)
Carter, Robert 1839 wb-7-207 (Wi)
Carter, Robert 1848 rb-l-145 (Mt)
Carter, Robert 1857 wb-h-167 (Hn)
Carter, Samuel 1812 wb-a-111 (St)
Carter, Samuel 1813 wb-#7 (Mu)
Carter, Samuel 1845 wb-d-158 (Hd)
Carter, Samuel W. 1860 wb-f-401 (G)
Carter, Sarah 1827 rb-6-316 (Ru)
Carter, Sarah 1852 wb-10-218 (Wi)
Carter, Stephen H. 1849 wb-13-59 (Rb)
Carter, Theodrick 1839 wb-7-32 (Wi)
Carter, Thompson 1857 wb-6-450 (Ma)
Carter, Troy 1858 wb-12-536 (K)
Carter, W. 1854 wb-i-256 (O)
Carter, William 1815 wb-2-206 (K)
Carter, William 1837 wb-10-32 (Rb)
Carter, William 1839 wb-10-267 (Rb)
Carter, William 1840 wb-12-89* (D)
Carter, William 1850 wb-14-363 (Rb)
Carter, William 1851 wb-2-210 (La)
Carter, William 1856 wb-j-170 (O)
Carter, William C. 1839 wb-2-51# (Ge)
Carter, William O. 1848 wb-1-250 (Fr)
Carter, William W. 1831 wb-#92 (Wl)
Carter, Williamson 1849 wb-1-393* (W)
Carthel, Joseph M. 1849 wb-d-195 (G)
Carthell, Josiah 1825 wb-#166 (Mu)
Cartmell, Henry T. 1855 wb-#117 (Wl)
Cartright, Hezekiah 1817 wb-#33 (Wl)
Cartright, John 1840 wb-#30 (Mc)
Cartright, Josua 1842 wb-1-451 (W)
Cartright, Patience 1838 wb-11-253 (D)
Cartright, Peter 1808 wb-#5 (Wl)
Cartright, Robert 1829 wb-1-44 (We)
Cartright, Thomas 1814 wb-1-202 (Bo)
Cartwright, Adison 1855 wb-7-0 (Sm)
Cartwright, Bennajah 1843 wb-c-108 (G)
Cartwright, Caleb 1799 wb-2-148 (D)
Cartwright, David 1814 wb-4-283 (D)
Cartwright, David 1819 wb-7-296 (D)
Cartwright, David 1836 wb-10-559 (D)
Cartwright, David 1860 wb-13-215 (Wi)

Cartwright, David 1860 wb-13-286 (Wi)
Cartwright, Edward 1860 rb-20-520 (Ru)
Cartwright, Edward W. 1842 wb-#136 (Wl)
Cartwright, Elizabeth 1851 wb-#178 (Wl)
Cartwright, Elizabeth 1857 wb-17-225 (D)
Cartwright, Jac 1844 wd-13-29 (D)
Cartwright, Jacob 1828 wb-9-247 (d)
Cartwright, Jacob 1838 wb-11-170 (D)
Cartwright, Jane 1834 wb-10-332 (D)
Cartwright, Jefferson 1833 wb-10-236 (D)
Cartwright, John 1825 wb-#64 (Wl)
Cartwright, M. T. 1843 wb-#139 (Wl)
Cartwright, Mathew 1811 wb-#11 (Wl)
Cartwright, Mathew T. 1845 wb-#158 (Wl)
Cartwright, Matthew 1825? wb-#55 (Wl)
Cartwright, P. A. 1845 wb-#147 (Wl)
Cartwright, Pembroke 1826 wb-8-557 (D)
Cartwright, Peter G. 1853 wb-e-14 (Hy)
Cartwright, Richard 1842 wb-#147 (Wl)
Cartwright, Robert 1816 wb-4-471 (D)
Cartwright, Robert 1816 wb-7-27 (D)
Cartwright, Robt. 1810 wb-4-82 (D)
Cartwright, Thomas 1825? wb-#56 (Wl)
Cartwright, Thomas 1843 wb-12-448* (D)
Cartwright, Thomas N. 1820 wb-#44 (Wl)
Cartwright, Vincent 1815 wb-4-352 (D)
Carty, B. W. D. 1856 wb-2-135 (Li)
Caruth, A. C. 1833 wb-#101 (Wl)
Caruth, E. S. 1861 wb-#133 (Wl)
Caruth, James 1854 wb-#115 (Wl)
Caruth, Rachel 1823 wb-3-459 (K)
Caruth, Walter 1838 wb-#122 (Wl)
Caruth, William S. 1837 wb-#119 (Wl)
Caruthers, Ab 1862 wb-#136 (Wl)
Caruthers, Edmund 1827 rb-7-2 (Ru)
Caruthers, Elizabeth 1845 wb-a2-243 (Mu)
Caruthers, James 1800 wb-#7 (Wa)
Caruthers, John 1845 wb-4-300 (Ma)
Caruthers, Robert 1830 wb-#216 (Mu)
Caruthers, Samuel 1814 wb-1-0 (Sm)
Caruthers, Samuel 1825 wb-2-0 (Sm)
Caruthers, Thomas J. 1836 wb-b-125 (G)
Caruthers, William 1845 wb-4-300 (Ma)
Caruthers, William 1855 wb-a-371 (Ms)
Caruthers, William B. 1851 wb-15-11 (D)
Carver, Cornelius 1840 wb-1-26 (Bo)
Carver, Cornelius 1852 wb-a-186 (Cr)
Carver, Isaac 1859 wb-#128 (Wl)
Carver, Samuel 1844 wb-#145 (Wl)
Carver, Thomas 1821 wb-#40 (Wl)
Carver, Thomas no year wb-1-28 (Bo)

Carver, William 1856 wb-#118 (Wl)
Carvin, William 1808 wb-4-2 (D)
Carvin, William 1826 wb-8-561 (D)
Cary, James 1848 rb-14-247 (Ru)
Cary, James 1855 wb-i-242 (O)
Cary, James B. 1850 wb-10-452 (K)
Cary, William 1854 wb-e-204 (G)
Casada, Reuben 1847 wb-#30 (Mc)
Casada, Wesley 1841 wb-#30 (Mc)
Case, John 1855 wb-16-568 (D)
Casens, Louis 1859 rb-20-47 (Ru)
Casey, David 1861 wb-13-520 (K)
Casey, Dennis 1839 wb-6-475 (K)
Casey, Hiram 1829 wb-1-92 (Hr)
Casey, Hiram 1847 wb-4-235 (Hr)
Casey, James 1849 wb-14-452 (D)
Casey, James 1851 wb-14-643 (D)
Casey, Joshua M. 1856 wb-6-307 (Ma)
Casey, Joshua M. 1857 wb-6-491 (Ma)
Casey, Randolph 1814 wb-1-0 (Sm)
Casey, Riley 1840 wb-b-219 (Hd)
Casey, Sims 1847 wb-14-21 (D)
Cash, Elisha 1802 Wb-1-97 (Wi)
Cash, Howard 1845 wb-c-178 (Wh)
Cash, James 1807 wb-#11 (Wa)
Cash, James 1861 wb-e-441 (Wh)
Cash, Joel 1850 wb-#24 (Mo)
Cash, Sampson 1850 wb-c-390 (Wh)
Cash, Simpson 1845 wb-c-178 (Wh)
Cash, Thomas 1829 wb-4-437 (Wi)
Cash, Thomas P. 1856 ib-1-407 (Wy)
Cashion, James L. 1857 wb-j-232 (O)
Cashion, Richard W. 1854 wb-i-160 (O)
Cason, Edward N. 1845 wb-g-20 (Hn)
Cason, John 1806 rb-2-18 (Ru)
Cason, Joseph 1835 wb-#109 (Wl)
Cass, John F. 1838 wb-a-25 (Ms)
Cassada, David 1849 wb-#30 (Mc)
Cassady, Joseph 1850 wb-e-260 (Ro)
Cassellman, Jacob 1791 wb-1-194 (D)
Casselman, Benjamin 1826 wb-8-512 (D)
Casselman, Jacob 1806 wb-3-125 (D)
Casselman, John L. 1837 wb-#117 (Wl)
Cassels, William 1854 wb-e-218 (G)
Casteel, David 1832 wb-a-134 (R)
Casteel, Edmond 1831 wb-#30 (Mc)
Casteel, Francis 1833 wb-5-206 (K)
Casteel, Jane 1833 wb-a-168 (R)
Casteel, John 1841 wb-a-475 (R)
Casteel, Peter 1833 wb-2-42# (Ge)
Casteel, Zachariah 1821 wb-1-6# (Ge)

Castelbury, Paul 1815 rb-b-265 (Mt)
Castellow, Henry D. 1856 wb-c-31 (L)
Castiller, Miles 1829 wb-3-56 (Je)
Castillow, John D. 1859 wb-e-104 (Hy)
Castleberry, Joseph 1822 wb-3-493 (Rb)
Castleberry, Sampson 1836 rb-g-388 (Mt)
Castlebury, Paul 1815 rb-b-281 (Mt)
Castleman, Andrew 1845 wb-13-145 (D)
Castleman, Anna 1848 wb-#156 (Wl)
Castleman, Arthur L. 1850 rb-15-557 (Ru)
Castleman, B. F. 1850 wb-g-298 (St)
Castleman, Benjamin 1847 wb-#156 (Wl)
Castleman, Benjamin F. 1852 wb-xx-75 (St)
Castleman, David 1846 as-b-325 (Di)
Castleman, Henry 1850 wb-14-489 (D)
Castleman, Jacob 1847 wb-#155 (Wl)
Castleman, John 1821 wb-8-15 (D)
Caswell, Henry 1860 as-c-175 (Ms)
Caswell, Richard W. 1811 rb-2-136 (Ru)
Caswell, Richard W. 1826 rb-6-213 (Ru)
Casy, H. 1845 wb-3-229 (Hr)
Catchings, Meredith J. jr. 1857 wb-1-352 (Fr)
Catchum, Martha 1816 wb-2-229 (K)
Cate, Charles 1824 wb-#31 (Mc)
Cate, John 1822 wb-2-351 (Je)
Cate, John 1840 wb-0-12 (Cf)
Cate, John 1840 wb-3-552 (Je)
Cate, John 1851 wb-5-237 (Je)
Cate, Martha 1841 wb-e-309 (Hn)
Cate, Perry 1852 mr-2-477 (Be)
Cate, Rolen 1813 wb-4-256 (D)
Cate, Simon 1841 wb-#31 (Mc)
Cate, Thomas 1843 wb-f-180* (Hn)
Cate, Thomas 1859 wb-h-315 (Hn)
Cate, William 1839 wb-#31 (Mc)
Cate, William H. 1823 wb-3-666 (Wi)
Cates, Charles 1850 33-3-230 (Gr)
Cates, Eliza 1846 rb-13-715 (Ru)
Cates, Ezra 1853 wb-3-129 (La)
Cates, John 1848 rb-14-486 (Ru)
Cates, Joshua 1838 rb-10-216 (Ru)
Cates, Moses 1839 wb-5-29 (Gr)
Cates, Nancy 1857 rb-18-389 (Ru)
Cates, William (Rev.) 1859 wb-#63 (Wa)
Cates, William 1844 wb-a2-80 (Mu)
Cathcart, Joseph 1814 wb-2-134 (K)
Cathey, Andrew 1823 wb-a-42 (Hn)
Cathey, George 1835 wb-6-50 (Wi)
Cathey, George 1843 wb-1-226 (Li)
Cathey, George sr. 1840 wb-d-445 (St)
Cathey, Griffith 1854 wb-f-49 (Mu)

Cathey, Honor B. 1845 A-468-6 (Le)
Cathey, James 1845 wb-a2-320 (Mu)
Cathey, James D. 1849 A-468-119 (Le)
Cathey, James D. 1849 A-468-123 (Le)
Cathey, John 1821 wb-#69 (Mu)
Cathey, John 1846 wb-f-311 (St)
Cathey, Margaret 1857 as-c-33 (Ms)
Cathey, Wiley 1843 wb-d-57 (O)
Cathey, William G. 1856 wb-f-118 (Mu)
Cathon, Barbra 1817 wb-1-0 (Sm)
Cathorn, Lemuel 1851 wb-14-545 (Rb)
Cathron, John 1831 wb-#93 (Wl)
Cathy, Cyrus 1843 wb-1-217 (Li)
Cathy, George W. 1856 wb-h-176 (St)
Cato, Daniel 1814 wb-a-243 (St)
Cato, Henry 1859 wb-i-137 (St)
Cato, Robert 1816 wb-7-67 (D)
Cato, Roland 1816 wb-7-83 (D)
Cato, Rowland 1854 wb-16-238 (D)
Caton, Jessee 1842 wb-1-525 (W)
Cator, Levin 1848 wb-9-69 (Wi)
Cator, Martha 1839 wb-7-27 (Wi)
Cator, Moses E. sr. 1853 wb-11-45 (Wi)
Catron, Felix 1843 wb-12-393* (D)
Catron, Jacob W. 1854 wb-12-53 (K)
Catron, John 1859 gs-1-456 (F)
Catron, Susan M. 1848 wd-14-208 (D)
Catron, Valentine 1832 wb-2-40# (Ge)
Catron, Valentine 1858 149-1-100 (Ge)
Catton, John M. 1859 39-2-310 (Dk)
Cattrell, Elvira 1851 wb-11-17 (K)
Caudle, Aaron 1837 wb-9-427 (Rb)
Caudle, Jesse 1827 wb-#151 (Mu)
Caughran, Alexander 1853 wb-2-58 (Li)
Caughran, Andrew 1853 wb-2-46 (Li)
Caughron, James P. 1863 wb-2-369 (Li)
Caughron, William 1821 wb-3-430 (Je)
Causby, James 1817 wb-A-176 (Li)
Causey, Aaron 1825 wb-a-86 (Hn)
Causey, Zebulon 1848 wb-b-222 (Mu)
Cautas?, Peter 1827 wb-1-9 (W)
Cauthon, Thomas 1819 wb-#35 (Wl)
Cauthron, Jane 1838 wb-0-8 (Cf)
Cavener, John sr. 1848 wb-2-67# (Ge)
Cavener, William 1816 wb-2-37# (Ge)
Cavenor, James 1861 149-1-234 (Ge)
Caves, George 1855 wb-#31 (Mc)
Cavett, George W. 1846 wb-b-184 (We)
Cavett, Michal 1821 wb-1-325 (Sn)
Cavett, Moses 1802 wb-0-35 (K)
Cavett, Moses 1818 wb-3-42 (K)

Caviness, Isaiah 1849 wb-4-555 (Hr)
Cavit, Alexander 1793 wb-1-11 (K)
Cavit, John 1818 rb-4-111 (Ru)
Cavite, A. 1839 wb-2-129 (Hr)
Cavitt, A. 1840 wb-2-183 (Hr)
Cavitt, Andrew 1841 wb-2-262 (Hr)
Cavitt, Joseph 1832 wb-c-43 (Hn)
Cavnar, Edward 1859 wb-5-102 (Hr)
Cavner, Hugh 1825 wb-1-3# (Ge)
Cawley, Milly 1847 lr (Sn)
Cawley, Signee 1823 wb-#64 (Mu)
Cawood, Mosses 1801 wb-1-25 (Bo)
Cawthon, Joseph W. 1852 wb-#178 (Wl)
Cayce, Elizabeth 1823 wb-1-0 (Sm)
Cayce, Fleming 1819 wb-1-0 (Sm)
Cayce, Shad. 1832 wb-1-38 (La)
Cayee, Geo. B. 1849 wb-4-510 (Hr)
Cazort, James W. 1840 wb-3-165 (Ma)
Cearnall, Hubbard 1852 wb-h-27 (Hu)
Cearnall, John W. 1853 wb-h-188 (Hu)
Cecil, John W. 1849 A-468-127 (Le)
Cecil, Samuel 1856 wb-f-116 (Mu)
Center, Francis K. 1838 wb-c-9 (Ro)
Center, James C. 1842 wb-c-83 (G)
Center, Milton 1848 wb-e-77 (Ro)
Center, Susana 1819 wb-a-115 (Ro)
Cerncue?, David C. 1845 wb-f-257* (Hn)
Cernell, Richard 1855 wb-2-122 (Li)
Cerry?, Samuel 1835 wb-b-194 (Wh)
Cerry?, Thomas 1831 wb-b-59 (Wh)
Cersay, John 1834 wb-1-68 (Gr)
Chaddock, George 1831 wb-#223 (Mu)
Chadwell, A. J. C. 1858? ib-2-421 (Cl)
Chadwell, George 1860 wb-18-398 (D)
Chadwell, Thomas G. 1847 wb-14-61 (D)
Chadwell, Valentine 1831 wb-5-1 (Wi)
Chadwell, William 1857 ib-2-425 (Cl)
Chadwick, Charles Y. 1848 wb-b-369 (Mu)
Chadwick, James 1849 wb-g-110 (St)
Chaffin, Coleman 1845 wb-b-27 (Mu)
Chaffin, Edward H. 1856 wb-f-118 (Mu)
Chaffin, Littleberry 1835 wb-x-289* (Mu)
Chaffin, Moses 1820? wb-#40 (Mu)
Chafin, Robert 1832 wb-1-80 (La)
Chaires, Jo. 1846 wb-4-62 (Hr)
Chaires, Joseph 1844 wb-3-142 (Hr)
Chalders, R. B. 1854 rb-17-30 (Ru)
Chalfin, Robert 1817 wb-#26 (Wl)
Chalk, William 1853 6-2-116 (Le)
Chalmers, James R. 1825 wb-a-59 (G)
Chamberlain, A. 1836 wb-1-210 (Gr)

Chamberlain, Andrew 1793 wb-1-12 (Je)
Chamberlain, Andrew 1834 wb-1-90 (Gr)
Chamberlain, David 1852 wb-e-1 (G)
Chamberlain, Hanah 1811 wb-1-16 (Bo)
Chamberlain, Jane J. 1842 wb-c-151 (O)
Chamberlain, Jeremiah 1834 wb-1-66 (Gr)
Chamberlain, John 1794 wb-1-13 (K)
Chamberlain, Ninian 1798 wb-1-32 (Je)
Chamberlain, Ninian 1798 wb-4-47 (Je)
Chamberlain, Ninian 1811 wb-1-252 (Bo)
Chamberlain, Ninian 1837 wb-3-435 (Je)
Chamberlain, Thos. 1838 wb-b-246 (G)
Chambers, Alexander 1821 wb-#39 (Wl)
Chambers, Daniel 1853 wb-1-125 (Hw)
Chambers, Edmund 1837 wb-#31 (Mc)
Chambers, Edward O. 1849 wb-a-139 (T)
Chambers, Galbreth 1840 wb-1-191 (Fr)
Chambers, George W. 1854 wb-1-36 (Dy)
Chambers, Henry R. 1842 wb-a-117 (L)
Chambers, James 1833 wb-#1 (Mo)
Chambers, James 1837 lw (Ct)
Chambers, James 1856 wb-#121 (Wl)
Chambers, John 1816 wb-3-204 (St)
Chambers, John 1819 wb-1-0 (Sm)
Chambers, John 1842 wb-a-110 (Cr)
Chambers, John A. 1839 abl-1-132 (T)
Chambers, John C. 1843 wb-3-0 (Sm)
Chambers, John P. 1843 wb-11-390 (Rb)
Chambers, John sr. 1819 wb-1-0 (Sm)
Chambers, Moses 1837 wb-1-136 (Li)
Chambers, Sarah A. 1859 wb-8-0 (Sm)
Chambers, Thomas 1837 wb-a-247 (O)
Chambers, William 1834 wb-3-0 (Sm)
Chambers, William L. 1854 wb-b-260 (L)
Chambless, James 1851 wb-14-533 (Rb)
Chambless, Jno. J. 1861 wb-a-224 (Ce)
Chambless, Mark 1841 rb-i-103 (Mt)
Chambless, Mark 1841 rb-i-105 (Mt)
Chambless, Nicholas R. 1835 wb-10-28 (Rb)
Chambless, Robert 1835 wb-9-118 (Rb)
Chambless, Robert 1845 wb-#147 (Wl)
Chambless, Ruth 1859? wb-a-339 (Cr)
Chambless, Thos. G. 1809 wb-4-57 (D)
Chamell, Thomas F. 1854 wb-n-457 (Mt)
Champ, Asahel 1819 wb-7-311 (D)
Champ, John 1810 wb-1-223 (Wi)
Champ, John 1821 Wb-3-242 (Wi)
Champe, A. K. 1857 wb-12-411 (K)
Champion, Daniel jr. 1853 wb-1-314 (Fr)
Champion, John 1818 wb-1-30 (Fr)
Champion, Jordon 1836 wb-d-26 (St)

Champion, Joseph 1838 wb-d-274 (St)
Chance, John B. 1855 wb-16-52 (Rb)
Chance, Thomas 1855 wb-g-685 (Hn)
Chandler, Andrew 1859 wb-h-328 (Hn)
Chandler, Betsy 1836 wb-6-9 (K)
Chandler, Daniel 1844 wb-5-294 (Gr)
Chandler, David 1842 wb-a-99 (F)
Chandler, E. C. 1853 wb-b-209 (L)
Chandler, E. T. 1847 wb-4-229 (Hr)
Chandler, Edward T. 1846 wb-4-96 (Hr)
Chandler, Ekelles 1852 wb-#180 (Wl)
Chandler, Henry 1818 wb-#42 (Wl)
Chandler, Isaac B. 1840 wb-e-4 (St)
Chandler, Ivey 1860 wb-k-167 (O)
Chandler, Ivey S. 1860 wb-k-237 (O)
Chandler, Ivy 1859 wb-c-272 (L)
Chandler, James 1810 wb-#8 (Wl)
Chandler, James H. 1849 wb-g-46 (O)
Chandler, Josiah 1834 wb-#103 (Wl)
Chandler, M. E. 1853 wb-#110 (Wl)
Chandler, Parkes 1845 wb-5-1 (Ma)
Chandler, Parks 1855 wb-6-155 (Ma)
Chandler, R. B. 1854 rb-17-48 (Ru)
Chandler, Richard 1833 wb-1-18 (Bo)
Chandler, Robert 1805 wb-#3 (Wl)
Chandler, Robert B. 1856 rb-18-29 (Ru)
Chandler, Ryland 1835 wb-2-20 (Ma)
Chandler, Ryland 1855 ib-h-449 (F)
Chandler, Shadrack 1838 wb-y-167 (Mu)
Chandler, Thomas 1814 wb-1-0 (Sm)
Chandler, William 1851 wb-14-648 (D)
Chaney, Ezekiel 1840 wb-7-223 (Wi)
Chaney, H. W. 1858 wb-12-599 (Wi)
Chaney, Houston W. 1860 wb-13-241 (Wi)
Chaney, W. T. 1850 wb-9-594 (Wi)
Chaney, Wilkins T. 1852 wb-10-445 (Wi)
Chaney, William 1846 wb-4-18 (Je)
Chaney, William T. 1850 wb-9-602 (Wi)
Chanlers, Green 1851 wb-d-339 (G)
Channaberry, George T. 1859 wb-13-157* (K)
Channel, Elisha J. 1855 wb-n-680 (Mt)
Channell, Elisha 1806 rb-a-302 (Mt)
Channell, Elisha 1853 wb-m-646 (Mt)
Channell, Henry S. 1852 wb-m-464 (Mt)
Channing, Penina P.? 1860 wb-18-379 (D)
Chaplin, Elizabeth 1844 wb-8-177 (Wi)
Chaplin, Elizabeth M. 1845 wb-8-245 (Wi)
Chapman, Benjamin 1832 rb-g-68 (Mt)
Chapman, Benjamin 1836 wb-9-267 (Rb)
Chapman, Benjamin 1846 wb-8-482 (Wi)
Chapman, Charles W. 1857 as-c-70 (Ms)

Chapman, Daniel 1847 wb-13-188 (Rb)
Chapman, Edmund W. 1836 wb-#32 (Mc)
Chapman, Elijah 1853 r39-1-263 (Dk)
Chapman, Elizabeth 1856 wb-12-288 (Wi)
Chapman, Fayette W. 1854 wb-12-3 (K)
Chapman, Isaac 1841 wb-11-28 (Rb)
Chapman, J. 1838 wb-1-578 (Hr)
Chapman, J. H. 1847 ib-1-53 (Cl)
Chapman, James 1800 lr (Sn)
Chapman, James 1824 wb-4-270 (Rb)
Chapman, James L. 1842 wb-#138 (Wl)
Chapman, John 1827 wb-a-36 (R)
Chapman, John 1842 lr (Sn)
Chapman, John S. 1856 wb-#118 (Wl)
Chapman, Joseph 1861 wb-17-253 (Rb)
Chapman, Joshua H. 1847 5-3-235 (Cl)
Chapman, Joshua M. 1840 abl-1-170 (T)
Chapman, Lemuel 1848 wb-#32 (Mc)
Chapman, Miles 1816 wb-2-273 (K)
Chapman, Robert 1795 wb-0-12 (K)
Chapman, Robert H. 1833 wb-a-15 (T)
Chapman, Samuel 1811 wb-#10 (Wl)
Chapman, Samuel 1826 wb-9-59 (D)
Chapman, Shadrick 1860 wb-4-364 (La)
Chapman, Silas 1847 wb-#176 (Wl)
Chapman, Thomas 1804 wb-1-157 (K)
Chapman, Thomas 1845 wb-1-259 (Li)
Chapman, Thomas E. 1857 as-c-33 (Ms)
Chapman, Vincent 1841 wb-11-28 (Rb)
Chapman, William 1838 lr (Gi)
Chapman, William 1852 as-b-63 (Ms)
Chapman, William 1858 ib-C-176 (C)
Chapouil, Pater 1836 wb-11-98 (D)
Chappalain, Samuel 1815 wb-A-89 (Li)
Chappel, Dickie 1856 wb-f-90 (Mu)
Chappell, Alexander 1833 wb-x-112 (Mu)
Chappell, John 1812 wb-1-0 (Sm)
Chappell, John L. 1857 wb-6-355 (Ma)
Chappell, Phebe 1803 wb-#7 (Wl)
Chappell, Samuel 1844 wb-#143 (Wl)
Chappell, Thomas B. 1835 wb-#108 (Wl)
Charles, Elvira 1854 wb-16-284 (D)
Charles, Etheldridge 1842 wb-1-123 (Hw)
Charles, Sarah 1839 wb-1-113 (Hw)
Charles, Solomon 1859 wb-e-308 (Wh)
Charleton, Pointen 1822 wb-#19 (Wa)
Charlton, Benjamin F. 1850 wb-14-556 (D)
Charlton, Jacob 1834 wb-1-107 (Hw)
Charlton, John 1840 wb-11-628 (D)
Charlton, Rebecca 1824 wb-#21 (Wa)
Charnell, Henry S. 1838 rb-h-87 (Mt)

Charter, Booker R. 1838 wb-y-210* (Mu)
Charter, James 1810 wb-1-319 (K)
Charter, John N. 1848 wb-9-39 (Wi)
Charter, John O. P. 1843 wb-8-74 (Wi)
Chase, Isaac M. 1859 wb-3e-99 (Sh)
Chase, John 1822 wb-2-359 (Je)
Chase, Walter 1836 wb-#32 (Wa)
Chastain, Elisha 1854 wb-#113 (Wl)
Chaudoin, Joel 1844 wb-12-229 (Rb)
Chauvin, William 1834 wb-10-316 (D)
Chavannes, Adrien 1855 wb-12-144 (K)
Chavis, Francis 1841 wb-12-156* (D)
Cheairs, John J. 1852 wb-5-32 (Hr)
Cheairs, Joseph 1843 wb-3-8 (Hr)
Cheairs, Nathaniel 1846 wb-a2-485 (Mu)
Cheairs, Sarah 1858 wb-f-152 (Mu)
Cheairs, V. S. 1842 wb-a-83 (F)
Chears, Frances 1841 wb-12-128* (D)
Chears, V. T. 1854 ib-h-58 (F)
Cheatham, A. 1825 wb-5-100 (Rb)
Cheatham, Archer 1800 wb-1-50 (Rb)
Cheatham, Francis A. 1828 wb-6-259 (Rb)
Cheatham, James 1828 wb-1-19 (Li)
Cheatham, Joel 1841 wb-a-28 (Dk)
Cheatham, John L. 1833 wb-8-360 (Rb)
Cheatham, John L. 1843 wb-12-43 (Rb)
Cheatham, Mary B. 1861 wb-b*-3 (O)
Cheatham, Paulinia 1835 rb-9-195 (Ru)
Cheatham, Prudence 1853 wb-f-18 (Mu)
Cheatham, R. C. 1845 mr-2-140 (Be)
Cheatham, Richard 1845 wb-12-486 (Rb)
Cheatham, Robert 1858 wb-f-142 (Mu)
Cheatham, Thomas 1834 rb-9-90 (Ru)
Cheatham, Thomas 1853 wb-15-315 (Rb)
Cheatham, Thomas R. 1843 mr-2-54 (Be)
Cheatham, Thomas Sr. 1854 wb-15-641 (Rb)
Cheatham, Thomas jr. 1853 wb-15-411 (Rb)
Cheatham, William 1833 wb-x-111 (Mu)
Cheek, Abraham 1814 wb-2-160 (Rb)
Cheek, Corbin 1838 5-2-26 (Cl)
Cheek, Eli 1847 wb-b-89 (Mu)
Cheek, Elijah 1820 wb-3-181 (Rb)
Cheek, Elisha 1818 wb-2-378 (Rb)
Cheek, Elizabeth 1833 wb-8-213 (Rb)
Cheek, Elizabeth C. 1837 wb-3-0 (Sm)
Cheek, F. M. 1858 wb-h-298 (Hn)
Cheek, Granville A. 1857 ib-2-369 (Cl)
Cheek, James W. 1840 wb-a-61 (L)
Cheek, Jesse 1829 wb-#181 (Mu)
Cheek, Joel 1837 wb-d-130* (Hn)
Cheek, Mary 1853 as-b-136 (Ms)

Cheek, William 1827 wb-2-568 (Je)
Cheek, William H. 1827 wb-3-0 (Sm)
Cheek?, Henry 1856 wb-f-3 (G)
Cheeks, Francis 1855 wb-2-182 (Sh)
Cheers, John 1793 wb-1-238 (Je)
Cheishur, J. 1844 wb-3-170 (Hr)
Chenoweth, Richard 1859 wb-13-242 (K)
Chenoweth, Richard jr. 1861 wb-13-514 (K)
Cheny, Eli 1845 wb-13-204 (D)
Cherchill, John 1824 wb-3-102* (St)
Cherry, Albert 1856 wb-g-719 (Hn)
Cherry, Caleb 1825 wb-8-496 (D)
Cherry, Charles 1819 rb-c-82 (Mt)
Cherry, Charles 1822 rb-d-74 (Mt)
Cherry, Daniel 1843 wb-3-216 (Hy)
Cherry, Daniel 1855 wb-h-168 (St)
Cherry, Daniel 1857 wb-h-352 (St)
Cherry, Eli 1842 wb-12-376* (D)
Cherry, Eli 1843 wb-b-465 (Hd)
Cherry, Isham 1836 wb-b-33 (Hd)
Cherry, Jeremiah 1821 wb-#95 (Mu)
Cherry, Joel 1853 ib-1-281 (Ca)
Cherry, Merina 1854 wb-h-47 (St)
Cherry, Nancy 1807 wb-#5 (Wl)
Cherry, Nancy 1808 wb-1-0 (Sm)
Cherry, Noal 1836 wb-b-33 (Hd)
Cherry, Pierce W. 1852 wb-15-213 (D)
Cherry, S. M. 1855 wb-n-689 (Mt)
Cherry, Soloman 1834 wb-1-556 (Ma)
Cherry, W. N. 1861 wb-13-439 (Wi)
Cherry, Wilee 1800 wb-#12 (Wl)
Cherry, Wiley 1804 wb-#3 (Wl)
Cherry, Wilie 1806 wb-1-0 (Sm)
Cherry, William 1826 wb-b-110 (St)
Cherry, William 1860 wb-13-262 (Wi)
Cherry, William B. 1859 wb-i-44 (St)
Cherry, William W. 1849 wb-g-125 (St)
Cherry, Willie 1819? wb-#32 (Wl)
Cherry, Willis 1835 wb-2-2 (Ma)
Chesher, Jonathan 1847 wb-4-140 (Hr)
Chesher, Thomas 1859 wb-3-563 (Gr)
Cheshier, J. sr. 1849 wb-4-558 (Hr)
Cheshier, Tennison 1848 wb-4-286 (Hr)
Cheshire, Jonathan 1841 wb-2-255 (Hr)
Chesier, William 1856 as-b-254 (Ms)
Chesnutt, Henry 1849 wb-#10 (Mo)
Chesnutt, James 1854 wb-#25 (Mo)
Chessenhall, Meredith 1857 rb-o-514 (Mt)
Chester, Ezra 1831 wb-1-63 (W)
Chester, John 1832 wb-1-106 (Hw)
Chester, John 1842 wb-1-432 (Su)

Chester, Mary 1861 wb-#64 (Wa)
Chester, Minerva 1859 rb-p-54 (Mt)
Chester, William P. 1827 wb-1-121 (Ma)
Cheswell, Samuel 1862 wb-1-139 (Hw)
Chevellette, Louisa 1839 wb-a-41 (F)
Chewning, Nancy 1844 wb-4-250 (Ma)
Cheyne, Abel R. 1854? wb-#26 (Mo)
Chickering, John 1858 wb-17-492 (D)
Chilcutt, B. F. 1860 wb-18-243 (D)
Chilcutt, B. P. 1859 wb-18-53 (D)
Chilcutt, George 1843 wb-f-182* (Hn)
Child, Francis 1823 wb-a-188 (Ro)
Childers, James Zecheriah 1848 mr-2-278 (Be)
Childers, Pleasant 1842 wb-f-75 (Hn)
Childres, Ann Harrison 1861 wb-13-447 (K)
Childres, Ayers 1861 wb-13-447 (K)
Childres, Loden 1861 wb-13-447 (K)
Childress, Benj. 1841 wb-b-401 (G)
Childress, Charles 1846 wb-4-33 (Hr)
Childress, Creed 1849 wb-10-290 (K)
Childress, David 1850 wb-g-377 (Hu)
Childress, David 1850 wb-g-434 (Hu)
Childress, David 1851 wb-h-91 (Hu)
Childress, E. 1859 ib-2-146 (Wy)
Childress, Elizabeth 1823 wb-8-198 (D)
Childress, Elizabeth 1859 ib-2-183 (Wy)
Childress, George 1841 wb-10-577 (Rb)
Childress, George 1845 rb-13-385 (Ru)
Childress, George S. 1861 wb-1-137 (Hw)
Childress, Henry 1814 Wb-2-42 (Wi)
Childress, James 1815 wb-2-159 (K)
Childress, James B. 1843 wb-z-492 (Mu)
Childress, Jesse 1856 wb-c-29 (L)
Childress, Joel 1820 rb-4-192 (Ru)
Childress, John 1811 wb-4-137 (D)
Childress, John 1821 wb-8-54 (D)
Childress, John 1849 wb-10-123 (K)
Childress, Lindsay 1840 wb-7-10 (K)
Childress, Loton 1851 wb-11-52 (K)
Childress, Major 1827 wb-a-81 (G)
Childress, Mary 1855 wb-16-538 (D)
Childress, Mitchell 1844 wb-8-351 (K)
Childress, Nancy 1843 wb-a-169 (L)
Childress, Nancy 1860 wb-f-344 (G)
Childress, Nelson 1846 wb-5-24 (Ma)
Childress, Rebecca 1843 wb-12-44 (Rb)
Childress, Rebecca J. 1842 wb-11-237 (Rb)
Childress, Robert L. 1849 wb-10-211 (K)
Childress, Sarah 1856 wb-2-146 (Li)
Childress, Stephen 1829 wb-a-7 (T)
Childress, Stephen S. 1835 wb-1-162 (Hy)

Childress, Thomas 1841 wb-1-190 (Li)
Childress, Thomas M. 1829 wb-4-432 (Wi)
Childress, Usley 1847 wb-9-310 (K)
Childress, William 1831 wb-5-64 (K)
Childress, William 1840 wb-a-13 (Dk)
Childress, William G. 1846 wb-8-477 (Wi)
Childs, Francis 1813 wb-1-0 (Sm)
Childs, George E. 1852 wb-5-109 (Ma)
Childs, Lois 1848 rb-14-389 (Ru)
Chiles, Hannah 1850 wb-1B-178 (A)
Chiles, Hendy Ann 1855 wb-n-712 (Mt)
Chiles, Henry 1836 rb-g-503 (Mt)
Chiles, Henry 1855 wb-12-143 (K)
Chiles, Henry 1856 wb-12-217 (K)
Chiles, Henry T. 1836 rb-g-476 (Mt)
Chiles, John 1817 wb-7-125 (D)
Chiles, John 1849? wb-1B-100 (A)
Chiles, Joseph 1860 rb-p-311 (Mt)
Chiles, Paul 1861 lr (Gi)
Chiles, Roland 1850? wb-1B-176 (A)
Chiltom, John N. 1844 5-3-9 (Cl)
Chilton, James 1852 wb-a-290 (Ms)
Chilton, John 1840 wb-2-149 (Hy)
Chilton, Mary 1853 wb-a-188 (Cr)
Chilton, Thomas 1807 wb-1-192 (Je)
Chiltum, Jno. N. 1853 ib-2-65 (Cl)
Chinoweth, Richard 1828 wb-4-259 (K)
Chinowth, Nicholas 1850? wb-#50 (Wa)
Chisenall, John 1846 rb-13-542 (Ru)
Chisenhall, John 1825 rb-6-149 (Ru)
Chisenhall, Reuben 1829 rb-e-509 (Mt)
Chisenhall, Virlen 1855 wb-n-599 (Mt)
Chisholm, Jamimah F. 1842 wb-a-121 (L)
Chism, Edmund 1847 rb-14-4 (Ru)
Chism, Elizabeth 1851 wb-5-13 (Hr)
Chism, Gain 1837 wb-2-241 (Ma)
Chism, James (Maj.) 1835 wb-1-389 (Hr)
Chism, Obadiah 1837 wb-9-344 (Rb)
Chism, William H. 1832 wb-1-319 (Ma)
Chisom, John 1854 wb-d-158 (Wh)
Chissom, John 1834 wb-1-526 (Ma)
Chisum, Elijah 1828 wb-b-68 (Wh)
Chisum, Elijah jr. 1811 wb-a-12 (Wh)
Chisum, Elijah sr. 1818 wb-a-116 (Wh)
Chisum, James 1839 wb-2-91 (Hr)
Chisum, James S. 1836 wb-1-482 (Hr)
Chisum, John W. 1842 wb-3-578 (Ma)
Chisum, William 1832 wb-1-227 (Ma)
Choat, Arthur 1855 ib-1-349 (Wy)
Choat, Edward 1831 wb-7-482 (Rb)
Choat, Gabriel 1845 wb-12-437 (Rb)

Choat, James W. 1835 wb-9-112 (Rb)
Choat, James Westly 1840 wb-10-523 (Rb)
Choat, Martin 1859 wb-16-712 (Rb)
Choat, Simpson 1856 ib-1-404 (Wy)
Choat, Steptoe? 1854 wb-15-505 (Rb)
Choat, Thomas 1837 wb-1-187 (La)
Choat, Thomas 1848 wb-2-18 (La)
Choat, Valuntine 1829 wb-1-12 (La)
Choate, Eleanor 1845 as-b-260 (Di)
Choate, John 1835 wb-a-114 (Di)
Choate, Squire 1852 wb-f-3? (Mu)
Choates, Joseph 1850 wb-2-77 (Sh)
Chowning, John 1831 wb-7-386 (Rb)
Chowning, Richard 1846 wb-12-563 (Rb)
Chriesman, Mary 1854 wb-11-182 (Wi)
Chrisman, Abraham 1822 wb-3-593 (Wi)
Chrisman, Aron 1817 wb-2-309 (Wi)
Chrisman, James J. 1860 wb-13-322 (Wi)
Chrisman, Samuel S. 1861 wb-13-453 (Wi)
Christain, Sarah 1857 wb-3-330 (W)
Christenberry, Joshua 1858 wb-f-138 (Ro)
Christian, Christopher 1828 wb-9-196 (D)
Christian, Drury 1842 as-b-79 (Di)
Christian, Elijah jr. 1828 wb-a-338 (Wh)
Christian, Frederick 1845 wb-1-121 (Sh)
Christian, Isaam 1811 wb-#3 (Mu)
Christian, Isham 1831 wb-#225 (Mu)
Christian, Jackson P. 1852 wb-h-84 (Hu)
Christian, John 1845 wb-1-115 (Hw)
Christian, Lewis 1830 wb-1-96 (Hw)
Christian, Lewis 1849 wb-#32 (Mc)
Christian, Margarett 1853 wb-h-101 (Hu)
Christian, Nathaniel 1830 wb-1-17 (La)
Christian, Nathaniel 1845 wb-1-374 (La)
Christian, William 1836 wb-1-217 (Hy)
Christian, William L. 1861 wb-1-138 (Hw)
Christian, Wyatt 1846 wb-1-133 (Sh)
Christianbury, John 1802 wb-a-1 (Ro)
Christie, Hannon 1852 as-c-171 (Di)
Christie, Thornton 1860 wb-b-49 (Dk)
Christie, Thornton 1860 wb-b-58 (Dk)
Christman, David 1841 wb-7-373 (Wi)
Christmas, Abraham 1822 wb-3-586 (Wi)
Christmas, William 1812 wb-1-264 (Wi)
Christmas, William 1822 wb-3-352 (Wi)
Christy, William 1828 wb-b-312 (St)
Chriswell, Abel 1851 wb-9-673 (Wi)
Chriswell, Andrew 1842 wb-7-559 (Wi)
Chriswell, Martha F. 1853 wb-10-597 (Wi)
Chriswelll, Laban 1857 wb-12-384 (Wi)
Chronister, Philip 1852 wb-3-16 (La)

Chumbley, Joseph 1843 wb-f-186* (Hn)
Chumbly, William 1832 wb-#97 (Wl)
Chumley, Ballard 1849 wb-#164 (Wl)
Chumley, Daniel 1846 wb-#150 (Wl)
Chumley, John 1850? ib-1-186 (Cl)
Chumley, Richard 1861 wb-#133 (Wl)
Chun, Bowlin 1840 wb-e-166 (Hn)
Chun, Henry 1835 wb-x-268 (Mu)
Chun, Obediance 1848 as-a-185 (Ms)
Chunn, Silvester 1841 wb-a-99 (Ms)
Church, Henry 1844 wb-1-114 (Hw)
Church, John Christian 1813 wb-1-88 (Hw)
Church, Seth 1852 wb-#32 (Mc)
Church, Thomas 1849 wb-9-288 (Wi)
Church, Thomas 1860 wb-f-203 (Mu)
Churchill, Chas. 1845 wb-a-255 (F)
Churchman, Edith 1852 wb-3-54 (Gr)
Churchman, Edward 1836 wb-1-115 (Gr)
Churchman, Edward 1840 wb-5-61 (Gr)
Churchman, Edward 1854 wb-3-185 (Gr)
Churchman, Elizabeth 1848 33-3-73 (Gr)
Churchman, Mary 1852 wb-3-70 (Gr)
Churchman, Matilda 1841 wb-5-145 (Gr)
Churchwell, Charles 1858 gs-1-199 (F)
Churchwell, Daniel B. 1860 ib-2-219 (Wy)
Churchwell, Ephraim 1811? wb-#37 (Mu)
Churchwell, John 1815 wb-#11 (Mu)
Churchwell, Pleasant 1858 ib-2-102 (Wy)
Churchwell, Richard 1807 wb-#1 (Mu)
City, London 1827 wb-4-253 (K)
Clabough, John 1860 wb-1-11 (Br)
Clack, James 1832 wb-10-40 (D)
Clack, Missourie 1856 wb-1-100 (R)
Clack, Spencer 1854 lr (Gi)
Clack, William 1801 wb-1-79 (K)
Claiborne, Alegernon 1850 wb-d-222 (G)
Claiborne, Alexander 1857 wb-e-81 (Hy)
Claiborne, Augustine 1856 wb-b-24 (Ms)
Claiborne, George R. 1834 wb-b-44 (G)
Claiborne, Myra 1859 wb-18-59 (D)
Claiborne, Phil 1829 wb-9-356 (D)
Claiborne, Sarah 1827 wb-9-137 (D)
Claiborne, Thomas A. 1835 wb-10-524 (D)
Claiborne, William F. L. 1832 wb-9-566 (D)
Claibourn, C. M. 1851 wb-e-263 (Ro)
Clampitt, Ezekiel 1832 lr (Sn)
Clampitt, William 1848 lr (Sn)
Clandennon, James A. 1853 148-1-425 (Ge)
Clanton, Josiah F. 1857 wb-6-489 (Ma)
Clapier, Lewis 1844 wb-8-291 (K)
Clapp, Adam 1843 wb-8-105 (K)

Clapp, Lewis 1848 wb-10-51 (K)
Clardy, Benjamin 1842 wb-3-0 (Sm)
Clardy, James 1841 rb-k-300 (Mt)
Clardy, Lucinda B. 1852 wb-7-0 (Sm)
Clardy, Micheal 1847? wb-1B-46 (A)
Clardy, P. J. 1858 wb-17-495 (D)
Clardy, Thomas 1830 rb-8-148 (Ru)
Clark, Abagail 1818 wb-1-301 (Sn)
Clark, Abigail 1854 rb-16-688 (Ru)
Clark, Abigail H. 1851 rb-16-120 (Ru)
Clark, Absolum 1849 wb-2-322 (W)
Clark, Absolum sr. 1849 wb-2-334 (W)
Clark, Allison 1846 wb-d-22 (G)
Clark, Amy (Mrs.) 1849 wb-4-399 (Hr)
Clark, Amy W. 1848 wb-4-367 (Hr)
Clark, Anthony 1827 rb-7-333 (Ru)
Clark, Arch 1842 wb-2-534 (Hy)
Clark, Archibald 1819 wb-3-53 (Rb)
Clark, Archibald 1837 wb-b-146 (G)
Clark, Avoma 1859 wb-f-164 (Mu)
Clark, B. G. 1841 wb-f-160 (Hn)
Clark, Benjamin 1850 wb-e-248 (Ro)
Clark, Benjamin 1852 as-c-169 (Di)
Clark, Christiana 1841 wb-c-13 (G)
Clark, Christopher 1854 wb-g-560 (Hn)
Clark, Daniel 1821 wb-8-46 (D)
Clark, Daniel B. 1831 wb-a-176 (G)
Clark, Darias sr. 1859 wb-e-269 (Wh)
Clark, David 1824 wb-a-2 (Cr)
Clark, E. T. 1858 rb-19-150 (Ru)
Clark, E. Y. 1855 rb-17-526 (Ru)
Clark, Edward W. 1860 wb-#63 (Wa)
Clark, Elenor 1843 rb-12-416 (Ru)
Clark, Elisha 1846 wb-1-129 (Sh)
Clark, Elizabeth 1850 33-3-268 (Gr)
Clark, Erastus Y. 1858 rb-19-203 (Ru)
Clark, Frederick 1860 wb-i-223 (St)
Clark, Fredrick H. 1860 wb-i-246 (St)
Clark, G. F. 1839 wb-e-80 (Hn)
Clark, George 1791 wb-1-238 (D)
Clark, George 1837 wb-#130 (Wl)
Clark, George 1839 wb-10-263 (Rb)
Clark, George 1843 as-b-146 (Di)
Clark, George 1849 rb-l-450 (Mt)
Clark, George C. 1859 wb-f-313 (G)
Clark, George H. 1851 wb-15-61 (D)
Clark, George S. 1833 wb-8-265 (Rb)
Clark, Green W. 1854 lr (Gi)
Clark, Hampton 1847 wb-2-22 (Sh)
Clark, Hu M. 1837 wb-6-141 (K)
Clark, Isaac 1838 wb-b-301 (Wh)

Clark, Isaac 1854 wb-a-324 (Ms)
Clark, Isaac 1859 rb-p-57 (Mt)
Clark, Isaac E. 1855 wb-e-559 (Ro)
Clark, J. B. 1823 wb-A-351 (Li)
Clark, James 1809 lr (Sn)
Clark, James 1831 wb-b-47 (Wh)
Clark, James 1833 wb-10-264 (D)
Clark, James 1842 rb-12-82 (Ru)
Clark, James 1850 wb-1-18 (Bo)
Clark, James 1855 39-2-86 (Dk)
Clark, James 1856 wb-f-9 (Ro)
Clark, James R. 1843 wb-3-18 (Hr)
Clark, Jane 1844 wb-#144 (Wl)
Clark, Jesse 1801 wb-#9 (Wa)
Clark, Jesse 1817 wb-A-195 (Li)
Clark, Jesse 1818 wb-3-14 (Rb)
Clark, Jesse 1819 wb-#35 (Wl)
Clark, John 1823 wb-3-432 (K)
Clark, John 1829 rb-7-167 (Ru)
Clark, John 1838 wb-2-312 (Ma)
Clark, John 1842 rb-12-238 (Ru)
Clark, John 1849 wb-e-139 (Ro)
Clark, John 1851 wb-a-165 (Cr)
Clark, John 1857 rb-19-13 (Ru)
Clark, John 1858 wb-2-257 (Li)
Clark, John A. 1848 wb-e-113 (Ro)
Clark, John C. 1851 wb-2-104 (Sh)
Clark, John C. 1855 wb-e-38 (Hy)
Clark, John E. 1854 wb-h-299 (Hu)
Clark, John James 1811 wb-#33 (Wl)
Clark, John M. 1844 wb-f-263 (Hn)
Clark, Joseph 1834 wb-1-83 (W)
Clark, Joseph 1845 A-468-15 (Le)
Clark, Joseph 1856 wb-2-152 (Li)
Clark, Joseph 1857 wb-b-44 (F)
Clark, Kelso 1847 wb-d-342 (Hd)
Clark, L. F. (Rev.) 1840 wb-7-112 (K)
Clark, L. F. 1840 wb-7-100 (K)
Clark, Lardner 1802 wb-2-252 (D)
Clark, Lemuel 1848 wb-4-264 (Hr)
Clark, Littleberry 1835 wb-c-395 (St)
Clark, Littleberry 1856 wb-h-285 (St)
Clark, Louisa L. 1847 wb-9-313 (K)
Clark, Lucinda P. 1833 wb-8-270 (Rb)
Clark, Lydia 1850 wb-14-390 (Rb)
Clark, Martha 1855 wb-a-191 (V)
Clark, Martin 1859 wb-18-103 (D)
Clark, Mary 1819 wb-#97 (Mu)
Clark, Mary 1824 wb-#78 (Mu)
Clark, Mary 1838 rb-10-124 (Ru)
Clark, Mary 1850 wb-#165 (Wl)

Clark, Mary 1857 rb-o-289 (Mt)
Clark, Mary Ann 1851 wb-11-114 (K)
Clark, Moses 1853 wb-2-153 (Sh)
Clark, Nancy 1858 wb-16-561 (Rb)
Clark, Nancy 1858 wb-16-634 (Rb)
Clark, Nathan 1811 wb-1-402 (Rb)
Clark, Nathan 1840 wb-10-502 (Rb)
Clark, Nathaniel 1838 wb-10-145 (Rb)
Clark, Patrick 1855 wb-h-164 (St)
Clark, Polly 1854 wb-15-580 (Rb)
Clark, R. 1861 wb-k-391 (O)
Clark, Richard 1815 wb-2-190 (Rb)
Clark, Richard 1831 wb-7-461 (Rb)
Clark, Robert 1837 wb-a-57 (T)
Clark, Robert 1848 wb-a-135 (T)
Clark, Sabrina 1855 wb-15-750 (Rb)
Clark, Samuel 1807 wb-1-166 (Wi)
Clark, Samuel 1818 wb-2-377 (Wi)
Clark, Samuel 1827 wb-3-0 (Sm)
Clark, Sarah 1851 wb-g-465 (St)
Clark, Sarah 1855 as-c-403 (Di)
Clark, Sarah Catharine 1843 wb-3-255 (Hy)
Clark, Silas 1836 wb-3-0 (Sm)
Clark, Thomas 1806 wb-3-49 (D)
Clark, Thomas 1812 wb-1-27 (Bo)
Clark, Thomas 1833 wb-5-228 (K)
Clark, Thomas 1843 lr (Gi)
Clark, Thomas D. 1843 as-a-80 (Ms)
Clark, Thomas H. 1853 wb-15-559 (D)
Clark, William 1793 wb-1-261 (D)
Clark, William 1837 wb-1-229 (Gr)
Clark, William 1841 wb-7-477 (Wi)
Clark, William 1845 wb-b-127 (We)
Clark, William A. 1839 wb-d-400 (St)
Clark, William H. 1851 wb-g-401 (Hn)
Clark, William J. 1842 wb-7-311 (K)
Clark, William J. 1861 wb-13-450 (K)
Clark, William S. 1833 wb-10-162 (D)
Clark, Wm. 1857 wb-h-706 (Hu)
Clark, Wm. M. 1857 wb-h-678 (Hu)
Clarke, Elizabeth 1837 wb-1-202 (W)
Clarke, Henry 1856 rb-o-210 (Mt)
Clarke, Henry C. 1860 wb-3e-134 (Sh)
Clarke, Jesse 1824 wb-#78 (Mu)
Clarkson, David 1836 wb-1A-160 (A)
Claton, John 1844 wb-b-55 (We)
Claud, Eldridge 1848 wb-9-118 (Wi)
Claud, Francis 1851 rb-16-141 (Ru)
Claud, Francis M. 1849 rb-15-185 (Ru)
Claud, Joshua D. 1836 wb-6-276 (Wi)
Claud, Philip 1848 wb-9-32 (Wi)

Claud, Susan 1854 wb-11-257 (Wi)
Clausell?, William W. B. 1835 wb-d-78 (Hn)
Clay, Armstead 1841 rb-11-241 (Ru)
Clay, Dennis 1818 rb-4-174 (Ru)
Clay, Green 1851 wb-10-36 (Wi)
Clay, John 1837 rb-10-36 (Ru)
Clay, John M. 1838 wb-11-213 (D)
Clay, John M. 1838 wb-11-262 (D)
Clay, John W. 1859 gs-1-523 (F)
Clay, Joshua 1859 gs-1-362 (F)
Clay, Larkin 1817 wb-7-166 (D)
Clay, Matthew 1815 wb-a-40 (Wh)
Clay, Rebecca 1850 33-3-303 (Gr)
Clay, William 1842 wb-5-187 (Gr)
Clay, William 1851 33-3-339 (Gr)
Clay, Woodson 1824 wb-8-373 (D)
Claybrook, Lucia 1850 wb-c-378 (Wh)
Claybrooks, Charles 1812 wb-#11 (Wl)
Claybrooks, George 1841 wb-1-359 (W)
Clayton, Hannah 1845 wb-#5 (Mo)
Clayton, John 1843 wb-12-86 (Rb)
Clayton, John 1859 6-1-9 (Le)
Clayton, Phebe 1848 wb-#166 (Wl)
Clayton, Stephen 1839 as-a-18 (Ms)
Clayton, Thomas 1834 wb-1-329 (Hr)
Clayton, William 1855 wb-12-94 (K)
Clayton, William 1861 wb-e-437 (Wh)
Clayton, William F. 1854 wb-12-55 (K)
Cleamons?, John 1856 ib-1-465 (Wy)
Clear, Peter 1855 wb-1C-204 (A)
Cleary, John R. 1855 wb-3e-12 (Sh)
Cleaveland, Mary 1843 wb-12-472* (D)
Cleaves, Ann 1856 wb-b-21 (F)
Cleaves, Michael 1840 wb-a-124 (L)
Cleaves, William 1853 wb-a-433 (F)
Cleek, Ezekel 1850 as-b-4 (Ms)
Cleek, William J. 1860 wb-b-97 (Ms)
Cleghorn, John H. 1856 wb-h-602 (Hu)
Clemans, William 1811 wb-4-129 (D)
Clement, Mary P. 1848 wb-b-264 (We)
Clement, Sophia 1856 wb-3e-25 (Sh)
Clements, Agnes 1820 rb-c-361 (Mt)
Clements, Charles A. 1853 wb-a-198 (T)
Clements, Christopher C. 1845 wb-f-275 (St)
Clements, James Madison 1841 wb-a-88 (T)
Clements, Sally 1835 wb-c-443 (St)
Clements, William 1822 rb-d-33 (Mt)
Clements, William 1838 wb-d-282 (St)
Clemm, James S. 1826 wb-4-143 (Wi)
Clemments, Benjamin 1837 wb-9-389 (Rb)
Clemmons, Abgail 1824 wb-8-374 (D)

Clemmons, Allen 1840 wb-#130 (Wl)
Clemmons, Edwin 1858 wb-#126 (Wl)
Clemmons, Isom 1854 wb-3-234 (La)
Clemmons, James (Jr.) 1860 wb-#131 (Wl)
Clemmons, Jeptha 1829 wb-#80 (Wl)
Clemmons, John 1859 wb-#127 (Wl)
Clemmons, John B. 1843 wb-#140 (Wl)
Clemmons, Samuel 1829 wb-#81 (Wl)
Clemmons, Samuel T. 1824 wb-#52 (Wl)
Clemmons, Samuel T. 1842 wb-#139 (Wl)
Clemmons, Thompson 1837 wb-#119 (Wl)
Clemmons, William 1826 wb-#69 (Wl)
Clemmons, William 1827 wb-#67 (Wl)
Clemons, Isaac 1853 wb-15-483 (D)
Clemons, James 1857 wb-17-232 (D)
Clemons, John 1856 ib-2-4 (Wy)
Clemons, William 1785 wb-1-6# (Ge)
Clendenen, James 1841 wb-1-365 (W)
Clendenen, John 1834 wb-3-248 (Je)
Clendenen, John 1841 wb-e-278 (Hn)
Clendenin, Griffin 1842 wb-1-510 (W)
Clendenin, James 1857 wb-3-366 (W)
Clendenin, James sr. 1843 wb-1-535 (W)
Clendening, James 1811 wb-1-312 (Sn)
Clendening, John 1786 wb-1-43 (D)
Clendennen, William 1835 wb-d-58 (Hn)
Clendenon, Charles 1848 A-468-98 (Le)
Clenny, Henry 1836 wb-2-202 (Sn)
Clenny, Jonathan 1853 wb-d-154 (Wh)
Cleveland, Albert M. 1858 wb-3-470 (Gr)
Cleveland, Eli 1856 wb-#17 (Mo)
Cleveland, Green F. 1858 wb-3-418 (Gr)
Cleveland, H. H. 1854 wb-#26 (Mo)
Cleveland, Joseph A. 1840 wb-3-0 (Sm)
Cleveland, Martin 1848 wb-2-336 (Gr)
Cleveland, Presley 1856 wb-#17 (Mo)
Clevenger, George 1837 wb-3-455 (Je)
Clevinger, Isaac 1840 wb-3-550 (Je)
Cliborne, Skelton 1832 wb-5-142 (K)
Clibourn, John 1836 wb-6-19 (K)
Clibourn, Jubal 1838 wb-6-320 (K)
Clibourne, Madison 1854 wb-#25 (Mo)
Click, Henry 1849 wb-#12 (Mo)
Click, Lewis 1853 wb-1-127 (Hw)
Click, Malachi 1840 wb-2-54# (Ge)
Click, Maleki 1858 149-1-124 (Ge)
Click, Martin sr. 1853 148-1-423 (Ge)
Click, Michael 1814 wb-1-90 (Hw)
Clifford, Patrick 1829 wb-9-354 (D)
Clifft, Thomas 1833 wb-1-280 (Hr)
Clift, Alfred B. 1862 wb-#19 (Mo)

Clift, David 1854 ib-H-194 (F)
Clift, Henry 1854 wb-2-84 (Li)
Clift, James 1855 wb-12-150 (K)
Clifton, Benjamin 1830 wb-#85 (Wl)
Clifton, Edwin 1826 rb-e-2 (Mt)
Clifton, Henry E. 1846 rb-k-253 (Mt)
Clifton, Jesse 1823 wb-#44 (Wl)
Clifton, Joshua H. 1820 wb-#40 (Wl)
Climer, Christina 1833 wb-#103 (Wl)
Climer, John 1833 wb-#99 (Wl)
Clinard, John 1853 wb-15-540 (D)
Clinard, Philip 1829 wb-6-494 (Rb)
Cline, Emery Dent 1854 wb-g-703 (Hn)
Cline, Michael 1859 wb-#61 (Wa)
Cline, P. A. 1855? wb-g-702 (Hn)
Clingan, David 1831 wb-a-91 (R)
Clinghan, George W. 1830 wb-a-76 (R)
Clingon, George W. 1853 wb-1-25 (R)
Clinton, Elizabeth 1860 rb-p-471 (Mt)
Clinton, Isaac 1851 wb-14-597 (D)
Clinton, Thomas 1812 wb-a-200 (St)
Cloar, Absalom 1813 wb-1-162 (Sn)
Cloar, J. C. 1852 wb-h-May (O)
Clopton, Eleanor 1835 wb-#108 (Wl)
Clopton, Jesse B. 1837 wb-#122 (Wl)
Clopton, Martha H. 1846 wb-12-584 (Rb)
Clopton, W. A. 1840 wb-#132 (Wl)
Clopton, Walter (Jr.) 1835 wb-#112 (Wl)
Clopton, Walter (Sr.) 1835 wb-#106 (Wl)
Clopton, William E. 1848 wb-g-29 (St)
Cloud, A. M. 1842 5-2-252 (Cl)
Cloud, Benjamin 1842 5-2-276 (Cl)
Cloud, Daniel 1846 5-3-105 (Cl)
Cloud, G. B. 1852 ib-2-63 (Cl)
Cloud, Jason 1827 eb-1-224 (C)
Cloud, Jeremiah 1849 wb-14-415 (D)
Cloud, Joseph 1850 ib-1-188 (Cl)
Cloud, Standwix 1842 5-2-282 (Cl)
Cloud, William 1847 wb-14-7 (D)
Clough, Robert 1853 wb-e-409 (Ro)
Clouse, Adam 1838 wb-b-317 (Wh)
Clow, Mary 1821 wb-7-507 (D)
Clowney, James L. 1826 wb-b-8 (Ro)
Cloyd, Ezekiel 1847 wb-#176 (Wl)
Cloyd, James M. 1839 wb-2-110 (Hr)
Cloyd, James W. 1861 wb-#60 (Wa)
Cloyd, John 1824 wb-#54 (Wl)
Cloyd, Samuel G. 1848 wb-c-300 (Wh)
Cloyd, Stephen 1819 wb-#31 (Wl)
Cloyd, William P. 1858 lr (Sn)
Cloyde, James B. 1861 wb-#64 (Wa)

Cloyed, Ezekiel 1847 wb-14-108 (D)
Cluck, Henry 1802 wb-1-88 (Je)
Cluck, Henry 1832 wb-3-336 (Je)
Cluck, Henry 1841 wb-#136 (Wl)
Cluck, Henry H. 1861 wb-#134 (Wl)
Cluck, Peter 1844 wb-4-13 (Je)
Cluck, William 1835 wb-#112 (Wl)
Cluff, Robert 1856 wb-f-76 (Ro)
Cluts, John 1804 as-1-55 (Ge)
Cluts?, John 1804 wb-1-5# (Ge)
Clyne, Mathew 1851 wb-15-207 (D)
Coachman, J.? D. 1840 wb-a-78 (L)
Coale, Thomas 1814 wb-4-311 (D)
Coates, Thompson C. 1855 wb-5-59 (Hr)
Coates, Will. 1849 wb-4-524 (Hr)
Coates, William sr. 1846 wb-4-103 (Hr)
Coats, A. M. 1833 wb-c-212 (Hn)
Coats, Barton 1838 mr-1-43 (Be)
Coats, Benjamin 1850 wb-7-0 (Sm)
Coats, Charles 1814 wb-#30 (Mu)
Coats, James T. 1827 wb-#32 (Mc)
Coats, John 1837 abl-1-43 (T)
Coats, John 1839 wb-11-540 (D)
Coats, William 1859 wb-#33 (Mc)
Cobb, D. J. 1857 wb-#33 (Mc)
Cobb, Diana H. 1854 wb-12-60 (K)
Cobb, Diana T. 1851 wb-11-115 (K)
Cobb, Elizabeth 1854 wb-b-340 (We)
Cobb, Frederick 1838 wb-10-4 (Rb)
Cobb, Frederick 1839 wb-10-258 (Rb)
Cobb, Hannah 1828 rb-e-259 (Mt)
Cobb, James H. 1860 wb-2-305 (Li)
Cobb, Jesse B. 1855 ib-h-264 (F)
Cobb, Jesse H. 1855 ib-h-337 (F)
Cobb, Joel 1861 wb-1-135 (Hw)
Cobb, John 1814 wb-A-60 (Li)
Cobb, John 1837 wb-#33 (Mc)
Cobb, John 1854 ib-h-229 (F)
Cobb, Joseph Sr. 1840 wb-#34 (Mc)
Cobb, Lewis 1807 wb-1-0 (Sm)
Cobb, Lewis 1832 wb-8-22 (Rb)
Cobb, Milton 1850 wb-10-479 (K)
Cobb, Pharoah 1841 wb-1-142 (Hw)
Cobb, Robert W. 1856 wb-e-45 (Hy)
Cobb, Samuel T. 1849 wb-10-153 (K)
Cobb, Thomas M. 1852 wb-5-114 (Ma)
Cobb, Wiley 1857 wb-1-131 (Hw)
Cobb, William 1803 rb-a-168 (Mt)
Cobb, William 1803 wb-0-43 (K)
Cobb, William 1836 wb-1-28 (Sh)
Cobb, William H. 1850 wb-14-293 (Rb)

Cobb, William P. 1828 wb-4-263 (K)
Cobble, Phillip 1861 wb-2-93# (Ge)
Cobbs, John H. 1834 rb-g-65 (Mt)
Cobbs, William A. 1851 wb-14-609 (D)
Cobler, Davis 1838 wb-11-407 (D)
Cochran, Alpha T. 1846 wb-b-171 (We)
Cochran, Ammon 1844 wd-13-31 (D)
Cochran, Benjamin 1825 wb-1-0 (Sm)
Cochran, David 1831 wb-3-0 (Sm)
Cochran, David 1842 wb-3-0 (Sm)
Cochran, Eli 1861 wb-b-155 (Ms)
Cochran, Ezekiel 1853 wb-3-160 (La)
Cochran, George 1829 wb-2-30# (Ge)
Cochran, George 1844 wb-#42 (Wa)
Cochran, James 1812 wb-1-0 (Sm)
Cochran, James 1851 wb-1-21 (Bo)
Cochran, James 1859 as-c-157 (Ms)
Cochran, Jesse 1835 wb-1-392 (Hr)
Cochran, Jno. 1861 wb-a-220 (Ce)
Cochran, John 1825 wb-4-1 (Wi)
Cochran, John 1833 wb-8-238 (Rb)
Cochran, John 1841 wb-a-68 (L)
Cochran, John 1843 wb-3-0 (Sm)
Cochran, John 1844 wb-7-0 (Sm)
Cochran, John 1856 wb-12-219 (Wi)
Cochran, Lewis 1851 wb-15-5 (D)
Cochran, Luther B. 1848 wb-b-287 (We)
Cochran, Margaret 1853 wb-f-19 (Mu)
Cochran, Marshall 1845 ib-2-98 (Ge)
Cochran, Martha 1860 wb-4-374 (La)
Cochran, Mary 1845 wb-a2-251 (Mu)
Cochran, Paul 1822 wb-1-192 (Bo)
Cochran, Reuben 1855 wb-f-56 (Mu)
Cochran, Samuel 1842 lr (Sn)
Cochran, Silas 1839 wb-1-22 (Bo)
Cochran, Simeon 1851 wb-m-193 (Mt)
Cochran, Susan 1856 wb-12-189 (Wi)
Cochran, William 1801 wb-1-64 (Sn)
Cochran, William 1819 wb-2-278 (Je)
Cochran, William 1842 wb-11-265 (Rb)
Cock, Hartwell B. 1836 rb-g-444 (Mt)
Cock, Henry 1847 rb-k-370 (Mt)
Cock, John 1823 wb-#45 (Wl)
Cock, John Sr. 1822 wb-#44 (Wl)
Cock, Mary 1845 rb-j-300 (Mt)
Cock, Nancy 1836 rb-g-344 (Mt)
Cock, Nancy 1842 rb-12-227 (Ru)
Cock, Sarah G. 1837 rb-g-619 (Mt)
Cock, Wm. 1835 rb-9-230 (Ru)
Cockburn, A. (Mrs.) 1840 wb-2-182 (Hr)
Cockburn, Averilla 1842 wb-2-328 (Hr)

Cockburn, Hamilton 1828 wb-1-66 (Hr)
Cocke, Abraham 1815 rb-b-75 (Mt)
Cocke, Abraham 1817 rb-b-456 (Mt)
Cocke, Abraham 1830 rb-f-18 (Mt)
Cocke, Benjamin 1858 wb-b-67 (F)
Cocke, Elizabeth 1817 rb-b-454 (Mt)
Cocke, Elizabeth B. 1819 rb-c-264 (Mt)
Cocke, James R. 1840 wb-7-85* (K)
Cocke, James R. 1853 wb-11-420 (K)
Cocke, John 1857 wb-12-391 (K)
Cocke, L. Laurie 1861 wb-13-518 (K)
Cocke, Nancy 1837 rb-g-512 (Mt)
Cocke, Peter 1803 rb-a-198 (Mt)
Cocke, Richard 1823 rb-d-155 (Mt)
Cocke, Singleton 1845 wb-e-53 (O)
Cocke, Solomon D. 1856 wb-b-26 (F)
Cocke, Stephen 1829 rb-f-4 (Mt)
Cocke, Susan 1836 rb-g-443 (Mt)
Cocke, Thomas 1849 wb-1-121 (Hw)
Cocke, Thomas Jones 1845 wb-a-261 (F)
Cocke, William Batt 1814 rb-b-175 (Mt)
Cockerell, James 1854 wb-16-221 (D)
Cockerham, Henry 1834 wb-3-0 (Sm)
Cockram, John Y. 1841 wb-2-246 (Hr)
Cockran, John J. 1832 wb-1-227 (Hr)
Cockrans, Lynch 1836 wb-1-30 (Sh)
Cockreham, John 1845 wb-1-111 (Hw)
Cockrell, James 1833 wb-1-135* (Hy)
Cockrell, John 1838 wb-11-200 (D)
Cockrell, Richard H. 1838 wb-11-366 (D)
Cockrell, William N. 1838 wb-11-363 (D)
Cockrill, James 1826 wb-1-73 (Ma)
Cockrill, John 1840 lr (Gi)
Cockrill, John jr. 1841 wb-12-189* (D)
Cockrill, Nathaniel 1861 wb-18-420 (D)
Cockrum, Sarah 1855 wb-3-296 (Gr)
Cocks, William 1814 wb-a-28 (Wh)
Coddington, Benjamin 1803 Wb-1-91 (Wi)
Codey, William 1857 wb-12-298 (Wi)
Cody, Pierce 1850 33-3-192 (Gr)
Coe, Elizabeth 1834 wb-#105 (Wl)
Coe, Joseph 1857 wb-b-37 (F)
Coe, Margaret 1858 wb-b-60 (F)
Coes, Levin H. 1850 wb-2-78 (Sh)
Coffee, A. J. 1856 wb-3-280 (W)
Coffee, Ananias 1861 wb-e-416 (Wh)
Coffee, Ann 1839 wb-1-273 (W)
Coffee, David 1822 wb-1-0 (Sm)
Coffee, James 1807 wb-2-11 (Je)
Coffee, James 1844 wb-3-202 (Hr)
Coffee, James 1851 33-3-399 (Gr)

Coffee, James L. 1837 wb-a-13 (Ms)
Coffee, Jessee 1838 wb-1-288 (W)
Coffee, Jessee T. 1848 33-3-38 (Gr)
Coffee, Joel 1848 wb-3-0 (Sm)
Coffee, Joel 1851 33-3-399 (Gr)
Coffee, John 1846 wb-5-429 (Gr)
Coffee, Joshua M. 1842 wb-1-509 (W)
Coffee, Margarett 1818 wb-#98 (Mu)
Coffee, Mary 1850 r39-1-156 (Dk)
Coffee, Meredith 1838 wb-1-324 (Gr)
Coffee, Polly 1842 wb-#34 (Mc)
Coffer, Jonathan 1859 wb-f-274 (Ro)
Coffey, Chesley 1818 wb-#95 (Mu)
Coffey, Elijah 1860 wb-3e-152 (Sh)
Coffey, Hugh 1845 wb-a2-248 (Mu)
Coffey, James 1839 as-a-12 (Ms)
Coffey, John 1843 wb-a-107 (F)
Coffin, Charles H. 1855 wb-12-156 (K)
Coffin, Daniel L. 1854 wb-12-53 (K)
Coffman, Andrew 1845 wb-5-397 (Gr)
Coffman, Andrew 1846 wb-5-448 (Gr)
Coffman, G. P. F. 1855 wb-#35 (Mc)
Coffman, Nicholas 1845 148-1-96 (Ge)
Coffy, Nathan 1858 wb-f-146 (Mu)
Coffy, Oliver H. 1847 wb-b-150 (Mu)
Cofy, Solomon 1847 wb-1-38 (Jo)
Coggburn, John 1851 wb-2-74# (Ge)
Coggin, Willis 1860 39-2-378 (Dk)
Coglin, Edward 1821 wb-8-24 (D)
Cohea, Amos 1828 wb-6-350 (Rb)
Cohea, George 1859 wb-16-769 (Rb)
Cohea, Peter 1856 wb-16-226 (Rb)
Cohoon, George 1820 wb-3-177 (Wi)
Cohoon, William 1832 rb-f-307 (Mt)
Cohorn, Patsy 1824 wb-2-439 (Je)
Coke, James 1855 wb-h-115 (St)
Coke, Mary A. 1861 wb-17-255 (Rb)
Coker, Charles 1851 wb-11-132 (K)
Coker, William 1817 wb-2-292 (K)
Colbert, Stephen 1856 wb-2-159 (Li)
Colburn, Maria 1856 wb-12-228 (K)
Colby, Cyrus 1851 wb-14-606 (D)
Coldwell, Abram 1858 as-c-504 (Di)
Coldwell, Greenberry 1855 wb#23 (Gu)
Coldwell, John 1823 rb-d-254 (Mt)
Coldwell, Joseph 1823 wb-8-253 (D)
Coldwell, Martha 1858 wb-h-216 (Hn)
Cole, A. S. 1853 mr-2-525 (Be)
Cole, Ann 1827 wb-1A-6 (A)
Cole, Bennet 1859 ib-2-151 (Wy)
Cole, Caswell 1860 wb-1-324 (Be)

Cole, Charlotte 1823 lr (Sn)
Cole, Chesla O. 1826 as-A-124 (Di)
Cole, David L. 1850 mr-2-380 (Be)
Cole, Elbert C. 1836 wb-a-15 (F)
Cole, Hartwell 1857 ib-1-454 (Wy)
Cole, Henry A. 1851 wb-m-275 (Mt)
Cole, James 1837 wb-a-62 (Cr)
Cole, James M. 1857 wb-j-215 (O)
Cole, John 1826 wb-1-100 (Hw)
Cole, John 1844 wb-1-235 (Li)
Cole, John 1847 wb-d-347 (Hd)
Cole, John 1857 wb-2-211 (Li)
Cole, John 1857 wb-h-95 (Hn)
Cole, John 1860 wb-7-66 (Ma)
Cole, John 1861 as-c-246 (Ms)
Cole, Joseph 1810 wb-1-214 (Wi)
Cole, Joseph 1824 wb-#50 (Wl)
Cole, Joseph 1857 wb-h-99 (Hn)
Cole, Louisa T. 1855 wb-16-92 (Rb)
Cole, Martha 1844 wb-12-293 (Rb)
Cole, Moses E. 1849 wb-d-170 (G)
Cole, Moses H. 1844 wb-b-53 (We)
Cole, Mumford H. 1841 wb-a-80 (F)
Cole, Peter 1823 rb-d-253 (Mt)
Cole, Peter H. 1824 rb-d-300 (Mt)
Cole, Peter H. 1836 rb-g-409 (Mt)
Cole, Pilmore 1829 wb-9-275 (D)
Cole, Pilmore 1844 wb-13-67 (D)
Cole, R. G. 1852 wb-15-62 (Rb)
Cole, Reuben G. 1854 wb-15-617 (Rb)
Cole, Richard G. 1852 wb-15-138 (Rb)
Cole, Samuel F. 1861 wb-f-421 (G)
Cole, Sarah 1854 wb-#113 (Wl)
Cole, Stephen 1839 wb-10-484 (Rb)
Cole, Stephen 1841 wb-1-184 (Li)
Cole, Thomas 1815 Wb-2-164 (Wi)
Cole, Thomas 1827 wb-4-278 (Wi)
Cole, Thomas 1847 rb-14-172 (Ru)
Cole, Thomas H. 1855 rb-17-582 (Ru)
Cole, Wile 1829 wb-a-123 (G)
Cole, William 1822 wb-3-341 (Wi)
Cole, William 1827 wb-5-445 (Rb)
Cole, Wingfield 1858 wb-3e-76 (Sh)
Cole, Wm. Alex 1844 wb-12-121 (Rb)
Coleburn, Thomas F. 1833 wb-x-105 (Mu)
Coleburn, William F. 1842 wb-z-415 (Mu)
Coleburne, Isabella 1854 wb-f-41 (Mu)
Colelough, Grisby 1843 rb-i-451 (Mt)
Coleman, A. 1854 ib-h-40 (F)
Coleman, Alex 1855 ib-h-384 (F)
Coleman, Andrew J. 1843 wb-f-133 (Hn)

Coleman, Benjamin 1838 wb-3-485 (Je)
Coleman, Benjamin B. 1837 wb-3-453 (Je)
Coleman, Bolin 1845 wb-#148 (Wl)
Coleman, Braxton 1832 rb-f-447 (Mt)
Coleman, Clarissa 1860 wb-f-199 (Mu)
Coleman, Clarrissa 1852 wb-f-7 (Mu)
Coleman, David 1857 wb-j-269 (O)
Coleman, Elizabeth 1832 wb-5-133 (Wi)
Coleman, Elizabeth 1853 wb-#111 (Wl)
Coleman, James 1859 rb-p-245 (Mt)
Coleman, James C. 1835 wb-3-0 (Sm)
Coleman, James C. 1859 wb-f-247 (G)
Coleman, James J. 1855 wb-16-93 (Rb)
Coleman, Jas. J. 1855 wb-16-96 (Rb)
Coleman, Jesse 1835 wb-3-0 (Sm)
Coleman, Joel P. 1855 wb-16-95 (Rb)
Coleman, John 1838 rb-10-169 (Ru)
Coleman, John S. 1839 wb-#125 (Wl)
Coleman, Jones R. 1844 wb-8-187 (Wi)
Coleman, Joseph 1819 wb-7-312 (D)
Coleman, Joseph 1857 wb-12-386 (Wi)
Coleman, Joshua 1821 Wb-3-271 (Wi)
Coleman, Leathy 1852 wb-3-167 (Sn)
Coleman, Mary E. 1860 wb-3e-136 (Sh)
Coleman, Moses 1830 as-a-202 (Di)
Coleman, Moses 1842 as-b-88 (Di)
Coleman, Nancy 1860 wb-h-441 (Hn)
Coleman, Peggy 1846 wb-7-0 (Sm)
Coleman, Polly 1835 wb-c-436 (St)
Coleman, Rice 1853 wb-n-140* (Mt)
Coleman, Richard 1841 rb-11-286 (Ru)
Coleman, Robert S. 1859 wb-f-237 (G)
Coleman, S. K. 1860 wb-18-317 (D)
Coleman, Samuel 1847 wb-1-309 (Li)
Coleman, Sarah 1845 rb-13-170 (Ru)
Coleman, Sarah G. 1845 rb-13-115 (Ru)
Coleman, Spencer 1834 wb-#1 (Mo)
Coleman, Sutton 1858 wb-12-492 (Wi)
Coleman, Thomas 1826 wb-#166 (Mu)
Coleman, Turner 1836 rb-g-390 (Mt)
Coleman, William 1846 rb-13-690 (Ru)
Coleman, William A. 1849 rb-15-144 (Ru)
Coleman, William H. 1842 wb-3-29 (Hr)
Coleman, William sr. 1842 rb-13-117 (Ru)
Coleman, Wyott 1839 rb-10-402 (Ru)
Coles, R. N. 1848 wb-#163 (Wl)
Coles, Robert 1836 wb-#115 (Wl)
Coles, Robert N. 1836 wb-#121 (Wl)
Coley, Isham 1831 wb-b-130 (Hn)
Coley, James A. 1860 wb-h-402 (Hn)
Coley, M. W. 1857 wb-h-130 (Hn)

Coley, Sally 1807 wb-#35 (Mc)
Coley, Sally 1807 wb-1-83 (Hw)
Colgin, Charles 1852 wb-15-168 (Rb)
Colgin, Elizabeth 1854 wb-15-642 (Rb)
Colgin, Elizabeth 1854 wb-15-643 (Rb)
Colgin, Richard 1840 wb-10-470 (Rb)
Colhart, John 1859 wb-e-106 (Hy)
Colhoon, Charles 1822 wb-3-587 (Wi)
Coliar, Wiggins 1841 mr-1-359 (Be)
Colier, James 1846 mr-2-145 (Be)
Colin, Mary C. 1830 rb-8-82 (Ru)
Colishaw, John 1859 rb-p-33 (Mt)
Colker, Charles 1800 wb-1-71 (K)
Collaque, William 1856 wb-#27 (Mo)
Collen, John R. 1829 wb-1-200 (Ma)
Collet, Jacob 1860 wb-2-92# (Ge)
Collett, Alexander 1859 149-1-169 (Ge)
Collett, Isaac 1809 ib-1-275 (Ge)
Collett, Nancy 1856 149-1-37 (Ge)
Colley, George W. 1846 wb-b-140 (We)
Collier, Ardelia 1858 rb-o-604 (Mt)
Collier, Arthur 1812 wb-a-121 (St)
Collier, Benjamin 1856 wb-h-619 (Hu)
Collier, Charles 1833 wb-1-87 (Li)
Collier, Dabney 1844 wb-3-416 (Hy)
Collier, Dabney C. 1844 wb-3-415 (Hy)
Collier, Dabney C. 1855 ib-h-428 (F)
Collier, Dabny 1844 wb-a-222 (F)
Collier, Daniel 1821 rb-c-401 (Mt)
Collier, Ferriba 1826 wb-b-122 (St)
Collier, Harbert 1845 wb-g-16 (Hn)
Collier, Hurbard 1845 wb-f-269* (Hn)
Collier, Ingram B. 1842 rb-12-116 (Ru)
Collier, J. B. 1842 rb-12-105 (Ru)
Collier, James M. 1844 rb-j-82 (Mt)
Collier, John 1854 wb-3-261 (W)
Collier, John R. 1825 wb-1-47 (Ma)
Collier, Robert 1836? as-a-316 (Di)
Collier, Robert H. 1856 wb-#121 (Wl)
Collier, Thomas 1838 as-b-20 (Di)
Collier, Thomas 1857 rb-o-495 (Mt)
Collier, Thomas Sr. 1859 rb-p-271 (Mt)
Collier, William 1832 wb-2-0 (Sm)
Collier, William 1842 wb-a-101 (F)
Collier, William C. 1855 wb-3-272 (W)
Collier, Winneford 1855 wb-h-400 (Hu)
Collins, Aaron 1849 wb-1-300 (Me)
Collins, Abner 1846 wb-f-372 (St)
Collins, Andrew? 1855 wb-h-68 (St)
Collins, Barber 1843 wb-1-217 (Fr)
Collins, Daniel 1851 wb-h-319 (St)

Collins, Dowell 1857 wb-3-375 (Gr)
Collins, Durham 1834 wb-x-163 (Mu)
Collins, Francis 1844 wb-f-168 (St)
Collins, Gilson 1852 lw (Ct)
Collins, Hannah 1857 wb-1-362 (Fr)
Collins, Hodijah 1826 wb-4-145 (Wi)
Collins, Holland 1845 as-a-88 (Ms)
Collins, James 1794 wb-1-25 (K)
Collins, James 1838 wb-d-188* (Hn)
Collins, John 1840 lr (Gi)
Collins, John 1857 wb-2-360 (Me)
Collins, John H. 1840 wb-e-96 (Hn)
Collins, John R. 1825 rb-d-473 (Mt)
Collins, John R. 1825 rb-d-477 (Mt)
Collins, Jonathan 1852 wb-2-151 (Me)
Collins, Joseph T. 1843 wb-c-125 (Wh)
Collins, Joseph T. 1854 wb-d-158 (Wh)
Collins, Maria 1834 rb-g-25 (Mt)
Collins, Mary 1859 rb-p-279 (Mt)
Collins, Nathan 1838 rb-h-124 (Mt)
Collins, Peter A. 1857 wb-5-72 (Hr)
Collins, R. C. 1857 wb-2-368 (Me)
Collins, Rebecca D. 1847 as-a-147 (Ms)
Collins, Reuben C. 1860 wb-3-46 (Me)
Collins, Robert 1857 rb-o-380 (Mt)
Collins, Rosewell 1837 lr (Gi)
Collins, Sally 1846 5-3-125 (Cl)
Collins, Sally 1847 5-3-212 (Cl)
Collins, Simeon 1837? wb-1-110 (Hw)
Collins, Susannah 1828 wb-#35 (Mc)
Collins, Thomas 1845 wb-13-278 (D)
Collins, Thomas 1851 wb-10-41 (Wi)
Collins, William 1838 rb-h-112 (Mt)
Collins, William 1842 wb-1-206 (Li)
Collins, William 1861 wb-1-202 (R)
Collins, William H. 1861 wb-1-210 (R)
Collins, Wm. D. 1855 wb-2-252 (Me)
Collins, Zilpha 1847 wb-14-26 (D)
Collinsworth, Alice 1828 wb-9-171 (D)
Collinsworth, Covington C. 1830 wb-1-21 (La)
Collinsworth, Edmond 1816 wb-7-5 (D)
Collinsworth, Edward 1824 wb-8-392 (D)
Collinsworth, William 1795 wb-2-34 (D)
Collough, John 1859 wb-f-281 (G)
Collum, James N. 1855 wb-j-52 (O)
Colman, James 1850 wb-m-62 (Mt)
Colman, William H. 1856 wb-h-214 (St)
Colson, George E. 1856 wb-h-254 (St)
Colson, William K. 1856 wb-h-255 (St)
Colson, William R. 1857 wb-h-371 (St)
Colson, William S. 1858 wb-h-453 (St)

Coltard, William 1822 wb-8-150 (D)
Coltart, William 1840 wb-7-340 (Wi)
Colter, Anderson 1849 ib-1-65 (Ca)
Colter, John W. 1854 wb-1-28 (Bo)
Colter, Mary 1851 wb-1-15 (Bo)
Coltharp, Clayton 1814 wb-2-154 (Rb)
Coltharp, John 1856 wb-#15 (Mo)
Coltharp, William 1833 wb-10-96 (D)
Colthorp, Samuel 1838 wb-e-138 (Hu)
Colville, George 1853 wb-#35 (Mc)
Colville, Samuel 1830 wb-#36 (Mc)
Colville, Young 1826 wb-#36 (Mc)
Colvin, John 1850 33-3-199 (Gr)
Colwell, Elizabeth 1841 wb-2-254 (Hy)
Colwell, Mary 1819 wb-a-128 (Wh)
Colyor, Alexander 1856 wb-1-349 (Fr)
Combs, James 1858 wb-1-238 (Be)
Combs, James H. 1858 wb-1-250 (Be)
Combs, John 1808 wb-1-322 (Je)
Combs, Mary 1857 wb-1-160 (Be)
Combs, William 1837 mr-1-18 (Be)
Comer, Adam 1859 rb-20-303 (Ru)
Comer, George 1850 rb-15-376 (Ru)
Comer, R. E. 1825 as-A-97 (Di)
Comer, R. P. 1856 wb-3-303 (W)
Commons, Joseph 1858 wb-2-240 (Li)
Commons, Thomas 1822 wb-A-293 (Li)
Compton, Aaron 1849 wb-2-61 (Sh)
Compton, B. H. 1860 wb-4-395 (La)
Compton, Basil 1846 lr (Gi)
Compton, Charles 1827 wb-#71 (Wl)
Compton, Edward 1818 wb-#28 (Wl)
Compton, Eli 1855 ib-h-308 (F)
Compton, Eli R. 1851 wb-2-87 (Sh)
Compton, Henry 1856 wb-12-209 (K)
Compton, John (Sr.) 1835 wb-#150 (Wl)
Compton, Mathew 1854 wb-3-178 (W)
Compton, Richard 1857 wb-5-73 (Hr)
Compton, Robert M. 1842 wb-3-487 (Ma)
Compton, T. L. 1861 39-2-432 (Dk)
Compton, T. P. 1841 wb-2-291 (Hr)
Compton, Thomas 1815 wb-#17 (Wl)
Compton, Thomas 1857 lr (Gi)
Compton, William 1822? wb-#44 (Wl)
Compton, William 1845 wb-13-324 (D)
Comstock, Clark M. 1861 wb-13-561 (Wi)
Comway, Eugene 1854 wb-2-173 (Sh)
Conatzer, Andrew 1862 wb-1-78 (Se)
Conaway, Frederick 1836 wb-1-123 (Li)
Conaway, Timothy 1821 wb-1-0 (Sm)
Condon, Ann P. 1844 wb-12-224 (Rb)

Condon, James 1838 wb-11-241 (D)
Condon, Rose (Col) 1860 wb-18-326 (D)
Cone, Gilum 1856 wb-17-148 (D)
Cone, John 1837 wb-9-395 (Rb)
Cone, John W. 1854 wb-16-218 (D)
Conger, Isaac 1831 wb-2-0 (Sm)
Conger, John 1806 wb-1-0 (Sm)
Conger, Joshua 1831 wb-2-0 (Sm)
Conger, Stephen 1806 wb-3-116 (D)
Conger, William 1852 r39-1-236 (Dk)
Congo, John 1842 wb-3-0 (Sm)
Congo, Stephen 1806 wb-3-107 (D)
Conier, Thomas 1816 wb-#22 (Wl)
Conlan, Catharine A. 1857 wb-17-338 (D)
Conlee, Daniel 1854 wb-e-207 (G)
Conley, Russell 1849 wb-d-185 (G)
Conlon, James 1851 wb-15-70 (D)
Conlow, James 1848 wd-14-227 (D)
Conly, Nancy 1851 wb-#54 (Wa)
Conly, Polly Ann 1842 wb-#52 (Wa)
Conly, Thomas K. 1840 rb-11-80 (Ru)
Conn, Samuel 1810 lr (Sn)
Connally, C. C. 1840 wb-3-300 (Ma)
Connally, George Anderson 1854 wb-5-160 (Ma)
Connell, James 1826 wb-5-175 (Rb)
Connell, John T. 1839 wb-10-6 (Rb)
Connell, O. S. 1844 wb-12-331 (Rb)
Connell, Oliver S. 1844 wb-12-374 (Rb)
Connell, Parasade 1827 wb-5-444 (Rb)
Connell, Robert 1854 wb-1-331 (Fr)
Connell, Sally 1851 wb-14-435 (Rb)
Connell, Thomas J. 1857 wb-1-66 (Dy)
Connell, William A. 1840 wb-10-528 (Rb)
Connell, William P. 1852 wb-15-396 (D)
Conner, Abraham 1830 wb-b-10 (Wh)
Conner, Anna 1852 wb-b-166 (L)
Conner, Dennis 1795 wb-1-39 (K)
Conner, Isham 1853 wb-i-84 (O)
Conner, James 1818 wb-a-93 (Wh)
Conner, James 1849 wb-1-26 (Bo)
Conner, John 1840 wb-a-456 (R)
Conner, John 1853 wb-b-241 (L)
Conner, Lewis 1843 lr (Gi)
Conner, Samuel F. 1831 rb-f-238 (Mt)
Conner, Samuel T. 1832 rb-f-382 (Mt)
Conner, Seth 1853 wb-b-207 (L)
Conner, Tarence 1811 wb-1-29 (Bo)
Conner, William 1835 wb-1-481 (Hr)
Conner, William 1836 wb-6-70 (K)
Conner, William 1860 wb-13-368 (K)
Connery, Samuel T. 1831 rb-f-211 (Mt)

Conrad, Geo. O. 1849 wb-14-265 (Rb)
Conrad, Joseph 1795 rb-a-2 (Mt)
Conrad, Nicholas 1811 wb-1-400 (Rb)
Conrad, Nicholas 1825 wb-5-109 (Rb)
Conrad, W. W. 1854 wb-n-218 (Mt)
Conrad, William C. 1839 wb-10-166 (Rb)
Conrad, William C. 1839 wb-10-342 (Rb)
Conrad, William C. 1839 wb-e-246 (Hu)
Conway, Ann 1851 wb-14-490 (Rb)
Conway, Benjamin 1816 wb-2-338 (Rb)
Conway, George 1800 wb-1-4# (Ge)
Conway, James 1827 wb-4-245 (K)
Conway, Morris 1855 wb-2-189 (Sh)
Conway, William 1802 wb-1-5# (Ge)
Conway, William 1838 wb-2-50# (Ge)
Conwell, William 1819 wb-A-225 (Li)
Conwell, William B. 1847 wb-d-38 (G)
Conyar, Bartholomew 1832 wb-3-323 (Je)
Conyar, Sarah 1832 wb-3-323 (Je)
Conyers, Charles 1849 wb-#170 (Wl)
Conyers, James 1856 wb-g-722 (Hn)
Conyers, Joseph 1847 wb-#155 (Wl)
Conyers, Thomas 1853 wb-#108 (Wl)
Conyers, William 1844 wb-#145 (Wl)
Cook, Adam 1839 wb-10-311 (Rb)
Cook, Adam P. 1839 wb-10-331 (Rb)
Cook, Alexander 1817 wb-a-68 (Wh)
Cook, Alexander 1859 wb-f-271 (G)
Cook, Anderson 1843 rb-12-384 (Ru)
Cook, Anderson 1843 rb-12-388 (Ru)
Cook, Augustin 1821 wb-3-260 (Rb)
Cook, Charlott S. 1852 rb-16-346 (Ru)
Cook, Claibourn 1846 wb-b-8 (Mu)
Cook, Edmund 1809 Wb-1-54 (Wi)
Cook, Elizabeth 1858 wb-13-50 (K)
Cook, Francis 1859 wb-b-85 (Ms)
Cook, George 1815 wb-2-36# (Ge)
Cook, George 1815 wb-a-64 (Ro)
Cook, George 1850 wb-e-219 (Ro)
Cook, Gracey B. 1851 wb-9-654 (Wi)
Cook, Green 1840 rb-10-489 (Ru)
Cook, Henry 1833 wb-5-319 (Wi)
Cook, Henry 1859 wb-16-757 (Rb)
Cook, Henry 1860 149-1-179 (Ge)
Cook, Hugh 1841 wb-c-13 (Wh)
Cook, Hugh 1859 wb-e-294 (Wh)
Cook, Jacob 1817 wb-a-98 (Ro)
Cook, Jacob 1844 wb-12-246 (Rb)
Cook, Jacob 1859 wb-16-695 (Rb)
Cook, Jacob C. 1842 wb-2-292 (Sn)
Cook, James 1843 wb-5-260 (Gr)

Cook, James 1846 wb-f-287 (St)
Cook, James B. 1849 wb-b-550 (Mu)
Cook, James H. 1844 wb-13-72 (D)
Cook, James T. 1849 33-3-196 (Gr)
Cook, John 1805 Ir (Sn)
Cook, John 1834 wb-5-396 (Wi)
Cook, John 1836 wb-c-476 (St)
Cook, John 1842 wb-3-512 (Ma)
Cook, John 1851 wb-14-528 (Rb)
Cook, John 1854 wb-16-277 (D)
Cook, John 1858 Ir (Gi)
Cook, John H. 1858 wb-e-86 (Hy)
Cook, John H. 1859 wb-17-574 (D)
Cook, John H. 1860 wb-f-324 (Ro)
Cook, John S. 1837 rb-10-80 (Ru)
Cook, John T. 1848 wb-9-196 (Wi)
Cook, John Z. 1846 wb-8-432 (Wi)
Cook, John sr. 1817 wb-1-25 (Fr)
Cook, Joseph 1840 wb-12-57* (D)
Cook, Joseph S. 1839 wb-7-31 (Wi)
Cook, Jourdon 1841 wb-e-214 (Hn)
Cook, Martha 1849 wb-b-547 (Mu)
Cook, Mary 1860 rb-20-592 (Ru)
Cook, Michael 1825 eb-1-147 (C)
Cook, Payton S. 1852 wb-xx-83 (St)
Cook, R. A. 1860 wb-b-452 (We)
Cook, Robert 1841 wb-c-21 (Wh)
Cook, Robert 1855 wb-h-146 (St)
Cook, Robert C. 1854 wb-xx-367 (St)
Cook, Robert I. 1857 as-c-48 (Ms)
Cook, Rolen 1844 wb-c-190 (G)
Cook, Roling 1843 wb-c-104 (G)
Cook, Samuel A. 1836 wb-#114 (Wl)
Cook, Sarah 1843 wb-a-177 (L)
Cook, Sarah 1851 wb-15-196 (D)
Cook, Sidney C. 1857 wb-f-131 (Mu)
Cook, Thomas 1851 wb-#176 (Wl)
Cook, Thomas 1861 wb-17-282 (Rb)
Cook, Thomas sr. 1832 wb-a-30 (Cr)
Cook, Thornton H. 1836 wb-9-232 (Rb)
Cook, Will A. 1842 wb-12-355* (D)
Cook, William 1841 wb-2-197 (Hr)
Cook, William 1850 as-a-209 (Ms)
Cook, William 1858 rb-o-766 (Mt)
Cook, William A. 1842 wb-12-311* (D)
Cook, William A. 1854 wb-7-0 (Sm)
Cooke, Brim 1831 wb-1-320 (Ma)
Cooke, George 1797 wb-2-92 (D)
Cooke, George W. 1855 wb-#36 (Mc)
Cooke, Giles 1834 wb-d-14 (Hn)
Cooke, Hezekiah C. 1859 wb-#37 (Mc)

Cooke, I. S. W. 1829 wb-b-45 (Hn)
Cooke, Isaac S. W. 1830 wb-b-83 (Hn)
Cooke, Jacob 1842 wb-#36 (Mc)
Cooke, John A. 1850 wb-#36 (Mc)
Cooke, John D. 1854 rb-17-178 (Ru)
Cooke, John W. 1846 wb-g-35 (Hn)
Cooke, Joseph 1833 wb-x-111 (Mu)
Cooke, Matthias 1829 wb-#36 (Mc)
Cooke, William H. 1848 wb-#37 (Mc)
Cooke, William W. 1816 wb-7-90 (D)
Cooksey, Enoch 1853 wb-3-160 (W)
Cooksey, John 1822 wb-1-0 (Sm)
Cooley, Cornelius 1815 wb-3-57 (St)
Cooley, Eaton J. 1854 wb-h-284 (Hu)
Cooley, Henry C. 1851 wb-g-526 (Hu)
Cooley, James 1858 as-c-546 (Di)
Cooley, Jane 1854 wb-h-284 (Hu)
Cooley, Joel 1814 wb-a-236 (St)
Cooley, Simeon W. 1860 wb-i-174 (St)
Cooley, Thomas F. 1850 wb-g-208 (St)
Cooley, William M. 1824 wb-3-295 (St)
Cooley, William T. 1849 wb-g-251 (Hu)
Cooly, John 1841 wb-c-8 (Wh)
Cooly, Wood J. H. 1851 mr-2-414 (Be)
Coon, Conrad 1843 wb-12-424* (D)
Coon, Deverick 1854 wb-15-528 (Rb)
Coon, James 1836 rb-g-470 (Mt)
Coon, James 1850 wb-m-129 (Mt)
Coon, James W. 1853 wb-n-59 (Mt)
Coon, James sr. 1848 wb-m-63 (Mt)
Coon, Michael 1803 wb-2-38 (Je)
Coon, Shadrack 1836 wb-9-272 (Rb)
Coonrad, John 1837 wb-#119 (Wl)
Coonrod, Nicholas 1812 wb-#11 (Wl)
Coop, Horatio L. 1846 wb-c-339 (G)
Coop, Richard 1852 wb-d-415 (G)
Cooper, Alice G. 1858 rb-o-711 (Mt)
Cooper, Andrew 1840 wb-10-510 (Rb)
Cooper, Andrew 1857 lw (Ct)
Cooper, Belsent? 1861 wb-h-497 (Hn)
Cooper, Benjamin 1807 wb-1-0 (Sm)
Cooper, Benjamin 1820 rb-4-223 (Ru)
Cooper, Benjamin 1837 wb-b-142 (G)
Cooper, Benjamin 1859 wb-e-210 (Wh)
Cooper, Benjamin 1859 wb-e-274 (Wh)
Cooper, Blount 1845 wb-g-21 (Hn)
Cooper, Christopher 1832 wb-#102 (Wl)
Cooper, Christopher 1853 wb-A-97 (Ca)
Cooper, Coor? 1826 wb-b-13 (Hn)
Cooper, D. H. 1854 wb-11-391 (Wi)
Cooper, David 1860 wb-2-303 (Li)

Cooper, Delany 1858 wb-f-211 (G)
Cooper, Elizabaeth 1831 wb-2-0 (Sm)
Cooper, Elizabeth 1828 wb-1-101 (Hw)
Cooper, Elizabeth 1851 wb-g-391 (Hn)
Cooper, Elmira 1854 wb-#37 (Mc)
Cooper, Esther 1820 rb-c-315 (Mt)
Cooper, Francis L. 1859 wb-b-87 (Ms)
Cooper, G. W. 1851 ib-1-181 (Ca)
Cooper, Geo. F. 1858 wb-3e-59 (Sh)
Cooper, Henry 1823 wb-8-179 (D)
Cooper, Henry 1834 wb-#38 (Mc)
Cooper, Hiram 1829 rb-e-485 (Mt)
Cooper, Howard? 1830 rb-f-36 (Mt)
Cooper, Ira 1849 wb-g-329 (Hn)
Cooper, J. B. 1854 wb-g-588 (Hn)
Cooper, Jacob 1856 wb-a-275 (Cr)
Cooper, James 1842 wb-#38 (Mc)
Cooper, James 1854 wb-a-227 (T)
Cooper, James J. 1851 wb-d-298 (G)
Cooper, Joel 1825 lw (Ct)
Cooper, John 1809 rb-a-429 (Mt)
Cooper, John 1813 wb-1-167 (Sn)
Cooper, John 1829 wb-#80 (Wl)
Cooper, John 1832 wb-1-104 (Hw)
Cooper, John 1834 wb-1A-142 (A)
Cooper, John 1844 wb-7-0 (Sm)
Cooper, John 1844 wb-d-106 (Hd)
Cooper, John L. 1840 abl-1-190 (T)
Cooper, Jonathan 1837 wb-b-46 (Hd)
Cooper, Joseph 1845 wb-a-134 (Cr)
Cooper, Lucinda 1832 wb-#98 (Wl)
Cooper, Mansel 1848 wb-a-137 (T)
Cooper, Patience 1804 lw (Ct)
Cooper, Patsey 1846 wb-a-279 (F)
Cooper, Philip 1838 wb-#38 (Mc)
Cooper, Polly 1853 wb-f-17 (Mu)
Cooper, Powell 1849 wb-#171 (Wl)
Cooper, Richard 1857 rb-o-315 (Mt)
Cooper, Robert 1824 wb-3-281 (St)
Cooper, Robert 1833 rb-9-61 (Ru)
Cooper, Robert 1854 wb-n-433 (Mt)
Cooper, Samuel 1851 wb-a-154 (T)
Cooper, Sarah 1858 wb-A-135 (Ca)
Cooper, Silis 1840 wb-a-14 (Dk)
Cooper, Smith D. 1848 wb-d-387 (Hd)
Cooper, Susan Tennessee 1858 rb-o-775 (Mt)
Cooper, Tennesee 1858 rb-o-715 (Mt)
Cooper, Thomas 1810 wb-1-24 (Bo)
Cooper, Thomas 1843 as-b-106 (Ms)
Cooper, Thomas 1848 wb-a-180 (Ms)
Cooper, Thomas 1851 ib-1-181 (Ca)

Cooper, Vincent 1836 wb-d-35 (St)
Cooper, Vincent 1845 rb-j-392 (Mt)
Cooper, Whitmel H. 1853 wb-g-560 (Hn)
Cooper, William 1807 wb-3-161 (D)
Cooper, William 1817 wb-7-159 (D)
Cooper, William 1835 wb-x-256* (Mu)
Cooper, William 1838 wb-y-189 (Mu)
Cooper, William 1857 wb-2-192 (Li)
Cooper, William B. 1848 rb-14-362 (Ru)
Cooper, William M. 1848 wb-f-127+ (O)
Cooper, _____ 1844 wb-d-105 (Hd)
Coor, Jesse 1835 wb-1-377 (Hr)
Coor, John 1837 wb-1-565 (Hr)
Coor, Thomas 1816 wb-2-219 (Wi)
Coore, James H. 1824 wb-3-688 (Wi)
Coorpender, Elizabeth 1842 wb-3-556 (Ma)
Coorpender, John 1839 wb-3-15 (Ma)
Cooter, Phillip 1853 wb-2-79# (Ge)
Coots, Elizabeth 1826 wb-9-31 (D)
Coots, Frederick 1831 wb-b-62 (Wh)
Coots, John 1821 wb-8-15 (D)
Coots, John 1840 wb-12-97* (D)
Cope, Daniel 1854 wb-g-636 (Hn)
Cope, George 1825 wb-1-27 (Bo)
Cope, John W. 1853 wb-d-153 (Wh)
Cope, Richard 1845 lr (Sn)
Cope, William 1858 wb-e-207 (Wh)
Cope, William sr. 1859 wb-e-262 (Wh)
Copeland, Andrew C. 1850 wb-10-334 (K)
Copeland, David (Sr.) 1824 wb-#77 (Mu)
Copeland, David 1814? wb-#39 (Mu)
Copeland, David 1824? wb-#97 (Mu)
Copeland, James 1817 wb-3-81 (Wi)
Copeland, Jesse 1850 ib-1-71 (Wy)
Copeland, John 1840 wb-11-617 (D)
Copeland, Joseph 1816 wb-2-138 (Je)
Copeland, Mary 1852 wb-g-454 (Hn)
Copeland, Solomon 1826 wb-#38 (Mc)
Copeland, William 1835 wb-d-148 (Hn)
Copelin, Solomon 1845 wb-f-262* (Hn)
Copely, John 1847 wb-14-69 (D)
Coper, John 1859 wb-3-531 (Gr)
Copher, Robert 1816 wb-2-254 (K)
Copher, William 1842 wb-3-627 (Ma)
Copp, Jacob 1842 wb-#39 (Wa)
Coppack, Thomas 1807? wb-1-338 (Je)
Coppage, Charles (Jr.) 1849 wb-#171 (Wl)
Coppage, Charles 1848 wb-#166 (Wl)
Coppage, Thomas L. 1848 wd-14-215 (D)
Copton, R. M. 1844 wb-4-135 (Ma)
Coquett, Peter 1853 wb-i-128 (O)

Coram, A. O. 1858 wb-j-346 (O)
Corban, William 1827 rb-e-199 (Mt)
Corbell, Peter 1817 wb-A-187 (Li)
Corbell, Thomas 1815 rb-3-62 (Ru)
Corbet, John 1798 wb-1-68 (Je)
Corbett, William A. 1854 wb-16-362 (D)
Corbin, Alfred 1853 ib-2-59 (Cl)
Corbin, Charnall 1823 rb-d-124 (Mt)
Corbin, Joseph 1825 rb-d-448 (Mt)
Corbin, William jr. 1807 rb-a-458 (Mt)
Corbitt, William 1810 wb-4-99 (D)
Corbitt, Wm. 1810 wb-4-109 (D)
Corby, Timothy 1860 rb-p-354 (Mt)
Cordel, Elizabeth 1846 wb-8-410 (Wi)
Cordell, William 1846 wb-13-494 (D)
Cordene, John 1814 wb-1-0 (Sm)
Corder, Frances F. 1837 wb-#116 (Wl)
Corder, John 1815 wb-1-0 (Sm)
Corder, Richard 1861 iv-C-54 (C)
Cording, Jacob 1843 rb-j-17 (Mt)
Cordle, B. F. 1858 wb-16-678 (Rb)
Cordle, Francis 1859 wb-16-786 (Rb)
Core, William C. 1840 wb-7-326 (Wi)
Corely, Jucy? Jane 1855 wb-n-639 (Mt)
Corey, James 1853 wb-h-Apr (O)
Corlett, Robert 1827 wb-4-229 (Wi)
Corlew, William sr. 1841 rb-i-171 (Mt)
Corley, Austen 1841 wb-#134 (Wl)
Corley, Edmund B. 1830 wb-#92 (Wl)
Corley, George 1827 wb-#67 (Wl)
Corley, Nathan 1845 wb-#149 (Wl)
Corley, Nathaniel 1835 wb-3-0 (Sm)
Corley, Robert 1856 wb-f-1 (G)
Corley, William 1852 wb-#108 (Wl)
Corn, Samuel 1851 wb-1-290 (Fr)
Corner, George 1847 rb-14-172 (Ru)
Cornett, G. D. 1860 wb-f-386 (Ro)
Cornwell, Drury 1854 wb-7-0 (Sm)
Cornwell, Francis 1834 wb-3-0 (Sm)
Cornwell, Francis 1853 wb-7-0 (Sm)
Cornwell, Polly 1853 wb-#53 (Wa)
Cornwell, William 1834 wb-3-309 (Je)
Corothers, John 1816 wb-A-121 (Li)
Corpender, John 1838 wb-2-369 (Ma)
Corruthers, James 1843 wb-1-166 (Bo)
Corruthers, James M. 1853 wb-a-203 (T)
Corsey, James 1815 wb-A-98 (Li)
Corum, Robert 1860 wb-b*-40 (O)
Corum, Travis 1854 wb-3-213 (Gr)
Corum, William 1844 wb-5-340 (Gr)
Corum, Willson 1847 wb-5-505 (Gr)

Corum, Wilson A. 1845 wb-5-357 (Gr)
Corzine, Abel 1828 wb-4-343 (Wi)
Corzine, Abel 1842 wb-7-522 (Wi)
Corzine, Eli 1821 Wb-3-255 (Wi)
Corzine, Rees 1839 wb-7-176 (Wi)
Cosby, Hartwell 1838 rb-10-109 (Ru)
Cosby, James (Dr.) 1826 wb-1-1 (Hy)
Cosby, Mary A. 1840 rb-10-553 (Ru)
Cosby, Thomas W. 1840 wb-3-0 (Sm)
Cosby, William M. 1826 wb-b-92 (St)
Cosner, Jacob 1824 wb-1-23 (Bo)
Cossett, Lucinda 1848 rb-l-158 (Mt)
Cosson, John 1811 wb-#12 (Wa)
Costner, Michael 1802 wb-1-149 (Je)
Cothran, Martha 1858 wb-4-101 (La)
Cotner, Jacob 1840 wb-e-96 (Hn)
Cotner, Martin 1853 wb-3-108 (Gr)
Cotten, Solomon 1835 wb-d-77 (Hn)
Cotter, Catharine 1830 rb-8-151 (Ru)
Cotter, Edward J. 1836 wb-1-236 (Hy)
Cotter, James 1836 wb-2-47# (Ge)
Cotter, Jeremiah 1840 wb-a-60 (L)
Cotter, Margaret 1852 148-1-410 (Ge)
Cotter, Samuel 1855 wb-2-83# (Ge)
Cotter, William 1828 rb-7-49 (Ru)
Cotterell, Moses 1858 ib-2-443 (Cl)
Cottingham, Lewis 1852 mr-2-457 (Be)
Cottingham, Mary 1846 mr-2-230 (Be)
Cottingham, William 1852 mr-2-446 (Be)
Cotton, John 1851 lr (Sn)
Cotton, Joseph 1842 wb-1-77 (Sh)
Cotton, Mary 1861 wb-18-567 (D)
Cotton, Noah 1859 lr (Sn)
Cotton, Precilla 1852 wb-15-368 (D)
Cotton, Robert 1836 wb-a-15 (F)
Cotton, Thomas 1794 wb-1-37 (Sn)
Cotton, Thomas N. 1854 wb-16-348 (D)
Cottrell, William 1859 wb-13-182 (K)
Couch, Elijah 1839 wb-#125 (Wl)
Couch, Jacob 1797 wb-1-4# (Ge)
Couch, John 1846 wb-2-64# (Ge)
Couch, Jonathan 1847 wb-#38 (Mc)
Couch, Joseph 1841 wb-#39 (Mc)
Couch, Mary 1860 wb-#131 (Wl)
Couch, Peter 1850 148-1-311 (Ge)
Couch, Peter 1860 149-1-185 (Ge)
Coughorn, William 1819 wb-2-260 (Je)
Coughron, Lamuel 1837 wb-y-45 (Mu)
Coul, Daniel 1854 wb-0-123 (Cf)
Couldwell, Green 1857 wb#39 (Gu)
Coulson, David C. 1833 wb-0-14 (Cf)

Coulson, Elijah 1853 wb-2-77# (Ge)
Coulson, Enock 1840 wb-#38 (Wa)
Coulson, John 1848 wb-1-224 (Bo)
Coulson, Thomas 1837 wb-2-49# (Ge)
Coulson, Thomas 1855 149-1-15 (Ge)
Coulson, William 1852 148-1-406 (Ge)
Coulter, Anderson 1849 ib-1-78 (Ca)
Coulter, Andrew 1833 wb-1-20 (Bo)
Coulter, Francis 1818 wb-1-0 (Sm)
Coulter, Francis sr. 1818 wb-1-0 (Sm)
Coulter, Harriet 1855 ib-h-483 (F)
Coulter, R. 1843 wb-12-394* (D)
Coulter, Robert 1845 wb-13-159 (D)
Counce, John 1821 wb-1-62 (Fr)
Councel, Cyrus 1839 mr-1-299 (Be)
Councel, David 1823 rb-d-213 (Mt)
Council, Dudley 1848 rb-l-115 (Mt)
Council, Elizabeth 1852 wb-m-578 (Mt)
Council, Jesse 1831 wb-5-34 (K)
Council, Jordan T. 1858 wb-13-17 (K)
Council, Morris 1856 rb-o-250 (Mt)
Council, Willis 1848 rb-l-127 (Mt)
Councile, Rebecca 1825 as-A-113 (Di)
Counts, Patsey 1854 wb-3-159 (Gr)
Counts, Rachel 1836 wb-1-127 (Gr)
Countz, Nicholas 1838 wb-4-33 (Je)
Countz, Patsey 1843 wb-5-244 (Gr)
Countz, Peter 1799 wb-1-256 (Je)
Countz, Rachel 1835 wb-1-112 (Gr)
Coupland, Hugh S. 1853 wb-11-342 (K)
Coupland, William 1831 wb-5-26 (K)
Court, Charles 1815 wb-#10 (Mu)
Courtice(Curtis), Joshua 1842 mr-2-15 (Be)
Courtney, George 1853 148-1-428 (Ge)
Courtney, George sr. 1849 wb-2-70# (Ge)
Courtney, James 1836 wb-2-45# (Ge)
Courtney, James 1853 148-1-459 (Ge)
Courtney, James E. 1848 148-1-247 (Ge)
Courtney, John C. 1830 lr (Gi)
Courtney, Marsha 1848 wb-4-62 (Je)
Courtney, Robert 1859 wb-13-167 (Wi)
Courtney, William 1814 wb-2-118 (K)
Courtny, Nehimiah 1794 wb-2-4 (D)
Couser, John F. 1863 wb-2-372 (Li)
Cousins, Lewis 1859 rb-19-625 (Ru)
Couts, Albert W. 1857 wb-16-536 (Rb)
Couts, Archer 1833 wb-8-334 (Rb)
Couts, Archer 1846 wb-12-595 (Rb)
Couts, Archer B. 1850 wb-14-403 (Rb)
Couts, Jackson 1846 wb-12-582 (Rb)
Couts, John 1828 wb-6-345 (Rb)

Couts, Mary P. 1851 wb-15-3 (Rb)
Couts, William 1849 wb-14-116 (Rb)
Covey, Huldah 1848 wb-d-389 (Hd)
Covey, Leven L. 1842 wb-b-447 (Hd)
Covey, Wesley 1845 wb-d-146 (Hd)
Covington, David 1830 rb-8-131 (Ru)
Covington, David 1840 rb-11-102 (Ru)
Covington, Henry 1815 wb-2-229 (Rb)
Covington, John 1847 rb-14-39 (Ru)
Covington, Lafayette 1857 rb-18-298 (Ru)
Covington, M. L. 1847 rb-14-17 (Ru)
Covington, M. P. 1857 rb-18-296 (Ru)
Covington, William H. D. 1836 wb-a-143 (O)
Cowan, A. M. 1854 wb-5-338 (Je)
Cowan, Alexander 1817 wb-7-207 (D)
Cowan, Andrew 1799 wb-1-126 (Je)
Cowan, David A. 1853 wb-10-599 (Wi)
Cowan, David C. 1835 wb-d-54 (Hn)
Cowan, David Holway 1825 wb-a-208 (Wh)
Cowan, Elizabeth 1857 wb-2-382 (Me)
Cowan, Henry F. 1848 wb-d-138 (G)
Cowan, Hugh 1861 wb-1-64 (Se)
Cowan, James 1801 wb-1-81 (K)
Cowan, James 1814 wb-1-11 (Fr)
Cowan, James 1820 wb-0-198 (K)
Cowan, James 1841 wb-1-62 (Me)
Cowan, James W. 1825 wb-#39 (Mc)
Cowan, Joel W. 1853 wb-5-327 (Je)
Cowan, John 1813 wb-#13 (Wa)
Cowan, John 1837 wb-1-164 (Fr)
Cowan, John 1839 wb-#37 (Wa)
Cowan, John F. 1856 wb-e-461 (G)
Cowan, Joseph 1846 wb-8-392 (Wi)
Cowan, Nancy 1849 wb-#171 (Wl)
Cowan, Robert 1841 wb-1-199 (Fr)
Cowan, Samuel 1801 wb-1-84 (K)
Cowan, Samuel 1832 eb-1-270 (C)
Cowan, Sarah H. 1846 wb-8-490 (Wi)
Coward, Curtis M. 1840 abl-1-198 (T)
Coward, David 1820 rb-5-19 (Ru)
Coward, John 1853 wb-1C-79 (A)
Coward, Sarah E. L. 1858 wb-1C-430 (A)
Coward, William S. 1851? wb-1B-269 (A)
Cowden, Elizabeth 1856 as-b-242 (Ms)
Cowden, Joseph 1851 as-b-43 (Ms)
Cowden, Robert 1841 wb-a-76 (Ms)
Cowden, William 1839 wb-a-36 (Ms)
Cowdon, John B. 1843 as-a-82 (Ms)
Cowdon, William 1820 lr (Sn)
Cowen, Andrew 1840 wb-1-19 (Bo)
Cowen, Benjamin F. 1847 wb-d-98 (G)

Cowen, James 1838 wb-#122 (Wl)
Cowen, William 1815 wb-2-143 (K)
Cowen, William 1833 wb-#104 (Wl)
Cowen, William M. 1835 wb-#108 (Wl)
Cowgill, Abner 1826 wb-8-513 (D)
Cowgill, Abner 1826 wb-9-19 (D)
Cowhard, Jno. W. 1847 rb-k-745 (Mt)
Cowherd, R. C. 1850 wb-m-60 (Mt)
Cowin, James M. 1833 wb-#100 (Wl)
Cowley, Matthew 1859 wb-8-30 (Sm)
Cowley, William 1830 wb-1-51 (Li)
Cowley, William H. 1860 wb-18-294 (D)
Cowls, Jesse 1861 wb-13-423 (Wi)
Cowser, James A. 1858 wb-2-430 (Me)
Cowsert, Andrew 1824 wb-3-722 (Wi)
Cowsert, Jane 1832 wb-5-158 (Wi)
Cox, Abraham 1826 wb-3-0 (Sm)
Cox, Anderson 1856 wb-#120 (Wl)
Cox, Andrew 1805 rb-a-252 (Mt)
Cox, Ann M. 1856 wb-2-84# (Ge)
Cox, Asa 1858 wb-5-85 (Hr)
Cox, Asa sr. 1859 wb-h-375 (Hn)
Cox, Azariah 1836 wb-6-74 (K)
Cox, Benjamin 1791 wb-1-79 (Hw)
Cox, Benjamin 1824 as-A-1 (Di)
Cox, Charles 1810 wb-#10 (Wl)
Cox, Charles 1852 wb-#179 (Wl)
Cox, Charles 1854 wb-1-54 (R)
Cox, Curd 1853 wb-11-458 (K)
Cox, Daniel 1802 Wb-1-99 (Wi)
Cox, David E. 1847 wb-f-127+ (O)
Cox, Dudley 1812 wb-2-37 (Je)
Cox, Edward 1844 wb-1-113 (Sh)
Cox, Eli 1861 wb-5-108 (Hr)
Cox, Eliakum 1862 wb-1-133 (Hw)
Cox, Elijah 1840 rb-10-477 (Ru)
Cox, Elijah 1840 rb-10-480 (Ru)
Cox, Elizabeth 1819 wb-#43 (Mu)
Cox, Enos 1856 wb-e-464 (G)
Cox, Evaline 1849 wb-#171 (Wl)
Cox, Frances B. 1853 wb-16-61 (D)
Cox, Garner M. 1852 wb-10-193 (Wi)
Cox, George 1814 wb-1-0 (Sm)
Cox, George 1839 wb-6-462 (k)
Cox, George R. 1840 wb-7-216 (Wi)
Cox, George W. C. 1855 wb-12-184 (K)
Cox, Gova 1859 wb-h-344 (Hn)
Cox, Greenberry 1805 wb-3-6 (D)
Cox, H. 1849 rb-l-465 (Mt)
Cox, Henry 1809 wb-1-22 (Bo)
Cox, Herman 1861 wb-18-620 (D)

Cox, Isaac 1855 wb-e-549 (Ro)
Cox, Jacob 1809 wb-1-85 (Hw)
Cox, Jacob 1815 wb-2-208 (K)
Cox, James 1805 wb-1-164 (K)
Cox, James 1812 wb-#12 (Wa)
Cox, James 1848 ib-1-50 (Ca)
Cox, James 1849 wb-e-178 (Ro)
Cox, James M. 1857 wb-1-130 (Hw)
Cox, Jason 1855 wb-a-245 (Cr)
Cox, Jehu E. 1852 wb-2-130 (Me)
Cox, Jesse 1816 wb-4-457 (D)
Cox, Jesse 1816 wb-7-68 (D)
Cox, John 1777 wb-#2 (Wa)
Cox, John 1798 wb-1-82 (Hw)
Cox, John 1820 wb-1-91 (Hw)
Cox, John 1822 wb-a-1 (Cr)
Cox, John 1835 wb-1A-129 (A)
Cox, John 1840 wb-c-151 (Ro)
Cox, John A. 1853 ib-1-224 (Wy)
Cox, John A. 1856 ib-1-426 (Wy)
Cox, John E. 1860 wb-3-55 (Me)
Cox, John F. 1844 rb-12-574 (Ru)
Cox, Jonathan 1814 rb-2-306 (Ru)
Cox, Joseph 1857 wb-#39 (Mc)
Cox, Lewis 1834 wb-5-271 (K)
Cox, Loyd A. 1859 149-1-81 (Ge)
Cox, Mabry T. 1826 wb-a-127 (Hn)
Cox, Mary 1854 wb-1-54 (R)
Cox, Mary 1857 wb-#39 (Mc)
Cox, Matthew 1807 as-1-178 (Ge)
Cox, Matthew 1807 wb-1-5# (Ge)
Cox, Meredith 1836 wb-b-31 (Hd)
Cox, Moses 1855 wb-12-143 (K)
Cox, Nancy 1859 wb-13-179 (Wi)
Cox, Samuel 1808 wb-1-268 (K)
Cox, Samuel 1820 wb-0-213 (K)
Cox, Samuel 1840 wb-5-94 (Gr)
Cox, Tabitha 1831 wb-1-103 (Hw)
Cox, Thomas 1824 wb-#96 (Mu)
Cox, Thomas 1831 wb-9-483 (D)
Cox, Thomas 1833 wb-a-180 (R)
Cox, Thomas 1835 wb-b-269 (Ro)
Cox, Thomas 1837 wb-#117 (Wl)
Cox, Washington S. 1848 wb-14-248 (D)
Cox, Widow 1851 wb-#176 (Wl)
Cox, William (Jr.) 1847 wb-#153 (Wl)
Cox, William (Jr.) 1850 wb-#165 (Wl)
Cox, William 1836 rb-9-189 (Ru)
Cox, William 1843 wb-4-99 (Je)
Cox, William 1845 wb-#149 (Wl)
Cox, William sr. 1804 wb-1-25 (Je)

Cox, Zachariah 1831 wb-5-57 (K)
Coy, Thomas 1854 wb-1-328 (Fr)
Coyle, Francis 1850 rb-l-540 (Mt)
Cozart, Gilbert 1860 wb-7-76 (Ma)
Cozart, James W. 1842 wb-3-554 (Ma)
Cozart, Joshua 1851 wb-5-107 (Ma)
Crab, John 1830 lr (Sn)
Crabb, Fountain R. 1858 wb-4-169 (La)
Crabb, Henry 1828 wb-9-147 (D)
Crabb, Miriam 1846 wb-c-290 (G)
Crabtree, Barnet 1825 wb-1-3# (Ge)
Crabtree, Benjamin 1844 wb-12-120 (Rb)
Crabtree, Daniel 1853 148-1-439 (Ge)
Crabtree, Isaac 1817 wb-a-57 (Wh)
Crabtree, James 1820 wb-3-81 (Rb)
Crabtree, Job 1848 wb-e-76 (Ro)
Craddock, Armistead 1852 wb-15-280 (D)
Craddock, Asa 1835 wb-10-410 (D)
Craddock, Asa 1835 wb-10-486 (D)
Craddock, George 1833 wb-b-4 (G)
Craddock, George 1833 wb-b-5 (G)
Craddock, Martha G. 1838 wb-6-444 (Wi)
Craddock, Matthew R. 1836 wb-6-113 (Wi)
Craddock, Rachel 1802 as-1-1 (Ge)
Craddock, Richard C. 1829 wb-#80 (Wl)
Craddock, Richard M. 1826 wb-#63 (Wl)
Craddock, William 1849 wb-2-70# (Ge)
Cradock, John 1846 rb-13-688 (Ru)
Crafford, Charles 1853 wb-15-446 (Rb)
Crafford, William 1804 wb-2-397 (D)
Craft, Jessee 1830 as-a-191 (Di)
Craft, Rebecca 1818 wb-1-92 (Hw)
Craftin, Staples 1825 wb-#144 (Mu)
Crafton, Daniel W. 1860 wb-f-371 (G)
Crafton, James 1810 wb-1-209 (Wi)
Crafton, John 1816 wb-2-220 (Wi)
Crafton, Paul C. 1838 wb-b-223 (G)
Crafton, Robert 1823 wb-#129 (Mu)
Crafton, Robert W. 1833 wb-x-113 (Mu)
Crage, Ann 1844 wb-a-139 (Cr)
Craghead, Shelton 1823 wb-1-0 (Sm)
Craig, Alexander 1823 wb-#39 (Mc)
Craig, Alexander 1843 wb-f-165* (Hn)
Craig, Cynthia 1856 wb-6-277 (Ma)
Craig, David (Jr.) 1824 wb-#88 (Mu)
Craig, David 1812 wb-1-327 (Wi)
Craig, David 1825 wb-4-2 (Wi)
Craig, David 1827 wb-4-274 (Wi)
Craig, Easter M. 1846 wb-c-286 (G)
Craig, Elijah 1851 wb-g-509 (Hu)
Craig, F. E. 1859 wb-k-4 (O)

Craig, James 1829 wb-1-1 (La)
Craig, James 1843 lr (Gi)
Craig, James W. 1849 wb-10-165 (K)
Craig, James W. sr. 1847 wb-9-295 (K)
Craig, Jane I. 1858 wb-2-88# (Ge)
Craig, John 1814 rb-2-279 (Ru)
Craig, John 1815 wb-#29 (Mu)
Craig, John 1848 wb-10-21 (K)
Craig, John P. 1815 wb-#15 (Mu)
Craig, Johnathan 1856 wb-a-243 (T)
Craig, Johnston 1849 wb-2-51 (La)
Craig, Johnston sr. 1850 wb-2-150 (La)
Craig, Joseph Miles 1858 wb-f-137 (Mu)
Craig, Martha Jane 1860 wb-a-301 (T)
Craig, Martha S. 1857 wb-j-249 (O)
Craig, Mary 1826 wb-4-149 (Wi)
Craig, Moses 1814 wb-3-49 (St)
Craig, Robert 1848 wb-4-8 (Je)
Craig, Samuel 1807 as-1-203 (Ge)
Craig, Samuel 1840 wb-y-679 (Mu)
Craig, Samuel M. 1843 wb-z-470 (Mu)
Craig, Thomas 1854 mr-2-563 (Be)
Craig, William 1831 wb-#218 (Mu)
Craig, William 1840 wb-z-46 (Mu)
Craige, Daniel 1828 wb-4-357 (Wi)
Craighead, Elizabeth 1830 wb-9-362 (D)
Craighead, J. P. N. 1854 wb-12-54 (K)
Craighead, Jane 1851 wb-15-20 (D)
Craighead, John 1826 wb-4-182 (K)
Craighead, John B. 1854 wb-16-393 (D)
Craighead, John V. 1827 wb-4-248 (K)
Craighead, Robert 1821 wb-3-281 (K)
Craighead, Temperance 1843 wb-8-69 (K)
Craighead, William 1835 wb-5-351 (K)
Craighead, William jr. 1836 wb-6-10* (K)
Crain, Jessee 1853 wb-a-176 (V)
Crain, John 1836 wb-d-1 (St)
Crain, Lewis 1827 lr (Sn)
Crain, Russell T. 1850 wb-a-133 (V)
Crain, William 1816 wb-1-232 (Sn)
Cranford, Anderson 1853 wb-a-440 (F)
Cranford, Anderson 1859 gs-1-481 (F)
Crank, Elbert 1851 wb-d-348 (G)
Crank, W. H. 1848 wb-g-113 (Hu)
Crapper, William 1853 wb-#111 (Wl)
Crather, Joseph 1820 wb-#36 (Wl)
Cravans, Elizabeth 1845 wb-b-103 (We)
Cravans, William 1844 wb-b-43 (We)
Craven, John 1854 wb-i-209 (O)
Cravens, John 1803 wb-2-339 (D)
Cravens, William 1796 wb-1-4# (Ge)

Cravin, Thos. 1840 wb-b-314 (G)
Crawford, Alexander B. 1836 wb-x-358 (Mu)
Crawford, Andrew J. 1848 wb-e-92 (Ro)
Crawford, Ann 1846 wb-4-74b (Hr)
Crawford, Anthony 1857 wb-2-190 (Li)
Crawford, B. R. 1860 wb-h-488 (Hn)
Crawford, Barnes 1858 wb-13-1 (K)
Crawford, Benoni 1857 wb-f-115 (G)
Crawford, Betsy 1861 wb-13-408 (K)
Crawford, Charles B. 1845 rb-13-177 (Ru)
Crawford, David 1787? wb-#23 (Wa)
Crawford, George G. (Dr.) 1837 wb-2-49# (Ge)
Crawford, Isabel 1843 wb-2-59# (Ge)
Crawford, J. J. 1854 ib-H-111 (F)
Crawford, James 1860 rb-20-413 (Ru)
Crawford, James H. 1846 wb-1-90 (Ct)
Crawford, James W. 1852 wb-g-436 (Hn)
Crawford, John 1813 wb-1-341 (Wi)
Crawford, John 1840 wb-2-61# (Ge)
Crawford, John 1843 rb-12-306 (Ru)
Crawford, John 1846 wb-#39 (Mc)
Crawford, John 1847 wb-1-328 (Li)
Crawford, John C. 1860 wb-f-353 (G)
Crawford, John H. 1852 wb-g-447 (Hn)
Crawford, Lazarus 1818 rb-4-164 (Ru)
Crawford, Martha J. 1855 wb-15-751 (Rb)
Crawford, Moses 1820 wb-3-147 (K)
Crawford, Robert 1794 wb-1-4# (Ge)
Crawford, Robert 1797 wb-1-4# (Ge)
Crawford, Robert R. 1860 wb-h-509 (Hn)
Crawford, Robert sr. 1835 wb-x-283* (Mu)
Crawford, Saml. 1843 wb-z-506 (Mu)
Crawford, Samuel 1822 wb-3-385 (K)
Crawford, Samuel 1832? wb-#32 (Wa)
Crawford, Samuel 1837 wb-6-100 (K)
Crawford, Sims A. 1850 wb-10-352 (K)
Crawford, Solomon 1849 wb-#40 (Mc)
Crawford, Thomas 1821 wb-#43 (Mu)
Crawford, Thomas 1824 wb-#79 (Mu)
Crawford, Thomas 1843 wb-f-191* (Hn)
Crawford, William 1803 as-1-47 (Ge)
Crawford, William 1803 wb-1-5# (Ge)
Crawford, William 1804 wb-1-82 (Hw)
Crawford, William 1814 wb-1-9 (Fr)
Crawford, William 1851 wb-g-402 (Hn)
Crawford, William 1857 wb-2-290 (Li)
Crawford, William 1859 wb-f-282 (G)
Crawford, William A. 1803 wb-2-338 (D)
Crawford, William D. 1859 wb-13-189 (K)
Crawford, Willie W. 1839 wb-b-356 (Wh)
Crawley, Jackson 1852 wb-g-435 (Hn)

Crawley, Lemuel 1840 rb-10-556 (Ru)
Crawley, William sr. 1852 wb-g-446 (Hn)
Crawly, Asa 1825 wb-a-206 (Wh)
Crawly, Thomas 1843 wb-a-61 (V)
Crawsby, James 1816 wb-A-135 (Li)
Crawson, Robert 1831 wb-#236 (Mu)
Craycroft, Ruben 1791 wb-1-79 (Hw)
Creal, William 1845 wb-13-214 (D)
Creamer, Thomas 1855 149-1-6 (Ge)
Creary, Archibald 1814 wb-a-21 (Wh)
Creason, James 1852 wb-2-31 (Li)
Creath, Mary 1823 rb-d-208 (Mt)
Creath, Samuel 1823 rb-d-239 (Mt)
Creath, Samuel 1823 rb-d-251 (Mt)
Crecelias, Randolph 1787 wb-#2 (Wa)
Creech, Thomas 1861 wb-18-453 (D)
Creecy, Nancy 1829 wb-4-385 (Wi)
Creeves, Harriett 1855 wb-e-356 (G)
Crehshaw, William A. 1855 wb-2-183 (Sh)
Creighton, Samuel B. 1840 wb-3-206 (Ma)
Cremer, Daniel 1846 148-1-154 (Ge)
Crenshaw, Benjamin 1859 wb-f-253 (Ro)
Crenshaw, Charles 1853 wb-f-15 (Mu)
Crenshaw, Cornelius 1817 wb-2-262 (Wi)
Crenshaw, David 1831 lr (Sn)
Crenshaw, Elizabeth 1850 wb-4-81 (Mu)
Crenshaw, Elizabeth 1853 wb-f-20 (Mu)
Crenshaw, Joel 1850 wb-2-64 (Sh)
Crenshaw, John 1813 wb-2-9 (Wi)
Crenshaw, John C. 1817 wb-2-323 (Wi)
Crenshaw, K.? K.? 1835 wb-d-91 (Hn)
Crenshaw, Meredith 1818? lr (Sn)
Crenshaw, Nancy 1844 wb-a2-12 (Mu)
Crenshaw, Nathaniel 1859 wb-13-70 (Wi)
Crenshaw, Nathaniel K. 1837 wb-d-127* (Hn)
Crenshaw, Rebecca 1855 wb-b-9 (F)
Crenshaw, Sarah 1860 wb-13-283 (Wi)
Crenshaw, Susannah 1836 wb-d-231 (Hn)
Crenshaw, Thomas C. 1859 wb-3e-94 (Sh)
Crenshaw, _____ 1840 wb-b-217 (Hd)
Creson, Abraham 1850 wb-A-68 (Ca)
Creswell, Andrew 1816 wb-#23 (Wl)
Creswell, Halem 1826 wb-#64 (Wl)
Creswell, James 1815 rb-b-244 (Mt)
Creswell, John A. 1855 wb-i-245 (O)
Creswell, Joseph 1834 wb-5-319 (K)
Creswell, Rebecca H. 1858 wb-b-51 (Ms)
Creswell, Samuel 1812 rb-b-30 (Mt)
Creswell, Samuel 1853 wb-1-267 (Bo)
Creudson, William N. 1843 as-b-157 (Di)
Creuse, V. S. 1843 as-b-181 (Di)

Crews, Benja. 1826 as-a-161 (Di)
Crews, Benjamine 1841 wb-1-243 (La)
Crews, Gideon 1824 wb-4-30 (K)
Crews, Isham J. 1857 wb-f-125 (Mu)
Crews, James 1841 wb-7-213 (K)
Crews, James F. 1854 wb-5-154 (Ma)
Crews, Littleberry 1855 wb-6-126 (Ma)
Crews, William 1839 wb-1-362 (Gr)
Cribbs, John 1826 wb-a-66 (G)
Cribbs, William 1829 wb-a-136 (G)
Cribs, William H. 1854 wb-e-216 (G)
Crichfield, Charles 1855 wb-g-743 (Hn)
Crichfield, John 1847 wb-g-202 (Hn)
Crichfield, John 1851 wb-b-134 (L)
Crichfield, Phillip 1850 wb-b-99 (L)
Crichler, Branker 1839 wb-11-542 (D)
Crichloe, Thomas H. 1856 rb-17-610 (Ru)
Crichlow, Brasher? 1838 wb-11-161 (D)
Crichlow, Henry 1858 wb-12-596 (Wi)
Crichlow, Henry E. 1860 wb-13-449 (Wi)
Criddle, Alexander E. 1846 wb-8-370 (Wi)
Criddle, James 1861 wb-13-471 (Wi)
Criddle, James M. 1861 wb-13-487 (Wi)
Criddle, John 1822 wb-8-82 (D)
Criddle, John 1832 wb-9-619 (D)
Criddle, Livingston G. 1831 wb-9-478 (D)
Criddle, Smith 1846 wb-g-79 (Hn)
Criddle, Smith 1861 wb-19-31 (D)
Criddle, Susannah 1830 wb-9-366 (D)
Criddles, Sarah 1834 wb-10-353 (D)
Crider, George 1838 wb-b-210 (G)
Crider, Isaac 1847 wb-4-1 (Je)
Crihfield, Henry 1858 wb-c-267 (L)
Crilly, Collin 1793 wb-1-80 (Hw)
Crimm, Zion T. 1856 wb-h-476 (Hu)
Crippen, George 1860 wb-13-343 (K)
Crippen, John 1801 wb-0-30 (K)
Crippen, John F. 1854 wb-12-44 (K)
Crippen, John J. 1855 wb-11-521 (K)
Cripps, Christian 1791 wb-1-229 (D)
Crips, Henry S. 1855 39-2-50 (Dk)
Crisp, Ezekiel 1847 wb-14-26 (D)
Crisp, John 1842 wb-#40 (Mc)
Crisp, M. P. 1849 wb-4-558 (Hr)
Crisp, Moses C. 1844 wb-3-116 (Hr)
Crisp, Moses P. (Dr.) 1842 wb-2-302 (Hr)
Crisp, Moses P. 1839 wb-2-119 (Hr)
Crisp, Thomas 1835 wb-1-107 (W)
Cristenbery, W. M. 1860 wb-h-442 (Hn)
Cristman, James 1860 wb-13-287 (Wi)
Criswell, Andrew 1837 wb-6-408 (Wi)

Criswell, Joseph 1836 wb-6-20 (K)
Criswell, Martin 1847 wb-#154 (Wl)
Critchfield, George 1852 wb-e-3 (G)
Critenden, John 1846 wb-g-150 (Hn)
Critentum, William 1827 lr (Gi)
Crittenton, Paletier 1840 abl-1-210 (T)
Crittenton, Patatire 1840 wb-a-54 (F)
Critz, Jacob 1821 Wb-3-228 (Wi)
Critz, James M. 1852 wb-10-197 (Wi)
Critz, John C. 1834 wb-5-362 (Wi)
Critz, John C. 1836 wb-6-114 (Wi)
Critz, Susannah 1861 wb-1-132 (Hw)
Crobarger, George 1837? wb-1-110 (Hw)
Crobb, William 1857 wb-1-176 (Be)
Crocker, Edwin H. 1858 wb-f-201 (G)
Crocker, John T. 1840 rb-11-32 (Ru)
Crocker, Mark 1858 wb-f-155 (G)
Crocker, William 1855 wb-c-42 (L)
Crocket, Andrew 1838 wb-7-18 (Wi)
Crocket, David 1851 wb-d-337 (G)
Crockett, Abraham 1828 wb-4-285 (Wi)
Crockett, Andrew 1821 Wb-3-246 (Wi)
Crockett, Andrew 1852 wb-10-383 (Wi)
Crockett, Andrew 1855 wb-1-196 (Su)
Crockett, Ann B. 1861 wb-k-439 (O)
Crockett, Archibald no date lr (Gi)
Crockett, David 1828 wb-9-248 (d)
Crockett, Fountain P. 1838 rb-10-90 (Ru)
Crockett, Frances 1843 wb-11-364 (Rb)
Crockett, Gracy 1846 wb-f-5 (O)
Crockett, Isaac 1841 wb-c-79 (O)
Crockett, J. M. 1861 wb-b*-30 (O)
Crockett, James 1847 rb-k-437 (Mt)
Crockett, John 1834 wb-b-36 (G)
Crockett, John 1854 wb-#40 (Mc)
Crockett, John 1857 wb-h-638 (Hu)
Crockett, John 1859 wb-00-1 (Cf)
Crockett, John A. 1853 wb-#41 (Mc)
Crockett, John H. 1828 wb-4-289 (Wi)
Crockett, John H. 1842 wb-7-523 (Wi)
Crockett, Joseph 1853 wb-10-526 (Wi)
Crockett, Judge W. 1852 wb-m-432 (Mt)
Crockett, Nancy 1844 wb-8-168 (Wi)
Crockett, P. P? 1837 rb-9-457 (Ru)
Crockett, Patterson 1834 wb-b-39 (G)
Crockett, Robert 1824 lr (Gi)
Crockett, Robert H. 1844 wb-d-197 (O)
Crockett, Samuel 1827 wb-4-199 (Wi)
Crockett, Samuel 1841 wb-11-55 (Rb)
Crockett, Samuel J. 1845 wb-12-461 (Rb)
Crockett, William 1838 wb-e-59 (Hu)

Crockett, William 1842 wb-11-144 (Rb)
Crockett, William 1851 wb-14-473 (Rb)
Crockett, William 1854 lr (Sn)
Crockett, William 1854 wb-#41 (Mc)
Crockett, Wm. M. 1856 rb-18-97 (Ru)
Crofford, Alexander 1839 wb-y-390 (Mu)
Crofford, Alexander C. 1851 rb-4-244 (Mu)
Croft, David 1842 wb-e-229 (St)
Cromwell, Alexr. 1802 wb-1-80 (Rb)
Cromwell, Catharine L. 1846 rb-k-299 (Mt)
Cromwell, George W. 1860 ib-2-188 (Wy)
Cromwell, John 1806 wb-1-225 (Rb)
Cromwell, Oliver 1829 wb-#41 (Mc)
Cromwell, Winiferd 1808 wb-1-258 (Rb)
Crook, George W. 1849 wb-g-183 (St)
Crook, John 1838 wb-b-293 (Wh)
Crook, John 1838 wb-b-318 (Wh)
Crook, John sr. 1838 wb-b-297 (Wh)
Crook, Rebecca 1840 wb-b-407 (Wh)
Crook, William 1841 wb-c-7 (Wh)
Crooke, L. B. 1835 wb-d-56 (Hn)
Crookshanks, William 1836 wb-#33 (Wa)
Crooms, Isaac 1858 wb-e-89 (Hy)
Cropper, Elizabeth 1833 wb-#104 (Wl)
Cropper, James 1848 wb-#166 (Wl)
Cropper, William G. 1836 wb-#110 (Wl)
Crosby, Levi 1839 wb-7-95 (Wi)
Crosby, Peggy 1808 ib-1-229 (Ge)
Crosby, Peggy 1808 wb-1-4# (Ge)
Crosby, Robert 1838 wb-y-262* (Mu)
Crosby, Susanna 1806 wb-1-5# (Ge)
Crosby, Susannah 1806 as-1-148 (Ge)
Crosby, Uriel 1799 wb-1-4# (Ge)
Crosby, Uriel 1821 wb-1-4# (Ge)
Crosby, William 1817 wb-1-6# (Ge)
Crosier, Casander 1847 wb-1-117 (Hw)
Croson, John 1814 wb-1-89 (Hw)
Cross, Burrell 1851 wb-5-23 (Hr)
Cross, Coleman 1860 mr (Gi)
Cross, Edward 1794 wb-1-81 (Hw)
Cross, Edward 1838 wb-a-36 (F)
Cross, Elijah 1832 wb-1-263 (Hr)
Cross, George W. 1849 wb-d-176 (G)
Cross, Hanna 1839 wb-b-166 (O)
Cross, Jesse 1852 wb-1-191 (Su)
Cross, John 1832 wb-8-99 (Rb)
Cross, John 1835 rb-9-267 (Ru)
Cross, John 1851 wb-1B-244 (A)
Cross, John 1851 wb-g-400 (Hn)
Cross, John F. 1837 wb-b-148 (G)
Cross, Joseph C. 1839 wb-y-625 (Mu)

Cross, Joseph O. 1842 wb-z-315 (Mu)
Cross, Marlin 1798 wb-2-121 (D)
Cross, Micajah 1815 eb-1-52 (C)
Cross, Oliver 1834 wb-x-261 (Mu)
Cross, Reddick 1858 gs-1-35 (F)
Cross, Richard 1798 wb-2-121 (D)
Cross, Richard 1802 wb-2-262 (D)
Cross, Samuel 1840 wb-b-357 (G)
Cross, Shederick 1841 wb-1-71 (Sh)
Cross, William 1814 wb-A-41 (Li)
Cross, William 1826 wb-9-27 (D)
Cross, William 1853 wb-xx-323 (St)
Cross, William O. 1848 wb-2-34 (La)
Crosser, Henry W. 1846 wb-b-180 (We)
Crossland, Wright W. 1845 wb-12-517 (Rb)
Crosslin, William 1852 wb-7-0 (Sm)
Crossno, Elijah 1853 ib-1-226 (Wy)
Crossno, George 1849 ib-1-51 (Wy)
Crossno, Jane 1859 wb-1-307 (Be)
Crossno, Thomas 1849 ib-1-31 (Wy)
Crossno, Thomas 1861 ib-2-227 (Wy)
Crossthwait, Thomas 1816 rb-3-101 (Ru)
Crossway, John N. 1827 wb-9-113 (D)
Crossway, Livingston G. 1831 wb-9-484 (D)
Crossway, Nicholas 1823 wb-8-206 (D)
Crosswell, Nimrod 1853 wb-h-172 (Hu)
Crosswell, Nimrod 1854 wb-h-240 (Hu)
Crosswell, Richmond 1839 wb-d-322 (St)
Crosswhite, Abraham 1801 wb-1-5# (Ge)
Crosswhite, Jesse 1848 wb-1-46 (Jo)
Crosswhite, John 1847 wb-1-44 (Jo)
Crosswhite, William 1847 wb-1-41 (Jo)
Crosswy, Linnington 1832 wb-10-53 (D)
Crostick, Sherod 1844 wb-7-0 (Sm)
Crostwait, Shelton 1826 rb-6-223 (Ru)
Crotzer, Jacob 1844 rb-j-103 (Mt)
Crouch, Delcenia 1847 lw (Ct)
Crouch, Harden 1846 rb-k-113 (Mt)
Crouch, Jesse 1855 wb#24 (Gu)
Crouch, John 1814 Wb-2-66 (Wi)
Crouch, Joseph 1830? wb-#29 (Wa)
Crouse, Mathias 1855 wb-3-235 (Gr)
Crouse, Mathius 1831 rb-8-403 (Ru)
Crouse, Spencer 1860 rb-20-591 (Ru)
Crouse, William 1854 wb-h-10 (St)
Crow, Abel 1832 wb-b-203 (Ro)
Crow, Abel 1847 wb-e-45 (Ro)
Crow, Benjamin 1831 wb-#216 (Mu)
Crow, Benjamin S. 1858 wb-1-138 (R)
Crow, C. J. 1856 wb-j-102 (O)
Crow, Calvin J. 1858 wb-j-320 (O)

Crow, E. D. 1848 wb-b-259 (We)
Crow, Edwin D. 1848 wb-b-270 (We)
Crow, George 1832 wb-b-190 (Ro)
Crow, Isaac 1813 wb-2-32 (Wi)
Crow, James 1842 wb-c-235 (O)
Crow, Joanna 1822 wb-3-571 (Wi)
Crow, John 1827 wb-#41 (Mc)
Crow, Polly 1802 rb-a-158 (Mt)
Crow, Thomas 1854? wb-2-26 (Ct)
Crowder, Bartholomew 1854 wb-11-161 (Wi)
Crowder, George 1811 wb-1-0 (Sm)
Crowder, Isaac 1842 as-a-62 (Ms)
Crowder, Isaac 1848 wb-g-267 (Hn)
Crowder, John H. 1857 rb-o-336 (Mt)
Crowder, John R. 1854 as-b-146 (Ms)
Crowder, Joseph 1852 r39-1-228 (Dk)
Crowder, Miles 1837 rb-h-11 (Mt)
Crowder, Overstreet 1858 wb-#28 (Mo)
Crowder, Richard 1853 wb-d-157 (Wh)
Crowder, Richard 1854 wb-d-232 (Wh)
Crowder, William J. 1831 wb-5-81 (Wi)
Crowder, William R. 1857 wb-5-69 (Hr)
Crowell, Mathias 1853 wb-3-117 (Gr)
Crowley, Francis 1847 wb-4-251 (Hr)
Crowley, Lemuel 1840 rb-10-552 (Ru)
Crowson, Rhoda 1853 wb-a-427 (F)
Croxdale, Isham 1855 ib-2-145 (Cl)
Crozier, Hannah 1838 wb-6-293 (K)
Crozier, John 1838 wb-6-294 (K)
Crozier, John 1845 wb-1-116 (Hw)
Cruddock, Nancy 1846 wb-#150 (Wl)
Crudgington, John 1841 wb-1-44 (Me)
Crudupe, John 1809 wb-#7 (Wl)
Cruidson, Wm. N. 1845 as-b-276 (Di)
Cruise, Gilbert 1837 wb-#42 (Mc)
Crum, Eliza P. 1842 wb-7-590 (Wi)
Crum, Godfrey 1842 wb-a-95 (T)
Crum, Jacob 1858 wb-2-87# (Ge)
Crum, John 1810 wb-2-32# (Ge)
Crumbliss, James 1839 wb-c-70 (Ro)
Crumless, Ann 1858 wb-f-185 (Ro)
Crumley, George 1851 wb-1-10 (Su)
Crumley, George 1859 wb-1-10 (Su)
Crump, Adam 1817 lr (Sn)
Crump, Edmund 1801 wb-1-5# (Ge)
Crump, Findal 1824 wb-3-701 (Wi)
Crump, John O. 1849 wb-9-320 (Wi)
Crumpler, James 1847 wb-13-169 (Rb)
Crumpton, James 1847 wb-14-232 (Rb)
Crunk, John W. 1843 wb-#139 (Wl)
Cruse, Edmond 1819 wb-3-74 (K)

Cruse, Robert H. 1853 wb-n-107 (Mt)
Cruse?, Ephraim 1848 wb-g-266 (Hn)
Crutcher, Edmund 1847 wb-14-5 (D)
Crutcher, Foster G. 1851 wb-14-561 (D)
Crutcher, Mary Jane 1851 wb-14-660 (D)
Crutcher, Nancy 1844 wb-8-155 (Wi)
Crutcher, Preston L. 1845 wb-8-366 (Wi)
Crutcher, Samuel 1852 wb-15-192 (Rb)
Crutcher, Thomas 1844 wb-13-76 (D)
Crutcher, Thomas H. 1836 wb-10-626 (D)
Crutcher, Willis 1844 wb-8-138 (Wi)
Crutchfield, George 1823 wb-1-0 (Sm)
Crutchfield, H. C. (Dr.) 1834 wb-#104 (Wl)
Crutchfield, James 1854 wb-a-233 (Cr)
Crutchfield, James M. 1846 wb-#150 (Wl)
Crutchfield, John 1840 5-2-171 (Cl)
Crutchfield, John 1845 wb-g-10 (Hn)
Crutchfield, Martha E. 1861 wb-h-553 (Hn)
Crutchfield, O. F. (Dr.) 1840 wb-#128 (Wl)
Crutchfield, Orrand F. 1839 wb-#125 (Wl)
Crutchfield, Richard J. 1858 wb-#127 (Wl)
Crutchfield, Samuel 1841 wb-#136 (Wl)
Crutchfield, Samuel B. 1832 wb-#97 (Wl)
Crutchfield, Sarah 1827 rb-7-100 (Ru)
Crutchfield, Thomas 1833 wb-3-0 (Sm)
Crutchfield, Thomas 1849 wb-#42 (Mc)
Crutchfield, William 1812 wb-#12 (Wl)
Crye, William 1837 wb-#42 (Mc)
Cryer, John 1855 lr (Sn)
Cubbins, William 1849 r39-1-103 (Dk)
Cudgington, Abraham 1856 wb-f-7 (Ro)
Cuff, Ewell A. 1857 wb-h-638 (Hu)
Cuffman, Benjamin 1842 lr (Sn)
Culberson, Hiram 1837 wb-1-139 (Li)
Culberson, Joseph C. 1859 wb-k-69 (O)
Culbert, George 1823 wb-3-660 (Wi)
Culbertson, James B. 1849 wb-14-268 (Rb)
Culbertson, John W. 1860 wb-17-61 (Rb)
Culbertson, Samuel 1799 wb-#7 (Wa)
Cullender, G. D. 1850 wb#19 (Gu)
Cullendor, Joseph 1852 wb-3-135 (W)
Cullom, James N. 1852 wb-h-Nov (O)
Cullom, Jesse 1838 wb-11-202 (D)
Cullum, James 1859 wb-a-284 (T)
Cullum, Jessee 1838 wb-11-208 (D)
Cullum, Mary 1847 wb-f-127+ (O)
Cullum, Mary 1858 wb-j-380 (O)
Culp, Henry 1853 ib-1-253 (Wy)
Culp, Henry sr. 1853 ib-1-229 (Wy)
Culpepper, James H. 1857 wb-h-120 (Hn)
Cumings, Joseph 1847 wb-#161 (Wl)

Cumins, Samuel 1832 wb-5-202 (Wi)
Cummings, Aaron 1861 rb-p-556 (Mt)
Cummings, Andrew 1832 wb-1-18 (Bo)
Cummings, Andrew E. 1847 as-a-148 (Ms)
Cummings, Charles C. 1857 wb-1C-357 (A)
Cummings, David 1848 wb-c-291 (Wh)
Cummings, Elen 1847 wb-13-70 (Rb)
Cummings, James 1861 rb-p-556 (Mt)
Cummings, Joel 1845? wb-#149 (Wl)
Cummings, John 1818 wb-A-272 (Li)
Cummings, John 1843 wb-#140 (Wl)
Cummings, Lavena 1853 wb-15-398 (Rb)
Cummings, Mary 1861 wb-17-258 (Rb)
Cummings, Moses 1809 wb-1-127 (Sn)
Cummings, Robert E. 1861 wb-1D-7 (A)
Cummings, Silas 1823 wb-#48 (Wl)
Cummings, Thomas 1798 wb-1-46 (Sn)
Cummings, Virgil 1845 as-a-82 (Ms)
Cummings, William C. 1848 ib-1-35 (Ca)
Cummins, Benjamin 1857 wb-h-427 (St)
Cummins, David 1836 wb-6-200 (Wi)
Cummins, David H. 1834 rb-f-544 (Mt)
Cummins, Elisabeth 1842 wb-1-215 (Bo)
Cummins, Elisabeth 1844 wb-1-270 (Bo)
Cummins, Henry 1838 wb-7-3 (Wi)
Cummins, Jacob B. 1848 rb-l-180 (Mt)
Cummins, James 1818 wb-A-212 (Li)
Cummins, John 1804 rb-2-1 (Ru)
Cummins, Richard W. 1838 rb-10-130 (Ru)
Cummins, Sally 1833 rb-f-426 (Mt)
Cummins, Thomas 1860 wb-i-159 (St)
Cummins, Waller 1848 wb-9-43 (Wi)
Cummins, William 1838 wb-2-227 (Sn)
Cummins, William 1853 wb-15-476 (D)
Cumpton, Benjamin 1835 wb-x-255* (Mu)
Cumpton, Vinson 1807 wb-#5 (Wl)
Cuningham, William 1848 wb-f-127+ (O)
Cunningham, A. A. R. 1860 wb-k-483 (O)
Cunningham, Aaron 1845 wb-d-201 (Hd)
Cunningham, Abraham jr. 1840 wb-1-169 (Li)
Cunningham, Ann 1857 wb-3-429 (W)
Cunningham, Arabala 1798 wb-1-84 (Je)
Cunningham, Benjamin 1854 wb#23 (Gu)
Cunningham, Benjamin B. 1853 wb#21 (Gu)
Cunningham, Christopher 1783 wb-#2 (Wa)
Cunningham, D. C. 1858 wb-h-201 (Hn)
Cunningham, E. J. 1853 mr-2-526 (Be)
Cunningham, E. John 1812 wb-#12 (Wa)
Cunningham, E. T. 1851 mr-2-428 (Be)
Cunningham, Edmond 1858 wb-e-211 (Wh)
Cunningham, Enoch 1851 wb-15-10 (D)

Cunningham, Fleming 1860 wb-f-358 (G)
Cunningham, George 1814 wb-4-319 (D)
Cunningham, George 1854 wb-2-86 (Li)
Cunningham, Hugh 1857 wb-h-73 (Hn)
Cunningham, James 1819? wb-#42 (Mc)
Cunningham, James 1826 wb-4-194 (K)
Cunningham, James 1840 wb-a-141 (Di)
Cunningham, James 1845 wb-0-56 (Cf)
Cunningham, James A. 1852 wb-10-368 (Wi)
Cunningham, James H. 1857 wb-1-68 (Dy)
Cunningham, Jesse 1855 wb-#13 (Mo)
Cunningham, Jessee 1856 wb-12-305 (K)
Cunningham, John 1842 wb-1-450 (W)
Cunningham, John 1852 wb-g-441 (Hn)
Cunningham, John 1861 wb-18-429 (D)
Cunningham, John B. 1858 wb-16-646 (Rb)
Cunningham, John P. 1835 wb-6-26 (Wi)
Cunningham, Jonathan 1816 eb-1-56 (C)
Cunningham, Joseph 1822 wb-#70 (Wl)
Cunningham, Joseph 1859 wb-#28 (Mo)
Cunningham, Josiah 1827 wb-#71 (Wl)
Cunningham, Langston jr. 1836 wb-1-131 (W)
Cunningham, Lee 1858 wb-f-184 (G)
Cunningham, Margaret 1858 wb-1-42 (Se)
Cunningham, Martha 1824 wb-#20 (Wa)
Cunningham, Mathew 1841 wb-z-123 (Mu)
Cunningham, Melvina 1854 wb-3-200 (La)
Cunningham, Nancy 1842 wb-1-199 (Li)
Cunningham, Paul 1796 wb-1-53 (K)
Cunningham, Pleasant T. 1839 wb-#42 (Mc)
Cunningham, Robert sr. 1844 wb-1-242 (Li)
Cunningham, Samuel 1834 wb-x-206 (Mu)
Cunningham, Samuel 1857 wb-h-346 (St)
Cunningham, Samuel 1857 wb-h-351 (St)
Cunningham, Sarah 1847 as-b-378 (Di)
Cunningham, Valentine 1832 wb-b-202 (Ro)
Cunningham, William 1843 rb-12-312 (Ru)
Cunningham, William 1854 wb-0-131 (Cf)
Cunningham, William 1854 wb-3-216 (W)
Cunningham, William Henry Sr. 1843
    wb-#42 (Mc)
Cunningham, Willis 1857 as-c-443 (Di)
Cupboy, Timoty 1860 rb-p-385 (Mt)
Curd, Elizabeth 1841 wb-#133 (Wl)
Curd, John 1822 wb-#45 (Wl)
Curd, John 1837 rb-10-61 (Ru)
Curd, Richard 1844 wb-#143 (Wl)
Curd, Richard 1845 wb-#43 (Mc)
Curd, Thomas 1837 wb-#119 (Wl)
Curd, William 1842 wb-#138 (Wl)
Curd, William E. 1861 wb-#136 (Wl)

Curfman, William 1833 wb-10-157 (D)
Curl, Bryant 1852 mr-2-466 (Be)
Curl, John T. 1859 wb-3-520 (Gr)
Curl, John T. 1859 wb-4-14 (Gr)
Curl, Seth 1839 wb-11-556 (D)
Curl, Susannah 1861 wb-4-29 (Gr)
Curl, Wilson 1803 rb-a-167 (Mt)
Curle, John 1812 rb-2-210 (Ru)
Curlee, Calvin 1851 ib-1-183 (Ca)
Curlee, Rebecca 1857 wb-A-120 (Ca)
Curles, Lockey 1850 wb-2-67 (Sh)
Curley, John B. 1853 wb-15-484 (D)
Curlin, John 1858 wb-7-19 (Ma)
Curnut, William 1840 eb-1-422 (C)
Currey, Isaac N. 1840 wb-#131 (Wl)
Currey, John 1840 wb-#131 (Wl)
Currey, Samuel 1830 wb-1-102 (Hw)
Currie, James 1842 wb-2-524 (Hy)
Currie, John 1835 wb-c-394 (St)
Currie, Margarett 1838 mr-1-289 (Be)
Currie, Mary (Mrs) 1835 rb-9-226 (Ru)
Currin, Ann S. 1854 wb-16-417 (D)
Currin, Barsheba 1857 wb-12-464 (Wi)
Currin, James 1848 wb-a-331 (F)
Currin, Jas. D. 1859 gs-1-320 (F)
Currin, John 1830 wb-9-459 (D)
Currin, John 1858 wb-17-487 (D)
Currin, John M. 1852 wb-10-389 (Wi)
Currin, Jonathan 1843 rb-12-412 (Ru)
Currin, Robert P. 1857 wb-c-166 (L)
Curry, Isaac 1851 wb-2-208 (La)
Curry, James 1845 wb-a2-194 (Mu)
Curry, James sr. 1842 wb-z-338 (Mu)
Curry, John 1835 wb-2-201 (Sn)
Curry, Nancy 1848 wb-2-41 (La)
Curry, Robert B. 1849 wb-14-443 (D)
Curry, Robert B. 1861 wb-18-433 (D)
Curry, Samuel 1812 wb-1-94 (Hw)
Curry, Thomas 1818 lr (Sn)
Curry, Thomas 1858 wb-4-84 (La)
Curtain, John 1830 wb-1-143 (Su)
Curtis, Aaron D. 1825 wb-3-766 (Wi)
Curtis, Benjamin 1827 wb-4-211 (Wi)
Curtis, Benjamin 1828 wb-4-299 (Wi)
Curtis, Clement N. 1857 wb-1-70 (Dy)
Curtis, Daniel 1824 wb-3-292 (St)
Curtis, Fanny 1843 wb-12-424* (D)
Curtis, Francis 1827 wb-9-134 (D)
Curtis, Francis 1841 wb-12-147* (D)
Curtis, James 1829 wb-1-12 (La)
Curtis, James 1838 wb-a-38 (L)

Curtis, James 1867 wb-#15 (Mo)
Curtis, Joel 1839 wb-c-168 (Hu)
Curtis, John 1829 wb-1-50 (W)
Curtis, John 1830 wb-1-53 (W)
Curtis, John 1838 wb-y-330 (Mu)
Curtis, John 1844 wb-#43 (Mc)
Curtis, John jr. 1828 wb-1-33 (W)
Curtis, Joshua 1819 wb-7-325 (D)
Curtis, Joshua 1841 wb-z-249 (Mu)
Curtis, Joshua 1857 wb-1-179 (Be)
Curtis, Martha A. 1846 wb-a2-444 (Mu)
Curtis, Mary 1852 lw (Ct)
Curtis, Rice 1798 wb-2-139 (D)
Curtis, Thomas 1836 wb-b-230 (Wh)
Curtner, George 1852 wb-h-Nov (O)
Curton, Isaac 1856 wb-2-291 (Me)
Cusick, Samuel 1861 wb-1-76 (Se)
Cutchen, Joshua 1826 wb-9-37 (D)
Cutchen, Samuel 1830 wb-9-440 (D)
Cutchin, Mourning 1841 wb-12-175* (D)
Cuthbertson, Jessee 1854 wb-n-558 (Mt)
Cuthbertson, Jessee 1855 wb-n-569 (Mt)
Cuthbertson, John 1811 rb-b-8 (Mt)
Cutrell, Samuel 1817 wb-A-232 (Li)
Cutshall, Frederick 1845 148-1-128 (Ge)
Cutshall, John jr. 1858 149-1-130 (Ge)
Cutshall, John sr. 1856 149-1-51 (Ge)
Cuttshall, Frederick 1830 wb-2-32# (Ge)
Cypert, Jesse 1858 ib-2-101 (Wy)
Cypert, Robert 1851 ib-1-110 (Wy)
Cyrumn (Cynum?), Mark 1826 wb-#133 (Mu)

- D -

Dabbs, Henry B. 1851 wb-15-203 (D)
Dabbs, James 1844 wb-3-29 (Sn)
Dabbs, John 1857 6-2-128 (Le)
Dabbs, John R. 1847 wb-14-40 (D)
Dabbs, Joseph 1849 wb-4-483 (Hr)
Dabbs, Joseph 1850 wb-4-582* (Hr)
Dabbs, Richard 1825 wb-8-483 (D)
Dabney, Charles A. 1830 wb-4-472 (Wi)
Dabney, E. J. (Mrs.) 1856 rb-o-56 (Mt)
Dabney, E. J. 1855 wb-n-498 (Mt)
Dabney, Elizabeth 1852 wb-n-512 (Mt)
Dabney, Frances 1846 rb-k-326 (Mt)
Dabney, J. T. 1847 rb-k-578 (Mt)
Dabney, John 1831 wb-5-21 (Wi)
Dabney, John T. 1833 rb-f-520 (Mt)
Dabney, Mary E. 1837 wb-6-298 (Wi)
Dabney, Mildred 1846 rb-k-269 (Mt)

Dabney, Samuel (Dr.) 1835 rb-g-101 (Mt)
Dabney, Samuel 1829 rb-e-402 (Mt)
Dabney, William 1828 wb-4-338 (Wi)
Dabney, William 1828 wb-4-351 (Wi)
Dabney, William H. 1836 rb-g-389 (Mt)
Dacus, Alexander 1854 wb-a-213 (T)
Dade, Lucien 1855 wb-n-593 (Mt)
Daffin, James Thomas 1852 wb-2-117 (Sh)
Dagley, Grace 1859 iv-C-35 (C)
Dagley, Joseph 1836 eb-1-332 (C)
Dail, Abner 1843 wb-5-242 (Gr)
Dail, Ira 1854 wb-3-196 (Gr)
Dail, Jesse F. 1856 wb-3-308 (Gr)
Dailey, John H. 1830 wb-4-406 (K)
Dailey, Richard 1832 rb-f-336 (Mt)
Dailey, Richard 1848 rb-l-7 (Mt)
Dailey, Richard E. 1846 rb-k-118 (Mt)
Daimwood, Jacob 1846 wb-a2-421 (Mu)
Dairs, John 1830 wb-1-14 (La)
Dalaney, Henry Rozier 1852 wb-15-283 (D)
Dalaney, Henry Rozier 1852 wb-15-284 (D)
Dale, A. M. 1855 wb-5-39 (La)
Dale, Abel 1837 wb-1-243 (Gr)
Dale, Amelia 1854 wb-e-233 (G)
Dale, Francis H. 1847 wb-14-116 (D)
Dale, Henry 1838 wb-b-32 (O)
Dale, John 1833 wb-b-126 (Wh)
Dale, John 1847 wb-c-266 (Wh)
Dale, John H. 1849 wb-c-371 (Wh)
Dale, Nathaniel M. 1853 wb-3-129 (La)
Dale, Thomas 1815 wb-2-0 (Sm)
Dale, Thomas jr. 1832 wb-2-0 (Sm)
Dale, Thomas sr. 1812 wb-1-0 (Sm)
Dale, William 1845 wb-a-64 (Dk)
Daley, James Oneal 1839 wb-1-7# (Ge)
Daley, Nathan 1847 wb-d-70 (G)
Daley, William 1858 rb-o-542 (Mt)
Dallace, Robert 1838 wb-#124 (Wl)
Dallas, Joshua 1849 wb-g-152 (O)
Dallas, Martha 1849 wb-g-92 (O)
Dallas, Matilda 1849 wb-g-165 (O)
Dally, Joseph G. 1843 wb-13-2 (D)
Dalton, Andrew 1843 wb-d-64 (Ro)
Dalton, Bradly 1847 wb-4-158 (Hr)
Dalton, Carter T. 1856 wb-3-319 (Gr)
Dalton, Carter T. 1858 wb-4-8 (Gr)
Dalton, Charles 1823 wb-a-37 (Hn)
Dalton, David 1823 wb-A-328 (Li)
Dalton, Isaac 1829 wb-#174 (Mu)
Dalton, John 1833 lr (Sn)
Dalton, John 1858 wb-12-539 (Wi)

Dalton, Martin 1847 wb-a-149 (Cr)
Dalton, P. P. 1854 ib-H-128 (F)
Dalton, T. P. 1854 ib-H-198 (F)
Dalton, William 1819 wb-1-0 (Sm)
Dalton, William 1844 wb-d-226 (O)
Dalton, Wm. S. 1843 wb-1-257 (La)
Daly, William 1854 lr (Gi)
Dalzell, Francis 1823 wb-1-147 (Hw)
Dame, David 1851 wb-2-179 (La)
Dame, James M. 1859 wb-4-42 (La)
Dameron, Phebia 1851 rb-15-568 (Ru)
Dameron, Tegner 1824 rb-6-54 (Ru)
Dameron, Tigner 1824 rb-6-57 (Ru)
Dames, David 1857 wb-1-107 (R)
Damewood, Boston 1841 wb-10-592 (Rb)
Damewood, Boston 1841 wb-10-595 (Rb)
Damewood, Henry 1859 wb-13-132 (K)
Damewood, Jacob 1812 wb-2-37 (K)
Damewood, John 1841 wb-7-196 (K)
Damewood, Malachi 1836 wb-6-38 (K)
Damewood, Malachiah 1836 wb-6-7 (K)
Damrell, Joseph 1817 wb-A-193 (Li)
Dance, Jacob 1815 wb-A-83 (Li)
Dance, John 1829 rb-f-14 (Mt)
Dance, John E. 1858 wb-#125 (Wl)
Dance, Russell 1839 wb-11-574 (D)
Dance, Stephen M. 1853 wb-2-62 (Li)
Dance, Thomas 1849 wb-1-371 (Li)
Dancer, Ulric M. 1822 wb-8-96 (D)
Dandridge, Robert A. 1839 wb-2-136 (Hr)
Daniel, Alexander 1857 rb-19-71 (Ru)
Daniel, David 1858 wb-h-454 (St)
Daniel, Edward 1833 wb-1-14 (Gr)
Daniel, Edward 1854 wb-11-319 (Wi)
Daniel, Ezekiel 1839 as-a-4 (Ma)
Daniel, Isaac 1850 33-3-304 (Gr)
Daniel, Isaac W. 1849 lr (Gi)
Daniel, J. P. 1858 rb-19-320 (Ru)
Daniel, James 1817 wb-a-84 (Wh)
Daniel, James 1845 mr-2-157 (Be)
Daniel, James M. 1836 wb-d-240 (Hn)
Daniel, Jeabud 1856 rb-17-691 (Ru)
Daniel, John 1813 wb-A-26 (Li)
Daniel, John 1836 wb-1-215 (Gr)
Daniel, John 1849 lr (Sn)
Daniel, John 1853 wb-A-91 (Ca)
Daniel, Joseph 1842 wb-5-182 (Gr)
Daniel, Kisiah 1844 wb-e-620 (Hu)
Daniel, Mary 1847 wb-b-129 (Mu)
Daniel, Mary E. 1847 rb-14-174 (Ru)
Daniel, Meredith 1847 wb-a-125 (T)

Daniel, Noah 1858 wb-2-24 (Ct)
Daniel, R. H. C. 1858 rb-o-631 (Mt)
Daniel, R. T. 1859 wb-i-108 (St)
Daniel, Simon 1853 wb-f-25 (Mu)
Daniel, Simon 1857 wb-h-439 (St)
Daniel, Susannah O. 1839 5-2-98 (Cl)
Daniel, Teabud 1854 rb-17-2 (Ru)
Daniel, Thomas 1834 wb-c-147 (Hn)
Daniel, W. V. 1826 wb-1-156 (Ma)
Daniel, William 1800 wb-#8 (Wa)
Daniel, William 1814 wb-a-25 (Wh)
Daniel, William 1836 wb-0-3 (Cf)
Daniel, William R. 1849 ib-1-44 (Wy)
Daniel, William W. 1834 wb-x-187 (Mu)
Daniel, Wilson 1828 wb-b-252 (St)
Daniel, Woodard 1840 wb-e-107 (Hn)
Daniel, Woodrow 1827 wb-b-160 (St)
Daniel, Woodson 1827 wb-b-180 (St)
Daniels, Henry 1855 wb-16-595 (D)
Daniels, William 1857 rb-o-441 (Mt)
Daniels, William 1857 rb-o-442 (Mt)
Danill, William 1828 wb-#167 (Mu)
Danley, Sarah 1860 wb-17-60 (Rb)
Danly, William D. 1858 wb-h-218 (Hn)
Dannel, Eden 1828 rb-7-190 (Ru)
Dannell, Jessey 1827 lr (Sn)
Danner, David S. 1856 wb-12-230 (K)
Danniel, Ann 1852 wb-2-122 (Sh)
Dansey, William 1818 rb-4-157 (Ru)
Danson, O. P. 1847 wb-b-156 (Mu)
Dansy? (Dasy?), William S. 1814 rb-1-165 (Ru)
Darby, George W. 1842 wb-c-86 (G)
Darby, Hugh 1840 mr-1-316 (Be)
Darby, Hugh 1840 mr-2-5 (Be)
Darby, Thomas B. 1855 wb-g-707 (Hn)
Darden, Carr 1831 wb-7-338 (Rb)
Darden, Cindarella 1835 wb-9-174 (Rb)
Darden, Henry 1814 wb-2-152 (Rb)
Darden, Henry 1834 wb-8-422 (Rb)
Darden, Hezekiah 1841 wb-11-256 (Rb)
Darden, Hezekiah 1841 wb-11-69 (Rb)
Darden, Holland 1831 wb-7-322 (Rb)
Darden, Jesse 1860 wb-17-12 (Rb)
Darden, Jonathan 1814 wb-2-160 (Rb)
Darden, Martha 1844 wb-12-212 (Rb)
Darden, Patience 1829 rb-e-404 (Mt)
Darden, Williamson 1821 wb-3-353 (Rb)
Dardin, Ann 1798 wb-1-24 (Rb)
Dardis, Edward 1837 wb-6-126 (K)
Dardis, Margaret 1852 wb-11-229 (K)
Dardis, Thomas 1810 wb-1-317 (K)

Dardis, Thomas 1832 wb-5-135 (K)
Dardon?, Johnathan 1834 wb-b-42 (G)
Daren, Henry 1852 wb-11-218 (K)
Dark, Elijah 1853 wb-3-146 (W)
Dark, Henry E. 1854 as-b-151 (Ms)
Dark, Jas. 1855 as-b-196 (Ms)
Dark, Micajah 1820 wb-#98 (Mu)
Darnal, Jarrat 1826 lr (Sn)
Darnald, Morgan 1840 wb-b-18 (We)
Darnald, Nicholas 1810 wb-1-349 (Rb)
Darnall, Nicholas 1824 wb-a-42 (Hn)
Darnell, Benjamin 1815 rb-b-249 (Mt)
Darnell, Celia 1852 wb-g-433 (Hn)
Darnell, Celia 1854 wb-g-601 (Hn)
Darnell, Cornelius 1835 wb-1-120 (Li)
Darnell, Davis 1854 wb-3-174 (W)
Darnell, Elizabeth 1854 wb-3-208 (Sn)
Darnell, James 1860 wb-k-248 (O)
Darnell, T. L. 1853 wb-g-526 (Hn)
Darnell, Thomas P. 1853 wb-h-Mar (O)
Darnold, Elizabeth 1838 wb-2-295 (Ma)
Darnold, Nicholas sr. 1830 wb-b-102 (Hn)
Darr, Daniel 1831 rb-f-235 (Mt)
Darr, Henry 1814 wb-2-134 (Rb)
Darr, Henry sr. 1855 wb-6-142 (Ma)
Darrow, Christopher 1848 wb-14-1 (Rb)
Darrow, Mary 1848 wb-g-33 (St)
Dauge, Enock 1842 wb-12-322* (D)
Dauge, Enock 1842 wb-12-373* (D)
Daugharty, Mary Ann 1848 as-a-169 (Ms)
Daugherty, Asa 1838 wb-1-403 (Hy)
Daugherty, Dennis 1843 wb-f-17 (St)
Daugherty, Dennis 1845 wb-f-255 (St)
Daugherty, Edmond 1853 wb-3-145 (La)
Daugherty, James 1845 wb-1-122 (Sh)
Daugherty, John 1849 wb-#44 (Mc)
Daugherty, John 1857 wb-#12 (Mo)
Daugherty, Michael 1806 wb-1-578 (Hw)
Daughton, M. M. 1849 rb-l-505 (Mt)
Daughton, Molder M. 1850 rb-l-547 (Mt)
Daughty, George 1847 wb-14-36 (D)
Dauncy, Jonathan 1821 wb-#41 (Wl)
Dausy, William 1812 rb-2-265 (Ru)
Davenport, Absolem 1853 ib-1-262 (Ca)
Davenport, Hardy 1827 wb-#69 (Wl)
Davenport, Hughston 1831 wb-5-72 (Wi)
Davenport, Samuel W. 1856 wb-c-95 (L)
Davenport, William 1827 wb-4-212 (K)
Davenport, William 1856 wb-12-223 (K)
Davey, Gabriel 1853 wb-5-129 (Ma)
Davey, Richard 1839 wb-b-165 (Hd)

David L(!), Claudias 1817? wb-a-26 (Di)
David, Isaac 1844 wb-d-129 (Hd)
David, Isaiah 1815 wb-#18 (Wl)
David, James 1823 wb-8-278 (D)
David, Lewis 1837 eb-1-355 (C)
David, Sampson 1826 eb-1-156 (C)
Davids, Samuel 1795 wb-1-37 (K)
Davidson, A. F. 1858 wb-f-217 (G)
Davidson, A. S. 1840 wb-b-316 (G)
Davidson, Absolom 1856 rb-o-60 (Mt)
Davidson, Andrew W. 1834 wb-a-7 (O)
Davidson, Bryant 1841 wb-1-237 (La)
Davidson, E. 1834 wb-1-335 (Hr)
Davidson, Elihu 1835 wb-1-397 (Hr)
Davidson, Elizabeth 1848 wb-g-107 (Hu)
Davidson, Ephraim B. 1825 wb-b-43 (St)
Davidson, Francis 1832 wb-x-29 (Mu)
Davidson, George 1812 wb-#5 (Mu)
Davidson, George 1823 wb-#45 (Mu)
Davidson, George 1833 wb-a-101 (Di)
Davidson, George 1838 wb-y-248* (Mu)
Davidson, George 1845 as-b-227 (Di)
Davidson, George 1845 as-b-269 (Di)
Davidson, George 1861 wb-f-219 (Mu)
Davidson, Gilbreath 1823 wb-#99 (Mu)
Davidson, Green 1816 wb-3-154 (St)
Davidson, Hugh 1841 wb-0-23 (Cf)
Davidson, James 1809 wb-2-34 (Je)
Davidson, James 1816 rb-3-122 (Ru)
Davidson, James C. 1845 wb-9-49 (K)
Davidson, John 1802 rb-a-151 (Mt)
Davidson, John 1822 rb-5-185 (Ru)
Davidson, John 1824 wb-#139 (Mu)
Davidson, John 1833 wb-#102 (Wl)
Davidson, John D. 1853 wb-e-112 (G)
Davidson, John sr. 1839 wb-a-139 (Di)
Davidson, Malinda 1856 wb-3-333 (Gr)
Davidson, Malinda M. 1855 wb-3-264 (Gr)
Davidson, Nancy 1838 wb-2-358 (Ma)
Davidson, Racheal 1849 wb-2-51 (Sh)
Davidson, Rosanna 1835 wb-x-328 (Mu)
Davidson, Sarah 1859 6-2-146 (Le)
Davidson, Thomas 1816? wb-#36 (Mu)
Davidson, Thomas 1825? as-A-103 (Di)
Davidson, Thomas 1853 as-c-225 (Di)
Davidson, William 1817 wb-1-177 (Bo)
Davidson, William 1817 wb-A-172 (Li)
Davidson, William G. 1842 wb-c-44 (G)
Davidson, William R. 1844 wb-c-202 (G)
Davidson, Wilson L. 1833 wb-#99 (Wl)
Davidson, Wilson Y. 1835 wb-#107 (Wl)

Davie, George N. 1835 wb-2-53 (Ma)
Davie, James 1847 rb-k-651 (Mt)
Davie, James 1858 rb-o-572 (Mt)
Davie, John 1830 rb-f-21 (Mt)
Davie, Jones 1847 rb-k-431 (Mt)
Davie, Jones 1860 rb-p-337 (Mt)
Davie, Kendal 1834 rb-g-28 (Mt)
Davie, Kendal 1834 rb-g-61 (Mt)
Davie, Tabitha 1855 wb-6-120 (Ma)
Davie, Thomas 1798 wb-2-118 (D)
Davies, James 1796 wb-0-14 (K)
Davis (Davice?), William 1830 wb-#44 (Mc)
Davis, A. 1837 wb-d-136* (Hn)
Davis, A. H. 1848 wb-4-368 (Hr)
Davis, Abner N. 1860 wb-8-41 (Sm)
Davis, Absalom 1835 rb-g-108 (Mt)
Davis, Absalom 1854 wb-n-484 (Mt)
Davis, Adam 1839 wb-2-63 (Hr)
Davis, Alexander 1855 as-b-197 (Ms)
Davis, Ammon 1807 wb-1-27 (Wi)
Davis, Amos 1834 wb-1-105 (Li)
Davis, Andrew 1815 wb-4-392 (D)
Davis, Andrew 1816 wb-7-7 (D)
Davis, Andrew 1851 wb-5-102 (Ma)
Davis, Ann 1840 wb-e-147 (Hn)
Davis, Archibald 1825 wb-#55 (Wl)
Davis, Archibald 1835 wb-d-101 (Hn)
Davis, Asa 1844 as-b-206 (Di)
Davis, Asa 1858 wb-1-165 (Hw)
Davis, B. F. 1859 wb-f-303 (Ro)
Davis, Babby 1847 rb-14-40 (Ru)
Davis, Basil 1818 wb-a-109 (Ro)
Davis, Benjamin 1826 wb-b-2 (Hn)
Davis, Benjamin 1834 wb-3-317 (Je)
Davis, Benjamin 1843 wb-z-508 (Mu)
Davis, Benjamin 1845 wb-a2-310 (Mu)
Davis, Benjamin 1851 wb-d-299 (G)
Davis, Benjamin 1852 wb-5-19 (Je)
Davis, Benjamin 1859 wb-f-321 (G)
Davis, Benjamin sr. 1795 wb-1-204 (Je)
Davis, Benjamin sr. 1829 wb-3-43 (Je)
Davis, Betsy 1838? wb-#121 (Wl)
Davis, Bradford 1818 wb-3-24 (K)
Davis, Burgess B. 1853 wb-5-133 (Ma)
Davis, C. B. 1855 wb-a-383 (Ms)
Davis, C. R. 1857 ib-1-453 (Ca)
Davis, Charles 1826 rb-6-223 (Ru)
Davis, Charles 1850 rb-l-594 (Mt)
Davis, Charles 1861 wb-3e-177 (Sh)
Davis, Charles F. 1848 wb-9-90 (Wi)
Davis, Christen 1854 wb-a-337 (Ms)

Davis, Clement R. 1857 ib-1-458 (Ca)
Davis, Cyrus 1834 wb-c-218 (Hn)
Davis, Daniel 1820 wb-#42 (Mu)
Davis, Daniel 1827 wb-#160 (Mu)
Davis, Daniel S. 1851 wb-2-45 (Me)
Davis, David 1805 Wb-1-126 (Wi)
Davis, David 1831 wb-#236 (Mu)
Davis, David 1838 rb-h-150 (Mt)
Davis, David 1861 rb-p-619 (Mt)
Davis, Delila 1855 wb-7-0 (Sm)
Davis, E. S. 1851 wb-11-116 (K)
Davis, Edward 1859 wb-7-49 (Ma)
Davis, Elbert 1851 wb-11-76 (K)
Davis, Elijah L. 1858 wb-17-478 (D)
Davis, Elisha 1803 wb-2-297 (D)
Davis, Elisha 1821 wb-8-12 (D)
Davis, Elisha 1836 wb-6-153 (Wi)
Davis, Elizabeth 1809 rb-2-85 (Ru)
Davis, Elizabeth 1827 wb-2-580 (Je)
Davis, Elizabeth 1847 wb-f-127+ (O)
Davis, Elizabeth 1852 wb-4-551 (Mu)
Davis, Elizabeth 1854 rb-17-160 (Ru)
Davis, Elizabeth jr. 1812 rb-2-200 (Ru)
Davis, Elizabeth sr. 1812 rb-2-210 (Ru)
Davis, Enoch 1797 wb-2-95 (D)
Davis, Ephraim 1846 wb-c-230 (Wh)
Davis, F. M. 1856 wb-#119 (Wl)
Davis, Fields 1810 ib-1-302 (Ge)
Davis, Foster 1815 wb-1-0 (Sm)
Davis, Francis 1832 wb-9-619 (D)
Davis, Franklin R. 1847 r39-1-26 (Dk)
Davis, Fredrick 1831 wb-5-75 (Wi)
Davis, G. W. 1849 wb-g-344 (Hn)
Davis, Gabriel 1854 wb-h-38 (St)
Davis, Gardner 1836 wb-2-203 (Sn)
Davis, George 1849 wb-9-220 (Wi)
Davis, George 1856 wb-12-304 (K)
Davis, George 1856 wb-f-29 (Ro)
Davis, George W. 1859 wb-13-134 (K)
Davis, Gideon 1855 wb-g-657 (Hn)
Davis, H. 1855 wb-e-266 (G)
Davis, H. W. 1861 wb-1-385 (Be)
Davis, Hamelton W. 1838 wb-11-290 (D)
Davis, Hardy 1816 wb-3-186 (St)
Davis, Harvy 1847 wb-8-561 (Wi)
Davis, Hatch 1852 wb-15-249 (D)
Davis, Henry 1843 wb-#140 (Wl)
Davis, Henry 1851 wb-#175 (Wl)
Davis, Henry W. 1847 wb-b-142 (Mu)
Davis, Hezekiah 1843 as-a-69 (Ms)
Davis, Hezekiah 1852 wb-h-Feb (O)

Davis, Holcome 1836 wb-6-118 (Wi)
Davis, Hollon 1836 wb-6-163 (Wi)
Davis, Hollon 1836 wb-6-259 (Wi)
Davis, Howell Tatum 1860 wb-18-376 (D)
Davis, Hugh 1840 wb-3-210 (Ma)
Davis, Ira P. 1848 rb-14-435 (Ru)
Davis, Isaac 1830 as-a-202 (Di)
Davis, Isaac 1832 as-a-223 (Di)
Davis, Isaac 1839 rb-h-349 (Mt)
Davis, Isaac 1855 wb-3-254 (Gr)
Davis, Isaac 1855 wb-3-271 (Gr)
Davis, Isabella J. 1856 wb-1-25 (Se)
Davis, Isham 1837 wb-#120 (Wl)
Davis, Isham F. 1846 wb-c-328 (G)
Davis, J. H. 1859 lr (Sn)
Davis, James 1807 wb-#9 (Wl)
Davis, James 1829 wb-1-31 (Bo)
Davis, James 1831 wb-b-112 (Wh)
Davis, James 1837 wb-1A-172 (A)
Davis, James 1842 as-a-66 (Ms)
Davis, James 1842 rb-12-166 (Ru)
Davis, James 1846 wb-e-238 (O)
Davis, James 1847 rb-l-134 (Mt)
Davis, James 1855 wb-3-233 (Gr)
Davis, James 1857 rb-o-290 (Mt)
Davis, James 1859 wb-b-77 (F)
Davis, James 1859 wb-k-88 (O)
Davis, James G. 1847 wb-5-51 (Ma)
Davis, James H. 1848 wb-#167 (Wl)
Davis, James H. 1858 wb-f-205 (G)
Davis, James M. 1836 wb-#114 (Wl)
Davis, James M. 1842 rb-12-83 (Ru)
Davis, James M. 1856 wb-4-1 (La)
Davis, James R. 1837 wb-6-358 (Wi)
Davis, James R. 1839 wb-#44 (Mc)
Davis, James S. 1851? wb-1B-289 (A)
Davis, Jane (Mrs.) 1851 wb-d-336 (G)
Davis, Jane 1849 wb-10-149 (K)
Davis, Jerome B. 1861 wb-18-480 (D)
Davis, Jerry 1855 ib-h-448 (F)
Davis, Jesse 1817 wb-A-176 (Li)
Davis, Jesse 1823 wb-1-7# (Ge)
Davis, Jesse 1848 148-1-236 (Ge)
Davis, Jesse 1848 wb-14-46 (Rb)
Davis, Jesse S. 1854 wb-#112 (Wl)
Davis, Joel 1824 wb-2-442 (Je)
Davis, John 1797 wb-1-185 (Je)
Davis, John 1807 as-1-161 (Ge)
Davis, John 1815 wb-1-0 (Sm)
Davis, John 1820 rb-4-215 (Ru)
Davis, John 1824 wb-8-289 (D)

Davis, Thomas 1816 wb-2-225 (K)
Davis, Thomas 1826 wb-1-7# (Ge)
Davis, Thomas 1848 ib-1-86 (Cl)
Davis, Thomas 1848 wb-14-268 (D)
Davis, Thomas 1856 wb-2-84# (Ge)
Davis, Thomas 1858 149-1-125 (Ge)
Davis, Thomas 1859 wb-2-89# (Ge)
Davis, Thomas G. 1841 wb-a-22 (Dk)
Davis, Turner 1861 wb-13-402 (Wi)
Davis, William 1808 wb-1-179 (Wi)
Davis, William 1820 wb-7-454 (D)
Davis, William 1825 wb-a-203 (Wh)
Davis, William 1836 rb-9-297 (Ru)
Davis, William 1842 wb-z-418 (Mu)
Davis, William 1843 wb-1-253 (La)
Davis, William 1844 wb-#148 (Wl)
Davis, William 1847 wb-e-29 (Ro)
Davis, William 1850 wb-e-242 (Ro)
Davis, William 1853 wb#21 (Gu)
Davis, William 1855 wb-3-279 (Gr)
Davis, William 1856 as-c-34 (Ms)
Davis, William A. 1834 wb-1-109 (Li)
Davis, William A. 1840 wb-2-141 (Hr)
Davis, William C. 1856 wb-#122 (Wl)
Davis, William H. 1835 wb-#106 (Wl)
Davis, Wilson 1839 wb-7-53 (Wi)
Davis, Wilson B. 1839 wb-7-59 (Wi)
Davis, Wm. H. 1852 rb-16-323 (Ru)
Davis, Wm. L. 1838 rb-10-173 (Ru)
Davis?, John 1830 rb-f-84 (Mt)
Davy, Thomas 1797 wb-2-92 (D)
Dawsen, John 1800 wb-2-178 (D)
Dawson, Absolum 1854 wb-n-430 (Mt)
Dawson, Benjamin 1836 wb-2-101 (Ma)
Dawson, Daniel 1833 wb-c-301 (St)
Dawson, Dewit A. 1854 wb-xx-368 (St)
Dawson, Dewit A. 1854 wb-xx-397 (St)
Dawson, Elijah 1816 wb-3-211 (St)
Dawson, F. G. 1854 wb-g-574 (Hn)
Dawson, Fleming G. 1854 wb-g-557 (Hn)
Dawson, Isaac 1805 as-1-110 (Ge)
Dawson, James 1843 wb-3-13 (Hr)
Dawson, Jas. C. 1842 wb-2-388 (Hr)
Dawson, John 1841 wb-3-0 (Sm)
Dawson, John 1843 wb-z-567 (Mu)
Dawson, John 1851 wb-15-22 (D)
Dawson, L. 1832 rb-f-331 (Mt)
Dawson, Larkin 1823 as-A-60 (Di)
Dawson, O. P. 1847 wb-b-173 (Mu)
Dawson, Onis? P. 1849 wb-b-544 (Mu)
Dawson, Stephen N. 1856 rb-o-33 (Mt)

Dawson, Thomas 1815 wb-#15 (Mu)
Dawson, Willis L. 1828 rb-e-329 (Mt)
Dawson, Zacheriah 1800 wb-2-174 (D)
Day, Edward H. 1860 wb-7-63 (Ma)
Day, George N. 1836 wb-2-97 (Ma)
Day, Henson 1838 wb-1-168 (La)
Day, John 1842 5-2-286 (Cl)
Day, John 1854 ib-2-85* (Cl)
Day, John H. 1856 wb-6-283 (Ma)
Day, John sr. 1834 wb-3-285 (Je)
Day, Mary Ann 1850 wb-e-222 (Ro)
Day, Matthew 1819 wb-3-187 (Rb)
Day, Nathaniel 1810 wb-1-348 (Je)
Day, Phillip 1834 wb-3-0 (Sm)
Day, Samuel 1851 wb-11-21 (K)
Day, Sarah 1847 wb-9-312 (K)
Day, Stephen 1811 wb-2-1 (Je)
Day, Stephen 1811 wb-2-12 (Je)
Dayley, Elijah 1846 wb-d-20 (G)
Dazey, Amanda M. 1860 as-c-181 (Ms)
Dazey, Jasper 1849 wb-a-204 (Ms)
Dazey, Kindal 1854 wb-a-326 (Ms)
DeGraffenried, Metcalf 1839 wb-7-183 (Wi)
DeGrove, Q. C. 1861 wb-18-451 (D)
DeGrove, Quincy C. 1861 wb-18-533 (D)
DeLaHay, John H. 1860 wb-18-249 (D)
DeVault, Frederick 1847 wb-#47 (Wa)
Deaderick, David 1825 wb-#20 (Wa)
Deaderick, David 1837 wb-#44 (Mc)
Deaderick, George M. 1832 wb-10-56 (D)
Deaderick, William H. 1858 wb-#45 (Mc)
Deadman, William H. 1846 wb-a2-490 (Mu)
Deadrick, George M. 1817 wb-7-149 (D)
Deadrick, George M. 1851 wb-14-671 (D)
Deadrik, John 1798 wb-2-105 (D)
Deal, Eliza 1860 wb-18-161 (D)
Deal, Elizaeth 1855 wb-16-460 (D)
Deal, Joseph 1831 wb-#225 (Mu)
Deale, Henry 1838 wb-b-298 (O)
Dean, Aaron 1845 wb-#45 (Mc)
Dean, Benjamin 1819 wb-a-112 (Wh)
Dean, Charity 1839 wb-1-292 (W)
Dean, Francis 1801 wb-1-43 (Je)
Dean, Francis 1829 wb-4-445 (Wi)
Dean, Francis 1839 wb-1-275 (W)
Dean, James 1818 wb-7-224 (D)
Dean, James M. 1840 wb-1-174 (Li)
Dean, Jas. 1802 wb-2-229 (D)
Dean, Lucy 1849 wb-3-20 (W)
Dean, Luke H. 1814 wb-#9 (Mu)
Dean, Michael 1836 wb-1-153 (W)

Dean, Richard 1827 wb-4-159 (Wi)
Dean, William 1816 wb-#22 (Mu)
Dean, William 1837 abl-1-27 (T)
Deane, Alis 1837 wb-y-14 (Mu)
Dear, John 1799 rb-a-43 (Mt)
Dearing, Amelia 1846 wb-#150 (Wl)
Dearing, Quin M. 1857 wb-e-128 (Wh)
Dearing, Robert H. 1859 wb-3e-109 (Sh)
Dearman, Allen 1836? wb-#2 (Mo)
Dearman, George G. 1860 wb-f-402 (G)
Dearman, John 1834 wb-5-306 (K)
Dearmon, Allen 1841? wb-#4 (Mo)
Dearmond, David 1838 wb-6-358 (K)
Dearmond, James 1831 wb-b-131 (Ro)
Dearmond, James 1859 wb-13-190 (K)
Dearmond, John 1809 wb-1-296 (K)
Dearmond, John 1856 wb-#46 (Mc)
Dearmond, William 1836 wb-6-7 (K)
Dearmore, Wm. 1856 wb-1-60 (Dy)
Deason, Azariah 1833 wb-8-252 (Rb)
Deason, Isaac 1851 wb-b-248 (L)
Deason, Presley 1838 wb-y-139 (Mu)
Deason, Samuel 1843 wb-a-136 (L)
Deatherage, Abner 1839 wb-c-32 (Ro)
Deatherage, Allen 1836 wb-b-287 (Ro)
Deatheridge, John 1825 wb-8-506 (D)
Deathrige, Thomas 1812 wb-4-193 (D)
Deavenport, Rebecca 1846 rb-k-44 (Mt)
Deavenport, Sarah B. 1840 lr (Gi)
Deavenport, Thomas D. 1854 wb-3-213 (La)
Deberry, Absolom 1853 wb-5-139 (Ma)
Deberry, Allen 1847 wb-5-44 (Ma)
Deberry, Benjamin 1845 wb-d-173 (Hd)
Deberry, Elizabeth 1846 wb-5-29 (Ma)
Deberry, John D. 1852 wb-5-123 (Ma)
Deberry, Joseph 1842 wb-3-538 (Ma)
Deberry, Mathias 1839 wb-3-10 (Ma)
Deberry, _____ 1845 wb-d-172 (Hd)
Debord, George 1849 wb-#46 (Mc)
Debow, Arch 1836 wb-#111 (Wl)
Debow, Frederick 1809 wb-1-0 (Sm)
Debow, James B. 1855 wb-#117 (Wl)
Debrell, Andrew J. 1841 wb-b-400 (G)
Debusk, Elias no date wb-1-35 (Bo)
Debusk, Jonathan 1848 148-1-264 (Ge)
Deck, Heronomus 1811 wb-2-33# (Ge)
Deckard, C. W. 1856 wb-3-396 (La)
Decker, John 1840 wb-11-626 (D)
Deckie, William 1860 rb-20-467 (Ru)
Dedman, Bethel 1854 wb-7-0 (Sm)
Dedrie, William 1851 wb-2-101 (Sh)

Deen, Richard 1831 rb-8-400 (Ru)
Deen, Thos. 1861 wb-17-228 (Rb)
Deens, Richard 1831 rb-8-265 (Ru)
Deese, M. B. 1847 r39-1-24 (Dk)
Defrees, James 1827 lr (Sn)
Defreese, George 1840 wb-b-401 (Wh)
Degraffenreed, Baker 1853 wb-xx-241 (St)
Degraffenreid, Boswell B. 1855 wb-b-14 (F)
Degraffenreid, Joseph J. 1832 wb-2-146 (Ma)
Degraffenreid, Matcalf 1803 Wb-1-111 (Wi)
Degraffenreid, Metcalf 1806 wb-3-67 (Wi)
Dehart, Joab 1852 wb-a-196 (T)
Deiss, Daniel 1854 wb-16-432 (D)
Dejarnett, Daniel 1858 rb-20-20 (Ru)
Dejarnett, Daniel M. 1858 rb-19-426 (Ru)
Dejarnett, James 1834 rb-9-143 (Ru)
Dejarnett, James 1847 rb-14-189 (Ru)
Dejournette, A. 1857 39-2-220 (Dk)
Delaney, Daniel 1831 wb-1-101 (We)
Delaney, Edward 1838 wb-a-351 (R)
Delaney, Frances 1784 wb-1-6# (Ge)
Delaney, James 1784 wb-1-6# (Ge)
Delaney, John 1823 wb-1-7# (Ge)
Delany, McCane 1861 wb-a-383 (Cr)
Delashmet, Sarah 1857 wb-a-304 (Cr)
Delashunt, Elijah 1852 wb-d-404 (G)
Delavergne, John 1850 wb-c-397 (Wh)
Delbridge, Edward W. 1827 rb-6-326 (Ru)
Delbridge, Turner 1844 rb-12-434 (Ru)
Delee, John 1860 wb-18-214 (D)
Deleshment, John 1856 wb-e-424 (G)
Delishmet, Elija 1855 wb-e-313 (G)
Dell, Mary 1844 wb-2-61# (Ge)
Dellis, Phebe 1839 wb-#124 (Wl)
Dellis, Robert 1838 wb-#121 (Wl)
Deloach, Jerusha 1820? wb-#40 (Wl)
Deloach, John 1816 wb-#22 (Wl)
Deloach, Juralea 1824 wb-#52 (Wl)
Deloach, Samuel 1793 wb-1-263 (D)
Deloach, Samuel 1813 wb-4-223 (D)
Deloach, Solomon 1815 wb-#19 (Wl)
Delozier, Asa 1856 wb-1-22 (Se)
Delozier, George 1857 wb-f-74 (Ro)
Delp, Daniel 1860 wb-1-161 (Hw)
Delph, Daniel 1842 wb-c-24 (G)
Delph, Philip 1858 wb-f-168 (G)
Delzell, John 1807 wb-1-30 (Bo)
Delzell, John 1842 wb-1-31 (Bo)
Delzell, Mary 1841 wb-1-30 (Bo)
Delzell, William 1836 wb-1-36 (Bo)
Dement, Abner 1825 rb-6-127 (Ru)

Dement, Abner 1835 rb-9-209 (Ru)
Dement, C. 1861 rb-20-745 (Ru)
Dement, Cader 1849 rb-15-156 (Ru)
Dement, Catharine 1857 wb-f-56 (G)
Dement, Charles 1848 wb-b-258 (We)
Dement, Edmond P. 1844 rb-12-568 (Ru)
Dement, Edward 1844 rb-12-434 (Ru)
Dement, Edward T. 1846 rb-13-540 (Ru)
Dement, Francis 1850 rb-15-557 (Ru)
Dement, George W. 1856 rb-18-191 (Ru)
Dement, John S. 1856 wb-f-7 (G)
Dement, Lesenby 1854 rb-16-713 (Ru)
Dement, Mary (Nancy) 1856 rb-18-190 (Ru)
Dement, Mary 1854 rb-17-270 (Ru)
Dement, Nancy (Mrs) 1859 rb-20-206 (Ru)
Dement, Nancy 1857 as-c-30 (Ms)
Demonbrun, Timothy 1827 wb-9-94 (D)
Demoss, Abraham 1851 wb-15-70 (D)
Demoss, Abram 1850 wb-14-512 (D)
Demoss, Elizabeth K. 1861 wb-19-29 (D)
Demoss, James 1814 wb-4-276 (D)
Demoss, James 1850 wb-14-487 (D)
Demoss, Lewis 1820 wb-7-465 (D)
Demoss, S. P. 1860 wb-a-381 (Cr)
Demoss, Skelton T. 1824 wb-8-357 (D)
Demoss, Thomas 1853 wb-e-113 (G)
Dempsey, George 1852 lr (Sn)
Dempsey, Hugh 1849 wb-9-227 (Wi)
Dempsey, Melven 1853 lr (Sn)
Denby, John 1854 wb-3-219 (W)
Denham, Charles 1836 wb-#39 (Wa)
Denham, Elizabeth 1848 wb-b-270 (Mu)
Denham, Elizabeth C. 1849 wb-b-363 (Mu)
Denham, Robt. F. 1847 wb-b-161 (Mu)
Denham, Samuel W. 1847 wb-b-54 (Mu)
Denley, John 1852 wb-3-120 (W)
Denney, Robert 1848 rb-14-324 (Ru)
Dennie, Felicity 1858 wb-3e-80 (Sh)
Denning, N. A. 1860 rb-p-441 (Mt)
Dennington, Stephen 1857 wb-j-197 (O)
Dennis, David 1844 wd-13-46 (D)
Dennis, David S. 1856 wb-12-222 (K)
Dennis, Isaac H. 1849 wb-#170 (Wl)
Dennis, John 1827 wb-#46 (Mc)
Dennis, John 1833 wb-1-37 (Gr)
Dennis, Marmaduke D. O. 1854 wb-n-378 (Mt)
Dennis, Pryor L. 1854 wb-e-458 (Ro)
Dennis, Sarah 1850 33-3-272 (Gr)
Dennis, Zebedee 1839 rb-h-347 (Mt)
Dennison, Ellen Mary 1845 rb-j-429 (Mt)
Dennisson, Isaac 1841 rb-i-168 (Mt)

Denny, Benjamin 1844 wb-7-0 (Sm)
Denny, Elizabeth 1814 wb-4-317 (D)
Denny, John 1847 wb-7-0 (Sm)
Denny, William 1851 wb-a-154 (V)
Denny, William 1852 wb-7-0 (Sm)
Denson, Jesse 1816 wb-3-179 (St)
Denson, John 1854 wb-1-327 (Fr)
Dent, William 1834 wb-1-534 (Ma)
Denton, David 1846 r39-1-11 (Dk)
Denton, Edward 1850 wb-#172 (Wl)
Denton, Isaac 1795 wb-#5 (Wa)
Denton, Isaac 1826 wb-2-539 (Je)
Denton, Isaac 1826 wb-2-556 (Je)
Denton, Jacob 1816 wb-2-135 (Je)
Denton, Jacob 1816 wb-2-144 (Je)
Denton, Jacob sr. 1833 wb-3-240 (Je)
Denton, Jacob sr. 1840 wb-4-63 (Je)
Denton, Jeremiah 1835 wb-b-189 (Wh)
Denton, John 1817 wb-2-194 (Je)
Denton, John 1820 wb-2-295 (Je)
Denton, John 1843 wb-11-46 (Rb)
Denton, Joseph 1820? wb-#42 (Mu)
Denton, Joseph 1824 wb-#79 (Mu)
Denton, Joseph 1859 gs-1-409 (F)
Denton, Samuel 1814 wb-#13 (Wa)
Denton, Thomas 1807 wb-1-320 (Je)
Denton, Thomas 1839 wb-#124 (Wl)
Denton, Thomas 1853 wb-b-206 (L)
Denton, Thomas D. 1859 wb-8-0 (Sm)
Denton, William 1856 wb-#27 (Mo)
Depew, John 1850 148-1-306 (Ge)
Depriest, Green 1831 wb-1-26 (La)
Depriest, Horatio 1820? wb-#43 (Mu)
Depriest, Joseph C. 1828 wb-1-83 (Hr)
Depriest, Moses 1835 wb-5-349 (K)
Depuise, George 1845 wb-c-199 (Wh)
Derch?, Henry 1844 wb-f-296 (Hn)
Derham, David 1835 wb-a-13 (O)
Derr, James 1856 mr (Gi)
Derrett, Rhoda 1838 wb-4-41 (Je)
Derrett?, Henry 1833 wb-1A-60 (A)
Derrick, Cornelius 1852 wb-#46 (Mc)
Derrick, Jacob L. 1848 wb-#46 (Mc)
Derrick, Michael 1839 wb-#46 (Mc)
Derryberry, H. W. 1840 wb-z-42 (Mu)
Derryberry, J. H. 1855 wb-f-74 (Mu)
Derryberry, Jacob 1857 wb-f-124 (Mu)
Desern, Elisha 1854 wb-12-24 (K)
Desha, Robert 1816 lr (Sn)
Deshazo, Edmond 1847 wb-4-201 (Hr)
Deshazo, William 1833 wb-10-172 (D)

Deshon, Clarissa 1834 wb-10-280 (D)
Deshough, Henderson 1860 wb-4-388 (La)
Detherage, Abner 1850 wb-e-218 (Ro)
Detherage, Andrew J. 1849 wb-c-140 (Ro)
Dethridge, Allen 1823 wb-a-194 (Ro)
Deus?, Jane 1846 wb-4-110 (Hr)
Devan, Elizabeth 1848 as-a-156 (Ms)
Devault, John 1815 wb-4-378 (D)
Devault, John 1842 wb-5-214 (Gr)
Devault, Mary 1849 33-3-132 (Gr)
Devenport, Granville 1848 mr-2-297 (Be)
Devenport, William R. 1842 wb-2-291 (Sn)
Dever, James H. 1853 lr (Gi)
Dever, Jane 1847 wb-4-170 (Hr)
Dever, William 1812 wb-#6 (Mu)
Dever, William 1843 wb-3-9 (Hr)
Devin, James A. 1850 as-a-212 (Ms)
Devorix, William C. 1815 Wb-2-130 (Wi)
Devoux, William C. 1814 Wb-2-109 (Wi)
Dew, Arthur 1844 wb-#145 (Wl)
Dew, John (Sr.) 1824 wb-#51 (Wl)
Dew, John 1823 wb-#50 (Wl)
Dew, John 1859 wb-e-316 (Wh)
Dew, John H. 1844 wb-a2-15 (Mu)
Dew, Joseph A. 1828 wb-#73 (Wl)
Dew, Matthew 1832 wb-#97 (Wl)
Dew, R. James 1846 wb-12-593 (Rb)
Dew, Robert 1858 wb-1C-399 (A)
Dew, Thomas Bradley 1849 wb-#171 (Wl)
Dewalt, Daniel 1859 wb-c-297 (L)
Dewbery, W. H. 1850 wb-4-591 (Hr)
Deweese, William 1847 wb-c-269 (Wh)
Dewitt, Frederick 1829 wb-2-31# (Ge)
Dewitt, Margaret Ann 1855 wb-#26 (Mo)
Dezaine, Elisha 1856 wb-12-299 (K)
Dial, James 1825 wb-4-30 (Wi)
Dial, Joseph 1819 wb-#99 (Mu)
Dial, Joseph 1827 wb-1-2 (W)
Dial, Philip 1839 wb-1-285 (W)
Dial, W. 1848 wb-4-379 (Hr)
Diamond, David 1839 wb-6-423 (K)
Dice, Henry 1829 wb-#82 (Wl)
Dice, Henry 1834 wb-3-0 (Sm)
Dice, Jacob 1844 wb-7-0 (Sm)
Dick, James 1849 wb-3e-104 (Sh)
Dick, William 1851 wb-m-388 (Mt)
Dickens, Ann 1829 wb-#82 (Wl)
Dickens, B. B. 1860 wb-1-39 (Cf)
Dickens, Henry 1828 wb-3-0 (Sm)
Dickens, John 1808 wb-1-30 (Wi)
Dickens, Samuel 1840 wb-3-214 (Ma)

Dickens, William 1845 wb-5-7 (Ma)
Dickenson, David 1859 gs-1-421 (F)
Dickenson, James 1839 5-2-99 (Cl)
Dickenson, Martha 1860 wb-7-70 (Ma)
Dickenson, Thomas J. 1847 rb-14-8 (Ru)
Dickenson, Wiley 1853 lr (Sn)
Dickerson, Eleanor 1837 wb-10-39 (Rb)
Dickerson, James 1849 lr (Sn)
Dickerson, John 1823 lr (Sn)
Dickerson, John 1851 wb-14-465 (Rb)
Dickerson, John R. 1840 wb-2-272 (Sn)
Dickerson, Jorden 1846 wb-c-330 (G)
Dickerson, Leonard 1843 wb-1-526 (W)
Dickerson, Lewis 1856 wb-h-492 (Hu)
Dickerson, Martha 1856 wb-3-280 (W)
Dickerson, Moses 1858 ib-2-98 (Wy)
Dickerson, Moses 1859 ib-2-61 (Wy)
Dickerson, Sarah 1851 wb-#177 (Wl)
Dickey, Alfred C. 1863 wb-2-375 (Li)
Dickey, David 1840 wb-b-341 (G)
Dickey, Ephraim 1840 wb-1-173 (Li)
Dickey, Ephraim 1847 wb-d-53 (G)
Dickey, George 1847 wb-b-158 (Mu)
Dickey, James 1846 wb-4-88 (Je)
Dickey, James 1857 ib-2-68 (Wy)
Dickey, John 1814 wb-#16 (Mu)
Dickey, John 1841 wb-b-378 (G)
Dickey, John D. 1848 wb-b-279 (We)
Dickey, Mary 1857 as-c-108 (Ms)
Dickey, Michael 1846 wb-c-338 (G)
Dickey, N. B. 1858 wb-4-329 (La)
Dickey, S. G. 1841 wb-z-245 (Mu)
Dickey, Samuel 1836 wb-#47 (Mc)
Dickey, Samuel 1841 wb-z-365 (Mu)
Dickey, Samuel E. 1836 wb-x-303* (Mu)
Dickey, Sarah W. 1845 wb-a2-254 (Mu)
Dickey, T. G. 1842 wb-z-419 (Mu)
Dickey, William H. 1837 wb-a-245 (O)
Dickie, William 1860 rb-20-463 (Ru)
Dickings, James 1807 wb-#5 (Wl)
Dickins, Christopher 1835 wb-1-484 (Hr)
Dickins, F. H. (Mrs.) 1855 ib-h-358 (F)
Dickins, Fanny H. 1855 ib-h-368 (F)
Dickins, Lunsford 1837 wb-b-204 (G)
Dickinson, Barbary 1845 rb-13-419 (Ru)
Dickinson, Catharine R. 1848 wd-14-214 (D)
Dickinson, Charles 1807 wb-3-141 (D)
Dickinson, David 1848 rb-14-411 (Ru)
Dickinson, David W. 1845 rb-13-177 (Ru)
Dickinson, Elizabeth 1824 lr (Sn)
Dickinson, George 1816 wb-a-56 (Wh)

Dickinson, Griffith 1818 lr (Sn)
Dickinson, Henry 1807 wb-3-147 (D)
Dickinson, Henry 1846 wb-13-414 (D)
Dickinson, Isaac 1840 wb-2-58 (Hy)
Dickinson, Isaac 1849 5-3-276 (Cl)
Dickinson, Jacob 1822 wb-8-71 (D)
Dickinson, Jacob 1836 wb-10-619 (D)
Dickinson, Jacob sr. 1816 wb-7-58 (D)
Dickinson, Jane 1807 wb-3-147 (D)
Dickinson, John 1815 wb-4-366 (D)
Dickinson, Johnathon 1854 ib-h-260 (F)
Dickinson, Sarah 1846 rb-13-531 (Ru)
Dickinson, Thomas J. 1844 rb-13-11 (Ru)
Dickinson, William 1816 rb-3-97 (Ru)
Dickinson, William 1860 rb-20-465 (Ru)
Dickinson, William G. 1845 wb-13-183 (D)
Dickinson, William T. 1842 wb-12-310* (D)
Dickison, Martha 1853 wb-15-237 (Rb)
Dickson, Alexander L. 1840 wb-#132 (Wl)
Dickson, Asahel 1856 wb-a-264 (Cr)
Dickson, David B. 1859 wb-f-319 (G)
Dickson, Elizabeth 1819 wb-#42 (Mu)
Dickson, Elizabeth 1842 wb-b-421 (Hd)
Dickson, Elizabeth 1852 ib-1-152 (Wy)
Dickson, Enoch 1841 rb-11-148 (Ru)
Dickson, Enoch 1841 rb-11-151 (Ru)
Dickson, Enos H. 1841 rb-11-105 (Ru)
Dickson, Enos H. 1841 rb-11-111 (Ru)
Dickson, Ezekiel 1859 gs-1-319 (F)
Dickson, F. H. 1848 rb-k-794 (Mt)
Dickson, Francis 1851 rb-15-589 (Ru)
Dickson, H. S. 1860 wb-b-86 (F)
Dickson, Hugh 1839 rb-h-195 (Mt)
Dickson, Hugh 1841 rb-i-92 (Mt)
Dickson, Hugh 1847 as-b-362 (Di)
Dickson, James 1844 rb-12-573 (Ru)
Dickson, James 1849 ib-1-37 (Wy)
Dickson, James D. 1849 wb-2-69# (Ge)
Dickson, Janah (Mrs) 1844 rb-12-477 (Ru)
Dickson, John 1819 wb-#98 (Mu)
Dickson, John 1823 as-A-90 (Di)
Dickson, John 1823 rb-5-258 (Ru)
Dickson, John 1825? as-a-156 (Di)
Dickson, John 1836 wb-b-117 (G)
Dickson, John 1837 wb-b-197 (G)
Dickson, John 1855 wb-2-81# (Ge)
Dickson, John 1856 as-c-420 (Di)
Dickson, John M. 1838 wb-b-110 (Hd)
Dickson, John P. 1845 wb-13-351 (D)
Dickson, Joseph (Genl.) 1825 rb-6-143 (Ru)
Dickson, Joseph 1804 wb-a-1 (Di)

Dickson, Joseph 1818 wb-7-223 (D)
Dickson, Joseph 1825 rb-6-114 (Ru)
Dickson, Joseph 1839 rb-h-349 (Mt)
Dickson, Levin 1815 wb-a-17 (Di)
Dickson, Mary 1816 wb-7-94 (D)
Dickson, Micheal M. 1855 wb-a-234 (T)
Dickson, Molton 1861 wb-a-318 (T)
Dickson, Monford S. 1853 wb-1-78 (Jo)
Dickson, Polly 1828 rb-7-305 (Ru)
Dickson, Robert 1834 wb-1-508 (Ma)
Dickson, Robert 1857 wb-1-267 (Bo)
Dickson, Robert A. 1851 as-c-142 (Di)
Dickson, Sarah 1838 wb-b-243 (G)
Dickson, Sarah 1851 wb-15-191 (D)
Dickson, Thomas 1833 wb-10-226 (D)
Dickson, Thomas sr. 1828 rb-7-300 (Ru)
Dickson, William 1816 wb-4-454 (D)
Dickson, William 1816 wb-7-86 (D)
Dickson, William 1824 wb-#10 (Mo)
Dickson, William 1826 wb-9-39 (D)
Dickson, William 1830 wb-1-165 (Hr)
Dickson, William 1837 rb-9-407 (Ru)
Dickson, William 1840 abl-1-208 (T)
Dickson, William 1847 rb-k-661 (Mt)
Dickson, William E. 1845 wb-13-351 (D)
Dickson, William F. 1849 A-468-125 (Le)
Dickson, William S. 1853 wb-1-154 (Hw)
Dicus, Oze 1856 ib-1-403 (Wy)
Diel, Henry 1853 wb-#53 (Wa)
Diel, Riley 1854 wb-5-46 (Hr)
Digg, John M. 1836 wb-a-58 (Cr)
Diggs, Elisha 1860 wb-h-383 (Hn)
Diggs, Elizabeth 1852 wb-g-461 (Hn)
Diggs, Harris 1854 wb-g-602 (Hn)
Diggs, John 1849 wb-g-327 (Hn)
Diggs, John H. 1848 wb-g-273 (Hn)
Diggs, Pleasant 1841 wb-e-314 (Hn)
Diggs, Thomas 1859 wb-h-378 (Hn)
Dikes, John 1813 rb-b-112 (Mt)
Dikus, John 1812 rb-a-73 (Mt)
Dill, Gilly 1854 rb-17-321 (Ru)
Dill, Isaac 1846 rb-13-535 (Ru)
Dill, Isaac 1857 rb-18-266 (Ru)
Dill, Joseph 1826 rb-6-255 (Ru)
Dill, Joseph jr. 1819 wb-1-0 (Sm)
Dill, Joseph sr. 1819 wb-1-0 (Sm)
Dill, Newton C. 1855 rb-17-495 (Ru)
Dill, Samuel 1804 wb-#2 (Wl)
Dill, William 1847 rb-14-164 (Ru)
Dill, William C. 1847 rb-14-135 (Ru)
Dillaha, John W. 1852 ib-1-186 (Wy)

Dillahunty, Edmond 1852 wb-4-288 (Mu)
Dillahunty, John 1798 wb-2-115 (D)
Dillahunty, John 1816 wb-4-463 (D)
Dillahunty, John 1816 wb-7-19 (D)
Dillahunty, John 1817 wb-7-143 (D)
Dillahunty, Lewis 1826 wb-1-29 (Hr)
Dillahunty, Silas 1829 wb-9-304 (D)
Dillahunty, Silas 1842 wb-12-334* (D)
Dillahunty, W. 1840 wb-e-177 (Hn)
Dillahunty, William 1838 wb-d-242* (Hn)
Dillard, George 1816 wb-#25 (Wl)
Dillard, James 1835 rb-h-435 (Mt)
Dillard, James A. 1837 wb-2-246 (Ma)
Dillard, John 1833 wb-1-395 (Ma)
Dillard, Martha 1838 rb-10-171 (Ru)
Dillard, Owen 1818 lr (Sn)
Dillard, Thomas 1784 wb-#3 (Wa)
Dillard, Thomas 1859 wb-b-81 (F)
Dillard, William 1826 wb-#69 (Wl)
Dillard, Zachary 1813 wb-#12 (Wl)
Dillehay, Edmond 1828 wb-3-0 (Sm)
Dillehay, Nancy 1852 as-c-161 (Di)
Dillehay, Nathan 1836 as-a-296 (Di)
Dillian, Carter 1818 wb-a-94 (Wh)
Dillians, Nimbrod 1816? wb-#35 (Mu)
Dilliard, Ally 1833 rb-f-464 (Mt)
Dilliard, Luke 1817 rb-b-418 (Mt)
Dilliard, Luke 1828 rb-e-305 (Mt)
Dilliha, Sterling 1851 wb-g-546 (Hu)
Dillingham, Margaret 1850 wb-g-310 (Hu)
Dillingham, Spencer 1837 wb-1-510 (Hr)
Dillion, Matilda 1847 wb-c-261 (Wh)
Dillon, Alexander 1844 wb-c-128 (Wh)
Dillon, Elizabeth C. 1860 lr (Sn)
Dillon, James 1834 wb-2-44# (Ge)
Dillon, John 1843 rb-12-405 (Ru)
Dillon, Peter sr. 1829 wb-2-30# (Ge)
Dillon, Thomas 1814 wb-4-273 (D)
Dillon, William 1819 wb-1-0 (Sm)
Dillon, William sr. 1847 wb-7-0 (Sm)
Dinkin, William 1842 wb-f-50 (Hn)
Dinning, John 1837 wb-2-225 (Sn)
Dinsmore, Samuel 1845 148-1-106 (Ge)
Dinwiddie, Adam 1807 as-1-156 (Ge)
Dinwiddie, James 1800 wb-1-6# (Ge)
Dinwiddie, James 1841 wb-b-406 (G)
Dinwiddie, James 1842 wb-f-96 (Hn)
Dinwiddie, James 1843 wb-f-135 (Hn)
Dinwiddie, James 1846 wb-2-64# (Ge)
Dinwiddie, James 1860 wb-h-484 (Hn)
Dinwiddie, James sr. 1806 as-1-139 (Ge)

Dinwiddie, Robert C. 1851 wb-m-391 (Mt)
Dinwiddie, Sarah 1843 wb-f-160* (Hn)
Dirickson, Isaiah 1812 wb-4-187 (D)
Dirkson, John 1832 wb-5-161 (K)
Dishough, R. 1845 wb-3-234 (Hr)
Dishough, Redick 1843 wb-3-84 (Hr)
Dismukes, Daniel 1855 lr (Sn)
Dismukes, E. E. 1850 wb-1-383 (Li)
Dismukes, John T. 1847 wb-14-36 (D)
Dismukes, Paul 1838 wb-11-439 (D)
Dismukes, Paul 1845 wb-13-196 (D)
Dismukes, Sarah 1839 wb-12-4 (D)
Dismukes, Stephen C. 1859 wb-h-379 (Hn)
Ditmore, John 1830 wb-#47 (Mc)
Ditto?, Elijah 1819 wb-1-0 (Sm)
Ditty, John 1847 wb-c-247 (Wh)
Ditty, John sr. 1853 wb-d-203 (Wh)
Ditty?, Mary Ann 1850 wb-c-434 (Wh)
Diver, Jane 1846 wb-4-116 (Hr)
Divine, John 1847 wb-#47 (Mc)
Divine, Thomas 1856 wb-#28 (Mo)
Divinny, Charles 1805 wb-1-163 (K)
Dixon, Anne 1857 wb-1-353 (Fr)
Dixon, Charles W. 1856 lr (Sn)
Dixon, Eli Jr. 1859 wb-#47 (Mc)
Dixon, George 1823 wb-#98 (Mu)
Dixon, George 1824 wb-#78 (Mu)
Dixon, Joshua 1817 wb-1-0 (Sm)
Dixon, Mary M. 1836 wb-2-67 (Ma)
Dixon, Nicholas 1836 wb-d-252 (Hn)
Dixon, Polly 1824 wb-4-269 (Rb)
Dixon, Tabitha H. 1826 wb-5-383 (Rb)
Dixon, Thomas 1810 wb-1-338 (Rb)
Dixon, Thomas 1821 wb-3-243 (Rb)
Dixon, Thomas 1851 rb-4-257 (Mu)
Dixon, Tilman 1807 wb-#43 (Wl)
Dixon, Tilmon 1816 wb-1-0 (Sm)
Dixon, William 1849 wb-a-206 (Ms)
Dixson, Reuben 1848 wb-f-475 (St)
Dixson, Reuben 1848 wb-f-477 (St)
Doak, Ann 1834 wb-#104 (Wl)
Doak, David 1828 eb-1-225 (C)
Doak, Edmond T. 1835 wb-x-324 (Mu)
Doak, Harriet D. 1844 wb-#141 (Wl)
Doak, Jane 1849 wb-#44 (Wa)
Doak, Jane A. 1838 wb-#35 (Wa)
Doak, John 1815 wb-#19 (Wl)
Doak, John 1815 wb-A-91 (Li)
Doak, John W. 1820 wb-#17 (Wa)
Doak, John sr. 1828 rb-7-201 (Ru)
Doak, John sr. 1828 rb-7-321 (Ru)

Doak, Jonathan 1820 wb-#36 (Wl)
Doak, Margaret 1831 rb-8-212 (Ru)
Doak, Robert 1820 wb-#42 (Wl)
Doak, Robert 1821 wb-1-1 (Ma)
Doak, Samuel 1813 wb-4-237 (D)
Doak, Samuel 1818 wb-2-39# (Ge)
Doake, Edmond V.? 1837 wb-y-113 (Mu)
Doakes, Sarah 1823 eb-1-135 (C)
Doan, Jesse 1837 wb-3-426 (Je)
Doane, John T. 1856 wb-4-65 (Je)
Dobbin, David 1860 wb-f-196 (Mu)
Dobbin, John 1857 rb-18-588 (Ru)
Dobbins, Alexander B. 1844 wb-12-213 (Rb)
Dobbins, Andrew 1849 rb-15-206 (Ru)
Dobbins, Hugh 1833 wb-c-14 (Hn)
Dobbins, James 1831 wb-3-0 (Sm)
Dobbins, James 1836 wb-y-62 (Mu)
Dobbins, Jane 1842 wb-7-489 (Wi)
Dobbins, John 1833 wb-c-54 (Hn)
Dobbins, John 1839 wb-2-249 (Sn)
Dobbins, L. 1851 wb-14-433 (Rb)
Dobbins, Lavina C. 1854 wb-15-460 (Rb)
Dobbins, Nancy 1848 lr (Sn)
Dobbins, R. S. 1860 wb-h-499 (Hn)
Dobbins, Richard 1861 wb-h-530 (Hn)
Dobbins, Samuel 1841 wb-1-185 (Li)
Dobbins, Solomon 1853 ib-2-67 (Cl)
Dobbins, Susanah 1849 wb-2-27 (Li)
Dobbins, William 1831 wb-5-43 (Wi)
Dobbs, Chesly 1838? 5-2-75 (Cl)
Dobkins, Andrew 1852 wb-2-76# (Ge)
Dobkins, George 1837 5-2-5 (Cl)
Dobrowskie, P. M. 1861 rb-21-94 (Ru)
Dobson, Benjamin 1836? wb-#116 (Wl)
Dobson, Charlotte 1855 149-1-8 (Ge)
Dobson, Henry 1824 wb-3-702 (Wi)
Dobson, John 1812 wb-#4 (Mu)
Dobson, John 1854 wb-16-340 (D)
Dobson, Joseph 1844 wb-1-183 (Bo)
Dobson, Robert 1828 wb-2-43# (Ge)
Dobson, Robert 1830 wb-1-151 (Hw)
Dobson, William 1839 wb-#127 (Wl)
Dobson, William 1860 wb-18-216 (D)
Dockerty, William 1852 wb-15-321 (D)
Dockery, Abel 1815 wb-A-94 (Li)
Dockery, John 1855 as-b-189 (Ms)
Dockery, William 1849 wb-#48 (Mc)
Dockery, William R. 1845 wb-a2-204 (Mu)
Dockny, John 1853 wb-a-308 (Ms)
Dodd, Elizabeth 1860 wb-k-338 (O)
Dodd, German 1844 wb-#145 (Wl)

Dodd, Griffen 1840 rb-11-82 (Ru)
Dodd, Griffen 1840 rb-11-85 (Ru)
Dodd, Henry P. 1846 wb-8-487 (Wi)
Dodd, Jane 1843 wb-8-101 (Wi)
Dodd, Joel 1857 as-c-55 (Ms)
Dodd, John 1840 wb-b-350 (G)
Dodd, John 1860 wb-2-91# (Ge)
Dodd, John Sr. 1855 wb-#48 (Mc)
Dodd, John sr. 1847 wb-1-7# (Ge)
Dodd, Josiah 1809 wb-1-284 (K)
Dodd, Margaret 1858 rb-19-227 (Ru)
Dodd, Peggy 1858 rb-19-222 (Ru)
Dodd, Samuel 1823 wb-#49 (Wl)
Dodd, Samuel 1837 wb-6-399 (Wi)
Dodd, Serena 1842 wb-7-556 (Wi)
Dodd, Thomas 1850 wb-m-30 (Mt)
Dodd, Thomas 1855 wb-j-51 (O)
Dodd, Thomas sr. 1850 wb-m-87 (Mt)
Dodd, Wilkins 1848 wb-9-164 (Wi)
Dodd, William 1845 wb-3-46 (Sn)
Dodd, William 1861 wb-2-93# (Ge)
Dodson, Abner J. 1826 wb-#130 (Mu)
Dodson, Allen 1822 wb-8-148 (D)
Dodson, Archabald 1846 wb-b-168 (We)
Dodson, Beverly 1852 rb-4-281 (Mu)
Dodson, Caleb 1848 wd-14-231 (D)
Dodson, David 1826 wb-#49 (Mc)
Dodson, David W. 1856 wb-f-85 (Mu)
Dodson, Eli 1828 wb-a-323 (Wh)
Dodson, Eli 1831 wb-b-67 (Wh)
Dodson, Frederick 1841 wb-12-124* (D)
Dodson, Gerome 1839 as-a-449 (Di)
Dodson, Henry 1829 wb-a-313 (Wh)
Dodson, I. J. 1853 wb-#111 (Wl)
Dodson, James E. 1859 gs-1-343 (F)
Dodson, James M. 1847 wb-a-181 (Di)
Dodson, John 1838 wb-1-152 (Hw)
Dodson, John 1852 wb-1-153 (Hw)
Dodson, John R. 1855 wb-11-504 (Wi)
Dodson, Joseph Y. 1856 wb-e-399 (G)
Dodson, Martha 1855 wb-1-163 (Hw)
Dodson, Martin 1861 wb-f-210 (Mu)
Dodson, Mary 1854 wb-11-116 (Wi)
Dodson, Nancy 1860 wb-b-111 (Ms)
Dodson, Nimrod 1840 wb-1-302 (W)
Dodson, Presley 1838 wb-y-161 (Mu)
Dodson, Presley 1840 wb-7-222 (Wi)
Dodson, Presley 1850 wb-9-393 (Wi)
Dodson, Raleigh 1793 wb-1-145 (Hw)
Dodson, Raleigh 1844 wb-a2-113 (Mu)
Dodson, Rawley 1836 wb-6-247 (Wi)

Dodson, Rebecca 1861 wb-1-165 (Hw)
Dodson, S. E. 1848 33-3-97 (Gr)
Dodson, Samuel 1848 33-3-96 (Gr)
Dodson, Samuel 1860 wb-4-22 (Gr)
Dodson, Samuel E. 1855 wb-3-298 (Gr)
Dodson, Thomas 1826? wb-1-149 (Hw)
Dodson, Thomas 1854 ib-H-186 (F)
Dodson, Timothy 1856 wb-17-99 (D)
Dodson, W. G. 1849 wb-4-547 (Hr)
Dodson, W. T. 1861 wb-5-121 (Hr)
Dodson, Wilford 1858 wb-#49 (Mc)
Dodson, William R. 1841 wb-z-248 (Mu)
Doggett, Jesse 1834 wb-3-390 (Je)
Doggett, Jesse 1836 wb-3-430 (Je)
Doggett, Miller 1807 wb-1-303 (Je)
Doherty, George 1833 wb-3-247 (Je)
Doherty, James T. 1832 wb-3-322 (Je)
Doherty, John 1828 wb-3-40 (Je)
Doherty, Joseph 1802 wb-1-31 (Je)
Doherty, Mary 1836 wb-6-208 (Wi)
Doherty, Robert 1857 wb-1-152 (Be)
Doherty, William 1851 wb-15-82 (D)
Doil, Kintchen 1815 Wb-2-136 (Wi)
Dolan, Timothy 1846 wb-a-146 (Cr)
Doland, Henry 1859 wb-f-310 (G)
Doland, John J. 1854 wb-e-228 (G)
Dolanson, Robert (Sr.) 1849 wb-2-63 (Sh)
Dollahite, Cornelius 1838 wb-d-197* (Hn)
Dollar, Calvin W. 1857 wb-6-491 (Ma)
Dollar, Nancy C. 1858 wb-2-257 (Li)
Dollar, William 1832 wb-5-178 (Wi)
Dollins, Joel 1844 wb-2-6 (Li)
Dollins, John J. 1855 wb-2-108 (Li)
Dollins, Tyre 1820? wb-#42 (Mu)
Dollins, Tyree 1824 wb-#79 (Mu)
Dolph, Daniel 1840 wb-b-351 (G)
Dolton, Bradley 1844 wb-3-162 (Hr)
Dolton, Carter 1834 wb-1-96 (Gr)
Dolton, Charles 1859 wb-1-303 (Be)
Dolton, Delpha 1849 33-3-148 (Gr)
Dolton, John 1846 as-a-134 (Ms)
Dolton, L. B. 1859 wb-1-315 (Be)
Dolton, Meredith 1851 33-3-346 (Gr)
Dolton, Merideth 1834 wb-1-101 (Gr)
Dolton, Samuel 1857 wb-1-178 (Be)
Dolton, Thomas S. 1846 wb-13-45 (Rb)
Dolun, Elizabeth 1859 rb-p-208 (Mt)
Domidion, Therisa 1843 wb-12-423* (D)
Domidion, Tresed 1847 wb-14-149 (D)
Donaho, Henry 1852 wb-3-41 (Gr)
Donald, David P. 1855 as-b-179 (Ms)

Donald, Nathaniel W. 1844 wb-d-154 (O)
Donaldson, A. 1833 wb-3-283 (Je)
Donaldson, Andrew 1828 wb-2-632 (Je)
Donaldson, Burkley 1843 wb-3-2 (Hr)
Donaldson, Daniel 1843 wb-#140 (Wl)
Donaldson, Elizabeth 1860 wb-#133 (Wl)
Donaldson, John 1852 wb-d-408 (G)
Donaldson, John 1856 wb-#118 (Wl)
Donaldson, Robert (Jr.) 1846 wb-#152 (Wl)
Donaldson, Robert 1849 wb-#164 (Wl)
Donaldson, William 1819 wb-2-231 (Je)
Donaldson, William 1822 wb-a-170 (Wh)
Donall, Thos. 1854 rb-16-773 (Ru)
Donalson, James 1796 wb-2-45 (D)
Donalson, James sr. 1842 wb-f-80 (Hn)
Donell, B. F. sr. 1843 wb-z-532 (Mu)
Donelson, Alexander 1816 wb-7-11 (D)
Donelson, Alexander 1834 wb-10-345 (D)
Donelson, Andrew 1806 wb-#4 (Wl)
Donelson, Charity 1828 wb-9-166 (D)
Donelson, Edward B. 1852 wb-15-439 (D)
Donelson, Eliza Eleanor 1851 wb-15-195 (D)
Donelson, Elizabeth 1828 wb-9-272 (D)
Donelson, George 1848 wb-14-238 (D)
Donelson, George S. 1851 wb-15-68 (D)
Donelson, Jacob D. 1853 rb-16-711 (Ru)
Donelson, James 1851 wb-#176 (Wl)
Donelson, John 1789 wb-1-109 (D)
Donelson, John 1830 wb-9-418 (D)
Donelson, Lemuel 1833 wb-5-229 (Wi)
Donelson, Lemuel 1842 rb-12-252 (Ru)
Donelson, Levin 1833 wb-10-238 (D)
Donelson, Mary 1849 wb-14-471 (D)
Donelson, Mary J. 1843 wb-12-440* (D)
Donelson, Severn 1819 wb-7-330 (D)
Donelson, Severn 1838 wb-12-21 (D)
Donelson, Stockly 1789 wb-1-91 (D)
Donelson, Thomas 1798 wb-2-130 (D)
Donelson, William 1808 wb-#6 (Wl)
Donelson, William 1823 wb-#47 (Wl)
Donelson, William 1829 wb-9-284 (D)
Donelson, William sr. 1820 wb-7-404 (D)
Donley, Isabel 1838 wb-11-294 (D)
Donley, James 1831 wb-9-479 (D)
Donley, John 1836 wb-10-551 (D)
Donnald, Eli 1829 wb-1-107 (Hr)
Donnel, Edin 1828 rb-7-289 (Ru)
Donnel, Elizabeth 1834 rb-9-118 (Ru)
Donnell, Adlai 1847 wb-#155 (Wl)
Donnell, Adnah 1838 wb-#121 (Wl)
Donnell, Allen 1838 wb-#122 (Wl)

Donnell, Amelia 1852 wb-#180 (Wl)
Donnell, Elizabeth 1850 wb-#173 (Wl)
Donnell, Elizabeth E. (Mrs.) 1849 wb-#169 (Wl)
Donnell, George 1831 wb-#94 (Wl)
Donnell, George 1848 wb-#161 (Wl)
Donnell, James 1846 wb-#177 (Wl)
Donnell, James E. 1852 wb-#178 (Wl)
Donnell, James Sr. 1815 wb-#26 (Wl)
Donnell, John H. 1861 lr (Sn)
Donnell, John W. 1848 wb-#167 (Wl)
Donnell, Leo L. (Dr.) 1833 wb-#102 (Wl)
Donnell, Nancy 1855 wb-#117 (Wl)
Donnell, Persis 1835 wb-2-185 (Sn)
Donnell, Robert E. 1844 wb-#144 (Wl)
Donnell, Robert M. 1857 wb-#123 (Wl)
Donnell, Robert S. 1847 rb-14-1 (Ru)
Donnell, Samuel 1817 wb-#26 (Wl)
Donnell, Samuel 1824 wb-#53 (Wl)
Donnell, Thomas 1816 wb-1-0 (Sm)
Donnell, Thomas 1840 wb-#133 (Wl)
Donnell, Thomas 1842 lr (Sn)
Donnell, Thos. 1853 rb-16-671 (Ru)
Donnell, Thos. 1854 rb-16-703 (Ru)
Donnell, William 1835 wb-#107 (Wl)
Donnell, William 1838 wb-#151 (Wl)
Donnell, William 1839 wb-#126 (Wl)
Donnell, William 1844 wb-#153 (Wl)
Donnell, William 1848 wb-#163 (Wl)
Donnell, William L.? 1849 wb-#164 (Wl)
Donnell, William P. 1839 wb-#127 (Wl)
Donnell, _____ 1831 wb-#92 (Wl)
Donnelly, James 1830 wb-9-456 (D)
Donnelson, Robert 1837 wb-6-409 (Wi)
Donoho, Albert G. 1855 wb-7-0 (Sm)
Donoho, Edward 1808 wb-1-0 (Sm)
Donoho, Edward 1827 rb-7-136 (Ru)
Donoho, G. 1857 lr (Sn)
Donoho, James 1820 lr (Sn)
Donoho, John 1802 wb-1-61 (Sn)
Donoho, Patrick 1835 wb-3-0 (Sm)
Donoho, Robert 1838 rb-10-161 (Ru)
Donoho, Robt. D. 1836 rb-9-337 (Ru)
Donoho, William 1856 rb-18-96 (Ru)
Donohos, Samuel 1818 wb-A-266 (Li)
Dooley, Gilbert W. 1842 wb-z-488 (Mu)
Dooley, James 1824 wb-#146 (Mu)
Dooley, James 1825 wb-#128 (Mu)
Dooley, James B. 1856 wb-2-165 (Li)
Dooley, James B. 1858 wb-2-219 (Li)
Dooley, Paris F. 1830 wb-#213 (Mu)
Dooley, Paris F. 1846 wb-a2-478 (Mu)

Dooley, William 1823 wb-#81 (Mu)
Doolittle, Henry 1861 wb-13-401 (K)
Dooton, Christian 1790 wb-1-172 (D)
Doran, Alexander 1814 lw (Ct)
Doran, John 1823 wb-1-0 (Sm)
Doran, Mary 1839 rb-10-381 (Ru)
Doran, William 1834 rb-9-220 (Ru)
Doran, William 1835 rb-9-161 (Ru)
Dorch, Henry 1847 wb-g-200 (Hn)
Dorch, William H. 1836? as-a-319 (Di)
Doren, James G. 1840 wb-b-261 (Hd)
Dorherty, George 1793 lr (Gi)
Dorothy, Asa 1840 wb-2-25 (Hy)
Dorris, Elizabeth 1844 wb-13-87 (D)
Dorris, Isaac 1825 wb-5-55 (Rb)
Dorris, Jackson J. 1856 wb-16-294 (Rb)
Dorris, John 1824 wb-4-251 (Rb)
Dorris, Narcissa 1856 wb-16-273 (Rb)
Dorris, S. L. 1854 wb-15-569 (Rb)
Dorris, Samuel 1837 wb-2-219 (Sn)
Dorris, Simpson L. 1854 wb-15-576 (Rb)
Dorris, W. B. 1853 wb-15-399 (Rb)
Dorris, William 1826 wb-5-323 (Rb)
Dorris, William 1829 lr (Sn)
Dorsey, Dimmon 1836 wb-#49 (Mc)
Dorsey, John 1839 wb-#50 (Mc)
Dortch, Isaac 1828 rb-e-271 (Mt)
Dortch, Isaac 1849 wb-14-113 (Rb)
Dortch, Isaac H. 1848 wb-14-62 (Rb)
Dortch, J. B. 1847 rb-k-680 (Mt)
Dortch, James M. 1846 rb-k-207 (Mt)
Dortch, James N. 1846 rb-k-274 (Mt)
Dortch, James jr. 1848 rb-l-104 (Mt)
Dortch, John B. 1833 rb-f-485 (Mt)
Dortch, John B. 1834 rb-g-72 (Mt)
Dortch, Martha 1855 wb-n-637 (Mt)
Dortch, Norfleet 1840 wb-10-445 (Rb)
Dortch, Norflett 1854 wb-n-431 (Mt)
Dortch, Robert 1842 wb-11-118 (Rb)
Dortch, Willis R. 1858 wb-13-4 (Wi)
Doruty, Dennis 1836 wb-d-23 (St)
Doshier, Enoch jr. 1851 wb-15-18 (D)
Doss, Avarilla 1852 wb-g-455 (Hn)
Doss, Ayres 1813 wb-#6 (Mu)
Doss, James 1848 wb-13-219 (Rb)
Doss, John T. 1851 wb-14-636 (D)
Doss, Jonathan C. 1855 39-2-50 (Dk)
Doss, Matthew 1829 wb-7-7 (Rb)
Doss, Stewart 1855 wb-b-4 (Dk)
Doss, William 1819 lr (Sn)
Dosset, Willis 1813 wb-2-108 (Rb)

Dotey, Jobe P. 1854 as-c-368 (Di)
Dotson, Catey 1825 lr (Sn)
Dotson, Charles 1797 ib-1-314 (Ge)
Dotson, Charles 1797 wb-1-6# (Ge)
Dotson, Eli 1828 wb-a-350 (Wh)
Dotson, Elijah 1848 wb-g-12 (Hu)
Dotson, Fountain 1856 wb-1-84 (R)
Dotson, George 1794 wb-1-1 (Ct)
Dotson, Hightower 1823 wb-3-613 (Wi)
Dotson, J. C. 1855 wb-h-418 (Hu)
Dotson, James 1854 as-c-360 (Di)
Dotson, John 1843 rb-i-508 (Mt)
Dotson, Jonathan 1812 wb-1-431 (Rb)
Dotson, Moses 1842 wb-2-59# (Ge)
Dotson, Moses 1855 wb-2-82# (Ge)
Dotson, Samuel 1841 wb-5-105 (Gr)
Dotson, Samuel E. 1858 wb-3-421 (Gr)
Dotson, Unity 1827 wb-4-174 (Wi)
Dotson, William 1828 wb-#75 (Wl)
Dotson, William 1858 wb-3-433 (Gr)
Dotty, Mary Ann 1851 wb-d-5 (Wh)
Doubelin, Henry 1854 wb-b-334 (We)
Dougan, Jno. T. 1843 wb-3-1 (Hr)
Dougan, John L. 1839 wb-2-139 (Hr)
Dougan, Robert 1837 wb-1-163 (Fr)
Dougherty, Edward 1848 wb-2-15 (Sh)
Doughton, Charles 1832 rb-f-370 (Mt)
Doughty, James 1856 wb-2-325 (Me)
Doughty, John L. 1837 wb-#117 (Wl)
Doughty, Martha 1858 wb-2-405 (Me)
Doughty, Robert 1845 wb-#149 (Wl)
Doughty, Thompson 1858 wb-2-381 (Me)
Douglas, David 1835 wb-3-0 (Sm)
Douglas, Elizabeth 1854 wb-16-295 (D)
Douglas, Elmore 1820 wb-1-0 (Sm)
Douglas, Elmore 1824 wb-2-0 (Sm)
Douglas, Jane C. 1861 wb-1D-5 (A)
Douglas, John 1805 wb-1-0 (Sm)
Douglas, John 1840 wb-4-48 (Je)
Douglas, Luke 1821 rb-5-129 (Ru)
Douglas, Thomas B. 1860 wb-k-252 (O)
Douglass, Alexander 1851 wb-11-78 (K)
Douglass, Alfred 1822 lr (Sn)
Douglass, Alfred 1849 lr (Sn)
Douglass, Alfred H. 1835 wb-2-197 (Sn)
Douglass, Andrew 1799 wb-1-68 (K)
Douglass, B. 1849 wb-a-368 (F)
Douglass, Burchette 1854 ib-H-197 (F)
Douglass, Charles S. 1861 wb-13-462 (K)
Douglass, Edward 1795 wb-1-33 (Sn)
Douglass, Edward 1825 lr (Sn)

Douglass, Elizabeth 1838 wb-#50 (Mc)
Douglass, Elizabeth 1839 wb-0-36 (Cf)
Douglass, Ennis 1848 wb-#156 (Wl)
Douglass, Hugh 1860 wb-f-202 (Mu)
Douglass, James 1856 lr (Gi)
Douglass, James sr. 1851 lr (Sn)
Douglass, Jemima 1845 wb-13-310 (D)
Douglass, John 1845 wb-9-144 (K)
Douglass, John 1848 wb-3-4 (W)
Douglass, John 1849 wb-3-19 (W)
Douglass, John W. 1856 wb-g-726 (Hn)
Douglass, Malissa 1833 lr (Sn)
Douglass, Mathew 1847 wb-2-254 (W)
Douglass, Mathew 1848 wb-2-326 (W)
Douglass, Nancy D. B.? 1846? wb-#50 (Mc)
Douglass, Nancy D. Bishop 1849 wb-#51 (Mc)
Douglass, Oscar E. 1858 wb-#28 (Mo)
Douglass, Reuben 1832 lr (Sn)
Douglass, Robert 1837 wb-#51 (Mc)
Douglass, Robert 1860 rb-p-406 (Mt)
Douglass, Rufus 1841 wb-#138 (Wl)
Douglass, Sarah 1797 wb-1-43 (Sn)
Douglass, Sarah 1852 lr (Sn)
Douglass, Tabitha L. 1857 wb-17-269 (D)
Douglass, Thomas L. 1843 wb-8-45 (Wi)
Douglass, William 1814 lr (Sn)
Douglass, William 1823 wb-8-192 (D)
Douglass, William 1834 wb-1-88 (W)
Douglass, William 1844 wb-2-29 (W)
Douglass, William H. 1834 lr (Sn)
Douglass, William H. 1834? lr (Sn)
Doulard, Henry 1858 wb-f-194 (G)
Douthet, Gincy 1844? wb-#5 (Mo)
Douthet, Samuel 1853 wb-#24 (Mo)
Douthit, John 1861 wb-2-333 (Li)
Douthitt, John W. 1859 wb-2-271 (Li)
Dove, John 1851 wb-15-60 (D)
Dovicy, William 1813 rb-2-209 (Ru)
Dow, Nathan H. 1854 wb-e-154 (G)
Dowd, John 1812 wb-1-283 (Wi)
Dowdall, Edward 1818 wb-1-146 (Hw)
Dowdy, Charles 1853 as-b-118 (Ms)
Dowdy, John 1845 wb-8-282 (Wi)
Dowdy, Martha 1851 wb-a-406 (F)
Dowdy, William 1845 wb-f-216 (St)
Dowdy, William 1859 wb-b-77 (Ms)
Dowell, B. F. 1843 wb-z-536 (Mu)
Dowell, B. F. sr. 1844 wb-a2-11 (Mu)
Dowell, Benjamin F. 1843 wb-z-575 (Mu)
Dowell, Elijah 1855 wb-12-148 (K)
Dowell, Nehemiah 1842 wb-3-0 (Sm)

Dowell, Robert 1850 wb-7-0 (Sm)
Dowing, Charles 1838 wb-#52 (Mc)
Dowler, Francis 1835 wb-c-430 (St)
Dowler, John 1808 wb-a-27 (Ro)
Dowlin, Harris 1855 wb-16-93 (Rb)
Dowlin, Harris 1857 wb-a-21 (Ce)
Downey, T. M. 1840 wb-z-57 (Mu)
Downey, Tabitha J. 1842 wb-c-287 (O)
Downey, Thomas M. 1840 wb-z-60 (Mu)
Downey, William 1823 wb-3-616 (Wi)
Downing, Jackson 1841 wb-c-18 (Wh)
Downing, John 1816 wb-A-132 (Li)
Downing, John 1858 as-c-131 (Ms)
Downing, Milton H. 1847 wb-9-25 (Wi)
Downing, Robert J. 1842 wb-c-54 (Wh)
Downing, William 1839 wb-b-294 (G)
Downs, David 1834 wb-c-381 (St)
Downs, James P. 1819 wb-7-360 (D)
Downs, John 1860 wb-18-418 (D)
Downs, Lewis 1857 wb-h-306 (St)
Downs, Richard 1819 wb-A-285 (Li)
Downs, Susan 1859 wb-i-99 (St)
Downs, Thomas 1854 wb-h-26 (St)
Downs, Thomas G. 1848 wb-f-499 (St)
Downs, William 1859 wb-i-38 (St)
Downs, William B. 1846 wb-13-483 (D)
Downs, William H. 1854 wb-16-382 (D)
Downs, William S. 1821 lr (Sn)
Downy, Jonathan 1822 wb-#41 (Wl)
Dowson?, James C.. 1844 wb-3-209 (Hr)
Doxey, Jeremiah 1833 wb-1-296 (Hr)
Doxey, Jeremiah 1842 wb-2-339 (Hr)
Doxy, James 1838 wb-b-244 (G)
Doyl, Willis 1845 A-468-57 (Le)
Doyle, Daniel M. 1855 wb-d-273 (Wh)
Doyle, Dinnis John 1850 wb-2-77 (Sh)
Doyle, Edward 1848 wb-2-32 (Sh)
Doyle, Jane 1856 wb-h-592 (Hu)
Doyle, John 1844 wb-8-315 (K)
Doyle, John 1850 wb-10-393 (K)
Doyle, Michael 1843 wb-8-10 (Wi)
Doyle, Simon 1843 wb-c-90 (Wh)
Doyle, Wm. T. 1857 as-c-101 (Ms)
Dozier, A. S. 1859 wb-16-751 (Rb)
Dozier, Enoch 1849 wb-14-390 (D)
Dozier, Margaret 1859 wb-17-564 (D)
Dozier, Philip 1855 wb-e-300 (G)
Dozier, William N. 1846 wb-13-456 (D)
Dozier, Zechoriah 1841 wb-10-548 (Rb)
Draffin, Agnes 1857 wb-a-257 (T)
Drain, Benjamin 1840 wb-#40 (Wa)

Drake, A. 1860 wb-a-321 (V)
Drake, B. W. 1859 wb-17-623 (D)
Drake, Benjamin 1831 wb-9-513 (D)
Drake, Blunt W. 1841 wb-12-222* (D)
Drake, Brittain 1846 wb-#152 (Wl)
Drake, Eley 1824 wb-#77 (Mu)
Drake, Eli 1831 wb-9-524 (D)
Drake, Elijah 1853 wb-3-162 (W)
Drake, Eliza 1851 wb-2-17 (Ct)
Drake, Emila 1820 wb-7-457 (D)
Drake, Ephraim 1816 wb-1-22 (Fr)
Drake, Ephraim 1817 wb-7-123 (D)
Drake, Isaac 1815 wb-4-357 (D)
Drake, Isaac 1816 wb-7-52 (D)
Drake, Isaac 1853 wb-15-480 (D)
Drake, J. F. 1838 wb-11-271 (D)
Drake, James 1849 wb-d-164 (G)
Drake, James F. 1838 wb-11-488 (D)
Drake, James L. 1858 wb-12-607 (Wi)
Drake, John 1835 wb-10-410 (D)
Drake, John H. 1859 wb-#128 (Wl)
Drake, Jonathan 1801 wb-2-213 (D)
Drake, Jonathan 1834 wb-10-375 (D)
Drake, Jonathan 1837 wb-11-36 (D)
Drake, Joseph 1816 wb-7-11 (D)
Drake, Joshua 1857 wb-17-165 (D)
Drake, Lewis J. 1858 wb-2-88# (Ge)
Drake, Martha F. 1849 wb-#169 (Wl)
Drake, Mary 1853 wb-15-273 (Rb)
Drake, Mary 1853 wb-15-277 (Rb)
Drake, Moore 1861 wb-e-168 (Hy)
Drake, Moses 1842 abl-1-262 (T)
Drake, Nicholas F. A. M. 1849 wb-#169 (Wl)
Drake, Peter W. 1846 wb-a-285 (F)
Drake, Rhoda 1839 wb-7-186 (Wi)
Drake, Sevier 1828 wb-9-216 (D)
Drake, Zachariah 1822 wb-3-297 (Wi)
Draper, D. H. 1850 wb-g-399 (Hu)
Draper, Daniel H. 1839 wb-e-169 (Hu)
Draper, Philip 1856 wb-7-0 (Sm)
Draper, Robert 1824 wb-2-581 (Je)
Draper, Samuel 1838 wb-e-139 (Hu)
Draughn, James W. 1851 wb-14-437 (Rb)
Draughon, John 1856 wb-16-133 (Rb)
Draughon, Miles 1857 wb-16-349 (Rb)
Draughon, Robert 1854 wb-15-507 (Rb)
Draughon, W. 1853 wb-15-306 (Rb)
Dredden, James M. 1853 wb-h-122 (Hu)
Dredden, Moses 1837 wb-e-1 (Hu)
Drennan, John 1816 wb-#21 (Wl)
Drennan, Thomas 1833 wb-#109 (Wl)

Drennan, Thomas 1849 wb-#168 (Wl)
Drewry, Nicholas 1817 wb-#24 (Wl)
Dreyfous, Felix 1859 wb-13-194 (K)
Dreyfous, Isaac 1852 wb-15-356 (D)
Dreyfus, Leccy (Lucy?) 1851 wb-14-607 (D)
Drinnen, Richard 1810 wb-1-339 (Je)
Driskell, George W. 1840 wb-b-345 (G)
Driver, Abner P. 1853 wb-16-174 (D)
Driver, Benjamin 1850 wb-a-101 (Dk)
Driver, Eli M. 1851 wb-2-110 (Sh)
Driver, Moses 1815 wb-A-80 (Li)
Driver, Sally 1856 as-b-207 (Ms)
Drolinger, John 1822 wb-#43 (Wl)
Drummer, Henry 1859 wb-13-127* (K)
Drummond, Tobitha 1849? ib-1-177 (Cl)
Drummonds, Thomas 1844 as-b-209 (Di)
Dryden, Nancy 1840 as-a-24 (Ms)
Dryden, William 1847 as-a-143 (Ms)
DuRey, Eprain 1849 wb-d-207 (G)
Duberry, William 1859 wb-5-95 (Hr)
Dubois, Elisha 1848 wb-4-278 (Hr)
Duboise, Elisha 1836 wb-1-462 (Hr)
Duckworth, John 1841 wb-#52 (Mc)
Dudley, Benjamin Howard 1833 rb-f-503 (Mt)
Dudley, Guilford 1833 wb-5-264 (Wi)
Dudley, J. B. 1860 rb-p-514 (Mt)
Dudley, John 1850 wb-10-428 (K)
Dudley, John 1857 wb-2-212 (Li)
Dudley, John B. 1861 rb-p-548 (Mt)
Dudley, R. B. 1860 rb-p-428 (Mt)
Dudley, Thomas E. 1838 wb-11-505 (D)
Dudley, Watson 1836 wb-2-46# (Ge)
Dudley, William 1860 wb-#131 (Wl)
Dudley, William P. 1839 wb-6-381 (K)
Dudney, Arthur 1824 wb-A-416 (Li)
Duff, Barny 1819 rb-c-77 (Mt)
Duff, George W. 1858 wb-1-118 (Jo)
Duff, James (Col.) 1845 wb-1-276 (Li)
Duff, Mary 1834 rb-g-21 (Mt)
Duff, Robert 1854 wb-3-209 (Gr)
Duff, Robert K. 1857 wb-3-410 (Gr)
Duff, Robert L. 1833 wb-10-240 (D)
Duff, Robert R. 1849 33-3-138 (Gr)
Duff, William R. 1832 wb-1-228 (Ma)
Duffer, Edward 1836 wb-#112 (Wl)
Duffer, Tabitha 1844 wb-f-236 (Hn)
Duffield, Elizabeth 1828 mr (Gi)
Duffield, John 1807 mr (Gi)
Duffield, John 1813 wb-4-234 (D)
Duffy, Francis 1858 lr (Sn)
Duffy, Hetty 1840 wb-11-615 (D)

Duffy, John 1844 wb-4-155A (Ma)
Duffy, Patrick M. 1846 wb-5-11 (Ma)
Dugan, Thomas 1835 wb-1-102 (W)
Dugar, Mary M. 1845 wb-a-259 (F)
Duggar, Daniel R. 1841 wb-c-212 (Ro)
Duggar, William 1839? wb-1-84 (Ct)
Dugger, Daniel 1840 wb-c-93 (Ro)
Dugger, Francis 1843 wb-3-15 (Sn)
Dugger, John 1845 wb-a2-281 (Mu)
Dugger, Joseph 1849 wb-b-560 (Mu)
Dugger, Leonard 1817 lr (Sn)
Dugger, Sarah 1843 wb-d-82 (Ro)
Dugger, Thomas 1815 wb-1-215 (Sn)
Dugger, Thomas B. 1852 wb-4-578 (Mu)
Duglass, John 1835 wb-1-108 (W)
Duke, A. H. 1837 rb-h-17 (Mt)
Duke, Amos H.? 1832 rb-f-367 (Mt)
Duke, E. L. 1856 rb-o-188 (Mt)
Duke, Elias G. 1835 rb-g-186 (Mt)
Duke, Elizabeth 1849 A-468-135 (Le)
Duke, Elizabeth S. 1853 wb-n-98 (Mt)
Duke, G. W. 1860 wb-a-166 (Ce)
Duke, George W. 1860 wb-3e-130 (Sh)
Duke, John 1819 rb-c-215 (Mt)
Duke, Louisa S. 1860 rb-p-334 (Mt)
Duke, Merit 1855 ib-h-313 (F)
Duke, Philip 1835 rb-g-234 (Mt)
Duke, Phillip 1837 rb-g-581 (Mt)
Duke, Prudence P. 1838 rb-h-120 (Mt)
Duke, Prudence P. 1851 wb-m-217 (Mt)
Duke, Rebecca 1815 rb-b-298 (Mt)
Duke, Robert 1845 rb-j-406 (Mt)
Duke, Robert 1845 wb-a-167 (Di)
Duke, Sarah 1859 rb-p-34 (Mt)
Duke, W. L. 1847 wb-#155 (Wl)
Duke, William 1816 wb-1-0 (Sm)
Duke, William P. 1848 wb-g-239 (Hn)
Dukes, John 1803 rb-a-178 (Mt)
Dukes, Sion 1833 wb-#100 (Wl)
Dukins, J. B. B. 1860 wb-00-7 (Cf)
Dulaney, W. R. 1854 wb-1-49 (Su)
Dulin, John 1838 wb-10-220 (Rb)
Dulin, John 1839 wb-10-266 (Rb)
Dulin, John G. 1847 wb-13-128 (Rb)
Dumas, Edward 1837 wb-d-178* (Hn)
Dumas, Francis M. 1854 wb-g-557 (Hn)
Dumas, Jeremiah 1858 wb-h-181 (Hn)
Dun, Richard 1834 rb-9-94 (Ru)
Dun, William 1844 wb-3-153 (Hr)
Dunagan, John 1837? as-a-401 (Di)
Dunahoe, William 1847 wb-2-2 (Sh)

Dunam, Henry 1803 wb-2-289 (D)
Dunam, John 1790 wb-1-136 (D)
Dunaway, James G. 1837 wb-6-359 (Wi)
Dunaway, Samuel 1817 rb-4-93 (Ru)
Dunaway, Samuel 1851 rb-15-631 (Ru)
Dunaway, Thomas 1861 rb-20-782 (Ru)
Dunbar, Ann 1824 rb-d-296 (Mt)
Dunbar, Ann 1836 wb-c-504 (St)
Dunbar, James 1830 wb-c-76 (St)
Dunbar, Sarah 1857 wb-h-431 (St)
Dunbar, Thomas 1810 rb-a-491 (Mt)
Dunbar, Thomas 1824 rb-d-396 (Mt)
Dunbar, Thomas E. 1847 wb-f-439 (St)
Dunbar, William 1832 wb-c-225 (St)
Dunbar, William 1852 wb-xx-95 (St)
Duncan, A. B. 1857 wb-12-480 (Wi)
Duncan, A. D. 1839 wb-c-47 (Ro)
Duncan, A. D. 1843 wb-3-1 (Hr)
Duncan, Abner 1847 wb-0-73 (Cf)
Duncan, Albert D. 1840 wb-2-151 (Hr)
Duncan, Andrew 1790? wb-#23 (Wa)
Duncan, Anthony 1839 wb-2-51# (Ge)
Duncan, Augusta 1861 wb-17-173 (Rb)
Duncan, Charles 1818 wb-#16 (Wa)
Duncan, Edwin 1852 wb-#179 (Wl)
Duncan, Elizabeth 1837 wb-9-452 (Rb)
Duncan, F. A. 1859 wb-k-2 (O)
Duncan, Frank 1859 wb-16-689 (Rb)
Duncan, Franklin 1861 wb-17-174 (Rb)
Duncan, George W. 1848 wb-10-34 (K)
Duncan, George W. 1850 lw (Ct)
Duncan, James 1831 wb-1-32 (Bo)
Duncan, James 1855 wb-12-156 (K)
Duncan, James F. 1857 wb-f-118 (Ro)
Duncan, James H. 1853 wb-h-192 (Hu)
Duncan, Jeremiah H. 1856 wb-#12 (Mo)
Duncan, Joab 1839 as-a-2 (Ms)
Duncan, John 1816 wb-a-89 (Ro)
Duncan, John 1827 wb-1-38 (Hr)
Duncan, John 1832 wb-1-38 (Bo)
Duncan, John 1844 wb-2-35 (W)
Duncan, John 1856 wb-6-221 (Ma)
Duncan, Joseph (Sr.) 1860 wb-#63 (Wa)
Duncan, Joseph 1836 wb-1-32 (Bo)
Duncan, Joseph 1838 wb-2-260 (Ma)
Duncan, Joseph 1845 wb-a-77 (Ms)
Duncan, Josiah 1827 wb-3-0 (Sm)
Duncan, Josiah 1856 wb-b-16 (Ms)
Duncan, Letty 1815 wb-A-95 (Li)
Duncan, Margret 1843 wb-1-192 (Bo)
Duncan, Marshall 1833 rb-9-64 (Ru)

Duncan, Marshall 1839 wb-b-361 (Wh)
Duncan, Martin 1828 wb-6-334 (Rb)
Duncan, Matilda N. 1858 wb-13-38 (K)
Duncan, Micajah 1839 as-a-16 (Ms)
Duncan, Nancy 1839 wb-3-31 (Ma)
Duncan, Norman 1851 wb-g-407 (Hn)
Duncan, O. C. 1857 ib-1-424 (Ca)
Duncan, Oliver 1853 ib-1-285 (Ca)
Duncan, Peter 1809 ib-1-275 (Ge)
Duncan, Rachael 1845 rb-13-116 (Ru)
Duncan, Robert 1823 wb-a-197 (Ro)
Duncan, Robert 1828 wb-1-100 (Ma)
Duncan, Robert A. 1860 wb-f-182 (Mu)
Duncan, Robert B. 1853 wb-1-315 (Fr)
Duncan, Robert W. 1834 wb-x-178 (Mu)
Duncan, S? H. 1855 ib-1-362 (Ca)
Duncan, Samuel 1839 wb-#3 (Mo)
Duncan, Tabitha 1842 wb-e-510 (Hu)
Duncan, Thomas 1832 wb-b-100 (Wh)
Duncan, Thomas 1855 wb-j-24 (O)
Duncan, Thomas W. 1843 wb-a-41 (Dk)
Duncan, Thomas W. 1853 r39-1-306 (Dk)
Duncan, William 1824 wb-4-259 (Rb)
Duncan, William 1836 wb-b-223 (Wh)
Duncan, William 1837 wb-a-20 (Ms)
Duncan, William 1841 wb-e-447 (Hu)
Duncan, William 1849 ib-1-19 (Wy)
Duncan, William 1853 wb-1-315 (Fr)
Duncan, William 1854 as-b-146 (Ms)
Duncan, William L. 1853 wb-#109 (Wl)
Duncomb, Benjamin 1856 wb-4-2 (Gr)
Dungan, John 1857 wb-1-104 (R)
Dungan, William 1853 wb-5-135 (Ma)
Dungey, John 1843 wb-12-432* (D)
Dunham, Allen 1835 wb-a-304 (R)
Dunham, Daniel A. 1837 wb-a-51 (T)
Dunham, David A. 1839 abl-1-157 (T)
Dunham, James 1857 wb-3-358 (W)
Dunham, John 1817 wb-2-359 (Wi)
Dunivant, Daniel 1854 wb-16-451 (D)
Dunken, Joseph 1833 wb-2-42# (Ge)
Dunkin, Benjamin 1860 wb-3e-146 (Sh)
Dunkin, Craven 1801 wb-1-133 (Je)
Dunkin, Elijah 1841 wb-a-23 (Dk)
Dunkin, John 1853 wb-5-234 (Je)
Dunkin, Judge 1854 wb-2-99 (Li)
Dunlap, A. L. 1851 wb-g-457 (Hu)
Dunlap, A. L. R. 1857 wb-h-710 (Hu)
Dunlap, Adam 1796 wb-1-243 (Bo)
Dunlap, Allen 1861 wb-h-531 (Hn)
Dunlap, Caroline 1852 wb-2-75# (Ge)

Dunlap, Charlotte 1841 wb-e-51 (St)
Dunlap, George 1835 wb-5-365 (K)
Dunlap, George W. 1859 wb-f-259 (G)
Dunlap, George W. C. 1860 149-1-203 (Ge)
Dunlap, H. J. 1859 wb-f-313 (G)
Dunlap, James 1839 wb-1-35 (Bo)
Dunlap, James 1860 wb-2-327 (Li)
Dunlap, James 1861 wb-#18 (Mo)
Dunlap, James 1861 wb-1D-9 (A)
Dunlap, John 1815 wb-2-176 (K)
Dunlap, John 1841 148-1-16 (Ge)
Dunlap, Joseph sr. 1844 148-1-90 (Ge)
Dunlap, Moses 1823 wb-3-438 (K)
Dunlap, Moses 1841 wb-e-206 (Hn)
Dunlap, Robert 1838 wb-d-257 (St)
Dunlap, S. L. G. 1850 wb-g-280 (Hu)
Dunlap, Samuel 1828 wb-#178 (Mu)
Dunlap, Samuel 1854 wb-e-194 (G)
Dunlap, Samuel A. 1840 wb-e-357 (Hu)
Dunlap, W. F. 1854 wb-h-283 (Hu)
Dunlap, William 1820 wb-1-190 (Bo)
Dunlap, William 1854 wb-e-185 (G)
Dunlap, William D. 1846 wb-c-271 (G)
Dunlap, William F. 1854 wb-h-303 (Hu)
Dunlap, William Y. 1853 wb-h-175 (Hu)
Dunlavy, Sallie 1858 rb-o-538 (Mt)
Dunn, Albartus 1848 wb-13-220 (Rb)
Dunn, Azariah 1833 wb-8-217 (Rb)
Dunn, B. H. 1857 wb-h-114 (Hn)
Dunn, Daniel 1822 wb-2-145# (Ge)
Dunn, Daniel 1844 wb-1-256 (Bo)
Dunn, David 1837 wb-1-35 (Sh)
Dunn, David L. 1861 wb-3e-186 (Sh)
Dunn, Dudley 1848 wb-2-6 (Sh)
Dunn, Godfrey 1860 wb-1-146 (Jo)
Dunn, Henry F. 1838 rb-10-115 (Ru)
Dunn, Henry T. 1836 rb-9-304 (Ru)
Dunn, Jane 1853 wb-15-326 (Rb)
Dunn, Jane 1853 wb-15-330 (Rb)
Dunn, John 1835 rb-9-222 (Ru)
Dunn, Joseph 1846 wb-#52 (Mc)
Dunn, Joseph 1855 wb-d-272 (Wh)
Dunn, Joseph Whitson 1861 wb-e-404 (Wh)
Dunn, Levi 1842 wb-11-144 (Rb)
Dunn, Lewis 1845 wb-13-168 (D)
Dunn, Michael C. 1854 wb-16-216 (D)
Dunn, Paulina A. 1857 wb-3e-52 (Sh)
Dunn, Samuel 1858 wb-e-206 (Wh)
Dunn, Samuel 1859 wb-e-270 (Wh)
Dunn, Samuel 1862 wb-1D-10 (A)
Dunn, Samuel G. 1846 wb-1-141 (Sh)

Dunn, Sophia 1856 wb-16-239 (Rb)
Dunn, Thomas 1839 5-2-112 (Cl)
Dunn, Thomas D. 1851 rb-15-586 (Ru)
Dunn, William A. 1839 rb-10-357 (Ru)
Dunn, William A. 1854 wb-16-217 (D)
Dunnagan, B. B. 1853 as-c-211 (Di)
Dunnagan, James 1811 as-a-129 (Di)
Dunnagan, W. S. 1858 as-c-496 (Di)
Dunnaway, Nancy 1855 rb-17-586 (Ru)
Dunnegan, James 1818 wb-a-31 (Di)
Dunneway, Opie 1830 wb-9-447 (D)
Dunnigan, John 1841 as-a-512 (Di)
Dunnigan, Sherwood 1840 as-a-33 (Ms)
Dunning, N. A. 1860 rb-p-348 (Mt)
Dunnington, J. P. 1859 wb-16-713 (Rb)
Dunnington, J. P. 1859 wb-16-772 (Rb)
Dunnington, John P. 1859 wb-16-750 (Rb)
Dunsmore, William D. 1853 ib-2-2 (Cl)
Dunwiddie, Andrew 1844 wb-a-129 (Cr)
Dunwoody, Adam 1794 wb-1-6# (Ge)
Dunwoody, Adam M. C. 1852 148-1-404 (Ge)
Dunwoody, Samuel 1827 wb-1-7# (Ge)
Dupey (Deprey?), Mary 1793 wb-3-0 (Sm)
Dupree, Henry 1860 wb-b-92 (F)
Dupree, James 1819 wb-3-102 (Wi)
Dupuy, James H. 1855 wb-a-465 (F)
Durand, Timothy 1852 wb-15-232 (D)
Durant, James 1835 wb-1-116 (W)
Durant, Silvius S. 1851 wb-b-121 (L)
Durard, R. 1859 wb-a-135 (Ce)
Durard, T. V. R. 1857 wb-a-28 (Ce)
Durard, Timothy 1851 wb-15-121 (D)
Durden, Jonathan 1861 wb-1-385 (Be)
Durden, Thomas 1857 wb-1-130 (Be)
Duren, John 1821 wb-3-221 (K)
Durett, John 1859 wb-5-59 (La)
Durham, Abraham 1843 wb-a-44 (Dk)
Durham, Elizabeth 1845 wb-a-258 (F)
Durham, Ezra 1858 wb-c-266 (L)
Durham, James 1855 wb-3-246 (W)
Durham, James A. 1858 39-2-259 (Dk)
Durham, John 1855 wb-e-522 (Ro)
Durham, Ruffin 1853 mr-2-523 (Be)
Durham, S. M. 1848 wb-4-342 (Hr)
Durham, Salatha James 1859 wb-3e-121 (Sh)
Durham, Stephen 1849 wb-a-349 (F)
Durham, Thomas 1823 wb-1-0 (Sm)
Durham, Thomas 1843 lr (Sn)
Durham, Thomas 1857 39-2-217 (Dk)
Durham, W. W. 1852 lr (Sn)
Durham, William R. 1832 wb-a-14 (T)

Durley, George 1852 wb-d-406 (G)
Durley, Jno. 1842 wb-2-384 (Hr)
Durr, Daniel 1831 rb-f-155 (Mt)
Durrett, J. W. 1858 rb-o-633 (Mt)
Durrett, James W. 1858 rb-o-686 (Mt)
Durrett, John G. 1836 wb-1A-152 (A)
Durrett, W. H. 1858 rb-o-663 (Mt)
Durrett, William 1813 wb-a-84 (Ro)
Dury, James A. 1857 wb-1-351 (Fr)
Dusenberry, John 1850 wb-2-3 (Li)
Dutton, David 1854 wb-e-513 (Ro)
Duty, Joseph 1830 wb-b-128 (Hn)
Duty, William 1830 wb-1-208 (Ma)
Duvall, Benjamin F. 1855 wb-6-67 (Ma)
Duvall, Brook 1831 wb-7-375 (Rb)
Duvall, Zebulam M. 1841 wb-11-86 (Rb)
Dyche, Henry 1848 148-1-221 (Ge)
Dyche, Jacob 1845 148-1-130 (Ge)
Dyche, Thomas 1853 148-1-427 (Ge)
Dycus, Edward 1858 rb-o-676 (Mt)
Dycus, John 1830 rb-f-140 (Mt)
Dye, B. R. 1861 rb-p-629 (Mt)
Dye, Benson W. 1859 rb-p-152 (Mt)
Dye, George W. 1850 wb-m-121 (Mt)
Dyer, Abraham 1828 wb-2-27# (Ge)
Dyer, Anderson T. 1844 wb-5-327 (Gr)
Dyer, Charlton 1845 wb-2-10 (Gr)
Dyer, Charlton jr. 1844 wb-5-303 (Gr)
Dyer, David 1829 wb-#179 (Mu)
Dyer, Famey 1841 wb-5-105 (Gr)
Dyer, Fanny 1838 wb-1-329 (Gr)
Dyer, Felix F. 1846 as-a-122 (Ms)
Dyer, George 1841 wb-5-158 (Gr)
Dyer, George Washington 1841 wb-5-117 (Gr)
Dyer, Isaac 1836 wb-1-116 (Gr)
Dyer, Isaac 1849 wb-2-269 (Gr)
Dyer, Isaiah 1857 rb-18-390 (Ru)
Dyer, Jackson 1849 wb-a-131 (V)
Dyer, Jacob 1831 wb-1-34 (Bo)
Dyer, James 1805 wb-1-0 (Sm)
Dyer, James 1858 wb-4-10 (Gr)
Dyer, James sr. 1858 wb-3-477 (Gr)
Dyer, Joel 1825 wb-1-47 (Ma)
Dyer, Joel 1839 wb-e-170 (Hu)
Dyer, Joel 1839 wb-e-224 (Hu)
Dyer, John 1818 wb-2-390 (Wi)
Dyer, John 1831 wb-b-92 (Wh)
Dyer, John 1841 wb-#2 (Mo)
Dyer, John 1844 wb-a-50 (Dk)
Dyer, John 1849 wb-#52 (Mc)
Dyer, Joseph 1828 wb-1-137 (Hy)

Dyer, Josiah 1859 rb-19-607 (Ru)
Dyer, Lea 1858 wb-3-427 (Gr)
Dyer, Margaret 1860 wb-7-67 (Ma)
Dyer, Mary 1860 wb-#16 (Mo)
Dyer, Obedyer 1856 wb-1-345 (Fr)
Dyer, Robert H. 1826 wb-1-99 (Ma)
Dyer, Samuel L. 1857 wb-e-171 (Wh)
Dyer, Samuel L. 1858 wb-e-200 (Wh)
Dyer, William 1837 lr (Gi)
Dyer, William 1839 wb-1-358 (Gr)
Dyer, William 1839 wb-5-9 (Gr)
Dyer, William 1841 wb-5-103 (Gr)
Dyer, William 1851 wb-5-100 (Ma)
Dykes, John 1858 wb-1-164 (Hw)
Dykes, William 1825 wb-1-148 (Hw)
Dyks, John 1858 wb-1-30 (Gu)
Dyournette, Harriett 1855 39-2-48 (Dk)
Dyre, George 1840 wb-5-52 (Gr)
Dysart, Assenath 1860 as-c-208 (Ms)
Dysart, Francis 1858 as-c-136 (Ms)
Dysart, R. E. 1856 as-b-203 (Ms)
Dyson, Aquilla 1835 wb-2-5 (Ma)
Dyson, Josiah H. 1855 wb-6-64 (Ma)
Dyson, Mark 1846 wb-7-0 (Sm)

- E -

Eagan, Barnaba 1822 wb-#43 (Wl)
Eagan, Barney 1846 wb-#150 (Wl)
Eagan, Hugh 1835 wb-#112 (Wl)
Eagan, Irvin 1851 wb-#175 (Wl)
Eagan, Jesse 1838 wb-#120 (Wl)
Eagan, Patrick 1849 wb-2-60 (Sh)
Eagan, William 1814 wb-#14 (Wl)
Eagen, John 1855 wb-2-181 (Sh)
Eagleton, David 1827 wb-1-42 (Bo)
Eagleton, Elijah M. (Rev.) 1838 wb-#1 (Mo)
Eagleton, W. W. 1852 wb-1-210 (Bo)
Eakin, David 1815 wb-#19 (Wl)
Eakin, Isabella 1853 wb-15-574 (D)
Eakin, John 1844 as-a-71 (Ms)
Eakin, Moses 1818 wb-7-257 (D)
Eakin, Spencer 1841 wb-12-189* (D)
Eakin, William 1834 wb-1-39 (Bo)
Eakin, William 1851 wb-14-642 (D)
Ealy, Adam 1854 148-1-512 (Ge)
Ealy, Elizabeth 1860 149-1-183 (Ge)
Ealy, Henry 1818 wb-2-213 (Je)
Ealy, John 1859 149-1-144 (Ge)
Ealy, Nicholas 1853 wb-2-76# (Ge)
Ealy, Philip 1844 148-1-78 (Ge)

Earhart, Abraham 1854 wb-16-297 (D)
Earhart, David 1817 wb-7-168 (D)
Earhart, Elijah 1820 wb-7-469 (D)
Earhart, Nimrod 1846 wb-13-378 (D)
Earheart, David 1843 wb-e-245 (St)
Earheart, Philip 1818 wb-7-218 (D)
Earles, Martain 1854 wb-a-184 (V)
Earles, McGregor 1853 wb-d-152 (Wh)
Earles, Nancy Ann 1860 wb-e-352 (Wh)
Earles, Pleasant 1845 wb-c-160 (Wh)
Early, Caleb 1853 rb-16-707 (Ru)
Early, George 1848 wb-c-275 (Wh)
Early, Harriet J. 1860 wb-13-224 (Wi)
Early, Joshua 1860 wb-13-338 (Wi)
Early, Richard S. 1836 wb-1-152 (Fr)
Earnest, Andrew sr. 1818 wb-1-8# (Ge)
Earnest, Felix 1842 wb-1-8# (Ge)
Earnest, Henry 1855 149-1-8 (Ge)
Earnest, Henry sr. 1809 ib-1-260 (Ge)
Earnest, Henry sr. 1809 wb-1-8# (Ge)
Earnest, Jacob 1840 wb-2-54# (Ge)
Earnest, Lawrence 1838 wb-#37 (Wa)
Earnest, Thomas W. 1844 wb-2-61# (Ge)
Earp, Jonathan 1855 mr-2-595 (Be)
Earthman, A. J. 1838 wb-11-321 (D)
Earthman, Isaac 1835 wb-10-459 (D)
Earthman, Isaac F. 1829 wb-9-353 (D)
Earthman, Jas. 1835 rb-9-199 (Ru)
Earthman, John 1828 wb-9-191 (D)
Earthman, Lewis 1828 wb-9-255 (D)
Easley, Daniel 1836 wb-1-244 (Hy)
Easley, Daniel 1848 33-3-37 (Gr)
Easley, Isaac 1818 wb-#29 (Wl)
Easley, James 1814 lr (Sn)
Easley, John B. 1846 wb-f-37 (O)
Easley, John V. 1846 wb-d-24 (G)
Easley, Millar W. 1844 wb-5-296 (Gr)
Easley, Miller W. 1834 wb-1-96 (Gr)
Easley, Miller W. 1858 wb-3-479 (Gr)
Easley, Nancy 1846 wb-1-231 (Fr)
Easley, Peter 1839 wb-e-159 (Hu)
Eason, Alexander 1808 wb-#7 (Wl)
Eason, Carter T. 1840 wb-b-340 (G)
Eason, Carter T. 1846 wb-e-226 (O)
Eason, Eli B. 1860 wb-#131 (Wl)
Eason, Howell D. 1837 wb-1-34 (Sh)
Eason, Ira E. 1834 wb-#105 (Wl)
Eason, Jesse 1832 wb-#96 (Wl)
Eason, Joseph 1840 wb-a-53 (F)
Eason, Mills 1815 as-A-77 (Di)
Eason, Robert 1823 wb-#49 (Wl)

East, Addison 1838 wb-11-454 (D)
East, Benjamin 1809 wb-4-78 (D)
East, Henry 1859 wb-17-607 (D)
East, Henry C. 1853 wb-15-546 (D)
Eastep, Samuel 1836 wb-6-225 (Wi)
Easter, Booker B. 1816 wb-A-331 (Li)
Easter, Peter 1829 wb-a-56 (R)
Easterly, George 1828 wb-2-29# (Ge)
Easterly, George 1853 148-1-469 (Ge)
Easterly, John 1855 wb-3-273 (Gr)
Eastes, John W. 1850 wb-7-0 (Sm)
Eastes, Tempy 1843 wb-1-551 (W)
Eastham, William 1831 wb-#217 (Mu)
Eastland, Davis 1838 wb-1-133 (Li)
Eastland, Thomas 1859 wb-e-316 (Wh)
Eastman, E. G. 1861 wb-18-431 (D)
Eastus, Elisha 1819 wb-a-117 (Ro)
Eastwood, Esquire 1857 wb-12-393 (Wi)
Eastwood, Lydie 1828 wb-#180 (Mu)
Eatherly, A. R. 1848 wb-#165 (Wl)
Eatherly, Elizabeth W. 1851 wb-#175 (Wl)
Eatherly, Frank 1859 wb-17-571 (D)
Eatherly, Isaac 1855 wb-#117 (Wl)
Eatherly, John (Sr.) 1860 wb-#130 (Wl)
Eatherly, William 1840 wb-#133 (Wl)
Eaton, Elizabeth 1843 wb-8-110 (Wi)
Eaton, Isaac 1813 rb-2-243 (Ru)
Eaton, John 1817 wb-2-364 (Wi)
Eaton, John W. 1851 wb-2-45 (Me)
Eaton, Joseph H. 1859 rb-19-566 (Ru)
Eaton, Lucy 1849 33-3-108 (Gr)
Eaton, Nathan 1828 rb-7-43 (Ru)
Eaton, William 1844 wb-#53 (Mc)
Eblen, Isaac 1860 wb-f-335 (Ro)
Eblen, John 1828 wb-b-22 (Ro)
Eblen, William 1843 wb-d-75 (Ro)
Echols, David 1808 wb-#6 (Wl)
Echols, Elizabeth 1821 wb-#40 (Wl)
Echols, Elkanah 1805 wb-#3 (Wl)
Echols, Frances 1840 wb-7-314 (Wi)
Echols, Joel 1823 wb-#44 (Wl)
Echols, John 1816? wb-2-304 (Wi)
Echols, John 1823 wb-#46 (Wl)
Echols, Larkin 1813 wb-#13 (Wl)
Echols, Thomas H. 1839 wb-e-165 (Hu)
Eckel, Peter 1844 wb-4-108 (Je)
Eckes, William 1854 wb-2-165 (Sh)
Eckford, John 1833 wb-a-27 (T)
Eckols, Abram 1823 lr (Sn)
Edde, James 1857 wb-2-7 (Li)
Eddings, Joseph 1848 wb-14-48 (Rb)

Eddings, Joseph 1848 wb-14-80 (Rb)
Eddings, Osbourn 1846 wb-d-25 (G)
Eddings, Sarah 1854 wb-#114 (Wl)
Eddings, William 1840 wb-#130 (Wl)
Eddington, James 1838 wb-6-352 (K)
Eddington, James H. 1844 wb-#53 (Mc)
Eddington, Joseph 1838 wb-6-263 (K)
Eddington, William 1816 wb-2-254 (K)
Eddins, Hannah 1856 wb-2-132 (Li)
Eddins, John 1852 wb-2-123 (Sh)
Eddins, Lewis T. 1855 wb-6-41 (Ma)
Eddins, Washington 1855 ib-h-296 (F)
Eddins, William 1841 wb-#133 (Wl)
Eddy, Joseph 1840 wb-1-313 (W)
Edens, James 1855 wb-2-18 (Ct)
Edes, Jessee 1844 rb-j-65 (Mt)
Edes, John 1827 wb-1-69 (Ma)
Edgar, Andrew 1849 wb-4-80 (Je)
Edgar, George 1811 wb-2-2 (Je)
Edgar, George 1837 wb-3-534 (Je)
Edgar, Isabella 1826 wb-2-561 (Je)
Edgar, Isabella 1826 wb-2-635 (Je)
Edgar, Isabella 1837 wb-3-473 (Je)
Edgar, Jno. T. 1861 wb-18-566 (D)
Edgar, John 1843 wb-8-64 (Wi)
Edge, Moses 1815 wb-2-250 (Rb)
Edgeman, Thomas 1860 wb-#53 (Mc)
Edington, James M. 1855 wb-12-101 (K)
Edington, Luke T. 1817 wb-1-0 (Sm)
Edington, Nicholas 1814 wb-2-120 (K)
Edleman, John 1826 wb-#134 (Mu)
Edminson, Cullen 1836 wb-2-143 (Ma)
Edminson, John 1812 wb-2-1 (K)
Edminson, Solomon 1818 wb-3-20 (K)
Edmiston, Alice 1840 wb-12-94* (D)
Edmiston, Andrew 1816 wb-A-149 (Li)
Edmiston, David 1816 wb-7-12 (D)
Edmiston, James E. 1815 wb-2-150 (Wi)
Edmiston, John 1816 wb-7-5 (D)
Edmiston, John 1824 wb-3-673 (Wi)
Edmiston, John 1839 wb-7-182 (Wi)
Edmiston, John B. 1844 wb-8-159 (Wi)
Edmiston, Nicholas P. 1835 wb-10-504 (D)
Edmiston, Robert 1816 wb-7-51 (D)
Edmiston, Samuel 1821 Wb-3-263 (Wi)
Edmiston, Thomas 1834 wb-10-290 (D)
Edmiston, William 1793 wb-1-233 (Je)
Edmiston, William 1853 wb-2-149 (Sh)
Edmon, Moses 1855 ib-2-193 (Cl)
Edmond, John 1843 wb-11-343 (Rb)
Edmonds, A. A. (Widow) 1857 wb-j-341 (O)

Edmonds, Benjamin 1854 wb-n-434 (Mt)
Edmonds, David W. 1816 wb-7-68 (D)
Edmonds, David W. 1818 wb-7-222 (D)
Edmonds, Howel 1855 wb-g-655 (Hn)
Edmonds, James L. 1843 wb-1-97 (Sh)
Edmonds, John J. 1850 wb-g-365 (Hn)
Edmonds, Mary A. 1859 wb-k-110 (O)
Edmonds, Samuel 1844 wb-d-136 (O)
Edmonds, William 1850 wb-9-437 (Wi)
Edmonds, William 1855 wb-j-54 (O)
Edmondson, Benjamin 1823 wb-1-44 (Bo)
Edmondson, Benjamin 1855 wb-n-525 (Mt)
Edmondson, James 1852 wb-15-435 (D)
Edmondson, James M. 1841 wb-z-260 (Mu)
Edmondson, John 1827 wb-4-165 (Wi)
Edmondson, John 1838 wb-y-150 (Mu)
Edmondson, Michael 1849 wb-d-162 (G)
Edmondson, Moses 1855 ib-2-364 (Cl)
Edmondson, Robert 1816 wb-4-449 (D)
Edmondson, Robert E. 1861 wb-2-340 (Li)
Edmondson, Thomas 1824 wb-8-365 (D)
Edmondson, Thomas 1825 wb-8-435 (D)
Edmondson, Thomas 1853 wb-16-78 (D)
Edmondson, William 1832 wb-5-182 (Wi)
Edmondson, William 1837 wb-1-206 (W)
Edmondson, William 1844 wb-8-193 (Wi)
Edmondson, William 1849 wb-1-40 (Bo)
Edmonson, Eliza V. 1851 wb-15-29 (D)
Edmonson, John 1828 wb-a-114 (G)
Edmonson, Robert 1822 wb-1-16 (Ma)
Edmonston, Andrew J. 1855 wb-11-499 (Wi)
Edmonston, Ardas? 1830 rb-f-17 (Mt)
Edmonston, Robert 1799 rb-a-31 (Mt)
Edmundson, John S. 1854 lr (Gi)
Edmundson, Robert 1850 wb-d-238 (G)
Edmundson, Wiley 1855 wb-6-76 (Ma)
Edmunson, Joseph 1851 wb-2-110 (Sh)
Edney, Alson 1816 wb-2-270 (Wi)
Edney, Amanda 1846 wb-13-413 (D)
Edney, Elevin 1853 wb-15-514 (D)
Edney, Levin 1852 wb-15-302 (D)
Edney, Newton 1835 wb-10-501 (D)
Edney, Polly 1824 wb-3-700 (Wi)
Edrington, Prior 1857 wb-f-106 (G)
Edson, Nancy 1854 wb-15-610 (D)
Edson, Samuel 1834 wb-8-413 (Rb)
Edson, Samuel 1854 wb-15-592 (Rb)
Edward, Debby 1836 wb-#53 (Mc)
Edward, Edmund 1826 wb-5-268 (Rb)
Edward, Olive C. 1845 wb-f-265* (Hn)
Edwards, Adonijah 1832 as-b-94 (Di)

Edwards, Alford 1832 as-a-223 (Di)
Edwards, Alford 1832 as-a-271 (Di)
Edwards, Alfred 1844 as-b-257 (Di)
Edwards, Andrew 1838 wb-a-70 (Cr)
Edwards, Arther M. 1854 rb-17-275 (Ru)
Edwards, Arthur 1806 wb-3-71 (D)
Edwards, Augustus 1841 wb-#135 (Wl)
Edwards, Benjamin 1851 lr (Sn)
Edwards, Celia 1831 wb-#229 (Mu)
Edwards, Cely 1841 wb-z-116 (Mu)
Edwards, Charles F. 1850 wb-g-317 (St)
Edwards, Edward 1849 wb-14-110 (Rb)
Edwards, Eli 1836 wb-#112 (Wl)
Edwards, Elias 1845 wb-b-105 (We)
Edwards, Elizabeth 1852 wb-a-166 (T)
Edwards, Francis 1842 wb-3-559 (Ma)
Edwards, Francis C. 1839 wb-3-10 (Ma)
Edwards, Frank M. 1855 wb-6-12 (Ma)
Edwards, Gravet 1851 wb-14-414 (Rb)
Edwards, Gray 1803 mr (Gi)
Edwards, Gray 1846 wb-12-533 (Rb)
Edwards, Hannah 1851 wb-1-290 (Fr)
Edwards, Henry 1824 wb-b-158 (St)
Edwards, Henry 1825 wb-b-20 (St)
Edwards, Henry 1848 ib-1-27 (Ca)
Edwards, Hiram 1828 wb-#74 (Wl)
Edwards, Hiram 1859 as-c-564 (Di)
Edwards, Isaac 1816 wb-7-97 (D)
Edwards, James 1829 wb-7-41 (Rb)
Edwards, James 1850 wb-#175 (Wl)
Edwards, James L. 1843 wb-2-10 (Sh)
Edwards, James P. 1834 wb-c-328 (St)
Edwards, Jessee 1855 wb-h-85 (St)
Edwards, John 1822 wb-3-329 (Wi)
Edwards, John 1833 wb-#102 (Wl)
Edwards, John 1850 wb-14-363 (Rb)
Edwards, John 1858 lr (Gi)
Edwards, John 1858 wb-16-678 (Rb)
Edwards, John J. 1848 wb-g-270 (Hn)
Edwards, John N. 1858 wb-12-592 (Wi)
Edwards, John S. 1859 wb-7-40 (Ma)
Edwards, John W. 1847 rb-14-204 (Ru)
Edwards, Jonathan 1852 wb-15-171 (Rb)
Edwards, Joseph 1854 wb-15-590 (Rb)
Edwards, Joseph B. 1849 wb-g-155 (St)
Edwards, Joseph S. 1823 wb-a-173 (Wh)
Edwards, Justin L. 1852 wb-5-116 (Ma)
Edwards, Kiturea 1840 wb-e-357 (Hu)
Edwards, Littleberry 1859 lr (Sn)
Edwards, Maddison 1845 wb-f-274* (Hn)
Edwards, Maria 1842 wb-#136 (Wl)

Edwards, Mary 1836 wb-1-180 (Gr)
Edwards, Mary 1849 wb-#171 (Wl)
Edwards, Matthew 1821 rb-5-61 (Ru)
Edwards, Nathan 1831 lr (Sn)
Edwards, Nathan 1860 wb-a-344 (Cr)
Edwards, Nicholas 1835 wb-#144 (Wl)
Edwards, Owen 1821 rb-5-90 (Ru)
Edwards, P. George 1835 wb-3-340 (Je)
Edwards, Ransom 1825 wb-#58 (Wl)
Edwards, Rebecca 1838 wb-10-150 (Rb)
Edwards, Richardson 1857 wb-a-308 (Cr)
Edwards, Robert 1831 wb-#87 (Wl)
Edwards, Robert 1832 wb-#93 (Wl)
Edwards, Sarah 1844 wb-#142 (Wl)
Edwards, Sarah 1853 wb-xx-287 (St)
Edwards, Spencer 1848 ib-1-78 (Cl)
Edwards, Stephen 1830 wb-#228 (Mu)
Edwards, Susan 1848 wb-9-184 (Wi)
Edwards, Thomas 1814 wb-#9 (Mu)
Edwards, Thomas 1849 wb-#45 (Wa)
Edwards, Thomas 1850 rb-15-236 (Ru)
Edwards, Thomas 1856 wb-e-443 (G)
Edwards, Thomas M. 1852 rb-16-320 (Ru)
Edwards, Thomas R. 1821 wb-A-311 (Li)
Edwards, W. D. 1861 wb-a-212 (Ce)
Edwards, West 1815 wb-1-264 (Sn)
Edwards, William 1814 lr (Sn)
Edwards, William 1824 rb-6-53 (Ru)
Edwards, William 1828 lr (Sn)
Edwards, William 1834 wb-#103 (Wl)
Edwards, William 1836 wb-9-221 (Rb)
Edwards, William 1837 wb-9-414 (Rb)
Edwards, William 1839 wb-2-248 (Sn)
Edwards, William 1844 wb-d-139 (Ro)
Edwards, William 1847 wb-b-235 (We)
Edwards, William 1850 wb-9-465 (Wi)
Edwards, William sr. 1827 lr (Sn)
Eesley, Christian 1829 eb-1-241 (C)
Eggleston, George P. 1860 wb-d-71 (L)
Eggman, Lott 1841 wb-10-547 (Rb)
Eggnew, James 1849 wb-4-511 (Hr)
Egman, Mary 1861 wb-17-252 (Rb)
Egmon, Sol 1840 wb-10-527 (Rb)
Egnew, Jesse W. 1852 wb-4-531 (Mu)
Ehrhart, John 1861 wb-18-430 (D)
Eicheson, Martha 1851 wb-d-312 (G)
Eidson, Nancy 1854 wb-15-631 (Rb)
Eidson, Samuel 1854 wb-15-629 (Rb)
Eidson, William sr. 1859 wb-1-176 (Hw)
Elam, Ann V. 1861 wb-i-350 (St)
Elam, Catharine 1839 wb-11-543 (D)

Elam, Daniel 1829 rb-7-168 (Ru)
Elam, Daniel 1829 rb-7-308 (Ru)
Elam, Edward 1830 wb-4-492 (Wi)
Elam, Edward 1846 wb-8-436 (Wi)
Elam, Elizabeth 1850 wb-g-200 (St)
Elam, Gilbert 1842 wb-a-102 (L)
Elam, Jane 1846 wb-8-434 (Wi)
Elam, John M. 1856 wb-h-178 (St)
Elam, Samuel 1853 wb-xx-170 (St)
Elam, Stephen 1813 wb-2-9 (Wi)
Elam, William C. 1858 wb-3-450 (W)
Elder, Andrew 1834 wb-1-100 (Gr)
Elder, C. 1845 wb-e-68 (O)
Elder, Elizabeth 1855 wb-3-298 (Gr)
Elder, Elizabeth 1856 wb-3-257 (Gr)
Elder, James 1824 rb-6-67 (Ru)
Elder, James 1826 rb-e-82 (Mt)
Elder, James 1854 wb-i-137 (O)
Elder, John 1853 wb-e-17 (Hy)
Elder, Robt. 1853 wb-e-33 (G)
Elder, William 1823 wb-2-413 (Je)
Elder, William 1842 wb-c-26 (G)
Eldridge, Alfred 1858 wb-3e-81 (Sh)
Eldridge, Edwin H. 1858 rb-o-603 (Mt)
Eldridge, Simeon 1851 wb-#54 (Mc)
Eldridge, Thomas 1857 wb-3e-35 (Sh)
Elean, George H. 1855 wb-b-1 (F)
Eleazer, George 1815 rb-b-273 (Mt)
Eleazer, John 1819 rb-c-78 (Mt)
Eleazer, Stephen 1837? as-a-394 (Di)
Eleazor, Catharine 1843 rb-i-551 (Mt)
Elerson, Jas. R. 1847 wb-13-165 (Rb)
Elgin, E. A. (Mrs.) 1841 wb-2-243 (Hr)
Elgin, Elizabeth 1835 wb-1-413 (Hr)
Elgin, Elizabeth 1836 wb-1-466 (Hr)
Elgin, Elizabeth A. 1837 wb-1-515 (Hr)
Elgin, Elizabeth Ann 1835 wb-1-479 (Hr)
Elgin, James 1827 wb-3-0 (Sm)
Elgin, John 1804 wb-#2 (Wl)
Elgin, John 1823 wb-#49 (Wl)
Elgin, Saml. 1849 rb-15-186 (Ru)
Elgin, W. B. 1834 wb-1-371 (Hr)
Elison, Hanah 1857 wb-1-176 (Be)
Elison, Joseph 1829 wb-2-0 (Sm)
Elkins, Alsey 1830 wb-b-72 (Hn)
Elkins, David 1836 wb-1-113 (Gr)
Elkins, Indamon L. 1848 ib-1-44 (Ca)
Elkins, John 1830 wb-#54 (Mc)
Elkins, Joseph 1834 wb-1-81 (Gr)
Elkins, William 1838 wb-d-238* (Hn)
Ellace, Robert 1818 lr (Sn)

Elledge, William 1825 wb-2-456 (Je)
Ellege, Wm. F. 1850 ib-1-113 (Ca)
Ellenor, Etheldred 1839 wb-e-31 (Hn)
Ellet, Patrick 1831 wb-#30 (Wa)
Ellington, Chasteen 1846 wb-5-28 (Ma)
Ellington, Paskal W. 1848 as-a-163 (Ms)
Ellington, Wm. 1859 gs-1-344 (F)
Ellinor, E. 1837 wb-d-300 (Hn)
Elliot, Hugh 1801 lr (Sn)
Elliot, John 1800 wb-2-176 (D)
Elliot, Knacy H. 1840 wb-7-243 (Wi)
Elliot, William 1836 rb-g-320 (Mt)
Elliott, A. B. 1854 as-b-150 (Ms)
Elliott, Alexander N. 1852 wb-10-261 (Wi)
Elliott, Allen 1848 wb-9-205 (Wi)
Elliott, Catharine 1839 rb-10-462 (Ru)
Elliott, Deborah 1829 rb-7-303 (Ru)
Elliott, Elizabeth 1854 wb-n-554 (Mt)
Elliott, Exum 1827 wb-4-233 (Wi)
Elliott, Hiram 1861 rb-21-48 (Ru)
Elliott, Isaac 1839 wb-d-379 (St)
Elliott, James 1816 rb-b-267 (Mt)
Elliott, James 1836 rb-9-390 (Ru)
Elliott, James 1856 ib-1-422 (Wy)
Elliott, James 1856 ib-2-1 (Wy)
Elliott, James D. 1845 wb-a2-248 (Mu)
Elliott, James sr. 1845 wb-12-368 (Rb)
Elliott, John 1828 wb-6-299 (Rb)
Elliott, John 1833 wb-3-257 (Je)
Elliott, John 1858 wb-b-58 (Ms)
Elliott, Jonathan C. 1857 ib-1-470 (Wy)
Elliott, Jonathan C. 1857 ib-2-7 (Wy)
Elliott, Joseph M. C. 1837 wb-6-396 (Wi)
Elliott, Knacey 1838 wb-6-469 (Wi)
Elliott, Lewis 1810 rb-a-435 (Mt)
Elliott, Margarett 1837 rb-g-498 (Mt)
Elliott, Nacy 1849 rb-15-61 (Ru)
Elliott, Nancy 1811 rb-b-36 (Mt)
Elliott, Richard R. 1859 rb-19-528 (Ru)
Elliott, Robert 1833 eb-1-274 (C)
Elliott, Samuel J. 1859 rb-19-527 (Ru)
Elliott, Thomas 1830 wb-4-388 (K)
Elliott, Thomas 1850 wb-14-405 (Rb)
Elliott, Thomas 1850 wb-14-409 (Rb)
Elliott, Thomas S. 1852 wb-xx-81 (St)
Elliott, William 1822 rb-d-16 (Mt)
Elliott, William 1832 rb-f-333 (Mt)
Elliott, William 1835 rb-9-248 (Ru)
Elliott, William 1855 wb-n-694 (Mt)
Elliott, Wm. J. 1846 rb-k-81 (Mt)
Ellis, Abner 1849 wb-10-236 (K)

Ellis, Abraham 1811 wb-2-0 (Sm)
Ellis, Abraham 1827 wb-2-0 (Sm)
Ellis, Azariah 1853 wb-16-86 (D)
Ellis, Caleb 1828 wb-b-241 (St)
Ellis, Caleb 1859 wb-f-265 (Ro)
Ellis, Duncan H. 1850 wb-g-219 (St)
Ellis, E. B. 1836 as-a-373 (Di)
Ellis, Edward 1800 wb-2-175 (D)
Ellis, Ellis 1808 ib-1-219 (Ge)
Ellis, Ephrim 1834 as-a-248 (Di)
Ellis, Ezekiel 1869 wb-#54 (Mc)
Ellis, Francis 1839 wb-c-62 (Ro)
Ellis, George T. 1848 wb-9-178 (Wi)
Ellis, Henry 1855 wb-#26 (Mo)
Ellis, Hicks 1860 rb-20-339 (Ru)
Ellis, Hicks 1860 rb-20-344 (Ru)
Ellis, Ira 1859 wb-h-303 (Hn)
Ellis, Jacob 1834 wb-#31 (Wa)
Ellis, Jacob 1858 wb-2-87# (Ge)
Ellis, James 1817 wb-A-208 (Li)
Ellis, James 1833 wb-#101 (Wl)
Ellis, James 1840 wb-7-295 (Wi)
Ellis, James 1849 wb-1-349 (Li)
Ellis, Jeremiah 1845 wb-13-218 (D)
Ellis, Jesse S. 1855 wb-15-719 (Rb)
Ellis, John 1815 wb-#22 (Wl)
Ellis, John 1828 wb-1-160 (Ma)
Ellis, John 1845 wb-g-79 (Hn)
Ellis, John H. 1851 wb-14-572 (D)
Ellis, John sr. 1844 wb-1-171 (Hw)
Ellis, Jonathan 1844 148-1-71 (Ge)
Ellis, Joshua 1840 wb-12-8* (D)
Ellis, Lucretia 1843 wb-11-458 (Rb)
Ellis, Mead 1837 wb-e-27 (Hu)
Ellis, Nancy 1853 as-c-213 (Di)
Ellis, Nancy 1858 wb-12-483 (K)
Ellis, Nancy W. 1853 as-c-240 (Di)
Ellis, Nathan 1830 wb-#87 (Wl)
Ellis, Ransom 1833 wb-a-100 (Di)
Ellis, Ransom 1852 as-c-193 (Di)
Ellis, Rebecca 1837 wb-#119 (Wl)
Ellis, Samuel 1835 wb-2-45# (Ge)
Ellis, Simion 1815 wb-#18 (Wl)
Ellis, Sims 1842 wb-11-154 (Rb)
Ellis, Sophia B. 1859 rb-20-187 (Ru)
Ellis, Stephen 1826 wb-5-417 (Rb)
Ellis, T. T. 1856 wb-#118 (Wl)
Ellis, Thomas 1788 wb-1-8# (Ge)
Ellis, Thomas 1798 wb-2-145# (Ge)
Ellis, Thomas 1841 as-b-18 (Di)
Ellis, Thomas 1861 wb-1-8# (Ge)

Ellis, W. A. 1855 rb-17-450 (Ru)
Ellis, William 1809 wb-#11 (Wa)
Ellis, William 1828 wb-b-255 (St)
Ellis, William 1831 wb-7-494 (Rb)
Ellis, William 1837 rb-9-409 (Ru)
Ellis, William 1859 wb-i-115 (St)
Ellis, Willis P. jr. 1833 wb-3-0 (Sm)
Ellis, Wyatt 1855 wb-11-565 (Wi)
Ellis, Wyott H. 1847 rb-14-5 (Ru)
Ellis, _____ (Mr.) 1844 wb-12-171 (Rb)
Ellison, Amos 1816 wb-1-0 (Sm)
Ellison, Andrew 1846 wb-13-33 (Rb)
Ellison, Charles 1851 wb-14-472 (Rb)
Ellison, James 1853 wb-m-645 (Mt)
Ellison, John 1857 wb-2-85# (Ge)
Ellison, Joseph 1826 wb-3-0 (Sm)
Ellison, Margaret 1837 wb-d-167* (Hn)
Ellison, Thomas 1855 wb-1-175 (Hw)
Ellison, William 1812 wb-#11 (Wl)
Ellison, William 1846 wb-g-135 (Hn)
Elliston, Charles M. 1857 wb-17-380 (D)
Elliston, John 1823 wb-8-171 (D)
Elliston, Joseph J. 1857 wb-17-367 (D)
Ellitt, John P. 1849 wb-b-483 (Mu)
Elmore, Alfred 1855 wb-e-43 (Hy)
Elmore, Archelus 1833 wb-3-211 (Je)
Elmore, Archibald 1834 wb-3-284 (Je)
Elmore, Calvin 1857 wb-4-9 (Je)
Elmore, Henry 1847 wb-13-126 (Rb)
Elmore, James 1850 wb-14-408 (Rb)
Elmore, Joel 1802 wb-1-36 (Je)
Elmore, Joel 1855 wb-5-393 (Je)
Elmore, John 1858 wb-16-618 (Rb)
Elmore, Nancy 1841 wb-4-69 (Je)
Elmore, Thomas 1842 wb-4-527 (Mu)
Elmore, Thomas 1844 wb-3-461 (Hy)
Elmore, Thomas 1845 wb-4-60 (Je)
Elmore, Thomas sr. 1832 wb-3-197 (Je)
Elmore, Traviss 1816 wb-2-373 (Rb)
Elrod, Adam 1857 ib-1-420 (Ca)
Elrod, Calaway 1861 wb-1-152 (Jo)
Elrod, James 1839 wb-3-118 (Ma)
Elrod, Jeremiah 1841 rb-12-45 (Ru)
Elrod, Jeremiah 1841 rb-12-74 (Ru)
Elrod, John 1857 ib-1-464 (Ca)
Elsea, Isaac 1840 wb-a-443 (R)
Elsey, Thomas 1826 wb-#22 (Wa)
Elsom, Elizabeth 1849 wb-#55 (Mc)
Elston, Eliel 1860 wb-7-78 (Ma)
Elston, Jesse C. 1855 wb-6-16 (Ma)
Elston, William 1818 wb-1-0 (Sm)

113

Elston, William 1843 wb-3-694 (Ma)
Elswick, Stephen 1824 eb-1-142 (C)
Elum, John D. 1849 wb-d-186 (G)
Ely, Elizabeth 1861 wb-e-163 (Hy)
Ely, George 1813 wb-2-35# (Ge)
Ely, George T. 1854 wb-h-220 (Hu)
Ely, Jas. A. G. 1854 ib-2-202 (Cl)
Ely, Jessee 1847 rb-k-390 (Mt)
Ely, Thomas 1836 wb-e-50 (Hu)
Elzey, Sarah 1855 as-b-182 (Ms)
Elzey, William 1855 as-b-182 (Ms)
Emberson, Allen 1841 wb-#55 (Mc)
Embree, Elbert L. 1851 wb-#50 (Wa)
Embree, Elihu 1821 wb-#18 (Wa)
Embrey, Baley 1832 wb-1-107 (Fr)
Embrey, Martha 1853 wb-1-319 (Fr)
Embrey, Merrell 1844 wb-1-219 (Fr)
Embrey, Peter 1848 wb-1-252 (Fr)
Embrey, Reuben 1835 wb-1-381 (Hr)
Embry, Amelia 1852 wb-1-300 (Fr)
Embry, Jessee 1848 wb-1-256 (Fr)
Embry, Reuben 1845 wb-3-286 (Hr)
Embry?, P. J. 1833 wb-1-103 (Hy)
Emerson, Benjamin 1848 as-a-163 (Ms)
Emerson, Rebecca 1851 wb-14-436 (Rb)
Emerson, Susan 1851 wb-f-8 (Mu)
Emerson, William 1851 wb-14-489 (Rb)
Emert, Jacob 1855 wb-2-253 (Me)
Emmerson, Catharine 1858 wb-#61 (Wa)
Emmerson, Eli 1838 wb-b-95 (Hd)
Emmerson, Jesse 1859 as-c-192 (Ms)
Emmerson, John 1844 wb-4-273 (Ma)
Emmerson, Thomas 1837 wb-#36 (Wa)
Emmert, William 1856 wb-1-105 (Jo)
Emmery, Frederick 1829 wb-1-5 (Sh)
Emmet?, Mary 1854? wb-2-26 (Ct)
Emmett, George W. 1846 wb-#55 (Mc)
Empson, Gregory 1830 wb-7-212 (Rb)
Empson, Thomas 1803 wb-#1 (Wl)
Endaley, Jas. 1831 rb-8-214 (Ru)
Endsley, Hugh 1833 wb-#103 (Wl)
Endsley, James 1848 wb-1-40 (Bo)
Endsley, John 1855 wb-a-354 (Ms)
Endsley, Mary 1856 as-c-22 (Ms)
England, Alcy 1855 wb-d-292 (Wh)
England, Alexander W. 1846 wb-2-127 (W)
England, Anderson 1860 as-c-577 (Di)
England, Daniel 1848 mr-2-294 (Be)
England, Daniel G. 1837 wb-2-216 (Ma)
England, David G. 1837 wb-2-228 (Ma)
England, E. G. 1859 wb-1C-479 (A)

England, Elijah 1828 wb-a-333 (Wh)
England, F. 1854 wb-1C-181 (A)
England, Frederick 1857 wb-1C-359 (A)
England, Isabella 1850 wb-c-420 (Wh)
England, James 1834 wb-8-397 (Rb)
England, James 1848 wb-1B-79 (A)
England, James C. 1839 wb-6-419 (K)
England, James S. 1861 wb-c-441 (Wh)
England, Jesse 1846 wb-c-240 (Wh)
England, Lydia 1844 wb-12-206 (Rb)
England, Mary Elizabeth 1861 wb-c-406 (Wh)
England, Rebecca 1838 mr-1-31 (Be)
England, William M. 1853 wb-15-376 (Rb)
England, Wm. C. 1859 gs-1-473 (F)
England, Zepporiah 1851 wb-1B-197 (A)
Engleman, Joseph 1816 wb-4-430 (D)
Engleman, Joseph 1816 wb-7-13 (D)
English, Abraham 1836 wb-1-171 (W)
English, Alexander 1858 wb-2-86# (Ge)
English, Andrew (esq) 1861 wb-2-92# (Ge)
English, Andrew 1795 wb-1-8# (Ge)
English, Anthony 1839 eb-1-407 (C)
English, Edward 1848 wb-b-289 (Mu)
English, Edward W. 1831 wb-#230 (Mu)
English, James 1804 as-1-57 (Ge)
English, James 1804 wb-1-8# (Ge)
English, James 1834 wb-c-374 (St)
English, James B. 1839 wb-1-161 (Li)
English, John (Sr.) 1807 wb-#11 (Wa)
English, John 1852 wb-2-74# (Ge)
English, John 1858 wb-#60 (Wa)
English, Joshua 1829 eb-1-239 (C)
English, Nancy 1822 wb-a-163 (Ro)
English, Stephen 1826 wb-b-95 (St)
English, Susan 1849 ib-1-58 (Ca)
English, Thomas 1816 wb-#14 (Wa)
English, Thomas 1829 wb-#180 (Mu)
Engster, John W. 1857 wb-17-150 (D)
Enoch, David 1809 wb-1-0 (Sm)
Enoch, John 1842 wb-3-0 (Sm)
Enoch, Stokely H. 1826 wb-a-8 (Cr)
Enright, Robert 1841 wb-3-477 (Ma)
Ensor, William T. 1847 wb-#46 (Wa)
Enyart, John 1806 wb-1-329 (Je)
Ephland, Elijah E. 1854 wb-i-182 (O)
Ephland, Elijah G. 1859 wb-k-46 (O)
Epperson, Anthony 1839 wb-3-0 (Sm)
Epperson, John 1852 wb-3-52 (Gr)
Epperson, Joseph 1814 wb-1-167 (Hw)
Epperson, Littleberry 1812 wb-1-288 (Wi)
Epperson, Samuel 1856 wb-6-297 (Ma)

Epperson, William 1823 wb-1-169 (Hw)
Eppes, Elizabeth 1840 wb-7-304 (Wi)
Epps, Daniel 1813 rb-b-106 (Mt)
Epps, David A. 1862 as-c-234 (Ms)
Epps, Edward 1813 rb-2-226 (Ru)
Epps, Edward 1841 wb-7-178 (K)
Epps, Freeman 1855 as-b-191 (Ms)
Epps, George 1849 wb-9-294 (Wi)
Epps, John P. 1844 wb-3-471 (Hy)
Epps, Peter 1841 wb-7-425 (Wi)
Epps, Rebecca 1856 rb-18-235 (Ru)
Erasly?, Thomas 1820 rb-4-263 (Ru)
Erskine, Thomas W. 1850 wb-14-551 (D)
Ervin, Francis 1833 eb-1-308 (C)
Ervin, John 1844 wb-f-211 (St)
Ervin, Patrick 1855 wb-#26 (Mo)
Ervin, Samuel 1850 wb-4-562 (Hr)
Ervin, William 1849 ib-1-71 (Ca)
Erving, John 1827 wb-1-41 (Bo)
Erwin, Alexander 1789 wb-1-7# (Ge)
Erwin, Alexander 1843 wb-z-544 (Mu)
Erwin, Alexander S. 1843 wb-z-546 (Mu)
Erwin, Andrew 1838 wb-a-350 (R)
Erwin, David 1826 wb-4-127 (Wi)
Erwin, Edward 1794 wb-1-166 (Hw)
Erwin, Francis 1841 wb-c-249 (Ro)
Erwin, Isaac N. 1859 wb-e-210 (Wh)
Erwin, Isaac Newton 1859 wb-e-274 (Wh)
Erwin, J. L. 1859 gs-1-257 (F)
Erwin, James sr. 1861 wb-18-589 (D)
Erwin, John 1822 lr (Sn)
Erwin, John 1845 wb-3-264 (Hr)
Erwin, John E. 1845 wb-a-60 (Ms)
Erwin, Jonas 1831 wb-#226 (Mu)
Erwin, Jonathan 1859 gs-1-206 (F)
Erwin, Joseph 1845 wb-13-356 (D)
Erwin, Joseph 1851 rb-4-273 (Mu)
Erwin, Rachel 1825 wb-a-213 (Wh)
Erwin, Robert A. 1846 as-a-128 (Ms)
Erwin, Samuel A. 1834 lw (Ct)
Erwin, William 1838 wb-11-368 (D)
Erwin, William 1850 wb-c-379 (Wh)
Erwin, William 1850 wb-c-400 (Wh)
Erwin, William 1852 wb-a-287 (Ms)
Erwin, William F. 1855 as-b-219 (Ms)
Erwin, Wm. 1859 gs-1-495 (F)
Escue, Samuel C. 1840 wb-#133 (Wl)
Eskew, Alexander 1841 wb-#135 (Wl)
Eskew, Alexander 1851 wb-#176 (Wl)
Eskew, Andrew 1854 wb-#113 (Wl)
Eskew, Benjamin 1843 wb-#139 (Wl)

Eskew, Benjamin 1848 wb-#163 (Wl)
Eskew, Eliza 1842 wb-#136 (Wl)
Eskew, James 1839 wb-#125 (Wl)
Eskridge, Parthenia 1859 wb-7-44 (Ma)
Eskridge, Samuel 1853 wb-e-373 (Ro)
Eskridge, Sophia 1857 wb-f-127 (Ro)
Eskridge, Thomas 1852 wb-a-418 (F)
Eslinger, Andrew 1820 wb-2-297 (Je)
Eslinger, Andrew 1837 wb-3-472 (Je)
Espey, George 1818 lr (Sn)
Espey, James 1813 rb-2-235 (Ru)
Espey, John 1855 ib-1-373 (Ca)
Espey, W. R. 1859 wb-c-305 (L)
Espy, Robert A. 1858 rb-19-223 (Ru)
Espy, Wm. R. 1859 wb-c-320 (L)
Ess, Mary 1819 wb-1-187 (Bo)
Esselman, James C. 1845 lr (Gi)
Essex, John 1860 wb-1-164 (R)
Essex, Thomas (Dr.) 1833 lr (Sn)
Essman, Thomas 1824 wb-#55 (Mc)
Estabrook, Joseph 1855 wb-e-540 (Ro)
Esters, Francis 1842 wb-f-105* (Hn)
Estes, Bartlet 1836 wb-11-106 (D)
Estes, Benjamin 1844 wb-#144 (Wl)
Estes, Benjamin H. 1843? wb-#142 (Wl)
Estes, George W. 1832 wb-1-58 (Gr)
Estes, Henry C. 1837 wb-1-345 (Hy)
Estes, Henry W. 1861 wb-f-409 (G)
Estes, J. B. 1842 wb-3-116 (Hy)
Estes, Joel 1833 wb-1-95 (Hy)
Estes, John 1840 wb-5-53 (Gr)
Estes, John 1853 wb-3-167 (La)
Estes, John 1855 wb-3-230 (Gr)
Estes, John 1855 wb-6-32 (Ma)
Estes, Lewis 1844 wb-#145 (Wl)
Estes, Mary 1840 wb-#129 (Wl)
Estes, Moses 1815 wb-#19 (Wl)
Estes, Richard B. 1836 wb-#115 (Wl)
Estes, Robert 1840 wb-#137 (Wl)
Estes, Samuel ca. 1832 wb-1-229 (Ma)
Estes, Tempy 1846 wb-2-132 (W)
Estes, Thomas 1833 wb-1-46 (La)
Estes, William 1834 wb-b-43 (G)
Estill, John 1837 wb-11-46 (D)
Estill, Jonathan 1823 wb-A-347 (Li)
Estill, Samuel 1837 wb-b-357 (Ro)
Estill, Wallis 1847 wb-1-244 (Fr)
Estill, Wallis sr. 1834 wb-1-128 (Fr)
Estis, Burris 1830 wb-b-61 (Hn)
Estis, David 1834 wb-d-166 (Hn)
Estis, Henson 1840 wb-12-40* (D)

Estis, Martha 1847 wb-14-81 (D)
Estis, William 1815 wb-1-0 (Sm)
Estus, L. B. (Dr.) 1815 wb-#31 (Mu)
Estus, L. B. 1815 wb-#17 (Mu)
Estus, Sarah 1814 wb-#29 (Mu)
Etheradge, Caleb 1856 wb-e-457 (G)
Etherage, Michael 1837 wb-A-7 (Ca)
Etheredy, Ann 1855 wb-e-344 (G)
Etheridge, David T. 1823 wb-8-178 (D)
Etheridge, John 1852 wb-d-388 (G)
Etheridge, Thomas 1844 wb-b-52 (We)
Etherly, Rufus 1852 wb-2-130 (Sh)
Ethridge, Bassett 1824 rb-6-23 (Ru)
Ethridge, Polly 1837 wb-d-150 (St)
Ethridge, Thomas 1856 wb-3-353 (La)
Ethrige, David T. 1828 wb-b-237 (St)
Etter, F. W. 1858 wb-#55 (Mc)
Etter, John 1851 rb-15-585 (Ru)
Etter, Phebe 1861 wb-2-93# (Ge)
Eubank, Ambrose 1860 wb-18-140 (D)
Eubank, Elijah 1845 wb-12-367 (Rb)
Eudaly, William 1852 wb-11-174 (K)
Evans, Abraham 1848 wb-2-324 (W)
Evans, Ann 1847 wb-8-533 (Wi)
Evans, Benjamin 1820 wb-3-123 (Wi)
Evans, Benjamin 1835 wb-b-247 (Ro)
Evans, Bird 1814 wb-4-292 (D)
Evans, Brastus 1843 wb-2-60# (Ge)
Evans, Caleb 1838? as-a-434 (Di)
Evans, Charles 1844 wb-7-0 (Sm)
Evans, Charles 1847 wb-f-127+ (O)
Evans, Charles C. 1848 wb-A-61 (Ca)
Evans, Cornelius 1831? wb-1A-43 (A)
Evans, Dale 1824 wb-1-0 (Sm)
Evans, Daniel 1826 wb-#150 (Mu)
Evans, Daniel 1853 wb-e-56 (G)
Evans, David 1831 wb-b-75 (Wh)
Evans, David 1843 rb-12-416 (Ru)
Evans, Edward 1861 39-2-472 (Dk)
Evans, Elijah 1842 5-2-264 (Cl)
Evans, Elisha 1836 wb-9-173 (Rb)
Evans, Elizabeth 1820 wb-7-434 (D)
Evans, Elizabeth 1844 wb-a2-13 (Mu)
Evans, Etheldred 1843 wb-z-493 (Mu)
Evans, Evan 1825 wb-a-6 (R)
Evans, Ezekiel 1855 rb-17-494 (Ru)
Evans, George 1830 rb-8-64 (Ru)
Evans, Hannah 1841 wb-2-57# (Ge)
Evans, Hannah 1845 wb-1-289 (Li)
Evans, Isaac H. 1859 rb-p-200 (Mt)
Evans, Isham 1814 Wb-2-107 (Wi)

Evans, Jacob 1842 wb-a-155 (Di)
Evans, James 1840 eb-1-427 (C)
Evans, James 1857 wb-1-175 (Be)
Evans, James D. 1841 rb-12-52 (Ru)
Evans, James H. 1854 wb-2-78# (Ge)
Evans, Jane 1832 wb-b-86 (Wh)
Evans, Jesse 1805 wb-1-14 (Wi)
Evans, Jesse 1830 wb-4-499 (Wi)
Evans, John 1809 wb-4-56 (D)
Evans, John 1833 wb-x-46 (Mu)
Evans, John 1836 lr (Gi)
Evans, John 1837 wb-a-241 (O)
Evans, John 1840 5-2-185 (Cl)
Evans, John 1842 wb-c-22 (G)
Evans, John 1843 wb-1-292 (La)
Evans, John 1844 rb-13-42 (Ru)
Evans, John 1853 ib-1-309 (Cl)
Evans, John 1854 as-2-324 (Ge)
Evans, John 1856 ib-h-476 (F)
Evans, John 1856 wb-12-206 (Wi)
Evans, John L. 1848 148-1-231 (Ge)
Evans, John S. 1861 wb-1-209 (R)
Evans, John W. 1833 wb-b-3 (G)
Evans, John W. 1850 wb-9-593 (Wi)
Evans, John jr. 1853 wb-11-69 (Wi)
Evans, John jr. 1856 wb-12-255 (Wi)
Evans, John sr. 1851 wb-9-660 (Wi)
Evans, Jonathan A. 1849 148-1-276 (Ge)
Evans, Jonathan sr. 1813 wb-2-35# (Ge)
Evans, Joseph 1831 wb-5-33 (K)
Evans, Joseph 1852 r39-1-229 (Dk)
Evans, Joseph S. 1860 wb-18-399 (D)
Evans, Josiah 1839 wb-3-59 (Ma)
Evans, Lewis 1821 as-A-80 (Di)
Evans, Lewis 1851 wb-d-16 (Wh)
Evans, Margret D. C. 1853 wb-16-91 (D)
Evans, Martha 1812 wb-1-282 (Wi)
Evans, Mary 1849? ib-1-146 (Cl)
Evans, Nancy 1858 rb-19-401 (Ru)
Evans, Nancy H. 1857 wb-e-171 (Wh)
Evans, Nathan 1797 wb-0-20 (K)
Evans, Parson 1858 ib-2-127 (Wy)
Evans, Rebecca 1833 wb-#99 (Wl)
Evans, Robert 1818 wb-3-29 (K)
Evans, Robert 1819 wb-7-312 (K)
Evans, Robert 1840 wb-2-55# (Ge)
Evans, Robert 1855? wb-#26 (Mo)
Evans, Robert H. 1845 148-1-99 (Ge)
Evans, Russel 1818 wb-1-0 (Sm)
Evans, S. T. 1859 wb-c-305 (L)
Evans, Sally B. 1860 wb-A-162 (Ca)

Evans, Samuel 1799 wb-1-67 (K)
Evans, Samuel Sr. 1851 wb-#55 (Mc)
Evans, Sanford 1861 149-1-208 (Ge)
Evans, Sarah (Mrs.) 1832 wb-3-204 (Je)
Evans, Sarah 1860 39-2-397 (Dk)
Evans, Sevier 1848 wb-c-290 (Wh)
Evans, Sherwood 1842 wb-3-0 (Sm)
Evans, Thomas 1816 wb-2-222 (K)
Evans, Thomas 1820 rb-4-209 (Ru)
Evans, Thomas F. 1854 148-1-503 (Ge)
Evans, W. G. 1841 wb-12-140* (D)
Evans, Walter 1827 wb-3-0 (Sm)
Evans, Walter 1837 wb-3-466 (Je)
Evans, William 1843 148-1-49 (Ge)
Evans, William 1853 wb-5-304 (Je)
Evans, William 1857 wb-e-74 (Hy)
Evans, William D. 1852 wb-7-0 (Sm)
Evans, William G. 1842 wb-12-350* (D)
Evans, William H. 1852 as-b-111 (Ms)
Evans, William H. 1857 wb-3e-54 (Sh)
Evans, William R. 1857 wb-e-171 (Wh)
Evans, William W. 1844 wb-1-331 (La)
Evens, Joseph 1837 wb-2-240 (Ma)
Evens, L. J. 1829 rb-7-229 (Ru)
Evens, Swail O. 1834 wb-3-0 (Sm)
Everett, Daniel 1852? wb-#24 (Mo)
Everett, David 1858 wb-7-0 (Sm)
Everett, James 1818 wb-7-275 (D)
Everett, Jesse 1860 wb-18-172 (D)
Everett, Jesse jr. 1820 wb-3-147 (K)
Everett, Jessee J. 1853 wb-16-117 (D)
Everett, John D. 1848 rb-k-757 (Mt)
Everett, John H. 1837 wb-#118 (Wl)
Everett, Kinchen 1835 wb-10-516 (D)
Everett, Phillip 1850 wb-1-8# (Ge)
Everett, Simon 1830 wb-9-435 (D)
Everett, Thomas H. 1854 wb-16-412 (D)
Everett, William R. 1860 wb-f-354 (G)
Everhart, Catharine 1847 wb-2-67# (Ge)
Everhart, Chrisley 1853 wb-1-169 (Hw)
Everhart, Nicholas 1854 wb-2-79# (Ge)
Everhart, Polly 1852 wb-1-176 (Hw)
Everhart, Polly Ann 1858 wb-2-88# (Ge)
Everit, John 1821 rb-c-430 (Mt)
Everly, Jacob 1836 wb-6-128 (Wi)
Everson, John 1857 wb-3e-46 (Sh)
Everson, John 1857 wb-3e-49 (Sh)
Evins, David 1814 Wb-2-78 (Wi)
Ewell, Conner 1837 wb-a-60 (T)
Ewell, James B. sr. 1847 wb-a-303 (F)
Ewell, William C. 1817 wb-7-207 (D)

Ewens, Robert 1853 as-b-113 (Ms)
Ewers, William 1851 wb-14-562 (D)
Ewin, Robert M. 1833 wb-b-118 (Wh)
Ewin, Watts D. 1857 wb-17-383 (D)
Ewing, Alexander 1822 wb-8-98 (D)
Ewing, Alexander 1824 wb-8-405 (D)
Ewing, Alexander 1850 wb-9-447 (Wi)
Ewing, Alexander C. 1834 wb-5-393 (Wi)
Ewing, Andrew 1813 wb-4-235 (D)
Ewing, Andrew F. 1829 wb-#181 (Mu)
Ewing, Andrew F. 1829? wb-#173 (Mu)
Ewing, Beedy 1845 wb-12-518 (Rb)
Ewing, C. B. 1860 as-c-190 (Ms)
Ewing, Chloe R. 1839 wb-7-162 (Wi)
Ewing, George 1838 wb-1-42 (Bo)
Ewing, H. L? 1858 rb-o-637 (Mt)
Ewing, H. Q? 1859 rb-p-258 (Mt)
Ewing, James 1810 wb-1-0 (Sm)
Ewing, James 1854 as-b-155 (Ms)
Ewing, James 1854 wb-#16 (Mo)
Ewing, James 1860 wb-b-104 (Ms)
Ewing, James L. 1845 wb-#147 (Wl)
Ewing, John L. 1816 wb-4-457 (D)
Ewing, John L. 1846 wb-#150 (Wl)
Ewing, John M. 1852 wb-2-39 (Li)
Ewing, John O. 1826 wb-9-49 (D)
Ewing, Joseph D. 1836 wb-x-401 (Mu)
Ewing, Joseph L. 1860 wb-18-383 (D)
Ewing, Joseph P. 1833 wb-x-119 (Mu)
Ewing, Joshua 1847 wb-1-326 (Li)
Ewing, Lile A. 1853 wb-a-300 (Ms)
Ewing, M. P. 1838 wb-11-286 (D)
Ewing, M. P. 1838 wb-11-305 (D)
Ewing, Margret 1846 wb-1-42 (Bo)
Ewing, N. E. (or A.) 1858 wb-h-220 (Hn)
Ewing, Nathan 1830 wb-9-404 (D)
Ewing, Nathan 1852 wb-15-414 (D)
Ewing, Nathaniel 1812 wb-1-29 (Fr)
Ewing, Randall M. 1853 wb-16-130 (D)
Ewing, Sarah 1840 wb-12-31 (D)
Ewing, Sarah 1841 wb-12-74 (D)
Ewing, Sarah 1855 wb-16-592 (D)
Ewing, Sarah S. 1859 wb-17-577 (D)
Ewing, Susannah 1819 wb-7-292 (D)
Ewing, T. J. H. 1855 as-b-183 (Ms)
Ewing, William 1795 wb-1-40 (K)
Ewing, William 1846 wb-13-369 (D)
Exum, Arther P. 1854 wb-i-136 (O)
Exum, Arthur 1819 wb-7-332 (D)
Exum, Dred 1860 39-2-389 (Dk)
Exum, Green 1846 wb-b-170 (We)

Exum, John 1850 wb-a-383 (F)
Exum, John 1858 wb-7-20 (Ma)
Exum, Martha 1860 wb-7-62 (Ma)
Exum, Robert 1852 wb-5-113 (Ma)
Ezell, Balaam 1833 wb-5-295 (Wi)
Ezell, Balaam 1850 wb-9-387 (Wi)
Ezell, Burnet M. 1849 as-a-194 (Ms)
Ezell, Charles G. 1852 wb-3-71 (La)
Ezell, Frederick 1859 wb-13-36 (Wi)
Ezell, George M. G. 1859 wb-17-621 (D)
Ezell, Henry 1859 rb-p-279 (Mt)
Ezell, Jephtha 1855 wb-a-370 (Ms)
Ezell, Jeremiah 1838 wb-11-378 (D)
Ezell, Jeremiah 1852 wb-10-374 (Wi)
Ezell, Joseph 1857 as-c-52 (Ms)
Ezell, Keziah 1851 as-b-41 (Ms)
Ezell, Lafayette 1852 wb-15-466 (D)
Ezell, Lameck W. 1854 lr (Gi)
Ezell, Littleberry R. 1852 as-b-53 (Ms)
Ezell, Micajah 1844 lr (Gi)
Ezell, Parham 1845 wb-f-293 (Hn)
Ezell, Thomas 1861 wb-4-433 (La)

- F -

Fagan, Henry 1855 rb-17-579 (Ru)
Fagan, Henry W. 1855 rb-17-525 (Ru)
Fagan, Peter 1843 wb-8-129 (K)
Fagan, Peter 1858 wb-f-154 (G)
Fagans, John 1820 rb-5-58 (Ru)
Fagg, Charles 1826 rb-6-218 (Ru)
Fagg, Ivel 1843 wb-z-518 (Mu)
Fagg, Joel 1843 wb-z-548 (Mu)
Fagg, William 1857 wb-b-94 (F)
Failing, Thomas 1837 wb-b-145 (G)
Fain, John 1788 wb-#2 (Wa)
Fain, John 1852 wb-5-100 (Je)
Fain, Nicholas 1847 wb-1-193 (Hw)
Fain, Nicholas S. 1830 wb-3-109 (Je)
Fain, William 1816 wb-#14 (Wa)
Fairall, Denis 1840 wb-z-95 (Mu)
Fairfax, Walter 1813 wb-4-253 (D)
Fairmon, John 1810 rb-a-350 (Mt)
Faison, Wright 1859 wb-5-97 (Hr)
Falconer, John 1811 wb-#9 (Wl)
Falk, Nancy 1848 wb-f-500 (St)
Falkener, Archabald 1842 wb-1-436 (W)
Falkner, David 1852 wb-11-282 (K)
Falkner, John 1820 rb-c-336 (Mt)
Fallen, Edmond 1824 wb-#76 (Mu)
Falls, James 1834 wb-10-275 (D)

Falwell, Elisha 1859 as-c-147 (Ms)
Fan, Elijah 1813 rb-2-249 (Ru)
Fancy, Henry 1847 wb-1-233 (Fr)
Fann (Tann?), Raleigh 1828 as-a-179 (Di)
Fanning, Middleton 1861 wb-2-344 (Li)
Fanville, Zachariah 1836 wb-#112 (Wl)
Fare, Jonathan sr. 1821 wb-1-0 (Sm)
Farear, William 1810 rb-a-364 (Mt)
Fargason, Dixon 1861 wb-8-67 (Sm)
Faribaugh, James 1859 wb-h-341 (Hn)
Faris, Alexander 1824 wb-#71 (Mu)
Faris, James 1840 wb-1-60 (Sh)
Faris, Jane 1840 abl-1-160 (T)
Faris, John 1840 wb-z-65 (Mu)
Faris, John A. 1816 wb-#101 (Mu)
Faris, John T. 1852 wb-4-382 (Mu)
Faris, Mary 1841 wb-z-244 (Mu)
Faris, Robert 1820? wb-#100 (Mu)
Faris, Robert 1821 wb-#71 (Mu)
Faris, William 1853 wb-1-313 (Fr)
Faris, William 1857 wb-0-149 (Cf)
Fariss, Jefferson 1850 A-468-144 (Lc)
Farley, Eliza 1859 gs-1-520 (F)
Farley, Isham 1848 wb-c-303 (Wh)
Farley, Isham F. 1846 wb-c-208 (Wh)
Farley, John 1823 wb-a-184 (Wh)
Farley, John 1838 wb-b-292 (Wh)
Farley, John sr. 1817 wb-a-81 (Wh)
Farley, Pleasant C. 1851 wb-a-114 (Dk)
Farley, Stephen 1838 wb-b-308 (Wh)
Farley, Thomas 1849 r39-1-108 (Dk)
Farley, William 1841 rb-i-74 (Mt)
Farley, William M. 1839 rb-h-195 (Mt)
Farly, John 1856 ib-1-407 (Ca)
Farmbrough, Stewart 1816 wb-7-30 (D)
Farmer, Anna 1845 wb-b-89 (We)
Farmer, Aquilla 1854 ib-2-83 (Cl)
Farmer, Bailey W. 1850 rb-15-491 (Ru)
Farmer, Braswell 1827 wb-6-152 (Rb)
Farmer, Caroline V. 1845 wb-b-88 (We)
Farmer, Dew 1833 wb-8-344 (Rb)
Farmer, E. C. 1840 wb-1A-280 (A)
Farmer, Elizabeth 1848 wb-14-72 (Rb)
Farmer, Elizabeth 1859 as-c-215 (Ms)
Farmer, Enoch 1858 rb-19-219 (Ru)
Farmer, Enoch J. 1858 rb-19-155 (Ru)
Farmer, Hannah 1815 wb-#20 (Wl)
Farmer, Irvine 1847 wb-b-216 (We)
Farmer, James 1837 wb-9-408 (Rb)
Farmer, James J. 1853 mr-2-532 (Be)
Farmer, James J. 1853 mr-2-550 (Be)

Farmer, Jane 1857 wb-12-468 (Wi)
Farmer, John 1847 wb-1-268 (Bo)
Farmer, John 1847 wb-1B-25 (A)
Farmer, John 1856 ib-2-370 (Cl)
Farmer, Joseph A. 1839 rb-10-430 (Ru)
Farmer, Josiah 1858 wb-16-561 (Rb)
Farmer, Luke 1835 wb-1A-140 (A)
Farmer, Mary 1860 wb-3e-164 (Sh)
Farmer, Moses 1827? wb-1A-11 (A)
Farmer, Moses E. 1841 wb-7-468 (Wi)
Farmer, Peter 1827 wb-1-68 (Fr)
Farmer, Polly 1848 wb-10-25 (K)
Farmer, Reynard 1823 wb-1-0 (Sm)
Farmer, Reynold 1823 wb-2-0 (Sm)
Farmer, Richard 1860 as-c-225 (Ms)
Farmer, Stephen 1815 wb-1-0 (Sm)
Farmer, Thomas 1835 rb-9-250 (Ru)
Farmer, Thomas G. 1860 as-c-214 (Ms)
Farmer, Thomas H. 1853 wb-15-229 (Rb)
Farmer, Thomas L. 1856 as-b-203 (Ms)
Farmer, Thomas S. 1855 wb-2-254 (Me)
Farmer, William 1811 wb-#9 (Wl)
Farney, Eliza C. 1860 wb-f-207 (Mu)
Farnsworth, Agnes 1839 wb-2-52# (Ge)
Farnsworth, Benjamin 1813 wb-2-35# (Ge)
Farnsworth, Caroline M. 1857 wb-2-86# (Ge)
Farnsworth, Henry 1850 wb-2-73# (Ge)
Farnsworth, Henry A. 1859 wb-1-9# (Ge)
Farnsworth, Jane 1845 wb-2-63# (Ge)
Farnsworth, Jeremiah 1854 wb-2-80# (Ge)
Farnsworth, John R. 1856 wb-2-84# (Ge)
Farnsworth, Rebecca 1848 148-1-262 (Ge)
Farnsworth, Thomas 1858 wb-2-88# (Ge)
Farnsworth, William G. 1836 wb-2-47# (Ge)
Farquharson, Robert 1857 wb-17-284 (D)
Farr, Ephraim 1842 rb-12-84 (Ru)
Farr, Ephraim 1842 rb-12-86 (Ru)
Farr, James Ephraim 1803 wb-#1 (Wl)
Farr, William 1803 wb-#1 (Wl)
Farrar, Daniel 1857 wb-2-201 (Li)
Farrar, Edward 1854 wb-2-189 (Me)
Farrar, Elizabeth 1853 wb-1-45 (R)
Farrar, Field 1837 as-a-351 (Di)
Farrar, George G. 1838 wb-y-190 (Mu)
Farrar, Jane 1854 wb-0-129 (Cf)
Farrar, John 1830 wb-1-51 (Li)
Farrar, John 1851 wb-a-147 (T)
Farrar, John 1852 wb-0-102 (Cf)
Farrar, Landon C. 1829 wb-9-293 (D)
Farrar, William 1848 wb-b-256 (Mu)
Farrar, William B. 1846 wb-a2-424 (Mu)

Farrar, William James 1857 wb-12-461 (Wi)
Farras, Frankey 1847 wb-2-203 (W)
Farrer, John 1823 wb-8-275 (D)
Farrer, John 1855 wb#24 (Gu)
Farrier, Mary 1813 rb-b-340 (Mt)
Farrier, Mary 1824 rb-d-391 (Mt)
Farrington, Jacob F. 1851 wb-2-91 (Sh)
Farrington, Johnathan F. 1851 wb-2-106 (Sh)
Farris, Caleb 1838 wb-y-183 (Mu)
Farris, Hezekiah 1844 wb-a-110 (F)
Farris, Hezekiah 1856 ib-h-501 (F)
Farris, James 1815 wb-#20 (Mu)
Farris, James A. 1824 wb-#145 (Mu)
Farris, James W. 1833 wb-1-287 (Hr)
Farris, John 1841 wb-z-149 (Mu)
Farris, John 1850 wb-2-79 (Sh)
Farris, John B. 1849 as-a-195 (Ms)
Farris, John M. 1857 wb-f-119 (Mu)
Farris, Josiah 1831 wb-#225 (Mu)
Farris, Lewis B. 1841 wb-c-26 (Wh)
Farris, Linias B. 1838 wb-b-321 (Wh)
Farris, May 1839 wb-y-309 (Mu)
Farris, Samuel 1816 wb-A-121 (Li)
Farris, William 1825 wb-#131 (Mu)
Farris, William 1836 wb-x-296* (Mu)
Farris, William 1839 abl-1-124 (T)
Farris, William 1854 wb-1-410 (Fr)
Farris, William 1861 wb-1-411 (Fr)
Farris, William D. 1860 wb-1-399 (Fr)
Farriss, Jane 1854 wb-f-36 (Mu)
Farriss, R? L. 1840 wb-b-356 (G)
Farriss, Thomas 1845 wb-a-236 (F)
Farrow, Sebina 1825 wb-8-499 (D)
Farthing, Richard 1861 wb-17-283 (Rb)
Fathera, J. C. 1858 rb-19-355 (Ru)
Fatio, P. (Dr.) 1861 wb-13-417 (K)
Faucet, Richard 1834 wb-c-347 (St)
Faucett, Franklin W. 1843 wb-f-38 (St)
Faucett, James L. 1857 rb-18-437 (Ru)
Faucett, James S. 1857 rb-18-391 (Ru)
Faulk, Alford 1836 rb-g-403 (Mt)
Faulk, William 1830 rb-f-142 (Mt)
Faulkenberry, David 1841 rb-12-30 (Ru)
Faulkner, Edward P. 1836 wb-#115 (Wl)
Faulkner, John (Capt) 1818 rb-c-11 (Mt)
Faulkner, John sr. 1818 rb-b-511 (Mt)
Faulkner, Tobias 1856 wb-e-51 (Hy)
Faulkner, William 1822 rb-d-47 (Mt)
Faulkner, William 1827 rb-e-254 (Mt)
Faulkner, William 1832 rb-f-355 (Mt)
Faulkner, William 1851 wb-14-575 (D)

119

Faulks, C. G. 1855 wb-i-247 (O)
Faulks, Charles G. 1858 wb-j-344 (O)
Fausett, Richard 1857 wb-b-50 (Ms)
Fausett, William 1847 as-a-136 (Ms)
Fawley, Elizabeth 1831 rb-f-206 (Mt)
Fawley, William 1828 rb-e-368 (Mt)
Feagan, John 1839 wb-3-0 (Sm)
Feas, Charles 1798 rb-a-26 (Mt)
Feasly, Lucy 1848 rb-l-86 (Mt)
Featherston, Edmond 1857 wb-f-86 (G)
Featherston, Henry 1815 wb-A-85 (Li)
Featherston, Mary E. 1851 wb-14-532 (Rb)
Featherston, Presley 1816 rb-3-216 (Ru)
Featherstone, Daniel M. 1816 wb-1-0 (Sm)
Featherstone, Henry 1828 wb-3-0 (Sm)
Feeland, Polly 1817 wb-7-164 (D)
Feeland, William 1817 wb-7-124 (D)
Feels, David 1827 wb-#66 (Wl)
Feerr?, George 1828 rb-7-9 (Ru)
Feeson, Sophrona A. 1857 ib-1-470 (Wy)
Feezel, Henry 1860 wb-2-90# (Ge)
Feild, Edward R. 1858 lr (Gi)
Feland, William 1815 wb-4-346 (D)
Felcknor, Henry 1810 wb-1-179 (Hw)
Felker, Mary 1838 wb-#124 (Wl)
Felker, Mrs. 1842 wb-#56 (Mc)
Felker, William 1859 wb-1-49 (Se)
Felkner, George 1830 wb-1-183 (Hw)
Felkner, Jacob 1821 wb-3-257 (Rb)
Fellers, Abraham G. 1858 wb-2-108# (Ge)
Fellers, Adam G. 1813 wb-2-34# (Ge)
Fellow, Martha 1858 wb-b-64 (F)
Felows, Thomas J. G. 1841 wb-b-330 (Hd)
Felts, Boling 1812 wb-1-0 (Sm)
Felts, Carey 1840 wb-12-50 (D)
Felts, Drury 1832 wb-8-83 (Rb)
Felts, George 1826 wb-5-371 (Rb)
Felts, George 1837 wb-10-58 (Rb)
Felts, Harris D. 1861 wb-17-256 (Rb)
Felts, Isham 1825 wb-8-457 (D)
Felts, Sally 1834 wb-8-418 (Rb)
Felts, Sarah Jane (Lones) 1853 wb-11-345 (K)
Felts, William 1859 wb-18-90 (D)
Felts, William G. 1860 wb-18-214 (D)
Fencher, E. 1838 wb-1-571 (Hr)
Fender, Michael 1858 wb-#21 (Mo)
Fenell, James B. 1849 wb-#56 (Mc)
Fenneal, James C. 1810 wb-#28 (Mu)
Fenner, Ann 1851 wb-5-98 (Ma)
Fenner, J. M. 1847 wb-5-39 (Ma)
Fenner, Junius P. 1834 wb-1-423 (Ma)

Fenner, Richard 1828 wb-1-76 (Ma)
Fenner, Richard H. 1836 wb-2-188 (Ma)
Fenney, Robert A. 1847 wb-2-14 (Sh)
Fenton, John H. 1860 wb-3e-162 (Sh)
Fentress, Absolam 1841 wb-e-121 (St)
Fentress, George W. 1839 wb-b-74 (O)
Fentress, James 1843 rb-i-550 (Mt)
Ferebee, Henry 1823 wb-8-183 (D)
Ferebee, Thomas 1847 wb-14-5 (D)
Fergason, Robert 1857 wb-1-109 (R)
Fergason, Wm. 1832 wb-a-230 (G)
Fergerson, Isabel 1833 wb-3-0 (Sm)
Fergerson, James A. 1858 wb-12-481 (K)
Fergus, Francis 1841 wb-c-17 (Wh)
Fergus, James 1806 wb-3-69 (Wi)
Fergus, James 1837 wb-a-65 (Cr)
Ferguson, Alexander 1828 wb-4-327 (K)
Ferguson, Archibald Pagen 1836 wb-3-0 (Sm)
Ferguson, Benjamin 1847 wb-9-391 (K)
Ferguson, David S. 1843 wb-8-10 (Wi)
Ferguson, Edward 1832 lr (Sn)
Ferguson, Elizabeth 1845 wb-12-507 (Rb)
Ferguson, Elizabeth 1856 rb-o-244 (Mt)
Ferguson, George 1835 wb-1-480 (Hr)
Ferguson, Henry 1816 wb-2-351 (Rb)
Ferguson, Henry 1847 wb-14-110 (D)
Ferguson, James 1854 wb-2-162 (Sh)
Ferguson, James 1857 wb-16-536 (Rb)
Ferguson, Joel 1841 wb-7-409 (Wi)
Ferguson, John 1807 wb-#11 (Wa)
Ferguson, John 1831 wb-#93 (Wl)
Ferguson, John 1833 rb-9-85 (Ru)
Ferguson, John G. 1860 wb-18-212 (D)
Ferguson, John W. 1855 wb-15-752 (Rb)
Ferguson, John sr. 1835 wb-a-282 (R)
Ferguson, Jonathan 1814 wb-2-163 (Rb)
Ferguson, Mary 1833 wb-5-217 (K)
Ferguson, Mary E. 1856 wb-16-293 (Rb)
Ferguson, Pemelia L. 1857 wb-3e-50 (Sh)
Ferguson, Robert 1799 wb-1-70 (K)
Ferguson, Robert 1825 wb-a-4 (R)
Ferguson, Robert 1844 wb-#5 (Mo)
Ferguson, Royal 1838 wb-y-424 (Mu)
Ferguson, Samuel 1815 wb-#17 (Wl)
Ferguson, Thomas 1848 wb-#47 (Wa)
Ferguson, William M. 1859 wb-17-573 (D)
Fergusson, John 1835 wb-x-288* (Mu)
Feris, Isaac 1839 wb-y-624 (Mu)
Ferman, John 1809 rb-a-470 (Mt)
Ferrel, Martha 1811 lr (Sn)
Ferrell, Elizabeth 1849 ib-1-83 (Ca)

Ferrell, Elizabeth 1858 wb-#124 (Wl)
Ferrell, James 1828 wb-2-609 (Je)
Ferrell, James 1834 wb-a-244 (R)
Ferrell, James 1850 ib-1-139 (Ca)
Ferrell, James W. 1853 wb-#110 (Wl)
Ferrell, Leighton 1835 wb-1-190 (W)
Ferrell, Levi 1821 wb-#193 (Mu)
Ferrell, Razey? 1832 mr-1-48 (Be)
Ferrell, T. Y. 1837 wb-1-230 (W)
Ferrell, Vezy 1840 mr-1-334 (Be)
Ferrell, William 1855 ib-1-358 (Ca)
Ferrell, William W. 1846 wb-#151 (Wl)
Ferrell, Wm. 1853 ib-1-275 (Ca)
Ferrell, Zadia 1851 lr (Sn)
Ferrill, Bazzill 1851 wb-15-141 (D)
Ferrill, John 1850 wb-g-260 (St)
Ferris, G. P. 1861 wb-18-588 (D)
Ferris, Mary J. 1859 rb-20-154 (Ru)
Ferriss, Josiah 1842 rb-12-278 (Ru)
Ferriss, Josiah sr. 1841 rb-11-109 (Ru)
Ferror, Edward P. 1856 wb-2-292 (Me)
Fetchur, James 1841 wb-e-155 (St)
Fetherston, John B. 1838 wb-10-159 (Rb)
Fetting, Albertine 1856 wb-12-315 (K)
Fetting, House 1856 wb-12-315 (K)
Fewell, James 1840 wb-2-25 (Hy)
Fewtrell, John D. 1853 wb-5-38 (Hr)
Field, Aleas 1821 wb-#39 (Wl)
Field, Alex 1859 gs-1-410 (F)
Field, Jeremiah 1853 wb-3-172 (La)
Field, John 1853 rb-16-436 (Ru)
Field, John 1855 wb-5-51 (Hr)
Field, Joseph 1833 wb-#56 (Mc)
Field, William Gibson 1821 wb-#39 (Wl)
Fielden, Berry G. 1852 wb-5-141 (Je)
Fielder, John 1807 wb-3-140 (D)
Fielder, John 1818 wb-7-279 (D)
Fielder, Nancy 1856 ib-1-443 (Wy)
Fielder, Samuel 1854 wb-e-157 (G)
Fielder, Samuel 1856 wb-1-51 (Dy)
Fielder, W. P. S. 1856 wb-1-57 (Dy)
Fielding, William L. 1858 wb-h-516 (St)
Fielding, William L. jr. 1861 wb-i-347 (St)
Fields, Absolam 1841 wb-b-22 (We)
Fields, Bennett 1818 wb-2-379 (Wi)
Fields, David 1825 wb-#57 (Wl)
Fields, Eli 1834 wb-10-351 (D)
Fields, Elizabeth 1859 rb-20-276 (Ru)
Fields, James 1855 wb-1-41 (Dy)
Fields, John 1845 wb-a2-170 (Mu)
Fields, John 1854 wb-g-547 (Hn)

Fields, Nelson 1839 wb-7-94 (Wi)
Fields, Robert 1842 wb-5-182 (Gr)
Fields, William 1841 wb-z-234 (Mu)
Fields, William 1860 wb-k-226 (O)
Fields, Winney 1817 rb-4-17 (Ru)
Figuers, Thomas N. 1854 wb-11-243 (Wi)
Figures, Mary 1839 wb-#177 (Wl)
Figures, Matthew 1827 wb-#70 (Wl)
Fike, Ferdinand 1860 wb-3e-152 (Sh)
Fike, John 1821 wb-a-144 (Ro)
Fillers, Jacob 1861 149-1-227 (Ge)
Fillows, T. J. C. 1841 wb-b-329 (Hd)
Fin, Edmond 1850 wb-c-380 (Wh)
Fin, Edmund 1850 wb-c-387 (Wh)
Finch, A. 1859 rb-20-242 (Ru)
Finch, Absalom 1850 rb-4-16 (Mu)
Finch, Adam 1859 rb-20-320 (Ru)
Finch, Calvin 1830 wb-#29 (Wa)
Finch, Cliff 1840 wb-b-20 (We)
Finch, Edward 1831 wb-1-92 (Fr)
Finch, Edward 1832 wb-9-595 (D)
Finch, J. W. 1857 wb-j-299 (O)
Finch, John 1827 rb-7-77 (Ru)
Finch, John W. 1830 rb-8-75 (Ru)
Finch, John W. 1846 wb-b-181 (We)
Finch, M. E. C. 1846 wb-b-169 (We)
Finch, M. T. C. 1845 wb-b-113 (We)
Finch, Sarah 1853 rb-16-709 (Ru)
Fincher, Ephraim 1836 wb-1-464 (Hr)
Fincher, John 1841 148-1-11 (Ge)
Fincher, Joshua 1841 148-1-10 (Ge)
Findley, James 1856 wb-f-18 (Ro)
Findley, John 1817 wb-2-342 (K)
Findley, Samuel 1849 as-a-187 (Ms)
Findley, Thomas 1851 wb-g-394 (Hn)
Fine, Abraham 1843 wb-#41 (Wa)
Fine, Elijah 1848 wb-#47 (Wa)
Fine, John 1855 wb-#12 (Mo)
Fine, John 1860 wb-1-164 (R)
Fine, Peter 1848 wb-1-240 (Me)
Fine, Polly 1857 wb-#28 (Mo)
Finger, John L. 1857 wb-3-346 (W)
Finlay, George 1817 wb-#26 (Wl)
Finley, Alexander 1850 ib-1-144 (Ca)
Finley, Anthony 1847 wb-14-81 (D)
Finley, Elizabeth 1849 wb-c-358 (Wh)
Finley, Harriet 1851 wb-a-253 (Ms)
Finley, James 1850 as-c-86 (Di)
Finley, John 1844 wb-a2-65 (Mu)
Finley, John 1850 ib-1-124 (Ca)
Finley, Sarah 1859 wb-b-76 (Ms)

Finley, William 1819 wb-2-279 (Je)
Finley, William 1848 wb-a-178 (Ms)
Finley, William 1855 wb-a-253 (Cr)
Finn, John 1852 wb-15-316 (D)
Finn, Thomas 1833 wb-10-64 (D)
Finn, Thomas 1860 wb-i-159 (St)
Finney, Andrew 1835 rb-9-198 (Ru)
Finney, Andrew 1845 rb-13-76 (Ru)
Finney, Thomas 1820 wb-7-490 (D)
Finney, William 1836 wb-10-620 (D)
Finney, William 1854 rb-17-211 (Ru)
Finney, William 1854 rb-17-225 (Ru)
Firestone, Eve 1828 wb-#56 (Mc)
Firestone, Mathias 1850 wb-#56 (Mc)
Firestone, William 1836 wb-#57 (Mc)
Firestone?, Eve 1836 wb-1-150 (Gr)
Fisackerly, John 1837 wb-1-333 (Hy)
Fiser, Benjamin E. 1849 wb-14-251 (Rb)
Fiser, H. 1859 wb-16-786 (Rb)
Fiser, James L. 1849 wb-14-251 (Rb)
Fiser, Joseph 1845 wb-12-457 (Rb)
Fiser, Martin 1842 wb-11-266 (Rb)
Fiser, Michael 1854 wb-15-467 (Rb)
Fiser, Michael D. 1838 wb-10-75 (Rb)
Fiser, Peter 1825 wb-5-122 (Rb)
Fiser, Peter L. 1850 wb-14-340 (Rb)
Fiser, William 1848 wb-g-81 (O)
Fiser, William T. 1845 wb-12-332 (Rb)
Fiser, Willis 1843 wb-b-42 (We)
Fish, James D. 1815 wb-4-355 (D)
Fishback, Elijah 1800 wb-2-179 (D)
Fisher, Christian 1848 wb-#57 (Mc)
Fisher, Eli A. 1839 wb-7-200 (Wi)
Fisher, Elizabeth 1856 wb-3-389 (La)
Fisher, Ensly 1840 wb-a-442 (R)
Fisher, Frederick 1848 as-a-162 (Ms)
Fisher, Frederick E. 1857 wb-17-295 (D)
Fisher, George 1850 wb-d-236 (G)
Fisher, George W. 1837 wb-a-64 (Cr)
Fisher, J. H. 1851 wb-#178 (Wl)
Fisher, J. W. 1860 wb-17-102 (Rb)
Fisher, J. W. 1860 wb-17-65 (Rb)
Fisher, Jackson 1849 wb-5-72 (Ma)
Fisher, James F. 1842 as-a-60 (Ms)
Fisher, James R. 1852 as-b-48 (Ms)
Fisher, Jno. 1820 rb-4-216 (Ru)
Fisher, John 1827 wb-1-230 (Ma)
Fisher, John 1837 wb-1-198 (W)
Fisher, John 1838 wb-2-352 (Ma)
Fisher, John 1857 wb-a-281 (Cr)
Fisher, Mary 1848 as-a-166 (Ms)

Fisher, Nancy 1858 wb-e-212 (Wh)
Fisher, Nancy 1859 wb-c-315 (L)
Fisher, Noah 1852 wb-1-16 (R)
Fisher, Peter 1827 wb-2-75 (Sn)
Fisher, Pleasant 1855 wb-e-369 (G)
Fisher, Polley 1847 wb-f-127+ (O)
Fisher, Richerson 1815 wb-#20 (Wl)
Fisher, Susanah 1854 wb-e-142* (G)
Fisher, Thomas 1841 wb-11-87 (Rb)
Fisher, Thomas 1841 wb-11-95 (Rb)
Fisher, William 1831 wb-b-29 (Wh)
Fisher, William 1841 wb-7-234* (K)
Fisher, William 1843 wb-d-87 (O)
Fisk, Ebenezer 1853 wb-16-133 (D)
Fisk, Madison 1855 wb-d-230 (Wh)
Fiske, Barlow 1859 wb-e-302 (Wh)
Fiske, Burton 1857 wb-e-198 (Wh)
Fiske, Madison 1855 wb-d-219 (Wh)
Fitch, James 1846 wb-1-147 (Me)
Fitch, Robert M. 1855 wb-12-71 (K)
Fite, Henry 1861 39-2-414 (Dk)
Fite, Jacob 1857 wb-4-131 (La)
Fite, Leonard 1842 wb-a-32 (Dk)
Fite, Peter 1844 wb-#57 (Mc)
Fite, Sarah A. 1847 wb-d-66 (G)
Fitts, R. D. 1860 wb-a-159 (Ce)
Fittspatrick, Andrew 1822 wb-#52 (Mu)
Fittz, Ulysses 1841 wb-7-376 (Wi)
Fitz, Clement P. 1855 wb-6-18 (Ma)
Fitz, Marshall G. 1844 wb-4-215 (Ma)
Fitzgerald, C. B. 1841 wb-1-51 (Me)
Fitzgerald, Christopher 1829 wb-#193 (Mu)
Fitzgerald, Edmond 1856 wb-f-100 (Mu)
Fitzgerald, James 1853 wb-f-20 (Mu)
Fitzgerald, Jno. M. 1841 wb-12-160* (D)
Fitzgerald, John 1848 wb-b-213 (Mu)
Fitzgerald, John Sr. 1858 wb-12-499 (Wi)
Fitzgerald, William 1816 wb-a-77 (Wh)
Fitzhugh, Aramenta 1860 wb-7-69 (Ma)
Fitzhugh, Edmund 1832 wb-1-251 (Hr)
Fitzhugh, Ezekiel 1824 wb-8-359 (D)
Fitzhugh, Lydia 1840 wb-12-1* (D)
Fitzhugh, Samuel 1832 wb-10-12 (D)
Fitzhugh, Samuel 1832 wb-9-580 (D)
Fitzpatrick, Morgan 1860 wb-b-94 (Ms)
Fitzpatrick, William G. 1846 wb-a2-401 (Mu)
Fitzugh, James 1840 wb-e-7 (St)
Fiveash, William 1847 wb-7-0 (Sm)
Flack, Alvis 1855 wb-2-109 (Li)
Flack, Rufus K. 1860 wb-2-328 (Li)
Flaherty, George 1858 wb-3e-80 (Sh)

Flanekin, James M. 1856 wb-3e-27 (Sh)
Flaniken, Samuel 1836 wb-6-61 (K)
Flanikin, James W. 1840 wb-7-119 (K)
Flanikin, Samuel sr. 1843 wb-8-40 (K)
Flankin, Adlah 1845 wb-#148 (Wl)
Flannegan, Martin 1860 wb-18-286 (D)
Flatford, Eleven 1859 iv-C-45 (C)
Flatt, William 1847 wb-d-374 (Hd)
Fleman, Jacob 1831 rb-8-269 (Ru)
Fleming, Andrew 1849 rb-15-53 (Ru)
Fleming, Andrew J. 1849 rb-14-520 (Ru)
Fleming, David 1801 wb-1-78 (K)
Fleming, David 1853 wb-1-41 (R)
Fleming, David B. 1859 wb-13-65 (Wi)
Fleming, David H. 1855 wb-1-82 (R)
Fleming, David N. 1854 wb-1-52 (R)
Fleming, Elizabeth 1806 wb-1-187 (K)
Fleming, J. M. 1859 rb-20-129 (Ru)
Fleming, James 1826 wb-4-143 (Wi)
Fleming, James 1844 wb-4-249 (Ma)
Fleming, James 1844 wb-4-256 (Ma)
Fleming, Josiah 1853 wb-11-80 (Wi)
Fleming, Ralph 1821 Wb-3-258 (Wi)
Fleming, Robert F. S. 1848 wb-10-36 (K)
Fleming, Samuel 1833 wb-5-209 (K)
Fleming, Sarah Ann 1852 mr-2-474 (Be)
Fleming, Thomas S. 1849 wb-14-590 (D)
Fleming, Warren 1846 wb-b-146 (We)
Fleming, William N. 1828 wb-1-79 (Hr)
Flemming, David 1815 rb-3-10 (Ru)
Flemming, Edward 1849 wb-g-317 (Hn)
Flemming, George F. 1856 as-c-18 (Ms)
Flemming, Joseph B. 1824 rb-d-294 (Mt)
Flemming, Samuel W. 1833 wb-c-21 (Hn)
Flemming, Thomas F. 1839 wb-y-478 (Mu)
Flemmings, John 1860 wb-a-319 (V)
Fleniken, Caroline (Badget) 1859 wb-13-241 (K)
Flenniken, Elizabeth 1848 wb-10-22 (K)
Flenniken, Mary 1836 wb-6-17 (K)
Flenniken, Samuel 1811 wb-1-357 (K)
Fleshart, Francis 1809 wb-1-288 (K)
Fletcher, Abram 1855 wb-n-672 (Mt)
Fletcher, Abram 1855 wb-n-679 (Mt)
Fletcher, Ann 1852 rb-16-342 (Ru)
Fletcher, Catharine 1858 rb-o-744 (Mt)
Fletcher, Henrietta 1846 rb-j-469 (Mt)
Fletcher, Henry 1859 rb-p-296 (Mt)
Fletcher, James 1816 wb-3-158 (St)
Fletcher, James H. 1814 wb-4-271 (D)
Fletcher, James H. 1815 wb-4-373 (D)
Fletcher, Jeremiah W. 1842 rb-12-83 (Ru)

Fletcher, John 1814 rb-b-219 (Mt)
Fletcher, John 1826 wb-2-0 (Sm)
Fletcher, John 1827 wb-6-127 (Rb)
Fletcher, John 1839 lw (Ct)
Fletcher, John 1845 wb-1-192 (Hw)
Fletcher, John 1845 wb-a-132 (Cr)
Fletcher, John 1849 rb-15-110 (Ru)
Fletcher, John H. 1850 wb-2-366 (W)
Fletcher, Josiah 1859 wb-f-299 (G)
Fletcher, Leanner 1854 wb-e-183 (G)
Fletcher, Lydia M. V. 1861 rb-p-614 (Mt)
Fletcher, M. H. 1835 rb-9-260 (Ru)
Fletcher, M. V. (Mrs.) 1859 rb-p-40 (Mt)
Fletcher, Mary J. 1847 rb-14-78 (Ru)
Fletcher, Mary Jane 1847 rb-14-271 (Ru)
Fletcher, Mary V. 1859 rb-p-16 (Mt)
Fletcher, Mouthford H. 1836 rb-9-351 (Ru)
Fletcher, Paul 1845 wb-c-214 (G)
Fletcher, Peyton 1854 wb-2-163 (Sh)
Fletcher, Thomas 1835 rb-g-67 (Mt)
Fletcher, Thomas 1835 rb-g-71 (Mt)
Fletcher, Thomas 1853 wb-e-45 (G)
Fletcher, Thomas A. 1841 wb-1-189 (Hw)
Fletcher, William 1844 wb-c-162 (G)
Fletcher, William 1845 rb-j-404 (Mt)
Fletcher, William T. 1845 rb-j-353 (Mt)
Fletcher, Winney 1857 wb-h-427 (St)
Fletcher, Winnie 1859 rb-p-282 (Mt)
Flewellin, William 1835 wb-a-49 (Cr)
Flim, John W. 1846 wb-a-116 (T)
Flimmon, Joseph B. 1826 rb-d-532 (Mt)
Flinn, Chloe 1853 wb-e-80 (G)
Flinn, Isaiah 1838 wb-2-32 (Hr)
Flinn, William 1839 wb-#58 (Mc)
Flintoff, Thomas 1852 wb-15-165 (Rb)
Flippen, John 1840 wb-a-51 (L)
Flippin, H. G. 1857 wb-17-417 (D)
Flippin, Jacob 1839 wb-7-122 (Wi)
Flippin, Jesse 1824? lr (Sn)
Flippin, Jesse S. 1854 ib-h-77 (F)
Flippin, Robert 1853 wb-11-35 (Wi)
Flippin, Thomas 1830 wb-b-87 (Hn)
Flippins, Joseph 1838 wb-1-174 (Fr)
Flippo, Henry 1858 wb-4-143 (La)
Flood, Abner 1851 wb-14-490 (Rb)
Flood, Judith 1811 wb-#9 (Wl)
Flood, Seth 1833 wb-8-265 (Rb)
Flood, Thomas 1811 wb-#9 (Wl)
Flora, Daniel 1838 wb-1-188 (Hw)
Flora, Daniel 1840 wb-1-189 (Hw)
Floriday, Patrick 1853 wb-#111 (Wl)

123

Flournoy, William 1818 lr (Gi)
Flournoy, William C. 1836 lr (Gi)
Flowers, Alexander 1847 rb-k-412 (Mt)
Flowers, Asher 1849 wb-d-154 (G)
Flowers, Barnabas 1855 wb-e-331 (G)
Flowers, Bryant 1836 wb-b-134 (G)
Flowers, C. 1853 wb-n-3 (Mt)
Flowers, Clarkey 1838 wb-b-256 (G)
Flowers, Deborah 1851 wb-d-327 (G)
Flowers, Hardy 1859 ib-2-196 (Wy)
Flowers, Henry 1854 wb-e-205 (G)
Flowers, Hilory 1862 wb-f-435 (G)
Flowers, Jacob 1855 wb-e-342 (G)
Flowers, John 1856 wb-f-94 (Mu)
Flowers, John W. 1858 wb-f-214 (G)
Flowers, Joseph 1849 rb-15-118 (Ru)
Flowers, Orlando 1845 rb-j-324 (Mt)
Flowers, Ralph 1821 wb-1-0 (Sm)
Flowers, Valentine 1838 wb-e-125 (Hu)
Flowers, Waitman 1856 wb-e-452 (G)
Flowers, William 1844 wb-7-0 (Sm)
Floyd, Alexander 1831 wb-1-149 (Fr)
Floyd, Andrew 1840 abl-1-191 (T)
Floyd, Elizabeth 1846 wb-#58 (Mc)
Floyd, J. M. 1855 wb-3-258 (La)
Floyd, James M. 1857 wb-4-43 (La)
Floyd, James R. 1861 wb-4-412 (La)
Floyd, John M. 1855 wb-3-265 (La)
Floyd, Jones 1857 wb-12-331 (Wi)
Floyd, Josiah 1850 wb-9-378 (Wi)
Floyd, Rebecca 1849 rb-15-109 (Ru)
Floyd, Richd. J. 1853 rb-16-566 (Ru)
Floyd, William 1821 wb-1-44 (Fr)
Floyd, William A. 1861 wb-4-433 (La)
Fly, Caleb 1852 wb-4-576 (Mu)
Fly, Elisha 1841 wb-b-23 (We)
Fly, Elizabeth 1847 wb-b-241 (We)
Fly, George W. 1852 wb-4-640 (Mu)
Fly, John 1854 wb-5-149 (Ma)
Fly, John D. 1814 wb-4-294 (D)
Fly, Mary J. 1854 wb-e-229 (G)
Fly, Sarah 1836 wb-10-548 (D)
Flyn, Cornelius O. 1825 rb-6-172 (Ru)
Flynn, Cornelius O. 1860 rb-20-640 (Ru)
Flynt, J. B. 1850 wb-4-579 (Hr)
Flynt, Joseph B. 1847 wb-4-234 (Hr)
Flynt, Martin 1818 wb-A-245 (Li)
Flynt, Martin 1818 wb-A-270 (Li)
Flynt, Richard 1844 wb-3-187 (Hr)
Foalk, William 1830 rb-f-108 (Mt)
Fochee, Sidney 1857 wb-1-74 (Dy)

Fogg, Charles 1822 rb-5-248 (Ru)
Fogg, James sr. 1836 lr (Gi)
Fogg, Milcy 1861 lr (Gi)
Fogleman, Michael 1826 wb-#140 (Mu)
Foland, Jacob 1853 wb-5-204 (Je)
Foley, Catharine (Mrs) 1860 wb-3e-163 (Sh)
Foley, Daniel 1853 wb-2-151 (Sh)
Folk, William 1855 wb-h-128 (St)
Folk, William 1855 wb-h-133 (St)
Folks, Martha 1827 rb-e-68 (Mt)
Follis, Mary 1850 wb-14-383 (Rb)
Follis, Nancy 1860 wb-f-345 (G)
Follis, William 1839 wb-10-311 (Rb)
Folly, Ham 1855 wb-#57 (Wa)
Folwell, Samuel 1854 ib-h-7 (F)
Fondron, James 1858 wb-4-199 (La)
Fong?, George R. 1846 wb-13-487 (D)
Fontain, Thomas B. 1850 wb-14-340 (Rb)
Fonville, Jeremiah 1850 wb-4-73 (Mu)
Fonville, John B. 1855 wb-e-267 (G)
Fooshee, John 1845 wb-1-130 (Me)
Foote, Richard 1837 wb-9-402 (Rb)
Forbank, James 1859 wb-#58 (Mc)
Forbes, Alexander 1828 wb-#58 (Mc)
Forbes, Alexander 1846 wb-1-288 (Li)
Forbes, Benjamin 1855 ib-h-315 (F)
Forbes, John 1819 wb-#34 (Wl)
Forbes, Robert 1815 wb-#13 (Wa)
Forbes, Robert 1861 wb-5-117 (Hr)
Forbess, Arthur 1848 wb-#167 (Wl)
Forbs, Benjamin S. 1837 wb-11-73 (D)
Ford, A. J. 1851 wb-15-11 (D)
Ford, Addison J. 1851 wb-15-18 (D)
Ford, Daniel 1818 wb-1-0 (Sm)
Ford, Edward M. 1848 wb-a-335 (F)
Ford, Elisha 1839 wb-6-490 (K)
Ford, Francis P. 1823 wb-8-170 (D)
Ford, Henrey 1844 wb-2-62# (Ge)
Ford, Henry 1845 wb-A-43 (Ca)
Ford, Jacob 1854 wb-e-159 (G)
Ford, James 1808 rb-a-102 (Mt)
Ford, James 1840 lr (Gi)
Ford, James 1846 wb-#44 (Wa)
Ford, James H. 1854 wb-15-593 (Rb)
Ford, John 1809 rb-1-72 (Ru)
Ford, John 1809 rb-2-65 (Ru)
Ford, John 1819 wb-2-275 (Je)
Ford, John 1832 ib-2-62 (Ge)
Ford, John 1838 wb-#43 (Wa)
Ford, John 1840 as-a-460 (Di)
Ford, John L. 1853 wb-15-576 (D)

Ford, John P. 1812 rb-b-52 (Mt)
Ford, Joseph M. 1831 wb-5-93 (K)
Ford, Joshua 1844 rb-12-500 (Ru)
Ford, Judah 1812 rb-b-83 (Mt)
Ford, Judith 1812 rb-b-118 (Mt)
Ford, Judith 1840 rb-10-479 (Ru)
Ford, L. S. 1857 ib-1-464 (Ca)
Ford, Larkin 1847 wb-0-78 (Cf)
Ford, Lewis 1833 wb-3-0 (Sm)
Ford, Lloyd 1847 wb-2-3 (Sh)
Ford, Mary 1855 ib-1-374 (Ca)
Ford, Mary 1860 149-1-188 (Ge)
Ford, Mary 1860 wb-1-135 (Jo)
Ford, Mumford 1848 wb-g-121 (Hu)
Ford, Nathan 1828 rb-7-200 (Ru)
Ford, Nathan 1845 rb-13-150 (Ru)
Ford, Robert 1841 wb-a-92 (L)
Ford, Samuel 1859 gs-1-314 (F)
Ford, William B. 1846 wb-1-146 (Me)
Fore, A. P. 1839 wb-#58 (Mc)
Fore, Nancy 1858 wb-#58 (Mc)
Fore, Thomas 1809 wb-#37 (Mu)
Fore, Thomas 1819 wb-#28 (Mu)
Forehand, John 1837 wb-6-385 (Wi)
Forest, Armstead W. 1845 wb-g-27 (Hn)
Forest, Brittain H. 1848 wb-a-182 (Ms)
Forest, Green 1848 wb-f-127+ (O)
Forest, Josiah 1854 mr-2-584 (Be)
Forest, Nancy 1855 wb-g-709 (Hn)
Forester, Charles 1825 wb-1-0 (Sm)
Forester, William 1836 wb-A-4 (Ca)
Forester, William B. C. 1855 wb-3-285 (Gr)
Forester, Wm. C. 1860 wb-17-58 (Rb)
Forgerson, John 1834 wb-1-84 (Gr)
Forgey, Andrew 1809 wb-1-178 (Hw)
Forgey, Andrew 1820 wb-#99 (Mu)
Forgey, Andrew 1830 wb-1-182 (Hw)
Forgey, James 1834 wb-1-183 (Hw)
Forgey, James 1836 wb-x-324* (Mu)
Forgey, James R. 1854 wb-1-196 (Hw)
Forgey, Margaret 1846 wb-1-190 (Hw)
Forgey, Rachael 1837 wb-1-187 (Hw)
Forgey, Rachael 1856 wb-1-202 (Hw)
Forgison, William 1796 wb-2-58 (D)
Forist, George 1848 wb-g-69 (O)
Forister, Charles jr. 1826 wb-2-0 (Sm)
Forkner, John 1814 rb-b-174 (Mt)
Forkner, Lewis 1814 wb-#20 (Mu)
Forkner, Lewis 1829 wb-#197 (Mu)
Forknor, Henrietta 1846 rb-13-712 (Ru)
Formwalt, John 1815 wb-2-142 (K)

Forrest, Henry 1852 wb-g-452 (Hn)
Forrest, James 1856 wb-h-503 (Hu)
Forrest, James 1869 wb-#58 (Mc)
Forrest, Nathan 1854 wb-a-331 (Ms)
Forrest, Samuel 1861 wb-e-146 (Hy)
Forrest, William M. 1850 wb-14-553 (D)
Forrester, Alexr. 1813 wb-2-73 (Rb)
Forrester, Charles 1815 wb-1-0 (Sm)
Forrester, James 1858 wb-2-253 (Li)
Forrester, James J. 1858 39-2-243 (Dk)
Forrester, Joel 1816 wb-2-362 (Rb)
Forrester, John 1815 wb-2-240 (Rb)
Forrester, John 1840 wb-1-9 (Jo)
Forrester, John 1857 wb-a-280 (Cr)
Forrester, John B. 1846 wb-2-125 (W)
Forrester, Jonathan 1813 wb-2-76 (Rb)
Forrester, Richard 1843 wb-c-121 (G)
Forrist, Nathan A. 1858 as-c-129 (Ms)
Forrister, Charles 1851 wb-d-371 (G)
Forshee, Jesse 1853 wb-#9 (Mo)
Forshee, Joseph 1855 wb-#10 (Mo)
Forshee, Mary 1858 wb-#28 (Mo)
Forst?, James 1859 wb-h-368 (Hn)
Forsyth, George R. 1844 wb-13-78 (D)
Forsythe, John 1814 wb-#20 (Mu)
Forsythe, John 1843 rb-i-516 (Mt)
Forsythe, John 1847 as-b-395 (Di)
Fort, Catharine O. 1830 wb-7-207 (Rb)
Fort, Charles 1845 rb-k-27 (Mt)
Fort, Charles W. 1860 wb-17-62 (Rb)
Fort, Dorothy 1856 wb-16-275 (Rb)
Fort, Elias 1820 wb-3-118 (Rb)
Fort, Elias 1827 wb-5-435 (Rb)
Fort, Elizabeth 1819 wb-3-96 (Rb)
Fort, Elizabeth 1820 wb-3-93 (Rb)
Fort, Jacob H. 1845 rb-j-322 (Mt)
Fort, James 1819 rb-c-182 (Mt)
Fort, James 1845 rb-j-322 (Mt)
Fort, Jeremiah 1808 wb-1-263 (Rb)
Fort, John 1836 rb-g-428 (Mt)
Fort, John D. 1830 rb-f-19 (Mt)
Fort, Josiah 1848 wb-14-23 (Rb)
Fort, Owen B. 1824 wb-4-201 (Rb)
Fort, Thomas J. 1860 wb-17-184 (Rb)
Fort, Thomas W. 1824 wb-4-254 (Rb)
Fort, William (Dr.) 1811 wb-1-393 (Rb)
Fort, William 1796 wb-1-4 (Rb)
Fort, William 1802 wb-1-78 (Rb)
Fort, William A. 1817 rb-b-386 (Mt)
Fort, William A. 1844 rb-j-442 (Mt)
Fortner, John 1844 wb-3-262 (Hr)

Fortner, Lewis 1821 wb-#169 (Mu)
Fortner, Richard 1842 abl-1-244 (T)
Fortson, Catharine 1857 rb-o-353 (Mt)
Fortson, John 1832 rb-f-386 (Mt)
Fortson, Marshall 1824 rb-d-397 (Mt)
Fortson, Mildred 1822 rb-d-93 (Mt)
Fortson, Richard 1832 rb-f-400 (Mt)
Fortson, Stephen 1823 wb-a-231 (Ro)
Fortson, William 1843 rb-i-547 (Mt)
Fortunal, Solomon 1841 wb-2-56# (Ge)
Fortune, A. R. 1842 rb-i-303 (Mt)
Fortune, William A. 1861 wb-a-229 (Ce)
Fosset, John 1835 rb-9-187 (Ru)
Foster, A. T. 1846 wb-b-137 (We)
Foster, Abednego 1832 wb-1-75 (Li)
Foster, Allen 1846 wb-a2-346 (Mu)
Foster, Andrew 1858 wb-#58 (Mc)
Foster, Ann Augusta 1852 wb-15-298 (D)
Foster, Anthony 1831 wb-9-491 (D)
Foster, Anthony 1835 wb-1-408 (Hr)
Foster, Anthony C. 1816 rb-b-333 (Mt)
Foster, Booker 1831 wb-#221 (Mu)
Foster, Charles G. 1853 wb-3-170 (W)
Foster, David 1827 wb-#161 (Mu)
Foster, David 1834 wb-c-216 (Hn)
Foster, Davis 1814 wb-1-0 (Sm)
Foster, E. J. 1847 wb-a2-534* (Mu)
Foster, Emsley D. 1832 wb-#97 (Wl)
Foster, Enoch 1850 wb-1B-172 (A)
Foster, Ephraim H. 1854 wb-16-425 (D)
Foster, George 1799 wb-2-159 (D)
Foster, George 1809 wb-4-78 (D)
Foster, George 1853 wb-15-485 (D)
Foster, H. B. 1854 wb-n-225 (Mt)
Foster, Hiram 1857 rb-o-467 (Mt)
Foster, James 1827 wb-#68 (Wl)
Foster, John 1839 wb-y-429 (Mu)
Foster, John D. 1838 wb-#121 (Wl)
Foster, John F. 1856 wb-3-371 (La)
Foster, John L. 1852 wb-15-377 (D)
Foster, Lott 1861 wb-5-119 (Hr)
Foster, Mercy 1851 148-1-375 (Ge)
Foster, Phebe 1842 wb-z-321 (Mu)
Foster, Phela 1843 wb-z-517 (Mu)
Foster, R. B. 1849 wb-b-401 (Mu)
Foster, R. C. 1845 wb-13-151 (D)
Foster, Richard 1825 rb-6-127 (Ru)
Foster, Richard 1837 wb-#117 (Wl)
Foster, Robert 1815 wb-#42 (Mu)
Foster, Robert 1818 wb-#27 (Wl)
Foster, Robert 1829 wb-#80 (Wl)

Foster, Robert 1843 148-1-66 (Ge)
Foster, Robert 1845 wb-#159 (Wl)
Foster, Robert C. 1845 wb-13-200 (D)
Foster, Samuel 1855 wb-e-347 (G)
Foster, Sarah 1855 rb-17-531 (Ru)
Foster, Septemus W. 1839 wb-11-577 (D)
Foster, Shelton C. 1836 wb-6-132 (Wi)
Foster, Stephen 1835 wb-5-346 (K)
Foster, Thomas 1815 wb-#17 (Wl)
Foster, Thomas 1829 wb-1-46 (W)
Foster, Thomas 1846 wb-#59 (Mc)
Foster, Thomas 1854 wb-2-17 (Ct)
Foster, W. B. 1860 wb-f-359 (G)
Foster, William 1816 wb-#22 (Wl)
Foster, William 1827 rb-7-109 (Ru)
Foster, William 1828 rb-7-315 (Ru)
Foster, William 1830 wb-1-82 (Fr)
Foster, William 1838 wb-1-161 (La)
Foster, William 1862 wb-#137 (Wl)
Foster, William M. 1838 wb-#122 (Wl)
Foster, Wm. H. 1857 wb-h-680 (Hu)
Fouler, Elizabeth 1848 wb-b-251 (We)
Foulks, Craddock 1819 wb-7-294 (D)
Foulks, Thomas 1818 wb-7-235 (D)
Fournier, N. S. 1809 wb-1-292 (K)
Fournier, Nicholas Honore S. 1800 wb-0-27 (K)
Foust, Amanda 1852 wb-11-293 (K)
Foust, Daniel 1855 wb-1C-226 (A)
Foust, Daniel 1858 wb-13-39 (K)
Foust, George 1851 wb-11-16 (K)
Foust, George sr. 1849 wb-10-113 (K)
Foust, Jacob 1832 wb-5-167 (K)
Foust, Jacob 1854 wb-11-497 (K)
Foust, Jacob 1854 wb-12-6 (K)
Foust, Jacob 1855 wb-1-79 (R)
Foust, John 1848 wb-9-439 (K)
Foust, Joseph 1824 wb-#53 (Wl)
Foust, Lewis L. 1861 wb-13-404 (K)
Foust, Sophia 1859 wb-13-219 (K)
Foutch, William 1856 39-2-126 (Dk)
Foute, Jacob 1831 wb-b-150 (Ro)
Fow, Jacob 1830 wb-9-372 (D)
Fowkes, John 1823 rb-d-153 (Mt)
Fowler, A. J. 1850 wb-b-110 (L)
Fowler, Abijah 1793 wb-1-9 (Je)
Fowler, Benjamin 1838 wb-b-241 (G)
Fowler, Bullard A. 1846 wb-b-149 (We)
Fowler, Calvin C. 1852 wb-g-440 (Hn)
Fowler, David 1835 wb-1-433 (Hr)
Fowler, Francis F. 1852 148-1-414 (Ge)
Fowler, Henry 1839 wb-e-50 (Hn)

Fowler, Hiram D. 1838 wb-d-236 (St)
Fowler, Isaac 1858 wb-f-226 (G)
Fowler, James 1856 rb-o-39 (Mt)
Fowler, John 1817 wb-A-172 (Li)
Fowler, Judith 1843 wb-f-110 (St)
Fowler, Marcilious 1848 as-a-179 (Ms)
Fowler, Nancy 1809 rb-a-470 (Mt)
Fowler, O. L. 1860 as-c-182 (Ms)
Fowler, Phebe 1845 wb-b-95 (We)
Fowler, Robert 1785 wb-#3 (Wa)
Fowler, Sarah 1858 as-c-88 (Ms)
Fowler, Sterling H. 1857 wb-h-625 (Hu)
Fowler, Thomas 1845 wb-b-104 (We)
Fowler, Thomas 1849 r39-1-120 (Dk)
Fowler, Thos. J. 1857 wb-h-658 (Hu)
Fowler, Wiley 1815 wb-4-377 (D)
Fowler, Will 1854 wb-g-592 (Hn)
Fowler, William 1815 rb-b-296 (Mt)
Fowler, William 1828 wb-9-232 (D)
Fowler, William 1830 rb-8-129 (Ru)
Fowlkes, John 1860 wb-f-344 (G)
Fowlkes, Mary 1827 wb-9-136 (D)
Fowlkes, Nancy Jane 1857 wb-12-401 (Wi)
Fowlkes, Thomas 1828 wb-9-163 (D)
Fox, Andrew 1819 wb-1-9# (Ge)
Fox, Andrew 1847 148-1-215 (Ge)
Fox, Austin 1841 wb-7-160 (K)
Fox, Edward 1852 wb-d-58 (Wh)
Fox, Elijah 1861 wb-13-589 (Wi)
Fox, Elizabeth 1850 rb-15-415 (Ru)
Fox, G. T. 1847 wb-4-200 (Hr)
Fox, Geo. T. 1848 wb-4-372 (Hr)
Fox, Henry 1849 wb-2-58# (Ge)
Fox, Henry 1861 149-1-240 (Ge)
Fox, Hugh 1841 wb-7-460 (Wi)
Fox, Hugh 1853 wb-11-44 (Wi)
Fox, J. W. 1859 wb-13-186 (K)
Fox, Jacob 1831 rb-8-175 (Ru)
Fox, Jacob 1844 rb-13-75 (Ru)
Fox, James 1838 wb-#59 (Mc)
Fox, James 1840 wb-1-314 (W)
Fox, John 1840 wb-7-108 (K)
Fox, John 1850 wb-a-234 (Ms)
Fox, John 1857 wb-1-28 (Se)
Fox, Joseph 1842 wb-z-426 (Mu)
Fox, Joseph W. 1857 wb-12-410 (K)
Fox, Joshua 1841 wb-c-3 (Wh)
Fox, Lance 1824 wb-#70 (Mu)
Fox, Philip 1841 wb-1-182 (Li)
Fox, Samuel 1826 wb-#135 (Mu)
Fox, Samuel 1832 wb-c-159 (St)

Fox, Samuel C. 1860 wb-13-388 (K)
Fox, Valencia 1854 wb-12-32 (K)
Fox, Valentine 1854 wb-12-10 (K)
Fox, William 1830 wb-#213 (Mu)
Foxall, Mary 1846 lr (Sn)
Foxall, Thomas 1835 wb-2-188 (Sn)
Frailey, Marton 1848 wb-d-394 (Hd)
Fraker, Christian 1828 wb-4-307 (K)
Fraker, Christian 1841 wb-7-275 (K)
Fraker, John A. 1847 wb-14-29 (D)
Fraker, Michael 1822 wb-1-9# (Ge)
Fraker, Robert 1834 wb-5-310 (K)
Fraker, William 1837 wb-6-129 (K)
Fraley, Henderson G. 1838 wb-b-115 (Hd)
Fraley, Martin 1838 wb-b-127 (Hd)
Frame, Theofilus 1815 wb-#18 (Mu)
Frame, William 1813 wb-A-27 (Li)
Frame, William 1841 wb-1-210 (Fr)
Frances, Ephraim 1852 wb-#52 (Wa)
Frances, Moses B. 1819 wb-3-104 (Wi)
Francesco, John 1849 wb-1-254 (Me)
Francis, Andrew 1835 wb-#108 (Wl)
Francis, Benjamin 1855 wb-1-334 (Fr)
Francis, Corbin H. 1845 wb-b-124 (We)
Francis, Mary 1832 wb-#99 (Wl)
Francis, Micajah 1825 wb-#55 (Wl)
Francis, Polly 1832 wb-#99 (Wl)
Francis, Widow 1825 wb-#57 (Wl)
Francisco, George 1860 wb-3-37 (Me)
Franklin, Andrew J. 1853 wb-0-117 (Cf)
Franklin, Benjamin 1855 wb-#59 (Mc)
Franklin, Benjamin 1856 wb-5-61 (Hr)
Franklin, David 1844 wb-#59 (Mc)
Franklin, Edmund 1831 wb-#59 (Mc)
Franklin, Elizabeth 1839 wb-e-249 (Hu)
Franklin, Elizabeth 1843 wb-d-72 (O)
Franklin, Henry 1828 wb-2-628 (Je)
Franklin, Henry M. 1837 wb-2-223 (Sn)
Franklin, Isaac 1846 wb-3-79 (Sn)
Franklin, James 1852 wb-h-Mar (O)
Franklin, James sr. 1829 lr (Sn)
Franklin, Joseph 1858 wb-1-378 (Fr)
Franklin, L. D. 1861 wb-5-540 (Je)
Franklin, Michal 1859 as-c-152 (Ms)
Franklin, Owen 1831 wb-3-133 (Je)
Franklin, P. O. 1850 rb-4-8 (Mu)
Franklin, Peachy 1840 wb-a-81 (F)
Franklin, Robert J. 1838 wb-3-480 (Je)
Franklin, Smith C. 1838 wb-2-229 (Sn)
Franks, John 1838 wb-1-149 (La)
Franks, John W. 1855 wb-d-294 (Wh)

Franks, Sarah 1856 wb-4-87 (La)

Frantham, John R. 1851 wb-10-2 (Wi)

Fraser, F. R. 1854 ib-H-108 (F)

Fraser, Fred R. 1859 gs-1-295 (F)

Frazer, Alexander 1837 wb-#119 (Wl)

Frazer, James 1830 wb-#97 (Wl)

Frazer, John 1828 wb-9-271 (D)

Frazer, William 1828 wb-9-273 (D)

Frazier, Abner 1855 as-2-358 (Ge)

Frazier, Beriah 1858 wb-1-141 (R)

Frazier, Betsy Ann 1843 wb-f-118* (Hn)

Frazier, George W. 1831 wb-a-93 (R)

Frazier, Hartwell 1860 wb-e-319 (Wh)

Frazier, Jacob H. 1857 wb-6-459 (Ma)

Frazier, James 1837 wb-1-36 (Sh)

Frazier, John 1859 wb-7-51 (Ma)

Frazier, John 1860 wb-e-320 (Wh)

Frazier, John W. 1847 wb-1B-31 (A)

Frazier, Julian 1837 wb-d-304 (Hn)

Frazier, Julian 1847 wb-g-178 (Hn)

Frazier, N. G. 1855 wb-1-76 (R)

Frazier, N. S. 1853 wb-1-35 (R)

Frazier, Nancy 1860 wb-a-161 (Ce)

Frazier, Robert N. 1855 wb-h-432 (Hu)

Frazier, S. S. 1858 wb-4-188 (La)

Frazier, Samuel 1839 wb-6-495 (K)

Frazier, Samuel 1854 wb-1-67 (R)

Frazier, Sarah Isabella J. 1852 wb-h-Dec (O)

Frazier, Stephen 1858 wb-4-164 (La)

Frazier, Thomas 1835 wb-d-224 (Hn)

Frazier, Thomas W. 1847 rb-k-503 (Mt)

Frazior, Mahala C. 1851 wb-14-627 (D)

Frazor, Daniel 1819 wb-7-333 (D)

Frazor, Mary D. 1853 lr (Sn)

Frazor, Rebecca 1836 wb-10-552 (D)

Frazor, William 1846 wb-3-58 (Sn)

Free, Mathew 1816 wb-3-142 (St)

Free, Philip 1838 wb-1-345 (Gr)

Freech, John 1856 wb-f-8 (Ro)

Freeland, Isaac 1861 wb-17-183 (Rb)

Freeland, James 1784 wb-1-16 (D)

Freeland, James 1820? wb-#100 (Mu)

Freeland, James 1825 wb-1-0 (Sm)

Freeland, John G. 1844 wb-a-115 (F)

Freeland, Joseph 1823 wb-#52 (Mu)

Freeland, Samuel 1811 wb-4-156 (D)

Freeland, William 1858 wb-b-57 (Ms)

Freeman (B), Andrew 1839 rb-10-337 (Ru)

Freeman, Abner 1854 wb-2-85 (Li)

Freeman, Alfred 1854 wb-6-45 (Ma)

Freeman, Andrew 1825 rb-6-121 (Ru)

Freeman, Andrew 1825 rb-6-132 (Ru)

Freeman, Arthur 1809 Wb-1-85 (Wi)

Freeman, Asa 1861 rb-21-128 (Ru)

Freeman, Berkley 1859 gs-1-353 (F)

Freeman, Carney 1851 wb-15-206 (D)

Freeman, Carra 1850 wb-14-479 (D)

Freeman, Gideon 1840 wb-2-48 (Hy)

Freeman, Hartwell 1845 wb-f-306 (Hn)

Freeman, Henry 1831 wb-#92 (Wl)

Freeman, Henry 1845 wb-12-311 (Rb)

Freeman, Howell 1836 wb-a-126 (Di)

Freeman, James 1811 rb-2-153 (Ru)

Freeman, James 1827 wb-1-248 (Bo)

Freeman, James 1841 wb-e-296 (Hn)

Freeman, James 1842 wb-3-563 (Ma)

Freeman, James 1849 wb-e-145 (Ro)

Freeman, John 1839 wb-7-93 (Wi)

Freeman, John 1854 wb-e-445 (Ro)

Freeman, Joshua 1832 wb-5-162 (K)

Freeman, Mary 1852 wb-15-164 (Rb)

Freeman, Mathew 1861 wb-17-226 (Rb)

Freeman, Richard 1845 wb-#60 (Mc)

Freeman, Robert 1831 rb-8-169 (Ru)

Freeman, Robert 1841 wb-2-291 (Hy)

Freeman, Rowland 1811 wb-#11 (Wl)

Freeman, Solomon C. 1856 wb-6-244 (Ma)

Freeman, Spencer 1836 wb-1-237 (Hy)

Freeman, Susannah 1858 wb-f-143 (Ro)

Freeman, William 1838 wb-b-98 (Hd)

Freeman, William 1839 wb-c-54 (Ro)

Freeman, William 1847 wb-d-316 (Hd)

Freeman, William 1848 wb-d-375 (Hd)

Freeman, William H. 1847 wb-b-215 (We)

Freeman, William P. 1840 wb-b-247 (Hd)

Freeman, William T. 1842 wb-z-357 (Mu)

Freeman, York 1832 wb-9-596 (D)

Freer, William 1845 wb-b-96 (We)

Frees, Jacob 1817 wb-2-39# (Ge)

Freese, Mary 1847 148-1-210 (Ge)

French, J. B. 1833 rb-f-465 (Mt)

French, John 1796 rb-a-4 (Mt)

French, John 1829 rb-e-482 (Mt)

French, John B. 1833 rb-f-471 (Mt)

French, John sr. 1807 rb-a-449 (Mt)

French, Joseph 1791 wb-1-240 (D)

French, Lewis H. 1857 wb-12-462 (Wi)

French, Marshall 1836 wb-d-196 (Hn)

French, Martha 1834 wb-c-143 (Hn)

French, Mary 1850 wb-3-22 (W)

French, Noah 1849 wb-g-145 (St)

French, Peter 1849 wb-10-248 (K)

French, Samuel C. 1838 wb-d-208* (Hn)
French, Samuel S. 1816 rb-b-358 (Mt)
French, Susan 1854 wb-h-46 (St)
French, Thomas 1815 wb-3-59 (St)
French, Thomas J. 1841 rb-i-147 (Mt)
French, William 1808 wb-#6 (Wl)
Freshour, John sr. 1801 wb-1-9# (Ge)
Frey, Avelin 1858 wb-16-570 (Rb)
Frey, Eveline 1856 wb-16-127 (Rb)
Frey, Henry S. 1853 wb-15-230 (Rb)
Frey, Jacob 1847 wb-13-196 (Rb)
Frey, Jacob 1848 wb-14-6 (Rb)
Frey, Jno. 1851 rb-4-179 (Mu)
Frields, David 1858 wb-b-422 (We)
Friend, Edward T. 1855 wb-b-270 (L)
Frierson, David 1829 wb-#195 (Mu)
Frierson, Elizabeth M. 1860 wb-f-194 (Mu)
Frierson, Flavel 1839 wb-y-311 (Mu)
Frierson, Floral? 1836 wb-x-395 (Mu)
Frierson, George 1820 wb-#101 (Mu)
Frierson, James 1846 wb-a2-462 (Mu)
Frierson, James A. 1858 wb-f-140 (Mu)
Frierson, James H. (Dr.) 1846 wb-a2-391 (Mu)
Frierson, Jane C. 1827 wb-#161 (Mu)
Frierson, John 1841 wb-z-152 (Mu)
Frierson, John D. 1857 wb-f-119 (Mu)
Frierson, John Witherspoon 1828 wb-#172 (Mu)
Frierson, Mada 1848 wb-b-220 (Mu)
Frierson, Margaret A. 1861 wb-f-211 (Mu)
Frierson, Mary 1849 wb-b-552 (Mu)
Frierson, Moses G. 1813 wb-#8 (Mu)
Frierson, Moses G. 1829 wb-#197 (Mu)
Frierson, Moses J. 1820? wb-#145 (Mu)
Frierson, Robert 1808 wb-#4 (Mu)
Frierson, Robert 1824 wb-#145 (Mu)
Frierson, Robert Luther 1857 wb-f-121 (Mu)
Frierson, Samuel 1829 wb-#193 (Mu)
Frierson, Samuel Dodridge 1860 wb-f-190 (Mu)
Frierson, Samuel E. 1826 wb-#133 (Mu)
Frierson, Sarah 1824 wb-#74 (Mu)
Frierson, Theodore 1844 wb-a2-291 (Mu)
Frierson, Thomas J. 1847 wb-a2-569 (Mu)
Frierson, William 1820 wb-#50 (Mu)
Frierson, William 1820 wb-#75 (Mu)
Frierson, William James 1834 wb-x-166 (Mu)
Frierson, William T. 1842 wb-z-399 (Mu)
Frith, A. 1844 wb-#146 (Wl)
Frith, Mary 1846 wb-#159 (Wl)
Frizzell, Isaac 1844 wb-b-75 (We)
Frost, Ebenezer 1825 rb-d-469 (Mt)
Frost, James 1848 wb-1-340 (Li)

Frost, John 1836 wb-6-228 (Wi)
Frost, John 1846 wb-9-188 (K)
Frost, Robert 1819 wb-1-181 (Hw)
Frost, Samuel 1837 wb-1A-166 (A)
Frost, Thomas 1806 rb-2-11 (Ru)
Frow, Archible 1829 wb-1-45 (Bo)
Fruman, James 1844 wb-4-184 (Ma)
Frunton, Mary 1854 wb-15-550 (Rb)
Fry, Elizabeth 1853 148-1-455 (Ge)
Fry, Frederick 1832 wb-9-618 (D)
Fry, John J. 1829 wb-#194 (Mu)
Fry, Joseph 1842 mr-2-16 (Be)
Fry, Joseph 1858 wb-b-70 (Ms)
Fry, Joseph H. 1837 wb-6-396 (Wi)
Fry, Philip 1853 wb-#60 (Mc)
Fry, Wesley 1858 wb-3-412 (Gr)
Fryar, William 1814 wb-2-129 (K)
Fryer, John 1842 wb-f-113 (Hn)
Fryers, John A. 1839 wb-b-348 (Wh)
Fryerson, Joshua 1817 wb-#25 (Mu)
Fryerson, Samuel 1815 wb-#34 (Mu)
Fudge, James 1855 wb-16-458 (D)
Fugate, Benjamin 1864 ib-2-555 (Cl)
Fugate, Henly 1840 5-2-181 (Cl)
Fugate, Rachael 1838 5-2-28 (Cl)
Fugate, William 1856? ib-2-272 (Cl)
Fugett, Jane H. 1856 wb-A-114 (Ca)
Fulcher, Elizabeth D. 1832 as-a-220 (Di)
Fulcher, Jesse 1836 wb-9-216 (Rb)
Fulcher, Lurana 1852 wb-15-52 (Rb)
Fulerton, Margaret 1839 wb-b-277 (G)
Fulgem, A. 1848 wb-4-331 (Hr)
Fulgham, Benjamin 1826 wb-1-27 (Hr)
Fulghum, R. 1858 wb-a-74 (Ce)
Fulghum, Theophilus 1857 wb-17-229 (D)
Fulk, Samuel 1860 rb-20-623 (Ru)
Fulkerson, James 1861 wb-d-118 (L)
Fulkerson, James L. 1849 wb-1-192 (Hw)
Fulks, John 1845 rb-13-178 (Ru)
Fulks, John 1856 rb-18-159 (Ru)
Fulks, John D. 1843 rb-12-311 (Ru)
Fulks, Samuel 1845 rb-13-387 (Ru)
Fulks, Samuel 1860 rb-20-622 (Ru)
Fulks, William 1848 rb-14-320 (Ru)
Fullen, William 1840 wb-a-48 (L)
Fuller, Arthur 1815 rb-3-83 (Ru)
Fuller, Ellison P. 1851 wb-b-125 (L)
Fuller, Emily 1845 wb-d-173 (Hd)
Fuller, Ezekiel 1861 wb-7-96 (Ma)
Fuller, George 1848 wb-e-83 (Ro)
Fuller, John 1852 rb-16-148 (Ru)

129

Fuller, Joshua 1859 wb-f-240 (Ro)
Fuller, Levi 1837 rb-10-7 (Ru)
Fuller, Susan 1846 rb-13-689 (Ru)
Fullerton, William 1857 wb-1-175 (Be)
Fulps, Michael S. 1846 5-3-114 (Cl)
Fulps, Michal S. 1852 ib-2-399 (Cl)
Fulps, Solomon 1856 ib-2-346 (Cl)
Fulsom, Benjamin 1832 wb-1-66 (Hy)
Fulton, Abe 1835 wb-9-99 (Rb)
Fulton, Archibald 1826 wb-#196 (Mu)
Fulton, H. F. 1849 as-a-188 (Ms)
Fulton, James 1831 wb-#234 (Mu)
Fulton, James 1856 wb-2-143 (Li)
Fulton, James C. 1846 as-a-126 (Ms)
Fulton, John G. 1834 wb-x-165 (Mu)
Fulton, Nathaniel 1833 wb-8-358 (Rb)
Fulton, Tinsley 1846 r39-1-17 (Dk)
Fulton, Tyre 1848 wb-14-61 (Rb)
Fulton, _____ 1833 wb-8-247 (Rb)
Fults, Alfred 1857 wb#39 (Gu)
Fults, Daniel 1860 wb#8 (Gu)
Fults, Ephriam 1836 wb-1-216 (W)
Fults, Isaac 1840 wb-1-309 (W)
Fults, Jessee 1846 wb-2-169 (W)
Funk, Henry 1839 rb-h-266 (Mt)
Fuqua, Elizabeth L. 1854 wb-a-226 (Cr)
Fuqua, Gabriel 1823 wb-8-204 (D)
Fuqua, John C. 1852 wb-15-376 (D)
Fuqua, Rebecca 1853 wb-15-519 (D)
Fuqua, Samuel 1850 wb-14-389 (Rb)
Fuqua, Thomas 1860 wb-18-328 (D)
Fuqua, William 1856 wb-h-199 (St)
Fuqua, William 1857 wb-16-537 (Rb)
Fuquay, William E. 1848 wb-#60 (Mc)
Fuqueway, A. G. 1861 wb-#60 (Mc)
Furgas, John 1836 wb-1-45 (Bo)
Furgason, L. L. 1857 wb-f-44 (G)
Furgerson, H. S. 1854 39-1-348 (Dk)
Furgerson, Hubberd S. 1854 39-2-36 (Dk)
Furgerson, Nelson 1825 lr (Sn)
Furgerson, William 1819 wb-1-0 (Sm)
Furguson, John F. 1853 as-b-78 (Ms)
Furguson, Mary F. 1859 wb-13-139 (Wi)
Furguson, Nathaniel 1849 wb-g-161 (Hu)
Furgusson, Hugh 1854 wb-1-45 (Bo)
Furlong, Robert 1814 wb-1-0 (Sm)
Furr, George 1830 rb-8-41 (Ru)
Fusley, James 1814 wb-1-181 (Hw)
Fuson, Bethel 1855 ib-1-359 (Wy)
Fuson, Sophrona A. 1857 ib-2-6 (Wy)
Fussell, Harrison 1829 rb-7-217 (Ru)

Fussell, James 1855 wb-a-252 (Cr)
Fuston, John 1820 wb-#36 (Wl)
Fuston, John Sr. 1812 wb-#11 (Wl)
Fuston, Samuel 1853 wb-#110 (Wl)
Futh, Wm. C. 1851 wb-3-103 (W)
Futrell, D. L. 1858 wb-h-179 (Hn)
Futrell, Isaac 1836 wb-d-29 (St)
Futrell, Isaac 1861 wb-i-325 (St)
Futrell, James 1852 wb-xx-78 (St)
Futrell, James E. 1852 wb-xx-85 (St)
Futrell, Joel 1834 wb-c-380 (St)
Futrell, Wiley 1856 wb-6-227 (Ma)
Futrill, Martha 1853 wb-xx-205 (St)
Fuzell, John 1839 rb-10-455 (Ru)
Fyffe, Isaac W. 1829 wb-#60 (Mc)
Fyke, Elkin 1819 wb-3-24 (Rb)
Fyke, Elkin 1821 wb-3-310 (Rb)
Fyke, John 1827 wb-5-433 (Rb)
Fyke, Mary 1861 wb-17-206 (Rb)
Fykes, Nathan 1833 wb-8-216 (Rb)
Fyles, James F. 1849 wb-g-151 (O)

- G -

Gabbe, James 1857 rb-o-503 (Mt)
Gabel, Barneybas 1844 wb-1-357 (La)
Gable, Barnabas 1858 wb-2-86# (Ge)
Gable, Jacob 1850 wb-m-105 (Mt)
Gable, William 1818 rb-4-107 (Ru)
Gaby, William 1848 rb-k-711 (Mt)
Gadd, Miriam 1857 wb-5-72 (Hr)
Gadd, William 1848 wb-#6 (Mo)
Gaddy, Elijah 1817 wb-#38 (Wl)
Gage, John 1818 wb-A-205 (Li)
Gage, John 1837 rb-h-13 (Mt)
Gainer, James C. 1842 wb-f-125 (Hn)
Gainer, John 1803 rb-a-182 (Mt)
Gainer, John S. 1857 wb-h-154 (Hn)
Gainer, Obadiah 1824 rb-6-50 (Ru)
Gainer, Sally 1819 rb-c-181 (Mt)
Gaines, A. B. 1852 wb-b-191 (L)
Gaines, Edmond P. 1853 wb-2-140 (Sh)
Gaines, Gideon 1833 wb-#101 (Wl)
Gaines, Henry P. 1861 wb-a-375 (Cr)
Gaines, James T. 1820 wb-1-211 (Hw)
Gaines, John 1803 rb-a-198 (Mt)
Gaines, John F. 1854 wb-15-464 (Rb)
Gaines, Larkin 1854 wb-b-259 (L)
Gaines, William Humprey 1832 wb-#86 (Wl)
Gains, Abraham C. 1857 rb-o-366 (Mt)
Gains, Charlotte 1846 wb-b-182 (We)

Gains, Fountain H. 1816 wb-4-468 (D)
Gains, Fountain H. 1816 wb-7-10 (D)
Gains, Ira 1862 wb-d-130 (L)
Gains, Philip 1817 wb-a-94 (Ro)
Gains, Robert 1836 wb-1-148 (Gr)
Gains, William S. 1816 wb-4-449 (D)
Gains, William S. 1816 wb-7-62 (D)
Gairland, Samuel 1824 lw (Ct)
Gaither, Brice 1828 rb-7-132 (Ru)
Gaither, Brice M. 1831 rb-8-183 (Ru)
Gaither, Edward 1856 wb-A-115 (Ca)
Gaither, Martin 1836 wb-1-113 (La)
Gaitherall, Alfred M. 1839 abl-1-128 (T)
Galbraith, Andrew 1860 wb-1-231 (Hw)
Galbraith, Arthur 1818 wb-1-210 (Hw)
Galbraith, John 1832 wb-1-219 (Hw)
Galbraith, John 1845 rb-j-462 (Mt)
Galbraith, John S. 1841 wb-12-43 (D)
Galbraith, Joseph 1811 wb-1-207 (Hw)
Galbraith, Joseph 1848 wb-1B-89 (A)
Galbraith, Miller D. 1841 wb-1A-336 (A)
Galbraith, Robert 1848 wb-1B-80 (A)
Galbraith, Samuel 1850 wb-1B-234 (A)
Galbraith, William 1802 lr (Sn)
Galbraith, William 1835 wb-b-256 (Ro)
Galbreath, Isabella 1859 wb-13-189 (K)
Galbreath, John 1814 wb-2-119 (K)
Galbreath, John 1855 wb-12-155 (K)
Galbreath, Robert 1841 wb-1A-339 (A)
Galbreath, William 1799 wb-2-145# (Ge)
Gale, Josiah 1795 wb-1-0 (Sm)
Galespie, James 1855 wb-2-180 (Sh)
Gallagher, Joseph 1825 wb-4-88 (K)
Gallagly, Darchus 1824 wb-#52 (Wl)
Gallagy, Gardner 1815 wb-#20 (Wl)
Gallaher, George 1837 wb-6-103 (K)
Gallaher, John 1848 ib-1-14 (Wy)
Gallant, Daniel 1835 wb-#61 (Mc)
Gallaspie, David 1803 wb-2-326 (D)
Galleghy, John S. 1859 ib-2-127 (Wy)
Galleher, James 1792 wb-#4 (Wa)
Gallemore, Abraham 1840 wb-2-53# (Ge)
Galley, John S. 1859 ib-2-184 (Wy)
Gallien, Geo. C. 1853 as-c-319 (Di)
Galliher, Joseph A. 1856 wb-12-271 (K)
Gallion, Mitchell M. 1851 wb-d-353 (G)
Gallion, Thomas 1858 wb-12-501 (K)
Gallope, Edmond (Edward) 1845 wb-e-47 (O)
Gallope, Edmond 1844 wb-d-291 (O)
Galloway, James 1855 wb-1-126 (Su)
Galloway, James E. 1834 wb-x-167 (Mu)

Galloway, James P. 1854 ib-h-80 (F)
Galloway, Jessee T. 1840 wb-y-684 (Mu)
Galloway, John 1855 wb-1-249 (Su)
Galloway, John 1851 rb-4-272 (Mu)
Galloway, John 1858 wb-3c-74 (Sh)
Galloway, John T. 1838 wb-y-164 (Mu)
Galloway, Robert M. 1840 wb-z-45 (Mu)
Galloway, Samuel 1829 wb-#194 (Mu)
Galloway, Thos. 1861 wb-b-102 (F)
Galoway, Glidwell O. 1844 wb-b-47 (We)
Galoway, William 1830 wb-#207 (Mu)
Gambel, Robert 1784 wb-1-9# (Ge)
Gambell, H. H. 1837 wb-1-558 (Hr)
Gambell, Hiram 1836 wb-1-531* (Hr)
Gambell, James 1843 wb-11-453 (Rb)
Gambell, John K. 1845 rb-13-163 (Ru)
Gambill, Alice 1841 wb-11-28 (Rb)
Gambill, Alice A. 1841 wb-11-55 (Rb)
Gambill, Bradley 1806 rb-2-21 (Ru)
Gambill, Elizabeth 1848 wb-13-26 (Rb)
Gambill, Frances 1840 wb-10-355 (Rb)
Gambill, James 1846 wb-13-25 (Rb)
Gambill, John 1843 rb-12-380 (Ru)
Gambill, Matilda 1840 wb-10-355 (Rb)
Gambill, Nancy 1840 wb-10-355 (Rb)
Gambill, Rubania 1841 wb-11-28 (Rb)
Gambill, T. J. 1856 wb-16-290 (Rb)
Gamble, Alexander 1803 wb-a-4 (Ro)
Gamble, Charles R. 1859 wb-e-270 (Wh)
Gamble, Elizabeth 1846 wb-d-231 (Ro)
Gamble, John N. 1819 wb-3-60 (K)
Gamble, John N. 1834 wb-#61 (Mc)
Gamble, John N. 1849 wb-#61 (Mc)
Gamble, Moses 1830 wb-1-51 (Bo)
Gamble, Samuel 1856 wb-2-284 (Me)
Gamble, Thomas 1838 wb-c-4 (Ro)
Gamble, William 1825 wb-a-2 (R)
Gamble, William 1841 abl-1-163 (T)
Gamble, William 1853 wb-1C-100 (A)
Gamble, William P. 1847 wb-#62 (Mc)
Gamble, Wm. 1853 wb-1B-328 (A)
Gamblin, J. W. 1849 wb-b-457 (Mu)
Gambling, James 1843 lr (Sn)
Gambling, John 1808 wb-1-180 (Wi)
Gambril, John R. 1854 rb-17-279 (Ru)
Gammel, David 1801 wb-1-9# (Ge)
Gammill, Elisha 1841 wb-b-355 (Hd)
Gammill, James T. 1844 wb-d-111 (Hd)
Gammill, Samuel 1817 rb-4-80 (Ru)
Gammon, Edward 1852 wb-2-132 (Sh)
Gammon, Harris 1844 wb-8-253 (K)

Gammon, Harris 1857 wb-12-420 (K)
Gammon, John 1848 wb-e-90 (Ro)
Gammon, Mary 1852 wb-2-132 (Sh)
Gammon, Sarah 1854 148-1-496 (Ge)
Gammon, William 1841 wb-c-260 (Ro)
Gammons, Ivey 1843 148-1-57 (Ge)
Gammons, Nicholas 1842 wb-c-87 (G)
Ganaway, Robert 1836 wb-2-181 (Ma)
Gandolfo, Sarah 1851 wb-2-99 (Sh)
Ganer?, Sarah C. 1845 wb-g-56 (Hn)
Gann, Adam 1811 wb-2-18 (Je)
Gannaway, Burrel 1853 rb-16-646 (Ru)
Gannaway, Elijah R. 1852 rb-16-335 (Ru)
Ganoway, Money 1815 wb-#22 (Mu)
Gant, Benjamin R. 1853 wb-10-547 (Wi)
Gant, Elizabeth 1849 as-a-193 (Ms)
Gant, Jeremiah 1855 wb-a-378 (Ms)
Gant, Thomas 1861 as-c-247 (Ms)
Gant, William 1816 wb-#25 (Mu)
Gant, William 1829 wb-#174 (Mu)
Ganter, John 1851 wb-m-390 (Mt)
Gantt, Fredrick G. 1844 wb-a2-107 (Mu)
Gantt, George H. 1860 wb-f-189 (Mu)
Gantt, J. B. 1846 wb-d-264 (Hd)
Gantt, Jesse B. 1845 wb-d-184 (Hd)
Gantt, John 1847 wb-d-328 (Hd)
Gantt, Jonathan 1847 wb-d-349 (Hd)
Gantt, Jonathan W. 1847 wb-d-329 (Hd)
Gantt, William C. 1844 wb-d-73 (Hd)
Garaway, John 1812 rb-2-204 (Ru)
Garaway, Robt. 1812 rb-2-203 (Ru)
Garber, Michael 1847 wb-#45 (Wa)
Gardiner, Pleasant 1855 ib-h-305 (F)
Gardner, Alfred J. 1845 wb-d-198 (Ro)
Gardner, Brittain 1854 wb-f-32 (Mu)
Gardner, Demsey 1839 wb-10-352 (Rb)
Gardner, George 1826 wb-5-378 (Rb)
Gardner, Henry 1837 wb-9-415 (Rb)
Gardner, James 1803 lr (Sn)
Gardner, James 1833 wb-8-339 (Rb)
Gardner, James 1859 wb-i-137 (St)
Gardner, Jane 1808 wb-1-33 (Wi)
Gardner, Jane 1818 wb-2-388 (Wi)
Gardner, Jane 1819 wb-3-15 (Wi)
Gardner, John 1828 wb-2-86 (Sn)
Gardner, John 1841 wb-e-139 (St)
Gardner, John 1842 wb-e-167 (St)
Gardner, John 1856 wb-12-231 (Wi)
Gardner, Joshua 1846 wb-12-600 (Rb)
Gardner, Mary Ann 1815 wb-1-217 (Sn)
Gardner, Mary L. 1850 rb-l-628 (Mt)

Gardner, Mary L. 1850 rb-l-629 (Mt)
Gardner, Mourning 1828 lr (Sn)
Gardner, Richard W. 1851 wb-15-2 (Rb)
Gardner, S. C. 1859 wb-f-300 (G)
Gardner, Shadrach 1842 wb-a-94 (F)
Gardner, Uriah 1830 rb-8-83 (Ru)
Gardner, Uriah 1830 rb-8-96 (Ru)
Gardner, Warren 1839 wb-11-336 (Mt)
Gardner, William 1806 wb-1-19 (Wi)
Gardner, William 1819 wb-3-1 (Wi)
Garey, James 1852 wb-10-271 (Wi)
Garey, Thomas W. 1846 wb-a2-337 (Mu)
Garland, Elisha 1837 wb-11-14 (D)
Garland, H. S. 1845 rb-j-414 (Mt)
Garland, James 1824 wb-a-46 (Hn)
Garland, Kinchen 1837 wb-2-210 (Ma)
Garland, Moses H. 1847 wb-e-59 (Ro)
Garland, P. 1818 lr (Gi)
Garland, Samuel 1860 wb-18-376 (D)
Garland, Sarah 1839 wb-3-105 (Ma)
Garmany, Margaret 1837 wb-#116 (Wl)
Garner, Abram 1856 wb-3-381 (La)
Garner, Benjamin 1850 wb-3-21 (W)
Garner, Elizabeth 1846 wb-d-268 (Hd)
Garner, Henry 1836 wb-b-47 (Hd)
Garner, Henry G. 1838 wb-b-87 (Hd)
Garner, Henry sr. 1838 wb-b-85 (Hd)
Garner, Henry sr. 1845 wb-d-153 (Hd)
Garner, James 1853 mr-2-521 (Be)
Garner, John 1817 rb-4-96 (Ru)
Garner, John 1855 wb-1C-313 (A)
Garner, John 1857 db-R-246 (A)
Garner, John F. 1835 wb-1-53 (Bo)
Garner, John N. 1847 rb-14-170 (Ru)
Garner, Josiah 1815 wb-2-182 (K)
Garner, M. W. 1860 wb-1-400 (Fr)
Garner, Obadiah 1822 rb-5-176 (Ru)
Garner, Thomas 1853 wb-3-188 (W)
Garner, Wm. S. 1859 wb-3e-88 (Sh)
Garner, _____ 1838 wb-b-93 (Hd)
Garnett, James H. 1853 wb-10-502 (Wi)
Garratt, Henry 1859 rb-20-82 (Ru)
Garren, Peter 1861 wb-b-118 (Ms)
Garret, Isaac 1825 rb-d-428 (Mt)
Garret, Jacob 1838 wb-2-49# (Ge)
Garrett, Aggathy 1830 lr (Gi)
Garrett, Caleb 1841 wb-7-478 (Wi)
Garrett, Catlet 1815 wb-a-62 (Ro)
Garrett, David 1835 wb-#109 (Wl)
Garrett, Edward 1801 wb-1-80 (Sn)
Garrett, Eli 1824 wb-A-412 (Li)

Garrett, Geo. W. 1853 wb-a-435 (F)
Garrett, Henry 1845 wb-8-346 (Wi)
Garrett, Jacob 1796 wb-1-46 (Je)
Garrett, James 1854 wb-f-42 (Mu)
Garrett, James 1861 wb-b*-1 (O)
Garrett, Jane 1818 wb-2-392 (Wi)
Garrett, John 1806 wb-1-139 (Wi)
Garrett, John L. 1845 wb-13-309 (D)
Garrett, Johnson Harris 1846 wb-0-66 (Cf)
Garrett, Kenneth 1852 wb-2-133 (Sh)
Garrett, Lewis R. 1842 wb-12-359* (D)
Garrett, Martin 1818 rb-b-509 (Mt)
Garrett, Matthew 1838 wb-e-55 (Hu)
Garrett, Thomas 1816 wb-7-99 (D)
Garrett, Thomas 1832 wb-10-1 (D)
Garrett, Thomas 1837 wb-6-329 (Wi)
Garrett, William 1851 wb-a-226 (Di)
Garrett, William 1854 wb-16-350 (D)
Garrett, William H. 1855 wb-6-40 (Ma)
Garrett, William W. 1832 wb-9-609 (D)
Garrett, William sr. 1857 wb-17-365 (D)
Garrison, Baily 1816 wb-#24 (Wl)
Garrison, Delila 1823 wb-#62 (Mu)
Garrison, E. M. 1854 39-2-4 (Dk)
Garrison, Hannah 1838 wb-a-365 (R)
Garrison, Isaiah 1851 ib-1-111 (Wy)
Garrison, J. M. 1857 wb-j-253 (O)
Garrison, James 1856 39-2-180 (Dk)
Garrison, Jane 1827 wb-#69 (Wl)
Garrison, John 1826 wb-#143 (Mu)
Garrison, John 1847 wb-b*-13 (O)
Garrison, John 1847 wb-f-127+ (O)
Garrison, John C. 1854 as-b-154 (Ms)
Garrison, Logan 1860 39-2-389 (Dk)
Garrison, Lucinda 1850 wb-g-330 (O)
Garrison, M. A. 1854 wb-6-318 (Ma)
Garrison, Nehemiah 1815 wb-1-0 (Sm)
Garrison, Peter 1824 rb-6-44 (Ru)
Garrison, Rosanna 1857 wb-b-36 (F)
Garrison, Samuel 1850 wb-g-284 (O)
Garrison, Samuel C. 1853 as-b-117 (Ms)
Garrison, Thos. S. 1851 wb-a-392 (F)
Garrison, William 1852 ib-1-187 (Wy)
Garrison, William 1856 wb-h-174 (St)
Garrison, William B. S. 1849 wb-2-43 (Sh)
Garrison, William F. 1852 ib-1-199 (Wy)
Garrisone?, John 1840 wb-d-451 (St)
Garriston, Job 1850 33-3-226 (Gr)
Garritt, Levi 1855 wb-3-270 (La)
Garrot, Jacob 1826 rb-e-49 (Mt)
Garrott, Pleasant 1829 wb-3-63 (Je)

Garth, W. A. 1844 rb-j-144 (Mt)
Garton, J. W. 1842 wb-z-293 (Mu)
Garton, John 1844 as-b-253 (Di)
Garton, Martin 1847 as-b-389 (Di)
Garwood, Joseph 1852 wb-d-412 (G)
Garwood, Joseph 1853 wb-e-122 (G)
Gary, James 1847 wb-9-8 (Wi)
Gary, Rebecca M. 1841 wb-c-10 (G)
Gary, Thomas W. 1849 wb-b-427 (Mu)
Gasaway, John 1813 rb-2-216 (Ru)
Gasaway, Robert 1814 rb-3-15 (Ru)
Gaskill, Robert 1856 wb-f-97 (Mu)
Gass, Charles B. 1858 wb-j-416 (O)
Gass, David 1826 wb-2-484 (Je)
Gass, Hezekiah B. 1841 148-1-9 (Ge)
Gass, Jacob 1799 wb-1-10# (Ge)
Gass, James 1842 wb-2-58# (Ge)
Gass, John 1845 wb-2-54# (Ge)
Gass, John sr. 1845 wb-2-63# (Ge)
Gass, Margaret 1861 wb-k-409 (O)
Gass, Samuel 1839 wb-4-64 (Je)
Gass, William 1809 ib-1-297 (Ge)
Gass, William 1847 wb-2-67# (Ge)
Gass, William 1861 wb-2-93# (Ge)
Gaston, Joseph 1841 148-1-19 (Ge)
Gaston, Joseph 1852 wb-#62 (Mc)
Gate, Robert S. 1851 wb-14-533 (Rb)
Gately, J. H. 1843 wb-f-181 (Hn)
Gately, John 1852 wb-5-117 (Ma)
Gately, Joseph H. 1841 wb-e-192 (Hn)
Gates, Benjamin 1822 wb-1-0 (Sm)
Gates, John 1835 wb-#31 (Wa)
Gates, Joseph 1857 wb-c-134 (L)
Gates, Lydia (Mrs.) 1853 wb-15-289 (Rb)
Gates, Wm. 1847 rb-14-226 (Ru)
Gates, Wm. M. 1846 rb-13-693 (Ru)
Gatewood, Sarah 1853 rb-16-466 (Ru)
Gather, Brice 1830 rb-8-146 (Ru)
Gather, Buie 1828 rb-7-119 (Ru)
Gatley, William 1824 wb-3-293 (St)
Gatlin, Ephraim 1837 wb-d-126 (St)
Gatlin, Ephraim C. 1854 wb-h-44 (St)
Gatlin, James 1836 wb-1-499 (Hr)
Gatlin, John M. C. 1853 wb-15-528 (D)
Gatlin, Lazerous 1808 wb-4-5 (D)
Gatlin, Martha E. 1856 wb-h-252 (St)
Gatlin, Mary 1824 rb-6-42 (Ru)
Gatlin, Nathan 1856 wb-16-613 (D)
Gatlin, Susannah C. 1853 wb-h-185 (Hu)
Gatlin, Winston C. 1844 lr (Gi)
Gattis, Isaac 1841 wb-1-195 (Li)

Gatton, Joseph H. 1856 wb-#120 (Wl)
Gatwood, Jane 1839 wb-1-56 (Sh)
Gaulling, John 1825 wb-#62 (Mc)
Gault, James 1837 wb-6-399 (Wi)
Gault, John 1821 wb-1-191 (Bo)
Gault, Thomas 1847 wb-9-358 (K)
Gault, William 1830 wb-1-50 (Bo)
Gault, William 1859 wb-13-118* (K)
Gaultell, John 1852 wb-h-Mar (O)
Gauntt, Mark 1859 149-1-159 (Ge)
Gauntt, Samuel 1831 wb-2-40# (Ge)
Gauntt, Samuel 1843 148-1-68 (Ge)
Gauntt, Susannah 1858 149-1-133 (Ge)
Gaut (Gault), Thomas 1819 wb-3-104 (K)
Gaut, John 1833 wb-3-212 (Je)
Gavin, John F. 1854 wb-h-228 (Hu)
Gay, Benjamin 1830 wb-1-172 (Hr)
Gay, H. H. 1848 r39-1-71 (Dk)
Gay, James 1806 wb-1-145 (Wi)
Gay, William 1854 wb-#25 (Mo)
Gaylor, William 1842 wb-2-557 (Hy)
Gaylord, John D. 1860 wb-18-299 (D)
Gear, Gilly 1832 wb-b-101 (Wh)
Gearin, David 1858 wb-1-134 (R)
Gearmany, Hugh 1826 wb-#69 (Wl)
Gee (B), George 1850 wb-1-378 (Li)
Gee (B), George 1850 wb-1-385 (Li)
Gee, Claiborn 1845 wb-a2-200 (Mu)
Gee, David 1823 wb-a-2 (Cr)
Gee, John 1829 wb-9-302 (D)
Gee, John 1847 wb-14-25 (D)
Gee, John 1848 wb-14-278 (D)
Gee, John H. 1860 as-c-205 (Ms)
Gee, Jonathan 1793 wb-1-274 (D)
Gee, Joseph 1823 rb-d-244 (Mt)
Gee, Joseph C. 1847 wb-14-161 (D)
Gee, Joshua J. 1852 wb-15-351 (D)
Gee, Mary W. 1847 wb-9-9 (Wi)
Gee, Nelson W. 1859 wb-13-69 (Wi)
Gee, Robert F. 1854 wb-a-214 (T)
Gee, Samuel M. 1840 wb-12-32 (D)
Gee, William O. 1843 wb-8-52 (Wi)
Gee, William W. 1840 wb-11-615 (D)
Geer, David 1821 wb-a-153 (Wh)
Geisler, Edward 1858 wb-17-478 (D)
Gelligher, John 1827 rb-e-225 (Mt)
Gen?, Gilly 1831 wb-b-30 (Wh)
Gensty?, William 1844 wb-c-167 (Wh)
Gent, Charles 1843 wb-11-455 (Rb)
Gentle, John 1855 wb-1-339 (Fr)
Gentry, Aaron 1852 wb-11-273 (K)

Gentry, Aaron G. 1850 wb-10-485 (K)
Gentry, Allen D. 1853 wb-#24 (Mo)
Gentry, Charlotte 1849 wb-10-119 (K)
Gentry, Elizabeth 1844 wb-f-152 (St)
Gentry, Elizabeth 1848 wb-9-474 (K)
Gentry, J. S. 1856 as-c-14 (Ms)
Gentry, Joseph 1847 wb-0-75 (Cf)
Gentry, Martin 1833 wb-3-235 (Je)
Gentry, Martin F. 1837 wb-3-451 (Je)
Gentry, Nancy 1861 wb-#18 (Mo)
Gentry, Nicholas 1784 wb-1-5 (D)
Gentry, Reuben A. 1841 wb-7-435 (Wi)
Gentry, Robert 1811 wb-2-8 (Je)
Gentry, Ruth T. 1852 wb-10-525 (Wi)
Gentry, Samuel R. 1816 wb-2-231 (Wi)
Gentry, Silas 1815 wb-2-128 (Je)
Gentry, Susan 1856 wb-#27 (Mo)
Gentry, Tho. 1847 wb-a-172 (Di)
Gentry, Thomas G. 1833 wb-5-280 (Wi)
Gentry, W. W. 1858 wb-b-65 (Ms)
Gentry, Watson 1844 wb-8-167 (Wi)
Gentry, William 1840 as-a-472 (Di)
Gentry, William E. 1849 wb-10-118 (K)
Gentry, William W. 1860 as-c-231 (Ms)
Genway, Charles 1817 wb-2-190 (Je)
George, Benjamin 1839 wb-2-17 (Hy)
George, Britain 1857 wb-1-116 (Be)
George, David W. 1854 wb-2-88 (Li)
George, Edward 1798 wb-1-65 (Je)
George, Isaac 1845 wb-#151 (Wl)
George, J. J. 1854 wb-1-332 (Fr)
George, James 1810 wb-1-309 (K)
George, James 1832 wb-#98 (Wl)
George, James F. 1855 wb-#116 (Wl)
George, Jesse 1849 wb-14-269 (Rb)
George, Jessee 1847 wb-d-46 (G)
George, Mary 1852 wb-e-15 (G)
George, Polly 1853 wb-#109 (Wl)
George, Presley 1821 wb-A-359 (Li)
George, Reverand 1845 wb-#148 (Wl)
George, Robert 1837 wb-A-8 (Ca)
George, Samuel 1839 wb-1-48 (Bo)
George, Solomon 1831 wb-5-55 (K)
George, Travis 1834 wb-5-282 (K)
George, Travis 1856 wb-j-143 (O)
George, William 1846 wb-2-63# (Ge)
George, William 1859 wb-16-812 (Rb)
George, William C. C. C. 1841 wb-#3 (Mo)
Geran, Hyram 1800 wb-1-71 (K)
Geren, Hiram 1818 wb-3-52 (K)
Geren, Solamon 1842 wb-d-14 (Ro)

Gerg, Youst 1804 wb-1-10# (Ge)
German, Daniel sr. 1859 wb-13-24 (Wi)
German, Elizabeth 1824 wb-3-719 (Wi)
German, Elizabeth 1827 wb-4-235 (Wi)
German, Joseph 1819 wb-3-1 (Wi)
German, P. 1855 ib-h-397 (F)
Geron, Andrew C. 1857 wb-f-95 (Ro)
Gerrin, Susannah 1805 wb-1-176 (K)
Getor, Argolas 1792 wb-1-252 (D)
Geurin, Joshua 1855 wb-h-130 (St)
Ghent, Charles 1845 wb-12-365 (Rb)
Gholson, John 1817 wb-2-334 (Wi)
Gholson, Sarah J. 1857 wb-6-429 (Ma)
Gholston, Benjamin 1841 wb-3-387 (Ma)
Ghost, Christopher 1856 ib-2-283 (Cl)
Gibbert, William 1837 rb-g-618 (Mt)
Gibbins, R. B. 1852 wb-3-72 (La)
Gibbons, A. B. 1861 wb-a-383 (Cr)
Gibbons, Abbigail 1840 wb-1-188 (Fr)
Gibbons, John 1858 wb-1-225 (Hw)
Gibbons, Samuel G. 1830 wb-#214 (Mu)
Gibbons, Thomas 1809 wb-1-205 (Hw)
Gibbons, Thomas 1857 wb-h-713 (Hu)
Gibbs, Anna E. 1849 wb-1B-210 (A)
Gibbs, Benjamin 1826 wb-a-221 (Wh)
Gibbs, C. C. 1844 wb-d-120 (Hd)
Gibbs, Daniel 1852 wb-11-194 (K)
Gibbs, David 1847 wb-9-364 (K)
Gibbs, David 1857 wb-12-412 (K)
Gibbs, Huldah 1856 wb-12-225 (K)
Gibbs, Jacob 1852 wb-11-290 (K)
Gibbs, John 1840 wb-1A-292 (A)
Gibbs, John 1841 wb-12-244* (D)
Gibbs, John 1845 wb-d-148 (Hd)
Gibbs, Nicholas jr. 1814 wb-2-120 (K)
Gibbs, Nicholas sr. 1817 wb-2-343 (K)
Gibbs, Rachel 1847 wb-9-327 (K)
Gibbs, Sally 1857 wb-12-412 (K)
Gibbs, Samuel 1828 wb-1-17 (W)
Gibbs, William 1828 wb-#62 (Mc)
Gibson, Alexander 1835 rb-g-223 (Mt)
Gibson, Amos 1847 wb-1-39 (Jo)
Gibson, Ann 1852 wb-3-9 (La)
Gibson, Edwin 1829 rb-f-2 (Mt)
Gibson, Edwin 1830 rb-f-53 (Mt)
Gibson, Edwin 1845 rb-j-298 (Mt)
Gibson, Elizabeth 1858 wb-h-262 (Hn)
Gibson, Felix G. 1857 wb-2-13 (Li)
Gibson, George 1835 lr (Gi)
Gibson, George 1835 wb-d-150 (Hn)
Gibson, Hannah 1847 wb-5-51 (Ma)

Gibson, James 1806 wb-1-191 (K)
Gibson, James 1831 wb-5-58 (Wi)
Gibson, James 1835 rb-9-258 (Ru)
Gibson, Jane 1849 wb-2-86 (La)
Gibson, John 1828 rb-e-369 (Mt)
Gibson, John 1835 wb-5-359 (K)
Gibson, John 1843 wb-#62 (Mc)
Gibson, John 1844 wb-1-231 (Li)
Gibson, John 1846 wb-#150 (Wl)
Gibson, John 1858 lr (Gi)
Gibson, John B. 1824 wb-3-742 (Wi)
Gibson, John B. 1848 wb-g-82 (St)
Gibson, John C. 1827 wb-#66 (Wl)
Gibson, John D. 1856 wb-12-203 (K)
Gibson, John jr. 1835 wb-5-347 (K)
Gibson, Joseph 1815 rb-3-171 (Ru)
Gibson, Joseph 1826 wb-b-5 (Hn)
Gibson, Joshua 1838 wb-1-151 (Li)
Gibson, Josiah B. 1856 wb-2-161 (Li)
Gibson, Louisa 1848 wb-#163 (Wl)
Gibson, Maranda 1858 wb-1-235 (Be)
Gibson, Margarett 1821? wb-#118 (Mu)
Gibson, Mary 1832 rb-f-327 (Mt)
Gibson, Mary 1840 wb-#38 (Wa)
Gibson, Partrick 1850 wb-9-384 (Wi)
Gibson, Patrick 1817 wb-2-291 (Wi)
Gibson, Philander 1841 rb-i-187 (Mt)
Gibson, Sarah A. 1846 wb-8-491 (Wi)
Gibson, Shepard 1842 wb-1-224 (Hw)
Gibson, Stephen 1848 wb-1-48 (Jo)
Gibson, Susan 1828 rb-e-378 (Mt)
Gibson, Thomas 1830 wb-#28 (Wa)
Gibson, Thomas 1852 wb-#51 (Wa)
Gibson, Thomas 1852 wb-3-72 (La)
Gibson, Thornton 1833 wb-8-221 (Rb)
Gibson, Travis 1858 iv-C-8 (C)
Gibson, William 1817 wb-#118 (Mu)
Gibson, William 1828 wb-9-217 (D)
Gibson, William 1838 wb-e-54 (Hu)
Gibson, William 1843 wb-12-396* (D)
Gibson, William 1848 wb-g-17 (Hu)
Gibson, William R. 1828 rb-e-328 (Mt)
Gibson, Wilson 1829 rb-f-2 (Mt)
Giddens, Francis sr. 1830 wb-4-531 (Wi)
Giddens, James 1820 lr (Gi)
Giddens, William 1829 lr (Gi)
Gideon, Aaron 1861 wb-13-429 (K)
Gideon, Mary 1836 wb-6-36 (K)
Gideous, James 1823 wb-1-213 (Hw)
Giets (Kitts), John 1802 wb-1-75 (Rb)
Giffin, Pryor L. 1855 wb-12-163 (K)

Gifford, William 1839 as-a-20 (Ms)
Giger, George 1821 wb-2-557 (Je)
Gilbert, Ann Eliza 1858 wb-h-219 (Hn)
Gilbert, B. 1843 wb-f-163 (Hn)
Gilbert, Charlotte H. A. 1858 wb-h-219 (Hn)
Gilbert, Ebenezer 1853 wb-#107 (Wl)
Gilbert, James Z. 1855 mr-2-636 (Be)
Gilbert, Jesse 1815 wb-3-71 (St)
Gilbert, Jesse 1815 wb-3-95 (St)
Gilbert, Jesse 1851 wb-g-398 (St)
Gilbert, John 1857 wb-16-553 (Rb)
Gilbert, Mary 1847 rb-k-389 (Mt)
Gilbert, Samuel 1840 lr (Gi)
Gilbert, Samuel 1844 wb-g-1 (Hn)
Gilbert, William 1837 rb-g-567 (Mt)
Gilbert, William 1861 wb-i-345 (St)
Gilbreath, Absalom M. 1859 wb-f-160 (Mu)
Gilbreath, Alexander 1855 wb-12-158 (K)
Gilbreath, James 1845 wb-a2-315 (Mu)
Gilbreath, John 1831 wb-#220 (Mu)
Gilbreath, John 1840 wb-z-17 (Mu)
Gilbreath, John 1857 wb-12-355 (K)
Gilbreath, Joseph 1827 wb-#62 (Mc)
Gilbreath, Joseph B. 1857 wb-#28 (Mo)
Gilbreath, Mary 1822 wb-3-340 (K)
Gilchrist, Allen 1846 wb-c-344 (G)
Gilchrist, Archibald 1851 wb-4-290 (Mu)
Gilchrist, Malcolm (Sr.) 1821 wb-#75 (Mu)
Gilchrist, Sarah Ellen 1851 wb-14-563 (D)
Gilcrist, Malcolm 1821 wb-#116 (Mu)
Gildusky, Julius 1853 wb-16-79 (D)
Giles, Edward 1800 lr (Sn)
Giles, Edward 1858 wb-12-504 (Wi)
Giles, Edward J. 1857 wb-12-401 (Wi)
Giles, James 1853 wb-a-310 (Ms)
Giles, Josiah E. 1827 wb-9-133 (D)
Giles, Josiah E. 1828 wb-4-309 (Wi)
Giles, Lewis L. 1838 wb-2-389 (Ma)
Giles, Newton C. 1856 wb-12-226 (Wi)
Giles, Patrick G. 1846 wb-8-452 (Wi)
Giles, Robertson 1851 wb-10-47 (Wi)
Giles, William 1844 wb-8-193 (Wi)
Gilespie, James D. 1860 wb-1-402 (Be)
Gilky, John 1796 wb-2-57 (D)
Gill, Caleb T. 1834 wb-5-358 (Wi)
Gill, Elizabeth 1857 wb-6-487 (Ma)
Gill, Geo. 1851 wb-d-347 (G)
Gill, George W. 1854 wb-e-155 (G)
Gill, J. J. 1854 wb-16-214 (D)
Gill, James 1822 wb-1-0 (Sm)
Gill, James B. 1861 wb-2-360 (Li)

Gill, James J. 1855 wb-16-586 (D)
Gill, John 1822 wb-1-0 (Sm)
Gill, John G. 1837 wb-a-66 (Cr)
Gill, Joseph 1858 wb-7-16 (Ma)
Gill, Rhoda 1846 wb-a-272 (F)
Gill, Robert sr. 1845 wb-5-10 (Ma)
Gill, Sarah 1839 wb-y-400 (Mu)
Gill, Thomas 1839 wb-y-410 (Mu)
Gill, Thomas 1846 wb-5-427 (Gr)
Gill, Thomas 1854 wb-7-0 (Sm)
Gill, W. C. 1852 wb-4-583 (Mu)
Gill, William B. 1858 wb-#131 (Wl)
Gillam, Danl. 1809 wb-4-58 (D)
Gillam, Gray 1846 wb-b-163 (We)
Gillam, John B. 1811 lr (Sn)
Gillaspie, David A. 1861 wb-13-488 (Wi)
Gillaspie, Elizabeth 1855 wb-c-378 (G)
Gillaspie, Isaac 1828 wb-4-349 (Wi)
Gillaspie, Jacob 1842 wb-7-343 (K)
Gillaspie, James 1807 wb-3-65 (Wi)
Gillaspie, Jane 1849 wb-4-501 (Hr)
Gilleland, James 1815 rb-3-6 (Ru)
Gilleland, James 1853 wb-1-82 (Jo)
Gilleland, John 1852 wb-b-167 (L)
Gilleland, Samuel V. 1847 wb-b-162 (L)
Gillentine, John W. 1858 wb-a-290 (V)
Gillenwaters, John 1806 wb-3-65 (D)
Gillenwaters, Mary 1855 wb-1-229 (Hw)
Gillenwaters, Thomas 1841 wb-1-223 (Hw)
Gillenwaters, William 1857 wb-1-230 (Hw)
Gillespey, James 1859 rb-20-146 (Ru)
Gillespie, Allen 1842 wb-2-58# (Ge)
Gillespie, Ann 1830 wb-1-51 (Bo)
Gillespie, Ann 1858 149-1-136 (Ge)
Gillespie, David 1861 wb-13-438 (Wi)
Gillespie, Elizabeth 1854 wb-e-232 (G)
Gillespie, George 1794 wb-#5 (Wa)
Gillespie, George 1818 lr (Sn)
Gillespie, George 1834 wb-5-448 (Wi)
Gillespie, George 1840 wb-a-446 (R)
Gillespie, George 1847 as-a-137 (Ms)
Gillespie, George H. 1846 wb-2-65# (Ge)
Gillespie, George H. 1858 149-1-135 (Ge)
Gillespie, Isaac 1828 wb-4-310 (Wi)
Gillespie, James 1817 rb-b-458 (Mt)
Gillespie, James 1857 rb-18-499 (Ru)
Gillespie, John 1812 wb-2-34# (Ge)
Gillespie, John 1839 wb-1-47 (Bo)
Gillespie, John 1841 wb-z-243 (Mu)
Gillespie, John 1857 lr (Sn)
Gillespie, Jonathan 1832 wb-#236 (Mu)

Gillespie, Julia 1858 wb-2-254 (Li)
Gillespie, Martha (Marthew) 1811 wb-2-33# (Ge)
Gillespie, Mary 1831 rb-8-402 (Ru)
Gillespie, Mary 1846 wb-8-397 (Wi)
Gillespie, Mary 1851 wb-2-72# (Ge)
Gillespie, R. M. 1851 rb-4-205 (Mu)
Gillespie, Reubin 1801 wb-1-82 (K)
Gillespie, Robert 1851 wb-10-94 (Wi)
Gillespie, Sarah 1846 wb-2-64# (Ge)
Gillespie, Sophia 1830 lr (Sn)
Gillespie, Thomas 1824 wb-3-448 (K)
Gillespie, Thomas 1830 wb-4-533 (Wi)
Gillespie, Thomas J. 1857 wb-1-129 (R)
Gillespie, William 1817 wb-1-252 (Sn)
Gillespie, William 1825 wb-1-250 (Bo)
Gillespie, Wm. 1833 wb-1-52 (Bo)
Gillespy, John 1796 wb-1-239 (Bo)
Gilley, Edward 1844 wb-A-35 (Ca)
Gilley, Gideon 1859 wb#6 (Gu)
Gilley, James 1831 wb-#224 (Mu)
Gilley, James M. 1832 wb-#236 (Mu)
Gilley, Jesse 1856 wb-A-113 (Ca)
Gilley, Simeon 1852 wb-0-106 (Cf)
Gillham, Jacob 1840 wb-z-23 (Mu)
Gilliam, Anthony 1851 wb-10-119 (Wi)
Gilliam, Charles 1803 wb-2-303 (D)
Gilliam, Devereaux 1809 wb-1-305 (K)
Gilliam, Harrison 1808 rb-2-60 (Ru)
Gilliam, Isham 1848 rb-14-251 (Ru)
Gilliam, James 1821 lr (Sn)
Gilliam, John 1802 wb-2-230 (D)
Gilliam, John 1825 wb-1-58 (Fr)
Gilliam, Nathaniel 1838 wb-11-287 (D)
Gilliam, Richard 1842 rb-12-195 (Ru)
Gilliam, Spencer 1810 wb-1-324 (K)
Gilliam, Stephen R. 1857 lr (Sn)
Gilliam, Susan 1828 wb-9-218 (D)
Gilliam, Thomas 1793 wb-1-11 (K)
Gilliam, Thomas 1822 wb-1-48 (Fr)
Gilliam, Thomas 1853 wb-15-509 (D)
Gilliam, William 1835 wb-x-301* (Mu)
Gilliam, William 1842 rb-12-107 (Ru)
Gilliam, William 1852 wb-15-387 (D)
Gilliam, William 1859 wb-00-3 (Cf)
Gilliam, William 1860 rb-20-686 (Ru)
Gilliam, Wm. 1804 wb-2-343 (D)
Gilliland, Joel 1847 wb-d-60 (G)
Gilliland, John 1795 wb-1-1 (Je)
Gilliland, Robert 1796 wb-1-50 (K)
Gilliland, Samuel 1857 wb-3e-38 (Sh)

Gilliland, Wm. 1800 wb-2-188 (D)
Gillis, Alexander 1834 wb-1-85 (W)
Gillis, John 1845 wb-e-139 (O)
Gillispie, David 1835 wb-6-67 (Wi)
Gillispie, George 1834 wb-6-17 (Wi)
Gillispie, George A. 1836 wb-6-44 (Wi)
Gillispie, Thomas R. 1847 lr (Gi)
Gillmore, James 1857 wb-3-353 (Gr)
Gillum, Charles 1827 wb-#81 (Wl)
Gillum, John 1844 wb-f-155 (St)
Gillum, John A. 1844 wb-f-169 (St)
Gilly, Samuel 1855 wb-#63 (Mc)
Gilman, Timothy W. 1850 wb-14-480 (D)
Gilmer, Nathaniel 1803 wb-1-75 (Sn)
Gilmore, Josephue 1842 wb-e-519 (Hu)
Gilmore, Peter 1858 rb-19-293 (Ru)
Gilmore, Thomas 1850 lr (Sn)
Gilmore, William 1837 rb-10-2 (Ru)
Gilmore, William A. M. 1851 wb-a-154 (T)
Gilreath, John 1856 wb-1C-469 (A)
Ginnan, Benjamin 1837 wb-3-489 (Je)
Ginnings, James A. 1841 as-a-43 (Ms)
Ginnings, William 1851 wb-14-418 (Rb)
Gipson, George 1837 wb-a-244 (O)
Gipson, George W. 1837 wb-a-263 (O)
Gipson, John 1855 wb-d-220 (Wh)
Gipson, John 1855 wb-d-227 (Wh)
Gipson, William 1816 wb-#21 (Mu)
Girdner, David 1809 wb-1-11# (Ge)
Girdner, Michael 1815 wb-2-36# (Ge)
Gist, John 1853 wb-d-156 (Wh)
Gist, Joseph 1861 wb-e-438 (Wh)
Gist, Thomas 1850 ib-1-58 (Wy)
Givan, George 1814 wb-1-0 (Sm)
Givan, Robert J. 1852 wb-a-232 (Dk)
Givan, William J. 1848 wb-a-78 (Dk)
Given, Sophia E. 1860 wb-b-52 (Dk)
Given, William 1861 39-2-401 (Dk)
Givens, Berryman 1856 wb-h-489 (Hu)
Givens, Hannah 1853 wb-n-163 (Mt)
Givens, Henry R. 1854 wb-11-313 (Wi)
Givens, James 1845 wb-c-268 (G)
Givens, Margaret 1826 wb-1-94 (Ma)
Givens, Margaret 1861 wb-2-347 (Li)
Givens, Samuel 1814 wb-2-92 (K)
Givens, Samuel A. 1856 wb-c-62 (L)
Givens, William 1823 wb-1-0 (Sm)
Givens, William 1850 rb-4-57 (Mu)
Givens, William 1857 wb-2-205 (Li)
Givins, Hannah 1853 wb-n-161 (Mt)
Givins, James 1846 wb-d-26 (G)

Givins, John W. 1856 wb-#63 (Mc)
Givins, Joseph 1849 wb-2-359 (W)
Gladson, Levin 1858 wb-1-234 (Hw)
Glasgow, Elias H. 1847 wb-b-243 (We)
Glasgow, Isaac 1848 wb-b-275 (We)
Glasgow, Isaac 1861 wb-18-470 (D)
Glasgow, Jesse 1838 wb-11-399 (D)
Glasgow, John (Capt.) 1840 wb-2-173 (Hr)
Glasgow, John 1835 wb-c-453 (St)
Glasgow, John C. 1843 wb-12-423* (D)
Glasgow, Robert 1854 ib-H-145 (F)
Glass, Hiram 1852? wb-#54 (Wa)
Glass, James S. 1856 wb-5-63 (Hr)
Glass, John 1848 wb-4-289 (Hr)
Glass, John Sr. 1847 wb-4-221 (Hr)
Glass, Nancy 1860 wb-b-454 (We)
Glass, Robert 1838 abl-1-85 (T)
Glass, Robert 1850 wb-9-451 (Wi)
Glass, Samuel 1808 wb-1-46 (Bo)
Glass, Samuel F. 1860 wb-18-212 (D)
Glass, William 1854 wb-#25 (Mo)
Glasscock, John 1843 wb-2-60# (Ge)
Glasscock, Nancy 1854 wb-e-134 (G)
Glasscock, Peter 1823 wb-#58 (Mu)
Glasscock, Sarah 1840 wb-#36 (Wa)
Glaster, Mary H. 1854 wb-a-467 (F)
Glaves, Michael 1811 wb-4-155 (D)
Glaze, Henry 1837 wb-#63 (Mc)
Gleason, Edward 1824 wb-a-193 (Wh)
Gleaves, Absalom 1834 wb-10-394 (D)
Gleaves, Elizabeth 1850 wb-a-224 (Di)
Gleaves, James 1841 wb-12-250* (D)
Gleaves, James M. 1844 wb-13-65 (D)
Gleaves, John 1822 wb-#45 (Wl)
Gleaves, John G. 1855 wb-16-483 (D)
Gleaves, Mathew 1805 wb-3-4 (D)
Gleaves, Mathew 1835 as-a-286 (Di)
Gleaves, Mathew 1842 wb-12-345* (D)
Gleaves, Michael 1811 rb-a-514 (Mt)
Gleaves, Michael 1814 wb-4-315 (D)
Gleaves, Michael 1834 wb-10-313 (D)
Gleaves, Michael H. 1854 wb-16-432 (D)
Gleaves, Rachel 1836 wb-10-607 (D)
Gleaves, Robert H. 1853 wb-16-116 (D)
Gleaves, Thomas 1831 wb-9-519 (D)
Gleaves, Thomas 1841 rb-12-4 (Ru)
Gleaves, Thomas 1850 wb-14-490 (D)
Gleaves, William 1840 wb-12-15 (D)
Gleaves, William B. 1857 wb-1-80 (Dy)
Gleaves, William D. 1841 wb-12-124* (D)
Gleaves, William P. 1841 wb-#134 (Wl)

Gleen, James 1837 wb-1-279 (Hy)
Gleeson, Edward 1835 wb-b-161 (Wh)
Gleeson, John W. 1831 wb-b-109 (Wh)
Gleghorn, Andrew 1850 wb-1-391 (Li)
Glen, Thomas (Jr.) 1838 wb-#4 (Mo)
Glenn, Abram 1851 wb-10-30 (Wi)
Glenn, Alexander 1818 wb-a-100 (Wh)
Glenn, Alexander 1828 wb-a-302 (Wh)
Glenn, Benjamin H. 1853 lr (Sn)
Glenn, David 1844 wb-a-85 (Ms)
Glenn, E. S. U. 1834 wb-x-181 (Mu)
Glenn, Giles H. 1831 wb-#92 (Wl)
Glenn, Hugh H. 1860 as-c-221 (Ms)
Glenn, James 1842 wb-2-313 (Hr)
Glenn, Jesse 1822 wb-a-166 (Wh)
Glenn, Jesse 1823 wb-a-183 (Wh)
Glenn, John 1829 wb-9-349 (D)
Glenn, John F. 1855 wb-a-360 (Ms)
Glenn, John R. 1840 wb-b-386 (Wh)
Glenn, Joseph 1845 wb-c-185 (Wh)
Glenn, N. A. 1861 as-c-260 (Ms)
Glenn, Nancy 1856 wb-e-81 (Wh)
Glenn, Nathan 1839 rb-h-323 (Mt)
Glenn, Nathan 1858 wb-#128 (Wl)
Glenn, Robert 1839 wb-b-337 (Wh)
Glenn, Robert 1840 eb-1-432 (C)
Glenn, Robert sr. 1820 wb-a-140 (Wh)
Glenn, Samuel 1858 wb-b-68 (Ms)
Glenn, Samuel 1861 as-c-244 (Ms)
Glenn, Thompson 1822 wb-#44 (Wl)
Glenn, William 1836 wb-6-184 (Wi)
Glenn, William 1836 wb-b-246 (Wh)
Glenn, William 1841 rb-i-154 (Mt)
Glenn, William 1857 wb-e-129 (Wh)
Glenn, William J. 1861 wb-e-442 (Wh)
Glenn, William sr 1856 wb-e-103 (Wh)
Glenn, William sr. 1856 wb-e-48 (Wh)
Glesson, James 1848 wb-g-235 (Hn)
Glidewell, Arthur 1815 wb-2-182 (K)
Glidewell, Mark 1839 wb-a-45 (L)
Glimph, George 1829 wb-4-433 (Wi)
Glisson, George R. 1852 wb-h-Oct (O)
Glisson, George Rufus 1852 wb-h-Dec (O)
Glisson, Henry 1819 wb-3-11 (Rb)
Glisson, Henry 1820 wb-3-121 (Rb)
Glisson, Nancy 1852 wb-h-Sep (O)
Glisson, Sarah 1847 wb-#154 (Wl)
Glisson, Stephen H. 1852 wb-h-Sep (O)
Glover, Banister 1837 wb-3-0 (Sm)
Glover, Eleanor C. 1821 wb-#60 (Mu)
Glover, Francis (Mrs.) 1859 wb-h-309 (Hn)

Glover, Jesse 1861 wb-k-504 (O)
Glover, John 1818 wb-1-0 (Sm)
Glover, John 1843 wb-11-391 (Rb)
Glover, Jones 1803 Wb-1-105 (Wi)
Glover, Jones 1806 wb-3-78 (Wi)
Glover, Joshua 1821? wb-#118 (Mu)
Glover, Joshua 1843 wb-f-178* (Hn)
Glover, Phineas T. 1858 wb-j-371 (O)
Glover, Spicy 1831 wb-#225 (Mu)
Glover, W. B. 1852 wb-3-47 (La)
Glover, William 1830 lr (Sn)
Glover, Wm. B. 1855 wb-5-36 (La)
Glover, Wm. B.. 1839 wb-1A-314 (A)
Glymph, James B. 1856 rb-17-614 (Ru)
Glympth, James 1856 rb-18-106 (Ru)
Goad, Edward 1829 wb-a-65 (R)
Goad, Isham 1815 wb-a-36 (Wh)
Goad, Joshua 1855 wb-7-0 (Sm)
Goad, William 1830 wb-a-70 (R)
Goan, Andrew 1816 wb-#14 (Mu)
Goan, Daniel H. 1852 wb-5-160 (Je)
Goard, Robert 1835 wb-b-195 (Wh)
Gocey, James 1854 wb-11-365 (Wi)
Gocey, Lew? R. 1847 wb-8-559 (Wi)
Godard, Moses 1836 wb-b-218 (Wh)
Godbehere, Sibbella 1860 wb-1-166 (R)
Goddard, Ann 1857 wb-12-334 (K)
Goddard, Francis 1828 wb-1-218 (Hw)
Goddard, James 1838 wb-b-296 (Wh)
Goddard, John 1826 wb-4-176 (K)
Goddard, John 1843 wb-8-38 (K)
Goddard, Sampson 1837 wb-b-269 (Wh)
Goddard, Thomas G. 1854 wb-e-486 (Ro)
Goddard, William 1836 wb-6-1 (K)
Godfrey, James 1844 wb-#146 (Wl)
Godsay, Lacy 1858 wb-j-337 (O)
Godsey, Bartlet B. 1834 wb-1-23 (Gr)
Godsey, Burley 1826 wb-a-13 (R)
Godsey, S. P. 1857 wb-2-364 (Me)
Godsey, Stephen J. 1857 wb-2-369 (Me)
Godwin, Caroline 1856 wb-3-327 (Gr)
Godwin, Jacob 1852 wb-3-39 (Gr)
Godwin, Mariah S. 1845 wb-5-389 (Gr)
Godwin, Mary M. B. 1859 wb-7-38 (Ma)
Godwin, Theophilus 1848 33-3-59 (Gr)
Godwin, William P. 1848 wb-5-56 (Ma)
Goff, Andrew 1827 wb-4-260 (Wi)
Goff, Andrew 1831 wb-5-74 (Wi)
Goff, Andrew 1849 wb-9-228 (Wi)
Goff, Felix 1843 wb-1-303 (La)
Goff, James 1850 wb-9-355 (Wi)

Goff, Thomas 1817 wb-2-345 (Wi)
Goff, Thomas 1851 wb-2-205 (La)
Goff, William 1849 wb-9-308 (Wi)
Goforth, Andrew 1810 wb-#3 (Mu)
Goforth, Andrew H. 1821 wb-#118 (Mu)
Goforth, Della 1851 ib-1-136 (Wy)
Goforth, Hiram 1823 wb-#49 (Mu)
Goforth, Zacariah 1858 ib-2-63 (Wy)
Goin, Susannah 1816 wb-2-155 (Je)
Goin, Thomas 1858 wb-3-419 (Gr)
Goin, Thomas S. 1854 wb-3-193 (Gr)
Going, William 1827 wb-1-216 (Hw)
Goins, Andrew 1827 wb-#153 (Mu)
Goins, Pleasant 1853 ib-2-507 (Cl)
Goins, Robert 1839 wb-5-5 (Gr)
Gold, William 1850 wb-g-217 (St)
Golding, Thomas 1853 wb-b-224 (L)
Goldman, John 1836 wb-x-422 (Mu)
Goldsberry, Sarah 1858 lr (Gi)
Goldsby, Edward 1843 wb-f-115* (Hn)
Goldsby, Edward T. 1840 wb-e-163 (Hn)
Goldsby, Richard 1840 wb-1-59 (Sh)
Goldsmith, William 1839 wb-b-137 (Hd)
Goldston, Charles M. 1849 wb-#163 (Wl)
Golladay, Isaac 1846 wb-#166 (Wl)
Gollahorn, Asa 1819 wb-3-105 (K)
Golliday, Gorge 1817 rb-b-460 (Mt)
Golsten, Lewis 1858 wb-17-459 (D)
Gonsalus, Daniel 1804 rb-a-231 (Mt)
Gonzer?, Daniel 1853 wb-e-102 (G)
Gooch, David 1831 wb-5-70 (Wi)
Gooch, David 1844 wb-8-144 (Wi)
Gooch, David R. 1854 wb-16-338 (D)
Gooch, Dick 1854 wb-d-158 (Wh)
Gooch, Edward J. 1851 wb-10-137 (Wi)
Gooch, F. R. 1861 wb-17-268 (Rb)
Gooch, Franklin R. 1861 wb-17-281 (Rb)
Gooch, Gideon 1829 wb-7-230 (Rb)
Gooch, James 1853 wb-15-362 (Rb)
Gooch, James A. 1861 wb-a-393 (Cr)
Gooch, Jane 1841 wb-12-249* (D)
Gooch, John 1857 rb-18-359 (Ru)
Gooch, John C. 1854 rb-16-713 (Ru)
Gooch, Joseph 1847 wb-c-263 (Wh)
Gooch, Nathaniel 1841 rb-12-53 (Ru)
Gooch, Nathaniel 1841 rb-12-55 (Ru)
Gooch, Samuel 1857 rb-18-351 (Ru)
Gooch, Thomas 1817 wb-2-342 (Wi)
Gooch, William 1833 wb-x-36 (Mu)
Gooch, William 1834 wb-1-506 (Ma)
Gooch, William 1852 wb-10-210 (Wi)

Goocher, Henry 1843 wb-0-35 (Cf)
Good, David 1856 149-1-33 (Ge)
Good, Elizabeth 1834 rb-9-145 (Ru)
Good, Elizabeth 1836 rb-9-115 (Ru)
Good, Henry 1840 rb-10-508 (Ru)
Good, Henry 1855 rb-17-358 (Ru)
Good, Hugh 1845 rb-13-364 (Ru)
Good, James O. 1854 rb-17-273 (Ru)
Good, John 1834 rb-9-169 (Ru)
Good, John 1855 wb-j-55 (O)
Good, John F. 1833 rb-9-46 (Ru)
Good, John T. 1833 rb-9-15 (Ru)
Good, Mary 1834 rb-9-167 (Ru)
Good, Sarah 1845 rb-13-163 (Ru)
Good, Thomas 1847 wb-a-120 (T)
Good, William 1848 wb-c-286 (Wh)
Goodall, Charles 1853 lr (Sn)
Goodall, Frances M. 1851 wb-#177 (Wl)
Goodall, Hardin 1837 wb-#118 (Wl)
Goodall, James T. 1848 wb-#162 (Wl)
Goodall, John L. 1858 wb-7-0 (Sm)
Goodall, Park 1826 wb-#64 (Wl)
Goodall, Parks 1826 wb-#70 (Wl)
Goodall, Patsy 1858 lr (Sn)
Goodall, William 1812 wb-1-0 (Sm)
Goodall, William 1827 wb-2-0 (Sm)
Goodall, Zachariah G. 1844 lr (Sn)
Goode, John 1823 wb-a-27 (Hn)
Goode, John W. 1851 wb-2-108 (Sh)
Goode, William 1828 wb-9-219 (D)
Gooden, Delila 1839 wb-c-23 (Ro)
Gooden, James 1846 148-1-159 (Ge)
Gooden, John 1839 wb-c-23 (Ro)
Goodgen, William 1839 wb-y-473 (Mu)
Goodin, J. F. 1851 wb-b-141 (L)
Goodin, Samuel B. 1846 wb-b-135 (We)
Goodlett, A. G. 1850 rb-15-377 (Ru)
Goodlett, Adam G. 1850 rb-15-412 (Ru)
Goodlett, Robert 1858 wb-17-489 (D)
Goodlink, Michel 1840 wb-1-167 (Bo)
Goodlink, Samuel 1855 wb-1-53 (Bo)
Goodloe, Henry 1846 rb-13-646 (Ru)
Goodloe, John 1830 rb-8-58 (Ru)
Goodloe, Mary 1861 wb-b-112 (F)
Goodloe, Rebecca 1852 rb-16-350 (Ru)
Goodloe, T. W. 1847 rb-14-173 (Ru)
Goodloe, Thompson 1847 rb-14-173 (Ru)
Goodloe, Thompson W. 1849 rb-15-231 (Ru)
Goodloe, William H. 1834 wb-x-270 (Mu)
Goodlow, Hannah 1857 rb-19-120 (Ru)
Goodlow, John M. 1816 wb-#25 (Mu)

Goodman, Albert G. 1854 rb-17-159 (Ru)
Goodman, Alferd 1854 rb-17-328 (Ru)
Goodman, Alfred 1854 wb-c-28 (Hy)
Goodman, Ansel 1841 wb-#135 (Wl)
Goodman, Asy 1834 wb-1-57 (Hy)
Goodman, Benijah 1820 wb-3-179 (Wi)
Goodman, Boswell 1838 wb-2-49 (Hr)
Goodman, Claiborne 1848 wb-#174 (Wl)
Goodman, Daniel W. 1838 wb-#120 (Wl)
Goodman, Edmond 1840 wb-#130 (Wl)
Goodman, Edmond H. 1839 wb-#127 (Wl)
Goodman, Edmund 1845 rb-13-216 (Ru)
Goodman, George 1815 rb-3-34 (Ru)
Goodman, George 1833 rb-9-26 (Ru)
Goodman, Henry 1835 wb-1A-128 (A)
Goodman, J. C. 1859 wb-#130 (Wl)
Goodman, James M. 1858 wb-3-532 (Gr)
Goodman, James W. 1858 wb-3-469 (Gr)
Goodman, John 1821 wb-1-42 (Fr)
Goodman, John 1845 A-468-42 (Le)
Goodman, Lucinda 1837 wb-e-62 (Hu)
Goodman, Robert 1859 wb-#127 (Wl)
Goodman, Robert D. 1845 wb-#147 (Wl)
Goodman, Solomon K. 1827 wb-1-65 (Fr)
Goodman, Stephen 1855 wb-#123 (Wl)
Goodman, William 1850 rb-15-502 (Ru)
Goodman, William 1858 wb-f-221 (G)
Goodman, William sr. 1850 rb-15-438 (Ru)
Goodner, Cyrus 1857 39-2-217 (Dk)
Goodrich, Dorothy 1838 wb-d-215 (St)
Goodrich, Ed 1857 wb-17-418 (D)
Goodrich, George J. 1832 as-a-218 (Di)
Goodrich, J. C. 1844 wb-4-273 (Ma)
Goodrich, James 1848 as-b-457 (Di)
Goodrich, Jane 1843 wb-a-160 (Di)
Goodrich, Jane M. 1859 wb-7-55 (Ma)
Goodrich, John 1817 wb-7-214 (D)
Goodrich, John 1837 wb-11-32 (D)
Goodrich, John 1840 wb-3-162 (Ma)
Goodrich, Martha 1849 wb-#165 (Wl)
Goodrich, R. 1838 wb-11-456 (D)
Goodrich, William 1847 wb-14-151 (D)
Goodrich, William 1859 wb-7-42 (Ma)
Goodrum, Allen 1822 wb-3-293 (Wi)
Goodrum, Jane 1825 wb-4-17 (Wi)
Goodrum, Thomas 1825 wb-4-13 (Wi)
Goodrum, Thomas 1836 wb-x-349 (Mu)
Goodson, Andrew 1854 wb-d-238 (Wh)
Goodson, Joseph W. 1849 wb-2-66 (La)
Goodwin, Ann 1835 wb-10-465 (D)
Goodwin, Ann 1835 wb-10-501 (D)

Goodwin, Beal 1828 as-a-172 (Di)
Goodwin, Beal 1834 as-a-242 (Di)
Goodwin, Britain 1811 wb-a-46 (Ro)
Goodwin, George 1808 wb-4-9 (D)
Goodwin, George 1838 wb-11-121 (D)
Goodwin, J. U. J. 1847 wb-14-91 (D)
Goodwin, James 1835 wb-10-424 (D)
Goodwin, Jane T. 1838 wb-11-280 (D)
Goodwin, Jesse 1810 wb-4-119 (D)
Goodwin, Jesse 1848 wb-b-273 (We)
Goodwin, Jessee 1825 wb-1-60 (Fr)
Goodwin, John L. 1825 wb-8-408 (D)
Goodwin, John W. 1835 wb-1-384 (Hr)
Goodwin, Michael 1849 A-468-132 (Le)
Goodwin, Peter 1836 wb-a-118 (Di)
Goodwin, Samuel 1823 wb-1-23 (Ma)
Goodwin, Thomas E. 1847 wb-14-13 (D)
Goodwin, Thomas F. 1854 wb-d-218 (Wh)
Goodwin, William 1832 wb-9-604 (D)
Goodwin, William 1853 wb-5-122 (Ma)
Goodwin, William 1863 wb-#63 (Mc)
Goodwin, William C. 1846 A-468-59 (Le)
Goodwin, William W. 1851 wb-15-138 (D)
Gooldsby, Nancy 1845 wb-b-117 (We)
Goolsby, John K. 1816 wb-a-62 (Wh)
Gord?, John 1852 wb-h-Mar (O)
Gordan, David 1836 wb-b-126 (G)
Gordan, Robert B. 1854 wb-n-434 (Mt)
Gorden, Charles H. 1846 rb-k-216 (Mt)
Gorden, George H. 1852 ib-1-241 (Ca)
Gorden, John 1851 wb-d-292 (G)
Gorden, Robert 1854 wb-3-232 (W)
Gordian, Sarah 1839 wb-b-289 (G)
Gordon, Alexander 1831 wb-7-480 (Rb)
Gordon, Elizabeth 1852 6-2-97 (Le)
Gordon, Elizabeth 1857 wb-7-0 (Sm)
Gordon, George 1851 wb-e-357 (Ro)
Gordon, James 1859 wb-18-104 (D)
Gordon, Jesse M. 1824 wb-#88 (Mu)
Gordon, John 1834 lr (Gi)
Gordon, John 1841 wb-z-174 (Mu)
Gordon, John 1850 A-468-146 (Le)
Gordon, John 1860 wb-8-44 (Sm)
Gordon, John sr. 1838 wb-y-183* (Mu)
Gordon, Louisa 1853 wb-e-40 (G)
Gordon, Margaret T. 1834 wb-10-380 (D)
Gordon, Moses 1849 A-468-88 (Le)
Gordon, O. 1840 wb-#131 (Wl)
Gordon, Patrick 1853 wb-e-124 (G)
Gordon, Robert 1855 lr (Gi)
Gordon, Robert C. 1845 148-1-125 (Ge)

Gordon, Thomas 1821 Wb-3-271 (Wi)
Gordon, William 1814 rb-b-206 (Mt)
Gore, Adaline 1861 wb-k-505 (O)
Gorham, William B. 1851 wb-15-30 (Rb)
Gorin, Gladen 1832 wb-c-156 (St)
Gorin, Nancy 1832 wb-c-231 (St)
Gorman, Ann B. (Mrs.) 1860 gs-1-608 (F)
Gorman, Paris A. 1857 wb-b-42 (F)
Gose, Cristopher 1854 ib-2-86 (Cl)
Gosey, Rebecca 1860 wb-13-290 (Wi)
Goslen, Elihew 1842 wb-#136 (Wl)
Goss, Charles B. 1856 wb-j-112 (O)
Goss, Elijah 1846 rb-13-714 (Ru)
Goss, Elijah 1853 wb-i-52 (O)
Goss, Elijah jr. 1850 wb-g-324 (O)
Goss, Elijah sr. 1852 wb-h-Nov (O)
Goss, Frederick 1822 rb-d-65 (Mt)
Goss, Fredrick 1811 rb-b-4 (Mt)
Gosset, Jacob 1853 wb-xx-291 (St)
Gosset, John 1822 wb-#118 (Mu)
Gosset, John 1823 wb-#49 (Wl)
Gossett, Elijah 1821 wb-3-381 (Rb)
Gossett, Elizabeth 1815 wb-3-98 (St)
Gossett, Henry 1853 wb-16-202 (D)
Gossett, Joel 1858 wb-13-57 (K)
Gossett, John W. 1840 wb-10-514 (Rb)
Gossett, John W. 1840 wb-11-18 (Rb)
Gossett, Louisa C. 1843 wb-11-496 (Rb)
Goswick, George 1848 wb-g-70 (Hu)
Gott, Anthony 1812 wb-#12 (Wa)
Gott, John 1843 wb-#41 (Wa)
Gounds, William 1858 wb-12-493 (K)
Gourley, Elizabeth 1849 lr (Sn)
Gourley, James 1848 lw (Ct)
Gourley, Margaret 1855 wb-7-0 (Sm)
Gowan, Alford P. 1857 rb-18-437 (Ru)
Gowan, William 1790 wb-1-168 (D)
Gowans, John 1830 rb-f-93 (Mt)
Gowen, Allen 1800 wb-2-166 (D)
Gowen, Allen 1800 wb-2-171 (D)
Gowen, Harriet 1839 rb-10-432 (Ru)
Gowen, James F. 1836 rb-9-336 (Ru)
Gowen, John 1835 wb-10-503 (D)
Gowen, Obediah 1858 wb-f-198 (Ro)
Gowen, Pleasant 1838 5-2-33 (Cl)
Gowen, Reuben 1849 wb-14-118 (Rb)
Gowen, William 1816 wb-2-192 (Wi)
Gowen, William 1852 wb-A-77 (Ca)
Gowen, William D. 1852 ib-1-207 (Ca)
Gower, Abel B. 1847 wb-14-88 (D)
Gower, Alexander K. 1815 wb-4-394 (D)

Gower, Charlotte 1860 wb-18-349 (D)
Gower, Edith 1822 wb-8-73 (D)
Gower, Elijah 1795 wb-2-34 (D)
Gower, Elijah 1807 wb-3-161 (D)
Gower, Elisha 1853 wb-16-132 (D)
Gower, L. F. 1854 wb-16-225 (D)
Gower, Manoah 1847 wb-14-24 (D)
Gower, Matthew 1848 wb-2-24 (La)
Gower, Noah 1847 wb-14-36 (D)
Gower, Rebecca 1851 wb-2-230 (La)
Gower, Thomas 1815 wb-2-143 (K)
Gower, William 1852 wb-15-349 (D)
Gower, William E. 1815 wb-4-354 (D)
Gower, William E. 1831 wb-9-556 (D)
Gower, William L. 1830 wb-9-426 (D)
Gowin, Pleasant 1838 5-2-45 (Cl)
Gowine, David 1784 wb-1-7 (D)
Gowins, Daniell 1810 wb-1-341 (Je)
Goyne, James 1838 rb-h-93 (Mt)
Grace, Betsy 1817 wb-2-192 (Je)
Grace, James 1819 wb-a-127 (Wh)
Grace, Richard 1816 wb-2-148 (Je)
Grace, Richard 1827 wb-2-576 (Je)
Grace, Soloman sr. 1829 rb-e-403 (Mt)
Gracey, Hugh 1854 wb-d-165 (Wh)
Gracy, John 1838 lr (Gi)
Gracy, William 1828 wb-a-297 (Wh)
Gracy, William N. R. 1854 lr (Gi)
Grady, Ann (Warfield) 1840 rb-h-472 (Mt)
Grady, Dawson 1848 wb-d-116 (G)
Grady, Dennis 1851 wb-2-99 (Sh)
Grady, Kinney 1834 wb-1-31 (Gr)
Graff, Samuel 1840 wb-a-18 (Dk)
Grafton, R. L. 1861 rb-p-560 (Mt)
Gragg, John 1842 wb-1-211 (Li)
Gragg, Robert 1793 wb-1-9# (Ge)
Graham, Alexander 1857 lr (Sn)
Graham, Andrew 1822 wb-8-150 (D)
Graham, Anson B. 1859 wb-#63 (Mc)
Graham, Daniel 1858 wb-1-209 (Be)
Graham, David 1857 wb-1-159 (Be)
Graham, Francis 1831 wb-5-62 (Wi)
Graham, Francis 1845 A-468-34 (Le)
Graham, George 1833 wb-3-214 (Je)
Graham, George 1834 wb-3-291 (Je)
Graham, George 1844 wd-13-13 (D)
Graham, George 1844 wd-13-47 (D)
Graham, George 1853 wb-15-484 (D)
Graham, George jr. 1834 wb-3-406 (Je)
Graham, George sr. 1838 wb-3-482 (Je)
Graham, J. B. 1842 mr-2-9 (Be)

Graham, James 1813 wb-2-35# (Ge)
Graham, Jane 1858 wb-12-496 (K)
Graham, Jane 1858 wb-13-4 (K)
Graham, John 1836 wb-6-118 (Wi)
Graham, John 1842 wb-#63 (Mc)
Graham, John B. 1842 mr-2-25 (Be)
Graham, John H. 1848 wb-9-118 (Wi)
Graham, Margaret 1829 wb-#178 (Mu)
Graham, Margaret 1847 5-3-266 (Cl)
Graham, Margaret C. 1855 wb-12-121 (K)
Graham, Nancy 1813 lr (Sn)
Graham, Nathaniel 1822 wb-3-331 (K)
Graham, Patrick 1853 wb-1-27 (R)
Graham, Richard 1833 wb-5-279 (Wi)
Graham, Robert 1825 wb-1-48 (Ma)
Graham, Robert 1829 wb-4-468 (Wi)
Graham, Susanna F. 1838 wb-11-494 (D)
Graham, Susanna F. 1838 wb-2-393 (Ma)
Graham, Thomas 1815 wb-1-0 (Sm)
Graham, Thomas 1821 wb-3-232 (K)
Graham, William 1839 wb-10-313 (Rb)
Graham, William 1841 5-2-208 (Cl)
Graham, William 1848 ib-1-64 (Cl)
Graham, William 1858 wb-5-523 (Je)
Graham, William P. 1861 wb-18-450 (D)
Grainger, J. L. 1860 wb-17-21 (Rb)
Grainger, James L. 1860 wb-17-93 (Rb)
Grainger, John 1853 wb-g-540 (Hn)
Grainger, William 1860 lr (Sn)
Grammar, Joseph 1853 wb-e-425 (Ro)
Grammer, John 1859 wb-2-277 (Li)
Granade, John A. 1808 wb-#5 (Wl)
Granade, John A. 1818 wb-#28 (Wl)
Granade, William 1818 wb-1-0 (Sm)
Grandstaff, David 1852 wb-#178 (Wl)
Grange, Nancy 1859 wb-h-313 (Hn)
Granger, Benjamin 1859 wb-h-386 (Hn)
Granger, Lucilla 1838 wb-2-245 (Sn)
Grant, Alexander 1789 wb-1-204 (Hw)
Grant, Burrel 1824 rb-d-399 (Mt)
Grant, Catharine 1857 wb-f-24 (G)
Grant, Charles 1824 rb-d-298 (Mt)
Grant, Charles 1824 rb-d-300 (Mt)
Grant, Charles 1852 wb-m-500 (Mt)
Grant, David 1832 lw (Ct)
Grant, James 1814 wb-A-58 (Li)
Grant, James 1841 wb-1-179 (Li)
Grant, James 1859 rb-p-123 (Mt)
Grant, James 1859 rb-p-130 (Mt)
Grant, John 1842 wb-1-52 (Bo)
Grant, Joshua 1849 rb-l-511 (Mt)

Grant, Joshua D. 1850 wb-m-126 (Mt)
Grant, Jubal 1848 wb-#165 (Wl)
Grant, Mary M. 1853 wb-n-168 (Mt)
Grant, Mary R. 1860 rb-p-329 (Mt)
Grant, Thomas 1841 as-a-51 (Ms)
Grant, Thomas 1849 wb-1-360 (Li)
Grantham, Richard 1846 wb-5-451 (Gr)
Grantham, Richard 1857 wb-3-401 (Gr)
Grasty, William 1850 wb-c-416 (Wh)
Grates, David 1822 wb-#19 (Wa)
Graves, A. B. 1855 wb-a-228 (T)
Graves, Alvina 1854 wb-d-206 (Wh)
Graves, Azariah 1836 wb-d-216 (Hn)
Graves, Bacholer? 1827 wb-#66 (Wl)
Graves, Balias 1817 wb-#32 (Mu)
Graves, Benjamin 1851 wb-#176 (Wl)
Graves, Benjamin 1858 wb-#124 (Wl)
Graves, Boston 1845 5-3-77 (Cl)
Graves, Christopher 1839 wb-#64 (Mc)
Graves, Daniel 1838 wb-6-359 (K)
Graves, Francis 1798 wb-2-102 (D)
Graves, Francis M. 1861 wb-#133 (Wl)
Graves, George 1861 wb-13-433 (K)
Graves, George C. 1838 wb-6-291 (K)
Graves, Henry 1826 wb-9-38 (D)
Graves, Henry 1848 wb-c-312 (Wh)
Graves, Henry M. 1851 wb-#64 (Mc)
Graves, J. G. B. 1854 wb-#115 (Wl)
Graves, John 1825 wb-8-443 (D)
Graves, John 1838 wb-11-467 (D)
Graves, John 1844 5-3-1 (Cl)
Graves, John B. 1837 wb-#116 (Wl)
Graves, John B. 1847 wb-#115 (Wl)
Graves, John P. 1839 wb-11-570 (D)
Graves, John P. 1858 wb-e-173 (Wh)
Graves, John P. 1858 wb-e-204 (Wh)
Graves, John R. 1859 wb-7-48 (Ma)
Graves, Joseph Lafayette 1854 wb-d-206 (Wh)
Graves, Lewis 1837 wb-d-111* (Hn)
Graves, Lewis 1837 wb-d-299 (Hn)
Graves, Lorenzo 1835 wb-#105 (Wl)
Graves, Nathaniel 1824 wb-#128 (Mu)
Graves, Peter 1796 wb-1-45 (K)
Graves, Rhoda 1829 wb-#79 (Wl)
Graves, Sabastian 1845 5-3-81 (Cl)
Graves, Sally 1838 wb-11-172 (D)
Graves, Samuel A. 1857 wb-17-162 (D)
Graves, Shirwood W. 1849 wb-a-187 (Ms)
Graves, Sterling 1837 wb-a-17 (F)
Graves, Susan 1845 wb-#147 (Wl)
Graves, Thomas 1829 wb-1-230 (Ma)

Graves, Thomas 1836 wb-x-353 (Mu)
Graves, Thomas 1843 lr (Gi)
Graves, U. 1853 wb-15-541 (D)
Graves, William 1839 lr (Gi)
Graves, William 1846 wb-#64 (Mc)
Graves, William 1860 wb-#65 (Mc)
Graves, William H. 1861 wb-18-587 (D)
Graves, William L. 1855 wb-6-190 (Ma)
Gray, A. 1857 wb-e-66 (Hy)
Gray, Absalom 1802 wb-1-10# (Ge)
Gray, Alexander 1812 wb-A-16 (Li)
Gray, Benajah 1837 wb-11-43 (D)
Gray, Benjamin 1837 wb-2-48# (Ge)
Gray, Benjamin 1859 149-1-141 (Ge)
Gray, Claudius B. 1861 wb-b-108 (F)
Gray, Coalby 1852 wb-2-42 (Li)
Gray, David 1827 wb-b-18 (Hn)
Gray, David 1831 wb-b-134 (Hn)
Gray, David S. 1855 wb-2-103 (Li)
Gray, E. T. 1842 wb-e-480 (Hu)
Gray, Edward 1835 wb-a-301 (R)
Gray, Eleanor 1860 wb-18-383 (D)
Gray, Elisha M. 1829 lr (Sn)
Gray, Eliza K. 1857 wb-f-132 (Mu)
Gray, Elizabeth 1853 wb-16-166 (D)
Gray, George 1847 rb-k-591 (Mt)
Gray, George 1859 wb-1-390 (Fr)
Gray, Hardy P. 1845 wb-8-258 (Wi)
Gray, Henrietta 1838 wb-11-457 (D)
Gray, Henry H. 1852 wb-10-428 (Wi)
Gray, Hermanus 1798 wb-1-10# (Ge)
Gray, Isaac 1845 148-1-119 (Ge)
Gray, Isaac 1850 r39-1-172 (Dk)
Gray, James 1809 wb-1-48 (Wi)
Gray, James 1816 rb-b-332 (Mt)
Gray, James 1820 rb-c-352 (Mt)
Gray, James 1836 wb-x-360 (Mu)
Gray, James 1848 wb-#165 (Wl)
Gray, James 1859 wb-f-180 (Mu)
Gray, Jean 1848 wb-#165 (Wl)
Gray, Jeremiah 1854 wb-3-174 (W)
Gray, Jessee 1848 wb-b-329 (Mu)
Gray, John 1798 wb-2-100 (D)
Gray, John 1828 wb-4-296 (Wi)
Gray, John 1834 wb-1-33 (Gr)
Gray, John 1837 wb-1-143 (Li)
Gray, John 1837 wb-11-53 (D)
Gray, John 1838 wb-7-1 (Wi)
Gray, Joseph 1847 wb-1-413 (La)
Gray, Joseph M. 1844 wb-7-0 (Sm)
Gray, Joseph sr. 1813 wb-a-193 (St)

Gray, Levin 1838 wb-a-1 (Dk)
Gray, Mary J. 1861 wb-13-391 (Wi)
Gray, Matthew 1849 wb-b-381 (Mu)
Gray, Orson 1857 wb-b-45 (Ms)
Gray, Peter F. 1860 wb-i-226 (St)
Gray, Phebe 1840 wb-#130 (Wl)
Gray, Price 1855 wb-11-506 (Wi)
Gray, Rachel 1849 wb-1-375 (Li)
Gray, Robert 1797 wb-1-10# (Ge)
Gray, Robert 1837 wb-2-48# (Ge)
Gray, Robert 1860 wb-13-358 (K)
Gray, Robert 1861 149-1-236 (Ge)
Gray, Sally 1838 wb-11-466 (D)
Gray, Sally L. R. 1813 wb-1-336 (Wi)
Gray, Samuel 1830 wb-5-17 (K)
Gray, Samuel 1835 wb-#135 (Wl)
Gray, Samuel 1837 wb-a-8 (Ms)
Gray, Sarah 1838 wb-11-182 (D)
Gray, Sidney 1857 wb-6-369 (Ma)
Gray, Simon 1836 wb-c-474 (St)
Gray, Simon 1836 wb-c-478 (St)
Gray, Thomas 1860 as-c-188 (Ms)
Gray, William 1820 wb-#36 (Wl)
Gray, William 1831 wb-#222 (Mu)
Gray, William 1831 wb-b-41 (Wh)
Gray, William 1835 rb-g-285 (Mt)
Gray, William 1845 wb-#159 (Wl)
Gray, William 1851 ib-1-172 (Ca)
Gray, William 1855 wb-#11 (Mo)
Gray, William F. 1834 rb-g-69 (Mt)
Gray, William M. 1842 wb-#138 (Wl)
Gray, William M. 1844 wb-#157 (Wl)
Grayer, James M. 1830 wb-a-160 (G)
Grayer, Sarah 1830 wb-a-160 (G)
Grayham, Margaret 1856 wb-12-294 (K)
Grear, Margaret C. 1857 wb-1-92 (Bo)
Grear, Mary 1824 wb-3-723 (Wi)
Greathouse, John 1844 wb-4-10 (Hr)
Greaver, Voluntine 1862 wb-1-154 (Jo)
Greaves, Francis 1797 wb-2-90 (D)
Greaves, Henry K. 1852 wb-d-71 (Wh)
Greaves, Rachel 1861 wb-e-159 (Hy)
Green, A. G. 1855 wb-16-34 (Rb)
Green, Abraham 1834 wb-1-86 (W)
Green, Abram L. 1837 wb-1-330 (Hy)
Green, Anderson 1849 wb-#168 (Wl)
Green, Ann 1820 rb-c-360 (Mt)
Green, Ann 1856 wb-a-240 (T)
Green, Ann C. 1844 wb-3-435 (Hy)
Green, Aron 1827 wb-a-11 (Cr)
Green, Benjamin 1838 wb-11-376 (D)

Green, C. O. 1861 wb-h-530 (Hn)
Green, Catharine 1845 rb-j-351 (Mt)
Green, Clinton 1860 wb-17-123 (Rb)
Green, Daniel 1856 wb#41 (Gu)
Green, David 1855 as-b-174 (Ms)
Green, David 1857 wb-a-311 (Cr)
Green, Edward 1841 wb-2-288 (Hr)
Green, Elisabeth J. 1847 wb-a-329 (F)
Green, Elisha 1853 ib-1-211 (Wy)
Green, Elizabeth E. 1839 wb-y-440 (Mu)
Green, Ephraim 1856 as-c-27 (Ms)
Green, Evan 1815 wb-4-338 (D)
Green, Francis M. 1857 wb-a-253 (T)
Green, Green B. 1842 wb-12-331* (D)
Green, Greenberry 1842 wb-12-363* (D)
Green, Harriet 1861 wb-3e-168 (Sh)
Green, Henry R. 1854 wb-11-262 (Wi)
Green, Ira 1847 wb-#46 (Wa)
Green, Isaac 1836 wb-d-292 (Hn)
Green, Isaac 1856 wb-#122 (Wl)
Green, Isaiah D. 1833 wb-10-214 (D)
Green, J. A. L. (Miss) 1852 wb-b-194 (L)
Green, James 1853 wb-0-120 (Cf)
Green, James 1860 as-c-224 (Ms)
Green, James M. 1855 wb-16-466 (D)
Green, James S. 1857 wb-#65 (Mc)
Green, Jane 1860 wb-#66 (Mc)
Green, John 1828 rb-7-22 (Ru)
Green, John 1844 rb-13-1 (Ru)
Green, John 1844 wb-#42 (Wa)
Green, John 1854 wb-d-210 (Wh)
Green, John 1860 wb-k-144 (O)
Green, John G. 1861 wb-#135 (Wl)
Green, Lewis 1806 wb-3-138 (D)
Green, Lewis 1845 wb-8-248 (Wi)
Green, Littleton 1814 wb-4-289 (D)
Green, Lucy K. 1859 wb-7-45 (Ma)
Green, M. C. 1858 wb-a-271 (T)
Green, Mary 1817 wb-#32 (Mu)
Green, Mastan C. 1843 wb-1-225 (Bo)
Green, Moses 1852 wb-a-192 (Cr)
Green, Nancy C. 1860 wb-b-99 (Ms)
Green, Nathan 1841 wb-e-198 (Hn)
Green, Oliver 1832 wb-10-10 (D)
Green, Oliver 1848 wb-14-286 (D)
Green, Priscilla 1855 wb-11-575 (Wi)
Green, R. W. 1859 wb-16-756 (Rb)
Green, Robert 1804 wb-2-395 (D)
Green, Robert E. 1852 wb-xx-1 (St)
Green, Robert W. 1859 wb-17-16 (Rb)
Green, Sam W. 1860 wb-a-160 (Ce)

Green, Sherwood 1840 wb-7-292 (Wi)
Green, Simon W. 1840 wb-2-185 (Hr)
Green, Thomas 1846 wb-c-212 (Wh)
Green, Thomas C. 1837 wb-y-122 (Mu)
Green, Thomas C. 1844 rb-12-563 (Ru)
Green, Wesley 1835 rb-g-249 (Mt)
Green, William (Sr.) 1836 wb-#115 (Wl)
Green, William 1809 wb-1-40 (Wi)
Green, William 1812? wb-#4 (Mu)
Green, William 1834 wb-#106 (Wl)
Green, William 1842 wb-a-96 (F)
Green, William B. 1859 wb-3e-124 (Sh)
Green, William L. 1850 lr (Sn)
Green, Zacariah 1840 wb-2-272 (Sn)
Greene, Joshua 1853 wb-#53 (Wa)
Greene, Josiah D. 1851 wb-15-117 (D)
Greene, Mastin 1859 wb-f-271 (Ro)
Greene, Morris 1816 rb-3-191 (Ru)
Greene, Thomas 1843 wb-d-34 (Ro)
Greene, William 1793 wb-1-230 (Je)
Greene, William 1836 wb-10-552 (D)
Greene, William 1841 148-1-22 (Ge)
Greenfield, G. T. (Dr.) 1852 wb-4-430 (Mu)
Greenfield, G. T. 1849 wb-b-511 (Mu)
Greenfield, Gerard T. 1847 wb-b-42 (Mu)
Greenfield, William 1835 rb-g-215 (Mt)
Greenhaw, Gabriel 1843 wb-1-96 (Sh)
Greenlee, Elizabeth 1821 wb-1-37 (Fr)
Greenlee, James 1857 wb-3-390 (Gr)
Greenlee, John 1858 wb-3-473 (Gr)
Greenlee, Samuel 1849 rb-14-501 (Ru)
Greenway, Richard 1849 wb-#48 (Wa)
Greenway, William 1839 wb-#35 (Wa)
Greer, Alexander 1858 wb-7-27 (Ma)
Greer, Andrew 1817 wb-1-0 (Sm)
Greer, Arthur 1838 wb-1-170 (Bo)
Greer, Benjamin 1838 wb-11-380 (D)
Greer, Benjamin 1851 mr-2-427 (Be)
Greer, David A. 1859 wb-f-246 (G)
Greer, George 1833 wb-10-71 (D)
Greer, Jackson 1840 wb-12-9* (D)
Greer, James 1833 wb-a-43 (Cr)
Greer, James 1845 wb-5-4 (Ma)
Greer, James 1855 wb-e-265 (G)
Greer, John 1803 wb-2-301 (D)
Greer, John 1828 rb-7-307 (Ru)
Greer, John 1847 wb-14-150 (D)
Greer, John M. 1857 wb-f-83 (G)
Greer, John P. 1851 mr-2-397 (Be)
Greer, Joseph 1831 wb-1-60 (Li)
Greer, Martin 1822 wb-8-123 (D)

Greer, Mary 1850 wb-9-366 (Wi)
Greer, Mary A. 1857 wb-2-214 (Li)
Greer, Nancy 1850 wb-#173 (Wl)
Greer, Nathan 1836 wb-d-189 (Hn)
Greer, Nathan 1856 rb-18-127 (Ru)
Greer, Nathan 1856 rb-18-182 (Ru)
Greer, Robert D. 1856 as-b-241 (Ms)
Greer, Samuel (Sr.) 1826 wb-#32 (Wa)
Greer, Vincent 1829 wb-1-137 (Ma)
Greer, William 1852 wb-g-439 (Hn)
Greer, William F. 1856 wb-e-48 (Wh)
Greer, Wm. 1851 as-c-135 (Di)
Greeson, Henry 1857 ib-1-439 (Wy)
Greg, Yoste 1804 as-1-64 (Ge)
Gregg, John 1847 wb-2-66# (Ge)
Gregg, John 1855 wb-3e-2 (Sh)
Gregory, Ambrose 1827 wb-3-0 (Sm)
Gregory, Barbary 1840 rb-11-54 (Ru)
Gregory, Brown 1858 wb-1-380 (Fr)
Gregory, Cydia 1834 wb-8-375 (Rb)
Gregory, Edna G. 1849 wb-b-456 (Mu)
Gregory, Edward 1842 rb-12-105 (Ru)
Gregory, Edward 1842 rb-12-113 (Ru)
Gregory, Edwin 1836 rb-9-393 (Ru)
Gregory, Fenton 1849 wb-1-375 (Li)
Gregory, Frances 1842 rb-12-223 (Ru)
Gregory, Francis 1853 rb-16-576 (Ru)
Gregory, George 1815 wb-1-0 (Sm)
Gregory, Herron 1844 wb-c-131 (G)
Gregory, J. T. 1855 ib-h-435 (F)
Gregory, John 1821 wb-#38 (Wl)
Gregory, John 1841 wb-7-362 (Wi)
Gregory, John 1861 wb-#66 (Mc)
Gregory, Joseph 1816 wb-1-0 (Sm)
Gregory, Major 1830 wb-7-261 (Rb)
Gregory, Margaret 1844 wb-#148 (Wl)
Gregory, Martha 1833 wb-8-151 (Rb)
Gregory, Milly 1845 wb-a2-193 (Mu)
Gregory, Osborne 1828 wb-1-68 (Hr)
Gregory, Peggy 1837 wb-10-52 (Rb)
Gregory, Smith 1848 wb-7-0 (Sm)
Gregory, Tapley 1857 wb-#66 (Mc)
Gregory, Thomas 1818 wb-1-0 (Sm)
Gregory, Thomas 1841 wb-#134 (Wl)
Gregory, Thomas 1845 wb-7-0 (Sm)
Gregory, Thos. 1840 wb-y-662 (Mu)
Gregory, William 1836 wb-3-453 (Je)
Gregory, William 1840 wb-1-58 (Sh)
Gregory, Wright 1816 wb-7-92 (D)
Gremmer, Dorcas M. 1852 wb-10-194 (Wi)
Gremmer, Jacob 1843 wb-8-123 (Wi)

Gremmer, Jacob 1844 wb-8-135 (Wi)
Grenade, John A. 1853 wb-g-500 (Hn)
Grenade, Silas 1842 wb-3-0 (Sm)
Grennon, Patrick 1798 wb-1-65 (K)
Gresham, Austin 1837 wb-11-79 (D)
Gresham, George W. 1855 wb-e-327 (G)
Gresham, Thomas 1804 wb-#9 (Wa)
Gresham, Wm. A. 1861 rb-20-800 (Ru)
Gribble, Samuel 1841 wb-1-366 (W)
Gribble, Samuel 1852 wb-3-141 (W)
Gribble, Thomas Sr. 1849 wb-3-11 (W)
Gribble, W. E. 1857 wb-3-341 (W)
Grice, James 1855 rb-o-16 (Mt)
Grice, Lewis 1845 rb-j-467 (Mt)
Grice, Patrick 1857 wb-h-321 (St)
Gricham, William 1819 wb-A-258 (Li)
Grider, Tobias 1854 ib-h-83 (F)
Grier, Ann 1810 wb-1-135 (Sn)
Grier, David 1797 wb-1-17 (Je)
Grier, James 1816 wb-#23 (Wl)
Grier, James 1835 wb-#107 (Wl)
Grier, James 1850 wb-#174 (Wl)
Grier, Permelia A. 1852 wb-e-2 (G)
Griffen, James 1840 rb-11-21 (Ru)
Griffen, Lewis 1840 wb-3-191 (Ma)
Griffeth, Moses 1861 wb-b-76 (Dk)
Griffeth, Thomas 1823 eb-1-134 (C)
Griffey, Marget 1810 wb-1-368 (Rb)
Griffin, Anderson 1856 lr (Gi)
Griffin, Arthur 1824 wb-3-323 (St)
Griffin, Benjamin 1826 wb-b-123 (St)
Griffin, Derham 1850 wb-14-497 (D)
Griffin, Elijah 1845 wb-1-108 (Sh)
Griffin, G. A. 1856 wb-3e-27 (Sh)
Griffin, Jackson A. 1841 wb-a-79 (F)
Griffin, James 1853 rb-16-479 (Ru)
Griffin, James C. 1859 wb-b-105 (F)
Griffin, James M. 1851 wb-d-324 (G)
Griffin, John B. 1854 ib-h-81 (F)
Griffin, Joseph 1836 wb-x-361 (Mu)
Griffin, Joseph E. 1853 wb-f-25 (Mu)
Griffin, Joshua 1828 wb-1-164 (Ma)
Griffin, Margaret 1832 wb-8-105 (Rb)
Griffin, Mathew 1841 wb-a-27 (Dk)
Griffin, Micajah 1853 as-b-112 (Ms)
Griffin, Patchence (Patience) 1849
    wb-b-490 (Mu)
Griffin, Peter 1838 wb-6-301 (K)
Griffin, Pleasant 1846 wb-1-125 (Sh)
Griffin, Reubin 1846 wb-13-14 (Rb)
Griffin, Sarah 1853 rb-16-375 (Ru)

Griffin, Sarah C. 1850 rb-15-491 (Ru)
Griffin, Sion 1844 wb-#143 (Wl)
Griffin, Solomon W. 1840 wb-2-111 (Hy)
Griffin, Thomas 1839 wb-e-69 (Hn)
Griffin, William 1810 wb-1-13 (Fr)
Griffin, William 1819 wb-3-6 (Rb)
Griffin, William 1834 wb-8-429 (Rb)
Griffin, William D. 1846 rb-k-42 (Mt)
Griffis, Doiley 1857 wb-2-3 (Li)
Griffis, Durham 1850 wb-14-497 (D)
Griffis, Elizabeth 1860 as-c-223 (Ms)
Griffis, John O. 1843 wb-1-218 (Li)
Griffis, Pleasant 1816 wb-A-133 (Li)
Griffis, William 1812 wb-2-26 (K)
Griffis, William 1848 wb-1-342 (Li)
Griffith, D. 1850 wb-14-497 (D)
Griffith, Donald 1855 wb-6-114 (Ma)
Griffith, Elizabeth 1854 39-2-5 (Dk)
Griffith, James C. 1858 wb-3e-86 (Sh)
Griffith, Jane 1858 wb-#14 (Mo)
Griffith, John 1819 wb-#117 (Mu)
Griffith, John 1828 wb-#67 (Mc)
Griffith, John 1829 wb-#198 (Mu)
Griffith, John 1837 wb-2-225 (Ma)
Griffith, John 1840 wb-b-411 (Wh)
Griffith, Jonathan 1848 wb-a-85 (Dk)
Griffith, Samuel 1833 wb-x-44 (Mu)
Griffith, Sarah R. 1832 wb-1-343 (Ma)
Griffith, William 1822 wb-1-16 (Ma)
Griffith, William 1834 wb-1A-92 (A)
Griffon, Nathaniel 1837 wb-6-326 (Wi)
Grigg, Frederick 1841 wb-e-284 (Hn)
Grigg, Joel 1844 wb-#67 (Mc)
Grigg, Lewis 1836 rb-9-392 (Ru)
Grigg, Persilla 1838 wb-d-172 (St)
Grigg, Samuel 1856 wb-f-113 (Mu)
Grigg, _____ 1839 wb-e-72 (Hn)
Griggs, George 1856 ib-1-463 (Wy)
Griggs, George sr. 1860 ib-2-161 (Wy)
Griggs, John 1821 wb-a-158 (Wh)
Griggs, Thomas J. 1854 wb-11-191 (Wi)
Griggs, Thomas J. 1856 wb-12-210 (Wi)
Grigory, George 1856 wb-2-342 (Me)
Grigory, Margaret 1851 wb-#20 (Mo)
Grigory, Martha A. 1852 rb-16-240 (Ru)
Grigsby, Ashley 1860 wb-f-493 (Ro)
Grigsby, James 1840 wb-c-182 (Ro)
Grigsby, James A. 1841 wb-c-194 (Ro)
Grigsby, John 1826 wb-1-214 (Hw)
Grigsby, Nathaniel 1859 wb-1-234 (Hw)
Grigsby, William 1839 wb-1-222 (Hw)

Grills, Harriett W. 1857 wb-#67 (Mc)
Grills, John 1803 wb-0-39 (K)
Grills, Philadelphia 1789 wb-1-206 (Hw)
Grills, Philadelphia 1803 wb-1-115 (K)
Grim, Charles 1852 wb-2-116 (Sh)
Grimes, A. A. 1851 wb-d-367 (G)
Grimes, Alexander 1841 wb-z-262 (Mu)
Grimes, Alvis C. 1856 ib-1-394 (Wy)
Grimes, Anna 1852 wb-4-497 (Mu)
Grimes, Benjamin 1844 wb-f-192 (St)
Grimes, Catharine 1851 wb-15-10 (Rb)
Grimes, Catharine 1852 wb-15-86 (Rb)
Grimes, Charlotte 1849 ib-1-43 (Wy)
Grimes, E. S. 1850 ib-1-68 (Wy)
Grimes, Elihu 1858 ib-2-76 (Wy)
Grimes, Elihu S. 1855 ib-1-370 (Wy)
Grimes, Henry 1824 as-A-110 (Di)
Grimes, Henry 1850 ib-1-78 (Wy)
Grimes, Jacob 1825 wb-5-153 (Rb)
Grimes, James 1829 wb-#192 (Mu)
Grimes, James 1831 rb-f-182 (Mt)
Grimes, James 1836 wb-6-276 (Wi)
Grimes, James 1840 wb-z-93 (Mu)
Grimes, James 1849 ib-1-28 (Wy)
Grimes, James B. 1842 wb-d-1 (Hd)
Grimes, John 1842 5-2-260 (Cl)
Grimes, John 1842 wb-z-407 (Mu)
Grimes, John 1851 wb-4-154 (Mu)
Grimes, John 1852 wb-4-498 (Mu)
Grimes, Luke 1812 wb-#5 (Mu)
Grimes, Luke 1825 wb-#131 (Mu)
Grimes, Robert A. 1855 ib-1-367 (Wy)
Grimes, Thomas W. 1849 6-2-26 (Le)
Grimes, William 1813 wb-4-225 (D)
Grimes, William 1816 wb-#26 (Mu)
Grimes, William 1856 ib-1-467 (Wy)
Grimes, William 1856 ib-2-5 (Wy)
Grimes, William B. 1848 wb-b-249 (Mu)
Grimes, William S. 1855 ib-1-334 (Wy)
Grimes, William W. 1851 ib-1-122 (Wy)
Grimm, Isaac 1828 lr (Sn)
Grimmett, Benjamin E. 1853 wb-4-597 (Mu)
Grinder, Joshua 1826 wb-#139 (Mu)
Grindstaff, Isaac 1840 wb-#132 (Wl)
Grindstaff, Isaac 1854 wb-1-87 (Jo)
Grindstaff, James D. 1846 r39-1-16 (Dk)
Grindstaff, Nicholas 1853 wb-1-74 (Jo)
Grindstaff, Reason 1860 39-2-399 (Dk)
Grisham, George W. 1854 wb-e-217 (G)
Grisham, Isaac 1838 wb-1-174 (La)
Grisham, J. W. 1861 wb-19-34 (D)

Grisham, James W. 1861 wb-#67 (Mc)
Grisham, Jesse 1852 wb-#67 (Mc)
Grisham, John M. 1856 wb-#67 (Mc)
Grisham, Thomas 1830 wb-#68 (Mc)
Grisham, William 1836 rb-9-370 (Ru)
Grisham, William 1848 rb-14-365 (Ru)
Grisham, William T. 1829 wb-#68 (Mc)
Grissard, Carter 1815 wb-2-228 (Rb)
Grissard, Hardy 1826 wb-5-325 (Rb)
Grissard, Hardy 1826 wb-5-334 (Rb)
Grissim, Elijah 1845 wb-#148 (Wl)
Grissim, R. W. 1831 wb-#98 (Wl)
Grissim, Rowland 1831 wb-#90 (Wl)
Grissim, Rowland W. 1830 wb-#99 (Wl)
Grissom, Bloomfield 1844 mr-2-76 (Be)
Grissom, James P. 1837 wb-y-121 (Mu)
Grissom, Peter 1843 wb-3-0 (Sm)
Grissom, William 1860 wb-b-460 (We)
Grissom, William B. 1819 wb-A-222 (Li)
Grissum, Stephen 1851 wb-d-361 (G)
Griswold, Wiley P. 1855 wb#23 (Gu)
Grizard, Edney 1853 wb-16-69 (D)
Grizzard, Jeremiah 1832 wb-9-574 (D)
Grizzard, Jeremiah V. 1848 wb-14-73 (Rb)
Grizzard, Joel 1830 rb-f-94 (Mt)
Grizzard, Sally 1836 rb-g-333 (Mt)
Grizzard, William M. 1857 wb-e-80 (Hy)
Grizzle, Daniel 1844 wb-1-615 (W)
Groce, John 1857 wb-2-216 (Li)
Grogan, James 1823 wb-1-0 (Sm)
Grogan, James H. 1850 rb-15-394 (Ru)
Groom, James 1854 wb-a-260 (Dk)
Groom, Leroy T. 1860 wb-h-442 (Hn)
Groom, Robert 1855 wb-a-239 (Cr)
Groom, Samuel 1861 wb-h-551 (Hn)
Grooms, Isaac 1848 wb-2-16 (Sh)
Grooms, John 1841 lr (Sn)
Grooms, Stephen H. 1833 wb-1-135 (We)
Grose, Chrisley 1809 wb-1-205 (Hw)
Gross, Adam 1835 wb-1-137 (Fr)
Gross, Eveline 1859 wb-17-608 (D)
Gross, Frederick 1836 wb-d-38 (St)
Gross, George S. 1857 wb-17-458 (D)
Gross, Jacob W. 1858 iv-C-3 (C)
Gross, Milton B. 1855 wb-e-19 (Wh)
Gross, William 1828 wb-1-216 (Hw)
Grosse, Martin 1844 wb-1-613 (W)
Grove, Elizabeth 1805 wb-1-204 (Hw)
Grove, George 1860 wb-13-370 (K)
Grove, Henson 1842 wb-z-390 (Mu)
Grove, Jacob 1847 wb-4-169 (Hr)

Grove, Jacob 1849 wb-4-439 (Hr)
Grove, William 1815 wb-2-178 (K)
Groves, Christian 1837 wb-#33 (Wa)
Groves, David 1845 wb-12-268 (Rb)
Groves, Fanny 1843 wb-z-511 (Mu)
Groves, Jacob B. 1837 wb-1-220 (Hw)
Groves, Joseph 1851 wb-a-225 (Di)
Groves, O. H. P. 1859 as-c-549 (Di)
Groves, Reubin jr. 1860 wb-3-601 (Gr)
Groves, Thomas 1814 lr (Sn)
Groves, William 1808 wb-1-3 (Fr)
Grubb, Allen Burd 1821 wb-#68 (Mc)
Grubb, John 1846 5-3-195 (Cl)
Grubb, John W. 1849 wb-g-139 (Hu)
Grubb, William 1846 wb-#68 (Mc)
Grubbs, Amos 1841 148-1-14 (Ge)
Grubbs, Austin W. 1837 wb-10-14 (Rb)
Grubbs, Elizabeth 1855 wb-2-81# (Ge)
Grubbs, Mary B. 1854 wb-15-640 (Rb)
Grubs, Edwin 1839 wb-2-51# (Ge)
Grundy, Ann P. (Nancy?) 1847 wb-14-66 (D)
Grundy, Felix 1841 wb-12-98* (D)
Grundy, Felix 1856 wb-17-77 (D)
Grymes, C. 1839 as-a-472 (Di)
Grymes, Catharine 1840 as-b-15 (Di)
Grymes, John 1859 as-c-561 (Di)
Guardner, Shadrack 1841 wb-a-71 (F)
Gubbins, Wm. 1786 wb-1-59 (D)
Gueren, J. B. 1857 wb-h-148 (Hn)
Guerin, J. J. B. 1857 wb-h-128 (Hn)
Guerin, Jonas 1852 wb-xx-66 (St)
Guerin, Jonas 1852 wb-xx-69 (St)
Guest, Jane 1849 wb-1-270 (Fr)
Guest, John B. 1837 wb-e-40 (Hu)
Guest, Moses 1843 wb-1-2 (Gu)
Guest, Moses 1857 wb#39 (Gu)
Guest, William 1844 wb-2-58 (W)
Guest, William 1856 wb#25 (Gu)
Guilchrist, Malcom 1860 ib-2-188 (Wy)
Guill, Bird 1827 wb-#69 (Wl)
Guill, James 1854 wb-#112 (Wl)
Guill, John H. 1854 wb-g-590 (Hn)
Guill, Josiah 1841 wb-#135 (Wl)
Guin, Daniel 1803 as-1-43 (Ge)
Guin, Daniel 1803 wb-1-10# (Ge)
Guin, James 1824 wb-1-11# (Ge)
Guin, Jane 1816 wb-2-32# (Ge)
Guin, Jinny 1816 wb-2-37# (Ge)
Guin, John 1829 wb-2-31# (Ge)
Guinn, Bartholemew 1848 wb-1-233 (Me)
Guinn, Duke A. 1858 wb-h-342 (Hn)

Guinn, Isaac 1849 wb-#168 (Wl)
Guinn, John 1852 148-1-383 (Ge)
Guinn, Lydia 1853 wb-5-187 (Je)
Guinn, Rebecca 1853 148-1-449 (Ge)
Guinn, Robert 1838 wb-e-55 (Hu)
Guinn, Thomas 1855 wb-#56 (Wa)
Gulden, William 1836 wb-3-0 (Sm)
Gulledge, Jeptha 1842 wb-a-111 (Cr)
Gulledge, Nancy 1849 wb-b-497 (Mu)
Gulledge, William 1825 wb-8-452 (D)
Gullett, James 1831 wb-#218 (Mu)
Gullett, Robert J.? 1845 wb-a2-295 (Mu)
Gullett, Samuel 1831 wb-#218 (Mu)
Gulley, Jesse 1814 Wb-2-107 (Wi)
Gulley, Lazarus 1837 wb-1-221 (Hw)
Gullick, J. C. 1858 ib-2-103 (Wy)
Gullick, J. C. 1858 ib-2-146 (Wy)
Gullick, Nancy 1845 wb-7-0 (Sm)
Gulliford, James 1849 wb-14-468 (D)
Gully, R. J. 1852 as-b-76 (Ms)
Gun, John 1815 wb-2-260 (Rb)
Gunn, Alexander 1853 wb-15-237 (Rb)
Gunn, Anderson 1837 wb-9-442 (Rb)
Gunn, James 1849 wb-14-237 (Rb)
Gunn, John 1840 wb-#135 (Wl)
Gunn, John A. 1839 wb-10-314 (Rb)
Gunn, Miles 1821 wb-3-324 (Rb)
Gunn, Pinkney 1837 wb-9-431 (Rb)
Gunn, Sarah 1848 wb-10-23 (K)
Gunn, Thomas 1859 wb-16-794 (Rb)
Gunn, Wilson 1838 wb-#120 (Wl)
Gunter, Clabourn 1835 wb-1-99 (W)
Gunter, Frances 1850 wb-9-397 (Wi)
Gunter, Francis 1840 wb-7-278 (Wi)
Gunter, John P. 1851 wb-4-96 (Mu)
Gunter, Joshua 1844 wb-1-254 (Li)
Gunter, William 1840 wb-1-168 (Li)
Gupton, Abner 1859 wb-a-127 (Ce)
Gupton, Cooper 1819 rb-4-211 (Ru)
Gurganus, Benjamin 1852 wb-d-380 (G)
Gurley, Jeremiah 1814 wb-#38 (Mu)
Gutherie, Mary 1845 wb-f-280* (Hn)
Guthrie, Andrew 1856 wb-6-211 (Ma)
Guthrie, David C. 1833 wb-5-271 (Wi)
Guthrie, David H. 1833 wb-5-229 (Wi)
Guthrie, Henry 1838 wb-11-291 (D)
Guthrie, Henry 1852 wb-15-394 (D)
Guthrie, James 1832 wb-2-31# (Ge)
Guthrie, James B. 1838 wb-2-283 (Ma)
Guthrie, James G. 1853 wb-1-227 (Hw)
Guthrie, John 1845 wb-a2-203 (Mu)

Guthrie, John 1848 wb-2-17 (Li)
Guthrie, R. F. 1854 wb-3-188 (La)
Guthrie, Robert 1838 wb-6-492 (Wi)
Guthrie, Sally V. 1843 wb-8-86 (Wi)
Guthrie, Thomas 1849 wb-#171 (Wl)
Guthrie, Wm. F. 1855 wb-g-708 (Hn)
Guthrie, Wm. H. 1852 rb-16-323 (Ru)
Gutlett, John 1856 wb-j-128 (O)
Guy, A. L. 1858 wb-j-333 (O)
Guy, James H. 1853 wb-h-Apr (O)
Guy, John 1824 wb-3-745 (Wi)
Guy, John W. 1832 wb-5-121 (Wi)
Guy, William H. 1861 wb-k-499 (O)
Guy, Willis 1853 ib-1-283 (Ca)
Guyan, Patrick 1861 rb-p-595 (Mt)
Guyder, John 1830 wb-1-45 (Li)
Gwaltney, Elias 1827 wb-3-0 (Sm)
Gwathmey, John B. 1818 wb-7-256 (D)
Gwin, Alexander 1852 wb-h-79 (Hu)
Gwin, Alexander sr. 1856 wb-h-478 (Hu)
Gwin, Joseph 1847 wb-2-309 (W)
Gwin, Ruth 1847 wb-b-149 (Mu)
Gwin, Sally 1855 wb-h-403 (Hu)
Gwin, William 1827 lr (Sn)
Gwin, William M. 1849 wb-g-138 (Hu)
Gwin?, Lewis 1785 wb-1-26 (D)
Gwinn, Ann 1856 39-2-170 (Dk)
Gwinn, Ann M. 1856 39-2-178 (Dk)
Gwinn, John 1833 wb-3-285 (Je)
Gwynn, Hugh (Jr.) 1826 wb-#65 (Wl)
Gwynn, Hugh 1828 wb-#79 (Wl)
Gwynn, Ransom 1848 wb-#166 (Wl)
Gwynn, Rebecca 1858 wb-#127 (Wl)
Gwynn, William 1840 wb-#132 (Wl)
Gyre, Catrina 1828 wb-#27 (Wa)

- H -

Haas, Philip 1829 wb-1-37 (W)
Haas, Philip 1849 wb-a-89 (Dk)
Haas, Simeon 1841? wb-#135 (Wl)
Hacker, Jacob 1844 wb-#4 (Mo)
Hacker, Joseph 1859 wb-f-282 (Ro)
Hackler, George Sr. 1860 wb-#69 (Mc)
Hackney, Aaron 1828 wb-1-55 (Bo)
Hackney, Allen 1839 as-a-15 (Ms)
Hackney, Benj. R. 1839 wb-1A-238 (A)
Hackney, Danl. 1803 wb-2-330 (D)
Hackney, Frances 1843 rb-j-46 (Mt)
Hackney, Hugh 1814 wb-1-201 (Bo)
Hackney, Jane 1841 wb-1-58 (Bo)

Hackney, John 1809 wb-1-66 (Bo)
Hackney, John 1855 wb-1-63 (Bo)
Hackney, John T. 1854 wb-e-464 (Ro)
Hackney, Joseph 1829 wb-#179 (Mu)
Hackney, Joseph 1849 wb-b-492 (Mu)
Hackney, Joseph 1849 wb-b-530 (Mu)
Hackney, Margaret Mulherin 1856 wb-f-98 (Mu)
Hackney, Newton 1850 wb-4-72 (Mu)
Hackney, Thomas 1845 rb-j-379 (Mt)
Hackney, Thomas 1845 rb-j-381 (Mt)
Hackney, William 1816 wb-2-231 (K)
Hackney, William C. 1850 wb-4-435 (Mu)
Haddin, George 1842 wb-1-66 (Bo)
Haden, Joseph 1833 wb-1-82 (W)
Hadley, Ambrose 1839 wb-y-607 (Mu)
Hadley, James H. 1836 wb-6-217 (Wi)
Hadley, John P. 1840 wb-z-56 (Mu)
Hadley, Louisa 1842 wb-z-383 (Mu)
Hadley, Noah 1839 wb-a-30 (Ms)
Hadley, William 1842 wb-12-334* (D)
Hadley, William 1842 wb-12-368* (D)
Hadley, William 1845 wb-13-140 (D)
Haffy, Hugh 1842 wb-7-582 (Wi)
Hagan, Edward 1827 wb-1-1 (W)
Hagan, James 1829 wb-1-244 (Hw)
Hagar, George 1858 wb-17-533 (D)
Hagar, George W. 1859 wb-18-88 (D)
Hagarty, Patrick 1842 wb-#136 (Wl)
Hager, Henry 1847 wb-14-46 (D)
Hager, William 1835 rb-9-251 (Ru)
Haggard, Henry 1829 wb-3-392 (Je)
Haggard, John 1793 wb-1-283 (D)
Haggard, John 1794 wb-2-4 (D)
Haggard, John 1836 wb-b-329 (Ro)
Haggard, Noel 1814 wb-a-206 (St)
Haggert, John 1803 wb-2-309 (D)
Hagie, Solomon 1845 rb-j-419 (Mt)
Hagler, Benjamin 1841 wb-c-246 (Ro)
Hagler, Daniel T. 1857 wb-h-326 (St)
Hagler, Delila 1854 wb-h-61 (St)
Hagler, Delly 1853 wb-xx-289 (St)
Hagler, Isaac 1815 wb-3-117 (St)
Hagler, Isaac 1840 wb-#6 (Mo)
Hagler, Isaac 1852 wb-#24 (Mo)
Hagler, John L. 1857 wb-h-156 (Hn)
Hagler, Thomas 1841 wb-c-264 (Ro)
Hagler, William 1841 wb-e-132 (St)
Hagood, James 1833 wb-1-249 (Hw)
Hague, James 1847 wb-1-305 (Li)
Hague, John 1846 wb-c-272 (G)
Hague, John H. 1859 wb-f-338 (G)

Hagy, William 1845 wb-d-119 (Hd)
Hail, Aaron P. 1860 wb-4-268 (La)
Hail, Charles 1843 148-1-63 (Ge)
Hail, G. W. 1852 wb-2-132 (Me)
Hail, George 1853 wb-2-175 (Me)
Hail, George I. 1835 wb-#34 (Wa(
Hail, George W. 1853 wb-2-183 (Me)
Hail, Green O. L. 1841 wb-b-372 (G)
Hail, James E. 1829 wb-1-10 (La)
Hail, John 1824 wb-#76 (Mu)
Hail, John 1843 wb-c-103 (G)
Hail, John A. 1853 wb-3-100 (La)
Hail, John C. 1858 wb-4-193 (La)
Hail, Michael P. 1856 wb-f-47 (Ro)
Hail, Powel 1826 wb-#150 (Mu)
Hail, Thomas 1814 wb-4-272 (D)
Hail, W. 1833 rb-f-510 (Mt)
Hail, William E. 1840 wb-b-308 (G)
Hail, William jr. 1859 wb-3e-99 (Sh)
Haile, Meshach 1813 wb-4-243 (D)
Haile, Meshack 1834 wb-2-43# (Ge)
Hailey, Henderson 1855 wb-3e-1 (Sh)
Hailey, Jessee 1826 wb-a-223 (Wh)
Hailey, John 1838 wb-b-288 (Wh)
Hailey, John S. 1861 wb-f-408 (G)
Hailey, Plesent 1813 wb-#12 (Wl)
Hailey, Wyatt 1855 wb-b-11 (Ms)
Haily, John A. 1834 wb-b-45 (G)
Haily, Sarah 1836 wb-2-85 (Ma)
Haily, Thomas 1821 wb-1-0 (Sm)
Haines, Abraham 1857? wb-4-10 (Je)
Haines, Joseph 1841 wb-3-467 (Ma)
Hainey, George 1841 wb-e-408 (Hu)
Hainline, John 1843 wb-3-119 (Hr)
Hains, Calvin M. 1851 wb-4-378 (Mu)
Haire, James A. 1861 wb-#18 (Mo)
Hairgrove, Bennett 1854 wb-11-371 (Wi)
Hairgrove, David B. 1854 wb-11-258 (Wi)
Hairston, Robert 1841 wb-1-204 (Li)
Haislet, James 1794 wb-1-25 (K)
Haislip, Elizabeth 1860 as-c-189 (Ms)
Haislip, James 1858 as-c-114 (Ms)
Haithcock, D. A. 1853 wb-10-526 (Wi)
Haithcock, Dempsey A. 1855 wb-11-490 (Wi)
Halbert, Daniel 1845 wb-1-271 (Li)
Halbert, Joel 1817 wb-A-235 (Li)
Halbrook, Noah W. 1833 wb-#101 (Wl)
Halbrooks, Noah H. 1835 wb-#109 (Wl)
Hale, Archibald 1855 wb-#55 (Wa(
Hale, Arthur 1845 wb-1-255 (Hw)
Hale, Benjamin 1853 ib-1-262 (Ca)

Hale, Bird S. 1852 wb-4-491 (Mu)
Hale, C. T. 1853 as-c-237 (Di)
Hale, Canday 1849 wb-#47 (Wa(
Hale, Elijah J. T. 1839 wb-b-282 (G)
Hale, Elizabeth 1827 wb-#26 (Wa(
Hale, Elizabeth 1855 39-2-91 (Dk)
Hale, Emanuel 1842 wb-2-398 (Hr)
Hale, Francis 1847 wb-14-81 (D)
Hale, Frederick 1825 wb-#69 (Mc)
Hale, George (Sr.) 1805 wb-#10 (Wa(
Hale, Harvy 1852 148-1-413 (Ge)
Hale, Henry 1822 wb-#18 (Wa(
Hale, Henry 1850 wb-#50 (Wa(
Hale, Jackson 1839 wb-#35 (Wa(
Hale, James 1827 wb-#69 (Mc)
Hale, James R. 1852 wb-1-300 (Fr)
Hale, Joab 1843 wb-a-46 (Dk)
Hale, John 1846? wb-#44 (Wa(
Hale, John 1857 wb-f-53 (G)
Hale, Joseph 1822 wb-#18 (Wa(
Hale, Joseph 1844 wb-#41 (Wa(
Hale, M. T. 1858 wb-a-60 (Ce)
Hale, Martha 1856 wb-#57 (Wa(
Hale, Meshack 1847 wb-14-70 (D)
Hale, Nicholas (Sr.) 1818 wb-#16 (Wa(
Hale, Nicholas 1828 lr (Sn)
Hale, Nicholas 1843 wb-12-389* (D)
Hale, Ogbon 1848 wb-1-253 (Hw)
Hale, Patrick H. 1847 148-1-214 (Ge)
Hale, Philip 1820 wb-1-14# (Ge)
Hale, Thomas 1838 wb-2-363 (Ma)
Hale, Thomas 1862 wb-8-0 (Sm)
Hale, Thomas J. 1845 wb-13-169 (D)
Hale, Thos. C. 1855 wb-e-302 (G)
Hale, William 1819 wb-#35 (Wl)
Hale, William 1822 lr (Sn)
Hale, William 1843 rb-17-100 (Ru)
Hale, William 1852 r39-1-244 (Dk)
Hale, William 1855 wb-#56 (Wa(
Hale, William C. 1848 wd-14-216 (D)
Hale, Williamson 1824 wb-2-0 (Sm)
Hales, Linton 1849 r39-1-145 (Dk)
Hales, Richard 1828 wb-#199 (Mu)
Hales, William 1859 39-2-319 (Dk)
Haley, B. W. 1851 as-b-28 (Ms)
Haley, Banister 1848 wb-9-176 (Wi)
Haley, Benjamin 1846 wb-e-210 (O)
Haley, Claibourn 1859 wb-4-20 (Gr)
Haley, David 1806 eb-1-3 (C)
Haley, David 1839 wb-c-81 (Ro)
Haley, Elijah G. 1810 wb-a-38 (Ro)

Haley, Elizabeth 1847 wb-e-11 (Ro)
Haley, Frances 1849 wb-#170 (Wl)
Haley, Henderson L. 1851 wb-g-504 (Hn)
Haley, Isaiah 1822 wb-1-7 (Ma)
Haley, James 1824 wb-1-40 (Ma)
Haley, James 1838 wb-2-267 (Ma)
Haley, James 1847 wb-#155 (Wl)
Haley, John 1845 wb-7-0 (Sm)
Haley, John C. 1840 wb-c-176 (Ro)
Haley, Nancy 1851 wb-#176 (Wl)
Haley, Nancy 1856 wb-h-97 (Hn)
Haley, Overton 1846 wb-8-462 (Wi)
Haley, Richard 1843 wb-8-1 (Wi)
Haley, Robert 1838 wb-c-8 (Ro)
Haley, Sarah 1838 wb-2-320 (Ma)
Haley, Ward 1847 wb-c-47 (Ro)
Haley, William 1845 wb-13-179 (D)
Haley, William 1851 wb-15-54 (D)
Haley, William B. 1859 wb-f-299 (Ro)
Haley, William R. 1832 wb-1-315 (Ma)
Haley, Wm. P. 1836 wb-2-162 (Ma)
Haley, Wyatt 1848 wb-9-72 (Wi)
Halfacre, Andrew 1836 wb-6-116 (Wi)
Halfacre, David 1848 wb-9-40 (Wi)
Halfacre, David 1859 wb-13-180 (Wi)
Halfacre, Elizabeth 1836 wb-6-102 (Wi)
Halfacre, Elizabeth 1857 wb-12-421 (Wi)
Halfacre, Henry 1854 wb-11-162 (Wi)
Halfacre, Jacob 1849 wb-9-318 (Wi)
Halfacre, Jacob 1859 wb-13-80 (Wi)
Halfacre, Tom 1855 wb-11-486 (Wi)
Halford, Bradly 1837 wb-b-203 (G)
Hall, A. 1851 rb-4-276 (Mu)
Hall, A. C. 1858 wb-13-8 (K)
Hall, A. T. 1857 wb-12-346 (K)
Hall, Absalom 1806 wb-1-96 (Sn)
Hall, Alexander 1855 149-1-10 (Ge)
Hall, Alfred G. 1846 rb-13-693 (Ru)
Hall, Anderson 1849 wb-9-299 (Wi)
Hall, Andrew 1854 rb-17-209 (Ru)
Hall, Andrew 1854 rb-17-226 (Ru)
Hall, Britten 1858 wb-b-423 (We)
Hall, Charles M. 1827 wb-9-98 (D)
Hall, Clem 1824 wb-8-387 (D)
Hall, Clement 1852 wb-e-317 (Ro)
Hall, Corban 1843 wb-11-349 (Rb)
Hall, Corban 1843 wb-11-498 (Rb)
Hall, Cullen 1859 wb-i-137 (St)
Hall, David 1851 wb-1B-228 (A)
Hall, Dickenson 1815 wb-2-220 (Rb)
Hall, Edward 1858 wb-17-491 (D)

Hall, Eliza Ann 1850 wb-#49 (Wa(
Hall, Elizabeth 1855 rb-17-584 (Ru)
Hall, Garet 1849 as-b-424 (Di)
Hall, George 1862 wb-2-354 (Li)
Hall, Gideon B. 1861 rb-21-14 (Ru)
Hall, Hampton 1856 wb-17-84 (D)
Hall, Henry 1843 mr-2-49 (Be)
Hall, Hopkins N. 1848 wb-b-252 (We)
Hall, Hugh M. 1839 wb-e-285 (Hn)
Hall, Jacob 1844 rb-12-527 (Ru)
Hall, Jacob sr. 1844 rb-12-525 (Ru)
Hall, James 1848 wb-2-107# (Ge)
Hall, James 1854 wb-b-337 (We)
Hall, James 1858 wb-#28 (Mo)
Hall, James G. 1849 wb-3-6 (W)
Hall, James S. 1847 as-b-385 (Di)
Hall, James T. 1852 wb-d-382 (G)
Hall, Jesse 1857 wb-b-39 (F)
Hall, Jesse D. 1848 mr-2-280 (Be)
Hall, Jessee 1854 wb-1-34 (Dy)
Hall, John 1816 rb-3-187 (Ru)
Hall, John 1823 as-A-125 (Di)
Hall, John 1830 wb-#30 (Wa(
Hall, John 1833 wb-3-0 (Sm)
Hall, John 1841 wb-b-390 (G)
Hall, John 1846 rb-13-692 (Ru)
Hall, John 1853 rb-16-396 (Ru)
Hall, John 1853 wb-b-310 (We)
Hall, John C. 1815 wb-a-31 (Wh)
Hall, John G. 1845 wb-a2-208 (Mu)
Hall, John H. 1841 wb-12-168* (D)
Hall, John sr. 1854 rb-17-346 (Ru)
Hall, Jonathan 1815 wb-2-143 (K)
Hall, Joseph 1815 wb-2-153 (Wi)
Hall, Joseph A. 1850 as-a-210 (Ms)
Hall, Levi 1834 lr (Sn)
Hall, Margaret 1853 148-1-439 (Ge)
Hall, Margret 1836 wb-a-38 (T)
Hall, Mary 1835 wb-9-180 (Rb)
Hall, Matilda 1844 wb-f-272 (Hn)
Hall, Nancy B. 1830 wb-9-376 (D)
Hall, Obadiah 1851 wb-11-167 (K)
Hall, Perry 1851 wb-1B-243 (A)
Hall, Philip 1847 wb-f-419 (St)
Hall, R. B. 1848 rb-14-399 (Ru)
Hall, Randolph 1848 rb-14-325 (Ru)
Hall, Randolph B. 1849 rb-15-232 (Ru)
Hall, Rchd. 1851 wb-1B-213 (A)
Hall, Rhoda 1857 6-1-4 (Le)
Hall, Richard 1816 lr (Sn)
Hall, Robert P. 1826 wb-4-112 (Wi)

Hall, Samuel 1852 wb-7-0 (Sm)
Hall, Samuel 1852 wb-a-278 (Ms)
Hall, Susannah 1855 149-1-9 (Ge)
Hall, Thomas 1830 wb-4-494 (Wi)
Hall, Thomas 1832 rb-8-500 (Ru)
Hall, Thomas 1832 wb-1-214 (Hr)
Hall, Thomas 1833 wb-5-246 (K)
Hall, Thomas A. 1846 as-a-124 (Ms)
Hall, Thomas B. 1816 wb-2-338 (Rb)
Hall, W. M. 1830 rb-8-134 (Ru)
Hall, W. S. 1858 wb-b-434 (We)
Hall, Warren 1837 wb-b-201 (G)
Hall, William 1819 wb-#33 (Wl)
Hall, William 1822 wb-1-0 (Sm)
Hall, William 1831 wb-#93 (Wl)
Hall, William 1843 mr-2-49 (Be)
Hall, William 1852 r39-1-235 (Dk)
Hall, William 1856 lr (Sn)
Hall, William B. 1843 wb-c-93 (Wh)
Hall, William Q. 1823 wb-1-22 (Ma)
Hall, William S. 1838 wb-1-148 (Li)
Hall, William W. 1857 wb-1-138 (Be)
Hall, William Willis 1844 wb-d-123 (O)
Hall, William sr. 1846 wb-2-64# (Ge)
Hall, Willis 1841 wb-c-105 (O)
Hall, Winny 1843 wb-1-574 (W)
Halley, Francis 1846 wb-a-296 (F)
Halliburton, Robert 1853 as-c-262 (Di)
Halliday, Alexander 1858 wb-i-8 (St)
Hallmark, Thomas 1806 wb-1-205 (K)
Halloman, Nathan 1848 wb-5-56 (Ma)
Halloway, Nathan 1846 wb-5-20 (Ma)
Hallowell, Caroline M. 1857 lr (Gi)
Hallowell, D. S. 1854 ib-h-249 (F)
Hallowell, W. D. S. 1859 gs-1-278 (F)
Hallum, Elizabeth 1826 wb-#65 (Wl)
Hallum, George 1827 wb-#65 (Wl)
Hallum, James 1817 wb-#25 (Wl)
Hallum, John 1810 wb-#8 (Wl)
Hallum, John 1822 wb-1-0 (Sm)
Hallum, William 1834 wb-3-0 (Sm)
Hallums, Josiah 1821 wb-1-0 (Sm)
Hallyburton, Richd. 1853 rb-16-565 (Ru)
Hallyburton, Susan 1855 rb-18-125 (Ru)
Hallyburton, Susannah 1855 rb-17-526 (Ru)
Hallyburton, William H. 1854 rb-17-188 (Ru)
Halsel, Elizabeth (Mrs.) 1834 rb-g-80 (Mt)
Halsel, Elizabeth 1834 rb-g-27 (Mt)
Halsel, Elizabeth 1834 rb-g-30 (Mt)
Halsel, Oney W. 1835 rb-g-81 (Mt)
Halsel, Thomas 1826 rb-d-526 (Mt)

Halsel, Thomas 1835 rb-g-133 (Mt)
Halsul, J. B. 1846 rb-k-148 (Mt)
Haltom, Ebenezer 1835 wb-2-59 (Ma)
Haltom, William G. 1843 wb-3-700 (Ma)
Halton, Mary 1859 gs-1-365 (F)
Halton, Wm. 1859 gs-1-365 (F)
Ham, B. H. 1853 wb-3-122 (La)
Ham, Berry W. 1851 wb-2-184 (La)
Ham, Buckley 1856 ib-1-383 (Wy)
Ham, Charity 1822 wb-a-172 (Ro)
Ham, Eber S. 1851 ib-1-94 (Wy)
Ham, Henry 1839 wb-y-455 (Mu)
Ham, Jacob 1845 wb-d-159 (Hd)
Ham, James 1859 wb-f-248 (G)
Ham, Jesse 1846 wb-8-454 (Wi)
Ham, John 1835 wb-1-409 (Hr)
Ham, Samuel 1848 ib-1-15 (Wy)
Ham, Samuel 1855 wb-16-480 (D)
Ham, William M. 1854 ib-1-320 (Wy)
Hamblen, Hezekiah 1855 wb-1-259 (Hw)
Hamblet, Berry 1837 wb-b-257 (Wh)
Hamblet, John 1835 wb-c-455 (St)
Hamblet, Littleberry 1817 wb-#39 (Mu)
Hamblet, Nicy 1844 wb-#142 (Wl)
Hambleton, Joseph 1839 wb-b-197 (Hd)
Hambleton, Thomas 1847 ib-1-72 (Cl)
Hamblett, Benjamin 1840 wb-b-380 (Wh)
Hamblett, Berry 1837 wb-b-267 (Wh)
Hamblett, Joshua 1838 wb-d-214 (St)
Hamblett, Littleberry 1827 wb-#159 (Mu)
Hamblin, Hamus 1855 wb-j-13 (O)
Hambrick, M. 1861 wb-k-502 (O)
Hambright, John Sr. 1829 wb-#70 (Mc)
Hambright, Nancy 1845 wb-#70 (Mc)
Hambright, Peter 1838 wb-#70 (Mc)
Hamby, Robert 1856 wb-g-716 (Hn)
Hamby, Robert J. 1853 wb-g-569 (Hn)
Hamel, James W. 1838 wb-1-355 (Hy)
Hamel, John 1830 wb-b-58 (Hn)
Hamel?, William 1835 wb-1-379 (Hr)
Hamelton, George 1849 ib-1-136 (Cl)
Hamelton, James 1839 wb-d-321 (St)
Hamelton, Samuel 1847 rb-k-372 (Mt)
Hamens, Saml. 1847 wb-4-164 (Hr)
Hamer, Daniel H. 1840 wb-2-188 (Hr)
Hamer, Daniel H. 1840 wb-7-307 (Wi)
Hamer, Emily H. 1858 wb-13-4 (Wi)
Hamer, Harris H. 1858 wb-13-26 (Wi)
Hamer, Miranda 1849 wb-9-307 (Wi)
Hamersley, William 1844 wb-f-252 (Hn)
Hames, Charles 1844 wb-d-88 (Hd)

Hames, Shelton G. 1860 wb-a-368 (Cr)
Hamil, John 1823 wb-1-71 (Bo)
Hamil, R. H. 1852 wb-b-168 (L)
Hamilton, Alexander 1805 wb-1-169 (K)
Hamilton, Alexander 1840 rb-h-416 (Mt)
Hamilton, Alexander 1852 wb-3-1 (Gr)
Hamilton, Alexander G. 1832 wb-a-197 (G)
Hamilton, Andrew 1815 wb-1-211 (Sn)
Hamilton, Andrew 1829 wb-1-87 (Ma)
Hamilton, David 1841 wb-c-9 (G)
Hamilton, David W. 1860 wb-f-357 (G)
Hamilton, Eleazor 1793 wb-1-282 (D)
Hamilton, Elijah 1826 wb-4-68 (Wi)
Hamilton, Elizabeth 1863 wb-2-368 (Li)
Hamilton, G. W. 1854 as-b-165 (Ms)
Hamilton, George 1796 wb-2-45 (D)
Hamilton, George 1798 wb-2-114 (D)
Hamilton, George 1846 wb-d-5 (G)
Hamilton, George 1858 wb-#131 (Wl)
Hamilton, Hance 1816 rb-3-186 (Ru)
Hamilton, Hance 1842 wb-z-406 (Mu)
Hamilton, Hugh R. 1854 wb-2-87 (Li)
Hamilton, Isaiah 1792 wb-1-1 (K)
Hamilton, Jacob 1852 wb-2-21 (Li)
Hamilton, James A. 1827 wb-#71 (Mc)
Hamilton, James 1816 wb-4-456 (D)
Hamilton, James 1816 wb-7-46 (D)
Hamilton, James 1832 wb-a-25 (Cr)
Hamilton, James 1839 5-2-78 (Cl)
Hamilton, James 1851 wb-14-624 (D)
Hamilton, James 1854 wb-n-207 (Mt)
Hamilton, James W. 1859 wb-f-324 (G)
Hamilton, John 1832 lr (Sn)
Hamilton, John 1857 wb-17-383 (D)
Hamilton, John C. 1833 wb-c-91 (Hn)
Hamilton, John H. 1854 wb-5-44 (Hr)
Hamilton, John W. 1829 wb-4-439 (Wi)
Hamilton, Joseph 1839 wb-1-488 (Hy)
Hamilton, Joseph 1849 ib-1-161 (Cl)
Hamilton, Joseph D. 1857 wb-17-197 (D)
Hamilton, Joseph sr. 1819 wb-3-431 (Je)
Hamilton, Joseph sr. 1834 wb-3-310 (Je)
Hamilton, Joshua 1848 ib-1-51 (Cl)
Hamilton, Margarett 1855 wb-e-336 (G)
Hamilton, Martha L. 1830 wb-4-515 (Wi)
Hamilton, Mary 1830 rb-8-152 (Ru)
Hamilton, Mary 1830 wb-4-476 (Wi)
Hamilton, Mary 1845 rb-j-303 (Mt)
Hamilton, Milton S. 1834 wb-5-398 (Wi)
Hamilton, Nancy 1833 wb-5-337 (Wi)
Hamilton, Nancy J. 1859 wb-17-618 (D)

Hamilton, Nicholas 1854 wb-n-345 (Mt)
Hamilton, Patrick 1809 wb-1-124 (Sn)
Hamilton, Peter 1834 wb-1-63 (Gr)
Hamilton, Rebecca 1820 wb-#104 (Mu)
Hamilton, Robert 1820 wb-3-177 (Rb)
Hamilton, Robert 1833 wb-3-246 (Je)
Hamilton, Robert W. 1848 wb-1-173 (Me)
Hamilton, Robert W. 1858 wb-#71 (Mc)
Hamilton, Robert sr. 1801 wb-1-236 (Hw)
Hamilton, Sally B. 1854 wb-16-284 (D)
Hamilton, Samuel 1853 wb-n-39 (Mt)
Hamilton, Samuel 1855 ib-2-351 (Cl)
Hamilton, Sarah 1849? ib-1-165 (Cl)
Hamilton, Sarah R. 1853 lr (Sn)
Hamilton, Thomas 1834 rb-9-162 (Ru)
Hamilton, Thomas 1847 5-3-242 (Cl)
Hamilton, Thomas 1853 ib-2-333 (Cl)
Hamilton, Thomas 1854 rb-16-706 (Ru)
Hamilton, William 1802 lr (Sn)
Hamilton, William 1834 wb-1-40 (Gr)
Hamilton, William 1840 wb-#132 (Wl)
Hamilton, William 1847 wb-14-92 (D)
Hamilton, William 1853 wb-2-51 (Li)
Hamilton, William G. 1854 wb-2-79 (Li)
Hamilton, William N. 1854 wb-5-144 (Ma)
Hamilton, William S. 1829 wb-4-379 (Wi)
Hamis, Rebecca 1847 wb-4-176 (Hr)
Hamlen, Daniel 1801 wb-1-238 (Hw)
Hamlet, Robertson 1842 wb-e-179 (St)
Hamlet, William 1832 wb-b-194 (Ro)
Hamlet, William 1844? wb-#143 (Wl)
Hamlet, William G. 1835 wb-x-251* (Mu)
Hamlett, Joshua 1841 wb-e-95 (St)
Hamlin, James 1857 wb-j-200 (O)
Hamlin, John 1846 wb-4-42 (Hr)
Hamm, Nancy 1851 ib-1-115 (Wy)
Hammack, Daniel 1829 wb-3-0 (Sm)
Hammell, Mary 1856 wb-j-184 (O)
Hammer, Daniel H. 1845 wb-3-240 (Hr)
Hammer, Elisha 1836 wb-1-195 (W)
Hammer, Enos sr. 1847 wb-5-502 (Gr)
Hammer, Hannah 1838 wb-1-314 (Gr)
Hammer, Isaac 1836 wb-2-45# (Ge)
Hammer, Jacob 1841 wb-#35 (Wa(
Hammer, John 1818 wb-#15 (Wa(
Hammer, Jonathan 1828 wb-#26 (Wa(
Hammer, Margaret 1827 wb-#26 (Wa(
Hammer, Rachel 1852 wb-2-75# (Ge)
Hammers, Enos 1846 wb-5-469 (Gr)
Hammers, Joel 1834 wb-1-78 (Gr)
Hammitt, William 1855 ib-h-317 (F)

Hammock, Lemuel A. 1860 wb-8-0 (Sm)
Hammon, Leroy 1843 wb-1-565 (W)
Hammond, William 1824 lr (Sn)
Hammond, William 1832 wb-1-397 (Ma)
Hammonds, Howel 1836 wb-1-143 (La)
Hammonds, Jesse 1847 wb-1-414 (La)
Hammonds, Moses 1832 wb-3-196 (Je)
Hammonds, Thomas 1835 wb-#31 (Wa(
Hammonds, Thomas D. 1858 wb-5-77 (Hr)
Hammonds, Wm. G. 1845 wb-1-351 (La)
Hammons, Jesse 1852 wb-d-385 (G)
Hammons, Saml. 1849 wb-4-431 (Hr)
Hammons, William 1839 wb-1-277 (W)
Hammons, Willis 1856 wb-3-378 (La)
Hammontree, Jeremiah 1813 wb-1-203 (Bo)
Hamner, Austin M. 1849 wb-b-489 (Mu)
Hamner, William 1851 wb-2-100 (Sh)
Hamontree, James 1831 wb-1-72 (Bo)
Hamontree, John 1840 wb-1-68 (Bo)
Hamontree, William 1815 wb-1-65 (Bo)
Hampston, Reuben E. 1836 wb-3-420 (Je)
Hampton, Abner V. 1823 rb-d-159 (Mt)
Hampton, Abner V. 1825 rb-d-467 (Mt)
Hampton, Andrew 1838 wb-b-291 (Wh)
Hampton, David 1841 wb-7-377 (Wi)
Hampton, Elizabeth 1839 wb-7-139 (Wi)
Hampton, Elizabeth 1850 wb-9-410 (Wi)
Hampton, Henry 1858 wb-12-585 (Wi)
Hampton, Jeremiah 1824 wb-3-673 (Wi)
Hampton, Jerry 1838 wb-6-476 (Wi)
Hampton, John 1818 rb-4-128 (Ru)
Hampton, John 1822 wb-3-374 (Rb)
Hampton, John 1854 wb-n-251 (Mt)
Hampton, John W. 1852 wb-h-Mar (O)
Hampton, Johnson 1854 wb-2-6 (Ct)
Hampton, Judith 1847 lr (Sn)
Hampton, Latitia 1853 wb-d-170 (Wh)
Hampton, Mary N. 1813 rb-b-156 (Mt)
Hampton, Mary Y.? 1813 rb-b-91 (Mt)
Hampton, Nancy 1851 wb-10-161 (Wi)
Hampton, Robert 1796 wb-#6 (Wa(
Hampton, Robert C. 1832 wb-5-184 (Wi)
Hampton, Rufus S. 1854 wb-11-304 (Wi)
Hampton, Sally B. 1861 wb-18-596 (D)
Hampton, Sarah Jane 1858 wb-13-8 (Wi)
Hampton, Waide 1851 wb-#71 (Mc)
Hampton, William 1827 wb-#71 (Mc)
Hampton, William 1829 wb-4-434 (Wi)
Hamrick, Jeremiah 1808 wb-#105 (Mu)
Hancock, Benjamin 1815 wb-#21 (Wl)
Hancock, Burrel A. 1858 rb-o-765 (Mt)

Hancock, David G. 1855 wb-n-626 (Mt)
Hancock, Dawson 1856 wb-#122 (Wl)
Hancock, E. H. 1856 wb-f-4 (G)
Hancock, Enoch 1859 lr (Gi)
Hancock, Francis 1851 rb-16-44 (Ru)
Hancock, G. D. 1860 wb-1-38 (Cf)
Hancock, George D. 1860 wb-00-6 (Cf)
Hancock, James 1839 wb-#125 (Wl)
Hancock, James 1839 wb-#127 (Wl)
Hancock, John 1817 wb-7-207 (D)
Hancock, Martin 1831 wb-#108 (Wl)
Hancock, N. K. 1846 wb-4-167 (Hr)
Hancock, Robert 1842 wb-2-361 (Hr)
Hancock, Samuel 1810 wb-#12 (Wl)
Hancock, Sean 1828 wb-#78 (Wl)
Hancock, Simon 1825 wb-#57 (Wl)
Hancock, Simon 1849 wb-#169 (Wl)
Hancock, Thomas 1817 rb-b-470 (Mt)
Hancock, Thomas 1851 rb-15-619 (Ru)
Hancock, Thos. G. 1852 wb-m-543 (Mt)
Hancock, Verlinda 1825 wb-#58 (Wl)
Hancock, William 1846 lr (Gi)
Hancock, _____ 1823 wb-#63 (Mu)
Hand, Jane 1814 rb-b-173 (Mt)
Hand, Jean 1814 rb-b-213 (Mt)
Hand, Levy 1813 rb-b-97 (Mt)
Handcock, Simon (Jr.) 1825 wb-#55 (Wl)
Handlin, John 1820 rb-c-355 (Mt)
Hanes, Thomas G. 1856 wb-17-101 (D)
Haney, Emanuel 1854 wb-#71 (Mc)
Haney, Martha 1837 wb-10-108 (Rb)
Hankins, A. G. 1852 wb-#107 (Wl)
Hankins, Abel 1844 wb-9-23 (K)
Hankins, Abraham 1841 wb-7-158 (K)
Hankins, Absolom 1820 wb-a-136 (Ro)
Hankins, Arthur 1835 wb-#114 (Wl)
Hankins, Charles 1818 wb-#28 (Wl)
Hankins, D. B. 1835 wb-#111 (Wl)
Hankins, Dandridge B. 1837 wb-#118 (Wl)
Hankins, Edward 1836 wb-3-502 (Je)
Hankins, Edward 1844 wb-5-320 (Gr)
Hankins, Edward sr. 1836 wb-3-426 (Je)
Hankins, George 1818 wb-a-113 (Ro)
Hankins, Grief B. 1835 wb-#111 (Wl)
Hankins, John 1824 wb-4-28 (K)
Hankins, John 1856 wb-#11 (Mo)
Hankins, John 1859 wb-#130 (Wl)
Hankins, John E. 1840 ib-2-78 (Ge)
Hankins, Joseph 1822 wb-a-175 (Ro)
Hankins, Matthew 1827 wb-#51 (Wl)
Hankins, Phebe 1853 wb-5-232 (Je)

Hankins, Richard 1800 wb-1-59 (Je)
Hankins, Richard 1843? wb-#142 (Wl)
Hankins, Robert 1794 wb-0-6 (K)
Hankins, Samuel 1803 wb-#1 (Wl)
Hankins, Samuel W. 1843 wb-a-132 (L)
Hankins, Sarah 1849 wb-10-210 (K)
Hankins, Sarah 1858 wb-2-86# (Ge)
Hankins, Thomas 1858 wb-f-166 (Ro)
Hankins, William 1824 rb-d-328 (Mt)
Hankins, William 1833 wb-1-20 (Gr)
Hankins, William A. 1851 wb-2-72# (Ge)
Hankins, William sr. 1821 wb-1-13# (Ge)
Hankins, Wilmoth 1839 wb-1-462 (Hy)
Hankins, Wm. 1830 rb-8-145 (Ru)
Hanks, Beauford 1835 wb-x-278* (Mu)
Hanks, John 1861 wb-#72 (Mc)
Hanks, Moses 1831 wb-#227 (Mu)
Hanks, R. H. 1853 wb-16-61 (D)
Hanks, Robert T. 1842 wb-#72 (Mc)
Hanks, Theophilus W. 1842 wb-2-551 (Hy)
Hanley, Crawford 1838 rb-10-91 (Ru)
Hanna, James 1817 wb-7-167 (D)
Hanna, James 1833 lr (Sn)
Hanna, James 1854 wb-f-47 (Mu)
Hanna, John 1813 wb-1-193 (Bo)
Hanna, John L. 1814 wb-1-183 (Sn)
Hanna, Nancy 1835 wb-2-184 (Sn)
Hanna, Samuel 1834 wb-x-255 (Mu)
Hanna, Samuel W. 1846 rb-13-465 (Ru)
Hanna, Susanna 1840 lr (Sn)
Hanna?, James 1841 wb-12-44 (D)
Hannah, Alexander 1836 wb-b-25 (Hd)
Hannah, Andrew 1835 wb-a-5 (O)
Hannah, Andrew 1843 wb-#40 (Wa(
Hannah, H. W. 1859 wb-a-132 (Ce)
Hannah, Jane 1847 wb-#47 (Wa(
Hannah, John 1837 wb-b-45 (Hd)
Hannah, John 1854 wb-16-312 (D)
Hannah, John D. 1845 wb-c-206 (G)
Hannah, John Mitchell 1831 wb-3-0 (Sm)
Hannah, Joseph 1810 wb-4-120 (D)
Hannah, Richard 1856 ib-1-389 (Ca)
Hannah, Sarah 1852 wb-d-386 (G)
Hannen, Jorden 1856 ib-1-399 (Ca)
Hanner, Avery 1858 wb-2-413* (Me)
Hanner, George W. 1853 wb-h-Apr (O)
Hannis, Rebecca 1848 wb-4-334 (Hr)
Hannis?, E. P. 1847 wb-4-168 (Hr)
Hannum, Henry 1845 wb-1-247 (Bo)
Hansard, Louisa 1854 ib-2-69 (Cl)
Hansard, Robert 1854 ib-2-69 (Cl)

Hansard, William 1846 wb-9-246 (K)
Hansbrough, D. 1835 wb-d-149 (Hn)
Hansbrough, Daniel 1833 wb-c-96 (Hn)
Hansbrough, Marcus 1838 rb-h-126 (Mt)
Hansel, James 1844 mr-2-113 (Be)
Hantz, Washington 1861 wb-#72 (Mc)
Haragis, Isabella 1857 wb-6-466 (Ma)
Haralson, Lea 1837 wb-#144 (Wl)
Harben, Wm. B. 1846 r39-1-40 (Dk)
Harber, Jacob 1858 wb-c-236 (L)
Harber, Silvy 1855 wb-b-7 (Ms)
Harbert, George W. 1860 as-c-219 (Ms)
Harbert, N. 1833 wb-#72 (Mc)
Harbert, Thomas 1817 wb-a-65 (Wh)
Harbeson, Robert 1851 wb-14-636 (D)
Harbison, Aaron 1860 wb-13-275 (K)
Harbison, Arthur 1857 wb-f-133 (Mu)
Harbour, James 1844 wb-c-189 (G)
Harbour, Samuel 1841 wb-d-250 (Hd)
Hardage, Andrew J. 1856 wb-6-253 (Ma)
Hardage, William T. 1856 wb-6-252 (Ma)
Hardage, Zachariah 1840 wb-3-256 (Ma)
Hardaway, James P. 1846 wb-1-134 (Sh)
Hardaway, Joseph 1851 wb-14-516 (Rb)
Hardcastle, Robert 1816 wb-1-24 (Fr)
Hardeman, Bailey 1838 wb-6-506 (Wi)
Hardeman, Constantine 1850 rb-15-439 (Ru)
Hardeman, George W. L. 1836 wb-6-242 (Wi)
Hardeman, Mary 1859 rb-19-624 (Ru)
Hardeman, Nicholas P. 1818 wb-2-387 (Wi)
Hardeman, Nicholas W. 1845 wb-8-343 (Wi)
Hardeman, Peter 1820 wb-3-193 (Wi)
Hardeman, Seth L. 1830 wb-4-537 (Wi)
Hardeman, Thomas 1836 wb-6-270 (Wi)
Harden, Asa 1814 wb-#14 (Wl)
Harden, Jeremiah 1829 wb-4-365 (Wi)
Harden, Tollison 1847 wb-1B-42 (A)
Harder, John N. 1819 wb-3-3 (Wi)
Harder, John N. 1831 wb-5-31 (Wi)
Harder, William 1826 wb-4-138 (Wi)
Hardgrave, Francis 1828 wb-9-246 (d)
Hardgraves, Samuel 1829 wb-4-447 (Wi)
Hardgraves, Sarah 1832 wb-10-38 (D)
Hardgraves, Skelton 1828 wb-9-204 (D)
Hardgraves, Skelton 1830 wb-1-233 (Ma)
Hardgraves, Susan 1829 wb-1-234 (Ma)
Hardgrove, Johnson 1825 wb-4-58 (Wi)
Hardgroves, John 1828 wb-1-82 (Ma)
Hardgroves, John 1832 wb-1-481 (Ma)
Hardiman, Constantine H. 1848 wb-b-250 (We)
Hardiman, Jane 1836 wb-3-376 (Je)

Hardin, Amos 1840 wb-7-92* (K)
Hardin, Amos 1853 wb-11-464 (K)
Hardin, Benjamin W. 1851 wb-2-24 (Li)
Hardin, Burgess 1848 wb-a-175 (Ms)
Hardin, Gabriel S. 1819 eb-1-93 (C)
Hardin, Gibson 1847 wb-d-332 (Hd)
Hardin, Giles 1847 wb-2-274 (W)
Hardin, Isaac B. 1819 wb-#106 (Mu)
Hardin, Isaac B. 1824? wb-#75 (Mu)
Hardin, Jacob 1852 wb-2-76# (Ge)
Hardin, James 1861 39-2-402 (Dk)
Hardin, Jeremiah 1798 wb-2-117 (D)
Hardin, Joab 1852 wb-a-257 (Di)
Hardin, John 1802 wb-1-94 (Rb)
Hardin, John 1846 wb-2-63# (Ge)
Hardin, John G. 1858 ib-2-50 (Wy)
Hardin, Letisha 1861 wb-13-486* (K)
Hardin, Lewis 1857 ib-1-475 (Wy)
Hardin, Lewis 1857 ib-2-8 (Wy)
Hardin, Mary 1846 wb-9-167 (K)
Hardin, Moses 1849 wb-1-370 (Li)
Hardin, Pleasant 1848 wb-b-183 (Mu)
Hardin, Pleasant G. 1839 wb-y-479 (Mu)
Hardin, Robert 1850 148-1-315 (Ge)
Hardin, Swan B. 1819? wb-#110 (Mu)
Hardin, W. E. 1812 lr (Sn)
Hardin, William 1810 wb-#77 (Mu)
Hardin, William P. 1816 wb-A-124 (Li)
Harding, Amelia E. 1860 wb-18-223 (D)
Harding, David M. 1854 wb-16-427 (D)
Harding, Elizabeth 1816 wb-7-57 (D)
Harding, F. Jefferson 1861 wb-18-451 (D)
Harding, George 1850 wb-14-526 (D)
Harding, George 1859 wb-7-35 (Ma)
Harding, Giles 1810 wb-4-105 (D)
Harding, Giles 1843 wb-12-405* (D)
Harding, Henry 1850 wb-14-525 (D)
Harding, Henry P. 1848 wb-14-251 (D)
Harding, John 1836 wb-1-170 (W)
Harding, Thomas 1805 wb-3-35 (D)
Harding, William 1833 wb-10-72 (D)
Harding, William 1848 wd-14-232 (D)
Hardison, Asa 1840 wb-z-71 (Mu)
Hardison, Charlotte 1859 wb-i-57 (St)
Hardison, James 1847 wb-b-104 (Mu)
Hardison, James M. 1843 wb-a-69 (Ms)
Hardison, John R. 1857 wb-5-77 (Hr)
Hardison, Joseph 1837 wb-y-119 (Mu)
Hardison, Joseph 1856 wb-h-291 (St)
Hardison, Joshua 1860 wb-b-89 (Ms)
Hardison, Mark 1853 wb-f-26 (Mu)

Hardison, Mary J. 1855 wb-5-55 (Hr)
Hardison, William 1831 wb-#224 (Mu)
Hardley, W. P. 1857 wb-16-355 (Rb)
Hardway, Nancy 1835 wb-y-116 (Mu)
Hardwick, Benjamin 1836 as-a-308 (Di)
Hardwick, William H. 1857 wb-#123 (Wl)
Hardy, Anne 1811 wb-4-126 (D)
Hardy, Catherine 1854 wb-#113 (Wl)
Hardy, Elizabeth 1822 wb-8-72 (D)
Hardy, Henson 1816 wb-4-423 (D)
Hardy, Henson 1816 wb-7-23 (D)
Hardy, James 1839 mr-1-298 (Be)
Hardy, James 1849 5-3-272 (Cl)
Hardy, Jinny 1811 wb-4-126 (D)
Hardy, Nehemiah 1839 wb-2-94 (Hy)
Hardy, O. 1859 rb-p-57 (Mt)
Hardy, Obadiah 1859 rb-p-69 (Mt)
Hardy, Rebecca K. 1827 wb-9-117 (D)
Hardy, Samuel 1850 wb-#72 (Mc)
Hardy, Thomas 1816 wb-4-408 (D)
Hardy, Thomas 1816 wb-7-18 (D)
Hardy, William 1850 wb-#174 (Wl)
Hardyman, George W. 1851 wb-14-434 (Rb)
Hare, Bryant 1825 rb-6-123 (Ru)
Hare, Starkey 1850 wb-2-82 (Sh)
Harelson, Burgess 1822 rb-d-47 (Mt)
Harelson, Burgess 1833 rb-f-536 (Mt)
Harelson, Ezekiel 1854 wb-i-234 (O)
Hargett, Benjamin W. 1840 wb-2-154 (Hy)
Hargett, Benjamin W. 1841 wb-2-239 (Hy)
Hargis, T. J. 1845 wb-4-281 (Ma)
Hargrave, John 1799 wb-2-144 (D)
Hargraves, Amy 1838 wb-2-234 (Sn)
Hargrove, Bennett 1843 wb-8-3 (Wi)
Hargrove, Bennett 1856 wb-12-288 (Wi)
Hargrove, Etheldred 1850 wb-m-128 (Mt)
Hargrove, John 1815 wb-1-214 (Sn)
Hargrove, John 1840 wb-2-115 (Hy)
Hargrove, Samuel 1827 wb-4-213 (Wi)
Hargroves, Thomas 1802 rb-a-160 (Mt)
Hargus, Jonathan 1837 abl-1-38 (T)
Harkins, Daniel sr. 1832 wb-1-340 (Ma)
Harkins, Joseph P. 1861 wb-2-349 (Li)
Harkins, William 1834 wb-1-375 (Hr)
Harkins, William C. 1859 wb-5-92 (Hr)
Harkleroads, Daniel 1845 wb-1-112 (Sh)
Harkreader, John 1835 wb-#108 (Wl)
Harkreader, John 1845 wb-#172 (Wl)
Harkreader, John W. 1837 wb-#117 (Wl)
Harkrider, Jacob 1858 wb-16-635 (Rb)
Harlan, Aaron 1854 ib-h-227 (F)

Harlan, Elizabeth 1837 wb-y-55 (Mu)
Harlan, John 1860 wb-1-261 (Hw)
Harland, Nathan 1860 wb-f-372 (G)
Harland, Samuel 1854 ib-h-202 (F)
Harle, Baldwin 1845 wb-4-104 (Je)
Harle, Leonard 1835 wb-3-410 (Je)
Harley, Elijah 1824 wb-A-387 (Li)
Harlin, Joseph 1841 wb-b-407 (G)
Harlin, Thomas 1823 wb-1-239 (Hw)
Harlin, Thomas 1856 wb-#119 (Wl)
Harlow, Lucus 1854 ib-1-298 (Wy)
Harlsfield, A. 1848 wb-4-242 (Hr)
Harly, Josiah 1842 wb-3-21 (Hr)
Harmack, Traves 1808 wb-#2 (Mu)
Harman, Isaac 1842 wb-2-539 (Hy)
Harman, Martin 1856 wb-#73 (Mc)
Harmand, Anthony 1793 wb-1-274 (D)
Harmon, Adam 1814 rb-b-187 (Mt)
Harmon, Adam 1844 wb-#42 (Wa(
Harmon, Adam jr. 1814 rb-b-154 (Mt)
Harmon, Elisha 1851 wb-g-379 (Hn)
Harmon, Harvey 1852 wb-11-283 (K)
Harmon, Henry 1848 wb-g-111 (Hu)
Harmon, Henry 1853 wb-h-167 (Hu)
Harmon, Henry L. 1854 wb-h-220 (Hu)
Harmon, Isaac 1847 wb-2-66# (Ge)
Harmon, Jacob 1844 wb-2-60# (Ge)
Harmon, Jacob 1852 wb-11-232 (K)
Harmon, Jacob 1855 148-1-521 (Ge)
Harmon, Jacob sr. 1848 148-1-255 (Ge)
Harmon, John 1798 wb-1-13# (Ge)
Harmon, John 1837 wb-1-13# (Ge)
Harmon, John 1857 149-1-64 (Ge)
Harmon, John 1860 iv-C-1 (C)
Harmon, Moses 1851 148-1-358 (Ge)
Harmon, Nancy 1846 wb-g-127 (Hn)
Harmon, Philip 1825 wb-a-7 (R)
Harmon, Reuben S. 1843 wb-e-543 (Hu)
Harn, Joseph 1857 wb-A-132 (Ca)
Harner, Christian 1817 wb-2-364 (K)
Harner, Christopher 1818 wb-3-19 (K)
Harness, Elizabeth J. 1859 wb-17-619 (D)
Harney, A. L. 1861 lr (Gi)
Harney, Elihu Ersken 1861 lr (Gi)
Harney, George W. 1805 rb-2-8 (Ru)
Harney, Sarah 1851 wb-15-119 (D)
Harney, Silby 1801 wb-2-117 (Sn)
Harp, Claiborn 1846 wb-0-64 (Cf)
Harp, William W. 1850 wb-c-376 (Wh)
Harpending, Andrew 1834 wb-5-346 (Wi)
Harper, Albert G. 1829 wb-1-128 (Hr)

Harper, Alfred W. 1863 wb-2-367 (Li)
Harper, Asa 1856 wb-16-321 (Rb)
Harper, Henry 1846 wb-g-193 (Hn)
Harper, James 1839 wb-b-72 (O)
Harper, James B. 1853 wb-i-114 (O)
Harper, John 1813 wb-a-19 (Wh)
Harper, Josiah sr. 1838 wb-3-0 (Sm)
Harper, Matthew 1839 wb-3-0 (Sm)
Harper, P. W. 1859 wb-2-278 (Li)
Harper, Richard 1851 ib-1-217 (Cl)
Harper, Robert 1807 wb-1-0 (Sm)
Harper, Robert B? 1839 abl-1-101 (T)
Harper, Saml. 1836 wb-2-86 (Hr)
Harper, T. J. 1859 wb-k-7 (O)
Harper, Thomas M. 1836 wb-a-61 (O)
Harper, Thomas M. 1846 wb-e-215 (O)
Harper, William 1822 wb-8-75 (D)
Harper, William 1836 wb-2-207 (Sn)
Harper, William B. 1842 wb-f-59 (Hn)
Harper, Williamson 1818 wb-7-219 (D)
Harpole, Abner 1827 wb-#66 (Wl)
Harpole, Abner 1827 wb-#76 (Wl)
Harpole, Adam (Sr.) 1828 wb-#120 (Wl)
Harpole, Barbra 1840 wb-#129 (Wl)
Harpole, George 1853 wb-#109 (Wl)
Harpole, John 1820 wb-#36 (Wl)
Harpole, Solomon 1808 wb-#6 (Wl)
Harr, Isaac 1824 wb-1-69 (Bo)
Harrald, John 1860 wb-b-458 (We)
Harraldson, Ephraim 1833 wb-#99 (Wl)
Harrel, L. D. 1856 wb-3e-13 (Sh)
Harrel, L. D. 1856 wb-3e-26 (Sh)
Harrel, William M. 1848 33-3-93 (Gr)
Harrell, Drewry 1839 5-2-114 (Cl)
Harrell, Eli 1804 wb-#2 (Wl)
Harrell, Henry 1851 rb-16-138 (Ru)
Harrell, J. C. 1858 wb-3-412 (Gr)
Harrell, James 1817 wb-2-286 (Wi)
Harrell, Lewis 1853 rb-16-708 (Ru)
Harrell, William 1844 wb-a-138 (Cr)
Harrell, William 1845 wb-a-321 (Cr)
Harrell, William sr. 1859 wb-3-599 (Gr)
Harrigan, Michael 1861 wb-13-464 (K)
Harrington, Birdsong 1845 wb-#148 (Wl)
Harrington, Charles 1795? wb-1-35 (Sn)
Harrington, Peter 1860 wb-#63 (Wa(
Harrington, Thomas 1815 wb-#65 (Wl)
Harrington, Thomas 1827 wb-#66 (Wl)
Harris, Abner 1826 rb-e-1 (Mt)
Harris, Abner 1846 wb-e-233 (O)
Harris, Adam G. 1841 wb-12-146* (D)

Harris, Alfred 1818 wb-#35 (Wl)
Harris, Alsea 1847 rb-14-196 (Ru)
Harris, Amelia 1861 wb-#133 (Wl)
Harris, Andrew 1812 wb-1-326 (Wi)
Harris, Andrew 1851 wb-7-0 (Sm)
Harris, Anne 1822 wb-8-107 (D)
Harris, Archer 1828 rb-e-275 (Mt)
Harris, Archer 1832 rb-f-408 (Mt)
Harris, Archibald 1823 rb-5-315 (Ru)
Harris, Arthur 1854 wb-n-342 (Mt)
Harris, Augustin 1849 rb-l-228 (Mt)
Harris, Augustus 1848 rb-l-99 (Mt)
Harris, Augustus A. 1848 rb-l-100 (Mt)
Harris, Benjamin 1814 rb-b-179 (Mt)
Harris, Benjamin 1834 wb-b-178 (Wh)
Harris, Beverly 1850 rb-15-370 (Ru)
Harris, Beverly sr. 1849 rb-14-500 (Ru)
Harris, Buckner 1848 as-b-392 (Di)
Harris, Buckner 1848 wb-a-198 (Di)
Harris, Burgess 1816 as-A-33 (Di)
Harris, Carey A. 1842 wb-7-575 (Wi)
Harris, Carey A. 1842 wb-7-583 (Wi)
Harris, Charles 1851 wb-14-474 (Rb)
Harris, Cheedle 1827 wb-6-65 (Rb)
Harris, Chubb 1821 wb-3-355 (Rb)
Harris, Coleman 1852 wb-15-62 (Rb)
Harris, Daniel 1828 as-a-170 (Di)
Harris, David 1827 wb-9-120 (D)
Harris, David P. 1829 wb-1-132 (Hr)
Harris, David V. 1827 wb-1-51 (Hr)
Harris, Deborah 1830 wb-#73 (Mc)
Harris, Edmond Kearney 1802 wb-1-254 (Rb)
Harris, Edmund 1835 wb-x-259* (Mu)
Harris, Edmund K. 1805 wb-1-169 (Rb)
Harris, Edward 1820 wb-#37 (Wl)
Harris, Edward 1839 wb-1-163 (Li)
Harris, Edward 1840 wb-#129 (Wl)
Harris, Edwin 1840 wb-10-536 (Rb)
Harris, Edwin 1847 wb-14-59 (D)
Harris, Eli M. 1858 wb-#126 (Wl)
Harris, Eli R. 1853 wb-#108 (Wl)
Harris, Elizabeth 1854 wb-16-276 (D)
Harris, Ephraim G. 1828 wb-#77 (Wl)
Harris, Ephraim Thomas 1832 rb-f-232 (Mt)
Harris, Eprim 1827 wb-#70 (Wl)
Harris, Errand? 1852 wb-#107 (Wl)
Harris, Evan 1836 wb-1-184 (Gr)
Harris, Ezra 1846 wb-13-451 (D)
Harris, Fergus S. 1859 wb-#129 (Wl)
Harris, Frances 1849 wb-#171 (Wl)
Harris, G. W. 1848 wd-14-219 (D)

Harris, George W. 1849 wb-14-421 (D)
Harris, Harrison H. 1835 rb-g-239 (Mt)
Harris, Hartwell 1813 wb-a-18 (Wh)
Harris, Henry 1821 Wb-3-213 (Wi)
Harris, Henry 1821 Wb-3-230 (Wi)
Harris, Henry 1829 wb-#191 (Mu)
Harris, Henry 1858 wb-b-51 (F)
Harris, Howell 1809 wb-4-49 (D)
Harris, Howell 1839 wb-d-304 (St)
Harris, Isaac 1858 wb-4-12 (Gr)
Harris, Isham 1844 wb-f-264 (Hn)
Harris, Jacob 1813 wb-4-209 (D)
Harris, James 1830 wb-1-89 (Fr)
Harris, James 1834 wb-c-348 (St)
Harris, James 1845 wb-a-66 (Ms)
Harris, James 1848 as-b-443 (Di)
Harris, James G. 1838 wb-2-335 (Ma)
Harris, James R. 1841 rb-12-6 (Ru)
Harris, James R. 1848 wb-9-29 (Wi)
Harris, Jeremiah 1829 wb-1-197 (Ma)
Harris, Jno. H. 1861 wb-18-565 (D)
Harris, John 1813 wb-A-38 (Li)
Harris, John 1814 wb-#17 (Wl)
Harris, John 1826 wb-#65 (Wl)
Harris, John 1827 wb-#71 (Wl)
Harris, John 1829 wb-3-0 (Sm)
Harris, John 1848 A-468-84 (Le)
Harris, John 1854 wb-11-474 (K)
Harris, John B. 1824 wb-#54 (Wl)
Harris, John C. 1842 wb-#40 (Wa(
Harris, John H. 1848 wb-2-39 (Sh)
Harris, John W. 1843 wb-b-41 (We)
Harris, John W. 1852 wb-4-577 (Mu)
Harris, Jonathan 1843 wb-c-98 (Wh)
Harris, Lewis 1853 as-b-120 (Ms)
Harris, Littleberry 1848 wb-14-100 (Rb)
Harris, Littleberry 1848 wb-14-74 (Rb)
Harris, Lucian J. 1845 lr (Sn)
Harris, Lucinda 1847 wb-14-150 (D)
Harris, Lucy 1856 wb-7-0 (Sm)
Harris, Maria 1808 wb-1-284 (Rb)
Harris, Mark 1840 as-a-27 (Ms)
Harris, Mark 1856 as-c-444 (Di)
Harris, Martha A. 1860 wb-a-161 (Ce)
Harris, Martha S. 1840 wb-2-269 (Sn)
Harris, Mary 1836 wb-x-362 (Mu)
Harris, Mary 1861 wb-a-214 (Ce)
Harris, Mary L. (Polly) 1853 wb-#107 (Wl)
Harris, Mathew 1826 wb-1-49 (Ma)
Harris, Mathew 1842 wb-11-311 (Rb)
Harris, Mathew 1844 as-b-199 (Di)

Harris, Michael 1832? wb-#96 (Wl)
Harris, Moody 1819 wb-7-357 (D)
Harris, Moses B. 1851 wb-14-657 (D)
Harris, Nathan 1814 wb-#15 (Wl)
Harris, Peter 1834 wb-1-27 (Gr)
Harris, Polly 1813 wb-#15 (Wl)
Harris, Pyre 1809 wb-4-28 (D)
Harris, R. F. 1856 rb-o-101 (Mt)
Harris, R. T. 1855 wb-n-570 (Mt)
Harris, Ransum 1857 rb-o-510 (Mt)
Harris, Rebecca L. 1851 wb-10-32 (Wi)
Harris, Reuben 1855 lr (Gi)
Harris, Reuben 1859 gs-1-251 (F)
Harris, Richard W. 1848 wb-#107 (Wl)
Harris, Richd. 1820 wb-3-131 (Rb)
Harris, Richmond 1825 wb-5-73 (Rb)
Harris, Richmond P. 1838 wb-1-182 (Fr)
Harris, Robert 1806 wb-1-107 (Sn)
Harris, Robert 1842 wb-5-220 (Gr)
Harris, Robert S. 1847 lr (Gi)
Harris, Rosana C. 1852 wb-15-364 (D)
Harris, Ruth 1837 wb-a-11 (Ms)
Harris, S. C. 1853 wb-15-488 (Rb)
Harris, Samuel 1824 rb-d-295 (Mt)
Harris, Samuel 1828 wb-1-51 (Hr)
Harris, Sarah 1858 wb-b-64 (Ms)
Harris, Sharderce? 1846 wb-b-158 (We)
Harris, Simpson 1833 rb-9-70 (Ru)
Harris, Simpson 1852 rb-16-322 (Ru)
Harris, Spencer 1852 wb-15-145 (Rb)
Harris, Stephen 1855 wb-12-187 (K)
Harris, Thomas 1852 as-b-70 (Ms)
Harris, Thomas 1855 wb-a-255 (Cr)
Harris, Thomas A. 1828 rb-8-121 (Ru)
Harris, Thomas F. 1852 wb-15-210 (D)
Harris, Thomas G. 1857 wb-17-158 (D)
Harris, Thomas K. 1816 wb-7-1 (D)
Harris, Thomas T. 1827 wb-1-73 (Fr)
Harris, Thomas W. 1860 wb-a-177 (Ce)
Harris, Timothy 1831 wb-b-54 (Wh)
Harris, Turner R. 1840 wb-2-174 (Hr)
Harris, Tyre 1813 wb-4-209 (D)
Harris, Tyree 1802 wb-2-266 (D)
Harris, Urbane 1853 wb-h-181 (Hu)
Harris, W. B. 1853 wb-#108 (Wl)
Harris, West 1819 wb-#66 (Mu)
Harris, West 1824? wb-#74 (Mu)
Harris, West 1851 wb-#177 (Wl)
Harris, Wilie 1840 wb-3-226 (Ma)
Harris, William 1815 wb-2-183 (K)
Harris, William 1820 wb-A-302 (Li)

Harris, William 1833 wb-8-271 (Rb)
Harris, William 1846 wb-13-365 (D)
Harris, William 1848 wb-5-55 (Ma)
Harris, William 1848 wd-14-227 (D)
Harris, William 1855 wb-n-491 (Mt)
Harris, William 1857 wb-f-120 (Mu)
Harris, William B. 1834 wb-1-127 (Fr)
Harris, William C. 1846 wb-a-281 (F)
Harris, William F. 1836 wb-#124 (Wl)
Harris, William F. 1849 wb-#171 (Wl)
Harris, William G. 1819 rb-4-208 (Ru)
Harris, William P. 1849 wb-#171 (Wl)
Harris, William Sr. 1855 wb-16-25 (Rb)
Harris, William sr. 1848 wb-14-177 (D)
Harris, Willis 1840 wb-3-271 (Ma)
Harris, Wm. 1831 wb-1-8 (Sh)
Harris, Wyatt 1853 wb-15-529 (D)
Harris, Zepheniah H. 1847 wb-b-232 (We)
Harrison, Andrew W. 1849 wb-5-60 (Ma)
Harrison, Answorth 1834 wb-#106 (Wl)
Harrison, Audly 1852 wb-3-126 (W)
Harrison, Bedee A. 1849 rb-l-259 (Mt)
Harrison, Benjamin 1818 wb-3-51 (K)
Harrison, Benjamin 1838 wb-e-55 (Hu)
Harrison, Charles C. 1858 wb-12-533 (Wi)
Harrison, Charles R. 1835 rb-g-104 (Mt)
Harrison, D. A. 1857 rb-19-17 (Ru)
Harrison, David 1821 rb-c-493 (Mt)
Harrison, David 1821 rb-c-518 (Mt)
Harrison, David 1822 rb-d-83 (Mt)
Harrison, David 1831 rb-f-158 (Mt)
Harrison, Doctor B. 1852 wb-f-7 (Mu)
Harrison, Dorothy 1840 rb-11-4 (Ru)
Harrison, Elizabeth 1857 wb-16-503 (Rb)
Harrison, Frankey 1851 wb-15-6 (D)
Harrison, G. W. 1849 ib-1-44 (Wy)
Harrison, George W. 1839 wb-2-264 (Sn)
Harrison, Henry 1857 wb-3e-42 (Sh)
Harrison, James 1811 wb-2-6 (Je)
Harrison, James 1830 lr (Sn)
Harrison, James A. 1848 rb-14-370 (Ru)
Harrison, Jeremiah 1793 wb-1-12# (Ge)
Harrison, Jessee 1855 wb-j-32 (O)
Harrison, John 1794 wb-1-313 (D)
Harrison, John 1810 wb-1-346 (Je)
Harrison, John 1829 wb-1-39 (Li)
Harrison, John 1833 wb-3-239 (Je)
Harrison, John 1838 wb-1-146 (La)
Harrison, John 1838 wb-11-309 (D)
Harrison, John 1839 mr-1-266 (Be)
Harrison, John 1847 wb-#154 (Wl)

Harrison, John 1856 wb-f-28 (Ro)
Harrison, John W. 1859 wb-3e-101 (Sh)
Harrison, Jordan 1860 wb-13-196 (Wi)
Harrison, Joseph 1851 wb-m-222 (Mt)
Harrison, Joshua 1826 rb-6-261 (Ru)
Harrison, Landsdon 1838 wb-#123 (Wl)
Harrison, Leonard 1849 wb-14-145 (Rb)
Harrison, Letes 1827 wb-#67 (Wl)
Harrison, Letice M. 1827 wb-#72 (Wl)
Harrison, Mary 1838 rb-h-149 (Mt)
Harrison, Mary 1840 wb-e-126 (Hn)
Harrison, Mary 1854 wb-n-296 (Mt)
Harrison, Mary H. 1829 rb-e-485 (Mt)
Harrison, Moses 1845 wb-#150 (Wl)
Harrison, Nancy 1844 mr-2-86 (Be)
Harrison, Nancy 1856 wb#25 (Gu)
Harrison, Oliver 1840 wb-e-101 (Hn)
Harrison, Peter 1845 wb-4-77 (Je)
Harrison, Peyton 1849 wb-2-47 (Sh)
Harrison, Reuben 1821 wb-3-238 (Rb)
Harrison, Reuben 1856 wb-h-246 (St)
Harrison, Richard 1795 wb-2-14 (D)
Harrison, Richard 1855 wb-3-219 (Sn)
Harrison, Richard R. 1850 wb-14-528 (D)
Harrison, Rolla 1858 wb-17-453 (D)
Harrison, Sophia (Mrs) 1856 rb-17-719 (Ru)
Harrison, Sophia 1855 rb-17-470 (Ru)
Harrison, Stephen S. 1815 wb-2-124 (Je)
Harrison, Sterling 1830 wb-#87 (Wl)
Harrison, Steth 1822 wb-#43 (Wl)
Harrison, Thomas 1821 wb-7-513 (D)
Harrison, Thomas 1838 wb-0-11 (Cf)
Harrison, Thomas 1846 wb#18 (Gu)
Harrison, Thomas 1856? wb#26 (Gu)
Harrison, Thos. 1809 wb-4-46 (D)
Harrison, Thweatt 1823 wb-#49 (Wl)
Harrison, Travis 1857 rb-o-359 (Mt)
Harrison, William 1811 wb-#4 (Mu)
Harrison, William 1830 wb-#1 (Mo)
Harrison, William 1833 rb-g-442 (Mt)
Harrison, William 1845 wb-12-547 (Rb)
Harrison, William 1855 wb#23 (Gu)
Harrison, William 1857 149-1-108 (Ge)
Harrison, William H. 1852 wb-15-210 (Rb)
Harrison, William P. 1842 wb-7-577 (Wi)
Harrison, William sr. 1855 wb-15-773 (Rb)
Harrison, Wm. P. 1833 wb-b-15 (G)
Harriss, David 1832 wb-1-233 (Hr)
Harriss, Eiphraim 1831 rb-f-198 (Mt)
Harriss, Joel 1854 wb-5-46 (Hr)
Harriss, John 1815 rb-b-79 (Mt)

Harriss, John 1858 wb-5-81 (Hr)
Harriss, Rebecca 1845 wb-d-198 (Hd)
Harriss, Rebecca 1847 wb-4-221 (Hr)
Harriss, Rice 1845 wb-d-198 (Hd)
Harriss, West 1835 wb-1-364 (Hr)
Harrisson, Jeremiah 1808 ib-1-230 (Ge)
Harrisson, Jesse 1856 wb-b-27 (F)
Harrisson, Lewis 1819 wb-7-360 (D)
Harrisson, Mildred 1846 rb-k-50 (Mt)
Harriway, Nancy 1826 wb-#135 (Mu)
Harrod, James 1784? wb-1-16 (D)
Harrod, William 1848 wb-#73 (Mc)
Harrold, Asa P. 1854 wb-e-182 (G)
Harrold, Peter 1826? wb-#151 (Mu)
Harston, Barbara 1841 wb-2-291 (Hy)
Hart, Alexander 1857 wb-#28 (Mo)
Hart, Anthony 1795 wb-2-19 (D)
Hart, Barnaby 1851 wb-14-445 (Rb)
Hart, Benjamin 1839 wb-#74 (Mc)
Hart, Cyrus 1854 lr (Sn)
Hart, E. F. 1852? wb-1B-292 (A)
Hart, Elijah 1854 ib-H-185 (F)
Hart, Elizabeth 1855 ib-h-433 (F)
Hart, George 1841 wb-12-130* (D)
Hart, George 1861 wb-h-548 (Hn)
Hart, George A. 1839 abl-1-122 (T)
Hart, Gilbert 1855 wb-a-1 (Cr)
Hart, Gilbert 1855 wb-a-241 (Cr)
Hart, Harrison D. 1854 lr (Gi)
Hart, Henry 1847 r39-1-26 (Dk)
Hart, Henry 1857 wb-16-378 (Rb)
Hart, James 1819 wb-1-297 (Sn)
Hart, James 1832 wb-1-214 (Hr)
Hart, James F. 1845 rb-13-145 (Ru)
Hart, James H. 1833 wb-x-86 (Mu)
Hart, John 1816 wb-A-125 (Li)
Hart, John 1842 wb-12-320* (D)
Hart, Joseph 1797 wb-1-8 (Rb)
Hart, Joseph 1828 wb-#175 (Mu)
Hart, Joseph 1832 wb-8-79 (Rb)
Hart, Mark 1835 rb-9-202 (Ru)
Hart, Mark 1846 rb-13-503 (Ru)
Hart, Moses 1831 wb-#218 (Mu)
Hart, Philemon 1853 wb-e-94 (G)
Hart, Robert M. 1857 lr (Sn)
Hart, S. A. M. 1856 as-b-245 (Ms)
Hart, Sampson 1790 wb-1-6 (Sn)
Hart, Samuel 1822 lr (Sn)
Hart, Samuel 1832 wb-10-36 (D)
Hart, Samuel 1838 wb-1-446 (Hy)
Hart, Sarah 1823 lr (Sn)

Hart, Sarah 1857 wb-#13 (Mo)
Hart, Thomas 1821 wb-1-0 (Sm)
Hart, Thomas D. 1849 wb-b-45 (L)
Hart, W. J. 1855 wb-h-91 (St)
Hart, William 1852 wb-f-9 (Mu)
Hart, William 1853 wb-n-67 (Mt)
Hart, William G. 1858 rb-19-490 (Ru)
Hart, William H. 1826 lr (Sn)
Hart, William J. 1855 wb-h-106 (St)
Hart, William W. 1848 wb-2-36 (Sh)
Hartier, G. A. 1851 as-b-7 (Ms)
Hartin, James 1816 wb-1-235 (Sn)
Hartless, William 1838 rb-10-200 (Ru)
Hartley, Laban 1844 wb-8-137 (Wi)
Hartley, Laban 1856 wb-12-242 (Wi)
Hartley, Laban 1857 wb-12-332 (Wi)
Hartley, Peter 1831 wb-b-147 (Ro)
Hartman, George 1840 wb-12-49* (D)
Hartman, Henry 1838 wb-#36 (Wa(
Hartman, John 1844 rb-12-533 (Ru)
Hartman, Joseph 1859 wb-2-88# (Ge)
Harton, Daniel 1827 wb-1-70 (Ma)
Harton, John J. 1838 wb-2-377 (Ma)
Harton, John P. 1838 wb-2-368 (Ma)
Harton, Joseph 1835 wb-b-192 (Wh)
Hartsell, Abraham 1860 wb-1D-3 (A)
Hartwell, Armstead 1855 rb-17-469 (Ru)
Hartwick, Coonrod 1837 wb-1-111 (La)
Hartwick, Coonrod 1848 wb-2-43 (La)
Harty, Dennis 1810 wb-2-32# (Ge)
Harvell, William 1849 r39-1-100 (Dk)
Harvey, Berry 1849 rb-l-479 (Mt)
Harvey, Elizabeth 1813 rb-b-144 (Mt)
Harvey, J. B. 1849 rb-l-508 (Mt)
Harvey, James 1815 rb-b-218 (Mt)
Harvey, Landon 1858 wb-3e-72 (Sh)
Harvey, M. D. 1845 wb-3-210 (Hr)
Harvey, Mark D. 1845 wb-3-228 (Hr)
Harvey, Nathan 1851 wb-11-3 (K)
Harvey, O. T. 1846 wb-4-36 (Hr)
Harvey, Richard 1853 wb-e-65 (G)
Harvey, Sarah V. 1860 wb-f-387 (G)
Harvey, Selby (Col.) 1828 wb-3-0 (Sm)
Harvey, Telitha 1852 wb-3-45 (Gr)
Harvey, Thomas 1838 wb-6-299 (K)
Harvey, William 1812 rb-b-60 (Mt)
Harvey, Zachariah 1815 rb-b-283 (Mt)
Harvey?, Daniel H. 1846 wb-4-114 (Hr)
Harvie, Wm. 1859 rb-p-297 (Mt)
Harvis, Benony 1829 wb-1-246 (Hw)
Harvy, Jonathan 1859 wb-1-7 (Br)

Harwell, Absalom 1818 lr (Gi)
Harwell, Buckner 1819 lr (Gi)
Harwell, Coleman 1841 lr (Gi)
Harwell, Elizabeth 1859 wb-3e-97 (Sh)
Harwell, Featherston 1843 lr (Gi)
Harwell, Gardner M. 1856 lr (Gi)
Harwell, Gilliam 1838 lr (Gi)
Harwell, Harbert 1822 wb-3-482 (Rb)
Harwell, Littleberry S. 1821 rb-5-166 (Ru)
Harwell, Sally 1841 lr (Gi)
Harwell, Samuel 1837 lr (Gi)
Harwell, Samuel 1849 lr (Gi)
Harwell, Sarah 1839 lr (Gi)
Harwell, Sterling 1819 wb-3-144 (Rb)
Harwell, Thomas 1854 wb-2-172 (Sh)
Harwell, Washington D. 1837 wb-10-140 (Rb)
Harwell, William H. 1850 ib-1-80 (Wy)
Harwell, William P. 1857 wb-b-35 (F)
Harwood, Henry 1851 as-c-108 (Di)
Harwood, John 1823 wb-8-169 (D)
Harwood, Richard W. 1860 mr (Gi)
Harwood, W. M. 1856 wb-e-414 (G)
Harwood, William A. 1856 wb-e-450 (G)
Hasel, Elisha M. 1816 Wb-2-188 (Wi)
Hash, William 1851 wb-3-110 (W)
Hashbarger, John 1845 wb-9-26 (K)
Hasket, John 1842 wb-4-15 (Je)
Haskew, John W. 1831 wb-5-50* (K)
Haskins, Chancy T. 1838 wb-11-323 (D)
Haskins, Ed 1820 wb-2-0 (Sm)
Haskins, Edmond 1825 wb-2-0 (Sm)
Haskins, Eman 1827 wb-2-0 (Sm)
Haskins, John 1835 wb-5-329 (K)
Haskins, John 1859 wb-1D-1 (A)
Haskins, Mary 1829 wb-1A-5 (A)
Haskins, Thomas C. 1831 wb-3-0 (Sm)
Haslam, Samuel 1858 wb-17-555 (D)
Haslerig, Conley F. 1828 wb-a-44 (R)
Haslerig, Richard 1827 wb-a-27 (R)
Haslerig, Thomas J. 1831 wb-a-79 (R)
Haslet, William 1819 wb-3-68 (K)
Haslett, William 1835 wb-5-362 (K)
Hason, Asa 1821 wb-a-147 (Ro)
Hassel, Cary 1850 wb-g-404 (Hu)
Hassell, Abraham 1807 lr (Sn)
Hassell, Amelia 1825 wb-4-12 (Wi)
Hassell, Amillian 1825 wb-3-757 (Wi)
Hassell, Asa 1860 lr (Sn)
Hassell, Dianah 1856 wb-e-446 (G)
Hassell, Isaac 1848 ib-1-12 (Wy)
Hassell, John 1806 lr (Sn)

Hassell, John 1827 lr (Sn)
Hassell, Presley 1842 wb-c-75 (G)
Hassler, Michael 1853 wb-e-419 (Ro)
Hastin, John 1843 wb-a-120 (Cr)
Hastings, Henry 1859 wb-h-327 (Hn)
Hastings, John 1830 wb-1-77 (Fr)
Hastings, William 1844 wb-12-250 (Rb)
Haston, David 1860 wb-a-317 (V)
Hasty, Benjamin 1840 wb-1-186 (Fr)
Hatch, Durant 1846 wb-1-130 (Sh)
Hatch, Henderson 1845 wb-1-56 (Br)
Hatch, Lemuel 1804 wb-2-397 (D)
Hatch, Peggy 1813 wb-2-73 (Rb)
Hatcher, Amos 1836 rb-g-332 (Mt)
Hatcher, Benjaman 1857 rb-o-349 (Mt)
Hatcher, Eli 1831 wb-b-135 (Hn)
Hatcher, Ethelbert H. 1853 wb-f-20 (Mu)
Hatcher, Henry 1830 rb-f-20 (Mt)
Hatcher, Henry 1857 rb-o-470 (Mt)
Hatcher, Henry H. 1834 wb-3-0 (Sm)
Hatcher, John 1850 rb-l-533 (Mt)
Hatcher, John B. 1857 wb-12-410 (Wi)
Hatcher, John R. 1857 wb-12-452 (Wi)
Hatcher, Nelson J. 1843 wb-d-34 (O)
Hatcher, Octavius C. 1856 wb-12-226 (Wi)
Hatcher, Octavius C. 1856 wb-12-238 (Wi)
Hatcher, Polly B. 1846 rb-k-115 (Mt)
Hatcher, R. N. 1860 rb-p-394 (Mt)
Hatcher, Ward 1841 wb-12-209* (D)
Hatcher, William 1847 wb-#154 (Wl)
Hatchett, C. F. 1854 wb-a-333 (Ms)
Hatchett, John 1850 as-a-206 (Ms)
Hathaway, David 1851 wb-5-89 (Ma)
Hathaway, George 1827 wb-9-111 (D)
Hathaway, John 1855 wb-3e-5 (Sh)
Hathaway, Lenard 1861 wb-b-74 (Dk)
Hathcock, Howel 1848 wb-0-84 (Cf)
Hathfield, Mathias 1847 wb-4-221 (Hr)
Hatler, Alexander 1846 wb-b-155 (We)
Hatley, Edwards 1861 wb-1-382 (Be)
Hatley, Hardy 1837 mr-1-27 (Be)
Hatley, Jackson 1860 wb-1-370 (Be)
Hatley, James 1845 wb-4-25 (Hr)
Hatley, Josiah 1842 wb-2-365 (Hr)
Hatley, Richard 1845 wb-a-256 (F)
Hatley, Sherrod 1838 mr-1-31 (Be)
Hatley, Sherrod 1839 wb-b-183 (Hd)
Hatsel, John B. 1845 rb-j-426 (Mt)
Hatton, Ebenezer 1837 wb-2-250 (Ma)
Hatton, Mary 1837 wb-2-221 (Ma)
Hatton, Robert 1862 wb-#136 (Wl)

Haughner, Coleman T. 1843 wb-c-119 (G)
Haughton, J. C. 1836 wb-a-134 (O)
Haul, Joel 1836 wb-1-62 (Bo)
Haun, Abraham 1847 wb-1-253 (Hw)
Haun, Adam 1823 lw (Ct)
Haun, Andrew B. 1853 wb-5-302 (Je)
Haun, Catharine 1851 wb-2-73# (Ge)
Haun, Christopher 1844 wb-2-62# (Ge)
Haun, Jacob 1846 148-1-142 (Ge)
Haun, John 1815 wb-2-113 (Je)
Haun, John 1854 lw (Ct)
Haun, Matthias 1814 lw (Ct)
Hauser, Harmon 1854 wb-i-180 (O)
Hauser, John H. 1855 wb-16-534 (D)
Havener, Peter 1850 148-1-312 (Ge)
Haw, William 1830 wb-3-0 (Sm)
Hawk, Abraham 1854 wb-12-1 (K)
Hawk, Jeremiah 1842 wb-7-569 (Wi)
Hawk, MadisonC. 1849? wb-#74 (Mc)
Hawk, Palser 1847 wb-2-66# (Ge)
Hawk, William 1857 149-1-92 (Ge)
Hawke, Thomas 1819 wb-3-294 (St)
Hawkings, Grant 1815 wb-#11 (Mu)
Hawkins, Allen 1821 wb-#102 (Mu)
Hawkins, Amosa 1818 wb-2-392 (Wi)
Hawkins, Anna 1846 wb-5-426 (Gr)
Hawkins, Benjamin 1827 wb-#74 (Mc)
Hawkins, Benjamine H. 1850 wb-2-69 (Sh)
Hawkins, Borden 1798 lr (Sn)
Hawkins, E. O. 1858 rb-p-15 (Mt)
Hawkins, Edward 1836 wb-3-362 (Je)
Hawkins, Elizabeth 1820 wb-a-132 (Ro)
Hawkins, Elizabeth 1858 wb-12-548 (Wi)
Hawkins, Elizabeth M. 1851 wb-14-615 (D)
Hawkins, George W. 1836 wb-b-224 (Wh)
Hawkins, James 1852 wb-15-88 (Rb)
Hawkins, James A. 1855 wb-#117 (Wl)
Hawkins, James O. 1840 wb-b-334 (Hd)
Hawkins, John 1821 wb-#105 (Mu)
Hawkins, John 1842 wb-z-430 (Mu)
Hawkins, John 1849 wb-9-295 (Wi)
Hawkins, John M. 1852 wb-a-234 (Cr)
Hawkins, John T. 1839 wb-b-161 (Hd)
Hawkins, Joseph J. 1850 wb-m-57 (Mt)
Hawkins, Maria 1839 lr (Gi)
Hawkins, Martha Jane 1842 wb-3-610 (Ma)
Hawkins, Mary 1834 wb-8-281 (Rb)
Hawkins, Moses 1845 wb-c-218 (G)
Hawkins, Moses B. 1846 wb-c-302 (G)
Hawkins, N. M. 1836 wb-x-346 (Mu)
Hawkins, Noah M. 1837 wb-x-480 (Mu)

Hawkins, Peter (B) 1839 wb-c-50 (Ro)
Hawkins, Reuben 1851 ib-1-175 (Ca)
Hawkins, Robert 1840 lr (Sn)
Hawkins, Robert Z. 1838 wb-1-177 (Fr)
Hawkins, Samuel 1822 rb-d-91 (Mt)
Hawkins, Samuel 1834 wb-8-298 (Rb)
Hawkins, Samuel B. 1854 wb-2-164 (Sh)
Hawkins, Samuel C. 1829 rb-e-405 (Mt)
Hawkins, Sarah 1885 wb-1-11# (Ge)
Hawkins, Stephen 1832 wb-5-197 (Wi)
Hawkins, Thomas A. 1852 wb-a-197 (Cr)
Hawkins, Uriah E. 1854 wb-e-164 (G)
Hawkins, Uzzell 1821 wb-#103 (Mu)
Hawkins, William (Rev.) 1814 wb-#29 (Mu)
Hawkins, William 1814 wb-#103 (Mu)
Hawkins, William 1834 wb-1-369 (Hr)
Hawkins, Willis N. 1850 wb-14-536 (D)
Hawks, George W. 1846 wb-b-186 (We)
Hawks, John 1855 wb-#110 (Wl)
Hawks, John 1860 wb-8-65 (Sm)
Hawks, Thomas H. 1848 wb-#156 (Wl)
Hawks, William 1837 wb-#117 (Wl)
Hawley, Crawford 1838 rb-10-145 (Ru)
Hawn, Jacob 1846 wb-9-171 (K)
Haworth, Absalom 1827 wb-1-12# (Ge)
Haworth, Ann 1834 wb-2-44# (Ge)
Haworth, Ann 1844 148-1-90 (Ge)
Haworth, Ann 1858 149-1-115 (Ge)
Haworth, Mary 1846 wb-2-65# (Ge)
Haworth, Nathaniel 1839 wb-2-51# (Ge)
Haworth, Richard 1807 wb-1-334 (Je)
Haworth, Richard 1813 wb-2-54 (Je)
Hawser, Elizabeth 1848 wb-10-1 (K)
Hawser, John 1849 wb-10-110 (K)
Hawthorn, Robert H. 1861 wb-1-389 (Be)
Hay, Ann 1814 wb-4-291 (D)
Hay, Ann 1826 wb-9-21 (D)
Hay, Balaam 1832 wb-5-157 (Wi)
Hay, Balaam 1836 wb-6-156 (Wi)
Hay, Benjamin 1819 wb-#106 (Mu)
Hay, Charles 1793 wb-#4 (Wa(
Hay, David 1801 wb-2-205 (D)
Hay, Edith 1807 wb-1-172 (Wi)
Hay, Elijah 1837 wb-a-239 (O)
Hay, Enos 1835 wb-a-23 (O)
Hay, Isaac 1838 wb-a-5 (Dk)
Hay, James 1844 wb-8-152 (Wi)
Hay, John 1808 wb-4-14 (D)
Hay, John 1827 wb-4-234 (Wi)
Hay, John 1856 wb-12-259 (Wi)
Hay, John G. 1835 wb-10-513 (D)

Hay, Lucy 1857 wb-12-423 (Wi)
Hay, Martha 1843 wb-8-69 (Wi)
Hay, Rebecca 1797 wb-1-13# (Ge)
Hay, Richard 1859 wb-13-76 (Wi)
Hay, William 1841 wb-7-397 (Wi)
Hay, William H. 1849 wb-9-307 (Wi)
Hayes, Adam 1833 rb-9-16 (Ru)
Hayes, Anderson S. 1859 as-c-196 (Ms)
Hayes, Archerbald 1845 rb-13-145 (Ru)
Hayes, Jacob 1843 wb-8-164 (K)
Hayes, James T. 1840 wb-b-366 (Wh)
Hayes, Jane 1839 wb-7-89 (Wi)
Hayes, Mary R. 1846 wb-a-152 (Ms)
Hayes, Oliver B. 1859 wb-17-631 (D)
Hayes, Robert 1839 wb-e-30 (Hn)
Hayes, Robert 1860 wb-13-176 (Wi)
Hayes, Samuel 1815 rb-3-53 (Ru)
Hayes, Sarah 1831 wb-9-560 (D)
Hayes, Thomas 1845 wb-5-405 (Gr)
Hayes, William 1811 wb-4-125 (D)
Hayes, William 1811 wb-4-157 (D)
Hayes, William 1857 wb-3-332 (W)
Haymes, Daniel D. 1843 wb-#75 (Mc)
Haymes, Reuben 1824 wb-#75 (Mc)
Haymes, William 1835 wb-#75 (Mc)
Hayn, Emand? 1839 mr-1-262 (Be)
Haynes, Abraham 1838 rb-10-195 (Ru)
Haynes, Anderson 1831 wb-5-79 (Wi)
Haynes, Andrew J. 1859 rb-20-78 (Ru)
Haynes, Anthony 1819 rb-c-213 (Mt)
Haynes, Christopher 1830 wb-1-248 (Hw)
Haynes, David N. 1855 lw (Ct)
Haynes, David O. 1844 rb-j-268 (Mt)
Haynes, F. B. 1854 wb-11-328 (Wi)
Haynes, Francis 1855 wb-1-261 (Hw)
Haynes, Franklin B. 1854 wb-11-395 (Wi)
Haynes, George 1846 wb-c-348 (G)
Haynes, Harbert 1846 mr-2-213 (Be)
Haynes, Henry 1830 wb-1-11 (Sh)
Haynes, Henry G. 1836 wb-d-195 (Hn)
Haynes, Herbert 1832 wb-1-244 (Hr)
Haynes, Ira 1857 wb-2-352 (Me)
Haynes, James 1824 wb-#76 (Mu)
Haynes, James 1848 wb-g-269 (Hn)
Haynes, James 1853 lw (Ct)
Haynes, James M. 1854 rb-17-64 (Ru)
Haynes, John 1834 wb-#75 (Mc)
Haynes, John D. 1843 wb-3-0 (Sm)
Haynes, John S. 1852 rb-16-335 (Ru)
Haynes, John W. 1856 rb-18-161 (Ru)
Haynes, Joseph 1843 wb-4-102 (Ma)

Haynes, Joseph 1845 wb-a2-247 (Mu)
Haynes, Josiah 1839 wb-y-487 (Mu)
Haynes, Josiah 1852 wb-4-530 (Mu)
Haynes, Louis 1857 wb-a-258 (T)
Haynes, Margaret A. 1855 rb-17-527 (Ru)
Haynes, Mildred 1847 wb-d-82 (G)
Haynes, Nancy 1830 rb-f-116 (Mt)
Haynes, Nathan 1856 wb-3-305 (Gr)
Haynes, Nathaniel 1852 rb-16-319 (Ru)
Haynes, Philadelphia 1829 rb-7-277 (Ru)
Haynes, Robert 1845 wb-1-349 (La)
Haynes, Sarah 1831 lr (Sn)
Haynes, Sterling 1851 33-3-412 (Gr)
Haynes, Thomas 1859 wb-h-345 (Hn)
Haynes, Thos. G. 1852 wb-e-16 (G)
Haynes, William 1841 rb-i-58 (Mt)
Haynes, William 1847 33-3-1 (Gr)
Haynes, William C. 1829 wb-1-112 (Hr)
Haynie, Elijah 1846 wb-7-0 (Sm)
Haynie, Jesse 1842 wb-2-293 (Sn)
Haynie, Jesse 1852 wb-a-194 (T)
Haynie, John N. 1823 wb-8-172 (D)
Haynie, Mary J. 1855 wb-12-73 (K)
Haynie, Samuel 1838 wb-6-281 (K)
Haynie, Samuel 1854 wb-12-15 (K)
Haynie, Spencer 1825 wb-4-50 (K)
Haynie, Spencer 1839 wb-6-392 (K)
Haynie, Stephen 1816 wb-2-213 (K)
Haynie, William 1826 lr (Sn)
Haynie, William 1826 wb-3-0 (Sm)
Hays, A. C. 1824 wb-1-32 (Ma)
Hays, A. F. 1856 wb-h-67 (Hn)
Hays, Andrew C. 1840 wb-y-682 (Mu)
Hays, Annie 1856 wb-2-83# (Ge)
Hays, Archer 1845 rb-13-205 (Ru)
Hays, Blackman 1847 wb-14-105 (D)
Hays, Carter 1844 wb-#75 (Mc)
Hays, Charles 1805 as-1-124 (Ge)
Hays, Charles 1820 wb-1-0 (Sm)
Hays, Charles 1854 wb-16-385 (D)
Hays, Cullen 1855 wb-6-344 (Ma)
Hays, Edward 1840 wb-1-352 (W)
Hays, H. P. 1842 wb-#137 (Wl)
Hays, Henry 1836 wb-b-131 (G)
Hays, Henry P. 1844 wb-#143 (Wl)
Hays, Hugh 1845 wb-#147 (Wl)
Hays, Isaac 1856 wb-j-140 (O)
Hays, J. W. 1856 as-c-457 (Di)
Hays, James 1812 wb-1-0 (Sm)
Hays, James 1816 wb-1-14# (Ge)
Hays, James 1820? wb-#104 (Mu)

Hays, James 1828 wb-2-626 (Je)
Hays, James 1832 wb-10-32 (D)
Hays, James 1853 wb-5-228 (Je)
Hays, James 1857 wb-2-170 (Li)
Hays, James P. 1848 wb-2-37 (Sh)
Hays, Jane (Mrs) 1836 wb-2-199 (Ma)
Hays, Jane 1834 wb-1-428 (Ma)
Hays, Jesse 1807 wb-#1 (Mu)
Hays, John 1811 wb-#9 (Wl)
Hays, John 1814 wb-1-0 (Sm)
Hays, John 1822 wb-A-290 (Li)
Hays, John 1826 as-A-123 (Di)
Hays, John 1832 wb-5-119 (Wi)
Hays, John 1836 wb-#116 (Wl)
Hays, John 1841 wb-12-34 (D)
Hays, John M. 1858 as-c-127 (Ms)
Hays, Joseph 1831 wb-3-187 (Je)
Hays, Joseph 1846 wb-b-142 (We)
Hays, Joseph 1846 wb-d-3 (G)
Hays, Joseph 1857 wb-2-85# (Ge)
Hays, Joseph L. 1847 wb-2-66# (Ge)
Hays, Judy 1841 wb-e-286 (Hn)
Hays, Mary 1851 wb-A-76 (Ca)
Hays, Nicholas 1800 wb-1-188 (Je)
Hays, P. H. 1847 wb-#154 (Wl)
Hays, P. P. 1849 wb-#165 (Wl)
Hays, Peter 1841 wb-b-397 (G)
Hays, Polly 1829 wb-#83 (Wl)
Hays, Rebecca 1819 wb-#33 (Wl)
Hays, Robert 1834 wb-1-332 (Hr)
Hays, Robert 1841 wb-2-55# (Ge)
Hays, Robert 1859 149-1-153 (Ge)
Hays, Sally 1826 wb-9-58 (D)
Hays, Sam 1793 wb-1-286 (D)
Hays, Sampson 1853 wb-#180 (Wl)
Hays, Samuel 1852 wb-4-594 (Mu)
Hays, William 1836 wb-10-537 (D)
Hays, William 1858 wb-f-212 (Ro)
Hays, William 1858 wb-f-216 (Ro)
Hays, William F. 1858 39-2-242 (Dk)
Hays, William P. 1836 wb-6-90 (Wi)
Hays, William S. 1861 wb-18-605 (D)
Hays, Wm. 1787 wb-1-67 (D)
Hays, Zachariah 1816 wb-7-52 (D)
Hayse, Jacob 1856 wb-j-161 (O)
Hayse, Ruben 1846 wb-7-0 (Sm)
Hayse, William H. 1854 wb-1-91 (Jo)
Hayter, Abraham 1829 eb-1-248 (C)
Hayter, Abraham 1829 eb-1-255 (C)
Hayter, Enos 1860 iv-C-36 (C)
Haywood, Edmond 1837 mr-1-256 (Be)

Haywood, George W. 1846 wb-a-154 (Ms)
Haywood, J. D. S. 1856 wb-b-20 (Ms)
Haywood, John 1827 wb-9-82 (D)
Haywood, John 1859 as-c-555 (Di)
Haywood, John sr. 1797 wb-1-13# (Ge)
Haywood, William 1842 wb-7-339 (K)
Hazard, John 1852 wb-#178 (Wl)
Hazard, Lewis 1844 wb-7-0 (Sm)
Haze, Shadrick 1854 wb-1-67 (R)
Hazel, Samuel K. 1833 wb-10-157 (D)
Hazlegrove, Mary 1861 wb-5-115 (Hr)
Hazlet, Kindler 1815 wb-#13 (Wa(
Hazlewood, Benjamin 1847 wb-9-406 (K)
Hazlewood, James 1838 wb-6-512 (Wi)
Hazlewood, Joshua 1862 wb-4-30 (Gr)
Hazlewood, Mary Ann 1849 wb-10-107 (K)
Hazlewood, Richard C. 1837 wb-a-201 (O)
Hazlewood, Thomas 1858 wb-4-93 (Je)
Head, Henry 1840 wb-b-244 (O)
Head, Henry 1852 Ir (Sn)
Head, Martha 1854 wb-15-446 (Rb)
Head, Robert 1854 wb-15-446 (Rb)
Head, Thurston 1827 wb-9-118 (D)
Headerick, John 1847 wb-1-256 (Hw)
Headley, Noah 1838 wb-a-24 (Ms)
Headon, John 1805 wb-1-86 (Sn)
Headrick, James S. 1853 wb-5-189 (Je)
Headrick, John B. 1862 wb-1-264 (Hw)
Headrick, William C. 1847 wb-e-28 (Ro)
Headrick, William W. 1852 wb-5-137 (Je)
Heald, H. O. T. 1854 39-1-340 (Dk)
Heald, Harrison O. T. 1854 39-2-26 (Dk)
Heard, Abraham 1822 wb-#75 (Mc)
Heard, Armstrong 1830 rb-8-107 (Ru)
Heard, John D. 1828 wb-#75 (Mc)
Hearn, Ebenezer 1835 wb-10-420 (D)
Hearn, Ebenezer 1844 wb-#143 (Wl)
Hearn, Edward 1829 wb-#80 (Wl)
Hearn, Elizabeth 1853 wb-#109 (Wl)
Hearn, George 1850 wb-#173 (Wl)
Hearn, James W. 1848 wb-#156 (Wl)
Hearn, James W. 1862 wb-#137 (Wl)
Hearn, John 1826 wb-#64 (Wl)
Hearn, John 1838 wb-#122 (Wl)
Hearn, L. 1860 gs-1-551 (F)
Hearn, Milbrey 1841 wb-#132 (Wl)
Hearn, N. N. 1860 gs-1-551 (F)
Hearn, Nancy 1838 wb-#123 (Wl)
Hearn, Purnel 1827 wb-3-0 (Sm)
Hearn, Purnel 1831 wb-#92 (Wl)
Hearn, Rachel C. 1845 wb-#159 (Wl)

Hearn, Stephen L. 1858 gs-1-69 (F)
Hearn, Susan 1841 wb-#135 (Wl)
Hearn, Susan 1841 wb-3-0 (Sm)
Hearn, Tabitha 1856 wb-#119 (Wl)
Hearn, Thomas 1829 wb-#180 (Wl)
Hearn, Thomas A. 1840 wb-b-250 (O)
Hearn, William F. 1852 wb-#107 (Wl)
Heart, Lenard 1852 wb-1-118 (Ct)
Heart, Leonard 1849 wb-1-134 (Ct)
Heartston, William 1841 wb-7-260 (K)
Heartwell, Alfred 1835 rb-9-256 (Ru)
Heath, Abner C. 1838 wb-1-147 (Li)
Heath, Chappel B. 1849 wb-g-237 (O)
Heath, Chappell 1849 wb-g-212 (O)
Heath, George 1828 wb-1-18 (Li)
Heath, Henry 1838 wb-#123 (Wl)
Heath, John 1843 wb-a-39 (D)
Heath, Pamelia (Jr.) 1848 wb-#167 (Wl)
Heath, Richard 1852 rb-16-351 (Ru)
Heath, William 1836 wb-6-68 (K)
Heathcock, John 1855 wb-n-627 (Mt)
Heathcock, Young 1841 rb-i-116 (Mt)
Heathenan, James sr. 1846 rb-k-308 (Mt)
Heathman, Elizabeth 1859 rb-p-152 (Mt)
Heathman, Elizabethh F. 1861 rb-p-616 (Mt)
Heathman, James 1832 rb-f-401 (Mt)
Heathman, James 1848 rb-l-195 (Mt)
Heathman, Joseph 1844 rb-j-123 (Mt)
Heaton, Amos 1795 wb-2-13 (D)
Heaton, Amos 1814 wb-4-308 (D)
Heaton, Amos 1860 wb-18-263 (D)
Heaton, Dickson 1841 wb-7-408 (Wi)
Heaton, Elizabeth 1805 wb-3-33 (D)
Heaton, Enoch 1836 wb-6-100 (Wi)
Heaton, Mary 1839 wb-7-184 (Wi)
Heaton, Robert 1844 wb-13-9 (D)
Heaton, Thomas 1853 wb-15-534 (D)
Hebron, John 1837 wb-11-78 (D)
Hedgcock, Mary H. 1853 wb-h-101 (Hu)
Hedge, William C. 1854 wb-h-318 (Hu)
Hedge, Wm. 1858 as-c-533 (Di)
Hedgecock, Lewis 1838 wb-e-149 (Hu)
Hedgecock, Moses H. 1853 wb-h-121 (Hu)
Hedgecock, Thomas 1817 wb-A-202 (Li)
Hedgepatch, Jesse 1821 rb-5-163 (Ru)
Hedgepeth, Jeremiah 1857 wb-2-9 (Li)
Hedger, William 1835 wb-1-139 (Fr)
Hedgpeth, John 1835 rb-9-263 (Ru)
Hedlon, Enoch 1835 wb-6-69 (Wi)
Heffington, William 1850 ib-1-63 (Wy)
Hefley, William 1851 wb-5-90 (Ma)

Heflin, Absalom 1833 rb-f-510 (Mt)
Heflin, Hawkins 1856 wb-7-0 (Sm)
Heflin, Simon 1861 rb-p-546 (Mt)
Heflin, Susan 1859 rb-p-33 (Mt)
Hegarty, P. H. 1844 wb-#140 (Wl)
Heggio, Solomon 1845 rb-k-35 (Mt)
Heidle, Charles F. 1857 wb-3e-51 (Sh)
Heiflen, William C.? 1818 rb-4-132 (Ru)
Heifler, William 1817 rb-4-92 (Ru)
Heire?, Joseph 1836 wb-b-133 (G)
Hellen, Mary 1798 wb-1-44 (Sn)
Hellman (B), Charles 1854 wb-xx-410 (St)
Helm, Susanna 1854 wb-11-98 (Wi)
Helmantoller, Michael 1815 wb-1-0 (Sm)
Helms, Charles E. 1851 wb-g-502 (Hu)
Helms, George 1816 wb-2-231 (K)
Helms, James 1841 as-a-53 (Ms)
Helms, Jozedeck 1833 wb-5-210 (K)
Helms, Mary J. 1861 wb-13-410 (K)
Helms, William 1840 wb-#76 (Mc)
Helterbran, Absalom 1837 wb-9-438 (Rb)
Helterbran, Henry 1823 wb-4-83 (Rb)
Helterbrand, Conrad 1835 wb-9-188 (Rb)
Helterbrand, Eli 1839 wb-10-242 (Rb)
Helton, A. G. 1857 wb-3-393 (Gr)
Helton, Henry 1828 wb-4-336 (K)
Helton, Peter 1849 rb-15-117 (Ru)
Helton, Robert 1840 rb-11-23 (Ru)
Hemley, Wilson 1831 wb-1-235 (Ma)
Hemphill, James 1839 wb-a-28 (Ms)
Hemphill, Joseph 1834 wb-#76 (Mc)
Henderson, Adam 1853 wb-15-538 (D)
Henderson, Alexander 1822 wb-#103 (Mu)
Henderson, Alexander 1840 wb-2-52# (Ge)
Henderson, Alexander 1842 wb-1-63 (Bo)
Henderson, Alexander A. 1856? wb-#15 (Mo)
Henderson, Ann B. 1854 wb-h-10 (St)
Henderson, Ann B. 1854 wb-h-24 (St)
Henderson, B. E. 1860 rb-p-410 (Mt)
Henderson, B. H. 1849 wb-a-378 (F)
Henderson, Benjamin 1852 wb-xx-3 (St)
Henderson, Benjamin Franklin 1849 lr (Gi)
Henderson, Bennet E. 1860 rb-p-414 (Mt)
Henderson, Charles 1831 wb-3-148 (Je)
Henderson, Daniel 1825 wb-4-57 (Wi)
Henderson, Daniel 1836 rb-g-427 (Mt)
Henderson, Edward H. 1852 wb-4-494 (Mu)
Henderson, Elizabeth 1860 wb-1-61 (Se)
Henderson, Ellender 1848 lr (Gi)
Henderson, Ezekiel 1828 wb-#194 (Mu)
Henderson, Ezekiel 1839 wb-y-304 (Mu)

Henderson, Hezekiah 1859 wb-c-327 (L)
Henderson, Hugh 1815 wb-2-293 (Wi)
Henderson, James 1793 wb-1-12# (Ge)
Henderson, James 1815 rb-3-28 (Ru)
Henderson, James 1831 wb-#217 (Mu)
Henderson, James 1857 rb-18-474 (Ru)
Henderson, James C. 1838 wb-#76 (Mc)
Henderson, James H. 1836 wb-2-101 (Ma)
Henderson, James M. 1831 wb-a-23 (Cr)
Henderson, Jane 1841 lr (Sn)
Henderson, Jeramiah 1856 ib-2-213 (Cl)
Henderson, Jesse 1836 wb-2-101 (Ma)
Henderson, Jesse B. 1835 wb-2-261 (Ma)
Henderson, John 1804 Wb-1-132 (Wi)
Henderson, John 1826 wb-1-11# (Ge)
Henderson, John 1828 rb-8-4 (Ru)
Henderson, John 1846 wb-1-304 (Li)
Henderson, John 1849 rb-l-422 (Mt)
Henderson, John 1856 wb-#26 (Mo)
Henderson, John 1860 rb-20-624 (Ru)
Henderson, John L. 1840 rb-11-32 (Ru)
Henderson, John L. 1855 wb-2-112 (Li)
Henderson, John sr. 1836 wb-2-46# (Ge)
Henderson, Joseph 1834 wb-2-43# (Ge)
Henderson, Joseph 1856 wb-j-134 (O)
Henderson, L. B. 1858 rb-o-789 (Mt)
Henderson, Logan 1847 rb-13-743 (Ru)
Henderson, Lucy 1843 wb-8-85 (Wi)
Henderson, Margaret 1854 rb-17-301 (Ru)
Henderson, Marrion 1856 rb-o-68 (Mt)
Henderson, Mary 1830 wb-3-129 (Je)
Henderson, Mary 1855 wb-3-202 (Gr)
Henderson, Mary H. 1854 wb-2-173 (Sh)
Henderson, Mary Susan 1849 33-3-142 (Gr)
Henderson, N. Lucinda C. 1849 lr (Gi)
Henderson, Noden 1831 wb-3-150 (Je)
Henderson, Pleasant 1837 wb-1-255 (W)
Henderson, Preston 1858 wb-#124 (Wl)
Henderson, Rebecca 1853 wb-2-83 (Li)
Henderson, Richard 1857 wb-1-78 (Dy)
Henderson, Richard H. 1845 wb-13-191 (D)
Henderson, Robert 1834 wb-5-426 (Wi)
Henderson, Robert 1836 wb-2-48# (Ge)
Henderson, Robert 1836 wb-6-122 (Wi)
Henderson, Samuel 1816 wb-1-19 (Fr)
Henderson, Samuel 1821 rb-5-96 (Ru)
Henderson, Samuel 1829 wb-4-367 (Wi)
Henderson, Samuel 1843 wb-1-254 (Hw)
Henderson, Samuel 1861 wb-#14 (Mo)
Henderson, Selena B. 1856 rb-o-166 (Mt)
Henderson, Susanah 1846 wb-1-70 (Bo)

Henderson, Thomas 1820 wb-2-289 (Je)
Henderson, Thomas 1836 wb-2-132 (Ma)
Henderson, Thomas 1838 wb-1-321 (Gr)
Henderson, Thomas 1857? ib-2-405 (Cl)
Henderson, W. B. 1819 wb-3-12 (Rb)
Henderson, William 1806 wb-1-102 (Sn)
Henderson, William 1814 wb-2-64 (Je)
Henderson, William 1822 wb-#66 (Mu)
Henderson, William 1823 rb-5-283 (Ru)
Henderson, William 1824 wb-#75 (Mu)
Henderson, William 1829 lr (Gi)
Henderson, William 1835 wb-1-64 (Bo)
Henderson, William 1836 wb-x-354 (Mu)
Henderson, William 1854 wb-5-358 (Je)
Henderson, William 1859 wb-#16 (Mo)
Henderson, William 1860 wb-1-56 (Se)
Henderson, William A. 1839 wb-2-18 (Hy)
Henderson, William B. 1819 wb-3-15 (Rb)
Henderson, William D. 1853 wb-1-44 (R)
Henderson, William L. 1847 wb-8-548 (Wi)
Henderson, William S. 1832 wb-#244 (Mu)
Henderson, William Steele sr. 1860
   wb-f-195 (Mu)
Henderson, William Y. 1849 33-3-143 (Gr)
Henderson, William Y. 1858 wb-17-487 (D)
Henderson, Wilson 1816? wb-#21 (Mu)
Henderson, Wilson 1843 wb-4-70 (Ma)
Henderson, Wilson 1859 wb-f-162 (Mu)
Henderson, Wilson B. 1844 wb-4-149 (Ma)
Henderson, Wm. 1835 rb-9-187 (Ru)
Hendley, Charles R. 1841 wb-10-547 (Rb)
Hendley, G. S. 1845 wb-a2-285 (Mu)
Hendley, G. S. H. 1845 wb-a2-256 (Mu)
Hendley, George S. H. 1845 wb-a2-264 (Mu)
Hendley, James 1852 wb-4-573 (Mu)
Hendley, Kezziah 1854 wb-15-592 (Rb)
Hendley, Mary S. 1852 wb-4-592 (Mu)
Hendley, T. B. 1857 wb-16-491 (Rb)
Hendley, William 1836 wb-9-273 (Rb)
Hendley, William 1854 wb-15-576 (Rb)
Hendon, David 1849 wb-g-148 (St)
Hendon, Francis 1847 wb-a-325 (F)
Hendon, William 1822 wb-1-40 (Fr)
Hendren, John 1860 wb-13-333 (K)
Hendrick, Jas. 1850 wb-m-52 (Mt)
Hendrick, William 1836 wb-d-197 (Hn)
Hendrick, William M. 1826 wb-a-53 (G)
Hendricks, Jno. B. 1847 wb-4-251 (Hr)
Hendricks, John 1838 wb-b-255 (G)
Hendricks, Joseph 1804 wb-#1 (Wl)
Hendricks, Uriah 1837 wb-d-138* (Hn)

Hendricks, William P. 1854 wb-16-226 (D)
Hendrix, Adam 1836 wb-6-277 (Wi)
Hendrix, Anderson 1848 wb-g-18 (Hu)
Hendrix, Andrew 1849 wb-g-162 (Hu)
Hendrix, Catherine 1838 rb-10-130 (Ru)
Hendrix, Edmund 1866 wb-1-11# (Ge)
Hendrix, Garret 1852 wb-11-319 (K)
Hendrix, Garrett 1808 wb-1-263 (K)
Hendrix, Henry 1830 wb-1-49 (We)
Hendrix, Isaac 1848 wb-g-131 (Hu)
Hendrix, Isaac 1853 wb-a-291 (Ms)
Hendrix, Joseph 1855 wb-11-510 (Wi)
Hendrix, Lee 1849 wb-g-266 (Hu)
Hendrix, Morgan 1843 wb-8-53 (K)
Hendrix, Solomon 1841 lw (Ct)
Hendrix, Thomas 1819 wb-3-100 (Wi)
Hendrix, Thomas 1857 rb-18-320 (Ru)
Hendrix, William 1841 wb-b-29 (We)
Hendry, William 1838 wb-2-50# (Ge)
Hendry, William 1855 149-1-13 (Ge)
Hendsley, Robert 1860 wb-4-391 (La)
Henegar, Henry 1832 wb-2-52# (Ge)
Henessee, James 1846 wb-c-215 (Wh)
Heney, Oney S. 1849 wb-4-432 (Hr)
Henkel, Phillip 1834 wb-2-43# (Ge)
Henley, Isaac 1840 wb-#44 (Wa(
Henley, James 1799 wb-#7 (Wa(
Henley, John J. 1842 lr (Sn)
Henley, John M. 1857 lr (Sn)
Henley, John M. 1860 lr (Sn)
Henley, Martha 1858 gs-1-194 (F)
Henley, William 1836 wb-9-297 (Rb)
Henly, Arthur H. 1849 wb-#6 (Mo)
Henly, George 1820 wb-3-123 (Rb)
Henly, George 1820 wb-3-61 (Rb)
Henly, Thomas 1860 rb-p-410 (Mt)
Henly, Turner B. 1836 wb-1-29 (Sh)
Hennegar, Henry 1860 149-1-177 (Ge)
Hennessee, James 1851 wb-3-65 (W)
Henning, John 1853 wb-b-231 (L)
Henning, Lewis 1857 wb-f-41 (G)
Hennon, James 1821 wb-7-509 (D)
Hennon?, James 1831 wb-9-559 (D)
Henry, Ann 1842 wb-3-497 (Ma)
Henry, Charles 1840 wb-#145 (Wl)
Henry, Cornelius 1856 wb-16-290 (Rb)
Henry, David 1846 wb-13-57 (Rb)
Henry, Earnest 1855 148-1-519 (Ge)
Henry, Elizabeth 1852 wb-a-281 (Ms)
Henry, George 1817 wb-a-80 (Wh)
Henry, George sr. 1836 wb-a-305 (R)

Henry, Hugh 1808 wb-1-291 (Rb)
Henry, Hugh 1832 wb-1-73 (Bo)
Henry, Hugh 1834 wb-8-385 (Rb)
Henry, Hugh 1855 wb-5-377 (Je)
Henry, Isaac 1814 wb-2-115 (Rb)
Henry, James 1806 as-1-143 (Ge)
Henry, James 1806 wb-1-14# (Ge)
Henry, James 1828 rb-e-258 (Mt)
Henry, James 1834 wb-1-13# (Ge)
Henry, James 1835 wb-2-43# (Ge)
Henry, James 1859 wb-#76 (Mc)
Henry, James B. 1856 wb-12-198 (K)
Henry, John 1802 wb-1-70 (Rb)
Henry, John 1834 wb-b-27 (G)
Henry, John S. 1861 wb-17-260 (Rb)
Henry, Joseph 1835 wb-b-190 (Wh)
Henry, Joseph 1847 wb-c-257 (Wh)
Henry, Lane 1836 wb-b-89 (G)
Henry, Levinia 1824 wb-4-254 (Rb)
Henry, Lewis W. 1839 wb-2-132 (Hr)
Henry, Margaret 1859 wb-13-218* (K)
Henry, Mary 1810 wb-1-344 (Rb)
Henry, Polly 1810 wb-1-348 (Rb)
Henry, Rebecca L. 1861 rb-21-105 (Ru)
Henry, Robert 1837? wb-2-53# (Ge)
Henry, Robert 1849 148-1-281 (Ge)
Henry, Saml. 1832 wb-a-227 (G)
Henry, Samuel C. 1860 wb-k-294 (O)
Henry, Silas 1838 wb-4-41 (Je)
Henry, Thomas 1823 wb-3-526 (Rb)
Henry, Thomas 1823 wb-4-4 (Rb)
Henry, Thomas 1835 wb-a-281 (R)
Henry, Thomas 1853 wb-a-212 (Cr)
Henry, Wiley K. 1853 lr (Sn)
Henry, William 1830 wb-3-73 (Je)
Henry, William 1844 wb-13-108 (D)
Henry, William 1851 wb-9-661 (Wi)
Henry, William 1851 wb-d-4 (Wh)
Henry, William 1856 wb-g-771 (Hn)
Henry, William 1859 lr (Sn)
Henry, William 1859 wb-k-34 (O)
Henry, William sr. 1839 wb-y-442 (Mu)
Hensely, Catharine 1830 rb-f-20 (Mt)
Henshaw, Uriah 1843 wb-1-78 (Bo)
Henshaw, William 1847 wb-a-300 (F)
Hensley, Cyprus 1825 rb-d-446 (Mt)
Hensley, Henry 1858 wb-3-410 (W)
Hensley, Henry C. 1849 wb-1-388* (W)
Hensley, Mary 1849 ib-1-33 (Wy)
Henson, Rachel 1844 wb-2-31 (W)
Henson, William 1801 wb-0-30 (K)

Henson, William 1816 lr (Sn)
Heraldson, Burges 1821 rb-c-402 (Mt)
Herbert, John B. 1848 wb-9-68 (Wi)
Herbert, Nath 1832 wb-1-255 (Hr)
Herbert, Nathaniel 1821 wb-8-25 (D)
Herbert, Richard 1834 wb-5-422 (Wi)
Herd, Jo 1861 wb-e-450 (Wh)
Herd, William 1820 wb-3-158 (Rb)
Hereford, Henry 1813 wb-1-8 (Fr)
Heriges, John J. 1858 wb-17-456 (D)
Hering, Joel 1843 wb-1-89 (Sh)
Herington, Anderson 1859 wb-f-294 (G)
Hern, Aquilla 1828 wb-1-196 (Ma)
Herndon, Anderson 1859 wb-f-290 (G)
Herndon, Benjamin 1818 wb-#62 (Mu)
Herndon, Benjamin 1842 wb-e-224 (St)
Herndon, Benjamin 1852 wb-xx-36 (St)
Herndon, George 1850 wb-g-309 (Hu)
Herndon, Joseph 1860 wb-18-144 (D)
Herndon, Joseph 1860 wb-18-166 (D)
Herndon, Pamphert 1820 wb-1-34 (Fr)
Herndon, Philip 1848 wb-f-508 (St)
Herndon, Sarah E. 1859 ib-2-104 (Wy)
Herndon, William 1831 wb-c-144 (St)
Herndon, Willis 1856 ib-1-468 (Wy)
Herod, Thomas 1833 wb-c-237 (St)
Herod, William sr. 1836 wb-3-0 (Sm)
Heron, John C. 1832 wb-1-232 (Hr)
Heron, John E. 1836 wb-1-502 (Hr)
Herral, James 1837 wb-1-335 (Hy)
Herral, Mallissa J. 1859 rb-19-625 (Ru)
Herrald, Lewis 1856 rb-18-179 (Ru)
Herrall, Henry 1851 rb-15-631 (Ru)
Herralson, Vincent 1846 wb-1-277 (Li)
Herran, James W. 1845 wb-1-124 (Sh)
Herrel, John 1815 wb-1-240 (Hw)
Herrell, William 1819 wb-#32 (Wl)
Herriford, James 1851 wb-1-279 (Fr)
Herriford, John W. 1832 wb-c-207 (St)
Herrin, Beverly 1858 wb-1-236 (Be)
Herrin, Elisha 1856 wb-1-81 (Be)
Herrin, Francis 1834 wb-x-181 (Mu)
Herrin, James W. 1860 39-2-398 (Dk)
Herrin, John F. 1851 wb-15-176 (D)
Herrin, Milley 1858 wb-1-198 (Be)
Herrin, William 1854 wb-16-239 (D)
Herrin, William 1861 iv-C-53 (C)
Herring, Abraham 1845 wb-e-84 (O)
Herring, Benjamin 1838 rb-h-153 (Mt)
Herring, Benjamin 1860 rb-p-490 (Mt)
Herring, Brite 1828 rb-e-256 (Mt)

Herring, David 1860 wb-17-47 (Rb)
Herring, Haywood 1845 wb-12-365 (Rb)
Herring, Jesse 1837 wb-10-73 (Rb)
Herring, Jesse 1839 wb-10-260 (Rb)
Herring, Solomon 1825 wb-#145 (Mu)
Herring, Solomon 1826 wb-#139 (Mu)
Herring, Stephen 1845 wb-12-345 (Rb)
Herring, Susan 1858 rb-o-780 (Mt)
Herring, Susan 1859 wb-16-796 (Rb)
Herrington, M. W. 1859 wb-16-754 (Rb)
Herrington, Phillip 1854 ib-h-60 (F)
Herrod, Henry 1851 rb-16-130 (Ru)
Herron, A. H. 1857 wb-3e-36 (Sh)
Herron, Andrew 1847 wb-5-38 (Ma)
Herron, Andrew 1849 wb-2-60 (Sh)
Herron, Isaac A. 1845 wb-1-109 (Sh)
Herron, James G. 1841 wb-#135 (Wl)
Herron, John 1806 wb-1-204 (K)
Herron, Susan G. C. 1847 wb-8-540 (Wi)
Herron, Thomas 1823 wb-3-664 (Wi)
Hertt, R. S. 1856 wb-#76 (Mc)
Hervey, M. D. 1847 wb-4-224 (Hr)
Hervey, Oney S. 1839 wb-2-103 (Hr)
Hervey, Zachariah 1815 rb-b-255 (Mt)
Heslip, Joseph 1833 wb-10-116 (D)
Hessey, John 1857 wb-#124 (Wl)
Hesson, Mary 1841 wb-3-0 (Sm)
Hester, Abram 1838 wb-d-154 (St)
Hester, Isaac W. 1859 wb-2-280 (Li)
Hester, James 1855 wb-n-625 (Mt)
Hester, John 1839? wb-#128 (Wl)
Hester, Joseph 1842 wb-1-214 (Li)
Hester, Marion H. 1858 rb-p-15 (Mt)
Hester, Minerva 1859 rb-p-273 (Mt)
Hester, R. B. 1847 wb-4-177 (Hr)
Hester, R. H. 1849 wb-4-413 (Hr)
Hester, Robert 1854 wb-n-393 (Mt)
Hester, Robert sr. 1841 rb-i-215 (Mt)
Hester, W. H. 1849 wb-4-416 (Hr)
Hetzel, George 1851 wb-14-643 (D)
Heuson, John 1817 wb-1-241 (Hw)
Hewett, Elizabeth 1829 rb-f-3 (Mt)
Hewett, Hazael 1859 wb-7-57 (Ma)
Hewett, Robert 1832 wb-#117 (Wl)
Hewett, Robert 1841 wb-b-438 (Wh)
Hewitt, Caleb 1817 wb-7-141 (D)
Hewitt, Patrick 1845 wb-c-172 (Wh)
Hewitt, Reed 1849 wb-b-412 (Mu)
Hewitt, Richard 1846 wb-a2-346 (Mu)
Hewlett, George 1822 wb-8-72 (D)
Hewlett, William 1834 wb-10-338 (D)

Hewley, Cyrena 1848 wb-2-291 (W)
Hewlitt, Edmond 1819 wb-7-330 (D)
Hewston, Sarah 1836 as-a-306 (Di)
Heydelberg, Richard 1843 wb-4-101 (Ma)
Heydons, Joseph 1819 rb-c-135 (Mt)
Heytton, Robert 1837 rb-10-58 (Ru)
Hibbett, Nancy 1854 lr (Sn)
Hibbitt, Joseph F. 1824 wb-2-0 (Sm)
Hibbitts, James 1821 wb-1-0 (Sm)
Hibbs, H. W. 1856 rb-o-50 (Mt)
Hibbs, W. W. 1855 wb-n-698 (Mt)
Hickerson, Charles 1854 wb-0-134 (Cf)
Hickerson, Daniel 1845 as-b-278 (Di)
Hickerson, David 1833 wb-1-122 (Fr)
Hickerson, David 1852 wb-0-104 (Cf)
Hickerson, Ezekiel 1831 wb-c-151 (St)
Hickerson, John 1845 wb-0-53 (Cf)
Hickerson, Joshua G. 1856 wb-3-328 (W)
Hickerson, Leander 1857 wb-0-156 (Cf)
Hickey, Baker 1854 wb-12-42 (K)
Hickey, Cornelius 1843 wb-8-195 (K)
Hickey, Cornelius 1853 wb-11-478 (K)
Hickey, John 1826 wb-a-63 (G)
Hickey, John 1836 wb-6-13 (K)
Hickey, Joshua 1844 wb-c-151 (Wh)
Hickey, Judah 1853 wb-11-463 (K)
Hickey, Thomas D. 1856 wb-4-11 (Je)
Hickle, Catharine 1854 wb-3-189 (Gr)
Hickle, John 1853 wb-3-130 (Gr)
Hickman, Amanda 1837 as-a-453 (Di)
Hickman, Andrew J. 1852 lr (Gi)
Hickman, Edwin 1791 wb-1-223 (D)
Hickman, Edwin 1808 wb-3-197 (D)
Hickman, Francis 1820 wb-2-575 (Je)
Hickman, Henry 1828 wb-3-42 (Je)
Hickman, Isaac B. 1847 wb-2-23 (Sh)
Hickman, James H. 1861 wb-k-480 (O)
Hickman, John 1845 wb-5-360 (Gr)
Hickman, John 1849 33-3-186 (Gr)
Hickman, John D. 1842 wb-5-222 (Gr)
Hickman, John P. 1841 wb-12-27 (D)
Hickman, John R. 1852 wb-15-458 (D)
Hickman, Joshua 1831 wb-3-176 (Je)
Hickman, Joshua 1837 wb-3-436 (Je)
Hickman, Lemuel 1855 lr (Gi)
Hickman, Noah 1818 wb-#29 (Wl)
Hickman, Snoden 1834 wb-#152 (Wl)
Hickman, Snowden (Sr.) 1846 wb-#152 (Wl)
Hickman, Snowdon 1848 wb-#163 (Wl)
Hickman, Thomas 1851 wb-15-144 (D)
Hickman, Thomas 1853 wb-16-113 (D)

Hickman, William 1811 wb-4-132 (D)
Hickman, Wright 1856 wb-#121 (Wl)
Hickory, Horace 1834 wb-#77 (Mc)
Hicks, Archabald 1861 wb-A-165 (Ca)
Hicks, Charles 1840 wb-b-307 (G)
Hicks, Edward D. 1840 wb-12-60* (D)
Hicks, Elias 1847 wb-f-404 (St)
Hicks, Elijah 1844 wb-8-206 (Wi)
Hicks, Elisha 1857 wb-#27 (Mo)
Hicks, Gideon E. 1859 wb-h-302 (Hn)
Hicks, Isaac 1856 wb-#27 (Mo)
Hicks, James 1847 wb-f-421 (St)
Hicks, James 1857 wb-#77 (Mc)
Hicks, James S. 1851 wb-g-391 (St)
Hicks, James sr. 1852 wb-g-469 (Hn)
Hicks, John W. 1839 wb-d-324 (St)
Hicks, John W. 1856 wb-h-289 (St)
Hicks, Mary 1804 wb-2-388 (D)
Hicks, Mary 1853 wb-#77 (Mc)
Hicks, Mary Ann 1803 wb-#1 (Wl)
Hicks, Matthew 1852 wb-2-291 (La)
Hicks, Reden 1855 wb-e-362 (G)
Hicks, Robert 1857 wb-#78 (Mc)
Hicks, Robert W. 1856 wb-#11 (Mo)
Hicks, Stephen 1854 wb-#78 (Mc)
Hicks, William 1836 wb-1-482 (Hr)
Hicks, William 1846 wb-4-101 (Hr)
Hicks, William 1851 wb-2-88 (Me)
Hicks, William 1854 wb-#78 (Mc)
Hicks, William R. 1843 wb-f-24 (St)
Hicks, Willis 1839 wb-a-72 (Cr)
Hickshaw, Vesta 1850 wb-3-42 (W)
Hide, Hartwell B. 1838 wb-6-478 (Wi)
Hider, Michael 1790 wb-#3 (Wa(
Hiers, Martin 1828 wb-3-0 (Sm)
Hiett, Joseph P. 1856 wb-7-0 (Sm)
Hiett, Moses 1833 wb-10-161 (D)
Higdon, Andrew 1839 wb-#127 (Wl)
Higdon, James 1835 lr (Gi)
Higgason, Edmund 1855 wb-b-12 (F)
Higgason, Josiah 1860 wb-b-86 (F)
Higgason, Richard P. 1849 lr (Sn)
Higgenbotham, Elijah 1851 rb-16-107 (Ru)
Higginbotham, John 1842 wb-12-277* (D)
Higginbothom, John 1855 rb-17-585 (Ru)
Higgins, Aaron D. 1853 wb-10-549 (Wi)
Higgins, Aaron D. 1853 wb-11-10 (Wi)
Higgins, Hannah 1861 wb-18-593 (D)
Higgins, James 1840 wb-1-41 (Me)
Higgins, James 1858 wb-2-242 (Li)
Higgins, John 1809 wb-1-51 (Wi)

Higgins, John 1838 wb-A-10 (Ca)
Higgins, John P. 1837 wb-1-165 (Fr)
Higgins, Martha 1837 wb-b-367 (Ro)
Higgins, Mary 1844 wb-c-199 (G)
Higgins, Mary 1848 ib-1-41 (Ca)
Higgins, Noah 1830 wb-4-521 (Wi)
Higgins, Noah 1845 wb-8-260 (Wi)
Higgins, William 1812 wb-1-274 (Wi)
Higgins, William 1840 wb-b-361 (G)
Higgs, Alfred 1846 wb-b-150 (We)
Higgs, Reuben 1845 wb-4-13 (Hr)
Higgs, Simon 1845 wb-1-361 (La)
Higgs, Winnaford A. 1850 wb-4-564 (Hr)
High, James 1858 wb-7-0 (Sm)
High, John W. 1849 rb-l-449 (Mt)
High, William 1817 wb-1-0 (Sm)
High, William 1840 wb-2-169 (Hr)
Highfield, Bennett 1844 wb-3-261 (Hr)
Highfil, Bennett 1847 wb-4-211 (Hr)
Highsaw, George 1843 wb-a-114 (Cr)
Highsmith, Daniel 1814 wb-2-101 (Rb)
Highsmith, Daniel 1814 wb-2-117 (Rb)
Hight, Archibald 1817? wb-#105 (Mu)
Hightower, Delia S. 1846 wb-8-368 (Wi)
Hightower, E. 1842 wb-5-193 (Gr)
Hightower, Epaph. 1852 wb-3-33 (Gr)
Hightower, Epaphroditus 1849 33-3-112 (Gr)
Hightower, John 1802 wb-1-7 (Wi)
Hightower, John 1833 wb-5-339 (Wi)
Hightower, John Q. A. 1856 wb-g-735 (Hn)
Hightower, Joseph 1839 wb-1-358 (Gr)
Hightower, Joseph B. 1837 wb-6-341 (Wi)
Hightower, Nancy L. 1849 wb-9-302 (Wi)
Hightower, Richard 1821 Wb-3-254 (Wi)
Hightower, Stephen 1840 wb-2-272 (Hy)
Hightower, Steth 1849 wb-#178 (Wl)
Hightower, William 1842 wb-a-153 (Di)
Hightower, William 1845 wb-8-336 (Wi)
Hignight, John 1816 rb-b-254 (Mt)
Hignight, Thomas 1804 lw (Ct)
Hignite, Peter 1845 mr-2-152 (Be)
Hiland, James 1794 wb-1-313 (D)
Hill, Adelphia 1853 wb-1-318 (Fr)
Hill, Amos 1843 wb-b-39 (We)
Hill, Andrew 1848 wb-3-0 (Sm)
Hill, Benjamin 1827 wb-4-170 (Wi)
Hill, Benjamin 1852 wb-3-131 (W)
Hill, Charles A. 1841 wb-3-485 (Ma)
Hill, Dan 1826 wb-4-116 (Wi)
Hill, Daniel 1850 mr-2-391 (Be)
Hill, David 1843 wb-8-111 (Wi)

Hill, David 1851 lr (Gi)
Hill, Duncan 1819 wb-#106 (Mu)
Hill, Elijah 1854 wb-a-148 (V)
Hill, Elizabeth 1838 wb-3-513 (Je)
Hill, Ervin 1846 wb-2-161 (W)
Hill, Franklin 1848 wb-g-16 (O)
Hill, George 1815 wb-2-267 (Rb)
Hill, Green 1826 wb-4-66 (Wi)
Hill, Green 1834 wb-1-470 (Ma)
Hill, H. R. W. 1854 wb-16-448 (D)
Hill, Hinton A. 1835 wb-#106 (Wl)
Hill, Isaac P. 1837 wb-#120 (Wl)
Hill, J. J. K. 1848 wb-4-331 (Hr)
Hill, James 1815 wb-a-30 (Wh)
Hill, James 1821 rb-5-160 (Ru)
Hill, James 1823 wb-1-24 (Ma)
Hill, James 1830 wb-#223 (Mu)
Hill, James 1832 wb-1-58 (Gr)
Hill, James 1836 wb-a-48 (T)
Hill, James 1841 wb-c-24 (Wh)
Hill, James C. 1831 wb-5-79 (Wi)
Hill, James E. 1860 wb-f-204 (Mu)
Hill, James F. 1847 wb-f-127+ (O)
Hill, James G. 1841 wb-7-476 (Wi)
Hill, James L. 1834 wb-5-344 (Wi)
Hill, James W. 1829 wb-#190 (Mu)
Hill, Jane 1819 wb-1-32 (Fr)
Hill, Joab 1853 wb-d-153 (Wh)
Hill, John (Major) 1814 wb-#14 (Wl)
Hill, John 1803 rb-a-193 (Mt)
Hill, John 1810 wb-#26 (Wl)
Hill, John 1835 wb-a-1 (Ms)
Hill, John 1840 wb-5-42 (Gr)
Hill, John 1841 wb-5-114 (Gr)
Hill, John 1850 wb-b-605 (Mu)
Hill, John 1851 33-3-353 (Gr)
Hill, John 1852 wb-e-2 (Hy)
Hill, John 1858 ib-2-524 (Cl)
Hill, John 1859 wb-17-630 (D)
Hill, John A. 1860 wb-1-403 (Fr)
Hill, John D. 1818 wb-2-410 (Wi)
Hill, John D. 1845 wb-8-268 (Wi)
Hill, John L. 1852 wb-#179 (Wl)
Hill, John L. 1856 wb-12-215 (Wi)
Hill, John R. 1860 wb-18-134 (D)
Hill, John S. 1823 wb-1-245 (Hw)
Hill, John S. 1851 wb-d-291 (G)
Hill, John T. 1854 wb-n-248 (Mt)
Hill, John jr. 1837 wb-1-231 (Gr)
Hill, Joseph 1823 wb-2-402 (Je)
Hill, Joseph 1834 wb-1-99 (Gr)

Hill, Joseph 1836 wb-x-373 (Mu)
Hill, Joseph 1858 wb-3-411 (Gr)
Hill, Joshua 1829 wb-a-64 (R)
Hill, Joshua 1844 wb-b-54 (We)
Hill, Joshua 1850 mr-2-392 (Be)
Hill, Joshua C. 1827 wb-4-226 (Wi)
Hill, Joshua C. 1839 wb-7-54 (Wi)
Hill, Joshua S. 1852 mr-2-463 (Be)
Hill, Lemiza 1860 wb-13-169 (Wi)
Hill, Louvica 1849 wb-1-395* (W)
Hill, M. P. 1856 wb-3-358 (W)
Hill, Margaret 1856 wb-a-237 (T)
Hill, Martha 1830 wb-a-9 (T)
Hill, Martha 1845 wb-8-293 (Wi)
Hill, Martha 1854 wb-c-14 (Wh)
Hill, Martha D. 1859 wb-f-334 (G)
Hill, Martin 1832 wb-1A-74 (A)
Hill, Mary James 1838 wb-7-5 (Wi)
Hill, Matthew 1862 wb-#136 (Wl)
Hill, Nancy 1832 wb-5-152 (Wi)
Hill, Nancy 1848 as-a-178 (Ms)
Hill, Pleasant 1851 wb-1-282 (Fr)
Hill, Reuben 1833 wb-x-33 (Mu)
Hill, Reuben S. 1858 wb-17-509 (D)
Hill, Richard 1833 wb-x-57 (Mu)
Hill, Richard 1833 wb-x-87 (Mu)
Hill, Richard 1839 wb-6-479 (K)
Hill, Richard 1843 wb-a-98 (Ms)
Hill, Robert 1834 wb-2-41# (Ge)
Hill, Robert 1844 wb-#149 (Wl)
Hill, Robert 1850 wb-9-430 (Wi)
Hill, Robert F. 1859 wb-13-121 (Wi)
Hill, Robert J. 1838 wb-1-155 (La)
Hill, Saml. S. 1857 wb-f-78 (G)
Hill, Samuel 1812 wb-2-52 (Je)
Hill, Samuel 1816 wb-2-156 (Je)
Hill, Samuel 1844 wb-#144 (Wl)
Hill, Samuel 1857 wb-17-226 (D)
Hill, Sarah B. 1857 wb-12-299 (Wi)
Hill, Spencer 1816 wb-2-213 (Wi)
Hill, Spencer 1861 wb-h-529 (Hn)
Hill, Theopolus 1835 wb-x-251* (Mu)
Hill, Thomas 1824 wb-8-303 (D)
Hill, Thomas 1841 wb-z-178 (Mu)
Hill, Thomas 1853 ib-1-252 (Wy)
Hill, Thomas J. 1855 wb-12-34 (Wi)
Hill, Thomas S. 1845 wb-#154 (Wl)
Hill, Thomas W. 1834 wb-1-105 (Li)
Hill, Walter M. 1844 wb-z-583 (Mu)
Hill, Whitmel 1828 wb-1-35 (W)
Hill, William 1816 rb-3-125 (Ru)

Hill, William 1822 wb-#125 (Mu)
Hill, William 1824 wb-#77 (Mu)
Hill, William 1830 wb-9-396 (D)
Hill, William 1838 wb-11-212 (D)
Hill, William 1840 wb-b-407 (Wh)
Hill, William 1842 wb-7-497 (Wi)
Hill, William 1849 lr (Sn)
Hill, William 1854 wb-g-588 (Hn)
Hill, William C. 1812 wb-1-300 (Wi)
Hill, William G. 1854 wb-g-644 (Hn)
Hill, William H. 1834 wb-x-165 (Mu)
Hill, William H. 1853 wb-10-611 (Wi)
Hill, William H. sr. 1853 wb-11-248 (Wi)
Hill, William N. 1856 wb-3-391 (La)
Hill, Winkfield 1851 wb-d-3 (Wh)
Hillard, David 1845 wb-c-266 (G)
Hilliard, Anderson W. 1851 wb-4-152 (Mu)
Hilliard, Ezekiel 1856 wb-a-261 (Cr)
Hilliard, Henry 1847 wb-a2-557 (Mu)
Hilliard, Isaac 1832 wb-5-185 (Wi)
Hilliard, James 1839 wb-b-278 (G)
Hilliard, Mary 1848 wb-9-160 (Wi)
Hilliard, Rightman 1840 wb-a-88 (Cr)
Hilliard, Rightman 1855 wb-a-257 (Cr)
Hilliard, William 1833 rb-f-427 (Mt)
Hilliard, William H. 1833 wb-5-240 (Wi)
Hilliard, Zadok 1844 wb-a-120 (F)
Hillis, James 1859 wb-a-286 (V)
Hillis, Levi 1840 as-a-36 (Ms)
Hillis, Mary 1841 wb-a-35 (V)
Hillsman, John 1851 wb-11-32 (K)
Hilsman, Reddick 1857 wb-a-292 (Cr)
Hilton, John 1851 wb-10-2 (Wi)
Hilton, John B. 1853 wb-11-20 (Wi)
Hilton, William 1820 wb-2-288 (Je)
Hinant, Berry 1854 mr-2-548 (Be)
Hind, James 1815 rb-3-117 (Ru)
Hinds, Abigail 1839 wb-c-59 (Ro)
Hinds, John 1811 wb-1-358 (K)
Hinds, John 1858 wb-f-202 (Ro)
Hinds, Joseph 1846 wb-d-252 (Ro)
Hinds, Joseph 1859 wb-f-275 (Ro)
Hinds, Joseph S. 1850 wb-e-224 (Ro)
Hinds, Susannah 1858 wb-f-139 (Ro)
Hines, David 1814? wb-#39 (Mu)
Hines, David 1824? wb-#76 (Mu)
Hines, George 1823 wb-#47 (WI)
Hines, James 1842 wb-5-263 (Gr)
Hines, James D. 1846 wb-13-466 (D)
Hines, John 1860 gs-1-626 (F)
Hines, Sarah C. 1860 wb-13-196 (Wi)

Hines, William 1810 wb-1-327 (K)
Hinkel, William 1838 wb-3-481 (Je)
Hinkle, Catharine 1856 wb-16-326 (Rb)
Hinkle, George 1853 wb-5-162 (Je)
Hinshaw, Washington 1853 wb-2-77# (Ge)
Hinshaw, William 1807 wb-1-273 (Je)
Hinson, John 1858 6-2-138 (Le)
Hinson, Joshua 1834 wb-x-249 (Mu)
Hinson, Tilmon D. 1861 wb-13-493 (Wi)
Hinton, James 1807 wb-3-157 (D)
Hinton, John H. 1843 rb-i-452 (Mt)
Hinton, Kimbrough 1822 rb-d-35 (Mt)
Hinton, Richard B. 1851 wb-a-229 (Di)
Hippenstall, Joseph 1816 wb-2-268 (K)
Hipshare, William 1855 wb-3-277 (Gr)
Hipsher, Henry 1859 wb-3-535 (Gr)
Hipshire, Elijah 1834 wb-1-65 (Gr)
Hisan, Mary J. 1846 wb-b-139 (We)
Hise, Conrad 1859 wb-1-389 (Fr)
Hise, James 1853 wb-2-77# (Ge)
Hitch, Archible 1848 wb-1-68 (Bo)
Hitch, Eleven 1837 wb-1-67 (Bo)
Hitchcock, Daniel 1794 wb-1-25 (K)
Hitchcock, Elijah 1814 wb-a-20 (Wh)
Hitchcock, Enos J. 1844 148-1-87 (Ge)
Hitchcock, Henry 1831 wb-b-66 (Wh)
Hitchcock, Robert 1852 wb-d-93 (Wh)
Hitchcock, Robert 1852 wb-d-97 (Wh)
Hitchcock, William 1846 wb-4-125 (Hr)
Hitchcock, William 1848 wb-c-336 (Wh)
Hitchens, Joseph 1857 wb-17-160 (D)
Hitt, Burrell G. 1846 rb-k-268 (Mt)
Hitt, Nancy 1858 rb-o-761 (Mt)
Hitt, Reuben S. 1857 wb-17-231 (D)
Hitt, Susan Grant 1841 wb-10-592 (Rb)
Hitt, Susan Grant 1841 wb-10-594 (Rb)
Hix, Isaac 1842 wb-#3 (Mo)
Hix, William C. 1848 wb-d-122 (G)
Hixon, John 1850 mr-2-381 (Be)
Hixon, William 1834 wb-1-72 (Gr)
Hixson, Joseph 1803 wb-1-13# (Ge)
Hixson, Joseph 1804 as-1-49 (Ge)
Hoalman, Benjamin 1828 wb-6-307 (Rb)
Hoard, Jesse 1816 wb-1-0 (Sm)
Hoard, Thomas 1831 wb-5-101 (K)
Hoard, Thomas J. 1831 wb-5-90 (K)
Hobb, Joel A. 1848 wb-g-103 (Hu)
Hobbs, C. S. 1849 wb-14-432 (D)
Hobbs, Collin S. 1831 wb-9-493 (D)
Hobbs, Collin S. 1854 wb-16-375 (D)
Hobbs, Edward D. 1833 wb-10-178 (D)

Hobbs, Esther 1845 wb-#148 (Wl)
Hobbs, Eupha 1851 wb-d-358 (G)
Hobbs, Frances 1858 wb-#127 (Wl)
Hobbs, Hartwell 1844 wb-8-154 (Wi)
Hobbs, Hartwell H. 1844 wb-8-203 (Wi)
Hobbs, Huchia? 1828 wb-1-76 (Hr)
Hobbs, James 1845 wb-#177 (Wl)
Hobbs, James B. 1844 wb-#144 (Wl)
Hobbs, James M. 1855 wb-e-256 (G)
Hobbs, John 1843 mr-2-38 (Be)
Hobbs, Redin 1846 wb-c-307 (G)
Hobbs, Richard 1854 wb-11-394 (Wi)
Hobbs, Richard 1855 wb#24 (Gu)
Hobbs, Samuel H. 1856 wb-2-166 (Li)
Hobbs, Thomas 1829 wb-#83 (Wl)
Hobbs, Thomas 1851 wb-15-89 (D)
Hobbs, Thomas W. 1860 wb-18-297 (D)
Hobbs, Vincent 1850 wb-3-55 (W)
Hobbs, William 1837 wb-1-141 (Li)
Hobby, Alexander 1853 wb-a-294 (Ms)
Hobday, John 1855 lr (Sn)
Hobday, Richard D. 1851 lr (Sn)
Hobday, Robert 1797 wb-1-42 (Sn)
Hobdy, Burwell 1815 wb-3-126 (St)
Hobdy, Sydney 1854 wb-2-166 (Sh)
Hobdy, William 1857 lr (Sn)
Hobson, Agnes 1849 wb-#169 (Wl)
Hobson, Ben 1838 wb-#123 (Wl)
Hobson, Benjamin 1826 wb-#69 (Wl)
Hobson, Henry 1841 wb-#134 (Wl)
Hobson, Jeremiah 1822 wb-#50 (Mu)
Hobson, John 1838 wb-11-119 (D)
Hobson, Joseph (Sr.) 1824 wb-#53 (Wl)
Hobson, Joseph 1815 wb-#20 (Wl)
Hobson, Joseph 1843 wb-12-415* (D)
Hobson, Joseph 1844 wb-#157 (Wl)
Hobson, Lawson 1836 lr (Gi)
Hobson, Nicholas 1837 wb-#118 (Wl)
Hobson, Norman L. 1852? wb-#179 (Wl)
Hobson, Thomas 1824 wb-#61 (Wl)
Hobson, William 1816 wb-4-451 (D)
Hobson, William 1816 wb-7-37 (D)
Hobson, William 1841 wb-#133 (Wl)
Hoch, Eugene 1857 wb-12-422 (K)
Hockaday, John W. 1847 wb-d-34 (G)
Hockins, John 1822 wb-#81 (Mu)
Hodge, Ada B. 1852 wb-4-431 (Mu)
Hodge, Agnes 1816 wb-#36 (Mu)
Hodge, Andrew 1856 wb-1-47 (Dy)
Hodge, Asa B. 1849 wb-b-322 (Mu)
Hodge, David M. 1844 5-2-371 (Cl)

Hodge, Elizebeth 1859 wb-1-94 (Dy)
Hodge, Francis 1828 wb-9-195 (D)
Hodge, Francis L. 1852 wb-4-380 (Mu)
Hodge, George 1834 wb-10-381 (D)
Hodge, George 1835 wb-10-423 (D)
Hodge, Hop. 1849 wb-4-485 (Hr)
Hodge, James 1818 wb-7-234 (D)
Hodge, James 1835 rb-9-181 (Ru)
Hodge, James 1853 rb-16-669 (Ru)
Hodge, James 1859 wb-#61 (Wa(
Hodge, John 1814 Wb-2-56 (Wi)
Hodge, John 1814? wb-#29 (Mu)
Hodge, John 1826 wb-#140 (Mu)
Hodge, John 1850 ib-1-198 (Cl)
Hodge, John W. 1855 wb-12-1 (Wi)
Hodge, Louisa 1854 wb-11-327 (Wi)
Hodge, Permelia M. 1856 wb-3e-29 (Sh)
Hodge, Robert 1847 lr (Sn)
Hodge, Robert 1853 wb-10-414 (Wi)
Hodge, Saml. 1852 wb-d-374 (G)
Hodge, Samuel 1815 wb-A-118 (Li)
Hodge, Samuel 1855 wb-12-169 (K)
Hodge, Samuel H. 1846 rb-13-531 (Ru)
Hodge, Susan 1852 wb-g-456 (Hn)
Hodge, William 1853 wb-e-371 (Ro)
Hodge, William A. 1850 wb-e-196 (Ro)
Hodges, Aaron 1844 lr (Sn)
Hodges, Abner 1839 wb-b-324 (Wh)
Hodges, Allen 1843 5-2-333 (Cl)
Hodges, Asa 1823 lr (Sn)
Hodges, Charles 1805 wb-#3 (Wl)
Hodges, Charles 1832 rb-f-369 (Mt)
Hodges, Charles 1832 rb-f-386 (Mt)
Hodges, Charles 1836 wb-3-415 (Je)
Hodges, Charles 1845 wb-e-55 (O)
Hodges, Charles S. 1857 rb-o-514 (Mt)
Hodges, Edmond 1836 wb-a-53 (O)
Hodges, Edmond 1857 wb-1-30 (Se)
Hodges, Edward 1858 wb-4-8 (Gr)
Hodges, Eli 1838 wb-1-295 (Gr)
Hodges, Eli 1846 wb-5-461 (Gr)
Hodges, Hannah 1829 wb-#81 (Wl)
Hodges, Henry 1837 wb-6-327 (Wi)
Hodges, Hiram K. 1850 wb-c-412 (Wh)
Hodges, Hoss 1850 wb-4-602 (Hr)
Hodges, Isham 1839 wb-2-258 (Sn)
Hodges, Isham jr. 1826 lr (Sn)
Hodges, James 1814 wb-1-0 (Sm)
Hodges, James 1829 wb-4-438 (Wi)
Hodges, James C. 1812 wb-#11 (Wl)
Hodges, Jemima 1833 lr (Sn)

Hodges, Jessee 1838 wb-1-303 (Gr)
Hodges, John 1841 5-2-231 (Cl)
Hodges, John 1861 wb-1-153 (Jo)
Hodges, Louisa Ann Cornelia 1859
   wb-3-598 (Gr)
Hodges, Mack 1860 rb-p-479 (Mt)
Hodges, Mariah 1839 rb-10-410 (Ru)
Hodges, Milton 1845 wb-1-293 (Li)
Hodges, Olive 1858 rb-o-543 (Mt)
Hodges, Oliver 1857 rb-o-476 (Mt)
Hodges, Olivie 1858 rb-o-705 (Mt)
Hodges, Richard 1858 wb-7-0 (Sm)
Hodges, Roland 1845 wb-#45 (Wa(
Hodges, Rowland T. 1839 wb-2-262 (Sn)
Hodges, Welcom 1807 wb-1-22 (Wi)
Hodges, William 1854 wb-a-186 (V)
Hodges, Willis 1834 wb-3-0 (Sm)
Hoffer, Daniel 1827 wb-4-253 (K)
Hoffman, Christian 1853 wb-2-144 (Sh)
Hoffman, Christopher 1842 wb-c-49 (Wh)
Hoffman, Mary 1850 wb-c-421 (Wh)
Hofman, William 1861 wb-d-115 (L)
Hogan, David 1834 lr (Gi)
Hogan, David 1848 rb-l-176 (Mt)
Hogan, David 1853 wb-h-Feb (O)
Hogan, Edmond 1838 wb-d-183* (Hn)
Hogan, Henry G. 1837 wb-d-119* (Hn)
Hogan, Humphrey 1794 rb-a-36 (Mt)
Hogan, James 1851 wb-10-116 (Wi)
Hogan, John 1801 rb-a-137 (Mt)
Hogan, John 1819 rb-c-81 (Mt)
Hogan, John 1843 wb-z-543 (Mu)
Hogan, John 1860 wb-18-224 (D)
Hogan, Martha C. 1860 lr (Sn)
Hogan, Robert 1854 wb-16-451 (D)
Hogan, S. E. 1859 gs-1-377 (F)
Hogan, Sarah 1846 wb-8-491 (Wi)
Hogan, Sarah E. 1859 rb-p-265 (Mt)
Hogan, Thomas 1844 wb-13-127 (D)
Hogan, Wilie 1856 rb-o-126 (Mt)
Hogan, William 1815 wb-1-0 (Sm)
Hogan, William 1835 rb-g-148 (Mt)
Hogan, William B. 1835 rb-g-74 (Mt)
Hogan, William P. 1845 as-b-329 (Di)
Hoge, Edward 1841 wb-1-455 (W)
Hoge, Henry 1853 wb-f-30 (Mu)
Hoge, Moses 1858 wb-f-154 (Mu)
Hogg, David 1854 wb-7-0 (Sm)
Hogg, Guilford 1819 wb-#30 (Wl)
Hogg, James 1808 wb-1-56 (Bo)
Hogg, James 1840 wb-e-27 (St)

Hogg, James 1858 wb-1-257 (Be)
Hogg, Samuel 1843 rb-12-307 (Ru)
Hogg, Susannah 1849 wb-g-341 (Hn)
Hogg, Thomas 1856 wb-1-110 (Be)
Hoggatt, Abraham 1825 wb-8-428 (D)
Hoggatt, Diana 1828 wb-9-218 (D)
Hoggatt, Dianna 1829 wb-9-337 (D)
Hoggatt, John 1824 wb-8-381 (D)
Hoggatt, Samuel 1836 wb-3-372 (Je)
Hogge, James 1837 wb-a-185 (O)
Hogge, William 1837 wb-a-5 (Ms)
Hogge, Willis A. 1856 wb-j-172 (O)
Hogins, M. H. 1854 as-c-353 (Di)
Hogins, Morgan H. 1841 as-b-19 (Di)
Hogins, William 1840 wb-a-142 (Di)
Hogins, William W. 1840 as-a-466 (Di)
Hogsett, E. 1854 wb-1C-117 (A)
Hogsett, Elizabeth 1857 wb-1C-373 (A)
Hogsett, Thomas P. 1852 wb-b-197 (L)
Hogshead, William 1847 wb-1B-21 (A)
Hogshead, Wm. 1828 wb-1A-1 (A)
Hogson, Honey 1812 wb-#5 (Mu)
Hogue, Archibald C. 1859 wb-k-28 (O)
Hogue, Burrel H. 1829 wb-#78 (Mc)
Hogue, James L. 1860 wb-k-363 (O)
Hogue, Samuel & Malinda 1860 wb-#79 (Mc)
Hogue, Willis A. 1858 wb-j-418 (O)
Hogue, Willis G. 1861 wb-b*-36 (O)
Hogwood, Ransom 1827 rb-7-95 (Ru)
Holbert, Enos 1834 wb-1-70 (W)
Holcomb, Kinchin 1829 wb-1-37 (Li)
Holcomb, Mary 1854 wb-a-464 (F)
Holcomb, Thomas J. 1852 wb-4-430 (Mu)
Holcombe, John 1826 wb-#143 (Mu)
Holcum, James 1842 wb-c-316 (Ro)
Holden, Biddy 1851 ib-1-107 (Wy)
Holden, Charles 1861 rb-20-801 (Ru)
Holden, Dennis 1845 rb-13-225 (Ru)
Holden, William 1858 rb-19-353 (Ru)
Holder, Berry G. 1842 wb-c-77 (G)
Holder, John W. 1841 wb-1-194 (Fr)
Holder, Ransom 1860 wb-13-310 (K)
Holder, William 1831 wb-3-132 (Je)
Holdridge, William 1822 wb-#105 (Mu)
Holdway, Timothy 1833 wb-3-296 (Je)
Holeman, Daniel 1820 wb-3-213 (Rb)
Holeman, Daniel 1833 wb-8-130 (Rb)
Holeman, Jeremiah 1823 wb-#79 (Mc)
Holeman, John 1848 wb-14-276 (D)
Holeman, Patrick 1828 wb-6-398 (Rb)
Holeman, Pendleton 1851 wb-14-532 (Rb)

Holgon, Robert 1825 wb-#198 (Mu)
Holladay, Benjamin 1815 wb-1-0 (Sm)
Holladay, David 1819 wb-1-0 (Sm)
Hollaman, Larry 1831 wb-1-239 (Ma)
Hollanback, William 1855 wb-d-281 (Wh)
Holland, Alexander G. 1833 wb-#101 (Wl)
Holland, Alston 1840 wb-b-405 (Wh)
Holland, Amos J. 1849 wb-b-441 (Mu)
Holland, Anthony 1853 wb-7-0 (Sm)
Holland, Benjamin 1854 wb-h-315 (Hu)
Holland, Benjamin jr. 1854 wb-h-324 (Hu)
Holland, Daniel 1849 wb-14-238 (Rb)
Holland, Danl. 1801 wb-1-81 (Rb)
Holland, Dudley M. 1831 wb-7-457 (Rb)
Holland, Edward T. 1857 wb-e-67 (Hy)
Holland, Eliza 1852 wb-h-85 (Hu)
Holland, Enos 1817 wb-#39 (Mu)
Holland, Garret 1828 wb-6-300 (Rb)
Holland, Green 1855 mr-2-610 (Be)
Holland, Green B. 1855 mr-2-645 (Be)
Holland, Gustavus A. 1852 wb-10-387 (Wi)
Holland, Hardy 1853 wb-h-191 (Hu)
Holland, Harrison 1854 wb-d-218 (Wh)
Holland, James 1823 wb-#60 (Mu)
Holland, James 1823 wb-4-79 (Rb)
Holland, James 1824 wb-#70 (Mu)
Holland, James 1835 wb-a-112 (Di)
Holland, James 1836 mr-1-1 (Be)
Holland, James 1836 wb-x-385 (Mu)
Holland, James 1837 wb-#116 (Wl)
Holland, James 1841 wb-c-27 (Wh)
Holland, James 1848 wb-#162 (Wl)
Holland, Joel 1808 wb-1-0 (Sm)
Holland, John 1841 wb-2-237 (Hr)
Holland, John 1855 ib-1-344 (Ca)
Holland, John A. 1845 wb-8-346 (Wi)
Holland, John B. 1855 as-b-198 (Ms)
Holland, John M. 1861 wb-1-199 (R)
Holland, Kemp 1825 wb-3-758 (Wi)
Holland, Levi 1836 wb-#115 (Wl)
Holland, Levi 1837 wb-#115 (Wl)
Holland, M. B. 1855 wb-15-726 (Rb)
Holland, Margaret 1842 wb-7-584 (Wi)
Holland, Merritt 1836 mr-1-1 (Be)
Holland, Nancy 1845 wb-#147 (Wl)
Holland, Nancy 1848 wb-#162 (Wl)
Holland, Needham 1843 wb-c-102 (G)
Holland, Peggy 1833 rb-f-494 (Mt)
Holland, R. 1841 wb-#134 (Wl)
Holland, Richard 1836 wb-1-146 (Fr)
Holland, Richard 1839 mr-1-260 (Be)

Holland, Richard 1839 mr-1-275 (Be)
Holland, Richard A. 1828 wb-#77 (Wl)
Holland, Robert 1854 wb-h-317 (Hu)
Holland, Thomas 1847 wb-d-392 (Hd)
Holland, Thomas 1849 wb-14-151 (Rb)
Holland, Thomas H. 1812 wb-#5 (Mu)
Holland, Washington L. 1847 wb-b-159 (Mu)
Holland, William 1841 wb-1-235 (La)
Holland, William J. 1856 as-c-449 (Di)
Holland, William M. 1859 wb-1-301 (Be)
Holland, William W. 1857 wb-1-130 (Be)
Holland, Wm. T. 1857 wb-h-639 (Hu)
Hollandsworth, Isaac 1859 ib-2-144 (Wy)
Hollandsworth, J. B. 1860 ib-2-216 (Wy)
Hollandsworth, Jacob B. 1860 ib-2-220 (Wy)
Hollandsworth, John 1854 ib-1-410 (Ca)
Hollanworth, Elizabeth 1856 ib-1-402 (Ca)
Hollenback, William 1855 wb-d-220 (Wh)
Hollensworth, Stephen 1857 wb-a-269 (V)
Holliday, Alexander 1856 wb-h-269 (St)
Holliday, Jno. 1850 wb-4-565 (Hr)
Holliday, Jno. M. 1849 wb-4-546 (Hr)
Hollier, Christopher 1841 wb-7-373 (Wi)
Hollier, Christopher A. 1841 wb-7-408 (Wi)
Hollingsworth, James 1822 wb-1-46 (Fr)
Hollingsworth, James 1825 eb-1-149 (C)
Hollingworth, John 1852 ib-1-217 (Ca)
Hollinsworth, Charles 1833 wb-10-238 (D)
Hollinsworth, Elizabeth 1856 wb-17-280 (D)
Hollinsworth, James 1811 wb-#9 (Wl)
Hollinsworth, John G. 1847 rb-k-511 (Mt)
Hollis, A. 1860 rb-p-470 (Mt)
Hollis, Amos D. 1856 ib-1-387 (Ca)
Hollis, David 1852 ib-1-203 (Ca)
Hollis, James 1814 Wb-1-180 (Sn)
Hollis, James B. 1850 ib-1-120 (Ca)
Hollis, Jesse 1834 lr (Sn)
Hollis, Jesse 1852 wb-a-414 (F)
Hollis, Jesse 1859 wb-k-145 (O)
Hollis, John 1857 ib-1-474 (Wy)
Hollis, John H. 1858 ib-2-60 (Wy)
Hollis, Joshua 1798 wb-2-110 (D)
Hollis, Richard S. B. 1831 wb-9-542 (D)
Hollis, Samuel 1813 wb-2-60 (Rb)
Hollis, W. L. 1861 wb-17-261 (Rb)
Hollis, William 1846 wb-A-44 (Ca)
Hollman, Yancy 1820 wb-1-0 (Sm)
Holloman, Josiah 1832 wb-a-194 (G)
Holloman, Lewis 1853 wb-e-105 (G)
Holloman, William 1852 wb-h-Dec (O)
Holloway, Billy 1828 wb-1-74 (Bo)

Holloway, Crowder 1853 wb-e-13 (Hy)
Holloway, Harriett 1854 ib-H-172 (F)
Holloway, Hinsly 1843 mr-2-34 (Be)
Holloway, Isaac 1837 rb-10-10 (Ru)
Holloway, James 1834 wb-b-234 (Ro)
Holloway, John 1836 wb-10-609 (D)
Holloway, John 1855 wb-e-41 (Hy)
Holloway, Levi 1862 wb-#135 (Wl)
Holloway, Obediah 1854 wb-1-330 (Fr)
Holloway, W. B. 1855 ib-h-363 (F)
Holloway, William 1846 rb-k-283 (Mt)
Hollowell, Hensly? 1838 mr-1-303 (Be)
Hollowell, J. R. B. 1856 rb-18-237 (Ru)
Hollowell, James J. 1850 rb-15-235 (Ru)
Hollowell, Robt. B. 1854 rb-17-273 (Ru)
Hollowell, W. D. S. 1855 ib-h-467 (F)
Holman, Andrew 1837 wb-9-411 (Rb)
Holman, Daniel 1838 wb-1-153 (Li)
Holman, Dicey 1853 wb-15-237 (Rb)
Holman, Elizabeth 1859 wb-2-282 (Li)
Holman, Esther 1849 wb-c-357 (Wh)
Holman, German Y. 1846 wb-#154 (Wl)
Holman, Polly 1838 wb-10-118 (Rb)
Holman, Robert M. 1844 wb-#144 (Wl)
Holman, Thomas J. 1850 wb-#174 (Wl)
Holman, Thomas P. 1850 wb-#175 (Wl)
Holman, Willis H. 1857 wb-2-199 (Li)
Holmes, A. G. 1849 wb-g-218 (Hu)
Holmes, Albert 1840 wb-e-16 (St)
Holmes, Albert G. 1849 wb-g-233 (Hu)
Holmes, Edward 1833 wb-b-117 (Wh)
Holmes, Gabriel 1845 wb-f-301 (Hn)
Holmes, Hannah 1830 wb-9-359 (D)
Holmes, James 1852 wb-1-258 (Bo)
Holmes, John 1840 wb-b-355 (G)
Holmes, John jr. 1817 wb-1-0 (Sm)
Holmes, Lenora 1849 wb-g-334 (Hn)
Holmes, Mary N. 1851 wb-5-96 (Ma)
Holmes, Moses 1843 wb-z-515 (Mu)
Holmes, Robert 1838 wb-2-235 (Sn)
Holmes, Robert 1845 mr-2-166 (Be)
Holmes, Robert 1846 wb-c-333 (G)
Holmes, Sarah 1841 wb-12-16 (D)
Holmes, Thomas 1860 wb-a-353 (Cr)
Holmes, W. N. 1838 wb-1-443 (Hy)
Holmes, William 1826 rb-6-216 (Ru)
Holmes, William 1830 wb-9-401 (D)
Holmes, William 1834 wb-1-155 (Hy)
Holmes, William 1851 wb-10-614 (Wi)
Holmes, William A. 1837 wb-1-298 (Hy)
Holms, James 1844 wb-a-116 (Cr)

Holms, John 1815 wb-1-0 (Sm)
Holowell, B. 1833 wb-1-105 (Hy)
Holstead, Elisabeth 1814 Wb-2-95 (Wi)
Holston, Henry 1853 wb-5-248 (Je)
Holston, John 1853 wb-#24 (Mo)
Holston, William 1840 wb-c-128 (Ro)
Holt, Chacy 1850 wb-m-36 (Mt)
Holt, Charles 1841 wb-3-466 (Ma)
Holt, Chasey (Sanders) 1849 rb-l-367 (Mt)
Holt, Chasey W. 1848 rb-l-14 (Mt)
Holt, David 1836 wb-1-14# (Ge)
Holt, David 1854 wb-3-221 (Gr)
Holt, Elizabeth 1847 rb-k-593 (Mt)
Holt, Elizabeth 1853 wb-3-162 (La)
Holt, Enoch E. 1857 lr (Gi)
Holt, George 1831 rb-f-225 (Mt)
Holt, Hannah 1848 rb-l-12 (Mt)
Holt, Harden P. 1816 wb-2-277 (Wi)
Holt, Herrod 1861 wb-f-425 (G)
Holt, Irby 1830 wb-#79 (Mc)
Holt, Issabel 1854 as-b-153 (Ms)
Holt, J. W. 1861 wb-4-413 (La)
Holt, Jacob 1804 wb-2-378 (D)
Holt, Jacob 1804 wb-2-381 (D)
Holt, Jacob 1846 wb-#43 (Wa(
Holt, James 1853 lr (Sn)
Holt, Jesse 1844 wb-#146 (Wl)
Holt, John 1842 wb-7-497 (Wi)
Holt, John 1843 wb-d-45 (Hd)
Holt, John W. 1841 wb-b-336 (Hd)
Holt, Jordan C. 1851 wb-5-101 (Ma)
Holt, Kemp 1840 wb-3-120 (Ma)
Holt, Laban 1859 wb-b-70 (F)
Holt, Mary Ann 1857 lr (Gi)
Holt, Micheal 1809 rb-2-75 (Ru)
Holt, Mildred 1832 wb-#80 (Mc)
Holt, Nicholas P. 1840 wb-7-329 (Wi)
Holt, Peter 1816 wb-a-91 (Ro)
Holt, Rebecca S. 1855 rb-17-360 (Ru)
Holt, Reuben 1856 rb-o-86 (Mt)
Holt, Reuben sr. 1839 rb-h-268 (Mt)
Holt, Robert 1821 wb-3-277 (K)
Holt, Robin 1856 rb-o-158 (Mt)
Holt, William (Esq.) 1820 wb-#58 (Mu)
Holt, William 1836 wb-x-304* (Mu)
Holt, William 1849 lr (Sn)
Holt, William 1850 ib-1-91 (Wy)
Holt, Wilson 1860 wb-4-411 (La)
Holt, Wm. 1860 rb-p-480 (Mt)
Holton, Abel 1845 rb-13-412 (Ru)
Holton, Abel B. 1846 rb-13-515 (Ru)

Holton, Samuel 1853 wb-16-90 (D)
Holyfield, Elisha 1836 wb-2-57 (Ma)
Homer?, David 1852 wb-3-55 (Gr)
Homes, Alijah 1813 wb-A-37 (Li)
Homes, John 1832 wb-9-578 (D)
Homes, William 1831 wb-9-499 (D)
Hommedien, Richard F. L. 1847 wb-14-67 (D)
Hone?, John 1837 abl-1-7 (T)
Honeycutt, Uriah 1842 5-2-270 (Cl)
Hood, Aaron 1843 wb-8-67 (K)
Hood, Alexander 1854 wb-a-476 (F)
Hood, Allen 1852 wb-h-Sep (O)
Hood, Chesley 1829 rb-8-57 (Ru)
Hood, Edward 1840 wb-7-271 (Wi)
Hood, James M. 1832 wb-a-119 (R)
Hood, James W. 1839 wb-a-372 (R)
Hood, John 1814 wb-#24 (Mu)
Hood, John 1817 wb-2-279 (Wi)
Hood, John 1829 wb-#194 (Mu)
Hood, John 1845 wb-b-107 (We)
Hood, John 1861 wb-k-408 (O)
Hood, John H. 1856 rb-18-236 (Ru)
Hood, Johnson 1845 wb-8-349 (Wi)
Hood, Mary 1847 wb-b-48 (Mu)
Hood, McDaniel 1847 wb-f-127+ (O)
Hood, Parker 1851 wb-#8 (Mo)
Hood, Robert 1784 wb-1-12# (Ge)
Hood, Robert 1808 ib-1-224 (Ge)
Hood, Samuel H. 1857 wb-j-246 (O)
Hood, Sterling 1860 gs-1-620 (F)
Hood, William B. 1842 wb-a-109 (Cr)
Hood, William H. 1859 rb-19-555 (Ru)
Hood, William McDaniel 1846 wb-f-43 (O)
Hoods, W. H. 1857 rb-18-401 (Ru)
Hoofman, Jacob 1840 wb-e-133 (Hn)
Hoofman, Milly 1840 wb-e-151 (Hn)
Hoofman, Thomas 1857 wb-h-165 (Hn)
Hook, Robert 1849 wb-1-55 (Bo)
Hooker, Anne 1808 wb-3-199 (D)
Hooker, Benjamin 1833 wb-#104 (Wl)
Hooker, James M. 1842 wb-f-109 (Hn)
Hooker, W. G. 1861 wb-3e-186 (Sh)
Hooks, A. G. 1855 ib-h-409 (F)
Hooks, Charles 1827 wb-b-175 (St)
Hooks, Ferrill 1835 wb-c-471 (St)
Hooks, John F. 1835 wb-c-434 (St)
Hooks, Lenard 1849 wb-a-376 (F)
Hooper, A. W. 1845 wb-12-388 (Rb)
Hooper, Absolem 1839 wb-e-242 (Hu)
Hooper, Absolom 1813 wb-4-246 (D)
Hooper, Bailey 1855 wb-h-352 (Hu)

Hooper, Bailey 1855 wb-h-409 (Hu)
Hooper, C. Y. 1849 wb-14-472 (D)
Hooper, Churchell 1808 wb-4-19 (D)
Hooper, Churchwell 1808 wb-4-17 (D)
Hooper, Claborne G. 1848 wb-14-259 (D)
Hooper, Ennis 1801 wb-2-200 (D)
Hooper, Isaac N. 1856 wb-16-239 (Rb)
Hooper, James 1832 wb-10-51 (D)
Hooper, James 1857 wb-4-141 (La)
Hooper, James A. 1855 wb-16-541 (D)
Hooper, James H. 1841 wb-12-10 (D)
Hooper, Jesse 1841 wb-12-242* (D)
Hooper, John J. 1859 wb-a-96 (Ce)
Hooper, John L. 1844 wb-e-624 (Hu)
Hooper, John Q. 1848 wb-10-5 (K)
Hooper, Joseph 1825 wb-8-454 (D)
Hooper, Joseph 1842 wb-2-367 (Hr)
Hooper, Margery 1852 wb-g-434 (Hn)
Hooper, Martha 1825 wb-8-462 (D)
Hooper, Miles N. 1844 5-3-28 (Cl)
Hooper, Thomas 1826 wb-8-556 (D)
Hooper, Thomas 1826 wb-9-35 (D)
Hooper, William 1827 rb-e-81 (Mt)
Hooper, William C. 1847 wb-14-39 (D)
Hooper, William G. 1845 5-3-64 (Cl)
Hooper, William J. 1854 wb-e-25 (Hy)
Hooper, William sr. 1843 5-2-352 (Cl)
Hooser, Anthoney 1849 wb-g-62 (O)
Hoover, A. J. 1838 rb-10-140 (Ru)
Hoover, Abel 1835 wb-x-273* (Mu)
Hoover, Andrew J. 1847 rb-14-174 (Ru)
Hoover, Christopher 1844 rb-12-527 (Ru)
Hoover, George 1817 eb-1-64 (C)
Hoover, Jacob 1844 wb-0-46 (Cf)
Hoover, Jacob 1845 wb-0-62 (Cf)
Hoover, John 1845 rb-13-220 (Ru)
Hoover, Julius 1860 rb-20-401 (Ru)
Hoover, Martin 1840 rb-11-51 (Ru)
Hoover, Martin L. 1840 rb-11-89 (Ru)
Hoover, Philip 1831 wb-9-519 (D)
Hoover, William K. 1837 wb-1-188 (W)
Hope, Adam 1842 wb-12-258* (D)
Hope, Adam 1842 wb-12-274* (D)
Hope, Adam 1842 wb-12-364* (D)
Hope, Ann 1838 wb-11-270 (D)
Hope, D. B. 1842 wb-f-102* (Hn)
Hope, D. P. 1840 wb-e-159 (Hn)
Hope, James (esq.) 1841 wb-c-198 (Ro)
Hope, John 1805 wb-3-17 (D)
Hope, John 1816 wb-7-91 (D)
Hope, John 1830 wb-b-72 (Ro)

Hope, John 1849 wb-e-174 (Ro)
Hope, John 1851 wb-11-154 (K)
Hope, Robert 1861 iv-C-52 (C)
Hope, Samuel W. 1848 wd-14-187 (D)
Hope, Thomas 1811 wb-1-239 (Wi)
Hope, Thomas 1821 wb-3-263 (K)
Hopewood, Willis M. 1854 as-b-142 (Ms)
Hopkins, Ally (Mrs.) 1854 wb-5-51 (Hr)
Hopkins, David 1789 wb-1-12# (Ge)
Hopkins, George W. 1837 wb-b-142 (G)
Hopkins, Hampton 1828 wb-1-67 (Hr)
Hopkins, Isaac L. 1859 wb-f-337 (G)
Hopkins, James 1800 wb-1-1 (Wi)
Hopkins, Jesse 1846 wb-c-220 (Wh)
Hopkins, John 1848 wb-b-255 (We)
Hopkins, John A. 1841 wb-10-568 (Rb)
Hopkins, Joseph 1830 wb-4-426 (K)
Hopkins, Josiah 1859 wb-3e-118 (Sh)
Hopkins, Martha A. 1861 wb-19-2 (D)
Hopkins, Nancy 1861 wb-e-153 (Hy)
Hopkins, Samuel 1840 wb-b-15 (We)
Hopkins, William 1854 wb-3-256 (W)
Hopkins, William D. 1835 wb-6-18 (Wi)
Hopper, Absalom 1852 wb-d-377 (G)
Hopper, George 1823 wb-A-349 (Li)
Hopper, Gilliam 1851 wb-d-340 (G)
Hopper, Harmon 1844 5-3-39 (Cl)
Hopper, Harmon 1850 ib-1-149 (Cl)
Hopper, James 1853 wb-e-69 (G)
Hopper, Joel 1852 wb-a-197 (T)
Hopper, John 1823 wb-A-321 (Li)
Hopper, Mary An 1823 as-A-106 (Di)
Hopper, Thomas 1856 wb-e-413 (G)
Hopper, Z. (D.?) 1825? as-a-138 (Di)
Hoppers, George 1843 wb-4-72 (Ma)
Hopsan, Tomsey 1849 5-3-274 (Cl)
Hopson, Elizabeth 1820 rb-c-370 (Mt)
Hopson, Elizabeth 1821 rb-c-479 (Mt)
Hopson, George B. 1847 rb-k-423 (Mt)
Hopson, Jeremiah 1823 wb-#68 (Mu)
Hopson, Joseph 1831 rb-f-224 (Mt)
Hopson, Joseph 1831 rb-f-244 (Mt)
Hopson, Joseph 1842 wb-f-79 (Hn)
Hopson, Joseph 1847 rb-k-564 (Mt)
Hopson, Sally Ann 1849 rb-1-356 (Mt)
Hopton, Aaron 1853 148-1-467 (Ge)
Hopton, John 1796 wb-1-12# (Ge)
Hopwood, F. M. 1860 as-c-204 (Ms)
Hopwood, Willis 1850 wb-a-242 (Ms)
Hord, John 1837 wb-a-145 (O)
Hord, Nancy 1837 wb-1-252 (Hw)

Hord, Robert 1848 rb-l-13 (Mt)
Hord, Stanwix 1826 wb-#80 (Mc)
Hord, Thomas 1834 wb-5-318 (K)
Horn, Andrew 1793 wb-1-14 (Je)
Horn, Axiom 1848 rb-l-149 (Mt)
Horn, Elizabeth 1856 rb-o-89 (Mt)
Horn, Etheldred P. 1814 wb-#14 (Wl)
Horn, Etheldred P. 1835 wb-#110 (Wl)
Horn, Jacob S. 1860 wb-#131 (Wl)
Horn, John 1848 wb-2-36 (La)
Horn, John 1853 mr-2-540 (Be)
Horn, John 1859 wb-1-6 (Su)
Horn, Matthew J. 1841 wb-#134 (Wl)
Horn, Moses 1842 wb-1-76 (Sh)
Horn, Nancy 1833 wb-1-41 (La)
Horn, Samuel 1789 wb-1-77 (Je)
Horn, Thomas P. 1857 lr (Sn)
Horn, Vincent 1855 mr-2-626 (Be)
Horn, William 1851 wb-#176 (Wl)
Horn, William P. 1852 wb-3-23 (La)
Horn?, Thomas 1849 ib-1-85 (Ca)
Hornback, John 1807 wb-1-278 (Je)
Hornbarger, Jacob 1837 wb-2-48# (Ge)
Hornbarger, Jacob 1859 wb-#61 (Wa(
Hornbarger, Phillip 1832 wb-c-194 (St)
Hornberger, G. A. 1859 wb-i-43 (St)
Hornberger, Jacob sr. 1843 148-1-47 (Ge)
Horne, Elizabeth 1828 rb-7-302 (Ru)
Horne, John 1838 abl-1-98 (T)
Horne, Nicholas 1835 wb-5-368 (K)
Horne, Sarah M. 1854 wb-e-185 (G)
Horne, Sherod 1821 wb-a-156 (Wh)
Horne, Simeon 1829 rb-7-208 (Ru)
Horne, W. P. 1852 wb-2-244 (La)
Horner, Catharine 1850 wb-d-258 (G)
Horner, Cavalier 1834 wb-3-503 (Je)
Horner, David 1847 33-3-17 (Gr)
Horner, Elizabeth 1852 148-1-391 (Ge)
Horner, Harriet E. 1849 rb-l-258 (Mt)
Horner, William 1834 wb-3-360 (Je)
Horner, William sr. 1824 wb-2-431 (Je)
Hornsby, Jemima 1836 wb-#80 (Mc)
Hornsby, Kimbrough 1850 wb-5-1 (Hr)
Hornsby, William 1829 wb-a-55 (R)
Horny, Elizabeth 1858 rb-o-638 (Mt)
Horsely, William 1852 wb-4-397 (Mu)
Horsley, James 1839 wb-2-261 (Sn)
Horsley, Stephen 1848 wb-g-33 (Hu)
Horten, John E. 1837 wb-y-12 (Mu)
Horton, Amos 1860 wb-1-397 (Fr)
Horton, Archabald 1844 wb-b-51 (We)

Horton, C. M. 1858 wb-3e-86 (Sh)
Horton, Clabon 1847 wb-9-13 (Wi)
Horton, Claiban 1837 wb-6-325 (Wi)
Horton, Elizabeth 1826 wb-4-99 (Wi)
Horton, George 1815 wb-3-67 (St)
Horton, Isaac 1853 wb-#107 (Wl)
Horton, Isaac 1854 ib-1-287 (Wy)
Horton, Isaac 1856 wb-2-84# (Ge)
Horton, James 1861 wb-18-503 (D)
Horton, James D. 1852 wb-10-231 (Wi)
Horton, John 1835 wb-2-44# (Ge)
Horton, John D. 1849 wb-9-317 (Wi)
Horton, John W. 1859 wb-2-1 (Li)
Horton, Joseph 1813 wb-a-57 (Ro)
Horton, Joseph W. 1847 wb-14-51 (D)
Horton, Joshua 1856 wb#25 (Gu)
Horton, Josiah 1828 wb-9-168 (D)
Horton, Nathaniel 1848 ib-1-2 (Wy)
Horton, W. J. 1857 wb-f-62 (G)
Horton, William 1849 ib-1-41 (Wy)
Hosea, James 1854 wb-e-138 (G)
Hosford, Cailer? 1853? ib-2-52 (Cl)
Hosford, Matthew 1837 wb-6-331 (Wi)
Hosford, Richd. 1851 wb-d-369 (G)
Hoskins, Daniel 1848 rb-14-249 (Ru)
Hoskins, George 1849 wb-1B-142 (A)
Hoskins, Jane 1848 wb-7-0 (Sm)
Hoskins, Jehu sr. 1841 rb-i-169 (Mt)
Hoskins, John 1834 wb-1-337 (Hr)
Hoskins, John 1837 wb-1-559 (Hr)
Hoskins, John A. 1859 wb-f-280 (Ro)
Hoskins, Mary Jane 1845 wb-7-0 (Sm)
Hoskins, Thomas C. 1839 rb-10-394* (Ru)
Hoss, Jacob 1817 wb-#15 (Wa(
Hoss, Peter 1812 wb-#13 (Wa(
Hotchkiss, Betsy 1847 wb-e-27 (Ro)
Hotchkiss, Holt 1839 wb-3-98 (Ma)
Hotchkiss, Jared 1838 wb-c-8 (Ro)
Hough, Joseph H. 1844 wd-13-16 (D)
Houghs, Samuel C. 1842 wb-c-90 (G)
Hounshell, David 1842 wb-1-69 (Me)
Hounshell, Jacob 1847 wb-#81 (Mc)
Housch, Rachael 1861 wb-2-351 (Li)
Housden, Benjamin 1853 wb-g-500 (Hn)
House, Baliss 1806 wb-1-98 (Sn)
House, Claiborne 1851 rb-16-111 (Ru)
House, Elisebeth 1823 lr (Sn)
House, Elizabeth 1858 wb-12-509 (Wi)
House, Elizabeth M. 1860 wb-13-194 (Wi)
House, George 1822 wb-a-11 (Hn)
House, George A. 1847 wb-8-597 (Wi)

House, George W. 1851 wb-15-116 (D)
House, Green 1813 wb-1-333 (Wi)
House, Green 1857 wb-7-0 (Sm)
House, Hardy 1850 wb-d-226 (G)
House, Isaac 1851 wb-9-647 (Wi)
House, Isaac 1857 wb-7-0 (Sm)
House, Isaac 1858 wb-12-556 (Wi)
House, Isaac H. 1851 wb-9-646 (Wi)
House, Isham 1806 rb-a-440 (Mt)
House, Jacob 1805 wb-#2 (Wl)
House, Jacob 1860 wb-17-111 (Rb)
House, James 1797 rb-a-17 (Mt)
House, James 1825 wb-4-28 (Wi)
House, John 1832 wb-5-188 (Wi)
House, John 1836 wb-6-151 (Wi)
House, John B. 1848 wb-g-276 (Hn)
House, John C. 1857 rb-18-455 (Ru)
House, Joshua B. 1853 wb-10-494 (Wi)
House, L. S. 1856 rb-o-38 (Mt)
House, Lewis 1838 wb-a-39 (F)
House, Mansfield 1835 wb-6-73 (Wi)
House, Nicholis J. 1857 wb-b-32 (Ms)
House, R. 1859 wb-18-60 (D)
House, R. M. 1859 rb-p-58 (Mt)
House, Rosa 1861 wb-18-548 (D)
House, William D. 1849 wb-a-219 (Ms)
House, William F. 1842 wb-b-45 (We)
House, William M. 1848 wb-9-171 (Wi)
House?, James A. 1854 wb-15-576 (Rb)
Houser, Anthony 1848 wb-g-83 (O)
Houser, Charles A. 1827 wb-#162 (Mu)
Houser, Elizabeth 1851 wb-11-35 (K)
Houser, George 1843 wb-8-88 (K)
Houser, Harmon J. 1852 wb-h-Jul (O)
Houser, Henry 1824 wb-3-478 (K)
Houser, J. G. 1851 wb-15-127 (D)
Houser, James A. 1858 wb-2-436 (Me)
Houser, Johanna C. 1857 wb-17-355 (D)
Houser, John G. 1853 wb-16-124 (D)
Houston, Christopher 1837 wb-a-16 (Ms)
Houston, Elizabeth 1844 wb-a-75 (Ms)
Houston, Hugh 1858 ib-2-584 (Cl)
Houston, James 1820 wb-1-14# (Ge)
Houston, James 1839 wb-1-58 (Bo)
Houston, James 1842 as-a-67 (Ms)
Houston, James B. 1824 wb-8-359 (D)
Houston, James B. 1837 wb-11-39 (D)
Houston, John 1824 wb-4-9 (K)
Houston, John 1835 wb-1-61 (Bo)
Houston, John Moore 1841 as-a-52 (Ms)
Houston, Jonathan 1849 wb-1-264 (Fr)

Houston, Margaret 1848 wb-9-454 (K)
Houston, Robert 1834 wb-5-308 (K)
Houston, Robert 1835 wb-5-366 (K)
Houston, Robert 1842 wb-7-321 (K)
Houston, Samuel 1809 wb-1-196 (Wi)
Houston, Samuel 1851 wb-c-447 (Wh)
Houston, Sarah 1836 as-b-77 (Di)
Houston, Shadrack L. 1860 rb-p-385 (Mt)
Houston, William 1815 wb-1-208 (Bo)
Houston, William 1831 as-a-204 (Di)
Houston, William 1841 wb-1-11# (Ge)
Houston, William 1859 wb-#62 (Wa(
Houston, William M. 1854 wb-a-347 (Ms)
Houston, William sr. 1843 148-1-51 (Ge)
Houston, _____ 1837 wb-b-60 (Hd)
Houts, Christopher 1842 wb-2-57# (Ge)
Houts, Mary Ann (Magdalene) 1850
    wb-2-71# (Ge)
Houts, Mary Magdalene 1854 wb-2-80# (Ge)
Hoving, Michael 1819 wb-3-97 (K)
Hovis, John 1860 wb-2-326 (Li)
How, Catharine 1854 mr-2-540 (Be)
How?, A. Z. 1853 mr-2-495 (Be)
Howard, Abraham 1795 wb-1-70 (Je)
Howard, Abraham 1827 wb-a-19 (R)
Howard, Amelia 1858 wb-17-490 (D)
Howard, America 1849 wb-d-212 (G)
Howard, Asa 1833 wb-b-209 (Ro)
Howard, Barnet 1821 wb-1-39 (Fr)
Howard, Benjamin 1810 wb-#3 (Mu)
Howard, Benjamin 1840? wb-1-62 (Bo)
Howard, C. T. 1847 wb-4-143 (Hr)
Howard, Chas. T. 1848 wb-4-373 (Hr)
Howard, Christopher 1853 wb-2-45 (Li)
Howard, Edward 1854 wb-n-245 (Mt)
Howard, Eliza 1844 wb-12-257 (Rb)
Howard, Elizabeth 1842 wb-11-143 (Rb)
Howard, Elizabeth 1848 wb-14-73 (Rb)
Howard, George 1840 wb-1-60 (Bo)
Howard, George Walter 1854 wb-#81 (Mc)
Howard, Henry 1849 as-b-410 (Di)
Howard, Henry 1859 wb-3e-117 (Sh)
Howard, J. 1853 wb-#116 (Wl)
Howard, James 1827 wb-a-285 (Wh)
Howard, James 1855 wb-n-674 (Mt)
Howard, James M. 1855 wb-2-185 (Sh)
Howard, Jane 1842 wb-f-27 (Hn)
Howard, John 1797 wb-2-145# (Ge)
Howard, John 1810 wb-1-326 (K)
Howard, John 1828 wb-#177 (Mu)
Howard, John 1832 wb-#53 (Wa(

Howard, John B. 1842 lr (Sn)
Howard, John H. 1830 rb-f-138 (Mt)
Howard, John H. 1830 rb-f-144 (Mt)
Howard, John P. 1859 wb-00-2 (Cf)
Howard, Joseph 1859 wb-#61 (Wa(
Howard, M. S. 1859 wb-h-339 (Hn)
Howard, Mantion 1827 wb-a-17 (R)
Howard, Martain 1830 wb-c-73 (St)
Howard, Mary 1844 wb-c-129 (Wh)
Howard, Mary 1857 wb-e-172 (Wh)
Howard, Parmenes 1823 wb-#46 (Mu)
Howard, Parmenus 1810 wb-#21 (Mu)
Howard, Peola 1850 wb-a-145 (T)
Howard, Robert 1832 wb-b-100 (Wh)
Howard, Samuel 1833 wb-c-12 (Hn)
Howard, Samuel 1859 wb-1-1 (Br)
Howard, Sarah 1854 wb-0-135 (Cf)
Howard, Sarah A. 1846 wb-4-106 (Hr)
Howard, William 1814 wb-#17 (Wl)
Howard, William 1835 wb-1-117 (Li)
Howard, William 1854 wb-n-215 (Mt)
Howard, William 1857 wb-e-172 (Wh)
Howard, William B. 1828 wb-a-99 (G)
Howard, William H. 1848 wb-e-95 (Ro)
Howard, William H. 1857 lr (Gi)
Howard, William J. 1850 wb-4-67 (Mu)
Howard, Wm. 1830 wb-a-152 (G)
Howcott, Nathaniel 1856 wb-3e-33 (Sh)
Howdeshelt, 1838 1838 wb-2-233 (Sn)
Howe, William 1843 mr-2-59 (Be)
Howel, John 1820 wb-1-242 (Hw)
Howel, Phillip 1812 wb-#11 (Wl)
Howel, Thomas 1843 wb-5-275 (Gr)
Howel, Thomas K. 1843 wb-5-284 (Gr)
Howell, Abner 1809 wb-1-328 (Rb)
Howell, Addison W. 1845 wb-2-92 (W)
Howell, Arch 1858 wb-f-210 (G)
Howell, Archibald 1845 148-1-111 (Ge)
Howell, Benjamin 1834 wb-1-101 (Gr)
Howell, Caleb 1836 wb-b-93 (G)
Howell, Catharine F. 1854 rb-17-2 (Ru)
Howell, David 1815 wb-A-128 (Li)
Howell, David W. 1814 wb-2-90 (K)
Howell, Duke 1847 wb-9-388 (K)
Howell, Edward 1796 wb-1-39 (Sn)
Howell, Edward 1849 wb-#168 (Wl)
Howell, Elizabeth 1822 wb-1-43 (Fr)
Howell, Elizabeth 1859 wb-2-295 (Li)
Howell, Francis 1854 rb-17-46 (Ru)
Howell, Gwin 1812 rb-3-109 (Ru)
Howell, James H. 1861 wb-13-498 (K)

Howell, Jane O. 1850 33-3-192 (Gr)
Howell, Jethro 1850 rb-4-8 (Mu)
Howell, John 1808 rb-2-49 (Ru)
Howell, John 1815 wb-2-235 (Rb)
Howell, John 1860 wb-e-378 (Wh)
Howell, John H. 1858 wb-e-211 (Wh)
Howell, Malaciah 1850 wb-e-227 (Ro)
Howell, Mary 1851 wb-11-20 (K)
Howell, Mary 1857 wb-3-354 (Gr)
Howell, Moses 1794 wb-1-15 (K)
Howell, Paul 1813 wb-a-163 (St)
Howell, Philip jr. 1846 148-1-171 (Ge)
Howell, Philip sr. 1847 148-1-201 (Ge)
Howell, Ralph 1847 wb-4-199 (Hr)
Howell, Rosina B. 1854 wb-2-90 (Li)
Howell, Sterling 1852 wb-h-Jul (O)
Howell, Thomas 1845 wb-3-226 (Hr)
Howell, William 1814 rb-2-269 (Ru)
Howell, William 1844 wb-3-420 (Hy)
Howell, William H. 1859 wb-18-51 (D)
Howell, William S. 1838 wb-6-279 (K)
Howell, Zealous 1834 Ir (Gi)
Howerey, Daniel 1858 wb-f-464 (Ro)
Howerton, Eldred 1857 wb-17-172 (D)
Howerton, William 1835 wb-#119 (Wl)
Howerton, William 1835 wb-1-27 (Sh)
Howerton, William 1853 ib-1-295 (Cl)
Howlett, Green C. 1851 wb-5-91 (Ma)
Howlett, Isaac H. 1834 wb-10-304 (D)
Howlett, James 1831 wb-9-550 (D)
Howlett, Stockley H. 1835 wb-10-420 (D)
Howlett, William 1831 wb-9-535 (D)
Howlett, William 1832 wb-9-590 (D)
Hows, Racy 1859 wb-17-629 (D)
Howse, Ambrose 1855 rb-17-498 (Ru)
Howse, Hezekiah 1844 rb-12-558 (Ru)
Howse, Isaac L. 1841 rb-11-309 (Ru)
Howse, Isaac L. 1841 rb-11-313 (Ru)
Howse, John C. 1855 rb-17-497 (Ru)
Howse, John C. 1856 rb-17-786 (Ru)
Howse, Keziah 1844 rb-13-129 (Ru)
Howse, Robert 1840 rb-11-260 (Ru)
Howse, Robert C. 1840 rb-11-54 (Ru)
Howse, Susan 1860 rb-20-415 (Ru)
Howser, Daniel 1839 wb-6-406 (K)
Howser, John 1833 wb-5-261 (K)
Hoxan, John 1856 wb-1-63 (Be)
Hoy, John 1850 148-1-313 (Ge)
Hoyl, David 1838 wb-#81 (Mc)
Hoyl, John 1857 wb-#81 (Mc)
Hoyl, Nancy 1852 wb-#82 (Mc)

Hoysette?, Samuel 1837 wb-a-3 (L)
Hubbard, Benjamin H. 1853 wb-5-138 (Ma)
Hubbard, Clark 1859 wb-A-138 (Ca)
Hubbard, Edward 1824 wb-#52 (Wl)
Hubbard, James 1852 wb-h-Jun (O)
Hubbard, James F. 1852 wb-h-Mar (O)
Hubbard, John 1814 wb-1-0 (Sm)
Hubbard, John 1857 rb-18-276 (Ru)
Hubbard, Joseph & Susannah 1841
    wb-#134 (Wl)
Hubbard, Lee 1835 wb-#109 (Wl)
Hubbard, Moses 1850 wb-10-368 (K)
Hubbard, Patrick 1849 wb-3-0 (Sm)
Hubbard, Peter 1851 wb-7-0 (Sm)
Hubbard, Prudence 1853 wb-7-0 (Sm)
Hubbard, Reuben 1839 wb-#126 (Wl)
Hubbard, Susan B. 1842 wb-3-0 (Sm)
Hubbard, Thomas 1841 wb-3-0 (Sm)
Hubbard, William 1813 wb-a-184 (St)
Hubbard, William 1814 rb-b-172 (Mt)
Hubbard, William 1854 ib-H-97 (F)
Hubbard, William jr. 1854 ib-h-263 (F)
Hubbard, Woodson 1835 wb-b-68 (G)
Hubbard, Woodson 1856 wb-12-218 (Wi)
Hubbert, Sarah 1835 wb-2-198 (Sn)
Hubbs, James 1813 wb-2-64 (K)
Hubbs, John 1845 wb-5-350 (Gr)
Hubbs, John sr. 1844 wb-5-328 (Gr)
Hubbs, Martin B. 1853 wb-11-413 (K)
Hubert, John 1836 wb-a-90 (O)
Hubert, William 1824 Ir (Sn)
Huchinson, Lewis H. 1849 wb-g-68 (O)
Huckaby, John 1820 wb-#103 (Mu)
Huddleston, Anthony W. 1850 wb-#173 (Wl)
Huddleston, Bennet 1838 wb-10-163 (Rb)
Huddleston, David 1850 ib-1-118 (Cl)
Huddleston, Elizabeth 1821 wb-3-235 (Rb)
Huddleston, Isaac 1845 wb-c-168 (Wh)
Huddleston, Isaac L. 1842 wb-c-49 (Wh)
Huddleston, J. W. 1843 wb-11-394 (Rb)
Huddleston, James L. 1850 wb-c-386 (Wh)
Huddleston, Joseph 1846 wb-1-230 (Fr)
Huddleston, Josiah 1841 wb-10-549 (Rb)
Huddleston, Martha 1820 wb-#36 (Wl)
Huddleston, William 1813 wb-2-62 (Rb)
Huddleston, William W. 1855 wb-#117 (Wl)
Huddlestone, Robert 1842 wb-5-175 (Gr)
Hudeburgh, Thomas A. 1852 wb-11-219 (K)
Hudgen, T. F. 1858 wb-c-225 (L)
Hudgen, W. D. 1852 wb-15-353 (D)
Hudgens, G. 1861 wb-a-225 (Ce)

Hudgens, Gabriel 1839 wb-10-263 (Rb)
Hudgens, James 1847 wb-c-267 (Wh)
Hudgens, K. D. 1858 wb-h-261 (Hn)
Hudgens, Mary 1835 wb-9-69 (Rb)
Hudgens, Patcy 1845 wb-12-310 (Rb)
Hudgens, Polly J. 1861 wb-a-218 (Ce)
Hudgens, R. D. 1858 wb-h-295 (Hn)
Hudgens, Rebecca 1858 wb-7-25 (Ma)
Hudgeons, Wm. 1841 wb-1-54 (Bo)
Hudgings, Gabriel 1834 wb-8-387 (Rb)
Hudgings, Samuel 1834 wb-8-410 (Rb)
Hudgins, Abner 1836 as-a-360 (Di)
Hudgins, Edward 1841 wb-10-590 (Rb)
Hudgins, Gabriel G. 1835 wb-9-29 (Rb)
Hudgins, James 1815 wb-2-189 (Rb)
Hudgins, James 1858 wb-a-84 (Ce)
Hudgins, Mary T. 1861 wb-a-228 (Ce)
Hudgins, Moses 1841 wb-10-558 (Rb)
Hudgins, Susannah 1846 wb-13-15 (Rb)
Hudgins, W. D. 1858 wb-17-433 (D)
Hudibagh, Lewis 1839 wb-6-414 (K)
Hudleberg, R. 1844 wb-4-218 (Ma)
Hudlow, George 1812 wb-1-285 (Wi)
Hudson, Aaron 1827 wb-6-149 (Rb)
Hudson, Andrew G. 1848 lr (Sn)
Hudson, Baker 1859 gs-1-493 (F)
Hudson, Burel 1819 wb-a-133 (Wh)
Hudson, C. 1825 as-a-152 (Di)
Hudson, Cuthbert 1822 as-A-24 (Di)
Hudson, Cuthbert 1853 wb-16-210 (D)
Hudson, Enoch M. 1843 rb-12-419 (Ru)
Hudson, Francis 1847 wb-e-59 (Ro)
Hudson, George 1849 wb-1-1 (Se)
Hudson, Harry 1857 wb-17-258 (D)
Hudson, Henry M. 1823 rb-5-294 (Ru)
Hudson, Hubbord 1850 wb-#12 (Mo)
Hudson, Isaac 1850 wb-14-489 (D)
Hudson, J. Thomas 1846 wb-1B-172 (A)
Hudson, James 1833 wb-#102 (Wl)
Hudson, Jesse 1841 wb-e-50 (St)
Hudson, John 1820 wb-3-185 (Rb)
Hudson, John 1826 rb-d-536 (Mt)
Hudson, John 1827 wb-a-36 (R)
Hudson, John 1830 lr (Sn)
Hudson, John 1830 wb-4-481 (Wi)
Hudson, John 1831 wb-#91 (Wl)
Hudson, John 1837? as-a-367 (Di)
Hudson, John 1839 wb-a-411 (R)
Hudson, John 1843 wb-11-324 (Rb)
Hudson, John 1857 wb-16-462 (Rb)
Hudson, Joseph G. 1843 wb-d-65 (Hd)

Hudson, Joseph S. 1862 wb-2-364 (Li)
Hudson, Judith 1853 wb-16-201 (D)
Hudson, Nancy 1845 wb-#148 (Wl)
Hudson, Obadiah 1840 wb-#131 (Wl)
Hudson, Peter jr. 1838 wb-c-23 (Ro)
Hudson, Polly 1850 wb-e-235 (Ro)
Hudson, Richard H. 1838 wb-d-182* (Hn)
Hudson, Thomas 1840 wb-e-351 (Hu)
Hudson, W. W. 1858 wb-1-237 (Be)
Hudson, William 1821 wb-a-34 (Di)
Hudson, William 1841 wb-#134 (Wl)
Hudspeth, James 1840 wb-z-134 (Mu)
Hudspeth, Sarah 1850 wb-4-64 (Mu)
Hudspeth, Thomas 1817 wb-1-26 (Fr)
Hudspeth, Thomas 1835 wb-x-283* (Mu)
Hudspeth, Thomas 1845 wb-f-273* (Hn)
Hudwall, N. B. 1854 mr-2-585 (Be)
Huey, James 1839 wb-y-363 (Mu)
Huey, John 1816 wb-2-337 (Rb)
Huey, William 1813 wb-2-63 (Rb)
Huff, John 1831 wb-b-93 (Ro)
Huff, Joseph 1852 wb-2-75# (Ge)
Huff, Rebecca 1855 lr (Gi)
Huff, Sterling 1855 lr (Gi)
Huff, Urial 1850 wb-1-358 (Me)
Huff, W. D. 1848 wb-g-71 (Hu)
Huff, Wiley 1855 rb-17-412 (Ru)
Huffaker, John 1839 wb-6-428 (K)
Huffaker, John 1856 wb-12-295 (K)
Huffaker, Peter 1846 5-3-188 (Cl)
Huffman, Archebald Y. 1855 wb-#116 (Wl)
Huffman, Balsor 1843 wb-12-433* (D)
Huffman, Burrell 1834 wb-#105 (Wl)
Huffman, Leonard 1839 wb-#124 (Wl)
Huffman, Mary 1844 wb-c-135 (Wh)
Huffmaster, Goodleff 1844 wb-1-247 (Hw)
Huflen, Absalom 1841 rb-i-115 (Mt)
Hufstutter, George 1854 wb-i-140 (O)
Hugely, Henry A. 1851 wb-10-30 (Wi)
Huggins, C. G. 1853 wb-15-577 (D)
Huggins, Carter 1851 wb-#21 (Mo)
Huggins, Eli C. 1858 wb-17-506 (D)
Huggins, Elizabeth 1859 rb-19-570 (Ru)
Huggins, John 1855 wb-16-542 (D)
Huggins, Robert D. 1836 rb-9-375 (Ru)
Huggins, William 1840 wb-b-7 (We)
Huggins, William 1857 wb-17-280 (D)
Hugh, J. H. 1846 wb-13-422 (D)
Hugh, Kirk 1851 rb-16-57 (Ru)
Hughes, Aaron 1799 wb-1-258 (Je)
Hughes, Albert G. 1843 wb-8-9 (Wi)

Hughes, Archilus 1834 wb-c-144 (Hn)
Hughes, Archilus 1854 wb-11-246 (Wi)
Hughes, Brice M. 1845 wb-e-146 (O)
Hughes, Edward P. 1824 wb-1-0 (Sm)
Hughes, Farley B. 1847 wb-7-0 (Sm)
Hughes, George 1859 149-1-143 (Ge)
Hughes, George R. 1833 wb-5-337 (Wi)
Hughes, George W. 1838 wb-7-1 (Wi)
Hughes, J. Bev 1838? wb-a-133 (Di)
Hughes, James 1841 wb-7-459 (Wi)
Hughes, James 1858 wb-12-594 (Wi)
Hughes, John 1795 wb-1-12# (Ge)
Hughes, John 1819 wb-A-260 (Li)
Hughes, John 1827 wb-3-0 (Sm)
Hughes, John 1860 wb-13-380 (Wi)
Hughes, John Bev. 1841 as-a-502 (Di)
Hughes, John L. 1855 wb-16-467 (D)
Hughes, John S. 1823 wb-A-355 (Li)
Hughes, Kibble T. 1838 wb-y-173 (Mu)
Hughes, Mary E. 1854 wb-5-50 (Hr)
Hughes, Moses 1833 wb-2-145# (Ge)
Hughes, Nicholas 1840 wb-7-327 (Wi)
Hughes, Richard 1827 wb-4-209 (Wi)
Hughes, Richard E. 1855 wb-15-717 (Rb)
Hughes, Robert 1856 wb-1-72 (Bo)
Hughes, Simon 1823 wb-1-0 (Sm)
Hughes, Tarlton 1850 wb-7-0 (Sm)
Hughes, Thomas 1830 wb-1-140 (Hr)
Hughes, Thomas B. 1827 wb-1-55 (Hr)
Hughes, William 1854 lr (Gi)
Hughes, William E. 1852 wb-10-204 (Wi)
Hughes, William H. 1855 lr (Sn)
Hughes, William J. 1861 wb-170 (Su)
Hughes, William no date wb-1-59 (Bo)
Hughey, Alexander 1843 wb-1-224 (Li)
Hughey, Edward 1838 wb-e-133 (Hu)
Hughey, Elizabeth 1837 wb-1-127 (Li)
Hughey, Henry 1832 wb-1-84 (Li)
Hughey, Joseph 1845 wb-12-366 (Rb)
Hughey, William B. 1848 wb-g-111 (Hu)
Hughlet, James 1838 wb-10-160 (Rb)
Hughlett, Leroy 1828 wb-6-305 (Rb)
Hughley, Alfed 1847 wb-#156 (Wl)
Hughs, Elijah 1828 wb-6-360 (Rb)
Hughs, Francis 1837 wb-b-353 (Ro)
Hughs, Gideliah 1822 wb-#41 (Wl)
Hughs, Gideliah 1836 wb-#114 (Wl)
Hughs, Gideon 1817 wb-#53 (Wl)
Hughs, Gideon 1828 wb-#71 (Wl)
Hughs, James 1826 wb-#58 (Wl)
Hughs, James M. 1851 wb-b-121 (L)

Hughs, Nancy W. 1847 wb-d-52 (G)
Hughs, Polly 1826 wb-4-75 (Wi)
Hughs, Powel? 1830? wb-1A-53 (A)
Hughs, Powell 1827? wb-1A-8 (A)
Hughs, Robert M. 1844 wb-f-209 (Hn)
Hughs, Thomas 1837 wb-1-280 (Hy)
Hughs, William 1852 wb-15-171 (Rb)
Hughy, William 1825 wb-5-5 (Rb)
Hugueley, Charles 1861 wb-#133 (Wl)
Huguely, Abraham 1849 wb-#119 (Wl)
Huguley, James 1830 wb-#85 (Wl)
Hulgan, Robert 1826 wb-#137 (Mu)
Hulgan, Stephen 1845 wb-9-146 (K)
Huling, George 1825 wb-b-23 (St)
Hull, David 1853 wb-5-34 (Hr)
Hull, John 1836 wb-2-47# (Ge)
Hull, John sr. 1847 148-1-199 (Ge)
Hull, Joseph 1835 wb-1-424 (Hr)
Hull?, Thomas 1831 wb-1-188 (Hr)
Hullet, William 1838 wb-a-6 (Dk)
Hullmark, Thomas 1809 wb-1-295 (K)
Hullum, D. W. sr. 1851 wb-5-10 (Hr)
Hulme, George W. 1834 wb-5-400 (Wi)
Hulme, George W. 1836 wb-6-119 (Wi)
Hulme, John C. 1818 wb-2-376 (Wi)
Hulme, Mary E. 1853 wb-10-461 (Wi)
Hulme, Robert 1844 wb-8-173 (Wi)
Hulme, Robert 1858 wb-12-553 (Wi)
Hulme, William 1817 wb-2-265 (Wi)
Hulsey, John 1860 wb-17-107 (Rb)
Humbard, Aidin 1853 148-1-447 (Ge)
Humberd, Jonathan 1841 wb-2-56# (Ge)
Humble, Mac 1860 wb-18-287 (D)
Hume, Alfred 1854 wb-16-277 (D)
Hume, Jesse W. 1854 rb-17-274 (Ru)
Hume, William 1833 wb-10-179 (D)
Humes, Thomas 1816 wb-2-272 (K)
Humes, Thomas 1833 wb-5-188 (K)
Humphrey, Charles 1837 rb-g-514 (Mt)
Humphrey, Dennis 1854 wb-12-19 (K)
Humphrey, James 1845 wb-#83 (Mc)
Humphrey, Riverious B. 1857 wb-5-74 (Hr)
Humphrey, William 1845 wb-c-260 (G)
Humphreys, Adaline 1854 wb-#10 (Mo)
Humphreys, Asa 1839 wb-e-61 (Hn)
Humphreys, Benjamin 1815 Wb-2-161 (Wi)
Humphreys, Charles L. 1823 wb-3-610 (Wi)
Humphreys, Daniel 1850 rb-4-15 (Mu)
Humphreys, David 1851 wb-d-4 (Wh)
Humphreys, Elijah 1816 lr (Sn)
Humphreys, George 1836 rb-g-446 (Mt)

Humphreys, Henry 1843 wb-f-134 (Hn)
Humphreys, Jesse 1830 lw (Ct)
Humphreys, John H. 1843 wb-e-619 (Hu)
Humphreys, John H. 1844 wb-e-621 (Hu)
Humphreys, N. T. 1856 wb-#27 (Mo)
Humphreys, Thomas 1859 wb-h-374 (Hn)
Humphreys, William 1835 wb-1-73 (Bo)
Humphreys, William C. 1853 wb-#24 (Mo)
Humphries, John 1851 wb-14-660 (D)
Humphries, Richard 1810 rb-a-486 (Mt)
Humphries, Solomon 1817 wb-2-312 (Wi)
Humphrys, Daniel J. 1839 wb-3-25 (Ma)
Hundley, James 1856 wb-6-421 (Ma)
Hundley, Jordan 1853 wb-1-258 (Hw)
Hundley, Margarett 1841 wb-12-117* (D)
Hungerford, Jane 1838 wb-a-70 (T)
Hunley, J. Y. 1840 wb-b-230 (Hd)
Hunnell, William 1809 Wb-1-57 (Wi)
Hunnicutt, Lewis 1849 lr (Gi)
Hunt (Hale), Elizabeth 1855 39-2-94 (Dk)
Hunt, A. J. 1854 wb-16-313 (D)
Hunt, Adam P. 1851 148-1-355 (Ge)
Hunt, Archibald 1862 wb-#136 (Wl)
Hunt, Benjamin 1831 wb-#102 (Wl)
Hunt, Christena 1841 rb-11-149 (Ru)
Hunt, Christopher 1836 wb-a-4 (F)
Hunt, Enoch J. 1852 wb-15-247 (D)
Hunt, George 1807 wb-1-130 (Sn)
Hunt, George 1815 wb-#18 (Mu)
Hunt, Gershom 1839 wb-7-29 (Wi)
Hunt, Green W. 1844 wb-8-192 (Wi)
Hunt, Hardy 1829 lr (Sn)
Hunt, Hardy 1860 wb-f-394 (G)
Hunt, Henry 1825 wb-#58 (Wl)
Hunt, Henry 1843 wb-11-344 (Rb)
Hunt, Henry 1862 wb-f-431 (G)
Hunt, Henson 1854 wb-2-5 (Ct)
Hunt, James 1805 wb-1-139 (Rb)
Hunt, James 1815 wb-#12 (Mu)
Hunt, James 1829 rb-7-167 (Ru)
Hunt, James W. 1861 wb-a-180 (Ce)
Hunt, Jno. W. 1849 wb-4-551 (Hr)
Hunt, John 1842 as-a-59 (Ms)
Hunt, John 1847 wb-4-230 (Hr)
Hunt, John 1856 wb-a-1 (Ce)
Hunt, John H. 1841 wb-a-93 (T)
Hunt, Jonathan S. 1861 wb-f-208 (Mu)
Hunt, Letha 1834 wb-#107 (Wl)
Hunt, Lucy 1815 wb-#11 (Mu)
Hunt, Margaret A. 1860 39-2-380 (Dk)
Hunt, Martha 1847 lr (Sn)

Hunt, Mary 1840 wb-e-140 (Hn)
Hunt, Mary Ann 1849 wb-4-419 (Hr)
Hunt, Mary Ann 1850 wb-4-600 (Hr)
Hunt, Mathew 1849 rb-15-232 (Ru)
Hunt, Mathew 1858 wb-b-39 (Dk)
Hunt, Matthew 1832 rb-8-421 (Ru)
Hunt, Nancy 1843 rb-14-220 (Ru)
Hunt, Nancy T. 1843 wb-c-126 (G)
Hunt, Narcissa Cintha 1859 wb-a-140 (Ce)
Hunt, Patience 1844 wb-#144 (Wl)
Hunt, Samuel 1848? wb-#51 (Wa(
Hunt, Sarah 1836 wb-a-14 (F)
Hunt, Sarah 1849 wb-9-313 (Wi)
Hunt, Sarah 1852? wb-#51 (Wa(
Hunt, Shadrick 1847 wb-13-186 (Rb)
Hunt, Simon 1814 wb-#14 (Wa(
Hunt, Sion 1827 wb-4-177 (Wi)
Hunt, Sion? 1851 wb-14-440 (Rb)
Hunt, Solomon 1841 rb-i-190 (Mt)
Hunt, Spencer T. 1844 wb-e-630 (Hu)
Hunt, Susanah 1845 wb-c-251 (G)
Hunt, Thomas 1831 lr (Sn)
Hunt, Thomas 1836 wb-#114 (Wl)
Hunt, Thomas 1842 wb-11-341 (Rb)
Hunt, Tibman S. 1838 wb-11-333 (D)
Hunt, Wilkins J. 1842 wb-2-300 (Hr)
Hunt, William 1834 wb-8-397 (Rb)
Hunt, William C. 1860 wb-13-286 (Wi)
Hunt, William G. 1834 wb-10-314 (D)
Hunt, William Hasell 1841 wb-12-230* (D)
Hunt, Wm. 1844 wb-12-90 (Rb)
Hunter, Adam 1824 lr (Sn)
Hunter, Albert G. 1841 wb-2-363 (Hy)
Hunter, Allen 1820 rb-c-366 (Mt)
Hunter, Andrew 1838 eb-1-333 (C)
Hunter, Ann 1835 wb-#109 (Wl)
Hunter, Aron 1815 wb-#10 (Mu)
Hunter, Catharine 1831 wb-5-43 (Wi)
Hunter, Celina Tate 1857 wb-f-126 (Mu)
Hunter, Cynthia 1854 wb-2-101 (Li)
Hunter, David 1859 wb-18-87 (D)
Hunter, David 1861 wb-18-579 (D)
Hunter, Dudley 1860 wb-e-451 (Wh)
Hunter, E. W. 1850 wb-m-7 (Mt)
Hunter, Edwin C. 1841 as-a-41 (Ms)
Hunter, Elijah 1817 wb-2-309 (Wi)
Hunter, Elijah 1836 wb-x-387 (Mu)
Hunter, Elisha 1829 wb-4-386 (Wi)
Hunter, Elizabeth 1829 wb-4-392 (Wi)
Hunter, Elizabeth W. 1849 rb-l-498 (Mt)
Hunter, Ephraim 1861 as-c-240 (Ms)

Hunter, Franklin G. 1845 wb-a2-262 (Mu)
Hunter, Henry 1833 wb-1-398 (Ma)
Hunter, Henry 1856 ib-2-366 (Cl)
Hunter, Henry H. 1857 lr (Gi)
Hunter, Jacob 1807 wb-3-159 (D)
Hunter, Jacob 1824 wb-#87 (Mu)
Hunter, James 1828 wb-#71 (Wl)
Hunter, James 1847 5-3-217 (Cl)
Hunter, James A. 1828 wb-#74 (Wl)
Hunter, James A. 1844 wb-8-147 (Wi)
Hunter, James H. 1830 wb-#207 (Mu)
Hunter, John 1789 wb-1-95 (D)
Hunter, John 1823 wb-#20 (Wa(
Hunter, John 1850 wb-#49 (Wa(
Hunter, John 1851 wb-f-11 (Mu)
Hunter, John 1858 149-1-112 (Ge)
Hunter, Jos. C. 1851 wb-d-330 (G)
Hunter, Joseph 1841 wb-c-19 (Wh)
Hunter, Joseph 1843 wb-c-95 (Wh)
Hunter, Joseph 1854 wb-11-307 (Wi)
Hunter, Joseph 1855 wb-e-314 (G)
Hunter, Joseph C. 1851 wb-d-321 (G)
Hunter, Joseph C. 1855 wb-e-318 (G)
Hunter, Lucy 1850 rb-l-625 (Mt)
Hunter, M. R. 1849 rb-l-500 (Mt)
Hunter, Martin R. 1848 rb-l-44 (Mt)
Hunter, Mary 1842 wb-c-64 (Wh)
Hunter, Mathew 1846 rb-k-345 (Mt)
Hunter, Mathew B. 1846 rb-k-282 (Mt)
Hunter, Mathew R. 1846 rb-k-251 (Mt)
Hunter, Nancy 1853 ib-1-303 (Cl)
Hunter, Needham 1844 lr (Sn)
Hunter, Phebe 1840 wb-7-46 (K)
Hunter, R. H. 1855 as-b-201 (Ms)
Hunter, Reubin 1833 wb-1-96 (Li)
Hunter, Samuel 1852 wb-2-121 (Me)
Hunter, Samuel 1859 wb-7-0 (Sm)
Hunter, Sarah 1853 wb-2-179 (Me)
Hunter, Sylvester M. 1855 as-b-200 (Ms)
Hunter, Tabitha 1861 iv-C-49 (C)
Hunter, Thomas 1836 rb-g-342 (Mt)
Hunter, Thomas 1842 wb-1-56 (Bo)
Hunter, Thomas 1842 wb-11-266 (Rb)
Hunter, Thomas 1844 wb-d-264 (O)
Hunter, Thomas 1845 148-1-102 (Ge)
Hunter, Thomas 1849 wb-1-340 (Me)
Hunter, Thomas J. 1841 wb-1-365 (W)
Hunter, Thos. sr. 1852 wb-2-103 (Me)
Hunter, Tirza 1855 as-b-181 (Ms)
Hunter, William 1836 wb-#110 (Wl)
Hunter, William 1845 wb-c-178 (Wh)

Hunter, William 1845 wb-c-182 (Wh)
Hunter, William H. 1827 wb-#72 (Wl)
Hunter, William H. 1830 wb-#207 (Mu)
Hunter, Wright 1853 wb-#111 (Wl)
Huntington, Willis 1855 wb-6-168 (Ma)
Huntsman, George T. 1859 wb-3e-109 (Sh)
Huntsman, John 1808 wb-1-246 (K)
Huntsman, Nancy 1858 wb-7-32 (Ma)
Hurd, William 1820 rb-c-324 (Mt)
Hurdle, Sarah 1851 wb-11-1 (K)
Hurdle, Truman 1837 wb-6-141 (K)
Hurley, A. B. 1859 gs-1-338 (F)
Hurley, Ann 1843 148-1-42 (Ge)
Hurley, Canada? 1857 lw (Ct)
Hurley, Moses 1818 wb-1-30 (Fr)
Hurley, Thomas 1841 wb-b-333 (Hd)
Hurley, Zechariah 1852 148-1-389 (Ge)
Hurst, Aaron 1839 5-2-54 (Cl)
Hurst, Andrew 1839 5-2-105 (Cl)
Hurst, Arthur R. 1856 rb-o-276 (Mt)
Hurst, E. (Mrs.) 1859 rb-p-24 (Mt)
Hurst, Elijah 1816 wb-7-13 (D)
Hurst, Elijah 1844 wb-#83 (Mc)
Hurst, Elizabeth 1858 rb-o-662 (Mt)
Hurst, Jesse 1843 5-2-331 (Cl)
Hurst, John 1838 5-2-28 (Cl)
Hurst, John 1840 5-2-186 (Cl)
Hurst, Milton 1853 ib-1-292 (Cl)
Hurst, R. R. 1838 wb-1-172 (La)
Hurst, Silva 1855 ib-2-355 (Cl)
Hurst, Sina 1854 ib-2-74 (Cl)
Hurst, Thomas 1847 5-3-265 (Cl)
Hurst, Thomas 1850 ib-1-153 (Cl)
Hurst, W. R. 1838 wb-1-173 (La)
Hurst, William 1816 wb-7-11 (D)
Hurt, Arthur H. 1854 wb-n-208 (Mt)
Hurt, Benjamin 1860 wb-18-145 (D)
Hurt, Bird S. 1836 wb-x-419 (Mu)
Hurt, Elisha 1853 wb-a-317 (Ms)
Hurt, Floyd 1842 wb-12-299* (D)
Hurt, Floyd 1855 wb-16-539 (D)
Hurt, Gillington A. 1858 wb-f-142 (Ro)
Hurt, Hiram 1817 wb-7-206 (D)
Hurt, Jane N. 1851 lr (Gi)
Hurt, Josiah 1818 wb-7-239 (D)
Hurt, Josiah 1835 wb-10-429 (D)
Hurt, Moses 1836 wb-x-291* (Mu)
Hurt, Phillip 1845 lr (Sn)
Hurt, Robert 1842 wb-a-98 (Cr)
Hurt, Spencer T. 1855 wb-a-233 (T)
Husk, Joseph 1812 rb-b-50 (Mt)

Hust, Elizabeth 1860 rb-p-459 (Mt)
Hust, Joseph 1812 rb-b-82 (Mt)
Hust, Rebecca 1855 rb-17-469 (Ru)
Hust, William 1843 rb-i-528 (Mt)
Huston, Nancy R. 1855 wb-b*-38 (O)
Huston, William M. 1845 wb-#84 (Mc)
Hutchenson, Sarah 1832 rb-8-467 (Ru)
Hutcheons, Tucker 1845 wb-c-258 (G)
Hutcher, Henry 1857 rb-o-490 (Mt)
Hutcherson, J. B. 1855 wb-c-67 (L)
Hutcherson, James B. 1854 wb-b-269 (L)
Hutcherson, John T. 1854 wb-n-344 (Mt)
Hutcherson, Joshua P. 1828 rb-e-274 (Mt)
Hutcherson, L. M. 1849 wb-g-114 (O)
Hutcherson, Mary 1854 wb-i-204 (O)
Hutcherson, Matilda 1860 wb-c-331 (L)
Hutcherson, William 1840 wb-a-427 (R)
Hutcherson, William 1859 lr (Sn)
Hutcheson, Asa 1844 wb-b-56 (We)
Hutcheson, Charles 1842 wb-1-86 (Me)
Hutcheson, Robert 1855 wb-#11 (Mo)
Hutchings, Aaron 1854 wb-d-266 (Wh)
Hutchings, Christopher 1854 wb-5-158 (Ma)
Hutchings, John 1860 rb-p-441 (Mt)
Hutchings, Thomas 1805 wb-3-5 (D)
Hutchins, Henry 1860 gs-1-603 (F)
Hutchins, John 1840 wb-b-390 (Wh)
Hutchins, Sarah 1848 wb-d-113 (G)
Hutchins, Webster 1837 wb-b-285 (Wh)
Hutchinson, Thomas 1808 rb-2-71 (Ru)
Hutchinson, William 1849 wb-g-184 (O)
Hutchinson, William B. 1849 wb-g-214 (O)
Hutchison, B. 1853 wb-#108 (Wl)
Hutchison, James 1800 wb-1-13# (Ge)
Hutchison, James 1836 wb-x-376 (Mu)
Hutchison, James 1850 wb-m-110 (Mt)
Hutchison, Jane 1857 lr (Sn)
Hutchison, Jas. 1850 wb-m-60 (Mt)
Hutchison, John 1822 rb-d-106 (Mt)
Hutchison, John 1836 wb-9-291 (Rb)
Hutchison, John 1860 wb-17-56 (Rb)
Hutchison, John sr. 1826 rb-d-524 (Mt)
Hutchison, Samuel 1854 wb-e-31 (Hy)
Hutchison, Welmouth 1844 wb-f-196* (Hn)
Hutchisson, Benjamin 1849 wb-1-257 (Hw)
Hutson, Abel 1845 wb-c-195 (Wh)
Hutson, Abel 1845 wb-c-198 (Wh)
Hutson, George 1859 wb-e-312 (Wh)
Hutson, James M. 1861 wb-e-438 (Wh)
Hutson, Jane 1839 wb-#84 (Mc)
Hutson, Jessee 1804 wb-2-344 (D)

Hutson, John 1821 rb-c-530 (Mt)
Hutson, Pleasant 1860 wb-e-374 (Wh)
Hutton, Charles 1814 wb-4-269 (D)
Hutton, John M. 1833 wb-5-320 (Wi)
Hutton, Thomas W. 1847 wb-14-115 (D)
Hutton, William D. 1858 wb-a-64 (Ce)
Huzza, John 1856 wb-j-190 (O)
Hyde, Alexander F. 1840 rb-i-49 (Mt)
Hyde, Alexander H. 1840 rb-i-4 (Mt)
Hyde, C. H. 1855 wb-16-525 (D)
Hyde, Christiana H. 1857 wb-17-342 (D)
Hyde, Edmund 1851 wb-14-560 (D)
Hyde, Edmund J. 1845 wb-13-324 (D)
Hyde, Hartwell 1833 wb-5-291 (Wi)
Hyde, Henry 1812 wb-4-200 (D)
Hyde, Henry 1825 wb-8-422 (D)
Hyde, Henry 1831 wb-7-476 (Rb)
Hyde, John 1839 wb-10-171 (Rb)
Hyde, John 1839 wb-10-2* (Rb)
Hyde, Jordan 1828 wb-9-154 (D)
Hyde, L. C. 1860 wb-18-381 (D)
Hyde, Mary D. 1836 wb-10-541 (D)
Hyde, Rebecca 1829 wb-9-347 (D)
Hyde, Richard 1859 wb-17-598 (D)
Hyde, Richard W. 1836 wb-6-200 (Wi)
Hyde, Richard sr. 1859 wb-18-44 (D)
Hyde, Taswell 1838 wb-11-401 (D)
Hyder, John 1833 wb-1-78 (Ct)
Hyder, Michael Sr. 1860 wb-2-27 (Ct)
Hyer, Randolph 1846 wb-g-111 (Hn)
Hynds, George W. 1846 wb-b-177 (We)
Hynds, Robert H. 1856 wb-5-398 (Je)
Hynes, Andrew 1849 wb-14-469 (D)
Hynes, John B. 1860 wb-1-142 (Jo)
Hynes, William 1839 wb-1-49 (Sh)

- I -

Idol, Adam 1854 wb-3-151 (Gr)
Ikard, Anthony 1847 wb#18 (Gu)
Iles, William 1819 wb-#16 (Wa(
Ils, Jean 1822 lw (Ct)
Ingle, Jacob 1813 wb-A-27 (Li)
Ingle, John 1848 wb-1-187 (Me)
Ingle, John jr? 1850 wb-2-2 (Me)
Ingle, Michael 1849 wb-1-268 (Me)
Ingle, William 1807 wb-#13 (Wa(
Ingle, William 1831 wb-1-63 (Li)
Ingles, Michael 1809 wb-#11 (Wa(
Inglish, A. J. 1858 rb-19-381 (Ru)
Ingram, Bealey 1854 wb-3-183 (La)

Ingram, Benjamin 1835 wb-a-3 (O)
Ingram, Cythia 1856 rb-o-227 (Mt)
Ingram, George 1860 wb-#84 (Mc)
Ingram, Hendleton 1857 wb-f-84 (G)
Ingram, Henry 1818 wb-2-379 (Wi)
Ingram, John 1807 wb-1-152 (Wi)
Ingram, John 1850 wb-10-322 (K)
Ingram, Joseph 1843 wb-z-536 (Mu)
Ingram, Merritt 1859 wb-13-152 (Wi)
Ingram, Merritt 1859 wb-13-154 (Wi)
Ingram, Moses 1852 wb-m-602 (Mt)
Ingram, Samuel 1850 wb-g-374 (Hn)
Ingram, Samuel B. 1858 wb-17-427 (D)
Ingram, Santill 1849 wb-g-326 (Hn)
Ingram, Sterling 1823 rb-d-206 (Mt)
Ingram, Thomas 1807 wb-3-175 (D)
Ingram, Thomas 1851? wb-1B-274 (A)
Ingram, W. J. 1859 wb-f-272 (G)
Ingram, William 1840 wb-7-98* (K)
Ingram, William P. 1837 wb-a-22 (F)
Ingram, Zaney 1860 wb-13-311 (Wi)
Inman, Abednego 1831 wb-3-132 (Je)
Inman, Alexander 1851 wb-2-167 (La)
Inman, David 1851 wb-2-165 (La)
Inman, J. R. 1859 ib-2-154 (Wy)
Inman, James R. 1859 ib-2-185 (Wy)
Inman, Jeremiah 1839 wb-4-35 (Je)
Inman, John 1838 wb-a-21 (L)
Inman, John 1859 wb-13-86 (Wi)
Inman, John C. 1852 wb-3-71 (La)
Inman, John C. 1858 lr (Gi)
Inman, Joseph 1855 lr (Gi)
Inman, Shadrach 1832 wb-3-205 (Je)
Inman, Shadrach 1833 wb-3-229 (Je)
Inman, Shadrach 1852 wb-5-25 (Je)
Irby, Carter 1837 wb-1-329 (Hy)
Irby, Charles 1833 lr (Sn)
Irby, Gerald 1837 wb-1-32 (Sh)
Irby, Henry 1859 gs-1-209 (F)
Irby, Nancy 1860 wb-#131 (Wl)
Irby, O. E. (Mrs.) 1859 gs-1-498 (F)
Irby, Olive G. 1860 gs-1-632 (F)
Irby, William 1848 wb-2-45 (Sh)
Iredale, John 1842 wb-12-260* (D)
Ireland, Benjamin W. 1858 lr (Sn)
Ireland, Daniel 1861 wb-17-225 (Rb)
Ireon, John P. 1857 wb-h-112 (Hn)
Ireson, James 1788 wb-1-69 (D)
Iron, Fredrick W. 1816 Wb-2-188 (Wi)
Iron, Sarah 1815 wb-2-151 (Wi)
Irons, Philip Jacob 1815 wb-2-150 (Wi)

Irons, V. R. 1856 ib-h-515 (F)
Irons, William 1851 wb-a-395 (F)
Irvin, Andrew 1854 wb-h-75 (St)
Irvin, Christopher 1823 wb-3-629 (Wi)
Irvin, Christopher 1840 wb-y-692 (Mu)
Irvin, George S. 1851 wb-b-137 (L)
Irvin, John 1840 wb-d-412 (St)
Irvin, William 1852 ib-1-205 (Ca)
Irvin, William 1855 ib-h-445 (F)
Irvine, George 1838 wb-3-497 (Je)
Irvine, Isaac L. J. Harber 1810 wb-1-350 (Je)
Irvine, J. P. J. H. 1815 wb-2-114 (Je)
Irvine, James H. 1828 rb-e-376 (Mt)
Irvine, James L. 1850 wb-b-597 (Mu)
Irvine, Rebecca 1834 wb-#31 (Wa(
Irwin, Adaline B. B. 1851 wb-m-217 (Mt)
Irwin, David 1824 wb-3-723 (Wi)
Irwin, David 1856 wb-h-253 (St)
Irwin, Isaac 1831 wb-a-171 (G)
Irwin, James 1796 wb-#6 (Wa(
Irwin, James 1836 wb-d-21 (St)
Irwin, John 1816 wb-7-19 (D)
Irwin, Joseph M. 1849 rb-l-205 (Mt)
Irwin, Lewis 1845 wb-a-260 (F)
Irwin, Martha 1836 wb-a-45 (T)
Irwin, Montgomery 1857 wb-#59 (Wa(
Irwin, Penelope E. 1852 wb-#84 (Mc)
Irwin, Rachel 1828 wb-a-330 (Wh)
Irwin, Rachel 1861 wb-18-635 (D)
Irwin, Robert 1823 wb-3-614 (Wi)
Irwin, Samuel 1840 wb-4-19 (Je)
Irwin, Thomas 1844 wb-c-135 (Wh)
Irwine, Robert 1808 ib-1-219 (Ge)
Isbell, George 1794 wb-1-313 (Rb)
Isbell, George 1855 wb-n-685 (Mt)
Isbell, George 1855 wb-n-686 (Mt)
Isbell, George sr. 1857 rb-o-350 (Mt)
Isbell, John M. 1853 wb-#25 (Mo)
Isbell, W. J. 1861 wb-b-72 (Dk)
Iseminger, William R. 1839 rb-10-267 (Ru)
Isenberg, Jacob 1861 wb-1-264 (Hw)
Isenberger, Henry 1809 wb-#24 (Wa(
Ish, Jacob 1844 wb-1-100 (Sh)
Ish, John 1794 wb-1-23 (K)
Isham, Carlin? 1836 wb-#116 (Wl)
Isham, Charles 1816 wb-#25 (Mu)
Isham, Henry 1860 wb-f-370 (Ro)
Isham, James 1823 wb-a-190 (Wh)
Isham, James 1837 wb-b-265 (Wh)
Isham, Jonathan 1813 wb-#40 (Mu)
Isham, Jonathan 1813 wb-#7 (Mu)

Isham, William 1813 wb-#6 (Mu)
Isley, Christian 1812 eb-1-23 (C)
Isom, Elizabeth 1849 A-468-116 (Le)
Isom, Elizabeth 1849 A-468-122* (Le)
Isom, George W. 1850 A-468-135 (Le)
Isom, James 1825 wb-#148 (Mu)
Isom, John 1813 wb-#24 (Mu)
Isom, V. C. 1862 wb-2-366 (Li)
Ivey, David 1848 wb-9-151 (Wi)
Ivey, Frederick 1856 wb-12-74 (Wi)
Ivey, Henry 1836 wb-1-153 (Gr)
Ivey, William B. 1848 wb-14-68 (Rb)
Ivie, Sterling 1830 rb-8-62 (Ru)
Ivy, Bengamin 1853 wb-3-107 (Gr)
Ivy, Burrell 1842 wb-#3 (Mo)
Ivy, John H. 1857 wb-3-367 (Gr)
Ivy, John Hamilton 1858 wb-3-437 (Gr)
Ivy, Louisa D. 1849 wb-9-301 (Wi)
Ivy, R. M. W. 1854 wb-a-459 (F)

- J -

Jack, Andrew 1835 wb-b-259 (Ro)
Jack, Andrew 1835 wb-b-263 (Ro)
Jack, Andrew 1859 wb-f-166 (Mu)
Jack, George 1820 wb-2-287 (Je)
Jack, James 1836 wb-1-15# (Ge)
Jack, Jeremiah 1833 wb-5-241 (K)
Jack, Jeremiah 1851 148-1-382 (Ge)
Jack, John F. 1834 wb-1-32 (Gr)
Jack, Mary 1856 wb-1-86 (R)
Jack, Saml. 1803 wb-1-156 (Je)
Jack, William 1819 eb-1-89 (C)
Jacks, Richard 1831 wb-3-174 (Je)
Jackson, Aaron 1846 wb-d-29 (G)
Jackson, Abel 1857 wb-h-685 (Hu)
Jackson, Anderson 1840 rb-11-26 (Ru)
Jackson, Andrew 1845 wb-13-291 (D)
Jackson, Andrew 1862 ib-1-476 (Wy)
Jackson, Ann? 1857 wb-f-117 (G)
Jackson, Archibald 1856 rb-o-219 (Mt)
Jackson, Bins 1843 wb-f-117* (Hn)
Jackson, Branch 1824 wb-#78 (Mu)
Jackson, Brice 1832 rb-f-335 (Mt)
Jackson, Burrell 1855 wb-#115 (Wl)
Jackson, Burris 1845 wb-g-78 (Hn)
Jackson, Carril 1829 wb-9-296 (D)
Jackson, Chesterfield 1827 wb-6-108 (Rb)
Jackson, Corban 1850 33-3-220 (Gr)
Jackson, Craven 1821 wb-8-33 (D)
Jackson, Daniel 1818 wb-1-0 (Sm)

Jackson, Daniel 1856 wb-h-614 (Hu)
Jackson, Daniel 1857 wb-f-68 (G)
Jackson, David 1824 wb-1-37 (Ma)
Jackson, David C. 1840 wb-1-231 (La)
Jackson, Durant K. 1838 abl-1-82 (T)
Jackson, Duron K. 1861 wb-13-482 (Wi)
Jackson, Edna E. 1848 33-3-36 (Gr)
Jackson, Elisha 1833 wb-c-264 (St)
Jackson, Elisha 1847 mr-2-235 (Be)
Jackson, Epps 1850 wb-a-210 (Di)
Jackson, Francis 1839 wb-7-26 (Wi)
Jackson, Francis 1845 rb-13-229 (Ru)
Jackson, Francis sr. 1845 rb-13-144 (Ru)
Jackson, G. J. (Dr.) 1860 wb-13-353 (K)
Jackson, G. J. 1861 wb-13-449 (K)
Jackson, George 1851 wb-#50 (Wa)
Jackson, George 1858 wb-2-87# (Ge)
Jackson, George J. 1856 wb-12-316 (K)
Jackson, Gilla (Mrs.) 1855 wb-16-45 (Rb)
Jackson, Gilliam 1813 rb-b-92 (Mt)
Jackson, Green 1857 as-c-431 (Di)
Jackson, H. B. 1860 wb-f-317 (Ro)
Jackson, Henry 1818 wb-7-218 (D)
Jackson, Hezekiah 1815 wb-a-62 (Ro)
Jackson, Hezekiah 1815 wb-a-67 (Ro)
Jackson, Isham 1816 wb-#35 (Wl)
Jackson, Isham 1823 wb-#46 (Wl)
Jackson, Isham 1854 wb-f-37 (Mu)
Jackson, J. B. 1858 wb-4-7 (Gr)
Jackson, J. B. 1861 rb-p-649 (Mt)
Jackson, J. M. 1839? wb-#125 (Wl)
Jackson, J. M. 1846 rb-k-329 (Mt)
Jackson, James 1816 wb-2-307 (Wi)
Jackson, James 1837 wb-d-131 (St)
Jackson, James 1852 wb-a-276 (Ms)
Jackson, James 1854 wb-d-166 (Wh)
Jackson, James M. 1844 wb-d-280 (O)
Jackson, James T. 1860 wb-2-308 (Li)
Jackson, Jesse 1827 wb-1-5 (Hy)
Jackson, Jesse 1850 wb-#172 (Wl)
Jackson, Jesse B. 1859 wb-h-349 (Hn)
Jackson, Jessee 1811 wb-4-163 (D)
Jackson, Joe Berry 1861 rb-p-623 (Mt)
Jackson, John 1803 wb-2-277 (D)
Jackson, John 1814 wb-1-77 (Bo)
Jackson, John 1840 wb-c-149 (Ro)
Jackson, John 1841 rb-i-95 (Mt)
Jackson, John 1848 as-a-168 (Ms)
Jackson, John 1855 ib-1-372 (Wy)
Jackson, John A. W. 1840 rb-i-6 (Mt)
Jackson, John B. 1816 wb-7-50 (D)

Jackson, John B. 1858 wb-3-427 (Gr)
Jackson, John M. 1838 wb-#123 (Wl)
Jackson, John M. 1847 rb-k-383 (Mt)
Jackson, John T. 1851 wb-15-88 (D)
Jackson, John sr. 1855 ib-1-349 (Wy)
Jackson, Johnathan 1855 wb-16-50 (Rb)
Jackson, Jonathan 1841 wb-7-234* (K)
Jackson, Jordan 1848 wb-d-146 (G)
Jackson, Joseph 1857 rb-o-493 (Mt)
Jackson, Josiah 1804 wb-1-96 (Je)
Jackson, Josiah 1816 wb-a-87 (Ro)
Jackson, Leona? 1838 wb-y-132 (Mu)
Jackson, Letitia 1859 149-1-155 (Ge)
Jackson, Lewis C. 1842 wb-3-609 (Ma)
Jackson, Lewis E. 1838 wb-2-374 (Ma)
Jackson, Margaret 1852 lr (Sn)
Jackson, Mark 1839 wb-y-359 (Mu)
Jackson, Mark 1858 wb-h-310 (Hn)
Jackson, Mark L. 1826 wb-#150 (Mu)
Jackson, Martha 1839 wb-7-169 (Wi)
Jackson, Martha J. 1853 wb-m-633 (Mt)
Jackson, Martha J. 1853 wb-m-640 (Mt)
Jackson, Martha Jane 1856 rb-o-65 (Mt)
Jackson, Mary 1841 wb-#141 (Wl)
Jackson, Mary 1843 as-b-165 (Di)
Jackson, Mary 1846 wb-5-26 (Ma)
Jackson, Mary Jane 1856 wb-12-222 (Wi)
Jackson, Mary W. 1847 wb-14-137 (D)
Jackson, Miles 1851 wb-15-1 (Rb)
Jackson, Nancy 1857 wb-f-130 (Mu)
Jackson, Nancy 1859 wb-#130 (Wl)
Jackson, Nelson P. 1831 wb-9-505 (D)
Jackson, Peter 1852 wb-#52 (Wa)
Jackson, Rebecca 1856 wb-3-326 (Gr)
Jackson, Rebecca 1858 wb-1-379 (Fr)
Jackson, Reuben 1832 wb-a-192 (G)
Jackson, Reuben 1844 wb-d-276 (O)
Jackson, Richard 1845 as-b-260 (Di)
Jackson, Richardson 1821 lr (Sn)
Jackson, Robert 1845 wb-a-263 (F)
Jackson, Robert 1847 wb-#153 (Wl)
Jackson, Robert 1858 wb-1-227 (Be)
Jackson, S. B. 1837 wb-1-522 (Hr)
Jackson, S. D. 1859 wb-h-367 (Hn)
Jackson, Sally 1839 wb-#124 (Wl)
Jackson, Samuel 1825 wb-b-76 (St)
Jackson, Samuel 1838 wb-b-307 (Wh)
Jackson, Sandal 1859 wb-f-327 (G)
Jackson, Sarah 1803 wb-2-276 (D)
Jackson, Stephen 1813 wb-4-249 (D)
Jackson, Thomas 1817 wb-1-266 (Hw)

Jackson, Thomas 1843 wb-7-0 (Sm)
Jackson, Thomas 1847 wb-a2-553 (Mu)
Jackson, Thomas W. 1853 wb-e-123 (G)
Jackson, Vincent 1857 wb-2-86# (Ge)
Jackson, Wesley 1854 wb-11-366 (Wi)
Jackson, William 1810 lw (Ct)
Jackson, William 1817 wb-2-340 (Wi)
Jackson, William 1833 wb-10-197 (D)
Jackson, William 1838 wb-#37 (Wa)
Jackson, William 1840 wb-11-616 (D)
Jackson, William 1844 wb-a2-171 (Mu)
Jackson, William 1850 wb-14-523 (D)
Jackson, William 1853 wb-10-493 (Wi)
Jackson, William F. 1853 wb-e-423 (Ro)
Jackson, William H. 1853 wb-h-May (O)
Jackson, Willis 1832 as-a-214 (Di)
Jackson, Zebulon 1841 wb-3-333 (Ma)
Jacobs, Allen 1850 rb-15-494 (Ru)
Jacobs, Alvin 1850 rb-15-441 (Ru)
Jacobs, E. G. 1848 wb-#156 (Wl)
Jacobs, Edmund 1850 wb-#172 (Wl)
Jacobs, Edward (Sr.) 1848 wb-#163 (Wl)
Jacobs, Jackson 1847 rb-14-136 (Ru)
Jacobs, Jeremiah 1850 rb-15-487 (Ru)
Jacobs, John 1818 wb-2-205 (Je)
Jacobs, John 1851 rb-16-138 (Ru)
Jacobs, John 1852 rb-16-233 (Ru)
Jacobs, John A. 1856 wb-0-136 (Cf)
Jacobs, John H. 1851 wb-a-153 (T)
Jacobs, Nancy 1861 rb-21-146 (Ru)
Jacobs, W. B. 1860 wb-i-222 (St)
Jacobs, William 1821 wb-#44 (Mu)
Jacobs, William 1824 wb-#77 (Mu)
Jadwin, Solomon 1809 wb-#6 (Wl)
Jaggars, Thomas J. 1841 wb-z-232 (Mu)
Jamerson, Samuel 1860 wb-a-365 (Cr)
James, Abarilla 1844 as-b-197 (Di)
James, Abraham 1834 wb-1-100 (Gr)
James, Abraham 1836 wb-1-127 (Gr)
James, Allen 1851 rb-15-582 (Ru)
James, Anderson 1836 rb-9-93 (Ru)
James, Bartlet 1857 wb-b-23 (Dk)
James, Bartlett 1845 wb-7-0 (Sm)
James, Buchanan 1851 wb-#175 (Wl)
James, Cary 1848 rb-14-339 (Ru)
James, David 1844 wb-f-234 (Hn)
James, David T. 1833 wb-b-123 (Wh)
James, Doritha 1859 rb-20-47 (Ru)
James, E. H. 1857 wb-f-87 (G)
James, Edmond 1844 wb-d-223 (O)
James, Edmund sr. 1857 wb-7-0 (Sm)

James, Edward 1819 wb-1-0 (Sm)
James, Eligah 1848 wb-f-127+ (O)
James, Elizabeth 1846 rb-13-464 (Ru)
James, Elizabeth 1851 wb-15-167 (D)
James, Emanuel 1840 wb-e-11 (St)
James, Enos 1831 as-a-208 (Di)
James, Enos 1845 as-b-227 (Di)
James, Frances 1852 rb-16-289 (Ru)
James, George H. 1815 Wb-2-128 (Wi)
James, George W. 1851 wb-14-635 (D)
James, Henry F. 1834 wb-1-19 (Sh)
James, Henry F. 1842 wb-12-308* (D)
James, Hester M. N. 1855 wb-1-101 (Jo)
James, Jesse 1814 wb-1-75 (Bo)
James, John 1839 wb-7-73 (Wi)
James, John 1840 wb-1A-285 (A)
James, John 1852 wb-xx-33 (St)
James, John P. 1841 rb-11-145 (Ru)
James, John P. sr. 1840 rb-11-83 (Ru)
James, John sr. 1840 rb-11-61 (Ru)
James, Joshua 1842 as-b-68 (Di)
James, Lewis B. 1856 wb-16-238 (Rb)
James, Martha (Mrs) 1851 rb-16-74 (Ru)
James, Martha 1851 rb-15-581 (Ru)
James, Mary 1846 rb-13-709 (Ru)
James, Mary T. 1851 wb-15-166 (D)
James, Matilda 1859 wb-3e-90 (Sh)
James, Perley 1860 wb-a-286 (T)
James, Philip 1813 rb-b-90 (Mt)
James, Philip H. 1813 rb-b-188 (Mt)
James, Richard 1844 wb-12-150 (Rb)
James, Samuel 1839 wb-a-134 (Di)
James, Samuel 1856 wb-e-470 (G)
James, Sarah 1818 rb-4-154 (Ru)
James, Thomas 1825 wb-8-500 (D)
James, Thomas 1836 wb-b-35 (Hd)
James, Thomas 1851 wb-d-314 (G)
James, Thomas 1854 rb-17-238 (Ru)
James, Unacy 1846 wb-c-287 (G)
James, William 1828 wb-b-57 (Hn)
James, William 1834 wb-1-101 (Li)
James, William 1841 lr (Gi)
James, William 1848 33-3-93 (Gr)
James, William 1852 rb-16-342 (Ru)
James, William R. 1842 wb-d-30 (Hd)
James, William R. 1844 wb-f-195 (St)
James, Wm. W. 1841 wb-2-295 (Hr)
James, _____ 1843 wb-d-72 (Hd)
Jameson, Benjamin 1816 wb-2-37# (Ge)
Jameson, James 1852 wb-2-137 (Sh)
Jameson, Samuel 1834 wb-#2 (Mo)

Jameson, Samuel 1858 rb-19-490 (Ru)
Jamison, Andrew 1839 wb-e-74 (Hn)
Jamison, Eleanor 1835 rb-g-181 (Mt)
Jamison, Henry D. 1859 rb-19-629 (Ru)
Jamison, James 1858 wb-a-283 (T)
Jamison, John 1811 wb-#5 (Mu)
Jamison, John 1824 wb-3-741 (Wi)
Jamison, John B. 1860 wb-13-195 (Wi)
Jamison, Thomas 1826 wb-3-0 (Sm)
Jamison, Thomas 1857 wb-16-452 (Rb)
Jamison, W. A. 1861 wb-17-257 (Rb)
Jamison, William Caldwell 1821 rb-c-532 (Mt)
Jamison, Wm. C. 1835 rb-g-198 (Mt)
Jane, Wiley 1837 wb-2-51# (Ge)
January, David 1847 wb-5-510 (Gr)
Jaquerod, John 1859 wb-13-94 (K)
Jaquerod, John L. 1859 wb-13-140 (K)
Jaratt, M. 1841 wb-f-10 (Hn)
Jared, William 1861 wb-e-407 (Wh)
Jarman, Amous 1856 rb-18-186 (Ru)
Jarman, Shadrack 1824 wb-1-2 (Hr)
Jarman, Susannah 1852 wb-#180 (Wl)
Jarmon, Robert 1849? wb-#169 (Wl)
Jarnagan, Benjamin 1815 wb-2-125 (Je)
Jarnagan, John 1857 wb-4-5 (Gr)
Jarnagin, Caswell 1840 wb-#86 (Mc)
Jarnagin, Chesley 1826 wb-2-496 (Je)
Jarnagin, Hilliam Calvin 1833 wb-3-237 (Je)
Jarnagin, John 1857 wb-3-393 (Gr)
Jarnagin, Mary 1829 wb-3-393 (Je)
Jarnagin, Noah 1849 33-3-128 (Gr)
Jarnagin, P. B. 1828 wb-3-10 (Je)
Jarnagin, Pleasant 1833 wb-3-214 (Je)
Jarnagin, Prator? B. 1838 wb-1-265 (Je)
Jarnagin, Preston B. 1828 wb-2-625 (Je)
Jarnagin, Spencer 1852 wb-#86 (Mc)
Jarnagin, Thomas 1802 wb-1-102 (Je)
Jarnagin, William C. 1833 wb-3-263 (Je)
Jarnigan, Benjamin 1818 wb-2-204 (Je)
Jarnigan, W. C. 1857 as-c-517 (Di)
Jarratt, Archibald 1832 rb-9-8 (Ru)
Jarratt, Archilus 1831 rb-8-239 (Ru)
Jarratt, Deveraux 1845 wb-#146 (Wl)
Jarratt, John F. W. 1861 wb-#133 (Wl)
Jarratt, Joseph 1825 rb-6-103 (Ru)
Jarratt, Mary 1860 rb-20-528 (Ru)
Jarratt, Rhoda 1852 rb-16-190 (Ru)
Jarratt, Thomas 1855 rb-17-565 (Ru)
Jarratt, Thomas S. 1858 rb-19-153 (Ru)
Jarratte, Thomas 1828 rb-7-37 (Ru)
Jarrell, Fountain 1862 wb-#136 (Wl)

Jarrell, Richard 1836 wb-#114 (Wl)
Jarrell, Wm. 1861 rb-p-623 (Mt)
Jarret, Wade 1826 wb-1-59 (Ma)
Jarrett, Amelia A. 1859 wb-13-206 (Wi)
Jarrett, John 1855 wb-6-140 (Ma)
Jarrett, Lyddy 1827 wb-a-13 (Cr)
Jarrett, R. F. 1836 wb-#114 (Wl)
Jarrett, William 1840 wb-a-47 (F)
Jarrison, Pearson 1839 wb-#128 (Wl)
Jarrott, John 1843 wb-#166 (Wl)
Jarrott, Martha 1851 wb-#175 (Wl)
Jarvis, F. R. 1855 wb-e-20 (Wh)
Jarvis, Foster R. 1857 wb-e-124 (Wh)
Jarvis, William 1816 wb-a-52 (Wh)
Jay, Richard G. 1838 wb-b-288 (Wh)
Jayroe, Andrew B. 1850 wb-b-102 (L)
Jeana?, James G. 1848 as-a-170 (Ms)
Jefferis, James 1816 rb-b-335 (Mt)
Jeffers, John A. 1836 wb-b-34 (Hd)
Jeffreys, David 1834 wb-1-503 (Ma)
Jeffreys, Osborne jr. 1821 wb-1-0 (Sm)
Jeffreys, Thomas M. 1834 wb-#104 (Wl)
Jeffries, William 1827 wb-1-78 (Bo)
Jeley?, George 1861 wb-h-531 (Hn)
Jelks, Jarrett M. 1829 wb-1-101 (Ma)
Jemison, Ephraim 1843 wb-11-497 (Rb)
Jenie, Eber 1860 wb-k-238 (O)
Jenkens, Aaron 1819 wb-#16 (Wa)
Jenkins, A. 1861 wb-18-473 (D)
Jenkins, A. C. C. 1840 wb-a-446 (R)
Jenkins, A. F. 1859 wb-k-138 (O)
Jenkins, Aaron 1828 wb-1A-12 (A)
Jenkins, Alexander 1861 wb-19-2 (D)
Jenkins, Charles T. 1858 wb-#126 (Wl)
Jenkins, Duke 1855 wb-12-10 (Wi)
Jenkins, Freeman 1846 wb-g-156 (Hn)
Jenkins, G. P. 1859 wb-3e-91 (Sh)
Jenkins, Geo. W. 1836 wb-a-40 (T)
Jenkins, Grace 1849 wb-1-49 (Jo)
Jenkins, Green 1841 wb-7-424 (Wi)
Jenkins, Hiram 1857 rb-19-68 (Ru)
Jenkins, Hugh sr. 1836 wb-1-5 (Jo)
Jenkins, Jeremiah 1845 wb-8-252 (Wi)
Jenkins, Jesse 1852 wb-h-Nov (O)
Jenkins, Jesse 1856 wb-0-137 (Cf)
Jenkins, John 1828 rb-e-363 (Mt)
Jenkins, John 1850 wb-#174 (Wl)
Jenkins, Joseph 1815 wb-1-0 (Sm)
Jenkins, Nimrod 1837 rb-10-18 (Ru)
Jenkins, Nimrod 1856 rb-17-614 (Ru)
Jenkins, Oliver 1822 wb-3-344 (Rb)

Jenkins, Philip 1835 wb-x-264* (Mu)
Jenkins, Roderick 1799 lr (Sn)
Jenkins, Rodrick 1823 wb-1-0 (Sm)
Jenkins, Samuel 1832 wb-1-70 (Li)
Jenkins, Samuel 1841 abl-1-230* (T)
Jenkins, Susannah 1856 wb-1-115 (Jo)
Jenkins, Thomas 1835 wb-c-437 (St)
Jenkins, Thomas H. 1817 wb-#111 (Mu)
Jenkins, Wiatt 1842 wb-a-36 (Dk)
Jenkins, William 1855 wb-#116 (Wl)
Jenkins, Williams 1806 lw (Ct)
Jenkins, Wilson 1830 wb-3-0 (Sm)
Jenkins, Winneford 1855 wb-b-356 (We)
Jenkins, Witton F. L. 1839 lr (Gi)
Jenney, Able 1807 rb-a-462 (Mt)
Jennings, Anderson 1853 ib-2-259 (Cl)
Jennings, Anderson H. 1846 wb-b-132 (We)
Jennings, Ashel 1844 wb-#145 (Wl)
Jennings, B. G. 1833 wb-x-37 (Mu)
Jennings, Benjamin G. 1833 wb-x-90 (Mu)
Jennings, Clem 1837 wb-#117 (Wl)
Jennings, Clem 1852 wb-#180 (Wl)
Jennings, Elizabeth 1852 wb-3-128 (W)
Jennings, Elizabeth 1857 wb-2-11 (Li)
Jennings, George 1837 wb-1-232 (Gr)
Jennings, George W. 1847 wb-a2-542 (Mu)
Jennings, J. A. 1860 wb-#133 (Wl)
Jennings, J. B. 1861 wb-3e-188 (Sh)
Jennings, Jacob 1835 wb-#112 (Wl)
Jennings, James W. 1843 wb-#141 (Wl)
Jennings, Joel 1860 wb-#132 (Wl)
Jennings, John 1849 wb-#170 (Wl)
Jennings, John A. 1850 wb-#171 (Wl)
Jennings, Jonathan 1784 wb-1-7 (D)
Jennings, Lewis T. S. 1837 wb-6-355 (Wi)
Jennings, Lewis T. S. 1843 wb-8-121 (Wi)
Jennings, Martha 1845 wb-a2-207 (Mu)
Jennings, Nancy C. 1836 wb-y-17 (Mu)
Jennings, Obadiah 1830 wb-1-52 (W)
Jennings, Obadiah 1832 wb-10-58 (D)
Jennings, Obediah 1840 wb-1-307 (W)
Jennings, R. B. 1856 wb-#119 (Wl)
Jennings, Robert 1861 wb-#134 (Wl)
Jennings, Robert H. 1859 wb-f-176 (Mu)
Jennings, Royal 1839 wb-5-1 (Gr)
Jennings, Samuel 1829 wb-#195 (Mu)
Jennings, Sophia 1851 wb-14-680 (D)
Jennings, Thomas 1808 wb-#6 (Wl)
Jennings, William 1839 wb-b-284 (G)
Jennings, William 1841 wb-#133 (Wl)
Jennings, William 1851 wb-15-102 (D)

Jennings, William 1858 wb-c-230 (L)
Jennings, William D. 1837 wb-1-237 (Gr)
Jernegan, W. H. 1854 wb-h-288 (Hu)
Jernegin, Henry B. 1839 wb-y-624 (Mu)
Jernigan, Amelia 1861 wb-b-99 (F)
Jernigan, David 1842 wb-a-89 (F)
Jernigan, H. B. 1848 wb-b-199 (Mu)
Jernigan, J. B. 1840 wb-y-650 (Mu)
Jernigan, Jesse 1816 wb-3-188 (St)
Jernigan, Jesse sr. 1816 wb-3-219 (St)
Jernigan, Jessee 1816 wb-3-178 (St)
Jernigan, Milley 1853 wb-15-417 (Rb)
Jernigan, Thomas P. 1855 wb-g-720 (Hn)
Jernigan, William 1834 wb-8-427 (Rb)
Jerow, George Fredrick 1819 wb-7-319 (D)
Jervis, Alexander 1803 wb-#9 (Wa)
Jesse, Jacob 1848 wb-10-50 (K)
Jester, Ebenezer 1841 wb-3-396 (Ma)
Jeter, Bryant 1847 wb-13-143 (Rb)
Jeter, Fielding 1852 wb-2-120 (Sh)
Jeter, George A. 1846 wb-b-185 (We)
Jeter, Robert 1838 wb-1-174 (We)
Jeter, William B. 1847 wb-b-247 (We)
Jett, Asa H. 1847 rb-k-451 (Mt)
Jett, Edward 1854 wb-n-364 (Mt)
Jett, Edward jr. 1861 rb-p-557 (Mt)
Jett, Edward sr. 1861 rb-p-557 (Mt)
Jett, John 1840 wb-b-406 (Wh)
Jett, Mary 1860 wb-e-315 (Wh)
Jetton, Andrew 1843 rb-12-296 (Ru)
Jetton, Andrew J. 1843 rb-12-315 (Ru)
Jetton, Elizabeth 1852 rb-16-378 (Ru)
Jetton, James 1852 rb-16-258 (Ru)
Jetton, James L. 1850 rb-15-562 (Ru)
Jetton, James M. 1849 rb-15-144 (Ru)
Jetton, Jas. S. 1851 rb-16-53 (Ru)
Jetton, John L. 1854 rb-17-182 (Ru)
Jetton, John S. 1831 rb-8-199 (Ru)
Jetton, John S. 1858 rb-19-314 (Ru)
Jetton, John W. 1839 rb-10-267 (Ru)
Jetton, John White 1839 rb-10-276 (Ru)
Jetton, Mary S. 1850 rb-15-297 (Ru)
Jetton, Nancy 1855 rb-17-525 (Ru)
Jetton, Robert 1841 rb-11-106 (Ru)
Jetton, Robert 1857 rb-18-352 (Ru)
Jetton, William 1850 rb-15-519 (Ru)
Jetton, William M. 1850 rb-15-415 (Ru)
Jetton, Wilson B. F. 1845 rb-13-215 (Ru)
Jewel, Mary 1851 wb-#108 (Wl)
Jewel, Seburn 1858 149-1-120 (Ge)
Jewell, E. 1846 wb-#150 (Wl)

Jewell, John 1814 wb-4-270 (D)
Jewell, Joseph 1822 wb-8-131 (D)
Jewell, William 1856 wb-#120 (Wl)
Jimerson, Benedeck 1852 wb-xx-97 (St)
Jimmerson, Andrew 1838 wb-d-186* (Hn)
Jinings, Daniel 1836 wb-1A-143 (A)
Jinkens, John 1815 wb-#22 (Mu)
Jinkens, John 1842 abl-1-254 (T)
Jinkins, John 1812 rb-a-69 (Mt)
Jinkins, John 1814? wb-#31 (Mu)
Jinnings, Benjamin 1837 wb-3-457 (Je)
Jinnings, Ryol 1841 wb-5-156 (Gr)
Job, Abigail 1819 wb-#16 (Wa)
Job, Enoch 1850 wb-#62 (Wa)
Job, Samuel 1859 wb-b-73 (Ms)
Job?, James 1837 wb-d-132° (Hn)
John, Thomas 1854 wb-#87 (Mc)
John, William 1840 wb-#87 (Mc)
John, Wm. E. H. 1836 wb-d-154 (Hn)
Johns, Abner 1825 rb-6-152 (Ru)
Johns, Ann 1813 rb-2-221 (Ru)
Johns, Benjamin 1813 wb-1-0 (Sm)
Johns, Benjamin 1826 wb-1-0 (Sm)
Johns, Benjamin 1826 wb-3-0 (Sm)
Johns, Daniel 1852 wb-15-87 (Rb)
Johns, Edmund 1812 rb-2-158 (Ru)
Johns, Edmund 1825 rb-6-162 (Ru)
Johns, Edward 1826 rb-6-288 (Ru)
Johns, Elizabeth 1844 rb-13-81 (Ru)
Johns, Franklin 1845 rb-13-248 (Ru)
Johns, Franklin A. 1845 rb-13-163 (Ru)
Johns, Frederick 1843 rb-12-295 (Ru)
Johns, Isaac 1809 wb-1-0 (Sm)
Johns, Isaac 1858 rb-19-402 (Ru)
Johns, Jacob 1857 rb-19-117 (Ru)
Johns, John 1837 rb-9-412 (Ru)
Johns, John 1860 wb-18-237 (D)
Johns, John Sr. 1827 wb-9-83 (D)
Johns, Joseph B. 1839 rb-10-462 (Ru)
Johns, Joseph P. 1861 rb-21-148 (Ru)
Johns, Margaret W. 1849 rb-15-185 (Ru)
Johns, Mary 1820 rb-5-14 (Ru)
Johns, Oscar D. 1857 wb-3e-43 (Sh)
Johns, Rebecca 1852 wb-15-171 (Rb)
Johns, Reise 1853 wb-15-425 (Rb)
Johns, Rice 1852 wb-15-87 (Rb)
Johns, Robert 1862 wb-#135 (Wl)
Johns, Samuel 1852 wb-11-257 (K)
Johns, Susan 1857 wb-16-355 (Rb)
Johns, William 1840 wb-#133 (Wl)
Johns, William 1857 wb-2-358 (Me)

Johns, William R. 1830 rb-8-79 (Ru)
Johnson, A. C. 1854 wb-#114 (Wl)
Johnson, A. F. 1861 rb-p-650 (Mt)
Johnson, Abel 1831 rb-f-197 (Mt)
Johnson, Abel 1849 rb-l-386 (Mt)
Johnson, Abram 1861 wb-1-151 (Jo)
Johnson, Agnes 1846 as-b-340 (Di)
Johnson, Alexander 1811 wb-#9 (Wl)
Johnson, Alexander 1832 wb-x-47 (Mu)
Johnson, Alexander 1857 wb-f-122 (Mu)
Johnson, Allen 1836 wb-6-117 (Wi)
Johnson, Allen 1859 39-2-332 (Dk)
Johnson, Ambrose 1849 ib-1-89 (Cl)
Johnson, Amos 1830 wb-#208 (Mu)
Johnson, Andrew 1860 wb-#132 (Wl)
Johnson, Anna 1853 wb-h-198 (Hu)
Johnson, Aquilla 1835 rb-g-182 (Mt)
Johnson, Archibald 1851 rb-16-137 (Ru)
Johnson, Benjamin 1818 wb-1-60 (Fr)
Johnson, Benjamin 1848 rb-14-441 (Ru)
Johnson, Benjamin 1858 wb-12-535 (Wi)
Johnson, Burrel 1860 rb-p-446 (Mt)
Johnson, Cader 1830 wb-#213 (Mu)
Johnson, Carol L. 1838 wb-#121 (Wl)
Johnson, Charles 1815 Wb-2-162 (Wi)
Johnson, Charles 1852 wb-xx-114 (St)
Johnson, Charles L. 1849 wb-1B-122 (A)
Johnson, Claiborn 1850 wb-e-227 (Ro)
Johnson, Clement 1817 wb-#28 (Wl)
Johnson, Clemuel P. D. 1829 wb-2-615 (Je)
Johnson, Coleman 1835 wb-#111 (Wl)
Johnson, D. W. 1853 mr-2-526 (Be)
Johnson, Daniel 1819 wb-3-142 (Rb)
Johnson, Daniel 1845 wb-12-333 (Rb)
Johnson, Daniel H. 1857 rb-18-339 (Ru)
Johnson, David B. 1857 wb-b-40 (F)
Johnson, David R. 1860 wb-2-92# (Ge)
Johnson, Drury 1831 wb-1-190 (Hr)
Johnson, Duncan 1813 wb-#13 (Wl)
Johnson, Duncan 1823 wb-#46 (Wl)
Johnson, Ebenezer 1839 wb-#7 (Mo)
Johnson, Edmond 1853 wb-e-395 (Ro)
Johnson, Edward 1853 rb-16-403 (Ru)
Johnson, Edward M. 1849 rb-15-17 (Ru)
Johnson, Edwin M. 1852 wb-m-459 (Mt)
Johnson, Eldridge 1853 wb-15-275 (Rb)
Johnson, Eleanor 1841 wb-#113 (Wl)
Johnson, Elenor 1858 wb-17-537 (D)
Johnson, Elijah 1801 wb-0-33 (K)
Johnson, Elijah 1840 wb-7-60 (K)
Johnson, Elijah jr. 1860 wb-13-335 (K)

Johnson, Elizabeth 1814 wb-2-141 (Rb)
Johnson, Elizabeth 1834 wb-1A-95 (A)
Johnson, Elizabeth 1839 wb-#126 (Wl)
Johnson, Elizabeth 1848 wb-7-0 (Sm)
Johnson, Elizabeth 1852 wb-m-444 (Mt)
Johnson, Elizabeth 1855 wb-2-86# (Ge)
Johnson, Elizabeth 1861 wb-#65 (Wa)
Johnson, Elizabeth Malinda 1839 wb-#125 (Wl)
Johnson, Fauntley 1815 rb-b-148 (Mt)
Johnson, G. B. 1858 wb-#126 (Wl)
Johnson, George 1852 wb-11-208 (K)
Johnson, Georoge S. 1853 wb-b-230 (L)
Johnson, Gideon 1844 wb-8-142 (Wi)
Johnson, Gilbert 1852 wb-1B-300 (A)
Johnson, Grizzy 1855 wb-b-6 (F)
Johnson, H. T. 1858 wb-1-121 (Jo)
Johnson, Hardy 1854 wb-a-244 (Dk)
Johnson, Hardy 1857 wb-j-233 (O)
Johnson, Harrison sr. 1857 wb-6-469 (Ma)
Johnson, Haywood 1844 wb-3-412 (Hy)
Johnson, Henrietta 1858 wb-2-264 (Li)
Johnson, Henry 1834 wb-#87 (Mc)
Johnson, Henry 1836 rb-h-172 (Mt)
Johnson, Henry 1856 wb-16-277 (Rb)
Johnson, Henry H. 1836 rb-g-338 (Mt)
Johnson, Henry sr. 1859 wb-16-792 (Rb)
Johnson, Hinty? 1815 rb-b-286 (Mt)
Johnson, Hudson 1828 as-a-182 (Di)
Johnson, Hugh 1836 wb-b-150 (Hd)
Johnson, Hugh 1860 wb-1-55 (Su)
Johnson, Isaac 1822 as-A-43 (Di)
Johnson, Isaac 1824 as-a-156 (Di)
Johnson, Isaac 1826 wb-4-159 (K)
Johnson, Isaac 1838 wb-a-69 (Cr)
Johnson, Isaac 1839 wb-11-593 (D)
Johnson, Isham 1832 wb-#100 (Wl)
Johnson, Jacob 1815 wb-3-116 (St)
Johnson, James 1791 wb-1-14# (Ge)
Johnson, James 1794 wb-1-73 (Je)
Johnson, James 1809 wb-1-199 (Wi)
Johnson, James 1810 wb-#8 (Wl)
Johnson, James 1816 wb-#19 (Mu)
Johnson, James 1820 wb-#36 (Wl)
Johnson, James 1824 rb-d-293 (Mt)
Johnson, James 1824 wb-3-697 (Wi)
Johnson, James 1828 rb-7-334 (Ru)
Johnson, James 1828 wb-2-27# (Ge)
Johnson, James 1828 wb-a-329 (Wh)
Johnson, James 1832 wb-1-267 (Hw)
Johnson, James 1835 wb-#110 (Wl)
Johnson, James 1839 wb-3-6 (Ma)

Johnson, James 1848 wb-#156 (Wl)
Johnson, James 1850 wb-5-86 (Ma)
Johnson, James 1851 148-1-363 (Ge)
Johnson, James 1853 wb-e-399 (Ro)
Johnson, James 1855 wb-g-705 (Hn)
Johnson, James 1861 149-1-224 (Ge)
Johnson, James H. 1854 wb-#117 (Wl)
Johnson, James R. 1840 wb-#130 (Wl)
Johnson, James S. 1848 wb-#47 (Wa)
Johnson, James sr. 1860 wb-1-270 (Hw)
Johnson, Jane D. 1838 wb-1-429 (Hy)
Johnson, Jane Deborah 1836 wb-1-235 (Hy)
Johnson, Jas. 1861 wb-#87 (Mc)
Johnson, Jeremiah 1841 wb-#135 (Wl)
Johnson, Jeremiah 1859 wb-13-205 (K)
Johnson, Jesse 1826 lr (Sn)
Johnson, Jesse 1856 wb-#122 (Wl)
Johnson, Joel 1833 wb-1-97 (Li)
Johnson, John 1807 wb-1-0 (Sm)
Johnson, John 1812 wb-a-117 (St)
Johnson, John 1813 wb-#9 (Mu)
Johnson, John 1815 rb-b-297 (Mt)
Johnson, John 1815 wb-2-291 (Rb)
Johnson, John 1835 wb-a-116 (Di)
Johnson, John 1837 wb-3-0 (Sm)
Johnson, John 1839 rb-h-332 (Mt)
Johnson, John 1840 wb-3-270 (Ma)
Johnson, John 1843 wb-d-56 (Hd)
Johnson, John 1851 rb-4-238 (Mu)
Johnson, John 1852 wb-f-6 (Mu)
Johnson, John 1853 mr-2-496 (Be)
Johnson, John 1855 wb-2-81# (Ge)
Johnson, John 1858 wb-3-482 (Gr)
Johnson, John 1858 wb-4-128 (La)
Johnson, John 1859 as-c-165 (Ms)
Johnson, John A. 1848 rb-l-10 (Mt)
Johnson, John B. 1815 wb-1-212 (Sn)
Johnson, John B. 1860 wb-5-107 (Hr)
Johnson, John M. 1839 wb-3-32 (Ma)
Johnson, John P. 1837 wb-1-160 (We)
Johnson, John R. 1857 wb-16-535 (Rb)
Johnson, John S. 1847 rb-k-567 (Mt)
Johnson, Jonathan 1816 wb-7-41 (D)
Johnson, Jonathan 1836 rb-g-439 (Mt)
Johnson, Joseph 1824 wb-1-81 (Bo)
Johnson, Joseph 1832 rb-f-324 (Mt)
Johnson, Joseph 1832 wb-5-126 (K)
Johnson, Joseph 1838 wb-11-245 (D)
Johnson, Joseph 1844 wb-12-230 (Rb)
Johnson, Joseph 1851 rb-4-176 (Mu)
Johnson, Joseph 1860 wb-f-495 (Ro)

Johnson, Joseph H. 1841 wb-12-51 (D)
Johnson, Joseph N. 1841 rb-i-189 (Mt)
Johnson, Joshua 1839 rb-10-361 (Ru)
Johnson, Joshua 1857 wb-12-300 (Wi)
Johnson, Josiah 1826 rb-d-548 (Mt)
Johnson, Josiah 1840 wb-#130 (Wl)
Johnson, Josiah 1858 wb-12-583 (Wi)
Johnson, Julius 1850 rb-l-588 (Mt)
Johnson, L. 1834 wb-1-355 (Hr)
Johnson, Levi 1850 wb-g-402 (Hu)
Johnson, Lewis 1838 wb-y-202 (Mu)
Johnson, Lewis jr. 1850 rb-15-455 (Ru)
Johnson, Lewis sr. 1853 rb-16-366 (Ru)
Johnson, Littleton 1835 wb-1-393 (Hr)
Johnson, Love C. 1852 wb-a-411 (F)
Johnson, Lucy 1839 wb-1-51 (Sh)
Johnson, Lucy 1857 rb-19-82 (Ru)
Johnson, M. B. 1850 wb-2-33 (Me)
Johnson, Margaret 1850 wb-g-394 (Hu)
Johnson, Mark 1831 wb-a-116 (R)
Johnson, Martha 1830 wb-7-258 (Rb)
Johnson, Martha 1853 wb-#112 (Wl)
Johnson, Martha 1861 wb-8-269 (Sm)
Johnson, Mary J. 1843 wb-3-711 (Ma)
Johnson, Matilda 1847 wb-b-213 (We)
Johnson, Matthew 1798 wb-1-24 (Rb)
Johnson, Matthew 1840 wb-#131 (Wl)
Johnson, Matthew 1850 wb-#174 (Wl)
Johnson, Michael 1849 wb-4-512 (Hr)
Johnson, Nancy 1842 wb-1-269 (Hw)
Johnson, Nathan B. 1860 wb-2-92# (Ge)
Johnson, Neal 1858 wb-h-475 (St)
Johnson, Needham 1815 rb-3-62 (Ru)
Johnson, Obadiah 1859 wb-2-89# (Ge)
Johnson, Oliver 1816 wb-4-466 (D)
Johnson, Oliver 1859 rb-20-241 (Ru)
Johnson, Othial 1859 wb-8-27 (Sm)
Johnson, Parmenas 1853 wb-e-98 (G)
Johnson, Philip 1822 rb-d-104 (Mt)
Johnson, Philip 1831 rb-8-270 (Ru)
Johnson, Philip 1839 wb-#126 (Wl)
Johnson, Polly 1849 wb-#87 (Mc)
Johnson, R. M. 1860 wb-1-138 (Jo)
Johnson, Reuben 1825 wb-#88 (Mc)
Johnson, Richard 1825? as-a-134 (Di)
Johnson, Richard 1844 wb-13-12 (D)
Johnson, Richard 1849 lr (Sn)
Johnson, Richard H. 1835 wb-#108 (Wl)
Johnson, Richard M. 1848 wb-2-69# (Ge)
Johnson, Robert 1809 wb-4-31 (Je)
Johnson, Robert 1815 wb-#14 (Mu)

Johnson, Robert 1842 wb-#143 (Wl)
Johnson, Robert 1849 wb-10-245 (K)
Johnson, Robert 1861 wb-1-272 (Hw)
Johnson, Samuel 1856 wb-#123 (Wl)
Johnson, Samuel 1859 rb-20-103 (Ru)
Johnson, Samuel C. 1845 wb-13-348 (D)
Johnson, Samuel R. 1849 wb-1B-122 (A)
Johnson, Sarah 1840 wb-a-47 (L)
Johnson, Sarah 1845 wb-5-10 (Ma)
Johnson, Sarah 1858 wb-h-452 (St)
Johnson, Sarah 1861 wb-17-213 (Rb)
Johnson, Sarah Ann 1851 ib-1-154 (Ca)
Johnson, Seth 1857 wb-f-62 (Ro)
Johnson, Simon 1822 wb-1-15 (Ma)
Johnson, Stephen 1849 33-3-101 (Gr)
Johnson, Stephen 1856 wb-e-53 (Hy)
Johnson, Susan 1838 rb-h-148 (Mt)
Johnson, Susannah 1842 wb-#137 (Wl)
Johnson, Swanson 1831 wb-5-73 (Wi)
Johnson, Tarlton 1852 wb-a-178 (Cr)
Johnson, Thomas 1807 as-1-163 (Ge)
Johnson, Thomas 1825 wb-5-53 (Rb)
Johnson, Thomas 1836 wb-2-88 (Ma)
Johnson, Thomas 1837 rb-10-12 (Ru)
Johnson, Thomas 1837 wb-1-2 (Jo)
Johnson, Thomas 1838 wb-2-312 (Ma)
Johnson, Thomas 1840 wb-a-86 (Cr)
Johnson, Thomas 1842 wb-12-361* (D)
Johnson, Thomas 1844 wb-5-293 (Gr)
Johnson, Thomas 1847 rb-14-14 (Ru)
Johnson, Thomas 1848 rb-k-721 (Mt)
Johnson, Thomas 1854 148-1-471 (Ge)
Johnson, Thomas 1861 wb-1-271 (Hw)
Johnson, Thomas C. 1859 wb-1-161 (R)
Johnson, Thomas D. 1819 wb-1-0 (Sm)
Johnson, Thomas D. 1840 wb-4-16 (Je)
Johnson, Thomas F. 1850 wb-4-72 (Mu)
Johnson, Thomas J. 1815 wb-#15 (Mu)
Johnson, Thomas J. 1843 wb-1-122 (Me)
Johnson, Thomas J. 1858 ib-2-411 (Cl)
Johnson, Thomas sr. 1838 wb-2-305 (Ma)
Johnson, Thompson H. 1844 wb-f-117 (St)
Johnson, W. B. 1853 wb-15-284 (Rb)
Johnson, Waddy P. 1841 wb-7-424 (Wi)
Johnson, Washington 1849 ib-1-26 (Wy)
Johnson, Watkins 1827 wb-#70 (Wl)
Johnson, Wellington D. W. 1851 wb-d-363 (G)
Johnson, Wilie B. 1853 wb-15-274 (Rb)
Johnson, Will. 1849 wb-4-436 (Hr)
Johnson, William 1814 wb-2-111 (Rb)
Johnson, William 1816 rb-3-126 (Ru)

Johnson, William 1816 rb-3-147* (Ru)
Johnson, William 1816 wb-2-142 (Je)
Johnson, William 1826 wb-5-314 (Rb)
Johnson, William 1828 wb-9-228 (D)
Johnson, William 1836 wb-2-47# (Ge)
Johnson, William 1837 wb-1-350 (Hy)
Johnson, William 1840 lr (Gi)
Johnson, William 1840 wb-#131 (Wl)
Johnson, William 1841 wb-#135 (Wl)
Johnson, William 1847 wb-d-56 (G)
Johnson, William 1848 wb-d-383 (Hd)
Johnson, William 1849 wb-#170 (Wl)
Johnson, William 1850 ib-1-156 (Cl)
Johnson, William 1854 wb-1-69 (R)
Johnson, William A. 1817? wb-#111 (Mu)
Johnson, William A. 1834 wb-1-484 (Ma)
Johnson, William C. 1844 wb-1-103 (Sh)
Johnson, William H. 1852 wb-15-389 (D)
Johnson, William H. 1854 mr-2-563 (Be)
Johnson, William W. 1857 wb-16-487 (Rb)
Johnson, Willie B. 1853 wb-15-374 (Rb)
Johnson, Willis 1839 wb-1-193 (We)
Johnson, Wineford 1839 wb-#125 (Wl)
Johnson, Winfield V. 1832 wb-9-122 (Rb)
Johnson, Winiford 1835 wb-#113 (Wl)
Johnson, Winifred 1822 wb-2-352 (Je)
Johnson, Wm. 1813 wb-2-107 (Rb)
Johnson, Wm. A. 1852 wb-e-24 (G)
Johnson?, Madison 1849 wb-1-313 (Me)
Johnston, Andrew 1850 wb-9-376 (Wi)
Johnston, Benjamin 1846 wb-a2-474 (Mu)
Johnston, D. C. 1860 wb-17-11 (Rb)
Johnston, Daniel C. 1860 wb-17-53 (Rb)
Johnston, David 1829 wb-4-383 (Wi)
Johnston, David 1856 rb-18-162 (Ru)
Johnston, E. C. 1858 wb-f-134 (Ro)
Johnston, Edward M. 1855 ib-2-293 (Cl)
Johnston, Ermin 1824 wb-8-340 (D)
Johnston, Exum 1814 wb-4-280 (D)
Johnston, Exum 1816 wb-4-422 (D)
Johnston, Exum 1816 wb-7-14 (D)
Johnston, Frances 1857 wb-16-356 (Rb)
Johnston, Francis 1817 wb-1-204 (Bo)
Johnston, George 1841 wb-z-116 (Mu)
Johnston, George 1847 wb-g-216 (Hn)
Johnston, H. R. 1852 wb-15-323 (D)
Johnston, Henrietta P. 1858 wb-12-481 (Wi)
Johnston, James 1814? wb-#31 (Mu)
Johnston, James 1850 wb-14-345 (Rb)
Johnston, James 1855 wb-e-558 (Ro)
Johnston, James M. 1860 wb-17-62 (Rb)

Johnston, John 1816 wb-2-210 (Wi)
Johnston, John 1825 rb-6-112 (Ru)
Johnston, John 1831 wb-b-43 (Wh)
Johnston, John 1857 wb-17-185 (D)
Johnston, John F. 1850 mr-2-362 (Be)
Johnston, Joseph K. 1861 wb-#18 (Mo)
Johnston, Lazarus 1861 wb-5-118 (Hr)
Johnston, Lewis 1842 abl-1-252 (T)
Johnston, Lewis 1849 rb-15-186 (Ru)
Johnston, Lewis 1849 rb-15-202 (Ru)
Johnston, Lucy 1850 wb-d-221 (G)
Johnston, Mary 1846 wb-#149 (Wl)
Johnston, Mary 1856 wb-5-63 (Hr)
Johnston, Michael 1850 wb-14-556 (D)
Johnston, Oliver 1816 wb-7-69 (D)
Johnston, Robert 1797 wb-0-18 (K)
Johnston, Robert 1827 wb-4-205 (Wi)
Johnston, Robert 1838 wb-2-315 (Ma)
Johnston, Robert 1849 as-a-180 (Ms)
Johnston, Samuel 1805 wb-1-168 (Rb)
Johnston, Samuel 1817 wb-a-19 (Di)
Johnston, Samuel 1832 wb-#95 (Wl)
Johnston, Sarah 1854 ib-h-13 (F)
Johnston, Stephen 1819 wb-3-42 (Wi)
Johnston, Thomas 1806 wb-1-15# (Ge)
Johnston, William 1826 wb-#133 (Mu)
Johnston, William 1837 wb-#1 (Mo)
Johnston, William 1841 wb-7-263 (K)
Johnston, William 1844 wb-3-206 (Hr)
Johnston, William 1845 wb-8-345 (Wi)
Johnston, William 1854 wb-#25 (Mo)
Johnston, William 1856 lr (Gi)
Johnston, William J. 1849 wb-f-184 (Mu)
Johnston, William S. 1854 ib-h-16 (F)
Johnstone, Elizabeth 1848 lr (Gi)
Joice, Robert 1847 wb-d-71 (G)
Joiner, Elisha 1840 wb-7-34 (K)
Joiner, Jepha 1815 wb-3-111 (St)
Joiner, Roderick 1832 wb-c-195 (St)
Joiner, Solomon 1859 wb-1-406 (Fr)
Joines, Alexander 1861 39-2-455 (Dk)
Jolly, James 1861 wb-f-408 (Ro)
Jolly, James 1861 wb-f-434 (Ro)
Jolly, John 1860 wb-1-198 (R)
Jolly, Nancy 1842 wb-c-296 (Ro)
Jolly, William 1836 wb-b-281 (Ro)
Jones, A. G. 1852 as-b-58 (Ms)
Jones, A. S. 1860 wb-18-226 (D)
Jones, Abbrigton 1834 rb-f-542 (Mt)
Jones, Abner 1815 wb-2-161 (K)
Jones, Abraham 1810 wb-1-345 (Rb)

Jones, Abraham 1834 wb-1A-58 (A)
Jones, Acheles 1841 wb-1-75 (Sh)
Jones, Agness 1858 wb-a-37 (Ce)
Jones, Albrighton 1837 rb-g-549 (Mt)
Jones, Albrighton 1838 rb-h-33 (Mt)
Jones, Alexander G. 1846 wb-1-130 (Sh)
Jones, Alfred H. 1848 148-1-259 (Ge)
Jones, Allen 1843 wb-4-92 (Ma)
Jones, Allen 1846 wb-4-71 (Hr)
Jones, Amelia 1828 wb-b-20 (Ro)
Jones, Amy? 1842 wb-#137 (Wl)
Jones, Amzi 1843 wb-12-436* (D)
Jones, Andrew 1814 wb-#15 (Wl)
Jones, Anthony 1842 rb-12-253 (Ru)
Jones, Anthony 1843 rb-12-312 (Ru)
Jones, Anthony 1843 wb-11-454 (Rb)
Jones, Aquilla 1809 wb-1-266 (Hw)
Jones, Armour 1859 wb-18-64 (D)
Jones, Asa 1842 wb-3-110 (Hy)
Jones, Asa J. 1844 wb-3-430 (Hy)
Jones, Atlas (Col.) 1842 wb-3-641 (Ma)
Jones, Atlas 1841 wb-3-478 (Ma)
Jones, Austacy 1860 wb-f-395 (G)
Jones, Bedford 1848 rb-14-397 (Ru)
Jones, Bedford C. 1846 rb-13-689 (Ru)
Jones, Benjamin 1840 wb-3-0 (Sm)
Jones, Benjamin 1848 wb-9-33 (Wi)
Jones, Benjamin H. 1835 wb-1-166 (Hy)
Jones, Benjn. W. 1844 as-b-206 (Di)
Jones, Benton 1841 as-a-45 (Ms)
Jones, Berry 1856 wb-e-49 (Wh)
Jones, Berthier 1837 wb-1-38 (Sh)
Jones, C. A. 1846 wb-13-433 (D)
Jones, Caesar A. 1850 wb-2-67 (Sh)
Jones, Calvin (Genl.) 1848 wb-4-360 (Hr)
Jones, Calvin 1846 wb-4-112 (Hr)
Jones, Cassius C. 1836 wb-1-199 (Hy)
Jones, Catharine 1860 wb-f-373 (G)
Jones, Cawalender? 1834 wb-x-237 (Mu)
Jones, Cecelia A. 1847 wb-14-10 (D)
Jones, Charles 1814 wb-1-0 (Sm)
Jones, Charles 1851 wb-b-111 (L)
Jones, Charles P. 1842 as-b-115 (Di)
Jones, Clericy 1858 ib-1-512 (Ca)
Jones, Coleman 1843 wb-f-179* (Hn)
Jones, Cooper B. 1852 wb-b-178 (L)
Jones, Daniel 1815 wb-4-384 (D)
Jones, Daniel 1845 5-3-52 (Cl)
Jones, Daniel 1853 ib-1-311 (Cl)
Jones, Daniel H. 1853 wb-#9 (Mo)
Jones, Daniel sr. 1854 lr (Gi)

Jones, Darling 1849 wb-#45 (Wa)
Jones, Darling 1852 wb-g-430 (Hn)
Jones, David 1806 wb-3-98 (D)
Jones, David 1815 wb-#12 (Mu)
Jones, David 1820 rb-5-20 (Ru)
Jones, David 1840 rb-h-388 (Mt)
Jones, David 1840 wb-2-158 (Hy)
Jones, David 1841 wb-11-88 (Rb)
Jones, David 1841 wb-11-93 (Rb)
Jones, David G. 1835 wb-6-75 (Wi)
Jones, David L. 1848 lr (Gi)
Jones, David Monroe 1861 lr (Gi)
Jones, Delilah 1855 rb-17-495 (Ru)
Jones, Dicy 1837 lr (Gi)
Jones, Drury 1849 wb-g-44 (O)
Jones, Edmond 1838 wb-2-274 (Ma)
Jones, Edmond 1851 wb-15-89 (D)
Jones, Edward 1837 wb-2-219 (Sn)
Jones, Edward 1851 wb-15-123 (D)
Jones, Edward sr. 1848 wb-g-250 (Hn)
Jones, Eldridge W. 1841 wb-1-74 (Sh)
Jones, Eleanor 1855 wb-3e-10 (Sh)
Jones, Eli 1818 wb-3-15 (Rb)
Jones, Eli S. 1845 wb-e-164 (O)
Jones, Elisha 1843 wb-z-440 (Mu)
Jones, Elisha 1850 wb-g-367 (Hn)
Jones, Elizabeth 1816 wb-4-424 (D)
Jones, Elizabeth 1816 wb-7-19 (D)
Jones, Elizabeth 1838 rb-10-189 (Ru)
Jones, Elizabeth 1838 wb-11-194 (D)
Jones, Elizabeth 1843 wb-3-86 (Hr)
Jones, Elizabeth 1845 wb-#149 (Wl)
Jones, Elizabeth 1855 wb-6-7 (Ma)
Jones, Elizabeth 1856 wb-h-615 (Hu)
Jones, Elizabeth 1857 wb-h-153 (Hn)
Jones, Elizabeth A. 1853 wb-b-329 (We)
Jones, Elizabeth D. 1840 wb-b-317 (G)
Jones, Elizabeth D. 1841 wb-b-375 (G)
Jones, Evan sr. 1808 ib-1-210 (Ge)
Jones, Ezekial 1850 wb-m-76 (Mt)
Jones, Ezekiel 1822 rb-d-8 (Mt)
Jones, Ezekiel 1832 rb-f-332 (Mt)
Jones, Ezra 1839 rb-10-358 (Ru)
Jones, Ezra 1839 rb-10-362 (Ru)
Jones, Ezra 1859 rb-20-140 (Ru)
Jones, Flemmin 1848 r39-1-81 (Dk)
Jones, Francis 1837 wb-1-81 (Bo)
Jones, Francis 1854 wb-1-76 (Bo)
Jones, Francis B. 1860 wb-k-359 (O)
Jones, George 1846 wb-2-65# (Ge)
Jones, George W. (Dr.) 1819 wb-#32 (Wl)

Jones, Gideon 1835 wb-1-209 (Hy)
Jones, Gideon 1838 wb-1-370 (Hy)
Jones, H. H. 1847 wb-#161 (Wl)
Jones, Hardy 1859 wb-f-230 (Ro)
Jones, Henderson 1842 wb-a-101 (L)
Jones, Henry 1847 rb-14-167 (Ru)
Jones, Henry 1849 lr (Sn)
Jones, Henry 1860 wb-h-445 (Hn)
Jones, Henry 1861 wb-5-109 (Hr)
Jones, Henry H. 1835 wb-#110 (Wl)
Jones, Henry L. 1856 wb-h-58 (Hn)
Jones, Hezekiah 1849 lr (Gi)
Jones, Ignaticious 1824 wb-#53 (Wl)
Jones, Isaac 1801 wb-0-34 (K)
Jones, Isaac 1848 lr (Gi)
Jones, Isaac 1857 wb-17-228 (D)
Jones, Isaac M. 1852 wb-15-61 (Rb)
Jones, Isaac M. 1855 wb-16-567 (D)
Jones, Isaiah 1848? wb-#173 (Wl)
Jones, Isam 1846 mr-2-188 (Be)
Jones, Israel 1860 wb-b-447 (We)
Jones, J. D. 1857 wb-h-164 (Hn)
Jones, J. R. 1855 wb-g-682 (Hn)
Jones, Jacob 1861 lr (Gi)
Jones, Jacob D. 1855 wb-12-24 (Wi)
Jones, James 1820 lr (Gi)
Jones, James 1820 wb-2-31# (Ge)
Jones, James 1823 wb-#63 (Mu)
Jones, James 1827 wb-4-220 (Wi)
Jones, James 1836 rb-g-401 (Mt)
Jones, James 1837 wb-d-306 (Hn)
Jones, James 1840 wb-2-207 (Hr)
Jones, James 1843 wb-1-565 (W)
Jones, James 1846 148-1-165 (Ge)
Jones, James 1847 lr (Gi)
Jones, James 1847 wb-13-116 (Rb)
Jones, James 1853 wb-g-533 (Hn)
Jones, James 1855 rb-17-530 (Ru)
Jones, James 1855 wb-3-294 (Gr)
Jones, James 1857 wb-4-1 (Gr)
Jones, James 1860 149-1-196 (Ge)
Jones, James 1861 39-2-454 (Dk)
Jones, James B. 1840 wb-a-90 (Cr)
Jones, James C. 1859 wb-3e-122 (Sh)
Jones, James D. 1858 wb-h-259 (Hn)
Jones, James E. 1857 rb-18-637 (Ru)
Jones, James H. 1849 wb-4-100 (Je)
Jones, James J. 1848 wb-14-82 (Rb)
Jones, James P. 1839 wb-3-0 (Sm)
Jones, James S. 1834 rb-g-60* (Mt)
Jones, James S. 1858 wb-f-185 (G)

Jones, James T. 1854 ib-H-115 (F)
Jones, James W. 1848 wb-b-182 (Mu)
Jones, Jarvis 1844 wd-13-46 (D)
Jones, Jeremiah 1846 wb-d-317 (Hd)
Jones, Jesse 1846 wb-#151 (Wl)
Jones, Jesse 1854 wb-h-280 (Hu)
Jones, Jesse W. 1814 wb-A-65 (Li)
Jones, Jno. 1843 5-2-330 (Cl)
Jones, Joanna 1853 148-1-447 (Ge)
Jones, Joel 1840 wb-d-461 (St)
Jones, Joel 1841 wb-e-35 (St)
Jones, Joel L. 1854 wb-a-444 (F)
Jones, John 1803 wb-1-133 (K)
Jones, John 1815 wb-#20 (Wl)
Jones, John 1819 wb-1-15# (Ge)
Jones, John 1828 wb-b-243 (St)
Jones, John 1836 wb-#114 (Wl)
Jones, John 1838 wb-1-0 (Sm)
Jones, John 1839 wb-1-367 (Gr)
Jones, John 1842 wb-2-391 (Hr)
Jones, John 1845 wb-12-503 (Rb)
Jones, John 1845 wb-g-8 (Hn)
Jones, John 1846 wb-a2-506 (Mu)
Jones, John 1849 wb-5-70 (Ma)
Jones, John 1850 wb-2-76 (Sh)
Jones, John 1853 wb-e-92 (G)
Jones, John 1856 wb-#58 (Wa)
Jones, John 1857 wb-12-346 (K)
Jones, John 1858 wb-h-481 (St)
Jones, John B. 1847 wb-b-248 (We)
Jones, John B. 1859 wb-13-74 (Wi)
Jones, John C. 1847 wb-2-209 (W)
Jones, John J. 1852 wb-7-0 (Sm)
Jones, John M. 1842 wb-z-384 (Mu)
Jones, John T. 1834 wb-1-324 (Hr)
Jones, John W. 1823 wb-#47 (Mu)
Jones, Johnathan 1840 wb-a-58 (L)
Jones, Johnston 1831 wb-1-76 (Bo)
Jones, Jonathan 1851 ib-1-173 (Ca)
Jones, Jordan 1840 rb-h-456 (Mt)
Jones, Joseph 1826 wb-1-15# (Ge)
Jones, Joseph 1853 ib-1-250 (Ca)
Jones, Joseph 1854 wb-1-79 (Bo)
Jones, Joshua 1833 rb-f-512 (Mt)
Jones, Joshua 1834 rb-f-570 (Mt)
Jones, Judith 1857 wb-12-363 (Wi)
Jones, Kimbro 1815 wb-2-248 (Rb)
Jones, Kinchen 1815 wb-2-222 (Rb)
Jones, Kiziah 1846 wb-8-489 (Wi)
Jones, Laban 1848 wb-1-248 (Fr)
Jones, Lafayette 1843 wb-1-97 (Sh)

Jones, Larkin 1854 wb-a-453 (F)
Jones, Lemuel 1845 wb-a2-302 (Mu)
Jones, Lewallen 1838 rb-10-92 (Ru)
Jones, Lewis 1821 wb-1-3 (Ma)
Jones, Lucy 1847 rb-14-168 (Ru)
Jones, Lura C. 1854 wb-b-252 (L)
Jones, Margaret 1826 wb-1-66 (Fr)
Jones, Margaret 1853 ib-1-304 (Cl)
Jones, Marshall 1861 wb-e-149 (Hy)
Jones, Martha 1847 wb-#156 (Wl)
Jones, Martin 1859 lr (Gi)
Jones, Martin B. 1846 wb-c-337 (G)
Jones, Mary B. 1857 wb-b-31 (Ms)
Jones, Milly 1832 wb-b-170 (Ro)
Jones, Minerva A. 1855 wb-15-751 (Rb)
Jones, Moody 1839 wb-2-265 (Sn)
Jones, Morton 1840 wb-0-25 (Cf)
Jones, Moses 1826 lr (Sn)
Jones, Nancy 1827 wb-4-248 (Wi)
Jones, Nancy 1838 rb-10-214 (Ru)
Jones, Nancy 1842 wb-f-123 (Hn)
Jones, Nancy 1843 rb-j-57 (Mt)
Jones, Nancy 1845 148-1-129 (Ge)
Jones, Nancy 1858 wb-5-82 (Hr)
Jones, Nathaniel 1821 rb-5-136 (Ru)
Jones, Nathaniel 1853 wb-g-503 (Hn)
Jones, Obadiah 1860 wb-f-206 (Mu)
Jones, Patsy 1842 rb-12-200 (Ru)
Jones, Peter 1813 wb-#13 (Wl)
Jones, Peter 1813 wb-1-0 (Sm)
Jones, Philip E. 1826 wb-1-154 (Ma)
Jones, Phineas 1857 wb-2-85# (Ge)
Jones, Polly 1840 wb-#127 (Wl)
Jones, Pricilla 1849 lr (Sn)
Jones, R. H. 1837 wb-1-318 (Hy)
Jones, Rebecca 1830 rb-f-114 (Mt)
Jones, Reuben 1815 wb-a-18 (Di)
Jones, Reuben 1857 rb-o-396 (Mt)
Jones, Reuben 1857 rb-o-423 (Mt)
Jones, Reubin 1827 rb-e-92 (Mt)
Jones, Richard (B) 1805 wb-1-144 (Rb)
Jones, Richard 1835 rb-9-262 (Ru)
Jones, Richard 1836 rb-9-203 (Ru)
Jones, Richard 1837 wb-2-224 (Sn)
Jones, Richard 1849 wb-#172 (Wl)
Jones, Richard 1853 wb-f-23 (Mu)
Jones, Richard H. 1837 wb-1-329 (Hy)
Jones, Richard R. 1823 wb-8-186 (D)
Jones, Richard W. 1851 wb-2-101 (Sh)
Jones, Robert 1834 wb-x-195 (Mu)
Jones, Robert 1843 wb-f-37 (St)

Jonte, Peter 1840 wb-12-90* (D)
Joplin, Elihu 1842 wb-#137 (Wl)
Joplin, Robert 1822 wb-#42 (Wl)
Joplin, Sarah 1850 wb-#173 (Wl)
Jordan, Alice 1854 wb-g-572 (Hn)
Jordan, Archer 1835 wb-6-66 (Wi)
Jordan, Benjamin W. 1846 rb-k-49 (Mt)
Jordan, Blount 1851 rb-15-618 (Ru)
Jordan, Drewry 1836 wb-10-632 (D)
Jordan, Eliza B. 1859 wb-f-158 (Mu)
Jordan, Elizabeth 1838 wb-y-192* (Mu)
Jordan, G. W. 1851 wb-m-371 (Mt)
Jordan, Grizzle 1851 wb-m-374 (Mt)
Jordan, Henry 1823 wb-3-653 (Wi)
Jordan, J. B. 1859 rb-19-569 (Ru)
Jordan, James B. 1861 rb-21-6 (Ru)
Jordan, John 1804 Wb-1-120 (Wi)
Jordan, John 1850 rb-15-248 (Ru)
Jordan, John J. 1849 rb-15-78 (Ru)
Jordan, John L. 1858 wb-f-140 (G)
Jordan, Laban 1858 wb-f-135 (Mu)
Jordan, Lewis 1847 wb-#45 (Wa)
Jordan, Louisa 1857 wb-17-161 (D)
Jordan, Marcellus 1841 rb-i-186 (Mt)
Jordan, Mary E. G. 1858 wb-#59 (Wa)
Jordan, Meredith 1831 wb-9-486 (D)
Jordan, Nancy 1852 rb-16-236 (Ru)
Jordan, Richard 1842 wb-2-525 (Hy)
Jordan, Sally 1844 wb-8-138 (Wi)
Jordan, Samuel 1850 wb-m-79 (Mt)
Jordan, Sarah 1859 wb-18-86 (D)
Jordan, Stephen 1850 wb-9-356 (Wi)
Jordan, Stephen B. 1848 wb-d-143 (G)
Jordan, Susannah 1847 wb-13-208 (Rb)
Jordan, Thomas 1855 wb-11-557 (Wi)
Jordan, Thomas C. 1863 wb-#88 (Mc)
Jordan, Thompson W. 1832 wb-a-215 (G)
Jordan, William 1815 rb-b-165 (Mt)
Jordan, William 1822 wb-3-583 (Wi)
Jordan, William 1838 wb-a-25 (L)
Jordan, Williamson 1847 wb-14-163 (D)
Jorden, Harris 1838 wb-2-351 (Ma)
Jorden, William 1815 wb-#11 (Mu)
Jordon, Alexander 1824 rb-6-63 (Ru)
Jordon, Benjamin 1847 wb-14-103 (D)
Jordon, Elizabeth 1844 lr (Gi)
Jordon, Hezekiah 1839 wb-1-166 (Li)
Jordon, Nancy 1831 wb-7-277 (Rb)
Jordon, Samuel 1834 lr (Gi)
Joslin, Gabriel 1858 as-c-547 (Di)
Joslin, Henderson 1841 as-a-503 (Di)

Joslin, James 1843 wb-a-159 (Di)
Joslin, Lewis 1856 wb-17-126 (D)
Joslin, Richard 1829 wb-9-355 (D)
Joslin, W. B. 1856 as-c-374 (Di)
Joslin, Willis 1846 wb-d-13 (G)
Jossey, James 1832 wb-#241 (Mu)
Jost, Christiana 1850 wb-14-511 (D)
Jost, John 1822 wb-#117 (Mu)
Jost, Thomas 1850 wb-14-522 (D)
Josy, James 1834 wb-x-248 (Mu)
Jouett?, William F. 1843 wb-f-180* (Hn)
Jourdan, Meredith 1831 wb-9-468 (D)
Jourdan, Richard 1828 wb-6-333 (Rb)
Jourdin, Mary 1858 wb-#88 (Mc)
Journey, James C. 1840 wb-e-146 (Hn)
Joy, Levi 1839 wb-2-44 (Hr)
Joyce, Joseph T. 1852 wb-15-417 (D)
Joyce, Thomas 1824 wb-A-375 (Li)
Joyce, Thomas 1838 wb-11-116 (D)
Joyner, Drewry 1823 wb-#48 (Wl)
Joyner, E. B. 1857 wb-j-245 (O)
Joyner, Henry 1843 wb-5-26 (Hr)
Joyner, Jesse 1847 lr (Sn)
Joyner, John 1859 wb-k-54 (O)
Joyner, Matthew 1856 wb-h-58 (Hn)
Joyner, Richard 1853 wb-h-Mar (O)
Joyner, Thomas 1824 lr (Sn)
Joyner, Thomas 1850 wb-4-563 (Hr)
Joyner, Whitehead 1821 rb-c-440 (Mt)
Judd, Daniel 1860 ib-2-190 (Wy)
Judge, John 1859 wb-4-220 (La)
Judkins, James 1845 wb-#88 (Mc)
Judkins, James M. 1861 39-2-472 (Dk)
Jugg, Priscilla 1841 wb-e-152 (St)
Julian, Drury P. 1858 wb-13-30 (K)
Julian, John 1851 wb-d-3 (Wh)
Julian, Nancy 1853 wb-11-408 (K)
Julin, John 1851 wb-d-6 (Wh)
Jurdon, Charles 1831 wb-1-243 (Ma)
Justice, A. J. 1850 wb-14-331 (Rb)
Justice, Alfred 1847 wb-13-144 (Rb)
Justice, Allen A. 1861 wb-1-102 (Dy)
Justice, Armstead 1849 wb-14-232 (Rb)
Justice, Francis W. 1851 wb-5-21 (Hr)
Justice, Henry 1815 wb-2-84 (Je)
Justice, Jack A. 1854 wb-15-643 (Rb)
Justice, Jacob 1808 lw (Ct)
Justice, James S. 1849 wb-14-270 (Rb)
Justice, John 1855 wb-1-15# (Ge)
Justice, John sr. 1855 wb-2-81# (Ge)
Justice, Nancy 1855 wb-16-96 (Rb)

Keener, Ullrich 1828 wb-#31 (Wa)
Keeney, Allison 1846 148-1-168 (Ge)
Keeney, Michael 1849? wb-1B-125 (A)
Keeney, William 1841 wb-1A-319 (A)
Keenum, Elizabeth 1856 wb-2-294 (Me)
Keenum, George 1851 wb-2-93 (Me)
Keeny, Jo 1857 wb-1C-352 (A)
Keer, Wilson 1827 rb-7-127 (Ru)
Keesee, Agnes 1829 lr (Sn)
Keesee, George 1825 lr (Sn)
Keesee, R. C. 1845 rb-j-363 (Mt)
Keesling, David 1838 wb-1A-187 (A)
Keeton, Allen 1850 wb-#89 (Mc)
Keeton, George 1834 wb-1-72 (La)
Keeton, Julis 1841 eb-1-440 (C)
Keeton, Littleton 1860 wb-#89 (Mc)
Keith, Alexander 1831 wb-#89 (Mc)
Keith, Britian 1845 wb-1-359 (La)
Keith, Charles F. 1857 wb-#89 (Mc)
Keith, Danl. 1836 rb-9-126 (Ru)
Keith, James S. 1861 wb-2-341 (Li)
Keith, Jemima 1837 wb-b-358 (Ro)
Keith, John 1801 wb-1-180 (Je)
Keith, John J. 1848? wb-1B-72 (A)
Keith, Malinda 1820 wb-3-205 (K)
Keith, Marion 1858 wb-1C-444 (A)
Keith, Mary 1818 wb-3-50 (K)
Keith, Nancy 1857 wb-7-0 (Sm)
Keith, P. H. 1856 wb-#89 (Mc)
Keith, Sarah 1853 wb-11-409 (K)
Keith, William 1854 wb-12-52 (K)
Keith, William Fleming 1857 wb-#90 (Mc)
Kellam, Lucian M. 1860 wb-k-366 (O)
Kellam, R. G. 1860 wb-k-368 (O)
Kellar, John 1807 as-1-186 (Ge)
Keller, Conrad 1821 rb-5-118 (Ru)
Keller, Daniel sr. 1840 wb-2-54# (Ge)
Keller, Imri 1841 wb-a-66 (L)
Keller, Jerry? 1838 wb-a-20 (L)
Keller, Phillip 1869 wb-#15 (Mo)
Keller, Samuel 1858 wb-2-145# (Ge)
Keller, Wesley 1840 wb-a-55 (L)
Kelley, Barnabas 1852 wb-1-297 (Hw)
Kelley, Cary T. 1854 wb-a-328 (Ms)
Kelley, Charles 1834 wb-3-393 (Je)
Kelley, Eleanor B. 1848 rb-l-118 (Mt)
Kelley, Eleanor B. 1848 wb-14-27 (Rb)
Kelley, John R. 1843 wb-3-0 (Sm)
Kelley, John R. 1851 r39-1-188 (Dk)
Kelley, Joshua 1831? wb-1-114 (Hy)
Kelley, Polly 1836 wb-2-45# (Ge)

Kelley, Sarah Jane 1852 wb-5-69 (Je)
Kelley, Turner D. 1859 wb-2-89# (Ge)
Kelley, Vincent P. 1860 wb-a-295 (T)
Kelley, William 1833 wb-3-233 (Je)
Kelley, William S. 1824 wb-1-56 (Fr)
Kellough, Robert H. 1843 rb-12-350 (Ru)
Kellough, S. D. 1859 wb-k-8 (O)
Kellough, Samuel 1842 rb-12-123 (Ru)
Kellough, Samuel D. 1860 wb-k-470 (O)
Kellow, Thomas 1834 wb-5-400 (Wi)
Kellum, Henry 1799 wb-2-154 (D)
Kellum, John 1826 wb-9-56 (D)
Kellum, John 1837 wb-x-479 (Mu)
Kellum, William 1811 wb-4-165 (D)
Kelly, A. M. 1860 wb-h-458 (Hn)
Kelly, Albert G. 1853 as-b-138 (Ms)
Kelly, Anthony 1801 wb-2-34# (Ge)
Kelly, Bartholomew 1853 lr (Sn)
Kelly, Benjamin 1836 wb-d-31 (St)
Kelly, Benjamin 1836 wb-d-36 (St)
Kelly, Cary C. 1861 as-c-237 (Ms)
Kelly, Cullin 1841 wb-#136 (Wl)
Kelly, Dennis 1825 wb-#61 (Wl)
Kelly, Dennis 1832 wb-#105 (Wl)
Kelly, Dr. 1826 wb-#64 (Wl)
Kelly, Edmond 1837 wb-d-73 (St)
Kelly, Edward 1828 wb-b-223 (St)
Kelly, Elizabeth 1839 wb-#125 (Wl)
Kelly, Francis 1851 wb-15-58 (D)
Kelly, George 1860 wb-4-370 (La)
Kelly, George P. 1851 as-b-61 (Ms)
Kelly, J. S. 1859 wb-18-49 (D)
Kelly, Jabez W. J. 1849 148-1-284 (Ge)
Kelly, James 1856 wb-f-5 (G)
Kelly, John 1793 wb-1-7 (K)
Kelly, John 1823 as-A-51 (Di)
Kelly, John 1831 wb-1-91 (Fr)
Kelly, John M. 1856? ib-2-328 (Cl)
Kelly, John sr. 1818 wb-A-246 (Li)
Kelly, Joseph 1834? wb-1-142 (Hy)
Kelly, Joseph 1840 wb-7-6 (K)
Kelly, Joshua 1859 wb-f-269 (G)
Kelly, Kinchen 1840 wb-#38 (Wa)
Kelly, Nimrod 1850 wb-a-164 (Cr)
Kelly, Patrick 1855 ib-2-294 (Cl)
Kelly, Redmund H. 1842 wb-e-511 (Hu)
Kelly, Rhoda 1839 wb-10-312 (Rb)
Kelly, Saml. L. 1825 rb-6-124 (Ru)
Kelly, Samuel 1835 wb-1-398 (Hr)
Kelly, Samuel 1836 wb-1-103 (La)
Kelly, Samuel W. 1854 wb-h-27 (St)

Kelly, Samuel W. 1854 wb-h-31 (St)
Kelly, Spencer 1844 wb-7-0 (Sm)
Kelly, Stephen 1856 rb-17-718 (Ru)
Kelly, Thomas 1834 wb-a-255 (R)
Kelly, William 1796 wb-1-52 (K)
Kelly, William 1815 wb-#11 (Mu)
Kelly, William 1816 wb-2-346 (Rb)
Kelly, William 1859 wb-i-37 (St)
Kelsay, John 1850 wb-#49 (Wa)
Kelsey, Samuel 1795? wb-#22 (Wa)
Kelsey, William 1806 wb-#10 (Wa)
Kelsick, Mary 1837 rb-g-606 (Mt)
Kelsick, Will R. 1825 rb-d-498 (Mt)
Kelsick, William 1827 rb-e-132 (Mt)
Kelso, Charles 1853 wb-#9 (Mo)
Kelso, Henry 1832 wb-1-81 (Li)
Kelso, James W. 1868 wb-#15 (Mo)
Kelsoe, David 1857 wb-#27 (Mo)
Keltner, James S. 1856 wb-c-82 (L)
Keltner, Solomon 1854 wb-e-37 (Hy)
Kelton, Elizabeth 1830 rb-8-130 (Ru)
Kelton, James 1847 rb-14-168 (Ru)
Kelton, James 1854 wb-15-590 (Rb)
Kelton, James L. 1858 ib-1-495 (Ca)
Kelton, Robert 1829 rb-7-169 (Ru)
Kelton, Robert E. 1860 rb-20-621 (Ru)
Kelton, Samuel 1840 rb-11-80 (Ru)
Kelton, Samuel B. 1841 rb-11-222 (Ru)
Kelton, William 1813 rb-1-150 (Ru)
Kelton, William 1844 rb-13-43 (Ru)
Kelton, William R. 1844 rb-13-152 (Ru)
Kemp, Barnett 1847 wb-c-266 (Wh)
Kemp, Burris 1827 wb-#69 (Wl)
Kemp, Lucretia 1844 wb-7-0 (Sm)
Kenady, Elias M. 1835 wb-1-422 (Hr)
Kenady, John B. 1823 wb-#66 (Mu)
Kenady, Joseph 1848 wb-4-350 (Hr)
Kendall, Cynthia 1825 wb-a-118 (Hn)
Kendall, James 1846 wb-g-145 (Hn)
Kendall, John 1860 wb-h-462 (Hn)
Kendall, Peter 1862 wb-h-554 (Hn)
Kendall, W. T. 1861 wb-h-543 (Hn)
Kendall, William T. 1859 wb-h-314 (Hn)
Kendrick, Austin 1849 wb-4-440 (Hr)
Kendrick, D. D. (D. L.?) 1828 rb-e-396 (Mt)
Kendrick, Dennis L. 1835 rb-g-152 (Mt)
Kendrick, Dennis L. 1842 rb-i-230 (Mt)
Kendrick, James 1815? wb-#33 (Mu)
Kendrick, James 1847 rb-k-568 (Mt)
Kendrick, Jones 1819? wb-#111 (Mu)
Kendrick, William 1844 wb-4-258 (Ma)

Kenedy, Alanon? 1853 wb-#113 (Wl)
Kenedy, Ann 1798 wb-1-25 (Rb)
Kenedy, Henry 1802 wb-2-239 (D)
Kenedy, James 1802 wb-2-262 (D)
Kenedy, James 1839 as-a-19 (Ms)
Kenedy, Obediance 1848 rb-14-425 (Ru)
Kenedy, Sampson 1845 wb-b-97 (We)
Kenedy, Thomas sr. 1832 wb-2-85 (Fr)
Kenley, Richard M. 1853 wb-i-104 (O)
Kenley, Thomas 1851 wb-d-346 (G)
Kenly, Richard 1853 wb-h-May (O)
Kennady, Elias 1835 wb-1-405 (Hr)
Kennard, Hannah 1825 wb-4-4 (Wi)
Kennedy, Adam M. 1832 wb-5-150 (K)
Kennedy, Allen J. 1833 wb-1-92 (Li)
Kennedy, Ann 1856 wb-2-84# (Ge)
Kennedy, Daniel 1802 as-1-1 (Ge)
Kennedy, E. S. 1837 wb-2-87 (Hr)
Kennedy, Enoch 1836 wb-1-496 (Hr)
Kennedy, Enoch S. 1841 wb-2-330 (Hr)
Kennedy, Esther 1823 wb-A-318 (Li)
Kennedy, Francis H. 1826? wb-#144 (Mu)
Kennedy, Isaac 1813 wb-#36 (Wl)
Kennedy, Isaac 1841 wb-e-204 (Hn)
Kennedy, J. V. W. S. 1840 wb-7-64 (K)
Kennedy, James 1826 wb-#90 (Mc)
Kennedy, James 1826 wb-4-165 (K)
Kennedy, James 1831 wb-#217 (Mu)
Kennedy, James 1836 wb-#90 (Mc)
Kennedy, James 1838 wb-6-270 (K)
Kennedy, James 1855 wb-12-151 (K)
Kennedy, James G. 1839? wb-#124 (Wl)
Kennedy, John 1785 wb-1-39 (D)
Kennedy, John 1823 lr (Sn)
Kennedy, John 1835 as-a-294 (Di)
Kennedy, John 1854 wb-f-52 (Mu)
Kennedy, John 1861 149-1-227 (Ge)
Kennedy, John M. 1842 wb-8-13 (K)
Kennedy, John M. 1855 wb-3-281 (La)
Kennedy, Joseph 1841 wb-1-193 (Li)
Kennedy, Joseph 1851 wb-2-72# (Ge)
Kennedy, Joseph C. 1851 148-1-374 (Ge)
Kennedy, Lemuel 1822 wb-8-112 (D)
Kennedy, Martin 1856 wb-3e-17 (Sh)
Kennedy, Mary 1853 wb-11-435 (K)
Kennedy, Nancy 1837 wb-6-127 (K)
Kennedy, O. G. 1854 wb-2-154 (Sh)
Kennedy, Patrick 1841 wb-7-363 (Wi)
Kennedy, Patsy M. 1853 lr (Gi)
Kennedy, Robert C. 1815 wb-A-67 (Li)
Kennedy, Thomas R. 1847 wb-#45 (Wa)

Kennedy, Walter 1857 wb-12-326 (K)
Kennedy, Walter jr. 1854 wb-12-44 (K)
Kennedy, Wiliam H. 1843 wb-1-87 (Sh)
Kennedy, William 1809 wb-1-128 (Sn)
Kennedy, William 1853 wb-11-83 (Wi)
Kennedy, William B. 1840? wb-#131 (Wl)
Kenner, Frank D. 1832 wb-2-0 (Sm)
Kenner, Howson 1824 wb-1-581 (Hw)
Kenner, Jacob 1843 148-1-45 (Ge)
Kenner, Judith 1819 wb-1-279 (Hw)
Kenner, Judith 1829 wb-1-282 (Hw)
Kenner, Malinda 1835 wb-1-291 (Hw)
Kenner, Wiley B. 1862 wb-1-302 (Hw)
Kennerly, John P. 1847 wb-1-237 (Fr)
Kenney, James 1821 wb-1-16# (Ge)
Kenney, James 1859 wb-2-88# (Ge)
Kenney, John 1855 wb-2-182 (Sh)
Kenney, Lucy J. 1861 wb-3e-176 (Sh)
Kennon, Hughs 1835 wb-1-199 (Gr)
Kennon, Hughs O. 1836 wb-1-221 (Gr)
Kennon, William 1850 wb-1-404 (Li)
Kenny, James 1816 wb-2-194 (Wi)
Kenny, Jeremiah 1827 wb-#67 (Wl)
Kent, Peter 1842 wb-2-60# (Ge)
Kent, Sarah Ann 1848 wb-2-68# (Ge)
Keon, Mary Jane 1845 wb-1-132 (Sh)
Keor, Saml. 1809 wb-4-38 (D)
Kephart, Samuel 1841 abl-1-231 (T)
Keplinger, Jacob 1824 wb-#20 (Wa)
Kerbaugh, John 1856 wb-2-83# (Ge)
Kerbough, George 1805 as-1-104 (Ge)
Kerby, Bennet 1840 wb-y-670 (Mu)
Kerby, Ezekiel 1832 wb-x-60 (Mu)
Kerby, George H. 1858 rb-19-219 (Ru)
Kerby, James 1829 wb-1-86 (Bo)
Kerby, James 1845 wb-12-343 (Rb)
Kerby, Miles 1816 wb-2-352 (Rb)
Kerby, Richard 1811 wb-1-87 (Bo)
Kerby, William 1840 wb-a-19 (Dk)
Kerby, Wright 1826 wb-#141 (Mu)
Kerchervall, Sally Ann 1825 rb-d-496 (Mt)
Kerchival, Samuel 1843 lr (Gi)
Kerfall, William S. 1848 wb-b-275 (Mu)
Kerk, Samuel 1828 rb-e-387 (Mt)
Kerley, C. W. 1855 39-2-85 (Dk)
Kerley, Clayborn W. 1855 39-2-87 (Dk)
Kern, David 1814 wb-2-58 (Je)
Kerney, Vincent 1844 wb-13-89 (D)
Kernon, James 1861 wb-f-211 (Mu)
Kerns, Charles 1815 wb-2-205 (K)
Kerns, Michael 1814 wb-2-132 (K)

Kerr, Alexdr. 1831 wb-b-63 (Wh)
Kerr, Andrew 1804 wb-1-137 (Je)
Kerr, Andrew 1845 wb-d-169 (Hd)
Kerr, Andrew M. 1847 wb-a2-534* (Mu)
Kerr, Andrew M. jr. 1844 wb-a2-100 (Mu)
Kerr, D. 1815 wb-2-87 (Je)
Kerr, David 1816 wb-2-153 (Je)
Kerr, David 1841 wb-1-85 (Bo)
Kerr, Henry 1856 lr (Gi)
Kerr, James 1820 wb-#111 (Mu)
Kerr, James 1824 wb-#77 (Mu)
Kerr, James 1825 wb-a-205 (Wh)
Kerr, Jane 1837 wb-b-44 (Hd)
Kerr, John 1854 wb-d-168 (Wh)
Kerr, Mary 1842 wb-1-87 (Bo)
Kerr, Richard 1857 wb-e-169 (Wh)
Kerr, Samuel 1811 wb-4-164 (D)
Kerr, William 1815 rb-b-277 (Mt)
Kerr, William 1829 wb-4-387 (K)
Kerr, William 1839 wb-y-334 (Mu)
Kerr, William 1854 wb-f-32 (Mu)
Kerr, William A. 1857 wb-3e-55 (Sh)
Kerr, William N. 1847 wb-b-397 (Mu)
Kerr, William sr. 1806 wb-1-202 (K)
Kerr, Wilson 1814 rb-1-166 (Ru)
Kersey, Elizabeth 1849 ib-1-59 (Ca)
Kersey, Hannibal 1858 39-2-225 (Dk)
Kersey, Hightower 1827 wb-2-566 (Je)
Kersey, Hiram 1843 wb-1-529 (W)
Kesee, Rewben 1844 rb-j-266 (Mt)
Kesterson, Charles 1843 148-1-59 (Ge)
Kesterson, David 1839 5-2-135 (Cl)
Kesterson, William sr. 1821 wb-1-16# (Ge)
Ketcherside, Chesley C. 1854 wb-d-222 (Wh)
Ketchum, Ezekiel 1860 wb-f-319 (Ro)
Ketchum, Ezekiel W. 1858 wb-f-158 (Ro)
Ketner, Henry 1818 wb-2-208 (Je)
Ketrell, Salomon 1830 rb-f-121 (Mt)
Ketrell, Wm. 1834 rb-9-167 (Ru)
Ketring, Francis 1819 lr (Sn)
Ketron, John 1853 wb-1-361 (Su)
Ketsick, William R. 1828 rb-e-285 (Mt)
Kettner, Solomon G. 1848 wb-2-32 (La)
Kettrell, John 1838 rb-10-164 (Ru)
Kettrell, Soloman A. 1818 rb-b-389 (Mt)
Keuthman, H. A. 1843 wb-12-439* (D)
Keuthman, Henry A. 1846 wb-13-365 (D)
Key, Amos T. 1821 wb-1-0 (Sm)
Key, Daniel 1840 wb-2-54# (Ge)
Key, David 1845 148-1-131 (Ge)
Key, Elizabeth 1830 wb-9-368 (D)

Key, James D. 1857 wb-f-47 (G)
Key, Jefferson 1828 wb-1-52 (Hr)
Key, Job 1851 wb-a-404 (F)
Key, John 1838 wb-1-171 (Fr)
Key, John 1854 wb-#25 (Mo)
Key, Jonathan 1826 wb-3-0 (Sm)
Key, Landon P. 1853 wb-b-204 (L)
Key, Logan D. 1858 wb-7-0 (Sm)
Key, M. G. 1861 wb-k-382 (O)
Key, Martin 1858 wb-7-8 (Ma)
Key, Mary 1842 wb-2-59# (Ge)
Key, Mary 1849 wb-2-70# (Ge)
Key, Peter 1849 wb-1-195 (Bo)
Key, Richard W. 1820 lr (Sn)
Key, Solomon 1833 wb-3-0 (Sm)
Key, Thomas T. 1838 wb-d-234* (Hn)
Key, William 1830 wb-9-366 (D)
Key, William W. 1820 wb-7-481 (D)
Key, William sr. 1833 lr (Sn)
Keyes, James A. 1860 wb-13-271 (Wi)
Keykendall, Jessee 1835 wb-d-49 (Hn)
Keys, Alexander D. 1859 wb-#90 (Mc)
Keys, David 1842 wb-2-58# (Ge)
Keys, Harrison 1817 wb-2-378 (K)
Keys, James 1854 wb-1-92 (Jo)
Keys, John 1816 rb-3-173 (Ru)
Keys, William 1835 wb-10-401 (D)
Kezer, Timothy 1845 wb-13-296 (D)
Kias, Harry 1821 wb-#40 (Wl)
Kicker, Conrad (Sr.) 1826 wb-#25 (Wa)
Kidd, A. W. 1837 wb-a-19 (L)
Kidd, Archibald 1861 wb-2-335 (Li)
Kidd, Benjamin 1832 wb-5-200 (Wi)
Kidd, David L. 1855 wb-12-97 (K)
Kidd, George 1843 wb-1-271 (La)
Kidd, George W. 1850 wb-2-91 (La)
Kidd, George W. 1851 wb-2-190 (La)
Kidd, Hezakiah 1859 wb-13-152 (K)
Kidd, James 1840 wb-a-48 (Ms)
Kidd, John 1855 wb-12-159 (K)
Kidd, Margaret 1841 wb-a-86 (Ms)
Kidwell, Elizabeth 1853 148-1-454 (Ge)
Kidwell, John 1827 wb-2-568 (Je)
Kidwell, John 1846 wb-5-462 (Gr)
Kiellough, Samuel 1813 rb-2-215 (Ru)
Kierman, Allice 1860 wb-3e-137 (Sh)
Kies, Henry 1821 wb-#41 (Wl)
Kiger, Peter 1820 wb-3-171 (Rb)
Kilabrew, Bryan W. 1850 wb-g-322 (St)
Kilburn, John M. 1850 wb-2-130 (La)
Kilchrist, Francis 1850 wb-b-618 (Mu)

Kilcrease, John 1843 wb-z-541 (Mu)
Kilcrease, W. W. 1838 wb-y-184* (Mu)
Kilcrease, William 1840 wb-y-686 (Mu)
Kilcrease, William 1843 wb-z-514 (Mu)
Kilger, James B. 1856 wb-e-447 (G)
Kilgore, Charles 1822 wb-1-16# (Ge)
Kilgore, James 1835 ib-2-69 (Ge)
Kilgore, James 1860 149-1-206 (Ge)
Kilgore, William 1826 wb-a-15 (R)
Killebrew, Buckner 1824 rb-d-372 (Mt)
Killebrew, Buckner 1846 rb-k-191 (Mt)
Killebrew, Buckner 1846 rb-k-77 (Mt)
Killebrew, Edithy O. 1854 wb-n-209 (Mt)
Killebrew, Edwin 1847 rb-k-669 (Mt)
Killebrew, Elias 1835 wb-1-149 (We)
Killebrew, Elias 1847 wb-b-223 (We)
Killebrew, Eliza 1849 rb-l-384 (Mt)
Killebrew, Eliza Jane 1851 wb-m-329 (Mt)
Killebrew, Glidewell 1829 rb-e-491 (Mt)
Killebrew, Margaret 1856 rb-o-193 (Mt)
Killebrew, Margaret Ann 1856 rb-o-228 (Mt)
Killebrew, Whitfield 1859 rb-p-120 (Mt)
Killin, John M. 1840 wb-z-64 (Mu)
Killough, John 1808 rb-2-60 (Ru)
Killough, John 1855 wb-a-249 (Cr)
Killough, Mary 1850 rb-15-301 (Ru)
Kilpatrick, Franklin 1836 wb-x-303* (Mu)
Kilpatrick, Robert 1856 lr (Sn)
Kilpatrick, Thomas D. 1857 wb-a-261 (T)
Kimberland, Jacob 1801 wb-1-83 (K)
Kimberland, Jacob 1811 wb-1-357 (K)
Kimble, James 1827 wb-#153 (Mu)
Kimble, Joseph 1842 as-b-101 (Di)
Kimbro, George 1845 wb-c-270 (G)
Kimbro, John 1852 wb-15-413 (D)
Kimbro, Joseph 1860 rb-20-686 (Ru)
Kimbro, W. W. 1853 rb-16-646 (Ru)
Kimbro, William 1816 rb-3-224 (Ru)
Kimbro, William 1833 rb-9-55 (Ru)
Kimbro, William G. 1825 rb-6-87 (Ru)
Kimbro, William G. 1839 rb-10-339 (Ru)
Kimbro, Wm. W. 1858 rb-19-142 (Ru)
Kimbrough, George 1809 wb-1-3 (Fr)
Kimbrough, Henry T. 1858 lr (Gi)
Kimbrough, James 1833 wb-1-15 (Sh)
Kimbrough, John 1822 wb-2-367 (Je)
Kimbrough, Lydia 1846 wb-1-127 (Sh)
Kimbrough, Margaret 1835 wb-1-26 (Sh)
Kimbrough, W. G. 1861 wb-e-163 (Hy)
Kimbrough, William 1836 wb-#2 (Mo)
Kimes, Elenor 1857 wb-2-197 (Li)

Kimes, Elizabeth 1863 wb-2-374 (Li)
Kincade, John 1862 wb-b-117 (F)
Kincade, Nancy 1822 eb-1-120 (C)
Kincaid, John 1818 eb-1-81 (C)
Kincaid, Joseph 1824 wb-#129 (Mu)
Kincaid, Landon 1855 wb-3-302 (La)
Kincaid, Thomas 1830 eb-1-261 (C)
Kincaid, William 1855 ib-2-148 (Cl)
Kincannon, A. 1846 wb-1-150 (Me)
Kincannon, Andrew 1847 wb-1-153 (Me)
Kincannon, David 1836 wb-b-34 (Hd)
Kincannon, Francis 1838 wb-b-110 (Hd)
Kincannon, Thomas H. 1854 wb-2-211 (Me)
Kincanon, Elizabeth 1854 wb-2-244 (Me)
Kincanon, George 1854 wb-2-192 (Me)
Kincheloe, Elijah 1833 wb-1-287 (Hw)
Kincheloe, George E. 1840 wb-#38 (Wa)
Kincheloe, John 1852 wb-#52 (Wa)
Kincheloe, Sarah 1842 wb-#39 (Wa)
Kincheloe, William 1840 wb-#35 (Wa)
Kindal, George 1796 wb-#6 (Wa)
Kinder, Jacob 1854 wb-3-206 (Gr)
Kinder, Mary 1858 wb-3-435 (Gr)
Kinder, Peter 1837 wb-#91 (Mc)
Kinder, Rachel 1853 wb-#91 (Mc)
Kindle, Guston 1848 ib-1-10 (Wy)
Kindle, Moses 1832 wb-c-11 (Hn)
Kindred, Thomas 1833 wb-#102 (Wl)
Kindrick, Austin 1849 wb-4-459 (Hr)
Kindrick, John 1821 wb-#45 (Mu)
Kindrick, John 1830 wb-1-23 (La)
Kindrick, Margaret (Mrs.) 1857 wb-f-68 (Ro)
Kindrick, Samuel 1851 wb-e-287 (Ro)
Kindrick, Samuel sr. 1854 wb-e-470 (Ro)
Kindrick, Thomas 1833 rb-9-62 (Ru)
King, Aaron 1849 wb-1-267 (Me)
King, Abner 1814? wb-#32 (Mu)
King, Alexander 1844 rb-j-84 (Mt)
King, Alexander 1856 wb-h-247 (St)
King, Alvin 1841 wb-c-11 (G)
King, Andrew 1831 wb-1-284 (Hw)
King, Ann 1836 wb-d-55 (St)
King, Armour 1839 wb-e-167 (Hu)
King, Aron 1860 wb-3-67 (Me)
King, Augustus W. 1855 wb-e-337 (G)
King, Barbary 1848 wb-1-292 (Hw)
King, Benjamin 1797 wb-1-15 (Rb)
King, Benjamin 1822 wb-3-368 (Rb)
King, Benjamin 1822 wb-3-566 (Wi)
King, Benjamin 1847 rb-k-457 (Mt)
King, Boling 1856 as-b-210 (Ms)

King, C. C. 1858 wb-i-6 (St)
King, Charles 1843 wb-f-94 (St)
King, Davis 1813 lr (Sn)
King, Delia C. 1858 wb-17-520 (D)
King, Drury 1841 wb-c-15* (G)
King, Edm. 1802 wb-1-136 (Je)
King, Edward H.. 1858 wb-12-552 (Wi)
King, Elenor 1852 ib-1-191 (Wy)
King, Elick 1856 wb-h-288 (St)
King, Elijah 1858 wb-3e-75 (Sh)
King, Elizabeth 1843 wb-4-98 (Ma)
King, Elizabeth 1851 wb-10-42 (Wi)
King, Enoch 1849 wb-4-397 (Hr)
King, Ephraim 1845 wb-1-268 (Li)
King, Francis 1840 5-2-146 (Cl)
King, Garrison 1855 as-c-418 (Di)
King, George 1846 wb-#151 (Wl)
King, George H. 1855 wb-6-244 (Ma)
King, H. R. 1840 rb-i-44 (Mt)
King, H. R. jr. 1849 rb-l-391 (Mt)
King, Henry 1816 rb-3-181 (Ru)
King, Henry 1825 wb-#21 (Wa)
King, Henry 1843 wb-3-676 (Ma)
King, Henry B. 1833? wb-1-88 (Hy)
King, Henry sr. 1844 wb-4-125 (Ma)
King, Holcom R. 1849 rb-l-351 (Mt)
King, Holcomb 1840 rb-i-23 (Mt)
King, Hugh M. 1848 wb-f-127+ (O)
King, Isaac 1808 wb-1-0 (Sm)
King, J. 1836 wb-3-389 (Je)
King, James 1820 as-A-79 (Di)
King, James 1836 wb-3-505 (Je)
King, James 1838 wb-6-277 (K)
King, James 1847 wb-14-165 (D)
King, James 1855 wb-1-300 (Hw)
King, James G. 1831 lr (Sn)
King, James P. 1856 wb-g-755 (Hn)
King, Jeremiah 1828 wb-4-335 (K)
King, Jesse 1847 wb-4-175 (Hr)
King, Jessee 1834 wb-1-367 (Hr)
King, John 1798 wb-1-54 (Je)
King, John 1805 rb-a-309 (Mt)
King, John 1810 wb-1-342 (Je)
King, John 1825 rb-d-419 (Mt)
King, John 1825 wb-b-6 (St)
King, John 1841 wb-z-254 (Mu)
King, John 1847 wb-9-397 (K)
King, John 1855 wb-3e-7 (Sh)
King, John 1857 wb-2-213 (Li)
King, John 1860 wb-13-344 (K)
King, John D. 1848 ib-1-13 (Wy)

King, John M. 1825 rb-6-141 (Ru)
King, John M. 1847 wb-d-74 (G)
King, John T. 1851 wb-11-95 (K)
King, John Ten. 1845 wb-9-113 (K)
King, John W. 1839 5-2-138 (Cl)
King, John W. 1860 wb-#131 (Wl)
King, Jonathan 1847 wb-1-97 (Su)
King, Joshua 1861 wb-4-450 (La)
King, Lewis 1827 wb-9-122 (D)
King, Lucinda 1844 wb-8-164 (Wi)
King, M. B. 1854 wb-g-613 (Hn)
King, M. M. (Mrs.) 1860 rb-p-512 (Mt)
King, Madison 1835 rb-g-214 (Mt)
King, Martha J. 1851 wb-2-65 (Me)
King, Mary 1852 wb-10-422 (Wi)
King, Mary 1855 wb-h-358 (Hu)
King, Mary E. 1856 wb-16-327 (Rb)
King, Mary J. 1847 wb-9-316 (K)
King, Michael 1832 wb-5-151 (K)
King, Nancy L. 1849 wb-14-143 (Rb)
King, Peter 1788 wb-1-15# (Ge)
King, Peter 1821 wb-2-316 (Je)
King, Peter sr. 1825 wb-1-0 (Sm)
King, Philip 1836 wb-1-185 (W)
King, Ralph 1833 wb-c-126 (Hn)
King, Richard 1834 lr (Sn)
King, Robert 1806 wb-1-91 (Sn)
King, Robert 1845 wb-9-38 (K)
King, Robert 1856 ib-1-431 (Wy)
King, Robert 1856 ib-2-5 (Wy)
King, Robert 1860 wb-18-132 (D)
King, Robert A. 1840 lr (Sn)
King, Rufus 1860 wb-e-135 (Hy)
King, Sanders 1862 wb-f-475 (Ro)
King, Sarah 1857 wb-17-414 (D)
King, Sarah 1861 wb-18-531 (D)
King, Susana 1840 wb-e-17 (St)
King, Tabitha 1858 wb-a-66 (Ce)
King, Thomas 1815 wb-#14 (Wa)
King, Thomas 1831 rb-f-196 (Mt)
King, Thomas 1850 wb#19 (Gu)
King, Thomas 1852 wb-15-235 (D)
King, Thomas 1852 wb-3-139 (W)
King, Thomas 1856 wb-#57 (Wa)
King, Thomas A. 1858 rb-o-614 (Mt)
King, Thomas C. 1846 wb-b-192 (We)
King, Thomas J. 1854 wb-3-218 (W)
King, Thomas S. 1852 wb-15-256 (D)
King, Thomas Sr. 1821 wb-#39 (Wl)
King, Thomas sr. 1840 wb-0-9 (Cf)
King, W. 1836 rb-g-301 (Mt)

King, W. B. 1852 wb-m-565 (Mt)
King, Walter 1830 wb-b-80 (Ro)
King, William 1800 lw (Ct)
King, William 1808 wb-1-0 (Sm)
King, William 1808 wb-1-118 (Sn)
King, William 1808 wb-1-275 (Hw)
King, William 1808 wb-4-16 (D)
King, William 1810 rb-a-357 (Mt)
King, William 1811 eb-1-20 (C)
King, William 1817 wb-A-153 (Li)
King, William 1825 wb-b-28 (St)
King, William 1832 wb-#33 (Wa)
King, William 1842 wb-3-4 (Sn)
King, William 1846 lr (Sn)
King, William 1848 wd-14-196 (D)
King, William 1852 as-b-68 (Ms)
King, William 1854 wb-1C-127 (A)
King, William 1860 wb-k-172 (O)
King, William H. 1844 wb-8-166 (Wi)
King, Wm. R. 1852 rb-16-293 (Ru)
Kingston, William 1840 wb-d-438 (St)
Kinkead, William 1860 wb-1-303 (Hw)
Kinnard, C. W. 1856 wb-12-249 (Wi)
Kinnard, Christopher W. 1854 wb-11-247 (Wi)
Kinnard, David 1852 wb-d-86 (Wh)
Kinnard, Gabriel H. 1859 wb-13-180 (Wi)
Kinnard, George 1845 wb-8-342 (Wi)
Kinnard, George C. 1858 wb-13-14 (Wi)
Kinnard, James 1829 wb-4-378 (K)
Kinnard, Michael 1810 wb-1-222 (Wi)
Kinnard, Michael 1813 rb-1-161 (Ru)
Kinnard, Michael 1847 wb-9-18 (Wi)
Kinnard, Michael 1851 wb-9-695 (Wi)
Kinnard, Samuel 1830 wb-b-92 (Hn)
Kinnard, Widow 1852 wb-d-123 (Wh)
Kinney, Manerva G. 1861 wb-#65 (Wa)
Kinnon, George 1855 wb-2-276 (Me)
Kinser, Jacob 1816 wb-2-38# (Ge)
Kinslow, W. E. 1849 as-c-14 (Di)
Kinzel, John C. 1857 wb-12-370 (K)
Kirbie, Daniel 1842? wb-2-58# (Ge)
Kirby, Archer 1836 wb-9-306 (Rb)
Kirby, Benjamin 1839 wb-10-3* (Rb)
Kirby, Francis jr. 1844 wb-8-244 (K)
Kirby, Hardy 1839 wb-10-3 (Rb)
Kirby, Henry 1830 wb-3-0 (Sm)
Kirby, Isaac 1839 wb-a-79 (Cr)
Kirby, James A. 1852 wb-g-440 (Hn)
Kirby, John M. 1849 wb-14-457 (D)
Kirby, Malakiah 1838 wb-6-492 (Wi)
Kirby, Miles 1826 wb-5-236 (Rb)

Kirby, Thomas 1854 wb-15-641 (Rb)
Kirchevall, Sally Ann 1845 rb-j-345 (Mt)
Kirk, Elijah 1837 wb-1A-169 (A)
Kirk, Goodwin 1842 as-b-87 (Di)
Kirk, Henry 1845 wb-a-237 (F)
Kirk, Hezekiah 1857 lr (Sn)
Kirk, Hugh 1850 rb-15-479 (Ru)
Kirk, James 1825 as-A-47 (Di)
Kirk, James 1860 rb-21-39 (Ru)
Kirk, Jane 1860 rb-20-341 (Ru)
Kirk, John 1822 rb-5-250 (Ru)
Kirk, John 1854 wb-12-46 (K)
Kirk, John 1855 wb-1-15# (Ge)
Kirk, Joseph 1839 wb-1-57 (Sh)
Kirk, Lucy A. 1859 wb-a-349 (Cr)
Kirk, Nancy M. 1847 rb-14-180 (Ru)
Kirk, Pamela 1861 wb-18-427 (D)
Kirk, Patience 1813 wb-#28 (Mu)
Kirk, Robert 1856 lr (Sn)
Kirk, Samuel 1827 rb-e-54 (Mt)
Kirk, Thomas 1854 wb-i-145 (O)
Kirk, William 1831 lr (Sn)
Kirk, William 1848 as-b-434 (Di)
Kirkham, Esther 1850 wb-10-401 (K)
Kirkham, Wm. 1845 wb-2-56 (Gr)
Kirkland, Levi 1852 wb-g-574 (Hu)
Kirkland, Levi sr. 1855 wb-h-459 (Hu)
Kirkland, Mary 1859 wb-h-382 (Hn)
Kirkland, Spias 1816 wb-1-0 (Sm)
Kirkman, Thomas 1827 wb-9-127 (D)
Kirkpatrick, Alexander 1824 lr (Sn)
Kirkpatrick, Caroline 1838 wb-#123 (Wl)
Kirkpatrick, Charles 1826 wb-1-83 (Bo)
Kirkpatrick, David 1816 wb-#25 (Wl)
Kirkpatrick, David 1827 wb-#68 (Wl)
Kirkpatrick, Emiline 1853 wb-#109 (Wl)
Kirkpatrick, Henry 1845 wb-8-336 (Wi)
Kirkpatrick, Henry A. 1851 wb-10-46 (Wi)
Kirkpatrick, Hugh 1810 wb-1-319 (Je)
Kirkpatrick, Hugh L. 1852 wb-1-297 (Hw)
Kirkpatrick, Hyram 1800 wb-1-76 (K)
Kirkpatrick, James 1816 wb-#23 (Wl)
Kirkpatrick, James 1852 lr (Sn)
Kirkpatrick, John 1806 wb-3-136 (D)
Kirkpatrick, John 1808 wb-#6 (Wl)
Kirkpatrick, John 1828 lr (Sn)
Kirkpatrick, John 1837 wb-#91 (Mc)
Kirkpatrick, John 1846 wb-1-294 (Hw)
Kirkpatrick, John 1846 wb-5-19 (Ma)
Kirkpatrick, John 1856 wb-12-268 (K)
Kirkpatrick, John O. 1847 wb-8-594 (Wi)

Kirkpatrick, Joseph 1849 wb-#178 (Wl)
Kirkpatrick, Martin 1838 wb-6-242 (K)
Kirkpatrick, Rachel 1859 wb-13-213 (K)
Kirkpatrick, Robert 1799 wb-1-160 (Je)
Kirkpatrick, Robert 1803 wb-a-3 (Ro)
Kirkpatrick, Robert 1815 wb-a-64 (Ro)
Kirkpatrick, Robert 1859 wb-13-145 (K)
Kirkpatrick, Stewart 1844 lr (Sn)
Kirkpatrick, Thomas J. 1844 wb-4-155A (Ma)
Kirkpatrick, Wilkins 1837 wb-3-494 (Je)
Kirkpatrick, William A. 1848 wb-#166 (Wl)
Kirkpatrick, Wilson 1852 wb-5-68 (Je)
Kirksey, Bryant 1825 wb-1-2 (Hy)
Kirksey, Bryant H. 1828 wb-1-32 (Hy)
Kirksey, Gideon 1816? wb-#32 (Mu)
Kirksey, Stephen 1824 wb-4-276 (Rb)
Kirksey, William 1815 wb-3-28 (St)
Kirksey, William H. 1848 wb-2-24 (La)
Kirksey, Wm. 1849 ib-1-82 (Ca)
Kirl, John W. 1847 wb-1-154 (Me)
Kirtner, George 1853 wb-h-Mar (O)
Kiser, Lewis 1851 wb-1-66 (Jo)
Kitchen, John 1856 wb-#92 (Mc)
Kitchen, William 1832 wb-b-89 (Wh)
Kitching, James 1818 wb-1-0 (Sm)
Kite, John 1851 wb-1-296 (Hw)
Kite, Richard 1810 lw (Ct)
Kitrell, Isham 1846 wb-#148 (Wl)
Kitrell, John 1836 rb-9-339 (Ru)
Kitrell, John A. 1831 wb-#220 (Mu)
Kitrell, Ruth 1848 wb-b-324 (Mu)
Kitrell, Wilie 1833 rb-9-25 (Ru)
Kitt, Solomon 1818 wb-5-79 (Rb)
Kittrell, Isaac 1811 rb-b-12 (Mt)
Kittrell, James 1811 rb-b-25 (Mt)
Kittrell, John F. 1858 wb-#127 (Wl)
Kittrell, Joseph 1839 wb-4-87 (Je)
Kittrell, Pleasant 1854 wb-#13 (Mo)
Kittrell, Ruth 1848 wb-b-264 (Mu)
Kittrell, Samuel 1845 wb-a2-211 (Mu)
Kittrell, Samuel K. 1835 wb-x-287* (Mu)
Kitts (Giets), John 1802 wb-1-75 (Rb)
Kitts, John 1850 33-3-252 (Gr)
Kitzmiller, Martin (Sr.) 1859 wb-#64 (Wa)
Kizer, John 1846 wb-f-370 (St)
Kizer, John 1850 wb-g-203 (St)
Klepper, Joseph 1838 wb-2-196 (Fr)
Kline, Jacob jr. 1807 wb-1-274 (Hw)
Klutts, Tobias 1845 wb-b-80 (We)
Klyce, Adam 1841 wb-2-472 (Hy)
Klyce, Eve E. 1854 wb-e-27 (Hy)

Klyne, Martha 1850 wb-g-396 (Hu)
Kneel, Samuel 1839 wb-a-34 (V)
Kneeland, John W. 1855 wb-1-298 (Hw)
Knight, A. 1837 mr-1-264 (Be)
Knight, Absalom 1837 mr-1-283 (Be)
Knight, Eveline D. 1843 rb-12-351 (Ru)
Knight, Graves 1838 wb-11-403 (D)
Knight, Graves 1838 wb-11-409 (D)
Knight, James 1846 wb-1-225 (Fr)
Knight, John 1832 rb-8-420 (Ru)
Knight, John 1833 wb-10-205 (D)
Knight, Joshua J. 1856 wb-h-619 (Hu)
Knight, Lucretia 1843 wb-e-580 (Hu)
Knight, Margaret 1836 wb-11-33 (D)
Knight, Moses 1836 wb-10-618 (D)
Knight, Nicholas 1856 wb-17-85 (D)
Knight, Robert 1814 wb-#14 (Wl)
Knight, Sarah 1824 wb-#54 (Wl)
Knight, Thomas 1820 wb-#52 (Wl)
Knight, Thomas 1838 wb-1-193 (Fr)
Knight, Thomas A. 1842 wb-c-308 (Ro)
Knight, Thomas P. 1854 ib-H-148 (F)
Knight, William 1832 wb-1-106 (Fr)
Knight, William 1840 wb-1-347 (W)
Knight, William M. 1853 wb-7-0 (Sm)
Knighton, William 1840 wb-e-9 (St)
Knighton, William H. 1853 wb-xx-236 (St)
Kniton, Susan 1839 wb-d-378 (St)
Knomis?, William G. 1849 wb-a-189 (Ms)
Knott, C. S. 1861 wb-i-335 (St)
Knott, John W. 1853 wb-n-166 (Mt)
Knott, William 1839 wb-y-459 (Mu)
Knott, William F. 1841 wb-z-115 (Mu)
Knowes, Sarah 1847 as-a-152 (Ms)
Knowes, William G. 1852 as-b-46 (Ms)
Knowis, Elijah A. 1853 as-b-110 (Ms)
Knowles, Benjamin 1845 wb-1-269 (Li)
Knowles, Daniel 1818 wb-1-0 (Sm)
Knowles, John 1854 wb-d-217 (Wh)
Knowles, John W. 1848 wb-c-333 (Wh)
Knowles, Thomas 1861 wb-e-443 (Wh)
Knowles, William W. 1860 wb-e-357 (Wh)
Knowlin, A. S. 1861 wb-e-439 (Wh)
Knox, Benjamin 1806 wb-3-51 (D)
Knox, Franklin 1856 rb-18-235 (Ru)
Knox, George 1812 wb-#5 (Mu)
Knox, J. C. 1847 rb-k-600 (Mt)
Knox, James 1812 wb-#5 (Mu)
Knox, James 1826 wb-9-35 (D)
Knox, James 1859 wb-1-160 (R)
Knox, John 1847 wb-#155 (Wl)

Knox, John L. 1861 wb-13-469 (K)
Knox, Joseph 1816 rb-3-170 (Ru)
Knox, Joseph 1835 rb-9-257 (Ru)
Knox, Joseph 1843 lr (Gi)
Knox, Joseph 1857 wb-A-121 (Ca)
Knox, Joseph C. 1846 rb-k-256 (Mt)
Knox, Mary C. 1829 wb-9-298 (D)
Knox, Naoma 1850 wb-#174 (Wl)
Knox, R. 1859 gs-1-263 (F)
Knox, Robert 1826 wb-4-180 (K)
Knox, Squire 1816 rb-3-132 (Ru)
Knox, Thomas 1821 rb-5-122 (Ru)
Knox, Walter 1815 wb-#10 (Mu)
Knox, William 1814 rb-2-268 (Ru)
Knox, William F. 1854 rb-17-190 (Ru)
Koehn, David D. 1801 wb-1-63 (Rb)
Koen, Abraham 1802 wb-1-76 (Rb)
Koen, Daniel 1812 wb-4-198 (D)
Koen, Lemuel 1805 wb-3-30 (D)
Koen, Ruben 1802 wb-2-252 (D)
Koger, Nicholas 1824 eb-1-141 (C)
Kooch, John N. 1852 wb-a-184 (Cr)
Koonce, Daniel 1859 wb-e-116 (Hy)
Koonce, Henry 1836 wb-x-360 (Mu)
Koonce, James H. 1816 wb-4-420 (D)
Koonce, John 1807 wb-3-175 (D)
Koonce, John 1826? wb-1-4 (Hy)
Koonce, Philip 1842 wb-1-203 (Li)
Koonce, Wright 1858 wb-c-241 (L)
Koons, Philip 1817 wb-2-341 (K)
Kopman, William 1842 wb-e-528 (Hu)
Kornegay, George 1808 wb-1-0 (Sm)
Korty, John 1850 wb-#49 (Wa)
Kraft, John H. 1857 wb-3e-50 (Sh)
Krantz, Thomas 1827 wb-6-188 (Rb)
Krisel, Ephraim 1849 wb-14-189 (Rb)
Krisle, Henry 1856 wb-16-327 (Rb)
Krisle, John 1842 wb-11-190 (Rb)
Krisle, John 1860 wb-17-58 (Rb)
Krisle, M. 1856 wb-16-322 (Rb)
Krisle, Malakiah 1856 wb-16-324 (Rb)
Krisle, Nancy 1860 wb-17-63 (Rb)
Krisle, Robert 1860 wb-17-159 (Rb)
Krouse, Michael 1851 wb-#50 (Wa)
Kuhn, Christopher 1844 wb-c-150 (Wh)
Kuhn, Francis 1853 wb-16-134 (D)
Kuhn, Mary Catharine 1828 wb-#29 (Wa)
Kussee, R. C. 1847 rb-k-532 (Mt)
Kuykendall, Peter 1783 wb-#2 (Wa)
Kyle, Barshaba 1855 wb-1-299 (Hw)
Kyle, Daniel 1839 rb-h-296 (Mt)

Kyle, George T. 1855 wb-12-175 (K)
Kyle, Hugh 1843 wb-#92 (Mc)
Kyle, Robert 1820 wb-1-280 (Hw)
Kyle, Robert P. 1861 wb-1-301 (Hw)
Kyser, John 1801 wb-1-80 (K)
Kysor, Philip 1853 wb-2-56 (Li)

- L -

LaPrade, William Washington 1858
  wb-16-572 (Rb)
Labath, Elizabeth 1842 wb-2-286 (Sn)
Lacey, Scelton 1832 wb-5-119 (Wi)
Lackey, A. R. 1857 rb-18-557 (Ru)
Lackey, Alexr. 1853 rb-16-620 (Ru)
Lackey, John 1815 wb-A-101 (Li)
Lackey, Solomon 1843 148-1-58 (Ge)
Lackey, Theodore 1839 wb-2-60 (Hr)
Lackey, Thomas 1829 wb-#28 (Wa)
Lackey, W. K. 1858 rb-19-459 (Ru)
Lackey, William 1825 wb-#57 (Wl)
Lackey, William S. 1852 wb-11-302 (K)
Lackland, Nancy 1826 wb-1-17# (Ge)
Lacky, Alexander R. 1857 rb-19-24 (Ru)
Lacky, Robert 1838 wb-1-170 (Fr)
Lacy, George W. 1848 wb-1-120 (Ct)
Lacy, Hugh R. 1843 wb-3-657 (Ma)
Lacy, Jesse 1841 wb-3-324 (Ma)
Lacy, John B. 1835 wb-1-406 (Hr)
Lacy, John B. 1845 wb-4-19 (Hr)
Lacy, Stephen 1831 wb-1-248 (Ma)
Lacy, Stephen 1853 wb-5-124 (Ma)
Lacy, Thomas 1807 wb-1-0 (Sm)
Lacy, Thomas 1831 wb-1-244 (Ma)
Lacy, Thomas 1853 wb-5-129 (Ma)
Ladd, Benjamine 1827 wb-a-8 (Cr)
Ladd, Jehosaphat 1820? wb-#145 (Mu)
Ladd, Nelson 1857 wb-f-99 (Ro)
Ladd, Noble 1855 wb-1-332 (Fr)
Ladd, Thomas 1815 wb-#16 (Mu)
Ladd, William H. 1846 wb-8-447 (Wi)
Ladd, William H. 1846 wb-8-455 (Wi)
Laden, George 1838 wb-b-116 (Hd)
Lady, John 1857 wb-1-329 (Hw)
Lafevre, William 1852 wb-g-473 (Hn)
Lagron, John A. 1817 wb-2-311 (Wi)
Lain, James M. 1835 wb-c-447 (St)
Lain, John 1849 wb-#169 (Wl)
Lain, John Sr. 1815 wb-#16 (Wl)
Lain, Mary 1828 wb-#77 (Wl)
Lain, Noah 1854 rb-17-2 (Ru)

Lain, Noah W. 1854 rb-17-51 (Ru)
Lain, Robert 1824 wb-#53 (Wl)
Lain, Samuel 1852 wb-e-323 (Ro)
Lain, Thomas 1851 wb-g-540 (Hu)
Lain, William J. 1860 wb-#132 (Wl)
Laine, George M. 1843 wb-1-583 (W)
Laine, Molly 1815 wb-#21 (Wl)
Laine, William 1858 wb-13-21 (K)
Laine, William H. 1853 wb-#108 (Wl)
Lainey, Johnathan 1858 wb-c-247 (L)
Lair, Kinchen 1839 wb-2-251 (Sn)
Laird, Robert 1839 wb-y-601 (Mu)
Lake, Elijah 1861 wb-e-151 (Hy)
Lake, Elizabeth 1861 wb-e-162 (Hy)
Lake, Jacob 1818 wb-1-0 (Sm)
Lake, Justus 1850 wb-5-3 (Hr)
Lake, Rob H. 1836 wb-2-191 (Ma)
Lake, Robt. M. 1857 wb-c-171 (L)
Lake, Samuel 1817 wb-1-0 (Sm)
Laman, Mary 1848 wb-d-141 (G)
Lamar, John K. 1853 wb-1C-74 (A)
Lamar, Polly 1856 wb-1C-275 (A)
Lamar, Thos. J. 1855 wb-1C-241 (A)
Lamar, William 1831 wb-1A-22 (A)
Lamar, William 1836 wb-1A-162 (A)
Lamar, Zachariah 1855 wb-#92 (Mc)
Lamaster, John 1840 wb-7-347 (Wi)
Lamaster, Lucinda 1860 wb-17-63 (Rb)
Lamb, Alexander S. 1840 wb-7-306 (Wi)
Lamb, David 1848 rb-14-325 (Ru)
Lamb, Davis 1861 wb-13-467 (Wi)
Lamb, John 1851 wb-d-2 (Wh)
Lamb, John 1851 wb-m-270 (Mt)
Lamb, Jonathan 1848 wb-g-260 (Hn)
Lamb, Mary (Mrs.) 1861 wb-a-316 (T)
Lamb, Mary 1852 wb-2-118 (Sh)
Lamb, Mary Jane 1851 wb-d-2 (Wh)
Lamb, Meablen? E. 1858 rb-o-602 (Mt)
Lamb, Robert T. 1849 wb-2-56 (Sh)
Lamb, Thomas 1821 Wb-3-249 (Wi)
Lamb, Thomas 1840 wb-e-139 (Hn)
Lamb, William 1848 wb-9-177 (Wi)
Lambdin, Mary 1855 wb-3-241 (Gr)
Lambe, Joseph 1859 wb-c-307 (Wh)
Lamberson, Dewitt? C. 1855 39-2-91 (Dk)
Lamberson, Jesse 1815 wb-1-0 (Sm)
Lamberson, Leonard 1852 wb-a-122 (Dk)
Lambert, Aaron 1820 wb-#35 (Wl)
Lambert, Aaron Sr. 1820 wb-#35 (Wl)
Lambert, Ephraim C. 1841 wb-b-371 (G)
Lambert, Jarvis 1846 rb-13-463 (Ru)

Lambert, Joseph 1844 wb-4-178 (Ma)
Lambert, Martha 1858 wb-1-370 (Fr)
Lambert, Mathew 1848 wb-14-234 (D)
Lambert, Thomas 1816 wb-#24 (Wl)
Lambert, William S. 1828 wb-1-82 (Hy)
Lambeth, Aaron 1818 wb-#29 (Wl)
Lambeth, Susan 1840 rb-h-439 (Mt)
Lambeth, Thomas 1837 rb-h-21 (Mt)
Lambeth, William 1812 wb-#12 (Wl)
Lambs, J. 1849 wb-g-382 (Hn)
Lamma, George 1840 wb-7-50 (K)
Lamon, David 1830 wb-#28 (Wa)
Lamon, Payton T. 1827 wb-3-0 (Sm)
Lamons, Abraham 1854 148-1-506 (Ge)
Lamons, Jane 1803 wb-2-28# (Ge)
Lamons, Orran 1835 wb-3-0 (Sm)
Lampklings, Robert 1816 wb-#32 (Mu)
Lampley, Jacob 1855 wb-a-293 (Di)
Lampley, Joseph 1853 as-c-259 (Di)
Lampley, William 1851 wb-g-426 (Hn)
Lancaster, Ephram 1857 wb-h-432 (St)
Lancaster, John 1813 wb-1-0 (Sm)
Lancaster, John 1840 wb-7-346 (Wi)
Lancaster, Orren D. 1847 wb-f-464 (St)
Lancaster, Samuel 1859 wb-7-41 (Ma)
Lancaster, Susanah 1837 wb-#92 (Mc)
Lancaster, William 1820 wb-1-0 (Sm)
Lancaster, William 1843 ib-h-213 (F)
Lancaster, William 1844 wb-d-243 (O)
Lancaster, William 1855 ib-h-375 (F)
Lancaster, William Allen 1860 wb-8-52 (Sm)
Lancaster, Wm. 1853 wb-a-427 (F)
Lance, Elizabeth 1820 wb-a-139 (Wh)
Lance, John 1859 wb-e-269 (Wh)
Lance, Thomas J. 1857 wb-e-198 (Wh)
Land, William P. 1853 wb-2-76 (Li)
Landers, William 1803 wb-1-112 (Rb)
Landess, Henry 1844 wb-1-252 (Li)
Landess, Henry 1862 wb-2-362 (Li)
Landis, John 1845 wb-g-40 (Hn)
Landiss, Jacob 1832 wb-1-84 (Li)
Landreth, N. F. 1859 gs-1-327 (F)
Landreth, Newton F. 1860 gs-1-583 (F)
Landreth, V. F. 1855 ib-h-317 (F)
Landreth, Wm. H. 1860 gs-1-583 (F)
Landrum, Benjamin 1839 wb-7-91 (Wi)
Landrum, Joannah 1844 148-1-93 (Ge)
Landrum, Mary 1843 wb-8-88 (Wi)
Landrum, Merriman 1826 wb-4-138 (Wi)
Landrum, Perlina 1853 wb-5-313 (Je)
Landrum, Robert M. 1852 wb-5-47 (Je)

Landrum, Thomas 1844 wb-8-358 (K)
Landrum, Thomas 1844 wb-b-78 (We)
Landrum, Thos. 1855 wb-1C-234 (A)
Landsden, Hugh B. 1850 wb-A-66 (Ca)
Lane, Anna 1854 as-b-141 (Ms)
Lane, Aquila 1819 wb-2-215 (Je)
Lane, Benjamin 1846 rb-13-671 (Ru)
Lane, Benjamin W. 1844 rb-12-435 (Ru)
Lane, Caroline M. 1849 rb-15-145 (Ru)
Lane, Denny 1846 wb-13-399 (D)
Lane, Denny 1847 wb-14-34 (D)
Lane, Emily 1848 wb-b-246 (Mu)
Lane, George W. 1854 ib-2-297 (Cl)
Lane, Granville 1846 wb-f-9 (O)
Lane, Isaac 1849 wb-#93 (Mc)
Lane, Jacob A. 1849 wb-c-357 (Wh)
Lane, James W. 1845 wb-a2-294 (Mu)
Lane, Joel 1855 wb-a-362 (Ms)
Lane, John 1823 wb-1-313 (Hw)
Lane, John 1855 wb-e-254 (G)
Lane, John 1858 wb-f-142 (G)
Lane, John W. 1854 wb-5-332 (Je)
Lane, John Y. 1842 wb-c-224 (O)
Lane, Joseph B. 1853 148-1-444 (Ge)
Lane, Lewis 1858 wb-1C-446 (A)
Lane, Millington J. 1839 as-a-441 (Di)
Lane, Molly 1856 wb-12-216 (K)
Lane, Nathan 1838 wb-y-201 (Mu)
Lane, Nathaniel G. 1826 wb-#93 (Mc)
Lane, Rebecca 1844 rb-13-10 (Ru)
Lane, Sally 1834 rb-9-187 (Ru)
Lane, Samuel 1847 wb-4-102 (Je)
Lane, Susan 1844 wb-4-256 (Ma)
Lane, Tandy A. 1845 wb-c-169 (Wh)
Lane, Thomas 1825 wb-8-441 (D)
Lane, Thomas 1837 wb-11-20 (D)
Lane, Tidence 1849 148-1-297 (Ge)
Lane, Tidence C. 1855 wb-#93 (Mc)
Lane, Turner sr. 1840 wb-b-399 (Wh)
Lane, William 1839 lr (Gi)
Lane, William 1846 wb-5-434 (Gr)
Lane, William 1848 wb-b-219 (Mu)
Lane, William T. 1844 wb-d-124 (Hd)
Lane, Woodson 1832 wb-#107 (Wl)
Lane?, Robert 1849 wb-a-198 (Ms)
Lanel, Tidence 1805 wb-1-90 (Je)
Lanes, Jacob jr. 1847 wb-9-329 (K)
Laney, Jeremiah 1829 wb-2-30# (Ge)
Lang, James 1799 wb-0-25 (K)
Lang, John 1835 wb-3-535 (Je)
Lang, Stephen 1834 wb-1-116 (Hy)

Lang, William 1853 wb-1-328 (Hw)
Langdon, Jonathan 1818 wb-2-210 (Je)
Langdon, Joseph 1841 wb-4-56 (Je)
Langford, Hiram 1861 wb-a-226 (Ce)
Langford, James 1845 wb-1-218 (Bo)
Langford, Jesse 1827 wb-3-0 (Sm)
Langford, John 1850 wb-14-351 (Rb)
Langford, John 1861 wb-17-293 (Rb)
Langford, Nancy 1859 wb-18-52 (D)
Langforth, David 1848 wb-#94 (Mc)
Langham, John 1809 wb-4-74 (D)
Langley, Elijah M. 1856 wb-1-105 (Be)
Langston, James 1822 wb-1-0 (Sm)
Langston, Obediah 1815 wb-#41 (Mu)
Langston, Richard 1849 wb-5-73 (Ma)
Langston, William 1855 wb-n-605 (Mt)
Lanham, Abel 1838 5-2-33 (Cl)
Lanham, Eldridge H. 1856 ib-2-357 (Cl)
Lanham, James L. 1847 wb-#154 (Wl)
Lanier, Benjamin B. 1849 wb-a-213 (Ms)
Lanier, Buchanan H. 1830 wb-9-443 (D)
Lanier, Charles J. 1849 wb-a-157 (Cr)
Lanier, Kenneth 1836 wb-1-253 (Hy)
Lanier, Lemuel 1817 rb-4-72 (Ru)
Lanier, Lovick 1856 wb-e-57 (Hy)
Lanier, Mathew P. 1857 wb-4-99 (La)
Lanier, Nicholas 1839 wb-7-92 (Wi)
Lanier, Renitt? 1833 wb-1-77 (Hy)
Lankford, Elisha 1838 wb-2-399 (Ma)
Lankford, Gibson 1848 wb-#94 (Mc)
Lankford, Hiram 1844 rb-j-288 (Mt)
Lankford, James 1845 wb-#94 (Mc)
Lankford, Jarret 1855 wb-h-420 (Hu)
Lankford, Jarrett 1857 wb-h-716 (Hu)
Lankford, John 1851 wb-g-443 (St)
Lankford, Matthew 1838 wb-1-350 (Hy)
Lankford, Nicholas 1848 rb-l-94 (Mt)
Lankford, Parish 1830 as-a-194 (Di)
Lankford, Thomas 1836 wb-c-503 (St)
Lankford, William 1836 wb-c-503 (St)
Lannam, William 1854 rb-17-186 (Ru)
Lanning, Elizabeth 1858 wb-13-40 (K)
Lanning, Ezekiel 1836 wb-3-358 (Je)
Lanning, John 1854 wb-5-352 (Je)
Lannom, A. F. 1857 rb-18-537 (Ru)
Lannom, Artilla 1854 rb-17-274 (Ru)
Lannom, Levi L. 1857 rb-18-592 (Ru)
Lannom, William 1856 rb-18-124 (Ru)
Lannon, Levi 1849 rb-15-185 (Ru)
Lannum, Joseph 1823 rb-5-259 (Ru)
Lannum, Thomas 1839 wb-#125 (Wl)

Lansden, Robert 1816 wb-#23 (Wl)
Lansdon, Robert W. 1855 wb-a-254 (Cr)
Lansum?, E. D. 1847 A-468-74 (Le)
Lantern, Joseph 1841 rb-11-309 (Ru)
Lantern, Joseph 1841 rb-11-311 (Ru)
Lapsley, Catharine R. 1844 wb-13-122 (D)
Lapsley, Thomas 1831 wb-5-23 (Wi)
Laramore, Edward 1781 wb-1-6 (D)
Larence, Charles 1806 wb-1-101 (Sn)
Larew, Abraham 1815 wb-2-145 (K)
Larew, George 1829 wb-4-372 (K)
Large, John 1855 wb-3-293 (Gr)
Largent, James 1857 wb-h-367 (St)
Largent, William 1856 wb-h-175 (St)
Larimore, Isaac G. 1856 ib-2-285 (Cl)
Larimore, Thomas 1816 wb-#32 (Mu)
Lark, Dennis 1851 rb-15-623 (Ru)
Larken, William T. 1854 wb-16-417 (D)
Larkin, Henry 1843 wb-1-323 (Hw)
Larkin, Margaret 1795 wb-1-16# (Ge)
Larkin, Roger 1829 wb-b-53 (Hn)
Larkin, Thomas 1829 wb-1-318 (Hw)
Larkins, Catherine 1858 as-c-548 (Di)
Larkins, John 1825 as-A-116 (Di)
Larkins, John Sr. 1842 as-b-102 (Di)
Larkins, Joseph 1836? as-a-376 (Di)
Larkins, Joseph 1841 as-a-494 (Di)
Larkins, Mary 1847 wb-g-1 (Hu)
Larkins, W. L. 1853 wb-3-133 (Gr)
Larmen, Isaac G. 1856 ib-2-330 (Cl)
Larrance, Richard 1852 wb-5-133 (Je)
Lasater, Abner 1859 wb-1-387 (Fr)
Lasater, Elizabeth 1847 wb-1-232 (Fr)
Lasater, Hardy 1842 wb-#138 (Wl)
Lasater, Hardy 1852 wb-#179 (Wl)
Lasater, Hezekiah 1842 wb-1-205 (Fr)
Lasater, John Jameson? 1853 wb-1-320 (Fr)
Lasater, Jotham 1849 ib-1-81 (Ca)
Lasater, Thomas J. 1838 wb-1-175 (Fr)
Lasater, Wiley 1858 wb-#94 (Mc)
Lash, George 1859 wb-#129 (Wl)
Lash, George W. 1849 wb-#169 (Wl)
Lash, John C. 1847 wb-#155 (Wl)
Lashlee, Burwell 1838 wb-e-71 (Hu)
Lashlee, Mary 1845 mr-2-163 (Be)
Lasiter, Thomas 1839 rb-10-270 (Ru)
Lasser?, Exeme 1859 wb-f-271 (G)
Lasseter, Francis 1835 wb-c-454 (St)
Lasseter, Willis 1835 wb-c-455 (St)
Lassiter, Daniel 1860 39-2-398 (Dk)
Lassiter, Enoch 1860 wb-f-400 (G)

Lassiter, Enos 1845 wb-f-271 (St)
Lassiter, Jesse 1844 wb-f-121 (St)
Lassiter, Lazarus 1837 wb-d-72 (St)
Lassiter, Rachel 1859 wb-17-628 (D)
Lassiter, Thomas 1855 wb-6-195 (Ma)
Lassiter, William 1836 wb-10-550 (D)
Lathem, John 1797 wb-1-232 (Je)
Lathem, John 1838 wb-1-326 (Gr)
Lathim, John 1851 33-3-306 (Gr)
Lathim, W. L. 1853 wb-3-290 (Gr)
Lathim, Wily L. 1853 wb-3-146 (Gr)
Latimer, Charles 1827 lr (Sn)
Latimer, Daniel 1856 wb-3-238 (Sn)
Latimer, George S. 1845? wb-#157 (Wl)
Latimer, Hugh 1815 wb-2-187 (Rb)
Latimer, Jacob 1855 wb-3-221 (Sn)
Latimer, James 1856 wb-h-603 (Hu)
Latimer, John 1802 wb-1-99 (Sn)
Latimer, Jonathan 1846 lr (Sn)
Latimer, Lynde 1844 wb-e-638 (Hu)
Latimer, Robert 1811 wb-1-152 (Sn)
Latimore, Mary 1854 wb-h-319 (Hu)
Latta, James 1815 wb-#10 (Mu)
Latta, James 1826 wb-#150 (Mu)
Latta, John (Sr.) 1826? wb-#160 (Mu)
Latta, John 1827 wb-#161 (Mu)
Latta, John H. 1842 wb-f-39 (Hn)
Latta, Samuel 1855 wb-f-75 (Mu)
Lattimore, George L. 1836 wb-#112 (Wl)
Lattimore, Jemima 1823 wb-#94 (Mc)
Lattimore, John 1833 wb-#94 (Mc)
Laudeback, Henry 1854 wb-1-326 (Hw)
Laudeback, Isaac 1847 wb-1-324 (Hw)
Lauderdale, Clarissa H. 1841 wb-a-89 (T)
Lauderdale, James 1796 wb-1-39 (Sn)
Lauderdale, John sr. 1822 wb-1-17# (Ge)
Lauderdale, Nancy 1860 wb-1-197 (R)
Lauderdale, Samuel W. 1847 lr (Sn)
Lauderdale, William 1838 wb-2-235 (Sn)
Laudermilk, Jacob 1850 wb-1-4 (Su)
Laugherty, James 1846 wb-1B-34 (A)
Laughery, James 1849 wb-1B-94 (A)
Laughlin, James Y. 1823 rb-6-12 (Ru)
Laughlin, Jane 1817 rb-4-83 (Ru)
Laughlin, Jean 1813 rb-2-241 (Ru)
Laughlin, John R. 1842 rb-12-118 (Ru)
Laughlin, Samuel H. 1850 wb-3-35 (W)
Laughlin, William 1856 wb-h-581 (Hu)
Laughmiller, George 1798 wb-1-305 (Hw)
Laughmiller, John 1814 wb-1-309 (Hw)
Laurance, Elizabeth 1814 wb-2-137 (Rb)

Laurence, Jesse 1821 wb-3-339 (Rb)
Laurence, Lemuel 1799 wb-#3 (Wl)
Laurence, Mary 1852 lr (Sn)
Laurence, Penina 1832 wb-8-103 (Rb)
Laurence, Timothy D. 1830 wb-9-397 (D)
Laurence, William 1840 wb-a-10 (Dk)
Laurents, Alexander 1853 wb-16-163 (D)
Lavender, Allen 1853 as-b-121 (Ms)
Lavender, Anthony 1854 wb-11-259 (Wi)
Lavender, George 1846 wb-8-476 (Wi)
Lavender, Nancy 1848 wb-9-64 (Wi)
Law, John S. 1844 wb-a2-14 (Mu)
Lawhon, William D. 1842 as-a-79 (Ms)
Lawhorn, Wm. 1850 wb-b-630 (Mu)
Lawler, Martin 1851 wb-b-317 (We)
Lawless, Jesse 1843 wb-8-203 (K)
Lawrance, David 1854 wb-a-340 (Ms)
Lawrance, James 1818 wb-2-195 (Je)
Lawrance, James 1820 wb-2-303 (Je)
Lawrance, John 1836 rb-9-324 (Ru)
Lawrence, Alexander 1851 wb-15-77 (D)
Lawrence, Amanda E. 1861 wb-18-545 (D)
Lawrence, Ann E. 1859 wb-18-52 (D)
Lawrence, Archerbald 1845 rb-13-416 (Ru)
Lawrence, Benjamin 1845 wb-A-41 (Ca)
Lawrence, Charles 1813 wb-1-0 (Sm)
Lawrence, Edmund 1860 wb-13-178 (Wi)
Lawrence, George 1842 wb-8-5 (K)
Lawrence, Henry 1842 as-b-89 (Di)
Lawrence, J. B. 1847 wb-#153 (Wl)
Lawrence, James F. 1856 wb-6-243 (Ma)
Lawrence, James H. 1854 39-2-35 (Dk)
Lawrence, Jane 1846 rb-13-715 (Ru)
Lawrence, Joanna (Mrs.) 1853 rb-17-255 (Ru)
Lawrence, Johanna 1853 rb-16-708 (Ru)
Lawrence, John 1833 wb-#101 (Wl)
Lawrence, John 1843 wb-#141 (Wl)
Lawrence, Jonathan 1804 wb-1-138 (K)
Lawrence, Jonathan 1826 rb-6-214 (Ru)
Lawrence, Joseph 1840 rb-11-79 (Ru)
Lawrence, Joseph 1841 wb-z-201 (Mu)
Lawrence, Joseph B. 1847 wb-#153 (Wl)
Lawrence, Levi 1815 wb-1-0 (Sm)
Lawrence, Lydia 1853 wb-#109 (Wl)
Lawrence, Mary 1841 rb-12-26 (Ru)
Lawrence, Mary 1856 wb-b-11 (Dk)
Lawrence, Nancy 1841 wb-z-202 (Mu)
Lawrence, Pharris 1852 r39-1-244 (Dk)
Lawrence, Ricks 1829? wb-#173 (Mu)
Lawrence, Robert 1828 lr (Sn)
Lawrence, Turner B. 1862 wb-#135 (Wl)

Lawrence, William (Sr.) 1848 wb-#162 (Wl)
Lawrence, William 1830 wb-1-1 (Sh)
Lawrence, William 1842 wb-#151 (Wl)
Lawrence, William 1854 wb-2-153 (Sh)
Lawrence, William P. 1853 wb-16-73 (D)
Laws, Aaron 1825? as-a-137 (Di)
Lawson, Drury 1847 5-3-271 (Cl)
Lawson, Edmond 1828 eb-1-234 (C)
Lawson, Edward 1832 wb-1-321 (Hw)
Lawson, Elizabeth 1826 wb-5-270 (Rb)
Lawson, Hugh 1858 wb-#95 (Mc)
Lawson, Isham 1841 wb-#95 (Mc)
Lawson, James 1852 wb-g-468 (Hn)
Lawson, James 1857 wb-3-338 (W)
Lawson, Moses 1852 wb-h-Dec (O)
Lawson, Peter 1834 wb-#95 (Mc)
Lawson, Ruthy 1858 wb-3-441 (W)
Lawton, Henry 1855 wb-h-423 (Hu)
Lax, Abijah 1842 wb-f-61 (Hn)
Lay, James 1845 wb-4-18 (Hr)
Lay, John 1841 wb-12-200* (D)
Lay, John D. 1859 ib-C-177 (C)
Lay, Thomas 1836 wb-10-599 (D)
Lay, Vincent 1836 wb-1-96 (La)
Lay, William 1856 wb-2-159 (Li)
Layman, Abraham 1841 wb-c-12* (G)
Layman, James 1841 wb-c-14* (G)
Laymon, David 1817 wb-2-182 (Je)
Layne, Ann Z. 1850 rb-l-616 (Mt)
Layne, George 1849 wb-2-319 (W)
Layne, John 1838 wb-6-461 (Wi)
Layne, John 1840 rb-h-455 (Mt)
Layne, Robert 1848 rb-14-370 (Ru)
Layne, Thomas 1859 wb-13-87 (Wi)
Layne, William 1833 wb-5-272 (Wi)
Layne, William K. 1851 wb-10-7 (Wi)
Layton, Thomas 1838 wb-b-256 (Hd)
Lazenby, Alexander 1839 wb-11-530 (D)
Lea, Hiram 1839 wb-#125 (Wl)
Lea, James 1836 wb-2-86 (Ma)
Lea, John 1831 wb-a-94 (R)
Lea, John 1851 wb-15-203 (D)
Lea, John 1857 wb-b-29 (Ms)
Lea, Lavinia 1849 33-3-145 (Gr)
Lea, Major 1821 wb-2-350 (Je)
Lea, Martha E. 1857 wb-f-95 (G)
Lea, Mary 1854 wb-e-26 (Hy)
Lea, Permit 1860 wb-13-279 (K)
Lea, Thomas D. 1839 wb-#125 (Wl)
Lea, Thomas J. 1838 wb-6-292 (K)
Lea, W. W. 1858 wb-3-455 (Gr)

Lea, William H. H. 1853 wb-#111 (Wl)
Lea, Willis 1849 wb-4-497 (Hr)
Leach, Calvin 1854 wb-1C-185 (A)
Leach, David 1826 wb-#151 (Mu)
Leach, James M. 1849 33-3-121 (Gr)
Leach, Jane 1855? wb-1C-258 (A)
Leach, John 1827 wb-#72 (Wl)
Leach, John 1847 wb-1B-18 (A)
Leach, John 1848 wb-1B-70 (A)
Leach, William 1854 wb-a-231 (Cr)
Leak, Williamm P. 1857 wb-f-46 (G)
Leake, Joseph C. 1860 wb-18-249 (D)
Leake, Richard 1850 wb-2-74 (Sh)
Leake, Samuel 1856 wb-3e-14 (Sh)
Leake, Sarah 1860 wb-18-194 (D)
Leaky, Levi 1809 wb-1-289 (K)
Leamans, Jane 1805 as-1-87 (Ge)
Leath, Charles A. 1849 wb-2-52 (Sh)
Leath, Peter 1839 wb-#130 (Wl)
Leath, Peter C. 1845 wb-f-279* (Hn)
Leath, Richard 1848 wb-9-146 (Wi)
Leath, Sarah H. 1858 wb-3e-56 (Sh)
Leatherdale, Robert 1858? wb-1-91 (Bo)
Leatherman, Martha 1850 wb-1-382 (Li)
Leathers, Anderson A. 1841 rb-12-20 (Ru)
Leatherwood, John B. 1843 wb-1-227 (Li)
Leatherwood, Jonas 1844 wb-1-241 (Li)
Leaton, Hugh 1853 wb-11-52 (Wi)
Leaton, Reuben 1853 wb-11-51 (Wi)
Leaton, Susan 1845 wb-8-338 (Wi)
Leaton, William 1840 wb-7-221 (Wi)
Leaves, Clarisa M. 1853 wb-2-187 (Me)
Leavin?, P. H. 1815 rb-3-49 (Ru)
Lebough, Henry 1834 wb-1-84 (W)
Lebow, John 1840 wb-5-54 (Gr)
Lebow, John D. 1853 wb-11-354 (K)
Lebow, Katherine 1848 33-3-36 (Gr)
Ledbetter, Ann 1861 ib-2-244 (Wy)
Ledbetter, Charles 1844 wb-7-0 (Sm)
Ledbetter, David 1824 rb-6-61 (Ru)
Ledbetter, Elenor C. 1838 rb-10-133 (Ru)
Ledbetter, Isaac 1820 rb-5-52 (Ru)
Ledbetter, Jesse 1856 wb-c-78 (L)
Ledbetter, William R. 1850 wb-b-105 (L)
Ledden, Benjamin 1814 rb-1-168 (Ru)
Leddon, Benjamin 1815 wb-4-328 (D)
Ledford, David 1827 wb-1-35 (Hr)
Ledon, Sarah 1838 rb-10-215 (Ru)
Lee, Aaron 1858 ib-2-62 (Wy)
Lee, Anthony 1841 wb-e-43 (St)
Lee, Augustine 1848 wb-c-337 (Wh)

Lee, Benjamin 1802 wb-1-9 (Wi)
Lee, Benjamin D. 1837 rb-g-625 (Mt)
Lee, Blan? H.? 1851 wb-b-117 (L)
Lee, Braxton 1841 wb-12-151* (D)
Lee, Catharine 1856 wb-17-144 (D)
Lee, Charles W. 1820 rb-c-338 (Mt)
Lee, Chloe 1855 wb-e-42 (Hy)
Lee, Daniel 1853 wb-2-74 (Li)
Lee, David 1842 wb-1-507 (W)
Lee, Edmond P. 1838 wb-a-23 (L)
Lee, Elizabeth 1855 lr (Gi)
Lee, George P. 1848 wb-g-234 (Hn)
Lee, H. A. G. 1841 wb-a-87 (L)
Lee, H. W. 1856 wb-h-173 (St)
Lee, Henry 1838 5-2-44 (Cl)
Lee, James 1843 wb-f-193 (Hn)
Lee, James B. 1830 wb-2-0 (Sm)
Lee, James sr. 1840 wb-e-137 (Hn)
Lee, Jane Virginia 1857 wb-f-132 (Mu)
Lee, John 1809 wb-1-306 (Hw)
Lee, John 1815 wb-4-339 (D)
Lee, John 1820 wb-7-469 (D)
Lee, John 1828 rb-7-190 (Ru)
Lee, John 1828 wb-b-46 (Hn)
Lee, John 1835 wb-1-380 (Hr)
Lee, John 1842 wb-z-330 (Mu)
Lee, John 1856 wb-h-260 (St)
Lee, John A. 1850 wb-g-247 (St)
Lee, John H. 1839 5-2-87 (Cl)
Lee, John sr. 1853 wb-xx-210 (St)
Lee, Jubal 1849 ib-1-156 (Cl)
Lee, Jubel 1846 5-3-178 (Cl)
Lee, L. P. 1841 wb-f-118 (Hn)
Lee, Lewis H. 1815 wb-4-341 (D)
Lee, Major 1837 5-2-9 (Cl)
Lee, Major Guy 1833 wb-3-0 (Sm)
Lee, Martena S. 1850 wb-d-255 (G)
Lee, Mary 1821 wb-1-312 (Hw)
Lee, Mary 1859 rb-p-143 (Mt)
Lee, Mary J. 1851 wb-b-113* (L)
Lee, Mary J. 1854 wb-b-263 (L)
Lee, Pleasant 1850 wb-4-69 (Mu)
Lee, Richard 1814 rb-b-192 (Mt)
Lee, Richard 1834 wb-9-63 (Rb)
Lee, Richard D. 1849 as-a-201 (Ms)
Lee, Robert 1817 wb-A-170 (Li)
Lee, Robert 1834 wb-1-322 (Hw)
Lee, Robert L. 1842 rb-i-266 (Mt)
Lee, Robert S. 1844 rb-j-164 (Mt)
Lee, Samuel L. 1857 149-1-62 (Ge)
Lee, Shaderick 1842 rb-i-443 (Mt)

Lee, Simpson 1837 wb-b-68 (Hd)
Lee, Susan (Mrs.) 1852 wb-b-156 (L)
Lee, Susannah E. 1844 lr (Gi)
Lee, Thomas 1816 wb-1-311 (Hw)
Lee, Thomas 1828 wb-1-317 (Hw)
Lee, Thomas 1839 5-2-52 (Cl)
Lee, W. B. 1852 mr-2-479 (Be)
Lee, Washington 1835 rb-g-138 (Mt)
Lee, William 1839 mr-1-53 (Be)
Lee, William 1848 wb-#95 (Mc)
Lee, William 1850 mr-2-398 (Be)
Lee, William C. 1843 wb-d-55 (Hd)
Lee, William R. 1851 wb-g-452 (St)
Lee, William W. 1855 mr-2-632 (Be)
Lee, Willis 1847 wb-4-195 (Hr)
Leech, Henry 1820? wb-#43 (Mu)
Leech, James L. 1838 wb-#123 (Wl)
Leech, John (Captain) 1824 wb-#51 (Wl)
Leech, John 1823 wb-#49 (Wl)
Leech, John 1823 wb-#50 (Wl)
Leech, Thomas 1839 rb-10-311 (Ru)
Leech, Thomas 1848 ib-1-29 (Ca)
Leeck, Halcomb H. 1828 wb-#78 (Wl)
Leek, Henry 1833 wb-a-147 (Di)
Leek, Henry 1833 wb-c-289 (St)
Leek, John M. 1840 rb-11-55 (Ru)
Leek, Randolph 1828 wb-b-318 (St)
Leek, Samuel 1816 wb-1-0 (Sm)
Leek, Samuel W. 1847 wb-9-346 (K)
Leeper, Allen 1839 wb-a-40 (Ms)
Leeper, Elizabeth 1851 wb-1-327 (Hw)
Leeper, James 1826 wb-1-315 (Hw)
Leeper, John W. 1852 wb-5-169 (Je)
Leeper, Matthew 1853 wb-5-306 (Je)
Leetch, James 1835 wb-x-374 (Mu)
Leetch, James C. 1842 wb-z-400 (Mu)
Leetch, William 1837 wb-y-169 (Mu)
Lefever, Cathrine 1785 wb-1-41 (D)
Lefever, John 1841 wb-0-21 (Cf)
Lefevre, William 1853 wb-g-544 (Hn)
Leffew, Joseph 1840 wb-5-46 (Gr)
Leffew, Uriah 1817 wb-a-61 (Wh)
Lefland, James S. 1855 wb-n-645 (Mt)
Lefler, Jacob 1854 wb-1-88 (Jo)
Leftwich, Jack H. 1847 wb-1-312 (Li)
Leftwich, William 1823 wb-a-180 (Ro)
Legan (Ligon), Henry A. 1856 wb-b-381 (We)
Legan, Richard 1817 wb-#26 (Wl)
Legate, Charles M. 1857 wb-j-208 (O)
Legate, Howe 1843 wb-d-29 (O)
Legate, Howell 1845 wb-e-64 (O)

Legate, William 1841 wb-c-67 (O)
Legate, William 1855 wb-h-412 (Hu)
Legett, Alexander 1842 wb-2-495 (Hy)
Legg, Edward 1835 wb-5-331 (K)
Legg, James 1856 wb-12-264 (K)
Legg, John 1812 wb-2-24 (Je)
Legg, Wesley 1859 wb-13-152 (K)
Legg, Wiley 1834 wb-#96 (Mc)
Leggate, Lemuel 1846 wb-f-390 (St)
Leggett, Daniel 1845 wb-4-4 (Hr)
Leggett, Henry R. 1850 rb-l-592 (Mt)
Leggett, John 1846 wb-4-33 (Hr)
Leigh, Benjamin 1831 wb-5-18 (Wi)
Leigh, John R. 1822 wb-1-42 (Hy)
Leigh, Martha 1844 wb-8-154 (Wi)
Leigh, Mary 1857 rb-o-482 (Mt)
Leigh, Polly (Mary) 1860 rb-p-310 (Mt)
Leigh, Polly 1857 rb-o-445 (Mt)
Leigh, Rachael 1827 rb-e-64 (Mt)
Leigh, Richard 1828 rb-e-345 (Mt)
Leigh, Richard 1829 rb-e-509 (Mt)
Leigh, Richard 1859 wb-a-351 (Cr)
Leigh, Washington 1826 rb-e-40 (Mt)
Leighton, Patrick 1820 wb-3-193 (K)
Leinart, Jacob 1849? wb-1B-113 (A)
Leinart, William 1847 wb-1B-14 (A)
Leiper, Holly 1854 wb-b-258 (L)
Leister, Elizabeth 1839 wb-10-259 (Rb)
Lemar, William 1811 wb-4-157 (D)
Lemar, William B. 1812 wb-1-308 (Hw)
Lemarr, Polley 1851 ib-1-191 (Cl)
Lemaster, Joseph 1827 wb-4-185 (Wi)
Lemaster, Nancy 1853 wb-15-416 (Rb)
Lemasters, John 1856 wb-16-227 (Rb)
Lemay, Richard U. 1862 wb-A-167 (Ca)
Lemay, Thomas S. 1859 iv-1-579 (Ca)
Leming, Daniel 1857 149-1-66 (Ge)
Lemming, Mary 1858 149-1-138 (Ge)
Lemmon, Sheldon 1853 wb-a-202 (T)
Lemmons, Peter 1817 lr (Sn)
Lemmons, William 1860 wb-f-398 (G)
Lemon, Charles P. 1847 wb-a-319 (F)
Lemon, John 1836 wb-a-1 (F)
Lemonds, Robert 1855 wb-g-702 (Hn)
Lemons, C. P. 1860 gs-1-638 (F)
Lemons, Geored? 1858 wb-4-154 (La)
Lenam, George 1855 wb-3-371 (La)
Lenear, — 1856 wb-3-397 (La)
Lenear, William 1814 wb-4-314 (D)
Lenhart, John W. 1851 wb-4-609 (Mu)
Lennard, W. W. 1839 wb-2-49 (Hr)

Lenoir, Betsy 1856 wb-f-36 (Ro)
Lenoir, William B. 1853 wb-e-365 (Ro)
Lenom, Thomas 1841 rb-11-148 (Ru)
Lenore, William N. 1859 rb-19-562 (Ru)
Lenox, John 1840 wb-b-9 (We)
Lenox, Samuel 1822 wb-8-145 (D)
Lenox, William 1834 wb-9-51 (Rb)
Lenster, Mary 1859 rb-20-77 (Ru)
Lentz, George 1845 A-468-13 (Le)
Lentz, Jacob 1851 wb-15-61 (D)
Leonard, Edy 1854 wb-1-331 (Hw)
Leonard, Hezekiah 1817 wb-A-156 (Li)
Leonard, James T. 1857 as-c-83 (Ms)
Leonard, John 1831 wb-b-130 (Ro)
Leonard, John G. 1854 ib-h-50 (F)
Leonard, John W. 1846 wb-1-297 (Li)
Leonard, L. R. 1841 wb-2-424 (Hy)
Leonard, Michael 1849 wb-2-51 (Sh)
Leonard, Thomas 1832 wb-1-79 (Li)
Leonard, William 1854 wb-e-245 (G)
Leonard, William 1855 wb-e-262 (G)
Leonard, William B. 1835 wb-1-377 (Hr)
Lesley, Peter 1848 wb-14-241 (D)
Lester, Alexander 1859 wb-7-49 (Ma)
Lester, Barnet 1836 wb-6-260 (Wi)
Lester, Elizabeth 1830 lr (Gi)
Lester, G. W. 1861 wb-17-259 (Rb)
Lester, German 1850 wb-14-511 (D)
Lester, Harrison 1854 wb-#114 (Wl)
Lester, Henry 1826 wb-4-71 (Wi)
Lester, Henry 1851 wb-10-160 (Wi)
Lester, Henry D. 1840 wb-#129 (Wl)
Lester, James 1840 lr (Gi)
Lester, John 1820 wb-7-370 (D)
Lester, John 1858 wb-#127 (Wl)
Lester, John M. 1824 wb-a-65 (Hn)
Lester, Joshua 1841 wb-#143 (Wl)
Lester, Joshua 1858 wb-#125 (Wl)
Lester, Manson B. 1853 wb-#108 (Wl)
Lester, Nathanel 1837 wb-a-24 (F)
Lester, Presley 1839 wb-#126 (Wl)
Lester, Rebecca 1857 wb-12-306 (Wi)
Lester, Richard S. 1855 wb-6-152 (Ma)
Lester, Robert 1852 wb-10-200 (Wi)
Lester, Robert H. 1853 wb-10-532 (Wi)
Lester, Susan 1837 wb-2-197 (Ma)
Lester, T. J. 1861 wb-17-259 (Rb)
Lester, Thomas J. 1861 wb-17-291 (Rb)
Lester, William 1792 wb-1-16# (Ge)
Lester, William 1840 wb-#138 (Wl)
Lester, William 1840 wb-#141 (Wl)

Lester, William 1850 wb-#165 (Wl)
Lester, William H. 1849 wb-2-58 (Sh)
Letsinger, Andrew 1837 wb-y-21 (Mu)
Letsinger, D. B. 1858 wb-13-24 (K)
Letsinger, Daniel 1854 wb-12-57 (K)
Letsinger, Daniel B. 1854 wb-12-41 (K)
Letsinger, Philip 1839 wb-6-466 (K)
Letten, Lemuel 1814 wb-4-319 (D)
Letton, Lemuel 1815 wb-4-337 (D)
Leuty, John 1835 wb-a-280 (R)
Leuty, William S. 1829 wb-a-57 (R)
Leuty, William T. 1840 wb-a-429 (R)
Levan, Alexander 1837 wb-6-117 (K)
Levan, P. H. 1857 wb#40 (Gu)
Leverton, Thomas 1817 wb-7-160 (D)
Levingston, Duncan 1851 lr (Sn)
Levingston, William 1839 wb-11-602 (D)
Levy, Enoch W. 1841 wb-3-470 (Ma)
Levy, Henry C. 1855 wb-e-298 (G)
Levy, William 1824 wb-8-335 (D)
Levy, William C. 1843 wb-3-678 (Ma)
Lewallen, John 1841 wb-1A-317 (A)
Lewallen, Josiah 1831 wb-x-89 (Mu)
Lewellin, Charles 1827 wb-#154 (Mu)
Lewellin, Thos. 1826 wb-#136 (Mu)
Lewin, Mary 1857 wb-f-97 (Ro)
Lewis, Aaron 1829 wb-3-61 (Je)
Lewis, Absalom 1853 wb-5-238 (Je)
Lewis, Agness 1824 wb-4-124 (Rb)
Lewis, Allen 1815 wb-2-273 (Rb)
Lewis, Benjamin 1844 rb-12-573 (Ru)
Lewis, Benjamin 1845 wb-4-23 (Hr)
Lewis, Benjamin 1858 wb-b-36 (Dk)
Lewis, Benjamin 1860 wb-7-71 (Ma)
Lewis, Benjamin 1860 wb-e-322 (Wh)
Lewis, Benjamin F. 1828 wb-9-228 (D)
Lewis, Benjamin F. 1839 wb-11-612 (D)
Lewis, Benjamin F. 1844 rb-13-23 (Ru)
Lewis, Charles 1832 wb-#94 (Wl)
Lewis, Charles A. 1829 wb-#82 (Wl)
Lewis, Charles W. 1826 wb-2-524 (Je)
Lewis, Charles W. 1846 wb-1-139 (Sh)
Lewis, Crowel 1825 wb-#57 (Wl)
Lewis, Daniel 1843 wb-f-25 (St)
Lewis, David 1814 Wb-2-97 (Wi)
Lewis, David C.? 1852 wb-1-296 (Fr)
Lewis, David L. 1858 wb-e-173 (Wh)
Lewis, Elam 1840 rb-10-487 (Ru)
Lewis, Elam 1850 rb-15-556 (Ru)
Lewis, Elam H. 1841 wb-7-440 (Wi)
Lewis, Evan 1823 wb-2-383 (Je)

Lewis, Fielding 1852 ib-1-296 (Cl)
Lewis, Gabriel 1852 rb-16-237 (Ru)
Lewis, Gabriel F. 1854 rb-17-32 (Ru)
Lewis, George 1807 wb-1-283 (Je)
Lewis, George 1852 as-c-146 (Di)
Lewis, George sr. 1832 wb-3-221 (Je)
Lewis, Gravil 1833 wb-5-335 (Wi)
Lewis, Henry 1815 wb-#18 (Wl)
Lewis, Henry 1851 as-2-203 (Ge)
Lewis, Hiram 1833 lr (Sn)
Lewis, Isaac 1829 wb-a-58 (R)
Lewis, Jacob 1816 wb-2-327 (Rb)
Lewis, Jacob 1816 wb-2-347 (Rb)
Lewis, James 1837 wb-9-428 (Rb)
Lewis, James 1849 wb-1-273 (Fr)
Lewis, James 1850 wb-1-281 (Fr)
Lewis, James M. 1822 wb-#83 (Mu)
Lewis, Joel 1817 wb-7-139 (D)
Lewis, John 1811 wb-#10 (Wl)
Lewis, John 1847 wb-f-409 (St)
Lewis, John 1850 wb-g-390 (Hu)
Lewis, John D. 1846 wb-f-363 (St)
Lewis, John H. 1853 wb-h-Mar (O)
Lewis, John N. 1841 wb-1-65 (Sh)
Lewis, John R. 1842 wb-e-192 (St)
Lewis, Joseph 1854 rb-16-787 (Ru)
Lewis, Judith 1839 wb-d-368 (St)
Lewis, Lupsley J. 1850 wb-1-346 (Me)
Lewis, Mahalah 1849? wb-1B-141 (A)
Lewis, Margret 1833 wb-a-21 (T)
Lewis, Martha (Patsey) 1844 rb-12-499 (Ru)
Lewis, Martha 1860 wb-7-86 (Ma)
Lewis, Mary 1855 rb-17-414 (Ru)
Lewis, Mary Ann 1837 wb-1-554 (Hr)
Lewis, Mary C. 1858 wb-1-368 (Fr)
Lewis, Mary C. B. 1850 wb-9-381 (Wi)
Lewis, Micajah G. 1826 wb-8-530 (D)
Lewis, Mordecai 1861 wb-i-302 (St)
Lewis, Nathaniel 1837 wb-#116 (Wl)
Lewis, Obediah 1834 wb-b-40 (G)
Lewis, Parson 1839 wb-10-167 (Rb)
Lewis, Patsey (Martha) 1844 rb-12-498 (Ru)
Lewis, Richard 1823? wb-2-428 (Je)
Lewis, Richard 1857 wb-17-156 (D)
Lewis, Robert N. 1859 wb-k-44 (O)
Lewis, Samuel 1793 wb-1-292 (D)
Lewis, Samuel 1828 wb-1-59 (Hr)
Lewis, Samuel 1844 rb-12-501 (Ru)
Lewis, Shaderick 1842 wb-f-94 (Hn)
Lewis, T. W. 1855 wb-h-86 (St)
Lewis, Thomas 1838 wb-1-572 (Hr)

Lloyd, Amelia 1842 as-b-122 (Di)
Lloyd, Berry H. 1855 wb-6-29 (Ma)
Lloyd, Lewis 1836 wb-6-235 (Wi)
Lloyd, Thomas 1849 lr (Sn)
Lloyd, Thomas 1857 wb-4-4 (Gr)
Lock, Charles 1839? wb-#125 (Wl)
Lock, Charles 1850 wb-2-65 (Sh)
Lock, Francis 1859 as-c-171 (Ms)
Lock, George 1842 wb-c-25 (G)
Lock, James 1843 wb-f-428 (St)
Lock, John 1840 wb-a-457 (R)
Lock, John 1853 wb-2-52 (Li)
Lock, Richard S. 1816 wb-2-217 (Wi)
Lock, Sarah 1843 rb-12-311 (Ru)
Lock, Stephen 1819 wb-7-356 (D)
Lock, William 1850 wb-1-344 (Me)
Lockard, Francis 1796 lw (Ct)
Lockard, John 1839 wb-a-42 (L)
Lockbey, James 1851 wb-15-14 (D)
Locke, Alexander 1822 lr (Gi)
Locke, B. F. 1854 wb-2-214 (Me)
Locke, Charles 1823 wb-#106 (Wl)
Locke, David C. 1837 wb-a-19 (F)
Locke, George 1859 gs-1-426 (F)
Locke, Green W. 1854 wb-11-373 (Wi)
Locke, John 1851 wb-2-37 (Me)
Locke, John W. 1821 wb-#40 (Wl)
Locke, Mary J. 1858 wb-f-143 (G)
Locke, Matthew 1843 wb-c-243 (St)
Locke, Pliney 1848 wb-1-231 (Me)
Locke, R. C. 1853 wb-#111 (Wl)
Locke, Richard 1826 wb-#65 (Wl)
Locke, Richard 1853 wb-#112 (Wl)
Locke, Robert 1839 wb-a-394 (R)
Locke, Robert 1853 wb-1-37 (R)
Locke, William (Col.) 1833 rb-9-53 (Ru)
Locke, William 1832 rb-8-495 (Ru)
Locke, William 1840 wb-1-31 (Me)
Locker, James 1858 wb-2-248 (Li)
Locker, William R. 1859 wb-2-276 (Li)
Lockert, Charles 1847 wb-13-135 (Rb)
Lockert, Charles 1847 wb-13-146 (Rb)
Lockert, Moses 1818 rb-c-21 (Mt)
Lockert, Sarah 1821 wb-3-340 (Rb)
Locket, Benjamin 1834 wb-1A-94 (A)
Lockett, Pleasant 1794 wb-2-8 (D)
Lockett, Thomas 1795 wb-2-18 (D)
Lockhart, Benjamin 1837 wb-a-255 (O)
Lockhart, Elijah 1857 wb-1-178 (Be)
Lockhart, James 1842 wb-1-443 (W)
Lockhart, James 1843 wb-a-37 (Dk)

Lockhart, John 1842 wb-12-270* (D)
Lockhart, John 1844 wb-4-45 (Je)
Lockhart, Joseph 1851 wb-g-446 (St)
Lockhart, Mary 1859 wb-18-117 (D)
Lockhart, Samuel 1857 wb-h-441 (St)
Lockhart, Thomas 1848 wb-b-271 (Mu)
Lockman, Felix 1846 wb-#149 (Wl)
Lockort, Clayton 1848 wb-14-62 (Rb)
Lockridge, Ann 1851 rb-4-277 (Mu)
Lockridge, C. H. 1853 wb-f-29 (Mu)
Lockridge, Henry? W. 1853 wb-f-22 (Mu)
Lockridge, James 1840 wb-y-690 (Mu)
Lockridge, James H. 1847 wb-b-226 (Mu)
Lockridge, R. H. 1854 ib-h-30 (F)
Lockridge, R. P. 1854 ib-h-78 (F)
Lockridge, Samuel 1850 rb-4-59 (Mu)
Lofland, James L. 1857 rb-o-287 (Mt)
Lofland, James S. 1856 rb-o-46 (Mt)
Loften, Lavinea 1826 rb-6-280 (Ru)
Loftin, Augustine 1851 wb-9-646 (Wi)
Loftin, Eldridge 1853 rb-16-566 (Ru)
Loftin, John 1848 wb-b-283 (Mu)
Loftin, Longfield 1839 wb-y-459 (Mu)
Loftin, Mary 1853 wb-f-16 (Mu)
Loftin, Mr. 1828 rb-7-44 (Ru)
Loftin, Thomas 1835 wb-2-6 (Ma)
Loftis, Martin 1849 as-b-449 (Di)
Loftis, Milton 1854 as-c-381 (Di)
Loftis, Phereby 1849 as-c-29 (Di)
Loftless, Susan 1854 wb-a-448 (F)
Lofton, Thomas 1835 wb-2-22 (Ma)
Lofton, William 1811 rb-2-152 (Ru)
Lofton, William 1811 rb-2-184 (Ru)
Logan, Benjamin T. 1851 as-b-25 (Ms)
Logan, Catharine 1827 wb-4-181 (Wi)
Logan, Charles 1825 wb-1-92 (Bo)
Logan, David 1826 wb-1-90 (Bo)
Logan, David 1849 wb-2-70# (Ge)
Logan, David 1852 as-b-72 (Ms)
Logan, Elizabeth 1848 rb-14-424 (Ru)
Logan, George 1814 wb-1-190 (Sn)
Logan, James 1827 wb-1-93 (Bo)
Logan, John H. 1849 as-a-198 (Ms)
Logan, Mariah 1838 wb-2-246 (Sn)
Logan, Mary 1852 as-b-73 (Ms)
Logan, Thomas 1825 wb-8-487 (D)
Logan, William 1823 wb-3-659 (Wi)
Loggins, Susannah 1837 wb-y-12 (Mu)
Loggins, William 1817 rb-b-419 (Mt)
Logue, Eleanor 1831 wb-9-497 (D)
Logue, John 1793 wb-1-293 (D)

Logue, Manassah 1852 wb-4-380 (Mu)
Logwood, John H. 1856 ib-h-472 (F)
Loller, Lawrence 1793 wb-1-285 (D)
Lomay, T. S. 1859 ib-1-567 (Ca)
Londer, Hannah 1854 as-b-135 (Ms)
London, John 1833 wb-x-61 (Mu)
London, Joseph 1833 wb-x-80 (Mu)
Lones, Elizabeth 1854 wb-12-42 (K)
Lones, Henry 1848 wb-10-15 (K)
Lones, Henry sr. 1848 wb-10-98 (K)
Lones, Jacob 1853 wb-11-337 (K)
Lones, Jacob sr. 1857 wb-12-430 (K)
Lones, Jacob sr. 1859 wb-13-166 (K)
Lones, Jesse H. 1857 wb-12-329 (K)
Lones, Jessee 1854 wb-12-45 (K)
Long, Andrew 1861 rb-p-559 (Mt)
Long, Arther 1862 wb-1-94 (Gu)
Long, Azariah 1837 wb-b-278 (Wh)
Long, Daniel 1845 wb-d-128 (Hd)
Long, Daniel 1856 wb-3-331 (Gr)
Long, David 1845 wb-a2-182 (Mu)
Long, Elizabeth 1835 wb-9-177 (Rb)
Long, G. L. 1856 as-b-268 (Ms)
Long, G. W. 1837 wb-a-277 (O)
Long, George 1823 wb-a-177 (Wh)
Long, George 1840 wb-a-9 (V)
Long, George 1853 wb-#9 (Mo)
Long, George H. 1839 wb-b-159 (O)
Long, George H. 1847 as-a-142 (Ms)
Long, George H. jr 1837 wb-a-256 (O)
Long, George H. sr. 1837 wb-a-274 (O)
Long, George Jr. 1842 wb-#96 (Mc)
Long, George Sr. 1835 wb-#97 (Mc)
Long, Hardy 1852 wb-3-73 (Gr)
Long, Henry 1847 wb-1-88 (Bo)
Long, Israel 1858 ib-1-514 (Ca)
Long, J. 1858 ib-1-495 (Ca)
Long, Jacob 1854 148-1-490 (Ge)
Long, James 1820 wb-3-125 (Rb)
Long, James 1820 wb-3-84 (Rb)
Long, James 1852 wb-d-414 (G)
Long, Jesse? 1822 wb-a-169 (Wh)
Long, Joel 1853 wb-1-31 (R)
Long, John 1830 wb-b-106 (Wh)
Long, John 1837 wb-1-166 (Fr)
Long, John 1845 wb-e-159 (O)
Long, John 1850 33-3-219 (Gr)
Long, John J. (Dr.) 1817 wb-#84 (Mu)
Long, John Joseph 1816 wb-#24 (Mu)
Long, Jonathan 1839 wb-1-323 (Hw)
Long, Joseph 1838 wb-1-150 (Li)

Long, Joseph 1857 rb-19-79 (Ru)
Long, Josiah 1858 rb-19-178 (Ru)
Long, Margaret 1815 wb-#15 (Mu)
Long, Mary 1845 wb-e-48 (O)
Long, Michael 1832 wb-5-181 (Wi)
Long, Michael 1838 wb-10-195 (Rb)
Long, Nicholas 1847 wb-b-130 (Mu)
Long, Nicholas J. 1823 wb-#47 (Mu)
Long, P. W. 1851 wb-15-183 (D)
Long, Richard 1850 wb-a-228 (Ms)
Long, Robert 1825 wb-4-299 (Rb)
Long, Robert 1857 wb-3-401 (Gr)
Long, Samuel 1852 wb-#97 (Mc)
Long, Sarah E. 1860 wb-17-65 (Rb)
Long, William 1814? wb-#31 (Mu)
Long, William 1828 rb-e-370 (Mt)
Long, William 1832 wb-b-191 (Ro)
Long, William 1848 wb-1-188 (Me)
Long, William 1854 wb-a-221 (Cr)
Long, William 1858 wb-16-654 (Rb)
Long, Wm. 1803 wb-2-306 (D)
Longacre, John 1813 wb-2-67 (Je)
Longley, Arther W. 1840 wb-b-280 (O)
Longley, James (Sr.) 1820 wb-#70 (Mu)
Longley, James 1821 wb-#84 (Mu)
Longley, John S. 1826 wb-#134 (Mu)
Longmire, Charles 1799 wb-#7 (Wa)
Longmire, Elijah 1836 wb-1A-155 (A)
Longmire, Elijah 1840 wb-1A-283 (A)
Longmire, Elijah 1848? wb-1B-53 (A)
Longmire, R. M. 1857 wb-1C-383 (A)
Longmire, Reuben M. 1857 wb-1C-371 (A)
Longmire, William 1816 wb-A-124 (Li)
Longstreet, W. S. 1835 wb-b-188 (Wh)
Longstreet, William 1834 wb-b-155 (Wh)
Longwell, Joseph M. 1841 wb-a-75 (F)
Longwith, Reuben 1852 wb-#97 (Mc)
Lonis, Charity 1851 wb-#97 (Mc)
Loomis, S. H. 1856 wb-17-104 (D)
Looney, Absalom D. 1863 wb-1-332 (Hw)
Looney, Espran? 1845 wb-b-109 (We)
Looney, Jesse 1841 wb-7-288 (K)
Looney, Jonathan 1824 wb-A-383 (Li)
Looney, Jonathan D. 1857 wb-h-147 (Hn)
Looney, Joseph 1817 wb-A-210 (Li)
Looney, Joseph 1840 wb-1-40 (Me)
Looney, Leroy 1855 wb-2-281 (Me)
Looney, Mary 1830 wb-1-320 (Hw)
Looney, Moses 1824 wb-4-17 (K)
Looney, Moses 1839 wb-6-438 (K)
Looney, Moses R. (of Moses) 1842 wb-7-309 (K)

Looney, Rachel 1835 wb-2-199 (Sn)
Looney, Sarah 1838 wb-6-289 (K)
Looney, Sarah 1849 wb-10-109 (K)
Looney, William G. 1847 148-1-182 (Ge)
Looney?, Mary 1857 wb#5 (Gu)
Loony, Joseph 1818 wb-a-109 (Ro)
Loots, Adam 1860 ib-2-187 (Wy)
Loprade, Richard 1859 wb-16-692 (Rb)
Lorance, John 1831 wb-#228 (Mu)
Lorance, William 1836 wb-a-54 (Cr)
Lorason, Thomas J. 1846 wb-#97 (Mc)
Lord, William 1850 wb-0-96 (Cf)
Lossin, Epphraditus 1814 wb-2-128 (Rb)
Losson, Epophroditus 1815 wb-2-279 (Rb)
Lotspeich, Christopher c. 1830 wb-2-32# (Ge)
Lotspeich, John 1845 wb-#5 (Mo)
Lott, Casper 1820 wb-#17 (Wa)
Louden, William 1861 as-c-248 (Ms)
Loug, James H. 1840 wb-#132 (Wl)
Loughran, Sylvania H. 1843 rb-j-25 (Mt)
Louis, Lapsley 1852 wb-2-127 (Me)
Lourey, Elijah 1844 wb-f-237 (Hn)
Lourey, Elijah M. 1846 wb-g-126 (Hn)
Loury, Jane 1845 wb-1-217 (Bo)
Loury, Joseph 1854 wb-b-259 (L)
Love, Albert G. 1851 wb-g-403 (Hn)
Love, Amelia 1855 wb-16-495 (D)
Love, Ann 1832 wb-2-41# (Ge)
Love, Anna 1843 lw (Ct)
Love, Charles 1840 rb-11-63 (Ru)
Love, Charles 1844 148-1-73 (Ge)
Love, Charles J. 1838 wb-11-210 (D)
Love, David 1827 wb-#159 (Mu)
Love, David 1830 rb-f-134 (Mt)
Love, David B. 1851 wb-15-172 (D)
Love, David B. 1851 wb-15-175 (D)
Love, Elizabeth 1833 wb-3-448 (Je)
Love, Emily (Mrs.) 1857 6-2-131 (Le)
Love, Henry 1816 wb-A-132 (Li)
Love, Henry J. 1824 wb-8-376 (D)
Love, Hezekiah 1841 wb-c-231 (Ro)
Love, Hiram 1860 lr (Sn)
Love, Hugh 1846 rb-13-605 (Ru)
Love, James 1796 wb-1-16# (Ge)
Love, James 1807 as-1-189 (Ge)
Love, James B. 1858 wb-h-254 (Hn)
Love, James T. 1851 wb-15-167 (D)
Love, James T. 1852 wb-15-319 (D)
Love, Jane 1832 wb-1-91 (Bo)
Love, John 1809 ib-1-256 (Ge)
Love, John 1811 wb-#4 (Mu)

Love, John 1824 wb-#82 (Mu)
Love, John 1834 wb-#97 (Mc)
Love, John 1835 wb-2-45# (Ge)
Love, John 1851 wb-#9 (Mo)
Love, John 1851 wb-11-126 (K)
Love, John B. 1856 wb-e-448 (G)
Love, John D. 1846 wb-g-131 (Hn)
Love, John J. 1852 lw (Ct)
Love, John M. 1836 wb-#98 (Mc)
Love, Joseph 1831 wb-9-558 (D)
Love, Joseph 1831 wb-a-110 (R)
Love, Joseph B. 1846 wb-5-25 (Ma)
Love, Josiah 1794 wb-0-6 (K)
Love, Luther G. 1860 39-2-356 (Dk)
Love, Mary 1840 wb-z-61 (Mu)
Love, Matthew 1849 wb-2-83 (La)
Love, Nathan 1836 wb-x-335* (Mu)
Love, Robert 1837 wb-b-375 (Ro)
Love, Robert 1853 wb-1-89 (Bo)
Love, Robert 1859 39-2-323 (Dk)
Love, Samuel 1818 wb-1-177 (Bo)
Love, Samuel 1824 wb-3-468 (K)
Love, Samuel 1840 wb-7-96* (K)
Love, Samuel 1846 wb-1-263 (Bo)
Love, Samuel jr. 1826 wb-4-142 (K)
Love, Samuel jr. 1859 wb-h-338 (Hn)
Love, Samuel sr. 1826 wb-4-138 (K)
Love, Saraphina C. 1846 wb-1-98 (Ct)
Love, Susan 1807 wb-1-29 (Wi)
Love, Thomas (General) 1844 wb-f-279 (Hn)
Love, Thomas 1810 ib-1-310 (Ge)
Love, Thomas 1810 wb-1-16# (Ge)
Love, Thomas 1832 wb-3-184 (Je)
Love, Thomas 1844 wb-f-244 (Hn)
Love, Thomas 1858 wb-h-292 (Hn)
Love, Thomas D. 1833 wb-1-81 (Ct)
Love, Thomas D. 1851 lw (Ct)
Love, William 1809 Wb-1-56 (Wi)
Love, William 1821 wb-1-0 (Sm)
Love, William 1826 wb-a-12 (R)
Love, William 1828 wb-b-4 (Ro)
Love, William 1845 wb-13-253 (D)
Love, William 1846 wb-4-66 (Je)
Love, William C. 1839 wb-3-59 (Ma)
Love, Wm. C. 1851 wb-d-330 (G)
Lovel, Jacob 1804 wb-2-373 (D)
Lovel, Jane 1856 lr (Sn)
Lovel, Markum 1846 rb-13-708 (Ru)
Lovelace, James M. 1860 wb-b-446 (We)
Lovelady, Elizabeth 1855 ib-h-450 (F)
Lovelady, James 1838 wb-3-0 (Sm)

Lovelady, Jane 1855 as-c-419 (Di)
Lovelady, John 1855 ib-h-332 (F)
Lovelady, Marshal 1792 wb-1-3 (Je)
Lovell, Benjamin P. 1859 wb-a-123 (Ce)
Lovell, Charles G. 1861 wb-a-209 (Ce)
Lovell, John M. 1855 wb-a-19 (Ce)
Lovell, John M. 1856 wb-16-612 (D)
Loven, William 1849 rb-15-206 (Ru)
Loven, William W. 1858 wb-b-55 (Ms)
Loving, Dolly 1839 wb-2-262 (Sn)
Loving, William (Sr.) 1824 wb-#131 (Mu)
Loving, William 1826 wb-#142 (Mu)
Low, Abraham 1830 wb-4-414 (K)
Low, Aquilla 1819 wb-3-99 (K)
Low, Elizabeth 1848 wb-2-343 (W)
Low, Hugh 1844 148-1-82 (Ge)
Low, John 1793 wb-1-291 (D)
Low, John C. 1851 wb-5-21 (Hr)
Lowder, John 1815 wb-2-183 (K)
Lowder, John 1836 wb-x-323* (Mu)
Lowe, A. 1853 wb-3-115 (Gr)
Lowe, Abner 1851 33-3-338 (Gr)
Lowe, Bridget 1858 wb-17-440 (D)
Lowe, Charles 1834 rb-9-198 (Ru)
Lowe, Charles 1836 rb-9-326 (Ru)
Lowe, George E. 1854 wb-a-209 (T)
Lowe, Gideon H. 1854 wb-16-366 (D)
Lowe, Henrietta 1832 rb-9-13 (Ru)
Lowe, John 1816 wb-4-441 (D)
Lowe, John 1816 wb-7-66 (D)
Lowe, John D. 1843 wb-f-324 (Hn)
Lowe, John S. 1838 rb-10-155 (Ru)
Lowe, Margaret H. 1848 wb-3-0 (Sm)
Lowe, Marvel 1834 wb-8-399 (Rb)
Lowe, Mary 1848 rb-14-241 (Ru)
Lowe, Mary 1848 wb-14-70 (Rb)
Lowe, Mary C. (Mrs.) 1861 rb-21-72 (Ru)
Lowe, Mary C. 1860 rb-20-386 (Ru)
Lowe, Robert W. 1858 rb-19-382 (Ru)
Lowe, Samuel 1856 wb-#98 (Mc)
Lowe, Walter 1827 rb-6-293 (Ru)
Lowe, Walter 1839 rb-10-410 (Ru)
Lowe, Walter S. 1844 rb-12-501 (Ru)
Lowe, William 1839 wb-1-286 (W)
Lowelling, Stephen W. 1851 wb-2-93 (Sh)
Lower, Andrew 1830 wb-b-77 (Ro)
Lower, Henry 1830 wb-b-73 (Ro)
Lowery, Catharine 1845 wb-f-250 (St)
Lowery, Elijah 1842 wb-f-107 (Hn)
Lowery, James 1837 rb-9-462 (Ru)
Lowery, James 1849 wb-g-119 (St)

Lowery, Overton 1842 wb-12-325* (D)
Lowrance, John 1808 wb-1-41 (Wi)
Lowrey, Alexander 1846 wb-c-229 (Wh)
Lowrey, T. T. 1854 ib-1-298 (Wy)
Lowrey, Vance C. 1857 wb-e-161 (Wh)
Lowry, Absolom 1811 wb-4-160 (D)
Lowry, David 1815 wb-3-68 (St)
Lowry, Elizabeth M. 1869 wb-#15 (Mo)
Lowry, Fanny L. 1869 wb-#15 (Mo)
Lowry, Frances L. 1869 wb-#16 (Mo)
Lowry, Isaac 1840 wb-#99 (Mc)
Lowry, James Sr. 1845 wb-#99 (Mc)
Lowry, John 1825 wb-#100 (Mc)
Lowry, John 1841 wb-b-383 (Hd)
Lowry, John 1863 wb-#100 (Mc)
Lowry, Mary 1845 rb-13-222 (Ru)
Lowry, Samuel 1840 wb-#100 (Mc)
Lowry, Samuel 1843 wb-d-90 (Hd)
Lowry, Susan 1853 wb-g-527 (Hn)
Lowry, Terry T. 1856 ib-1-462 (Wy)
Lowry, William 1845 wb-3-44 (Sn)
Lowry, William P. 1846 wb-b-167 (We)
Lowthen, George 1841 wb-12-165* (D)
Lowther, John W. 1810 rb-a-349 (Mt)
Lowther, William Lewis 1821 rb-d-3 (Mt)
Loy, John 1840 wb-1A-284 (A)
Loy, John M. 1838 wb-1A-179 (A)
Loyd, Abel 1816 wb-2-37# (Ge)
Loyd, Anderson 1849 wb-#170 (Wl)
Loyd, Elizabeth 1850 ib-1-71 (Wy)
Loyd, Ephraim 1820 wb-A-358 (Li)
Loyd, Erasmus 1860 149-1-210 (Ge)
Loyd, Henry H. 1853 ib-1-238 (Wy)
Loyd, James 1815 lw (Ct)
Loyd, James 1822 wb-1-17# (Ge)
Loyd, James 1840 wb-#107 (Wl)
Loyd, Jarrett 1835 wb-#128 (Wl)
Loyd, Jodan 1821 wb-#38 (Wl)
Loyd, John 1829 wb-b-45 (Ro)
Loyd, Lewis 1826 wb-4-96 (Wi)
Loyd, Lucy 1854 wb-#112 (Wl)
Loyd, Preston 1843 wb-5-239 (Gr)
Loyd, Stephen 1831 lr (Gi)
Loyd, Susan M. 1846 lr (Gi)
Loyd, Thomas 1789 wb-1-305 (Hw)
Loyons, John B. 1850 wb-14-486 (D)
Luallen, John 1838 wb-1A-230 (A)
Luallen, Richard 1833 wb-1A-85 (A)
Lucas, Abraham M. 1849 wb-g-267 (Hu)
Lucas, Alexander 1851 wb-15-17 (Rb)
Lucas, Andrew 1830 wb-9-371 (D)

Lucas, Charles 1818 wb-A-238 (Li)
Lucas, Charles 1839 wb-2-254 (Sn)
Lucas, David 1786 wb-1-46 (D)
Lucas, David 1840 wb-10-457 (Rb)
Lucas, David 1840 wb-10-469 (Rb)
Lucas, David sr. 1840 wb-10-456 (Rb)
Lucas, Edmund C. 1861 wb-18-427 (D)
Lucas, George 1815 wb-2-215 (Rb)
Lucas, George 1845 wb-9-89 (K)
Lucas, George W. 1856 wb-16-321 (Rb)
Lucas, Harriet 1837 wb-11-53 (D)
Lucas, Hugh 1827 wb-1-64 (Fr)
Lucas, Isaac 1849 wb-g-257 (Hu)
Lucas, John 1848 wb-g-11 (Hu)
Lucas, Margarett B. 1847 wb-13-218 (Rb)
Lucas, Oslin 1851 rb-16-33 (Ru)
Lucas, Parker 1843 wb-11-404 (Rb)
Lucas, Richmond 1852 wb-15-199 (Rb)
Lucas, Robert 1797 wb-2-64 (D)
Lucas, Samuel 1844 wb-12-222 (Rb)
Lucas, Sarah 1815 wb-2-192 (K)
Lucas, William 1813 wb-1-0 (Sm)
Luck, Henry 1812 wb-#37 (Mu)
Luck, Holcomb H. 1830 wb-#88 (Wl)
Luck, James 1835 wb-#110 (Wl)
Luck, John 1805 wb-#5 (Wl)
Luckado, Peter 1855 ib-h-390 (F)
Luckett, Davis sr. 1846 rb-13-633 (Ru)
Lucky, James M. 1842 wb-3-546 (Ma)
Lucky, S. R. 1858 wb-h-263 (Hn)
Lucky, Samuel R. 1858 wb-h-297 (Hn)
Lucus, A. H. 1854 wb-15-482 (Rb)
Lucy, Peyton 1817 wb-3-263 (St)
Lucy, Robert 1856 wb-f-39 (Ro)
Luggett, Benjamin 1834 wb-1-22 (Sh)
Luker, David 1855 wb-j-33 (O)
Luker, Elizabeth 1858 wb-j-362 (O)
Luker, George W. 1855 wb-i-245 (O)
Luker, James R. 1835 lr (Gi)
Luker, John B. 1859 wb-k-48 (O)
Luker, R. M. C. 1860 wb-k-220 (O)
Lumbrick, Abraham 1839 wb-e-42 (Hn)
Lumbrie, Abraham 1841 wb-e-311 (Hn)
Lumby, Benjamin 1812 wb-A-20 (Li)
Lumkins, George W. 1860 wb-c-335 (L)
Lumpkin, John W. 1832 wb-c-234 (St)
Lumpkin, Obadiah 1833 wb-#116 (Wl)
Lumpkins, Robert 1816 wb-#35 (Mu)
Lumsdale, William 1850 lr (Sn)
Lumsden, Margaret 1855 wb-h-458 (Hu)
Lumsden, Stephen P. 1855 wb-h-458 (Hu)

Luna, James G. 1846 wb-a-153 (Ms)
Luna, Peter 1851 wb-a-260 (Ms)
Lund, Peter 1861 wb-4-425 (La)
Lunday, Joshua C. 1850 wb-2-83 (Sh)
Lundy, William A. 1853 wb-e-12 (Hy)
Lunn, A. C. 1852 wb-a-289 (Ms)
Lunn, Nathan 1839 wb-a-38 (Ms)
Lunsford, Lewis Mc. W. 1843 wb-f-38 (St)
Luny, John C. 1848 r39-1-73 (Dk)
Luper, James 1784 wb-1-10 (D)
Lusk, Elias 1835 wb-x-243* (Mu)
Lusk, Elias 1845 A-468-50 (Le)
Lusk, Elizabeth 1860 wb-f-204 (Mu)
Lusk, Henry 1811 wb-#4 (Mu)
Lusk, James 1854 wb-f-39 (Mu)
Lusk, James G. 1854 wb-1-5 (Gu)
Lusk, John 1839 wb-1-270 (W)
Lusk, John 1855 wb-1-14 (Gu)
Lusk, John W. 1838 wb-y-192* (Mu)
Lusk, Rebecca 1854 wb#9 (Gu)
Lusk, Robert 1802 wb-1-21 (Ct)
Lusk, Robert 1860 wb-f-188 (Mu)
Lusk, Saml. 1852 wb-f-6? (Mu)
Lusk, Samuel (Sr.) 1824 wb-#76 (Mu)
Lusk, Samuel 1820 wb-#84 (Mu)
Lusk, Samuel 1837 lw (Ct)
Lusk, Samuel 1848 wb-#6 (Mo)
Lusk, Samuel 1855 wb-f-81 (Mu)
Lusk, Samuel sr. 1852 wb-4-602 (Mu)
Lusk, Theodrick W. 1838 wb-y-204* (Mu)
Lusk, Thomas R. 1845 wb-a2-287 (Mu)
Lusk, William 1848 wb-0-82 (Cf)
Lusk, William 1856 wb#25 (Gu)
Lust, J. M. 1858 wb-c-249 (L)
Luster, Josiah 1850 wb-g-299 (O)
Luster, Thos. J. 1838 wb-11-491 (D)
Luster, William 1834 wb-5-312 (K)
Luster, William 1846 148-1-178 (Ge)
Luten, Henry 1855 wb-h-452 (Hu)
Luten, Matthew 1832 wb-8-10 (Rb)
Luter, Elizabeth 1837 wb-9-456 (Rb)
Luter, Holland 1857 wb-16-350 (Rb)
Luter, James W. 1848 wb-14-49 (Rb)
Luter, Matthew 1834 wb-8-332 (Rb)
Luton, Clement 1827 wb-b-170 (St)
Luton, Clement H. 1827 wb-b-191 (St)
Luton, Henry 1855 wb-h-423 (Hu)
Luton, King 1837 wb-2-222 (Sn)
Luton, King 1861 wb-18-468 (D)
Luton, Read 1834 wb-c-330 (St)
Luton, Sally C. 1838 wb-d-295 (St)

Luton, Samuel 1831 wb-c-150 (St)
Lutrell, Mason 1848 wb-e-102 (Ro)
Lutterell, Nathan 1840 wb-2-157 (Hr)
Luttrell, Jackson 1856 wb-2-161 (Li)
Luttrell, James 1848 wb-10-92 (K)
Luttrell, James C. 1825 wb-4-56 (K)
Luttrell, John 1800 wb-1-73 (K)
Luttrell, John 1854 wb-12-25 (K)
Luttrell, John W. 1814 wb-2-74 (K)
Luttrell, Lewis 1855 wb-12-117 (K)
Luttrell, Nelson 1857 wb-f-98 (Ro)
Luttrell, Silas 1851 wb-e-269 (Ro)
Luttrell, Wesley 1856 wb-2-160 (Li)
Luttrell, William 1814 wb-2-72 (K)
Lyal, Catharine 1835 rb-g-156 (Mt)
Lyal, Robert M. 1832 rb-f-396 (Mt)
Lyan, James 1821 wb-1-0 (Sm)
Lyda, Rachael 1860 wb-e-314 (Wh)
Lyda, William 1840 wb-b-429 (Wh)
Lyle, Daniel 1856 wb-5-416 (Je)
Lyle, J. L. 1859 rb-p-265 (Mt)
Lyle, James L. 1859 rb-p-278 (Mt)
Lyle, Jesse 1816 wb-a-76 (Ro)
Lyle, Jordan 1843 rb-i-505 (Mt)
Lyle, Mary 1839 wb-4-12 (Je)
Lyle, Miram 1850 wb-5-183 (Je)
Lyle, Samuel R. 1835 wb-3-426 (Je)
Lyle, Samuel sr. 1834 wb-3-314 (Je)
Lyle, Thomas 1840 wb-3-548 (Je)
Lyle, Thomas 1850 rb-l-621 (Mt)
Lyle, Thomas 1850 wb-m-4 (Mt)
Lyle, William G. 1834 wb-1-90 (Bo)
Lyles, James L. 1848 wb-f-127+ (O)
Lyles, John 1821 rb-c-506 (Mt)
Lynch, Daniel 1848 wb-d-126 (G)
Lynch, David 1850 rb-l-624 (Mt)
Lynch, David 1850 rb-l-631 (Mt)
Lynch, Elizabeth 1854 ib-h-79 (F)
Lynch, Hugh 1830 wb-9-410 (D)
Lynch, Ira 1832 wb-#98 (Wl)
Lynch, John 1842 wb-3-620 (Ma)
Lynch, John 1845 wb-c-207 (G)
Lynch, John B. 1842 wb-12-325* (D)
Lynch, John B. 1842 wb-12-332* (D)
Lynch, Peter 1848 wb-f-481 (St)
Lyne, Lucy F. 1858 wb-b-62 (F)
Lynes, Samuel 1841 rb-i-194 (Mt)
Lynes, William J. 1833 rb-f-475 (Mt)
Lynn, Andrew 1850 wb-0-95 (Cf)
Lynn, Jacob 1851 wb-3-85 (W)
Lynn, Joseph 1860 wb-b-90 (F)

Lynn, Thomas 1849 wb-0-93 (Cf)
Lynn, William 1844 wb-2-36 (W)
Lynn, William 1844 wb-2-38 (W)
Lynus, Violetta S. 1859 rb-p-33 (Mt)
Lyon, Andrew 1841 wb-z-185 (Mu)
Lyon, Elizabeth 1857 rb-18-438 (Ru)
Lyon, Elizabeth 1857 rb-18-607 (Ru)
Lyon, Elly 1831 rb-f-239 (Mt)
Lyon, Ezekiel 1845 wb-#42 (Wa)
Lyon, James 1837 wb-#118 (Wl)
Lyon, James M. 1857 wb-17-181 (D)
Lyon, Merritt 1852 wb-15-460 (D)
Lyon, Nathan 1857 rb-18-390 (Ru)
Lyon, Nicholas P. 1837 rb-g-547 (Mt)
Lyon, Valentine 1835 wb-#111 (Wl)
Lyon, William 1846 wb-g-190 (Hn)
Lyon, Wm. H. 1854 rb-17-329 (Ru)
Lyons, Ameline 1859 rb-p-119 (Mt)
Lyons, Guthridge 1827 rb-e-84 (Mt)
Lyons, John 1808 wb-1-271 (K)
Lyons, Nathaniel 1848 wb-9-440 (K)
Lyons, Peter 1824 wb-#71 (Mu)
Lyons, Thomas 1806 wb-a-7 (Ro)
Lyons, Thomas sr 1848 wb-9-478 (K)
Lyons, W. W. 1854 wb-g-606 (Hn)
Lysles, John 1825 wb-4-54 (K)
Lyson, Uriah 1850 rb-l-513 (Mt)
Lytle, Archibald 1855 wb-11-431 (Wi)
Lytle, Elizabeth 1858 wb-12-590 (Wi)
Lytle, Elizabeth C. 1856 wb-12-284 (Wi)
Lytle, John 1841 rb-12-26 (Ru)
Lytle, John 1841 rb-12-28 (Ru)
Lytle, Mary 1847 rb-14-204 (Ru)
Lytle, Mary W. 1848 rb-14-217 (Ru)
Lytle, Nancy 1842 wb-a-127 (L)
Lytle, Peyton 1838 wb-2-181 (Hy)
Lytle, Peyton 1851 wb-g-461 (Hu)
Lytle, Sophia 1858 rb-19-489 (Ru)
Lytle, William 1829 rb-7-271 (Ru)
Lytle, William 1839 wb-11-538 (D)
Lytle, William 1851 wb-14-623 (D)
Lytle, William sr. 1830 rb-8-110 (Ru)

- M -

Mabane, George 1818 wb-2-407 (Wi)
Mabe, William 1854 wb-3-195 (La)
Maberry, Catharine 1859 ib-2-184 (Wy)
Maberry, Daniel 1850 ib-1-96 (Wy)
Maberry, John C. 1852 wb-4-514 (Mu)
Mabery, James 1859 wb-f-250 (Ro)

Mabias, Charles F. 1814 wb-1-0 (Sm)
Mabry, Alcy A. 1843 wb-8-128 (K)
Mabry, Benjamin S. 1838 wb-#121 (Wl)
Mabry, Francis E. 1853 wb-#110 (Wl)
Mabry, George 1801 wb-1-79 (K)
Mabry, George W. 1838 wb-#121 (Wl)
Mabry, George W. 1853 wb-16-185 (D)
Mabry, Hartwell 1856 wb-#123 (Wl)
Mabry, Joel 1844 wb-2-39 (W)
Mabry, John 1837 rb-10-19 (Ru)
Mabry, Joseph A. 1837 wb-6-110 (K)
Mabry, Joseph A. sr. 1858 wb-12-513 (K)
Mabry, Marthia M. 1842 wb-0-31 (Cf)
Mabry, Peter A. B. 1848 rb-14-409 (Ru)
Mabry, Thomas J. 1826 rb-6-184 (Ru)
Mabry, Thomas J. 1855 rb-17-613 (Ru)
Mabry, William 1831 wb-#90 (Wl)
Mace, Henry 1841 148-1-21 (Ge)
Mace, John 1839 wb-2-54# (Ge)
Mace, Thompson 1857 wb-#123 (Wl)
Mace, Thompson 1858 wb-#126 (Wl)
Macgowan, Ebenezer 1850 rb-15-346 (Ru)
Macgowan, William B. 1848 rb-14-465 (Ru)
Mack, John 1813 wb-#21 (Mu)
Mack, John 1855 wb-f-59 (Mu)
Mack, R. H. 1849 ib-1-34 (Wy)
Mack, Robert H. 1858 ib-2-65 (Wy)
Mackey, John 1821 rb-c-459 (Mt)
Mackey, Samuel 1841 wb-1-74 (Sh)
Mackey, William sr. 1835 wb-1-117 (W)
Mackleberry, James 1846 wb-1-132 (Sh)
Macklin, James 1820 rb-4-237 (Ru)
Maclin, Benj. 1827 wb-a-87 (G)
Maclin, James B. 1860 wb-a-292 (T)
Maclin, James C. 1803 wb-2-273 (D)
Maclin, William 1803 wb-2-275 (D)
Maclin, William sr. 1798 wb-2-121 (D)
Maclin, Zackfield 1803 wb-2-273 (D)
Maclom, George 1807 wb-1-345 (Je)
Macon, Betsy 1808 wb-3-191 (D)
Macon, Burchet 1851 rb-4-258 (Mu)
Macon, Gabriel 1841 wb-z-102 (Mu)
Macon, Gabriel L. 1843 wb-z-454 (Mu)
Macon, H. H. 1851 wb-3-83 (W)
Macon, J. T. 1855 ib-h-347 (F)
Macon, William 1857 wb-5-68 (Hr)
Madcaff, George 1800 wb-1-165 (Je)
Madden, Champness 1839 wb-3-86 (Ma)
Madden, James L. 1856 wb-1-71 (Be)
Madden, Minerva 1842 as-b-116 (Di)
Madden, William 1830 wb-#109 (Mc)

Maddin, Elisha 1856 wb-f-88 (Mu)
Maddin, Sarah 1856 wb-f-115 (Mu)
Maddin, William 1823 wb-#46 (Mu)
Madding, Joel 1824 wb-1-36 (Ma)
Maddox, Ann 1849 wb-14-150 (Rb)
Maddox, David 1843 wb-11-533 (Rb)
Maddox, Sarah 1851 rb-16-110 (Ru)
Maddox, Sarah H. 1851 rb-16-130 (Ru)
Maddox, Schoolfield 1811 wb-2-33# (Ge)
Maddox, Tapley 1815 wb-3-39 (St)
Maddox, William 1810 wb-4-106 (D)
Maddox, William M. 1855 wb-2-177 (Sh)
Maddux, T. M. 1852 wb-xx-126 (St)
Maddux, Taply 1830 wb-c-105 (St)
Madewell, James 1837 wb-b-274 (Wh)
Mading, Joel 1815 wb-1-0 (Sm)
Mading, Joel 1830 wb-2-0 (Sm)
Madison, Ambrose 1842 rb-12-223 (Ru)
Madole, John W. 1841 wb-12-156* (D)
Madox, Nolly 1816 wb-#25 (Wl)
Magby, Turner 1825 wb-b-36 (St)
Magee, Asa 1860 wb-k-242 (O)
Magee, Hugh 1846 lr (Sn)
Magee, W. W. 1861 wb-k-438 (O)
Magee, Zera 1836 wb-1-179 (Gr)
Magers, Samuel 1844 wb-a2-10 (Mu)
Magers, Sol L. 1844 wb-a2-277 (Mu)
Maget, G. C. 1851 wb-11-151 (K)
Maget, Hugh B. 1844 wb-8-295 (K)
Maget, Samuel W. 1847 wb-a-314 (F)
Magett, Gainum C. 1849 wb-10-266 (K)
Magett, Samuel 1849 wb-10-267 (K)
Maggeson, H. W. 1847 r39-1-22 (Dk)
Maghee, Thomas 1844 wb-4-281 (Ma)
Magill, Charles 1859 wb-f-273 (Ro)
Magill, Hugh 1838 wb-2-50# (Ge)
Magill, John 1842 wb-d-13 (Ro)
Magill, Samuel 1809 wb-1-18# (Ge)
Magill, Samuel 1810 ib-1-312 (Ge)
Magill, Samuel 1855 wb-#11 (Mo)
Magill, Samuel W. 1856 wb-#26 (Mo)
Magill, William 1806 as-1-150 (Ge)
Magill, William 1806 wb-1-18# (Ge)
Magner, Barnabas 1839 wb-d-301 (St)
Magness, B. C. 1846 r39-1-19 (Dk)
Magness, Bethel C. 1846 r39-1-20 (Dk)
Magruder, William 1850 wb-c-398 (Wh)
Maguire, Charles P. 1859 wb-17-620 (D)
Maguire, Judy 1851 wb-2-113 (Sh)
Maguire, Martha 1858 wb-f-157 (Mu)
Maguire, Patrick 1850 wb-4-74 (Mu)

Mahan, Archibald 1814 wb-2-96 (Rb)
Mahan, David 1822 lr (Sn)
Mahan, Sally 1842 lr (Sn)
Mahan, William A. sr. 1847 wb-b-228 (We)
Maholland, John 1830 wb-#115 (Wl)
Mahon, John 1849 wb-#168 (Wl)
Mahon, Thomas 1856 wb-f-105 (Mu)
Mahoney, Thomas 1861 wb-13-523 (K)
Mainard, Acril A. 1839 wb-3-60 (Hy)
Mainard, Morill? A. 1839 wb-2-18 (Hy)
Mainard, Willis W. 1836 wb-a-53 (Cr)
Mainor, Jethro 1836 wb-9-125 (Rb)
Mainor, Robert 1833 wb-8-237 (Rb)
Mainord, Elender 1854 wb-g-611 (Hn)
Mains, David 1849 wb-#48 (Wa)
Mairs, Samuel 1815 Wb-2-147 (Wi)
Major, Henry 1838 wb-#122 (Wl)
Major, John 1839 wb-#137 (Wl)
Major, John A. 1858 wb-#127 (Wl)
Major, Smith 1840 wb-7-84 (K)
Majors, Thomas 1832 wb-a-151 (R)
Makiff, Isaah 1834 wb-1-111 (Gr)
Malam?, Susanna Ann 1855 wb-n-646 (Mt)
Malcom, Alexander 1807 wb-1-111 (Bo)
Malcom, Silas 1819 wb-1-175 (Bo)
Malicoat, John 1833 wb-1-13 (Gr)
Malin, James 1842 mr-2-11 (Be)
Malin, Mary 1854 mr-2-548 (Be)
Malinn, William 1844 mr-2-96 (Be)
Mallard, John 1815 rb-3-51 (Ru)
Mallery, P. T. 1848 as-b-408 (Di)
Mallicoat, Deadman 1838 wb-1-315 (Gr)
Mallicoat, James 1845 wb-2-181 (Gr)
Mallory, Benjamin 1851 wb-14-530 (Rb)
Mallory, Frances 1832 rb-f-464 (Mt)
Mallory, Francis 1823 rb-d-111 (Mt)
Mallory, Francis D. 1848 wb-g-293 (Hn)
Mallory, George 1823 rb-d-241 (Mt)
Mallory, George S. 1823 rb-d-272 (Mt)
Mallory, J. T. 1851 as-c-131 (Di)
Mallory, James 1833 rb-f-463 (Mt)
Mallory, James H. 1857 wb-12-355 (Wi)
Mallory, James W. 1859 wb-13-336 (Wi)
Mallory, John 1860 wb-13-267 (Wi)
Mallory, Phillip 1857 wb-17-318 (D)
Mallory, Roger 1838 wb-6-477 (Wi)
Mallory, Stephen 1835 rb-g-225 (Mt)
Mallory, Stephen 1836 rb-g-265 (Mt)
Mallory, Stephen 1846 rb-k-292 (Mt)
Mallory, T. G. 1844 r39-1-1 (Dk)
Mallory, Thomas 1814 rb-b-201 (Mt)

Mallory, Thomas 1832 rb-f-387 (Mt)
Mallory, Thomas G. 1832 wb-5-161 (Wi)
Mallory, William 1839 wb-#124 (Wl)
Malloy, Gilliam 1814 rb-3-77 (Ru)
Malloy, Philip 1854 wb-16-392 (D)
Malone, Amzi 1860 wb-8-48 (Sm)
Malone, F. M. 1858 wb-2-374 (Me)
Malone, Fereby B. 1853 wb-#24 (Mo)
Malone, Fred 1860 rb-p-510 (Mt)
Malone, George 1845 lr (Gi)
Malone, George 1845 mr (Gi)
Malone, Humphrey 1845 148-1-126 (Ge)
Malone, J. J. 1861 wb-h-496 (Hn)
Malone, Leonard 1860 gs-1-592 (F)
Malone, Robert 1829 wb-#205 (Mu)
Malone, Wesley 1844 lr (Sn)
Malone, William 1846 148-1-163 (Ge)
Malone, William N. 1847 rb-14-138 (Ru)
Malone, William jr. 1847 148-1-185 (Ge)
Maloney, Edward 1833 wb-a-239 (R)
Maloney, George B. 1845 wb-9-137 (K)
Maloney, Hugh 1840 wb-2-55# (Ge)
Maloney, Patrick 1858 wb-3e-77 (Sh)
Maloney, Robert 1848 wb-2-68# (Ge)
Maloney, Thomas 1841 wb-2-56# (Ge)
Malry, Thomas J. 1828 rb-7-45 (Ru)
Maltbie, J. R. 1861 wb-3e-185 (Sh)
Maltsbargar, Philip 1808 ib-1-251 (Ge)
Maltsberger, John 1854 wb-2-79# (Ge)
Man, Mary 1854 wb-16-297 (D)
Manafee, J. M. 1854 wb-n-319 (Mt)
Manard, William 1842 wb-f-93 (Hn)
Manas, Jacob 1824 wb-1-348 (Hw)
Mancy, Joseph 1842 wb-7-380 (K)
Maneer, John William 1844 wb-a-72 (Ms)
Manees, James 1856 ib-h-480 (F)
Maness, Benaga 1843 wb-3-652 (Ma)
Maness, James 1849 wb-a-373 (F)
Maney, Thomas H. 1847 rb-14-67 (Ru)
Maney?, Bennett 1843 wb-3-735 (Ma)
Mangram, Edwin 1827 wb-#168 (Mu)
Mangram, _____ 1826 wb-#162 (Mu)
Mangrem, Martha 1852 wb-4-432 (Mu)
Mangrum, Henry 1827 wb-#154 (Mu)
Mangrum, Henry 1857 wb-f-124 (Mu)
Mangrum, Isham 1818 wb-#205 (Mu)
Mangrum, Littleberry B. 1843 wb-z-535 (Mu)
Mangrum, Pleasant 1858 wb-12-486 (Wi)
Mangrum, W. D. 1852 wb-4-577 (Mu)
Mangum, Silas 1851 wb-g-398 (Hn)
Manier, Rebecca 1857 wb-b-49 (Ms)

Manifee, Jonas 1822 wb-8-83 (D)
Manifee, Thomas 1816 wb-7-61 (D)
Manifee, William 1798 wb-0-23 (K)
Manifold, Benjamin 1816 wb-2-233 (K)
Manifold, Benjamin sr. 1816 wb-2-216 (K)
Manire, John 1809 wb-1-323 (Wi)
Manire, John 1849 wb-a-209 (Ms)
Manire, Lemuel 1837 wb-6-339 (Wi)
Manis, Jesse 1846 wb-1-365 (Hw)
Manis, John 1855 wb-1-372 (Hw)
Manis, Joseph 1858 wb-f-204 (G)
Manis, William 1842 wb-1-359 (Hw)
Mankin, Jeremiah 1858 rb-19-155 (Ru)
Mankin, William 1829 rb-7-172 (Ru)
Mankins, Hezekiah 1853 rb-16-625 (Ru)
Mankins, William 1850 rb-15-558 (Ru)
Manley, Ansel 1853? wb-1C-80 (A)
Manley, Caleb 1831 wb-5-69 (Wi)
Manley, Evaline G. 1835 wb-d-52 (Hn)
Manley, Evaline G. 1835 wb-d-57 (Hn)
Manley, F. L. 1860 wb-h-454 (Hn)
Manley, Hamblen F. 1846 wb-g-128 (Hn)
Manley, Jesse 1837 wb-1-296 (Hy)
Manley, Miles 1820 wb-0-192 (K)
Manley, Nicholas 1857 rb-o-491 (Mt)
Manley, Richard 1838 wb-a-105 (F)
Manley, Richard 1847 wb-9-5 (Wi)
Manley, Richard 1851 wb-g-405 (Hn)
Manlove, Christopher (Dr.) 1860 wb-17-64 (Rb)
Manlove, Christopher 1860 wb-17-99 (Rb)
Manly, E. G. 1836 wb-d-257 (Hn)
Manly, George 1850 mr-2-390 (Be)
Manly, John 1835 wb-d-76 (Hn)
Manly, John 1855 wb-11-563 (Wi)
Manly, John F. 1856 wb-g-757 (Hn)
Manly, Richard 1858 wb-h-240 (Hn)
Manly, Thomas J. 1861 wb-3e-179 (Sh)
Manly, Wilson 1816 wb-2-253 (K)
Mann, Eliza 1854 wb-e-23 (Hy)
Mann, Joel 1830 wb-c-80 (St)
Mann, Malchi 1824 wb-3-345 (St)
Mann, Nancy 1852 wb-xx-84 (St)
Mann, William C. 1827 wb-9-80 (D)
Mann, Wm. R. 1857 as-c-94 (Ms)
Mannen, William 1840 wb-c-154 (Ro)
Manner, Joseph 1840 abl-1-200 (T)
Manning, Edward 1815 rb-3-57 (Ru)
Manning, Edwin 1855 wb-2-179 (Sh)
Manning, Eliza 1856 wb-e-55 (Hy)
Manning, Eliza G. 1851 wb-14-603 (D)
Manning, Elizio G. 1848 wb-14-274 (D)

Manning, Exum 1845 wb-f-260* (Hn)
Manning, J. William 1828 wb-#78 (Wl)
Manning, James 1854 wb-a-229 (Cr)
Manning, John 1816 wb-2-363 (Rb)
Manning, John 1823 rb-5-312 (Ru)
Manning, John 1838 wb-1-372 (Hy)
Manning, John 1844 wb-f-186 (St)
Manning, John 1856 wb-7-0 (Sm)
Manning, John M. 1857 wb-j-252 (O)
Manning, Lawrence M. 1849 wb-g-172 (St)
Manning, Mary A. P. 1858 rb-19-380 (Ru)
Manning, Matthew 1844 wb-f-132 (St)
Manning, Milton 1859 wb-k-62 (O)
Manning, Olive 1853 wb-xx-286 (St)
Manning, Parthena 1858 rb-19-292 (Ru)
Manning, Prigeon 1844 wb-f-122 (St)
Manning, Richard 1853 wb-g-549 (Hn)
Manning, S. M. 1850 wb-g-248 (St)
Manning, W. D. 1860 wb-d-53 (L)
Manning, William 1816 rb-3-142 (Ru)
Manning, William 1832 wb-c-208 (St)
Manning, William 1836 wb-#114 (Wl)
Manning, William E. 1853 wb-xx-282 (St)
Manning, William W. 1833 wb-c-305 (St)
Manor, Mills 1848 rb-14-487 (Ru)
Manor, Nancy 1847 rb-14-2 (Ru)
Manord, Thomas 1843 wb-f-170 (Hn)
Mansell, Burrell 1825 wb-#109 (Mc)
Mansfield, Giley 1821 wb-#39 (Wl)
Mansfield, Granville 1861 wb-#133 (Wl)
Mansfield, Grasty 1859 wb-b*-28 (O)
Mansfield, John 1817 wb-#27 (Wl)
Mansfield, Nicholas 1831 wb-b-149 (Ro)
Mansfield, William T. 1841 wb-e-89 (St)
Mansker, Elizabeth 1841 wb-2-277 (Sn)
Mansker, Kasper 1821 wb-1-323 (Sn)
Manson, Nancy W. 1857 wb-12-328 (Wi)
Manson, Susan A. C. 1848 wb-9-58 (Wi)
Manson, Thomas 1855 wb-n-687 (Mt)
Manson, Thomas H. 1857 rb-o-408 (Mt)
Manuel, Green 1845 wb-9-139 (K)
Manuel, Payton 1859 wb-4-325 (La)
Manuel, William G. 1845 wb-9-152 (K)
Manuel, William P. 1853 wb-11-440 (K)
Manuell, Absolem 1859? wb-a-337 (Cr)
Maples, Henry 1857 wb-3-403 (Gr)
Maples, William 1855 wb-#109 (Mc)
Marable, A. H. 1834 rb-9-119 (Ru)
Marable, Ann J. 1860 rb-p-313 (Mt)
Marable, Elizabeth 1841 rb-11-104 (Ru)
Marable, Elizabeth 1841 rb-11-110 (Ru)

Marable, H. H. 1853 rb-16-399 (Ru)
Marable, Henry H. 1833 rb-9-72 (Ru)
Marable, Henry H. 1841 wb-e-370 (Hu)
Marable, Isaac 1831 rb-8-210 (Ru)
Marable, Isaac H. 1820 rb-4-245 (Ru)
Marable, Isaac M. 1829 rb-7-193 (Ru)
Marable, J. H. 1844 rb-j-217 (Mt)
Marable, James 1851 wb-15-43 (D)
Marable, John H. 1848 wb-g-35 (Hu)
Marable, John H. sr. 1844 rb-j-142 (Mt)
Marable, Mary M. 1843 rb-i-467 (Mt)
Marable, Silas 1850 wb-9-470 (Wi)
Marable, Travis 1825 rb-6-168 (Ru)
Marbee?, Barnett 1819 wb-#31 (Wl)
Marberry, Ann E. 1853 wb-g-515 (Hn)
Marberry, Jacob 1846 wb-g-125 (Hn)
Marberry, John 1859 wb-1-282 (Be)
March, Elizabeth 1861 as-c-260 (Ms)
March, John 1853 wb-1-304 (Fr)
Marchbanks, Reuben 1858 wb-1-221 (Be)
Marchbanks, William 1857 wb-1-177 (Be)
Marcom, William 1808 eb-1-8 (C)
Marcum (Markham), General S. 1863
   wb-2-371 (Li)
Marcum, John 1847 wb-9-396 (K)
Marcum, Josiah 1841 wb-#110 (Mc)
Marcum, Micajah 1848 ib-1-7 (Ca)
Marcum, Nathaniel 1849 wb-c-375 (Wh)
Marcum, William 1842 wb-A-27 (Ca)
Mardock, William 1811 wb-1-200 (Bo)
Marecle, George 1824 wb-#53 (Wl)
Mares, Joel 1836 wb-A-1 (Ca)
Mares, Joseph (MD) 1844 wd-13-17 (D)
Margowan, William B. 1848 rb-14-436 (Ru)
Marian, John W. 1849 as-a-183 (Ms)
Marine, Mary 1854 wb-e-135 (G)
Maritto, Richard W. 1842 wb-11-265* (Rb)
Mark, Lucy 1815 wb-4-332 (D)
Markham, J. P. 1859 wb-18-62 (D)
Markham, John P. 1859 wb-18-109 (D)
Markham, Pleasant M. 1844 wb-#146 (Wl)
Markland, Nathan B. 1817 wb-2-348 (K)
Marks, Bailey 1862 wb-#136 (Wl)
Marks, John 1848 wb-#168 (Wl)
Marks, John 1857 wb-#124 (Wl)
Marks, Lewis 1852 wb-#178 (Wl)
Marks, Thomas 1834 wb-#105 (Wl)
Marks, Thomas 1854 wb-#115 (Wl)
Marks, William 1838 wb-6-450 (Wi)
Markum, Mary 1858 ib-1-474 (Ca)
Markum, Samuel 1859 iv-1-577 (Ca)

Marler, Alfred Tate 1860 wb-#110 (Mc)
Marler, John 1856 wb-2-149 (Li)
Marler, Michael 1853 wb-1C-82 (A)
Marley, Adam 1831 wb-2-0 (Sm)
Marley, Robert 1806 rb-2-11 (Ru)
Marley, Robert 1828 wb-4-300 (K)
Marley, Robert 1842 wb-7-307 (K)
Marlin, Andrew 1857 wb-h-318 (St)
Marlin, George W. 1859 wb-18-52 (D)
Marlin, John 1827 wb-9-133 (D)
Marlin, John 1841 rb-i-138 (Mt)
Marlin, William 1799 wb-1-17 (Ct)
Marlin, William 1805 rb-2-5 (Ru)
Marling, George 1854 wb-11-310 (Wi)
Marling, John L. 1857 wb-17-350 (D)
Marlow, Edward 1805 wb-#3 (Wl)
Marlow, George 1809 wb-#10 (Wl)
Marlow, Judith 1850 wb-2-81 (Sh)
Marlow, Nathaniel 1834 wb-b-156 (Wh)
Marlow, Nathaniel 1860 wb-e-354 (Wh)
Marly, Adam 1841 wb-a-80 (L)
Marly, Susan C. 1840 wb-a-49 (L)
Marman, Thomas 1849 wb-7-0 (Sm)
Marney, Amos 1840 wb-c-61 (Ro)
Marney, Amos sr. 1855 wb-e-530 (Ro)
Marney, Rufus 1857 wb-f-55 (Ro)
Marney, Sarah 1858 wb-f-220 (Ro)
Maroney, James 1843 wb-4-77 (Ma)
Maroney, Patrick 1856 wb-3e-17 (Sh)
Marr, Alexander 1841 wb-2-273 (Hy)
Marr, Ann G. 1847 rb-k-371 (Mt)
Marr, Benjamin 1850 wb-c-379 (Wh)
Marr, Benjamin 1850 wb-c-402 (Wh)
Marr, C. H. P. 1854 wb-n-340 (Mt)
Marr, Constantine P. 1836 wb-a-161 (O)
Marr, Elizabeth 1835? wb-1-210 (Hy)
Marr, G. W. P. 1856 wb-j-152 (O)
Marr, John 1834 wb-1-112 (Li)
Marr, John 1840 wb-2-143 (Hy)
Marr, Nicholas L. 1858 wb-12-528 (Wi)
Marr, R. P. 1860 wb-k-214 (O)
Marr, Sarah 1843 wb-3-188 (Hy)
Marr, William 1837 wb-2-186 (Fr)
Marrow, James H. 1846 rb-k-352 (Mt)
Marrs, Hugh 1826 wb-#60 (Wl)
Marrs, Martin 1837 wb-#119 (Wl)
Marrs, Samuel E. 1858 wb-#124 (Wl)
Marrs, William 1832 wb-#98 (Wl)
Marrs, William C. 1827 wb-9-80 (D)
Marsh, A. O. 1860 rb-p-470 (Mt)
Marsh, Gravenor 1832 wb-1-20# (Ge)

Marsh, Henry 1846 wb-#43 (Wa)
Marsh, James 1858 149-1-102 (Ge)
Marsh, William 1851 wb-2-107 (Sh)
Marshal, John 1842 wb-e-164 (St)
Marshal, Thomas 1849 wb-7-0 (Sm)
Marshall, Abram 1827 wb-1-20# (Ge)
Marshall, Alexander D. 1850 rb-15-345 (Ru)
Marshall, Ann 1861 wb-13-407 (Wi)
Marshall, Ann 1861 wb-13-408 (Wi)
Marshall, Benjamin 1819 wb-A-269 (Li)
Marshall, Benjamin sr. 1819 wb-A-273 (Li)
Marshall, Carter 1823 rb-d-253 (Mt)
Marshall, Charles 1859 wb-h-364 (Hn)
Marshall, Daniel 1822 rb-5-177 (Ru)
Marshall, David 1833 wb-a-37 (Cr)
Marshall, David 1849 wb-a-213 (Cr)
Marshall, Eliga J. 1849 ib-1-64 (Ca)
Marshall, Elihu 1829 wb-9-351 (D)
Marshall, Elizabeth 1854 wb-11-88 (Wi)
Marshall, Elizabeth 1855 wb-11-500 (Wi)
Marshall, Ezekiel 1842 lr (Sn)
Marshall, Francis 1836 wb-2-208 (Sn)
Marshall, Francis H. 1851 wb-14-604 (D)
Marshall, Gilbert 1801 wb-2-209 (D)
Marshall, Gilbert 1857 wb-12-414 (Wi)
Marshall, Harriet D. 1853 wb-15-509 (D)
Marshall, Isaac C. 1856? wb-#27 (Mo)
Marshall, James 1837 wb-11-72 (D)
Marshall, John 1838 rb-h-122 (Mt)
Marshall, John 1849? wb-2-70# (Ge)
Marshall, John C. 1848 ib-1-53 (Ca)
Marshall, John H. 1829 wb-3-0 (Sm)
Marshall, Jonas 1857 wb-e-77 (Hy)
Marshall, Joseph H. 1845 wb-13-336 (D)
Marshall, Margaret 1855 wb-16-538 (D)
Marshall, Rachel 1845 wb-e-166 (O)
Marshall, Rebecca 1836 wb-a-60 (Cr)
Marshall, Robert 1803 wb-1-74 (Sn)
Marshall, Robert 1850 wb-5-81 (Ma)
Marshall, Sarah 1840 wb-3-0 (Sm)
Marshall, W. S. 1857 wb-12-375 (Wi)
Marshall, W. W. 1853 wb-h-Jan (O)
Marshall, William 1826 wb-4-92 (Wi)
Marshall, William 1855 wb-h-92 (St)
Marshall, William S. 1857 wb-12-376 (Wi)
Marshall, William W. 1853 wb-h-Feb (O)
Martan, James 1829 wb-1-48 (W)
Martin, A. W. 1857 ib-1-445 (Ca)
Martin, Abner 1854 wb-e-251 (G)
Martin, Abraham 1861 lr (Sn)
Martin, Abram 1846 lr (Sn)

Martin, Agness 1823 wb-1-369 (Sn)
Martin, Alexander 1812 wb-3-79 (Wi)
Martin, Alexander 1832 as-a-260 (Di)
Martin, Alexander T. 1851 wb-m-272 (Mt)
Martin, Ambrose 1851 wb-m-174 (Mt)
Martin, Ambrose jr. 1847 rb-k-625 (Mt)
Martin, Amzi W. 1855 wb-A-104 (Ca)
Martin, Andrew 1799 wb-1-68 (K)
Martin, Andrew 1857 wb-h-388 (St)
Martin, Armstead 1829 wb-1-112 (Hr)
Martin, Aserius G. 1824 wb-1-32 (Ma)
Martin, Austin 1859 wb-h-363 (Hn)
Martin, Bradley 1857 rb-o-415 (Mt)
Martin, Brice 1857 wb-17-401 (D)
Martin, Burges 1854 mr-2-577 (Be)
Martin, C. C. 1857 wb-j-323 (O)
Martin, C. Harris 1857 wb-j-310 (O)
Martin, Caswell 1860 wb-k-146 (O)
Martin, Daniel 1859 wb-13-55 (Wi)
Martin, Daniel G. 1859 wb-13-56 (Wi)
Martin, David 1832 wb-#241 (Mu)
Martin, David 1837 wb-#116 (Wl)
Martin, Edward 1840 wb-11-634 (D)
Martin, Elijah 1853 as-b-120 (Ms)
Martin, Elizabeth 1851 wb-a-270 (Ms)
Martin, Ezekiel M. 1839 wb-#126 (Wl)
Martin, Gabriel 1821 wb-3-342 (Rb)
Martin, George 1819 wb-#33 (Wl)
Martin, George 1824 wb-3-446 (K)
Martin, George 1831 wb-b-156 (Ro)
Martin, George 1843 wb-1-219 (Li)
Martin, George 1860 wb-18-318 (D)
Martin, George 1860 wb-18-348 (D)
Martin, George W. 1854 wb-f-43 (Mu)
Martin, Henry 1819 wb-#16 (Wa)
Martin, Henry 1842 wb-z-414 (Mu)
Martin, Henry 1848 wb-1-167 (Me)
Martin, Henry 1860 wb-3-56 (Me)
Martin, Hudson 1859 wb-13-26 (Wi)
Martin, Hugh 1838 wb-4-24 (Je)
Martin, Hugh E. 1836 wb-b-342 (Ro)
Martin, Hugh E. 1857 wb-#12 (Mo)
Martin, Isaac C. 1842 wb-11-191 (Rb)
Martin, James 1801 wb-#8 (Wa)
Martin, James 1825 wb-b-15 (St)
Martin, James 1832 wb-1-37 (La)
Martin, James 1836 rb-9-350 (Ru)
Martin, James 1838 as-a-387 (Di)
Martin, James 1844 wb-#139 (Wl)
Martin, James 1844 wb-d-107 (Ro)
Martin, James 1846 wb-13-368 (D)

Martin, James 1847 wb-1-239 (Fr)
Martin, James 1847 wb-1-336 (Li)
Martin, James 1848 wb-g-20 (O)
Martin, James 1853 wb-7-0 (Sm)
Martin, James M. 1835 wb-#111 (Wl)
Martin, James T. 1848 wb-#167 (Wl)
Martin, Jane 1842 wb-b-459 (Hd)
Martin, Jane 1861 wb-13-412 (K)
Martin, Jesse 1815 wb-1-205 (Bo)
Martin, Jesse 1820 rb-c-323 (Mt)
Martin, Jesse 1840 wb-1-36 (Me)
Martin, Jesse 1840 wb-e-253 (Hu)
Martin, John 1820 wb-#37 (Wl)
Martin, John 1821? wb-1-48 (Fr)
Martin, John 1825 wb-a-7 (Cr)
Martin, John 1827? wb-#117 (Wl)
Martin, John 1839 wb-#127 (Wl)
Martin, John 1840 rb-i-33 (Mt)
Martin, John 1841 wb-#110 (Mc)
Martin, John 1842 wb-c-265 (Ro)
Martin, John 1843 wb-1-185 (Bo)
Martin, John 1847 lr (Sn)
Martin, John 1851 wb-2-47 (Me)
Martin, John 1852 wb-#111 (Mc)
Martin, John 1854 wb-2-197 (Me)
Martin, John 1858 wb-e-97 (Hy)
Martin, John 1859 39-2-335 (Dk)
Martin, John 1859 rb-20-47 (Ru)
Martin, John D. 1860 wb-3e-154 (Sh)
Martin, John G. 1842 wb-c-269 (O)
Martin, John H. 1846 lr (Sn)
Martin, John H. 1857 as-c-116 (Ms)
Martin, John S. 1855 wb-a-286 (Di)
Martin, John Sr. 1853 wb-2-150 (Me)
Martin, John W. 1856 39-2-167 (Dk)
Martin, Jonathan W. 1843 wb-d-64 (Hd)
Martin, Joseph 1824 wb-#20 (Wa)
Martin, Joseph I. 1853 wb-#111 (Mc)
Martin, Josiah 1795 wb-1-211 (Bo)
Martin, Josiah 1816 wb-1-0 (Sm)
Martin, Josiah 1855 wb-2-274 (Me)
Martin, Josiah N. 1849 as-a-197 (Ms)
Martin, Josias 1835 rb-9-263 (Ru)
Martin, M. A. 1851 wb-m-328 (Mt)
Martin, M. N. 1856 rb-o-113 (Mt)
Martin, Madison 1859 lr (Sn)
Martin, Margaret 1855 wb-e-525 (Ro)
Martin, Martha A. 1856 wb-3e-32 (Sh)
Martin, Mary 1852 rb-16-319 (Ru)
Martin, Mary 1858 ib-2-442 (Cl)
Martin, Mary Ann 1840 wb-#136 (Wl)

Martin, Mortimer A. 1855 wb-16-53 (Rb)
Martin, Moses 1833 wb-b-208 (Ro)
Martin, Nathaniel 1819 wb-a-103 (Wh)
Martin, Nathaniel 1848 ib-1-16 (Wy)
Martin, Patrick 1852 wb-15-198 (Rb)
Martin, Patrick 1852 wb-15-258 (Rb)
Martin, Patrick H. 1815 wb-1-0 (Sm)
Martin, Peter H. 1849 lr (Sn)
Martin, Pleasant 1837 wb-#116 (Wl)
Martin, Prince 1816 wb-4-433 (D)
Martin, Prince 1816 wb-7-6 (D)
Martin, Pugh 1840 wb-#130 (Wl)
Martin, Richard 1846 lr (Sn)
Martin, Robert 1832 as-a-215 (Di)
Martin, Robert 1840 rb-11-52 (Ru)
Martin, Robert 1859 wb-k-128 (O)
Martin, Robert 1861 wb-h-497 (Hn)
Martin, Sally 1852 wb-15-200 (Rb)
Martin, Samuel 1793 wb-1-292 (D)
Martin, Samuel 1795 wb-1-30 (K)
Martin, Samuel 1844 wb-a-116 (F)
Martin, Samuel 1855 wb-12-168 (K)
Martin, Sarah 1843 wb-#111 (Mc)
Martin, Sarah S. (Thomas) 1814 wb-4-283 (D)
Martin, Scipio 1829 wb-4-374 (Wi)
Martin, Susan C. 1844 rb-j-265 (Mt)
Martin, Susannah 1827 wb-1-67 (Fr)
Martin, T. J. 1845 wb-1-133 (Me)
Martin, Thomas (Rev.) 1855 wb-16-49 (Rb)
Martin, Thomas 1802 wb-2-225 (D)
Martin, Thomas 1803 wb-1-330 (Hw)
Martin, Thomas 1808 wb-1-134 (Sn)
Martin, Thomas 1834 wb-1-91 (W)
Martin, Thomas 1836 wb-10-639 (D)
Martin, Thomas 1847 wb-1-367 (Hw)
Martin, Thomas 1854 wb-b-352 (We)
Martin, Thomas D. 1846 5-3-121 (Cl)
Martin, Thomas W. 1828? wb-#169 (Mu)
Martin, Thomas sr. 1817 wb-1-0 (Sm)
Martin, William H. 1852 wb-d-94 (Wh)
Martin, William 1816 wb-1-227 (Sn)
Martin, William 1820 wb-1-346 (Hw)
Martin, William 1828 wb-1-87 (Hr)
Martin, William 1832 wb-a-216 (G)
Martin, William 1843 wb-8-127 (Wi)
Martin, William 1846 wb-7-0 (Sm)
Martin, William 1846 wb-d-200 (Ro)
Martin, William 1855 wb-b-9 (Ms)
Martin, William 1857 wb-1-72 (Dy)
Martin, William 1860 wb-f-346 (G)
Martin, William B. 1860 wb-b-455 (We)

Martin, William E. 1834 rb-g-39 (Mt)
Martin, William E. 1844 rb-j-167 (Mt)
Martin, William H. 1858 wb-13-13 (Wi)
Martin, William M. 1860 wb-h-450 (Hn)
Martin, William P. 1846 wb-#152 (Wl)
Martin, William sr. 1859 wb-3-599 (Gr)
Martin, Wm. D. 1853 as-b-119 (Ms)
Martin, Zachariah 1854 ib-h-41 (F)
Martin?, Rebecca 1852 wb-#179 (Wl)
Martindale, William 1830 wb-1-165 (Hr)
Marton, Campbell 1836 wb-10-552 (D)
Marton, Quin 1807 wb-#6 (Wl)
Mase, Nicholas 1808 ib-1-236 (Ge)
Mase, Nicholas no date wb-1-18# (Ge)
Masen, Jno. A. 1858 wb-a-71 (Ce)
Mash, Obediah 1824 wb-#144 (Mu)
Mash, Roland 1834 wb-1-82 (W)
Mashburn, Reding 1848 wb-4-383 (Hr)
Mask, P. M. 1850 wb-4-570 (Hr)
Mask, Plesent M. 1848 wb-4-244 (Hr)
Maskal, Sarah 1855 wb-3-287 (Gr)
Masner, Teter 1853 148-1-464 (Ge)
Mason, Alexander 1835 wb-9-184 (Rb)
Mason, Alexis 1815 wb-2-186 (K)
Mason, Caleb 1838 wb-b-300 (Wh)
Mason, Caleb 1841 wb-12-178* (D)
Mason, Coleman 1820 rb-5-13 (Ru)
Mason, Daniel 1839 wb-c-53 (Ro)
Mason, Delita D. 1854 rb-17-274 (Ru)
Mason, Demsey 1839 wb-10-312 (Rb)
Mason, Eleanor 1822 wb-3-399 (K)
Mason, Elizabeth (Mrs.) 1855 wb-15-753 (Rb)
Mason, Gabriel L. 1840 wb-z-14 (Mu)
Mason, Guilford 1815 wb-2-251 (Rb)
Mason, Henriana 1848 wb-9-38 (Wi)
Mason, Huldah 1857 wb-0-154 (Cf)
Mason, Isaac 1846 wb-13-31 (Rb)
Mason, Isaac 1846 wb-13-67 (Rb)
Mason, James 1813 wb-2-73 (Rb)
Mason, James 1840 wb-1-58 (Sh)
Mason, John 1827 rb-e-174 (Mt)
Mason, John 1831 wb-2-0 (Sm)
Mason, Lucy 1829 wb-2-299 (Ma)
Mason, Martha E. 1854 rb-17-274 (Ru)
Mason, P. M. 1858 rb-19-177 (Ru)
Mason, Pleasant 1857 rb-19-82 (Ru)
Mason, Ralph 1808 wb-1-297 (Rb)
Mason, Reynear H. 1852 rb-16-145 (Ru)
Mason, Robert 1861 wb-2-93# (Ge)
Mason, Samuel 1824 wb-4-264 (Rb)
Mason, Wiley 1843 wb-3-0 (Sm)

Masoner, Mary 1856 wb-2-84# (Ge)
Massa, Antonia 1858 wb-3e-78 (Sh)
Massa, John sr. 1837 wb-b-277 (Wh)
Massa, Thomas 1814 wb-a-26 (Wh)
Massengale, Bennett 1848 ib-1-81 (Cl)
Massengill, Mary 1852 ib-2-58 (Cl)
Massengill, Michael 1834 wb-1-97 (Gr)
Massengill, William sr. 1852 wb-5-1 (Je)
Massey, Abraham A. 1856 wb-#122 (Wl)
Massey, Andrew 1846 wb-5-22 (Ma)
Massey, Benjamin 1814 wb-#14 (Wl)
Massey, Benjamin 1827 wb-#68 (Wl)
Massey, E. D. 1858 wb-17-561 (D)
Massey, Elizabeth 1856 wb-h-463 (Hu)
Massey, Isaac H. 1843 wb-e-605 (Hu)
Massey, John 1849 wb-g-260 (Hu)
Massey, Margaret Ann 1856 wb-#122 (Wl)
Massey, Mary J. 1858 wb-12-528 (Wi)
Massey, Reuben 1860 wb-3e-129 (Sh)
Massey, Stephen 1855 wb-6-22 (Ma)
Massey, T. R. 1854 ib-h-76 (F)
Massey, Thomas 1832 wb-5-167 (K)
Massey, Thomas 1845 wb-1-257 (Li)
Massey, William 1815 wb-1-0 (Sm)
Massey, William 1849 wb-g-225 (Hu)
Massey, William 1860 wb-8-40 (Sm)
Massie, Absalom 1842 as-b-42 (Di)
Massie, Thomas 1836? as-a-326 (Di)
Massie, Wilie 1857 wb-f-30 (G)
Massy, Adam 1849 wb-c-350 (Wh)
Massy, Anthony 1808 ib-1-244 (Ge)
Master, Agnes 1823 lr (Sn)
Masterson, Thomas 1812 wb-4-189 (D)
Mastin, Jemima 1859 wb-#111 (Mc)
Mastin, Thomas W. 1853 wb-#111 (Mc)
Mathena, Milly 1849 ib-1-38 (Wy)
Matheny, Elijah 1839 wb-c-68 (Ro)
Mathes, George A. 1846 wb-1-364 (Hw)
Mathes, Jane W. 1854 wb-5-332 (Je)
Mathes, Phebe 1854 wb-#53 (Wa)
Mathes, Thomas 1847 rb-k-493 (Mt)
Mathews, A. P. 1854 wb-h-285 (Hu)
Mathews, Charles 1819 wb-7-294 (D)
Mathews, Cornelius 1849 wb-9-247 (Wi)
Mathews, Drury 1847 rb-k-664 (Mt)
Mathews, Elisabeth 1842 wb-1-242 (La)
Mathews, Elizabeth 1851 wb-14-672 (D)
Mathews, George 1837 wb-3-455 (Je)
Mathews, Hortio 1834 wb-10-373 (D)
Mathews, James 1825 wb-#139 (Mu)
Mathews, James 1841 wb-3-482 (Ma)

Mathews, James S. 1853 wb-16-60 (D)
Mathews, Jesse 1856 wb-2-310 (Me)
Mathews, John 1831 wb-1-97 (Fr)
Mathews, John 1839 wb-y-432 (Mu)
Mathews, John 1843 rb-12-343 (Ru)
Mathews, John P. 1858 wb-j-350 (O)
Mathews, L. T. 1860 wb-17-55 (Rb)
Mathews, Lemuel 1851 wb-3-84 (W)
Mathews, Mary 1814 wb-1-338 (Hw)
Mathews, Mary 1853 lr (Sn)
Mathews, Nancy 1856 wb-16-277 (Rb)
Mathews, P. H. 1859 as-c-559 (Di)
Mathews, Richard 1827 wb-6-143 (Rb)
Mathews, Richard 1846 wb-12-613 (Rb)
Mathews, Sampson 1846 wb-13-44 (Rb)
Mathews, Samuel 1754 lr (Sn)
Mathews, Simon 1848 lr (Sn)
Mathews, William 1816 wb-4-456 (D)
Mathews, William 1839 wb-4-42 (Je)
Mathews, William R. 1849 rb-15-117 (Ru)
Mathias, Isiah 1818 wb-7-259 (D)
Mathis, Alexander (Sr.) 1806 wb-#10 (Wa)
Mathis, Allen 1848 wd-14-229 (D)
Mathis, Jackson 1850 wb-e-246 (Ro)
Mathis, James 1826 rb-7-326 (Ru)
Mathis, Joel 1856 wb-1-377 (Hw)
Mathis, William 1816 wb-7-53 (D)
Mathis, William 1826 rb-d-544 (Mt)
Mathis, William 1836 wb-1-154 (W)
Mathis, William 1846 wb-c-340 (G)
Mathis, William 1847 wb-d-103 (G)
Mathis, William 1856 wb-c-70 (L)
Mathis, William H. 1855 wb-16-563 (D)
Mathus, Thomas 1853 wb-h-186 (Hu)
Matison, Marget 1845 wb-1-269 (Bo)
Matlock, Caswell 1837 mr-1-22 (Be)
Matlock, Caswell 1837 wb-e-45 (Hu)
Matlock, Caswell 1850 wb-g-428 (Hu)
Matlock, Charles 1836 wb-#112 (Mc)
Matlock, Charles 1839 wb-#112 (Mc)
Matlock, Charles 1852 wb-#113 (Mc)
Matlock, David 1790 wb-#3 (Wa)
Matlock, Edmond D. 1857 wb-h-711 (Hu)
Matlock, George 1833 wb-#104 (Wl)
Matlock, Gideon C. 1851 wb-#177 (Wl)
Matlock, Henry 1861 wb-#113 (Mc)
Matlock, Henry Sr. 1847 wb-#113 (Mc)
Matlock, Jason 1847 wb-e-62 (Ro)
Matlock, John 1844 as-b-185 (Di)
Matlock, John 1848 wb-#114 (Mc)
Matlock, John P. 1858 wb-f-168 (Ro)

Matlock, Mary 1851 mr-2-423 (Be)
Matlock, Moore 1812 wb-a-48 (Ro)
Matlock, Moore 1842 wb-c-295 (Ro)
Matlock, Moore 1852 wb-e-320 (Ro)
Matlock, Rebecca 1852 wb-e-325 (Ro)
Matlock, William 1845 wb-#114 (Mc)
Matlock, William 1845 wb-13-250 (D)
Matlock, William 1848 wd-14-192 (D)
Matlock, William 1854 wb-a-275 (Di)
Matthew, Dudly 1814 rb-2-283 (Ru)
Matthew, John 1844 wb-3-121 (Hr)
Matthews, Aaron 1836 wb-#115 (Mc)
Matthews, Agness 1848 wb-b-184 (Mu)
Matthews, Alsa 1846 wb-d-238 (Hd)
Matthews, Isaac W. 1849 wb-2-57 (Sh)
Matthews, James B. 1857 wb-b-33 (F)
Matthews, James J. 1844 wb-f-125 (St)
Matthews, John 1851 wb-10-118 (Wi)
Matthews, John 1851 wb-g-445 (St)
Matthews, John D. 1853 ib-1-268 (Wy)
Matthews, John W. 1835 wb-x-267* (Mu)
Matthews, Joseph 1847 wb-b-84 (Mu)
Matthews, Lewis 1837 wb-a-1 (L)
Matthews, Richard 1799 wb-1-42 (Rb)
Matthews, Robert 1822 wb-#73 (Mu)
Matthews, Robert 1839 wb-y-394 (Mu)
Matthews, Robert 1843 wb-z-534 (Mu)
Matthews, Tho. 1844 wb-3-96 (Hr)
Matthews, Thomas 1835 wb-a-128 (Di)
Matthews, Thomas 1846 wb-13-400 (D)
Matthews, Thomas J. 1846 wb-1-403 (La)
Matthews, William 1823 rb-6-28 (Ru)
Matthews, William 1842 148-1-41 (Ge)
Matthews, William K. 1823 wb-#52 (Mu)
Matthews, William R. 1822 wb-#62 (Mu)
Matthews, William W. 1836 wb-1-100 (La)
Matthews, William W. 1846 wb-1-377 (La)
Matthewson, John 1836 wb-d-242 (Hn)
Mattock, William 1825 wb-1-66 (Ma)
Mattox, John 1839 lr (Sn)
Mauk, Abraham 1847 wb-#46 (Wa)
Maulden, Leroy 1857 wb-f-63 (G)
Mauldin, Harris 1851 as-b-19 (Ms)
Mauldin, July A. 1852 as-b-65 (Ms)
Maulsby, William 1806 wb-1-92 (Je)
Maupin, Amos 1858 iv-C-174 (C)
Maupin, Austin 1852 wb-h-Jul (O)
Maupin, John 1861 wb-k-498 (O)
Maurice, John 1845 148-1-107 (Ge)
Mauris, John 1828 wb-2-27# (Ge)
Maury, Abram 1825 wb-4-6 (Wi)

Maury, Abram P. 1848 wb-9-161 (Wi)
Maury, Elizabeth J. 1853 wb-10-487 (Wi)
Maury, Jefferson 1839 mr-1-277 (Be)
Maury, Josephine 1852 wb-10-192 (Wi)
Maury, Mary E. T. 1852 wb-10-396 (Wi)
Maury, Octavia 1852 wb-10-192 (Wi)
Maury, Philip 1840 wb-7-344 (Wi)
Maury, Richard L. 1839 wb-7-66 (Wi)
Maury, Thomas T. 1817 wb-2-329 (Wi)
Maury, Thomas T. 1837 wb-6-332 (Wi)
Mawhorter, Elizabeth 1854 wb-#54 (Wa)
Mawyer?, Thomas A. 1835 wb-d-142 (Hn)
Maxey, Allen 1857 wb-b-419 (We)
Maxey, Bennet 1843 wb-4-87 (Ma)
Maxey, James 1837 wb-9-328 (Rb)
Maxey, James 1851 wb-14-473 (Rb)
Maxey, Joseph 1838 wb-6-286 (K)
Maxey, Mary E. 1859 gs-1-221 (F)
Maxey, Nancy 1847 wb-f-127+ (O)
Maxey, Shadrack 1831 wb-5-94 (K)
Maxey, Stephen 1846 wb-e-212 (O)
Maxey, William 1823 wb-8-267 (D)
Maxey, William P. 1851 wb-14-588 (D)
Maxsey, Halloway 1838 wb-10-143 (Rb)
Maxwell, Francis 1861 wb-18-471 (D)
Maxwell, George 1821 wb-1-347 (Hw)
Maxwell, Henry J. 1847 A-468-70 (Le)
Maxwell, J. W. E. 1847 wb-b-87 (Mu)
Maxwell, James 1826 wb-9-40 (D)
Maxwell, James J. 1829 rb-7-163 (Ru)
Maxwell, James J. 1829 rb-7-278 (Ru)
Maxwell, Jesse 1857 wb-17-307 (D)
Maxwell, Jesse E. 1856 wb-3e-26 (Sh)
Maxwell, Jesse W. E. 1849 wb-4-332 (Mu)
Maxwell, Jno. W. 1830 rb-8-411 (Ru)
Maxwell, John 1807 wb-1-269 (Je)
Maxwell, John 1831 wb-1-94 (Bo)
Maxwell, John W. 1828 wb-b-88 (Hn)
Maxwell, Robert 1842 wb-a-108 (L)
Maxwell, Robert 1854 wb-#116 (Mc)
Maxwell, Samuel 1852 wb-#52 (Wa)
Maxwell, Susan 1853 mr-2-491 (Be)
Maxwell, William 1838 wb-#122 (Wl)
May, A. J. 1852 wb-15-211 (D)
May, Anthony F. 1826 wb-4-193 (K)
May, B. 1831 wb-1-30 (La)
May, Benjamin 1836 wb-1-31 (Sh)
May, Benjamin 1836 wb-b-114 (G)
May, Daniel 1833 wb-1-46 (La)
May, Eliza F. 1854 wb-16-309 (D)
May, Elizabeth 1850 wb-1-64 (Jo)

May, Francis 1818 wb-7-220 (D)
May, George 1824 wb-2-426 (Je)
May, James F. 1844 wd-13-32 (D)
May, John 1814 rb-2-303 (Ru)
May, John 1843 wb-#116 (Mc)
May, John 1843 wb-4-97 (Ma)
May, Joseph 1849 rb-15-76 (Ru)
May, M. 1860 wb-f-465 (Ro)
May, Magdalena 1836 wb-2-215 (Sn)
May, Mead 1841 wb-2-283 (Sn)
May, Milly 1850 ib-1-53 (Wy)
May, Obediah 1837 wb-2-259 (Ma)
May, Philip 1803 wb-2-346 (D)
May, Philip 1804 wb-2-374 (D)
May, Philip 1846 wb-f-332 (St)
May, Philip 1846 wb-f-346 (St)
May, Reuben 1834 wb-1-417 (Ma)
May, Richard 1843 wb-8-157 (K)
May, Robert 1857 rb-19-66 (Ru)
May, Thomas 1847 wb-9-347 (K)
May, William 1824 wb-2-452 (Je)
May, William 1839 wb-3-25 (Ma)
May, William M. 1845 wb-a-264 (F)
Mayberry, Job 1845 wb-8-210 (Wi)
Mayberry, John 1837 wb-y-107 (Mu)
Mayberry, John C. 1837 wb-y-110 (Mu)
Mayberry, Michael 1843 wb-a2-528 (Mu)
Maybourn, David H. 1818 wb-a-101 (Wh)
Mayers, Samuel 1801 wb-1-107 (Bo)
Mayes, David 1831 wb-#218 (Mu)
Mayes, Dudley 1844 wb-5-321 (Gr)
Mayes, Elizabeth 1847 wb-5-542 (Gr)
Mayes, James 1842 wb-5-228 (Gr)
Mayes, Joel 1857 wb-3e-54 (Sh)
Mayes, Nancy 1848 33-3-76 (Gr)
Mayes, Oscar 1859 wb-16-804 (Rb)
Mayes, Prescilla 1852 wb-3-31 (Gr)
Mayes, Samuel 1841 wb-z-216 (Mu)
Mayes, Shurad 1836 wb-1-152 (Gr)
Mayes, Shurrad 1834 wb-1-102 (Gr)
Mayes, William 1861 lr (Sn)
Mayes, William B. 1857 wb-16-491 (Rb)
Mayfield, Archibald 1823 wb-A-347 (Li)
Mayfield, Cartre 1850 wb-#116 (Mc)
Mayfield, Elijah 1843 wb-z-546 (Mu)
Mayfield, George 1848 wb-9-119 (Wi)
Mayfield, Isaac 1796 wb-2-44 (D)
Mayfield, Isaac 1796 wb-2-50 (D)
Mayfield, Isaac 1856 wb-17-108 (D)
Mayfield, Isaac 1856 wb-17-55 (D)
Mayfield, James 1807 wb-3-66 (Wi)

Mayfield, James 1808 wb-1-199 (Wi)
Mayfield, James 1840 wb-b-318 (G)
Mayfield, Jesse 1833 wb-#116 (Mc)
Mayfield, John 1851 wb-10-115 (Wi)
Mayfield, P. W. 1854 wb-h-299 (Hu)
Mayfield, Pearson B. 1832 wb-#117 (Mc)
Mayfield, Penelop 1848 wb-#117 (Mc)
Mayfield, Samuel 1843 wb-z-578 (Mu)
Mayfield, Sutherlin 1789 wb-1-94 (D)
Mayfield, Thomas 1846 rb-13-710 (Ru)
Mayfield, Thomas F. 1848 rb-14-358 (Ru)
Mayfield, Valentine 1834 wb-b-38 (G)
Mayfield, William T. 1838 wb-#117 (Mc)
Mayhall, William 1837 wb-0-6 (Cf)
Mayhew, John 1844 as-b-194 (Di)
Mayner, Edward 1841 wb-c-13* (G)
Mayo, Frederick 1856 wb-6-329 (Ma)
Mayo, Frederick 1858 wb-7-9 (Ma)
Mayo, Frederick W. 1853 wb-a-441 (F)
Mayo, Hardy 1855 wb-6-98 (Ma)
Mayo, Hardy 1857 wb-6-449 (Ma)
Mayo, James 1830 wb-b-59 (Hn)
Mayo, James 1848 wb-a-337 (F)
Mayo, John 1811 wb-4-163 (D)
Mayo, Lawrence 1840 wb-2-181 (Hr)
Mayo, Newsom B. 1860 wb-a-178 (Ce)
Mayo, Rheubin 1839 wb-1-357 (Hw)
Mayo, Rickey 1854 wb-2-154 (Sh)
Mayo, Samuel 1841 wb-12-13 (D)
Mayo, Sarah 1827 wb-#73 (Wl)
Mayo, Valentine 1859 wb-#16 (Mo)
Mayo, William 1827 wb-#72 (Wl)
Mays, Abraham 1831 wb-#219 (Mu)
Mays, Drury 1845 wb-c-211 (G)
Mays, Frances 1840 wb-7-303 (Wi)
Mays, Gooding sr. 1842 wb-z-405 (Mu)
Mays, Goodwin 1842 wb-z-408 (Mu)
Mays, James F. 1854 wb-16-404 (D)
Mays, John W. H. 1847 wb-d-99 (G)
Mays, Mucellus 1838 5-2-11 (Cl)
Mays, Rubin 1836 wb-b-121 (G)
Mays, Sally 1844 wb-f-188 (St)
Mays, Samuel 1838 wb-11-398 (D)
Mays, Samuel 1842 wb-#39 (Wa)
Mays, Samuel 1850 wb-g-408 (Hu)
Mays, Smith 1831 wb-5-77 (Wi)
Mays, Thomas 1846 5-3-163 (Cl)
Mays, Thomas 1848 ib-1-126 (Cl)
Mays, Thomas 1852 wb-5-166 (Je)
Mays, William W. 1853 wb-15-556 (D)
Mayse, John 1848 wb-2-300 (Gr)

Mayse, Jonathan 1853 ib-2-29 (Cl)
Mayson, F. M. 1846 wb-14-4 (D)
Maze, William 1819 wb-2-228 (Je)
McAdam, Thomas 1818 wb-#13 (Wa)
McAdams, Ann S. 1861 wb-#65 (Wa)
McAdams, Irwin 1861 wb-b-126 (Ms)
McAdams, Joseph 1823 wb-A-296 (Li)
McAdams, Joseph 1844 as-a-79 (Ms)
McAdams, Margaret 1832? wb-#29 (Wa)
McAdaw, John 1824 wb-#56 (Wl)
McAden, Henry 1841 Ir (Sn)
McAdoo, Alfred 1841 wb-e-199 (Hn)
McAdoo, Anna 1861 wb-13-434 (K)
McAdoo, David 1817 wb-a-22 (Di)
McAdoo, Elizabeth 1859 wb-1C-460 (A)
McAdoo, Erastus 1852 rb-16-223 (Ru)
McAdoo, Erastus Z. 1853 rb-16-573 (Ru)
McAdoo, Eratus B. 1852 rb-16-190 (Ru)
McAdoo, John 1854 wb-1C-191 (A)
McAdoo, John 1856 wb-h-463 (Hu)
McAdoo, John sr. 1829 wb-1A-39 (A)
McAdoo, Joseph S. 1861 rb-21-142 (Ru)
McAdoo, Mary 1860 rb-20-586 (Ru)
McAdoo, Nancy 1854 wb-2-195 (Me)
McAdoo, Samuel 1846 wb-1-148 (Me)
McAdoo, Samuel 1847 rb-14-63 (Ru)
McAdoo, Samuel 1857 wb-#100 (Mc)
McAdoo, Samuel P. 1856 rb-18-88 (Ru)
McAdoo, William 1853 wb-1C-82 (A)
McAdoo, _____ (Mrs.) 1830 as-a-199 (Di)
McAdow, Andrew 1797 wb-1-63 (Je)
McAdow, James 1834 wb-#103 (Wl)
McAdow, Jehu 1836 wb-#111 (Wl)
McAdow, John 1836 wb-#109 (Wl)
McAdow, Mary 1835 wb-#109 (Wl)
McAdow, Newbern S. 1835 wb-#110 (Wl)
McAdow, W. S. 1855 ib-1-378 (Ca)
McAfee, Archibald 1860 wb-2-101# (Ge)
McAfee, Ezeriah 1853 wb-2-57 (Li)
McAfee, John sr. 1854 wb-3-209 (W)
McAfee, Lisha 1848 wb-a-183 (Ms)
McAfee, Mills 1831 wb-#227 (Mu)
McAfee, Wills 1832 wb-#238 (Mu)
McAfforty, James 1836 wb-x-384 (Mu)
McAffrey, James W. 1864 wb-#100 (Mc)
McAffry, Terence 1830 wb-5-23 (K)
McAlelley, Richard 1854 wb-e-140 (G)
McAlelly, John 1835 wb-b-65 (G)
McAlhatton?, Mary 1830 rb-8-97 (Ru)
McAlister, Charles 1825 wb-4-44 (Wi)
McAlister, Hawkins 1858 wb-f-177 (G)

McAlister, James 1851 wb-#51 (Wa)
McAlister, John 1814 wb-#14 (Wa)
McAlister, John 1820 rb-c-301 (Mt)
McAlister, John 1826 rb-e-33 (Mt)
McAlister, John 1827 wb-4-231 (Wi)
McAlister, John R. 1857 wb-f-115 (G)
McAlister, Marcus 1834 rb-g-56 (Mt)
McAlister, Melton G. 1855 wb-16-514 (D)
McAlister, Sarah 1860 wb-13-358 (K)
McAllen, James 1845 wb-12-371 (Rb)
McAllister, Daniel E. 1856 wb-e-395 (G)
McAllister, Garland 1850 wb-7-0 (Sm)
McAllister, John 1827 rb-e-195 (Mt)
McAllister, Margaret E. 1850 wb-d-276 (G)
McAlpin, Alexander 1805 wb-1-18# (Ge)
McAlpin, Alexander 1806 as-1-134 (Ge)
McAmis, D. C. 1848 wb-#101 (Mc)
McAmis, Thomas 1849 wb-2-53# (Ge)
McAmis, Thomas 1859 wb-2-89# (Ge)
McAmish, William 1826 wb-1-20# (Ge)
McAnally, Abigal 1858 wb-4-9 (La)
McAnally, Ann 1841 wb-1-238 (La)
McAnally, Charles 1848 wb-2-308 (Gr)
McAnally, Charles 1849 33-3-130 (Gr)
McAnally, David 1836 wb-1-188 (Gr)
McAnally, David 1854 wb-3-190 (Gr)
McAnally, David 1854 wb-3-204 (Gr)
McAnally, F. M. 1859 wb-4-294 (La)
McAnally, James M. 1842 wb-5-233 (Gr)
McAnally, Jesse 1852 wb-3-47 (La)
McAnally, John 1836 wb-1-97 (La)
McAnally, Martin 1839 wb-1-171 (La)
McAnally, Thomas P. 1850 33-3-226 (Gr)
McAnally, Wm. 1861 wb-5-83 (La)
McAnulty, William 1836 wb-1-467 (Hr)
McAphen, Isaac 1844 as-a-76 (Ms)
McAsee, James 1855 wb-16-512 (D)
McAsee?, James 1851 wb-14-670 (D)
McAulay, William 1852 wb-xx-64 (St)
McAulay, William 1852 wb-xx-73 (St)
McAuley, Anne 1842 Ir (Sn)
McAuley, Daniel 1859 wb-i-43 (St)
McAuley, Roderick 1859 wb-i-56 (St)
McBass, Archa 1856 39-2-164 (Dk)
McBass, Rachael 1856 39-2-164 (Dk)
McBath, William sr. 1828 wb-4-310 (K)
McBay, Houston 1856 wb-2-160 (Li)
McBean, Daniel 1815 wb-4-385 (D)
McBee, Callaway 1850 wb-10-421 (K)
McBee, Eveline A. S. 1852 wb-11-271 (K)
McBee, James H. 1856? ib-2-299 (Cl)

McBee, Lemuel 1843 wb-5-255 (Gr)
McBee, Lemuel J. 1856 wb-4-72 (Je)
McBee, Mary Ann 1840 wb-7-118 (K)
McBee, Obediah 1827 wb-1-34 (Hr)
McBee, Risden H. 1851 wb-m-304 (Mt)
McBee, Silas 1861 wb-4-28 (Gr)
McBee, William 1826 wb-4-136 (K)
McBee, William 1840 wb-7-123 (K)
McBee, William 1840 wb-7-139 (K)
McBory?, John 1859 as-c-161 (Ms)
McBride, A. 1854 wb-n-317 (Mt)
McBride, Alfred 1854 wb-n-374 (Mt)
McBride, Andrew 1853 wb-d-153 (Wh)
McBride, Charlton J. 1849 wb-c-380 (Wh)
McBride, Francis 1809 rb-2-83 (Ru)
McBride, Isaac G. 1855 wb-a-226 (T)
McBride, Isaiah 1815 wb-#11 (Mu)
McBride, James 1821 wb-7-511 (D)
McBride, James 1823 wb-8-176 (D)
McBride, James 1841 wb-b-367 (G)
McBride, James 1857 wb-17-248 (D)
McBride, Jesse 1856? wb#44 (Gu)
McBride, John 1858 wb-f-134 (Mu)
McBride, Joseph 1815 wb-4-376 (D)
McBride, Joseph 1829 wb-9-353 (D)
McBride, Joseph 1841 wb-7-441 (Wi)
McBride, Joseph 1850 wb-a-249 (Ms)
McBride, Lucy 1845 wb-c-259 (G)
McBride, Marcus J. 1852 wb-5-133 (Je)
McBride, Paterson 1845 wb-c-194 (Wh)
McBride, Patterson E. 1848 wb-c-322 (Wh)
McBride, Thomas 1815 wb-A-89 (Li)
McBride, William 1837 wb-1-571 (Hr)
McBride, William 1856 149-1-36 (Ge)
McBride, William C. 1851 ib-1-141 (Wy)
McBride, William E. 1855 ib-h-332 (F)
McBride, William sr. 1854 148-1-474 (Ge)
McBroom, Andrew 1857 wb-#101 (Mc)
McBroom, John 1828 wb-1-352 (Hw)
McBroom, Thomas 1842 wb-5-200 (Gr)
McBroom, William 1826 wb-2-487 (Je)
McBurnie, James 1860 wb-18-229 (D)
McCabb, James K. 1846 wb-d-10 (G)
McCabe, Charles 1828 wb-4-306 (Wi)
McCabe, Hugh 1832 wb-x-60 (Mu)
McCabe, William P. A. 1836 wb-1-95 (La)
McCaffirty, Edward 1824 wb-#146 (Mu)
McCaffrey, James 1850 wb-#174 (Wl)
McCaffrey, Robert 1856 wb-#122 (Wl)
McCaib, Andrew 1828 rb-7-93 (Ru)
McCain, James M. 1858 wb-a-282 (T)

McCain, John 1798 wb-1-176 (Bo)
McCain, John 1817 wb-7-142 (D)
McCain, Robert 1812 wb-#27 (Mu)
McCain, William Ross 1860 wb-a-298 (T)
McCaleb, Andrew 1860 wb-1-174 (R)
McCaleb, Ann 1850 wb-d-274 (G)
McCaleb, Archibald 1814 wb-2-100 (K)
McCalister, Charles 1818 wb-2-407 (Wi)
McCall, A. W. 1861 wb-19-32 (D)
McCall, Alexander H. 1856 wb-2-326 (Me)
McCall, Ann 1835 wb-3-0 (Sm)
McCall, David 1851 wb-7-0 (Sm)
McCall, Francis 1808 wb-1-201 (Wi)
McCall, Joe (Sr.) 1821 wb-#18 (Wa)
McCall, John 1830 wb-4-413 (K)
McCall, John 1835 wb-5-389 (K)
McCall, Samuel 1837 wb-a-22 (Ms)
McCall, Thomas 1815 wb-1-0 (Sm)
McCalla, Margaret 1844 wb-8-359 (K)
McCalla, Robert 1861 wb-3e-180 (Sh)
McCallan, Andrew J. 1850 wb-1-350 (Me)
McCallay, Thomas 1850 wb-g-207 (St)
McCallester, John jr. 1820 rb-c-293 (Mt)
McCallie, John 1831 wb-1-95 (Bo)
McCallie, William T. 1850 wb-#101 (Mc)
McCallum, Daniel 1830 lr (Gi)
McCallum, Thrasher 1829 wb-#174 (Mu)
McCammon, John 1838 wb-6-254 (K)
McCammon, Thomas E. 1836 wb-d-220 (Hn)
McCammon, William 1851 wb-11-152 (K)
McCampbell, Andrew 1825 wb-4-63 (K)
McCampbell, Andrew L. 1839 wb-6-487 (K)
McCampbell, Ann 1841 wb-7-262 (K)
McCampbell, John 1821 wb-3-258 (K)
McCampbell, John 1853 wb-11-454 (K)
McCampbell, Samuel S. 1832 wb-5-161 (K)
McCampbell, William 1814 wb-2-113 (K)
McCampbell, William A. 1839 wb-6-420 (K)
McCan, John 1816 wb-2-135 (Je)
McCan, John 1841 wb-1-239 (La)
McCan, William 1855 wb-e-37 (Wh)
McCana, William N. 1852 wb-15-356 (D)
McCance, E. W. 1852 wb-15-462 (D)
McCanless, Samuel 1829 lr (Gi)
McCanlis, Daniel 1849 ib-1-113 (Cl)
McCann, James 1852 wb-#102 (Mc)
McCann, Sims 1852 wb-d-53 (Wh)
McCant, David 1815 wb-A-71 (Li)
McCardel, Philip 1827 wb-#26 (Wa)
McCarmack, George W. 1854 wb-16-335 (D)
McCarrel, James 1813 wb-2-61 (K)

McCarrell, James 1836 wb-6-21 (K)
McCarrell, Margaret 1819 wb-3-109 (K)
McCarrell, William 1815 wb-2-184 (K)
McCarrol, Keziah 1841 wb-3-0 (Sm)
McCarrol, Narcissa 1859 wb-1-89 (Dy)
McCarroll, Abner 1841 mr-1-352 (Be)
McCarroll, Francis 1860 wb-i-227 (St)
McCarry, Samuel 1814 wb-1-206 (Bo)
McCartee, Sarah 1795? wb-1-211 (Bo)
McCarter, Thomas 1857 wb-5-67 (Hr)
McCartland, William 1849 wb-g-143 (Hu)
McCartney, Andrew 1845 wb-1-295 (Li)
McCartney, Andrew J. 1845 wb-#147 (Wl)
McCartney, Jane 1841 wb-1-56 (Me)
McCartney, John B. 1834 wb-#106 (Wl)
McCartney, John Bell 1836 wb-#115 (Wl)
McCartney, Lewis 1806 wb-#5 (Wl)
McCartney, Lewis 1827 wb-#75 (Wl)
McCartney, Margaret 1840 rb-10-508 (Ru)
McCartney, Widow 1826 wb-#75 (Wl)
McCarty, Elizabeth 1848 33-3-74 (Gr)
McCarty, H. H. 1859 wb-h-350 (Hn)
McCarty, Jacob 1812 wb-a-120 (St)
McCarty, James 1815 wb-#16 (Mu)
McCarty, James 1848 wb-9-457 (K)
McCarty, John 1838 wb-6-287 (K)
McCarty, John L. 1860 wb-#102 (Mc)
McCarty, Lamos 1793 wb-0-3 (K)
McCarty, William 1841 wb-#102 (Mc)
McCarver, William 1856 wb-1-378 (Hw)
McCaskill, Allen 1855 wb-h-78 (St)
McCaskill, John 1851 wb-g-396 (St)
McCaskill, Taylor (Capt.) 1842 wb-2-327 (Hr)
McCasland, Andrew W. 1843 wb-z-513 (Mu)
McCasland, Isaac 1848 wb-g-11 (Hu)
McCasland, John 1848 wd-14-229 (D)
McCaucle?, Mary C. 1860 rb-p-479 (Mt)
McCaughan, A. 1855 wb-h-117 (St)
McCaughan, James 1842 rb-i-316 (Mt)
McCaughan, Kain A. 1855 wb-b-66 (F)
McCaughn, Kain A. 1855 wb-h-105 (St)
McCaul, Alexander 1833 wb-c-104 (Hn)
McCaul, James 1853 wb-10-588 (Wi)
McCauley, George 1860 rb-p-442 (Mt)
McCauley, James W. 1847 wb-a-322 (F)
McCauley, John 1843 rb-i-499 (Mt)
McCauley, John 1854 wb-6-5 (Ma)
McCauley, John sr. 1842 rb-i-362 (Mt)
McCauley, John sr. 1842 rb-i-405 (Mt)
McCauley, William 1822 rb-d-107 (Mt)
McCauly, Daniel 1833 wb-c-268 (St)

McCauly, Wm. 1852 as-c-173 (Di)
McCawley, James 1815 wb-#16 (Mu)
McCearly, Sally 1846 wb-4-65 (Hr)
McCeary, B. C. 1844 wb-5-300 (Gr)
McCerley, John 1852 wb-a-416 (F)
McChesney, Margaret 1824 wb-1-99 (Bo)
McChesney, William 1818 wb-7-232 (D)
McClain, Alfred 1852 wb-#107 (Wl)
McClain, Daniel 1842 wb-c-85 (Wh)
McClain, Elizabeth 1857 wb-#122 (Wl)
McClain, James 1838? wb-b-84 (Hd)
McClain, James 1850 wb-a-237 (Ms)
McClain, John 1852 as-b-75 (Ms)
McClain, Joseph 1843 wb-f-196 (Hn)
McClain, Joseph 1861 wb-i-304 (St)
McClain, Josiah S. 1854 wb-#115 (Wl)
McClain, Judith 1850 wb-c-445 (Wh)
McClain, Kiziah 1843 wb-d-51 (Hd)
McClain, Rufus H. 1835 wb-#115 (Wl)
McClain, Stephen 1830 wb-4-404 (K)
McClain, Stephen 1850 wb-10-400 (K)
McClain, Stephen jr. 1851 wb-11-44 (K)
McClain, Temperance 1841 wb-e-281 (Hn)
McClain, Thomas 1789 wb-1-95 (D)
McClain, Thomas 1842 5-2-284 (Cl)
McClain, Thomas 1847 ib-2-10 (Cl)
McClain, Thomas 1855 wb-2-82# (Ge)
McClain, Thos. 1843 5-2-311 (Cl)
McClain, W. J. 1859 wb-i-137 (St)
McClain, William 1818 wb-#29 (Wl)
McClain, William 1829 wb-#79 (Wl)
McClain, William P. 1852 wb-#179 (Wl)
McClanahan, F. P. 1860 wb-i-196 (St)
McClanahan, Henry 1858 wb-17-477 (D)
McClanahan, John 1806 wb-1-94 (Je)
McClanahan, Robert 1854 rb-16-716 (Ru)
McClanahan, Samuel 1798 wb-1-242 (Je)
McClanahan, Samuel 1847 rb-14-172 (Ru)
McClanahan, Sarah 1858 rb-19-383 (Ru)
McClane, James 1825 wb-a-211 (Wh)
McClane, Lewis 1856 rb-18-245 (Ru)
McClannahan, R. B. 1853 rb-16-709 (Ru)
McClaran, Alexander 1816 wb-2-275 (Wi)
McClaran, Clem 1849 wb-9-291 (Wi)
McClaran, Franklin 1858 gs-1-99 (F)
McClaran, Jno. D. 1851 rb-16-109 (Ru)
McClaran, Thomas 1827 wb-4-252 (Wi)
McClarine, Robert sr. 1846 mr (Gi)
McClarn, James 1824 wb-a-196 (Wh)
McClarney, Mary Elizabeth 1836 wb-d-42 (St)
McClary, Andrew 1848? ib-1-128 (Cl)

McClatchy, John 1840 wb-#103 (Mc)
McCleavis, Jesse 1848 as-a-177 (Ms)
McClelan, Robert 1850 wb-1-394 (Li)
McClellan, Andrew 1850 wb-7-0 (Sm)
McClellan, Catharine 1860 wb-7-85 (Ma)
McClellan, Isabella C. 1857 wb-7-2 (Ma)
McClellan, James D. 1852 wb-5-115 (Ma)
McClellan, John 1840 wb-3-273 (Ma)
McClellan, Margaret 1818 wb-1-0 (Sm)
McClellan, Samuel C. 1844 wb-4-251 (Ma)
McClellan, Sarah E. 1859 wb-13-70 (Wi)
McClellan, W. B. 1834 wb-1-131 (Hy)
McClellan, William 1852 wb-2-37 (Li)
McClellan, William B. 1838 wb-1-413 (Hy)
McClelland, Fargus 1802 wb-1-148 (Je)
McClelland, James 1819 wb-a-20 (Di)
McClelland, James M. 1861 wb-d-81 (L)
McClelland, John (Lt. Col.) 1855 wb-12-111 (K)
McClelland, John 1857 wb-12-346 (K)
McClelland, John F. 1858 wb-b-60 (Ms)
McClelland, Thomas 1859 wb-3e-96 (Sh)
McClelland, William G. 1858 wb-c-185 (L)
McClendon, Dennis 1844 wb-13-131 (D)
McClerkin, Robert L. 1840 wb-a-76 (T)
McClish, William 1803 wb-1-109 (Rb)
McClister, James 1837 wb-3-438 (Je)
McClod, William 1801 wb-0-29 (K)
McCloud, Anguish 1844 wb-A-37 (Ca)
McCloud, Daniel 1853 wb-g-541 (Hn)
McCloud, James 1824 wb-3-481 (K)
McCloud, Sollomon 1847 wb-g-4 (Hu)
McCloud, Thomas 1808 wb-1-1 (Fr)
McCloud, William 1816 wb-2-215 (K)
McCloud, William jr. 1801 wb-1-80 (K)
McClung, Calvin M. 1858 wb-12-539 (K)
McClung, Charles 1828 wb-4-287 (K)
McClung, Charles 1835 wb-5-388 (K)
McClung, Charles jr. 1830 wb-4-394 (K)
McClung, Hugh 1786 wb-1-18# (Ge)
McClung, Mathew 1844 wb-9-3 (K)
McClung, Matthew 1858 wb-12-470 (K)
McClung, Wm. 1836 wb-1-107 (Bo)
McClure, Elijah 1836 wb-1-125 (Li)
McClure, Halbert 1829 wb-1-104 (Bo)
McClure, Henry 1855 wb-11-578 (Wi)
McClure, Hugh 1828 rb-e-260 (Mt)
McClure, Hugh 1839 rb-h-269 (Mt)
McClure, James 1827 wb-b-22 (Hn)
McClure, James 1842 wb-e-462 (Hu)
McClure, James 1849 rb-l-302 (Mt)
McClure, James B. 1838 rb-h-30 (Mt)

McClure, James B. 1851 wb-m-282 (Mt)
McClure, John 1808 wb-#11 (Wa)
McClure, Thomas 1845 rb-j-352 (Mt)
McClure, William 1831 rb-f-226 (Mt)
McClure, William 1831 rb-f-238 (Mt)
McClure, William 1838 lr (Gi)
McClure, William 1854 lr (Gi)
McClure, William 1857 wb-a-287 (Cr)
McClure, William 1858 wb-2-246 (Li)
McClurey, W. A. 1860 rb-p-471 (Mt)
McCluskin, Robert L. 1840 abl-1-181 (T)
McCoferty, Edward 1824 wb-f-83 (Mu)
McColin, Alexander 1847 wb-1-254 (Bo)
McColloch, Sarah Ann 1854 rb-17-161 (Ru)
McCollough, Henry 1834 wb-1-354 (Hw)
McCollough, William 1864 wb-1-379 (Hw)
McCollum, Aaron 1856 wb-a-297 (Cr)
McCollum, Columbus M. 1856 as-b-245 (Ms)
McCollum, Daniel 1852 wb-11-231 (K)
McCollum, Elizabeth 1852 wb-10-392 (Wi)
McCollum, James 1860 wb-2-92# (Ge)
McCollum, James J. 1840 wb-b-248 (O)
McCollum, John 1841 wb-2-56# (Ge)
McCollum, John 1842 wb-7-577 (Wi)
McCollum, Mathew 1854 wb-a-327 (Ms)
McCollum, Patton S. 1835 as-a-245 (Di)
McCollum, Peter 1834 wb-1-518 (Ma)
McCollum, Sarah 1854 148-1-482 (Ge)
McCollum, Sarah L. 1857 wb-6-488 (Ma)
McCollum, Thomas 1806 as-1-149 (Ge)
McCollum, Thomas 1816 wb-2-38# (Ge)
McCollum, Thrasher 1815 wb-#13 (Mu)
McCollum, Thrasher 1827 wb-#159 (Mu)
McCollum, William 1815 wb-4-322 (D)
McColough, James 1819 wb-3-72 (K)
McComack, Elizabeth 1849 ib-1-59 (Ca)
McCombs, Alexander 1826 wb-8-546 (D)
McCombs, Elizabeth 1844 wb-8-136 (Wi)
McCombs, Jane 1828 rb-7-157 (Ru)
McCombs, Robert 1825 rb-6-165 (Ru)
McConehay, John 1842 wb-3-0 (Sm)
McConell, James 1830 wb-a-19 (Cr)
McConico, Christopher 1844 wb-a2-31 (Mu)
McConley, M. 1831 rb-8-174 (Ru)
McConnel, Archibald 1847 wb-a-191 (Ms)
McConnel, Elizabeth 1855 wb-b-141 (Ms)
McConnel, James 1815 wb-2-184 (K)
McConnell, Anna 1838 wb-1-146 (Li)
McConnell, F. 1843 wb-f-121* (Hn)
McConnell, Francis 1843 wb-f-178* (Hn)
McConnell, Jacob 1796 wb-1-227 (Bo)

McConnell, James 1833 wb-1-172 (Bo)
McConnell, James A. sr. 1855 wb-d-274 (Wh)
McConnell, Martha C. 1849 wb-1-374 (Li)
McConnell, Robert K. 1855 wb-2-111 (Li)
McConnell, Sarah P. 1821 wb-8-32 (D)
McConnell, Sarah T. 1821 wb-8-13 (D)
McConnell, William 1838 wb-b-297 (Wh)
McConnico, C. W. 1844 wb-a2-41 (Mu)
McConnico, Christopher W 1847 wb-b-119 (Mu)
McConnico, Frances W. 1848 wb-9-36 (Wi)
McConnico, Garner 1835 wb-6-47 (Wi)
McConnico, Jared 1803 Wb-1-102 (Wi)
McConnico, Jared 1816 wb-2-221 (Wi)
McConnico, Jared 1834 wb-5-346 (Wi)
McConnico, Keziah 1818 wb-2-377 (Wi)
McConnico, Mary 1839 wb-7-72 (Wi)
McCool, James 1856 rb-o-258 (Mt)
McCord, Abner 1832 wb-5-163 (Wi)
McCord, David 1819 wb-3-80 (Wi)
McCord, David 1834 wb-5-363 (Wi)
McCord, Elizabeth 1834 wb-5-361 (Wi)
McCord, George 1857 wb-12-400 (Wi)
McCord, Harvey B. 1838 wb-6-448 (Wi)
McCord, Henry B. 1836 wb-6-114 (Wi)
McCord, James 1851 wb-10-63 (Wi)
McCord, James H. 1840 148-1-1 (Ge)
McCord, John 1826 wb-4-99 (Wi)
McCord, Mary B. 1851 as-b-44 (Ms)
McCord, Mary Jane 1857 wb-b-35 (Ms)
McCord, Robert 1844 wb-a-103 (Ms)
McCord, William 1824 wb-#128 (Mu)
McCord, William 1854 wb-g-559 (Hn)
McCorkle, Alexander 1833 wb-c-65 (Hn)
McCorkle, James 1854 wb-g-583 (Hn)
McCorkle, James H. 1831 wb-b-130 (Hn)
McCorkle, James H. 1847 wb-g-196 (Hn)
McCorkle, Joseph 1803 rb-a-181 (Mt)
McCorkle, Lewis 1842 wb-f-38 (Hn)
McCorkle, Lilburn H. 1848 wb-1-214 (Me)
McCorkle, Nancy 1855 wb-g-659 (Hn)
McCorkle, Robert 1849 wb-1-292 (Me)
McCorkle, William 1818 rb-4-118 (Ru)
McCormac, Andrew 1820 wb-7-411 (D)
McCormack, D. 1842 wb-11-406 (Rb)
McCormack, Drury 1844 wb-12-254 (Rb)
McCormack, George 1851 wb-15-179 (D)
McCormack, John 1817 wb-2-346 (K)
McCormack, John 1827 wb-#153 (Mu)
McCormack, John P. 1854 wb-g-624 (Hn)
McCormack, Mary 1811 lw (Ct)
McCormack, Nathan D. 1845 wb-12-373 (Rb)

McCormack, Robert 1796 lw (Ct)
McCormick, James 1842 wb-12-277* (D)
McCormick, Samuel 1854 wb-a-217 (T)
McCormick, Thomas 1815 rb-b-260 (Mt)
McCortling, Isaac 1849 wb-g-140 (Hu)
McCowan, William 1850 wb-1-277 (Fr)
McCown, James 1795 wb-2-35 (D)
McCown, Malcom 1828 wb-1-16 (Li)
McCoy, Absalom 1861 wb-e-442 (Wh)
McCoy, Angus 1840 wb-2-57# (Ge)
McCoy, Beaty 1816 rb-3-118 (Ru)
McCoy, C. 1852 33-3-432 (Gr)
McCoy, Campbell 1852 wb-xx-138 (St)
McCoy, Claburn 1849 33-3-204 (Gr)
McCoy, Daniel 1838 wb-y-302 (Mu)
McCoy, E. B. 1838 wb-2-288 (Ma)
McCoy, Esther 1836 wb-2-100 (Ma)
McCoy, Ezekiel B. 1841 wb-3-316 (Ma)
McCoy, Francis B. 1837 wb-2-244 (Ma)
McCoy, Hugh 1819 wb-#32 (Wl)
McCoy, James 1832 wb-a-126 (R)
McCoy, John 1815 rb-3-70 (Ru)
McCoy, John 1829 wb-#103 (Mc)
McCoy, L. A. 1852 wb-b-177 (L)
McCoy, Margaret 1837 wb-1-140 (Li)
McCoy, Martha Ann 1844 wb-4-227 (Ma)
McCoy, R. 1844 wb-a-180 (L)
McCoy, Robert 1844 rb-12-430 (Ru)
McCoy, Sarah A. 1857 wb-6-444 (Ma)
McCoy, Sherard 1836 rb-9-162 (Ru)
McCoy, Sherod 1835 rb-9-197 (Ru)
McCoy, William 1825 wb-#103 (Mc)
McCoy, William 1836 wb-6-242 (Wi)
McCoy, William 1849 wb-9-242 (Wi)
McCrabb, Alexander 1811 rb-b-14 (Mt)
McCracken, George 1826 rb-6-274 (Ru)
McCracken, John 1820 wb-#30 (Wa)
McCracken, John 1859 wb-#62 (Wa)
McCracken, Joseph 1848 lr (Gi)
McCrackin, Calvin 1851 wb-2-174 (La)
McCrackin, Joseph G. 1835 wb-x-331 (Mu)
McCracking, David 1812 wb-A-8 (Li)
McCrady, Andrew 1839 wb-7-129 (Wi)
McCrae, William 1856 rb-17-638 (Ru)
McCrary, B. C. 1840 wb-5-125 (Gr)
McCrary, B. C. 1851 33-3-390 (Gr)
McCrary, George R. 1854 wb-h-318 (Hu)
McCrary, John 1856 rb-18-184 (Ru)
McCrary, Joseph 1839 wb-e-241 (Hu)
McCrary, Mary 1852 wb-g-595 (Hu)
McCraw, Gabriel 1860 wb-1-381 (Hw)

McCraw, William 1851 wb-a-146 (T)
McCray, Daniel 1819? wb-#23 (Wa)
McCray, Isaac 1830 wb-1-84 (Fr)
McCray, William 1857 rb-19-85 (Ru)
McCreary, Joel 1814 wb-A-52 (Li)
McCreary, Lucy 1845 wb-12-366 (Rb)
McCreary, Nathaniel 1827 wb-6-177 (Rb)
McCright, John R. 1853 wb-a-201 (T)
McCristion, James 1836 wb-3-391 (Je)
McCrory, Catharine 1847 wb-14-138 (D)
McCrory, Catharine 1859 wb-f-173 (Mu)
McCrory, John 1837 wb-y-108 (Mu)
McCrory, John 1858 wb-12-567 (Wi)
McCrory, John L. 1855 wb-6-96 (Ma)
McCrory, Robert 1795 wb-2-33 (D)
McCrory, Robert 1796 wb-2-44 (D)
McCrory, Robert E. 1843 wb-12-441* (D)
McCrory, Thomas 1819 wb-3-97 (Wi)
McCroskey, David 1860 wb-#103 (Mc)
McCroskey, John 1866 wb-#14 (Mo)
McCroskey, Samuel 1839 wb-6-382 (K)
McCroskey, William 1840 wb-#104 (Mc)
McCrosky, Samuel 1848 wb-#6 (Mo)
McCroy, Henry 1857 39-2-242 (Dk)
McCuistion, Isabella 1837 wb-3-439 (Je)
McCulla, Henry 1815 wb-#12 (Mu)
McCullagh, John 1858 wb-3e-62 (Sh)
McCullah, Joseph 1822 wb-2-368 (Je)
McCulloch, Benjamin 1848 rb-14-242 (Ru)
McCulloch, G. J. 1862 wb-f-443 (G)
McCulloch, John 1814 wb-1-205 (Bo)
McCulloch, Milas M. 1851 wb-d-315 (G)
McCulloch, Robert 1844 rb-12-497 (Ru)
McCulloch, Robert L. 1844 rb-12-498 (Ru)
McCulloch, Samuel 1821 rb-5-84 (Ru)
McCulloch, Samuel E. 1846 wb-d-23 (G)
McCullock, David 1818 wb-7-237 (D)
McCullock, Isabella 1846 wb-c-283 (G)
McCullock, James 1825 wb-b-16 (St)
McCullock, John 1825 wb-b-68 (St)
McCullock, Martha 1836 wb-3-422 (Je)
McCullock, Samuel 1809 rb-2-72 (Ru)
McCullough, Alexander 1850 rb-15-479 (Ru)
McCullough, Alexander 1857 wb-2-179 (Li)
McCullough, Allen 1839 wb-e-26 (Hn)
McCullough, James 1852 wb-0-107 (Cf)
McCullough, Thomas 1807 wb-2-33# (Ge)
McCully, Elizabeth 1849 wb-c-350 (Wh)
McCully, Miles 1855 wb-b-3 (F)
McCully, Rebecca 1858 gs-1-173 (F)
McCully, Samuel 1840 wb-c-122 (Ro)

McCully, Thomas J. 1850 wb-c-443 (Wh)
McCully, William 1838 wb-#104 (Mc)
McCulough, David 1818 wb-7-257 (D)
McCurdy, Ann H. 1831 wb-1-58 (Li)
McCurdy, David 1834 wb-5-423 (Wi)
McCurdy, John L. 1831 wb-9-515 (D)
McCurdy, Robert 1818 wb-1-179 (Bo)
McCurry, John 1852 wb-2-75# (Ge)
McCurry, John 1860 wb-2-91# (Ge)
McCurry, John sr. 1854 148-1-495 (Ge)
McCurry, Joseph (of Joseph) 1846
    148-1-143 (Ge)
McCutchen, Benjamin 1851 wb-9-669 (Wi)
McCutchen, Catharine 1857 wb-12-365 (Wi)
McCutchen, Catharine E. 1846 wb-8-499 (Wi)
McCutchen, Grizle 1822 wb-8-78 (D)
McCutchen, James 1810 wb-1-237 (Wi)
McCutchen, James 1836 wb-1-121 (La)
McCutchen, James 1836 wb-1-126 (La)
McCutchen, John 1789 wb-1-92 (D)
McCutchen, John 1828 wb-6-356 (Rb)
McCutchen, John 1833 rb-f-534 (Mt)
McCutchen, John B. 1855 wb-e-375 (G)
McCutchen, John E. 1838 wb-11-292 (D)
McCutchen, John H. 1859 wb-f-308 (G)
McCutchen, John W. 1831 wb-9-466 (D)
McCutchen, Mary M. 1844 wb-8-197 (Wi)
McCutchen, Patrick 1812 wb-1-307 (Wi)
McCutchen, Patrick 1841 wb-7-377 (Wi)
McCutchen, Robert 1839 wb-e-239 (Hu)
McCutchen, Samuel 1816 wb-2-243 (Wi)
McCutchen, Valentine 1815 rb-b-293 (Mt)
McCutchen, William 1789 wb-1-93 (D)
McCutchen, William H. 1835 wb-d-148 (Hn)
McCutchin, John 1842 wb-12-323* (D)
McCutchin, John 1842 wb-12-363* (D)
McCutchin, Valentine 1830 rb-f-30 (Mt)
McCuthin, John 1833 rb-f-473 (Mt)
McDade, Charles 1823 wb-a-35 (Hn)
McDaniel, A. K. 1847 mr-2-268 (Be)
McDaniel, Aron 1828? wb-#171 (Mu)
McDaniel, C. 1838 wb-2-2 (Hr)
McDaniel, Charles 1842 wb-1-202 (Fr)
McDaniel, Cornelius 1835 wb-1-412 (Hr)
McDaniel, Duncan 1840 wb-d-444 (St)
McDaniel, Effy 1812 wb-1-0 (Sm)
McDaniel, Elizabeth 1852 wb-e-25 (G)
McDaniel, Fielding sr. 1841 wb-1-175 (Li)
McDaniel, Francis 1860 as-c-213 (Ms)
McDaniel, George 1855 wb-n-683 (Mt)
McDaniel, Harriette E. 1839 rb-h-296 (Mt)

McDaniel, Hugh 1839 wb-b-298 (G)
McDaniel, James 1830 wb-a-70 (R)
McDaniel, James 1843 wb-#141 (Wl)
McDaniel, James 1847 wb-13-145 (Rb)
McDaniel, James 1853 wb-3-121 (Gr)
McDaniel, James W. 1850 wb-3-35 (Gr)
McDaniel, Joel 1828 wb-#171 (Mu)
McDaniel, Joel 1838 wb-b-119 (Hd)
McDaniel, John 1835 wb-#111 (Wl)
McDaniel, John 1837 wb-11-72 (D)
McDaniel, John 1840 wb-1-34 (Me)
McDaniel, John 1841 wb-b-290 (Hd)
McDaniel, John 1845 wb-5-414 (Gr)
McDaniel, John 1848 as-a-167 (Ms)
McDaniel, John 1861 wb-2-383 (Li)
McDaniel, John W. 1841 lr (Gi)
McDaniel, John sr. 1825 wb-1-0 (Sm)
McDaniel, Johnson 1806 rb-a-440 (Mt)
McDaniel, Joseph 1838 wb-1-11 (Me)
McDaniel, Lea 1848 33-3-39 (Gr)
McDaniel, Magness 1810 wb-#8 (Wl)
McDaniel, Mary 1855 wb-16-585 (D)
McDaniel, Mathew 1846 mr-2-27 (Be)
McDaniel, Neal 1826 wb-9-65 (D)
McDaniel, R. 1810 wb-#35 (Wl)
McDaniel, Rebecca 1849 wb-10-172 (K)
McDaniel, Riley 1850 wb-a-259 (Ms)
McDaniel, Rincher 1824 wb-#50 (Wl)
McDaniel, Samuel 1826 wb-#150 (Mu)
McDaniel, Samuel 1849 wb-1-299 (Me)
McDaniel, Sarah A. 1857 wb-2-194 (Li)
McDaniel, Susan 1848 33-3-86 (Gr)
McDaniel, Tabitha 1811 wb-#8 (Wl)
McDaniel, William 1833 wb-5-196 (K)
McDaniel, William R. 1853 lr (Sn)
McDannell, William 1820 lr (Sn)
McDanold, Alexander 1811 wb-2-16 (Je)
McDavid, William 1819 wb-A-228 (Li)
McDearman, Byren 1825 wb-#109 (Wl)
McDermott, Colonel William P.H. 1854
    wb-#104 (Mc)
McDermott, Paul 1807 wb-1-297 (Je)
McDonal, Henry 1847 wb-c-260 (Wh)
McDonald, A. C. 1860 wb-a-288 (T)
McDonald, Alen P. 1855 ib-1-481 (Wy)
McDonald, Alexander 1817 wb-A-152 (Li)
McDonald, Alexander 1832 wb-3-225 (Je)
McDonald, Charles W. 1848 wb-#104 (Mc)
McDonald, Daniel 1814 wb-#18 (Mu)
McDonald, Daniel 1837 wb-1-526 (Hr)
McDonald, David 1841 wb-2-231 (Hr)

McDonald, Donald 1814 wb-#41 (Mu)

McDonald, James 1849 wb-14-216 (Rb)

McDonald, James M. 1851 wb-e-280 (Ro)

McDonald, Jane 1842 wb-#137 (Wl)

McDonald, John 1807 wb-#1 (Mu)

McDonald, John 1834 wb-3-381 (Je)

McDonald, John 1835 wb-#111 (Wl)

McDonald, John 1842 148-1-31 (Ge)

McDonald, John 1860 149-1-191 (Ge)

McDonald, Joseph 1815 wb-#17 (Wl)

McDonald, Nathaniel 1846 wb-e-263 (O)

McDonald, Nathaniel M. 1844 wb-d-184 (O)

McDonald, Neil 1851 wb-g-343 (St)

McDonald, Neil 1854 wb-e-178 (G)

McDonald, Randal 1841 wb-#136 (Wl)

McDonald, Reuben 1830 wb-4-419 (K)

McDonald, Sarah 1855 wb-12-87 (K)

McDonald, Sarah 1857 wb-12-351 (K)

McDonald, Thomas 1859 wb-b-437 (We)

McDonald, William 1857 wb-7-0 (Sm)

McDonald, William 1858 wb-1-135 (R)

McDonald, William sr. 1851 148-1-364 (Ge)

McDonnald, A. P. 1852 ib-1-173 (Wy)

McDougal, Alexander 1842 wb-1-312 (La)

McDougal, Chainy 1852 wb-3-68 (La)

McDougal, Daniel 1856 ib-1-392 (Wy)

McDougal, Elenor 1854 wb-3-241 (La)

McDougal, James 1854 wb-3-182 (La)

McDougal, James L. 1848 wb-g-316 (Hn)

McDougal, Robert 1849 wb-g-173 (St)

McDougald, Allen 1856 wb-e-467 (G)

McDougald, Hezakiah 1848 wb-d-142 (G)

McDougle, Thomas 1850 rb-l-629 (Mt)

McDougle, Thomas 1850 rb-l-630 (Mt)

McDowel, John 1819 wb-a-126 (Wh)

McDowel, Susannah 1816 wb-2-227 (K)

McDowell, Andrew 1857 wb-3e-53 (Sh)

McDowell, John 1814 wb-2-123 (K)

McDowell, John 1824 wb-4-7 (K)

McDowell, John sr. 1836 wb-a-306 (R)

McDowell, Joseph 1822 wb-3-464 (Rb)

McDowell, Joseph 1837 wb-9-383 (Rb)

McDuffee, Edward 1856 wb-f-7 (Ro)

McDuffee, John 1841 wb-c-245 (Ro)

McDuffee, Neel 1823 wb-a-211 (Ro)

McDugal, Archibald 1834 wb-c-146 (Hn)

McDugald, Angus 1813 wb-1-0 (Sm)

McDugan, Manly 1846 wb-f-328 (St)

McEachern, Patrick 1818 wb-#35 (Wl)

McEachern, Patrick 1820 wb-1-0 (Sm)

McElhany, John 1819 wb-3-48 (Rb)

McElhatten, Stewart 1855 rb-17-581 (Ru)

McElmoyle, John S. 1861 wb-k-452 (O)

McElroy, Adam C. 1846 rb-13-641 (Ru)

McElroy, Archibald 1841 wb-1-189 (Li)

McElroy, D. O. 1856 wb-1-347 (Fr)

McElroy, James 1842 wb-c-144 (O)

McElroy, James 1847 rb-14-170 (Ru)

McElroy, James 1859 wb-h-310 (Hn)

McElroy, Jane 1848 rb-14-435 (Ru)

McElroy, John C. 1853 rb-16-650 (Ru)

McElroy, Lemuel 1837 wb-d-149 (St)

McElroy, Margaret 1816 wb-2-38# (Ge)

McElroy, Mary 1856 wb-2-164 (Li)

McElroy, Samuel 1847 rb-14-221 (Ru)

McElroy, William 1856 wb-2-128 (Li)

McElwee, Elizabeth 1859 wb-7-34 (Ma)

McElwee, James M. 1827 wb-1-60 (Ma)

McElwie, Margret 1846 wb-1-166 (Bo)

McElwrath, Joseph sr. 1825 lr (Sn)

McElyea, Daniel 1814 wb-#15 (Wl)

McElyea, Jesse 1853 wb-h-Feb (O)

McElyea, Robert 1837 wb-e-45 (Hu)

McElyea, Samuel 1836 wb-a-151 (O)

McErvin, James M. 1857 wb-e-146 (Wh)

McEwen, Alexander 1796? wb-#24 (Wa)

McEwen, Alexander 1827 rb-6-298 (Ru)

McEwen, Alexander 1853 rb-17-126 (Ru)

McEwen, Cyrus J. 1853 wb-10-463 (Wi)

McEwen, David 1822 wb-3-294 (Wi)

McEwen, Elizabeth 1842 wb-c-273 (Ro)

McEwen, Felix G. 1831 wb-5-56 (Wi)

McEwen, Hannah 1852 rb-16-350 (Ru)

McEwen, Hugh 1855 wb-e-325 (G)

McEwen, James 1815 rb-3-29 (Ru)

McEwen, James 1822 wb-3-296 (Wi)

McEwen, James 1828 wb-4-280 (Wi)

McEwen, Jas. A. 1854 rb-16-714 (Ru)

McEwen, John 1822 wb-a-164 (Ro)

McEwen, John 1824 rb-6-67 (Ru)

McEwen, John A. 1859 wb-17-627 (D)

McEwen, John C. 1839 wb-c-75 (Ro)

McEwen, Joseph H. 1857 wb-17-196 (D)

McEwen, Josiah 1848 ib-1-8 (Ca)

McEwen, Nancy M. 1842 wb-c-282 (Ro)

McEwen, Sarah 1851 wb-10-65 (Wi)

McEwen, William 1816 wb-2-216 (Wi)

McEwin, David F. 1839 wb-3-110 (Ma)

McEwin, James M. 1857 wb-e-159 (Wh)

McEwing, David 1839 wb-3-104 (Ma)

McEwing, John 1828 wb-#105 (Mc)

McEwing, John 1839 wb-3-104 (Ma)

McFadden, A. V. 1853 wb-m-648 (Mt)
McFadden, D. 1834 rb-g-22 (Mt)
McFadden, David sr. 1838 rb-h-42 (Mt)
McFadden, Francis W. 1842 rb-12-258 (Ru)
McFadden, Guy 1836 wb-10-582 (D)
McFadden, Jame 1857 rb-o-513 (Mt)
McFadden, James 1815 wb-2-153 (Wi)
McFadden, Jane 1851 wb-14-626 (D)
McFadden, Jane 1858 wb-a-274 (T)
McFadden, John 1833 wb-x-38 (Mu)
McFadden, Mary Jane 1848 wb-9-148 (Wi)
McFadden, Robert 1823 wb-3-640 (Wi)
McFadden, Robt. W. 1840 rb-11-51 (Ru)
McFadden, Saml. 1848 rb-14-369 (Ru)
McFadden, Samuel 1838 wb-d-213* (Hn)
McFaddin, Andrew 1853 wb-n-24 (Mt)
McFaddin, Candour 1832 wb-5-140 (Wi)
McFaddin, David 1834 rb-g-77 (Mt)
McFaddin, David 1835 rb-g-221 (Mt)
McFaddin, David 1851 wb-m-255 (Mt)
McFaddin, David jr. 1836 rb-g-402 (Mt)
McFaddin, John 1848 rb-k-718 (Mt)
McFaddin, Joseph 1828 wb-1-105 (Bo)
McFaddin, Mary 1848 rb-l-154 (Mt)
McFaddin, Thos. 1849 wb-a-364 (F)
McFaden, Candie 1855 ib-h-297 (F)
McFaden, Candour 1847 wb-a-311 (F)
McFaden, Edward 1836 wb-x-292* (Mu)
McFall, Henry 1850 wb-m-15 (Mt)
McFall, John 1829 wb-#205 (Mu)
McFall, Martha 1848 wb-b-183 (Mu)
McFall, Sally A. S. 1852 wb-m-619 (Mt)
McFall, Sally Ann S. 1855 wb-n-671 (Mt)
McFall, Samuel 1859 rb-p-260 (Mt)
McFall, Zany 1852 wb-m-620 (Mt)
McFalls, Daniel 1861 wb-1-216 (R)
McFarland, Anderson 1855 wb-16-479 (D)
McFarland, Benjamin 1824 wb-2-388 (Je)
McFarland, Charles 1861 wb-13-475 (Wi)
McFarland, Daniel 1817 wb-a-73 (Wh)
McFarland, James 1797 rb-b-70 (Mt)
McFarland, James 1856 wb-#120 (Wl)
McFarland, John 1807 wb-1-276 (Je)
McFarland, John 1824 wb-#52 (Wl)
McFarland, John 1839 wb-#125 (Wl)
McFarland, John 1853 wb-11-1 (Wi)
McFarland, John 1856 wb-#119 (Wl)
McFarland, John B. 1845 wb-g-72 (Hn)
McFarland, Louis 1860 wb-8-37 (Sm)
McFarland, Mary 1853 148-1-448 (Ge)
McFarland, Mathew 1824 wb-a-223 (Ro)

McFarland, Nancy 1835 wb-#146 (Wl)
McFarland, Robert P. 1822 wb-8-111 (D)
McFarland, Robert sr. 1837 wb-3-432 (Je)
McFarland, Sarah 1844 rb-12-489 (Ru)
McFarland, William 1840 wb-1-399 (W)
McFarlane, John 1833 wb-1-354 (Ma)
McFarlen, Charles J. 1861 wb-13-421 (Wi)
McFarlin, Benjamin 1818 wb-A-213 (Li)
McFarlin, Benjamin 1829 rb-7-348 (Ru)
McFarlin, Crissa 1861 wb-#134 (Wl)
McFarlin, John 1844 wb-4-257 (Ma)
McFarlin, Sarah 1854 rb-17-35 (Ru)
McFarlin, Thomas 1796 wb-2-40 (D)
McFarlin, William 1824 rb-6-43 (Ru)
McFarlin, William 1837 rb-9-403 (Ru)
McFarling, Sarah M. 1856 rb-18-190 (Ru)
McFerran, James 1832 wb-1-83 (Li)
McFerren, John 1809 rb-2-68 (Ru)
McFerrin, James 1840 abl-1-206 (T)
McGahee, Edwin 1843 wb-c-116 (G)
McGan, Eli 1855 wb-11-564 (Wi)
McGarrah, Thomas 1822 wb-a-162 (Wh)
McGaugh, John M. 1854 wb-i-205 (O)
McGaugh, Mathew 1860 as-c-217 (Ms)
McGaugh, Thomas H. 1856 wb-2-168 (Li)
McGaugh, William 1790 wb-1-128 (D)
McGaugh, William W. 1844 as-a-75 (Ms)
McGaughey, David R. 1851 as-2-220 (Ge)
McGaughey, Jane R. 1851 as-2-220 (Ge)
McGaughey, Richard W. 1856 149-1-36 (Ge)
McGavock, David 1838 wb-11-492 (D)
McGavock, David 1842 wb-12-315* (D)
McGavock, Hugh W. 1854 wb-16-296 (D)
McGavock, Lucinda 1848 wb-9-121 (Wi)
McGavock, Lysander 1855 wb-11-579 (Wi)
McGavock, Randal 1843 wb-8-108 (Wi)
McGee, Andrew L. 1841 wb-c-108 (O)
McGee, Ann 1851 rb-4-247 (Mu)
McGee, Ann 1851 wb-4-156 (Mu)
McGee, Anthony W. 1854 wb-11-93 (Wi)
McGee, Charles W. 1855 wb-5-53 (Hr)
McGee, Chiles 1838 wb-y-283 (Mu)
McGee, Elizabeth 1828 wb-3-0 (Sm)
McGee, George 1821 wb-1-0 (Sm)
McGee, George 1831 wb-2-0 (Sm)
McGee, Harmon 1856 wb-a-276 (Cr)
McGee, James 1819 wb-1-0 (Sm)
McGee, James 1830 wb-2-0 (Sm)
McGee, John 1836 wb-3-0 (Sm)
McGee, John 1844 wb-3-111 (Hr)
McGee, John 1846 wb-4-40 (Hr)

McGee, John A. 1860 wb-e-361 (Wh)
McGee, Joseph 1812 wb-#7 (Mu)
McGee, Joseph 1857 wb-4-96 (La)
McGee, Martha 1846 wb-f-329 (St)
McGee, Micager 1854 ib-1-324 (Wy)
McGee, Samuel 1855 wb-e-363 (G)
McGee, Thompson 1855 wb-1-375 (Hw)
McGee, William 1832 wb-5-183 (Wi)
McGehee, A. F. 1856 wb-5-64 (Hr)
McGehee, E. M. 1858 wb-h-294 (Hn)
McGehee, Elijah 1858 wb-h-259 (Hn)
McGehee, Fountain 1843 wb-1-86 (Sh)
McGehee, George W. 1830 wb-9-411 (D)
McGehee, Milton M. 1846 wb-b-191 (We)
McGehee, Thomas 1834 rb-f-614 (Mt)
McGehee, Thomas jr. 1836 rb-g-427 (Mt)
McGehee, William 1849 wb-g-335 (Hn)
McGhee, B. 1856? wb-#12 (Mo)
McGhee, John 1849 wb-#7 (Mo)
McGhee, John Westley 1843 wb-c-101 (Wh)
McGhee, Matthew W. 1832 wb-#2 (Mo)
McGill, Isaac 1848 rb-14-241 (Ru)
McGill, James 1834 rb-9-75 (Ru)
McGill, James P. 1857 ib-1-438 (Ca)
McGill, John 1843 wb-3-47 (Hr)
McGill, John sr. 1848 mr-2-283 (Be)
McGill, Nancy 1840 wb-A-21 (Ca)
McGill, Nancy 1858 rb-19-285 (Ru)
McGill, Rebecca 1860 wb-1-332 (Be)
McGill, Robert 1846 wb-1-236 (Bo)
McGill, Samuel 1833 rb-9-63 (Ru)
McGill, Thomas 1838 mr-1-57 (Be)
McGill, Thomas 1858 wb-1-259 (Be)
McGilvray, William 1831 wb-5-22 (Wi)
McGimpsey, Thomas 1837 wb-y-109 (Mu)
McGimpsey, William 1832 wb-#243 (Mu)
McGimsey, John 1821 wb-#97 (Mu)
McGinness, Elizabeth 1860 wb-b-56 (Dk)
McGinness, Richard 1856 wb-b-13 (Dk)
McGinnis, Aaron 1857 wb-3-354 (Gr)
McGinnis, Aaron 1857 wb-4-2 (Gr)
McGinnis, John S. 1856 wb-1-45 (Dy)
McGinnis, L. 1845 wb-5-365 (Gr)
McGinnis, Lettiticea 1845 wb-5-350 (Gr)
McGinnis, Robert 1836 wb-1-114 (Gr)
McGinnis, Robert 1839 wb-1-19 (Me)
McGirk, John 1821 wb-2-311 (Je)
McGladey, Samuel 1829 wb-A-368 (Li)
McGlamery, John 1858 ib-2-30 (Wy)
McGlohn, James 1855 wb-6-17 (Ma)
McGlothlin, Joseph 1839 wb-2-255 (Sn)

McGolrick, E. E. 1861 wb-13-517 (K)
McGowan, Ebenezer 1852 rb-16-247 (Ru)
McGowan, Florinda C. 1851 wb#20 (Gu)
McGowan, Francis (Mrs.) 1853 rb-16-456 (Ru)
McGowan, Francis 1852 rb-16-336 (Ru)
McGowan, William B. 1854 rb-17-82 (Ru)
McGowen, James 1840 wb-b-416 (Wh)
McGowen, James 1845 wb-3-249 (Hr)
McGowen, L. D. 1853 wb#22 (Gu)
McGowen, Lucy 1861 rb-21-69 (Ru)
McGowen, Lucy A. 1859 rb-20-154 (Ru)
McGowen, Robert 1820 rb-c-269 (Mt)
McGowen, T. H. 1859 rb-20-155 (Ru)
McGowen, Thomas H. 1861 rb-21-69 (Ru)
McGowen, William 1845 wb-f-283 (Hn)
McGowin, Andrew 1849 wb#19 (Gu)
McGown, John 1793 wb-1-71 (Je)
McGown, Margaret W. 1831 wb-1-96 (Fr)
McGraw, Lewis 1827 wb-#162 (Mu)
McGraw, Michael 1859 iv-C-47 (C)
McGree, Isabella 1835 wb-#130 (Wl)
McGreger, William 1839 wb-1-273 (W)
McGreggar, Bartlett 1843 wb-e-241 (St)
McGregor, Albert 1857 wb-a-250 (T)
McGregor, Ezekiel 1856 wb-3-302 (W)
McGregor, Flower 1849 wb-#164 (Wl)
McGregor, John 1835 rb-9-270 (Ru)
McGregor, John 1847 rb-14-188 (Ru)
McGregor, N? 1852 wb-3-134 (W)
McGregor, Nancy 1855 wb-3-241 (W)
McGregor, Sarah 1859 as-c-200 (Ms)
McGregor, Wm. 1855 as-b-202 (Ms)
McGrigor, Milberry 1846 rb-13-465 (Ru)
McGuiggin, Terrence A. 1822 wb-8-73 (D)
McGuire, Cornelius 1809 wb-1-335 (Je)
McGuire, Cornelius 1824 wb-2-482 (Je)
McGuire, David 1837 wb-2-241 (Ma)
McGuire, Francis 1848 rb-k-748 (Mt)
McGuire, James 1855 wb-6-74 (Ma)
McGuire, John 1803 wb-1-100 (Sn)
McGuire, John 1835 rb-g-108 (Mt)
McGuire, John 1835 rb-g-245 (Mt)
McGuire, Patrick 1831 wb-3-164 (Je)
McGuown, James W. 1853 wb-1-80 (Jo)
McHaffie, Andrew 1848 wb-9-436 (K)
McHaffie, Catherine 1859 wb-13-144 (K)
McHaffie, John 1832 wb-5-144 (K)
McHaffie, John sr. 1828 wb-4-322 (K)
McHaney, Andrew 1826 wb-#66 (Wl)
McHenry, Elizabeth 1858 wb-#124 (Wl)
McHenry, Jesse 1833 wb-#101 (Wl)

McHenry, John 1823 rb-5-332 (Ru)
McHenry, William 1855 ib-2-93 (Cl)
McHughs, Moses 1804 wb-1-133 (Wi)
McIlherian, John 1843 wb-1-214 (Fr)
McIlwain, Henry 1829 wb-9-276 (D)
McIlwin, James M. 1827 wb-1-104 (Ma)
McIndoe, Robert 1839 wb-11-569 (D)
McIntire, Ann 1820? wb-#43 (Mu)
McIntire, James 1844 wb-f-208 (St)
McIntire, James jr. 1828 wb-b-3 (Ro)
McIntire, James sr. 1828 wb-b-7 (Ro)
McIntire, John 1841 wb-z-232 (Mu)
McIntosh, Abel 1835 wb-2-45# (Ge)
McIntosh, Alexander 1799 wb-1-39 (Rb)
McIntosh, Anderson 1856 wb-16-288 (Rb)
McIntosh, Andrew 1855 wb-15-725 (Rb)
McIntosh, Candes 1857 wb-16-367 (Rb)
McIntosh, Charles 1836 wb-9-290 (Rb)
McIntosh, Charles 1854 wb-15-675 (Rb)
McIntosh, Donald 1837 wb-6-143 (K)
McIntosh, John 1836 wb-9-217 (Rb)
McIntosh, John 1860 wb-18-170 (D)
McIntosh, Mary 1843 wb-11-363 (Rb)
McIntosh, Nimrod 1844 wb-12-248 (Rb)
McIntosh, Thomas 1838 wb-d-193 (St)
McInturff, Christopher 1814 lw (Ct)
McInturff, John 1847 lw (Ct)
McInturff, John sr. 1811 lw (Ct)
McIntyer, John 1839 abl-1-131 (T)
McIntyre, Anney 1824 wb-#76 (Mu)
McIntyre, Charles 1855 wb-n-690 (Mt)
McIntyre, Daniel 1829 wb-1-2 (La)
McIver, Donald 1843 wb-4-101 (Ma)
McIver, Evander 1828 rb-7-118 (Ru)
McIver, Evander 1828 rb-7-283 (Ru)
McIver, John 1830 rb-8-153 (Ru)
McIver, John 1840 rb-11-25 (Ru)
McIver, John 1853 wb-16-203 (D)
McIver, Matilda 1856 wb-6-388 (Ma)
McKaig, John 1834 wb-1-76 (W)
McKain, John 1816 wb-7-42 (D)
McKamey, Andrew 1852 wb-1B-304 (A)
McKamey, Robert 1861 149-1-214 (Ge)
McKamey, William 1840 wb-1A-259 (A)
McKamy, Barton 1854 wb-1C-130 (A)
McKamy, Elizabeth 1854 wb-1C-169 (A)
McKamy, James 1826 wb-#105 (Mc)
McKamy, John 1830 wb-b-74 (Ro)
McKamy, John 1834 wb-b-230 (Ro)
McKamy, John P. 1855 wb-1C-229 (A)
McKamy, John P. 1859 wb-1C-478 (A)

McKamy, Robert H. 1852 wb-e-362 (Ro)
McKamy, William 1860 wb-#106 (Mc)
McKamy, William C. 1845 wb-d-195 (Ro)
McKaskill, Taylor 1844 wb-3-156 (Hr)
McKaughan, Forester 1848 wb-4-308 (Hr)
McKaughn, Christian 1849 wb-4-511 (Hr)
McKaw, Wm. 1809 wb-4-58 (D)
McKay, David 1837 rb-9-402 (Ru)
McKay, Dickinson 1846 wb-13-404 (D)
McKay, Duncan 1849 wb-14-399 (D)
McKay, Francis 1828 wb-9-177 (D)
McKay, George 1855 wb-1-106 (Bo)
McKay, Henry 1856 lr (Gi)
McKay, James M. 1836 wb-6-259 (Wi)
McKay, Mary 1846 wb-8-481 (Wi)
McKay, Mary 1854 wb-16-413 (D)
McKay, Milton R. 1839 wb-7-29 (Wi)
McKay, William 1836 wb-6-117 (Wi)
McKean, Robert 1812 wb-#4 (Mu)
McKee, Alexander 1812 wb-#13 (Wa)
McKee, Daniel 1837 wb-#119 (Wl)
McKee, Daniel 1855 as-b-182 (Ms)
McKee, Herndon 1833 wb-x-53 (Mu)
McKee, Jacob 1820? wb-#40 (Mu)
McKee, James 1819 wb-#44 (Mu)
McKee, James 1829 wb-a-131 (G)
McKee, James 1846 wb-a-291 (F)
McKee, John 1860 wb-2-91# (Ge)
McKee, Leven 1815 wb-#18 (Wl)
McKee, Lewis 1815 wb-#16 (Wl)
McKee, Robert 1808 wb-#7 (Wl)
McKee, Robert 1859 wb-#62 (Wa)
McKee, Samuel 1834 wb-x-174 (Mu)
McKee, William 1829 wb-b-53 (Hn)
McKeehan, James 1805 wb-1-18# (Ge)
McKeehen, James 1805 as-1-132 (Ge)
McKeen, A. D. 1840 wb-b-19 (We)
McKeen, Alexander 1825 rb-6-166 (Ru)
McKeen, J. H. 1831 rb-8-262 (Ru)
McKeen, John 1840 wb-z-72 (Mu)
McKeen, John H. 1836 rb-9-114* (Ru)
McKehen, John 1849 148-1-277 (Ge)
McKelvy, George 1853 mr-2-522 (Be)
McKelvy, Wm. 1850 wb-d-282 (G)
McKendree, Nancy D. 1842 lr (Sn)
McKendrie, William 1835 wb-2-191 (Sn)
McKenney, Samuel 1820 wb-2-44# (Ge)
McKenney, Samuel 1835 wb-2-52# (Ge)
McKenni?, Michl. 1842 wb-2-395 (Hr)
McKennie, William 1816 rb-b-363 (Mt)
McKennie, Zanina H. 1856 wb-17-273 (D)

McKennon, Daniel 1844 wb-f-187 (St)
McKeny, William C. 1836 wb-3-387 (Je)
McKenzie, Benjamin 1854 wb-2-242 (Me)
McKenzie, James 1831 wb-1-201 (Hr)
McKenzie, Mark 1848 wb-#6 (Mo)
McKenzie, Mary A. 1861 wb-#19 (Mo)
McKeon, Miles 1845 wb-13-192 (D)
McKeon, Nicholas 1843 wb-1-95 (Sh)
McKeown, Green B. 1854 wb-e-163 (G)
McKey, William 1837 wb-1-231 (W)
McKibben, John 1840 wb-z-68 (Mu)
McKillop, Ann 1820 wb-#17 (Wa)
McKinley, Samuel 1845 wb-9-35 (K)
McKinne, Charlotte 1861 wb-5-122 (Hr)
McKinne, Michael 1840 wb-2-178 (Hr)
McKinne, Sol. P. 1844 wb-3-109 (Hr)
McKinney, Andrew Thompson 1852 wb-#8 (Mo)
McKinney, David 1821 wb-#106 (Mc)
McKinney, Ebenezer 1816 wb-2-239 (Wi)
McKinney, Elisha 1857 wb-f-121 (Ro)
McKinney, George 1834 wb-4-30 (Je)
McKinney, James 1853 wb-2-61 (Li)
McKinney, Jeremiah 1816 wb-#23 (Wl)
McKinney, Joel T. 1850 wb-4-54 (Je)
McKinney, John 1816 wb-2-226 (Wi)
McKinney, John 1840 wb-7-313 (Wi)
McKinney, John 1848 wb-1-338 (Li)
McKinney, John V. 1849 wb-1-366 (Li)
McKinney, Joseph 1850 wb-g-287 (St)
McKinney, L. D. 1848 as-a-155 (Ms)
McKinney, Lucinda 1859 wb-4-271 (La)
McKinney, M. F. 1858 wb-4-181 (La)
McKinney, Randolph 1827 wb-4-269 (Wi)
McKinney, Robert 1817 wb-3-264 (St)
McKinney, Vincent 1833 wb-3-238 (Je)
McKinney, Willie 1856 wb-7-0 (Sm)
McKinnie, Arthur 1843 wb-3-108 (Hr)
McKinnie, John 1844 wb-3-194 (Hr)
McKinnie, John R. 1834 wb-1-354 (Hr)
McKinnie, P. 1848 wb-4-356 (Hr)
McKinnie, Solomon P. 1855 wb-5-54 (Hr)
McKinnie, William 1853 wb-5-42 (Hr)
McKinnis, Alexander 1840 wb-3-0 (Sm)
McKinnon, Elizabeth 1847 wb-b-102 (Mu)
McKinnon, Niel 1840 wb-2-155 (Hy)
McKinny, Jeremiah 1826 wb-#64 (Wl)
McKinny, John 1821 wb-a-145 (Ro)
McKinny, Robert 1830 wb-c-65 (St)
McKinrie, W. P. 1859 wb-5-92 (Hr)
McKinzie, J. H. 1858 wb-f-146 (G)
McKissack, Arabella 1855 wb-f-68 (Mu)

McKissick, Alfred 1860 wb-h-472 (Hn)
McKissick, Arabella 1856 wb-f-103 (Mu)
McKlemurray, Lewis 1847 wb-2-1 (Sh)
McKlin, P. 1829 wb-a-138 (G)
McKnight, Alexander 1859 wb-A-148 (Ca)
McKnight, Alfred W. no date lr (Gi)
McKnight, David 1809 wb-#8 (Wl)
McKnight, David 1842 wb-A-28 (Ca)
McKnight, David 1851 wb-2-102 (Sh)
McKnight, Eleanor 1828 rb-7-337 (Ru)
McKnight, Eliza Y. 1859 rb-20-152 (Ru)
McKnight, Elizabeth 1827 wb-1-115 (Ma)
McKnight, Ellenor 1848 rb-14-388 (Ru)
McKnight, James 1822 rb-5-220 (Ru)
McKnight, John 1815 wb-2-113 (Je)
McKnight, John 1823 rb-5-327 (Ru)
McKnight, John 1838 lr (Gi)
McKnight, John 1857 as-c-29 (Ms)
McKnight, John J. 1844 wb-c-197 (G)
McKnight, John M. 1844 wb-A-38 (Ca)
McKnight, Joseph 1845 wb-c-261 (G)
McKnight, Margaret R. 1852 wb-2-133 (Sh)
McKnight, Moses 1849 wb-A-64 (Ca)
McKnight, Robert M. 1848 mr-2-284 (Be)
McKnight, Samuel 1837 lr (Gi)
McKnight, Samuel A. 1856 wb-3-332 (W)
McKnight, Samuel F. 1841 rb-12-52 (Ru)
McKnight, Samuel Folle 1841 rb-12-99 (Ru)
McKnight, Silas M. 1843 wb-c-112 (G)
McKnight, William 1806 wb-1-148 (Wi)
McKnight, William 1831 rb-8-328 (Ru)
McKnight, William 1840 rb-11-15 (Ru)
McKnight, William 1857 wb-6-492 (Ma)
McKnight, William F. 1841 wb-c-8 (G)
McLain, Charles 1846 wb-b-154 (We)
McLain, Dorcas 1840 wb-7-220 (Wi)
McLain, Elizabeth 1856 wb-2-104# (Ge)
McLain, Jane 1841 wb-7-426 (Wi)
McLain, John 1846 wb-b-145 (We)
McLain, Joseph 1826 wb-4-169 (K)
McLain, Robert 1807 wb-1-231 (K)
McLain, Temperance 1841 wb-f-10 (Hn)
McLain, William 1818 wb-#30 (Wl)
McLamore, Abram 1844 wb-c-201 (G)
McLamore, Abram 1846 wb-c-335 (G)
McLanahan, Sarah 1858 rb-19-524 (Ru)
McLane, Findlay 1843 wb-a-109 (T)
McLaren, John 1850 wb-2-137 (La)
McLaren, John sr. 1841 wb-1-360 (La)
McLaren, Robert 1860 wb-4-384 (La)
McLaren, Sarah 1853 wb-3-137 (La)

McLarey, John 1837 wb-b-151 (G)
McLarin, Archibald 1829 wb-9-298 (D)
McLarin, John W. H. 1838 wb-#121 (Wl)
McLarne, James 1827 wb-a-242 (Wh)
McLary, Andrew 1832 wb-a-217 (G)
McLary, Emaly 1847 wb-d-105 (G)
McLary, James 1845 wb-c-242 (G)
McLary, Robert 1846 5-3-99 (Cl)
McLaughlin, John 1848 wb-14-260 (D)
McLaughlin, William H. 1854 wb-16-328 (D)
McLaughlon, Joseph 1814 rb-2-300 (Ru)
McLaurine, George W. 1832 wb-9-577 (D)
McLaurine, Robert 1846 lr (Gi)
McLaurine, Willis S. 1861 lr (Gi)
McLean (McClain?), Joseph 1827 wb-#106 (Mc)
McLean, Archibald 1840 wb-1-63 (Sh)
McLean, Charles 1826 rb-6-260 (Ru)
McLean, Charles 1847 rb-14-203 (Ru)
McLean, Charles G. 1853 rb-16-672 (Ru)
McLean, Daniel 1859 wb-f-258 (G)
McLean, Ephraim (Jr.) 1824 wb-#79 (Mu)
McLean, Ephraim 1833 wb-x-120 (Mu)
McLean, Henry M. 1842 wb-a-81 (Ms)
McLean, John 1831 wb-#222 (Mu)
McLean, John 1840 wb-2-171 (Hr)
McLean, Joseph 1839 wb-e-32 (Hn)
McLean, Laughlen 1816 wb-7-66 (D)
McLean, Lauhlin 1816 wb-4-469 (D)
McLean, Lewis 1854 rb-17-321 (Ru)
McLean, Marcia F. 1821 rb-c-494 (Mt)
McLean, Mary Ann 1829 wb-1-182 (Ma)
McLean, Peggy 1814 wb-#29 (Mu)
McLean, R. J. 1836 wb-1-124 (La)
McLean, Samuel 1823 wb-#58 (Mu)
McLean, Samuel 1850 wb-2-123 (La)
McLean, Sarah 1847 rb-14-202 (Ru)
McLean, William (Dr.) 1833 wb-8-202 (Rb)
McLean, William 1816 wb-#33 (Mu)
McLean, William 1826 wb-#142 (Mu)
McLean, William E. 1857 rb-18-626 (Ru)
McLearen, Daniel 1838 wb-1-164 (La)
McLeary, James 1851 wb-d-311 (G)
McLelland, John 1852 wb-15-329 (D)
McLemore, Atkins J. 1849 wb-9-303 (Wi)
McLemore, Atkins Jefferson 1805 wb-3-15 (D)
McLemore, Bethenia S. 1857 wb-12-429 (Wi)
McLemore, Edward 1829 wb-#176 (Mu)
McLemore, Edward J. 1826 wb-#151 (Mu)
McLemore, John 1844 wb-9-18 (K)
McLemore, Robert 1823 wb-3-625 (Wi)
McLemore, Robert 1836 wb-6-119 (Wi)

McLemore, Sally 1846 wb-c-346 (G)
McLemore, Sidney Smith 1860 wb-13-197 (Wi)
McLemore, Young 1804 wb-1-10 (Wi)
McLemore, Young 1823 wb-3-661 (Wi)
McLemore, Young 1824 wb-3-749 (Wi)
McLendon, Simon 1809 wb-4-44 (D)
McLeod, D. C. 1840 wb-a-48 (F)
McLeod, Olive 1857 wb-b-34 (Ms)
McLeroy, Isaac 1830 wb-2-38 (Fr)
McLery, Robert 1838 wb-b-236 (G)
McLester, W. W. 1854 wb-#106 (Mc)
McLin, Alexander 1820 wb-#23 (Wa)
McLin, Benjamin 1849 wb-#44 (Wa)
McLin, James 1820 rb-4-259 (Ru)
McLin, James Z. 1856 lr (Gi)
McLin, John 1849 lr (Sn)
McLin, John A. 1839 rb-10-360 (Ru)
McLin, Robert 1841 rb-11-205 (Ru)
McLin, Sarah 1851 wb-14-581 (D)
McLin, William 1825 wb-1-102 (Bo)
McLin, Wm. E. 1852 rb-16-151 (Ru)
McLoud, David 1855 wb-g-694 (Hn)
McLoud, Duncan 1838 wb-e-66 (Hu)
McLure, John H. 1860? wb-a-359 (Cr)
McLurkin, Robert 1840 abl-1-195 (T)
McMackin, Andrew 1853 wb-3-168 (La)
McMackin, Elizabeth S. 1853 mr-2-523 (Be)
McMackin, James 1821 wb-1-19# (Ge)
McMackin, Thomas sr. 1821 wb-1-19# (Ge)
McMackin, William 1860 149-1-174 (Ge)
McMackins, Michael 1841 wb-e-428 (Hu)
McMahan, Caswell 1835 wb-#106 (Mc)
McMahan, Daniel 1838 wb-7-3 (Wi)
McMahan, Esther & Mary Jane 1841
  wb-#107 (Mc)
McMahan, Francis 1838 wb-1-42 (Sh)
McMahan, James 1854 wb-16-385 (D)
McMahan, James A. 1832 wb-1-265 (Hr)
McMahan, James F. 1837 wb-b-64 (Hd)
McMahan, John Sr. 1837 wb-#107 (Mc)
McMahan, Seletha C. 1836 wb-a-55 (Cr)
McMahan, William R. 1824 wb-3-483 (K)
McMahan, William W. 1833 wb-1-296 (Hr)
McMahen, James 1815 wb-#19 (Mu)
McMahon, Andrew 1820 wb-#36 (Wl)
McMahon, Jas. A. 1849 wb-4-437 (Hr)
McManis, David 1845 rb-j-417 (Mt)
McMannery, John 1803 wb-1-65 (Sn)
McManus, James 1816 wb-4-472 (D)
McManus, John 1848 wb-b-308 (Mu)
McManus, Joseph 1831 wb-#107 (Mc)

McManus, William C. 1829? wb-#173 (Mu)
McMarth, John 1842 wb-a-40 (V)
McMasters, Hannah 1852 wb-2-273 (La)
McMasters, John 1834 wb-1-53 (La)
McMasters, John 1848 wb-2-42 (La)
McMasters, Jonathan 1840 wb-1-209 (La)
McMeans, John 1806 wb-3-132 (D)
McMeans, John 1838 wb-y-245* (Mu)
McMeans, Thomas 1807 wb-1-281 (Je)
McMeens, Mary M. 1849 wb-b-459 (Mu)
McMenaway, Alexander 1840 wb-#128 (Wl)
McMillan, Alexander 1837 wb-6-133 (K)
McMillan, Alexander 1855 wb-12-78 (K)
McMillan, Andrew 1838 wb-6-276 (K)
McMillan, Andrew 1849 wb-10-277 (K)
McMillan, Barbary 1845 wb-9-97 (K)
McMillan, Catharine 1828 wb-b-294 (St)
McMillan, Daniel 1814 wb-a-224 (St)
McMillan, Hugh 1847 wb-f-452 (St)
McMillan, J. D. 1858 wb-13-81 (K)
McMillan, John 1842 wb-7-355 (K)
McMillan, John 1845 wb-#149 (Wl)
McMillan, John D. 1858 wb-12-538 (K)
McMillan, Murdoch 1840 wb-1-62 (Sh)
McMillan, Robert 1822 wb-1-8 (Ma)
McMillan, Susan 1842 wb-7-316 (K)
McMillan, Thomas 1857 wb-12-423 (K)
McMillan, Thomas 1858 wb-13-60 (K)
McMillan, Thomas A. 1851 wb-11-13 (K)
McMillan, Thomas A. A. 1849 wb-10-150 (K)
McMillan, William 1842 wb-7-362 (K)
McMillen, Alexander 1860 wb-f-183 (Mu)
McMillen, Jane 1854 wb-2-167 (Sh)
McMillen, John 1814 wb-2-75 (K)
McMillen, John 1844 wb-1-246 (Li)
McMillen, Joseph 1859 wb-2-267 (Li)
McMillen, Martha 1828 wb-1-21 (Li)
McMillen, William 1817 wb-A-202 (Li)
McMillin, David 1827 wb-#107 (Mc)
McMillin, Robert W. 1825 wb-#107 (Mc)
McMillin, Thomas 1859 wb-3-554 (Gr)
McMillin, Thomas 1859 wb-4-18 (Gr)
McMillin, William 1794 wb-0-7 (K)
McMillion, Malcomb 1840 wb-e-342 (Hu)
McMillon, Andrew 1837 wb-#118 (Wl)
McMinas, Lawrence 1823 wb-#52 (Mu)
McMinn, Jehu 1836 wb-#136 (Wl)
McMinn, John 1837 wb-b-150 (G)
McMinn, Joseph 1824 wb-1-349 (Hw)
McMinn, Joseph 1835 wb-#107 (Mc)
McMinn, Nancy 1858 wb-17-477 (D)

McMinn, Robert 1845 wb-13-264 (D)
McMonin, Dominic 1802 wb-2-230 (D)
McMordie, Robert 1859 rb-p-278 (Mt)
McMorris, Alexander 1854 as-b-165 (Ms)
McMorris, Newton 1857 as-c-17 (Ms)
McMoss, Abram 1836 wb-6-118 (Wi)
McMullen, Andrew 1802 Wb-1-101 (Wi)
McMullen, James 1839 wb-c-29 (Ro)
McMullen, John C. 1860 wb-3-46 (Me)
McMullin, James 1828 wb-b-47 (Ro)
McMullin, John 1798 wb-1-65 (K)
McMullin, John 1858 wb-2-422 (Me)
McMullin, Marinda 1837 wb-#117 (Wl)
McMullin, William 1794 wb-1-28 (K)
McMunn, William 1837 wb-1A-164 (A)
McMurray, Charles 1845 wb-13-267 (D)
McMurray, David 1843 wb-11-363 (Rb)
McMurray, Elizabeth 1855 wb-16-40 (Rb)
McMurray, Jacob 1845 wb-12-460 (Rb)
McMurray, John 1852 wb-10-429 (Wi)
McMurray, Samuel 1859 wb-16-740 (Rb)
McMurray, Washington 1833 as-a-239 (Di)
McMurry, Archie D. 1861 wb-8-0 (Sm)
McMurry, Charles 1820 wb-1-0 (Sm)
McMurry, David 1840 wb-#132 (Wl)
McMurry, James 1845 wb-3-45 (Sn)
McMurry, James M. 1838 wb-#124 (Wl)
McMurry, John 1820 wb-1-314 (Sn)
McMurry, John C. 1847 lr (Sn)
McMurry, John L. 1844 wb-3-402 (Hy)
McMurry, Samuel 1819 wb-1-188 (Bo)
McMurry, Samuel 1827 rb-7-79 (Ru)
McMurry, Samuel 1828 wb-6-387 (Rb)
McMurry, Samuel 1839 wb-11-547 (D)
McMurry, Samuel 1856 lr (Sn)
McMurry, Thomas 1855 as-c-401 (Di)
McMurry, W. W. 1860 lr (Gi)
McMurry, William 1842 wb-12-295* (D)
McMurry, Wm. 1851 as-c-117 (Di)
McMurtry, James 1851 as-2-212 (Ge)
McMurtry, John 1841 wb-2-278 (Sn)
McMurtry, John 1846 148-1-176 (Ge)
McMury, James 1829 rb-7-257 (Ru)
McNabb, Baptist 1784 wb-#2 (Wa)
McNabb, D. 1826 lw (Ct)
McNabb, Elizabeth 1848 wb-#107 (Mc)
McNabb, James 1861 wb-#108 (Mc)
McNabb, L. D. 1861 wb-13-446 (K)
McNabb, William 1809 lw (Ct)
McNail, E. H. 1859 wb-f-282 (G)
McNair, Ann 1852 wb-e-349 (Ro)

McNair, James 1817 wb-2-351 (K)
McNair, Price 1816 wb-2-272 (K)
McNair, W. B. 1860 wb-17-64 (Rb)
McNair, William B. 1860 wb-17-100 (Rb)
McNairy, Boyd 1857 wb-17-369 (D)
McNairy, Francis 1812 wb-4-171 (D)
McNairy, James 1844 wb-13-123 (D)
McNairy, John 1838 wb-11-297 (D)
McNairy, John N. 1845 wb-13-318 (D)
McNairy, John S. 1851 wb-14-661 (D)
McNairy, Nathaniel A. 1852 wb-15-309 (D)
McNairy, Robert 1831 lr (Gi)
McNally, Michael 1859 wb-18-172 (D)
McNamara, Bryan M. 1854 wb-16-245 (D)
McNamara, John M. 1859 wb-3e-110 (Sh)
McNamara, Michael 1853 wb-2-142 (Sh)
McNamarra, Patrick 1820 wb-3-207 (K)
McNare, Martha 1817 wb-2-354 (K)
McNatt, Charles 1847 wb-2-2 (Li)
McNatt, David 1825 wb-b-25 (St)
McNatt, John 1848 wb-e-110 (Ro)
McNatt, Lucretia 1855 wb-e-527 (Ro)
McNatt, Mackey 1813 wb-a-140 (St)
McNatt, Matthew 1812 wb-a-139 (St)
McNatt, Solomon 1838 wb-d-262 (St)
McNeal, Clanssee? 1847 wb-4-148 (Hr)
McNeal, Clarasa 1847 wb-4-195 (Hr)
McNeal, Hector 1815 wb-1-0 (Sm)
McNeal, James 1859 gs-1-487 (F)
McNeal, Joseph 1821 wb-3-314 (Rb)
McNeal, Thomas 1830 wb-1-152 (Hr)
McNeal, Thomas 1847 wb-4-178 (Hr)
McNeece, Samuel 1860 149-1-196 (Ge)
McNeel, Miles M. 1850 wb-g-386 (Hu)
McNeel, Neel 1852 mr-2-457 (Be)
McNeeley, James 1844 wb-d-181 (O)
McNeeley, Mary 1834 wb-1-340 (Hr)
McNeely, Alexander 1816 wb-#23 (Wl)
McNeely, Elizabeth 1835? wb-#163 (Wl)
McNeely, Enoch 1831 wb-#91 (Wl)
McNeely, Enoch 1848 wb-#163 (Wl)
McNeely, James 1816 wb-#22 (Wl)
McNeely, Margaret 1824 wb-#56 (Wl)
McNeely, Michael 1840 wb-b-3 (We)
McNeely, Moses 1819 wb-#30 (Wl)
McNeely, Rebecca 1855 wb-6-75 (Ma)
McNeely, Robert 1817 wb-1-0 (Sm)
McNeely, Sarah 1832 wb-#96 (Wl)
McNeely, Seth 1822 wb-#42 (Wl)
McNeely, William 1814 wb-#14 (Wl)
McNees, Charity 1859 wb-2-96# (Ge)

McNees, Isaiah 1818 wb-1-19# (Ge)
McNees, Samuel 1838 wb-2-50# (Ge)
McNees, Samuel 1840 148-1-2 (Ge)
McNeese, James 1841 148-1-13 (Ge)
McNeese, James 1841 lr (Gi)
McNeese, Jonas 1845 wb-2-62# (Ge)
McNeese, Richard H. 1852 wb-5-33 (Hr)
McNeese, Samuel 1850 148-1-333 (Ge)
McNeese, William 1808 ib-1-253 (Ge)
McNeice, Samuel 1837 wb-1-273 (Gr)
McNeil, Archibald 1842 wb-2-558 (Hy)
McNeil, John 1838 wb-11-146 (D)
McNeil, Lemuel S. 1827 wb-4-174 (Wi)
McNeill, Alexr. 1857 wb-b-41 (F)
McNeill, Call 1827 wb-9-94 (D)
McNeill, John 1833 wb-5-255 (K)
McNeill, Joseph 1839 wb-10-222 (Rb)
McNeill, Joseph 1839 wb-10-284 (Rb)
McNeill, Neill 1821 wb-3-263 (Rb)
McNeill, Sarah 1851 wb-2-175 (La)
McNeill, Thomas J. 1841 wb-11-65 (Rb)
McNeill, William 1844 wd-13-42 (D)
McNelley, George H. 1854 wb-15-506 (Rb)
McNew, William 1839 5-2-94 (Cl)
McNew, William 1850 148-1-318 (Ge)
McNew, William 1856 ib-2-344 (Cl)
McNichols, Samuel 1846 rb-k-142 (Mt)
McNut, Susannah 1853 wb-#52 (Wa)
McNutt, Anthony 1818 wb-#16 (Wa)
McNutt, Benjamin 1855 wb-12-162 (K)
McNutt, George 1823 wb-3-407 (K)
McNutt, George A. 1824 wb-4-34 (K)
McNutt, James 1853 wb-11-356 (K)
McNutt, Martha 1855 wb-12-75 (K)
McNutt, Melinda H. 1849 wb-10-106 (K)
McNutt, Robert 1831 wb-5-40 (K)
McNutt, Thomas 1825 wb-1-0 (Sm)
McNutt, William 1794 wb-1-28 (K)
McNutt, William F. 1810 lr (Sn)
McOrd, William 1826 wb-#133 (Mu)
McPeak, Eliza A. 1857 rb-19-120 (Ru)
McPeak, James 1853 rb-16-651 (Ru)
McPeak, John 1853 rb-16-653 (Ru)
McPearn, Elizabeth 1848 wb-2-65# (Ge)
McPearson?, James 1827 wb-a-291 (Wh)
McPhail, Daniel 1846 wb-8-492 (Wi)
McPhail, Mary, Neil, & Doug. 1851
    wb-#109 (Mc)
McPhail, Sarah 1851 wb-10-48 (Wi)
McPheran, John 1821 wb-1-19# (Ge)
McPheran, William 1822 wb-1-19# (Ge)

McPheron, Andrew 1845 wb-2-62# (Ge)
McPheron, Samuel 1848 wb-2-68# (Ge)
McPherson, Cornelius 1838 wb-7-18 (Wi)
McPherson, Daniel 1846 wb-d-211 (Ro)
McPherson, Elizabeth 1854 wb-e-169 (G)
McPherson, George 1806 wb-a-9 (Ro)
McPherson, Henry 1817 wb-a-97 (Ro)
McPherson, Jonathan 1815 Wb-2-168 (Wi)
McPherson, Thomas 1857 wb-3e-47 (Sh)
McQueen, Barbary 1851 wb-1-86 (Jo)
McQueen, Thomas 1850 wb-1-60 (Jo)
McQueen, William 1860 wb-1-132 (Jo)
McQuiston, Archibald 1839 abl-1-159 (T)
McRae, Duncan 1814 wb-a-202 (St)
McRae, Lucinda 1859 as-c-158 (Ms)
McRae, Wm. 1855 rb-17-529 (Ru)
McRee, James 1850 wb-1-392 (Li)
McReynold, John 1822 wb-1-194 (Bo)
McReynold, Joseph sr. 1825 wb-1-100 (Bo)
McReynolds, Joseph 1852? wb-#24 (Mo)
McReynolds, Robert 1858 wb-#13 (Mo)
McSpadden, Archibald 1830 wb-3-112 (Je)
McSpadden, Cynthia 1855 ib-2-191 (Cl)
McSpadden, Esther 1835 wb-3-346 (Je)
McSpadden, Isabella 1837 wb-3-493 (Je)
McSpadden, James 1825 wb-2-460 (Je)
McSpadden, John 1799 wb-1-249 (Je)
McSpadden, Mathew 1847 wb-#6 (Mo)
McSwan, John 1838 wb-6-176 (K)
McSwine, John 1815 wb-2-150 (Wi)
McTeer, James 1825 wb-1-100 (Bo)
McTeer, Martin 1845 wb-1-102 (Bo)
McTeer, Robert 1823 wb-1-101 (Bo)
McTeer, William 1848 wb-1-110 (Bo)
McVey, E. W. 1836 wb-d-132 (Hn)
McVey, O. B. 1844 wb-f-286 (Hn)
McWherter, B. F. 1850 wb-g-321 (O)
McWherter, Benjamin F. 1852 wb-h-May (O)
McWherter, George 1847 wb-d-314 (Hd)
McWherter, Reuben 1849 wb-g-208 (O)
McWhirter, George M. 1836 wb-#116 (Wl)
McWhirter, Mary 1817 wb-7-167 (D)
McWhirter, William M. 1846 wb-c-329 (G)
McWhirton, S. C. (Dr.) 1856 rb-18-123 (Ru)
McWhorter, George H. 1857 as-c-31 (Ms)
McWhorter, James 1831 wb-#30 (Wa)
McWhorter, Jeremiah 1828 wb-a-111 (G)
McWilliams, Andrew 1835 wb-10-402 (D)
McWilliams, Hugh 1832 wb-a-229 (G)
McWilliams, Hugh 1844 wb-c-175 (G)
McWilliams, James 1850 wb-5-79 (Ma)

McWilliams, Jesse 1813 wb-1-342 (Hw)
McWilliams, John 1788 wb-1-74 (Je)
McWilliams, John 1855 wb-1-374 (Hw)
McWilliams, Martha 1819 wb-1-345 (Hw)
McWirter, S. C. 1856 rb-18-100 (Ru)
Mccollum, John 1843 148-1-56 (Ge)
Mcguire, Joseph 1839 wb-3-539 (Je)
Mcwhorter, Aaron 1837 wb-1-145 (Li)
Meacham, Elizabeth 1841 wb-3-463 (Ma)
Meacham, Elizabeth G. 1857 wb-7-8 (Ma)
Meacham, Green 1852 wb-10-423 (Wi)
Meacham, J. B. 1856 rb-o-92 (Mt)
Meacham, James 1846 rb-k-275 (Mt)
Meacham, James 1851 wb-10-35 (Wi)
Meacham, John 1860 rb-p-407 (Mt)
Meacham, John L. 1859 rb-p-284 (Mt)
Meacham, John S. 1860 rb-p-386 (Mt)
Meacham, Samuel L. 1838 wb-2-348 (Ma)
Mead, Martha 1851 wb-15-173 (D)
Mead, Michael 1852 wb-15-369 (D)
Mead, Stithe H. 1850? wb-2-28 (Li)
Mead, William 1831 wb-b-117 (Ro)
Mead, William 1839? wb-#35 (Wa)
Mead, William O. 1838 wb-c-16 (Ro)
Mead, William O. 1847 wb-e-5 (Ro)
Meador, Frances 1851 lr (Sn)
Meador, Jesse 1853 lr (Sn)
Meador, Jonas jr. 1815 wb-1-0 (Sm)
Meador, Joseph 1832 wb-5-156 (Wi)
Meador, Joseph R. 1848 wb-9-34 (Wi)
Meador, Sucky 1823 wb-1-0 (Sm)
Meador, William 1840 wb-7-297 (Wi)
Meadow, William 1837 wb-6-362 (Wi)
Meadows, Anderson 1827 wb-4-215 (Wi)
Meadows, James 1849 wb-g-154 (O)
Meadows, Jane 1849 wb-g-48 (O)
Meadows, Jeremiah 1854 wb-16-424 (D)
Meadows, Jonus B. 1850 wb-g-306 (O)
Meadows, Joseph 1821 wb-#115 (Mu)
Meadows, Joseph 1836 wb-a-138 (O)
Meadows, T. A. 1841 wb-e-278 (Hn)
Meads, William 1840 wb-e-111 (Hn)
Meaney, Jane 1838 wb-11-431 (D)
Meanley, William 1823 rb-d-188 (Mt)
Means, Ann 1838 wb-1-134 (Li)
Means, John 1852 wb-1-221 (Bo)
Means, William 1810 wb-1-200 (Bo)
Meany, Gregory F. 1818 wb-7-281 (D)
Mears, G. B. 1859 iv-1-572 (Ca)
Mears, Hugh 1818 wb-#126 (Mu)
Mears, Joseph 1844 wd-13-27 (D)

Menefee, Jonas 1824 wb-8-337 (D)
Menefee, Lavinia 1857 mr (Gi)
Menefee, Sarah J. 1856 wb-e-134 (Wh)
Menifee, Elizabeth 1830 wb-1-54 (W)
Menifee, John B. 1830 wb-9-418 (D)
Menifee, John N. 1858 rb-o-672 (Mt)
Menifee, William N. 1824 wb-8-366 (D)
Menifee, Willis 1831 wb-b-28 (Wh)
Mercer, Isaac 1851 wb-2-92 (Sh)
Mercer, Isaac 1851 wb-a-399 (F)
Mercer, Joseph 1854? wb-#25 (Mo)
Merden, Kiddy 1852 wb-xx-137 (St)
Mereck, Richard 1803 rb-a-184 (Mt)
Meredeth, David 1849 wb-g-207 (Hu)
Meredith, John D. 1852 wb-15-465 (D)
Meredith, Richard (Colonel) 1841 wb-2-219 (Hr)
Meredith, William 1808 wb-#6 (Wl)
Meride, George 1828 wb-#73 (Wl)
Meriman, Francis 1822 wb-3-397 (K)
Meriwether, Charles 1815 rb-b-72 (Mt)
Meriwether, Francis 1857 wb-6-443 (Ma)
Meriwether, James 1855 wb-6-345 (Ma)
Meriwether, Wm. H. 1839 wb-3-113 (Ma)
Meroney, James 1835 wb-2-174 (Ma)
Merrett, James M. 1854 ib-1-316 (Ca)
Merrett, Underhill 1846 wb-12-613 (Rb)
Merrick, Jacob 1808 ib-1-232 (Ge)
Merrick, James E. 1859 wb-1-283 (Be)
Merrick, Molton 1848 mr-2-274 (Be)
Merrick?, Peter 1835 wb-1-378 (Hr)
Merrill, Benjamin 1830 wb-1-46 (Li)
Merrill, Benjamin 1835 wb-1-148 (We)
Merrit, Harman 1850 ib-1-141 (Ca)
Merritt, Ann D. 1854 wb-11-268 (Wi)
Merritt, Benjamin 1844 wb-c-170 (G)
Merritt, James 1837 wb-6-353 (Wi)
Merritt, James 1837 wb-6-417 (Wi)
Merritt, John 1825 wb-#58 (Wl)
Merritt, John 1825 wb-#60 (Wl)
Merritt, John A. 1853 wb-11-47 (Wi)
Merritt, R. A. 1861 rb-p-614 (Mt)
Merritt, Shimmey 1856 wb-12-208 (Wi)
Merritt, Thomas 1857 wb-12-424 (Wi)
Merritt, Thomas F. 1840 wb-12-17 (D)
Merritt, Thomas J. 1838 wb-#125 (Wl)
Merritt, William B. 1836 wb-#110 (Wl)
Merriwether, Richard T. 1842 wb-c-161 (O)
Merriwether, William Hunter 1861
   wb-3e-179 (Sh)
Merryman, Alexander 1857 wb-17-181 (D)
Merryman, Eli 1851 ib-1-136 (Wy)

Merryman, Nancy 1853 wb-11-412 (K)
Merryman, William 1819 wb-7-297 (D)
Messer, Christian 1831 wb-1-353 (Hw)
Messer, Dennis 1843 mr-2-73 (Be)
Messey, William 1789 wb-1-18# (Ge)
Messick, John 1836 wb-0-1 (Cf)
Messimer, Susannah 1856 wb-#27 (Mo)
Metcalf, C. W. C. 1843 wb-11-339 (Rb)
Metcalf, Camelia 1860 wb-e-372 (Wh)
Metcalf, Ilai 1824 wb-5-170 (Rb)
Metcalf, Susannah 1849 wb-14-188 (Rb)
Metcalf, William C. 1859 wb-e-308 (Wh)
Metcalfe, George C. 1848 wb-#118 (Mc)
Metcalfe, Thomas J. 1843 wb-#118 (Mc)
Metheny, Jonathan 1840 wb-e-93 (Hn)
Mewell, John 1821 rb-c-499 (Mt)
Mews, S. H. 1836 wb-1-450 (Hr)
Mezell, Henry 1841 wb-e-117 (St)
Michael, William 1815 wb-#20 (Mu)
Michell, James 1854 rb-17-143 (Ru)
Michem, Spencer 1835 rb-g-190 (Mt)
Mickle, George 1842 rb-k-40 (Mt)
Mickle, John C. 1859 rb-p-208 (Mt)
Mickle, John C. 1859 rb-p-233 (Mt)
Middlecoff, Joseph 1847 wb-1-369 (Hw)
Middleton, B. F. 1856 wb-e-462 (G)
Middleton, Isaac 1835 wb-d-61 (Hn)
Middleton, John 1831 wb-#223 (Mu)
Middleton, John 1854 wb-#119 (Mc)
Middleton, Joseph H. 1845 wb-a2-182 (Mu)
Middleton, Smallwood 1824 wb-2-447 (Je)
Middlimist, John B. 1857 wb-h-125 (Hn)
Midkiff, Isaiah 1845 wb-5-346 (Gr)
Midkiff, Thomas 1794 wb-1-335 (Hw)
Midyett, Jesse 1840 wb-3-182 (Ma)
Midyett, Margaret 1861 wb-e-154 (Hy)
Mier, Thomas 1844 lr (Sn)
Miers, Humphrey 1853 lr (Sn)
Milam, Elam 1817 wb-3-237 (St)
Milam, James 1817 wb-a-162 (St)
Milam, Rolin 1826 wb-b-142 (St)
Milam, Thomas 1848 wb-b-277 (We)
Milam, Willis R. 1853 wb-2-70 (Li)
Milburn, John 1805 as-l-106 (Ge)
Milburn, Joseph 1825 wb-1-20# (Ge)
Miles, Bedford W. 1858 wb-17-486 (D)
Miles, Charles 1831 wb-7-431 (Rb)
Miles, E. G. 1861 wb-k-372 (O)
Miles, E. J. 1854 wb-i-228 (O)
Miles, Edward 1840 wb-10-529 (Rb)
Miles, Edward H. 1843 wb-11-387 (Rb)

Miles, Hardy D. 1846 wb-13-381 (D)
Miles, Hartwell 1840 rb-10-492 (Ru)
Miles, Jacob 1836 wb-9-289 (Rb)
Miles, James 1812 wb-1-433 (Rb)
Miles, John 1843 wb-1-294 (La)
Miles, Leonard 1835 wb-1-119 (Li)
Miles, S. D. 1859 wb-3-544 (Gr)
Miles, Sam H. 1857 wb-h-375 (St)
Miles, Samuel 1843 wb-12-391* (D)
Miles, Sarah A. 1862 rb-21-169 (Ru)
Miles, Thomas 1835 wb-9-113 (Rb)
Miles, Thomas 1839 rb-10-311 (Ru)
Miles, Thomas sr. 1838 rb-10-181 (Ru)
Miles, W. R. 1858 wb-16-677 (Rb)
Miles, William J. 1860 wb-17-46 (Rb)
Milican, James 1813 wb-#8 (Mu)
Miligan, James 1828 wb-#75 (Wl)
Millard, William 1856 wb-2-137 (Li)
Miller, Abraham 1830 lw (Ct)
Miller, Abraham 1837 wb-3-446 (Je)
Miller, Abraham 1841 wb-1-386 (W)
Miller, Abraham 1847 wb-#47 (Wa)
Miller, Adam 1848 wb-e-99 (Ro)
Miller, Albert S. 1855 wb-6-22 (Ma)
Miller, Allen S. 1859 wb-h-379 (Hn)
Miller, Andrew 1814 wb-#37 (Mu)
Miller, Andrew 1820 wb-#119 (Mc)
Miller, Andrew 1842 wb-c-70 (G)
Miller, Ann 1795? wb-#22 (Wa)
Miller, Caswell 1837 wb-b-144 (G)
Miller, Catharine 1848 wb-#44 (Wa)
Miller, Christopher 1822 wb-A-308 (Li)
Miller, Dovy B. 1843 wb-f-172 (Hn)
Miller, E. S. 1859 rb-19-569 (Ru)
Miller, Elias 1860 wb-f-357 (G)
Miller, Elizabeth 1821 rb-c-427 (Mt)
Miller, Elizabeth 1846 wb-d-12 (G)
Miller, Elizabeth 1854 rb-17-247 (Ru)
Miller, Elizabeth 1855 wb-e-529 (Ro)
Miller, Frederick 1852 wb-a-182 (Cr)
Miller, Gardner 1842 wb-a-98 (T)
Miller, Garland B. 1860 wb-2-316 (Li)
Miller, George 1837 wb-9-421 (Rb)
Miller, George W. 1839 wb-b-348 (Wh)
Miller, Hardy 1857 rb-19-42 (Ru)
Miller, Harman 1826 wb-#133 (Mu)
Miller, Harmon 1848 wb-b-364 (Mu)
Miller, Henry 1819 wb-a-120 (Ro)
Miller, Henry 1843 lr (Gi)
Miller, Henry 1855 ib-h-312 (F)
Miller, Isaac 1807 wb-1-1 (Fr)

Miller, Isaac 1828 wb-1-158 (Ma)
Miller, Isaac 1844 rb-13-7 (Ru)
Miller, Isaac 1851 rb-16-115 (Ru)
Miller, Isaac 1861 rb-21-141 (Ru)
Miller, Isaac J. 1841 rb-12-6 (Ru)
Miller, Jacob (Sr.) 1858 wb-#60 (Wa)
Miller, Jacob 1838 wb-e-54 (Hu)
Miller, Jacob 1840 148-1-5 (Ge)
Miller, Jacob 1843 wb-1-361 (Hw)
Miller, Jacob 1851 lr (Gi)
Miller, James 1817 wb-a-64 (Wh)
Miller, James 1819 wb-3-65 (K)
Miller, James 1820 wb-3-149 (K)
Miller, James 1840 wb-1-326 (W)
Miller, James 1854 wb-a-352 (Ms)
Miller, James A. 1850 wb-d-228 (G)
Miller, James R. 1846 rb-13-606 (Ru)
Miller, James T. 1852 wb-h-Jul (O)
Miller, Jefferson 1832 wb-c-210 (St)
Miller, Jeremiah 1825 wb-1-76 (Ct)
Miller, John 1805 rb-2-8 (Ru)
Miller, John 1820 rb-4-227 (Ru)
Miller, John 1820 wb-3-169 (K)
Miller, John 1821 wb-#57 (Mu)
Miller, John 1832 wb-5-170 (K)
Miller, John 1834 wb-b-47 (G)
Miller, John 1835 wb-#119 (Mc)
Miller, John 1837 wb-a-21 (F)
Miller, John 1841 wb-z-100 (Mu)
Miller, John 1843 wb-8-64 (K)
Miller, John 1847 rb-14-203 (Ru)
Miller, John 1847 wb-#119 (Mc)
Miller, John 1848 lr (Sn)
Miller, John 1848 wb-b-313 (Mu)
Miller, John 1857 wb-j-297 (O)
Miller, John 1858 wb-4-126 (La)
Miller, John 1860 iv-C-170 (C)
Miller, John 1860 wb-2-92# (Ge)
Miller, John A. 1847 rb-14-223 (Ru)
Miller, John B. 1830 wb-#213 (Mu)
Miller, John B. H. 1831 wb-#217 (Mu)
Miller, John C. 1839 rb-h-311 (Mt)
Miller, John L. 1856 wb-b-22 (Ms)
Miller, John M. 1848 wb-#173 (Wl)
Miller, John R. 1854 ib-H-173 (F)
Miller, John R. 1859 rb-20-196 (Ru)
Miller, John sr. 1833 wb-5-197 (K)
Miller, Joseph 1847 wb-14-126 (D)
Miller, Joseph 1850 wb-g-302 (St)
Miller, Joseph 1858 wb-1-372 (Fr)
Miller, Joseph sr. 1858 lr (Sn)

Miller, Khleber 1843 lr (Sn)
Miller, Lewis 1850 rb-15-414 (Ru)
Miller, Lucy 1857 wb-17-283 (D)
Miller, Margaret 1833 rb-9-78 (Ru)
Miller, Mark S. 1859 wb-f-318 (Ro)
Miller, Martin 1840 5-2-148 (Cl)
Miller, Mary 1834 wb-1A-64 (A)
Miller, Mary 1860 wb-3-59 (Me)
Miller, Mathew 1814 rb-1-167 (Ru)
Miller, Mathew 1837 rb-10-29 (Ru)
Miller, N. C. 1857 rb-19-18 (Ru)
Miller, Nathaniel 1816 wb-a-90 (Ro)
Miller, Nimrod 1839 eb-1-415 (C)
Miller, Oliver G. 1862 wb-1-382 (Hw)
Miller, Peter 1801? wb-#22 (Wa)
Miller, Peter 1809 wb-1-337 (Hw)
Miller, Pleasent M. 1849 wb-d-193 (G)
Miller, Prudence 1806 rb-2-20 (Ru)
Miller, Ralph 1801 rb-a-131 (Mt)
Miller, Ralph 1814 rb-b-189 (Mt)
Miller, Rebecca 1855 wb-1-38 (Dy)
Miller, Richard B. 1855 wb-e-376 (G)
Miller, Robert 1824 wb-4-36 (K)
Miller, Robert 1837 rb-10-43 (Ru)
Miller, Robert 1857 rb-18-429 (Ru)
Miller, Robert C. 1859 wb-k-6 (O)
Miller, Rutha 1857 wb-0-153 (Cf)
Miller, Samuel 1822 wb-#42 (Wl)
Miller, Samuel J. 1858 wb-a-326 (Cr)
Miller, Samuel jr. 1848 wb-c-312 (Wh)
Miller, Sarah 1839 5-2-113 (Cl)
Miller, Tabitha C. 1839 wb-1-358 (Hw)
Miller, Thomas 1822 wb-3-300 (Wi)
Miller, Thomas 1838 wb-#119 (Mc)
Miller, Thomas 1838 wb-1-46 (Sh)
Miller, Thomas 1855 wb-#56 (Wa)
Miller, Thomas 1858 wb-17-479 (D)
Miller, Thos. B. 1845 wb-g-168 (Hn)
Miller, Vincent 1848 wb-b-250 (Mu)
Miller, W. C. 1846 wb-2-191 (W)
Miller, Wallace 1845 wb-c-262 (G)
Miller, William 1827 wb-2-583 (Je)
Miller, William 1829 wb-a-61 (R)
Miller, William 1839 eb-1-412 (C)
Miller, William 1841 wb-2-367 (Hy)
Miller, William 1842 wb-e-217 (St)
Miller, William 1848 wb-g-277 (Hn)
Miller, William 1849 wb-1-320 (Me)
Miller, William 1851 wb-a-404 (F)
Miller, William 1853 wb-h-128 (Hu)
Miller, William 1857 wb-3-379 (W)

Miller, William 1858 lw (Ct)
Miller, William 1858 wb-1-380 (Hw)
Miller, William A. 1832 wb-a-12 (T)
Miller, William C. 1858 ib-1-477 (Ca)
Miller, William N. 1857 rb-19-130 (Ru)
Miller, William P. 1832 rb-8-501 (Ru)
Miller, William R. 1837 wb-y-50 (Mu)
Miller, William T. 1860 wb-18-416 (D)
Miller, Wm. B. 1846 wb-2-138 (W)
Miller, Wm. C. 1847 wb-2-262 (W)
Miller, Woods S. 1842 lr (Sn)
Millers, James 1854 wb-a-206 (T)
Millican, Moses S. 1850 wb-e-214 (Ro)
Milligan, William 1837 wb-b-56 (Hd)
Milliken, Amos 1856 wb-h-59 (Hn)
Milliken, Baxter 1831 wb-#218 (Mu)
Milliken, Ezekiel 1816 wb-2-230 (K)
Milliken, James 1826 wb-#171 (Mu)
Milliken, James 1854 ib-h-241 (F)
Milliken, John 1815 wb-A-92 (Li)
Milliken, William 1839 wb-1-351 (Gr)
Millikin, John W. 1855 wb-A-110 (Ca)
Million, John 1842 wb-#40 (Wa)
Million, Robert 1856 wb-#57 (Wa)
Milloway, John F. 1858 wb-2-434* (Me)
Milloway, John T. 1860 wb-3-54 (Me)
Mills, Aaron 1794 wb-1-78 (Je)
Mills, Alice 1853 wb-5-241 (Je)
Mills, Alice 1853 wb-5-397 (Je)
Mills, Andrew R. 1842 wb-c-261 (O)
Mills, Benjamin 1858 wb-1-269 (Bo)
Mills, Ellen 1844 wb-d-191 (O)
Mills, Gideon 1829 wb-#188 (Mu)
Mills, Jacob 1789 wb-1-95 (D)
Mills, James sr. 1847 wb-1-308 (Li)
Mills, Jessee 1834 wb-c-308 (St)
Mills, John 1815 wb-2-101 (Je)
Mills, John 1816 wb-#21 (Wl)
Mills, John 1856 lr (Sn)
Mills, Pinckney C. 1847 wb-f-127+ (O)
Mills, Richard 1817 wb-2-189 (Je)
Mills, Samuel 1844 wb-d-237 (O)
Mills, Sharod 1815 Wb-2-128 (Wi)
Mills, Sharod 1815 Wb-2-129 (Wi)
Mills, Zachariah 1851 wb-5-397 (Je)
Mills, Zachariah 1852 wb-5-45 (Je)
Milroy, John 1840 wb-a-33 (Ms)
Milsaps, Jesse 1845 wb-#5 (Mo)
Milstead, Zealos 1836 wb-1-131 (Li)
Milton, Daniel 1811 wb-1-141 (Sn)
Milton, Thomas 1822 wb-#44 (Wl)

Mincy, Philip 1857 wb-12-463 (Wi)
Mincy, Susan 1858 wb-12-545 (Wi)
Mingo, Jacob 1799 wb-1-18 (Ct)
Minis, James P. 1854? wb-#25 (Mo)
Minnefee?, William 1819 wb-#27 (Mu)
Minner, Peter 1836 wb-1-468 (Hr)
Minnick, Ann 1850 wb-14-493 (D)
Minnick, Joseph P. 1835 wb-10-514 (D)
Minnick, Samuel 1832 wb-a-119 (R)
Minor, Charles 1842 rb-i-442 (Mt)
Minor, John 1817 rb-b-421 (Mt)
Minor, John 1822 rb-d-66 (Mt)
Minor, Mary Ann 1835 rb-g-253 (Mt)
Minor, Thomas C. 1824 rb-d-391 (Mt)
Minor, Thomas Carr 1819 rb-c-130 (Mt)
Minor, Thomas O. 1819 rb-g-87 (Mt)
Minter, Franklin 1849 wb-4-536 (Hr)
Minter, Jeptha 1861 rb-21-93 (Ru)
Minter, John 1832 wb-1-252 (Hr)
Minton, A. E. 1857 wb-17-402 (D)
Minton, Catherine 1841 wb-c-73 (O)
Minton, Sabra 1853 wb-7-0 (Sm)
Minton, Shadrack 1841 wb-b-33 (We)
Minton, Thomas B. 1855 wb-16-563 (D)
Minton?, R. D. 1855 wb-n-551 (Mt)
Minze, Joseph 1848 wb-#120 (Mc)
Mires, G. B. 1859 wb-A-140 (Ca)
Mirick, Richard 1802 rb-a-162 (Mt)
Mirick, Richard 1826 rb-e-39 (Mt)
Missemer, Mary 1840 148-1-5 (Ge)
Missimer, Jacob 1814 wb-2-36# (Ge)
Missimer, John 1817 wb-2-38# (Ge)
Missimore, William 1832 wb-5-142 (K)
Mitchel, Aquilla 1836 wb-1-190 (Gr)
Mitchel, Aquilla 1847 wb-5-512 (Gr)
Mitchel, Daniel 1825 rb-d-500 (Mt)
Mitchel, Dorothy 1853 ib-1-276 (Ca)
Mitchel, James 1845 wb-A-40 (Ca)
Mitchel, John 1831 wb-7-495 (Rb)
Mitchel, John G. 1841 wb-e-427 (Hu)
Mitchel, Marget 1788 wb-1-77 (D)
Mitchel, Mary 1856 rb-18-92 (Ru)
Mitchel, Mesnier 1823 rb-d-211 (Mt)
Mitchel, Robert 1803 wb-2-317 (D)
Mitchel, Stephen 1853 wb-A-83 (Ca)
Mitchel, William 1806 wb-3-49 (D)
Mitchell (B), Major 1854 wb-2-96 (Li)
Mitchell, Adam 1802 wb-#9 (Wa)
Mitchell, Andrew 1824 wb-#71 (Mu)
Mitchell, Ann 1842 wb-c-81 (Wh)
Mitchell, Ann S. 1845 wb-c-191 (Wh)

Mitchell, Aquilla 1836 wb-1-121 (Gr)
Mitchell, Azariah 1855 rb-17-583 (Ru)
Mitchell, Benjamin 1850 33-3-230 (Gr)
Mitchell, Benjamin F. 1843 wb-d-102 (O)
Mitchell, Bernard 1859 wb-7-46 (Ma)
Mitchell, Constantine P. 1838 wb-3-0 (Sm)
Mitchell, Daniel 1830 rb-f-104 (Mt)
Mitchell, David 1827 wb-#25 (Wa)
Mitchell, David 1830 rb-f-100 (Mt)
Mitchell, David 1857 wb-1-106 (Bo)
Mitchell, David L. 1837 wb-b-255 (Wh)
Mitchell, Delphia 1821 rb-c-421 (Mt)
Mitchell, Evan 1810 wb-1-215 (Wi)
Mitchell, Frederick N. 1844 wb-7-0 (Sm)
Mitchell, George 1852 wb-a-254 (Di)
Mitchell, Greenbery 1860 wb-4-24 (Gr)
Mitchell, Hardy 1838 wb-11-389 (D)
Mitchell, Hiram 1830 wb-1-252 (Ma)
Mitchell, Isaac 1851 wb-g-542 (Hu)
Mitchell, Isaac 1857 wb-3e-35 (Sh)
Mitchell, James 1815 wb-A-99 (Li)
Mitchell, James 1835 wb-9-87 (Rb)
Mitchell, James 1843 rb-12-344 (Ru)
Mitchell, James 1843 wb-z-560 (Mu)
Mitchell, James 1854 ib-h-36 (F)
Mitchell, James 1854? wb-#25 (Mo)
Mitchell, James 1856 rb-17-682 (Ru)
Mitchell, James 1857 rb-o-418 (Mt)
Mitchell, James 1857 rb-o-422 (Mt)
Mitchell, James A. 1856 wb-2-299 (Me)
Mitchell, James C. 1846 wb-a2-480 (Mu)
Mitchell, Jesse 1830 lr (Gi)
Mitchell, Joab 1780 wb-#1 (Wa)
Mitchell, John 1815 wb-A-90 (Li)
Mitchell, John 1826? wb-#151 (Mu)
Mitchell, John 1852 wb-a-162 (V)
Mitchell, John 1852 wb-d-52 (Wh)
Mitchell, John B. 1842 wb-c-262 (O)
Mitchell, John H. 1856 wb-6-213 (Ma)
Mitchell, John T. 1859 wb-3-525 (Gr)
Mitchell, Manerva 1846 wb-b-159 (We)
Mitchell, Marcellus 1848 wb-3-0 (Sm)
Mitchell, Marcus 1836 lr (Gi)
Mitchell, Martha A. 1854 wb-f-33 (Mu)
Mitchell, May C. 1856 wb-g-726 (Hn)
Mitchell, Misenier 1823 rb-d-227 (Mt)
Mitchell, Nancy 1832 lr (Sn)
Mitchell, Peter 1847 wb-2-25 (Sh)
Mitchell, Rachel 1860 wb-e-379 (Wh)
Mitchell, Robert 1794 wb-#2 (Wl)
Mitchell, Robert 1794 wb-#26 (Wl)

Mitchell, Robert 1809 wb-#11 (Wa)
Mitchell, Robert 1839 wb-b-349 (Wh)
Mitchell, Robert 1853 rb-16-653 (Ru)
Mitchell, Robert S. 1858 wb-e-211 (Wh)
Mitchell, Robert sr. 1839 wb-b-350 (Wh)
Mitchell, Samuel C. 1852 ib-1-167 (Wy)
Mitchell, Samuel C. 1857 wb-1-21 (Br)
Mitchell, Solomon 1837 wb-1-355 (Hw)
Mitchell, Spence 1849 wb-c-354 (Wh)
Mitchell, Tabitha 1820 wb-3-214 (Rb)
Mitchell, Taswell 1821 wb-#42 (Wl)
Mitchell, Thomas 1784 wb-#2 (Wa)
Mitchell, Thomas 1812 wb-#10 (Wl)
Mitchell, Thomas 1821 wb-2-40# (Ge)
Mitchell, Thomas 1835 wb-d-89 (Hn)
Mitchell, Thomas 1847 148-1-198 (Ge)
Mitchell, Thomas 1850 wb-3-43 (W)
Mitchell, Thomas H. 1854 ib-h-54 (F)
Mitchell, Thomas R. 1843 wb-#142 (Wl)
Mitchell, Vachel 1855 wb-12-24 (Wi)
Mitchell, Wiley 1819 lr (Sn)
Mitchell, William 1816 wb-#24 (Wl)
Mitchell, William 1842 wb-#120 (Mc)
Mitchell, William 1842 wb-1-512 (W)
Mitchell, William 1854 wb-#54 (Wa)
Mitchell, William C. 1820 wb-#35 (Wl)
Mitchell, William H. 1837 rb-g-489 (Mt)
Mitchell, William J. 1859 wb-a-342 (Cr)
Mitchell, William S. 1819 rb-c-75 (Mt)
Mitchell, William S. 1822 rb-d-86 (Mt)
Mitchell, Wm. 1805 wb-3-42 (D)
Mitchell, Wm. 1854 rb-16-712 (Ru)
Mitchum, Robert 1854 wb-a-227 (Cr)
Mitts, Calvin 1859 wb-3-17 (Me)
Mitts, Thomas 1857 wb-2-357 (Me)
Mize, Henry 1816 rb-3-141 (Ru)
Mizell, Henry 1857 wb-1-177 (Be)
Mizell, Stephen 1848 wb-g-81 (St)
Mizles?, George ca. 1828 wb-1-176 (Ma)
Moad, James 1826 eb-1-154 (C)
Moake, Jacob 1822 wb-3-435 (Rb)
Moarning, Wyatt 1844 wb-#140 (Wl)
Mobley, Allen 1851 wb-g-416 (St)
Mobley, R. J. 1851 wb-2-226 (La)
Mobley, William 1829 wb-b-52 (Hn)
Mobly, Harbert 1846 wb-c-275 (G)
Mobly, William 1854 wb-e-206 (G)
Mockbee, Ann S. 1840 rb-h-462 (Mt)
Mockbee, John 1836 rb-g-289 (Mt)
Mockbee, John H. 1844 wb-f-154 (St)
Mockbee, Mary C. 1859 rb-p-19 (Mt)

Mockbee, Thomas D. 1852 wb-xx-115 (St)
Modgelin, William 1843 wb-#149 (Wl)
Moding, William (Jr.) 1793 wb-#5 (Wa)
Moffatt, James 1860 wb-k-162 (O)
Moffatt, John 1859 wb-k-141 (O)
Moffet, John 1835 wb-1-201 (Gr)
Mohlar, John 1801 wb-1-64 (Je)
Molder, John 1819 wb-2-280 (Je)
Moler, Henry 1837 wb-#36 (Wa)
Moles, Richard P. 1860 wb-18-298 (D)
Molloy, Fanny M. 1855 rb-17-529 (Ru)
Molloy, Fanny M. 1855 rb-17-533 (Ru)
Molloy, Gilliam 1830 rb-8-66 (Ru)
Molloy, Gwilliam 1817 rb-4-84 (Ru)
Molloy, John 1857 rb-19-64 (Ru)
Molloy, Thomas 1802 wb-2-245 (D)
Molloy, William 1855 rb-17-360 (Ru)
Molloy, Zillah R. 1859 lr (Gi)
Molsbee, William 1839 wb-1-359 (Hw)
Molsbee, William 1856 wb-1-376 (Hw)
Molton, Elijah 1833 wb-1-43 (La)
Molton, Sarah 1812 wb-a-11 (Di)
Moncrieff, James 1824 wb-8-380 (D)
Monday, Gilbert 1830 wb-9-433 (D)
Monday, J. P. 1858 wb-13-28 (K)
Monday, James W. 1858 wb-12-469 (K)
Monday, William 1818 wb-3-1 (K)
Monger, Peter 1843 wb-8-170 (K)
Monger, Thomas 1814 wb-4-321 (D)
Monks, Eli 1848 wb-2-8 (Li)
Monroe, Adeline 1855 wb-16-457 (D)
Monroe, John 1836 wb-1-165 (W)
Monroe, William 1842 rb-i-428 (Mt)
Monrow, James 1842 wb-7-353 (K)
Monrow, Robert 1836 wb-1-128 (Gr)
Monrow, Robert 1848 33-3-62 (Gr)
Montague, Clement? 1838 wb-d-239* (Hn)
Montague, Thomas 1860 ib-2-186 (Wy)
Montgomery, A. H. 1858 wb-17-455 (D)
Montgomery, Alexander 1830 wb-4-496 (Wi)
Montgomery, Andrew 1855 wb-a-232 (T)
Montgomery, Cyrus 1854 wb-11-377 (Wi)
Montgomery, David 1846 wb-0-69 (Cf)
Montgomery, Hannah 1806 wb-1-21 (Wi)
Montgomery, Hugh 1826 rb-6-251 (Ru)
Montgomery, Hugh 1841 wb-1-200 (Fr)
Montgomery, James 1809 wb-1-203 (Bo)
Montgomery, James 1828 wb-1-157 (Ma)
Montgomery, James 1841 wb-7-207 (K)
Montgomery, James 1853 wb-1-22 (R)
Montgomery, James 1857 wb-6-471 (Ma)

Montgomery, John 1802 wb-0-36 (K)
Montgomery, John 1813 wb-2-54 (K)
Montgomery, John 1818 wb-2-395 (Wi)
Montgomery, John 1830 wb-1-95 (Bo)
Montgomery, John 1840 wb-f-462 (Ro)
Montgomery, John 1846 wb-c-288 (G)
Montgomery, John 1860 wb-f-376 (Ro)
Montgomery, John A. 1822 wb-3-346 (K)
Montgomery, John B. 1858 wb-f-206 (G)
Montgomery, John S. 1851 wb-3-102 (W)
Montgomery, Jonathan 1852 wb-a-180 (Cr)
Montgomery, Joseph 1843 rb-12-289 (Ru)
Montgomery, Joseph A. 1840 rb-11-58 (Ru)
Montgomery, Lemuel P. (Esq.) 1814
    wb-A-49 (Li)
Montgomery, Lemuel P. 1814 eb-1-265 (C)
Montgomery, Lemuel P. 1814 wb-4-308 (D)
Montgomery, Lemuel P. 1837 wb-11-68 (D)
Montgomery, Martha 1856 wb-6-336 (Ma)
Montgomery, Mary M. 1843 rb-12-385 (Ru)
Montgomery, Moses 1817 wb-2-286 (Wi)
Montgomery, Rebecca 1847 wb-9-366 (K)
Montgomery, Robert 1830 wb-4-538 (Wi)
Montgomery, Samuel 1831 wb-1-200 (Hr)
Montgomery, Sarah 1839 wb-6-481 (K)
Montgomery, Silas 1854 wb-11-375 (Wi)
Montgomery, Stepney 1858 rb-19-218 (Ru)
Montgomery, Thomas 1827 wb-1-103 (Bo)
Montgomery, Thos. 1840 wb-1-229 (La)
Montgomery, William 1819 lr (Sn)
Montgomery, William 1822 wb-A-371 (Li)
Montgomery, William 1833 wb-5-248 (K)
Montgomery, William 1843 lr (Sn)
Montgomery, William 1859 wb-e-275 (Wh)
Montgumery, Stephen 1857 rb-19-126 (Ru)
Montieth, Robert 1839 wb-a-400 (R)
Mood, Ladawick 1844 5-3-1 (Cl)
Mood, R. W. 1849 ib-1-77 (Ca)
Moodey, Jeremiah 1849 wb-g-337 (Hn)
Moody, B. A. 1849 wb-g-281 (Hu)
Moody, B. W. 1856 wb-j-117 (O)
Moody, Benjamin 1811 wb-4-151 (D)
Moody, Benjamin 1849 wb-g-259 (Hu)
Moody, Benjn. 1811 wb-4-133 (D)
Moody, Elizabeth 1857 rb-o-375 (Mt)
Moody, Epps 1847 wb-4-252 (Hr)
Moody, George 1840 wb-5-90 (Gr)
Moody, George 1855 wb-3-236 (Gr)
Moody, George W. 1839 wb-e-22 (Hn)
Moody, Henry 1824 wb-3-285 (St)
Moody, Henry M. 1848 33-3-65 (Gr)

Moody, James 1846 rb-k-9 (Mt)
Moody, James J. 1853 wb-e-18 (Hy)
Moody, James W. 1845 rb-k-131 (Mt)
Moody, Marshall 1841 wb-2-355 (Hy)
Moody, Matilda J. 1844 wb-3-112 (Hr)
Moody, Philip 1826 wb-1-32 (Hr)
Moody, R. L. 1858 wb-e-99 (Hy)
Moody, Samuel 1816 rb-3-121 (Ru)
Moody, Theodrick 1853 wb-n-69 (Mt)
Moody, W. J. 1841 wb-12-114* (D)
Mooman, Rudolph 1820 wb-a-133 (Ro)
Moon, F. M. 1856 wb-h-489 (Hu)
Moon, James 1853 wb-h-199 (Hu)
Moon, Jane 1851 wb-g-525 (Hu)
Moon, R. W. 1849 ib-1-55 (Ca)
Moon, Samuel A. 1845 wb-c-195 (Wh)
Moon, Samuel J. 1840 wb-7-21 (K)
Moon, Thomas H. 1844 wb-3-154 (Hr)
Moones, Laudrick F. 1842 wb-f-146 (Hn)
Mooney, Daniel 1845 wb-b-100 (We)
Mooney, Samuel 1832 wb-1-354 (Hw)
Mooney, Sarah 1837 wb-1-356 (Hw)
Mooney, Thomas 1815 wb-1-344 (Hw)
Moor, George 1835 wb-1-110 (Bo)
Moor, John 1838 5-2-42 (Cl)
Moor, Patrick H. 1830 wb-c-72 (St)
Moor, Samuel 1826 rb-6-216 (Ru)
Moore (B), Ben 1853 wb-n-173 (Mt)
Moore, Abigail 1841 wb-z-104 (Mu)
Moore, Abraham 1841 wb-10-584 (Rb)
Moore, Abraham 1855 wb-2-83# (Ge)
Moore, Abram 1844 wb-12-190 (Rb)
Moore, Alexander 1813 wb-A-39 (Li)
Moore, Alexander 1823 wb-#51 (Wl)
Moore, Alexander 1837 wb-3-459 (Je)
Moore, Alexander 1851 rb-4-245 (Mu)
Moore, Alexander 1857 wb-e-172 (Wh)
Moore, Alexander S. 1832 wb-3-326 (Je)
Moore, Alfred 1837 wb-6-299 (Wi)
Moore, Alfred W. 1852 wb-d-400 (G)
Moore, Amos 1840 wb-10-530 (Rb)
Moore, Amos 1840 wb-10-532 (Rb)
Moore, Amos L. 1853 wb-15-327 (Rb)
Moore, Andrew K. 1858 rb-19-460 (Ru)
Moore, Anna 1844 wb-z-583 (Mu)
Moore, Armistead 1843 wb-3-0 (Sm)
Moore, Arthur 1821 wb-1-41 (Fr)
Moore, Ben 1853 wb-n-304 (Mt)
Moore, Benjamin 1827 wb-6-145 (Rb)
Moore, Benjamin 1844 wb-a-109 (T)
Moore, Benjamin 1849 wb-9-273 (Wi)

Moore, C. C. 1861 wb-18-511 (D)
Moore, C. J. 1854 wb-b-342 (We)
Moore, Carey H. 1834 wb-5-421 (Wi)
Moore, Catharine 1806 wb-1-156 (Wi)
Moore, Catherine 1815 wb-#29 (Mu)
Moore, Charity 1835 wb-1-25 (Sh)
Moore, Charles 1852 wb-0-109 (Cf)
Moore, Clara 1846 wb-a-145 (Cr)
Moore, Cleon 1862 wb-1-370 (Hw)
Moore, Daniel 1820 wb-#17 (Wa)
Moore, Daniel 1857 rb-o-512 (Mt)
Moore, Daniel A. 1843 wb-4-83 (Ma)
Moore, David 1822 rb-5-248 (Ru)
Moore, David 1822 wb-8-121 (D)
Moore, David 1837 wb-#121 (Mc)
Moore, David 1842 5-2-279 (Cl)
Moore, David 1846 rb-13-530 (Ru)
Moore, David 1850 148-1-338 (Ge)
Moore, David 1857 rb-o-531 (Mt)
Moore, David 1860 wb-i-251 (St)
Moore, David A. 1840 wb-3-291 (Ma)
Moore, David P. 1828 wb-1-9 (Li)
Moore, Edw. 1795 wb-1-229 (Je)
Moore, Edward 1813 wb-#13 (Wl)
Moore, Edward 1837 wb-2-53# (Ge)
Moore, Edward 1860 gs-1-630 (F)
Moore, Edwin S. 1838 wb-11-437 (D)
Moore, Eli 1855 wb-a-385 (Ms)
Moore, Elijah 1854 wb-5-354 (Je)
Moore, Elisha 1834 wb-3-396 (Je)
Moore, Elisha B. 1849 wb-d-191 (G)
Moore, Elizabeth 1825 wb-1-351 (Hw)
Moore, Elizabeth 1840 wb-b-2 (We)
Moore, Elizabeth 1844 wd-13-14 (D)
Moore, Ferdinand 1840 wb-7-359 (Wi)
Moore, Francis 1821 wb-a-151 (Wh)
Moore, Francis 1839 wb-d-374 (St)
Moore, George 1835 wb-d-91 (Hn)
Moore, George 1838 wb-1-444 (Hy)
Moore, George 1842 wb-d-4 (Ro)
Moore, George H. 1857 rb-o-396 (Mt)
Moore, George H. 1857 rb-o-424 (Mt)
Moore, George T. 1837 rb-9-405 (Ru)
Moore, George sr. 1843 wb-d-66 (Ro)
Moore, Gillum 1839 wb-d-355 (St)
Moore, Gilman 1842 wb-e-181 (St)
Moore, Gully 1825 rb-e-86 (Mt)
Moore, Henry 1840 wb-1-171 (Li)
Moore, Henry 1857 wb-a-266 (T)
Moore, Horace G. 1851 wb-4-171 (Mu)
Moore, Horace G. 1851 wb-m-324 (Mt)

Moore, Indimun B. 1859 wb-e-265 (Wh)
Moore, Isaac 1845 rb-13-227 (Ru)
Moore, Isaac 1856 wb-c-80 (L)
Moore, Isaac P. 1850 rb-15-418 (Ru)
Moore, Israel 1854 wb-#116 (Wl)
Moore, James 1786 wb-1-47 (D)
Moore, James 1805 Wb-1-121 (Wi)
Moore, James 1814 rb-2-252 (Ru)
Moore, James 1827 wb-2-611 (Je)
Moore, James 1829 wb-a-6 (T)
Moore, James 1833 wb-x-88 (Mu)
Moore, James 1836 wb-d-201 (Hn)
Moore, James 1838 wb-6-525 (Wi)
Moore, James 1839 rb-10-411 (Ru)
Moore, James 1841 wb-1A-311 (A)
Moore, James 1844 148-1-74 (Ge)
Moore, James 1845 wb-S-386 (Gr)
Moore, James 1846 wb-13-49 (Rb)
Moore, James 1846 wb-d-204 (Ro)
Moore, James 1849? wb-1B-156 (A)
Moore, James 1852 wb-1-370 (Hw)
Moore, James 1855 wb-#57 (Wa)
Moore, James 1857 wb-2-361 (Me)
Moore, James 1859 wb-7-55 (Ma)
Moore, James A. 1828 wb-1-125 (Ma)
Moore, James A. 1845 wb-e-175 (O)
Moore, James D. 1845 wb-13-258 (D)
Moore, James E. 1853 wb-16-174 (D)
Moore, James H. 1836 wb-#112 (Wl)
Moore, James M. 1855 149-1-20 (Ge)
Moore, James M. 1856 wb-2-167 (Li)
Moore, James jr. 1815 Wb-2-137 (Wi)
Moore, James sr. 1838 wb-1A-193 (A)
Moore, Jane 1843 wb-1-127 (Me)
Moore, Jane 1843 wb-a-108 (Ms)
Moore, Jane B. 1859 wb-2-273 (Li)
Moore, Jane W. 1847 wb-8-599 (Wi)
Moore, Jeremiah 1850 148-1-302 (Ge)
Moore, Jesse 1837 wb-3-456 (Je)
Moore, Jesse 1839 wb-e-36 (Hn)
Moore, Jesse 1849 wb-4-55 (Je)
Moore, Jesse 1860 wb-13-343 (K)
Moore, Joel 1852 wb-15-58 (Rb)
Moore, John 1798? wb-#22 (Wa)
Moore, John 1804 wb-1-29 (Je)
Moore, John 1808 wb-1-0 (Sm)
Moore, John 1821 wb-3-306 (K)
Moore, John 1827 wb-9-137 (D)
Moore, John 1832 wb-3-0 (Sm)
Moore, John 1834 rb-9-86 (Ru)
Moore, John 1835 wb-1-576 (Ma)

Moore, John 1835 wb-b-254 (Ro)
Moore, John 1837 wb-x-477 (Mu)
Moore, John 1838 wb-3-0 (Sm)
Moore, John 1844 wb-1-251 (Li)
Moore, John 1846 wb-b-176 (We)
Moore, John 1848 wb-2-280 (W)
Moore, John 1853 wb-b-206 (L)
Moore, John 1860 wb-1-163 (R)
Moore, John B. 1842 wb-3-100 (Hy)
Moore, John D. 1834 rb-9-186 (Ru)
Moore, John F. 1834 wb-x-461 (Mu)
Moore, John F. 1859 wb-h-400 (Hn)
Moore, John H. 1840 as-a-28 (Ms)
Moore, John L. 1841 rb-11-310 (Ru)
Moore, John P. 1846 wb-4-122 (Hr)
Moore, John T. 1832 wb-#242 (Mu)
Moore, John W. 1853 wb-11-52 (Wi)
Moore, John sr. 1827 wb-3-0 (Sm)
Moore, John sr. 1850 wb-1-380 (Li)
Moore, Jonathan 1839 wb-a-73 (Cr)
Moore, Joseph 1814 wb-#9 (Mu)
Moore, Joseph 1840 wb-b-241 (Hd)
Moore, Joseph 1842 wb-12-333* (D)
Moore, Joseph 1842 wb-12-359* (D)
Moore, Joseph 1855 wb-#118 (Wl)
Moore, Joseph B. 1850 wb-10-419 (K)
Moore, Josephus A. 1843 wb-13-1 (D)
Moore, L. F. 1847 wb-g-198 (Hn)
Moore, Lemuel 1859 39-2-321 (Dk)
Moore, Lemuel W. 1848 wb-a-344 (F)
Moore, Levi 1805 wb-1-173 (Rb)
Moore, Levi 1828 wb-1-75 (Hr)
Moore, Lewis 1832 rb-f-417 (Mt)
Moore, Lewis 1847 wb-4-213 (Hr)
Moore, Lewis 1847 wb-4-226 (Hr)
Moore, Magness 1849 33-3-130 (Gr)
Moore, Margaret 1825 rb-6-150 (Ru)
Moore, Martha R. 1858 rb-19-380 (Ru)
Moore, Mary 1834 wb-1-553 (Ma)
Moore, Mary 1843 wb-f-112 (St)
Moore, Mary 1849 rb-l-456 (Mt)
Moore, Mary 1850 wb-a-236 (Ms)
Moore, Mary 1858 rb-19-512 (Ru)
Moore, Mary 1860 39-2-392 (Dk)
Moore, Mary M. 1855 wb-5-412 (Je)
Moore, Matilda 1861 wb-18-513 (D)
Moore, Moses 1817 wb-2-204 (Wi)
Moore, Nancy 1842 rb-12-199 (Ru)
Moore, Nancy 1846 wb-a2-449 (Mu)
Moore, Nancy 1849 ib-1-73 (Ca)
Moore, Nancy 1860 39-2-392 (Dk)

Moore, Nathaniel 1829 wb-#189 (Mu)
Moore, Nathaniel 1849 wb-4-547 (Hr)
Moore, Noble 1857 rb-18-554 (Ru)
Moore, Noble 1860 rb-20-341 (Ru)
Moore, Patterson 1852 wb-15-198 (Rb)
Moore, Polly 1861 wb-3-79 (Me)
Moore, R. S. 1861 rb-p-592 (Mt)
Moore, Rebecca 1841 wb-b-315 (Hd)
Moore, Rice 1834 wb-1-62 (Gr)
Moore, Richard S. 1845 wb-f-224 (St)
Moore, Richard T. 1830 wb-3-52 (Hy)
Moore, Robert 1812 wb-#23 (Wl)
Moore, Robert 1817 wb-1-0 (Sm)
Moore, Robert 1823 wb-#46 (Wl)
Moore, Robert 1825 wb-1-40 (Ma)
Moore, Robert 1834 wb-#32 (Wa)
Moore, Robert 1836 wb-1-124 (Li)
Moore, Robert 1838 rb-10-128 (Ru)
Moore, Robert 1853 wb-5-301 (Je)
Moore, Robert B. 1826 wb-5-338 (Rb)
Moore, Robert J. 1849 wb-14-447 (D)
Moore, Robert J. 1851 wb-15-198 (D)
Moore, Russell 1858 wb-3e-58 (Sh)
Moore, Samuel 1851 wb-a-143 (V)
Moore, Samuel J. 1841 wb-7-183 (K)
Moore, Sarah 1836 wb-d-267 (Hn)
Moore, Sarah F. 1842 wb-12-312* (D)
Moore, Sarah T. 1861 wb-f-403 (G)
Moore, Stephen 1836 wb-1-2 (Me)
Moore, Stephenson 1818 wb-#28 (Wl)
Moore, Susan 1848 lr (Sn)
Moore, Susan 1854 wb-16-338 (D)
Moore, Susanah 1849 wb-1B-140 (A)
Moore, Sylvia 1847 wb-13-147 (Rb)
Moore, Sylvia 1859 wb-16-746 (Rb)
Moore, T. A. 1861 rb-21-158 (Ru)
Moore, Tabitha 1855 wb-7-0 (Sm)
Moore, Thomas 1836 rb-g-462 (Mt)
Moore, Thomas 1841 wb-a-30 (V)
Moore, Thomas 1847 rb-14-207 (Ru)
Moore, Thomas 1861 wb-3e-170 (Sh)
Moore, Thomas D. 1846 wb-4-50 (Hr)
Moore, Thomas J. 1829 wb-9-311 (D)
Moore, Thomas P. 1843 wb-#121 (Mc)
Moore, Thomas S. 1836 rb-g-429 (Mt)
Moore, Thos. H. 1843 wb-3-34 (Hr)
Moore, Travis 1835 wb-c-451 (St)
Moore, Walter O. 1837 rb-10-21 (Ru)
Moore, Wilburn 1853 wb-15-369 (Rb)
Moore, William (Col.) 1823 wb-1-0 (Sm)
Moore, William 1813 rb-b-133 (Mt)

Moore, William 1814 wb-2-80 (Je)
Moore, William 1820 wb-3-168 (Rb)
Moore, William 1825 wb-2-483 (Je)
Moore, William 1827 wb-1-8 (Li)
Moore, William 1836 wb-1-243 (Hy)
Moore, William 1838 wb-1-292 (Gr)
Moore, William 1843 wb-1-212 (Fr)
Moore, William 1844 rb-13-43 (Ru)
Moore, William 1845 wb-c-253 (G)
Moore, William 1851 wb-14-474 (Rb)
Moore, William 1854 wb-5-349 (Je)
Moore, William A. 1845 wb-1-110 (Sh)
Moore, William B. 1855 wb-b-1 (Dk)
Moore, William B. 1859 wb-e-214 (Wh)
Moore, William C. 1844 wb-13-49 (D)
Moore, William C. 1861 lr (Sn)
Moore, William F. 1845 wb-3-230 (Hr)
Moore, William H. 1826 wb-#130 (Mu)
Moore, William P. 1859 lr (Gi)
Moore, William R. 1841 wb-11-65 (Rb)
Moore, William R. 1863 wb-2-379 (Li)
Moore, William T. 1846 wb-f-307 (St)
Moore, Zachariah 1848 r39-1-101 (Dk)
Moore, Zadock 1844 wb-1-363 (Hw)
Moorefield, Hardin A. 1851 wb-e-273 (Ro)
Moorehead, Joseph 1852 wb-a-164 (T)
Moorehouse, J. B. 1857 rb-o-327 (Mt)
Mooreland, John 1846 wb-f-328 (St)
Moores, John W. 1856 wb-j-120 (O)
Moores, William 1828 wb-3-0 (Sm)
Moorhead, Joseph 1828? wb-#169 (Mu)
Mooring, Wyatt 1834 wb-#105 (Wl)
Moorman, Esther 1849 wb-a-351 (F)
Moran, James H. 1844 wb-b-44 (We)
Moran, John 1846 wb-8-449 (Wi)
More, George 1840 wb-a-57 (L)
More, Lewis 1819 rb-c-207 (Mt)
More, Nathaniel 1835 wb-1-24 (Sh)
More, Thomas C. 1845 A-468-28 (Le)
More, Wilson 1838 wb-e-127 (Hu)
Moreland, Charles 1846 lw (Ct)
Moreland, J. W. 1859 gs-1-217 (F)
Moreland, John W. 1860 gs-1-639 (F)
Moreland, Nicholas 1851 wb-1-67 (Jo)
Morell, Martha W. 1851 wb-g-394 (Hn)
Morelock, David 1841 wb-2-55# (Ge)
Morelock, David 1852 148-1-399 (Ge)
Morelock, George 1832 wb-2-41# (Ge)
Morelock, Jacob 1847 148-1-209 (Ge)
Morgan (B), Stephen 1850 wb-g-209 (St)
Morgan, Allen D. 1851 33-3-350 (Gr)

Morgan, Anderson 1830 wb-a-163 (G)
Morgan, Angelena 1848 wb-0-88 (Cf)
Morgan, Benjamin 1843 wb-12-442* (D)
Morgan, Cal Rufus 1847 wb-9-337 (K)
Morgan, Calvin 1851 wb-11-106 (K)
Morgan, Calvin R. 1845 wb-9-106 (K)
Morgan, Calvin sr. 1852 wb-11-216 (K)
Morgan, Charles 1860 lr (Sn)
Morgan, Daniel 1816 wb-A-144 (Li)
Morgan, Edward 1848 lr (Sn)
Morgan, Edward T. 1824 wb-a-212 (Ro)
Morgan, Elizabeth 1844 wb-f-129 (St)
Morgan, Fielding B. 1837 wb-a-216 (O)
Morgan, Frances 1842 wb-12-367* (D)
Morgan, Francis N. 1829 rb-f-5 (Mt)
Morgan, Franklin H. 1852 wb-11-244 (K)
Morgan, Franklin H. 1860 wb-13-367 (K)
Morgan, George W. 1861 wb-#19 (Mo)
Morgan, Gideon 1851 wb-#122 (Mc)
Morgan, Gideon sr. 1832 wb-b-198 (Ro)
Morgan, Hummer 1850 wb-14-389 (Rb)
Morgan, James 1852 wb-15-377 (D)
Morgan, James T. 1860 rb-p-385 (Mt)
Morgan, John 1816 wb-A-150 (Li)
Morgan, John 1825 wb-#122 (Mc)
Morgan, John 1840 wb-a-57 (F)
Morgan, John 1841 wb-c-117 (O)
Morgan, John 1843 wb-f-111* (Hn)
Morgan, John 1849 wb-d-175 (G)
Morgan, John 1850 wb-2-72 (Sh)
Morgan, Joseph 1824 wb-1-6 (Hr)
Morgan, Lemuel 1840 wb-e-127 (Hn)
Morgan, Lemuel A. 1843 wb-f-178* (Hn)
Morgan, Lewis 1828 wb-1-11 (Li)
Morgan, Mark 1852 wb-#9 (Mo)
Morgan, Mathew 1839 wb-d-397 (St)
Morgan, Plummer 1853 wb-15-309 (Rb)
Morgan, R. B. 1845 wb-12-342 (Rb)
Morgan, Richard 1831 wb-#122 (Mc)
Morgan, Robert F. 1846 wb-13-390 (D)
Morgan, Rolly 1861 rb-21-94 (Ru)
Morgan, Rufus (Col.) 1850 wb-10-451 (K)
Morgan, Rufus 1827 wb-b-12 (Ro)
Morgan, Rufus 1830 wb-#122 (Mc)
Morgan, Rufus 1839 wb-6-465 (K)
Morgan, Rufus 1841 wb-c-235 (Ro)
Morgan, Samuel 1826 wb-#144 (Mu)
Morgan, Theophilus 1843 wb-11-484 (Rb)
Morgan, Thomas 1819 wb-2-218 (Je)
Morgan, Thomas 1822 wb-3-481 (Rb)
Morgan, Thomas B. 1836 wb-10-635 (D)

Morgan, Thomas R. 1836 wb-10-631 (D)
Morgan, William B. 1860 wb-e-368 (Wh)
Morgan, Willis 1857 rb-o-526 (Mt)
Morgan, Willis Montgomery 1860 rb-p-330 (Mt)
Morgan, Willis sr. 1860 rb-p-410 (Mt)
Moring, William 1815 wb-4-353 (D)
Moris, James 1826 wb-#130 (Mu)
Morison, William 1833? wb-1-137* (Hy)
Morlan, Absalom 1814 wb-1-342 (Hw)
Morland, A. B. 1860 gs-1-580 (F)
Morphis, James 1859 wb-h-329 (Hn)
Morrell, Martha W. 1853 wb-g-549 (Hn)
Morris, Absalom 1829 eb-1-242 (C)
Morris, Adley 1811 rb-b-11 (Mt)
Morris, Allen 1827 wb-#160 (Mu)
Morris, Andrew 1814 wb-2-127 (K)
Morris, Ann E. 1859 wb-13-116 (Wi)
Morris, Aquilla 1827 rb-e-91 (Mt)
Morris, Araminta 1852 wb-15-88 (Rb)
Morris, Asa 1838 wb-d-272 (St)
Morris, Asa 1838 wb-d-275 (St)
Morris, Benjamin 1850 wb-#176 (Wl)
Morris, C. M. 1855 wb-3-293 (Gr)
Morris, Caroline 1856 wb-3-302 (Gr)
Morris, Caroline M. 1853 wb-3-125 (Gr)
Morris, Caroline S. 1858 wb-12-478 (K)
Morris, Charles P. 1861 rb-p-545 (Mt)
Morris, Christiana (widow) 1811 wb-2-7 (Je)
Morris, Daniel 1815 wb-4-345 (D)
Morris, Daniel 1816 wb-7-63 (D)
Morris, David 1861 wb-1-381 (Be)
Morris, Dempsey 1847 wb-7-0 (Sm)
Morris, E. C. 1851 wb-14-661 (D)
Morris, E. S. 1838 wb-11-509 (D)
Morris, Edward 1828 wb-#84 (Wl)
Morris, Eli 1854 wb-16-396 (D)
Morris, Fawny 1846 wb-b-141 (We)
Morris, Frances 1845 wb-b-128 (We)
Morris, Francis 1846 wb-b-197 (We)
Morris, Francis 1855 wb-1-48 (Be)
Morris, Gennett 1828 wb-2-614 (Je)
Morris, George 1858 wb-b*-21 (O)
Morris, Henry B. 1859 wb-18-107 (D)
Morris, Hezekiah 1823 wb-A-335 (Li)
Morris, Hillory 1836 as-a-337 (Di)
Morris, Hugh 1825 wb-#58 (Wl)
Morris, Isaac E. 1851 wb-15-83 (D)
Morris, Isaiah 1848 wb-14-82 (Rb)
Morris, J(esse) E. 1838 wb-11-120 (D)
Morris, Jacob 1858 wb-j-339 (O)
Morris, James 1816 wb-1-0 (Sm)

Morris, Jane 1855 wb-16-511 (D)
Morris, Jehu 1850 33-3-275 (Gr)
Morris, Jennet 1829 wb-2-618 (Je)
Morris, Jeptha 1833 wb-c-299 (St)
Morris, Jessee 1803 wb-2-309 (D)
Morris, Jessee 1845 wb-12-506 (Rb)
Morris, John 1843 mr-2-59 (Be)
Morris, John 1845? wb-13-26 (Rb)
Morris, John 1849 wb-f-272 (Fr)
Morris, John 1851 33-3-392 (Gr)
Morris, John 1859 wb-16-760 (Rb)
Morris, John D. 1849 wb-g-131 (St)
Morris, John Q. 1844 mr-2-104 (Be)
Morris, John T. 1859 rb-p-57 (Mt)
Morris, Joseph 1812 wb-4-181 (D)
Morris, Joseph 1841 as-a-478 (Di)
Morris, Joshua F. 1833 wb-x-112 (Mu)
Morris, Lucy G. 1841 as-a-487 (Di)
Morris, Malacki 1858 wb-b-53 (F)
Morris, Martha H. 1860 wb-18-401 (D)
Morris, Mary 1845 wb-f-270 (St)
Morris, Mary A. 1860 wb-k-334 (O)
Morris, Massey 1859 wb-16-711 (Rb)
Morris, Mathew 1825 wb-5-43 (Rb)
Morris, Mathew E. 1853 wb-10-466 (Wi)
Morris, Matthew 1814 wb-2-112 (Rb)
Morris, Matthew 1825 wb-5-71 (Rb)
Morris, Nancy 1831 wb-3-0 (Sm)
Morris, Nathan 1830 rb-f-65 (Mt)
Morris, Nathan 1830 wb-c-75 (St)
Morris, Nathan 1849 wb-9-252 (Wi)
Morris, Nathan D. 1852 wb-m-443 (Mt)
Morris, Nathan E. 1849 wb-9-266 (Wi)
Morris, Nimrod 1815 wb-1-0 (Sm)
Morris, Peter B. 1855 wb-16-558 (D)
Morris, Robert S. 1860 wb-b-444 (We)
Morris, Samuel 1855 lr (Sn)
Morris, Samuel H. 1847 wb-f-403 (St)
Morris, Sarah 1860 wb-k-358 (O)
Morris, Sarah H. 1860 wb-k-179 (O)
Morris, Simeon 1803 wb-2-301 (D)
Morris, Simeon L. 1852 wb-15-193 (Rb)
Morris, Simon 1804 wb-2-347 (D)
Morris, Smith L. 1858 wb-f-182 (Ro)
Morris, Susan 1850 wb-g-320 (St)
Morris, Thomas 1822 rb-d-20 (Mt)
Morris, Thomas 1828 wb-9-174 (D)
Morris, Thomas 1856 wb-4-98 (Je)
Morris, Will 1837 rb-h-18 (Mt)
Morris, William 1803 wb-1-116 (Rb)
Morris, William 1820 rb-4-233 (Ru)

Morris, William 1822 wb-3-570 (Wi)
Morris, William 1830 wb-b-91 (Hn)
Morris, William 1834 as-a-251 (Di)
Morris, William 1846 rb-13-711 (Ru)
Morris, William 1853 wb-n-175 (Mt)
Morris, William 1854 ib-h-328 (F)
Morris, William B. 1855 wb-j-72 (O)
Morris, William G. 1834 wb-1-483 (Ma)
Morris, William M. 1857 rb-o-430 (Mt)
Morris, William P. 1849 wb-14-398 (D)
Morris, Willis B. 1846 lr (Sn)
Morris, Wm. sr. 1835 rb-g-243 (Mt)
Morriset, Joseph 1812 wb-1-341 (Hw)
Morrisett, Joseph 1790 wb-1-334 (Hw)
Morrisette, Mary 1843 wb-1-362 (Hw)
Morrison, Andrew 1815 wb-1-38 (Fr)
Morrison, Andrew 1832 wb-10-35 (D)
Morrison, Asahel 1832 rb-f-312 (Mt)
Morrison, Charles 1831 wb-1-248 (Ma)
Morrison, Daniel 1853 wb-n-161 (Mt)
Morrison, Daniel 1853 wb-n-162 (Mt)
Morrison, David 1852 wb-2-131 (Sh)
Morrison, Elias 1805 wb-1-95 (Sn)
Morrison, James 1831 rb-f-300 (Mt)
Morrison, James 1856 rb-o-262 (Mt)
Morrison, John 1843 wb-2-59# (Ge)
Morrison, John A. 1805 wb-3-291 (Sn)
Morrison, John C. 1838 wb-e-61 (Hu)
Morrison, John W. 1861 wb-3e-181 (Sh)
Morrison, Mary 1817 wb-2-340 (Wi)
Morrison, Michael 1795 wb-1-335 (Hw)
Morrison, Patrick 1810 wb-#8 (Wl)
Morrison, Thomas 1831 wb-1-93 (Fr)
Morrison, William 1812 rb-b-37 (Mt)
Morrison, William 1835 wb-a-120 (Di)
Morrison, William 1837 wb-1-168 (Fr)
Morrison, William A. 1833 wb-1-153 (Hy)
Morrison, William P. 1839 wb-#126 (Wl)
Morriss, Gideon 1801 wb-1-175 (Je)
Morriss, Jessee 1803 wb-2-272 (D)
Morriss, Thomas 1811 wb-4-150 (D)
Morriss, William 1808 wb-1-336 (Hw)
Morrisson, David 1836 wb-1-499 (Hr)
Morrisson, Ezekiel 1847 wb-1-418 (La)
Morrisson, Samuel 1848 wb-2-310 (W)
Morrisson, William 1856 wb-3-316 (W)
Morrow, Adam 1794 wb-1-18# (Ge)
Morrow, Allen 1851 wb-d-362 (G)
Morrow, B. 1843 wb-3-140 (Hy)
Morrow, Benjamin 1852 wb-3-18 (La)
Morrow, Daniel 1815 wb-1-0 (Sm)

Morrow, Ebenezer 1815 wb-2-36# (Ge)
Morrow, Hugh 1856 wb-3-321 (W)
Morrow, Israel 1833 wb-2-43# (Ge)
Morrow, J. C. 1859 ib-2-89 (Wy)
Morrow, James 1816 wb-1-0 (Sm)
Morrow, James 1842 wb-7-364 (K)
Morrow, James 1843 wb-2-59# (Ge)
Morrow, James 1845 rb-j-394 (Mt)
Morrow, James H. 1843 rb-j-48 (Mt)
Morrow, John 1835 wb-1-190 (W)
Morrow, John 1836 wb-6-36 (K)
Morrow, John 1855 wb-3-250 (W)
Morrow, John 1857 wb-2-85# (Ge)
Morrow, Louisa 1861 rb-p-579 (Mt)
Morrow, Lovicie 1859 rb-p-283 (Mt)
Morrow, N. B. 1861 rb-p-642 (Mt)
Morrow, Robert 1835 wb-1-149 (Gr)
Morrow, Robert 1861 wb-13-522 (K)
Morrow, Sarah 1845 rb-j-394 (Mt)
Morrow, Susan Ann 1855 wb-n-704 (Mt)
Morrow, W. B. 1859 wb-7-44 (Ma)
Morrow, W. C. 1857 ib-2-116 (Wy)
Morrow, William 1816 wb-1-0 (Sm)
Morrow, William 1829 wb-1-40 (W)
Morrow, William 1830 wb-4-425 (K)
Morrow, William 1846 rb-k-684 (Mt)
Morrow, William 1852 wb-4-553 (Mu)
Morrow, William 1859 wb-2-108# (Ge)
Morrow, William C. 1857 ib-1-473 (Wy)
Morse, Elijah 1838 wb-6-280 (K)
Mortimer, Sally 1819 wb-#32 (Wl)
Morton, Abner W. 1830 wb-4-479 (Wi)
Morton, Abraham B. 1854 wb-11-320 (Wi)
Morton, Asa 1816 wb-7-21 (D)
Morton, Catharine 1827 rb-7-119 (Ru)
Morton, Catharine 1827 rb-7-338 (Ru)
Morton, Cicely 1842 rb-12-105 (Ru)
Morton, Cicely 1842 rb-12-116 (Ru)
Morton, Cynthia 1855 wb-11-488 (Wi)
Morton, David 1838 wb-1A-203 (A)
Morton, Elisha 1821 wb-3-281 (Wi)
Morton, Francis M. 1839 rb-10-357 (Ru)
Morton, Henry 1838 wb-11-473 (D)
Morton, Hughs 1845 wb-c-212 (G)
Morton, Jacob sr. 1854 wb-11-368 (Wi)
Morton, James 1808 rb-2-64 (Ru)
Morton, James 1827 rb-8-1 (Ru)
Morton, James 1847 rb-14-208 (Ru)
Morton, John 1841 wb-z-91 (Mu)
Morton, John 1851 wb-15-129 (D)
Morton, Joseph 1823 rb-5-273 (Ru)

Morton, Joseph 1837 rb-9-410 (Ru)
Morton, Leevicy 1833 wb-5-340 (Wi)
Morton, Nancy 1823 rb-5-336 (Ru)
Morton, Penisa 1853 wb-11-29 (Wi)
Morton, Robert M. 1856 ib-h-477 (F)
Morton, Samuel 1825 wb-4-52 (Wi)
Morton, Samuel 1836 wb-6-187 (Wi)
Morton, Samuel 1842 rb-12-67 (Ru)
Morton, Samuel 1846 rb-13-531 (Ru)
Morton, Samuel 1851 wb-9-665 (Wi)
Morton, Samuel M. 1845 rb-13-387 (Ru)
Morton, Samuel sr. 1846 rb-13-580 (Ru)
Morton, Sarah 1856 wb-3-283 (W)
Morton, Seth 1836 wb-6-280 (Wi)
Morton, Solomon G. 1859 rb-20-75 (Ru)
Morton, Step 1838 wb-7-13 (Wi)
Morton, Susan 1854 wb-11-401 (Wi)
Morton, Thomas 1815 wb-2-148 (Wi)
Morton, Thos. 1854 wb-1C-193 (A)
Morton, William 1822 wb-3-584 (Wi)
Morton, William 1833 wb-b-9 (G)
Morton, William 1843 wb-c-110 (G)
Morton, William 1852 wb-1-235 (Bo)
Morton, William B. 1859 wb-13-88 (Wi)
Morton, William C. 1837 wb-6-368 (Wi)
Morton, William E. 1850 wb-9-655 (Wi)
Moruing, Joshua 1824 wb-#53 (Wl)
Mosbey, John 1838 rb-10-84 (Ru)
Mosby, Jane 1833 rb-9-220 (Ru)
Moseby, David 1836 rb-9-286 (Ru)
Moseley, Edward 1846 wb-b-172 (We)
Moseley, H. W. 1856 rb-o-220 (Mt)
Moseley, Henry 1849 wb-4-8 (Je)
Moseley, Jephtha 1854 wb-16-434 (D)
Moseley, Jesse 1817 rb-b-399 (Mt)
Moseley, John 1837 wb-11-75 (D)
Moseley, John S. 1844 rb-j-261 (Mt)
Moseley, Martha 1846 wb-b-130 (We)
Moseley, Mary A. 1837 wb-#119 (Wl)
Moseley, Thomas 1820 wb-7-369 (D)
Mosely, A. C. 1857 wb-f-34 (G)
Mosely, B. F. 1860 wb-i-193 (St)
Mosely, B. K. 1857 wb-h-430 (St)
Mosely, Benjamin 1857 wb-h-324 (St)
Mosely, Burwell 1819 wb-#32 (Wl)
Mosely, Edward 1841 rb-i-195 (Mt)
Mosely, H. H. 1856 rb-o-91 (Mt)
Mosely, John 1836 rb-g-452 (Mt)
Mosely, John 1853 wb-m-634 (Mt)
Mosely, Missiniah 1861 lr (Gi)
Mosely, Samuel 1822 wb-#43 (Wl)

Mosely, Samuel 1854 lr (Gi)
Mosely, Thomas 1819 rb-c-179 (Mt)
Moser, Adam 1818 wb-#27 (Wl)
Moser, Adam 1862 iv-C-34 (C)
Moser, Daniel 1849 wb-#168 (Wl)
Moser, Henry 1858 wb-#126 (Wl)
Moser, Philip 1830 wb-3-116 (Je)
Moser, Samuel 1857 wb-5-420 (Je)
Moses, Abram R. 1822 wb-3-302 (Wi)
Moses, Albert J. 1844 wb-3-456 (Hy)
Moses, Festes 1848 r39-1-49 (Dk)
Moses, Henry 1808 wb-1-18# (Ge)
Moses, Isaac D. 1859 wb-13-143 (K)
Moses, William 1849 ib-1-25 (Wy)
Mosier, Sally 1845 wb-e-155 (O)
Mosier, Samuel 1842 wb-c-292 (O)
Mosier?, Hardisun J. 1854 wb-i-181 (O)
Mosley, G. B. 1859 wb-f-260 (G)
Mosley, Henry 1857 wb-5-330 (Je)
Mosley, John S. 1844 rb-j-125 (Mt)
Mosley, Jordan Y. 1845 wb-a-240 (F)
Mosley, Polly Ann 1837 wb-#118 (Wl)
Mosley, Samuel (Col.) 1805 rb-1-21 (Ru)
Mosley, Samuel 1822 wb-#53 (Wl)
Mosley, William 1841 wb-1-200 (We)
Mosley, Zaph 1815 wb-A-88 (Li)
Mosly, Isaac 1858? ib-2-426 (Cl)
Moss, Ann 1845 wb-b-93 (We)
Moss, Benjamin (B) 1816 wb-#21 (Wl)
Moss, Benjamin 1815 wb-4-364 (D)
Moss, Benjamin 1817 wb-7-169 (D)
Moss, Britton 1815 wb-1-0 (Sm)
Moss, Danl. 1783 wb-1-25 (D)
Moss, David 1844 wb-#122 (Mc)
Moss, David 1845 wb-13-160 (D)
Moss, David 1855 mr-2-630 (Be)
Moss, Edward 1855 wb-2-113 (Li)
Moss, Eli 1846 wb-#122 (Mc)
Moss, George W. 1847 wb-14-56 (D)
Moss, Gessom 1837 wb-1-524 (Hr)
Moss, H. 1854 wb-e-240 (G)
Moss, Henry 1857 wb-12-358 (Wi)
Moss, J. P. 1856 rb-o-137 (Mt)
Moss, James 1849 wb-g-171 (Hu)
Moss, James 1845 ib-2-82 (Cl)
Moss, James B. 1829 wb-3-0 (Sm)
Moss, John 1841 wb-#135 (Wl)
Moss, John 1857 wb-#122 (Mc)
Moss, John B. 1847 wb-13-115 (Rb)
Moss, John D. 1829 wb-a-122 (G)
Moss, John D. 1854 wb-n-394 (Mt)

Moss, M. S. 1854 wb-e-130 (G)
Moss, Marcellus 1840 5-2-169 (Cl)
Moss, Martin B. 1847 ib-1-266 (Cl)
Moss, Mary 1860 wb-2-323 (Li)
Moss, Mason 1847 wb-b-234 (We)
Moss, Nancy 1858 wb-5-87 (Hr)
Moss, Robert 1813 wb-#21 (Wl)
Moss, Robert 1857 ib-2-437 (Cl)
Moss, Spencer 1843 wb-11-402 (Rb)
Moss, Spencer A. 1843 wb-11-411 (Rb)
Moss, Thomas 1823 wb-#47 (Wl)
Moss, Thomas 1840 wb-#138 (Wl)
Moss, Thomas B. 1846 wb-#160 (Wl)
Moss, William 1859 wb-5-90 (Hr)
Moss, William W. 1843 wb-11-500 (Rb)
Moss, William W. sr. 1842 wb-11-284 (Rb)
Mossey, Isaac H. 1848 wb-g-8 (Hu)
Motes?, Henry 1808 ib-1-210 (Ge)
Motheral, James 1837 wb-a-302 (O)
Motheral, Jane 1833 wb-5-310 (Wi)
Motheral, John 1824 wb-3-724 (Wi)
Motheral, Joseph 1815 lr (Sn)
Motheral, Mary 1847 wb-f-127+ (O)
Motheral, Robert 1803 lr (Sn)
Motheral, Robert 1842 wb-c-150 (O)
Motheral, Sarah 1848 wb-#173 (Wl)
Motherall, Samuel 1838 wb-#129 (Wl)
Motherel, William 1850 wb-d-242 (G)
Mothershed, John Jett 1815 wb-4-338 (D)
Mothorn, John 1857 wb-2-25 (Ct)
Motley, B. L. 1849 wb-#168 (Wl)
Motley, James 1855 wb-e-277 (G)
Motley, John 1844 wb-c-195 (G)
Motlow, John 1855 wb-2-104 (Li)
Motly, Merrett 1855 wb-e-312 (G)
Mottley, John D. 1851 wb-#177 (Wl)
Mottley, Martha (Mrs.) 1849 wb-#170 (Wl)
Moulton, Thomas 1822 wb-3-577 (Wi)
Moultree, Mary 1855 wb-i-246 (O)
Moultrie, Moses 1853 wb-i-92 (O)
Moultrie, William 1843 wb-d-32 (O)
Mounger, Joseph J. 1850 wb-e-232 (Ro)
Mounger, Peter 1843 wb-8-201 (K)
Mounger, Sampson 1858 wb-f-141 (Ro)
Mounger, Williamson 1849 wb-e-122 (Ro)
Mount, Humphrey 1856 wb-4-70 (Je)
Mount, Mary 1860 wb-#132 (Wl)
Mountcastle, George E. 1849 wb-#123 (Mc)
Mourfield, Parker H. 1855 wb-e-516 (Ro)
Mourning, Samuel 1843 wb-#140 (Wl)
Mowery, Peter 1840 wb-7-17 (K)

Mowry, Henry 1855 wb-12-169 (K)
Mowry, John 1855 wb-#26 (Mo)
Moxley, James H. 1859 wb-#129 (Wl)
Moxley, Joseph (Sr.) 1842 wb-#140 (Wl)
Moxley, Joseph 1845 wb-#158 (Wl)
Moyers, Christopher 1815 wb-2-99 (Je)
Moyers, David 1836 wb-3-349 (Je)
Moyers, Henry 1849 ib-1-80 (Cl)
Moyers, John 1836 wb-3-375 (Je)
Moyers, Mathias 1812 wb-2-27 (Je)
Moyers, William 1855 wb-2-81# (Ge)
Moyers, William S. 1857 149-1-64 (Ge)
Mozly, A. 1836 wb-x-347 (Mu)
Muckleroy, Elizabeth 1847 wb#18 (Gu)
Muirhead, John 1813 wb-#8 (Mu)
Muirhead, John 1860 wb-#132 (Wl)
Mulhall, Jane 1860 wb-18-375 (D)
Mulherrin, James 1826 wb-9-29 (D)
Mulkey, Isaac 1855 wb-#56 (Wa)
Mulkey, Jesse 1848 wb-#46 (Wa)
Mulkey, Jonathan 1826? wb-#25 (Wa)
Mulky, James 1794 wb-1-1 (Ct)
Mulky, Josiah 1816 wb-a-91 (Ro)
Mullen, Elizabeth 1844 wd-13-43 (D)
Mullen, Jesse 1821 wb-8-17 (D)
Mullen, Jesse 1828 wb-4-352 (Wi)
Mullen, Jesse 1829 wb-4-373 (Wi)
Mullen, Jessee 1806 wb-3-136 (D)
Mullen, Josiah 1825 wb-8-501 (D)
Mullen, William Scott 1810 wb-4-108 (D)
Muller, James 1806 wb-1-225 (Rb)
Muller, Lewis 1853 rb-16-665 (Ru)
Mullican, Allen 1851 wb-3-103 (W)
Mullican, William 1853 wb-3-196 (W)
Mullin, Henry 1847 wb-9-8 (Wi)
Mullin, Joel 1836 rb-9-191 (Ru)
Mullin, William S. 1806 wb-1-192 (Wi)
Mullinax, Levi 1818 wb-#49 (Wl)
Mulliniks, Pleasant 1852 mr-2-439 (Be)
Mullins, Alexander 1839 wb-3-50 (Ma)
Mullins, Anthony 1836 wb-1-129 (Li)
Mullins, Asa 1851 wb-#8 (Mo)
Mullins, Giles C. 1827 rb-7-109 (Ru)
Mullins, Jesse 1842 rb-12-253 (Ru)
Mullins, Jessee 1857 rb-18-316 (Ru)
Mullins, Jillis C. 1829 rb-7-180 (Ru)
Mullins, Joel 1835 rb-9-188 (Ru)
Mullins, John 1845 rb-13-223 (Ru)
Mullins, John 1859 wb#40 (Gu)
Mullins, John 1861 wb-f-419 (G)
Mullins, Joseph 1848 ib-1-24 (Ca)

Mullins, L. B. 1854 ib-h-26 (F)
Mullins, Oney 1842 rb-12-223 (Ru)
Mullins, Sarah 1849 rb-l-503 (Mt)
Mullins, Thomas 1855 wb-e-375 (G)
Mullins, Washington 1859 wb#6 (Gu)
Mulloy, Daniel 1857 wb-16-453 (Rb)
Mumford, M. B. 1850 wb-m-148 (Mt)
Mumford, Marshall 1848 rb-l-133 (Mt)
Mumford, W. B. 1859 rb-p-200 (Mt)
Mumphrey, George W. 1851 wb-2-97 (Sh)
Mumpower, Jonathan 1834 wb-1-80 (Gr)
Muncy, Eli 1849 wb-3-18 (W)
Munday, Constantine 1861 wb-13-487 (K)
Munday, J. W. 1861 wb-13-490 (K)
Munday, John 1843 wb-8-206 (K)
Mundy, William 1860 wb-8-32 (Sm)
Munford, William 1837 wb-#117 (Wl)
Mungle, Daniel 1803 wb-1-0 (Sm)
Mungle, Nathan 1827 wb-3-0 (Sm)
Munson, Permelia Jane 1860 wb-3e-132 (Sh)
Murchison, John 1840 wb-3-119 (Ma)
Murchurson, Kenneth 1861 ib-2-246 (Wy)
Murdock, John 1844 wb-4-261 (Ma)
Murdock, John sr. 1836 wb-1-128 (Li)
Murdock, Sampson 1814 wb-2-113 (Rb)
Murdough, Sampson 1831 wb-8-65 (Rb)
Murdy, Stephen 1843 rb-i-536 (Mt)
Murfre, Edward 1828 as-a-170 (Di)
Murfree, Hardy 1807 wb-#26 (Wl)
Murfree, Hardy 1809 Wb-1-87 (Wi)
Murfree, Hardy 1818 wb-2-458 (Wi)
Murfree, Mary A. 1859 rb-20-145 (Ru)
Murfree, Mary Ann (Mrs.) 1857 rb-19-15 (Ru)
Murfree, Matthias B. 1854 rb-16-696 (Ru)
Murfree, William H. 1827 wb-4-208 (Wi)
Murison, James 1830 rb-f-92 (Mt)
Murphee, Mathew 1803 rb-a-174 (Mt)
Murphey, E. A. 1854 ib-h-79 (F)
Murphey, E. G. 1859 wb-a-103 (Ce)
Murphey, Ezekiel 1843 rb-12-296 (Ru)
Murphey, James 1859 wb-16-770 (Rb)
Murphey, John 1855 wb-12-161 (K)
Murphey, John D. 1841 wb-z-180 (Mu)
Murphey, John G. 1846 rb-13-465 (Ru)
Murphey, John M. 1815 wb-#17 (Mu)
Murphey, John S. 1839 wb-y-425 (Mu)
Murphey, Malachia 1841 wb-7-200 (K)
Murphey, Milley 1858 wb-16-678 (Rb)
Murphey, R. S. 1854 ib-1-325 (Ca)
Murphey, S. H. 1855 wb-c-50 (L)
Murphey, Sandy 1853 wb-15-230 (Rb)

Murphey, Stephen N. 1852 wb-d-383 (G)
Murphey, Thomas 1857 wb-1-20# (Ge)
Murphey, Thomas 1857 wb-2-85# (Ge)
Murphey, Wayne W. 1849 rb-15-2 (Ru)
Murphey, Wily B. 1842 wb-7-393 (K)
Murphrey, Jesse 1811 wb-a-10 (Wh)
Murphrey, John 1852 ib-1-176 (Wy)
Murphrey, Laurence 1816 wb-2-274 (Wi)
Murphrey, Miles P. 1854 rb-17-137 (Ru)
Murphry, Levi L. 1855 wb-e-45 (Wh)
Murphy, Aaron 1854 wb-#112 (Wl)
Murphy, Alexander 1840 wb-1-225 (La)
Murphy, Charles 1851 wb-4-290 (Mu)
Murphy, Dennis 1808 wb-1-247 (K)
Murphy, Dennis C. 1834 wb-a-261 (R)
Murphy, Edward 1835 wb-#123 (Mc)
Murphy, Elizabeth 1860 39-2-351 (Dk)
Murphy, George 1833 wb-8-151 (Rb)
Murphy, Hugh 1838 wb-1A-188 (A)
Murphy, James 1823 wb-#123 (Mc)
Murphy, James 1830 wb-7-259 (Rb)
Murphy, Jenkins 1847 rb-k-575 (Mt)
Murphy, Jenkins 1848 rb-k-484 (Mt)
Murphy, Jno. Jr. 1837 wb-1-531 (Hr)
Murphy, John 1823 wb-4-58 (Rb)
Murphy, John 1825 wb-#123 (Mc)
Murphy, John 1829 wb-1-116 (Hr)
Murphy, John 1851 wb-5-7 (Hr)
Murphy, John 1855 wb-#123 (Mc)
Murphy, John 1859 wb-13-136 (K)
Murphy, Joseph 1828 wb-1-82 (Hr)
Murphy, Joseph 1834 wb-1-83 (W)
Murphy, Joseph 1843 wb-a-160 (L)
Murphy, Martin H. 1844 wb-8-304 (K)
Murphy, Mary 1859 wb-16-712 (Rb)
Murphy, Nathaniel 1830 wb-#215 (Mu)
Murphy, Patrick 1800 rb-a-119 (Mt)
Murphy, Robert 1850 wb-10-377 (K)
Murphy, Robertson 1827 wb-6-142 (Rb)
Murphy, Samuel R. 1856 wb-e-66 (Hy)
Murphy, Theodore F. N. B. 1847 wb-9-377 (K)
Murphy, Tho. J. 1852 wb-15-129 (Rb)
Murphy, Thomas J. 1840 wb-10-528 (Rb)
Murphy, W. B. 1847 rb-k-592 (Mt)
Murphy, Warren B. 1847 rb-k-636 (Mt)
Murphy, Wayne 1854 rb-17-36 (Ru)
Murphy, Wayne W. 1849 rb-15-38 (Ru)
Murphy, William 1838 wb-11-476 (D)
Murphy, William M. 1857 wb-12-417 (K)
Murrah, Charles 1844 wb-12-227 (Rb)
Murray, Christopher 1824 eb-1-136 (C)

Murray, Debora 1845 wb-g-71 (Hn)
Murray, Deborah 1845 wb-f-278* (Hn)
Murray, Enoch 1799 wb-1-18# (Ge)
Murray, John 1837 eb-1-349 (C)
Murray, John 1850 wb-#65 (Wa)
Murray, Rosanna 1821 wb-7-506 (D)
Murray, Samuel 1847 rb-14-5 (Ru)
Murray, Stephen F. 1836 eb-1-348 (C)
Murray, Thomas 1822 wb-#43 (Wl)
Murray, Thomas 1843 rb-12-418 (Ru)
Murray, William 1858 wb-17-456 (D)
Murray, William C. 1834 wb-#106 (Wl)
Murrell, Jeffery 1825 wb-3-755 (Wi)
Murrell, Richard 1840 as-a-470 (Di)
Murrell, Sarah 1859 wb-7-39 (Ma)
Murrell, Zelpha 1839 wb-2-409 (Ma)
Murrey, Capel 1822 mr (Gi)
Murrey, Thomas 1805 wb-#10 (Wa)
Murrey, William 1803 Wb-1-111 (Wi)
Murrie, Charles 1833 wb-c-80 (Hn)
Murril, Susan 1832 wb-1-339 (Ma)
Murrin, Robert 1846 wb-1-219 (Bo)
Murry, Ellender 1824 wb-4-33 (K)
Murry, Henry 1804 wb-2-391 (D)
Murry, James 1837 eb-1-357 (C)
Murry, James 1853 wb-#109 (Wl)
Murry, John 1854 wb-#115 (Wl)
Murry, Margaret A. 1845 wb-1-110 (Sh)
Murry, Patrick 1808 wb-1-98 (Bo)
Murry, Pleasant 1860 wb-#124 (Mc)
Murry, Riley D. 1861 wb-13-472 (Wi)
Murry, Robert 1815 Wb-2-147 (Wi)
Murry, Simon 1815 wb-#17 (Wl)
Murry, Susan 1839 wb-e-161 (Hu)
Murry, William 1848 wb-#173 (Wl)
Murry, William 1861 wb-13-505 (K)
Muse, Alison 1857 wb-1-355 (Fr)
Muse, Catharine 1817 wb-#34 (Mu)
Muse, Dennis B. 1858 wb-1-377 (Fr)
Muse, Josiah 1836 wb-1-159 (Fr)
Muse, Kiziah 1848 wb-1-246 (Fr)
Muse, Omega 1861 wb-1-411 (Fr)
Muse, Richard T. 1858 rb-19-317 (Ru)
Muse, Richard T. 1858 rb-19-379 (Ru)
Muse, Samuel 1847 rb-14-175 (Ru)
Muse, Samuel O. 1848 rb-14-485 (Ru)
Muse, William B. Y. 1856 wb-1-348 (Fr)
Muse, William J. 1848 rb-14-433 (Ru)
Musgrave, James 1855 wb-e-360 (G)
Musgrave, John 1839 wb-1-8 (Jo)
Musgraves, Aaron 1847 wb-1-40 (Jo)

Musgrove, Everett 1847 wb-d-37 (G)
Musick, Aleackus 1826 wb-2-554 (Je)
Muzzall, Mary 1851 wb-g-399 (Hn)
Myars, Henry 1843 wb-2-60# (Ge)
Myatt, Burrell 1838 wb-a-132 (Di)
Myatt, Burrell 1857 as-c-463 (Di)
Myer, William 1823 wb-1-20# (Ge)
Myers (Moyers?), Adam 1824 wb-1-19# (Ge)
Myers, Catherine 1846 148-1-141 (Ge)
Myers, Charles W. 1850 wb-10-335 (K)
Myers, Elias 1847 wb-a-147 (Cr)
Myers, George 1842 wb-3-96 (Hy)
Myers, Harriet 1856 149-1-56 (Ge)
Myers, Henry 1847 148-1-205 (Ge)
Myers, Henry 1857 149-1-61 (Ge)
Myers, Hiram 1839 lr (Gi)
Myers, Martha A. 1860 rb-p-386 (Mt)
Myers, Nancy 1839 wb-2-52# (Ge)
Myers, Phillip 1847 wb-1-231 (Bo)
Mynatt, Alexander 1852 wb-11-292 (K)
Mynatt, Elizabeth 1856 wb-12-216 (K)
Mynatt, George 1803 wb-1-129 (K)
Mynatt, John 1827 wb-4-203 (K)
Mynatt, Joseph 1853 wb-11-415 (K)
Mynatt, Mary 1822 wb-3-396 (K)
Mynatt, Richard 1827 wb-4-210 (K)
Mynatt, Sabilla 1853 wb-11-386 (K)
Mynatt, William 1831 wb-5-52* (K)
Mynatt, William 1849 wb-10-187 (K)
Mynatt, William C. 1837 wb-6-100 (K)
Myrack, Green D. 1847 wb-g-189 (Hn)
Myres, Charles 1853 wb-3-171 (La)
Myrick, Eliza Jane 1852 wb-g-447 (Hn)
Myrick, Elizabeth 1847 wb-b-84 (Mu)
Myrick, Harrison 1834 wb-c-141 (Hn)
Myrick, Howell 1834 wb-1-327 (Hr)
Myrick, Martha A. 1848 wb-4-336 (Hr)
Myrick, Mathew 1841 wb-e-194 (Hn)
Myrick, Will. 1849 wb-4-409 (Hr)
Myrick, William 1846 wb-4-107 (Hr)

- N -

Nabers, Benjamin 1831 wb-1-185 (Hr)
Nabers, Benjamin 1846 wb-4-28 (Hr)
Naegle, Dedrick 1860 wb-3e-151 (Sh)
Naff, Jonathan 1855 149-1-22 (Ge)
Naff, Jonathan sr. 1853 wb-2-77# (Ge)
Nail, Andrew 1832 wb-1-257 (Ma)
Nail, Arche 1830 wb-1-155 (Hr)
Nail, Archibald 1831 wb-1-190 (Hr)

Nail, John 1829 wb-b-39 (Ro)
Nail, John 1859 wb-13-127* (K)
Nail, Nicholas 1828 wb-b-4 (Ro)
Nail, Samuel 1845 wb-5-3 (Ma)
Nailing, Nelson 1855 wb-b-371 (We)
Nailor, James 1845 wb-#158 (Wl)
Nall, John L. 1847 wb-14-119 (D)
Nall, Thomas 1842 wb-11-265 (Rb)
Nall, William 1843 wb-8-15 (Wi)
Nance, A. W. 1855 rb-17-584 (Ru)
Nance, Allen 1836 rb-9-327 (Ru)
Nance, Allen 1848 rb-14-386 (Ru)
Nance, Bird 1814 rb-3-110 (Ru)
Nance, Elizabeth V. 1844 wb-13-117 (D)
Nance, Isaac 1820 rb-4-247 (Ru)
Nance, Isham 1828 rb-7-23 (Ru)
Nance, James 1855 wb-e-508 (Ro)
Nance, Jane 1859 rb-19-571 (Ru)
Nance, John 1852 wb-5-39 (Je)
Nance, John S. 1841 wb-12-221* (D)
Nance, John sr. 1813 wb-2-56 (Je)
Nance, Joseph 1847 lr (Gi)
Nance, Philip 1850 wb-4-79 (Mu)
Nance, Thomas 1821 wb-3-268 (K)
Nance, W. A. J. 1851 mr-2-410 (Be)
Nance, William 1856 wb-g-732 (Hn)
Nance, William H. 1838 wb-11-362 (D)
Nance, William H. 1854 mr-2-551 (Be)
Nanny, Abel 1844 rb-j-250 (Mt)
Nanny, Henry 1839 wb-3-21 (Ma)
Nanteles?, Angalie 1849 wb-g-340 (Hn)
Nants, Peter R. 1857 wb-j-192 (O)
Nanys?, Henry 1836 wb-2-133 (Ma)
Napier, A. C. 1846 as-b-288 (Di)
Napier, Caleb 1827 wb-2-340 (Je)
Napier, E. W. 1848 wb-a-183 (Di)
Napier, H. A. C. 1848 as-b-350 (Di)
Napier, Mary 1821 rb-c-474 (Mt)
Napier, Richard Claiborne 1834 wb-a-106 (Di)
Napier, Richd. 1823 as-A-123 (Di)
Naron, John C. 1862 wb-h-556 (Hn)
Nash, Arrison 1843 mr-2-42 (Be)
Nash, Charles 1826 wb-4-111 (Wi)
Nash, Dempsey 1833 wb-5-278 (Wi)
Nash, Francis 1805 wb-3-1 (D)
Nash, Jno. 1802 wb-2-253 (D)
Nash, John 1836 rb-9-313 (Ru)
Nash, John 1857 wb-3-403 (Gr)
Nash, Thomas 1828 rb-7-24 (Ru)
Nash, Thornton 1853 wb-a-432 (F)
Nash, William 1811 wb-#10 (Wl)

Nations, Thomas 1816 wb-#19 (Mu)
Nave, Daniel 1835 wb-9-111 (Rb)
Nave, John 1857 lr (Gi)
Nave, Joseph 1840 wb-10-406 (Rb)
Nave, T. M. 1851 wb-15-27 (Rb)
Nave, Tilford 1851 wb-14-533 (Rb)
Nave, William 1843 wb-11-498 (Rb)
Naville, Henry 1795 wb-0-8 (K)
Naw, Nancy 1847 wb-4-165 (Hr)
Naylor, Sarah 1857 wb-j-296 (O)
Naylor, W. H. 1857 rb-19-119 (Ru)
Naylor, Wade H. 1857 rb-19-234 (Ru)
Neace, Mary 1845 wb-f-303 (Hn)
Neal, Archer 1828 wb-1-81 (Hr)
Neal, Benjamin 1823 wb-2-416 (Je)
Neal, C. F. 1859 wb-#130 (Wl)
Neal, Charles 1836 wb-1-220 (W)
Neal, Charles 1845 wb-#124 (Mc)
Neal, Creath 1845 lr (Sn)
Neal, Gracy 1857 rb-19-81 (Ru)
Neal, Gray 1858 rb-19-418 (Ru)
Neal, Hetty 1844 wb-a-228 (F)
Neal, Isaac 1854 lr (Gi)
Neal, Isaac? 1833 wb-#104 (Wl)
Neal, J. L. 1855 wb-3-254 (Gr)
Neal, James H. 1852 wb-h-Aug (O)
Neal, James J. 1849 wb-9-333 (Wi)
Neal, James L. 1854 wb-3-182 (Gr)
Neal, James P. 1838 wb-a-32 (F)
Neal, Jeremiah 1840 wb-7-92 (K)
Neal, John 1833 wb-c-82 (Hn)
Neal, John 1845 rb-13-146 (Ru)
Neal, John H. 1859 wb-#129 (Wl)
Neal, Lawson 1840 wb-2-32 (Hy)
Neal, Martha A. 1861 wb-18-616 (D)
Neal, Palles 1851 wb-#175 (Wl)
Neal, Peyton 1836 wb-#111 (Wl)
Neal, Richard P. 1840 wb-12-9* (D)
Neal, Robert 1840 wb-a-49 (F)
Neal, Sarah 1840 wb-#130 (Wl)
Neal, Thomas 1859 rb-20-204 (Ru)
Neal, William 1833 wb-5-274 (Wi)
Neal, William 1837 wb-#120 (Wl)
Neal, William 1845 wb-#167 (Wl)
Neal, William D. 1856 rb-18-231 (Ru)
Neal, William R. 1859 wb-a-302 (V)
Neal, William S. 1843 lr (Gi)
Neal, Zepheniah 1845 wb-#148 (Wl)
Nearn, Benjamin 1860 wb-d-57 (L)
Neas, Phillip 1856 wb-2-84# (Ge)
Nease, John 1844 148-1-79 (Ge)

Neber, Eliza 1852 mr-2-478 (Be)
Neblet, Elizabeth 1834 rb-9-117 (Ru)
Neblet, John sr. 1830 rb-f-115 (Mt)
Neblet, Josiah D. 1854 wb-n-442 (Mt)
Neblett, E. C. 1850 wb-m-127 (Mt)
Neblett, Edward 1845 rb-k-1 (Mt)
Neblett, Elizabeth N. 1858 rb-o-716 (Mt)
Neblett, Francis 1820 rb-c-346 (Mt)
Neblett, John 1837 rb-g-522 (Mt)
Neblett, John sr. 1830 rb-f-117 (Mt)
Neblett, Josiah (Doctor) 1842 rb-i-447 (Mt)
Neblett, Josiah 1842 rb-i-393 (Mt)
Neblett, Josiah D. 1848 rb-l-117 (Mt)
Neblett, R. A. 1859 rb-p-296 (Mt)
Neblett, Sally 1848 rb-k-716 (Mt)
Neblett, Stephen 1845 rb-j-416 (Mt)
Neblett, Sterling 1845 rb-j-326 (Mt)
Neblett, Sterling sr. 1844 rb-j-272 (Mt)
Neblett, Susanna 1837 rb-g-635 (Mt)
Neblett, William 1851 wb-m-317 (Mt)
Nedry, John 1847 wb-f-127+ (O)
Nedry, William 1856 wb-j-232 (O)
Neece, James K. 1843 wb-1-226 (Li)
Needham, Bailey 1838 wb-1-570 (Hr)
Needham, Franklin 1859 wb-f-338 (G)
Needham, Gardner 1852 wb-5-28 (Hr)
Needham, James 1840 wb-5-69 (Gr)
Needham, John 1851 33-3-363 (Gr)
Needham, John W. 1854 wb-e-197 (G)
Needham, John W. 1854 wb-e-211 (G)
Needham, John W. 1855 wb-e-311 (G)
Needham, Nancy 1857 wb-f-76 (G)
Needham, Solomon 1841 wb-2-307 (Hr)
Neel, Charles 1848 wb-a-132 (V)
Neel, Daniel 1812 wb-#6 (Mu)
Neel, Duncan 1843 wb-0-50 (Cf)
Neel, Gilbreth F. 1843 wb-3-702 (Ma)
Neel, Hector 1815 wb-1-0 (Sm)
Neel, James H. 1849 wb-g-38 (O)
Neel, Jane 1849 lr (Sn)
Neel, Sarah E. 1857 rb-18-327 (Ru)
Neel, William 1819 wb-#32 (Wl)
Neel, William Sr. 1819 wb-#32 (Wl)
Neeld, William 1858 wb-2-256 (Li)
Neele, Joseph 1833 wb-#101 (Wl)
Neeley, Elijah L. 1846 wb-8-451 (Wi)
Neeley, John 1845 rb-13-418 (Ru)
Neeley, John 1845 wb-a2-308 (Mu)
Neeley, John H. 1845 wb-a2-311 (Mu)
Neeley, Nancy 1849 rb-15-36 (Ru)
Neeley, Nancy C. 1853 wb-16-57 (D)

Neeley, Wesly G. 1838 wb-y-219* (Mu)
Neell, Richard G. 1855 wb-a-247 (Cr)
Neelly, George 1817 wb-2-353 (Wi)
Neelly, James 1819 wb-3-40 (Wi)
Neelly, James 1835 wb-6-68 (Wi)
Neelly, Jane 1842 wb-7-543 (Wi)
Neelly, John 1818 wb-2-411 (Wi)
Neelly, Robert 1815 wb-2-153 (Wi)
Neelly, Sophia 1831 wb-5-29 (Wi)
Neely, Charles 1822 wb-3-566 (Wi)
Neely, Elizabeth 1846 wb-13-44 (Rb)
Neely, George 1833 wb-5-309 (Wi)
Neely, George 1836 wb-6-130 (Wi)
Neely, George L. 1860 wb-13-223 (Wi)
Neely, J. A. 1847 wb-4-183 (Hr)
Neely, James 1834 wb-5-351 (Wi)
Neely, James 1836 wb-6-120 (Wi)
Neely, James W. 1844 wb-d-134 (O)
Neely, Jane 1827 wb-9-119 (D)
Neely, John 1816 wb-7-11 (D)
Neely, John 1816 wb-7-58 (D)
Neely, Nathan 1848 ib-1-45 (Ca)
Neely, Richard 1846 wb-13-44 (Rb)
Neely, Robert 1807 wb-#13 (Mu)
Neely, Samuel 1815 wb-#11 (Mu)
Neely, Samuel 1845 wb-13-193 (D)
Neely, Samuel 1856 wb-17-112 (D)
Neely, Thomas 1798 wb-2-131 (D)
Neely, Thomas 1841 wb-z-128 (Mu)
Neely, Thomas 1847 wb-14-161 (D)
Neely, Thos. 1802 wb-2-232 (D)
Neely, W. 1853 wb-#109 (Wl)
Neely, William 1790 wb-1-166 (D)
Neely, William 1827 wb-4-203 (Wi)
Neely, William 1842 wb-12-314* (D)
Neely, William 1845 wb-7-0 (Sm)
Neely, William L. 1840 wb-z-189 (Mu)
Neely, Wm. 1833 rb-f-428 (Mt)
Nees, Jesse 1847 wb-1-332 (Li)
Neese, Jane 1854 wb-16-252 (D)
Neese, Maretin 1849 wb-g-326 (Hn)
Neese, Sarah 1855 as-b-177 (Ms)
Neff, Jacob 1805 wb-1-164 (K)
Nehs (Neas), John 1846 wb-2-39# (Ge)
Nehs (Neas), Michael 1815 wb-2-36# (Ge)
Neighbors, Fleet 1835 wb-1-145 (Fr)
Neighbors, William 1840 wb-2-156 (Hr)
Neil, Charles R. 1840 wb-a-47 (Ms)
Neil, David 1854 lr (Gi)
Neil, Duncan 1840 wb-0-22 (Cf)
Neil, George 1810 wb-#9 (Wl)

Neil, George C. 1848 as-a-172 (Ms)
Neil, James H. 1849 wb-a-211 (Ms)
Neil, James H. L. 1857 wb-f-66 (G)
Neil, Jane 1850 as-b-30 (Ms)
Neil, John 1858 wb-#124 (Mc)
Neil, John R. 1858 wb-2-378 (Me)
Neil, Peter 1835 wb-#125 (Mc)
Neil, Stoddart 1856 149-1-43 (Ge)
Neil, William 1854 as-b-151 (Ms)
Neill, Ann 1852 wb-a-282 (Ms)
Neill, Call W. 1832 wb-10-20 (D)
Neill, George 1848 as-a-152 (Ms)
Neill, Jacob 1815 wb-#19 (Wl)
Neill, John W. 1833 wb-10-100 (D)
Neill, Robert 1840 wb-10-487 (Rb)
Neill, Samuel sr. 1860 wb-1-387 (Hw)
Neilly, Charles S. 1822 wb-3-598 (Wi)
Neilson, A. D. 1854 as-2-322 (Ge)
Neilson, Archibald D. 1847 148-1-191 (Ge)
Neilson, Eliza M. 1849 148-1-286 (Ge)
Neilson, H. D. 1860 wb-b-82 (F)
Neilson, Horatio 1850 148-1-330 (Ge)
Neilson, P. D. 1839 wb-2-138 (Hr)
Neilson, Lucy 1848 wb-10-9 (K)
Nelms, Ezekiel 1843 wb-z-537 (Mu)
Nelms, Richard 1861 wb-k-496 (O)
Nelms, Samuel 1852 wb-h-Apr (O)
Nelms, Sarah 1844 wb-a2-99 (Mu)
Nelson, A. 1859 wb-13-204 (K)
Nelson, Abraham 1858 wb-12-535 (K)
Nelson, Alexander M. 1822 wb-#19 (Wa)
Nelson, Alexr. 1800 wb-2-194 (D)
Nelson, Benj. B. 1835 rb-9-247 (Ru)
Nelson, Benjamin A. 1834 rb-9-147 (Ru)
Nelson, C. H. 1849 wb-9-253 (Wi)
Nelson, Charles 1836 wb-2-134 (Ma)
Nelson, Daniel 1845 rb-13-418 (Ru)
Nelson, David 1850 wb-2-1 (Ct)
Nelson, David 1852 wb-4-294 (Mu)
Nelson, Elizabeth M. 1854 wb-2-158 (Sh)
Nelson, Garrott 1852 wb-#179 (Wl)
Nelson, Geo. 1803 wb-2-328 (D)
Nelson, George B. 1838 rb-h-42 (Mt)
Nelson, Henry 1785 wb-#26 (Wa)
Nelson, Hugh F. 1860 wb-h-478 (Hn)
Nelson, Humphrey 1814 rb-2-248 (Ru)
Nelson, J. D. 1845 wb-a2-317 (Mu)
Nelson, James 1862 wb-2-356 (Li)
Nelson, James C. 1860 rb-20-587 (Ru)
Nelson, James L. 1830 wb-1-144 (Hr)
Nelson, James W. 1859 wb-13-244 (K)

Nelson, Jane 1807 wb-#10 (Wa)
Nelson, Janett 1853 wb-1-321 (Fr)
Nelson, Jarrot 1822 wb-8-150 (D)
Nelson, John (Sr.) 1824 wb-#72 (Mu)
Nelson, John 1833 wb-#34 (Wa)
Nelson, John 1837 lr (Gi)
Nelson, John 1843 wb-0-39 (Cf)
Nelson, John 1844 wb-1-333 (La)
Nelson, John 1856 wb-6-287 (Ma)
Nelson, John D. 1847 wb-b-111 (Mu)
Nelson, John J. (Dr.) 1854 wb-b-242 (L)
Nelson, John K. 1856 wb-3e-29 (Sh)
Nelson, John L. 1847 wb-9-294 (K)
Nelson, John R. 1856 wb-12-306 (K)
Nelson, Joshua 1853 wb-5-201 (Je)
Nelson, Judieth 1851 rb-15-629 (Ru)
Nelson, Levina 1804 wb-2-393 (D)
Nelson, Lewis sr. 1859 lr (Gi)
Nelson, Lucy 1848 wb-10-3 (K)
Nelson, M. A. 1839 rb-h-196 (Mt)
Nelson, Mary 1839 wb-y-381 (Mu)
Nelson, Mary 1848 rb-14-389 (Ru)
Nelson, Mathew 1852 wb-#9 (Mo)
Nelson, Mathew 1856 rb-18-211 (Ru)
Nelson, Matthew 1843 wb-z-564 (Mu)
Nelson, Matthew M. 1858 wb-13-5 (K)
Nelson, Nathan 1824 wb-#21 (Wa)
Nelson, Phoebe 1858 wb-#63 (Wa)
Nelson, Pleasant H. 1831 rb-8-327 (Ru)
Nelson, Robert 1808 rb-a-341 (Mt)
Nelson, Robert 1818 rb-c-55 (Mt)
Nelson, Robert 1840 abl-1-214 (T)
Nelson, Robert L. 1854 wb-h-298 (Hu)
Nelson, Samuel 1815 wb-#13 (Mu)
Nelson, Sarah 1847 wb-a2-562 (Mu)
Nelson, Thomas 1835 wb-#33 (Wa)
Nelson, Thomas 1836 wb-2-79 (Ma)
Nelson, Thomas 1851 rb-15-625 (Ru)
Nelson, William 1797 wb-1-58 (K)
Nelson, William 1820 rb-c-284 (Mt)
Nelson, William 1829 wb-#28 (Wa)
Nelson, William 1830 rb-f-138 (Mt)
Nelson, William 1832 wb-1-386 (Hw)
Nelson, William L. 1838 wb-y-311 (Mu)
Nelson, Williams D. 1836 wb-x-399 (Mu)
Nelton?, Edward 1849 wb-c-374 (Wh)
Nenney, Patrick (esq.) 1824 wb-2-468 (Je)
Nepper, William 1857 wb-16-470 (Rb)
Nesbitt, Jeremiah 1855 wb-a-290 (Di)
Nesbitt, John 1825 as-A-119 (Di)
Nesbitt, John 1841 wb-a-145 (Di)

Nesbitt, Joseph 1857 rb-19-127 (Ru)
Nesbitt, Nathan 1828 wb-a-15 (Cr)
Nesbitt, Robert 1847 wb-a-175 (Di)
Nestor, Jonathan 1840 wb-7-20 (K)
Neswanger, Jacob 1841 wb-a-72 (L)
Netherland, Dr. James W. 1848 wb-#125 (Mc)
Netherland, Margaret 1841 wb-1-149 (Su)
Nettle, John A. 1834 wb-#106 (Wl)
Nettles, Benjamin 1831 wb-#90 (Wl)
Nettles, Frances 1832 wb-#96 (Wl)
Nettles, Harvey 1850 wb-d-268 (G)
Nettles, William 1831 wb-#90 (Wl)
Nettles, Zachariah 1853 wb-#179 (Wl)
Neusom, William E. 1831 wb-9-494 (D)
Nevel, John 1830 rb-8-226 (Ru)
Nevell, Joseph B. 1855 wb-h-90 (St)
Nevell, Rachael 1845 rb-j-299 (Mt)
Nevil, James 1831 rb-8-243 (Ru)
Nevil, Rachel 1829 rb-e-492 (Mt)
Nevill, Benjamin O. 1849 wb#40 (Gu)
Nevill, George 1811 rb-a-56 (Mt)
Neville, George 1821 rb-c-403 (Mt)
Neville, John 1853 wb-n-189 (Mt)
Neville, John D. 1854 wb-a-454 (F)
Neville, Mary 1843 rb-j-18 (Mt)
Nevills, Booker 1841 wb-z-278 (Mu)
Nevills, Christiana T. 1859 wb-13-186 (Wi)
Nevils, Ann E. 1855 wb-11-577 (Wi)
Nevils, Clemant H. 1840 wb-z-5 (Mu)
Nevils, John 1830 wb-#207 (Mu)
Nevils, John C. 1850 wb-b-119 (L)
Nevils, Josiah 1854 wb-11-403 (Wi)
Nevils, Robert 1848 wb#18 (Gu)
Nevils, Sarah 1861 wb-f-216 (Mu)
Nevin, John 1806 wb-1-215* (K)
New, John 1833 wb-10-270 (D)
New, Martin 1848 wb-14-239 (D)
New, Milly 1846 wb-#160 (Wl)
New, Milly D. 1844 wb-#147 (Wl)
New, Nancy A. 1845 wb-3-307 (Hr)
New, Nancy N. 1845 wb-4-3 (Hr)
New, William 1820 wb-#44 (Wl)
New, William 1835 lr (Sn)
New, William 1835 wb-#108 (Wl)
New, William 1838 wb-#127 (Wl)
New, William 1841 wb-2-234 (Hr)
New, Wm. P. 1843 wb-3-7 (Hr)
Newbern, Acy (Asa) 1854 ib-1-288 (Wy)
Newbery, John W. 1845 wb-b-108 (We)
Newbury, James 1832 rb-f-366 (Mt)
Newby, Cyrena 1848 wb-2-294 (W)

Newby, John 1832 wb-#96 (Wl)
Newby, Judith Ann 1854 ib-h-214 (F)
Newby, Nancy 1856 wb-7-0 (Sm)
Newby, Oswell P. 1859 wb-3e-100 (Sh)
Newby, Samuel 1854 wb-a-447 (F)
Newby, Sarah 1833 wb-#100 (Wl)
Newby, Sarah C. 1835 wb-#110 (Wl)
Newby, Thomas 1846 wb-2-160 (W)
Newby, Thompson 1836 wb-1-166 (W)
Newby, Washington Z. W. 1844 wb-2-10 (W)
Newby, Whaly 1854 wb-7-0 (Sm)
Newby, William 1844 wb-7-0 (Sm)
Newby, William 1854 ib-h-216 (F)
Newby, William C. 1855 wb-3-247 (W)
Newel, Edward 1843 rb-j-23 (Mt)
Newell, E. W. 1857 wb-2-380 (Me)
Newell, Ephraim M. 1855 wb-2-277 (Me)
Newell, Ephriam 1856 wb-2-334 (Me)
Newell, Jane 1831 wb-9-481 (D)
Newell, John 1818 rb-c-52 (Mt)
Newell, Joseph 1816 wb-2-37# (Ge)
Newell, S. S. 1852 wb-m-430 (Mt)
Newell, Samuel 1794 wb-1-17 (K)
Newell, William 1844 rb-j-285 (Mt)
Newgent, William H. 1844 rb-12-488 (Ru)
Newgent, William H. jr. 1849 rb-14-509 (Ru)
Newgent, William jr. 1846 rb-13-714 (Ru)
Newland, Isaac 1838 wb-11-120 (D)
Newland, John 1851 wb-15-122 (D)
Newland, Mary 1845 wb-13-290 (D)
Newland, Susan 1847 wb-14-100 (D)
Newley, Mary 1851 wb-3-100 (W)
Newman, Alfred C. 1840 wb-#126 (Mc)
Newman, Allen 1859 rb-20-82 (Ru)
Newman, Andrew 1845 wb-12-461 (Rb)
Newman, Caroline H. 1858 wb-12-481 (K)
Newman, Cornelius 1823 wb-1-21# (Ge)
Newman, Edward 1859 wb-13-180 (K)
Newman, Henry B. 1848 wb-10-4 (K)
Newman, Hugh 1840 wb-7-33 (K)
Newman, Isaac 1832 wb-#126 (Mc)
Newman, Jacob 1834 wb-5-289 (K)
Newman, Jacob 1855 wb-12-135 (K)
Newman, James 1840 rb-11-50 (Ru)
Newman, Jared 1839 wb-3-541 (Je)
Newman, John 1836 wb-#126 (Mc)
Newman, John 1838 as-a-406 (Di)
Newman, John 1841 as-a-499 (Di)
Newman, John 1842 rb-12-106 (Ru)
Newman, John 1842 rb-12-111 (Ru)
Newman, John 1848 33-3-40 (Gr)

Newman, John F. 1836 wb-a-74 (T)
Newman, John F. 1839 abl-1-140 (T)
Newman, John sr. 1844 rb-12-575 (Ru)
Newman, Joseph 1849 rb-15-204 (Ru)
Newman, Robert M. 1854 wb-#126 (Mc)
Newman, Samuel 1851 wb-#127 (Mc)
Newman, Thomas 1836 wb-b-24 (Hd)
Newman, Wiley C. 1842 wb-1-210 (Li)
Newman, William 1841 wb-b-28 (We)
Newport, M. C. 1843 wb-f-119* (Hn)
News, William P. 1841 wb-2-199 (Hr)
Newsom, Balam 1841 wb-3-341 (Ma)
Newsom, Benjamin L. 1849 wb-9-226 (Wi)
Newsom, Eaton R. 1857 wb-5-76 (Hr)
Newsom, Eldridge 1827 wb-1-116 (Ma)
Newsom, Eliza H. 1833 wb-10-180 (D)
Newsom, Gilliam 1829 rb-e-494 (Mt)
Newsom, Harbert 1837 wb-2-225* (Ma)
Newsom, Herbert 1855 wb-6-121 (Ma)
Newsom, James 1838 wb-6-493 (Wi)
Newsom, John R. 1852 wb-10-375 (Wi)
Newsom, Lawrence 1816 wb-2-255 (Wi)
Newsom, Mary 1838 wb-6-539 (Wi)
Newsom, Nathaniel 1831 wb-5-9 (Wi)
Newsom, Priscilla 1849 wb-14-430 (D)
Newsom, Sarah 1841 wb-z-261 (Mu)
Newsom, Sarah B. 1852 rb-16-334 (Ru)
Newsom, Thomas J. 1836 rb-9-306 (Ru)
Newsom, William 1834 wb-x-145 (Mu)
Newsom, William 1855 wb-6-8 (Ma)
Newsom, William B. 1847 wb-14-102 (D)
Newsom, William E. 1845 wb-13-176 (D)
Newsome, Francis 1845 wb-13-171 (D)
Newton, Frederick 1844 wb-13-103 (D)
Newton, George 1807 wb-3-162 (D)
Newton, George 1807 wb-3-170 (D)
Newton, Henry 1834 wb-8-411 (Rb)
Newton, James 1840 wb-b-17 (We)
Newton, John 1855 wb-16-17 (Rb)
Newton, Mary 1822 wb-3-473 (Rb)
Newton, Nancy 1838 wb-10-90 (Rb)
Newton, Richard D. 1851 wb-m-273 (Mt)
Newton, Robert 1840 wb-10-540 (Rb)
Newton, Sarah 1852 wb-15-167 (Rb)
Niblet, John sr. 1832 rb-f-382 (Mt)
Niblet?, Jane 1855 wb-n-635 (Mt)
Niblett, Elija H. 1855 wb-n-635 (Mt)
Niblett, Jane R. 1853 wb-n-1 (Mt)
Niblett, William 1853 wb-n-134 (Mt)
Nice, Dr. William G. 1853 wb-#127 (Mc)
Niceler, Mary 1857 wb-1-124 (Be)

Nicely, Katharine 1859 wb-4-14 (Gr)
Nicely, Nicholas 1844 wb-5-302 (Gr)
Nichodemus, William 1837 wb-6-125 (K)
Nichol, Eli 1850 ib-1-99 (Ca)
Nichol, Henry A. 1847 wb-b-54 (Mu)
Nichol, Irvin O. 1856 wb-6-222 (Ma)
Nichol, John 1853 wb-16-68 (D)
Nichol, Josiah 1833 wb-10-175 (D)
Nichol, Josiah D. 1842 wb-12-300* (D)
Nichol, Mary E. 1845 wb-13-304 (D)
Nicholas, Joshua 1855 wb-a-377 (Ms)
Nichold, James 1828 wb-b-289 (St)
Nicholls, Nancy 1840 wb-b-208 (Hd)
Nichols, A. C. 1859 gs-1-413 (F)
Nichols, Allen 1848 wb-9-143 (Wi)
Nichols, Allen F. 1851 wb-10-4 (Wi)
Nichols, Benjamin 1843 wb-a-118 (Cr)
Nichols, Ferdinando S. 1859 wb-13-145 (Wi)
Nichols, George 1851 wb-15-83 (D)
Nichols, Irwin 1842 wb-3-536 (Ma)
Nichols, James 1852 rb-16-150 (Ru)
Nichols, Jefferson 1856 wb-a-259 (Cr)
Nichols, Jesse 1806 wb-1-0 (Sm)
Nichols, John 1817 wb-7-162 (D)
Nichols, John 1860 wb-18-235 (D)
Nichols, John c. 1820 wb-#112 (Mu)
Nichols, Joseph 1826 rb-6-182 (Ru)
Nichols, Laurence 1847 as-a-145 (Ms)
Nichols, Margaret 1859 wb-1-47 (Se)
Nichols, Mary 1842 wb-b-418 (Hd)
Nichols, Mathew 1859 wb-7-0 (Sm)
Nichols, Nancy 1854 ib-1-345 (Ca)
Nichols, Nancy Ann 1854 ib-1-324 (Ca)
Nichols, Richd. 1848 wb-14-9 (Rb)
Nichols, Robert 1850 wb-2-108 (La)
Nichols, Sarah 1821 wb-7-508 (D)
Nichols, Sarah 1847 wb-0-77 (Cf)
Nichols, William 1839 wb-e-18 (Hn)
Nichols, William 1845 wb-e-36 (O)
Nichols, William P. 1859 wb-00-5 (Cf)
Nicholson, Adkin 1838 wb-y-193* (Mu)
Nicholson, Alfred O. 1823 wb-#57 (Mu)
Nicholson, B. 1833 rb-f-494 (Mt)
Nicholson, Boyd M. 1856 wb-17-127 (D)
Nicholson, Brittian 1833 rb-f-486 (Mt)
Nicholson, Calvin H. 1824 wb-#212 (Mu)
Nicholson, Catharine B. 1854 wb-5-334 (Je)
Nicholson, David 1855 wb-6-137 (Ma)
Nicholson, E. M. 1849 wb-b-442 (Mu)
Nicholson, Edward M. 1849 wb-b-444 (Mu)
Nicholson, Edy 1841 wb-7-251 (K)

Nicholson, Elijah 1852 wb-15-226 (D)
Nicholson, Elisha 1849 wb-14-412 (D)
Nicholson, George 1820 wb-#69 (Mu)
Nicholson, Griffin 1828 rb-e-340 (Mt)
Nicholson, Griffin 1849 rb-l-483 (Mt)
Nicholson, James 1856 wb-16-142 (Rb)
Nicholson, Jane? 1846 wb-a2-452 (Mu)
Nicholson, John 1823 wb-#60 (Mu)
Nicholson, Joseph J. 1829 wb-1-186 (Ma)
Nicholson, Mala 1829 wb-4-435 (Wi)
Nicholson, Malachi 1829 wb-4-463 (Wi)
Nicholson, Malachi 1849 wb-9-233 (Wi)
Nicholson, Marmaduke N. 1836 wb-6-21 (Wi)
Nicholson, Mary 1844 rb-j-64 (Mt)
Nicholson, Nancy 1854 wb-5-147 (Ma)
Nicholson, Nathaniel 1833 wb-8-164 (Rb)
Nicholson, Osburne P. 1812 wb-#6 (Mu)
Nicholson, P. O. 1815 wb-#14 (Mu)
Nicholson, R. G. 1856 wb-17-107 (D)
Nicholson, R. M. sr. 1856 wb-17-106 (D)
Nicholson, Robert G. 1858 wb-17-464 (D)
Nicholson, Samuel 1831 wb-5-89 (K)
Nicholson, Sarah 1848 wb-9-161 (Wi)
Nicholson, William 1857 wb-17-227 (D)
Nickelson, John 1803 wb-1-223 (Bo)
Nickle, Matthias 1838 wb-6-249 (K)
Nickles, John 1816 wb-#19 (Mu)
Nickols, A. M. 1858 wb-4-207 (La)
Nicks, Doke 1857 wb-2-180 (Li)
Nickson, Charles 1835 wb-3-0 (Sm)
Nickson, William 1820 rb-4-232 (Ru)
Night, Jesse 1833 wb-8-268 (Rb)
Nightingale, George Cortes 1827? wb-#161 (Mu)
Nighton, W. H. 1852 wb-xx-95 (St)
Niman, Jacob 1793 wb-1-6 (K)
Nimmi, W. C. 1850 wb-14-384 (Rb)
Nimmo, Allen C. 1848 wb-d-136 (G)
Nimmo, William 1853 lr (Sn)
Nipper, Caleb 1820 wb-2-287 (Je)
Nipper, James 1858 wb-f-155 (Ro)
Nipper, Mary Ann E. 1853 wb-15-399 (Rb)
Nisbett, Alexander sr. 1853 rb-16-356 (Ru)
Nisbett, Alexr. 1852 rb-16-323 (Ru)
Nisler, Albert 1850 mr-2-168 (Be)
Nisler, David 1847 mr-2-243 (Be)
Nisler, Henry 1846 mr-2-179 (Be)
Nisler, Mary 1847 mr-2-267 (Be)
Nivins, Isaac 1860 wb-1-326 (Be)
Nivins, James 1852 rb-16-338 (Ru)
Nix, Jonathan 1845 wb-e-58 (O)
Nix, Joseph 1841 wb-b-328 (Hd)

Nix, Mark 1847 wb-g-176 (Hn)
Nix, Robert 1822 wb-A-305 (Li)
Nixon, George W. 1854 wb-e-441 (Ro)
Nixon, John 1826 wb-#168 (Mu)
Nixon, John 1840 wb-z-95 (Mu)
Nixon, John 1842 rb-12-238 (Ru)
Nixon, John B. 1842 rb-12-288 (Ru)
Nixon, John H. 1861 wb-d-95 (L)
Nixon, Jonathan J. 1835 wb-1-193 (Hy)
Nixon, Mary L. C. 1855 ib-1-359 (Wy)
Nixon, Mary W. 1842 wb-3-92 (Hy)
Noble, John 1809 wb-1-351 (Rb)
Nobles, Abner 1860 wb-d-48 (L)
Nobles, Emily 1856 wb-6-196 (Ma)
Nobles, James 1833 wb-b-12 (G)
Nobles, John 1843 mr-2-48 (Be)
Nobles, Josh 1841 abl-1-235 (T)
Nobles, Milly 1844 mr-2-77 (Be)
Noblet, Thomas 1824 wb-1-114 (Bo)
Nodding, John 1783 wb-#2 (Wa)
Nodding, William 1812 wb-#12 (Wa)
Noe, Jacob 1851 wb-3-337 (Gr)
Noe, John 1859 rb-19-633 (Ru)
Noe, John sr. 1856 wb-3-338 (Gr)
Noe, John sr. 1856 wb-4-1 (Gr)
Noe, Margaret 1858 wb-3-533 (Gr)
Noe, Margaret 1858 wb-4-9 (Gr)
Noel, Ewel 1854 wb-e-32 (Hy)
Noel, Reuben 1850 wb-14-494 (D)
Noell, Martha C. 1842 wb-3-8 (Hy)
Noell, Zachariah 1848 wb-g-278 (Hn)
Nokes, Thomas 1849 ib-1-74 (Ca)
Nolan, Benjamin 1839 wb-e-233 (Hu)
Noland, John 1807 wb-1-170 (Wi)
Nolen, Alen 1814 rb-b-162 (Mt)
Nolen, B. P. 1854 wb-h-48 (St)
Nolen, Berry 1850 wb-9-592 (Wi)
Nolen, Charles 1839 wb-3-0 (Sm)
Nolen, David 1839 wb-7-203 (Wi)
Nolen, David 1851 wb-10-123 (Wi)
Nolen, General L. 1851 wb-10-135 (Wi)
Nolen, General L. 1851 wb-10-322 (Wi)
Nolen, General Lee 1860 wb-13-349 (Wi)
Nolen, John 1857 wb-12-368 (Wi)
Nolen, Leanna L. 1856 wb-6-291 (Ma)
Nolen, Mary a. 1860 wb-13-353 (Wi)
Nolen, Purce G. 1840 rb-11-55 (Ru)
Nolen, Stephen 1851 wb-10-51 (Wi)
Nolen, Thomas 1851 wb-m-192 (Mt)
Nolen, Thomas J. 1853 wb-10-488 (Wi)
Nolen, William 1842 wb-7-575 (Wi)

Northern, Samuel 1854 as-c-372 (Di)
Northington (B), Peter 1856 wb-h-543 (Hu)
Northington, Atlas 1861 wb-17-257 (Rb)
Northington, David 1853 mr-2-491 (Be)
Northington, E. C. (Miss) 1860 rb-p-516 (Mt)
Northington, E. N. 1856 rb-o-127 (Mt)
Northington, Felix G. 1859 rb-p-171 (Mt)
Northington, Felix jr. 1856 rb-o-126 (Mt)
Northington, John 1836 rb-g-263 (Mt)
Northington, Samuel 1844 rb-j-61 (Mt)
Northington, Sterling 1818 wb-7-225 (D)
Norton, Alexander 1834 wb-1-115 (Bo)
Norton, Minerva 1854 wb-2-82# (Ge)
Norton, Nancy 1850 wb-1-257 (Bo)
Norton, William 1813 wb-2-30 (Wi)
Norton, William 1830 wb-4-501 (Wi)
Norton, William H. 1854 wb-3-153 (Gr)
Norvel, James J. 1846 5-3-125 (Cl)
Norvell, Dempsey 1852 wb-e-7 (Hy)
Norvell, H. J. H. 1854 wb-2-155 (Sh)
Norvell, Hendrick 1838 wb-11-206 (D)
Norvell, James J. 1851 ib-1-219 (Cl)
Norvell, Joseph 1847 wb-14-108 (D)
Norvell, Joseph 1860 wb-18-331 (D)
Norvell, Lipscomb 1843 wb-12-415* (D)
Norvell, Nancy B. 1850 rb-15-321 (Ru)
Norville, James 1836 wb-b-36 (Hd)
Norwood, Elizabeth P. 1841 rb-i-120 (Mt)
Norwood, John 1826 wb-1-113 (Bo)
Norwood, John 1846 wb-d-280 (Hd)
Norwood, John P. 1845 wb-d-194 (Hd)
Norwood, Nathaniel 1861 wb-18-619 (D)
Norworthy, Willis 1843 wb-e-543 (Hu)
Notgrass, Jacob S. 1858 wb-4-211 (La)
Notgrass, James 1834 wb-x-175 (Mu)
Notgrass, Thos. 1861 wb-b-109 (F)
Nothern, Edward 1810 wb-1-363 (Rb)
Nothern, Mary 1860 wb-1-391 (Hw)
Nourse, Lawson 1827 wb-a-229 (Wh)
Nowel, Barnabas 1842 wb-3-547 (Ma)
Nowland, Arminta S. 1861 wb-e-395 (Wh)
Nowland, Thos. 1788 wb-1-68 (D)
Nowlen, Benjamin 1858 wb-4-127 (La)
Nowlen, John 1811 wb-1-260 (Wi)
Nowlen, John S. 1829 wb-b-55 (Hn)
Nowlen, P. G. 1857 rb-18-294 (Ru)
Nowlin, Arabella 1844 wb-#142 (Wl)
Nowlin, B. W. 1861 wb-b-122 (Ms)
Nowlin, David 1861 wb-4-452 (La)
Nowlin, J. B. W. 1856 as-b-229 (Ms)
Nowlin, James D. 1842 wb-#137 (Wl)

Nowlin, Thomas 1855 wb-3-253 (La)
Nowne?, Lawson (Dr.) 1821 wb-a-146 (Wh)
Noy, Jacob 1803 wb-2-299 (D)
Noyes, Levi 1816 wb-2-324 (Rb)
Nuburn, Asa 1856 ib-1-419 (Wy)
Nucholds, Wm. 1852 wb-d-391 (G)
Nuckolls, Richard 1835 wb-9-85 (Rb)
Nuckolls, Starling 1860 wb-5-106 (Hr)
Nuell, S. S. 1854 wb-n-331 (Mt)
Nuell, William 1846 rb-k-360 (Mt)
Nugent, Nancy 1858 wb-1-389 (Hw)
Null, John 1831 wb-1-29 (La)
Numan, John 1839 wb-y-381 (Mu)
Numan, John H. 1835 wb-x-252* (Mu)
Nunley, Anderson 1849 ib-1-39 (Wy)
Nunley, Philip 1853 ib-1-204 (Wy)
Nunley, Wesley 1859 wb#5 (Gu)
Nunley, William 1856 wb#2 (Gu)
Nunly, Branch 1849 wb-7-0 (Sm)
Nunn, Francis 1816 Wb-2-182 (Wi)
Nunn, Francis 1837 wb-a-4 (L)
Nunn, Francis 1841 wb-7-368 (Wi)
Nunn, Francis 1848 wb-2-25 (La)
Nunn, John 1834? wb-1-52 (Hy)
Nunn, Mary G. 1852 wb-3-92 (La)
Nunn, William 1842 wb-2-554 (Hy)
Nunnely, John J. 1825 wb-1-0 (Sm)
Nurrel, Edward 1845 rb-k-21 (Mt)
Nurrel, Wm. 1845 rb-k-76 (Mt)
Nusom, Newett 1830 wb-1-256 (Ma)
Nutt, Thomas 1843 wb-1-96 (Sh)
Nye, Shadrack 1850 lr (Sn)

- O -

O'Briant, John 1827 wb-#70 (Wl)
O'Brien, William 1858 wb-12-467 (K)
O'Brien, William 1859 wb-13-156 (K)
O'Dell, Samuel W. 1836 wb-6-56 (K)
O'Donald, Maurice? 1829 wb-#128 (Mc)
O'Donnel, Matthew 1823 wb-3-609 (Wi)
O'Gwin, Stephen 1853 wb-h-174 (Hu)
O'Neal, Laban 1852 wb-5-112 (Ma)
O'Neal, Marmaduke 1808 wb-#43 (Mu)
O'Neal, Martin 1812 wb-#22 (Wl)
O'Neil, Jesse 1824 wb-#128 (Mc)
O'Neil, Robert 1851 wb-5-98 (Ma)
O'Reiley, J. C. jr. 1838 wb-y-187 (Mu)
O'Reilley, James C. 1850 wb-f-17 (Mu)
O'Reilly, James C. 1836 wb-x-382 (Mu)
O'Brien, Charles R. 1852 wb-15-243 (D)

O'Brien, John C. 1841 lw (Ct)
O'Gwin, Bryant 1848 wb-g-80 (Hu)
O'Neal, Elizabeth 1850 wb-#165 (Wl)
O'Neal, James L. 1852 wb-h-Mar (O)
O'Neil, John F. 1842 wb-12-354* (D)
Oakes, Isaac 1824 wb-3-673 (Wi)
Oakes, Isaac N. 1840 wb-2-168 (Hr)
Oakes, Isaac N. 1848 wb-4-260 (Hr)
Oakley, Elizabeth 1849 wb-b-458 (Mu)
Oakley, George 1824 wb-1-0 (Sm)
Oakley, James 1822 wb-#43 (Mu)
Oakley, James 1849 wb-b-387 (Mu)
Oakley, James sr. 1849 wb-b-457 (Mu)
Oakley, Stephen 1850 wb-4-97 (Mu)
Oakley, Thomas 1835 wb-x-254* (Mu)
Oakley, Thomas M. 1853 wb-4-638 (Mu)
Oakley, William 1822 wb-#113 (Mu)
Oakley, William 1846 wb-#152 (Wl)
Oakley, William 1851 rb-15-619 (Ru)
Oaks, Isaac 1824 wb-A-378 (Li)
Oaks, J. N. 1850 wb-4-631 (Hr)
Oaks, James 1841 wb-0-15 (Cf)
Oaks, Joshua 1833 eb-1-306 (C)
Oaks, Presly T. 1858 wb-a-281 (T)
Obar, James J. 1858 wb-i-1 (St)
Obarr, Daniel 1819 rb-c-80 (Mt)
Obars, Robert 1832 wb-1-328 (Ma)
Ochmig, Adam 1853 wb#41 (Gu)
Odam, Armstead? G. 1856 wb-A-112 (Ca)
Odam, Charlotte 1858 ib-1-492 (Ca)
Odam, James 1829 lr (Sn)
Odam, Lewis 1850 mr-2-373 (Be)
Odam, Wm. C. 1856 ib-1-383 (Ca)
Odell, Abraham 1829? wb-#28 (Wa)
Odell, David M. 1854 wb-f-38 (Mu)
Odell, Mary 1855 wb-#55 (Wa)
Odell, Samuel 1788 wb-1-45 (Je)
Odell, Samuel W. 1850 wb-10-338 (K)
Odell, William 1848 wb-10-7 (K)
Oden, John 1843 wb-4-78 (Je)
Oden, Solomon 1860 wb-13-273 (Wi)
Oden, Thomas A. 1827 rb-7-290 (Ru)
Odeneal, Tate (Lt.) 1816 rb-b-57 (Mt)
Odeneal, Tate 1816 rb-b-311 (Mt)
Odil, George B. 1853 wb-f-27 (Mu)
Odil, James M. 1842 wb-7-555 (Wi)
Odil, John 1843 wb-z-544 (Mu)
Odil, Mary E. 1853 wb-f-28 (Mu)
Odil, Samuel A. 1854 wb-f-41 (Mu)
Odle, Saml. 1798 wb-1-240 (Je)
Odneal, Sarah 1839 wb-2-112 (Hr)

Odom, James 1843 wb-A-31 (Ca)
Odom, Wiley 1819 wb-1-0 (Sm)
Odonneley, Henry 1849 wb-g-242 (Hu)
Officer, James 1848 wb-c-301 (Wh)
Officer, Robert 1847 wb-c-265 (Wh)
Officer, Robert H. 1854 wb-d-159 (Wh)
Offutt, Henry 1855 lr (Sn)
Offutt, William 1861 wb-f-220 (Mu)
Ogan, John 1836 wb-1-187 (Gr)
Ogan, John 1848 33-3-61 (Gr)
Ogburn, James M. 1858 rb-o-674 (Mt)
Ogburn, John 1854 wb-n-379 (Mt)
Ogburn, Josiah 1829 rb-f-1 (Mt)
Ogburn, Matthew 1839 rb-h-359 (Mt)
Ogburn, Sarah 1824 rb-d-299 (Mt)
Ogburn, Sarah 1824 rb-d-301 (Mt)
Ogburn, Sarah 1846 rb-k-52 (Mt)
Ogden, Benjamin Wesley 1854 wb-16-339 (D)
Ogden, George 1843 wb-c-112 (Wh)
Ogden, Joshua 1794 wb-1-14 (K)
Ogden, Titus 1793 wb-1-12 (K)
Oge, Moses 1815 wb-2-226 (Rb)
Ogg, Elizabeth 1861 rb-p-559 (Mt)
Ogg, Micajah 1853 wb-15-327 (Rb)
Ogg, Peter 1850 wb-10-425 (K)
Ogg, Wm. 1860 rb-p-409 (Mt)
Ogilsby, Elisha 1839 wb-b-175 (O)
Ogilvie, Cynthia M. 1854 wb-11-89 (Wi)
Ogilvie, Francis 1821 rb-5-81 (Ru)
Ogilvie, Harris 1824 wb-8-289 (D)
Ogilvie, Jason W. 1848 wb-9-134 (Wi)
Ogilvie, John 1822 wb-3-291 (Wi)
Ogilvie, Richard 1822 wb-3-588 (Wi)
Ogilvie, Smith 1812 rb-2-177 (Ru)
Ogilvie, William 1813 wb-1-313 (Wi)
Ogilvie, William 1860 wb-18-352 (D)
Ogle, Thomas 1861 wb-1-74 (Se)
Ogles, James 1830 wb-a-162 (G)
Ogles, James 1830 wb-a-166 (G)
Oglesby, Elisha 1783 wb-1-4 (D)
Oglesby, James 1811 wb-#28 (Mu)
Oglesby, James 1823 wb-#49 (Mu)
Oglesby, Robert W. 1857 wb-12-451 (K)
Oglevie, David 1816 wb-#35 (Mu)
Oglevie, Smith 1822 rb-5-239 (Ru)
Oguinn, William 1857 wb-h-441 (St)
Old, James 1851 wb-b-304 (We)
Old, James 1861 wb-b-116 (Ms)
Old, John E. 1828 wb-1-60 (Hr)
Old, Lew A. 1844 wb-b-74 (We)
Old, Nancy 1860 wb-2-324 (Li)

Old, Nancy Elizabeth 1859 wb-2-296 (Li)
Old, Thomas 1831 wb-5-23 (Wi)
Old, William 1852 ib-1-186 (Wy)
Old, William 1855 wb-2-125 (Li)
Old, William W. 1852 ib-1-192 (Wy)
Oldfield, James 1851 ib-1-182 (Ca)
Oldfield, James M. 1852 ib-1-207 (Ca)
Oldham, Bishop 1841 wb-7-380 (Wi)
Oldham, Charles 1817 wb-7-125 (D)
Oldham, Elizabeth 1841 wb-7-380 (Wi)
Oldham, George 1829 rb-e-535 (Mt)
Oldham, Isaac 1845 wb-b-101 (We)
Oldham, James 1859 wb-c-302 (L)
Oldham, James K. 1860 rb-p-518 (Mt)
Oldham, Jessee 1840 rb-h-374 (Mt)
Oldham, Jessee 1845 rb-j-318 (Mt)
Oldham, Joel R. 1810 rb-a-413 (Mt)
Oldham, Moses 1819 rb-c-85 (Mt)
Oldham, Moses 1860 rb-p-471 (Mt)
Oldham, Moses sr. 1818 rb-b-489 (Mt)
Oldham, Peter 1824 wb-8-339 (D)
Oldham, Richard 1846 wb-#150 (Wl)
Oldham, Samuel 1847 wb-7-0 (Sm)
Oldham, Samuel 1860 wb-e-138 (Hy)
Oldham, Virgenia 1846 wb-b-136 (We)
Olinger, David 1848 wb-2-68# (Ge)
Olinger, Jacob 1815 wb-2-192 (K)
Olinger, John 1823 wb-1-21# (Ge)
Oliphant, Henrietta N. 1855 wb-e-305 (G)
Oliphant, James 1849 rb-15-3 (Ru)
Oliphant, James 1855 wb-2-82# (Ge)
Oliphant, Samuel 1842 wb-z-429 (Mu)
Oliphant, William C. 1841 wb-z-263 (Mu)
Olive, Elizabeth 1858 wb-b-72 (F)
Olive, Elizabeth T. 1855 ib-1-346 (Wy)
Olive, Jessee 1856 wb-f-17 (G)
Olive, John 1859 wb-h-444 (Hn)
Olive, John jr. 1835 wb-d-170 (Hn)
Olive, Josey 1859 wb-h-451 (Hn)
Oliver, Edward 1809 wb-4-30 (D)
Oliver, Enoch 1816 wb-7-7 (D)
Oliver, Frederick 1815 wb-A-87 (Li)
Oliver, George 1833 lr (Gi)
Oliver, James 1847 wb-g-213 (Hn)
Oliver, Jane 1857 rb-19-27 (Ru)
Oliver, John 1834 wb-1-442 (Ma)
Oliver, John 1852 wb-b-190 (L)
Oliver, Kellis 1819 wb-1-0 (Sm)
Oliver, Peter 1856 wb-17-57 (D)
Oliver, Plesent 1846 wb-4-39 (Hr)
Oliver, Robert 1839 wb-y-431 (Mu)

Oliver, Thomas 1854 wb-a-223 (Cr)
Oliver, William 1847 wb-g-208 (Hn)
Oliver, William 1853 wb-3-150 (W)
Oliver, William 1855 wb-6-163 (Ma)
Oliver, William 1858 wb-4-214 (La)
Oliver, William 1859 as-c-143 (Ms)
Olliver, Isaac 1845 wb-b-90 (We)
Olliver, Stephen 1844 wb-b-62 (We)
Olliver, Thomas B. 1839 wb-1-50 (Sh)
Olwar, Plesent 1848 wb-4-257 (Hr)
Oneal, Arthur 1814 wb-3-3 (St)
Oneal, Briant 1825 wb-b-56 (St)
Oneal, John 1854 wb-xx-330 (St)
Oneal, Mary 1833 wb-x-30 (Mu)
Oneal, Mary 1850 wb-g-329 (St)
Oneal, Peter 1845 rb-k-38 (Mt)
Oneal, Zachariah 1833 wb-c-306 (St)
Only, Levi E. 1860 wb-#128 (Mc)
Oragan, John 1859 wb-i-151 (St)
Oram, Eliza P. 1841 wb-7-411 (Wi)
Oram, William H. 1841 wb-7-396 (Wi)
Orand, John 1854 wb-A-100 (Ca)
Orange, William 1815 wb-1-0 (Sm)
Ore, C. M. 1858 wb-3-483 (Gr)
Ore, Elizabeth 1845? wb-4-20 (Je)
Ore, Joseph 1854 wb-3-224 (Gr)
Ore, Nelson 1837 wb-3-450 (Je)
Ore, Wilson 1848 wb-4-89 (Je)
Orgain, Benjamin 1839 rb-h-351 (Mt)
Orgain, Benjamin 1841 rb-i-65 (Mt)
Orgain, James 1833 rb-f-510 (Mt)
Orgain, Susannah 1840 rb-h-466 (Mt)
Orgain, William D. 1840 rb-i-3 (Mt)
Organ, Enness 1850 wb-#172 (Wl)
Organ, Ennis 1832 wb-#96 (Wl)
Organ, Rolly 1830 wb-2-0 (Sm)
Organ, Upton 1838 rb-h-141 (Mt)
Orion, William 1851 wb-1-284 (Fr)
Orman, James 1858 as-c-85 (Ms)
Orman, Joseph 1857 wb-12-385 (Wi)
Ormand, David 1836 wb-2-204 (Sn)
Ormes, Elly 1852 wb-e-8 (G)
Ormond, Adam 1851 wb-10-54 (Wi)
Orms, Evan B. 1856 wb-12-75 (Wi)
Orms, Thomas 1841 wb-b-365 (G)
Orndorff, John W. 1855 wb-16-16 (Rb)
Orne, Richard Elwins 1860 wb-3e-153 (Sh)
Orr, Azariah 1838 wb-6-318 (K)
Orr, E. W. 1842 wb-z-416 (Mu)
Orr, Ebenezer W. 1845 wb-a2-224 (Mu)
Orr, G. W. 1855 wb-g-638 (Hn)

Orr, Griffin W. 1855 wb-g-660 (Hn)
Orr, H. B. 1859 rb-p-200 (Mt)
Orr, James 1838 wb-b-90 (Hd)
Orr, Jane (Mrs.) 1860 wb-17-168 (Rb)
Orr, John 1850 as-b-104 (Ms)
Orr, John K. 1854 ib-H-160 (F)
Orr, Joseph 1820 wb-1-189 (Bo)
Orr, Nelson 1852 wb-3-12 (Gr)
Orr, Robert 1817 wb-1-199 (Bo)
Orr, Robert 1855 wb-a-365 (Ms)
Orr, Thomas 1853 lr (Gi)
Orr, William 1822 wb-3-330 (Wi)
Orr, William 1830 wb-#129 (Mc)
Orr, William 1847 wb-g-232 (Hn)
Orr, William M. 1846 as-a-131 (Ms)
Orr, _____ 1837 wb-b-60 (Hd)
Orrand, Thomas 1833 wb-#102 (Wl)
Orrick, James 1856 wb-3-334 (W)
Orsburn, John 1860 wb-k-211 (O)
Ortin, Jane 1823 wb-3-610 (Wi)
Orton, Richard 1824 wb-3-720 (Wi)
Orton, Samuel R. 1838 wb-11-302 (D)
Orton, William 1803 wb-1-138 (Wi)
Orum, James 1853 wb-10-587 (Wi)
Osbern, John 1835 wb-d-49 (Hn)
Osborn, Thomas 1859 wb-f-282 (Ro)
Osborne, Edward 1816 wb-1-16 (Fr)
Osborne, Elizabeth 1835 rb-9-268 (Ru)
Osborne, John F. 1851 rb-4-260 (Mu)
Osborne, Phillips 1829 rb-7-182 (Ru)
Osborne, William 1817 wb-7-149 (D)
Osbourn, Jasper N. 1848 wb-e-68 (Ro)
Osburn, Berry J. 1854 wb-i-208 (O)
Osburn, John 1841 lr (Gi)
Osburn, John B. 1852 wb-m-510 (Mt)
Osburn, John sr. 1849 as-a-196 (Ms)
Osburn, Nancy 1851 wb-10-37 (Wi)
Osburne, Daniel 1817 wb-2-362 (K)
Osler, Orlander 1835 wb-8-460 (Rb)
Oslin, Lucus 1851 rb-15-568 (Ru)
Oslin, William 1826 wb-4-101 (Wi)
Ott, John 1854 rb-17-1 (Ru)
Ott, R. B. 1857 rb-19-80 (Ru)
Ottinger, Ellender 1861 wb-2-94# (Ge)
Ottinger, John 1846 148-1-166 (Ge)
Ottinger, Samuel 1861 149-1-217 (Ge)
Outland, Bryan 1843 wb-f-24 (St)
Outland, Enos 1835 wb-c-435 (St)
Outland, Josiah 1834 wb-c-329 (St)
Outlaw, Alexander B. 1831 wb-c-90 (St)
Outlaw, David 1849 wb-g-127 (St)

Outlaw, Davis 1809 rb-a-143 (Mt)
Outlaw, Eli 1855 wb-h-118 (St)
Outlaw, Eli A. 1857 wb-h-359 (St)
Outlaw, George 1843 rb-i-486 (Mt)
Outlaw, George sr. 1842 rb-i-240 (Mt)
Outlaw, J. A. 1846 rb-k-272 (Mt)
Outlaw, John A. 1846 rb-k-317 (Mt)
Outlaw, John A. jr. 1850 rb-l-602 (Mt)
Outlaw, John C. 1846 wb-f-60 (O)
Outlaw, Lewis 1841 wb-b-312 (Hd)
Outlaw, Thomas 1849 rb-l-380 (Mt)
Outlaw, Thomas B. 1847 rb-k-420 (Mt)
Outlaw, W. W. 1841 wb-e-83 (St)
Outlaw, William 1814 wb-3-48 (St)
Outlaw, William 1814 wb-3-9 (St)
Outlaw, William 1848 wb-g-78 (St)
Outlaw, William T. M. 1855 wb-#55 (Wa)
Outlaw, William W. 1826 wb-b-121 (St)
Outlaw, Wright 1813 rb-b-134 (Mt)
Outterbridge, Stephen 1852 wb-b-159 (L)
Overall, Abraham 1844 wb-a-52 (Dk)
Overall, Andrew J. 1848 rb-14-380 (Ru)
Overall, Isaac 1857 rb-19-17 (Ru)
Overall, Isaac H. 1859 rb-19-537 (Ru)
Overall, Jackson 1846 rb-13-697 (Ru)
Overall, Jackson M. 1845 rb-13-388 (Ru)
Overall, James G. 1848 rb-14-325 (Ru)
Overall, Nathaniel 1835 rb-9-258 (Ru)
Overall, Perlina Ann 1859 wb-k-5 (O)
Overall, Sarah E. 1854 rb-17-1 (Ru)
Overall, W. L. 1860 rb-20-704 (Ru)
Overall, William 1793 wb-1-283 (D)
Overall, William 1795 wb-2-17 (D)
Overall, William S. 1858 rb-19-507 (Ru)
Overby, Goodwin 1841 wb-a-59 (F)
Overdeer, Jacob 1836 rb-9-383 (Ru)
Overeall, Nace 1862 wb-f-430 (G)
Overfelt, John 1843 wb-#41 (Wa)
Overman, Nancy 1841 wb-12-121* (D)
Overstreet, Elijah H. 1851 wb-4-149 (Mu)
Overstreet, James 1846 wb-a2-505 (Mu)
Overstreet, James sr. 1847 wb-a2-536 (Mu)
Overton, Archibald W. 1857 wb-17-475 (D)
Overton, Benjamine 1848 wb-2-38 (Sh)
Overton, David 1836 wb-1-169 (W)
Overton, Eli 1858? wb-1-393 (Hw)
Overton, Gabriel 1814 wb-a-17 (Di)
Overton, George 1853 wb-5-41 (Hr)
Overton, James G. 1829 wb-9-303 (D)
Overton, John 1833 wb-10-149 (D)
Overton, Joseph 1840 wb-1A-279 (A)

Overton, Melborn 1857 ib-2-389 (Cl)
Overton, Milla 1858 wb-1-393 (Hw)
Overton, Penelope 1844 wb-13-11 (D)
Overton, Richard 1827 rb-e-175 (Mt)
Overton, Richard jr. 1832 rb-f-338 (Mt)
Overton, Richard sr. 1834 rb-f-572 (Mt)
Overton, Samuel 1823 wb-8-260 (D)
Overton, Samuel 1843 wb-z-518 (Mu)
Overton, Thomas 1824 wb-8-356 (D)
Overton, Willis 1860 wb-e-145 (Hy)
Owen, Aaron 1853 wb-5-236 (Je)
Owen, Alfred 1855 wb-h-431 (Hu)
Owen, Benjamin 1802 wb-2-225 (D)
Owen, Benjamin R. 1850 wb-#171 (Wl)
Owen, Caleb 1842 wb-a-96 (T)
Owen, Christopher 1840 rb-h-415 (Mt)
Owen, Daniel 1839 wb-b-174 (Hd)
Owen, Daniel 1840 wb-#129 (Mc)
Owen, David 1840 wb-b-252 (Hd)
Owen, Edmond 1822 wb-8-79 (D)
Owen, Edmund 1835 wb-10-525 (D)
Owen, Edward 1845 wb-3-250 (Hr)
Owen, Eliza A. 1857 wb-12-470 (Wi)
Owen, Everett 1859 wb-13-208 (Wi)
Owen, Frederick 1834 wb-10-384 (D)
Owen, Hannah 1861 wb-17-247 (Rb)
Owen, Hardy 1814 wb-2-70 (K)
Owen, Hardy 1860 wb-3e-145 (Sh)
Owen, Harrison 1817 wb-a-70 (Wh)
Owen, Jabez 1850 wb-9-431 (Wi)
Owen, James 1831 wb-5-72 (Wi)
Owen, James 1833 wb-8-248 (Rb)
Owen, James B. 1820 wb-7-377 (D)
Owen, James J. 1844 wd-13-22 (D)
Owen, James S. 1852 wb-10-197 (Wi)
Owen, Jane 1838 abl-1-69 (T)
Owen, Jesse 1835 wb-#112 (Wl)
Owen, John 1825 wb-1-0 (Sm)
Owen, John 1826 wb-3-0 (Sm)
Owen, John 1847 wb-2-3 (Sh)
Owen, Johnathan 1858 wb-j-336 (O)
Owen, Joshua 1820 wb-7-412 (D)
Owen, Margaret 1858 ib-1-488 (Ca)
Owen, Martha 1841 abl-1-227* (T)
Owen, Martha A. R. 1845 wb-13-182 (D)
Owen, Mary S. 1838 wb-11-183 (D)
Owen, Mary S. 1839 wb-11-553 (D)
Owen, Nathaniel R. 1846 wb-8-484 (Wi)
Owen, Nelson 1850 wb-A-73 (Ca)
Owen, Peter 1852 as-b-55 (Ms)
Owen, Peter 1852 wb-g-455 (Hn)

Owen, Peter 1855 wb-16-595 (D)
Owen, Philip 1854 wb-11-177 (Wi)
Owen, Richard 1839 wb-#126 (Wl)
Owen, Richard A. 1852 wb-10-390 (Wi)
Owen, Richard C. 1860 wb-13-225 (Wi)
Owen, Robert 1836 wb-#112 (Wl)
Owen, Robert 1841 wb-7-361 (Wi)
Owen, Robert C. 1828 wb-9-169 (D)
Owen, Samuel 1839 wb-7-34 (Wi)
Owen, Samuel 1840 wb-7-272 (Wi)
Owen, Sandy 1829 wb-9-351 (D)
Owen, Sandy G. 1858 wb-13-6 (Wi)
Owen, Sarah 1837 wb-11-22 (D)
Owen, Silas L. 1847 wb-14-170 (D)
Owen, Stephen 1844 wb-#156 (Wl)
Owen, Stephen W. 1851 wb-#176 (Wl)
Owen, Thomas 1822 lw (Ct)
Owen, Thomas 1838 wb-b-97 (Hd)
Owen, Thomas 1840 wb-#130 (Wl)
Owen, Thomas 1844 rb-12-488 (Ru)
Owen, Thomas 1860 rb-20-341 (Ru)
Owen, Thomas 1860 rb-20-343 (Ru)
Owen, Thomas A. 1855 wb-2-111 (Li)
Owen, William 1815 wb-1-392 (Hw)
Owen, William 1840 wb-2-67 (Hy)
Owen, William 1842 wb-f-89 (Hn)
Owen, William 1852 wb-10-425 (Wi)
Owen, William 1854 wb-e-35 (Hy)
Owen, _____ 1840 wb-b-272 (Hd)
Owenby, James 1823 wb-4-51 (Rb)
Owenby, James 1833 wb-8-248 (Rb)
Owenby, John R. 1847 wb-13-165 (Rb)
Owens, B. R. 1843 wb-f-146* (Hn)
Owens, Balitha 1849 wb-g-154 (Hu)
Owens, Benjamin 1843 wb-f-145* (Hn)
Owens, Christopher 1828 rb-e-203 (Mt)
Owens, Claiborne 1858 wb-f-160 (G)
Owens, David 1827 wb-1-115 (Bo)
Owens, Jackey 1838 wb-a-65 (T)
Owens, James 1844 wb-c-176 (G)
Owens, Jno. H. 1838 wb-11-158 (D)
Owens, John 1850 wb-#129 (Mc)
Owens, John D. 1838 wb-#121 (Wl)
Owens, John J. 1848 wb-g-85 (Hu)
Owens, Mary 1836 wb-a-149 (O)
Owens, Mary 1840 wb-b-232 (Hd)
Owens, Matthew H. 1841 wb-2-418 (Hy)
Owens, Peter 1853 wb-a-200 (T)
Owens, R. G. W. 1858 wb-1C-443 (A)
Owens, Samuel 1831 wb-3-0 (Sm)
Owens, Samuel 1839 wb-e-171 (Hu)

Owens, Samuel 1854 wb-h-338 (Hu)
Owens, Samuel P. 1855 wb-c-21 (L)
Owens, Sophia 1838 rb-h-94 (Mt)
Owens, William 1808 wb-1-0 (Sm)
Owens, William 1815 wb-2-149 (Wi)
Owens, William 1836 wb-a-149 (O)
Owens, William 1842 wb-f-73 (Hn)
Owin, Nancy 1857 wb-#129 (Mc)
Owings, Alfred 1856 wb-f-12 (Ro)
Owings, Edward 1857 wb-f-114 (Ro)
Owings, Elijah 1804 wb-1-13 (Wi)
Owings, William 1843 wb-d-48 (Ro)
Owsley, Jesse 1794 wb-1-19 (K)
Owsley, John 1845 5-3-92 (Cl)
Owsley, John 1850 ib-1-185 (Cl)
Owsley, Mary (widow of John) 1850 ib-1-157 (Cl)
Owsley, ____ (widow of John) 1849?
     ib-1-139 (Cl)
Ozbrooks, Michael 1804 lr (Sn)
Ozbrooks, Ruth 1809 lr (Sn)
Ozburn, James 1848 wb-9-27 (Wi)
Ozburn, Jane 1850 wb-9-422 (Wi)
Ozburn, Robert 1852 wb-10-390 (Wi)
Ozburn, Thomas 1849 wb-#168 (WI)
Ozburne, Richie 1848 wb-9-149 (Wi)
Ozier, John 1849 wb-a-379 (F)
Ozier, Sarah 1851 wb-a-405 (F)
Ozier, Willis 1845 wb-a-278 (F)
Ozment, H. L. 1843 wb-#145 (WI)
Ozment, Harris L. 1845 wb-#158 (WI)
Ozment, Jonathan 1825 wb-#57 (WI)

- P -

Pace, Alsey 1815 wb-2-272 (Rb)
Pace, Briton 1825 rb-6-100 (Ru)
Pace, Drury 1848 wb-g-102 (Hu)
Pace, James 1815 rb-3-59 (Ru)
Pace, Joel 1840 wb-2-57 (Hy)
Pace, John 1815 rb-3-105 (Ru)
Pace, Thomas 1859 wb-a-118 (Ce)
Pace, William 1845 rb-j-453 (Mt)
Pace, William 1850 wb-g-415 (Hu)
Pace, William jr. 1835 wb-9-209 (Rb)
Pack, B. D. 1858 wb-a-56 (Ce)
Pack, B. L. 1859 wb-a-98 (Ce)
Pack, Bartemus 1833 wb-8-263 (Rb)
Pack, Benjamin 1818 wb-7-284 (D)
Pack, Elisha 1859 27-lw (Hd)
Pack, Isaac 1854 39-2-46 (Dk)
Pack, Joseph 1848 r39-1-70 (Dk)

Pack, Thomas 1855 wb-16-594 (D)
Pack, Thomas L. 1855 wb-16-602 (D)
Packett, William 1851 wb-11-165* (K)
Paddocks, B. A. 1849 wb-b-100 (L)
Padgett, Henry G. 1853 wb-11-45 (Wi)
Padgett, Mary 1856 wb-12-49 (Wi)
Padgettt, Merit 1861 wb-i-289 (St)
Pafford, Thomas 1849 r39-1-141 (Dk)
Page, Absolom 1823 wb-8-205 (D)
Page, David D. 1817 wb-2-364 (Wi)
Page, David D. 1824 wb-3-672 (Wi)
Page, Elizabeth 1838 wb-d-260 (St)
Page, Frederick D. 1848 wd-14-213 (D)
Page, Giles H. 1851 wb-15-120 (D)
Page, Henrietta 1860 wb-18-241 (D)
Page, Jacob 1850 r39-1-156 (Dk)
Page, James 1801 wb-1-81 (K)
Page, John 1808 wb-1-185 (Wi)
Page, John 1847 wb-8-126 (Sm)
Page, John 1857 wb-h-129 (Hn)
Page, Martha 1853 wb-16-62 (D)
Page, Nathan 1856 wb-#58 (Wa)
Page, Nity J. 1860 lr (Gi)
Page, Robert O. 1859 wb-3e-110 (Sh)
Page, Samuel 1839 wb-b-76 (O)
Page, Vinson 1829 wb-c-7 (St)
Page, Vinson 1855 wb-h-136 (St)
Page, William 1843 wb-c-95 (G)
Page, William 1852 wb-h-28 (Hu)
Page, William 1853 wb-15-511 (D)
Page, William 1859 wb-a-345 (Cr)
Page, William B. 1857 wb-17-336 (D)
Page, William D. 1837 rb-10-8 (Ru)
Pain, Cyntha Ann 1857 rb-o-352 (Mt)
Paine, Ephraim T. 1813 wb-2-69 (Rb)
Paine, Harriet 1858 rb-o-584 (Mt)
Paine, James 1818 rb-d-90 (Mt)
Paine, James 1840 lr (Gi)
Paine, James 1860 wb-b-89 (F)
Paine, James E. 1852 wb-m-606 (Mt)
Paine, John 1846 wb-f-17 (O)
Paine, John L. 1853 wb-n-89 (Mt)
Paine, John T. 1855 wb-n-615 (Mt)
Paine, Mary A. J. 1846 rb-k-82 (Mt)
Paine, Orville 1860 wb-1-177 (R)
Paine, Solomon 1858 wb-e-86 (Hy)
Paine, Thomas 1846 rb-k-330 (Mt)
Paine, William 1836 wb-3-0 (Sm)
Painter, John 1851 rb-15-569 (Ru)
Painter, John 1856? ib-2-300 (Cl)
Painter, Marilla T. 1857 149-1-77 (Ge)

Painter, William 1856 149-1-47 (Ge)
Paisley, James 1845 lr (Gi)
Paisley, Thomas 1823 wb-4-95 (Rb)
Paisley, William 1833 wb-8-271 (Rb)
Pallett, Abraham 1812 rb-2-172 (Ru)
Pallett, James Y. 1850 ib-1-116 (Ca)
Palmer, Amanda M. F. 1853 wb-g-536 (Hn)
Palmer, Daniel 1822 wb-#43 (Wl)
Palmer, David 1854 wb-7-0 (Sm)
Palmer, Drucilla J. 1861 39-2-451 (Dk)
Palmer, Elizabeth 1852 wb-g-474 (Hn)
Palmer, Frances 1840 wb-#142 (Wl)
Palmer, Frances 1857 wb-#125 (Wl)
Palmer, H. S. 1849 wb-g-152 (St)
Palmer, Henry 1844 wb-#145 (Wl)
Palmer, Henry S. 1850 wb-g-259 (St)
Palmer, Iseah 1843 wb-f-165* (Hn)
Palmer, John B. 1825 wb-1-57 (Fr)
Palmer, John S. 1855 ib-h-387 (F)
Palmer, Lee 1858 wb-a-324 (Cr)
Palmer, Nancy 1845 wb-g-28 (Hn)
Palmer, Nancy 1858 wb-h-262 (Hn)
Palmer, Ophelia M. 1856 rb-18-131 (Ru)
Palmer, Palmer 1821 wb-1-0 (Sm)
Palmer, Philip sr. 1831 wb-3-0 (Sm)
Palmer, Phillip 1860 39-2-358 (Dk)
Palmer, R. A. W. 1846 wb-f-19 (O)
Palmer, Sarah E. 1861 wb-h-530 (Hn)
Palmer, Simeon 1825 wb-a-158 (Hn)
Palmer, Smith 1840 wb-1-195 (We)
Palmer, Smith 1843 wb-f-177 (Hn)
Palmer, Virginia 1855 wb-g-639 (Hn)
Palmer, William 1821 wb-a-157 (Wh)
Palmer, William 1846 wb-4-67 (Hr)
Palmer, William 1857 wb-#123 (Wl)
Palmer, William H. 1845 rb-13-180 (Ru)
Palmer, William H. 1854 wb-g-552 (Hn)
Palmer, William Russell 1860 wb-3e-126 (Sh)
Palmer, Wm. 1856 wb-g-727 (Hn)
Palmer, Wm. P. 1843 wb-a-230 (F)
Palmore, John S. 1859 gs-1-281 (F)
Palmore, Thomas 1860 wb-13-266 (Wi)
Palmore, W. P. 1855 ib-h-452 (F)
Pamer, W. H. 1850 wb-4-632 (Hr)
Pample, Elizabeth 1853 wb-5-99 (Je)
Pamplin, Armstead 1834 wb-1-100 (Li)
Pangle, Frederick 1836 wb-3-363 (Je)
Pangle, John 1852 wb-5-37 (Je)
Pankey, A. L. 1859 wb-k-64 (O)
Pankey, Danl 1803 wb-2-348 (D)
Pankey, H. A. 1836 wb-1-535 (Hr)

Pankey, Hampton 1835 wb-1-444 (Hr)
Pankey, John 1804 wb-2-369 (D)
Pankey, Mastin D. 1860 wb-5-105 (Hr)
Pankey, S. L. 1857 wb-j-288 (O)
Pankey, William Riley 1814 wb-2-83 (Je)
Parchmen, L. B. 1852 wb-xx-65 (St)
Parchment, John 1832 wb-c-159 (St)
Parchment, John 1832 wb-c-174 (St)
Pardue, Richard 1810 rb-a-396 (Mt)
Pare, William 1849 wb-4-421 (Hr)
Parham, Charles L? 1859 rb-p-220 (Mt)
Parham, Charles S. 1859 rb-p-209 (Mt)
Parham, Elizabeth 1845 wb-a-270 (F)
Parham, Elizabeth 1855 wb-12-26 (Wi)
Parham, Ephriam 1818 lr (Gi)
Parham, George 1850 wb-9-342 (Wi)
Parham, James 1808 wb-3-218 (D)
Parham, Lewis A. 1842 wb-7-318 (K)
Parham, M. P. 1855 wb-f-78 (Mu)
Parham, Nancy 1856 wb-6-448 (Ma)
Parham, Newsom 1840 wb-12-73* (D)
Parham, Peyton 1819 wb-7-324 (D)
Parham, Rebecca 1818 wb-2-362 (Wi)
Parham, Sion 1843 wb-1-98 (Sh)
Parham, Thomas 1832 wb-5-196 (Wi)
Parham, Thomas 1851 wb-b-297 (We)
Parham, Thomas 1854 ib-H-166 (F)
Parham, William 1815 wb-4-337 (D)
Parham, William 1839 wb-y-608 (Mu)
Paris, Robert H. 1846 wb-2-167 (W)
Parish, Any 1849 r39-1-148 (Dk)
Parish, Jessee 1834 wb-1-325 (Hr)
Parish, Joel 1798 wb-2-125 (D)
Parish, Jolly 1838 wb-11-499 (D)
Parish, Martha 1857 ib-1-452 (Wy)
Parish, Martha A. 1855 ib-1-343 (Wy)
Parish, Thos. S. 1856 wb-h-63 (Hn)
Park, Bartemus 1826 wb-5-424 (Rb)
Park, Hiram 1841 wb-2-201 (Hy)
Park, James 1853 wb-11-423 (K)
Park, Jane C. 1848 wb-9-443 (K)
Park, John 1857 lr (Gi)
Park, John M. 1845 wb-c-248 (G)
Park, Martha J. 1849 wb-9-277 (Wi)
Park, Rhoda 1852 wb-10-387 (Wi)
Park, Ro. 1850 wb-4-565 (Hr)
Park, Robt. 1847 wb-4-248 (Hr)
Park, Thomas 1845 wb-a-61 (Ms)
Park, Thomas 1852 wb-5-23 (Hr)
Park, William 1841 wb-2-245 (Hr)
Park, William 1846 wb-9-237 (K)

Park, William B. 1840 wb-2-153 (Hr)
Parker, A. G. 1846 wb-13-371 (D)
Parker, A. K. 1847 wb-a-71 (V)
Parker, Aaron 1849 wb-g-184 (St)
Parker, Allen 1828 wb-6-332 (Rb)
Parker, C. C. 1856 ib-1-481 (Wy)
Parker, Cader 1841 wb-e-283 (Hn)
Parker, Calvin 1852 mr-2-452 (Be)
Parker, Carrol S. 1844 wb-c-187 (G)
Parker, Charles C. 1856 ib-2-4 (Wy)
Parker, Charles G. 1853 ib-1-256 (Wy)
Parker, Charles L. 1848 wb-14-184 (D)
Parker, Charles Y. 1851 ib-1-126 (Wy)
Parker, Colman 1826 lr (Sn)
Parker, Daniel 1815 rb-3-82 (Ru)
Parker, Daniel 1835 rb-9-241 (Ru)
Parker, Daniel E. 1857 wb-1-63 (Dy)
Parker, David 1848 wb-14-174 (D)
Parker, David H. 1853 wb-15-416 (Rb)
Parker, Docton 1853 rb-16-643 (Ru)
Parker, Dolly 1837 rb-g-518 (Mt)
Parker, Elizabeth 1846 wb-c-209 (Wh)
Parker, Elizabeth 1847 wb-c-259 (Wh)
Parker, Elizabeth 1858 rb-19-292 (Ru)
Parker, Felix 1853 wb-e-55 (G)
Parker, Frances sr. 1824 wb-2-0 (Sm)
Parker, Francis 1829 wb-2-0 (Sm)
Parker, Francis S. 1858 wb-12-466 (K)
Parker, Francis jr. 1826 wb-2-0 (Sm)
Parker, Francis sr. 1807 wb-1-0 (Sm)
Parker, G. W. 1858 wb-h-251 (Hn)
Parker, George 1816 wb-2-274 (Wi)
Parker, George W. 1844 wb-8-150 (Wi)
Parker, Green W. 1860 wb-k-298 (O)
Parker, Hardey 1831 wb-1-263 (Ma)
Parker, Henry S. 1855 wb-6-73 (Ma)
Parker, Isaac 1846 lr (Sn)
Parker, Isaac 1852 rb-16-341 (Ru)
Parker, Isaac 1857 wb-h-310 (St)
Parker, Isaac E. 1850 wb-d-245 (G)
Parker, Isham A. 1821 wb-8-40 (D)
Parker, J. W. 1848 rb-l-202 (Mt)
Parker, James 1852 wb-e-335 (Ro)
Parker, James E. 1833 wb-10-229 (D)
Parker, Jehu 1838 rb-h-95 (Mt)
Parker, Jeremiah 1840 lr (Gi)
Parker, Jesse 1845 wb-13-245 (D)
Parker, Jesse 1845 wb-13-300 (D)
Parker, Jesse 1845 wb-4-22 (Hr)
Parker, Jesse J. 1857 wb-17-301 (D)
Parker, Jessee 1810 wb-1-312 (K)

Parker, Jno. L. 1849 wb-4-426 (Hr)
Parker, Joel 1836 rb-9-376 (Ru)
Parker, John 1814 wb-3-1 (St)
Parker, John 1817 wb-1-0 (Sm)
Parker, John 1825 lr (Sn)
Parker, John 1829 wb-2-0 (Sm)
Parker, John 1841 rb-i-224 (Mt)
Parker, John 1851 wb-9-682 (Wi)
Parker, John 1851 wb-g-357 (St)
Parker, John 1852 rb-16-241 (Ru)
Parker, John 1860 wb-13-268 (K)
Parker, John 1860 wb-8-62 (Sm)
Parker, John C. 1853 wb-15-229 (Rb)
Parker, John J. 1852 wb-h-64 (Hu)
Parker, John M. 1846 wb-2-204 (W)
Parker, Joseph 1836 wb-b-227 (Wh)
Parker, Joseph 1850 rb-15-414 (Ru)
Parker, Josiah 1855 wb-#55 (Wa)
Parker, King 1846 lr (Sn)
Parker, Lemuel 1815 wb-1-0 (Sm)
Parker, Levi 1851 ib-1-153 (Ca)
Parker, Lucy 1821 wb-1-0 (Sm)
Parker, M. C. (Dr.) 1859 wb-13-101 (K)
Parker, Marcus C. 1858 wb-12-537 (K)
Parker, Martha 1809 wb-4-32 (D)
Parker, Mary 1833 wb-10-70 (D)
Parker, Mary 1849 wb-A-64 (Ca)
Parker, Matha 1834 wb-1-55 (Hy)
Parker, Matthew 1834 wb-1-123 (Hy)
Parker, Moses 1852 wb-a-244 (Di)
Parker, Nathan 1814 wb-a-195 (St)
Parker, Nathan 1815 wb-#17 (Wl)
Parker, Nathaniel 1811 wb-1-156 (Sn)
Parker, Newman 1836 wb-1-251 (Hy)
Parker, Noah 1856 wb-3-390 (La)
Parker, O. F. 1855 wb-16-515 (D)
Parker, Page P. 1852 lr (Sn)
Parker, Priscilla 1846 rb-k-259 (Mt)
Parker, Richard 1838 wb-2-232 (Sn)
Parker, Richard A. W. 1845 wb-e-148 (O)
Parker, Sarah 1849 ib-1-58 (Ca)
Parker, Sarah E. 1858 wb-17-474 (D)
Parker, Sterling 1845 wb-e-170 (O)
Parker, Susan 1843 wb-c-118 (G)
Parker, Susan 1852 wb-15-437 (D)
Parker, T. W. 1848 rb-l-163 (Mt)
Parker, Thomas 1810 wb-1-150 (Sn)
Parker, Thomas 1817 wb-#25 (Mu)
Parker, Thomas 1819 rb-c-214 (Mt)
Parker, Thomas 1843 wb-b*-9 (O)
Parker, Thomas B. 1846 wb-c-310 (G)

Parker, Uriah F. 1852 wb-h-28 (Hu)
Parker, W. D. 1854 wb-h-324 (Hu)
Parker, William 1818 wb-1-0 (Sm)
Parker, William 1819 wb-7-306 (D)
Parker, William 1826 wb-3-0 (Sm)
Parker, William 1834 wb-b-152 (Wh)
Parker, William 1842 rb-12-84 (Ru)
Parker, William 1843 wb-12-461* (D)
Parker, William 1853 wb-g-550 (Hn)
Parker, William 1858 wb-1-220 (Be)
Parker, William 1859 wb-1-93 (Dy)
Parker, Zachariah 1810 wb-1-314 (K)
Parkerson, Sarah 1855 wb-3-226 (Gr)
Parkes, Charles 1848 wb-2-26 (La)
Parkes, Jefferson 1861 wb-A-164 (Ca)
Parkes, Thomas L. D. 1848 wb-1-351 (Li)
Parkhurst, Abrel 1810 wb-1-0 (Sm)
Parkinson, Thomas W. 1859 as-c-193 (Ms)
Parkison, Manuel 1847 wb-#129 (Mc)
Parkman, David 1835 wb-x-288* (Mu)
Parks, Aaron 1820 wb-A-359 (Li)
Parks, Allen 1854 wb-2-95 (Li)
Parks, Benjamin T. 1857 wb-2-174 (Li)
Parks, Frank 1838 5-2-27 (Cl)
Parks, Franklin 1838 5-2-43 (Cl)
Parks, George I. 1852 wb-1-301 (Fr)
Parks, Hiram 1835 wb-1-228 (Hy)
Parks, Jacob 1858 wb-#17 (Mo)
Parks, James N. 1856 ib-h-516 (F)
Parks, John 1823 wb-3-608 (Wi)
Parks, John 1830 rb-8-43 (Ru)
Parks, John 1830 rb-8-95 (Ru)
Parks, John 1836 wb-6-151 (Wi)
Parks, John 1837 wb-1-31 (Sh)
Parks, John 1845 rb-13-65 (Ru)
Parks, John 1850 wb-9-429 (Wi)
Parks, Joseph 1834 wb-10-376 (D)
Parks, Philip 1854 wb-#54 (Wa)
Parks, Rachael 1834 wb-5-403 (Wi)
Parks, Richard 1834 wb-b-396 (Hd)
Parks, Robert 1839 wb-b-276 (G)
Parks, Stephen N. 1858 wb-12-501 (Wi)
Parks, William 1815 wb-2-152 (Wi)
Parks, William 1819 wb-2-266 (Je)
Parks, William 1831 wb-b-114 (Ro)
Parks, Wm. 1855 wb-g-694 (Hn)
Parman, Emanuel 1857 149-1-91 (Ge)
Parmely, Giles 1803 wb-1-8 (Wi)
Parmenter, Elizabeth 1844 wb-f-263 (Hn)
Parmer, James H. 1848 wb-4-260 (Hr)
Parmer, Thomas J. 1824 wb-8-385 (D)

Parmer, W. 1848 wb-4-304 (Hr)
Parmer, William 1849 wb-4-489 (Hr)
Parmley, John 1840 wb-c-133 (Ro)
Parmontier, Nicholas S. 1835 wb-10-512 (D)
Parnell, Kinchen 1850 wb-g-404 (Hu)
Paron, Aaron 1819 wb-a-113 (Wh)
Parr, Allen 1845 wb-c-267 (G)
Parr, Arthur 1814 wb-A-54 (Li)
Parr, James M. 1844 wb-d-126 (O)
Parr, Mary 1831 wb-1-62 (Li)
Parr, Moses 1837 wb-a-203 (O)
Parr, Polly 1834 wb-a-55 (O)
Parradise, William 1833 wb-10-131 (D)
Parradise, William 1833 wb-10-81 (D)
Parran, Thomas 1844 wb-3-128 (Hr)
Parrett, Caleb 1843 wb-8-59 (Wi)
Parris, Jesse 1836 wb-1-469 (Hr)
Parris, Lemuel J. 1858 wb-#130 (Mc)
Parris, Obadiah 1856 wb-7-0 (Sm)
Parris, William Sr. 1869 wb-#130 (Mc)
Parrish, Abraham 1841 as-a-48 (Ms)
Parrish, Abram M. 1828 .wb-4-300 (Wi)
Parrish, Absalom 1836 wb-10-598 (D)
Parrish, Benjamin 1848 rb-k-720 (Mt)
Parrish, Benjamin 1860 lr (Sn)
Parrish, David W. 1845 wb-8-296 (Wi)
Parrish, Elijah R. 1840 wb-7-315 (Wi)
Parrish, Francis 1844 as-b-263 (Di)
Parrish, George 1849 rb-15-17 (Ru)
Parrish, George H. 1834 rb-g-23 (Mt)
Parrish, George W. 1833 rb-9-14 (Ru)
Parrish, George W. 1856 39-2-182 (Dk)
Parrish, Henry 1811 wb-#9 (Wl)
Parrish, Henry 1861 wb-b-115 (F)
Parrish, Hudson 1854 wb-xx-369 (St)
Parrish, Huel 1826 as-a-151 (Di)
Parrish, J. C. 1856 wb-#119 (Wl)
Parrish, James D. 1836 wb-6-258 (Wi)
Parrish, James H. 1850 wb-g-313 (St)
Parrish, James S. 1841 wb-12-161* (D)
Parrish, Jessey 1854 wb-16-237 (D)
Parrish, Joel 1812 wb-1-272 (Wi)
Parrish, John 1834 wb-1-143 (We)
Parrish, Johnson 1854 39-2-1 (Dk)
Parrish, Matilda G. 1860 lr (Sn)
Parrish, Matthew F. 1845 wb-8-296 (Wi)
Parrish, Nancy 1858 wb-#127 (Wl)
Parrish, Robert 1827 wb-4-254 (Wi)
Parrish, Robert E. 1845 wb-8-296 (Wi)
Parrish, Sarah J. 1857 wb-17-324 (D)
Parrish, Sarah P. 1845 wb-8-296 (Wi)

Parrish, Susanna 1845 wb-8-264 (Wi)
Parrish, Thomas H. 1851 wb-15-126 (D)
Parrish, William B. 1858 wb-7-31 (Ma)
Parrish, William R. 1860 wb-#132 (Wl)
Parrish, Woodson 1833 wb-10-154 (D)
Parrish, Wyatt 1823 as-A-57 (Di)
Parrot, Benjamin 1848 wb-4-49 (Je)
Parrot, Henry 1853 wb-5-366 (Je)
Parrott, Evan 1846 5-3-176 (Cl)
Parrott, Evan 1849 ib-1-114 (Cl)
Parrott, John 1820 as-A-61 (Di)
Parrott, Mary 1853 wb-5-232 (Je)
Parry, Andrew I. 1842 wb-2-59# (Ge)
Parshall, Anna 1849 wb-#131 (Mc)
Parshall, Dr. John 1848 wb-#131 (Mc)
Parshley, Stephen 1853 wb-#24 (Mo)
Parsley, Drury W. 1848 wb-9-211 (Wi)
Parsley, James 1861 wb-b-65 (Dk)
Parsley, John 1844 wb-8-197 (Wi)
Parsley, John L. 1857 wb-b-41 (Ms)
Parsley, William 1826 wb-4-155 (K)
Parson, John 1843 lr (Sn)
Parsons, Allen 1834 wb-1-341 (Hr)
Parsons, Henry 1844 wb-a-124 (Cr)
Parsons, Polly P. 1854 wb-5-48 (Hr)
Parsons, Sarah 1856 wb-16-274 (Rb)
Parsons, Vaden W. 1854 wb-15-484 (Rb)
Parsons, William 1821 wb-1-0 (Sm)
Partee, Abner 1843 wb-z-533 (Mu)
Partee, Abner H. 1835 wb-y-114 (Mu)
Partee, Charles 1833 wb-x-81 (Mu)
Partee, Locker 1814 wb-#30 (Mu)
Partee, Yearby 1816 wb-1-0 (Sm)
Parten*, William 1856 ib-1-416 (Ca)
Parten, David 1848 ib-1-35 (Ca)
Parthman, John 1826 wb-8-547 (D)
Partin, John 1845 wb-1-223 (Fr)
Partlow, Benjamin E. 1847 wb-#155 (Wl)
Partlow, Joshua 1859 wb-#130 (Wl)
Parton, Dovey 1844 wb-#141 (Wl)
Parum, William 1822 wb-a-168 (Wh)
Paschal, Alexander 1846 wb-b-160 (We)
Paschal, J. R. 1851 rb-4-205 (Mu)
Paschal, Jesse 1860 wb-h-440 (Hn)
Paschal, Samuel 1815 wb-1-0 (Sm)
Paschall, Ann 1854 wb-g-553 (Hn)
Paschall, Elisha 1844 wb-f-253 (Hn)
Paschall, Samuel 1847 wb-g-217 (Hn)
Paschell, Elisha 1838 as-a-386 (Di)
Pass, James H. 1850 wb-c-378 (Wh)
Pass, James H. 1850 wb-c-401 (Wh)

Pass, James H. 1858 wb-e-272 (Wh)
Passmore, David 1834 wb-a-103 (Di)
Patchen, H. H. 1854 wb-5-342 (Je)
Pate, Booker 1850 wb-7-0 (Sm)
Pate, Edward P. 1852 wb-7-0 (Sm)
Pate, Hugh 1837 wb-3-461 (Je)
Pate, Jeremiah 1849 wb-10-190 (K)
Pate, John W. 1861 wb-18-583 (D)
Pate, Matthew 1809 ib-1-298 (Ge)
Pate, Peter 1847 r39-1-39 (Dk)
Pate, Rosannah 1861 wb-13-419 (Wi)
Pate, Stephen 1846 wb-7-0 (Sm)
Pate, Thomas Sr. 1833 wb-5-266 (Wi)
Pate, William 1826 wb-3-136 (Je)
Paterson, J. M. 1855 wb-j-17 (O)
Paterson, Joab 1815 wb-#19 (Mu)
Patillo, David 1861 wb-13-494 (Wi)
Patillo, H. H. 1834 rb-9-163 (Ru)
Patillo, Harrison 1833 rb-9-42 (Ru)
Patillo, Robert H. 1847 wb-1-145 (Sh)
Patrick, Alex H. 1837 wb-b-154 (G)
Patrick, Eli 1857 wb-f-79 (G)
Patrick, Hamilton 1838 wb-b-225 (G)
Patrick, James D. 1831 rb-8-326 (Ru)
Patrick, Jesse 1820 rb-5-50 (Ru)
Patrick, John B. 1854 wb-h-236 (Hu)
Patrick, John sr. 1827 lr (Gi)
Patrick, Joseph 1824 wb-A-411 (Li)
Patrick, Levi 1835 wb-1-93 (W)
Patten, William 1861 wb-#20 (Mo)
Pattern, Isaac 1814 wb-#17 (Mu)
Patterson, Alex. P. 1838 wb-3-485 (Je)
Patterson, Alexander 1831 rb-8-214 (Ru)
Patterson, Alfred S. 1861 lr (Gi)
Patterson, Allen L. 1857 wb-7-1 (Ma)
Patterson, Andrew 1849 wb-a-201 (Ms)
Patterson, Burrell 1854 wb-#114 (Wl)
Patterson, C. R. 1858 wb-f-225 (G)
Patterson, Elizabeth 1849 as-b-440 (Di)
Patterson, Ellen 1858 wb-17-518 (D)
Patterson, Frances 1858 wb-f-227 (G)
Patterson, Gilbert 1838 wb-1-320 (Gr)
Patterson, Henry 1844 wb-1-236 (Li)
Patterson, I. W. 1856 rb-18-32 (Ru)
Patterson, Isaac W. 1850 rb-15-440 (Ru)
Patterson, Isham 1819 wb-#34 (Wl)
Patterson, J. A. 1849 wb-#171 (Wl)
Patterson, Jacob 1815 wb-#19 (Mu)
Patterson, James 1804 wb-1-21# (Ge)
Patterson, James 1808 ib-1-212 (Ge)
Patterson, James 1830 rb-8-164 (Ru)

Patterson, James 1832 wb-2-42# (Ge)
Patterson, James 1857 wb-h-633 (Hu)
Patterson, James E. 1851 wb-#131 (Mc)
Patterson, James M. 1858 wb-j-370 (O)
Patterson, Jane 1807 wb-3-161 (D)
Patterson, Jane 1842 wb-1-398 (Hw)
Patterson, Jarred 1827 wb-#190 (Mu)
Patterson, Jefferson W. 1854 rb-17-320 (Ru)
Patterson, Joel 1816 wb-#88 (Mu)
Patterson, John 1800 wb-1-46 (Rb)
Patterson, John 1819 wb-7-355 (D)
Patterson, John 1834 wb-3-0 (Sm)
Patterson, John 1835 wb-#121 (Wl)
Patterson, John 1838 eb-1-390 (C)
Patterson, John 1838 wb-11-442 (D)
Patterson, John 1843 wb-1-247 (La)
Patterson, John 1852 wb-h-94 (Hu)
Patterson, John 1854 lr (Sn)
Patterson, John 1856 rb-18-217 (Ru)
Patterson, John P. 1848 wd-14-188 (D)
Patterson, John S. 1854 wb-e-453 (Ro)
Patterson, John T. 1861 wb-i-276 (St)
Patterson, Joseph 1811 wb-2-13 (Je)
Patterson, Joseph 1836 wb-x-335* (Mu)
Patterson, Juliann 1815 wb-#20 (Wl)
Patterson, Louvica 1853 rb-16-404 (Ru)
Patterson, Malcomb 1821 wb-A-303 (Li)
Patterson, Mathew 1839 wb-11-531 (D)
Patterson, Nathan 1819 wb-7-311 (D)
Patterson, Nelson 1855 as-b-190 (Ms)
Patterson, Patrick 1837 wb-9-428 (Rb)
Patterson, Peggy 1821 wb-#40 (Wl)
Patterson, R. 1857 as-c-483 (Di)
Patterson, Richard P. 1860 wb-a-371 (Cr)
Patterson, Robert 1800 wb-2-164 (D)
Patterson, Robert 1828 wb-#131 (Mc)
Patterson, Robert 1836 wb-b-112 (G)
Patterson, Robert 1858 as-c-120 (Ms)
Patterson, Robt. 1844 wb-0-43 (Cf)
Patterson, S. N. 1856 wb-e-468 (G)
Patterson, Samuel 1815 wb-#18 (Wl)
Patterson, Samuel 1848 rb-14-447 (Ru)
Patterson, Samuel 1849 wb-#171 (Wl)
Patterson, Samuel 1850 wb-2-65 (Sh)
Patterson, Samuel 1860 rb-20-503 (Ru)
Patterson, Samuel P. 1853 wb-#111 (Wl)
Patterson, Sarah E. 1859 wb-f-312 (G)
Patterson, Sarah S. 1846 wb-13-430 (D)
Patterson, Thomas 1847 as-a-141 (Ms)
Patterson, William 1816 wb-2-202 (Wi)
Patterson, William 1835 wb-#110 (Wl)

Patterson, William 1835 wb-1-114 (Li)
Patterson, William 1846 wb-d-1 (G)
Patterson, William 1855 lr (Sn)
Patterson, William 1860 wb-k-218 (O)
Patterson, William N. 1819 wb-A-275 (Li)
Patterson, William N. 1823 wb-A-346 (Li)
Patterson, William S. 1860 wb-h-403 (Hn)
Patterson, William sr. 1823 wb-1-0 (Sm)
Patterson, Willis 1840 wb-#131 (Wl)
Pattie, James D. 1855 wb#23 (Gu)
Pattillo, Littleton 1842 rb-12-106 (Ru)
Pattillo, Littleton 1842 rb-12-115 (Ru)
Pattillo, Samuel 1841 rb-12-31 (Ru)
Pattison, Joseph C. E. 1861 wb-1-69 (Se)
Patton, Andrew J. 1854 wb-11-306 (Wi)
Patton, David 1844 wb-d-123 (Ro)
Patton, David M. 1853 ib-1-254 (Ca)
Patton, Elizabeth 1850 lr (Sn)
Patton, F. A. 1857 wb-#27 (Mo)
Patton, Francis A. 1846 wb-#5 (Mo)
Patton, George 1826? wb-#151 (Mu)
Patton, Isabella 1823 wb-3-412 (K)
Patton, James 1807 wb-1-150 (Wi)
Patton, James 1819 wb-3-108 (Wi)
Patton, James 1832 wb-5-199 (Wi)
Patton, James 1833 wb-5-221 (Wi)
Patton, James G. 1850 wb-#174 (Wl)
Patton, Jane H. 1841 wb-a-96 (Cr)
Patton, Jason 1841 wb-7-478 (Wi)
Patton, John & Mary 1846 wb-#153 (Wl)
Patton, John 1809 wb-1-203 (Wi)
Patton, John 1819 wb-3-31 (Wi)
Patton, John 1849 wb-#163 (Wl)
Patton, John 1859 lr (Sn)
Patton, John A. 1856 wb-16-326 (Rb)
Patton, Joseph 1859 wb-#130 (Wl)
Patton, Joseph C. 1856 rb-18-192 (Ru)
Patton, Mathew 1839 wb-11-583 (D)
Patton, Matthew 1808 rb-2-62 (Ru)
Patton, Robert 1805 wb-1-191 (Je)
Patton, Robert 1809 lr (Sn)
Patton, Robert 1813 wb-A-40 (Li)
Patton, Robert 1815 wb-2-192 (K)
Patton, Robert 1825 wb-4-93 (K)
Patton, Robert 1830 lr (Sn)
Patton, Robert 1832 wb-a-222 (G)
Patton, Robert 1832 wb-a-225 (G)
Patton, Robert 1834 wb-5-395 (Wi)
Patton, Robert 1835 wb-3-414 (Je)
Patton, Robert 1844 wb-8-203 (Wi)
Patton, Samuel 1839 rb-10-269 (Ru)

Patton, Samuel P. 1854 wb-#111 (Wl)
Patton, Sarah 1852 wb-10-205 (Wi)
Patton, Sarah F. 1852 wb-10-256 (Wi)
Patton, Thomas 1819 wb-1-292 (Sn)
Patton, Thomas 1832 wb-8-9 (Rb)
Patton, Thomas 1854 ib-h-66 (F)
Patton, Thomas W. 1848 wb-9-38 (Wi)
Patton, Tristram 1855 wb-11-580 (Wi)
Patton, William 1827 lr (Sn)
Patton, William 1846 wb-8-448 (Wi)
Patton, William 1847 wb-8-607 (Wi)
Patton, William 1850 wb-a-162 (Cr)
Patton, Wm. 1859 as-c-561 (Di)
Patton, Wm. M. 1852 wb-e-28 (G)
Pattrick, Thomas M. 1829 wb-1-122 (Hr)
Patty, James M. 1858 wb-#132 (Mc)
Patty, Josiah 1857 wb-f-84 (Ro)
Patty, Obed 1839 wb-#132 (Mc)
Patty, William H. 1846 wb-#132 (Mc)
Paty, Jesse 1816 wb-1-0 (Sm)
Paul, Asa 1818 rb-4-171 (Ru)
Paul, Audley 1831 wb-5-40 (K)
Paul, James 1793 wb-0-2 (K)
Paul, James S. 1859 wb-3-24 (Me)
Paul, John 1823 lr (Gi)
Paul, John M. 1845 wb-9-86 (K)
Paul, S. S. 1846 wb-c-289 (G)
Paul, Thomas R. 1835 wb-b-195 (Wh)
Pavatt, Isaac 1856 wb-h-591 (Hu)
Paveley, John 1782 wb-#1 (Wa)
Paxton, Addison 1824 wb-a-2 (T)
Paxton, James 1818 lr (Gi)
Paxton, John 1787 wb-1-119 (Bo)
Paxton, John 1846 wb-a-79 (Ms)
Paxton, Mary 1852 as-b-57 (Ms)
Payn, Chesley 1845 wb-9-118 (K)
Payn, Daniel 1839 wb-y-593 (Mu)
Payn, Henry 1857 wb-j-250 (O)
Payne, A. W. 1844 wb-#142 (Wl)
Payne, Albert G. 1861 wb-18-505 (D)
Payne, Alfred B. 1846 wb-#152 (Wl)
Payne, Andrew B. 1841 rb-12-36 (Ru)
Payne, Annes 1847 wb-13-127 (Rb)
Payne, Benjamin 1820 wb-1-0 (Sm)
Payne, Benona 1846 wb-9-185 (K)
Payne, Charity 1859 wb-2-281 (Li)
Payne, Collinson 1814 wb-1-0 (Sm)
Payne, David 1860 wb-17-145 (Rb)
Payne, Dorothea 1851 wb-15-184 (D)
Payne, Dudley 1861 wb-17-235 (Rb)
Payne, George 1813 wb-4-238 (D)

Payne, Greenwood 1798 wb-2-118 (D)
Payne, Harriet E. 1860 rb-p-405 (Mt)
Payne, Hiram 1847 wb-13-128 (Rb)
Payne, Isaac 1844 wb-#133 (Mc)
Payne, Isaac 1845 wb-7-0 (Sm)
Payne, Isaiah 1860 wb-k-292 (O)
Payne, J. J. 1849 wb-14-151 (Rb)
Payne, Jacob 1847 rb-14-139 (Ru)
Payne, James 1828 wb-1-129 (Ma)
Payne, James 1830 wb-7-243 (Rb)
Payne, Jesse 1829? wb-#29 (Wa)
Payne, Jesse 1846 wb-#152 (Wl)
Payne, John 1850 wb-14-390 (Rb)
Payne, John 1855 wb-1-39 (Dy)
Payne, John 1858 wb-17-443 (D)
Payne, John sr. 1807 wb-1-233 (Rb)
Payne, Joseph 1806 wb-1-0 (Sm)
Payne, Joseph 1822 wb-1-0 (Sm)
Payne, Joseph 1843 wb-#140 (Wl)
Payne, Joseph 1846 wb-13-43 (Rb)
Payne, Joseph 1860 wb-17-263 (Rb)
Payne, Josiah 1806 wb-3-80 (D)
Payne, Josiah 1824 wb-1-120 (Bo)
Payne, Levi 1860 wb-f-369 (G)
Payne, M. 1853 as-2-279 (Ge)
Payne, Margaret 1858 149-1-104 (Ge)
Payne, Martha 1822 rb-5-223 (Ru)
Payne, Martha 1824 wb-1-0 (Sm)
Payne, Mathew sr. 1806 wb-3-124 (D)
Payne, Merryman 1844 wb-2-61# (Ge)
Payne, Nancy 1858 wb-16-676 (Rb)
Payne, Nicholas 1859 lw (Ct)
Payne, Perleman 1848 wb-b-276 (We)
Payne, Philip 1831 wb-2-0 (Sm)
Payne, Phillip 1815 wb-1-0 (Sm)
Payne, Reuben S. 1853 wb-15-375 (Rb)
Payne, Rewben 1838 wb-11-471 (D)
Payne, Robert 1857 wb-3-251 (Sn)
Payne, Robert B. 1833 wb-a-41 (Cr)
Payne, Samuel D. 1861 rb-p-568 (Mt)
Payne, Sarah 1804 wb-2-397 (D)
Payne, Sarah 1814 wb-4-315 (D)
Payne, Sarah 1841 wb-12-164* (D)
Payne, Squire 1816 wb-7-51 (D)
Payne, Thomas 1828 wb-6-308 (Rb)
Payne, Thomas 1852 wb-xx-2 (St)
Payne, Thomas E. 1846 wb-#150 (Wl)
Payne, Thomas H. 1818 wb-1-0 (Sm)
Payne, Thomas H. 1829 wb-2-0 (Sm)
Payne, Thomas W. 1852 wb-15-170 (Rb)
Payne, Warren 1850 wb-14-407 (Rb)

Payne, William 1815 wb-4-383 (D)
Payne, William 1817 wb-A-174 (Li)
Payne, William 1831 wb-5-2 (Wi)
Payne, William 1858 wb-7-0 (Sm)
Paysinger, John 1815 wb-1-0 (Sm)
Payton, Henry 1813 wb-#7 (Mu)
Payton, John W. 1836 wb-#118 (Wl)
Payton, Thomas 1829 wb-#203 (Mu)
Payton, Thomas C. 1847 wb-#155 (Wl)
Payton, William 1805 wb-#2 (Wl)
Peabody, Edward 1847 wb-f-127+ (O)
Peabody, Enos 1847 wb-f-127+ (O)
Peabody, John 1822 wb-8-71 (D)
Peabody, John 1851 wb-15-90 (D)
Peace, Francis M. 1853 wb-#109 (Wl)
Peace, William H. 1852 wb-#179 (Wl)
Peach, James 1851 wb-15-87 (D)
Peach, John 1859 wb-13-73 (Wi)
Peach, John 1859 wb-13-83 (Wi)
Peack, Jacob (col) 1844 wb-a2-147 (Mu)
Peacock, James L. 1859 wb-3e-111 (Sh)
Peacock, Micajah 1844 wb-#144 (Wl)
Peacock, Rosey 1849 wb-#165 (Wl)
Peairs, Orran 1832 lr (Sn)
Peairs, William B. 1831 lr (Sn)
Peak, Booker 1859 wb-h-362 (Hn)
Peak, Evaline 1835 wb-#107 (Wl)
Peak, Jacob 1853 wb-1C-103 (A)
Peak, Jacob R. 1849 wb-c-360 (Wh)
Peak, James M. 1857 rb-18-326 (Ru)
Peak, John 1846 wb-#149 (Wl)
Peak, Sarah 1847 wb-#153 (Wl)
Peak, Simmons 1853 rb-16-438 (Ru)
Peak, Zechariah S. 1835 wb-#107 (Wl)
Peake, James 1826 wb-a-214 (Wh)
Pealer, Solomon 1848 wb-A-50 (Ca)
Pearce, Asa 1852 wb-3-49 (La)
Pearce, C. D. 1859 gs-1-352 (F)
Pearce, Caren Happuch 1830 lr (Sn)
Pearce, Daniel 1858 wb-#133 (Mc)
Pearce, E. G. 1852 wb-3-21 (La)
Pearce, George M. 1832 wb-1-336 (Ma)
Pearce, George W. 1833 wb-1-389 (Ma)
Pearce, Isaac 1844 wb-3-27 (Sn)
Pearce, John 1844 wb-#134 (Mc)
Pearce, Joseph M. 1860 wb-h-383 (Hn)
Pearce, Kesiah 1837 wb-#134 (Mc)
Pearce, L. B. 1849 wb-a-365 (F)
Pearce, Lacey J. 1853 mr-2-496 (Be)
Pearce, Lawrence C. 1849 wb-b-292 (We)
Pearce, Martin 1838 wb-11-400 (D)

Pearce, Neoma 1831 wb-1-29 (La)
Pearce, Obadiah 1862 wb-h-553 (Hn)
Pearce, Ruben 1854 wb-e-231 (G)
Pearce, S. P. 1856 wb-g-765 (Hn)
Pearce, Thomas 1826 wb-a-68 (G)
Pearce, William 1825 wb-b-50 (St)
Pearce, William F. 1840 wb-b-13 (We)
Pearcy, Algernon 1834 wb-5-390 (Wi)
Pearcy, Algernon 1836 wb-6-182 (Wi)
Pearcy, Maria 1805 wb-14-153 (D)
Pearcy, Robt. W. 1853 rb-16-581 (Ru)
Pearcy, Sherwood 1847 wb-#156 (Wl)
Pearcy, Thomas 1836 rb-9-360 (Ru)
Pearcy, Thomas T. 1836 rb-9-288 (Ru)
Pearman, William 1847 wb-#134 (Mc)
Pearre, James 1841 wb-7-403 (Wi)
Pearre, Joshua 1847 wb-9-20 (Wi)
Pearre, Joshua W. 1839 wb-7-145 (Wi)
Pearre, Milly Ann 1853 wb-11-81 (Wi)
Pearre, William W. 1850 wb-9-341 (Wi)
Pearson, Amos 1854 ib-h-225 (F)
Pearson, C. W. 1847 wb-#153 (Wl)
Pearson, Christian 1819 wb-1-395 (Hw)
Pearson, David 1824 rb-6-52 (Ru)
Pearson, David 1854 ib-h-223 (F)
Pearson, Doctor 1833 wb-#134 (Mc)
Pearson, Ellis 1850? wb#19 (Gu)
Pearson, George 1824 wb-#134 (Mc)
Pearson, Henry 1841 wb-1-397 (Hw)
Pearson, John 1855 lr (Sn)
Pearson, Michael 1856 ib-2-288 (Cl)
Pearson, Richard 1850 wb-e-226 (Ro)
Pearson, Thomas 1829 wb-1-115 (Hr)
Peas, Wm. B.? 1791 wb-1-217 (D)
Peay, Austin 1853 wb-n-63 (Mt)
Peay, Elias 1851 wb-14-620 (D)
Peay, George 1845 wb-13-216 (D)
Peay, J. L. 1853 wb-0-119 (Cf)
Peay, Mary 1822 wb-3-314 (Wi)
Peay, Nancy 1851 wb-14-593 (D)
Peay, Samuel 1854 wb-11-318 (Wi)
Peay, Samuel C. 1851 wb-g-385 (Hn)
Peay, Susannah 1857 wb-12-327 (Wi)
Peay, Thomas 1837 wb-6-416 (Wi)
Peay, Thomas 1838 wb-6-471 (Wi)
Peay, Thomas Sr. 1858 wb-12-547 (Wi)
Peay, William 1831 rb-f-195 (Mt)
Pebly, Isaac 1836 eb-1-352 (C)
Pebly, John 1840 eb-1-427 (C)
Peck, A. 1854 wb-1C-195 (A)
Peck, Adam 1817 wb-2-176 (Je)

Peck, Benjamin 1850 33-3-270 (Gr)
Peck, Caroline 1851 wb-15-56 (D)
Peck, D. A. 1858 wb-1C-415 (A)
Peck, Elizabeth 1832 wb-3-190 (Je)
Peck, Elliott 1843 wb-#134 (Mc)
Peck, Francis 1859 rb-p-209 (Mt)
Peck, James M. 1860 rb-20-646 (Ru)
Peck, Jeffery 1858 rb-19-489 (Ru)
Peck, Joseph 1847 rb-14-225 (Ru)
Peck, Mary 1841 wb-5-169 (Gr)
Peck, Simmons 1846 rb-13-585 (Ru)
Peden, Hosea 1856 lr (Sn)
Peden, Moses 1855 lr (Sn)
Peebles, Alexander 1831 wb-5-86 (Wi)
Peebles, Nathan 1813 wb-4-237 (D)
Peebles, Nathan 1818 wb-7-284 (D)
Peek, Anna 1830 lr (Sn)
Peek, Jeffery 1850 rb-15-453 (Ru)
Peek, Jeffery 1859 rb-19-571 (Ru)
Peek, John 1852 wb-b-320 (We)
Peek, Joseph 1847 rb-14-166 (Ru)
Peek, Norman 1815 lr (Sn)
Peek, Simmons 1845 rb-13-417 (Ru)
Peel, Elisha 1854 wb-g-619 (Hn)
Peel, William 1855 wb-e-388 (G)
Peeler, F. J. 1847 wb-#165 (Wl)
Peeples, Agathy 1817 rb-b-449 (Mt)
Peeples, Burrell H. 1819 rb-c-134 (Mt)
Peeples, David 1816 rb-b-374 (Mt)
Peeples, Nathan 1820 rb-c-359 (Mt)
Peercy, William 1841 wb-3-415 (Ma)
Peery, John 1843 wb-z-516 (Mu)
Pegram, Benjamin 1832 rb-f-494 (Mt)
Pegram, Francis 1855 wb-16-456 (D)
Pegram, George S. 1848 wd-14-191 (D)
Pegram, Thomas 1847 wb-14-35 (D)
Pegram, William 1840 wb-12-7* (D)
Peirce, Robert 1812 wb-2-30 (Je)
Peirce, Robert 1850 wb-2-22 (Me)
Peirce, Robert 1855 wb-5-415 (Je)
Pelham, John 1805 wb-1-163 (K)
Pelham, Levi 1855 ib-1-348 (Ca)
Pelham, Martha 1852 ib-1-219 (Ca)
Pemberton, Hutsen 1848 wb-3-27 (Gr)
Pemberton, William 1841 wb-12-226* (D)
Pendarvis, William 1851 wb-7-0 (Sm)
Pender, William 1861 wb-e-157 (Hy)
Pendergrass, M. P. 1849 as-b-425 (Di)
Pendergrass, Mary 1856 as-c-407 (Di)
Pendergrass, Mauly P. 1851 as-c-130 (Di)
Pendergrass, William E. 1852 wb-a-246 (Di)

Pendleton, R. L. 1858 ib-1-551 (Ca)
Penick, Adam 1815 wb-a-65 (Ro)
Penick, Adam 1832 wb-b-170 (Ro)
Penick, Henry M. 1840 wb-e-98 (Hn)
Penick, Jeremiah 1851 wb-b-152 (L)
Penick, John J. 1856 wb-1-83 (Be)
Penick, T. W. 1859 wb-h-378 (Hn)
Penington, Abraham 1829 wb-1-12 (La)
Penn, George 1826 rb-6-227 (Ru)
Penn, James 1832 wb-1-327 (Ma)
Penn, James 1845 wb-4-291 (Ma)
Penn, Jane 1833 wb-2-0 (Sm)
Penn, Martha 1828 rb-7-151 (Ru)
Penn, Martha 1828 rb-7-324 (Ru)
Penn, Robert A. 1827? wb-1-8 (Hy)
Penn, William 1851 wb-7-0 (Sm)
Pennegar, Matthias 1831 wb-b-46 (Wh)
Penner, Dempsey 1835 wb-b-184 (Wh)
Pennington, Caroline F. 1849 wb-2-79 (La)
Pennington, Clement S. 1854 wb-11-264 (Wi)
Pennington, Graves 1854 wb-16-295 (D)
Pennington, Isaac 1801 rb-a-143 (Mt)
Pennington, Isaac 1838 wb-1-151 (La)
Pennington, Jacob B. 1860 wb-4-301 (La)
Pennington, James T. 1854 wb-16-330 (D)
Pennington, John 1797 rb-a-19 (Mt)
Pennington, John 1867 wb-#15 (Mo)
Pennington, William A. 1854 wb-d-217 (Wh)
Pennington, William J. 1857 wb-4-118 (La)
Pennington, William R. 1855 wb-16-559 (D)
Pennis, John 1807 wb-3-162 (D)
Penny, David C. 1830 wb-7-288 (Rb)
Penny, Joseph 1830 wb-7-257 (Rb)
Penny, Joseph R. 1831 wb-7-492 (Rb)
Pennybaker, Samuel W. 1835 wb-#110 (Wl)
Pennybaker, Samuel W. 1835 wb-#111 (Wl)
Penrice, Joseph 1812 rb-b-41 (Mt)
Penrice, Sally 1826 rb-d-529 (Mt)
Pentecost, Mary 1823 wb-#48 (Wl)
Pentecost, Scarboro 1842 wb-3-534 (Ma)
Pentecost, Thomas 1813/14? wb-#13 (Wl)
Penticuff, Philip 1851 wb-2-204 (La)
Penuel, Hardy 1817 wb-#26 (Wl)
Peoples, John 1801 lw (Ct)
Peoples, Nathan 1857 wb-#59 (Wa)
Pepper, James R. 1860 wb-1-830 (Su)
Pepper, Sally 1852 wb-5-31 (Hr)
Pepper, W. W. 1861 wb-17-175 (Rb)
Percell, James 1822 wb-#86 (Mu)
Percy, Charles B. 1851 wb-15-205 (D)
Perdew, John 1856 wb-g-768 (Hn)

Perdue, Daniel 1856 lr (Sn)
Perdue, Luke 1832 lr (Sn)
Perkapile, Isaac 1847 wb-5-501 (Gr)
Perkins, Alvin 1860 wb-c-334 (L)
Perkins, Cornelia C. 1857 wb-h-369 (St)
Perkins, Daniel 1834 wb-5-424 (Wi)
Perkins, Daniel 1845 wb-8-325 (Wi)
Perkins, Gracy 1826 wb-1-61 (Fr)
Perkins, Jacob 1819 lw (Ct)
Perkins, Jesse 1823 wb-1-52 (Fr)
Perkins, John P. 1807 wb-1-162 (Wi)
Perkins, John P. 1820 wb-3-210 (Wi)
Perkins, Joseph 1825 rb-6-157 (Ru)
Perkins, Joseph I. 1848 wb-1-259 (Fr)
Perkins, Mary 1823 rb-5-325 (Ru)
Perkins, Mary 1833 wb-5-318 (Wi)
Perkins, Mary H. 1850 wb-4-623 (Hr)
Perkins, Mary Henry 1848 wb-4-241 (Hr)
Perkins, Nancy 1827 wb-#215 (Mu)
Perkins, Nicholas 1801 wb-2-199 (D)
Perkins, Nicholas 1848 wb-9-93 (Wi)
Perkins, Nicholas T. 1843 wb-8-102 (Wi)
Perkins, Partheny 1857 wb-1-198 (Be)
Perkins, Peter (Colonel) 1813 wb-1-310 (Wi)
Perkins, Peter 1816 wb-7-100 (D)
Perkins, Powhattan 1853 wb-15-558 (D)
Perkins, R. G. 1860 wb-1-147 (Jo)
Perkins, R. S.. 1856 ib-h-525 (F)
Perkins, Richard C. 1855 ib-h-353 (F)
Perkins, Samuel 1843 wb-8-48 (Wi)
Perkins, Samuel 1856 wb-b-13 (Ms)
Perkins, Samuel 1861 wb-13-409 (Wi)
Perkins, Susan 1836 wb-10-616 (D)
Perkins, Susannah 1836 wb-10-547 (D)
Perkins, Thomas H. 1820 wb-7-474 (D)
Perkins, Thomas H. 1827 wb-9-89 (D)
Perkins, Thomas H. 1839 wb-7-213 (Wi)
Perkins, Thomas Hardin 1834 wb-5-359 (Wi)
Perkins, U. S. 1860 wb-h-386 (Hn)
Perkins, William 1822 wb-8-104 (D)
Perkinson, Benjamin 1834 wb-a-32 (T)
Perkison, John 1821 wb-1-1 (Sh)
Perkypile, Michael 1845 wb-5-362 (Gr)
Perrey, Noah 1858 wb-1-83 (Dy)
Perrigin, William 1853 as-c-224 (Di)
Perrin, William 1857 wb-3-356 (Gr)
Perrington, Elizabeth J. 1848 rb-k-690 (Mt)
Perrington, T. A. U. 1852 wb-m-596 (Mt)
Perrington, Thomas A. 1850 wb-m-103 (Mt)
Perris, Charles 1830 wb-c-78 (Hn)
Perry, A. H. 1854 wb-n-448 (Mt)

Perry, Albert 1835 wb-1-576 (Ma)
Perry, Albert 1860 wb-A-156 (Ca)
Perry, Allen 1837 wb-d-147* (Hn)
Perry, Austin 1852 wb-g-454 (Hn)
Perry, Benjamin 1850 wb-7-0 (Sm)
Perry, Benjamin M. 1853 wb-5-128 (Ma)
Perry, Burrell 1852 wb-15-251 (D)
Perry, Daniel 1862 wb-h-560 (Hn)
Perry, Drury 1814 wb-#15 (Wl)
Perry, Elizabeth 1839 wb-2-264 (Sn)
Perry, Ester 1858 wb-17-429 (D)
Perry, George 1836 wb-6-35 (K)
Perry, George B. 1854 ib-h-32 (F)
Perry, H. C. (Miss) 1848 wb-4-297 (Hr)
Perry, Harry (Hardin?) 1859 wb-#135 (Mc)
Perry, Hepzebah Carolin 1847 wb-4-196 (Hr)
Perry, I. S. 1861 27-lw (Hd)
Perry, James 1838 wb-6-258 (K)
Perry, James 1842 wb-a-87 (F)
Perry, James 1851 wb-11-4 (K)
Perry, James W. 1859 wb-f-168 (Mu)
Perry, Jane 1858 wb-13-29 (K)
Perry, Jeremiah 1853 mr-2-483 (Be)
Perry, Jo. 1844 wb-12-237 (Rb)
Perry, John 1845 lr (Sn)
Perry, John 1852 wb-h-Mar (O)
Perry, Joseph 1822 wb-3-444 (Rb)
Perry, Joseph 1822 wb-3-468 (Rb)
Perry, Joseph 1833 wb-8-267 (Rb)
Perry, Joseph 1843 wb-8-182 (K)
Perry, Joseph 1852 wb-3-158 (W)
Perry, Josiah 1832 rb-f-4001 (Mt)
Perry, Kinchen 1851 wb-g-510 (Hu)
Perry, Martha 1842 wb-8-34 (K)
Perry, Mary 1858 wb-17-455 (D)
Perry, Nathaniel 1838 wb-2-273 (Ma)
Perry, Nathaniel 1846 wb-4-111 (Hr)
Perry, Nathaniel 1849 wb-1-391* (W)
Perry, Nathl. 1849 wb-4-406 (Hr)
Perry, Nicholas 1834 wb-1-430 (Ma)
Perry, Owen Seymore 1844 wb-4-156 (Ma)
Perry, Pamelia 1851 wb-15-114 (D)
Perry, R. H. 1835 wb-#110 (Wl)
Perry, Richard 1858 wb-e-191 (Wh)
Perry, Richardson 1816 Wb-2-189 (Wi)
Perry, Robert 1825 wb-8-495 (D)
Perry, Sarah 1828 wb-#203 (Mu)
Perry, Sarah 1828 wb-a-104 (G)
Perry, Simpson 1823 wb-#47 (Mu)
Perry, Simpson 1859 wb-f-174 (Mu)
Perry, Tho. C. 1849 wb-4-432 (Hr)

Perry, Thomas 1807 wb-1-115 (Sn)
Perry, Thos. 1858 wb-a-45 (Ce)
Perry, William 1807 rb-a-445 (Mt)
Perry, William 1822 wb-#86 (Mu)
Perry, William 1824 wb-#74 (Mu)
Perry, William 1848 wb-b-278 (Mu)
Perry, Wm. 1853 wb-e-38 (G)
Perry, _____ 1829 wb-#201 (Mu)
Perryman, Benoni 1827 wb-#158 (Mu)
Persise, John B. 1856 wb-16-163 (Rb)
Persley, Addison 1838 wb-6-239 (K)
Persney, B. P. 1861 rb-p-527 (Mt)
Person, B. P. 1861 rb-p-549 (Mt)
Person, Benjamin 1840 wb-3-121 (Ma)
Person, Benjamin E. 1843 wb-1-88 (Sh)
Person, John B. 1854 wb-2-158 (Sh)
Person, Michal 1855? ib-2-210 (Cl)
Person, Richard J. A. 1842 wb-1-84 (Sh)
Person, Turner 1851 wb-2-95 (Sh)
Person?, Walter 1814 wb-a-211 (St)
Pertle, Obediah H. 1847 wb-c-262 (Wh)
Pervis, Alexander 1842 wb-f-58 (Hn)
Pervis, Allen 1836 wb-c-474 (St)
Pervis, Allen B. 1836 wb-d-19 (St)
Pervis, George 1838 wb-1-463 (Hy)
Pesterfield, Henry 1838 wb-1-121 (Bo)
Peters, Christena 1853 wb-2-76# (Ge)
Peters, Christian 1851 wb-#135 (Mc)
Peters, Henry 1852 wb-g-578 (Hu)
Peters, James 1827 wb-#202 (Mu)
Peters, James 1829 wb-#205 (Mu)
Peters, John 1823 wb-3-440 (K)
Peters, Joseph 1840 wb-e-118 (Hn)
Peters, Joseph 1843 wb-f-151* (Hn)
Peters, Landon C. 1853 wb-#135 (Mc)
Peters, Lucy 1835 wb-d-81 (Hn)
Peters, Mylland 1823 wb-#67 (Mu)
Peters, Rachel 1834 wb-1A-60 (A)
Peters, Simon 1850 wb-g-375 (Hn)
Peters, Tobias 1831 wb-1A-21 (A)
Peters, Willard 1823 wb-#67 (Mu)
Peters, William (Major) 1807 wb-a-21 (Ro)
Peterson, Elizabeth 1836 wb-2-47# (Ge)
Peterson, George W. 1853 wb-11-427 (K)
Peterson, Rowland 1836 rb-g-290 (Mt)
Peterson, William 1818 wb-3-54 (K)
Petree, George 1838 eb-1-363 (C)
Petree, John 1849 wb-10-231 (K)
Petteree, Joseph B. 1846 wb-g-153 (Hn)
Petters, Sarah 1854 wb-a-445 (F)
Pettillo, John L. 1831 wb-#222 (Mu)

Pettit, Jonas 1837 wb-b-368 (Ro)
Pettit, Nehemiah 1824 wb-1-26# (Ge)
Pettitt, Francis P. 1852 wb-#135 (Mc)
Pettitt, Nehemiah 1830 wb-#135 (Mc)
Pettitt, Nesbitt 1857 wb-f-96 (G)
Pettus, Elizabeth O. 1856 wb-12-290 (Wi)
Pettus, Susannah 1861 wb-13-385 (Wi)
Pettus, Susannah 1861 wb-13-400 (Wi)
Pettus, Thomas B. 1851 wb-m-389 (Mt)
Pettus, William 1841 wb-2-397 (Hy)
Pettway, Edward 1848 wb-#156 (Wl)
Petty, Alexander 1850 wb-14-311 (Rb)
Petty, Charles 1860 rb-20-416 (Ru)
Petty, Delanson G. 1842 wb-3-61 (Hy)
Petty, George 1840 wb-d-415 (St)
Petty, George C. 1838 as-a-404 (Di)
Petty, John S. 1848 wb-g-30 (St)
Petty, Johnathan 1849 as-b-427 (Di)
Petty, Joshua 1845 as-b-328 (Di)
Petty, Margaret 1836 wb-A-2 (Ca)
Petty, Matthias 1832 lr (Gi)
Petty, Reece 1857 wb-h-421 (St)
Petty, Samuel 1842 as-b-65 (Di)
Petty, Solomon 1860 as-c-576 (Di)
Petty, Thomas 1841 mr-1-357 (Be)
Petty, Thomas 1841 mr-2-4 (Be)
Petway, Honchey 1857 wb-17-321 (D)
Petway, John S. 1833 wb-5-238 (Wi)
Petway, Mary 1833 wb-5-237 (Wi)
Petway, William 1826 wb-4-116 (Wi)
Pewett, Adam 1841 wb-2-474 (Hy)
Pewett, Catharine 1823 wb-3-630 (Wi)
Pewett, James 1822 wb-3-595 (Wi)
Pewett, James 1854 wb-11-100 (Wi)
Pewett, James B. 1854 wb-b-256 (L)
Pewett, Joel 1823 wb-3-641 (Wi)
Pewett, Joseph 1822 wb-3-333 (Wi)
Pewett, William B. 1861 wb-e-158 (Hy)
Pewit, Joseph 1840 wb-7-328 (Wi)
Pewitt, John 1846 wb-d-4 (G)
Pewitt, Susanna 1848 wb-9-177 (Wi)
Peyton, Frances 1851 wb-#179 (Wl)
Peyton, George W. 1858 wb-a-331 (Cr)
Peyton, James H. 1852 wb-#180 (Wl)
Peyton, John M. 1858 rb-19-319 (Ru)
Peyton, John Sr. 1816 wb-#24 (Wl)
Peyton, John W. 1848 wb-#170 (Wl)
Peyton, John sr. 1830 lr (Sn)
Peyton, Joseph M. 1857 wb-#123 (Wl)
Peyton, Sarah F. 1856 wb-3e-20 (Sh)
Peyton, Sarah Flelming 1859 wb-3e-123 (Sh)

Pfifer, Alexander 1849 mr-2-319 (Be)
Pfifer, Peter 1846 mr-2-205 (Be)
Phagan, Eleanor 1839 wb-2-247 (Sn)
Phagan, James 1828 wb-2-610 (Je)
Phagan, Philip 1849 wb-1-372 (Li)
Pharice, William 1805 wb-1-0 (Sm)
Pharis, John 1835 wb-a-284 (R)
Phelan, David 1862 wb-f-436 (G)
Phelp, Randolph 1826 wb-1-261 (Ma)
Phelps, Henry 1820 lr (Sn)
Phelps, Richard 1821 wb-#40 (Wl)
Phelps, Thomas 1816 wb-A-137 (Li)
Phelps, William 1844 wb-f-258 (Hn)
Phelps, William 1857 wb-17-152 (D)
Phifer, Feras 1848 wb-e-64 (Ro)
Phiffer, Joseph 1846 wb-c-220 (Wh)
Philbeck, William 1840 wb-1-348 (W)
Philips, A. P. 1857 wb-f-22 (G)
Philips, Benj. A. 1855 wb-16-597 (D)
Philips, Benjamin 1820 wb-7-397 (D)
Philips, Benjamin 1846 wb-#152 (Wl)
Philips, Bennett 1853 rb-16-656 (Ru)
Philips, Bethel 1853 wb-#107 (Wl)
Philips, Clabourn 1847 wb-f-451 (St)
Philips, David 1803 rb-a-171 (Mt)
Philips, David 1846 wb-#151 (Wl)
Philips, Eliza 1853 wb-n-75 (Wl)
Philips, Isaac M. 1839 wb-7-177 (Wi)
Philips, James William 1854 rb-17-186 (Ru)
Philips, Jessee H. 1852 wb-10-399 (Wi)
Philips, John 1818 wb-7-276 (D)
Philips, John 1844 wb-#146 (Wl)
Philips, Joseph 1833 wb-5-270 (Wi)
Philips, Joseph 1857 rb-19-78 (Ru)
Philips, Lydia 1851 wb-#177 (Wl)
Philips, Mark 1821 wb-8-16 (G)
Philips, Mary 1847 wb-b-229 (We)
Philips, Merrell 1831 wb-9-485 (D)
Philips, Nancy 1856 wb-#118 (Wl)
Philips, Nathan B. 1816 wb-1-17 (Fr)
Philips, Philip 1797 wb-2-85 (D)
Philips, Philip 1817 wb-7-120 (D)
Philips, Pleasant 1824 wb-3-476 (K)
Philips, Randolph 1829 wb-1-114 (Ma)
Philips, Reuben 1858 wb-2-415* (Me)
Philips, Samuel 1823 wb-8-273 (D)
Philips, Samuel 1839 wb-y-418 (Mu)
Philips, Samuel L. 1819 wb-7-331 (D)
Philips, Sterling 1855 ib-1-337 (Wy)
Philips, Thrower 1844 wb-d-105 (Ro)
Philips, William 1846 wb-b-199 (We)

Phillips, Abram sr. 1856 wb-h-302 (St)
Phillips, Archer 1851 wb-b-147 (L)
Phillips, Bennett 1842 rb-12-237 (Ru)
Phillips, Charles 1830 wb-a-149 (G)
Phillips, Charles 1832 wb-a-213 (G)
Phillips, Charles 1845 wb-#135 (Mc)
Phillips, Charles C. 1839 wb-b-296 (G)
Phillips, David 1798 wb-2-105 (D)
Phillips, David 1814 wb-A-45 (Li)
Phillips, E. J. 1855 wb-16-53 (Rb)
Phillips, Eliza G. 1849 rb-l-352 (Mt)
Phillips, Elizabeth 1814 wb-A-53 (Li)
Phillips, Elizabeth Ann 1850 mr (Gi)
Phillips, Ezekiel 1828 wb-1-74 (Fr)
Phillips, Gabriel 1812 wb-1-394 (Hw)
Phillips, George 1844 148-1-86 (Ge)
Phillips, Iredell 1854 wb-g-640 (Hn)
Phillips, James 1858 ib-2-126 (Wy)
Phillips, James J. 1858 ib-2-102 (Wy)
Phillips, James M. 1852 wb-h-Sep (O)
Phillips, John 1832 eb-1-275 (C)
Phillips, John 1849 wb-g-318 (Hn)
Phillips, Johnathan 1839 rb-h-194 (Mt)
Phillips, Johnson 1848 wb-0-81 (Cf)
Phillips, Joseph 1822 wb-8-119 (D)
Phillips, Man 1827 wb-b-164 (St)
Phillips, Merrell 1809 wb-4-43 (D)
Phillips, Nancy 1841 wb-12-2 (D)
Phillips, Ozwell 1816 wb-#22 (Wl)
Phillips, Pinkney P. 1844 wb-d-246 (O)
Phillips, Pleasant P. 1854 wb-i-216 (O)
Phillips, Robert 1849 wb-g-64 (O)
Phillips, Samuel 1836 wb-1-206 (Gr)
Phillips, Sarah 1859 lr (Sn)
Phillips, Thomas G. 1860 ib-2-186 (Wy)
Phillips, Walter 1860 wb-b-82 (F)
Phillips, William 1808 wb-3-224 (D)
Phillips, William 1819 wb-3-4 (Wi)
Phillips, William 1832 wb-c-3 (Hn)
Phillips, William 1840 wb-#132 (Wl)
Phillips, William J. 1861 wb-19-23 (D)
Philpot, John W. 1832 wb-1-220 (Hr)
Philpot, Samuel 1824 wb-a-225 (Ro)
Phipps, Dorcas 1853 wb-11-418 (K)
Phipps, Dudley 1851 wb-a-169 (Cr)
Phipps, Isaac 1857 wb-16-552 (Rb)
Phipps, John 1857 wb-16-535 (Rb)
Phipps, Jordan 1827 wb-4-234 (Wi)
Phipps, Joshua 1861 wb-1-404 (Hw)
Phipps, Lewellyn 1843 wb-12-3 (Rb)
Phipps, Lewelun 1843 wb-11-533 (Rb)

Phipps, Montgomery B. 1852 wb-10-401 (Wi)
Phipps, Nancy 1854 wb-16-298 (D)
Phipps, Richardson 1847 wb-14-39 (D)
Phipps, Robert W. 1844 wb-8-214 (Wi)
Phipps, William 1809 wb-1-132 (Sn)
Phipps, William 1850 wb-1-400 (Hw)
Phips, Ruth 1815 wb-4-333 (D)
Piatt, John H. 1844 wb-9-1 (K)
Pickard, Alexander 1854 wb-f-42 (Mu)
Pickard, Allen 1861 wb-a-306 (T)
Pickard, C. W. 1856 wb-4-1 (La)
Pickard, Elisha 1861 6-1-22 (Le)
Pickard, Ellen 1815 wb-#14 (Mu)
Pickard, George M. 1836 wb-6-232 (Wi)
Pickard, George M. 1848 A-468-76 (Le)
Pickard, H. S. 1861 wb-4-424 (La)
Pickard, Henderson C. 1852 wb-h-Aug (O)
Pickard, Henry 1834 wb-1-50 (La)
Pickard, Henry 1845 A-468-3 (Le)
Pickard, Henry 1847 wb-1-444 (La)
Pickard, Henry S. 1861 wb-4-449 (La)
Pickard, John 1827 wb-#154 (Mu)
Pickard, John 1829 wb-#201 (Mu)
Pickard, John H. 1848 A-468-90 (Le)
Pickard, John J. 1830 wb-#212 (Mu)
Pickard, Mrs. 1847 wb-1-442 (La)
Pickard, William 1857 wb-j-226 (O)
Pickards, Nancy 1839 wb-y-484 (Mu)
Pickel, Henry W. 1855 wb-e-514 (Ro)
Pickel, Peggy 1857 wb-f-123 (Ro)
Pickell, Edwin N. 1839 wb-6-391 (K)
Pickens, Abram 1827 wb-#153 (Mu)
Pickens, David 1825 wb-#146 (Mu)
Pickens, James 1851 wb-2-72# (Ge)
Pickens, John 1827 wb-#136 (Mc)
Pickens, John 1831 wb-1-117 (Bo)
Pickens, John 1861 wb-k-478 (O)
Pickens, William 1835 wb-x-331 (Mu)
Pickering, Benjamin 1806 wb-1-21# (Ge)
Pickering, Benjamin 1807 as-1-177 (Ge)
Pickering, Ellis 1836 wb-2-46# (Ge)
Pickering, Enos 1857 wb-2-86# (Ge)
Pickering, John 1851 148-1-370 (Ge)
Pickering, Rebecca 1824 wb-2-47# (Ge)
Pickering, Samuel 1829 wb-2-31# (Ge)
Pickering, Spencer 1846 rb-k-288 (Mt)
Picket, Charles 1807 rb-a-49 (Mt)
Picket, John 1835 as-a-263 (Di)
Pickett, Andrew 1861 wb-b-67 (Dk)
Pickett, Birdsay 1841 wb-7-164 (K)
Pickett, Edmund 1838 wb-6-354 (K)

Pickett, Edward 1838 wb-#121 (Wl)
Pickett, Reuben 1834 wb-1-119 (Hy)
Pickins, A. G. 1854 ib-h-29 (F)
Pickins, Abram 1815 wb-#33 (Mu)
Pickins, David 1813 wb-#7 (Mu)
Pickins, Elizabeth 1815 wb-#19 (Mu)
Pickins, Elizabeth C. 1856 ib-1-378 (Wy)
Pickins, John 1814 wb-a-239 (St)
Pickins, John G. 1857 wb-b-32 (F)
Pickins, John L. B. 1856 ib-1-379 (Wy)
Pickins, Jonathan R. 1840 wb-b-269 (Hd)
Pickins, Joseph 1820 rb-4-242 (Ru)
Pickle, Christian 1814 wb-2-112 (K)
Pickle, Christian 1836 wb-6-78 (K)
Pickle, James 1858 wb-13-21 (K)
Pickle, James N. 1858 wb-13-79 (K)
Pickle, Jesse 1848 wb-10-35 (K)
Pickle, Jonathan 1854 wb-#25 (Mo)
Pickle, Jonathan 1855 wb-12-74 (K)
Pickler, William 1842 mr-2-12 (Be)
Pierce, D. D. 1857 wb-f-120 (G)
Pierce, Elizabeth 1841 wb-12-119* (D)
Pierce, Elizabeth H. 1827 wb-3-0 (Sm)
Pierce, Ferney? W. 1855 wb-1-34 (Be)
Pierce, George 1826 wb-3-0 (Sm)
Pierce, Isaac 1847 rb-14-198 (Ru)
Pierce, Johnathan 1862 wb-2-94# (Ge)
Pierce, Jonathan 1829 lr (Sn)
Pierce, Martin 1838 wb-11-400 (D)
Pierce, Robert 1848 wb-1-198 (Me)
Pierce, Susanna 1854 wb-2-78# (Ge)
Pierce, Thomas L. K. 1855 wb-2-180 (Sh)
Pierce, William 1837 wb-1-9 (Me)
Piercey, Cader 1847 wb-5-49 (Ma)
Piercey, Thomas 1842 wb-1-63 (Me)
Piercy, John 1852 wb-5-121 (Ma)
Pigg, James 1847 wb-14-104 (D)
Pigg, John 1825 wb-1-0 (Sm)
Pigg, John 1852 ib-1-160 (Wy)
Pigg, Nancy 1845 wb-2-56 (W)
Pigg, Nelson W. G. 1833 wb-10-80 (D)
Pigg, Pierson P. 1835 wb-10-481 (D)
Pigg, Stephen 1827 wb-4-256 (Wi)
Pigg, William P. 1833 wb-10-160 (D)
Pigue, Mariah 1845 wb-13-187 (D)
Pike, James 1849 wb-#136 (Mc)
Pike, James M. 1836 wb-10-573 (D)
Pike, John 1825 wb-5-48 (Rb)
Pile, Thomas 1853 wb-1-26 (R)
Pilent, John 1822 wb-1-397 (Hw)
Piles, Newton 1828 wb-7-48 (Rb)

Pilkinton, Larkin 1858 wb-f-143 (Mu)
Pillow, Abner 1860 wb-f-205 (Mu)
Pillow, Gideon 1831 wb-#219 (Mu)
Pillow, John 1793 wb-1-292 (D)
Pillow, John 1794 wb-1-313 (D)
Pillow, William 1809 wb-#28 (Wl)
Pillow, William C. 1834 wb-#107 (Wl)
Pillows, Joseph B. 1846 wb-g-161 (Hn)
Pimmo, Elizabeth 1859 wb-17-635 (D)
Pinchum, John 1857 wb-17-178 (D)
Pinckard, Bailey 1859 rb-20-112 (Ru)
Pinegar, Leonard 1835 wb-a-111 (Di)
Pinhard, Thomas 1847 wb-14-41 (D)
Pinkard, Thomas 1859 wb-17-566 (D)
Pinkard, William 1853 rb-16-464 (Ru)
Pinkard?, William 1833 wb-c-123 (Hn)
Pinkerton, David 1842 wb-12-378* (D)
Pinkerton, Thomas 1816 wb-A-123 (Li)
Pinkley, John 1801 wb-1-65 (Rb)
Pinkston, David 1851 wb-9-709 (Wi)
Pinkston, Edward 1823 wb-2-399 (Je)
Pinkston, Francis 1860 wb-13-177 (Wi)
Pinkston, James 1845 wb-a-137 (Cr)
Pinkston, Peter 1840 wb-7-248 (Wi)
Pinkston, Turner 1842 wb-a-99 (T)
Pinkston, Zachariah 1827 wb-4-245 (K)
Pinner, John A. 1847 wb-f-416 (St)
Pinner, Joseph 1845 wb-f-245 (St)
Pinner, Renson B. 1840 wb-1-299 (W)
Pinner, S. A. 1849 wb-g-141 (St)
Pinnon, Isham 1856 wb-j-139 (O)
Pinser, S.? A.? 1858 wb-h-267 (Hn)
Pinson, Isaac J. 1852 wb-b-188 (L)
Pinson, Martha 1851 wb-a-168 (Cr)
Pinson, Nathaniel G. 1847 wb-f-105 (O)
Piper, Alexander 1821 wb-1-0 (Sm)
Piper, James 1816 wb-1-0 (Sm)
Piper, James 1833 wb-2-0 (Sm)
Piper, Jane Young 1857 wb-12-417 (K)
Piper, Samuel 1826 wb-a-119 (Hn)
Pipkin, Enis 1854 wb-e-160 (G)
Pipkin, Enos 1854 wb-e-142 (G)
Pipkin, Lewis 1814 wb-1-0 (Sm)
Pipkin, Thomas B. 1820 wb-7-413 (D)
Pippan, John 1842 mr-1-366 (Be)
Pirie, Alexander 1850 wb-14-554 (D)
Pirtle, George 1840 wb-b-410 (Wh)
Pirtle, Jacob 1837 wb-1-510 (Hr)
Pirtle, John 1843 wb-3-58 (Hr)
Pirtle, John 1845 wb-3-299 (Hr)
Pirtle, Michael 1828 wb-1-75 (Hr)

Pirtle, Robert 1858 wb-5-84 (Hr)
Pistole, Elizabeth 1853 r39-1-264 (Dk)
Pistole, John 1826 wb-a-226 (Wh)
Pistole, John H. 1831 wb-b-1 (Wh)
Pistole, John H. 1842 wb-c-72 (Wh)
Pitman, Thomas 1854 ib-1-317 (Ca)
Pitman, Thomas 1856 ib-1-403 (Ca)
Pitner, Adam 1841 wb-#136 (Mc)
Pitt, Arthur 1839 wb-10-268 (Rb)
Pitt, Arthur 1858 wb-1-222 (Be)
Pitt, Arthur 1858 wb-1-223 (Be)
Pitt, Henry 1840 lr (Sn)
Pitt, Susan 1855 wb-16-52 (Rb)
Pittman, Asa 1838 wb-11-206 (D)
Pittman, William 1826 lr (Sn)
Pitts, James 1862 wb-2-357 (Li)
Pitts, Jeremiah 1855 wb-15-725 (Rb)
Pitts, Joseph 1819 wb-3-26 (Rb)
Pitts, Joseph 1819 wb-3-65 (Rb)
Pitts, Joseph 1843 wb-11-503 (Rb)
Pitts, Joseph B. 1844 wb-12-91 (Rb)
Pitts, Lunsford 1813 wb-1-168 (Sn)
Pitts, Patty 1841 wb-11-94 (Rb)
Pitts, William 1852 rb-16-203 (Ru)
Pitts, William 1852 rb-16-213 (Ru)
Pivers, William 1825 rb-6-128 (Ru)
Plank, Christian B. 1858 wb-#136 (Mc)
Player, Thomas T. 1853 wb-16-274 (D)
Player, Thomson T. 1855 wb-16-528 (D)
Pledge, Archer 1858 wb-5-79 (Hr)
Plumlee, Isaac 1836 wb-b-198 (Wh)
Plumlee, Stephen 1847 wb-1-230 (Bo)
Plumley, Stephen J. 1838 wb-6-357 (K)
Plumley, Stephen L. 1844 wb-8-275 (K)
Plumley, William 1826 wb-4-191 (K)
Plummer, James R. 1859 wb-17-615 (D)
Plummer, Jesse 1856 27-lw (Hd)
Plummer, Nancy 1831 wb-#234 (Mu)
Plummer, William 1809 wb-1-311 (Rb)
Poe, B. H. 1859 wb-1-290 (Be)
Poe, David 1841 wb-f-37 (Hn)
Poe, Jonathan 1818 rb-4-126 (Ru)
Pofford, John 1851 mr-2-413 (Be)
Pofford, John 1854 mr-2-589 (Be)
Pofford, Thomas W. 1858 wb-1-226 (Be)
Pogue, Elizabeth 1841 rb-12-25 (Ru)
Pogue, James 1814 rb-1-164 (Ru)
Pogue, John 1814 wb-2-36# (Ge)
Pogue, Martha 1814 rb-1-164 (Ru)
Pogue, Nancy 1847 148-1-200 (Ge)
Poindexter, Andrew B. 1855 wb-n-566 (Mt)

Poindexter, C. C. 1859 gs-1-245 (F)
Poindexter, G. C. 1861 wb-18-473 (D)
Poindexter, James 1857 wb-#59 (Wa)
Poindexter, Joseph 1825 rb-6-139 (Ru)
Poindexter, Lewis T. 1859 rb-p-245 (Mt)
Poindexter, Nicholas J. 1846 wb-b-138 (We)
Poindexter, Thomas 1852 wb-1-403 (Hw)
Pointer, John 1851 rb-17-105 (Ru)
Pointer, John 1854 wb-16-219 (D)
Pointer, William 1859 wb-h-333 (Hn)
Pok, Thomas 1814 wb-2-158 (Rb)
Poland, Jemima 1805 lw (Ct)
Poland, John 1835 lw (Ct)
Polk, Abigail 1823 wb-4-86 (Rb)
Polk, Alexander F. 1838 wb-b-99 (O)
Polk, Benjamin 1840 abl-1-212 (T)
Polk, Charles T. 1839 wb-b-154 (Hd)
Polk, E. 1828 wb-6-306 (Rb)
Polk, Ezekiel 1824 wb-1-8 (Hr)
Polk, Ezekiel 1829 wb-6-486 (Rb)
Polk, Franklin E. 1831 wb-#221 (Mu)
Polk, Green W. 1842 wb-b-409 (Hd)
Polk, James J. 1857 wb-16-552 (Rb)
Polk, James K. 1851 wb-14-585 (D)
Polk, John 1805 wb-1-172 (Rb)
Polk, John 1836 wb-b-32 (Hd)
Polk, John 1837 wb-a-303 (O)
Polk, John 1845 wb-a2-281 (Mu)
Polk, John 1845 wb-f-141 (Mu)
Polk, John 1851 wb-10-323 (Wi)
Polk, John L. 1832 wb-#243 (Mu)
Polk, Mariah 1856 wb-3-352 (La)
Polk, Marshall T. 1831 wb-#226 (Mu)
Polk, Mary L. 1851 wb-4-154 (Mu)
Polk, Richard 1837 wb-6-343 (Wi)
Polk, Robert A. 1839 wb-z-388 (Mu)
Polk, Rufus K. 1843 wb-z-468 (Mu)
Polk, Samuel 1829 wb-#200 (Mu)
Polk, Samuel W. 1839 wb-y-393 (Mu)
Polk, Sarah 1843 wb-a2-120 (Mu)
Polk, Shelby 1839 wb-2-116 (Hr)
Polk, Sophia 1852 wb-5-25 (Hr)
Polk, Thomas 1815 wb-2-193 (Rb)
Polk, Thomas 1825 wb-1-21 (Hr)
Polk, William 1839 wb-d-94 (Hd)
Polk, William J. 1860 wb-f-200 (Mu)
Polk, _____ 1843 wb-d-69 (Hd)
Pollack, D. D. 1860 wb-k-352 (O)
Pollard, Elizabeth 1860 wb-e-370 (Wh)
Pollard, G. M. 1858 rb-o-606 (Mt)
Pollard, Isaac N. 1838 wb-a-68 (Cr)

Pollard, James 1839 wb-b-185 (Hd)
Pollard, John E. 1852 wb-m-520 (Mt)
Pollard, Joseph 1841 wb-7-421 (Wi)
Pollard, Margaret 1847 rb-k-614 (Mt)
Pollard, Rebecca 1855 wb-n-697 (Mt)
Pollard, Reuben 1851 wb-m-343 (Mt)
Pollard, Reubin 1843 rb-j-38 (Mt)
Pollard, Thomas P. 1816 rb-3-189 (Ru)
Pollock, Daniel 1846 wb-1-406 (La)
Polston, John 1815 wb-a-64 (Ro)
Poltz, Sally 1859 wb-18-49 (D)
Ponder, Nathaniel 1843 wb-f-158* (Hn)
Pool, Aaron 1839 wb-2-111 (Hr)
Pool, Alexander 1816 rb-4-3 (Ru)
Pool, George 1806 wb-1-217 (Rb)
Pool, John 1859 rb-p-95 (Mt)
Pool, John P. 1822 wb-#85 (Mu)
Pool, John W. 1844 wb-12-222 (Rb)
Pool, Lucretia 1847 rb-k-396 (Mt)
Pool, William 1848 wb-14-28 (Rb)
Pool, William P. 1849 wb-b-563 (Mu)
Pooley, William 1861 wb-3e-188 (Sh)
Poor, Elizabeth 1835 rb-g-229 (Mt)
Poor, Sarah E. 1835 rb-g-254 (Mt)
Poor, William M. 1854 wb-a-460 (F)
Poore, C. F. 1861 wb-17-257 (Rb)
Poore, Carroll F. 1861 wb-17-275 (Rb)
Pope, Abel H. 1843 wb-a-167 (L)
Pope, Adkins 1815 wb-1-0 (Sm)
Pope, Ann 1836 wb-6-278 (Wi)
Pope, Ann 1837 wb-6-297 (Wi)
Pope, Barnaby 1862 wb-f-428 (G)
Pope, C. 1860 rb-20-685 (Ru)
Pope, Charles 1860 rb-20-718 (Ru)
Pope, Clarissa 1859 wb-c-281 (L)
Pope, Elias 1834 wb-a-30 (T)
Pope, Elijah 1847 wb-b-238 (We)
Pope, Elijah 1852 6-2-133 (Le)
Pope, Elizabeth H. (Mrs.) 1852 wb-2-126 (Sh)
Pope, Ezekiel 1829 wb-4-368 (Wi)
Pope, Gustavus A. 1834 wb-5-383 (Wi)
Pope, Isac W. 1840 wb-7-217 (Wi)
Pope, Jahu 1802 wb-1-143 (Je)
Pope, Jane O. 1833 wb-5-293 (Wi)
Pope, John 1829 wb-4-436 (Wi)
Pope, John 1838 wb-11-474 (D)
Pope, John 1840 wb-7-268 (Wi)
Pope, John M. 1852 wb-15-172 (Rb)
Pope, John W. 1842 wb-7-512 (Wi)
Pope, Lemuel 1848 ib-1-3 (Wy)
Pope, Levander 1853 wb-3-169 (W)

Pope, Mary C. 1838 wb-6-491 (Wi)
Pope, Norfleet 1843 wb-11-392 (Rb)
Pope, Opie 1860 wb-18-267 (D)
Pope, Rebecca 1860 149-1-205 (Ge)
Pope, Simon 1841 mr-1-342 (Be)
Pope, Simon 1848 wb-2-69# (Ge)
Pope, Thadeus 1830 wb-9-400 (D)
Pope, William 1846 wb-12-587 (Rb)
Pope, William 1847 wb-13-1 (Rb)
Pope, William R. 1846 wb-8-409 (Wi)
Porch, Hartwell 1838 wb-y-348 (Mu)
Porch, Henry 1814 wb-A-59 (Li)
Portale?, John 1831 wb-b-31 (Wh)
Portale?, Martha 1831 wb-b-33 (Wh)
Porter, Alexander 1833 wb-10-186 (D)
Porter, Alexander 1853 wb-16-189 (D)
Porter, Benjamin 1852 wb-15-226 (Rb)
Porter, Benjamin 1853 wb-15-279 (Rb)
Porter, Benjamin sr. 1861 wb-17-262 (Rb)
Porter, Boyd 1861 wb-#137 (Mc)
Porter, Charles 1840 wb-e-13 (St)
Porter, Charles T. 1831 wb-3-154 (Je)
Porter, David 1860 wb-17-57 (Rb)
Porter, Dudley 1812 wb-1-287 (Wi)
Porter, Elizabeth A. 1848 wb-g-241 (Hn)
Porter, Francis W. 1850 wb-b-627 (Mu)
Porter, George 1823 wb-8-251 (D)
Porter, George M. 1845 wb-g-13 (Hn)
Porter, Henry H. 1843 wb-#137 (Mc)
Porter, Isaac N. 1826 wb-#130 (Mu)
Porter, James 1817 wb-7-210 (D)
Porter, James 1829 wb-9-320 (D)
Porter, James 1833 wb-x-30 (Mu)
Porter, James 1838 wb-3-0 (Sm)
Porter, James M. 1838 wb-b-69 (O)
Porter, Jemima 1850 wb-1-0 (Sm)
Porter, Jemima S. 1857 wb-b-47 (Ms)
Porter, Jessee 1824 wb-3-674 (Wi)
Porter, John (Dr.) 1821 wb-1-0 (Sm)
Porter, John 1786 wb-1-45 (D)
Porter, John 1828 wb-4-287 (Wi)
Porter, John 1831 wb-b-26 (Wh)
Porter, John 1851 as-c-105 (Di)
Porter, John 1859 wb-f-308 (Ro)
Porter, John B. 1848 wb-9-86 (Wi)
Porter, John R. 1860 wb-f-330 (Ro)
Porter, Joseph B. 1829 wb-#204 (Mu)
Porter, Joshua 1831 wb-b-13 (Wh)
Porter, Lucinda 1854 wb-15-599 (Rb)
Porter, Mary 1834 rb-f-615 (Mt)
Porter, Mary 1847 wb-7-0 (Sm)

Porter, Mary Ann 1854 wb-6-164 (Ma)
Porter, Mary E. 1859 wb-16-811 (Rb)
Porter, Miriam 1841 wb-7-407 (Wi)
Porter, Rees 1817 lr (Gi)
Porter, Robert 1833 wb-10-225 (D)
Porter, Robert J. 1861 27-lw (Hd)
Porter, Robert M. 1857 wb-17-294 (D)
Porter, Robert M. 1860 wb-f-378 (G)
Porter, Sarah 1835 wb-3-341 (Je)
Porter, Sarah 1836 wb-3-489 (Je)
Porter, Stephen 1855 wb-a-363 (Ms)
Porter, T. N. 1851 as-b-35 (Ms)
Porter, Thomas 1815 rb-b-314 (Mt)
Porter, Thomas 1859 wb-16-738 (Rb)
Porter, Thomas D. 1837 wb-6-384 (Wi)
Porter, Thomas J. 1851 wb-5-8 (Hr)
Porter, Thomas S. 1816 rb-b-251 (Mt)
Porter, W. 1834 wb-c-142 (Hn)
Porter, W. C. 1853 wb-15-416 (Rb)
Porter, William 1832 wb-c-37 (Hn)
Porter, William 1837 wb-b-63 (Hd)
Porter, William 1842 wb-z-430 (Mu)
Porter, William 1843 wb-f-152* (Hn)
Porter, William 1844 wb-z-566 (Mu)
Porter, William 1850 wb-#137 (Mc)
Porter, William 1851 wb-a-237 (Di)
Porter, William 1855 wb-6-130 (Ma)
Porter, William C. 1853 wb-15-443 (Rb)
Porter, William J. 1859 ib-2-183 (Wy)
Porter, William R. 1861 wb-f-212 (Mu)
Porter, William T. 1859 ib-2-129 (Wy)
Porter, William sr. 1837 wb-d-137* (Hn)
Porter, William sr. 1841 wb-z-246 (Mu)
Porter, Young G. 1833 wb-1-42 (La)
Porterfield, C. A. 1847 wb-#154 (Wl)
Porterfield, Charles A. 1849 wb-#165 (Wl)
Porterfield, Francis 1834 wb-10-271 (D)
Porterfield, James 1812 wb-#10 (Wl)
Porterfield, Richard 1852 wb-11-178 (K)
Porterfield, Robert R. 1846 wb-13-463 (D)
Porterfield, Samuel G. 1854 wb-A-95 (Ca)
Portwood, Page 1847? wb-1B-4 (A)
Posey, Allison 1840 wb-#132 (Wl)
Posey, D. Campbell 1853 ib-2-56 (Cl)
Posey, David P. 1853 wb-c-60 (L)
Posey, Elizabeth 1843 wb-#141 (Wl)
Posey, George W. 1855 ib-2-231 (Cl)
Posey, Marshall 1857 wb-c-174 (L)
Posey, Marshall A. 1859 wb-c-291 (L)
Posey, William S. 1854 rb-17-210 (Ru)
Posey, Zachariah 1844 rb-13-37 (Ru)

Post, George W. 1859 wb-17-578 (D)
Poston, John 1859 gs-1-255 (F)
Poston, John H. 1848 rb-l-146 (Mt)
Poston, Louisa J. 1858 gs-1-153 (F)
Poteet, A. J. 1858 wb-4-200 (La)
Poteet, Isaac 1837 wb-6-429 (Wi)
Poteet, John 1831 wb-5-45 (Wi)
Poteet, Sarah 1860 wb-e-318 (Wh)
Potter, Dave S. 1859 39-2-301 (Dk)
Potter, David 1858 39-2-261 (Dk)
Potter, Donnaldson 1849 wb-b-430 (Mu)
Potter, Frances 1844 wb-8-196 (Wi)
Potter, J. B. 1859 39-2-291 (Dk)
Potter, John 1790 wb-#3 (Wa)
Potter, John 1807 wb-a-16 (Ro)
Potter, John 1825 wb-b-26 (Ro)
Potter, John A. 1843 wb-d-88 (O)
Potter, Reuben 1850 wb-1-59 (Jo)
Potter, Thomas 1817 rb-b-420 (Mt)
Potter, Thomas S. 1815 rb-b-282 (Mt)
Potts, Daniel 1845 wb-8-309 (Wi)
Potts, Henry 1838 rb-10-183 (Ru)
Potts, Henry 1852 rb-16-204 (Ru)
Potts, James 1844 wb-8-207 (Wi)
Potts, John 1852 wb-d-80 (Wh)
Potts, John sr. 1850 wb-c-376 (Wh)
Potts, Joseph 1812 wb-1-277 (Wi)
Potts, Mary 1850 wb-c-380 (Wh)
Potts, Mary 1850 wb-c-403 (Wh)
Potts, Peter 1815 wb-2-147 (Wi)
Potts, Stephen 1852 wb-10-206 (Wi)
Potts, Willie 1854 wb-g-568 (Hn)
Pounds, Thomas 1846 wb-b-156 (We)
Powel, A. K. 1849 ib-1-40 (Wy)
Powel, Bennet 1856 ib-1-385 (Wy)
Powel, Exum 1815 wb-2-200 (Rb)
Powel, Francis M. 1850 wb-g-403 (Hu)
Powel, George 1855 wb-3-269 (Gr)
Powel, Harry 1845 wb-1-348 (La)
Powel, Henry 1844 wb-1-338 (La)
Powel, Rebecca 1827 rb-6-306 (Ru)
Powel, Thomas 1815 wb-#13 (Mu)
Powell, A. 1830 wb-b-114 (Hn)
Powell, A. J. 1861 wb-17-261 (Rb)
Powell, Albert H. 1857 wb-f-103 (G)
Powell, Alford D. 1857 wb-e-71 (Hy)
Powell, Allanson 1831 wb-b-135 (Hn)
Powell, Allen 1818 wb-1-0 (Sm)
Powell, Allen H. 1837 wb-y-49 (Mu)
Powell, Ambrose 1827 wb-#202 (Mu)
Powell, Andrew J. 1851 wb-14-547 (Rb)

Powell, Ann 1837 wb-11-76 (D)
Powell, Benjamin 1816 wb-2-364 (Rb)
Powell, Benjamin 1817 wb-2-332 (Rb)
Powell, Benjamin 1831 wb-#137 (Mc)
Powell, Benjamin R. 1838 wb-11-381 (D)
Powell, Charles 1818 wb-#39 (Mu)
Powell, Charles 1819 wb-3-163 (Rb)
Powell, Charles 1831 wb-#233 (Mu)
Powell, Charles 1832 wb-8-35 (Rb)
Powell, Charles 1857 rb-18-436 (Ru)
Powell, Charles S. 1855 wb-e-315 (G)
Powell, David 1817 rb-4-19 (Ru)
Powell, Dempsey 1832 wb-10-8 (D)
Powell, Edmund L. 1842 wb-12-307* (D)
Powell, Elias 1852 wb-10-400 (Wi)
Powell, Garston 1847 wb-1-37 (Jo)
Powell, George W. 1816 rb-3-185 (Ru)
Powell, Hampton 1852 wb-m-431 (Mt)
Powell, Henry 1813 wb-#13 (Wa)
Powell, Henry 1856 ib-1-387 (Ca)
Powell, Honor 1853 wb-4-624 (Mu)
Powell, J. 1830 wb-2-0 (Sm)
Powell, James 1832 wb-8-184 (Rb)
Powell, James 1841 rb-i-193 (Mt)
Powell, James 1846 wb-7-0 (Sm)
Powell, James C. 1854 wb-a-344 (Ms)
Powell, Jesse 1821 wb-1-0 (Sm)
Powell, John 1847 wb-#156 (Wl)
Powell, John 1853 wb-e-21 (Hy)
Powell, John 1854 wb-15-611 (Rb)
Powell, John T. 1860 wb-18-146 (D)
Powell, Joseph 1839 wb-1-80 (Ct)
Powell, Joseph 1839 wb-b-133 (O)
Powell, Joseph J. 1837 wb-a-214 (O)
Powell, Jourden 1858 ib-2-101 (Wy)
Powell, Lemuel B. 1857 wb-17-415 (D)
Powell, Mariah 1861 wb-3e-184 (Sh)
Powell, Martin 1858 wb-f-227 (Ro)
Powell, Mary 1843 wb-12-110 (Rb)
Powell, Mathew 1851 wb-14-470 (Rb)
Powell, Milton 1847 wb-8-551 (Wi)
Powell, Nancy H. Jr. 1860 wb-17-53 (Rb)
Powell, Nancy H. sr? 1860 wb-17-53 (Rb)
Powell, Nathan 1834 wb-#107 (Wl)
Powell, Rachel 1859 rb-20-83 (Ru)
Powell, Rebecca 1843 wb-12-43 (Rb)
Powell, Rhoda 1812 wb-1-0 (Sm)
Powell, Sarah 1828 wb-#200 (Mu)
Powell, Thomas 1859 rb-20-83 (Ru)
Powell, W. B. 1848 wb-g-98 (Hu)
Powell, William 1826 rb-6-260 (Ru)

Powell, William 1841 wb-10-596 (Rb)
Powell, William 1845 wb-f-296 (Hn)
Powell, William 1853 wb-b-241 (L)
Powell, Willie 1821 wb-3-235 (Rb)
Power, Holloway 1852 wb-#137 (Mc)
Power, James Miles 1860 wb-#138 (Mc)
Power, Samuel D. 1832 rb-f-346 (Mt)
Powers, George 1841 5-2-220 (Cl)
Powers, Green? 1854 wb-xx-410 (St)
Powers, John 1799 wb-1-19 (Ct)
Powers, Michael 1857 wb-3e-36 (Sh)
Powers, Morgan 1858 wb-#138 (Mc)
Powers, Nathaniel 1856 wb-h-592 (Hu)
Powers, R. C. 1860 rb-p-479 (Mt)
Powers, Travis 1854 wb-n-365 (Mt)
Poyner, Henry W. 1854 wb-16-352 (D)
Poyner, John O. 1862 wb-#135 (Wl)
Poyner, William 1830 wb-4-501 (Wi)
Poynor, Charles M. 1849 wb-9-277 (Wi)
Poynor, John 1852 wb-10-200 (Wi)
Poynor, Robert 1848 wb-9-144 (Wi)
Poynor, William J. 1856 wb-f-100 (Mu)
Poynter, William 1859 wb-h-346 (Hn)
Poyzer, Benjamin 1833 wb-10-85 (D)
Poyzer, George 1818 wb-7-283 (D)
Prall, P. M. 1837 wb-2-244 (Ma)
Prall, Peter M. 1840 wb-3-283 (Ma)
Prater, Archalous 1854 wb-3-207 (W)
Prater, Benjamin 1851 wb-e-293 (Ro)
Prater, Elizabeth 1858 rb-19-384 (Ru)
Prater, Mary A. 1854 wb-e-458 (Ro)
Prater, Mary A. 1854 wb-e-468 (Ro)
Prater, Philip 1855 rb-17-582 (Ru)
Prather, Thomas 1813 wb-2-35# (Ge)
Prather, William 1824 wb-4-26 (K)
Prator, Martha 1844 wb-b-59 (We)
Prator, Samuel 1840 wb-c-148 (Ro)
Prator, Thomas 1842 wb-d-18 (Ro)
Pratt, Ann 1860 wb-13-319 (Wi)
Pratt, John 1853 wb-3-120 (Gr)
Pratt, Samuel 1855 wb-16-453 (D)
Prescott, Simon 1833 lr (Sn)
Preson, Mary 1832 wb-1-338 (Ma)
Presson, John 1860 wb-1-327 (Be)
Presson, William 1840 mr-1-320 (Be)
Pressor, Mary 1829 wb-1-136 (Ma)
Preston, George 1808 wb-a-24 (Ro)
Preston, George 1826 wb-b-27 (Ro)
Preston, James 1840 wb-a-452 (R)
Preston, James 1853 wb-1-33 (R)
Preston, Jesse 1836 wb-b-337 (Ro)

Preston, Joel sr. 1829 wb-3-0 (Sm)
Preston, John 1840 wb-a-454 (R)
Preston, John 1854 ib-1-325 (Ca)
Preston, Sarah J. 1847 wb-14-27 (D)
Preston, Thomas 1810 lr (Sn)
Prewen, William 1836 rb-g-272 (Mt)
Prewet, Harris B. 1853 wb-e-89 (G)
Prewett, James 1856 wb-h-503 (Hu)
Prewett, James M. 1837 rb-9-409 (Ru)
Prewett, John 1837 rb-10-25 (Ru)
Prewett, John 1842 wb-e-517 (Hu)
Prewett, John 1849 wb-4-438 (Hr)
Prewett, Leroy 1835 wb-d-53 (Hn)
Prewett, Mary 1847 wb-4-250 (Hr)
Prewett, Mary E. 1846 wb-4-30 (Hr)
Prewett, Moses H. 1856 wb-6-357 (Ma)
Prewett, Smith 1837 rb-10-78 (Ru)
Prewett, Unity K. 1833 wb-x-56 (Mu)
Prewit, Thomas 1834 wb-b-33 (G)
Prewitt, John 1847 wb-4-234 (Hr)
Price, Bob (Col) 1860 wb-3e-143 (Sh)
Price, Daniel 1860 wb-k-208 (O)
Price, Drury 1824 as-A-95 (Di)
Price, Drury 1826 as-a-151 (Di)
Price, Edward 1833 wb-5-251 (K)
Price, Emily 1857 wb-#58 (Wa)
Price, Euagy 1852 wb-3-114 (W)
Price, Francis D. 1841 wb-1-206 (Fr)
Price, Francis Dennington 1830 rb-8-146 (Ru)
Price, George 1861 wb-e-413 (Wh)
Price, Haskew 1853 wb-15-238 (Rb)
Price, Haskew 1853 wb-15-239 (Rb)
Price, Henry 1857 wb-1-28 (Br)
Price, J. C. 1858 wb-2-438 (Me)
Price, J. F. 1857 wb-f-82 (Ro)
Price, James 1838 wb-6-356 (K)
Price, James 1844 wb-8-188 (Wi)
Price, James L. 1822 wb-1-7 (Ma)
Price, Jane 1852 wb-15-173 (Rb)
Price, Jno. 1849 wb-4-523 (Hr)
Price, Job 1806 wb-1-194 (K)
Price, John 1806 rb-2-16 (Ru)
Price, John 1815 wb-4-331 (D)
Price, John 1816 rb-3-218 (Ru)
Price, John 1836 wb-1-522 (Hr)
Price, John 1839 wb-2-51# (Ge)
Price, John 1847 wb-a-307 (F)
Price, John 1849 148-1-272 (Ge)
Price, John C. 1828 wb-7-80 (Rb)
Price, John C. 1854 wb-16-347 (D)
Price, John D. 1848 wb-c-326 (Wh)

Price, John L. 1846 wb-c-219 (Wh)
Price, John S. 1846 wb-c-216 (Wh)
Price, Lindsay 1835 wb-x-340 (Mu)
Price, Margaret 1852 wb-d-54 (Wh)
Price, Maria 1861 wb-18-428 (D)
Price, Mary 1858 wb-12-578 (Wi)
Price, Matthew 1843 wb-1-225 (Li)
Price, Meshack 1860 wb-d-69 (L)
Price, R. J. 1861 wb-00-10 (Cf)
Price, Reece 1835 wb-5-342 (K)
Price, Richard sr. 1833 wb-5-199 (K)
Price, Robert C. 1852 rb-16-332 (Ru)
Price, Sara Ann 1847 rb-k-606 (Mt)
Price, Silas 1851 wb-15-169 (D)
Price, Thomas 1832 wb-a-156 (R)
Price, Thomas 1837 wb-1-106 (La)
Price, Thomas 1837 wb-1-98 (La)
Price, William 1845 wb-c-183 (Wh)
Price, William 1853 wb-2-59 (Li)
Price, William 1855 wb-d-274 (Wh)
Price, William A. 1852 wb-10-389 (Wi)
Price, William B. 1860 wb-a-357 (Cr)
Price, William sr. 1842 wb-a-104 (L)
Price, Williamson sr. 1842 wb-a-114 (L)
Price, Willie 1861 wb-h-546 (Hn)
Price, Wm. M. 1859 gs-1-390 (F)
Price, Zachariah 1841 wb-1-208 (Fr)
Price, Zebadee 1855 wb-h-421 (Hu)
Prichard, Benjamin 1826 wb-8-554 (D)
Prichard, David 1824 rb-d-370 (Mt)
Prichard, Henry 1836 wb-1-93 (La)
Prichard, Isaac C. 1845 wb-8-229 (Wi)
Prichard, John 1821 rb-d-356 (Mt)
Prichard, Richard 1848 wb-a-203 (Di)
Prichard, Robert 1847 wb-8-532 (Wi)
Prichard, Sarah 1839 wb-11-517 (D)
Prichett, Singleton 1845 wb-#42 (Wa)
Priddy, William 1856 wb-3e-24 (Sh)
Pride, Allen 1859 wb-f-298 (Ro)
Pride, Benjamin 1817 wb-a-103 (Ro)
Pride, Francis 1818 wb-3-359 (Rb)
Pride, Francis 1850 wb-7-0 (Sm)
Pride, James 1848 wb-#167 (Wl)
Pride, John 1813 wb-4-254 (D)
Pride, Mary 1822 wb-3-351 (Rb)
Pride, Polly 1854 wb-#138 (Mc)
Prier, Frances 1846 wb-d-226 (Ro)
Priest, Francis 1855 wb-a-220 (V)
Priest, James 1825 wb-1-39 (Ma)
Priest, John T. 1810 wb-1-216 (Wi)
Priest, Nancy 1858 wb-12-569 (Wi)

Priestley, Franklin 1842 wb-12-362* (D)
Priestley, James 1821 wb-8-1 (D)
Priestley, James 1838 wb-e-151 (Hu)
Priestley, Joseph L. 1835 wb-c-410 (St)
Priestley, Matilda 1850 wb-m-77 (Mt)
Priestley, Sarah 1829 wb-9-303 (D)
Priestley, William 1820 wb-7-459 (D)
Priestly, John T. 1824 wb-4-274 (Rb)
Priestly, John T. 1835 wb-9-123 (Rb)
Priez, Thompson 1838 wb-1-167 (La)
Prigmore, Kiziah 1841 wb-#138 (Mc)
Prim, Abraham 1825 rb-6-105 (Ru)
Prim, Abram 1835 rb-9-208 (Ru)
Prim, James 1837 wb-#147 (Wl)
Prim, Kinsie 1836 wb-#114 (Wl)
Primm, James O. K. 1846 rb-13-464 (Ru)
Primm, Jeremiah 1860 wb-13-355 (Wi)
Primm, John 1819 wb-3-99 (Wi)
Primm, Sally 1838 wb-6-526 (Wi)
Prince, John 1850 wb-a-159 (Cr)
Prince, Robert 1813 rb-a-489 (Mt)
Prince, William 1858 lr (Sn)
Prine, Daniel 1841 wb-b-32 (We)
Pring, Nicholas 1859 wb-#61 (Wa)
Prior, Luke 1848 wb-9-172 (Wi)
Prior, Sy 1860 wb-1D-2 (A)
Prior, Zachariah B. 1838 wb-11-274 (D)
Pritchard, Benjamin 1826 wb-9-33 (D)
Pritchard, David 1824 rb-d-398 (Mt)
Pritchard, Jesse 1844 wb-a-130 (Cr)
Pritchard, Samuel N. 1859 wb-13-52 (Wi)
Pritchet, John 1847 rb-k-573 (Mt)
Pritchet, Nancy 1813 rb-b-150 (Mt)
Pritchett, Benjamin 1826 wb-9-47 (D)
Pritchett, Benjamin 1861 wb-#134 (Wl)
Pritchett, Ephraim 1822 wb-8-159 (D)
Pritchett, George 1832 wb-#95 (Wl)
Pritchett, John 1855 wb-e-516 (Ro)
Pritchett, Mary J. 1859 wb-h-361 (Hn)
Pritchett, Nathaniel 1828 wb-#88 (Wl)
Pritchett, Robert 1849 wb-9-327 (Wi)
Pritchett, Samuel 1853 rb-16-434 (Ru)
Pritchett, Susannah 1854 wb-g-548 (Hn)
Pritchett, Thomas J. 1848 wb-9-45 (Wi)
Pritchett, William 1816 wb-1-0 (Sm)
Pritchett, William C. 1830 rb-f-137 (Mt)
Probarts, William Y. 1820 wb-7-371 (D)
Proctor, Absalom 1835 wb-9-124 (Rb)
Proctor, Edmund 1835 wb-#109 (Wl)
Proctor, Edmund P. 1838 wb-#123 (Wl)
Proctor, Ellen 1859 as-c-556 (Di)

Proctor, Franklin 1839 wb-2-124 (Hr)
Proctor, James 1815 wb-A-91 (Li)
Proctor, John 1829 wb-7-75 (Rb)
Proctor, Judith 1836 wb-#115 (Wl)
Proctor, Thomas 1830 wb-#85 (Wl)
Proctor, William 1828 wb-#79 (Wl)
Proctor, William 1837 wb-2-226 (Sn)
Proffit, Elisha 1845 5-3-91 (Cl)
Proffit, William 1833 eb-1-300 (C)
Proham, John 1844 mr-2-130 (Be)
Prosser, James 1855 wb-2-107 (Li)
Prosson, Samuel 1829 wb-1-170 (Ma)
Proudfit, John H. 1840 rb-i-9 (Mt)
Proudfoot, Nancy 1855 wb-n-524 (Mt)
Provine, J. N. 1858 wb-h-211 (Hn)
Provine, John 1855 wb-#116 (Wl)
Prowell, Mary 1841 wb-1-53 (Me)
Prowell, Thomas 1840 wb-7-304 (Wi)
Prowell, Thomas 1855 wb-11-505 (Wi)
Prowell, Thomas 1855 wb-11-559 (Wi)
Pruden, David T. 1843 wb-4-89 (Ma)
Pruder?, Lodwick L. 1836 wb-2-100 (Ma)
Pruet, Joseph 1830 wb-3-0 (Sm)
Pruet, William 1815 wb-1-0 (Sm)
Pruett, Elizabeth 1855 wb-e-286 (G)
Pruett, Frances 1852 wb-#180 (Wl)
Pruett, Jacob 1828 wb-1-31 (Li)
Pruett, Richard 1850 wb-#173 (Wl)
Pruit, Abraham 1795 wb-1-30 (K)
Pruit, David 1854 wb-h-317 (Hu)
Pruit, John 1854 wb-h-319 (Hu)
Pruitt, Mary 1857 ib-1-472 (Wy)
Pruitt, Patrick H. 1858 wb-5-86 (Hr)
Pryer, William 1846 wb-c-218 (Wh)
Pryerson, Samuel 1816? wb-#33 (Mu)
Pryor, Eleanor 1851 wb-10-9 (Wi)
Pryor, Harris 1847 wb-e-28 (Ro)
Pryor, Henry 1854 wb-i-156 (O)
Pryor, John 1810 wb-1-240 (Wi)
Pryor, John 1841 wb-b-27 (We)
Pryor, John sr. 1842 wb-1-198 (Li)
Pryor, Nelly 1849 wb-9-335 (Wi)
Pryor, Saml. 1811 wb-4-130 (D)
Pryor, Samuel 1834 wb-1-352 (Hr)
Pryor, Thomas 1841 wb-b-31 (We)
Pucket, Cheatham 1811 wb-4-146 (D)
Pucket, Edward 1823 wb-#87 (Mu)
Pucket, Jacob 1849 as-b-437 (Di)
Puckett, Armstead A. 1861 wb-#134 (Wl)
Puckett, Arthur 1827 rb-6-308 (Ru)
Puckett, Avarella 1848 wb-g-236 (Hn)

Puckett, Benjamin 1860 wb-1-352 (Be)
Puckett, Cas 1854 rb-17-264 (Ru)
Puckett, Charles 1854 rb-16-796 (Ru)
Puckett, Douglas 1815 wb-2-116 (Je)
Puckett, Elizabeth (Mrs.) 1860 rb-20-542 (Ru)
Puckett, Elizabeth 1859 rb-20-113 (Ru)
Puckett, Fleming 1851 wb-#175 (Wl)
Puckett, Frances 1850 wb-#174 (Wl)
Puckett, Isham 1838 wb-#139 (Wl)
Puckett, Isham 1849 wb-#165 (Wl)
Puckett, John 1835 wb-#110 (Wl)
Puckett, John 1847 wb-g-211 (Hn)
Puckett, John S. 1853 wb-g-506 (Hn)
Puckett, Lemuel 1842 wb-f-145 (Hn)
Puckett, Leonard 1842 rb-12-256 (Ru)
Puckett, Leonard 1850 wb-g-374 (Hn)
Puckett, Lodwick 1860 rb-20-414 (Ru)
Puckett, Milly 1859 rb-20-235 (Ru)
Puckett, Nancy 1846 rb-13-687 (Ru)
Puckett, Nathaniel 1842 rb-12-177 (Ru)
Puckett, Rebeckah 1845 wb-a2-200 (Mu)
Puckett, Richard 1813 wb-2-30 (Wi)
Puckett, Ship A. 1836 wb-#113 (Wl)
Puckett, Thomas A. 1844 wb-#142 (Wl)
Puckett, Washington J. 1835 wb-#110 (Wl)
Puckett, Wiley 1853 wb-h-Apr (O)
Puckitt, Isham 1853 wb-e-127 (G)
Pue, Reese 1816 wb-#23 (Wl)
Pugh, Andrew J. 1847 wb-#138 (Mc)
Pugh, David 1851 lw (Ct)
Pugh, Elizabeth 1834 wb-10-350 (D)
Pugh, Fleming C. 1834 wb-#139 (Mc)
Pugh, Henry 1855 wb-h-65 (St)
Pugh, J. F. 1862 wb-#139 (Mc)
Pugh, Jesse 1845 wb-4-22 (Hr)
Pugh, John 1816 wb-4-410 (D)
Pugh, John 1816 wb-7-21 (D)
Pugh, John 1835 wb-10-434 (D)
Pugh, John 1859 wb-#139 (Mc)
Pugh, Joseph 1839 wb-#127 (Wl)
Pugh, Joseph 1858 6-2-137 (Le)
Pugh, Saml. 1834 wb-10-372 (D)
Pugh, Susannah 1812 lw (Ct)
Pugh, Willoughby 1853 ib-1-236 (Wy)
Pugh, Wiloughby Y. 1849 wb-4-546 (Hr)
Pugsley, Charles 1832 wb-9-596 (D)
Pullam, George W. 1840 rb-10-491 (Ru)
Pullen, Archibald 1848 wb-a-199 (Di)
Pullen, Jesse 1859 lr (Gi)
Pullen, Moses 1858 wb-4-169 (La)
Pullen, Thomas 1821 rb-5-173 (Ru)

Pullen, Thomas 1821 wb-1-41 (Ma)
Pulley, David 1819 wb-7-359 (D)
Pulley, Robert M. 1853 wb-16-191 (D)
Pulley, Thomas 1828 wb-1-24 (Li)
Pulliam, D. K. 1855 wb-b-2 (F)
Pulliam, John 1840 wb-b-261 (O)
Pulliam, Mary 1833 wb-5-220 (Wi)
Pulliam, Nancy 1844 wb-d-207 (O)
Pulliam, Temperance 1829 wb-1-192 (Ma)
Pullin, Leroy 1839 wb-1-352 (Gr)
Pully, James 1837 lr (Gi)
Pully, Jesse 1841 wb-b-24 (We)
Pully, William 1838 wb-e-139 (Hu)
Pulse, Fredrick 1845 wb-4-76 (Je)
Purcell, Daniel 1851 wb-#139 (Mc)
Purcell, Daniel 1852 wb-#140 (Mc)
Purcy, William 1842 wb-3-625 (Ma)
Purdam, John 1827 wb-1-11 (W)
Purdom, Alexander 1803 as-1-15 (Ge)
Purdue, Orren 1811 rb-b-22 (Mt)
Purdy, Robert 1832 wb-10-38 (D)
Purkins, Lewis 1840 wb-c-183 (Ro)
Purkins, William 1860 wb-i-160 (St)
Purnell, Lemuel 1825 wb-1-0 (Sm)
Purnell, M. T. 1849 wb-10-244 (K)
Purrington, T. A. 1851 wb-m-279 (Mt)
Purris, Elizabeth 1858 wb-#140 (Mc)
Purris, Henry S. 1844 wb-d-99 (Ro)
Purris, John 1830 wb-b-60 (Ro)
Pursell, George (Sr.) 1829 wb-#27 (Wa)
Purselley, William sr. 1857 wb-12-442 (K)
Purselly, Sarah 1857 wb-12-421 (K)
Pursley, Adison 1836 wb-6-1 (K)
Pursley, James 1856 wb-8-115 (Sm)
Pursley, William 1850 wb-10-336 (K)
Purvis, Charles 1826 wb-a-120 (Hn)
Purvis, Charles 1834 wb-d-135 (Hn)
Purvis, Miles 1836 wb-d-28 (St)
Purvis, William 1816 lr (Sn)
Puryear, David 1849 mr (Gi)
Puryear, Hezekiah 1816 wb-2-233 (Wi)
Puryear, Jordan R. H. 1847 wb-8-585 (Wi)
Puryear, Louisa 1856 lr (Gi)
Puryear, Matilda 1835 wb-6-77 (Wi)
Puryear, William Augustus 1849 wb-9-228 (Wi)
Putman, Jabin 1836 wb-6-279 (Wi)
Putman, James 1836 wb-6-248 (Wi)
Putman, Mark 1823 wb-#51 (Wl)
Putman, Solomon 1834 wb-a-47 (Cr)
Putnam, Jabin 1836 wb-6-115 (Wi)
Putney, David E. 1847 wb-a-317 (F)

Putney, David E. 1854 ib-h-94 (F)
Pybas, James 1817 wb-A-165 (Li)
Pybas, James 1843 wb-1-221 (Li)
Pybas, Stephen 1839 rb-10-312 (Ru)
Pybass, Nathaniel 1857 wb-f-89 (G)
Pyland, James 1851 wb-d-360 (G)
Pyle, Benjamin 1845 wb-13-148 (D)
Pyle, Sarah 1841 lr (Gi)
Pyles, D. W. 1856 as-b-248 (Ms)
Pyles, Levi G. 1851 wb-a-269 (Ms)
Pyron, Charles 1847 wb-8-588 (Wi)

- Q -

Qualls, Abner 1823 wb-3-498 (Rb)
Qualls, Anne 1826 wb-5-422 (Rb)
Qualls, George W. 1842 rb-12-83 (Ru)
Qualls, John 1842 5-2-283 (Cl)
Qualls, Judah 1844 5-2-399 (Cl)
Qualls, William 1835 wb-0-2 (Cf)
Quarles, Elilzabeth 1835 wb-#110 (Wl)
Quarles, Elizabeth 1848 wb-c-300 (Wh)
Quarles, Garret M. 1847 rb-k-391 (Mt)
Quarles, James 1817 wb-#24 (Wl)
Quarles, James 1831 wb-#89 (Wl)
Quarles, James M. 1838 wb-#126 (Wl)
Quarles, John B. 1814? wb-#14 (Wl)
Quarles, John B. 1824 wb-#52 (Wl)
Quarles, Mary 1823 wb-#49 (Wl)
Quarles, Roger 1817 wb-#27 (Wl)
Quarles, Roger 1820 wb-#37 (Wl)
Quarles, William 1814 wb-a-22 (Wh)
Quarles, William A. 1846 wb-#153 (Wl)
Quarles, Wm. P. 1809 wb-4-59 (D)
Quarlles, John W. 1845 rb-13-159 (Ru)
Queener, Jacob sr. 1838 eb-1-386 (C)
Queener, John 1832 wb-#140 (Mc)
Queener, S. D. 1858 iv-C-5 (C)
Quesenberry, John 1820 wb-#34 (Wl)
Quesenberry, Nicholas 1820 wb-#35 (Wl)
Quesenberry, Nicholas 1822 wb-#42 (Wl)
Quick, John 1812 wb-1-0 (Sm)
Quiett, William 1827 wb-a-36 (R)
Quigley, Patrick 1784 wb-1-17 (D)
Quin, Elliot 1833 wb-#98 (Wl)
Quinchett, Vivant 1838 wb-1-48 (Sh)
Quinley, Owen 1842 wb-3-639 (Ma)
Quinn, Enoch 1832 wb-5-155 (Wi)
Quinn, Lot? 1855 wb-n-597 (Mt)
Quinn, Michael 1841 wb-12-176* (D)
Quinn, Sarah 1823 wb-3-612 (Wi)

Quinner, Michael 1814 eb-1-38 (C)
Quisenberry, Henry 1831 wb-9-466 (D)
Quisenberry, Lucinda 1848 wb-14-279 (D)

- R -

Rabourn, Joseph 1858 wb-#140 (Mc)
Rabourn, Thomas 1843 wb-d-61 (Ro)
Racine, Eugene R. 1855 wb-3e-7 (Sh)
Rackle, Patsy? 1834 wb-1-66 (La)
Rackley, Fredrick 1829 wb-1-3 (La)
Rackley, Fredrick 1847 wb-2-11 (La)
Rackley, Silas 1832 wb-1-36 (La)
Rader, Adam 1812 wb-#12 (Wa)
Rader, Andrew 1859 149-1-150 (Ge)
Rader, Elizabeth Ann 1856 wb-2-84# (Ge)
Rader, Henry 1851 wb-2-73# (Ge)
Rader, John (of Henry) 1843 148-1-54 (Ge)
Rader, John 1842 148-1-38 (Ge)
Rader, Mary 1848 wb-2-67# (Ge)
Radford, Abner 1855 wb-g-672 (Hn)
Radford, Ann (Mrs) 1826 rb-d-551 (Mt)
Radford, Emily S. 1854 wb-11-181 (Wi)
Radford, James 1815 Wb-2-165 (Wi)
Radford, Jesse 1816 wb-#16 (Mu)
Radford, John 1815 wb-2-148 (Wi)
Radford, Nancy 1824 rb-d-301 (Mt)
Radford, William 1833 wb-5-228 (Wi)
Raebourn, Thomas 1799 rb-a-37 (Mt)
Ragan, J. B. 1859 rb-20-205 (Ru)
Ragan, Jesse 1837 as-a-366 (Di)
Ragan, Jno. B. 1860 rb-20-412 (Ru)
Ragan, John O. 1860 wb-i-159 (St)
Ragan, Larkin 1842 wb-1-211 (Fr)
Ragan, Lewis 1850 wb-g-328 (O)
Ragan, Marcus B. 1858 wb-3e-87 (Sh)
Ragan, Nathan 1835 as-a-253 (Di)
Ragan, W. B. 1849 wb-4-560 (Hr)
Ragan, W. B. 1850 wb-4-610 (Hr)
Ragen, Elizabeth 1853 as-b-135 (Ms)
Raggon, James 1828 wb-4-312 (K)
Ragland, Evan O. 1850 wb-#174 (Wl)
Ragland, James 1817 wb-1-0 (Sm)
Ragland, John D. 1840 wb-#133 (Wl)
Ragland, N. 1859 wb-3e-116 (Sh)
Ragland, Pettis 1843 wb-#140 (Wl)
Ragle, William K. 1857 wb-f-110 (Ro)
Ragsdale, Andrew 1848 wb-5-55 (Ma)
Ragsdale, Daniel 1821 wb-#37 (Wl)
Ragsdale, Daniel 1841 wb-7-401 (Wi)
Ragsdale, Daniel 1841 wb-7-403 (Wi)

Ragsdale, David 1853 wb-1-45 (R)
Ragsdale, Edward 1823 wb-3-628 (Wi)
Ragsdale, Edward 1836 wb-6-117 (Wi)
Ragsdale, J. M. 1857 wb-f-119 (G)
Ragsdale, J. P. 1855 wb-h-436 (Hu)
Ragsdale, James 1834 wb-1-52 (Gr)
Ragsdale, James 1850 wb-9-585 (Wi)
Ragsdale, John 1832 lr (Sn)
Ragsdale, L. B. 1853 wb-e-82 (G)
Ragsdale, Nancy 1827 wb-#66 (Wl)
Ragsdale, Penelope 1850 wb-9-416 (Wi)
Ragsdale, Sterling 1859 wb-#16 (Mo)
Ragsdale, Thomas 1858 wb-12-568 (Wi)
Ragsdale, William 1824 wb-4-193 (Rb)
Raigains, Thomas 1834 wb-5-420 (Wi)
Rail, Samuel 1838 wb-1-306 (Gr)
Raimy, John R. 1847 rb-k-396 (Mt)
Raines, Benjamin 1848 wb-c-303 (Wh)
Raines, Henry Y. 1838 rb-10-216 (Ru)
Raines, William M. 1835 wb-1-140 (Fr)
Rainey, Allen 1831 rb-8-400 (Ru)
Rainey, C. H. 1843 wb-z-530 (Mu)
Rainey, Jane 1860 rb-p-513 (Mt)
Rainey, John 1854 rb-17-224 (Ru)
Rainey, John 1854 wb-e-189 (G)
Rainey, John Jr. 1838 wb-#140 (Mc)
Rainey, John sr. 1856 rb-18-240 (Ru)
Rainey, Lemuel 1859 lr (Gi)
Rainey, Sarah 1842 lr (Gi)
Rainey, Wesley 1859 wb-c-303 (L)
Rainey, William 1860 rb-20-591 (Ru)
Rains, Benjamin 1860 wb-e-333 (Wh)
Rains, George 1855 wb-3-244 (W)
Rains, J. B. 1858 ib-1-549 (Ca)
Rains, James 1848 6-1-2 (Le)
Rains, James 1848 wb-2-323 (W)
Rains, James B. 1858 ib-1-554 (Ca)
Rains, John 1835 wb-10-404 (D)
Rains, John 1857 wb-17-154 (D)
Rains, John 1857 wb-A-126 (Ca)
Rains, Labon 1835 wb-x-270* (Mu)
Rains, Larkin 1853 wb-3-181 (W)
Rains, Martha 1837 wb-11-70 (D)
Rains, Naomi 1821 wb-8-18 (D)
Rains, Ursula 1857 wb-17-301 (D)
Rains, William 1812 wb-4-199 (D)
Rains, William 1827 wb-9-102 (D)
Rains, William C. 1852 wb-4-379 (Mu)
Rainwaters, Robert 1824 wb-3-102* (St)
Rainy, John 1854 rb-17-209 (Ru)
Rakes, James 1853 wb-#111 (Wl)

Ralph, Alexander 1854 wb-a-220 (T)
Ralph, Thomas 1837 rb-9-434 (Ru)
Ralph, Thomas 1857 wb-a-254 (T)
Ralston, David 1831 wb-9-546 (D)
Ralston, Elizabeth 1854 rb-17-318 (Ru)
Ralston, George 1837 rb-10-31 (Ru)
Ralston, George 1847 rb-14-160 (Ru)
Ralston, George 1858 rb-19-332 (Ru)
Ralston, Robert 1857 wb-12-474 (Wi)
Ramey, Benjamin 1861 wb-2-337 (Li)
Ramey, Jonathan 1850 wb-g-312 (St)
Ramey, Margaret 1853 wb-n-201 (Mt)
Ramey, Randolph 1841 rb-i-119 (Mt)
Ramsay, Jacob W. 1828 wb-9-167 (D)
Ramsey, David 1806 wb-3-116 (D)
Ramsey, David 1806 wb-3-135 (D)
Ramsey, David 1815 rb-3-54 (Ru)
Ramsey, David 1844 wb-a-70 (Ms)
Ramsey, Duncan B. 1851 rb-4-272 (Mu)
Ramsey, Francis A. 1821 wb-3-217 (K)
Ramsey, James 1859 wb-2-297 (Li)
Ramsey, John 1808 as-1-207 (Ge)
Ramsey, John 1843 wb-1-280 (La)
Ramsey, John 1852 wb-15-359 (D)
Ramsey, Lewis 1858 gs-1-84 (F)
Ramsey, Mary 1849 wb-d-205 (G)
Ramsey, Reynolds 1817 wb-2-322 (K)
Ramsey, Robert W. 1848 as-a-151 (Ms)
Ramsey, Samuel G. 1817 wb-2-357 (K)
Ramsey, Samuel G. 1827 wb-4-222 (K)
Ramsey, Samuel G. 1857 wb-j-247 (O)
Ramsey, Thomas 1845 wb-a2-279 (Mu)
Ramsey, William 1790 wb-1-169 (D)
Ramsey, William 1790 wb-1-176 (D)
Ramsey, William 1829 wb-#203 (Mu)
Ramsey, William 1833 rb-9-84 (Ru)
Ramsey, William 1834 wb-11-519 (D)
Ramsey, William 1855 lr (Sn)
Ramsey, William sr. 1840 wb-12-53* (D)
Ranch, Peter 1818 wb-#15 (Wa)
Randal, Aquila 1837 wb-11-6 (D)
Randal, George W. 1845 wb-#140 (Mc)
Randal, James sr. 1854 wb-d-162 (Wh)
Randal, Mearitt 1839 wb-a-75 (Cr)
Randall, Anna 1822 wb-8-77 (D)
Randall, James 1828 wb-1-18 (Li)
Randall, Jemima 1838 wb-y-189 (Mu)
Randall, Micha 1823 wb-8-201 (D)
Randall, Priestly M. 1835 wb-#109 (Wl)
Randals, Churchwell B. 1857 wb-e-146 (Wh)
Randals, Dosha 1852 wb-d-88 (Wh)

Randals, James sr. 1856 wb-e-91 (Wh)
Randell, P. M. 1833 wb-#102 (Wl)
Randle, Anna 1847 wb-f-402 (St)
Randle, Anna 1847 wb-f-430 (St)
Randle, George Davidson 1833 wb-a-126 (Cr)
Randle, Henry 1816 wb-3-210 (St)
Randle, John 1824 wb-3-290 (St)
Randle, John 1848 wb-g-46 (St)
Randle, John 1855 wb-h-185 (St)
Randle, Mary P. 1847 wb-g-215 (Hn)
Randle, Ozbern 1815 wb-3-18 (St)
Randle, Payton S. 1843 wb-f-160 (Hn)
Randle, Polly P. 1844 wb-f-285 (Hn)
Randle, Susan 1852 wb-g-444 (Hn)
Randle, Susan S. 1852 wb-g-470 (Hn)
Randle, T. S. 1858 rb-p-13 (Mt)
Randle, Thomas 1824 wb-3-348 (St)
Randle, Thomas W. 1858 rb-o-606 (Mt)
Randle, William 1841 wb-e-317 (Hn)
Randolp, John 1859 wb-3e-121 (Sh)
Randolph, Elizabeth 1840 wb-3-292 (Ma)
Randolph, Fanny 1837 wb-2-226 (Ma)
Randolph, G. R. 1831 rb-8-278 (Ru)
Randolph, Harrison 1835 rb-9-259 (Ru)
Randolph, Henry 1840 wb-1-312 (W)
Randolph, Henry 1845? wb-4-105 (Je)
Randolph, James 1794 wb-1-80 (Je)
Randolph, James 1804 wb-1-302 (Je)
Randolph, James 1815 wb-2-122 (Je)
Randolph, James 1845 wb-f-233 (St)
Randolph, James 1851 wb-5-88 (Ma)
Randolph, James A. 1859 rb-20-56 (Ru)
Randolph, James H. 1842 wb-e-219 (St)
Randolph, James M. 1827 wb-2-589 (Je)
Randolph, James W. 1839 wb-d-351 (St)
Randolph, John M. 1851 wb-3-109 (W)
Randolph, Martha 1855 ib-h-393 (F)
Randolph, Mary 1827 rb-7-329 (Ru)
Randolph, Mary 1853 wb-5-131 (Ma)
Randolph, Mary 1856 wb-1-94 (R)
Randolph, Nancy 1845 wb-5-2 (Ma)
Randolph, Olive 1814 wb-1-0 (Sm)
Randolph, Peter 1819 wb-7-359 (D)
Randolph, Peter 1856 rb-18-125 (Ru)
Randolph, R. B. B. 1849 wb-4-481 (Hr)
Randolph, Sarah 1858 rb-19-210 (Ru)
Randolph, Sarah J. 1852 rb-16-242 (Ru)
Randolph, William 1828 wb-a-45 (R)
Randolph, William Y. 1830 wb-9-410 (D)
Raney, Benjamin jr. 1856 wb-j-138 (O)
Raney, Jesse G. 1843 wb-z-540 (Mu)

Raney, John 1818 wb-1-0 (Sm)

Range, James sr. 1825 lw (Ct)

Rankin, Alexander 1835 rb-9-206 (Ru)

Rankin, Armina 1841 rb-11-109 (Ru)

Rankin, David 1831 rb-8-190 (Ru)

Rankin, David 1836 wb-2-46# (Ge)

Rankin, David 1853 148-1-450* (Ge)

Rankin, David sr. 1802 wb-1-22# (Ge)

Rankin, Elizabeth 1857 149-1-65 (Ge)

Rankin, George H. 1844 wb-b-63 (We)

Rankin, George W. 1836 wb-d-251 (Hn)

Rankin, George W. 1837 wb-d-110* (Hn)

Rankin, James 1824 wb-2-439 (Je)

Rankin, James 1827 lr (Sn)

Rankin, James 1844 rb-12-556 (Ru)

Rankin, James P. 1832 rb-8-428 (Ru)

Rankin, Jane 1844 wb-4-94 (Je)

Rankin, Jennet 1824 wb-2-420 (Je)

Rankin, John 1826 wb-1-123 (Bo)

Rankin, John 1828 wb-2-624 (Je)

Rankin, John 1847 wb-7-0 (Sm)

Rankin, P. R. 1847 wb-b-87 (Mu)

Rankin, Richard 1826 wb-2-594 (Je)

Rankin, Richard 1855 wb-a-368 (Ms)

Rankin, Richard D. 1857 as-c-19 (Ms)

Rankin, Robert 1837? wb-2-49# (Ge)

Rankin, Robert 1856 149-1-25 (Ge)

Rankin, Samuel K. 1847 wb-8-517 (Wi)

Rankin, Thomas 1810 wb-1-340 (Je)

Rankin, Thomas 1821 wb-2-306 (Je)

Rankin, Thomas C. 1851 wb-2-74# (Ge)

Rankin, William J. 1848 wb-b-178 (Mu)

Rankins, David 1814 wb-2-67 (Je)

Ransbarger, Nancy 1846 wb-1-231 (Bo)

Ransdale, James P. 1839 rb-h-267 (Mt)

Ransom, Benjamin 1845 rb-13-186 (Ru)

Ransom, Benjamin C. 1844 rb-13-31 (Ru)

Ransom, Elizabeth 1857 rb-19-42 (Ru)

Ransom, Gideon M. 1850 rb-15-487 (Ru)

Ransom, John 1849 rb-15-162 (Ru)

Ransom, Richard 1836 wb-6-115 (Wi)

Ransom, Richard 1847 rb-14-56 (Ru)

Ransom, William 1816 rb-3-146? (Ru)

Rape, Daniel 1838 wb-11-507 (D)

Rape, Gustavus 1852 wb-a-239 (Di)

Rape, Susanah M. 1846 wb-13-403 (D)

Rasberry, Lovick 1859 ib-2-130 (Wy)

Rascoe, Alexander 1857 wb-17-282 (D)

Rascoe, William 1813 wb-a-178 (St)

Rasford, Nancy 1824 rb-d-297 (Mt)

Rash, Robert 1844 wb-8-173 (Wi)

Rash, Stephen H. 1855 wb-12-13 (Wi)

Rash, Thomas A. 1838 wb-1-46 (Sh)

Ratcliff, Silas 1858 wb-#60 (Wa)

Ratcliffe, Cary M. 1841 wb-z-181 (Mu)

Ratcliffe, Gideon 1854 wb-11-179 (Wi)

Rather, James 1828 wb-#83 (Wl)

Rather, James 1844 wb-#157 (Wl)

Rather, Sally 1847 wb-e-17 (Ro)

Raules, Martha J. 1857 wb-a-16 (Ce)

Raulston, Alexander 1861 wb-b-471 (We)

Rausbarger, John 1839 wb-1-126 (Bo)

Ravenhill, Joseph 1803 wb-1-126 (K)

Rawling, Isaac 1839 wb-1-54 (Sh)

Rawling, William 1833 wb-#1 (Mo)

Rawlings, Alexander 1828 rb-e-260 (Mt)

Rawlings, Alexander H. (Dr.) 1828 rb-e-343 (Mt)

Rawlings, Benjamin 1825 lr (Sn)

Rawlings, Edwin 1844 wb-4-183 (Ma)

Rawlings, George W. 1833 lr (Sn)

Rawlings, Hip Juliett 1844 wb-1-105 (Sh)

Rawlings, John H. 1859 wb-3e-115 (Sh)

Rawlings, John 1840 rb-10-480 (Ru)

Rawlings, John S. 1838 wb-a-29 (F)

Rawlings, Sarah 1844 rb-13-30 (Ru)

Rawlings, Sarah R. 1848 rb-14-287 (Ru)

Rawlings, Thomas 1846 rb-13-715 (Ru)

Rawlings, William 1827 rb-7-2 (Ru)

Rawlings, William 1827 rb-7-347 (Ru)

Rawlins, William 1836 wb-1-150 (Fr)

Rawls, David L. 1860 wb-17-66 (Rb)

Rawls, Luke 1800 wb-1-59 (Rb)

Rawls, Shadrack 1831 wb-7-363 (Rb)

Rawly, Daniel 1852 wb-7-0 (Sm)

Raworth, Edward 1836 wb-10-587 (D)

Raworth, George F. 1853 as-c-278 (Di)

Ray, Alice 1852 wb-g-470 (Hn)

Ray, B. J. 1860 wb-00-9 (Cf)

Ray, Benjamin 1836 wb-1-181 (Gr)

Ray, Charles 1809 rb-2-77 (Ru)

Ray, Charles 1852 6-2-105 (Le)

Ray, David 1795 wb-1-29 (K)

Ray, Eaton 1852 ib-1-184 (Wy)

Ray, Ezekiel 1843 148-1-60 (Ge)

Ray, Henson 1859 ib-2-204 (Wy)

Ray, Jabel 1858 wb-1-376 (Fr)

Ray, James 1842 wb-f-93 (Hn)

Ray, James 1856 wb-e-425 (G)

Ray, John 1843 wb-1-259 (La)

Ray, Luke 1814 wb-#14 (Wl)

Ray, Luke 1829 wb-#84 (Wl)

Ray, M. 1854 ib-H-118 (F)

Ray, Nathan 1807 rb-a-333 (Mt)
Ray, Robert 1842 wb-5-238 (Gr)
Ray, Samuel 1838 wb-1-331 (Gr)
Ray, Samuel 1856 wb-3-321 (Gr)
Ray, Stephen S. 1852 ib-1-153 (Wy)
Ray, Thomas 1849 rb-15-119 (Ru)
Ray, Thomas 1855 wb-3-256 (La)
Ray, Thomas 1861 wb-d-128 (L)
Ray, W. F. 1855 wb-j-37 (O)
Ray, William 1820 wb-1-186 (Bo)
Ray, William 1849 wb-14-413 (D)
Rayburn, Adam 1849 wb-0-91 (Cf)
Rayburn, Elihu C. 1848 ib-1-2 (Wy)
Rayburn, Robt. S. 1845 wb-0-48 (Cf)
Raymer, Susan 1860 wb-18-402 (D)
Raymey, John 1852 wb-d-397 (G)
Raymond, N. T. 1851 wb-14-557 (D)
Raymond, Nicholas 1813 wb-4-257 (D)
Rayner, Catharine 1861 wb-b-118 (F)
Rea, John A. 1845 wb-d-193 (Hd)
Rea, John C. 1848 wb-d-395 (Hd)
Rea, John H. 1861 lr (Gi)
Rea, Tabitha 1855 wb-11-561 (Wi)
Rea, William 1837 wb-#116 (Wl)
Reach, John 1853 wb-e-47 (G)
Read, Benjamine A. 1830 wb-1-79 (Fr)
Read, Charles L. Jr. 1853 wb-b-216 (L)
Read, Edmund R. 1856 rb-17-694 (Ru)
Read, Edmund Randolph 1843 rb-12-413 (Ru)
Read, Edward Randolph 1856 rb-18-89 (Ru)
Read, Elijah 1845 rb-13-439 (Ru)
Read, Eliza 1845 rb-13-388 (Ru)
Read, Francis N. 1830 wb-9-417 (D)
Read, Hezekiah 1806 wb-3-118 (D)
Read, James 1839 rb-10-464 (Ru)
Read, Jane 1847 rb-k-562 (Mt)
Read, Jane 1849 wb-a-375 (F)
Read, John 1818 wb-a-199 (Ro)
Read, John 1845 rb-13-214 (Ru)
Read, John N. 1836 rb-9-298 (Ru)
Read, John Nash 1826 rb-6-179 (Ru)
Read, John Nash 1853 rb-16-537 (Ru)
Read, John R. 1842 wb-3-95 (Hy)
Read, Jones 1829 wb-9-346 (D)
Read, Jones 1839 wb-11-590 (D)
Read, Josiah 1842 wb-7-530 (Wi)
Read, Josiah 1842 wb-7-534 (Wi)
Read, Mary 1856 rb-17-663 (Ru)
Read, Mary 1861 rb-20-743 (Ru)
Read, Mordecai 1828 rb-e-391 (Mt)
Read, Nancy 1851 wb-14-575 (D)

Read, Nathaniel 1857 wb-2-198 (Li)
Read, P. F. A. 1852 rb-16-290 (Ru)
Read, Polly 1854 lr (Sn)
Read, Polly 1856 lr (Sn)
Read, Robert 1816 wb-4-429 (D)
Read, Robert A. 1849 rb-15-32 (Ru)
Read, Robert H. 1848 rb-14-357 (Ru)
Read, Samuel D. 1838 wb-2-229 (Sn)
Read, Sion S. 1845 wb-2-120 (W)
Read, Thomas 1834 wb-3-360 (Je)
Read, Wiats 1805 wb-3-34 (D)
Read, William 1816 as-A-69 (Di)
Read, William 1846 rb-13-523 (Ru)
Read, William 1854 wb-3-203 (Sn)
Read, William B. 1843 rb-12-417 (Ru)
Reade, William 1795 lr (Gi)
Reader (Rader), Jacob 1822 wb-1-22# (Ge)
Reader, Isaac 1844 wb-1-319 (La)
Reader, Racheal 1855 wb-3-303 (La)
Reads, David 1831 wb-1-72 (Li)
Ready, Charles sr. 1859 rb-20-148 (Ru)
Ready, Levin 1813 wb-A-31 (Li)
Reagan, Charles 1824 wb-1-5 (Hr)
Reagan, Charles C. 1834 wb-1-343 (Hr)
Reagan, Daniel 1860 wb-#17 (Mo)
Reagan, James 1828 wb-4-338 (K)
Reagan, John 1857 wb-12-344 (K)
Reagan, William 1859 wb-13-240 (K)
Real, William 1843 wb-f-163* (Hn)
Reams, Andrew D. 1840 wb-7-333 (Wi)
Reams, E. H. 1859 wb-1-269 (Be)
Reams, Henry 1836 wb-6-214 (Wi)
Reams, Henry 1836 wb-6-248 (Wi)
Reams, Henry 1846 wb-8-462 (Wi)
Reams, Jesse 1835 wb-c-448 (St)
Reams, Jesse 1835 wb-c-462 (St)
Reams, John 1853 wb-5-194 (Je)
Reams, John 1854 wb-3-240 (La)
Reams, Joshua 1859 wb-13-119 (Wi)
Reams, Nancy 1849 wb-9-285 (Wi)
Reams, Oscar 1861 wb-13-440 (Wi)
Reams, Robert 1860 wb-13-216 (Wi)
Reams, Robert 1860 wb-13-222 (Wi)
Reams, William 1841 wb-7-425 (Wi)
Rease, Henry 1838 wb-a-366 (R)
Reason, Bartholomew 1814 wb-1-416 (Hw)
Reasoner, George 1842 wb-c-76 (G)
Reasonover, Joseph 1833 wb-3-0 (Sm)
Reasonover, Joseph 1854 wb-7-0 (Sm)
Reasons, Alfred B. 1834 rb-f-540 (Mt)
Reasons, Alfred P. 1834 rb-f-584 (Mt)

Reasons, Charlotte 1849 rb-l-427 (Mt)
Reasons, James 1846 rb-k-110 (Mt)
Reasons, John 1828 rb-e-204 (Mt)
Reasons, Joseph 1840 rb-h-476 (Mt)
Reasons, Sarah 1840 rb-h-434 (Mt)
Reasons, William 1825 rb-d-449 (Mt)
Reasons, William 1825 rb-d-468 (Mt)
Reasons, William 1840 rb-h-385 (Mt)
Reavace, William 1824 as-a-160 (Di)
Reaves, B. H. 1851 wb-m-314 (Mt)
Reaves, Benjamin 1849 rb-l-353 (Mt)
Reaves, Daniel 1824 wb-8-375 (D)
Reaves, E. G. 1852 mr-2-480 (Be)
Reaves, Green 1855 as-b-190 (Ms)
Reaves, James M. 1856 wb-h-502 (Hu)
Reaves, John (Sr.) 1849 wb-2-47 (Sh)
Reaves, John 1803 wb-1-22# (Ge)
Reaves, Reubin 1821? wb-#115 (Mu)
Reaves, W. F. 1850 wb-g-316 (Hu)
Reaves, William 1850 wb-g-362 (Hu)
Reaves, William F. 1852 wb-g-613 (Hu)
Reavis, Francis 1829 wb-b-54 (Hn)
Reavis, John 1835 wb-d-107 (Hn)
Reavis, John H. 1856 wb-b-392 (We)
Reavis, John L. 1836 wb-d-228* (Hn)
Reavis, Samuel B. 1832 wb-x-58 (Mu)
Reavis, Thomas 1829 wb-b-41 (Hn)
Recer, Samuel jr. 1838 abl-1-75 (T)
Record, John 1814 wb-#22 (Mu)
Record, Sion 1826 wb-#150 (Mu)
Record, Sion 1839 as-a-13 (Ms)
Record, Sion 1859 wb-b-72 (Ms)
Record, Sion P. 1823 wb-#65 (Mu)
Rector, Daniel 1837 wb-#141 (Mc)
Rector, Enoch 1816 wb-a-79 (Ro)
Rector, Jesse 1860 wb-1-183 (R)
Rector, John 1858 149-1-106 (Ge)
Rector, John sr. 1856 wb-2-83# (Ge)
Rector, Landon 1839? wb-1A-237 (A)
Rector, Lewis 1831? wb-1A-55 (A)
Rector, Maximillian 1850 wb-#141 (Mc)
Redd, Jesse 1855 ib-h-396 (F)
Redd, John 1856 wb-2-136 (Li)
Redd, Mordecai 1826 rb-e-5 (Mt)
Redd, P. B. 1841 wb-2-383 (Hy)
Redd, Robert S. 1841 wb-7-368 (Wi)
Reddell, William 1846 wb-1-413 (La)
Reddett, William 1823 lr (Sn)
Reddick, John 1825 wb-b-69 (St)
Reddick, John 1835 lr (Sn)
Reddick, Kenneth 1831 wb-c-79 (Hn)

Reddick, Patsy 1834 wb-c-214 (Hn)
Reddick, Rice 1810 wb-a-140 (St)
Reddick, William R. 1832 wb-c-196 (St)
Redding, Robert 1820 wb-3-103 (Rb)
Redding, Samuel 1844 wb-d-74 (Hd)
Redding, Thomas 1838 wb-d-192* (Hn)
Redditt, M.D. 1857 lr (Sn)
Reddy, James 1826 wb-2-549 (Je)
Rede?, Tempy? 1843 wb-f-259* (Hn)
Redenhours, John 1841 148-1-8 (Ge)
Redfearn, Miami 1852 wb-15-166 (Rb)
Redfearn, Rhoda 1850 wb-14-405 (Rb)
Redfern, James 1824 wb-4-300 (Rb)
Redfern, John 1825 wb-5-157 (Rb)
Redfern, John 1840 wb-10-451 (Rb)
Redford, Sally 1818 wb-2-410 (Wi)
Redford, William 1832 wb-5-202 (Wi)
Reding, Stephen 1830 lr (Wi)
Redman, Benjamin 1826 wb-a-57 (G)
Redman, John 1806 wb-1-325 (Je)
Redman, John 1852 r39-1-230 (Dk)
Redmon, John 1816 wb-2-158 (Je)
Redmond, Arthur 1822 wb-8-140 (D)
Redmond, James 1849 wb-9-252 (Wi)
Redmond, John 1828 wb-a-46 (R)
Reece, Casuel T. 1856 wb-1-104 (Jo)
Reece, Charles 1837 wb-e-38 (Hu)
Reece, Daniel 1850 wb-1-51 (Jo)
Reece, Isaac 1856 wb-1-184 (Jo)
Reece, Valentine 1814 lw (Ct)
Reece, William 1849 wb-#171 (Wl)
Reece, William 1854 wb-h-323 (Hu)
Reed, Agnes Jane 1853 wb-a-316 (Ms)
Reed, Alexander 1825 wb-4-66 (Wi)
Reed, Alexander B. 1836 wb-a-4 (Ms)
Reed, Andrew 1836 wb-6-199 (Wi)
Reed, Archibald 1829 wb-1-188 (Ma)
Reed, Charles L. 1859 gs-1-329 (F)
Reed, Daniel 1861 wb-f-412 (G)
Reed, David 1818 rb-c-57 (Mt)
Reed, David 1838 wb-2-392 (Ma)
Reed, Edward 1816 Wb-2-191 (Wi)
Reed, Elizabeth 1836 wb-1-469 (Hr)
Reed, Felps 1835 wb-1-167 (Gr)
Reed, George G. 1837 wb-1-279 (Gr)
Reed, George G. 1850 33-3-236 (Gr)
Reed, Harmon 1862 wb-f-438 (G)
Reed, Henry 1816 wb-a-92 (Ro)
Reed, Holi 1840 wb-y-654 (Mu)
Reed, Hugh 1850 wb-d-284 (G)
Reed, Isaiah 1845 wb-c-269 (G)

Reed, James 1811 wb-1-137 (Sn)
Reed, James 1823 wb-#60 (Mu)
Reed, James 1848 wb-a-171 (Ms)
Reed, James 1851 wb-d-323 (G)
Reed, James H. 1852 wb-A-84 (Ca)
Reed, Jeremiah 1834 wb-#141 (Mc)
Reed, Jesse Y. 1837 wb-3-473 (Je)
Reed, Jessee 1797 wb-2-79 (D)
Reed, Jessee 1798 wb-2-111 (D)
Reed, John 1841 wb-e-142 (St)
Reed, John 1842 wb-3-70 (Hy)
Reed, John H. 1854 wb-3-241 (La)
Reed, John M. 1842 wb-f-115 (Hn)
Reed, John S. 1855 wb-2-82# (Ge)
Reed, John W. 1861 rb-21-49 (Ru)
Reed, L. L. 1858 wb-a-29 (Ce)
Reed, Mary 1824 wb-#69 (Mu)
Reed, Moses 1854 wb-n-318 (Mt)
Reed, Nancy 1819 wb-1-189 (Bo)
Reed, Nero 1834 wb-5-321 (K)
Reed, P. B. 1841 wb-2-391 (Hy)
Reed, R. A. 1848 rb-14-378 (Ru)
Reed, R. H. 1861 wb-k-374 (O)
Reed, Rebecca 1853 as-c-210 (Di)
Reed, Robert 1848 wb-#166 (Wl)
Reed, Samuel C. 1844 lr (Gi)
Reed, Sarah 1829 wb-2-29# (Ge)
Reed, Thomas 1817 wb-2-326 (K)
Reed, Thomas 1837 wb-3-494 (Je)
Reed, Thomas 1860 rb-20-642 (Ru)
Reed, Watson 1796 wb-0-16 (K)
Reed, William 1822 wb-A-310 (Li)
Reed, William 1849 wb-#170 (Wl)
Reed, William 1854 wb-15-544 (Rb)
Reed, William 1859 wb-3-9 (Me)
Reed, William Riley 1850 wb-2-151 (La)
Reed, Wm. B. 1858 gs-1-100 (F)
Reeder, Benjamin 1834 wb-#106 (Wl)
Reeder, John F. 1847 wb-#141 (Mc)
Reeder, Lydea 1842 wb-#137 (Wl)
Reeder, Mary D. 1859 rb-20-109 (Ru)
Reeder, Stephen K. 1852 wb-#141 (Mc)
Reems, Elisha 1848 wb-14-11 (Rb)
Rees, Henry 1823 wb-a-171 (Wh)
Rees, John 1846 148-1-164 (Ge)
Rees, John 1861 wb-2-93# (Ge)
Rees, John 1863 wb-2-381 (Li)
Rees, Moses 1837 wb-2-48# (Ge)
Rees, Phebe 1842 wb-2-57# (Ge)
Rees, William 1841 148-1-7 (Ge)
Reese, A. W. 1845 lr (Sn)

Reese, Hullum G. 1852 wb-2-115 (Sh)
Reese, James 1822 wb-#68 (Mu)
Reese, James 1828 wb-a-43 (R)
Reese, James 1839 wb-4-75 (Je)
Reese, Jordon 1813 wb-1-315 (Wi)
Reese, Jordon 1830 wb-1-47 (Li)
Reese, Joseph B. M. 1850 wb-5-171 (Je)
Reese, Mary 1849 rb-15-143 (Ru)
Reese, Moses jr. 1845 148-1-112 (Ge)
Reese, Sarah 1824 wb-3-698 (Wi)
Reese, Solomon 1834 wb-1-108 (Li)
Reese, William 1816 wb-2-28# (Ge)
Reese, William 1849 wb-#170 (Wl)
Reese, William 1854 as-2-334 (Ge)
Reese, William B. 1860 wb-13-387 (K)
Reese, William B. sr. 1860 wb-13-346 (K)
Reeser, Frederick 1827 wb-#142 (Mc)
Reeser, Jacob 1853 wb-2-77# (Ge)
Reeve, George W. 1860 wb-2-92# (Ge)
Reeve, Jesse 1841 wb-2-56# (Ge)
Reeve, Sarah 1855 wb-2-82# (Ge)
Reeves, Ann (Mrs.) 1844 wb-a-231 (F)
Reeves, Dudley G. 1846 wb-f-67 (O)
Reeves, Elanor 1852 wb-15-443 (D)
Reeves, Eli 1859 wb-16-754 (Rb)
Reeves, Elijah 1844 wb-d-287 (O)
Reeves, George 1814? wb-#25 (Wl)
Reeves, George 1840 wb-3-272 (Ma)
Reeves, George W. 1849 ib-1-71 (Ca)
Reeves, J. P. 1855 wb-i-244 (O)
Reeves, James 1860 wb-f-187 (Mu)
Reeves, Jesse 1853 148-1-434 (Ge)
Reeves, John 1835 wb-1-141* (Hy)
Reeves, John 1862 wb-#135 (Wl)
Reeves, John A. 1856 rb-18-234 (Ru)
Reeves, John C. 1856 rb-18-123 (Ru)
Reeves, John L. 1837 wb-d-136* (Hn)
Reeves, John P. 1857 wb-j-198 (O)
Reeves, Levi 1856 rb-18-215 (Ru)
Reeves, Mary 1853 as-b-114 (Ms)
Reeves, Moses G. 1861 rb-21-51 (Ru)
Reeves, Peter 1812 wb-1-288 (Wi)
Reeves, Peter 1822 wb-3-579 (Wi)
Reeves, Samuel 1850 wb-2-71# (Ge)
Reeves, Samuel P. 1842 wb-c-299 (O)
Reeves, Stephen 1852 wb-m-457 (Mt)
Reeves, Susannah 1823 wb-#48 (Wl)
Reeves, Thomas 1855 wb-b-2 (Dk)
Reeves, Thos. J. 1857 wb-f-80 (G)
Reeves, Urias 1844 wb-d-194 (O)
Reeves, William sr. 1839 wb-3-0 (Sm)

Reeves, Willis 1854 ib-H-189 (F)
Regan, Cornelius 1816 wb-1-416 (Hw)
Region, Joel 1842 wb-7-541 (Wi)
Register, Francis 1834? wb-#29 (Wa)
Register, James 1799 wb-1-22# (Ge)
Reid, Alexander 1816 wb-2-207 (Wi)
Reid, Anthony 1826 lr (Sn)
Reid, B. 1860 wb-3e-145 (Sh)
Reid, Clarissa 1860 wb-#142 (Mc)
Reid, David 1845 wb-f-299 (Hn)
Reid, David 1858 wb-7-27 (Ma)
Reid, J. R. 1843 wb-3-139 (Hy)
Reid, James 1820 rb-4-268 (Ru)
Reid, James 1834 wb-c-375 (St)
Reid, James J.? 1847 as-a-135 (Ms)
Reid, John 1816 wb-2-209 (Wi)
Reid, John 1827 wb-4-171 (Wi)
Reid, John 1839 eb-1-392 (C)
Reid, John R. 1845 wb-1-111 (Sh)
Reid, M. M. 1850 wb-g-249 (St)
Reid, M. M. 1860 wb-i-167 (St)
Reid, Marey 1838 wb-b-214 (G)
Reid, Mary 1850 wb-5-85 (Ma)
Reid, Richard 1811 wb-a-43 (Ro)
Reid, Samuel D. 1859 wb-b-61 (Ms)
Reid, Thos. P. 1851 as-b-41 (Ms)
Reid, William 1834 wb-1-67 (W)
Reinhardt, Charles E. 1848 wb-2-24 (Sh)
Rembert, Andrew 1845 wb-1-118 (Sh)
Rembert, James 1841 wb-1-64 (Sh)
Ren, Josiah 1851 wb-2-80# (Ge)
Ren, William 1826? wb-#145 (Mu)
Ren?, Jeremiah 1821 wb-3-338 (Rb)
Renegar, George 1857 wb-2-175 (Li)
Renegar, Henry 1859 wb-2-259 (Li)
Renfro, Elizabeth Ann 1852 wb-11-294 (K)
Renfro, John 1844 wb-a2-119 (Mu)
Renfro, Joshua 1856 wb-2-345 (Me)
Renfro, Stephen 1836 wb-6-2 (K)
Renfro, William 1830 wb-#214 (Mu)
Renfro, William 1846 wb-a2-475 (Mu)
Renfro, William 1852 wb-4-408 (Mu)
Renner, Jacob 1840 wb-2-54# (Ge)
Renner, John 1858 149-1-134 (Ge)
Rennolds, Fielding 1839 wb-1-51 (Sh)
Reno, John 1806 lw (Ct)
Renow, Anny 1847 wb-#142 (Mc)
Renshaw, Eligah 1837 wb-d-150* (Hn)
Renshaw, Isaah 1820 rb-4-269 (Ru)
Renshaw, Nancy 1841 wb-e-184 (Hn)
Renshaw, Nathan 1849 rb-15-1 (Ru)

Renshaw, Nathan L. 1851 rb-15-614 (Ru)
Renshaw?, E. 1838 wb-d-235* (Hn)
Rentfro, John 1855 wb-e-561 (Ro)
Rentfro, John 1860 wb-4-26 (Gr)
Rentfro, John 1860 wb-f-391 (G)
Rentfro, Stephen 1794 wb-1-25 (K)
Rentfroe, John 1839 wb-c-47 (Ro)
Rentphrow, Stephen 1804 wb-1-149 (K)
Replogle, Frederick 1857 wb-6-511 (Ma)
Retherford, Mary 1861 wb-13-470 (K)
Revel, Kinchen 1829 wb-4-371 (Wi)
Revel, Wilson 1850 rb-15-301 (Ru)
Reveley, James 1847 wb-#6 (Mo)
Revell, Edmund 1858 wb-e-99 (Hy)
Revell, Isham 1836 rb-9-365 (Ru)
Reves, Charlotte 1849 rb-l-359 (Mt)
Reves, Elisabeth 1812 wb-1-127 (Bo)
Reves, John 1803 as-1-33 (Ge)
Revis, Frances L. 1857 wb-h-658 (Hu)
Reynolds, Clement 1860 wb-2-74# (Ge)
Reynolds, Elijah 1831 wb-1-95 (Fr)
Reynolds, Gay 1829 wb-1-94 (Hr)
Reynolds, George 1813 Wb-2-38 (Wi)
Reynolds, George F. 1828 wb-4-261 (K)
Reynolds, George F. 1846 wb-9-212 (K)
Reynolds, George et al. 1847 wb-9-387 (K)
Reynolds, Green L. 1846 wb-#142 (Mc)
Reynolds, Guy 1832 wb-1-220 (Hr)
Reynolds, Henry 1834 wb-#142 (Mc)
Reynolds, Henry 1836 wb-b-36 (Hd)
Reynolds, Henry sr. 1835 wb-2-44# (Ge)
Reynolds, Hugh A. 1835 wb-1-405 (Hr)
Reynolds, Isham 1830 wb-3-123 (Je)
Reynolds, James 1826 wb-4-132 (K)
Reynolds, James 1831 wb-b-154 (Ro)
Reynolds, James 1847? wb-7-0 (Sm)
Reynolds, James B. 1851 wb-m-326 (Mt)
Reynolds, James W. 1860 wb-d-80 (L)
Reynolds, Jane 1859 wb-c-301 (L)
Reynolds, Joel J. 1838 wb-a-22 (L)
Reynolds, John 1814 wb-2-36# (Ge)
Reynolds, John 1837 wb-b-61 (Hd)
Reynolds, John 1840 wb-a-424 (R)
Reynolds, John 1843 as-b-147 (Di)
Reynolds, John 1848 wb-10-37 (K)
Reynolds, John 1851 wb-3-101 (W)
Reynolds, John 1851 wb-3-83 (W)
Reynolds, John G. 1858 wb-12-503 (Wi)
Reynolds, Joseph 1837 wb-2-52# (Ge)
Reynolds, Joseph 1841 wb-b-305 (Hd)
Reynolds, Josiah 1818 wb-1-0 (Sm)

Reynolds, Josiah 1834 wb-3-0 (Sm)
Reynolds, M. V. 1853 wb-b-240 (L)
Reynolds, Mary W. 1846 wb-8-456 (Wi)
Reynolds, Nancy 1845 wb-5-447 (Gr)
Reynolds, Prepare 1832 wb-5-203 (Wi)
Reynolds, Richard 1836 wb-6-168 (Wi)
Reynolds, Richard C. 1826 wb-4-94 (Wi)
Reynolds, Robert 1858 wb-3e-71 (Sh)
Reynolds, S. H. 1853 wb-3-198 (W)
Reynolds, Silas 1853 wb-3-210 (W)
Reynolds, Silas H. 1856 wb-3-336 (W)
Reynolds, Spencer 1830 wb-4-517 (Wi)
Reynolds, Spencer 1844 wb-8-176 (Wi)
Reynolds, Spencer 1845 wb-8-244 (Wi)
Reynolds, Spencer 1856 wb-12-95 (Wi)
Reynolds, Squire 1835 wb-c-447 (St)
Reynolds, Susan 1828 wb-4-337 (K)
Reynolds, Susan 1861 rb-p-628 (Mt)
Reynolds, Susanna 1821 Wb-3-274 (Wi)
Reynolds, Tabitha 1852 wb-#143 (Mc)
Reynolds, Thomas 1839 wb-7-173 (Wi)
Reynolds, Thomas 1857 wb-c-116 (L)
Reynolds, Thomas P. 1847 wb-8-517 (Wi)
Reynolds, William 1828 wb-3-2 (Je)
Reynolds, William 1834 wb-b-242 (Ro)
Reynolds, William 1840 wb-1-206 (La)
Reynolds, William 1856 wb-3e-15 (Sh)
Reynolds, William 1859 wb-13-240 (K)
Reynolds, _____ 1845 wb-d-228 (Hd)
Rhea (Ray?), Hiram 1846 wb-#143 (Mc)
Rhea, Archibald 1794 wb-1-14 (K)
Rhea, Archibald 1835 wb-#107 (Wl)
Rhea, B. M. G. 1852 wb-2-30 (Li)
Rhea, David 1794 wb-1-19 (K)
Rhea, James 1855 wb-1-389 (Su)
Rhea, Jessee 1858 wb-#16 (Mo)
Rhea, John 1805 wb-#2 (Wl)
Rhea, John 1839 wb-1-157 (Li)
Rhea, John 1840 wb-1A-272 (A)
Rhea, John 1851 wb-1B-228 (A)
Rhea, Joseph 1850 wb#20 (Gu)
Rhea, Joseph 1862 wb#44 (Gu)
Rhea, Nancy 1850 148-1-316 (Ge)
Rhea, Rebecca 1854 wb-12-17 (K)
Rhea, Ritter 1846 wb#18 (Gu)
Rhea, Sally 1847 wb-1-322 (Li)
Rhea, Susannah 1838 wb-#122 (Wl)
Rhea, William 1796 wb-1-50 (K)
Rhea, William R. 1862 wb-#65 (Wa)
Rhine, L. J. B. 1842 wb-a-84 (F)
Rhoads, John sr. 1808 wb-1-0 (Sm)

Rhode, Taylor 1837 abl-1-12 (T)
Rhodes, Abner 1833 wb-d-172 (Hn)
Rhodes, Abner 1835 wb-d-126 (Hn)
Rhodes, Arthur 1856 wb-g-757 (Hn)
Rhodes, Christian 1810 wb-1-315 (K)
Rhodes, Elisha 1816 wb-#36 (Mu)
Rhodes, John 1823 wb-3-409 (K)
Rhodes, John C. 1846 wb-a-283 (F)
Rhodes, Mary 1857 wb-a-268 (T)
Rhodes, Sarah 1816 wb-#35 (Mu)
Rhodes, Thomas 1822 wb-#46 (Wl)
Rhodes, William 1815 rb-3-62 (Ru)
Rhyne, V. M. 1857 wb-4-95 (La)
Riadon, George 1841 lr (Sn)
Riadon, Martha H. 1842 lr (Sn)
Riadon, Richard H. 1845 lr (Sn)
Rial, William 1841 wb-e-180 (Hn)
Rias, Henry 1821 wb-#41 (Wl)
Rice, Albert G. 1850 wb-#143 (Mc)
Rice, Calvin 1856 wb-2-290 (Me)
Rice, David 1839 wb-#129 (Wl)
Rice, Ebenezer (Jr.) 1832 wb-#237 (Mu)
Rice, Ebenezer 1831 wb-#227 (Mu)
Rice, Ebenezer sr. 1833 wb-x-52 (Mu)
Rice, Elisha 1807 wb-3-175 (D)
Rice, Fereby (Pherreby?) 1815 wb-#11 (Mu)
Rice, Francis 1860 wb-13-333 (Wi)
Rice, Henry 1828 wb-#73 (Wl)
Rice, Henry 1829 wb-#82 (Wl)
Rice, Henry 1829 wb-h-243 (Hn)
Rice, Hiram 1844 wb-12-231 (Rb)
Rice, Hiram 1857 wb-17-151 (D)
Rice, Horace 1830 wb-1-419 (Hw)
Rice, Isaac 1823 wb-#144 (Mc)
Rice, Isham 1855 wb-12-27 (Wi)
Rice, James 1829 eb-1-249 (C)
Rice, James 1835 wb-6-56 (Wi)
Rice, James 1838 wb-#123 (Wl)
Rice, James 1847 wb-8-540 (Wi)
Rice, James S. 1825 wb-#144 (Mc)
Rice, Jeremiah 1823 wb-4-72 (Rb)
Rice, Jesse 1855 wb-2-289 (Me)
Rice, John 1792 wb-1-249 (D)
Rice, John 1806 wb-3-107 (D)
Rice, John 1815 wb-a-60 (Ro)
Rice, John 1821 wb-#42 (Wl)
Rice, John 1838 wb-#144 (Mc)
Rice, John 1848 wb-g-20 (Hu)
Rice, John 1853 wb-#108 (Wl)
Rice, John 1854 wb-#145 (Mc)
Rice, John A. 1840 wb-b-275 (Hd)

Rice, John H. 1843 wb-#139 (Wl)
Rice, John Sr. 1811 wb-1-415 (Hw)
Rice, Joseph 1839 wb-6-419 (K)
Rice, Leatha (Lethe?) 1856 wb-#145 (Mc)
Rice, Martha 1850 wb-#145 (Mc)
Rice, Martha K. 1849 wb-14-150 (Rb)
Rice, Nancy K. 1858 wb-h-263 (Hn)
Rice, Nicholas 1856 wb-f-112 (Mu)
Rice, Samuel Sr. 1838 wb-a-67 (T)
Rice, Sarah P. 1861 wb-e-150 (Hy)
Rice, Susannah 1845 wb-#149 (Wl)
Rice, Theodorick B. 1840 wb-b-415 (Wh)
Rice, William 1818 wb-#93 (Wl)
Rice, William 1831 wb-#94 (Wl)
Rice, William B. sr. 1845 wb-a-68 (Dk)
Rich, Benjamin F. 1844 wb-4-112 (Ma)
Rich, C. 1854 ib-h-61 (F)
Rich, Charles 1856 wb-#120 (Wl)
Rich, Curtis 1854 ib-h-256 (F)
Rich, Henry S. 1835 wb-5-332 (K)
Rich, Henry S. 1835 wb-5-358 (K)
Rich, Jacob 1832 wb-1-359 (Fr)
Rich, Jacob 1838 wb-1-179 (Fr)
Rich, Joseph 1853 wb-3-142 (Gr)
Richards, Adam 1832 wb-#145 (Mc)
Richards, Edward M. 1857 wb-16-504 (Rb)
Richards, Elijah W. 1853 ib-1-267 (Cl)
Richards, Elizabeth 1855 wb-16-478 (D)
Richards, Gabriel 1826 wb-#145 (Mc)
Richards, Henry 1847 wb-14-90 (D)
Richards, James L. 1859 wb-18-54 (D)
Richards, Joaly 1847 wb-14-40 (D)
Richards, John 1855 wb-6-184 (Ma)
Richards, Joseph 1795 wb-1-227 (Je)
Richards, Richard 1834 wb-#146 (Mc)
Richardson, Alpia 1815 wb-#17 (Mu)
Richardson, Amos 1843 wb-z-565 (Mu)
Richardson, Austin 1836 as-a-305 (Di)
Richardson, Benjamin 1840 eb-1-436 (C)
Richardson, Bernard 1846 r39-1-21 (Dk)
Richardson, Canada 1841 abl-1-221 (T)
Richardson, Conrad 1857 wb-12-369 (Wi)
Richardson, David 1818 rb-4-109 (Ru)
Richardson, David M. 1828 wb-9-210 (D)
Richardson, Drury 1855 wb-2-121 (Li)
Richardson, Elizabeth 1821 wb-8-29 (D)
Richardson, Elizabeth 1848 wb-b-248 (Mu)
Richardson, Fisher 1815 wb-#16 (Wl)
Richardson, Francis 1825 wb-a-87 (Hn)
Richardson, Francis A. 1860 wb-4-250 (La)
Richardson, Hancel? C. 1847 as-a-146 (Ms)

Richardson, Isham 1829 rb-e-514 (Mt)
Richardson, Isham P. 1837 rb-g-624 (Mt)
Richardson, James 1824 wb-8-358 (D)
Richardson, James 1825 wb-#146 (Mc)
Richardson, James 1826 rb-6-279 (Ru)
Richardson, James 1846 rb-13-694 (Ru)
Richardson, James A. 1851 wb-a-109 (Dk)
Richardson, James B. 1853 wb-16-181 (D)
Richardson, James F. 1842 rb-12-239 (Ru)
Richardson, James M. 1848 wb-b-370 (Mu)
Richardson, James T. 1847 rb-14-29 (Ru)
Richardson, John 1794 wb-1-22# (Ge)
Richardson, John 1835 wb-a-276 (R)
Richardson, John 1836 wb-1-26 (Me)
Richardson, John 1839 wb-z-17 (Mu)
Richardson, John 1860 wb-13-164 (Wi)
Richardson, John M. 1853 wb-5-43 (Hr)
Richardson, Joseph 1849 wb-d-209 (G)
Richardson, Keziah 1848 wb-b-369 (Mu)
Richardson, Lawrence 1811 wb-1-148 (Sn)
Richardson, Lebius 1833 wb-a-104 (Di)
Richardson, Mary 1840 rb-10-608 (Ru)
Richardson, Milley 1842 wb-12-333* (D)
Richardson, Nancy 1840 wb-12-31 (D)
Richardson, Reuben 1830 wb-b-63 (Hn)
Richardson, Robert G. 1861 wb-13-420 (Wi)
Richardson, Samuel 1841 as-b-35 (Di)
Richardson, Sandy D. 1841 as-b-29 (Di)
Richardson, Thomas 1815 wb-#22 (Mu)
Richardson, Thomas 1817? wb-a-24 (Di)
Richardson, Thomas 1849 wb-b-469 (Mu)
Richardson, Thomas A. 1860 wb-4-301 (La)
Richardson, Wiley P. 1861 wb-f-410 (G)
Richardson, William 1827 wb-#158 (Mu)
Richardson, William 1840 wb-#146 (Mc)
Richardson, William 1847 wb-14-132 (D)
Richardson, William 1848 wb-2-30 (La)
Richardson, William 1850 wb-d-215 (G)
Richardson, William M. 1833 rb-9-47 (Ru)
Richardson, Willis 1838 wb-1-152 (La)
Richardson, Winneford 1842 as-b-77 (Di)
Richardson, Winneford 1855 as-c-393 (Di)
Richardson, Winneford 1855 wb-a-283 (Di)
Richason, James 1838 wb-#2 (Mo)
Richee, Davied 1861 wb-b-467 (We)
Richee, William 1834 wb-1-320 (Hr)
Richer, Lucy 1840 wb-3-0 (Sm)
Richerson, Green H. 1848 wb-b-285 (We)
Richeson, John R. 1841 wb-11-18 (Rb)
Richey, Joseph 1820 wb-2-298 (Je)
Richey, Robert 1811 wb-2-31 (Je)

Richey, William 1827 wb-2-561 (Je)
Richie, John 1842 as-a-58 (Ms)
Richie, N. D. 1827 wb-2-569 (Je)
Richison, Thomas 1851 wb-14-549 (Rb)
Richman, Robert D. 1854 wb-15-601 (Rb)
Richmond, Catharine 1861 wb-3e-167 (Sh)
Richmond, Daniel 1856 wb-#120 (Wl)
Richmond, Edmund 1854 wb-e-34 (Hy)
Richmond, James 1845 wb-#147 (Wl)
Richmond, Jesse 1822 wb-1-9 (Ma)
Richmond, John 1810 rb-2-87 (Ru)
Richmond, Josiah 1839 wb-a-43 (F)
Richmond, Winifred 1854 wb-16-397 (D)
Ricker, Peter 1814 wb-2-35# (Ge)
Rickets, James 1826 wb-a-55 (G)
Rickets, John 1815 wb-1-0 (Sm)
Ricketts, William 1852 wb-#179 (Wl)
Rickman, David Hardy 1822 lr (Sn)
Rickman, John 1849 wb-a-216 (Ms)
Rickman, L. H. 1854 as-b-166 (Ms)
Rickman, Mary 1829 lr (Sn)
Rickman, Susannah 1859 wb-b-80 (Ms)
Rickmon, Nathan 1816 lr (Sn)
Ricks, P. W. 1860 rb-p-427 (Mt)
Ridd, Jesse 1838 wb-a-26 (F)
Riddle, B. 1846 wb-4-55 (Hr)
Riddle, Bazell 1835 wb-1-96 (W)
Riddle, Benjamin 1822 wb-#146 (Mc)
Riddle, Benjamin 1846 wb-4-57 (Hr)
Riddle, Britton 1841 wb-b-353 (Hd)
Riddle, Harmon 1846 wb-#149 (Wl)
Riddle, James 1829 wb-2-0 (Sm)
Riddle, John 1830 wb-1-141 (Hr)
Riddle, Nathaniel 1841 wb-b-308 (Hd)
Riddle, Tarver 1832 wb-2-0 (Sm)
Riddle, Zachariah 1853 wb-5-311 (Je)
Ridenour, John sr. 1828 eb-1-229 (C)
Rider, John (Sr.) 1869 wb-#16 (Mo)
Rider, John 1834 wb-1-122 (Bo)
Ridgeway, James 1856 wb-h-60 (Hn)
Ridgeway, Madison H. 1846 wb-b-129 (We)
Ridgeway, Roseann? 1837 wb-d-275 (Hn)
Ridgway, James 1823 wb-a-34 (Hn)
Ridgway, Roseman 1839 wb-e-29 (Hn)
Ridgway, Samuel C. 1847 wb-b-219 (We)
Ridings, Joel 1850 wb-g-329 (Hu)
Ridings, Nicy 1855 wb-h-360 (Hu)
Ridings, Rebbecca 1848 wb-g-28 (Hu)
Ridings, Wyly 1846 wb-g-375 (Hu)
Ridley, Beverly 1845 wb-8-246 (Wi)
Ridley, Beverly 1845 wb-8-314 (Wi)

Ridley, Elizabeth 1858 rb-19-510 (Ru)
Ridley, Geo. 1793 wb-1-281 (D)
Ridley, George 1838 wb-11-139 (D)
Ridley, George G. 1845 wb-8-328 (Wi)
Ridley, George Granville 1860 rb-20-496 (Ru)
Ridley, Henry 1835 rb-9-233 (Ru)
Ridley, Henry 1854 rb-17-320 (Ru)
Ridley, Henry jr. 1854 rb-17-169 (Ru)
Ridley, James 1847 wb-14-131 (D)
Ridley, James 1857 wb-17-210 (D)
Ridley, Mary W. 1852 wb-f-4? (Mu)
Ridley, Moses 1854 rb-17-159 (Ru)
Ridley, Samuel J. 1828 wb-9-153 (D)
Ridley, Vincent 1853 wb-4-614 (Mu)
Ridley, William 1852 wb-10-220 (Wi)
Ridley, William B. 1852 wb-10-193 (Wi)
Ridley, Willis 1834 wb-x-231 (Mu)
Ridout, Rebecca 1862 wb-f-442 (G)
Ridout, William 1833 rb-9-32 (Ru)
Ridsdale, Jno. 1823 rb-d-273 (Mt)
Rieff, Henry 1824 wb-#50 (Wl)
Rieger, John 1815 wb-4-390 (D)
Rieves, Joel 1819 wb-#115 (Mu)
Rieves, John C. 1843 wb-z-536 (Mu)
Rife, Jacob 1794 wb-1-18 (K)
Rigg, Samuel A. 1861 wb-3-79 (Me)
Riggan, Daniel 1831 wb-1-202 (Hr)
Riggan, Frances 1849 wb-#170 (Wl)
Riggan, Martha A. 1850 wb-#172 (Wl)
Riggan, Samuel H. 1847 wb-#167 (Wl)
Riggby, S. 1856 ib-1-415 (Ca)
Riggins, Jane 1858 wb-#147 (Mc)
Riggins, Peter 1826 wb-a-99 (Hn)
Riggins, Ruth 1841 rb-i-63 (Mt)
Riggon, John 1857 wb-17-177 (D)
Riggs, Clisbe 1858 wb-3-427 (Gr)
Riggs, E. 1853 wb-5-212 (Je)
Riggs, Edward 1852 wb-5-159 (Je)
Riggs, Elizabeth 1855 wb-b-8 (Ms)
Riggs, Elizabeth B. 1857 as-c-104 (Ms)
Riggs, Ellis 1848 wb-2-210 (Gr)
Riggs, Ellis M. 1841 wb-#147 (Mc)
Riggs, James 1826 rb-d-524 (Mt)
Riggs, John 1849 wb-1-426 (Hw)
Riggs, Nenian 1837 wb-1-252 (Gr)
Riggs, Pleasant M. 1842 wb-4-85 (Je)
Riggs, Reuben 1833 lr (Gi)
Riggs, Samuel 1829 wb-#200 (Mu)
Riggs, Thomas H. 1861 wb-i-350 (St)
Riggs, Townsly 1860 wb-3-51 (Me)
Riggs, Wright 1812 wb-1-330 (Wi)

Riggs, Zadock 1816 wb-2-232 (Wi)
Righerson, Asa 1811? wb-#38 (Mu)
Right, G. W. 1852 wb-5-173 (Je)
Right, Paschal 1867 wb-3-0 (Sm)
Right, Perrian 1851 wb-2-183 (La)
Right, Robert 1831 wb-3-0 (Sm)
Right, Samuel 1853 wb-3-145 (Gr)
Rightsel, George 1803 wb-2-28# (Ge)
Rightsel, George 1805 as-1-103 (Ge)
Rigney, Isaac 1814 wb-4-270 (D)
Rigsby, Thomas 1859 ib-1-568 (Ca)
Riley, G. E. 1859 wb-k-32 (O)
Riley, George E. 1859 wb-k-52 (O)
Riley, John 1857 wb-2-104# (Ge)
Riley, John S. 1851 ib-1-301 (Cl)
Riley, L. C. 1847 wb-2-2 (Sh)
Riley, Moses 1856 wb-#118 (Wl)
Riley, Samuel 1853 ib-1-270 (Wy)
Rilley, James 1827 wb-#167 (Mu)
Rimal, Rebecca 1830 wb-2-56# (Ge)
Rinehart, Jacob 1854 wb-n-299 (Mt)
Rinehart, Michael 1854 wb-5-343 (Je)
Rineheart, John 1833 wb-3-237 (Je)
Rineheart, John 1855 wb-n-697 (Mt)
Rineheart, Sarah 1860 rb-p-446 (Mt)
Rineman, Susan 1833 wb-10-235 (D)
Rineman, Susan 1844 wb-13-62 (D)
Ring, Abraham 1830 wb-a-161 (G)
Ring, H. E. 1858 wb-i-18 (St)
Ring, Ralph 1837 wb-d-115* (Hn)
Ringo, Elijah M. 1857 wb-2-206 (Li)
Ringo, Polly 1857 wb-2-193 (Li)
Ringold, John 1862 wb-f-441 (G)
Riol, Tempy 1843 wb-f-156* (Hn)
Ripley, Eliza 1841 wb-7-407 (Wi)
Ripley, Henry 1859 wb-2-90# (Ge)
Ripley, Linza F. 1860 wb-2-92# (Ge)
Ripley, Samuel 1847 wb-2-65# (Ge)
Ripley, Samuel 1861 149-1-218 (Ge)
Rippy, James sr. 1861 lr (Sn)
Rippy, Josiah 1845 lr (Sn)
Rison, Ellery 1828 wb-3-0 (Sm)
Rison, Richard 1839 wb-3-0 (Sm)
Ritchie, Nathaniel D. 1829 wb-3-41 (Je)
Ritchie, Will 1835 wb-1-411 (Hr)
Rittenberry, John 1848 wb-f-127+ (O)
Ritter, Moses 1837 5-2-8 (Cl)
Ritter, Moses 1851 ib-1-306 (Cl)
River, Jacob 1851 wb-15-86 (D)
Rivers, Edmunds 1859 wb-5-100 (Hr)
Rivers, Ephraim 1851 wb-10-1 (Wi)

Rivers, James J. 1841 wb-7-363 (Wi)
Rivers, John F. 1861 wb-k-404 (O)
Rivers, John H. 1858 wb-j-361 (O)
Rivers, Mildred 1832 rb-f-368 (Mt)
Rivers, R. 1830 wb-1-157 (Hr)
Rivers, Robert 1829 wb-1-88 (Hr)
Rivers, Robert 1848 wb-9-186 (Wi)
Rivers, Thomas 1827 rb-e-173 (Mt)
Rives, Edmund 1841 wb-e-447 (Hu)
Rives, George 1845 wb-1-116 (Sh)
Rives, Green 1853 wb-a-308 (Ms)
Rives, James 1829 wb-1-39 (W)
Rives, Stephen 1836 rb-g-264 (Mt)
Rives, Stephen 1849 rb-l-458 (Mt)
Rives, Thomas 1855 39-2-415 (Dk)
Rives, Willis G. 1861 wb-2-332 (Li)
Roach, Aaron 1838 wb-11-297 (D)
Roach, Absalom 1840 wb-5-44 (Gr)
Roach, Ann 1836 wb-11-29 (D)
Roach, Charles L. 1844 wb-0-47 (Cf)
Roach, E. B. 1847 rb-k-583 (Mt)
Roach, Hannah 1835 wb-10-534 (D)
Roach, James C. 1850 wb-14-487 (D)
Roach, Jesse 1848 wd-14-198 (D)
Roach, John (Sr.) 1849 wb-#164 (Wl)
Roach, John 1840 wb-b-259 (Hd)
Roach, John 1846 wb-#154 (Wl)
Roach, Joshua 1828 eb-1-236 (C)
Roach, Lydia 1848 wb-14-173 (D)
Roach, Simon 1856 wb-12-76 (Wi)
Roach, Stephen 1816 wb-4-430 (D)
Roach, Stephen 1816 wb-7-8 (D)
Roach, William 1837 eb-1-396 (C)
Roach, William 1845 wb-13-231 (D)
Roach, William H. 1858 wb-3-482 (Gr)
Roads, Abner 1833 wb-c-23 (Hn)
Roads, Henderson 1845 wb-2-96 (W)
Roads, Henry 1794 wb-1-15 (K)
Roan, Archibald 1819 wb-3-72 (K)
Roan, Elizabeth 1816 wb-2-245 (K)
Roan, Hannah 1847 wb-#176 (Wl)
Roan, Hugh 1825 wb-#58 (Wl)
Roan, William 1812 wb-2-7 (K)
Roane, Ann 1831 wb-9-502 (D)
Roane, James 1833 wb-10-200 (D)
Roane, James 1833 wb-10-251 (D)
Roark, Michael 1839 wb-1-422 (Hw)
Roark, William 1832 wb-1-104 (Fr)
Rob, Reuben 1861 wb-1-149 (Jo)
Robards, Howell R. 1861 wb-3e-171 (Sh)
Robards, Nath J. 1856 wb-4-100 (La)

Robards, Nathaniel 1859 wb-4-229 (La)
Robards, Sarah 1848 wb-9-167 (Wi)
Robb, James 1833 wb-1-16 (Sh)
Robb, Joseph 1816 wb-#25 (Mu)
Robb, William 1859 rb-20-228 (Ru)
Robb, William sr. 1830 lr (Sn)
Robbins, Edward 1852 wb-h-Jan (O)
Robbins, Eligah 1848 wb-f-127+ (O)
Robbins, H. M. 1847 wb-#155 (Wl)
Robbins, Isaac 1834 wb-1A-57 (A)
Robbins, Isaac 1834 wb-1A-69 (A)
Robbins, John 1846 wb-f-21 (O)
Robbins, John G. 1821 rb-c-405 (Mt)
Robbins, Thomas 1832? rb-9-129 (Ru)
Robbins, William 1846 wb-f-65 (O)
Robbins, William 1861 149-1-236 (Ge)
Robbins, William C. 1857 wb-#125 (Wl)
Robbs, John 1828 wb-b-295 (St)
Robbs, John W. 1830 wb-c-65 (St)
Robenson, Jacob 1828 wb-b-59 (Wh)
Roberds, Enoch 1843 wb-a-106 (F)
Roberds, William 1820 wb-3-163 (Wi)
Roberson, Christopher T. 1831 lr (Gi)
Roberson, Isam 1861 wb-d-127 (L)
Roberson, James 1853 wb-e-383 (Ro)
Roberson, John 1839 wb-#126 (Wl)
Roberson, John 1847 wb-b-222 (We)
Roberson, John W. 1860 wb-f-337 (Ro)
Roberson, Michael 1839 wb-y-599 (Mu)
Roberson, Percy 1844 wb-c-192 (G)
Roberson, Starkey 1850 wb-1-385 (Li)
Roberson, William 1795 wb-1-36 (K)
Roberson, William 1861 rb-21-9 (Ru)
Robert, Milly 1847 wb-2-210 (W)
Robert, Peter P. 1833 rb-f-474 (Mt)
Robert, Walker 1840 wb-#181 (Mc)
Roberts, Aaron 1838 wb-e-149 (Hu)
Roberts, Aaron 1857 wb-h-628 (Hu)
Roberts, Adam 1802 wb-2-255 (D)
Roberts, Alexander 1861 wb-h-549 (Hn)
Roberts, Alfred M. 1859 wb-k-41 (O)
Roberts, Amos 1840 wb-b-14 (We)
Roberts, Andrew 1860 wb-13-274 (K)
Roberts, Anna 1853 wb#21 (Gu)
Roberts, Bede 1834 rb-g-26 (Mt)
Roberts, Bedee (Mrs.) 1835 rb-g-191 (Mt)
Roberts, Benjamin 1830 wb-4-515 (Wi)
Roberts, Benjamin 1846 wb-8-391 (Wi)
Roberts, Charles 1807 wb-a-19 (Ro)
Roberts, Charles 1820 wb-1-0 (Sm)
Roberts, Charles 1833 wb-c-63 (Hn)

Roberts, Cly 1806 wb-a-6 (Ro)
Roberts, Collin 1812 rb-a-75 (Mt)
Roberts, Cyrus 1844 rb-13-54 (Ru)
Roberts, Cyrus L. 1843 wb-A-33 (Ca)
Roberts, Dempsy 1826? as-A-127 (Di)
Roberts, E. 1815? wb-#38 (Mu)
Roberts, Elias 1807 wb-a-17 (Ro)
Roberts, Elijah 1816 wb-#22 (Mu)
Roberts, Emsly 1833 wb-x-124 (Mu)
Roberts, Ephraim 1853 wb-15-274 (Rb)
Roberts, Ephraim 1853 wb-15-282 (Rb)
Roberts, Fanny 1840 wb-10-527 (Rb)
Roberts, Franklin 1859 wb-k-51 (O)
Roberts, George (B) 1845 wb-#148 (Mc)
Roberts, George 1837 wb-e-38 (Hu)
Roberts, Granville 1855 rb-17-535 (Ru)
Roberts, H. F. 1847 wb-#148 (Mc)
Roberts, Hannah L. 1834 wb-5-354 (Wi)
Roberts, Hannah S. 1836 wb-6-158 (Wi)
Roberts, Henry 1813 wb-2-38 (K)
Roberts, Henry H. 1835 wb-b-81 (G)
Roberts, Hensley 1836 wb-x-296* (Mu)
Roberts, Hiram 1850 ib-1-69 (Wy)
Roberts, I. B. 1846 wb#18 (Gu)
Roberts, Ichabod 1859 wb-k-43 (O)
Roberts, Isaac (Gen.) 1816 wb-#43 (Mu)
Roberts, Isaac (General) 1816 wb-#22 (Mu)
Roberts, Isaac H. 1853 wb#21 (Gu)
Roberts, Izador 1844 wb-8-243 (K)
Roberts, J. F. 1859 wb-k-41 (O)
Roberts, Jacob 1825 wb-4-85 (K)
Roberts, James 1837 wb-6-129 (K)
Roberts, James 1844 wb-2-1 (W)
Roberts, James 1850 wb-c-397 (Wh)
Roberts, James 1854 148-1-501 (Ge)
Roberts, James M. 1854 wb-3-206 (W)
Roberts, James M. 1856 wb-#148 (Mc)
Roberts, James M. 1857 wb-h-372 (St)
Roberts, James M. 1857 wb-h-394 (St)
Roberts, James S. 1856 wb-h-56 (Hn)
Roberts, Jesse 1838 rb-10-108 (Ru)
Roberts, John 1805 wb-1-0 (Sm)
Roberts, John 1824 wb-3-677 (Wi)
Roberts, John 1846 wb-b-166 (We)
Roberts, John 1859 wb-13-163 (Wi)
Roberts, John O. 1861 ib-2-245 (Wy)
Roberts, John R. 1847 wb-#6 (Mo)
Roberts, Jonas 1837 abl-1-7 (T)
Roberts, Jonathan 1780 wb-1-413 (Hw)
Roberts, Jonathan E. 1841 abl-1-217 (T)
Roberts, Josadic 1838 wb-6-282 (K)

Roberts, Joseph 1810 wb-1-226 (Wi)
Roberts, Lemuel 1822 wb-3-594 (Wi)
Roberts, Letitia 1841 wb-1-232 (La)
Roberts, Linedus 1846 wb-g-202 (Hn)
Roberts, Lucy F. 1836 wb-6-218 (Wi)
Roberts, Mack 1850 wb-#174 (Wl)
Roberts, Minton C. 1853 as-b-122 (Ms)
Roberts, Moses 1822 wb-3-333 (K)
Roberts, Nunaley 1837 wb-y-66 (Mu)
Roberts, Peter P. 1833 rb-f-490 (Mt)
Roberts, Peter P. 1834 rb-f-603 (Mt)
Roberts, R. T. 1854 ib-h-69 (F)
Roberts, Rachel 1849 wb-a-353 (F)
Roberts, Rebecca 1859 wb-f-229 (Ro)
Roberts, Reuben 1841 wb-1-408 (W)
Roberts, Reuben 1857 wb-h-373 (St)
Roberts, Richard 1847 wb-f-127+ (O)
Roberts, Richard 1856 wb-b-395 (We)
Roberts, Richard W. 1857 wb-1-174 (Be)
Roberts, Samuel 1823 rb-d-89 (Mt)
Roberts, Samuel 1856 rb-o-67 (Mt)
Roberts, Samuel 1857 wb-h-160 (Hn)
Roberts, Sarah 1859 ib-2-194 (Wy)
Roberts, Thomas 1810 wb-a-7 (Wh)
Roberts, Thomas 1842 wb-1-424 (Hw)
Roberts, Thomas 1852 wb-d-123 (Wh)
Roberts, Wesley 1842 wb-3-476 (Hy)
Roberts, Wesley H. 1842 wb-3-122 (Hy)
Roberts, William 1812 rb-2-160 (Ru)
Roberts, William 1816 wb-2-223 (K)
Roberts, William 1835 wb-b-196 (Wh)
Roberts, William 1836 wb-1-150 (We)
Roberts, William 1837 wb-e-43 (Hu)
Roberts, William ca. 1850 wb-1-427 (Hw)
Roberts, Wright 1847 wb-e-17 (Ro)
Roberts, Zephaniah 1861 wb-a-387 (Cr)
Robertson, A. B. 1842 wb-12-265* (D)
Robertson, Bazel 1851 ib-1-118 (Wy)
Robertson, Benjamin 1848 wb-#167 (Wl)
Robertson, Benjamin 1848 wb-#167 (Wl)
Robertson, Burrell 1850 wb-14-555 (D)
Robertson, Burrell 1855 wb-1-53 (Dy)
Robertson, Catherine 1805 wb-#10 (Wa)
Robertson, Charles (Sr.) 1798 wb-#6 (Wa)
Robertson, Charles 1806 wb-3-67 (D)
Robertson, Charles 1829 wb-4-466 (Wi)
Robertson, Charles 1841 wb-2-307 (Hr)
Robertson, Christopher 1832 wb-10-54 (D)
Robertson, Darius 1815 wb-2-281 (Rb)
Robertson, David 1821 wb-1-37 (Fr)
Robertson, David 1821 wb-3-275 (Wi)

Robertson, David 1828 wb-2-0 (Sm)
Robertson, David 1837 wb-b-275 (Wh)
Robertson, David 1847 wb-7-0 (Sm)
Robertson, Duncan 1833 wb-10-225 (D)
Robertson, Edith 1840 wb-b-405 (Wh)
Robertson, Edward 1829 wb-4-423 (Wi)
Robertson, Elijah 1797 wb-2-77 (D)
Robertson, Elijah 1823 wb-#51 (Mu)
Robertson, Elijah 1831 lr (Sn)
Robertson, Elijah 1859 wb-17-615 (D)
Robertson, Elizabeth 1838 wb-b-235 (G)
Robertson, Ezekiel 1844 rb-12-526 (Ru)
Robertson, George 1854 ib-h-240 (F)
Robertson, H. 1860 rb-20-417 (Ru)
Robertson, Hardy 1835 wb-6-45 (Wi)
Robertson, Higdon 1844 wb-#142 (Wl)
Robertson, Higdon 1852 wb-#118 (Wl)
Robertson, Hugh 1805 wb-#2 (Wl)
Robertson, Hugh 1825 wb-#56 (Wl)
Robertson, James 1805 as-1-104 (Ge)
Robertson, James 1844 wb-a2-2 (Mu)
Robertson, James 1851 wb-14-474 (Rb)
Robertson, James E. 1853 rb-16-465 (Ru)
Robertson, James R. 1861 wb-f-496 (Ro)
Robertson, James T. 1837 wb-b-255 (Wh)
Robertson, James W. 1858 wb-h-451 (St)
Robertson, Jane 1857 6-2-140 (Le)
Robertson, Jararot 1855 wb-e-365 (G)
Robertson, Jesse 1821 wb-3-327 (Rb)
Robertson, Jessee 1831 lr (Sn)
Robertson, John 1814 wb-#15 (Wl)
Robertson, John 1818 wb-#30 (Wl)
Robertson, John 1821 wb-a-145 (Wh)
Robertson, John 1829 wb-1-190 (Ma)
Robertson, John 1853 wb-f-21 (Mu)
Robertson, John 1854 wb-5-339 (Je)
Robertson, John 1858 wb-f-214 (Ro)
Robertson, Jonathan F. 1815 wb-4-381 (D)
Robertson, Jordan 1849 wb-#171 (Wl)
Robertson, Joseph 1821 eb-1-113 (C)
Robertson, Joseph 1826 wb-5-233 (Rb)
Robertson, Lewis 1851 wb-#179 (Wl)
Robertson, Lewis 1856 wb-16-240 (Rb)
Robertson, Lewis 1860 wb-f-367 (G)
Robertson, Lydia 1833 wb-10-68 (D)
Robertson, Marcus 1838 wb-2-240 (Sn)
Robertson, Mark 1784 wb-1-53 (D)
Robertson, Mark 1816 wb-2-367 (Rb)
Robertson, Mark C. C. 1830 wb-9-417 (D)
Robertson, Mark C. C. 1841 wb-12-229* (D)
Robertson, Mary 1837 wb-6-138 (K)

Robertson, Mary 1843 wb-1-284 (La)
Robertson, Mary 1849 ib-1-33 (Wy)
Robertson, Mary 1850 wb-5-5 (Hr)
Robertson, Mary A. L. 1842 wb-7-585 (Wi)
Robertson, Mildred 1860 wb-f-183* (Mu)
Robertson, Nancy 1849 wb-3-13 (W)
Robertson, Nowell H. 1836 wb-10-546 (D)
Robertson, Richard 1831 wb-1-421 (Hw)
Robertson, Richard 1852 wb-10-193 (Wi)
Robertson, Robert 1819 wb-#32 (Wl)
Robertson, Robert 1849 wb-a-138 (T)
Robertson, Robertson? 1826 wb-#56 (Wl)
Robertson, S. G. 1853 wb-n-67 (Mt)
Robertson, S. G. 1858 wb-a-45 (Ce)
Robertson, Sarah 1847 wb-14-34 (D)
Robertson, Thomas 1825 rb-6-136 (Ru)
Robertson, Thomas 1831 rb-8-179 (Ru)
Robertson, Thomas 1854 wb-d-169 (Wh)
Robertson, Thomas 1861 wb-3e-167 (Sh)
Robertson, Thomas S. 1854 ib-H-136 (F)
Robertson, Wiatt 1860 wb-5-104 (Hr)
Robertson, William 1806 wb-1-224 (Rb)
Robertson, William 1808 rb-2-36 (Ru)
Robertson, William 1835 wb-1-150 (Gr)
Robertson, William 1838 wb-0-7 (Cf)
Robertson, William 1840 wb-3-166 (Ma)
Robertson, William 1858 rb-19-511 (Ru)
Robertson, William B. 1839 rb-10-272 (Ru)
Robertson, William R. 1827 wb-#159 (Mu)
Robertson, Willie 1826 wb-5-212 (Rb)
Robertson, Willoughby 1836 wb-6-40 (K)
Robertson, Winford 1823 wb-3-507 (Rb)
Robertson, Zachariah T. 1832 wb-1-14 (Sh)
Robeson, Alexander C. 1843 wb-#148 (Mc)
Robeson, Catherine 1846 wb-#149 (Mc)
Robeson, Elizabeth 1844 wb-#149 (Mc)
Robeson, Henry 1851 wb-g-499 (Hu)
Robeson, Henry P. 1851 wb-g-447 (Hu)
Robeson, John 1853 wb-5-229 (Je)
Robeson, R. W. 1850 wb-9-585 (Wi)
Robeson, Richard 1820 rb-4-239 (Ru)
Robeson, Thomas 1845 wb-#149 (Mc)
Robinett, Ezekiel 1855 wb-2-181 (Sh)
Robinett, Michael 1849 wb-#149 (Mc)
Robins, Alfred 1840 wb-e-346 (Hu)
Robins, George W. 1846 wb-4-78 (Hr)
Robins, John 1812 wb-1-7 (Fr)
Robins, Samuel 1829 wb-7-47 (Rb)
Robins, William 1838 wb-e-145 (Hu)
Robinson, —— 1848 wb-d-373 (Hd)
Robinson, A. L. 1847 wb-d-353 (Hd)

Robinson, A. M. 1855 39-2-69 (Dk)
Robinson, A. M. C.. 1855 39-2-96 (Dk)
Robinson, Abner 1852 wb-11-217 (K)
Robinson, Absalom L. 1841 wb-b-377 (Hd)
Robinson, Alexander 1791 wb-1-14 (Sn)
Robinson, Alexander F. 1839 wb-b-171 (Hd)
Robinson, Alexander M. 1847 wb-8-613 (Wi)
Robinson, Archibald 1854 39-2-36 (Dk)
Robinson, Asa 1848 wb-7-0 (Sm)
Robinson, C. A. 1852 wb-e-18 (G)
Robinson, Charles 1828 wb-4-286 (Wi)
Robinson, Charley 1852 wb-a-190 (T)
Robinson, Comfort 1848 ib-1-10 (Cl)
Robinson, David 1813 wb-2-34# (Ge)
Robinson, David 1824 wb-#77 (Mu)
Robinson, David 1830 wb-2-0 (Sm)
Robinson, David 1847 wb-d-355 (Hd)
Robinson, David R. 1839 wb-7-51 (Wi)
Robinson, David R. 1856 as-b-211 (Ms)
Robinson, Deborah 1835 wb-1-477 (Hr)
Robinson, Edward 1821 wb-1-0 (Sm)
Robinson, Elijah 1853 r39-1-314 (Dk)
Robinson, Elizabeth 1852 wb-a-286 (Ms)
Robinson, Elizabeth 1855 wb-#56 (Wa)
Robinson, Elizabeth D. 1847 wb-5-51 (Ma)
Robinson, Frances 1837 rb-10-39 (Ru)
Robinson, George 1823 wb-2-0 (Sm)
Robinson, Hannah 1851 wb-A-74 (Ca)
Robinson, Henry 1822 rb-5-209 (Ru)
Robinson, Horace 1860 rb-20-467 (Ru)
Robinson, Hugh 1848 ib-1-29 (Ca)
Robinson, Ica 1852 wb-15-62 (Rb)
Robinson, Isaac A. 1840 wb-y-693 (Mu)
Robinson, Isaiah 1859 rb-20-125 (Ru)
Robinson, Jacob 1838 wb-#36 (Wa)
Robinson, Jacob 1838 wb-b-310 (Wh)
Robinson, Jacob 1840 wb-#38 (Wa)
Robinson, James 1830 wb-1-161 (Hr)
Robinson, James 1837 wb-b-253 (Wh)
Robinson, James 1845 wb-d-160 (Ro)
Robinson, James 1848 as-a-173 (Ms)
Robinson, James 1849 wb-b-488 (Mu)
Robinson, James 1853 wb-#111 (Wl)
Robinson, James 1855 wb-5-52 (Hr)
Robinson, James 1856 ib-1-396 (Wy)
Robinson, James 1856 wb-b-20 (Dk)
Robinson, James 1856 wb-f-41 (Ro)
Robinson, James 1858 wb-1-374 (Fr)
Robinson, James C. 1852 wb-10-416 (Wi)
Robinson, James C. 1855 wb-2-121 (Li)
Robinson, James S. 1856 wb-12-55 (Wi)

Robinson, James T. 1852 wb-d-77 (Wh)
Robinson, Jane 1844 wb-a2-140 (Mu)
Robinson, Jane P. 1848 wb-14-182 (D)
Robinson, Jesse B. 1849 ib-1-81 (Ca)
Robinson, John 1826 lw (Ct)
Robinson, John 1834 wb-1-57 (La)
Robinson, John 1843 wb-d-109 (O)
Robinson, John 1848 as-a-150 (Ms)
Robinson, John 1849 wb-b-399 (Mu)
Robinson, John 1852 wb-2-76# (Ge)
Robinson, John 1854 148-1-511 (Ge)
Robinson, John 1856 wb-#27 (Mo)
Robinson, John 1861 wb-a-373 (Cr)
Robinson, John A. 1856 wb-#121 (Wl)
Robinson, John B. 1849 wb-5-70 (Ma)
Robinson, John D. 1860 wb-13-283 (Wi)
Robinson, John H. 1841 rb-11-149 (Ru)
Robinson, John W. 1857 wb-f-66 (Ro)
Robinson, Jonas 1853 wb-5-36 (Hr)
Robinson, Jonas 1856 39-2-194 (Dk)
Robinson, Joseph 1850 wb-a-222 (Ms)
Robinson, Joseph 1854 wb-1-83 (Jo)
Robinson, Josiah J. 1841 wb-2-212 (Hr)
Robinson, Malinda 1852 wb-h-Nov (O)
Robinson, Malinda B. 1855 wb-12-32 (Wi)
Robinson, Malinda M. 1854 wb-i-236 (O)
Robinson, Martha 1852 as-b-70 (Ms)
Robinson, Mary 1860 39-2-380 (Dk)
Robinson, Mathew 1831 wb-1-102 (Fr)
Robinson, Michael 1808 wb-1-201 (Wi)
Robinson, Michael 1840 wb-7-325 (Wi)
Robinson, Michael 1842 wb-z-309 (Mu)
Robinson, Michael 1851 wb-9-679 (Wi)
Robinson, Michael 1861 wb-2-346 (Li)
Robinson, Nancy L. 1844 rb-12-594 (Ru)
Robinson, Rebecca 1849 wb-2-63 (Sh)
Robinson, Robert 1828 wb-1-418 (Hw)
Robinson, Samuel 1827 wb-3-0 (Sm)
Robinson, Samuel 1835 wb-2-45# (Ge)
Robinson, Samuel 1836 wb-b-21 (Hd)
Robinson, Samuel 1848 148-1-226 (Ge)
Robinson, Stephen 1846 wb-7-0 (Sm)
Robinson, Stephen sr. 1835 wb-3-0 (Sm)
Robinson, T. F. 1857 wb-1-384 (Be)
Robinson, Thomas 1830 rb-8-133 (Ru)
Robinson, Thomas 1837 wb-a-54 (T)
Robinson, Thomas 1840 wb-b-213 (Hd)
Robinson, Thomas 1856 ib-2-354 (Cl)
Robinson, Thomas C. 1832 wb-9-595 (D)
Robinson, Thomas L. 1850 wb-9-378 (Wi)
Robinson, Thomas S. 1859 gs-1-325 (F)

Robinson, Thos. W. 1857 wb-b-44 (Ms)
Robinson, William 1826 wb-3-0 (Sm)
Robinson, William 1833 wb-10-237 (D)
Robinson, William 1848 wb-2-19 (Sh)
Robinson, William 1856 39-1-358 (Dk)
Robinson, William A. 1855 wb-2-117 (Li)
Robinson, William P. 1815 wb-4-344 (D)
Robinson, William P. 1825 wb-8-461 (D)
Robinson, William P. 1848 wb-14-241 (D)
Robinson, William P. 1852 wb-h-Dec (O)
Robinson, Willie H. 1848 ib-1-37 (Ca)
Robinson, Wm. B. 1842 5-2-272 (Cl)
Robison, George R. 1836 wb-6-228 (Wi)
Robison, James 1830 wb-2-39# (Ge)
Robison, James 1833 wb-x-85 (Mu)
Robison, John 1854 wb-d-163 (Wh)
Robison, Michael 1839 wb-y-602 (Mu)
Robison, Moses 1836 wb-2-79 (Ma)
Robison, Richard W. 1850 wb-9-602 (Wi)
Robison, Thomas 1815 wb-2-163 (K)
Robison, William 1848 wb-#150 (Mc)
Robley?, John 1834 wb-1-540 (Ma)
Robman, Henry 1838 wb-1-177 (Fr)
Roche, Edward B. 1844 rb-j-256 (Mt)
Rochell, Robert 1853 wb-h-127 (Hu)
Rock, John 1838 wb-#36 (Wa)
Rock, Nancy 1841 wb-#54 (Wa)
Rockhold, William 1861 wb-1-74 (Su)
Rodden, Jacob 1815 wb-3-92 (St)
Roddy, James 1800 wb-1-74 (K)
Roddy, James 1815 wb-2-163 (K)
Roddy, James 1823 wb-1-124 (Bo)
Roddy, James 1823 wb-2-380 (Je)
Roddy, James 1835 wb-a-33 (T)
Roddy, Jesse 1852 wb-1-15 (R)
Roddy, Jessee 1862 wb-1-218 (R)
Roddy, Lydia 1825 wb-a-1 (R)
Rodeny, Benjamin 1827 wb-#175 (Mu)
Rodeny, Benjamin 1829 wb-#200 (Mu)
Rodes, Tyree 1858 lr (Gi)
Rodgers, Andrew H. 1858 wb-12-508 (Wi)
Rodgers, Corder (Cordie) 1816 wb-1-0 (Sm)
Rodgers, George 1836 wb-3-388 (Je)
Rodgers, George 1837 wb-3-444 (Je)
Rodgers, George 1838 wb-3-538 (Je)
Rodgers, James 1794 wb-1-21# (Ge)
Rodgers, James 1794 wb-1-26# (Ge)
Rodgers, James 1808 wb-1-2 (Fr)
Rodgers, John 1839 rb-10-268 (Ru)
Rodgers, John B. 1851 wb-2-109 (Sh)
Rodgers, John H. 1852 wb-a-235 (Dk)

Rodgers, John M. 1854 wb-2-81# (Ge)
Rodgers, Joseph 1833 wb-5-240 (K)
Rodgers, Joseph 1836 wb-1-452 (Hr)
Rodgers, Joseph T. 1837 wb-a-208 (O)
Rodgers, Levi 1850 wb-3-22 (W)
Rodgers, Mary 1857 wb-3e-52 (Sh)
Rodgers, Mary 1857 wb-f-70 (Ro)
Rodgers, Mary O. 1841 wb-4-29 (Je)
Rodgers, Nathaniel 1837 wb-a-207 (O)
Rodgers, Reuben B. 1838 wb-6-261 (K)
Rodgers, Seth 1850 wb-4-14 (Je)
Rodgers, Thomas 1800 wb-#8 (Wa)
Rodgers, Thomas 1819 wb-2-236 (Je)
Rodgers, Thomas 1824 wb-#51 (Wl)
Rodgers, Thomas 1852 wb-e-352 (Ro)
Rody, Moses 1855 wb-12-96 (K)
Roe, Benjamin 1834 wb-3-0 (Sm)
Roe, James B. 1848 wb-13-224 (Rb)
Roe, William C. 1856 wb-7-0 (Sm)
Rogan, Nancy 1839 wb-2-252 (Sn)
Rogers, A. M. 1859 rb-p-297 (Mt)
Rogers, A. W. (Dr.) 1861 rb-p-591 (Mt)
Rogers, Abraham 1804 wb-#3 (Wl)
Rogers, Abraham 1807 wb-1-113 (Sn)
Rogers, Absalom 1839 rb-10-442 (Ru)
Rogers, Ann 1853 wb-1-28 (R)
Rogers, Armstead 1836 rb-g-267 (Mt)
Rogers, Armstead 1847 rb-k-615 (Mt)
Rogers, Armsted sr. 1835 rb-g-247 (Mt)
Rogers, Basel 1856 wb-a-270 (Cr)
Rogers, Benjamin 1799 wb-1-71 (Rb)
Rogers, Benjamin 1834 eb-1-310 (C)
Rogers, Brittain 1857 lr (Sn)
Rogers, Carey N. 1816 wb-#115 (Mu)
Rogers, Chany 1854 wb-h-225 (Hu)
Rogers, Charles 1825 wb-4-5 (Wi)
Rogers, Chasey 1852 wb-g-563 (Hu)
Rogers, Daniel 1802 wb-1-57 (Sn)
Rogers, David 1813 rb-2-239 (Ru)
Rogers, Elisha 1815 wb-#16 (Wl)
Rogers, Elizabeth 1820 lr (Sn)
Rogers, Ellen 1837 wb-1-424 (Hw)
Rogers, Emeline 1857 wb-1-428 (Hw)
Rogers, George Sr. 1853 wb-1-427 (Hw)
Rogers, Isaac 1814 rb-b-147 (Mt)
Rogers, Isaac 1824 rb-d-316 (Mt)
Rogers, Isaac 1824 rb-d-413 (Mt)
Rogers, Isabella O. 1854 wb-b-339 (We)
Rogers, Jacob 1849 wb-b-462 (Mu)
Rogers, James 1815 wb-2-149 (Wi)
Rogers, James 1821 wb-1-22# (Ge)

Rogers, James 1825 rb-d-472 (Mt)
Rogers, James 1834 wb-a-258 (R)
Rogers, James 1843 wb-1-561 (W)
Rogers, James 1853 wb-1-50 (R)
Rogers, James C. 1850 mr-2-379 (Be)
Rogers, James H. 1842 wb-3-626 (Ma)
Rogers, James K. 1849 wb-g-337 (Hn)
Rogers, James W. 1820 wb-#91 (Mu)
Rogers, Jefferson 1844 wb-b-57 (We)
Rogers, Jesse 1843 wb-e-606 (Hu)
Rogers, Job 1838 wb-1-179 (We)
Rogers, Joel 1854 wb-h-283 (Hu)
Rogers, John 1831 wb-1-40 (Hy)
Rogers, John 1837 wb-1-230 (W)
Rogers, John 1852 wb-#24 (Mo)
Rogers, John B. 1848 ib-1-30 (Ca)
Rogers, John D. 1847 wb-d-67 (G)
Rogers, Jonathan T. 1841 wb-b-31 (We)
Rogers, Joseph F. 1840 rb-11-64 (Ru)
Rogers, Jubilee 1855 wb-b-358 (We)
Rogers, Lucy M. 1835? wb-1-144 (Hy)
Rogers, Margaret 1809 wb-2-32# (Ge)
Rogers, Martha 1825 rb-d-473 (Mt)
Rogers, Martha 1825 rb-d-479 (Mt)
Rogers, Mary E. 1861 iv-C-55 (C)
Rogers, Matthew 1843 wb-f-98 (St)
Rogers, Michael 1861 wb-b*-16 (O)
Rogers, Nancy 1859 wb-i-150 (St)
Rogers, Nancy G. 1854 wb-5-143 (Ma)
Rogers, Nathaniel 1802 wb-1-95 (Rb)
Rogers, Peter 1858 as-c-90 (Ms)
Rogers, Pleasant 1848 wb-g-16 (Hu)
Rogers, Randolph 1836 wb-x-339* (Mu)
Rogers, Reuben 1797 wb-1-204 (Je)
Rogers, Robert 1815 as-A-64 (Di)
Rogers, Robert 1815 as-a-150 (Di)
Rogers, Robert 1819 wb-3-38 (Wi)
Rogers, Robert 1858 wb-1-430 (Hw)
Rogers, Russell 1844 wb-2-3 (W)
Rogers, Samuel 1816 Wb-2-183 (Wi)
Rogers, Shadrach 1825 wb-1-124 (Bo)
Rogers, T. W. 1858 wb-1-235 (Be)
Rogers, Thomas 1807 wb-1-177 (Wi)
Rogers, Thomas 1811 wb-1-414 (Hw)
Rogers, Tobias 1858 wb-1-263 (Be)
Rogers, W. J. 1860 rb-p-393 (Mt)
Rogers, William 1822 wb-a-163 (Wh)
Rogers, William 1839 5-2-107 (Cl)
Rogers, William 1842 wb-a-106 (Cr)
Rogers, William 1855 wb-h-430 (Hu)
Rogers, Willobe 1828 wb-1-121 (Bo)

Rogers, Wm. 1860 rb-p-423 (Mt)
Rogers, Wm. C. 1856 wb-g-760 (Hn)
Roland, Abijah 1820 wb-3-229 (Rb)
Roland, Elizabeth 1818 wb-7-232 (D)
Roland, George 1853 ib-2-43 (Cl)
Roland, Martha 1858 wb-4-199 (La)
Roland, Robert 1828 wb-1-0 (Sm)
Rolin, William 1856 wb-#150 (Mc)
Rolland, Jacob 1812 wb-2-10 (Wi)
Rolland, Robert 1845 wb-#146 (Wl)
Roller, Margaret 1858 wb-1-7 (Su)
Rollings, David 1827 wb-1-23# (Ge)
Rollings, James 1856 wb-7-0 (Sm)
Rollins, Mary 1851 wb-#178 (Wl)
Rollins, Thomas 1833 rb-9-39 (Ru)
Rollins, William 1861 149-1-218 (Ge)
Rollins, William sr. 1856 wb-2-83# (Ge)
Rolls, J. W. 1859 wb-h-320 (Hn)
Rolls, William B. 1858 wb-1-199 (Be)
Rolston, Franky 1817 wb-2-159 (Je)
Rolston, Moses 1850 wb-10-364 (K)
Romack, Madison 1835 wb-#150 (Mc)
Romines, Fanny 1848 wb-#150 (Mc)
Romines, Nancy 1858 wb-1C-407 (A)
Romins, Soloman 1859 wb-2-454 (Me)
Rone, George 1850 as-a-214 (Ms)
Rone, Harry 1859 as-c-144 (Ms)
Rone, Henry 1856 wb-b-25 (Ms)
Rone, James 1859 wb-7-43 (Ma)
Rone, Levi 1850 as-a-215 (Ms)
Roney, Benjamin 1803 lr (Sn)
Roney, Benjamin 1853 wb-h-May (O)
Roney, James 1844 lr (Sn)
Roney, James sr. 1835 wb-2-190 (Sn)
Roney, Margret 1860 wb-k-246 (O)
Roofs, James H. 1830 wb-1-18 (La)
Rook, Daniel 1824 rb-d-330 (Mt)
Rook, Daniel 1837 rb-g-494 (Mt)
Rook, Eaton T. 1849 wb-4-500 (Hr)
Rook, John 1826 rb-e-48 (Mt)
Rook, John sr. 1824 rb-d-385 (Mt)
Rook, John sr. 1825 rb-d-435 (Mt)
Rook, Susanna 1826 rb-e-4 (Mt)
Rooker, John 1854 wb-5-146 (Ma)
Rooks, James 1844 wb-3-452 (Hy)
Rooks, Joby 1843 wb-a-107 (T)
Rooks, Thomas 1842 wb-3-505 (Ma)
Roots, Elizabeth 1838 wb-6-285 (K)
Roper, David 1845 wb-8-337 (Wi)
Roper, David E. 1846 wb-8-372 (Wi)
Roper, Dinney 1845 lr (Gi)

Roper, Eliza 1846 wb-8-372 (Wi)
Roper, Eliza Ann 1848 wb-9-55 (Wi)
Roper, Elizabeth 1860 as-c-215 (Ms)
Roper, John 1831 wb-1-65 (Li)
Roper, John 1858 wb-5-464 (Je)
Roper, Martha B. 1846 wb-8-371 (Wi)
Roper, Martha P. 1848 wb-9-55 (Wi)
Roper, Sarah E. 1853 ib-1-258 (Wy)
Roper, Tennessee 1853 ib-1-201 (Wy)
Roper, Thomas 1816 wb-2-318 (Rb)
Roper, William 1852 ib-1-188 (Wy)
Rorax, Margaret 1821 wb-A-313 (Li)
Rorax, William 1816 wb-A-139 (Li)
Rorie, Ezekiah 1847 wb-f-416 (St)
Rosamond, Saml. 1838 wb-2-32 (Hr)
Rose (Ross?), Alexr. 1828? as-a-179 (Di)
Rose, A. 1823 as-A-94 (Di)
Rose, Benjamin 1833 wb-8-246 (Rb)
Rose, E. R. 1861 wb-17-258 (Rb)
Rose, Elias 1849 A-468-114 (Le)
Rose, Frances M. 1840 wb-a-89 (T)
Rose, Gilbert 1854 as-c-359 (Di)
Rose, James 1826 wb-5-214 (Rb)
Rose, James 1831 wb-1-420 (Hw)
Rose, John 1851 wb-c-447 (Wh)
Rose, Johnathan 1856 wb-a-277 (Cr)
Rose, Johnathan 1860 wb-a-354 (Cr)
Rose, Reubin 1860 wb-17-75 (Rb)
Rose, Richard 1846 wb-f-375 (St)
Rose, Robert H. 1833 wb-a-20 (T)
Rose, Roda 1856 wb-a-279 (Cr)
Rose, Samuel 1859 wb-3e-98 (Sh)
Rose, Sarah 1851 wb-g-401 (St)
Rose, Sarah 1851 wb-g-405 (St)
Rose, Sarah 1853 27-lw (Hd)
Rose, Virginia 1856 rb-o-226 (Mt)
Rose, Wiley 1844 rb-j-267 (Mt)
Rose, William R. 1847 wb-a2-563 (Mu)
Rose, William W. 1856 wb-1-96 (R)
Rose, Wm. 1861 rb-p-574 (Mt)
Rose, Wm. A. 1858 wb-3e-59 (Sh)
Rose?, James 1830 wb-1-140 (Hr)
Rose?, Littleberry 1816 wb-2-360 (Rb)
Roseberry, William 1794 wb-1-14 (K)
Roseborough, Samuel 1853 wb-1-305 (Fr)
Rosebrough, William 1811 wb-A-1 (Li)
Ross, Allen 1846 148-1-147 (Ge)
Ross, Benjamin 1838 wb-d-259 (St)
Ross, Benjamin W. 1840 wb-e-25 (St)
Ross, Catharine J. 1854 wb-1-329 (Fr)
Ross, Catherine 1850 wb-5-83 (Ma)

Ross, Daniel 1841 wb-a-95 (Cr)
Ross, Franklin 1850 wb-g-299 (Hu)
Ross, George 1849 ib-1-32 (Wy)
Ross, George D. 1826 wb-1-62 (Ma)
Ross, Harmon 1832 wb-c-30 (Hn)
Ross, Harmon 1842 wb-f-88 (Hn)
Ross, Hezekiah H. 1856 wb-6-340 (Ma)
Ross, Hugh 1814? wb-#37 (Mu)
Ross, James H. 1829 wb-1-13 (La)
Ross, James M. 1836 wb-a-290 (O)
Ross, James M. 1846 wb-d-11 (G)
Ross, Jesse S. 1853 ib-1-240 (Wy)
Ross, John 1839 wb-#124 (Wl)
Ross, John 1850 148-1-320 (Ge)
Ross, Lucy 1840 wb-1A-271 (A)
Ross, Maranda A. 1860 ib-2-213 (Wy)
Ross, Mary Ann 1851 148-1-362 (Ge)
Ross, Nancy 1841 wb-#134 (Wl)
Ross, Nancy 1854 rb-17-29 (Ru)
Ross, Nathan sr. 1834 wb-c-350 (St)
Ross, Reuben 1835 wb-c-450 (St)
Ross, Reuben 1835 wb-c-461 (St)
Ross, Robert 1845 rb-13-61 (Ru)
Ross, S. N. 1859 wb-#129 (Wl)
Ross, Thomas 1848 wb-b-288 (We)
Ross, William 1813 wb-a-176 (St)
Ross, William 1829 wb-c-28 (St)
Ross, William J. 1837 wb-y-48 (Mu)
Ross, William N. 1814 wb-a-236* (St)
Ross, William T. 1856 wb-2-162 (Li)
Ross, William sr. 1831 wb-2-49# (Ge)
Ross, William sr. 1849 148-1-290 (Ge)
Ross, Wilson Y. 1850 rb-15-235 (Ru)
Rosser, David 1853 wb-16-120 (D)
Rosson, Abner 1841 wb-2-272 (Hr)
Rosson, E. W. 1851 as-b-7 (Ms)
Rosson, John 1826 wb-5-273 (Rb)
Rosson, John 1835 wb-1-422 (Hr)
Rosson, John 1837 wb-9-333 (Rb)
Rosson, Joseph 1839 wb-a-52 (Ms)
Rosson, Milton 1849 wb-a-186 (Ms)
Rosson, William 1856 as-b-234 (Ms)
Rosson, William 1858 rb-o-569 (Mt)
Roswell, John 1848 mr-2-295 (Be)
Rotan, William 1841 wb-c-10 (Wh)
Rothwell, Gideon 1836 wb-1-184 (W)
Rottan, John M. 1837 wb-b-254 (Wh)
Rouden, Sally 1823 wb-3-658 (Wi)
Roudon, John 1817 wb-a-93 (Ro)
Roughton, Richard 1836 wb-#112 (Wl)
Roulhac, Francis 1852 rb-16-347 (Ru)

Roulhac, George 1840 rb-10-509 (Ru)
Roulhac, George G. 1839 rb-10-429 (Ru)
Roulston, David 1838 wb-11-334 (D)
Roulstone, George 1804 wb-1-159 (K)
Roulstone, Mathew 1800 wb-1-60 (Je)
Roundtree, Andrew 1841 wb-z-229 (Mu)
Roundtree, Cicero 1850 wb-9-458 (Wi)
Rounsaville, Amos 1839 wb-a-32 (L)
Rountree, Jeelsey? 1849 wb-b-555 (Mu)
Rountree, John 1842 wb-z-328 (Mu)
Rountree, Julay 1849 wb-b-498 (Mu)
Rountree, William 1843 wb-c-120 (G)
Rouse, Nancy 1842 wb-1-425 (Hw)
Routh, Edward 1844 wb-8-267 (K)
Routh, Edward 1858 wb-12-518 (K)
Routh, Isaac 1840 wb-5-98 (Gr)
Routh, Jacob 1826 wb-2-596 (Je)
Routon, Aaron F. 1853 wb-g-529 (Hn)
Routon, Mary 1849 wb-#167 (Wl)
Routon, Philip 1838 wb-d-243* (Hn)
Rovin, T. M. 1861 wb-a-315 (T)
Rowan, Daniel 1801 rb-a-123 (Mt)
Rowan?, Robert 1833 wb-1-75 (Hy)
Rowans, Daniel 1801 wb-2-223 (D)
Rowe, Anderson 1835 wb-x-288 (Mu)
Rowe, James S. 1836 wb-10-539 (D)
Rowe, Johnson 1858 wb-f-140 (Mu)
Rowe, Joseph 1845 lr (Gi)
Rowe, Thomas 1802 wb-1-20 (Ct)
Rowe, W. L. 1859 gs-1-438 (F)
Rowell, William 1844 wb-1-250 (Li)
Rowen, Mary Ann 1860 wb-3e-133 (Sh)
Rowland, Benjamin 1857 wb-3-350 (W)
Rowland, David 1838 wb-3-0 (Sm)
Rowland, J. T. 1849? wb-#12 (Mo)
Rowland, James 1835 wb-b-181 (Wh)
Rowland, James M. 1837 wb-b-260 (Wh)
Rowland, James M. 1853 wb-d-194 (Wh)
Rowland, John 1821 wb-1-332 (Sn)
Rowland, Joseph 1828 wb-9-179 (D)
Rowland, Margarett 1849 wb-c-358 (Wh)
Rowland, Robert 1828 wb-3-0 (Sm)
Rowland, William 1834 wb-c-137 (Hn)
Rowland, William B. 1861 wb-b*-2 (O)
Rowlet, John H. 1841 5-2-242 (Cl)
Rowlett, Benjamin 1858 wb-i-18 (St)
Rowlett, John 1827 wb-4-247 (Wi)
Rowlett, Leonard S. 1851 rb-15-564 (Ru)
Rowlett, Makness 1848 ib-1-52 (Cl)
Rowlett, Martin 1842 wb-7-529 (Wi)
Rowlett, Prudence 1833 wb-5-274 (Wi)

Rowlett, Rebecca 1858 rb-19-404 (Ru)
Rowlett, Rebecca J. 1858 rb-19-198 (Ru)
Rowlett, Thomas 1855 rb-17-516 (Ru)
Rowlett, Thomas 1855 rb-17-536 (Ru)
Rowley, M. 1842 rb-i-444 (Mt)
Rowlon, Peyton 1859 rb-20-113 (Ru)
Rowlon, William 1859 rb-19-541 (Ru)
Rowntree, Thomas 1828 wb-1-29 (Li)
Rowten, William 1829 rb-7-317 (Ru)
Rowton, Molloy 1855 rb-17-532 (Ru)
Rowton, Peyton 1861 rb-21-3 (Ru)
Rowton, William 1856 rb-18-121 (Ru)
Roy, Isaac 1849 wb-g-267 (Hu)
Roy, Joseph 1858 wb-#14 (Mo)
Royal, John 1824 wb-#72 (Mu)
Royal, John 1837 abl-1-9 (T)
Royal, Pamelia 1841 abl-1-239 (T)
Royale, William 1834 wb-x-178 (Mu)
Royster, David 1843 wb-1-93 (Sh)
Royster, George W. 1857 wb-7-0 (Sm)
Royster, Joseph G. 1853 wb-2-174 (Me)
Royster, Keturah 1840 wb-7-217 (Wi)
Royster, N. M. 1855 wb-n-511 (Mt)
Royster, Nathaniel 1853 lr (Sn)
Royster, Nathaniel M. 1838 rb-h-138 (Mt)
Royster, Phebe 1856 wb-2-338 (Me)
Royster, Richard W. 1854 wb-2-175 (Sh)
Royston, Grandison 1832 wb-5-142 (K)
Royston, Richard C. 1836 wb-1-486 (Hr)
Royston, Richard C. 1836 wb-1-489 (Hr)
Royston, Richard C. Sr. 1838 wb-2-36 (Hr)
Ruble, Catharine 1837 wb-#39 (Wa)
Rubman, Justice 1817 wb-1-0 (Sm)
Rucker, A. J. 1848 wb-#150 (Mc)
Rucker, Ann 1845 rb-13-416 (Ru)
Rucker, B. A. 1859 wb-#129 (Wl)
Rucker, Coalby 1852 wb-3-49 (Gr)
Rucker, Edmund M. 1859 rb-19-526 (Ru)
Rucker, Elizabeth 1845 wb-8-365 (Wi)
Rucker, G. L. 1827 rb-6-337 (Ru)
Rucker, Gideon 1842 wb-A-24 (Ca)
Rucker, Gideon S. 1829 rb-7-178 (Ru)
Rucker, James 1820 rb-4-199 (Ru)
Rucker, James 1830 rb-8-135 (Ru)
Rucker, James 1850 rb-15-451 (Ru)
Rucker, James Sr. 1837 wb-#150 (Mc)
Rucker, Joanna 1830 wb-#88 (Wl)
Rucker, John 1845 wb-8-342 (Wi)
Rucker, Lavinia 1844 rb-12-584 (Ru)
Rucker, Mary Eliza 1856 rb-18-96 (Ru)
Rucker, Mordecai 1855 wb-#151 (Mc)

Rucker, Samuel C. 1823 rb-5-265 (Ru)
Rucker, Samuel C. jr. 1827 rb-6-289 (Ru)
Rucker, Sarah 1845 wb-8-326 (Wi)
Rucker, Thomas 1845 rb-13-222 (Ru)
Rucker, Thomas D. 1853 wb-n-44 (Mt)
Rucker, Thomas sr. 1843 rb-12-309 (Ru)
Rucker, William 1846 wb-8-495 (Wi)
Rucker, William 1854 wb-3-196 (Gr)
Rucker, William sr. 1826 wb-4-140 (Wi)
Rucker, Williford 1845 rb-13-386 (Ru)
Rucks, Elizabeth 1857 wb-7-0 (Sm)
Rucks, Josiah 1836 wb-3-0 (Sm)
Rud, John 1842 wb-e-164 (St)
Rudd, Absalom 1840 wb-2-153 (Hy)
Rudd, Herrod 1828 wb-#151 (Mc)
Rudd, John 1859 wb-#151 (Mc)
Rudd, Sarah 1845 wb-#152 (Mc)
Rudd, Thomas 1840 wb-#152 (Mc)
Rudder, Elizabeth 1854 wb-b-253 (L)
Rudder, Epaphroditus 1845 wb-9-138 (K)
Rudder, Epaphroditus 1847 wb-8-535 (Wi)
Rudder, Manoah B. 1846 wb-8-491 (Wi)
Rudder, Richard H. 1853 wb-10-418 (Wi)
Rudder?, Samuel 1839 wb-a-44 (L)
Ruddie, Epaphroditus 1843 wb-8-156 (K)
Ruddle, Cornelius 1787 wb-1-54 (D)
Rudolph, Fredrick 1860 rb-p-445 (Mt)
Rudolph, Jacob 1838 rb-h-192 (Mt)
Rudolph, John 1845 rb-k-299 (Mt)
Rudolph, Thomas S. 1856 rb-o-247 (Mt)
Ruff, Bennett 1859 wb-3e-123 (Sh)
Ruffin, Etheldred 1824 wb-4-110 (Rb)
Ruffin, James 1848 wb-2-28 (Sh)
Ruffin, James F. 1846 wb-4-30 (Hr)
Ruffin, James F. 1853 wb-b-213 (L)
Ruffin, Mary 1842 wb-11-267 (Rb)
Ruffin, William 1857 wb-3e-48 (Sh)
Ruffo, Dominick 1860 wb-3e-137 (Sh)
Rule, George 1857 wb-12-426 (K)
Rule, George sr. 1857 wb-12-456 (K)
Rumage, William 1861 wb-a-389 (Cr)
Rumbley, Smith 1814 wb-a-198 (St)
Rumbley, Smith 1814 wb-a-230 (St)
Rumbley, William 1815 wb-3-136 (St)
Rumbly, Levin 1853 wb-g-532 (Hn)
Rumley, Thomas 1859 wb-h-304 (Hn)
Run, James 1829 wb-1-261 (Ma)
Runam?, George 1851 wb-2-90 (Me)
Runels, Joseph 1816 wb-2-37# (Ge)
Runels, Joseph 1850 wb-2-76# (Ge)
Runions, Charles W. 1847 5-3-222 (Cl)

Runnels, John 1830 wb-a-71 (R)
Runnels, Moses 1827 wb-1-69 (Fr)
Runnolds, Nancy 1844 wb-5-289 (Gr)
Runyan, Cyntha 1856 wb-h-303 (St)
Runyan, Turner 1849 wb-1-314 (Me)
Runyon, David L. 1851 wb-g-404 (St)
Ruple?, Mathew 1846 wb-g-110 (Hn)
Ruplee?, O. H. P. 1849 wb-g-341 (Hn)
Rush, Isaac 1846 wb-1-145 (Me)
Rush, William 1857 rb-o-505 (Mt)
Rushen, Philip 1842 wb-d-12 (Ro)
Rushing, Abel 1837 mr-1-13 (Be)
Rushing, Abel K. 1839 wb-d-300 (St)
Rushing, Abraham 1848 wb-g-31 (Hu)
Rushing, Clement 1838 wb-d-185 (St)
Rushing, D. C. 1859 wb-1-278 (Be)
Rushing, David L. 1854 wb-h-283 (Hu)
Rushing, Dennis 1860 wb-1-391 (Be)
Rushing, George W. 1854 mr-2-541 (Be)
Rushing, J. 1849 mr-2-330 (Be)
Rushing, Joel A. 1844 rb-12-489 (Ru)
Rushing, John 1857 wb-A-128 (Ca)
Rushing, John D. 1858 wb-1-232 (Be)
Rushing, John P. 1835 wb-c-434 (St)
Rushing, John P. 1853 wb-xx-248 (St)
Rushing, John P. 1854 wb-xx-420 (St)
Rushing, Mark 1858 wb-h-523 (St)
Rushing, Philip 1814 wb-a-194 (St)
Rushing, Robert 1855 mr-2-641 (Be)
Rushing, Robert T. 1854 mr-2-557 (Be)
Rushing, Sarah 1858 wb-h-186 (Hn)
Rushing, William A. 1850 wb-g-405 (Hu)
Rushing, Willis 1848 wb-g-33 (Hu)
Rushing, Willis 1853 mr-2-513 (Be)
Russ, David 1838 wb-y-333 (Mu)
Russan, Catharine 1859 ib-2-124 (Wy)
Russan, Catharine 1859 ib-2-126 (Wy)
Russel, Buckner 1836 wb-1-153 (We)
Russel, John 1825 rb-d-503 (Mt)
Russel, Melbry 1859 rb-20-155 (Ru)
Russel, Richard 1835 wb-x-342 (Mu)
Russell, A. 1854 wb-h-298 (Hu)
Russell, A. H. 1831 wb-#235 (Mu)
Russell, Alexander 1829 wb-#170 (Mu)
Russell, Alexander 1838 wb-b-93 (Hd)
Russell, Alfred H. 1844 wb-13-135 (D)
Russell, Andrew 1803 wb-1-124 (K)
Russell, Andrew 1842 wb-8-35 (K)
Russell, Andrew 1849 wb-10-283 (K)
Russell, Augustus 1854 wb-h-310 (Hu)
Russell, Benjamin 1845 wb-8-329 (Wi)

Russell, Benjamin B. 1840 wb-b-6 (We)
Russell, D. W. 1858 wb-17-532 (D)
Russell, Daniel 1805 wb-1-261 (Je)
Russell, David 1825 wb-#23 (Wa)
Russell, David 1854 148-1-476 (Ge)
Russell, David C. 1853 wb-b-201 (L)
Russell, Delilah 1837 wb-b-70 (Hd)
Russell, Elam 1849 wb-7-0 (Sm)
Russell, Elijah 1838 wb-1-396 (Hy)
Russell, Elizabeth 1827 wb-b-210 (St)
Russell, Hannah 1854 wb-16-263 (D)
Russell, Hezekiah 1854 wb-2-80# (Ge)
Russell, J. R. 1846 wb-d-247 (Hd)
Russell, James 1814 wb-2-96 (K)
Russell, James 1820 wb-7-370 (D)
Russell, James 1837 wb-b-71 (Hd)
Russell, James 1839 5-2-90 (Cl)
Russell, James 1839 wb-b-156 (O)
Russell, James 1842 wb-1-212 (Li)
Russell, James 1843 wb-12-436* (D)
Russell, James 1845 wb-#41 (Wa)
Russell, James 1846 wb-d-276 (Hd)
Russell, James 1854 as-2-318 (Ge)
Russell, James H. 1826 wb-b-136 (St)
Russell, Jane M. 1860 wb-3-62 (Me)
Russell, Jesse 1831 wb-1-179 (Hr)
Russell, John 1825 rb-d-497 (Mt)
Russell, John 1850 wb-b-90 (L)
Russell, John 1851 wb-7-0 (Sm)
Russell, John 1856 wb-1-344 (Fr)
Russell, John 1862 wb-1-21# (Ge)
Russell, John T. 1836 wb-b-22 (Hd)
Russell, Joseph 1816 wb-1-417 (Hw)
Russell, Lemuel 1853 as-c-249 (Di)
Russell, Louisa E. 1861 wb-#64 (Wa)
Russell, Martha 1854 wb-b-331 (We)
Russell, Mary 1855 wb-h-425 (Hu)
Russell, Mary A. 1842 wb-b-465 (Hd)
Russell, Mathew 1845 wb-f-319 (Hn)
Russell, Matthew 1833 wb-5-214 (K)
Russell, Richard 1819? wb-#114 (Mu)
Russell, Richard 1852 lr (Gi)
Russell, Robert 1855 wb-2-82# (Ge)
Russell, Robert Allison 1861 wb-#64 (Wa)
Russell, Sarah L. 1855 wb-h-424 (Hu)
Russell, Thomas 1824 wb-8-319 (D)
Russell, Thomas C. 1855 wb-h-459 (Hu)
Russell, W. B. 1859 wb-3-20 (Me)
Russell, William 1817 wb-A-183 (Li)
Russell, William 1824 wb-#53 (Wl)
Russell, William 1826 wb-#24 (Wa)

Russell, William 1834 wb-5-309 (K)
Russell, William C. 1823 wb-A-324 (Li)
Russell, William E. 1817 wb-A-195 (Li)
Russell, Wyatt 1841 wb-b-283 (Hd)
Russom, John 1851 wb-1-247 (Bo)
Rust, Azarilla 1841 wb-z-292 (Mu)
Rust, B. F. 1859 wb-k-15 (O)
Rust, Benedict 1852 wb-3-114 (W)
Rust, David B. 1846 wb-a2-412 (Mu)
Rust, David P. 1839 wb-y-346 (Mu)
Rust, Lemuel 1843 wb-a-121 (Cr)
Ruth, Mary A. (Mrs.) 1847 wb-2-4 (Sh)
Rutherford, Absalom 1841 wb-7-253 (K)
Rutherford, Absalom 1850 wb-10-329 (K)
Rutherford, Archibald 1824 wb-1-0 (Sm)
Rutherford, C. 1856 wb-1C-324 (A)
Rutherford, Calvin M. 1858 wb-#152 (Mc)
Rutherford, David 1826 wb-4-162 (K)
Rutherford, Elliot 1849 148-1-282 (Ge)
Rutherford, George S. 1848 wb-4-260 (Hr)
Rutherford, Griffith 1804? wb-1-87 (Sn)
Rutherford, Griffith W. 1846 wb-#152 (Wl)
Rutherford, James 1838 wb-2-230 (Sn)
Rutherford, James 1849 wb-#152 (Mc)
Rutherford, John 1817 wb-2-336 (K)
Rutherford, John 1828 wb-4-304 (K)
Rutherford, John 1838 wb-6-243 (K)
Rutherford, John R. 1839 wb-#126 (Wl)
Rutherford, John R. 1840 wb-#127 (Wl)
Rutherford, Joseph 1855 wb-e-537 (Ro)
Rutherford, Julius 1831 wb-1A-54 (A)
Rutherford, Julius 1835 wb-1A-132 (A)
Rutherford, L. Loyd 1851 wb-1B-224 (A)
Rutherford, Mary 1859 wb-13-198 (K)
Rutherford, Saml. 1849 wb-4-525 (Hr)
Rutherford, Samuel 1839 wb-2-126 (Hr)
Rutherford, William 1834 wb-5-291 (K)
Rutland, Blake 1815 wb-#16 (Wl)
Rutland, Jackson 1840 wb-e-2 (St)
Rutland, Martha 1831 wb-#87 (Wl)
Rutland, Rayford 1826 wb-b-80 (St)
Rutland, Rutherford 1856 wb-#122 (Wl)
Rutland, Willie N. 1853 wb-2-146 (Sh)
Rutledge, Bethena 1860 ib-2-186 (Wy)
Rutledge, Bethena R. 1860 ib-2-198 (Wy)
Rutledge, Henry M. 1844 wb-13-83 (D)
Rutledge, Henry M. 1844 wd-13-14 (D)
Rutledge, Isaac 1837 wb-1-126 (Li)
Rutledge, John 1828 wb-a-349 (Wh)
Rutledge, John 1833 wb-1-95 (Li)
Rutledge, John 1845 rb-13-416 (Ru)

Rutledge, John R. 1850 wb-#172 (Wl)
Rutledge, Marcia H. 1854 rb-16-701 (Ru)
Rutledge, Robert 1819 wb-3-26 (Wi)
Rutledge, Robert 1843 wb-1-96 (Su)
Rutledge, Robert 1853 wb-1-887 (Su)
Rutledge, Samuel J. 1855 ib-1-357 (Wy)
Rutledge, Thomas 1831 wb-#227 (Mu)
Rutledge, William 1807 wb-1-161 (Wi)
Rutledge, William 1809 Wb-1-55 (Wi)
Rutledge, William 1835 wb-1-198 (Hy)
Rutledge, William 1855 ib-1-366 (Wy)
Ruyle, Henry 1790 wb-1-4 (Sn)
Ryals, Noah 1835 wb-1-121 (Li)
Ryan, Darby 1852 wb-15-438 (D)
Ryan, Darby 1852 wb-15-441 (D)
Ryan, Fleming 1858 lr (Sn)
Ryan, James 1845 wb-f-242 (St)
Ryan, James 1850 wb-m-122 (Mt)
Ryan, John 1826 wb-1-22# (Ge)
Ryan, John 1828 wb-6-392 (Rb)
Ryan, John W. 1856 wb-16-142 (Rb)
Ryan, Nicholas H. 1849 wb-14-238 (Rb)
Ryan, Richard 1839 wb-7-29 (Wi)
Rybourn, Washington 1803 rb-a-172 (Mt)
Rye, Absalom 1823 rb-d-485 (Mt)
Rye, Benjamin 1859 rb-p-283 (Mt)
Rye, Francis 1847 rb-k-638 (Mt)
Rye, Henry 1849 wb-#169 (Wl)
Rye, Solomon 1819 wb-a-33 (Di)
Rys, Benjamin 1823 rb-d-243 (Mt)
Ryver, Jacob 1851 wb-14-644 (D)

- S -

Saddler, James 1851 wb-15-42 (D)
Sadler, Burwell 1810 wb-4-118 (D)
Sadler, James M. 1851 wb-15-66 (D)
Sadler, Jane 1849 wb-#169 (Wl)
Sadler, Jeremiah 1852 wb-15-315 (D)
Sadler, Lucy 1833 wb-10-238 (D)
Sadler, Mary 1833 wb-10-238 (D)
Sadler, Thomas 1815 wb-#17 (Wl)
Sadler, Thomas 1849 wb-14-287 (D)
Sadler, William B. 1859 lr (Sn)
Saffarans, Catharine 1856 wb-17-91 (D)
Saffarans, David 1853 wb-15-573 (D)
Saffle, Amos 1860 wb-A-163 (Ca)
Sage, John 1827 rb-7-349 (Ru)
Sain, George M. 1842 wb-1-515 (W)
Sain, Wm. 1849 wb-d-187 (G)
Sains, Noah 1854 rb-17-158 (Ru)

Saint John, Nathaniel 1841 wb-#153 (Mc)
Sale, H. B. 1854 ib-H-159 (F)
Sale, H. W. 1855 ib-h-387 (F)
Sale, Henry W. 1846 wb-a-275 (F)
Sale, Henry W. 1858 gs-1-195 (F)
Sale, James H. 1855 wb-n-619 (Mt)
Sale, James H. 1855 wb-n-622 (Mt)
Salisburry, M. L. 1858 wb-c-271 (L)
Salisburry, Micheal 1858 wb-c-261 (L)
Salisbury, James 1855 wb-c-11 (L)
Salisbury, Mary Ann (Mrs) 1857 wb-c-110 (L)
Salisbury, William 1807 wb-3-177 (D)
Sallee, William 1857 rb-o-342 (Mt)
Sallee, Wm. F. 1855 wb-n-525 (Mt)
Saller, Widon H. 1855 wb-n-502 (Mt)
Sallie, Samuel K. 1852 wb-g-455 (Hn)
Salliers, Western 1830 wb-3-118 (Je)
Sammons, James J. 1840 wb-b-305 (G)
Sammons, Sally 1844 wb-8-158 (Wi)
Sample, Hiram 1855 wb-j-80 (O)
Sample, James 1816 wb-2-233 (Wi)
Sample, Jared 1858 lr (Sn)
Sample, John 1817 wb-2-313 (Wi)
Sample, Matthew 1817 wb-A-191 (Li)
Sample, Moses 1824 wb-2-558 (Je)
Sample, Robert 1823 wb-8-268 (D)
Sample, William 1816 wb-2-219 (Wi)
Sampson, Richard 1818 wb-2-389 (Wi)
Sampson, Samuel 1846 wb-#153 (Mc)
Samson, Jesse 1815 wb-1-0 (Sm)
Samuel, Archibald 1841 wb-11-113 (Rb)
Samuel, Edwin 1834 rb-g-64 (Mt)
Samuel, Edwin G. 1836 rb-g-395 (Mt)
Samuel, James 1846 wb-12-585 (Rb)
Samuel, Richard 1851 wb-14-590 (D)
Samuels, S. H. 1857 wb-3e-38 (Sh)
Sandedge, Richard 1829 wb-A-79 (Ca)
Sanderlin, B. C. 1852 wb-2-137 (Sh)
Sanderlin, John 1853 wb-e-22 (Hy)
Sanderlin, Wilson 1852 wb-2-126 (Sh)
Sanders, Andrew 1822 wb-3-453 (Rb)
Sanders, B. H. 1848 wb-f-491 (St)
Sanders, B. H. 1858 wb-h-462 (St)
Sanders, Clemuel (Clement?) 1848
   wb-#153 (Mc)
Sanders, Cornelious 1854 rb-16-799 (Ru)
Sanders, Daniel 1857 wb-a-24 (Ce)
Sanders, Dollarson 1853 rb-16-672 (Ru)
Sanders, Donelson 1854 rb-16-719 (Ru)
Sanders, Edward 1819 wb-1-300 (Sn)
Sanders, Edward F. 1847 rb-14-174 (Ru)

Sanders, Elihu 1850 ib-1-114 (Ca)
Sanders, Ezekiel 1863 wb-2-352 (Li)
Sanders, Frederick 1801 wb-#8 (Wa)
Sanders, Harman T. 1847 wb-b-146 (Mu)
Sanders, Harmon? L.? 1846 wb-a2-364 (Mu)
Sanders, Harris 1847 wb-13-209 (Rb)
Sanders, Isaac 1845 5-3-43 (Cl)
Sanders, Isaac 1852 wb-b-167 (L)
Sanders, Isaac 1860 rb-20-436 (Ru)
Sanders, J. J. 1845 rb-13-438 (Ru)
Sanders, James 1845 wb-5-8 (Ma)
Sanders, James 1855 lr (Sn)
Sanders, James 1856 wb-h-544 (Hu)
Sanders, Jane 1813 wb-#9 (Mu)
Sanders, Joel 1857 wb-6-451 (Ma)
Sanders, Joel B. 1834 wb-1-19 (Sh)
Sanders, Joel B. 1835 wb-1-22 (Sh)
Sanders, John 1792 wb-1-79 (Je)
Sanders, John 1820 wb-7-370 (D)
Sanders, John 1827 wb-#78 (Wl)
Sanders, John 1829 rb-8-42 (Ru)
Sanders, John 1829 wb-4-377 (K)
Sanders, John 1834 wb-9-27 (Rb)
Sanders, John 1845 wb-c-241 (G)
Sanders, John 1849 wb-a-201 (Di)
Sanders, John 1852 mr-2-445 (Be)
Sanders, John 1854 wb-h-278 (Hu)
Sanders, John 1856 ib-2-539 (Cl)
Sanders, John 1859 wb-1-393 (Fr)
Sanders, John Q. A. 1858 wb-3e-77 (Sh)
Sanders, Joseph 1823 wb-#65 (Mu)
Sanders, Levi L. 1855 rb-17-378 (Ru)
Sanders, Levi S. 1854 rb-17-191 (Ru)
Sanders, Lewis 1852 wb-d-392 (G)
Sanders, Luke 1810 wb-1-364 (Rb)
Sanders, Mary 1831 wb-7-373 (Rb)
Sanders, Mary 1856 ib-2-232 (Cl)
Sanders, Mary 1858 lr (Sn)
Sanders, Mary L. 1860 wb-7-62 (Ma)
Sanders, Mirram L. 1846 wb-1-127 (Sh)
Sanders, Philip 1823 rb-5-316 (Ru)
Sanders, Philip 1840 rb-10-492 (Ru)
Sanders, R. 1861 wb-a-222 (Ce)
Sanders, R. D. 1858 rb-19-154 (Ru)
Sanders, Rebecca 1853 wb-b-214 (L)
Sanders, Richard 1835 wb-#106 (Wl)
Sanders, Richard D. 1836 wb-#113 (Wl)
Sanders, Richard D. 1858 rb-19-269 (Ru)
Sanders, Robert 1835 wb-#109 (Wl)
Sanders, Robert 1852 wb-15-210 (Rb)
Sanders, Robert 1852 wb-15-212 (Rb)

Sanders, Robert 1855 rb-17-583 (Ru)
Sanders, Robert 1858 as-c-498 (Di)
Sanders, Samuel 1843 wb-4-105 (Ma)
Sanders, Sterlin 1845 5-3-96 (Cl)
Sanders, Thomas 1807 rb-2-39 (Ru)
Sanders, Thomas 1812 wb-4-200 (D)
Sanders, Thomas 1839 wb-3-2 (Ma)
Sanders, Thomas 1845 rb-13-388 (Ru)
Sanders, Thomas 1855 wb#24 (Gu)
Sanders, Thomas F. 1851 wb-2-107 (Sh)
Sanders, Thomas W. 1860 rb-20-445 (Ru)
Sanders, William 1827 wb-#153 (Mc)
Sanders, William 1829 lr (Sn)
Sanders, William 1831 wb-7-392 (Rb)
Sanders, William 1853 wb-15-275 (Rb)
Sanders, William 1861 wb-13-463 (K)
Sanders?, James 1828? wb-1-36 (Hy)
Sanderson, Benjamin 1813 rb-b-93 (Mt)
Sanderson, Edward 1826 wb-9-64 (D)
Sanderson, Elizabeth 1837 wb-1-33 (Sh)
Sanderson, Jacob 1841 as-a-508 (Di)
Sanderson, James 1833 wb-1-569 (Ma)
Sanderson, Jesse 1813 rb-b-94 (Mt)
Sanderson, John 1847 wb-4-150 (Hr)
Sanderson, Nancy 1851 rb-4-246 (Mu)
Sanderson, Nathaniel 1825 wb-a-50 (G)
Sanderson, Robert 1814 rb-b-220 (Mt)
Sanderson, Robert 1825 wb-8-448 (D)
Sanderson, Thomas 1815 rb-b-302 (Mt)
Sanderson, Thomas 1817 wb-1-0 (Sm)
Sanderson, Thomas 1819 wb-#33 (Wl)
Sanderson, Wade 1849 wb-#180 (Wl)
Sanderson, William 1808 wb-3-211 (D)
Sanderson, William 1818 wb-#27 (Wl)
Sandford, James T. 1823 wb-#47 (Mu)
Sandford, James T. 1834 wb-x-196 (Mu)
Sandford, Joseph 1817 wb-#31 (Mu)
Sandford, Robert 1818 wb-2-409 (Wi)
Sandford, William 1855 wb-f-66 (Mu)
Sandford, Wineford 1831 wb-#232 (Mu)
Sandford, Wineford 1845 wb-a2-150 (Mu)
Sandford, Young S. 1838 wb-1-144 (La)
Sandhouse, Lambert 1857 wb-17-196 (D)
Sandifer, Richard 1842 wb-a-63 (Ms)
Sandlin, James 1833 wb-1-111 (Fr)
Sandlin, Randolph 1859 wb-b-47 (Dk)
Sandridge, Catharine 1850 wb-1-278 (Fr)
Sands, Robert 1847 148-1-189 (Ge)
Sands, Samuel W. 1823 wb-#60 (Wl)
Sands, William 1819 wb-#36 (Wl)
Sandy, William 1841 wb-12-127* (D)

Sanford, James 1845 wb-8-327 (Wi)
Sanford, James 1853 wb-5-134 (Ma)
Sanford, Jesse 1854 ib-1-299 (Wy)
Sanford, Margaret 1842 wb-#136 (Wl)
Sanford, Reuben 1846 wb-8-494 (Wi)
Sanford, Robert H. M. 1828 wb-#77 (Wl)
Sanford, Robert W. 1861 wb-a-311 (T)
Sanford, Stephen 1861 wb-b*-17 (O)
Sangster, John 1858 wb-e-104 (Hy)
Sansom, Dorrel N. (Dr.) 1821 wb-#48 (Mu)
Sansom, Dorrel N. 1834 wb-x-192 (Mu)
Santee, Michael 1810 wb-4-102 (D)
Sappington, Elizabeth 1840 wb-7-290 (Wi)
Sappington, Francis B. 1800 wb-2-178 (D)
Sappington, Francis B. 1818 wb-7-254 (D)
Sappington, Mark B. 1795 wb-2-28 (D)
Sargent, James 1825 wb-1-61 (Fr)
Sarrett, John 1834? mr-2-58 (Be)
Sarrett, John 1839 wb-e-166 (Hu)
Sarrett, N. H. 1861 wb-1-379 (Be)
Sarrett, William M. 1860 wb-1-327 (Be)
Sartain, James 1832 wb-1-108 (Fr)
Sartin?, Isaac 1831? wb-1A-45 (A)
Sasseen, R. 1826 wb-3-1 (Je)
Sasseen, Randolph 1838 wb-3-498 (Je)
Sasseen, Richard 1827 wb-2-572 (Je)
Sasser, J. T. 1854 ib-H-131 (F)
Sasser, Stephen 1827 wb-4-160 (Wi)
Sathern, Lee 1848 5-3-339 (Cl)
Satterfield, Alvis 1852 wb-4-502 (Mu)
Satterfield, Elizabeth 1834 wb-1-90 (Gr)
Satterfield, Green B. 1848 33-3-72 (Gr)
Satterfield, Jeremiah 1838 wb-b-88 (Hd)
Satterfield, John 1852 wb-10-211 (Wi)
Satterfield, Larry 1838 wb-d-174 (St)
Satterfield, Madison 1858 wb-f-153 (Mu)
Satterfield, Moses 1823 wb-A-298 (Li)
Satterfield, Nancy 1852 wb-5-94 (Je)
Satterfield, Unicy 1854 wb-5-342 (Je)
Satterlee, John 1834 wb-x-305 (Mu)
Satterwhite, Drucilla 1828 wb-1-68 (Hr)
Sauk, John K. 1848 ib-1-26 (Ca)
Saunders, Chloe 1850 lr (Sn)
Saunders, Edward 1822 wb-3-460 (Rb)
Saunders, Elihu 1844 rb-13-13 (Ru)
Saunders, Elizabeth 1847 wb-13-113 (Rb)
Saunders, Ferdinand L. 1857 wb-1-76 (Dy)
Saunders, Francis 1821 wb-7-510 (D)
Saunders, Francis 1826 wb-1-64 (Ma)
Saunders, Hubbard 1829 lr (Sn)
Saunders, J. James 1846 rb-13-640 (Ru)

Saunders, James 1825 lr (Sn)
Saunders, James 1844 rb-12-435 (Ru)
Saunders, John H. 1857 wb-h-103 (Hn)
Saunders, John 1807 wb-1-432 (Hw)
Saunders, John W. 1842 wb-12-335* (D)
Saunders, Lavisa 1850 wb-#176 (Wl)
Saunders, Mary 1849 rb-15-37 (Ru)
Saunders, T. W. 1859 rb-20-153 (Ru)
Saunders, William 1803 wb-1-0 (Sm)
Saunders, William 1847 wb-14-22 (D)
Saunders, William B. 1859 wb-#129 (Wl)
Saunders, William L. 1852 ib-1-174 (Wy)
Savage, A. M. 1858 39-2-225 (Dk)
Savage, George E. 1854 wb-16-313 (D)
Savage, James 1857 wb-17-378 (D)
Savage, Jeremiah 1852 wb-3-70 (Gr)
Savage, Jessee 1849 wb-3-1 (W)
Savage, Kendal 1835 wb-b-158 (Wh)
Savage, Robert 1854 wb-15-674 (Rb)
Savage, Starling 1854 wb#22 (Gu)
Savage, Sterling 1845 wb-2-70 (W)
Savage, Thomas 1830 wb-7-288 (Rb)
Savage, William 1857 ib-2-508 (Cl)
Sawyer, Dempsey 1860 wb-13-341 (Wi)
Sawyer, James 1836 wb-9-293 (Rb)
Sawyer, John 1854 wb-n-414 (Mt)
Sawyer, Rebecca 1851 wb-m-351 (Mt)
Sawyers, Betsy 1818 wb-#34 (Mu)
Sawyers, David 1820 wb-A-360 (Li)
Sawyers, Elijah 1824 wb-a-191 (Wh)
Sawyers, Elizabeth 1824 wb-A-380 (Li)
Sawyers, Hannah 1809 wb-1-282 (K)
Sawyers, James 1853 wb-15-415 (Rb)
Sawyers, James H. 1858 wb-13-38 (K)
Sawyers, John 1798 wb-1-67 (K)
Sawyers, John 1832 wb-5-103 (K)
Sawyers, John 1851 wb-11-146 (K)
Sawyers, Josiah 1847 wb-9-380 (K)
Sawyers, Nancy J. 1857 wb-12-382 (K)
Sawyers, Robert 1840 rb-h-377 (Mt)
Sayers, Robert A. 1856 wb-12-53 (Wi)
Sayle, William 1851 wb-14-487 (Rb)
Saylers, Thomas 1853 wb-d-152 (Wh)
Sayles, James S. 1844 mr-2-129 (Be)
Saylor, Godfrey 1848 wb-2-68# (Ge)
Saylor, Godfrey 1861 wb-#64 (Wa)
Saylor, Jacob 1853 148-1-465 (Ge)
Saylor, John 1854 wb-#56 (Wa)
Saylor, Rebecca 1858 wb-2-87# (Ge)
Sayre, Foster 1820 wb-7-453 (D)
Scales, Absalom 1832 wb-5-161 (Wi)

Scales, Absalom 1835 wb-6-46 (Wi)
Scales, Charlotte G. 1860 wb-13-300 (Wi)
Scales, Daniel 1836 wb-6-146 (Wi)
Scales, Daniel 1840 wb-7-263 (Wi)
Scales, Elizabeth 1847 wb-#161 (Wl)
Scales, Fanny 1827 wb-4-180 (Wi)
Scales, Henry 1845 wb-13-351 (D)
Scales, James 1848 wb-a-343 (F)
Scales, James T. 1855 wb-16-519 (D)
Scales, Joab 1848 wb-9-72 (Wi)
Scales, John 1859 wb-13-140 (Wi)
Scales, John M. 1839 wb-7-142 (Wi)
Scales, John M. 1839 wb-7-210 (Wi)
Scales, John M. 1839 wb-7-212 (Wi)
Scales, John M. 1840 wb-7-218 (Wi)
Scales, Joseph 1833 wb-10-261 (D)
Scales, Joseph H. 1856 wb-12-273 (Wi)
Scales, Nancy 1838 wb-6-494 (Wi)
Scales, Nicholas H. 1849 wb-14-457 (D)
Scales, Noah 1860 wb-13-236 (Wi)
Scales, Peter 1857 wb-4-97 (La)
Scales, Robert 1853 wb-16-115 (D)
Scales, Robert 1860 wb-13-299 (Wi)
Scales, Samuel 1837 wb-6-305 (Wi)
Scales, Sarah P. 1853 wb-16-127 (D)
Scales, William G. 1841 wb-7-397 (Wi)
Scales, William G. 1851 wb-9-674 (Wi)
Scalis, Joseph 1843 wb-1-90 (Sh)
Scarborough, Henderson B. 1854 wb-h-13 (St)
Scarborough, Henderson B. 1854 wb-h-25 (St)
Scarborough, James sr. 1848 wb-f-480 (St)
Scarborough, John 1824 wb-3-325 (St)
Scarborough, John 1837 wb-d-121 (St)
Scarborough, Robert 1846 wb-b-198 (We)
Scarborough, Theodore S. 1840 wb-e-5 (St)
Scarborough, Thomas 1840 wb-e-8 (St)
Scarborough, W. P. 1849 wb-g-112 (St)
Scarborough, Whitmell P. 1849 wb-g-175 (St)
Scarborough, William 1834 wb-1A-71 (A)
Scarborough, Wm. W. 1857 wb-h-304 (St)
Scarbrough, A. sr. 1852 wb-g-491 (Hn)
Scarbrough, Alexander 1852 wb-g-643 (Hn)
Scarbrough, David 1829 wb-c-8 (St)
Scarbrough, James 1853 wb-e-418 (Ro)
Scarbrough, John 1838 wb-c-21 (Ro)
Scarbrough, Naoma 1851 wb-b-308 (We)
Scarbrough, T. S. 1852 wb-xx-275 (St)
Scarbrough, William sr. 1830 wb-1A-20 (A)
Scarce, David 1854 rb-17-154 (Ru)
Scates, Albert N. 1840 wb-a-87 (Cr)
Scesson?, William 1857 ib-1-418 (Ca)

Scroggs, Miles F. 1851 148-1-360 (Ge)
Scruggs, Amelia 1851 wb-1B-201 (A)
Scruggs, Drury 1833 lr (Sn)
Scruggs, Drury 1850 wb-9-409 (Wi)
Scruggs, Edward 1847 wb-8-587 (Wi)
Scruggs, Edward 1859 wb-18-63 (D)
Scruggs, Elizabeth 1859 wb-#129 (Wl)
Scruggs, Emelia 1849 wb-1B-98 (A)
Scruggs, Frederick 1808 as-1-207 (Ge)
Scruggs, Gross 1828 wb-#108 (Wl)
Scruggs, James 1852 wb-2-114 (Sh)
Scruggs, James 1852 wb-5-95 (Je)
Scruggs, John 1831 wb-1A-46 (A)
Scruggs, John 1851 wb-10-90 (Wi)
Scruggs, John 1861 wb-1D-6 (A)
Scruggs, John B. 1845 wb-8-228 (Wi)
Scruggs, John H. 1855 wb-11-440 (Wi)
Scruggs, Keziah 1829 wb-4-381 (Wi)
Scruggs, Langhorn 1841 wb-12-106* (D)
Scruggs, R. M. 1850 33-3-198 (Gr)
Scruggs, Richard 1859 wb-2-89# (Ge)
Scruggs, Robert 1842 wb-1-86 (Sh)
Scruggs, Rufus M. 1840 wb-5-82 (Gr)
Scruggs, Thomas 1853 wb-1C-79 (A)
Scruggs, Thos. 1855 wb-1C-220 (A)
Scruggs, William 1859 wb-13-67 (Wi)
Scurlock, Dudly 1833 wb-#101 (Wl)
Seabolt, Andrew 1824 wb-4-31 (K)
Seaborn, Isaac R. 1842 wb-#137 (Wl)
Seaborn, John H. 1841 wb-12-235* (D)
Seaborne, John H. 1852 wb-15-255 (D)
Seabourn, Benjamin 1813 wb-4-245 (D)
Seal, Anthony 1822 wb-2-372 (Je)
Seal, Anthony 1824 wb-1-54 (Fr)
Seal, Charles 1832 wb-8-104 (Rb)
Seal, Willis 1819 wb-3-108 (K)
Seal, Zebedee 1839 wb-b-354 (Wh)
Seale, Agness 1851 wb-14-548 (Rb)
Seale, Rebecca 1844 wb-1-129 (Me)
Sealey, William 1846 wb-a2-402 (Mu)
Seals, Malinda 1848 wb-g-87 (Hu)
Seals, Palatira 1825 as-A-117 (Di)
Seals, Palatira 1842 as-b-98 (Di)
Seals, William J. 1847 wb-g-3 (Hu)
Seamands, Jonathan 1834 wb-3-320 (Je)
Searcy, Anderson 1832 rb-8-419 (Ru)
Searcy, Anderson 1845 rb-13-167 (Ru)
Searcy, Bennet 1818 rb-b-508 (Mt)
Searcy, Francis B. 1839 rb-10-312 (Ru)
Searcy, James D. 1853 wb-7-0 (Sm)
Searcy, John W. 1844 rb-12-430 (Ru)

Searcy, Lafayette M. 1852 rb-16-279 (Ru)
Searcy, M. L. 1852 rb-16-240 (Ru)
Searcy, Reuben 1862 wb-#136 (Wl)
Searcy, Richard 1804 rb-2-3 (Ru)
Searcy, Robert 1820 wb-7-470 (D)
Searcy, Robert E. 1823 wb-8-172 (D)
Searcy, Robert E. 1834 wb-10-308 (D)
Searcy, Robert W. 1850 rb-15-558 (Ru)
Searcy, Sarah 1842 wb-12-313* (D)
Searcy, W. M. 1856 rb-18-23 (Ru)
Searcy, W. W. 1856 rb-19-224 (Ru)
Searcy, William 1858 wb-#126 (Wl)
Searcy, William W. 1846 rb-13-496 (Ru)
Seargent, Tubal 1849 wb-14-190 (Rb)
Searight, George 1847 wb-8-604 (Wi)
Searight, Marcus 1860 wb-13-376 (Wi)
Sears, Andrew 1842 rb-i-392 (Mt)
Sears, George W. 1842 wb-f-94 (Hn)
Sears, Green H. 1847 wb-14-60 (D)
Sears, James 1857 wb-h-123 (Hn)
Sears, Washington 1842 wb-f-91 (Hn)
Sease, David 1852 rb-16-240 (Ru)
Seat, Hartwell 1827 wb-9-135 (D)
Seat, Herod 1824 wb-#52 (Wl)
Seat, John 1844 wb-12-80 (Rb)
Seat, Margaret 1823 rb-5-337 (Ru)
Seat, Nathl. 1802 wb-2-268 (D)
Seat, William B. 1854 wb-e-195 (G)
Seat, William P. 1853 wb-e-90 (G)
Seat, Wm. P. 1857 wb-f-48 (G)
Seates, William J. 1853 wb-h-114 (Hu)
Seaton, A. K. 1849 wb-4-559 (Hr)
Seaton, George 1846 wb-4-58 (Hr)
Seaton, James 1846 wb-4-97 (Hr)
Seaton, James 1852 wb-11-317 (K)
Seaton, James 1861 wb-2-334 (Li)
Seaton, William B. 1839 wb-3-13 (Ma)
Seaton, William M. 1841 wb-3-374 (Ma)
Seaton, Wm. 1842 wb-3-552 (Ma)
Seats, Isham 1845 wb-f-268 (St)
Seats, Joseph 1843 wb-11-532 (Rb)
Seats, Thomas 1860 wb-i-214 (St)
Seats, Thomas H. 1860 wb-i-228 (St)
Seats?, Peggy 1826 rb-6-215 (Ru)
Seawell, John 1801 wb-1-52 (Sn)
Seawell, Joseph 1824 wb-#52 (Wl)
Seawell, Joseph N. 1825 wb-#58 (Wl)
Seawell, Martha L. 1851 lr (Sn)
Seawell, Mary 1832 lr (Sn)
Seawell, Thomas 1825 lr (Sn)
Seawell, Thomas B. 1847 lr (Sn)

Seawell, William 1846 wb-#152 (Wl)
Seawright, Alexander 1854 wb-g-603 (Hn)
Seawright, John L. 1852 wb-g-438 (Hn)
Seay, Elizabeth W. 1836 wb-6-225 (Wi)
Seay, James W. 1828 wb-#76 (Wl)
Seay, John (Sr.) 1830 wb-#88 (Wl)
Seay, John 1812 wb-1-276 (Wi)
Seay, John 1833 wb-#98 (Wl)
Seay, Lewis 1849 wb-d-403 (Hd)
Sebastian, John W. 1846 wb-1-303 (Li)
Sebert, Thomas B. 1848 wb-f-127+ (O)
Seck, Simeon 1846 wb-13-400 (D)
Secrest, Jacob 1835 wb-#4 (Mo)
Secrest, John 1836 wb-6-124 (Wi)
Secrest, John 1847 wb-9-17 (Wi)
Secrest, Tyre 1850 wb-4-132 (Mu)
Sedberry, William 1856 wb-f-96 (Mu)
Sedwick, Solomon 1839 wb-1-192 (We)
Seet, William J. 1843 wb-e-606 (Hu)
Seet, William J. 1843 wb-e-608 (Hu)
Segraves, Kitchen (Kinchen) 1859 wb-4-39 (La)
Segraves, Thomas 1815 wb-#12 (Mu)
Sehorn, John 1831 wb-3-151 (Je)
Sehorne, James 1803 wb-#9 (Wa)
Seiber, Joseph 1858 wb-1C-440 (A)
Seibert, George 1859 wb-17-609 (D)
Seignor, John 1855 wb-2-80# (Ge)
Seitze, Thomas 1834 wb-1-86 (W)
Self, Elizabeth 1855 148-1-514 (Ge)
Self, Samuel 1850 wb-g-300 (Hu)
Self, Thomas 1851 wb-2-73# (Ge)
Selgreaves, Joseph A. 1792 wb-1-247 (D)
Sellar, Mathew 1861 wb-b-84 (Dk)
Sellars, A. J. 1841 wb-#133 (Wl)
Sellars, Alford 1842 wb-#142 (Wl)
Sellars, Alvis 1850 wb-#173 (Wl)
Sellars, Andrew J. 1846 wb-#160 (Wl)
Sellars, Francis M. 1853 wb-#116 (Wl)
Sellars, Isaiah 1841 wb-c-259 (Ro)
Sellars, James 1843 wb-5-247 (Gr)
Sellars, James B. 1854 wb-#113 (Wl)
Sellars, John 1825? wb-#149 (Mu)
Sellars, John C. 1855 wb-11-488 (Wi)
Sellars, Jordin 1847 wb-2-201 (W)
Sellars, Joseph 1849 wb-4-559 (Hr)
Sellars, Larkin 1858 wb-16-693 (Rb)
Sellars, Patience 1812 wb-#4 (Mu)
Sellars, Sarah 1838 wb-y-304 (Mu)
Sellers, Cain 1826 wb-b-13 (Ro)
Sellers, Flenie 1853 wb-3-202 (W)
Sellers, Flynn 1841 wb-1-396 (W)

Sellers, Henry 1840 wb-1-316 (W)
Sellers, Isaac 1848 wb-d-149 (G)
Sellers, John 1828 wb-1-46 (W)
Sellers, John 1853 wb-10-483 (Wi)
Sellers, Robert 1828? wb-#169 (Mu)
Sellers, Robert 1848 wb-d-125 (G)
Sellers, Samuel 1822 Ir (Sn)
Sellers, Samuel 1839 wb-3-540 (Je)
Sellers, William 1818? wb-#115 (Mu)
Selph, Mark 1845 wb-c-219 (G)
Selph, Peter 1859 wb-1-312 (Be)
Selvidge, George 1849 wb-#7 (Mo)
Selvidge, Jeremiah 1827 wb-b-14 (Ro)
Sensabaugh, David 1862 wb-1-456 (Hw)
Sensabaugh, Jacob 1841 wb-1-447 (Hw)
Sensing, M. G. 1853 as-c-221 (Di)
Sensing, McKindree Sensing 1852 wb-a-245 (Di)
Senter, E. 1854 wb-3-214 (Gr)
Senter, Elizabeth 1859 wb-3-552 (Gr)
Senter, Harriett T. 1848 33-3-77 (Gr)
Senter, James L. 1839 wb-#154 (Mc)
Senter, Joanna A. 1848. 33-3-77 (Gr)
Senter, Martin 1839 wb-#154 (Mc)
Senter, Nelson A. 1846 wb-5-467 (Gr)
Senter, Patsy 1851 Ir (Sn)
Senter, Stephen W. 1829 wb-2-337 (Gr)
Senter, William 1859 wb-f-239 (G)
Senter, William T. 1849 33-3-103 (Gr)
Serrett, Mary 1843 mr-2-69 (Be)
Sessam, W. 1858 ib-1-551 (Ca)
Sessoms, Benjamin W. 1854 wb-e-152 (G)
Sesson, Jesse 1855 ib-1-513 (Ca)
Settle, David 1859 wb-h-376 (Hn)
Settle, Edward 1839 wb-3-0 (Sm)
Settle, George W. 1854 mr-2-585 (Be)
Settle, Leroy B. 1861 wb-#134 (Wl)
Settle, Pendleton 1839 wb-d-399 (St)
Settle, William 1839 wb-#126 (Wl)
Settle, William 1845 wb-9-87 (K)
Settler, James W. 1826 wb-8-552 (D)
Seveir (sic), John 1816 wb-2-231 (K)
Sevier, James 1844 wb-#44 (Wa)
Sevier, Valentine 1799 lw (Ct)
Sevier, Valentine 1800 rb-a-114 (Mt)
Sevier, Valentine 1854 wb-2-78# (Ge)
Seward, David 1848 rb-14-246 (Ru)
Seward, John 1854 rb-17-275 (Ru)
Seward, John A. 1855 rb-17-551 (Ru)
Seward, Martha D. 1856 rb-18-189 (Ru)
Seward, Sarah P. 1849 rb-15-161 (Ru)
Sewel, Newton 1843(5?) wb-d-159 (Hd)

Sewell, Benjamin 1831 wb-b-16 (Wh)
Sewell, Benjamin 1847 ib-1-1 (Cl)
Sewell, Elizabeth 1826 wb-#155 (Mc)
Sewell, Ezekiel 1853 rb-16-379 (Ru)
Sewell, Wm. 1851 rb-15-588 (Ru)
Sexten, Henry 1838 wb-d-220* (Hn)
Sexten, James 1838 wb-d-180* (Hn)
Sexton, Anderson 1846 wb-f-362 (St)
Sexton, Britton 1848 wb-f-502 (St)
Sexton, Caroline 1855 wb-h-119 (St)
Sexton, Linfield 1851 wb-d-331 (G)
Sexton, Margaret 1858 wb-h-450 (St)
Sexton, Miller 1859 wb-2-101# (Ge)
Sexton, Nancy 1853 wb-xx-167 (St)
Sexton, Ransom 1851 wb-4-558* (Hr)
Sexton, Ransom N. 1849 wb-4-433 (Hr)
Sexton, Susan 1857 wb-b-404 (We)
Sexton, Tempe 1840 wb-e-89 (Hn)
Sexton, Tilman 1847 wb-f-429 (St)
Sexton, William 1847 wb-f-420 (St)
Seymour, G. W. 1854 ib-H-112 (F)
Shackleford, J. C. 1849 wb-4-523 (Hr)
Shackleford, John C. 1846 wb-4-83 (Hr)
Shackly, Thomas 1853 wb-a-182 (V)
Shadd, Thomas A. 1852 wb-5-36 (Je)
Shadden, Elizabeth 1832 wb-3-194 (Je)
Shadden, William A. 1856 wb-#27 (Mo)
Shafer, Andrew 1820 wb-a-138 (Wh)
Shaffer, Richd. 1793? wb-1-295 (D)
Shain, Morris 1821 wb-8-14 (D)
Shall, Wm. 1859 as-c-563 (Di)
Shamblin, William 1851 wb-#155 (Mc)
Shamwell, Joseph 1838 rb-k-774 (Mt)
Shamwell, Marion 1858 rb-o-780 (Mt)
Shancle, John 1837 wb-d-305 (Hn)
Shane, Elenor 1842 wb-12-251* (D)
Shane, Morris 1823 wb-8-282 (D)
Shane, Morris 1836 wb-11-109 (D)
Shane, Moses 1838 wb-11-331 (D)
Shane, Penelope 1843 wb-12-433* (D)
Shane, Rebecca B. 1853 wb-15-482 (D)
Shankle, Mary 1835 wb-d-288 (Hn)
Shankle, Voluntine 1841 wb-e-232 (Hn)
Shanklin, Andrew 1811 wb-1-370 (Rb)
Shanklin, Cinthia 1862 wb-17-297 (Rb)
Shanklin, Robert C. 1857 wb-16-354 (Rb)
Shanklin, Robert D. 1846 rb-13-544 (Ru)
Shanks, Christian 1859 wb-1-458 (Hw)
Shanks, David 1859 wb-1-462 (Hw)
Shanks, Holden 1831 wb-1-129 (Bo)
Shanks, John 1855 wb-1-457 (Hw)

Shanks, Michael 1833 wb-1-442 (Hw)
Shanks, Robert B. 1860 wb-#130 (Wl)
Shanks, William 1804 wb-#2 (Wl)
Shanks, William 1850 148-1-328 (Ge)
Shanks, William 1862 wb-1-463 (Hw)
Shannaberry, George P. 1856 wb-12-224 (K)
Shannon, Avy 1838 wb-10-164 (Rb)
Shannon, David 1821 Wb-3-261 (Wi)
Shannon, David 1839 wb-7-71 (Wi)
Shannon, Elijah 1855 wb-#56 (Wa)
Shannon, George 1836 wb-6-235 (Wi)
Shannon, Henry 1841 wb-#145 (Wl)
Shannon, Henry 1845 wb-#158 (Wl)
Shannon, Hugh 1836 wb-9-245 (Rb)
Shannon, J. C. 1861 wb-19-17 (D)
Shannon, John 1823 wb-4-20 (Rb)
Shannon, John 1831 wb-#30 (Wa)
Shannon, John R. 1851 rb-4-249 (Mu)
Shannon, Joseph 1859 wb-3-564 (Gr)
Shannon, Joseph 1859 wb-4-19 (Gr)
Shannon, Joseph N. 1852 wb-5-153 (Je)
Shannon, Michael 1840 lr (Sn)
Shannon, Quinton 1830 lr (Gi)
Shannon, Rebecca 1837 wb-#119 (Wl)
Shannon, Robert 1815 wb-#17 (Wl)
Shannon, Robert 1833 wb-#102 (Wl)
Shannon, Robert Mc(Knight) W. 1828
    wb-4-306 (Wi)
Shannon, Robert Washington 1861
    wb-13-458 (Wi)
Shannon, Samuel 1811 wb-4-161 (D)
Shannon, Samuel 1834 wb-9-27 (Rb)
Shannon, _____ 1839 wb-b-163 (Hd)
Shapard, John M. 1857 wb-6-507 (Ma)
Shapard, John T. 1861 lr (Gi)
Shapard, Thomas 1840 wb-2-16? (Hy)
Sharber, Jehu 1845 rb-13-453 (Ru)
Sharber, John 1845 rb-13-225 (Ru)
Sharber, John E. 1860 rb-20-563 (Ru)
Share, Thos. 1854 wb-h-45 (St)
Sharlock, James H. 1850 wb-a-176 (Cr)
Sharp, Adison S. 1858 wb-#155 (Mc)
Sharp, Alford 1836 wb-2-104 (Ma)
Sharp, Allice R. 1850 wb-1-401 (Li)
Sharp, Anthony 1812 wb-2-1 (Wi)
Sharp, Aron sr. 1822 eb-1-118 (C)
Sharp, Benjamin F. 1855 wb-2-118 (Li)
Sharp, Bluford 1834 wb-#155 (Mc)
Sharp, Conrad 1826 eb-1-168 (C)
Sharp, Conrad 1826 eb-1-169 (C)
Sharp, D. H. 1856 wb-2-302 (Me)

Sharp, Daniel 1809 eb-1-6 (C)
Sharp, Ezekiel 1828 wb-#74 (Wl)
Sharp, George A. 1859 wb-f-279 (G)
Sharp, Henry 1848 ib-1-48 (Cl)
Sharp, Jacob 1812 eb-1-25 (C)
Sharp, Jacob 1843 wb-#155 (Mc)
Sharp, James B. 1824 wb-2-436 (Je)
Sharp, James M. 1856 wb-a-244 (T)
Sharp, John 1828 wb-b-2 (Ro)
Sharp, John 1830 wb-1A-3 (A)
Sharp, John 1840 wb-#3 (Mo)
Sharp, John 1852 6-2-92 (Le)
Sharp, John 1856 wb-1C-286 (A)
Sharp, John 1857 wb-1-406 (Su)
Sharp, John 1857 wb-12-432 (K)
Sharp, John M. 1860 wb-k-357 (O)
Sharp, Joseph 1827 eb-1-224 (C)
Sharp, Mary 1831 rb-f-259 (Mt)
Sharp, Mary 1850 rb-15-480 (Ru)
Sharp, Mary 1856 149-1-52 (Ge)
Sharp, Matthias 1796 wb-0-13 (K)
Sharp, Patterson 1849 wb-1-50 (Jo)
Sharp, Rachel 1824 rb-6-60 (Ru)
Sharp, Richard 1852 wb-1-308 (Fr)
Sharp, Robert 1793 wb-1-4 (K)
Sharp, Robert 1849 rb-15-159 (Ru)
Sharp, Samuel 1859 wb-13-181 (K)
Sharp, Thomas 1808 wb-1-189 (Wi)
Sharp, Turner 1851 wb-#156 (Mc)
Sharp, Walter B. 1835 wb-1-115 (Li)
Sharp, William 1838 wb-1-169 (Fr)
Sharp, William 1840 5-2-151 (Cl)
Sharp, William 1840 5-2-156 (Cl)
Sharp, William T. 1855 ib-h-286 (F)
Sharpe, Benjamin 1848 wb-14-247 (D)
Sharpe, Cyrus 1826 rb-6-301 (Ru)
Sharpe, James 1811 rb-2-114 (Ru)
Sharpe, John 1825 rb-6-89 (Ru)
Sharpe, Theophilus A. 1831 rb-8-251 (Ru)
Sharrenburger, Caspar 1854 wb-16-398 (D)
Shauer, Martin 1827 wb-1-439 (Hw)
Shaugh, Nancy 1850 wb-1-455 (Hw)
Shaver, Jacob 1850 ib-1-154 (Cl)
Shaver, John 1791 wb-1-17 (Sn)
Shaver, Michael 1793 wb-1-19 (Sn)
Shaver, Michael 1854 wb-h-229 (Hu)
Shaw, A. B. 1861 wb-3e-184 (Sh)
Shaw, Abner 1822 wb-#43 (Wl)
Shaw, Alexander 1826 wb-4-103 (Wi)
Shaw, Alsey 1852 wb-#178 (Wl)
Shaw, Andrew 1848 wb-a-133 (T)

Shaw, Charles J. 1854 ib-H-196 (F)
Shaw, Daniel 1841 abl-1-241 (T)
Shaw, Daniel G. 1851 wb-g-451 (St)
Shaw, David 1803 as-1-27 (Ge)
Shaw, David 1848 wb-a-363 (F)
Shaw, David 1852 wb-xx-138 (St)
Shaw, E. H. 1847 wb-13-105 (Rb)
Shaw, Edmund B? 1848 wb-14-1 (Rb)
Shaw, Edmund W. 1846 wb-13-58 (Rb)
Shaw, Eliza 1848 wb-9-192 (Wi)
Shaw, Francis 1833 wb-1-131 (Bo)
Shaw, Gabriel 1807 wb-1-0 (Sm)
Shaw, H. W. 1848 wb-14-1 (Rb)
Shaw, Henry 1819 rb-c-206 (Mt)
Shaw, J. G. 1858 wb-17-425 (D)
Shaw, J. T. 1854 ib-H-135 (F)
Shaw, James 1823 wb-4-79 (Rb)
Shaw, James 1824 wb-4-208 (Rb)
Shaw, James 1837 wb-9-382 (Rb)
Shaw, James L. 1850 A-468-148 (Le)
Shaw, Jane 1819 wb-#116 (Mu)
Shaw, Jane 1824 wb-#78 (Mu)
Shaw, Jesse W. 1837 wb-#117 (Wl)
Shaw, John 1808 ib-1-230 (Ge)
Shaw, John 1808 wb-2-28# (Ge)
Shaw, John 1825 wb-5-38 (Rb)
Shaw, John 1841 wb-c-24 (Wh)
Shaw, John 1849 ib-1-20 (Wy)
Shaw, John 1851 wb-d-46 (Wh)
Shaw, John 1852 wb-3-116 (W)
Shaw, John A. 1839 wb-b-335 (Wh)
Shaw, John L. 1852 wb-3-134 (W)
Shaw, Leonard 1858 wb-i-31 (St)
Shaw, Levi 1826 wb-f-77 (Mu)
Shaw, Malcum 1852 wb-e-4 (Hy)
Shaw, Martha Ann 1848 wb-14-79 (Rb)
Shaw, Minor 1834 wb-b-34 (G)
Shaw, Nathaniel 1857 wb-12-408 (Wi)
Shaw, Robert 1831 lr (Sn)
Shaw, Samuel 1794 wb-#5 (Wa)
Shaw, Samuel 1807 wb-3-144 (D)
Shaw, Samuel 1818 wb-#78 (Mu)
Shaw, Samuel 1840 wb-#3 (Mo)
Shaw, Sarah 1835 wb-9-120 (Rb)
Shaw, Sarah 1847 wb-1-333 (Li)
Shaw, Sarah 1850 wb-14-402 (Rb)
Shaw, Simpson 1847 wb-d-94 (G)
Shaw, Simpson H. 1847 wb-d-88 (G)
Shaw, Temperance 1851 wb-d-318 (G)
Shaw, Theo? 1848 wb-4-240 (Hr)
Shaw, Thomas 1824 wb-4-278 (Rb)

Shaw, Thomas 1839 wb-10-402 (Rb)
Shaw, Thomas 1852 wb-xx-162 (St)
Shaw, Timothy 1830 wb-1-132 (Hr)
Shaw, Wiley B. 1857 gs-1-32 (F)
Shaw, William 1826 wb-#99 (Wl)
Shaw, William 1835 wb-10-525 (D)
Shaw, William J. 1844 wb-a-113 (T)
Shaw, Willie C. 1846 wb-4-74a (Hr)
Shaw, Wm. C. 1859 gs-1-475 (F)
Shaw, Zachariah 1836 wb-b-118 (G)
Shaw, Zechariah 1858 wb-h-521 (St)
Shawley, Luke 1792 wb-1-23# (Ge)
Shealds, William 1792 wb-#4 (Wa)
Sheals, James 1853 as-b-132 (Ms)
Shearin, Jarotte 1838 wb-1-435 (Hy)
Shearin, Jarret 1827 wb-1-31 (Hy)
Shearman, George W. 1844 wb-d-255 (O)
Shearman, Hetty 1817 wb-#32 (Mu)
Shearon, Aaron 1825 wb-#58 (Wl)
Shearon, Thomas W. 1854 wb-16-416 (D)
Shearron, Thomas 1854 wb-n-250 (Mt)
Shearwood, Hugh 1829 rb-7-306 (Ru)
Sheddan, Mary E. 1865 wb-#156 (Mc)
Shee, Godfort 1857 wb-17-198 (D)
Sheed, James 1856 wb-0-143 (Cf)
Sheegog, John 1852 wb-4-434 (Mu)
Sheehan, David 1861 wb-5-112 (Hr)
Sheeks, David 1837 wb-a-261 (O)
Sheeks, David 1837 wb-a-270 (O)
Sheeks, Jesse 1835 wb-a-38 (O)
Sheets, Jacob 1849 wb-#9 (Mo)
Sheets, John 1861 wb-#18 (Mo)
Sheets, Joseph 1859 wb-2-89# (Ge)
Sheffey, Lawrence B. 1856 lr (Gi)
Sheffield, Samuel T. 1854 ib-h-86 (F)
Shegog, James 1853 wb-10-408 (Wi)
Shehane, John F. 1857 as-c-46 (Ms)
Sheid, William 1840 wb-0-16 (Cf)
Sheilds, John 1848 wb-2-204 (Gr)
Shelburn, James 1813 wb-2-18 (Wi)
Shelburn, James 1839 wb-7-205 (Wi)
Shelburne, Parmelia 1858 wb-12-546 (Wi)
Shelby, David 1822 wb-1-352 (Sn)
Shelby, Evan 1784 wb-1-9 (D)
Shelby, Evan 1842 wb-c-302 (O)
Shelby, Even 1795 rb-a-5 (Mt)
Shelby, Hargey 1835 rb-g-237 (Mt)
Shelby, Harry 1843 rb-i-511 (Mt)
Shelby, Harvey 1837 rb-g-546 (Mt)
Shelby, Henry 1816 wb-#29 (Wl)
Shelby, Henry 1817 wb-#27 (Wl)

Shelby, Isaac 1813 rb-a-503 (Mt)
Shelby, Isaac 1835 rb-g-235 (Mt)
Shelby, Jenkin W. 1846 rb-k-119 (Mt)
Shelby, John (of Thomas) 1814 wb-#23 (Mu)
Shelby, John 1818 rb-b-384 (Mt)
Shelby, John 1823 rb-d-151 (Mt)
Shelby, John 1829 wb-3-0 (Sm)
Shelby, John 1860 wb-18-215 (D)
Shelby, John H. 1816 wb-#26 (Mu)
Shelby, Moses 1840 wb-A-19 (Ca)
Shelby, Moses 1844 wb-d-139 (Hd)
Shelby, Moses A. 1841 wb-b-346 (Hd)
Shelby, Sally 1821 rb-c-472 (Mt)
Shelby, Sally 1852 wb-15-464 (D)
Shelby, Smith 1855 wb-e-279 (G)
Shelby, Thomas 1816 rb-b-376 (Mt)
Shelby, Thomas 1822 wb-#64 (Mu)
Shelby, Thomas 1824 wb-#79 (Mu)
Shelby, Thomas P. 1817 rb-b-403 (Mt)
Shelby, William 1832 as-a-226 (Di)
Shelby, Wm. A. 1855 wb-2-179 (Sh)
Shelbys, Evan jr. 1806 rb-a-260 (Mt)
Sheldon, Malvina E. 1860 wb-3e-161 (Sh)
Shell, Andrew 1843 lw (Ct)
Shell, Christian 1820 wb-3-137 (K)
Shell, John 1854 wb-11-488 (K)
Shell, William H. 1847 wb-9-341 (K)
Shelly, Jeremiah 1797 wb-1-39 (Je)
Shelly, Nathan 1837 wb-3-461 (Je)
Shelly, Sally 1821 rb-c-400 (Mt)
Shelly, Thomas 1848 wb-d-119 (G)
Shelton, Abel 1836 as-a-305 (Di)
Shelton, Crispen E. 1836 wb-a-317 (R)
Shelton, Daviad 1860 gs-1-622 (F)
Shelton, David 1814 wb-A-55 (Li)
Shelton, David 1840 wb-#156 (Mc)
Shelton, David F. 1857 wb-#26 (Mo)
Shelton, E. F. 1859 gs-1-516 (F)
Shelton, Edmund 1846 lr (Gi)
Shelton, Eleanor 1856 wb-a-298 (Di)
Shelton, Eliphaz 1834 wb-1-60 (La)
Shelton, Elizabeth 1843 wb-12-425* (D)
Shelton, Elizabeth 1843 wb-12-438* (D)
Shelton, Franklin 1840 wb-12-39* (D)
Shelton, George 1825? as-a-144 (Di)
Shelton, Godfrey 1830 wb-9-445 (D)
Shelton, Henry 1836 wb-3-422 (Je)
Shelton, Hugh A. 1853 wb-i-115 (O)
Shelton, James 1836 wb-3-429 (Je)
Shelton, James 1850 wb-7-0 (Sm)
Shelton, James L. 1844 wb-12-91 (Rb)

Shetler, George 1840 5-2-148 (Cl)
Shetterly, George 1849 wb-10-251 (K)
Shetterly, Michael 1847 wb-9-345 (K)
Shield, E. J. 1846 wb-1-127 (Sh)
Shields, Amelia 1855 wb-16-477 (D)
Shields, David 1839 wb-5-27 (Gr)
Shields, David 1858 wb-3-472 (Gr)
Shields, Henry 1827 wb-1-23# (Ge)
Shields, James 1834 wb-2-55# (Ge)
Shields, James 1838 lr (Gi)
Shields, James 1847 148-1-190 (Ge)
Shields, Jane 1850 33-3-193 (Gr)
Shields, John 1820 wb-2-286 (Je)
Shields, John 1833 wb-1-42 (Gr)
Shields, John C. 1852 wb-#62 (Wa)
Shields, John N. 1849 ib-1-46 (Wy)
Shields, Joseph 1836 wb-x-402 (Mu)
Shields, Joseph S. 1861 wb-2-103# (Ge)
Shields, Thomas 1845 wb-13-319 (D)
Shields, William 1841 wb-12-168* (D)
Shields, William C. 1855 wb-16-476 (D)
Shields, William F. 1861 ib-2-241 (Wy)
Shifflett, George W. 1859 wb-3-30 (Me)
Shigley, Samuel 1815 wb-#18 (Mu)
Shillcut, Thomas 1851 wb-14-670 (D)
Shinalt, Walter 1845 wb-3-230 (Hr)
Shinault, Isaac 1841 wb-2-243 (Hr)
Shinault, William 1826 wb-1-26 (Hr)
Shinault, William 1846 wb-4-119 (Hr)
Shinault, Wm. 1838 wb-2-40 (Hr)
Shinliver, Charles 1851? wb-1B-206 (A)
Shinliver, Jane 1851 wb-1B-231 (A)
Shinnick, Jerry 1851 wb-15-81 (D)
Shinpack, Joseph 1841 wb-a-68 (F)
Shinpock, Henry 1816 wb-2-216 (K)
Ship, Joseph 1821 rb-5-133 (Ru)
Ship, Meakin 1844 wb-7-0 (Sm)
Ship, William 1814 wb-#14 (Wl)
Shipley, Benjamin 1803 wb-#9 (Wa)
Shipley, Benjamin 1815 wb-#33 (Mu)
Shipley, Christopher 1830 wb-#157 (Mc)
Shipley, Thomas 1835 wb-1-156 (Gr)
Shipman, J. D. 1861 wb-k-412 (O)
Shipman, John R. 1858 wb-a-318 (Cr)
Shipp, Benjamin 1850 rb-15-300 (Ru)
Shipp, Benjamin F. 1850 rb-15-362 (Ru)
Shipp, James sr. 1849 rb-15-51 (Ru)
Shires, D. B. F. 1856 as-b-224 (Ms)
Shires, John 1855 as-b-183 (Ms)
Shires, Peter 1842 wb-z-342 (Mu)
Shirley, Paul 1834 wb-10-327 (D)

Shirley, Uriah 1843 wb-3-241 (Hy)
Shive, Christian 1860 as-c-222 (Ms)
Shivers, Abagail 1844 wb-13-82 (D)
Shivers, Benjamin 1840 wb-1-61 (Sh)
Shivers, Clemant 1837 wb-2-259 (Ma)
Shivers, Noah 1833 wb-10-182 (D)
Shivers, Thomas 1829 wb-9-328 (D)
Shockley, Basmath 1860 as-c-216 (Ms)
Shockley, Isaiah 1855 wb-a-237 (V)
Shockley, Thomas 1856 as-c-37 (Ms)
Shoemake, Jourden 1829 eb-1-249 (C)
Shoemake, Tandy 1824 wb-1-0 (Sm)
Shoemaker, Elizabeth 1841 wb-#157 (Mc)
Shoemaker, S. S. 1857 wb-h-347 (St)
Shoemate, Fielding 1842 wb-c-85 (G)
Shook, Andrew J. 1840 wb-#158 (Mc)
Shook, John Sr. 1827 wb-#158 (Mc)
Shore, Wm. 1838 wb-2-22 (Hr)
Shores, Aberam 1843 wb-1-216 (Fr)
Shores, Cassey 1859 wb-a-124 (Ce)
Shores, Emanuel 1837 wb-a-249 (O)
Shores, Jacob 1848 wb-14-62 (Rb)
Shores, James 1859 wb-a-127 (Ce)
Shores, John 1815 wb-2-151 (Wi)
Shores, Joseph 1849 wb-g-218 (O)
Shores, Levi 1836 wb-1-148 (Fr)
Short, Benjamin 1839 as-a-6 (Ma)
Short, Burrel 1810 wb-a-1 (Wh)
Short, Burrill 1846 wb-c-246 (Wh)
Short, Isaac 1854 lr (Sn)
Short, Joshua 1811 rb-b-23 (Mt)
Short, Samuel 1828 wb-#158 (Mc)
Shorter, James 1860 wb-#131 (Wl)
Shoulders, Soloman 1855 lr (Sn)
Shoultz, Stuffle 1834 wb-1-443 (Hw)
Shoun, David H. 1850 wb-1-63 (Jo)
Shoun, Elihu A. 1852 wb-1-68 (Jo)
Shoun, Leonard 1845 wb-1-15 (Jo)
Shouse, Joseph 1856 wb-h-591 (Hu)
Shower, E. (Dr.) 1861 wb-18-431 (D)
Shrader, Daniel 1839 wb-1-282 (W)
Shrader, Henry 1850 wb-3-24 (W)
Shrader, Henry 1857 wb-f-65 (Ro)
Shrader, John D. 1855 wb-3-443 (W)
Shropshire, Joel 1825? as-A-100 (Di)
Shropshire, John 1837 wb-e-28 (Hu)
Shropshire, Sally 1837 wb-e-48 (Hu)
Shropshire, Winfield 1816 wb-1-17 (Fr)
Shrum, Nicholas W. 1833 wb-1-138 (We)
Shryock, Jacob 1840 wb-e-12 (St)
Shryock, Margaret 1861 wb-i-332 (St)

Shuff, James 1858 rb-o-601 (Mt)
Shuffield, Arthur 1841 as-a-39 (Ms)
Shuffield, Lucretia 1839 as-a-8 (Ms)
Shulch?, John 1830 wb-b-110 (Hn)
Shull, A. B. 1847 wb-1-317 (Li)
Shull, David 1856 ib-1-431 (Wy)
Shull, John 1850 wb-1-62 (Jo)
Shull, Samuel G. 1859 wb-f-170 (Mu)
Shull, William M. 1849 ib-1-20 (Wy)
Shults, David 1833 wb-#158 (Mc)
Shults, Jacob 1839 5-2-93 (Cl)
Shumate, James 1813 wb-2-33 (Wi)
Shumate, John 1808 wb-1-179 (Wi)
Shumate, John 18.5 ib-2-131 (Cl)
Shumate, Mark 18.8 5-2-1 (Cl)
Shumate, Sarah C. 1845 wb-13-271 (D)
Shumate, Willis L. 1824 wb-8-333 (D)
Shurley, Margaret 1795 wb-2-28# (Ge)
Shurley, Margaret 1803 as-1-45 (Ge)
Shurman, Squire 1823 wb-#50 (Mu)
Shute, Asa 1815 wb-4-360 (D)
Shute, Daniel 1849 rb-14-521 (Ru)
Shute, John 1844 wd-13-39 (D)
Shute, Philip 1811 wb-4-135 (D)
Shutt, George H. 1853 wb-#110 (Wl)
Shutte, Isaac 1811 wb-4-154 (D)
Siddel, Job 1820 wb-3-166 (Rb)
Sides, Margaret 1842 wb-1-455 (W)
Sieber, John 1847 wb-1B-45 (A)
Sieber, Philip 1848? wb-1B-59 (A)
Sigler, John 1819 wb-3-22 (Rb)
Sigman, O. K. 1859 wb-f-272 (G)
Sikes, Jonas 1844 wb-4-12⁸ (Ma)
Sikes, Joshua sr. 1823 wb-1-0 (Sm)
Sikes, Sampson 1826 wb-a-123 (Hn)
Silcox, James 1818 rb-b-517 (Wn)
Siler, John 1835 wb-1-446 (Hr)
Siler, John 1851 wb-a-158 (T)
Silleman, William 1824 wb-#129 (Mu)
Silliman, Thomas 1823 wb-#46 (Wl)
Sillivan, Fletcher 1816 wb-#27 (Wl)
Sills, Isaiah 1835 wb-c-422 (St)
Sills, Isham 1832 wb-c-199 (St)
Sills, Josiah 1847 wb-f-413 (St)
Sills, William 1847 wb-f-414 (St)
Sills, William 1848 wb-4-385 (Hr)
Sills, _____ 1834 wb-c-381 (St)
Silman, Thomas 1816 wb-1-12 (Fr)
Silvertooth, Jacob 1851 ib-1-162 (Ca)
Silvertooth, John 1860 wb-2-325 (Li)
Silvertooth, John 1861 wb-d-114 (L)

Simerley, John 1837 wb-1-213 (Bo)
Simmon, Samuel 1798 wb-1-45 (Sn)
Simmonds, Thomas H. 1856 wb-13-170 (Wi)
Simmons, Ann 1846 wb-4-48 (Hr)
Simmons, Anthony 1834 wb-b-46 (G)
Simmons, Charles 1825 wb-1-13 (Hr)
Simmons, E. C. 1857? ib-2-393 (Cl)
Simmons, Edmond 1816 wb-7-70 (D)
Simmons, Edward 1816 wb-7-13 (D)
Simmons, Edward 1847 wb-14-165 (D)
Simmons, Elizabeth 1843 wb-1-222 (Fr)
Simmons, Elizabeth 1857 wb-f-58 (G)
Simmons, Ezekiel 1847 wb-14-165 (D)
Simmons, Hardeman 1837 wb-6-296 (Wi)
Simmons, Hardy 1835 wb-6-52 (Wi)
Simmons, Harriet W. 1859 wb-7-53 (Ma)
Simmons, Henry J. 1853 rb-16-649 (Ru)
Simmons, Isaiah 1833 wb-c-122 (Hn)
Simmons, J. A. 1847 wb-1-311 (Li)
Simmons, Jahu 1836 wb-1-187 (Gr)
Simmons, James 1828 wb-1-25 (Li)
Simmons, James 1840 wb-12-78* (D)
Simmons, James 1844 5-3-39 (Cl)
Simmons, James 1851 ib-1-231 (Cl)
Simmons, James 1851 wb-1-452 (Hw)
Simmons, James 1852 wb#21 (Gu)
Simmons, James M. 1841 wb-b-376 (G)
Simmons, John 1807 wb-1-244 (Rb)
Simmons, John 1815 wb-4-362 (D)
Simmons, John 1842 wb-e-517 (Hu)
Simmons, John P. 1856 wb-16-227 (Rb)
Simmons, Josiah 1835 wb-d-128 (Hn)
Simmons, Margaret 1838 wb-e-153 (Hu)
Simmons, Margaret 1850 wb-14-391 (Rb)
Simmons, Margaret 1856 wb-16-115 (Rb)
Simmons, Martha 1859 wb#6 (Gu)
Simmons, Robert G. 1839 wb-3-1 (Ma)
Simmons, S. .R. 1860 wb-3e-165 (Sh)
Simmons, Sarah 1859 wb-f-335 (G)
Simmons, Smith 1824 wb-1-0 (Sm)
Simmons, Thomas 1794 wb-1-244 (Wi)
Simmons, Thomas A. 1841 wb-10-558 (Rb)
Simmons, Thomas A. 1841 wb-10-611 (Rb)
Simmons, Thomas I. 1851 wb-2-86 (Sh)
Simmons, Valentine 1854 wb-15-544 (Rb)
Simmons, Weleby D. 1855 wb-b-5 (F)
Simmons, Wilie 1862 wb-f-440 (G)
Simmons, William 1838 wb-11-382 (D)
Simmons, William 1853 ib-1-230 (Wy)
Simmons, William 1856 wb-1-408 (Fr)
Simmons, William 1857 wb-a-25 (Ce)

Simmons, William D. 1840 5-2-162 (Cl)
Simmons, Willie 1853 wb-h-184 (Hu)
Simms, B. J. L. 1855 wb-15-721 (Rb)
Simms, Elizabeth T. 1846 wb-#149 (Wl)
Simms, Milly 1858 wb-#28 (Mo)
Simms, Phebe 1844 wb-a-235 (F)
Simms, Sarah 1852 wb-e-10 (G)
Simms, Sylvia 1847 wb-5-50 (Ma)
Simonds, Joseph 1856 wb-g-773 (Hn)
Simons, Hardy 1837 wb-6-304 (Wi)
Simons, James 1842 wb-a-37 (V)
Simons, William 1819 wb-1-178 (Bo)
Simonson, G. Tucker 1853 wb-3-175 (La)
Simonton, Archibald M. 1842 abl-1-308 (T)
Simonton, Archibald M. 1843 wb-a-101 (T)
Simonton, Jane 1859 wb-4-222 (La)
Simonton, John 1840 wb-1-202 (La)
Simonton, William 1843 wb-a-104 (T)
Simpkins, Nancy 1860 wb-18-346 (D)
Simpkins, Orman A. 1857 wb-17-260 (D)
Simpkins, Thomas 1846 wb-13-375 (D)
Simpkins, Thomas 1858 wb-17-510 (D)
Simpkins, Thomas C. 1858 wb-17-545 (D)
Simpson, Andrew 1791 wb-1-181 (D)
Simpson, B. L. 1861 wb-19-20 (D)
Simpson, E. M. 1855 wb-n-595 (Mt)
Simpson, Hannah 1852 rb-16-192 (Ru)
Simpson, Hugh M. 1832 wb-1-210 (Hr)
Simpson, James 1819 wb-1-0 (Sm)
Simpson, James 1822 wb-3-350 (K)
Simpson, James 1827 wb-a-293 (Wh)
Simpson, James 1841 wb-a-24 (Dk)
Simpson, James 1842 abl-1-247 (T)
Simpson, James 1854 wb-d-159 (Wh)
Simpson, James 1855 wb-#55 (Wa)
Simpson, Jesse sr. 1850 wb-10-386 (K)
Simpson, Jessee 1854 ib-1-348 (Ca)
Simpson, John 1828 eb-1-229 (C)
Simpson, John 1834 lr (Sn)
Simpson, John 1844 wb-2-61# (Ge)
Simpson, John 1847 148-1-208 (Ge)
Simpson, John A. 1854 wb-d-217 (Wh)
Simpson, John C. 1860 wb-f-320 (Ro)
Simpson, Jones M. 1851 wb-c-450 (Wh)
Simpson, Joshua 1814 wb-A-46 (Li)
Simpson, Margaret 1858 wb#42 (Gu)
Simpson, Nathan 1829 wb-#82 (Wl)
Simpson, Nathaniel 1843 wb-e-605 (Hu)
Simpson, Nathaniel 1853 wb-h-179 (Hu)
Simpson, Newton 1853 wb-h-184 (Hu)
Simpson, Ricie 1847 wb-1-241 (Fr)

Simpson, Robt. 1852 rb-16-192 (Ru)
Simpson, Samuel 1844 wb-#158 (Mc)
Simpson, Thomas 1842 wb-e-470 (Hu)
Simpson, William 1788 wb-1-83 (D)
Simpson, William 1808 wb-4-14 (D)
Simpson, William 1835 wb-1-365 (Hr)
Simpson, William 1842 wb-a-117 (T)
Simpson, William 1842 wb-c-62 (Wh)
Simrell, William 1861 wb-e-411 (Wh)
Simrill?, William M. 1859 wb-e-213 (Wh)
Sims, Allen 1829 wb-1-113 (Hr)
Sims, Bartlet 1793 wb-1-440 (Hw)
Sims, Benj. 1846 as-b-330 (Di)
Sims, Benjamin 1831 wb-#90 (Wl)
Sims, Boyd M. 1849 wb-9-290 (Wi)
Sims, Chisley 1844 wb-#139 (Wl)
Sims, Elisha 1852 wb-1-298 (Fr)
Sims, Eliza M. 1855 wb-b-12 (Ms)
Sims, George B. 1821 rb-5-138 (Ru)
Sims, Gorge 1805 rb-a-244 (Mt)
Sims, Guilford D. 1854 wb-b-344 (We)
Sims, James 1830 wb-2-0 (Sm)
Sims, James 1837 wb-a-20 (F)
Sims, James 1846 wb-b-187 (We)
Sims, John 1827? wb-#161 (Mu)
Sims, John A. 1855 wb-6-105 (Ma)
Sims, John G. 1844 wb-8-189 (Wi)
Sims, Judith 1841 wb-z-363 (Mu)
Sims, Len Sanders 1861 wb-3e-169 (Sh)
Sims, Martin 1846 wb-a-290 (F)
Sims, Parrish 1812 wb-A-10 (Li)
Sims, Phebe 1846 wb-a-273 (F)
Sims, Polly 1846 rb-13-530 (Ru)
Sims, Rebecca 1848 wb-#171 (Wl)
Sims, Robert L. 1857 rb-18-439 (Ru)
Sims, Swepson 1850 rb-15-449 (Ru)
Sims, Walter 1820 wb-7-381 (D)
Sims, William 1813 wb-#7 (Mu)
Sims, William 1857 wb-3-357 (W)
Sims, William G. 1855 wb-d-274 (Wh)
Simson, Robert 1812 wb-A-23 (Li)
Sinclair, John 1848 ib-1-6 (Wy)
Sinclair, William 1858 ib-2-27 (Wy)
Sing, John 1859 wb-13-135 (K)
Singletary, Catherine 1817 wb-7-207 (D)
Singletary, John S. 1803 wb-2-318 (D)
Singleton, Chapel H. 1848 rb-14-368 (Ru)
Singleton, Chappell 1848 rb-14-478 (Ru)
Singleton, Eliza A. 1848 wb-g-29 (Hu)
Singleton, Jeremiah 1855 ib-2-207 (Cl)
Singleton, John 1825 wb-1-128 (Bo)

Singleton, John 1838 wb-b-258 (G)
Singleton, Randolph 1842 wb-f-133 (Hn)
Singleton, Rebecca 1856 wb-1-132 (Bo)
Singular, Samuel W. 1855 wb-e-293 (G)
Sinkler, Charles 1859 wb-k-86 (O)
Sinkler, Charles jr. 1853 wb-h-Apr (O)
Sinkler, John B. 1856 wb-j-174 (O)
Sinks, Powell 1826 as-A-88 (Di)
Sisk, James 1825 wb-1-63 (Fr)
Sisk, James 1828 wb-#159 (Mc)
Sisk, James 1844 wb-#159 (Mc)
Sisk, Martin 1823 wb-8-269 (D)
Sisk, Nancy 1837 wb-2-188 (Fr)
Sisk, William 1859 wb-e-259 (Wh)
Sissle, Freeman 1846 wb-f-286 (St)
Sissom, G. W. 1858 6-2-136 (Le)
Sitcoks?, James 1817 rb-b-397 (Mt)
Sitler, James W. 1833 wb-10-71 (D)
Sittler, Isaac 1838 wb-11-242 (D)
Sitton, John 1821 wb-1-0 (Sm)
Sitton, William 1823 wb-1-23# (Ge)
Sivily, John 1832 wb-1-76 (Li)
Sizemore, Owen 1836 wb-1-444 (Hw)
Skaggs, Eli 1833 wb-5-222 (K)
Skaggs, James 1840 wb-7-23 (K)
Skaggs, Stephen M. 1851 wb-11-87 (K)
Skeen, Jesse 1842 lr (Sn)
Skeen, John 1836 wb-3-380 (Je)
Skeen, John 1850 wb-#172 (Wl)
Skeggs, K. L. (Mrs.) 1856 ib-h-528 (F)
Skelley, James 1816 wb-2-207 (Wi)
Skelly, John 1834 wb-10-347 (D)
Skelton, Abel 1834 as-a-240 (Di)
Skelton, Alfred 1840 as-a-451 (Di)
Skelton, Archibald 1853 wb-a-262 (Di)
Skelton, James 1848 wb-1-453 (Hw)
Skelton, William 1851 wb-1-455 (Hw)
Skiles, Jacob 1857 wb-f-69 (G)
Skillern, William 1835 wb-2-72 (Ma)
Skinner, Emanuel 1819 wb-3-41 (Rb)
Skinner, Gilly G. 1858 wb-12-508 (Wi)
Skinner, James J. 1850 wb-m-104 (Mt)
Skinner, Jesse 1835 wb-9-116 (Rb)
Skinner, John 1824 wb-3-318 (St)
Skinner, Jonathan 1846 wb-f-356 (St)
Skinner, Jonathan jr. 1848 wb-g-28 (St)
Skinner, Josiah 1842 rb-i-265 (Mt)
Skinner, Leah (Mrs.) 1851 wb-m-279 (Mt)
Skinner, Leah (or Leor) Mrs. 1851
    wb-m-248 (Mt)
Skinner, Nathan 1827 wb-b-207 (St)

Skinner, Nathan 1846 wb-f-373 (St)
Skinner, Nathan 1846 wb-f-376 (St)
Skinner, Samuel 1824 wb-a-52 (Hn)
Skinner, Samuel 1846 wb-12-534 (Rb)
Skipper, Arthur 1853 wb-e-110 (G)
Skipper, Elizabeth 1827 eb-1-179 (C)
Skipper, Hardy 1822 eb-1-125 (C)
Skipper, Joseph 1845 wb-a2-208 (Mu)
Skippeth, Archibald 1842 lr (Sn)
Slack, Ephraim C. 1836 wb-#159 (Mc)
Slack, S. W. 1830 rb-8-103 (Ru)
Slacks, Abraham 1831 wb-#227 (Mu)
Slagal, Henry 1830 wb-#34 (Wa)
Slagle, George 1826 wb-1-23# (Ge)
Slagle, Henry 1849 wb-#48 (Wa)
Slagle, John 1856 wb-12-277 (K)
Slandridge, Richard 1837 rb-9-440 (Ru)
Slapes, Thomas 1821 eb-1-109 (C)
Slasy, William 1838 wb-1-445 (Hw)
Slate, Elizabeth 1839 rb-10-441 (Ru)
Slater, Charles 1837 wb-a-16 (F)
Slater, Cornelius N. 1854 wb-2-89 (Li)
Slater, Henry 1825 wb-5-142 (Rb)
Slater, John Toms 1832 wb-9-574 (D)
Slater, Mary 1854 wb-2-91 (Li)
Slater, Sarah 1823 wb-4-75 (Rb)
Slatery, Patrick 1824 wb-4-28 (K)
Slatery, Patrick 1834 wb-5-273 (K)
Slaton, Reuben 1845 wb-#151 (Wl)
Slatter, Polly P. 1844 wb-1-218 (Fr)
Slaughter, George 1823 wb-#61 (Mu)
Slaughter, George 1831 wb-b-9 (Wh)
Slaughter, Lucy B. 1848 wb-9-59 (Wi)
Slaughter, Matilda 1845 wb-b-106 (We)
Slaughter, Patsey 1823 wb-#81 (Mu)
Slaughter, Robert 1806 wb-3-116 (D)
Slaven, Alexander 1848 wb-9-30 (Wi)
Slaven, Daniel 1840 5-2-136 (Cl)
Slaven, Michael C. 1856 wb-17-139 (D)
Slayden, Benjamin 1841 wb-z-269 (Mu)
Slayden, Daniel E. 1843 as-b-218 (Di)
Slayden, Dilly? 1850 as-c-51 (Di)
Slayden, Edney 1852 as-c-163 (Di)
Slayden, Hartwell M. 1847 wb-a-177 (Di)
Slayden, Nicholas B. 1855 wb-16-593 (D)
Slaydon, Thomas 1859 wb-f-241 (G)
Slead, John 1856 wb-g-712 (Hn)
Sledd, John M. 1841 rb-12-44 (Ru)
Sledd, William 1827 rb-7-319 (Ru)
Sledge, Amos P. 1851 wb-5-20 (Hr)
Sledge, Jesse 1842 wb-2-368 (Hr)

Sledge, John 1823 wb-3-644 (Wi)
Sledge, John 1860 wb-13-218 (Wi)
Sledge, Washington A. 1843 wb-12-446* (D)
Slicker, George sr. 1828 wb-4-307 (Wi)
Sligar, Adam 1834 wb-#2 (Mo)
Slimp, A. B. 1861 wb-1-150 (Jo)
Slimp, John 1858 wb-1-120 (Jo)
Slimp, Michael 1846 wb-1-29 (Jo)
Slimp, Simeon 1859 wb-1-127 (Jo)
Slimpson?, James F. 1850 wb-g-226 (St)
Slipe, George 1841 wb-1-447 (Hw)
Sloan, Archibald 1836 wb-3-0 (Sm)
Sloan, Archibald 1858 wb-#21 (Mo)
Sloan, Frederick 1854 wb-16-278 (D)
Sloan, Jason R. 1858 wb-7-0 (Sm)
Sloan, John 1840 wb-3-0 (Sm)
Sloan, Johnson T. 1853 wb-5-40 (Hr)
Sloan, Patrick 1810 wb-1-0 (Sm)
Sloan, William sr. 1850 wb-7-0 (Sm)
Sloan?, John B. 1856 wb-e-434 (G)
Sloane, David 1802 rb-a-153 (Mt)
Sloop, Henry 1855 wb-#159 (Mc)
Sloop, James 1861 wb-#159 (Mc)
Sloss, John 1813 lr (Sn)
Sloss, Joseph L. 1847 wb-2-20 (Sh)
Slover, Aaron 1847 wb-1B-28 (A)
Slover, Abraham 1834 wb-3-315 (Je)
Slover, Elizabeth 1847 wb-1B-28 (A)
Sly, Jacob 1826 rb-d-550 (Mt)
Slyger, Henry 1834 wb-#30 (Wa)
Slyger, Henry 1834 wb-#34 (Wa)
Slyger, John 1818 wb-#16 (Wa)
Slyger, Jon 1830 wb-#30 (Wa)
Small, A. L. 1858 rb-o-782 (Mt)
Small, Jacob 1859 wb-3e-113 (Sh)
Small, Lewis 1858 rb-o-605 (Mt)
Small, Sarah jr. 1850 148-1-336 (Ge)
Small, William 1857 wb-2-365 (Me)
Small, Wilson 1857 wb-2-367 (Me)
Small, Wilson 1861 wb-#160 (Mc)
Smalling, Robert 1860 wb-1-171 (Su)
Smalling, Samuel (Sr.) 1857 wb-#13 (Mo)
Smallman, John 1827 wb-a-292 (Wh)
Smallwood, John 1829 wb-1-7 (La)
Smally, John H. 1850 wb-e-228 (Ro)
Smart, Elisha 1839 lr (Gi)
Smart, John Sr. 1822 wb-#41 (Wl)
Smartt, Francis (Frank) 1843 wb-1-535 (W)
Smartt, G. R. 1854 wb-3-235 (W)
Smartt, George K. 1854 wb-3-251 (W)
Smedley, William 1842 wb-7-308 (K)

Smelcer, George 1857 149-1-60 (Ge)
Smellige, Edward W. 1848 wb-f-127+ (O)
Smelser, Adam 1822 wb-1-23# (Ge)
Smelser, Adam 1855 wb-5-373 (Je)
Smelser, Adam 1855 wb-5-413 (Je)
Smelser, Frederick 1861 149-1-237 (Ge)
Smelser, George 1845 wb-2-63# (Ge)
Smelser, Jacob 1838 wb-2-49# (Ge)
Smiley, David sr. 1860 wb-18-404 (D)
Smiley, Emaline 1861 wb-18-449 (D)
Smiley, John L. 1859 wb-b-82 (Ms)
Smiley, Robert 1823 wb-8-272 (D)
Smiley, Tresea 1842 wb-12-378* (D)
Smiser, John 1840 wb-z-47 (Mu)
Smith (B), Jack 1855 wb-h-154 (St)
Smith, A. 1846 wb-13-382 (D)
Smith, Abraham 1810 wb-#11 (Wa)
Smith, Abraham 1853 wb-15-477 (D)
Smith, Absolem 1818 wb-2-207 (Je)
Smith, Absolum 1835 wb-3-423 (Je)
Smith, Albert 1842 wb-c-256 (O)
Smith, Albert 1847 wb-14-35 (D)
Smith, Albion R. 1853 wb-1-48 (R)
Smith, Alexander 1835 wb-a-36 (T)
Smith, Alexander 1841 wb-1-448 (Hw)
Smith, Alexander 1841 wb-7-411 (Wi)
Smith, Alexander 1850 wb-10-380 (K)
Smith, Alexander B. 1824 wb-#80 (Mu)
Smith, Alexander D. 1838 eb-1-376 (C)
Smith, Allen 1856 mr (Gi)
Smith, Alonzo P. 1841 wb-b-36 (We)
Smith, Alvin 1846 wb-1-389 (La)
Smith, Alvis 1853 wb-e-42 (G)
Smith, Aly 1837 eb-1-353 (C)
Smith, Andrew 1836 wb-6-200 (Wi)
Smith, Andrew G. 1836 wb-6-206 (Wi)
Smith, Ann 1821 rb-5-95 (Ru)
Smith, Ann 1830 wb-b-59 (Hn)
Smith, Anna 1857 wb-h-368 (St)
Smith, Anne 1856 6-2-132 (Le)
Smith, Anthony 1847 wb-e-4 (Ro)
Smith, Antoinette 1852 wb-10-369 (Wi)
Smith, Archibald L. 1852 wb-3-12 (La)
Smith, Archibald no date lr (Gi)
Smith, Barbara 1853 148-1-463 (Ge)
Smith, Barney 1841 wb-7-222 (K)
Smith, Bartholomew 1854 wb-a-271 (Di)
Smith, Benjamin 1828 wb-a-5 (T)
Smith, Benjamin 1830 wb-7-290 (Rb)
Smith, Benjamin 1839 abl-1-111 (T)
Smith, Benjamin 1839 wb-a-37 (L)

Smith, Benjamin 1841 wb-a-91 (T)
Smith, Benjamin 1852 ib-C-217 (C)
Smith, Benjamin A. 1838 wb-#123 (Wl)
Smith, Benjamin D. 1859 wb-1-143 (R)
Smith, Bennett 1848 rb-14-372 (Ru)
Smith, Buckner 1818 lr (Gi)
Smith, C. L. 1854 ib-H-125 (F)
Smith, C. M. 1827 wb-1-4 (Sh)
Smith, Catharine 1832 lw (Ct)
Smith, Cecily M. 1862 rb-21-166 (Ru)
Smith, Charles 1797 wb-2-28# (Ge)
Smith, Charles 1812 wb-2-28# (Ge)
Smith, Charles 1813 wb-2-35# (Ge)
Smith, Charles 1835 wb-1-418 (Hr)
Smith, Charles 1838 wb-a-362 (R)
Smith, Charles B. 1825 wb-#58 (Wl)
Smith, Charley 1816 wb-A-126 (Li)
Smith, Cornelius 1845 wb-2-62# (Ge)
Smith, Cunningham 1840 rb-11-82 (Ru)
Smith, Cyrena 1857 wb-2-5 (Li)
Smith, D. C. 1859 wb-f-314 (G)
Smith, D. R. 1853 as-c-269 (Di)
Smith, Daniel 1816 lr (Sn)
Smith, Daniel 1853 wb-7-0 (Sm)
Smith, Daniel 1860 wb-b-469 (We)
Smith, Daniel R. 1854 as-c-286 (Di)
Smith, Darling 1856 6-2-130 (Le)
Smith, David 1837 wb-d-154* (Hn)
Smith, David 1841 wb-7-193 (K)
Smith, David 1852 wb-5-136 (Je)
Smith, David 1854? wb-#25 (Mo)
Smith, Dean 1858 wb-3-424 (W)
Smith, Delilah J. 1860 wb-#161 (Mc)
Smith, Dier 1858 wb-3-424 (W)
Smith, Drury 1810 wb-4-110 (D)
Smith, Drury 1826 wb-a-228 (Wh)
Smith, Drury 1836 lr (Gi)
Smith, E. B. 1835 wb-1-414 (Hr)
Smith, E. B. 1855 wb-n-631 (Mt)
Smith, E. H. 1854 ib-h-88 (F)
Smith, Ebenezer 1826 wb-#136 (Mu)
Smith, Edward 1844 wb-#161 (Mc)
Smith, Edward 1845 as-b-228 (Di)
Smith, Edward J. 1815 as-a-148 (Di)
Smith, Edward W. 1815 rb-3-62 (Ru)
Smith, Edwin 1857 wb-12-471 (Wi)
Smith, Elijah 1848 lr (Gi)
Smith, Elijah H. 1836 wb-2-142 (Ma)
Smith, Elijah P. 1860 wb-k-348 (O)
Smith, Elisha 1818 as-A-66 (Di)
Smith, Elisha 1840 wb-#129 (Wl)

Smith, Elisha B. 1835 wb-1-400 (Hr)
Smith, Elisha D. 1852 wb-m-603 (Mt)
Smith, Eliza B. 1860 wb-k-354 (O)
Smith, Elizabeth 1838 wb-d-156 (St)
Smith, Elizabeth 1843 wb-f-177* (Hn)
Smith, Elizabeth 1847 wb-d-91 (G)
Smith, Elizabeth 1848 wb-#166 (Wl)
Smith, Elizabeth 1849 wb-10-288 (K)
Smith, Elizabeth 1850 wb-10-456 (K)
Smith, Elizabeth 1854 wb-#161 (Mc)
Smith, Elizabeth 1856 rb-17-611 (Ru)
Smith, Elizabeth 1860 wb-#131 (Wl)
Smith, Elizabeth V. 1858 wb-f-171 (G)
Smith, Ephraim F. 1856 rb-17-618 (Ru)
Smith, Erecus sr. 1850 wb-3-42 (W)
Smith, Ester B. 1854 ib-1-323 (Wy)
Smith, Esther 1860 lr (Gi)
Smith, Euracus 1850 wb-3-74 (W)
Smith, Evander B. 1860 ib-2-211 (Wy)
Smith, Ezekiel 1822 wb-8-160 (D)
Smith, Ezekiel 1837 as-a-390 (Di)
Smith, F. 1848 wb-14-242 (D)
Smith, Fielding 1826 rb-d-546 (Mt)
Smith, Francis 1835 wb-c-431 (St)
Smith, Francis M. 1852 wb-a-188 (T)
Smith, Frederick 1815 wb-3-65 (St)
Smith, Frederick 1854 148-1-486 (Ge)
Smith, Freeland 1816 wb-3-146 (St)
Smith, G. M. 1861 wb-17-283 (Rb)
Smith, Garland 1854 wb-#25 (Mo)
Smith, Garrut 1843 wb-8-114 (K)
Smith, Geo. A. 1858 gs-1-97 (F)
Smith, George 1833 wb-#102 (Wl)
Smith, George 1836 wb-2-205 (Sn)
Smith, George 1838 wb-a-64 (T)
Smith, George 1841 as-a-517 (Di)
Smith, George 1841 wb-12-167* (D)
Smith, George 1842 wb-1-431 (W)
Smith, George 1850 wb-1-114 (Ct)
Smith, George D. 1854 ib-H-178 (F)
Smith, George L. 1826 wb-#65 (Wl)
Smith, George S. 1842 wb-12-269* (D)
Smith, George W. 1848 rb-k-747 (Mt)
Smith, Gracey 1849 wb-a-142 (T)
Smith, Guy 1823 rb-5-288 (Ru)
Smith, H. H. 1842 wb-#137 (Wl)
Smith, H. P. 1840 wb-y-605 (Mu)
Smith, Hannah 1840 wb-#131 (Wl)
Smith, Hector 1849 ib-1-66 (Ca)
Smith, Henry 1838 abl-1-83 (T)
Smith, Henry 1850 wb-g-356 (Hn)

Smith, Henry 1856 wb-b-24 (Ms)
Smith, Henry B. 1840 wb-1-168 (Li)
Smith, Henry F. 1842 wb-f-140 (Hn)
Smith, Henry F. 1862 wb-#136 (Wl)
Smith, Henry P. 1852 wb-e-334 (Ro)
Smith, Howell 1820 rb-c-266 (Mt)
Smith, Hugh 1856 wb-2-342 (Me)
Smith, Isaac 1805 wb-#3 (Wl)
Smith, Isaac 1815 wb-#20 (Wl)
Smith, Isaac 1850 wb-9-437 (Wi)
Smith, Isaac jr. 1857 wb-3-364 (W)
Smith, Isabella 1852 rb-16-339 (Ru)
Smith, Isaiah 1859 wb-#161 (Mc)
Smith, Isham 1845 wb-3-224 (Hr)
Smith, J. 1845 wb-3-217 (Hr)
Smith, J. A. 1835 rb-g-204 (Mt)
Smith, J. B. 1858 wb-3-441 (Gr)
Smith, J. G. 1860 wb-a-167 (Ce)
Smith, J. M. 1861 wb-00-13 (Cf)
Smith, Jackson 1848 wb-#162 (Mc)
Smith, Jackson 1861 rb-20-801 (Ru)
Smith, Jacob (of Robert) 1851 148-1-367 (Ge)
Smith, Jacob 1838 wb-a-68 (T)
Smith, Jacob 1840 wb-#136 (Wl)
Smith, Jacob 1847 wb-2-66# (Ge)
Smith, Jacob 1849 lw (Ct)
Smith, James 1806 wb-#4 (Wl)
Smith, James 1815 wb-3-124 (St)
Smith, James 1828 rb-7-115* (Ru)
Smith, James 1828 wb-#77 (Wl)
Smith, James 1830 wb-#163 (Mc)
Smith, James 1835? wb-1-146 (Hy)
Smith, James 1840 wb-1A-257 (A)
Smith, James 1842 rb-i-434 (Mt)
Smith, James 1843 wb-2-69# (Ge)
Smith, James 1843 wb-3-200 (Hy)
Smith, James 1847 rb-14-206 (Ru)
Smith, James 1849 lw (Ct)
Smith, James 1851 wb-#8 (Mo)
Smith, James 1851 wb-3-0 (Sm)
Smith, James 1854 wb-a-461 (F)
Smith, James 1855 wb-16-528 (D)
Smith, James 1858 wb-5-89 (Hr)
Smith, James 1859 rb-20-46 (Ru)
Smith, James B. 1830 wb-1-163 (Hr)
Smith, James B. 1852 wb-3-68 (Gr)
Smith, James H. 1845 wb-13-322 (D)
Smith, James H. 1854 lr (Sn)
Smith, James Hudson 1850 wb-2-83 (Sh)
Smith, James K. 1859 39-2-299 (Dk)
Smith, James K. 1860 wb-a-178 (Ce)

Smith, James M. 1848 rb-14-338 (Ru)
Smith, James M. 1858 wb-a-279 (T)
Smith, James S. (B) 1858 rb-20-16 (Ru)
Smith, James S. 1841 rb-11-286 (Ru)
Smith, James S. 1855 ib-h-370 (F)
Smith, James S. 1858 rb-19-383 (Ru)
Smith, James W. 1838 wb-d-216 (St)
Smith, James W. 1859 gs-1-430 (F)
Smith, James Webb 1853 lr (Sn)
Smith, Jane 1840 wb-#138 (Wl)
Smith, Jane 1855 wb-12-170 (K)
Smith, Jane 1856 wb-3e-12 (Sh)
Smith, Jane 1856 wb-b-20 (F)
Smith, Jefferson 1857 wb-h-349 (St)
Smith, Jehu 1839 wb-#163 (Mc)
Smith, Jeremiah 1823 wb-1-53 (Fr)
Smith, Jeremiah 1842 mr-2-14 (Be)
Smith, Jeremiah 1847 as-b-338 (Di)
Smith, Jesse 1822 wb-8-75 (D)
Smith, Jesse 1849 wb-#167 (Wl)
Smith, Joel 1840 wb-a-5 (V)
Smith, Joel 1849 wb-g-232 (Hu)
Smith, Johannon Sr. 1857 wb-h-85 (Hn)
Smith, John 1795 wb-0-9 (K)
Smith, John 1811 wb-1-0 (Sm)
Smith, John 1813 rb-2-214 (Ru)
Smith, John 1813 rb-b-95 (Mt)
Smith, John 1815 wb-#16 (Wl)
Smith, John 1815 wb-2-86 (Je)
Smith, John 1819 wb-2-227 (Je)
Smith, John 1822 lr (Gi)
Smith, John 1824 wb-1-35 (Ma)
Smith, John 1825 rb-6-116 (Ru)
Smith, John 1825 wb-#21 (Wa)
Smith, John 1825 wb-4-54 (Wi)
Smith, John 1829 wb-#81 (Wl)
Smith, John 1831 wb-5-96 (K)
Smith, John 1833 wb-1-130 (Bo)
Smith, John 1835 rb-g-106 (Mt)
Smith, John 1839 wb-#124 (Wl)
Smith, John 1841 wb-c-193 (Ro)
Smith, John 1842 wb-5-219 (Gr)
Smith, John 1842 wb-b-467 (Hd)
Smith, John 1846 wb-9-181 (K)
Smith, John 1846 wb-g-76 (Hn)
Smith, John 1847 6-2-7 (Le)
Smith, John 1847 wb-b-246 (We)
Smith, John 1848 wb-1-353 (Li)
Smith, John 1851 wb-d-3 (Wh)
Smith, John 1856 wb-12-72 (Wi)
Smith, John 1858 wb-3-372 (W)

Smith, John 1858 wb-h-168 (Hn)
Smith, John 1861 rb-21-103 (Ru)
Smith, John A. 1830 wb-a-78 (R)
Smith, John A. 1835 rb-g-66 (Mt)
Smith, John A. 1836 wb-b-124 (G)
Smith, John A. 1836 wb-b-127 (G)
Smith, John A. 1841 wb-#135 (Wl)
Smith, John B. 1850 rb-15-345 (Ru)
Smith, John C. 1847 wb-f-405 (St)
Smith, John C. 1856 wb-h-55 (Hn)
Smith, John E. 1850 rb-15-439 (Ru)
Smith, John F. 1836 wb-6-95 (Wi)
Smith, John G. 1851 wb-a-150 (T)
Smith, John H. 1833 lr (Sn)
Smith, John H. 1834 wb-10-390 (D)
Smith, John H. 1846 wb-9-258 (K)
Smith, John H. 1854 wb-15-593 (Rb)
Smith, John L. 1845 wb-c-196 (Wh)
Smith, John L. 1857 wb-f-42 (G)
Smith, John L. 1861 wb-f-217 (Mu)
Smith, John M. 1814 wb-#14 (Wa)
Smith, John N. 1858 as-c-128 (Ms)
Smith, John P. 1853 rb-17-271 (Ru)
Smith, John P. 1854 wb-5-49 (Hr)
Smith, John P. 1859 wb-b-75 (F)
Smith, John T. 1843 wb-f-187* (Hn)
Smith, John T. 1855 rb-17-380 (Ru)
Smith, John W. 1837 lr (Gi)
Smith, John W. 1837 rb-10-25 (Ru)
Smith, John W. 1845 wb-#158 (Wl)
Smith, John Y. 1838 wb-y-208* (Mu)
Smith, John Y. 1861 wb-f-440 (Ro)
Smith, John sr. 1793 wb-1-196 (Je)
Smith, Jon A. 1827 wb-2-0 (Sm)
Smith, Jonathan 1822 wb-2-0 (Sm)
Smith, Jonathan 1854 wb-1-332 (Fr)
Smith, Jorham? 1834 wb-b-35 (G)
Smith, Joseph 1821 wb-1-0 (Sm)
Smith, Joseph 1829 rb-7-173 (Ru)
Smith, Joseph 1830 wb-c-54 (St)
Smith, Joseph 1834 wb-1-21 (Sh)
Smith, Joseph 1838 wb-11-217 (D)
Smith, Joseph 1839 wb-d-318 (St)
Smith, Joseph 1840 wb-#163 (Mc)
Smith, Joseph 1851 wb-#8 (Mo)
Smith, Joseph 1858 lr (Sn)
Smith, Joseph 1862 wb-1-413 (Fr)
Smith, Joseph M. 1828 wb-b-246 (St)
Smith, Joshua 1831 wb-#225 (Mu)
Smith, Joshua 1842 as-b-110 (Di)
Smith, Josiah 1816 rb-3-137 (Ru)

Smith, Josiah 1837 wb-1-262 (Gr)
Smith, Josiah 1847 wb-#170 (Wl)
Smith, Josiah 1849 33-3-115 (Gr)
Smith, Jourdan J. 1862 iv-C-15 (C)
Smith, Kinchen 1815 wb-#17 (Wl)
Smith, Kinchen 1827 wb-#68 (Wl)
Smith, L. Windser 1861 wb-1-29 (Br)
Smith, Larkin 1840 wb-3-0 (Sm)
Smith, Laura L. 1844 wb-8-207 (Wi)
Smith, Lavisa 1843 wb-#149 (Wl)
Smith, Lemuel 1817 rb-1-437 (Hw)
Smith, Lemuel 1844 wb-8-147 (Wi)
Smith, Leonard 1847 wb-a-126 (T)
Smith, Leonard 1851 wb-14-546 (Rb)
Smith, Levi 1819 rb-c-140 (Mt)
Smith, Levi 1854 wb-e-148 (G)
Smith, Louther 1821 wb-1-437 (Hw)
Smith, Lucy 1849 rb-l-406 (Mt)
Smith, Luke 1809 wb-1-52 (Wi)
Smith, Luke L. 1853 wb-10-489 (Wi)
Smith, Major Joseph 1855 wb-#163 (Mc)
Smith, Malcom 1827 wb-3-0 (Sm)
Smith, Margaret 1838 wb-#120 (Wl)
Smith, Margaret 1849 wb-#165 (Wl)
Smith, Mariah 1846 wb-f-317 (St)
Smith, Mariah 1846 wb-f-329 (St)
Smith, Mariah 1857 wb-h-365 (St)
Smith, Martha 1835 wb-2-30 (Ma)
Smith, Martha 1859 wb-f-178 (Mu)
Smith, Martha A. 1854 rb-17-158 (Ru)
Smith, Martin S. 1847 wb-14-90 (D)
Smith, Mary 1821 rb-5-93 (Ru)
Smith, Mary 1832 wb-#87 (Wl)
Smith, Mary 1839 rb-10-380 (Ru)
Smith, Mary 1844 wb-#140 (Wl)
Smith, Mary 1856 wb-a-238 (T)
Smith, Mary A. 1860 wb-f-187 (Mu)
Smith, Mary A. E. 1842 wb-7-498 (Wi)
Smith, Mary E. 1856 wb-6-413 (Ma)
Smith, Mary G. 1850 wb-14-524 (D)
Smith, Merewether 1840 wb-c-119 (Ro)
Smith, Michael 1842 wb-7-388 (K)
Smith, Millington 1836 rb-9-380 (Ru)
Smith, Moses 1855 149-1-7 (Ge)
Smith, Moses 1858 wb-1C-441 (A)
Smith, Mumford 1837? as-a-362 (Di)
Smith, Mumford 1844 wb-z-587 (Mu)
Smith, Mumford sr. 1830 wb-a-84 (R)
Smith, Nancy 1849 33-3-114 (Gr)
Smith, Nancy 1851 wb-m-245 (Mt)
Smith, Nancy Ann 1861 lr (Gi)

Smith, Nancy Ann 1863 wb-2-375 (Li)
Smith, Nathaniel 1828? wb-#27 (Wa)
Smith, Nathaniel 1838 wb-a-39 (Ms)
Smith, Nathaniel 1842 wb-#164 (Mc)
Smith, Nicholas P. 1833 wb-5-242 (Wi)
Smith, Noah 1836 wb-a-46 (T)
Smith, O. B. 1853 rb-16-467 (Ru)
Smith, Obadiah 1819 rb-5-10 (Ru)
Smith, Oliver 1812 wb-2-34# (Ge)
Smith, Parthia Q. 1858 wb-f-170 (G)
Smith, Patrick 1814 eb-1-46 (C)
Smith, Peggy 1836 wb-#112 (Wl)
Smith, Peggy 1853 wb-#111 (Wl)
Smith, Peter 1808 wb-1-433 (Hw)
Smith, Peter 1834 wb-#105 (Wl)
Smith, Peter 1841 wb-#164 (Mc)
Smith, Peter F. 1835 wb-#108 (Wl)
Smith, Peter N. 1836 wb-6-222 (Wi)
Smith, Peter P. 1855 wb-5-56 (Hr)
Smith, Pleasant 1851 wb-15-32 (D)
Smith, Polemna 1835 rb-9-248 (Ru)
Smith, Polly 1815 rb-b-68 (Mt)
Smith, Polly 1844 rb-12-588 (Ru)
Smith, Pryor 1857 wb-3-355 (Gr)
Smith, R. P. 1853 wb-15-487 (D)
Smith, R. W. 1852 wb-m-437 (Mt)
Smith, Rachel 1824 wb-A-397 (Li)
Smith, Rachel 1825 wb-3-765 (Wi)
Smith, Ralph 1845 wb-1-262 (Li)
Smith, Ralph 1853 wb-2-77 (Li)
Smith, Rebecca 1845 wb-a2-252 (Mu)
Smith, Reuben 1836 wb-#115 (Wl)
Smith, Reuben 1850 wb-b-581 (Mu)
Smith, Reuben M. 1850 wb-g-256 (St)
Smith, Reuben M. 1853 wb-n-62 (Mt)
Smith, Richard 1812 wb-a-1: 'St)
Smith, Richard 1814 Wb-2-55 (Wi)
Smith, Richard 1858 wb-17-562 (D)
Smith, Robert 1806 rb-2-12 (Ru)
Smith, Robert 1823 wb-#45 (Wl)
Smith, Robert 1832 wb-9-581 (D)
Smith, Robert 1834 rb-9-170 (Ru)
Smith, Robert 1838 wb-#120 (Wl)
Smith, Robert 1848 wb-#164 (Mc)
Smith, Robert 1849 rb-15-36 (Ru)
Smith, Robert 1849 rb-15-52 (Ru)
Smith, Robert 1851 wb-11-70 (K)
Smith, Robert 1852 148-1-402 (Ge)
Smith, Robert 1859 rb-p-298 (Mt)
Smith, Robert C. 1844? wb-#154 (Wl)
Smith, Robert C. 1847 wb-#153 (Wl)

Smith, Robert W. 1851 wb-m-327 (Mt)
Smith, Robert sr. 1826 rb-6-259 (Ru)
Smith, Robert sr. 1847 wb-2-65# (Ge)
Smith, Roscinda O. 1857 wb-b-32 (F)
Smith, Sally (Sarah?) 1854 wb-2-163 (Sh)
Smith, Sally 1857 wb-h-366 (St)
Smith, Saml. 1800 wb-2-166 (D)
Smith, Saml. 1800 wb-2-167 (D)
Smith, Samuel 1798 wb-1-432 (Hw)
Smith, Samuel 1809 rb-2-81 (Ru)
Smith, Samuel 1817 wb-2-310 (Wi)
Smith, Samuel 1829 wb-#190 (Mu)
Smith, Samuel 1829 wb-b-335 (St)
Smith, Samuel 1837 rb-g-519 (Mt)
Smith, Samuel 1842 rb-i-376 (Mt)
Smith, Samuel 1850 wb-9-459 (Wi)
Smith, Samuel 1851 rb-15-620 (Ru)
Smith, Samuel 1856 wb-3-303 (Gr)
Smith, Samuel 1859 wb-5-97 (Hr)
Smith, Samuel 1861 rb-21-84 (Ru)
Smith, Samuel G. 1836 wb-10-540 (D)
Smith, Samuel G. 1836 wb-x-397 (Mu)
Smith, Samuel H. 1843 wb-d-52 (Ro)
Smith, Samuel S. 1851 lr (Gi)
Smith, Sarah 1854 ib-h-12 (F)
Smith, Sarah 1855 149-1-4 (Ge)
Smith, Sarah J. 1843 wb-1-88 (Sh)
Smith, Shadrach 1844 mr-2-75 (Be)
Smith, Shadrack 1851 wb-#115 (Wl)
Smith, Sherwood 1851 wb-10-29 (Wi)
Smith, Sidney 1839 wb-2-122 (Hr)
Smith, Sidney 1843 rb-j-46 (Mt)
Smith, Sidney P. 1839 wb-3-8 (Ma)
Smith, Skelton 1838 wb-2-240 (Sn)
Smith, Solamon 1861 wb-1-17 (Su)
Smith, Solomon 1858 wb-2-88# (Ge)
Smith, Sparkman 1850 ib-1-157 (Cl)
Smith, Stephen 1844 wb-#164 (Mc)
Smith, Stephen 1844 wb-a2-118 (Mu)
Smith, Susanna 1844 wb-1-99 (Sh)
Smith, Susannah 1844 wb-2-62# (Ge)
Smith, Susannah 1852 wb-2-75# (Ge)
Smith, Temperance 1807 wb-1-0 (Sm)
Smith, Theophelus 1848 wb-#165 (Wl)
Smith, Thomas 1815 wb-#11 (Mu)
Smith, Thomas 1815 wb-A-117 (Li)
Smith, Thomas 1818 wb-7-283 (D)
Smith, Thomas 1821 wb-1-0 (Sm)
Smith, Thomas 1830 rb-f-137 (Mt)
Smith, Thomas 1835 rb-9-268 (Ru)
Smith, Thomas 1836 wb-1-220 (Gr)

Smith, Thomas 1836 wb-1-223 (W)
Smith, Thomas 1836 wb-x-374 (Mu)
Smith, Thomas 1840 rb-h-438 (Mt)
Smith, Thomas 1846 rb-13-694 (Ru)
Smith, Thomas 1854 wb-12-55 (K)
Smith, Thomas 1856 wb-17-70 (D)
Smith, Thomas 1859 wb-3-491 (Gr)
Smith, Thomas B. 1838 wb-7-6 (Wi)
Smith, Thomas J. 1847 wb-e-19 (Ro)
Smith, Thomas Lea 1851 wb-2-97 (Sh)
Smith, Thomas O. 1815 wb-#15 (Mu)
Smith, Thomas S. 1844 wb-8-152 (Wi)
Smith, Thomas S. 1856 wb-#120 (Wl)
Smith, Thomas W. 1844 rb-j-208 (Mt)
Smith, Thos. N. 1836 rb-g-404 (Mt)
Smith, Turner 1854 wb-2-79# (Ge)
Smith, W. P. 1861 wb-k-497 (O)
Smith, Wiley 1840 eb-1-422 (C)
Smith, William 1805 wb-1-451 (Hw)
Smith, William 1814 rb-2-273 (Ru)
Smith, William 1814 wb-#15 (Wl)
Smith, William 1815 Wb-2-165 (Wi)
Smith, William 1826 wb-#165 (Mc)
Smith, William 1829 wb-#165 (Mc)
Smith, William 1830 wb-1-43 (Li)
Smith, William 1832 wb-5-120 (Wi)
Smith, William 1832 wb-a-127 (R)
Smith, William 1833 rb-9-60 (Ru)
Smith, William 1833 wb-3-0 (Sm)
Smith, William 1833 wb-b-219 (Ro)
Smith, William 1834 wb-#30 (Wa)
Smith, William 1835 wb-#36 (Wa)
Smith, William 1840 wb-#138 (Wl)
Smith, William 1841 wb-1-55 (Me)
Smith, William 1841 wb-3-0 (Sm)
Smith, William 1845 wb-c-257 (G)
Smith, William 1848 wb-#166 (Mc)
Smith, William 1849 wb-7-0 (Sm)
Smith, William 1850 148-1-345 (Ge)
Smith, William 1850 mr-2-371 (Be)
Smith, William 1853 wb-n-65 (Mt)
Smith, William 1854 wb-12-67 (K)
Smith, William 1856 wb-16-616 (D)
Smith, William 1857 wb-2-183 (Li)
Smith, William 1857 wb-f-104 (G)
Smith, William 1859 wb-1-460 (Hw)
Smith, William 1860 wb-h-397 (Hn)
Smith, William B. 1858 6-2-142 (Le)
Smith, William C. (Dr.) 1858 wb-3-486 (Gr)
Smith, William C. 1854 wb-3-207 (Gr)
Smith, William D. 1860 wb-#133 (Wl)

Smith, William F. 1835 wb-a-36 (O)
Smith, William F. 1852 wb-1-17 (R)
Smith, William G. 1859 rb-20-110 (Ru)
Smith, William G. 1859 rb-20-196 (Ru)
Smith, William H. 1829 wb-1-85 (Ma)
Smith, William H. 1851 rb-15-565 (Ru)
Smith, William H. 1861 39-2-453 (Dk)
Smith, William M. 1847 wb-9-318 (K)
Smith, William M. 1850 rb-15-559 (Ru)
Smith, William P. 1847 wb-e-21 (Ro)
Smith, William Sharp 1820 wb-7-373 (D)
Smith, William W. 1857 wb-h-398 (St)
Smith, William Y. 1852 wb-4-495 (Mu)
Smith, William jr. 1821 wb-A-341 (Li)
Smith, William sr. 1855 wb-12-112 (K)
Smith, Wineyfred 1841 wb-1-128 (Bo)
Smith, Winney 1852 wb-7-0 (Sm)
Smith, Wm. A. 1853 rb-16-538 (Ru)
Smith, Wm. B. 1816 wb-2-139 (Je)
Smith, Wright 1854 wb-1-57 (R)
Smith, Zachariah 1852 wb-e-17 (G)
Smith, Zelpha 1857 wb-1-115 (R)
Smith?, Caswell D. 1858 wb-f-129 (G)
Smithe, Daniel 1837 wb-d-142* (Hn)
Smithpeter, Christenia 1855 wb-1-97 (Jo)
Smithpeter, Michael 1856 wb-1-109 (Jo)
Smithson, A. F. 1854 ib-h-236 (F)
Smithson, A. H. 1854 ib-h-14 (F)
Smithson, Clement 1814 Wb-2-105 (Wi)
Smithson, Elizabeth C. 1839 wb-7-71 (Wi)
Smithson, Francis 1851 rb-4-283 (Mu)
Smithson, Hiram 1853 ib-1-283 (Ca)
Smithson, J. P. 1857 as-c-42 (Ms)
Smithson, John 1837 wb-6-400 (Wi)
Smithson, John 1857 39-2-218 (Dk)
Smithson, Matilda 1859 wb-f-172 (Mu)
Smithson, Nathaniel B. 1859 wb-13-150 (Wi)
Smithson, Richard K. 1836 wb-6-216 (Wi)
Smithson, Samuel C. 1838 wb-6-441 (Wi)
Smithwick, B. 1835 wb-2-42 (Ma)
Smithwick, Bates 1843 wb-3-743 (Ma)
Smithwick, Humphrey 1857 wb-7-0 (Sm)
Smithwick, John A. 1842 wb-3-55 (Hy)
Smithwick, Luke 1828 wb-6-378 (Rb)
Smithwick, Shade 1839 rb-h-263 (Mt)
Smithwick, Slade 1836 rb-g-454 (Mt)
Smithwick, William 1848 wb-b-256 (We)
Smitzer, Peter 1823 wb-1-131 (Bo)
Smoot, Samuel D. 1835 wb-d-105 (Hn)
Smoot, W. J. 1846 rb-k-269 (Mt)
Smotherman, J. R. 1861 rb-20-744 (Ru)

Smotherman, John 1833 rb-9-48 (Ru)
Smotherman, John G. 1847 rb-14-171 (Ru)
Smotherman, Jonathan P. 1849 rb-15-51 (Ru)
Smotherman, Samuel 1842 rb-12-254 (Ru)
Smothers, Green B. 1856 wb-a-260 (Cr)
Smothers, James 1814 lr (Sn)
Smyth, Jacob 1841 wb-1-258 (Bo)
Smyth, Richie 1846 wb-b-148 (We)
Snapp, Abraham 1833 wb-#32 (Wa)
Snapp, John (Sr.) 1819 wb-#22 (Wa)
Snapp, John 1830 wb-2-39# (Ge)
Snapp, Samuel sr. 1859 wb-2-89# (Ge)
Snary, John 1829 wb-9-319 (D)
Snead, John S. 1841 wb-e-183 (Hn)
Snead, William 1835 rb-9-252 (Ru)
Sneed (Snell?), Charles E. 1853 rb-16-569 (Ru)
Sneed, A. W. H. 1858 39-2-258 (Dk)
Sneed, Alexander 1853 wb-10-458 (Wi)
Sneed, Alexander E. 1853 wb-10-532 (Wi)
Sneed, Charles E. 1838 rb-10-190 (Ru)
Sneed, Elizabeth 1860 wb-b-50 (Dk)
Sneed, James 1827 wb-#68 (Wl)
Sneed, James 1853 wb-11-37 (Wi)
Sneed, John 1854 rb-17-323 (Ru)
Sneed, John A. 1841 wb-#135 (Wl)
Sneed, Lucy 1839 rb-10-356 (Ru)
Sneed, Mark A. 1854 wb-11-173 (Wi)
Sneed, Stephen K. 1841 wb-a-65 (F)
Sneed, Stephen K. 1841 wb-a-67 (F)
Sneed, Susan 1861 wb-13-448 (Wi)
Sneed, Susan B. 1842 wb-#137 (Wl)
Sneed, Thomas 1858 wb-h-161 (Hn)
Sneed, William 1821 wb-1-0 (Sm)
Sneed, William 1838 wb-#120 (Wl)
Sneed, William 1858 wb-5-78 (Hr)
Snell, Elizabeth 1820 wb-#36 (Wl)
Snell, Hardy 1852 rb-16-229 (Ru)
Snell, Hardy T. 1850 rb-15-300 (Ru)
Snell, Hugh 1848 as-a-164 (Ms)
Snell, J. E. 1857 as-c-97 (Ms)
Snell, James 1838 rb-10-239 (Ru)
Snell, James E. 1860 as-c-218 (Ms)
Snell, Jesse L. 1853 as-b-124 (Ms)
Snell, John 1849 rb-l-332 (Mt)
Snell, Lewis 1860 rb-p-435 (Mt)
Snell, Sarah R. 1859 rb-20-304 (Ru)
Snell, Willis 1851 rb-15-587 (Ru)
Snider, Abraham 1850 wb-2-71# (Ge)
Snider, Adam 1859 wb-1-122 (Jo)
Snider, Alexander 1847 wb-1-43 (Jo)
Snider, Amy 1832 wb-#98 (Wl)

Snider, Charles 1796 rb-a-13 (Mt)
Snider, Frederick 1852 wb-#8 (Mo)
Snider, George 1846 wb-#5 (Mo)
Snider, Henry 1859 wb-2-269 (Li)
Snider, John 1842 wb-#3 (Mo)
Snider, Jonas 1840 wb-e-125 (Hn)
Snider, Michael 1811 lw (Ct)
Snider, Peter 1840 wb-e-161 (Hn)
Snider, Peter 1846 wb-1-131 (Bo)
Snider, Peter 1857 wb-h-86 (Hn)
Snider, Peter 1860 wb-1-148 (Jo)
Snider, Thomas J. 1853 mr-2-531 (Be)
Snipe, Susan 1840 wb-y-638 (Mu)
Snipes, Charity 1844 wb-z-566 (Mu)
Snipes, Jesse 1827 wb-b-40 (Hn)
Snipes, John 1834 lr (Gi)
Snipes, Willis L. 1842 wb-z-394 (Mu)
Snoddy, Carey 1852 wb-4-50 (Je)
Snoddy, David 1858 wb-2-258 (Li)
Snoddy, Glasgo 1859 wb-1-51 (Se)
Snoddy, Robert H. 1859 wb-13-168 (K)
Snoddy, Thomas 1839 wb-3-543 (Je)
Snoddy, William sr. 1812 wb-1-160 (Sn)
Snodgrass, David 1839 wb-4-68 (Je)
Snodgrass, James 1824 wb-#166 (Mc)
Snodgrass, James 1853 wb-d-95 (Wh)
Snodgrass, Joseph 1822 wb-2-379 (Je)
Snodgrass, Joseph 1858 wb-e-209 (Wh)
Snodgrass, Margaret 1858 wb-e-207 (Wh)
Snodgrass, Thomas 1852 wb-d-93 (Wh)
Snodgrass, Thomas sr. 1852 wb-d-98 (Wh)
Snodgrass, Walter J. 1859 wb-e-270 (Wh)
Snodgrass, William 1841 wb-c-8 (Wh)
Snodgrass, William G. 1858 wb-e-207 (Wh)
Snotterly, Henry 1837? wb-1A-171 (A)
Snow, Andrew J. 1860 ib-2-187 (Wy)
Snow, Anthony J. 1853 wb-16-166 (D)
Snow, Augustine 1854 wb-#114 (Wl)
Snow, David C. 1833 wb-10-242 (D)
Snow, Henry sr. 1849 wb-1-358 (Li)
Snow, John 1842 wb-1-78 (Sh)
Snow, Thomas 1818 wb-a-113 (Ro)
Snowden, Nathan 1847 wb-2-15 (Sh)
Snyder, Charles 1808 wb-3-222 (D)
Snyder, Jacob B. 1835 wb-5-333 (K)
Soape, William 1836 rb-9-354 (Ru)
Soloman, Avy 1857 wb-3-376 (W)
Soloman, Wm. H. 1860 wb-3-310 (Sn)
Solomon, John R. 1858 wb-16-661 (Rb)
Solomon, Samuel 1861 wb-17-227 (Rb)
Solomon, William 1845 wb-1-272 (Li)

Somerow, James H. 1851 wb-b-142 (L)
Somers, James Sr. 1821 wb-#39 (Wl)
Somers?, M. P. 1858 wb-4-11 (La)
Sommerset, Joseph 1834 wb-3-0 (Sm)
Sommerville, George W. 1824 wb-8-330 (D)
Sommerville, John 1846 wb-13-474 (D)
Sory, Horatio 1846 wb-13-30 (Rb)
Sory, Michael 1852 wb-7-0 (Sm)
Souell, W. P. 1850 wb-b-564 (Mu)
Soule, Dempsey 1832 wb-1-236 (Hr)
Souls, Abraham 1840 wb-A-17 (Ca)
Southall, James 1845 wb-8-344 (Wi)
Southall, Joseph J. B. 1853 wb-16-194 (D)
Southerlan, Gabriel H. 1841 wb-a-70 (F)
Southerland, Alvis 1840 wb-c-90 (Ro)
Southerland, Geo. 1857 as-c-516 (Di)
Southerland, Solomon 1823 wb-2-395 (Je)
Southern, Achillus M. 1815 wb-2-272 (Rb)
Southern, Burton 1852 ib-2-46 (Cl)
Southern, Isaah 1861 wb-f-214 (Mu)
Southern, James D. 1844 wb-a2-117 (Mu)
Southern, James P. 1845 wb-a2-208 (Mu)
Southern, Robert 1837 5-3-40 (Cl)
Southern, Robert 1850 ib-1-123 (Cl)
Southern, William 1821 wb-3-262 (Rb)
Southern, William B. 1838 wb-c-135 (Hu)
Southers, Jesse A. 1852 wb-d-389 (G)
Southgate, Gertrude Vanleer 1860 wb-18-360 (D)
Soward, Henry 1840 wb-c-63 (Ro)
Soward, John 1859 wb-c-290 (L)
Soward, Wilson N. 1842 wb-c-290 (Ro)
Sowder, Adam 1840 5-2-158 (Cl)
Sowell, Charles 1839 wb-y-490 (Mu)
Sowell, George 1833 wb-c-4 (Hn)
Sowell, Henry C. 1860 wb-f-192 (Mu)
Sowell, Joseph 1832 wb-#241 (Mu)
Sowell, Newton 1843 wb-d-7 (Hd)
Sowell, Thomas 1847 wb-a-312 (F)
Sowell, Thomas W. 1859 wb-f-159 (Mu)
Sowell, William P. 1848 wb-b-223 (Mu)
Sox, John 1854 wb-h-289 (Hu)
Spain, James 1833 wb-3-0 (Sm)
Spain, James 1852 wb-7-0 (Sm)
Spain, James 1853 wb-15-393 (Rb)
Spain, John 1823 wb-#48 (Wl)
Spain, John 1852 ib-1-189 (Wy)
Spain, John 1852 ib-1-194 (Wy)
Spain, John D. 1853 27-lw (Hd)
Spain, Lucy 1861 rb-21-157 (Ru)
Spain, Lucy N. 1836 wb-9-375 (Rb)
Spain, Martha S. 1851 wb-14-532 (Rb)

Spain, Martha S. K. 1851 wb-14-532 (Rb)
Spain, Stephen 1820 wb-7-454 (D)
Spain, Stephen 1840 rb-10-519 (Ru)
Spain, Stephen 1840 rb-10-553 (Ru)
Spain, Thomas P. 1835 wb-9-70 (Rb)
Spain, William 1809 wb-1-285 (K)
Spain, William K. 1856 ib-1-446 (Wy)
Spain, William R. 1854 ib-1-315 (Wy)
Spalding, Timothy 1834 wb-1-333 (Hr)
Span, William 1843 rb-12-385 (Ru)
Sparkman, Elizabeth 1849 wb-b-539 (Mu)
Sparkman, George 1816 wb-a-55 (Wh)
Sparkman, Humphreys W. 1838 wb-y-302 (Mu)
Sparkman, James 1845 wb-5-376 (Gr)
Sparkman, Jesse 1846 wb-8-392 (Wi)
Sparkman, John 1850 wb-2-71 (Sh)
Sparkman, Kinchen 1836 wb-6-213 (Wi)
Sparkman, Kinchen 1846 wb-8-472 (Wi)
Sparkman, Martha M. 1846 wb-8-463 (Wi)
Sparkman, William 1832 wb-5-153 (Wi)
Sparkman, William C. 1854 wb-11-95 (Wi)
Sparkman, Wm. 1848 wb-b-255 (Mu)
Sparks, James J. 1852 wb-g-562 (Hu)
Sparks, Nancy 1856 wb-#119 (Wl)
Sparks, Nathan 1844 wb-#145 (Wl)
Speakeman, William 1830 wb-a-10 (T)
Spear, James G. H. 1833 wb-8-218 (Rb)
Spear, S. 1859 wb-f-245 (G)
Spearman, John W. 1853 wb-1-303 (Fr)
Spearman, Wesley 1838 wb-#166 (Mc)
Spears, Edward A. 1855 wb-b-376 (We)
Spears, James 1859 wb-#127 (Wl)
Speciard, John 1834 wb-1A-82 (A)
Specks, George C. 1847 33-3-18 (Gr)
Speece, James N. 1835 wb-10-424 (D)
Speer, Burrell B. 1851 wb-2-102 (Sh)
Speer, George 1858 lr (Gi)
Speight, A. 1852 as-c-160 (Di)
Speight, Albert 1853 as-c-216 (Di)
Speight, Alsey 1831 as-a-212 (Di)
Speight, Alsey S. 1833 as-a-238 (Di)
Speight, Jesse M. 1852 as-c-184 (Di)
Speight, V. A. 1857 as-c-488 (Di)
Speight, William D. 1852 wb-a-252 (Di)
Speight, William H. 1859 wb-e-117 (Hy)
Spellman, N. J. 1859 wb-#167 (Mc)
Spence, Alanson 1860 rb-20-622 (Ru)
Spence, Alaxson 1860 rb-20-639 (Ru)
Spence, David 1817 wb-7-206 (D)
Spence, David 1840 wb-10-450 (Rb)
Spence, James 1808 wb-1-251 (K)

Spence, James 1821 wb-0-224 (K)
Spence, James 1826 wb-b-6 (Hn)
Spence, James 1844 wb-13-129 (D)
Spence, John 1825 wb-8-410 (D)
Spence, John 1845 wb-13-157 (D)
Spence, Joseph 1840 wb-12-10 (D)
Spence, Joseph 1841 wb-12-18 (D)
Spence, M. 1857 rb-19-74 (Ru)
Spence, Marmon 1847 rb-14-62 (Ru)
Spence, Nancy 1860 rb-20-564 (Ru)
Spence, Sarah 1857 rb-18-634 (Ru)
Spence, Sarah L. 1845 wb-13-158 (D)
Spence, Thomas 1841 wb-e-143 (St)
Spence, Thomas 1847 wb-e-24 (Ro)
Spence, William 1856 wb-b-390 (We)
Spence, William G. 1853 wb-2-60 (Li)
Spencer, Benjamin 1854 wb-e-172 (G)
Spencer, Britain 1830 rb-8-93 (Ru)
Spencer, Daniel 1852 as-c-200 (Di)
Spencer, David 1816 wb-4-438 (D)
Spencer, John 1825 wb-a-60 (G)
Spencer, John 1826 wb-1-108 (Ma)
Spencer, John 1860 wb-f-385 (G)
Spencer, Joseph 1818 rb-4-186 (Ru)
Spencer, Joseph 1833 rb-9-50 (Ru)
Spencer, Neace 1856 wb-a-278 (Cr)
Spencer, R. C. 1849 wb-#170 (Wl)
Spencer, Richard 1848 rb-14-218 (Ru)
Spencer, Thomas 1853 wb-2-82 (Li)
Spencer?, Edward 1847 wb-g-1 (Hu)
Sperry, John M. 1834 wb-b-146 (Wh)
Sperry, Lewis 1838 rb-10-165 (Ru)
Sperry, Thomas 1833 wb-b-128 (Wh)
Sperry, Thomas 1834 wb-#126 (Wl)
Spiceland, Sandford 1838 wb-d-212 (St)
Spicer, James 1850 wb-g-394 (Hu)
Spicer, James 1850 wb-g-421 (Hu)
Spicer, Winifred 1845 wb-1-114 (Sh)
Spickard, John 1853 wb-#107 (Wl)
Spillings, Britian 1835 wb-b-73 (G)
Spires, Elizabeth O. 1844 wb-3-26 (Sn)
Spivey, Jethro 1843 wb-8-87 (K)
Spivy, J. G. 1843 wb-3-190 (Hy)
Spivy, John 1853 wb-a-215 (Cr)
Spivy, Jonathan G. 1841 wb-2-392 (Hy)
Spivy?, T. 1836 wb-2-91 (Ma)
Spotswood, Julia A. 1860 wb-18-361 (D)
Spradley, Tarver 1822? wb-#42 (Wl)
Spradlin, Lucinda 1849 wb-g-248 (Hu)
Spradlin, Obediah 1823 wb-#87 (Wl)
Spradling, Charles 1841 wb-1-561 (W)

Spradling, J. U. 1858 wb-1-230 (Be)
Spralding, Andrew 1817 wb-A-157 (Li)
Spring, Aaron 1815 wb-#16 (Wl)
Spring, Abner 1840 wb-#173 (Wl)
Spring, Lawrence 1832 wb-1-345 (Ma)
Springer, Aaron 1852 wb-3-1 (La)
Springer, E. J. 1855 mr-2-628 (Be)
Springer, Frances 1862 wb-f-444 (G)
Springs, John 1837 wb-#119 (Wl)
Sprott, James A. 1859 wb-13-80 (Wi)
Sproule, Robert 1827 rb-e-55 (Mt)
Sprouse, Aaron 1829 wb-1-86 (Ma)
Sprouse, G. B. 1858 wb-16-608 (Rb)
Sprouse, James 1860 wb-17-109 (Rb)
Sprout, Alexander 1851 wb-b-314 (We)
Spurgin, Benjamin H. 1855 wb-2-183 (Sh)
Spurlock, Granderson 1855 wb-b-11 (F)
Spurock, Garrison 1859 gs-1-212 (F)
Squairs, Evington 1820 rb-5-15 (Ru)
Squibb, George 1852 wb-5-38 (Je)
Squier, David 1819 wb-3-3 (Wi)
Squier, Gurdon 1813 Wb-2-36 (Wi)
Squire, Solomon 1808 wb-1-306 (Rb)
Squires, Elizabeth 1834 wb-3-451 (Je)
Squires, George 1838 wb-y-159 (Mu)
Squires, Levi 1841 wb-3-0 (Sm)
Squires, Levi J. 1860 wb-8-42 (Sm)
Srigley, Samuel 1815 wb-#14 (Mu)
Srote, Peter 1854 wb-g-589 (Hn)
St Johns, Elizabeth 1843 rb-j-41 (Mt)
St. Clair, Albert J. 1859 wb-13-183 (K)
St. Clair, Lavelle 1837 rb-10-6 (Ru)
St. Clair, Wm. 1855 rb-17-528 (Ru)
St. John, George 1849 ib-1-63 (Ca)
St. John, Thos. 1854 ib-1-314 (Ca)
Stack, Adam 1849 wb-m-578 (Mt)
Stack, G. W. 1858 wb-a-63 (Ce)
Stack, Simon W. 1826 rb-6-266 (Ru)
Stacker, Samuel 1860 wb-i-183 (St)
Stacks, Abraham 1832 wb-#240 (Mu)
Stacy, Daniel B. 1831 wb-5-4 (Wi)
Stacy, Willis A. 1839 wb-2-110 (Hr)
Staffard, John 1859 wb-A-150 (Ca)
Stafford, Arthur 1841 wb-3-403 (Ma)
Stafford, Basel G. 1847 wb-a-306 (F)
Stafford, Caleb 1860 wb-k-341 (O)
Stafford, Jesse 1855 wb-b-13 (F)
Stafford, Joab 1853 wb-a-187 (Cr)
Stafford, Merrel 1858 wb-4-39 (La)
Stafford, Sampson 1861 wb-b-96 (F)
Stafford, Thomas 1858 wb-7-0 (Sm)

Stafford, Thomas J. 1859 gs-1-387 (F)
Stafford, William 1854 wb-b-336 (We)
Staggs, Felix 1826 wb-4-139 (Wi)
Staggs, John 1827 wb-4-156 (Wi)
Staggs, John N. 1851 ib-1-151 (Wy)
Staggs, Joseph 1855 ib-1-348 (Wy)
Staggs, Robert N. 1852 ib-1-172 (Wy)
Staggs, William 1854 wb-i-144 (O)
Staggs, William N. 1852 ib-1-188 (Wy)
Stagner, Barnabas 1836 wb-d-2 (St)
Stagner, Uriah 1851 mr-2-440 (Be)
Staily, Fredrick 1815 rb-b-272 (Mt)
Stainback, Robt. 1857 wb-16-543 (Rb)
Stair, Joseph 1859 wb-13-205 (K)
Stair, William 1797 wb-1-16 (Rb)
Stalcup, Swain 1820 lr (Sn)
Stalcup, William 1819 wb-1-0 (Sm)
Stalcup, William 1855 wb-7-0 (Sm)
Staley, Frederick 1825 rb-d-485 (Mt)
Stallings, Delila 1812 wb-1-0 (Sm)
Stallings, John 1859 wb-8-28 (Sm)
Stallings, Miles 1819 wb-1-0 (Sm)
Stallings, Mills 1822 wb-2-0 (Sm)
Stallings, Thomas R. 1848 wb-b-218 (Mu)
Stalls, James 1841 wb-e-90 (St)
Stalls, Jesse 1827 wb-b-145 (St)
Stalsworth, Amos 1845 wb-2-61 (Gr)
Stamper, A. W? 1855 wb-h-88 (St)
Stamper, Asa 1852 wb-xx-132 (St)
Stamper, Blount 1857 rb-o-288 (Mt)
Stamper, John W. 1860 wb-1-401 (Fr)
Stamper, John W. D. 1860 wb-1-401 (Fr)
Stamper, Mason 1848 wb-f-486 (St)
Stamper, Nicholas 1858 rb-o-704 (Mt)
Stamper, Robert 1832 rb-f-369 (Mt)
Stamps, Elizabeth 1850 as-a-208 (Ms)
Stamps, James 1841 wb-1-201 (Fr)
Stamps, James A. A. 1861 ib-2-227 (Wy)
Stamps, Sandford 1824 wb-a-197 (Wh)
Stamps, William 1833 wb-b-120 (Wh)
Stan, George W. 1853 wb-16-136 (D)
Stancel, John 1844 wb-f-178 (St)
Stancell, Elisha 1839 wb-1-272 (W)
Stancil, Elizabeth 1848 wb-9-168 (Wi)
Stancill, Nathan 1822 wb-3-326 (Wi)
Standback, Litlebery 1848 wb-4-347 (Hr)
Standfield, John 1856 wb-2-313 (Me)
Standfield, John A. 1857 wb-2-348 (Me)
Standley, Garland 1812 eb-1-24 (C)
Standley, Isaac 1840 wb-b-188 (O)
Standley, Joseph B. 1854 wb-e-147 (G)

Standley, Thomas 1858 wb-16-648 (Rb)
Standly, Matilda 1855 wb-e-355 (G)
Standly, Spencer 1854 wb-i-179 (O)
Standly, Thos. D. 1855 wb-e-296 (G)
Standridge, Elizabeth 1841 rb-11-309 (Ru)
Stanfield, Abram 1835 wb-2-194 (Sn)
Stanfield, Ashley 1839 wb-2-260 (Sn)
Stanfield, Ephraim 1815 wb-2-159 (Wi)
Stanfield, Goodlow 1838 wb-11-487 (D)
Stanfield, James 1812 wb-#5 (Mu)
Stanfield, James W. 1851 ib-1-141 (Wy)
Stanfield, James W. 1855 ib-1-369 (Wy)
Stanfield, John (Col.) 1813 wb-#8 (Mu)
Stanfield, John 1812 wb-#5 (Mu)
Stanfield, Robert G. 1855 wb-11-558 (Wi)
Stanfield, Sarah 1859 wb-7-59 (Ma)
Stanfield, Spivey 1842 wb-7-535 (Wi)
Stanfield, William 1861 149-1-220 (Ge)
Stanfill, John 1844 wb-f-130 (St)
Stankey, Abram 1854 wb-n-346 (Mt)
Stanley, John 1840 wb-1-304 (W)
Stanley, Joseph B. 1853 wb-e-84 (G)
Stanley, Martin 1822 wb-3-326 (Wi)
Stanley, Martin 1836 wb-6-264 (Wi)
Stanley, Moses 1816 wb-#26 (Wl)
Stanley, R. H. 1858 wb-3-425 (W)
Stanley, Samuel 1841 wb-2-286 (Hr)
Stanley, Thomas W. 1860 wb-d-57 (L)
Stanley, Wright 1833 wb-5-296 (Wi)
Stanley, Wright 1836 wb-6-161 (Wi)
Stanly, William D. 1860 as-c-228 (Ms)
Stansbury, I. N. 1857 wb-#167 (Mc)
Stansbury, Moses 1840 wb-7-86* (K)
Stanton, Benjamin 1846 wb-1-136 (Sh)
Stapleton, Michael 1855 wb-12-174 (K)
Star, Michael 1857 wb-#59 (Wa)
Starbuck, Peter 1803 wb-1-0 (Sm)
Stark, Alexander 1845 lr (Sn)
Stark, Amus 1859 wb-16-690 (Rb)
Stark, Annis 1861 wb-17-163 (Rb)
Stark, Ephraim 1839 wb-10-168 (Rb)
Stark, Jeremiah 1851 wb-14-415 (Rb)
Stark, John 1814 wb-1-181 (Sn)
Stark, John C. 1841 wb-12-14 (D)
Stark, Magdalene 1855 wb-16-66 (Rb)
Stark, Nancy 1857 wb-16-429 (Rb)
Stark, Peggy (Mrs.) 1853 wb-e-429 (Ro)
Stark, Sarah 1852 wb-15-192 (Rb)
Stark, Sarah 1858 wb-16-677 (Rb)
Stark, Thomas 1802 wb-1-91 (Rb)
Stark, Thomas 1824 lr (Sn)

Stark, Thomas B. 1854 wb-15-558 (Rb)
Stark, Thornton 1853 lr (Sn)
Stark, Walter 1832 wb-8-167 (Rb)
Stark, Walter W. 1832 wb-8-194 (Rb)
Stark, Walter W. 1859 wb-16-712 (Rb)
Starkey, Benjamin 1860 wb-18-381 (D)
Starkey, Joshua 1847 wb-2-5 (Sh)
Starkey, Rebecca 1854 wb-16-263 (D)
Starkie, Abraham 1846 rb-k-273 (Mt)
Starkie, Pleasant 1835 rb-g-213 (Mt)
Starks, Prudence 1827 lr (Sn)
Starks, Stephen G. 1860 wb-3c-127 (Sh)
Starky, Joel 1831 wb-1-277 (Ma)
Starnes, Adam 1834 wb-1-50 (Gr)
Starnes, Adam 1834 wb-1-83 (Gr)
Starnes, Moses 1852 wb-a-189 (T)
Starnes, Samuel 1850 wb-9-346 (Wi)
Starnes, Samuel S. 1842 wb-7-586 (Wi)
Starnes, Shubal 1851 wb-10-26 (Wi)
Starnes, Shubart? 1848 wb-9-165 (Wi)
Starnes, William 1850 148-1-307 (Ge)
Starr, George H. 1857 wb-17-381 (D)
Starrett, David 1854 wb-#26 (Mo)
Staten, Susan M. 1860 wb-7-82 (Ma)
Statham, Charles 1826 rb-6-237 (Ru)
Statham, Charles 1826 rb-6-252 (Ru)
Statham, Jane 1850 rb-15-321 (Ru)
Statham, Robert 1856 rb-18-97 (Ru)
Statham, William P. 1853 wb-h-Feb (O)
Staton, Elijah 1850 rb-15-323 (Ru)
Stavely, Eli J. jr. 1844 wb-f-211 (St)
Steane, John 1831 wb-9-486 (D)
Steane, Michael 1829 wb-9-352 (D)
Stearns, Sarah 1849 wb-14-237 (Rb)
Stedman, Nathan W. 1860 wb-7-60 (Ma)
Steed, John 1841 wb-#168 (Mc)
Steed, Justus 1851 wb-#168 (Mc)
Steed, Phebe 1846 wb-#168 (Mc)
Steed, Thomas 1863 wb-#169 (Mc)
Steel, David 1812 wb-2-11 (K)
Steel, James 1823 wb-#59 (Mu)
Steel, James 1824 wb-#69 (Mu)
Steel, John 1847 wb-a-160 (Ms)
Steel, John 1848 rb-l-173 (Mt)
Steel, Judiah H. 1859 wb-#127 (Wl)
Steel, Mary 1861 wb-f-421 (Ro)
Steel, Samuel F. 1828 wb-1-48 (Hr)
Steel, William 1834 wb-1-58 (Hy)
Steele, Aaron 1854 wb-a-335 (Ms)
Steele, Alexander 1846 wb-8-449 (Wi)
Steele, Andrew 1858 wb-17-439 (D)

Steele, Benjamin 1844 wb-3-355 (Hy)
Steele, Edward H. 1828 rb-e-330 (Mt)
Steele, John 1822 rb-d-14 (Mt)
Steele, John sr. 1822 rb-d-84 (Mt)
Steele, Mary 1859 wb-f-165 (Mu)
Steele, Miles R. 1831 wb-1-184 (Hr)
Steele, Moses 1844 wb-8-169 (Wi)
Steele, Ninian S. 1840 wb-2-150 (Hr)
Steele, Robert 1831 lr (Sn)
Steele, Sally 1843 rb-i-510 (Mt)
Steele, Samuel F. 1844 wb-3-131 (Hr)
Steele, Sarah R. 1853 wb-11-3 (Wi)
Steele, Thomas 1832 lr (Gi)
Steele, Thomas A. 1858 lr (Gi)
Steele, Thomas J. 1860 wb-18-319 (D)
Steele, William 1815 wb-2-144 (K)
Steele, William D. 1857 wb-f-120 (Mu)
Steelmoln?, Presley 1861 39-2-455 (Dk)
Steely, Benjamin 1860 wb-h-491 (Hn)
Steely, John 1843 wb-g-132 (Hn)
Steen, Ty? 1858 wb-4-198 (La)
Steerman, Thomas K. 1847 wb-4-17 (Je)
Stegall, A. 1852 wb-g-485 (Hn)
Stegall, Samuel J. 1855 as-b-184 (Ms)
Stegar, Francis 1854 rb-16-700 (Ru)
Stegar, William 1830 rb-f-116 (Mt)
Stegar, William 1842 rb-12-252 (Ru)
Stegar, William 1847 wb-14-104 (D)
Steger, Nancy 1855 wb-e-373 (G)
Stein, Joseph 1859 wb-17-601 (D)
Stem, James 1830 wb-b-86 (Hn)
Stembridge, John 1811 wb-#10 (Wl)
Stembridge, John 1848 wb-#162 (Wl)
Stenate, Geo. 1802 wb-2-266 (D)
Stephen, Martha 1858 wb-12-547 (Wi)
Stephens, Abram 1844 wb-c-200 (G)
Stephens, Daniel 1850 wb-5-6 (Hr)
Stephens, Dennis 1858 wb-12-548 (Wi)
Stephens, Edward 1827 wb-3-131 (Je)
Stephens, Edward 1836 wb-6-276 (Wi)
Stephens, Edwin 1814 wb-a-225 (St)
Stephens, Elvin? 1815 wb-3-135 (St)
Stephens, George 1855 wb-12-187 (K)
Stephens, Jacob 1843 wb-3-101 (Hr)
Stephens, James 1803 wb-a-312 (D)
Stephens, James 1848 as-a-184 (Ms)
Stephens, John 1803 wb-2-339 (D)
Stephens, John 1853 wb-2-76# (Ge)
Stephens, Lewis S. (B) 1847 5-3-301 (Cl)
Stephens, Lewis S. 1845 5-3-68 (Cl)
Stephens, Loami 1815 Wb-2-164 (Wi)

Stephens, Luraney 1839 wb-7-70 (Wi)
Stephens, Mary 1813 rb-2-245 (Ru)
Stephens, Mary B. 1815 rb-3-38 (Ru)
Stephens, Moses 1851 wb-15-51 (D)
Stephens, Nancy 1846 wb-d-2 (G)
Stephens, Nancy 1863 wb-2-377 (Li)
Stephens, Philip 1830 wb-b-69 (Ro)
Stephens, Rebecca 1860 wb-18-169 (D)
Stephens, Richard 1840 wb-#1 (Mo)
Stephens, Richard 1854? wb-#25 (Mo)
Stephens, Robert 1836 wb-A-3 (Ca)
Stephens, Robert 1837 wb-1-137 (Li)
Stephens, Samuel 1833 wb-b-7 (G)
Stephens, Silas 1838 wb-6-504 (Wi)
Stephens, Silas 1838 wb-7-25 (Wi)
Stephens, Simion 1847 wb-14-161 (D)
Stephens, Simon 1847 wb-14-137 (D)
Stephens, Squire 1820 rb-c-302 (Mt)
Stephens, Thomas 1854 wb-11-402 (Wi)
Stephens, William 1860 wb-b-83 (F)
Stephens, William sr. 1816 Wb-2-184 (Wi)
Stephenson, Adelia A. 1853 wb-7-0 (Sm)
Stephenson, Alexander Campbell 1860
    wb-#169 (Mc)
Stephenson, Andrew 1854 wb-#169 (Mc)
Stephenson, David 1849 wb-#48 (Wa)
Stephenson, Francis M. 1852 wb-#169 (Mc)
Stephenson, George 1849 wb-14-440 (D)
Stephenson, J. H. 1854 wb-i-186 (O)
Stephenson, James 1838 wb-6-268 (K)
Stephenson, James B. 1859 wb-13-87 (K)
Stephenson, James W. 1848 wb-9-145 (Wi)
Stephenson, John 1817 rb-4-57 (Ru)
Stephenson, John 1841 wb-#39 (Wa)
Stephenson, John 1854 wb-3-200 (La)
Stephenson, John E. 1856 wb-f-108 (Mu)
Stephenson, John J. 1838 wb-y-198* (Mu)
Stephenson, John W. 1848 wb-b-373 (Mu)
Stephenson, Jonathan 1851 wb-b-311 (We)
Stephenson, Joseph 1838 wb-1-141 (La)
Stephenson, Joshua M. 1857 wb-17-394 (D)
Stephenson, Margaret 1857 wb-12-320 (K)
Stephenson, Matthew 1838 wb-#37 (Wa)
Stephenson, Moore 1818 wb-#28 (Wl)
Stephenson, Nathaniel 1848 wb-9-38 (Wi)
Stephenson, Robert 1793 wb-1-8 (Je)
Stephenson, Robert 1844 wb-8-355 (K)
Stephenson, Robert 1845 wb-#169 (Mc)
Stephenson, Rosanna D. 1849 wb-9-289 (Wi)
Stephenson, Roseannah 1825 wb-#21 (Wa)
Stephenson, Samuel 1848 wb-b-272 (Mu)

Stephenson, Thomas 1848 wb-b-252 (Mu)
Stephenson, William 1796? wb-#23 (Wa)
Stephenson, William 1821 wb-1-0 (Sm)
Stephenson, William 1821 wb-3-292 (K)
Stephenson, William Sr. 1839 wb-#169 (Mc)
Stepp, Colby 1843 wb-3-0 (Sm)
Stepp, Frederick 1857 wb-3-366 (W)
Stepp, Richard M. 1861 wb#42 (Gu)
Sterblin, Obadiah 1835 wb-1-76 (La)
Sterling, Hannah 1815 wb-2-167 (K)
Sterling, John 1848 wb-2-14 (Sh)
Sterling, Margret 1845 wb-1-244 (Bo)
Sterling, Martha A. 1843 wb-8-78 (K)
Sterling, Martha E. 1838 wb-6-245 (K)
Sterling, Robert 1840 wb-1-182 (Bo)
Sterling, Samuel 1836 wb-6-66 (K)
Stern, James 1835 wb-d-58 (Hn)
Sterrett, William 1822 rb-5-211 (Ru)
Stevens, Abednego 1841 wb-12-150* (D)
Stevens, Ambrose 1853 wb-2-141 (Sh)
Stevens, Edward 1837 wb-6-330 (Wi)
Stevens, Elizabeth 1850 wb-4-68 (Mu)
Stevens, George W. 1838 wb-11-322 (D)
Stevens, Henry 1801 wb-#8 (Wa)
Stevens, Henry 1838 wb-b-92 (Hd)
Stevens, Henry C. 1840 wb-7-277 (Wi)
Stevens, Henry C. 1850 wb-9-581 (Wi)
Stevens, James 1857 wb-0-150 (Cf)
Stevens, James P. 1852 wb-10-266 (Wi)
Stevens, Joel 1847 wb-9-2 (Wi)
Stevens, John 1821 wb-2-0 (Sm)
Stevens, John sr. 1847 wb-a-130 (T)
Stevens, L. B. 1848 wb-#162 (Wl)
Stevens, Moses 1841 wb-12-148* (D)
Stevens, Polly 1844 wb-a2-50 (Mu)
Stevens, R. H. 1846 wb-a2-482 (Mu)
Stevens, Rachel 1854 wb-0-133 (Cf)
Stevens, Thomas E. 1851 wb-#176 (Wl)
Stevenson, E. D. 1851 wb-14-647 (D)
Stevenson, Isaac L. 1840 wb-#130 (Wl)
Stevenson, Isaac T. 1837 wb-#119 (Wl)
Stevenson, James W. 1847 wb-9-24 (Wi)
Stevenson, Robert 1843 wb-a-122 (Cr)
Stevenson, Washington Moore 1848
    wb-#162 (Wl)
Stevenson, William 1845 wb-#41 (Wa)
Steverson, James H. 1856 wb-j-168 (O)
Steverson, John 1815 wb-1-0 (Sm)
Stevins, Robt. 1850 rb-4-17 (Mu)
Steward, James 1815 wb-2-164 (K)
Steward, James 1819 wb-#32 (Wl)

Steward, William 1793 wb-1-284 (D)
Stewart, Alexander 1815 wb-a-72 (Ro)
Stewart, Alexander 1836 wb-1-156 (W)
Stewart, Alexander 1847 wb-1-209 (Bo)
Stewart, Allen 1855 wb-3-328 (La)
Stewart, Andrew 1815 wb-A-82 (Li)
Stewart, Andrew 1841 wb-12-33 (D)
Stewart, Andrew 1848 wb-1-243 (Me)
Stewart, Andrew 1850 wb-14-292 (Rb)
Stewart, Ann 1812 wb-1-277 (Wi)
Stewart, Archibald 1856 wb-j-180 (O)
Stewart, Barney 1840 lr (Sn)
Stewart, Bartholomew G. 1840 wb-3-192 (Ma)
Stewart, Charles 1817 rb-b-450 (Mt)
Stewart, Charles 1837 wb-2-216 (Ma)
Stewart, Charles 1860 wb-#132 (Wl)
Stewart, Cyrus 1860 lr (Sn)
Stewart, Duncan 1810 rb-a-510 (Mt)
Stewart, E. L. 1857 wb-a-12 (Ce)
Stewart, Edward 1857 wb-a-23 (Ce)
Stewart, Elijah R. 1838 wb-#121 (Wl)
Stewart, Elisha 1822 wb-a-162 (Wh)
Stewart, Elisha T. 1834 wb-1-554 (Ma)
Stewart, G. W. 1854 wb-15-461 (Rb)
Stewart, George 1846 wb-4-120 (Hr)
Stewart, Herbert 1836 wb-9-266 (Rb)
Stewart, James (Sr.) 1824 wb-#61 (Wl)
Stewart, James 1810 rb-a-511 (Mt)
Stewart, James 1815 wb-a-70 (Ro)
Stewart, James 1818 rb-c-62 (Mt)
Stewart, James 1826 rb-6-243 (Ru)
Stewart, James 1834 wb-10-272 (D)
Stewart, James 1858 wb-a-49 (Ce)
Stewart, Jane 1858 gs-1-29 (F)
Stewart, John 1800 wb-1-4 (Wi)
Stewart, John 1817 wb-a-78 (Wh)
Stewart, John 1826 wb-a-13 (R)
Stewart, John 1837 wb-e-26 (Hu)
Stewart, John 1840 wb-7-217 (Wi)
Stewart, John 1846 wb-1-406 (La)
Stewart, John 1849 lr (Sn)
Stewart, John D. 1846 as-a-130 (Ms)
Stewart, Joseph 1842 wb-#138 (Wl)
Stewart, Joseph 1844 wb-#142 (Wl)
Stewart, L. D. 1854 ib-H-102 (F)
Stewart, Lebert 1816 wb-2-322 (Rb)
Stewart, M. B. 1850 wb-5-88 (Ma)
Stewart, Peter 1851 wb-15-57 (D)
Stewart, R. L. 1853 as-c-267 (Di)
Stewart, Robert 1839 wb-1-167 (Li)
Stewart, Robert W. 1820 rb-c-356 (Mt)

Stewart, Robert W. 1854 wb-15-641 (Rb)
Stewart, Robt. L. 1838 as-b-17 (Di)
Stewart, Samuel 1854 wb-#111 (Wl)
Stewart, Sarah 1832 wb-1-68 (Li)
Stewart, Sarah 1844 wb-#145 (Wl)
Stewart, Sarah 1858 wb-3-440 (W)
Stewart, Thomas 1839 wb-7-83 (Wi)
Stewart, Thomas 1847 wb-7-0 (Sm)
Stewart, Thomas H. 1860 wb-i-159 (St)
Stewart, William 1816 wb-1-11 (Fr)
Stewart, William 1816 wb-2-335 (Rb)
Stewart, William 1829 wb-b-46 (Hn)
Stewart, William 1831 wb-b-45 (Wh)
Stewart, William 1837 wb-11-81 (D)
Stewart, William 1845 wb-13-147 (D)
Stewart, William 1845 wb-b-102 (We)
Stewart, William 1848 rb-l-171 (Mt)
Stewart, William 1851 wb-15-12 (D)
Stewart, William 1854 wb-#115 (Wl)
Stewart, William 1860 rb-p-514 (Mt)
Stewart, William P. 1846 wb-1-126 (Sh)
Stewart, William sr. 1834 wb-1-420 (Ma)
Sticklan, Joseph 1839 wb-#1 (Mo)
Stickley, Daniel 1797 wb-0-22 (K)
Stickly, Daniel 1816 wb-2-211 (K)
Stier, Cornelius 1849 mr-2-316 (Be)
Stiffy, John 1836 wb-1-140 (Gr)
Stiffy, Ruth 1834 wb-1-111 (Gr)
Stigall, Henry 1852 mr-2-476 (Be)
Stiles, Jesse 1849 wb-1-365 (Li)
Stiles, John 1844 wb-0-40 (Cf)
Still, John 1835 wb-6-63 (Wi)
Still, John 1851 wb-15-120 (D)
Still, John P. 1858 wb-12-573 (Wi)
Still, Joseph 1840 wb-7-270 (Wi)
Still, Josiah 1830 wb-4-535 (Wi)
Still, Josiah 1840 wb-7-258 (Wi)
Still, Rebecca 1849 wb-9-272 (Wi)
Still, Rhodam 1850 wb-14-554 (D)
Still, William 1820 rb-4-213 (Ru)
Still, William 1820 rb-5-39 (Ru)
Stilwell, E. A. 1857 as-c-57 (Ms)
Stilwell, Elias 1844 wb-a-117 (Ms)
Stilwell, Eliazer 1842 wb-a-113 (Ms)
Stilwell, James A. 1858 as-c-95 (Ms)
Stilwell, Jesse 1848 wb-a-177 (Ms)
Stimpson, James F. 1854 wb-h-11 (St)
Stimson, J. F. 1850 wb-g-265 (St)
Stine, Andrew 1858 wb-2-87# (Ge)
Stinnet, George 1809 wb-4-32 (D)
Stinson, James 1844 wb-a-227 (F)

Stinson, L. 1848 wb-f-127+ (O)
Stinson?, Willingto? 1851 as-b-38 (Ms)
Stirling, Henry 1806 wb-1-215* (K)
Stirling, James 1797 wb-1-60 (K)
Stirling, John 1797 wb-0-19 (K)
Stirling, John 1814 wb-2-90 (Je)
Stith, Abner 1855 wb-c-13 (L)
Stith, Ariana 1856 wb-b-31 (F)
Stith, Ferdinando 1856 wb-12-46 (Wi)
Stith, Henry 1833 wb-c-100 (Hn)
Stobaugh, Henry 1811 wb-4-143 (D)
Stockard, Camilla Ann 1850 rb-4-2 (Mu)
Stockard, Cyntha 1851 ib-1-127 (Wy)
Stockard, Isaac N. 1850 rb-4-25 (Mu)
Stockard, James 1831 wb-#219 (Mu)
Stockard, James R. 1832 wb-x-30 (Mu)
Stockard, John 1830 rb-8-167 (Ru)
Stockard, John 1846 rb-13-510 (Ru)
Stockard, Richard (esq.) 1850 wb-4-70 (Mu)
Stockard, S. A. 1837 wb-y-75 (Mu)
Stockard, Samuel 1843 wb-z-543 (Mu)
Stockard, Silas A. 1837 wb-y-598 (Mu)
Stockard, William 1838 wb-y-130 (Mu)
Stockdale, Matthew 1824 wb-a-40 (Hn)
Stockdon, Margaret 1818 lr (Gi)
Stockell, William 1847 wb-14-119 (D)
Stockett, Daniel 1836 wb-6-244 (Wi)
Stockett, Joseph H. 1821 Wb-3-228 (Wi)
Stockett, Joseph H. 1832 wb-5-172 (Wi)
Stockett, Noble 1803 Wb-1-108 (Wi)
Stockett, Thomas W. 1820 wb-3-118 (Wi)
Stockinger, John C. 1853 wb-a-438 (F)
Stockstill, David 1840 wb-1-308 (W)
Stockstill, Elisha 1848 wb-2-277 (W)
Stockstill, Jesse 1859 wb-2-275 (Li)
Stockstill, Rachel 1846 wb-2-155 (W)
Stockstule, David 1828 wb-1-16 (W)
Stockton, Benjamin 1820 wb-a-131 (Ro)
Stockton, D. H. 1836 wb-1-86 (La)
Stockton, Jehu 1846 wb-#170 (Mc)
Stockton, Sarah B. 1840 wb-#170 (Mc)
Stockton, Thomas 1840 wb-b-218 (Hd)
Stockton, Thomas 1858 wb-f-224 (Ro)
Stockwell, William 1847 wb-14-6 (D)
Stocton, Sarah 1838 wb-11-272 (D)
Stoddart, Matthew 1813 wb-a-145 (St)
Stoddert, William 1839 wb-3-9 (Ma)
Stoddert, William 1855 wb-6-83 (Ma)
Stoffle, William 1845 wb-g-65 (Hn)
Stogner, Sarah 1835 wb-10-513 (D)
Stoker, John 1837 wb-a-324 (O)

Stokes, Edmond 1854 wb-b-343 (We)
Stokes, H. B. 1853 as-b-107 (Ms)
Stokes, James S. 1837 abl-1-104 (T)
Stokes, John 1835 wb-c-450 (St)
Stokes, Josiah 1830 wb-4-518 (Wi)
Stokes, Robert 1839 wb-b-275 (G)
Stokes, Sil 1822 wb-2-0 (Sm)
Stokes, Silvanus 1818 wb-1-0 (Sm)
Stokes, Thomas 1815 wb-1-0 (Sm)
Stokes, Thomas 1827 wb-2-0 (Sm)
Stokes, Yonger 1854 as-b-163 (Ms)
Stokes, Young 1845 rb-13-406 (Ru)
Stokes, Young 1857 rb-19-57 (Ru)
Stolize, Mary 1861 wb-17-212 (Rb)
Stone, Barton W. 1841 wb-7-377 (Wi)
Stone, Claborn 1856 wb-b-379 (We)
Stone, Dillard G. 1857 wb-3-338 (W)
Stone, Emily 1858 wb-e-208 (Wh)
Stone, Esabius 1828 wb-#178 (Mu)
Stone, Fountain P. 1857 lr (Sn)
Stone, Geo. P. (Graville) 1851 wb-a-391 (F)
Stone, Hendley 1834 wb-5-425 (Wi)
Stone, Jacob F. 1856 wb-7-0 (Sm)
Stone, James 1853 wb-A-86 (Ca)
Stone, James Thomas 1859 lr (Sn)
Stone, Jane 1828 wb-4-345 (Wi)
Stone, Jane 1829 wb-4-374 (Wi)
Stone, Jeremiah 1837 wb-b-356 (Ro)
Stone, John 1827 wb-#70 (Wl)
Stone, John 1828 wb-1-25 (W)
Stone, John 1828 wb-6-334 (Rb)
Stone, John 1831 wb-5-20 (Wi)
Stone, John 1844 rb-12-435 (Ru)
Stone, John H. 1831 wb-5-41 (Wi)
Stone, John H. 1836 wb-6-142 (Wi)
Stone, Kindness 1858 wb-h-522 (St)
Stone, Kindness 1858 wb-h-526 (St)
Stone, Lawrence 1839 wb-5-34 (Gr)
Stone, Martha 1853 wb-3-264 (W)
Stone, Mary 1840 wb-7-340 (Wi)
Stone, Mary 1844 wb-#154 (Wl)
Stone, Micajah 1827 wb-1-3 (Li)
Stone, Moses 1847 wb-1-327 (Li)
Stone, Nicholas 1834 wb-8-417 (Rb)
Stone, Pickett 1815 wb-#16 (Wl)
Stone, Rachal (Rebecca?) 1847 wb-d-58 (G)
Stone, Randolph 1840 wb-b-191 (O)
Stone, Randolph 1843 wb-d-26 (O)
Stone, Richard 1831 wb-#225 (Mu)
Stone, Robert 1844 wb-5-341 (Gr)
Stone, Robert B. 1837 rb-g-636 (Mt)

Stone, Sarah A. 1841 wb-7-486 (Wi)
Stone, Sarah Ann 1842 wb-7-529 (Wi)
Stone, Thomas 1841 lr (Sn)
Stone, Thomas 1841 wb-c-4 (Wh)
Stone, Thomas 1843 wb-#142 (Wl)
Stone, Thomas C. 1844 lr (Gi)
Stone, Uriah 1833 wb-a-92 (Cr)
Stone, William 1805 wb-a-3 (Di)
Stone, William 1812 wb-1-285 (Wi)
Stone, William 1818 wb-#116 (Mu)
Stone, William 1820 wb-#170 (Mc)
Stone, William 1830 lr (Sn)
Stone, William 1831 wb-b-106 (Hn)
Stone, William 1833 wb-c-18 (Hn)
Stone, William 1848 wb-2-38 (Sh)
Stone, William 1856 as-c-25 (Ms)
Stone, William N. 1856 wb-#118 (Wl)
Stone, William P. 1859 wb-f-166 (Mu)
Stonecifer, Absalom 1858 149-1-138 (Ge)
Stonecypher, Absalom 1845 wb-2-74# (Ge)
Stonecypher, Alexander H. 1846 148-1-161 (Ge)
Stonecypher, Solomon 1844 wb-2-61# (Ge)
Stoneman, John 1802 wb-2-264 (D)
Stoner, Henry 1857 wb-b-26 (Dk)
Stons?, Margaret 1857 ib-1-461 (Ca)
Stooksbery, Robert 1857 wb-1C-366 (A)
Stormer, George 1851 wb-11-12 (K)
Stormin?, George 1838 wb-6-303 (K)
Stott, Eli T. 1851 wb-15-18 (Rb)
Stott, James H. 1843 wb-3-0 (Sm)
Stotts, E. E. 1854 wb-15-446 (Rb)
Stotts, J. S. 1857 wb-16-378 (Rb)
Stotts, Jacob 1857 wb-16-451 (Rb)
Stotts, Mary 1861 wb-17-254 (Rb)
Stotts, Solomon 1844 wb-12-181 (Rb)
Stout, Ann 1829 wb-b-44 (Ro)
Stout, Dr. Benjamin C. 1829 wb-#171 (Mc)
Stout, Godfrey Daniel sr. 1846 wb-1-27 (Jo)
Stout, Ira 1818 wb-7-237 (D)
Stout, Isaac 1815 wb-2-171 (K)
Stout, Isaiah 1858 ib-2-66 (Wy)
Stout, S. V. D. 1851 wb-15-75 (D)
Stovall, Byrd 1845 lr (Sn)
Stovall, George 1820 wb-1-33 (Fr)
Stovall, George 1840 wb-b-5 (We)
Stovall, James B. 1855 wb-1-338 (Fr)
Stovall, John 1816 rb-3-131 (Ru)
Stovall, Leroy M. 1860 rb-20-642 (Ru)
Stovall, William 1857 wb-j-270 (O)
Stover, Daniel 1849 lw (Ct)
Stover, David L. 1838 lw (Ct)

Stowel, George 1815 wb-2-168 (K)
Strain, M. D. 1861 wb-d-110 (L)
Strain, William B. 1833 wb-#31 (Wa)
Strange, Edmund G. 1855 wb-16-583 (D)
Strange, Henry 1843 wb-d-76 (Ro)
Strange, Nathaniel 1842 wb-z-285 (Mu)
Strange, Sarah 1844 wb-13-122 (D)
Strange, Willis 1833 wb-10-157 (D)
Stratton, James 1851 lr (Sn)
Stratton, John R. 1844 wb-d-135 (Hd)
Stratton, Margaret M. 1858 wb-3e-61 (Sh)
Stratton, Trifany 1833 wb-8-266 (Rb)
Straud, William 1841 wb-1-375 (W)
Straughan, Hiram L. 1826 wb-5-411 (Rb)
Straughn, Mary L. 1853 mr-2-505 (Be)
Strawbridge, Gray 1831 wb-c-108 (St)
Strawn, John 1824 wb-8-386 (D)
Strayhorn, David 1824 wb-#129 (Mu)
Strayhorn, David 1835 wb-x-246* (Mu)
Strayhorn, David 1841 wb-3-466 (Ma)
Strayhorn, David W. 1849 A-468-118 (Le)
Strayhorn, David W. 1849 A-468-122 (Le)
Strayhorn, James 1836 wb-x-319* (Mu)
Strayhorn, James C. 1836 wb-x-347 (Mu)
Strayhorn, John 1852 wb-5-119 (Ma)
Strayhorn, John D. 1836 wb-x-335* (Mu)
Strayhorn, Penelope 1849 A-468-115 (Le)
Street, Abram M. 1856 wb-h-602 (Hu)
Street, Abram M. 1856 wb-h-604 (Hu)
Street, Alexander 1837 wb-y-47 (Mu)
Street, Elizabeth 1853 lr (Sn)
Street, James E. 1843 wb-a-129 (L)
Street, Joseph 1818 wb-A-264 (Li)
Street, Joseph 1840 as-a-31 (Ms)
Street, Martha 1854 as-c-290 (Di)
Street, Mary 1850 wb-a-225 (Ms)
Street, Moses 1843 wb-a-156 (Di)
Street, William 1837 wb-1-160 (Fr)
Stribling, B. T. 1833 wb-1-45 (La)
Stribling, Thos. T. 1857 wb-h-659 (Hu)
Strickland, Alexander 1841 wb-a-73 (L)
Strickland, Charles Williams 1856 wb-1-84 (Be)
Strickland, Harman 1830 wb-3-0 (Sm)
Strickland, Jesse 1853 wb-15-451 (Rb)
Strickland, Jesse 1854 wb-15-485 (Rb)
Strickland, Joseph 1829 wb-4-465 (Wi)
Strickland, Sarah A. 1857 wb-4-81 (La)
Strickland, Thomas 1804 Wb-1-131 (Wi)
Stricklin, Jacob 1851 ib-1-108 (Wy)
Stricklin, James 1850 ib-1-80 (Wy)
Stricklin, John 1814 wb-2-127 (Rb)

Stricklin, John 1853 ib-1-271 (Wy)
Stricklin, Joseph 1827 wb-4-157 (Wi)
Stricklin, Thomas A. 1852 wb-4-557 (Mu)
Stringer, William B. 1815 wb-2-172 (K)
Stringfellow, Richard 1827 wb-9-111 (D)
Stringfellow, Robert 1815 wb-4-364 (D)
Stringfellow, Stephen W. 1841 wb-a-104 (Ms)
Stringfellow, William 1816 wb-2-203 (Wi)
Stringfellow, William 1847 wb-14-65 (D)
Strode, James 1830 lr (Sn)
Stron, John 1825 wb-8-412 (D)
Strong, Christopher 1850 wb-a-214 (Di)
Strong, Jane 1846 wb-9-261 (K)
Strong, John 1816 wb-4-439 (D)
Strong, John 1816 wb-7-53 (D)
Strong, John 1848 wb-1-346 (Li)
Strong, Joseph C. 1844 wb-9-12 (K)
Strong, William J. 1857 wb-a-245 (T)
Strong, Wm. M. 1858 wb-f-132 (G)
Strong?, Mary 1855 wb-1-36 (Be)
Strother, George 1816 wb-7-24 (D)
Strother, Gideon 1835 wb-b-65 (G)
Strother, John 1816 wb-4-431 (D)
Strother, John 1816 wb-7-20 (D)
Strother, Judd 1843 wb-3-0 (Sm)
Strother, Mary 1852 wb-h-Dec (O)
Strother, Richard 1813 lr (Sn)
Strothers, Samuel K. 1816 wb-2-287 (Rb)
Stroud, Ann E. 1853 wb-10-610 (Wi)
Stroud, Archibald 1836 wb-#141 (Wl)
Stroud, B. S. 1853 wb-3-177 (W)
Stroud, Bartlett S. 1853 wb-3-181 (W)
Stroud, Daniel M. 1852 ib-1-227 (Wy)
Stroud, David 1858 39-2-265 (Dk)
Stroud, Hannah 1851 wb-3-98 (W)
Stroud, Jesse 1834 wb-1-139 (We)
Stroud, Jesse 1842 as-b-105 (Di)
Stroud, Jessee 1831 as-a-206 (Di)
Stroud, Joseph 1841 rb-i-106 (Mt)
Stroud, Lucretia 1844 wb-#145 (Wl)
Stroud, Morris 1844 wb-f-192* (Hn)
Stroud, Sarah 1858 39-2-265 (Dk)
Stroud, Silus 1849 wb-g-220 (O)
Stroud, Thomas 1852 wb-3-121 (W)
Stroud, William sr. 1853 wb-3-189 (W)
Stroup, Jacob 1812 rb-2-205 (Ru)
Strutton, Joel H. 1853 wb-#25 (Mo)
Stuart, Archabald 1855 wb-i-235 (O)
Stuart, Hamilton 1850? wb-#171 (Mc)
Stuart, John 1822 rb-d-252 (Mt)
Stuart, John 1853 wb-#53 (Wa)

Stuart, John 1868 wb-#171 (Mc)
Stuart, Margaret 1808 wb-4-7 (D)
Stuart, Robert 1826 wb-#25 (Wa)
Stuart, Robert 1838 as-a-408 (Di)
Stuart, Robert 1844 wb-8-360 (K)
Stuart, Thomas 1818 wb-a-95 (Wh)
Stuart, Thomas 1838 wb-7-6 (Wi)
Stuart, William 1808 wb-3-191 (D)
Stuart, William 1812 wb-4-196 (D)
Stuart, William 1833 lr (Sn)
Stuart, Wm. 1794 wb-1-304 (D)
Stubbins, William 1837 wb-x-441 (Mu)
Stubblefield, Allen 1857 wb-2-204 (Li)
Stubblefield, Clement 1845 wb-13-191 (D)
Stubblefield, George 1847 wb-2-251 (W)
Stubblefield, Martin 1835 wb-4-44 (Je)
Stubblefield, Mary 1834 wb-#171 (Mc)
Stubblefield, Nancy 1850 lr (Sn)
Stubblefield, Peter 1849 ib-1-28 (Wy)
Stubblefield, Robert Loxly 1817 wb-1-434 (Hw)
Stubblefield, Thomas 1825 lr (Sn)
Stubblefield, Thomas 1833 wb-1-441 (Hw)
Stubblefield, William 1827 lr (Sn)
Stubblefield, William 1833 wb-#172 (Mc)
Stubblefield, Wyett 1824 wb-1-438 (Hw)
Stubbs, Everett 1817 wb-a-98 (Ro)
Stubbs, George 1849 wb-e-160 (Ro)
Stubbs, Jesse 1828 wb-b-1 (Ro)
Stuckey, James G. 1852 wb-b-185 (L)
Stuckey, Michael 1855 wb-c-28 (L)
Stuckey, Noah 1853 wb-b-199 (L)
Stucky, Samuel 1837 wb-1-342 (Hy)
Studart, Mathew 1829 wb-c-24 (St)
Studdard, Nancy 1827 wb-#172 (Mc)
Stull, George 1854 wb-16-361 (D)
Stull, Nancy (Mrs.) 1852 wb-15-212 (D)
Stull, Rachiel 1847 wb-14-111 (D)
Stull, Valentine 1827 wb-#73 (Wl)
Stull, Zacheriah 1819 wb-7-314 (D)
Stump, Albert G. 1836 wb-10-601 (D)
Stump, Albert G. 1853 wb-15-568 (D)
Stump, F. H. 1848 wb-14-243 (D)
Stump, Frederick 1820 wb-7-501 (D)
Stump, John 1854 wb-16-418 (D)
Stump, Jonathan 1806 wb-3-77 (D)
Stump, Nancy B. 1857 wb-17-298 (D)
Stump, Rachel 1860 wb-18-238 (D)
Stump, Rebecca W. 1853 wb-16-165 (D)
Stunston, John 1836 wb-1-155 (We)
Stuntston, Henry 1847 wb-b-221 (We)
Sturdevant, Henry W. 1826 wb-9-36 (D)

Sturdivant, Joseph 1853 wb-n-123 (Mt)
Sturdivant, Josiah M. 1830 wb-9-446 (D)
Sturen, Alcy 1850 wb-1-454 (Hw)
Sturgis, Joshua L. 1848 wb-2-35 (Sh)
Sturgis, Samuel 1848 wb-2-34 (Sh)
Stutts, Barberry 1861 wb-2-93# (Ge)
Stutts, Lewis 1854 wb-2-79# (Ge)
Stutts, Solomon 1844 wb-12-152 (Rb)
Sublett, George A. 1855 rb-17-497 (Ru)
Sublett, Rebecca 1855 wb-#118 (Wl)
Sublett, Volentine M. 1846 rb-13-529 (Ru)
Sublett, William A. 1839 rb-10-451 (Ru)
Sudbury, Shadrach R. 1859 wb-1-91 (Dy)
Sudbury, William D. 1836 wb-6-185 (Wi)
Sudbury, William D. 1846 wb-8-399 (Wi)
Suddath, B. F. 1855 wb-1-80 (R)
Suddath, Benjamin 1835 wb-b-272 (Ro)
Suddath, Benjamin sr. 1836 wb-b-339 (Ro)
Suddath, John 1847 wb-e-23 (Ro)
Sudduth, Benjamin 1857 wb-1-132 (R)
Sugg, Aquila 1789 wb-1-97 (D)
Sugg, Elijah 1854 wb-0-127 (Cf)
Sugg, Elizabeth 1832 rb-8-502 (Ru)
Sugg, Franklin 1857 wb-0-151 (Cf)
Sugg, H. H. 1853 wb-15-273 (Rb)
Sugg, Henry H. 1853 wb-15-277 (Rb)
Sugg, John H. 1833 rb-9-21 (Ru)
Sugg, Lemuel 1809 rb-a-452 (Mt)
Sugg, Lemuel 1814 wb-2-129 (Rb)
Sugg, Noah 1800 wb-1-44 (Rb)
Sugg, Solomon 1839 wb-#124 (Wl)
Sugg, William 1825? as-a-136 (Di)
Suggs, Isaac 1846 wb-1-140 (Sh)
Suggs, Noah 1798 wb-2-119 (D)
Suiitor, William 1824 wb-a-3 (Cr)
Suit, Solomon 1854 wb-h-146 (St)
Suit, William 1835 wb-2-196 (Sn)
Sulevan, Samuel W. 1855 wb-3-339 (La)
Sulivan, Jacob 1846 wb-b-179 (We)
Sulivan, Patrick 1831 rb-8-245 (Ru)
Sulivan, Thomas 1861 wb-13-465 (K)
Sullards, James 1812 wb-1-321 (Wi)
Sullins, Josiah 1847 wb-e-36 (Ro)
Sullivan, Azel 1836 wb-#113 (Wl)
Sullivan, Cornelius 1846 wb-1-302 (Li)
Sullivan, Eclemuel 1847 wb-#153 (Wl)
Sullivan, Ezekiel 1847 wb-1-450 (Hw)
Sullivan, Fletcher & Molly 1822 wb-#43 (Wl)
Sullivan, Fletcher 1822 wb-#49 (Wl)
Sullivan, Gilbert 1837 wb-#118 (Wl)
Sullivan, Harney 1857 ib-1-449 (Ca)

Sullivan, J. W. 1861 wb-#134 (Wl)
Sullivan, James 1818 rb-4-144 (Ru)
Sullivan, James 1831 rb-8-230 (Ru)
Sullivan, Jesse 1846 wb-#152 (Wl)
Sullivan, Jesse M. 1850 wb-c-433 (Wh)
Sullivan, John 1831 wb-b-64 (Wh)
Sullivan, John 1840 wb-#133 (Wl)
Sullivan, Lahoma 1857 iv-1-583 (Ca)
Sullivan, Lucian B. 1853 r39-1-281 (Dk)
Sullivan, Nancy 1834 as-a-269 (Di)
Sullivan, Owen 1830 lr (Sn)
Sullivan, Patrick 1817 rb-4-76 (Ru)
Sullivan, Reuben 1852 wb-#178 (Wl)
Sullivan, Thomas 1825 wb-#57 (Wl)
Sullivan, W. W. 1850 wb-14-646 (D)
Sullivan, W. W. 1851 wb-14-618 (D)
Sullivan, William 1808 wb-3-186 (D)
Sullivan, William 1827 wb-1-8 (W)
Sullivan, William 1835 wb-1-122 (W)
Sullivan, William 1854 wb-#112 (Wl)
Sullivan, William W. 1853 wb-#110 (Wl)
Sullivant, Samuel 1859 wb-4-276 (La)
Sullivant, Susannah 1841 wb-1-241 (La)
Sulser, Mathias 1793 wb-1-9 (K)
Sumerow, Henry 1853 wb-b-235 (L)
Sumerow, James H. 1853 wb-b-212 (L)
Summars, Alexander 1831 wb-#89 (Wl)
Summars, H. H. 1849 wb-#170 (Wl)
Summars, Harris H. 1849 wb-#171 (Wl)
Summer, Ad Eliza 1859 wb-i-127 (St)
Summer, James 1858 wb-A-136 (Ca)
Summer, James B. 1855 wb-A-108 (Ca)
Summer, Lohama 1858 ib-1-498 (Ca)
Summerhill, G. W. 1847 wb-#154 (Wl)
Summerhill, George W. 1847 wb-#155 (Wl)
Summerhill, William 1857 rb-18-637 (Ru)
Summerhill, William L. 1858 rb-19-223 (Ru)
Summers, Ann 1841 wb-3-404 (Ma)
Summers, Charles 1834 wb-c-373 (St)
Summers, Geo. 1834 rb-9-149 (Ru)
Summers, George 1853 rb-16-398 (Ru)
Summers, Matthew 1835 wb-#108 (Wl)
Summers, Robert 1851 rb-15-567 (Ru)
Summers, Thomas 1850 wb-14-346 (Rb)
Summers, Thomas 1852 rb-16-242 (Ru)
Summers, William 1844 rb-12-500 (Ru)
Summersett, Joseph 1834 lr (Sn)
Summerville, John 1835 wb-9-62 (Rb)
Summett, Sarah 1856 wb-#27 (Mo)
Summons, V. 1857 wb-16-364 (Rb)
Sumner, Duke William 1844 wb-13-103 (D)

Sumner, Exum P. 1852 wb-15-271 (D)
Sumner, Geo. D. 1852 rb-16-236 (Ru)
Sumner, Jacob B. 1815 wb-4-343 (D)
Sumner, John H. 1837 rb-10-23 (Ru)
Sumner, Mary 1849 wb-14-612 (D)
Sumner, Moses 1855 wb-a-472 (F)
Sumner, Thomas E. 1817 wb-3-90 (Wi)
Sumner, Thomas E. 1820 wb-3-112 (Wi)
Sumner, Thomas E. 1833 wb-5-283 (Wi)
Sumner, William 1801 wb-1-38 (Je)
Sumners, Abraham 1838 wb-1-152 (Li)
Sumners, James 1838 wb-2-263 (Ma)
Sumners, John 1845 wb-1-264 (Li)
Sumpter, Edward 1855 wb-12-73 (K)
Sunderland, Abraham 1852 wb-5-94 (Je)
Sunderland, Nathan 1816 wb-#35 (Mu)
Sunderland, Solomon 1824 wb-2-443 (Je)
Sures, Charles 1809 wb-4-47 (D)
Surles, Henry 1860 lr (Gi)
Surls, Frank 1836 wb-3-0 (Sm)
Susong, John sr. 1861 wb-2-101# (Ge)
Susong, Nicholas 1848 148-1-249 (Ge)
Susong, William 1855 149-1-12 (Ge)
Sut, Garret 1842 lr (Sn)
Sutherland, Andrew 1798 wb-1-253 (Je)
Sutherland, James 1855 wb-b-364 (We)
Sutherland, John 1817 wb-#32 (Mu)
Sutherland, John 1846 wb-1-33 (Jo)
Sutherland, Joseph 1859 wb-1-126 (Jo)
Sutherland, Joshua 1852 wb#21 (Gu)
Sutherland, Samuel 1849 wb#19 (Gu)
Sutherland, Solomon 1822 wb-2-356 (Je)
Sutlieve, James 1835 wb-3-352 (Je)
Suttie, Presley 1843 lr (Sn)
Suttle, Bushrod 1826 wb-a-220 (Wh)
Suttle, Henry 1854 wb-3-176 (W)
Suttle, Henry J. 1845 wb-2-93 (W)
Suttle, John 1851 wb-d-52 (Wh)
Suttle, William 1843 lr (Gi)
Suttle, William D. 1861 lr (Gi)
Sutton, Benjamin F. 1850 lr (Sn)
Sutton, Edmund 1825 rb-6-120 (Ru)
Sutton, Foster 1854 as-b-149 (Ms)
Sutton, James 1835 wb-3-0 (Sm)
Sutton, James 1844 wb-0-41 (Cf)
Sutton, John 1836 wb-b-135 (G)
Sutton, Lovey 1852 lr (Sn)
Sutton, Malichiah 1794 wb-2-3 (D)
Sutton, Stephen 1838 wb-11-218 (D)
Sutton, _____ (widow Sarah?) 1836 wb-b-116 (G)
Swain, Elizabeth 1836 wb-1-444 (Hw)

Swain, John 1853 wb-#173 (Mc)
Swan, Alexander 1837 wb-6-91 (K)
Swan, Andrew 1844 wb-#145 (Wl)
Swan, George 1832 wb-5-169 (K)
Swan, Harvey 1803 wb-1-129 (K)
Swan, John 1804 wb-1-155 (K)
Swan, John 1820 wb-0-210 (K)
Swan, John 1835 wb-#107 (Wl)
Swan, John A. 1832 wb-5-186 (K)
Swan, John McC. 1838 wb-6-238 (K)
Swan, Katherine 1847 wb-#168 (Wl)
Swan, Mathew 1824 wb-#127 (Mu)
Swan, Moses L. 1837 wb-6-123 (K)
Swan, Moses L. 1848 wb-10-85 (K)
Swan, Robert 1845 rb-13-116 (Ru)
Swan, Robert 1860 wb-13-310 (K)
Swan, Robert B. 1845 rb-13-205 (Ru)
Swan, Samuel 1813 wb-2-40 (Je)
Swan, Samuel 1818 wb-3-39 (K)
Swan, William (Maj.) 1859 wb-13-215 (K)
Swan, William 1859 wb-13-135 (K)
Swaner, John 1851 wb-#177 (Wl)
Swaney, John 1846 wb-8-394 (Wi)
Swann, James 1821 wb-3-244 (Rb)
Swann, Jane C. 1834 wb-10-379 (D)
Swann, John 1817 wb-3-18 (Rb)
Swann, Mathew 1860 wb-1-398 (Fr)
Swann, Thomas 1812 lr (Sn)
Swann, William 1854 wb-16-213 (D)
Swann, Willis 1832 wb-9-597 (D)
Swanner, Jesse 1856 wb-1-55 (Dy)
Swanson, Edward 1840 wb-7-342 (Wi)
Swanson, Edward 1843 wb-8-87 (Wi)
Swanson, James 1850 wb-9-426 (Wi)
Swanson, Mary 1845 wb-8-345 (Wi)
Swayne, James W. 1856 wb-6-228 (Ma)
Swayne, Joshua 1859 wb-a-343 (Cr)
Swearingen, Mary E. 1861 wb-18-581 (D)
Sweat, Anthony 1826 lr (Sn)
Sweat, Benjamin 1834 eb-1-313 (C)
Sweat, Virtue 1858 wb-h-208 (Hn)
Sweatt, Edward 1854 wb-#113 (Wl)
Sweatt, Edward C. 1849 wb-#168 (Wl)
Sweatt, Garrison 1839 wb-#125 (Wl)
Sweatt, George 1830 wb-#82 (Wl)
Sweatt, Martha 1844 wb-#146 (Wl)
Sweatt, Sarah 1839 wb-#125 (Wl)
Sweatt, William 1830 wb-#98 (Wl)
Sweeney, Hillory W. 1853 wb-g-639 (Hn)
Sweeney, William R. 1858 wb-h-161 (Hn)
Sweeny, B. F. 1861 wb-18-467 (D)

Sweet, Moses 1848 wb-9-72 (Wi)
Swenny, Margaret 1861 wb-a-309 (T)
Swenson, James M. 1857 wb-17-217 (D)
Swenson, John M. 1854 wb-16-275 (D)
Swift, Edward 1854 wb-g-561 (Hn)
Swift, John 1808 wb-3-218 (D)
Swift, John 1838 wb-e-1 (Hn)
Swift, Sarah J. 1847 wb-g-206 (Hn)
Swift, Thomas 1827 as-a-157 (Di)
Swift, William 1859 wb-b-75 (F)
Swigart, Christian 1826 wb-5-382 (Rb)
Swindle, Cason 1839 wb-b-334 (Wh)
Swindle, Holwell 1847 wb-d-76 (G)
Swindle, Job 1832 wb-#96 (Wl)
Swindle, Nathan 1860 wb-1-335 (Be)
Swindle, Thomas 1860 wb-1-325 (Be)
Swinebroad, Henry 1840 wb-1-172 (Li)
Swinfield, Barton 1856 rb-17-633 (Ru)
Swinford, James 1853 wb-#173 (Mc)
Swingley, Jonas 1854 wb-#114 (Wl)
Swingley, Joseph 1820 wb-#37 (Wl)
Swingston, Rachel 1845 wb-13-275 (D)
Swink, Elizabeth 1842 wb-7-357 (K)
Swink, George 1831 wb-1-101 (Fr)
Swink, Michael 1860 rb-20-589 (Ru)
Swink, Peter J. 1851 wb-5-104 (Ma)
Swink?, George 1818 wb-1-29 (Fr)
Swinney, Briant 1837 lr (Gi)
Swinney, Richmond 1854 ib-h-252 (F)
Swinney, William 1852 wb-#116 (Wl)
Swipes, John H. 1853 wb-10-462 (Wi)
Swipes, John R. 1853 wb-10-457 (Wi)
Swor, John 1859 wb-h-314 (Hn)
Swor, Joseph 1844 wb-f-278 (Hn)
Syester, Daniel 1821 wb-1-435 (Hw)
Syke, Sanford 1832 rb-f-308 (Mt)
Sykes, A. R. 1845 mr-2-165 (Be)
Sykes, H. H. 1840 wb-e-356 (Hu)
Sykes, Jacob 1822 rb-d-20 (Mt)
Sykes, James 1845 wb-4-291 (Ma)
Sykes, James M. 1846 wb-5-21 (Ma)
Sykes, Jonas 1843 wb-3-676 (Ma)
Sykes, Lunsford 1832 rb-f-348 (Mt)
Sykes, William 1857 wb-1-118 (Be)
Sylar, Jacob 1832 wb-b-184 (Ro)
Sylor, John 1851 wb-1-286 (Fr)
Symes, Charles 1857 wb-a-27 (Ce)
Sypert, Sally 1843 wb-#142 (Wl)
Sypert, Thomas 1831 wb-#89 (Wl)
Sypert, Thomas 1844 wb-#142 (Wl)
Sypert, William L. 1826 wb-#61 (Wl)

- T -

Tabb, James A. 1804 wb-2-384 (D)
Tacker, Andrew E. Y. 1859 lr (Gi)
Tacker, Joshua 1848 lr (Gi)
Tackett, David 1857 ib-2-96 (Wy)
Tackett, Will B. 1849 ib-1-45 (Wy)
Tadlock, John 1857 149-1-74 (Ge)
Tadlock, Lewis 1815 wb-#14 (Wa)
Tadlock, William 1858 wb-e-91 (Hy)
Taff, Elizabeth 1834 wb-3-291 (Je)
Taggart, John 1842 wb-2-326 (Hr)
Tailor, Berryman 1837 as-a-364 (Di)
Tailor, Thomas 1846 wb-f-69 (O)
Tait, Caleb 1822 wb-3-360 (Wi)
Tait, Franklin M. 1835 wb-9-109 (Rb)
Tait, Margaret 1816 wb-4-462 (D)
Tait, Robert 1804 wb-2-380 (D)
Tait, Robert 1836 wb-#119 (Wl)
Tait, William 1816 wb-4-458 (D)
Tait, William 1816 wb-7-42 (D)
Taite, Netherland 1857 A-468-152 (Le)
Talbert, Thomas 1847 wb-14-23 (D)
Talbot, Eli 1833 wb-10-229 (D)
Talbot, Elizabeth 1814 wb-2-133 (K)
Talbot, Jane 1809 wb-4-78 (D)
Talbot, Joseph H. 1849 wb-2-48 (Sh)
Talbot, Mathew 1804 wb-2-394 (D)
Talbot, Mathew 1815 wb-4-333 (D)
Talbot, Thomas 1833 wb-10-184 (D)
Talbot, Thomas 1858 wb-1-43 (Se)
Talbott, Mathew 1805 wb-3-8 (D)
Taliaferro, C. P. 1839 wb-1-482 (Hy)
Taliaferro, Charles 1856 wb-f-31 (Ro)
Taliaferro, Charles P. 1836 wb-1-240 (Hy)
Taliaferro, Garland 1859 wb-e-118 (Hy)
Taliaferro, Walker 1852 wb-g-446 (Hn)
Tallant, Jonathan 1839 wb-6-489 (K)
Tallant, Richard 1832 wb-#173 (Mc)
Tallent, Thomas 1855 wb-#26 (Mo)
Talley, C. A. 1857 wb-j-294 (O)
Talley, David 1853 wb-15-571 (D)
Talley, Nelson 1853 wb-16-70 (D)
Talley, Sarah 1860 wb-k-266 (O)
Talley, Thomas J. 1860 wb-1-96 (Dy)
Talley, William 1815 wb-1-10 (Fr)
Talley, Wm. W. 1858 wb-3e-78 (Sh)
Talley, Zachariah sr. 1832 lr (Sn)
Tallman, George 1850 wb-3-52 (W)
Tally, Catharine 1816 wb-1-18 (Fr)
Tally, Guilford 1859 rb-p-67 (Mt)

Tally, Haley 1835 wb-#140 (Wl)
Tally, Haley 1845 wb-#159 (Wl)
Tally, Hannah Webb 1838 wb-a-361 (O)
Tally, Henry 1834 wb-1-107 (Hy)
Tally, Henry 1834 wb-1-45 (Hy)
Tally, Peter 1814 wb-#15 (Wl)
Tally, Reuben 1852 wb-15-347 (D)
Tally, Spencer 1818 wb-#28 (Wl)
Tally, Spencer W. 1851 wb-#177 (Wl)
Tally, William 1840 wb-b-338 (G)
Tally, William 1845 wb-a-114 (T)
Tamberson, Jno. 1848 wb-4-272 (Hr)
Tame, Elijah 1844 148-1-80 (Ge)
Tamler?, Henry 1838 wb-d-198* (Hn)
Tankersley, Benjamin 1851 as-b-26 (Ms)
Tankesley, Francis 1847 wb-14-91 (D)
Tanksley, Louisa J. 1852 wb-15-424 (D)
Tann (Fann?), Raleigh 1828 as-a-179 (Di)
Tanner, Burrel S. 1849 wb-g-99 (O)
Tanner, Burwell 1849 wb-g-198 (O)
Tanner, Edward 1820 wb-1-35 (Fr)
Tanner, Elizabeth W. 1861 wb-3e-173 (Sh)
Tanner, George W. 1852 wb-h-Apr (O)
Tanner, John B. 1843 wb-d-58 (O)
Tanner, Lodwick 1841 wb-z-191 (Mu)
Tanner, Samuel Y. 1840 wb-a-52 (F)
Tanner, Thomas J. 1860 wb-b*-37 (O)
Tanner, William 1829 wb-#81 (Wl)
Tapley, John 1809 wb-1-196 (Wi)
Tapscott, Henry C. 1859 wb-c-319 (L)
Tapscott, James 1856 wb-c-83 (L)
Tarbet, Samuel 1839 wb-1-263 (Bo)
Tarkington, Jesse 1834 wb-5-355 (Wi)
Tarkington, Jesse 1836 wb-6-122 (Wi)
Tarkington, William 1833 wb-5-219 (Wi)
Tarkington, William 1836 wb-6-119 (Wi)
Tarkinton, Zabulon 1799 wb-2-141 (D)
Tarpley, Ezra 1844 lr (Gi)
Tarpley, James 1854 wb-e-141 (G)
Tarpley, James A. 1860 rb-20-387 (Ru)
Tarpley, Sterling & Lucretia 1857 wb-#126 (Wl)
Tarpley, Thomas 1861 rb-21-109 (Ru)
Tarpley, William 1828 wb-4-333 (Wi)
Tarply, Sterling 1848 wb-#167 (Wl)
Tarrant, Osillar R. 1850 wb-2-71# (Ge)
Tarrant, Samuel 1797 rb-a-14 (Mt)
Tarrant, Ursula 1828 wb-2-30# (Ge)
Tart, James 1855 wb-g-653 (Hn)
Tarter, Sarah 1860 wb-1-470 (Hw)
Tarver, Arthur H. 1844 wb-#143 (Wl)
Tarver, Benjamin 1804 wb-#1 (Wl)

Tarver, Benjamin 1817 wb-#40 (Wl)
Tarver, Jane W. 1857 wb-17-256 (D)
Tarver, Samuel 1830 wb-#99 (Wl)
Tarver, Silas 1862 wb-#136 (Wl)
Tarver, William 1840 wb-#129 (Wl)
Tarver, William 1848 wb-#168 (Wl)
Tarwater, Lewis 1831 wb-1-112 (Fr)
Tarwater, Peter 1849 wb-10-217 (K)
Tarwater, William 1857 wb-12-432 (K)
Tate, Alexander 1847 wb-2-225 (W)
Tate, Anderson 1856 as-c-460 (Di)
Tate, David 1838 wb-1-323 (Gr)
Tate, David 1848 33-3-42 (Gr)
Tate, George 1849 wb-4-494 (Hr)
Tate, George 1853 wb-f-28 (Mu)
Tate, George W. 1846 wb-4-104 (Hr)
Tate, Henry 1844 wb-a-125 (Cr)
Tate, Isaac 1839 wb-c-79 (Ro)
Tate, J. J. 1846 wb-d-6 (G)
Tate, J. W. 1857 wb-h-717 (Hu)
Tate, James 1842 wb-3-623 (Ma)
Tate, James 1848 wb#20 (Gu)
Tate, James A. 1848 wb-1-255 (Fr)
Tate, James K. 1855 wb-3-304 (La)
Tate, James L. 1859 wb-2-304 (Li)
Tate, John 1826 wb-9-31 (D)
Tate, John 1828 wb-3-0 (Sm)
Tate, John 1830 wb-#211 (Mu)
Tate, John 1836 wb-3-0 (Sm)
Tate, John 1841 wb-b-377 (G)
Tate, John 1845 wb-2-120 (W)
Tate, John A. 1848 r39-1-62 (Dk)
Tate, John G. 1831 wb-5-19 (Wi)
Tate, Letitia Ann 1852 wb-15-130 (Rb)
Tate, Milton (Dr.) 1856 wb-1C-305 (A)
Tate, Patsy 1843 wb-8-106 (K)
Tate, Rebecca 1835 wb-10-494 (D)
Tate, Robert S. 1854 wb-15-407 (Rb)
Tate, Samuel 1834 as-a-249 (Di)
Tate, Samuel 1848 wb-1-344 (Li)
Tate, Turner 1841 wb-3-405 (Ma)
Tate, William 1858 wb-f-155 (Mu)
Tate, William T. 1859 wb-3-586 (Gr)
Tatem, German Y. 1853 as-b-140 (Ms)
Tates, Chloe 1861 wb-3e-178 (Sh)
Tatom, Benjamin 1851 wb-g-522 (Hu)
Tatom, James 1850 as-c-78 (Di)
Tatom, John 1831 rb-f-311 (Mt)
Tatom, John M. 1831 rb-f-258 (Mt)
Tatum, B. S. 1858 gs-1-45 (F)
Tatum, Bartlett 1848 A-468-111 (Le)

Tatum, Benjamin 1845 wb-12-370 (Rb)
Tatum, Dabney 1856 wb-#120 (Wl)
Tatum, Howell 1823 wb-8-219 (D)
Tatum, Ira 1826 Ir (Sn)
Tatum, Ira 1830 wb-#85 (Wl)
Tatum, James 1821 wb-8-28 (D)
Tatum, Jesse 1834 rb-9-79 (Ru)
Tatum, John C. 1854 ib-h-62 (F)
Tatum, Jos? 1843 wb-12-39 (Rb)
Tatum, Mark 1832 rb-9-12 (Ru)
Tatum, Mathew 1832 wb-8-71 (Rb)
Tatum, Nathaniel 1819 wb-A-283 (Li)
Tatum, Nathaniel 1844 wb-13-78 (D)
Tatum, Stephen 1841 wb-a-72 (F)
Tatum, William 1819 wb-A-268 (Li)
Taul, Thomas Paine 1829 wb-1-77 (Fr)
Taurmon, John 1854 wb-2-161 (Sh)
Tawzer, Richard B. 1848 wb-10-19 (K)
Tayler, Samuel 1839 wb-1A-241 (A)
Tayler, Sarah Hoyland 1849 wb-g-404 (Hn)
Tayloe, John 1847 wb-f-474 (St)
Tayloe, Thomas B. 1840 wb-1-57 (Sh)
Taylor, Abram 1844 wb-8-197 (Wi)
Taylor, Abram 1861 wb-f-423 (G)
Taylor, Absolem 1815 Wb-2-145 (Wi)
Taylor, Alexander 1815 wb-#19 (Wl)
Taylor, Alfred W. 1856 wb-2-19 (Ct)
Taylor, Also 1840 wb-7-63 (K)
Taylor, Andrew 1787 wb-#2 (Wa)
Taylor, Andrew 1816 wb-2-242 (K)
Taylor, Andrew 1844 wb-d-253 (O)
Taylor, Andrew 1847 wb-1-101 (Ct)
Taylor, Andrew 1847 wb-1-136 (Ct)
Taylor, Anthony 1857 Ir (Gi)
Taylor, B. 1841 as-a-500 (Di)
Taylor, Benjamin 1849 wb-g-171 (O)
Taylor, Benjamin W. 1837 wb-d-105 (St)
Taylor, Berigrine 1827 wb-#66 (Wl)
Taylor, Berry 1830 wb-9-379 (D)
Taylor, Betsy 1833 rb-f-503 (Mt)
Taylor, Betty 1838 wb-3-484 (Je)
Taylor, Bitcy 1834 rb-f-576 (Mt)
Taylor, Cannon 1806 wb-1-0 (Sm)
Taylor, Carey J. 1854 wb-11-223 (Wi)
Taylor, Charles 1811 wb-1-257 (Wi)
Taylor, Charles 1841 wb-#134 (Wl)
Taylor, Charles D. 1847 wb-5-36 (Ma)
Taylor, Chesley 1840 wb-12-88* (D)
Taylor, Creed A. 1857 wb-e-169 (Wh)
Taylor, D. 1853 wb-15-419 (Rb)
Taylor, Daniel 1822 wb-3-486 (Rb)

Taylor, Daniel 1836 wb-1-130 (Gr)
Taylor, Daniel 1839 wb-e-164 (Hu)
Taylor, Daniel 1841 wb-a-146 (Di)
Taylor, David 1836 wb-a-137 (O)
Taylor, David 1843 wb-11-455 (Rb)
Taylor, David 1854 wb-a-250 (Dk)
Taylor, Dempsey 1858 ib-2-128 (Wy)
Taylor, Dempsey 1858 ib-2-88 (Wy)
Taylor, Dorman 1852 wb-#179 (Wl)
Taylor, Drury 1852 wb-g-563 (Hu)
Taylor, E. M. O. 1849 rb-k-767 (Mt)
Taylor, Edmond 1826 rb-e-2 (Mt)
Taylor, Edmond 1847 wb-A-45 (Ca)
Taylor, Edmond 1848 wb-g-98 (Hu)
Taylor, Edmond 1854 wb-a-348 (Ms)
Taylor, Edmund 1847 wb-b-218 (We)
Taylor, Edmund 1854 wb-e-246 (G)
Taylor, Edward 1825? as-a-133 (Di)
Taylor, Elizabeth 1816 wb-#25 (Wl)
Taylor, Elizabeth 1839 wb-2-253 (Sn)
Taylor, Elizabeth 1852 wb-5-116 (Ma)
Taylor, Elizabeth 1857 wb-3-376 (Gr)
Taylor, Elizabeth 1858 wb-4-15 (Gr)
Taylor, Esther (Cooper) 1825 rb-d-517 (Mt)
Taylor, F. B. 1861 wb-e-148 (Hy)
Taylor, Federick 1855 as-b-188 (Ms)
Taylor, Frederick 1826 wb-b-79 (St)
Taylor, Frederick 1843 wb-a-67 (Ms)
Taylor, Frederick 1843 wb-d-97 (O)
Taylor, Geo. W. 1836 wb-2-192 (Ma)
Taylor, George 1822 wb-1-12 (Ma)
Taylor, George 1829 rb-7-312 (Ru)
Taylor, George 1842 Ir (Gi)
Taylor, George W. 1834 wb-#173 (Mc)
Taylor, Goodwin 1841 rb-12-25 (Ru)
Taylor, Green B. 1832 wb-9-617 (D)
Taylor, H. O. 1852 wb-3-87 (Gr)
Taylor, Henry 1811 wb-4-158 (D)
Taylor, Henry 1830 wb-9-454 (D)
Taylor, Henry 1854 rb-17-126 (Ru)
Taylor, Henry 1855 wb-2-116 (Li)
Taylor, Henry 1856 wb-#58 (Wa)
Taylor, Henry C. 1831 rb-f-202 (Mt)
Taylor, Henry sr. 1847 wb-1-317 (Li)
Taylor, Hiram W. 1857 wb-e-169 (Wh)
Taylor, Howell 1858 wb-e-93 (Hy)
Taylor, Hughet O. 1852 wb-3-58 (Gr)
Taylor, Hughs O. 1837 wb-1-249 (Gr)
Taylor, Isaac (Major) 1856 wb-e-54 (Wh)
Taylor, Isaac 1790 wb-1-24# (Ge)
Taylor, Isaac 1840 wb-12-79* (D)

Taylor, Isaac 1854 wb-d-169 (Wh)
Taylor, Isaac 1854 wb-d-211 (Wh)
Taylor, Isaac 1862 wb-#19 (Mo)
Taylor, Isaac sr. 1816 wb-a-50 (Wh)
Taylor, J. B. 1856 wb-j-254 (O)
Taylor, J. M. 1856 wb-17-56 (D)
Taylor, Jabin S. 1857 wb-#173 (Mc)
Taylor, James 1818 wb-a-96 (Wh)
Taylor, James 1820 rb-4-205 (Ru)
Taylor, James 1820 wb-#36 (Wl)
Taylor, James 1829 rb-7-278 (Ru)
Taylor, James 1833 wb-5-220 (K)
Taylor, James 1839 wb-1-172 (Bo)
Taylor, James 1839 wb-1-184 (Fr)
Taylor, James 1846 wb-9-187 (K)
Taylor, James 1847 wb-8-520 (Wi)
Taylor, James 1848 wb-A-47 (Ca)
Taylor, James 1848 wb-A-59 (Ca)
Taylor, James 1850 wb-g-320 (St)
Taylor, James 1851 rb-17-127 (Ru)
Taylor, James 1853 mr-2-498 (Be)
Taylor, James 1857? wb-#27 (Mo)
Taylor, James A. 1856 wb-#120 (Wl)
Taylor, James B. 1845 wb-#147 (Wl)
Taylor, James M. 1844 rb-13-11 (Ru)
Taylor, James M. 1852 wb-h-Oct (O)
Taylor, James M. 1857 wb-17-370 (D)
Taylor, James P. 1833 lw (Ct)
Taylor, James P. 1841 wb-1-67 (Sh)
Taylor, James W. 1847 wb-g-183 (Hn)
Taylor, James W. 1847 wb-g-209 (Hn)
Taylor, James sr. 1834 wb-5-397 (Wi)
Taylor, Jane 1843 wb-5-283 (Gr)
Taylor, Jennetty 1840 wb-e-267 (Hu)
Taylor, Jesse W. 1848 r39-1-72 (Dk)
Taylor, Jessee W. 1849 r39-1-146 (Dk)
Taylor, Joel 1838 mr-1-45 (Be)
Taylor, Joel R. 1838 wb-11-174 (D)
Taylor, John (Sr.) 1845 wb-#147 (Wl)
Taylor, John 1820 wb-1-0 (Sm)
Taylor, John 1834 wb-x-187 (Mu)
Taylor, John 1836 wb-10-538 (D)
Taylor, John 1838 wb-d-171 (St)
Taylor, John 1838 wb-d-177 (St)
Taylor, John 1839 rb-10-447 (Ru)
Taylor, John 1847 wb-#155 (Wl)
Taylor, John 1847 wb-a-123 (T)
Taylor, John 1849 wb-g-147 (St)
Taylor, John B. 1856 wb-j-191 (O)
Taylor, John J. 1860 wb-k-334 (O)
Taylor, John L. 1836 rb-9-347 (Ru)

Taylor, John Y. 1839 abl-1-155 (T)
Taylor, John Y. 1857 wb-e-62 (Hy)
Taylor, Jonathan 1842 wb-1-132 (Ct)
Taylor, Jos. F. 1852 rb-16-295 (Ru)
Taylor, Jos. R. 1837 wb-11-5 (D)
Taylor, Joseph 1826 wb-3-0 (Sm)
Taylor, Joseph 1833 wb-0-3 (Cf)
Taylor, Joseph 1833 wb-1-119 (Fr)
Taylor, Joseph 1833 wb-1-291 (Hr)
Taylor, Joseph 1838 wb-2-28 (Hr)
Taylor, Joseph 1846 mr-2-232 (Be)
Taylor, Joseph 1847 rb-14-65 (Ru)
Taylor, Joseph 1851 wb-14-622 (D)
Taylor, Joseph M. 1837 wb-a-175 (O)
Taylor, Joseph jr. 1832 wb-1-247 (Hr)
Taylor, Joshua 1833 wb-#103 (Wl)
Taylor, Joshua V. 1836 wb-#110 (Wl)
Taylor, Josiah 1852 wb-15-464 (D)
Taylor, Josiah R. 1846 wb-#154 (Wl)
Taylor, Leeroy 1853 wb-5-242 (Je)
Taylor, Lenard 1856 wb-a-272 (Cr)
Taylor, Leroy 1813 wb-2-42 (Je)
Taylor, Leroy 1834 wb-#32 (Wa)
Taylor, Leroy 1837 wb-#2 (Mo)
Taylor, Lewis 1844 wb-0-44 (Cf)
Taylor, Margaret 1850 lr (Sn)
Taylor, Margaret O. 1849 wb-5-69 (Ma)
Taylor, Martha E. 1857 rb-18-587 (Ru)
Taylor, Martha M. 1857 rb-18-639 (Ru)
Taylor, Mary 1832 wb-#98 (Wl)
Taylor, Mary 1843 wb-#140 (Wl)
Taylor, Mary 1854 wb-2-8 (Ct)
Taylor, Mary C. 1844 lw (Ct)
Taylor, Matilda 1847 rb-14-38 (Ru)
Taylor, Micajah 1837 wb-b-277 (Wh)
Taylor, Mildred 1859 wb-8-43 (Sm)
Taylor, Mills 1861 wb-17-297 (Rb)
Taylor, Moses 1845 wb-#146 (Wl)
Taylor, Moses N. 1858 wb-7-18 (Ma)
Taylor, Nathaniel 1816 lw (Ct)
Taylor, Nathanil K. 1848 wb-1-103 (Ct)
Taylor, Parmenas 1827 wb-2-581 (Je)
Taylor, Parmenas 1838 wb-3-485 (Je)
Taylor, Paulina 1858 wb-#13 (Mo)
Taylor, Peregin 1827 wb-#66 (Wl)
Taylor, Rachel 1859 wb-18-48 (D)
Taylor, Rebecca 1827 wb-a-278 (Wh)
Taylor, Rebecca 1849 wb-1B-104 (A)
Taylor, Rebecca 1860 wb-#174 (Mc)
Taylor, Richard 1824 lr (Sn)
Taylor, Richard 1839 wb-d-369 (St)

Taylor, Richard 1848 ib-1-36 (Ca)
Taylor, Richard W. 1854 wb-11-260 (Wi)
Taylor, Robert 1799 wb-1-56 (Sn)
Taylor, Robert 1846 rb-13-686 (Ru)
Taylor, Robert 1847 wb-14-133 (D)
Taylor, Robert 1855 lr (Sn)
Taylor, Robert P. 1849 rb-1-454 (Mt)
Taylor, Rolly M. 1856 rb-17-611 (Ru)
Taylor, Samuel (B) 1838 wb-#174 (Mc)
Taylor, Samuel 1814 rb-b-191 (Mt)
Taylor, Samuel 1852 wb-b-324 (We)
Taylor, Samuel A. 1835 wb-1-173 (Hy)
Taylor, Sousannah 1832 wb-a-31 (Cr)
Taylor, Spencer 1844 wb-c-174 (G)
Taylor, Susan 1853 wb-#180 (Wl)
Taylor, Susanna 1840 wb-#127 (Wl)
Taylor, T. C. 1859 rb-p-111 (Mt)
Taylor, Temple 1851 wb-2-23 (Li)
Taylor, Thomas 1813 wb-1-465 (Hw)
Taylor, Thomas 1814 wb-1-187 (Sn)
Taylor, Thomas 1815 wb-4-393 (D)
Taylor, Thomas 1816 wb-2-205 (Wi)
Taylor, Thomas 1818 wb-a-92 (Wh)
Taylor, Thomas 1819 wb-#32 (Wl)
Taylor, Thomas 1827 wb-9-90 (D)
Taylor, Thomas 1840 lr (Sn)
Taylor, Thomas 1849 wb-g-234 (O)
Taylor, Thomas 1853 wb-16-59 (D)
Taylor, Thomas B. 1819 wb-#37 (Wl)
Taylor, Thomas C. 1859 rb-p-152 (Mt)
Taylor, Thomas M. 1854 ib-H-137 (F)
Taylor, Vincent 1861 rb-21-16 (Ru)
Taylor, Widow 1815 wb-#19 (Wl)
Taylor, William 1834 wb-3-313 (Je)
Taylor, William 1838 wb-d-223* (Hn)
Taylor, William 1840 wb-10-529 (Rb)
Taylor, William 1844 wb-#145 (Wl)
Taylor, William 1847 rb-k-619 (Mt)
Taylor, William 1850 wb-#7 (Mo)
Taylor, William 1851 wb-d-2 (Wh)
Taylor, William 1855 39-2-124 (Dk)
Taylor, William 1860 wb-a-355 (Cr)
Taylor, William D. 1852 wb-10-189 (Wi)
Taylor, William M. 1856 wb-1C-291 (A)
Taylor, William P. 1840 wb-2-26 (Hy)
Taylor, Willis 1835 wb-1-476 (Hr)
Taylor, Willis L. 1831 wb-1-198 (Hr)
Taylor, Wm. sr. 1855 wb-a-222 (T)
Taylor, Woody 1845 wb-1-298 (Li)
Tays, James C. 1844 wb-1-342 (La)
Teag, Elizabeth 1847 wb-1B-13 (A)

Teague, E. 1845 wb-#148 (Wl)
Teague, Edward 1844 wb-a-112 (F)
Teague, Israel 1859 wb-h-300 (Hn)
Teague, Stephen 1834 wb-1-81 (Gr)
Teague, William 1845 wb-#149 (Wl)
Teal, Albert 1851 wb-3-164 (W)
Teal, Edward 1823 wb-A-345 (Li)
Teal, Elias 1851 wb-3-165 (W)
Teal, Elias 1856 wb-0-145 (Cf)
Teas, Anna 1852 wb-g-564 (Hu)
Teas, Charles 1801 rb-a-118 (Mt)
Teas, James 1847 as-b-441 (Di)
Teas, James 1853 wb-h-105 (Hu)
Teas, William 1852 wb-g-565 (Hu)
Teasley, John 1816 rb-b-328 (Mt)
Teasley, John 1852 wb-m-608 (Mt)
Teasley, Lucy 1846 rb-k-301 (Mt)
Teater, Samuel L. 1838 wb-b-35 (O)
Tedder, James 1847 mr-2-253 (Be)
Tedder, James 1858 wb-1-240 (Be)
Tedder, Nancy 1856 ib-1-466 (Wy)
Tedford, David 1827 wb-1-45 (Hr)
Tedford, George 1823 wb-1-140 (Bo)
Tedford, James 1793 wb-1-11 (K)
Tedford, John 1825 wb-1-137 (Bo)
Teel, Henry 1812 wb-1-141 (Bo)
Teer, Richard V. 1845 rb-13-413 (Ru)
Teeter, Stout B. 1837 rb-10-33 (Ru)
Teeters, Isham 1858 wb-c-173 (Wh)
Telford, David 1827 wb-#67 (Wl)
Telford, Hugh 1832 wb-#100 (Wl)
Telford, James 1847 wb-#153 (Wl)
Telford, John 1858 wb-#124 (Wl)
Telford, Robert 1816 wb-#24 (Wl)
Telford, Sarah 1852 wb-15-244 (D)
Telford, Thomas 1816 wb-#15 (Wa)
Telford, Thomas 1857 wb-#123 (Wl)
Teller, Daniel 1830 wb-1A-38 (A)
Temple, Burrell 1844 wb-8-190 (Wi)
Temple, Elizabeth 1836 wb-6-110 (Wi)
Temple, Francis B. 1838 rb-h-142 (Mt)
Temple, G. B. 1842 wb-a-95 (L)
Temple, J. S. 1858 wb-13-53* (K)
Temple, James 1840 ib-2-81 (Ge)
Temple, Jane 1860 wb-2-91# (Ge)
Temple, Leston 1819 wb-7-354 (D)
Temple, Major 1816 wb-2-38# (Ge)
Temple, Mary 1820 wb-1-24# (Ge)
Temple, Mary A. 1843 rb-i-484 (Mt)
Temple, Thomas 1854 148-1-497 (Ge)
Temple, Thomas B. 1834 wb-5-405 (Wi)

Temple, William 1833 wb-a-28 (T)
Temple, William 1850 wb-9-591 (Wi)
Temple, William A. 1851 wb-9-669 (Wi)
Templen, Jacob 1840 lr (Gi)
Templeton, George W. 1855 wb-d-295 (Wh)
Templeton, Green 1854 wb-a-223 (V)
Templeton, James 1817 wb-a-63 (Wh)
Templeton, James 1821 Wb-3-270 (Wi)
Templeton, John H. 1859 wb-1-146 (R)
Templeton, L. 1857 wb-e-189 (Wh)
Templeton, William L. 1855 wb-e-21 (Wh)
Templin, Samuel 1852 wb-#52 (Wa)
Templin, William 1846 wb-#43 (Wa)
Tench, John R. 1835 rb-9-222 (Ru)
Tench, John R. 1853 rb-16-620 (Ru)
Tenison, Jerome B. 1852 wb-10-357 (Wi)
Tenison, Jerome R. 1851 wb-10-4 (Wi)
Tenison, Matthew 1850 wb-9-408 (Wi)
Tennain?, Lemuel 1837 wb-11-62 (D)
Tennin, John 1815 rb-b-264 (Mt)
Tennison, Abraham 1825 rb-6-169 (Ru)
Tennison, Alexander 1806 wb-1-215 (Rb)
Tennison, Jacob 1808 wb-#75 (Wl)
Tennison, John 1802 wb-1-93 (Rb)
Tennison, Joseph 1861 wb-19-32 (D)
Tennison, Washington 1852 wb-10-372 (Wi)
Tenny, E. H. 1861 wb-18-472 (D)
Tenor, John 1803 wb-1-118 (K)
Tenpenny, Daniel 1859 wb-A-141 (Ca)
Tenpenny, Richard 1850 wb-A-69 (Ca)
Terrell, Jephtha 1856 wb-b-383 (We)
Terrell, Jessee 1852 wb-10-189 (Wi)
Terrell, John 1844 wb-b-66 (We)
Terrell, McMerran? 1831 rb-f-159 (Mt)
Terrell, Meream 1830 rb-f-136 (Mt)
Terrell, Richard 1850 wb-#172 (Wl)
Terrell, Sally B. 1848 rb-l-132 (Mt)
Terrell, William 1804 wb-2-396 (D)
Terrell, William 1837 wb-a-2 (L)
Terrell?, George 1857 wb-f-59 (G)
Terrett, John 1847 wb-f-127+ (O)
Terrill, Buford 1828 wb-a-93 (G)
Terrill, Frances 1837 wb-a-205 (O)
Terrill, James 1827 wb-4-162 (Wi)
Terrill, Lewis 1836 rb-g-334 (Mt)
Terrill, Timothy 1859 wb-13-93 (Wi)
Terry, Alexander J. 1860 wb-f-185 (Mu)
Terry, Burrell 1852 wb-15-300 (D)
Terry, David 1815 Wb-2-137 (Wi)
Terry, David 1835 wb-x-287 (Mu)
Terry, E. W. sr. 1839 wb-3-112 (Ma)

Terry, Enoch W. 1839 wb-3-106 (Ma)
Terry, James 1820 wb-1-0 (Sm)
Terry, James 1831 wb-2-0 (Sm)
Terry, Jeremiah 1851 wb-15-55 (D)
Terry, Jesse 1810 wb-a-3 (Wh)
Terry, John 1831 wb-b-78 (Wh)
Terry, John sr. 1835 wb-b-177 (Wh)
Terry, Nancy B. 1856 wb-f-99 (Mu)
Terry, Susan M. 1858 wb-12-486 (Wi)
Terry, Thomas 1801 wb-1-81 (K)
Terry, Thomas 1840 wb-3-0 (Sm)
Terry, William C. 1842 wb-3-620 (Ma)
Terry, William D. 1838 wb-y-190* (Mu)
Teter, Shelby 1861 wb-b*-20 (O)
Tevoles, Joseph 1845 wb-2-69 (W)
Thacker, Jeremiah 1803 rb-2-6 (Ru)
Thacker, Larken 1842 rb-12-107 (Ru)
Thacker, Larkin 1855 rb-17-415 (Ru)
Thacker, Valentine 1858 wb-#28 (Mo)
Thacker, William 1835 wb-#37 (Wa)
Tharp, G. T. 1854 ib-H-121 (F)
Tharp, Joshua 1799 wb-1-214 (Bo)
Thatcher, Carey 1826 wb-4-153 (K)
Thatcher, James C. 1839 wb-1A-210 (A)
Thaxton, John B. 1855 wb-n-688 (Mt)
Thaxton, Martha 1843 wb-d-96 (Hd)
Thaxton, Nathaniel 1835 wb-#107 (Wl)
Thaxton, William W. 1830 wb-b-210 (Hd)
Thedford, John 1843 wb-c-115 (G)
Thedford, Josias 1835 wb-b-71 (G)
Thedford, W. A. 1859 wb-f-310 (G)
Theobald, William B. 1844 wb-a2-112 (Mu)
Thetford, Joseph 1824 wb-1-34 (Ma)
Thetford, Nancy 1850 wb-d-247 (G)
Thetford, Walter N. 1858 wb-f-219 (G)
Theven, J. B. A. (Dr.) 1834 wb-x-266 (Mu)
Thevenot, J. B. A. 1836 wb-x-260* (Mu)
Thining?, David 1815 rb-3-115 (Ru)
Thomas, A. S. 1859 wb-3e-101 (Sh)
Thomas, Abijah 1814 wb-4-321 (D)
Thomas, Adam 1855 wb-12-98 (K)
Thomas, Alexander 1814 wb-a-20 (Wh)
Thomas, Alexander 1833 wb-c-97 (Hn)
Thomas, Anthony H. 1815 Wb-2-167 (Wi)
Thomas, Benjamin 1849 wb-b-386 (Mu)
Thomas, Caleb 1834 wb-x-244 (Mu)
Thomas, Daniel 1842 wb-2-397 (Hr)
Thomas, David 1838 wb-2-292 (Ma)
Thomas, David D. 1843 wb-e-581 (Hu)
Thomas, Dr. A. 1852 wb-15-145 (Rb)
Thomas, Edward 1861 rb-20-802 (Ru)

Thomas, Elisha 1816 lr (Sn)
Thomas, Elisha 1860 wb-18-235 (D)
Thomas, Elizabeth 1809 wb-#8 (Wl)
Thomas, Elizabeth 1847 rb-k-382 (Mt)
Thomas, Francis 1828 wb-a-325 (Wh)
Thomas, Francis B. 1826 wb-a-227 (Wh)
Thomas, George 1833 wb-#174 (Mc)
Thomas, George 1836 wb-#112 (Wl)
Thomas, George G. (Dr.) 1808 wb-4-5 (D)
Thomas, Henry 1848 ib-1-38 (Ca)
Thomas, Henry 1857 wb-f-65 (G)
Thomas, Henson W. 1839 wb-1-22 (Me)
Thomas, Isiah 1858 wb-a-272 (V)
Thomas, J. R. 1852 mr-2-443 (Be)
Thomas, Jacob (Sr.) 1832? wb-#99 (Wl)
Thomas, Jacob 1804 wb-1-259 (Bo)
Thomas, Jacob 1831 wb-#90 (Wl)
Thomas, Jacob 1840 wb-7-121 (K)
Thomas, Jacob 1846 wb-c-306 (G)
Thomas, Jacob 1851 wb-11-47 (K)
Thomas, James 1827 wb-a-83 (G)
Thomas, James 1836 wb-3-0 (Sm)
Thomas, James 1838 wb-#122 (Wl)
Thomas, James 1850 wb-#174 (Wl)
Thomas, James 1857 wb-6-440 (Ma)
Thomas, James G. 1828 wb-4-336 (Wi)
Thomas, James Sr. 1838 wb-#174 (Mc)
Thomas, James sr. 1834 wb-b-48 (G)
Thomas, Jesse 1813 Wb-2-78 (Wi)
Thomas, Jesse W. 1816 wb-4-470 (D)
Thomas, Jesse W. 1816 wb-7-107 (D)
Thomas, Jno. 1803 wb-2-335 (D)
Thomas, Job H. 1860 wb-f-203 (Mu)
Thomas, John 1802 wb-#1 (Wl)
Thomas, John 1803 wb-2-334 (D)
Thomas, John 1804 wb-2-347 (D)
Thomas, John 1811 wb-1-5 (Fr)
Thomas, John 1816 wb-7-97 (D)
Thomas, John 1825 rb-6-135 (Ru)
Thomas, John 1828 rb-7-322 (Ru)
Thomas, John 1828 wb-b-59 (Hn)
Thomas, John 1833 wb-10-161 (D)
Thomas, John 1844 wb-13-115 (D)
Thomas, John 1851 wb-1-402 (Su)
Thomas, John 1858 wb-17-422 (D)
Thomas, John 1858 wb-f-156 (Mu)
Thomas, John jr. 1846 wb-b-173 (We)
Thomas, Jonas E. 1856 wb-f-110 (Mu)
Thomas, Jos. P. 1835 rb-g-236 (Mt)
Thomas, Joshua 1795 wb-2-13 (D)
Thomas, Joshua 1835 wb-x-281 (Mu)

Thomas, Lawson 1855 wb-12-100 (K)
Thomas, Luke 1826 wb-b-11 (Hn)
Thomas, Mark 1816 Wb-2-191 (Wi)
Thomas, Mary 1852 wb-#175 (Mc)
Thomas, Micah 1857 wb-17-379 (D)
Thomas, Micajah 1858 gs-1-94 (F)
Thomas, Nathan 1853 wb-xx-293 (St)
Thomas, Nottley 1852 wb-1-466 (Hw)
Thomas, Organ 1830 wb-b-115 (Hn)
Thomas, Philip 1835 wb-10-521 (D)
Thomas, R. C. 1857 wb-f-52 (G)
Thomas, Robert 1838 wb-11-453 (D)
Thomas, Samuel 1857 wb-4-90 (La)
Thomas, Sarah 1847 wb-13-128 (Rb)
Thomas, Sarah Ann 1861 wb-3e-172 (Sh)
Thomas, Thomas D. 1848 wb-d-131 (G)
Thomas, Thomas M. 1849 rb-l-454 (Mt)
Thomas, Tobitha 1858 wb-f-169 (G)
Thomas, W. P. 1844 wb-12-118 (Rb)
Thomas, W. P. 1844 wb-12-119 (Rb)
Thomas, William 1794 wb-1-13 (K)
Thomas, William 1798 wb-2-111 (D)
Thomas, William 1805 wb-#4 (Wl)
Thomas, William 1829 wb-1-132 (Bo)
Thomas, William 1838 wb-e-20 (Hn)
Thomas, William 1841 wb-7-477 (Wi)
Thomas, William 1847 wb-14-163 (D)
Thomas, William 1850 wb-7-0 (Sm)
Thomas, William 1854 ib-h-6 (F)
Thomas, William 1857 wb-f-100 (G)
Thomas, William A. 1849 wb-14-161 (Rb)
Thomas, Wilson 1856 rb-18-99 (Ru)
Thomas, Wm. 1832 rb-8-484 (Ru)
Thomason, Adam 1829 wb-3-0 (Sm)
Thomason, Elizabeth 1825 wb-b-70 (St)
Thomason, George 1843 wb-f-137 (Hn)
Thomason, George D. 1842 wb-f-86 (Hn)
Thomason, John M. 1848 wb-g-107 (Hu)
Thomason, John sr. 1847 148-1-195 (Ge)
Thomason, Pleasant 1840 wb-2-53# (Ge)
Thomason, William 1840 wb-z-94 (Mu)
Thomasson, Alfred 1852 wb-a-277 (Ms)
Thomasson, John 1845 wb-2-62# (Ge)
Thomasson, William 1856 wb-2-83# (Ge)
Thomerson, John 1859 wb-k-51 (O)
Thomerson?, Harriet 1841 wb-3-383 (Ma)
Thompson*, Neal 1814 wb-4-296 (D)
Thompson, A. C. 1858 wb-f-207 (G)
Thompson, Abraham 1805 wb-1-0 (Sm)
Thompson, Abram 1821 rb-5-113 (Ru)
Thompson, Adam 1861 lr (Sn)

Thompson, Alexander 1839 wb-3-96 (Ma)
Thompson, Alexander 1842 wb-z-413 (Mu)
Thompson, Alexander B. 1832 wb-#175 (Mc)
Thompson, Alfred 1831 wb-#175 (Mc)
Thompson, Alfred 1843 wb-13-1 (D)
Thompson, Allen 1852 wb-15-438 (D)
Thompson, Allen 1852 wb-15-455 (D)
Thompson, Almeda 1853 wb-15-577 (D)
Thompson, Amos G. 1843 wb-3-77 (Hr)
Thompson, Andrew (Jr.) 1854 wb-#112 (Wl)
Thompson, Andrew 1819 wb-#17 (Wa)
Thompson, Andrew 1829 wb-1-136 (Bo)
Thompson, Andrew 1842 wb-11-265* (Rb)
Thompson, Andrew 1853 wb-#112 (Wl)
Thompson, Andrew 1856 wb-#120 (Wl)
Thompson, Archibald 1856 wb-6-306 (Ma)
Thompson, Augustin 1835 wb-c-438 (St)
Thompson, Benjamin 1848 wb-a-164 (Ms)
Thompson, Burwell 1839 wb-1-188 (Fr)
Thompson, Catharine T. 1827 wb-a-271 (Wh)
Thompson, Charles 1824 wb-a-131 (Di)
Thompson, Charlotte S. 1853 wb-0-118 (Cf)
Thompson, Daniel 1840 wb-3-183 (Ma)
Thompson, David 1815 wb-1-138 (Bo)
Thompson, David 1831 lr (Gi)
Thompson, David 1858 rb-19-291 (Ru)
Thompson, David 1861 wb-13-487 (K)
Thompson, David N. 1845 lr (Gi)
Thompson, David S. 1850 rb-15-379 (Ru)
Thompson, David W. 1849 wb-4-397 (Hr)
Thompson, Elizabeth 1848 wb-g-73 (Hu)
Thompson, Elizabeth 1855 wb-16-532 (D)
Thompson, Elizabeth 1859 rb-p-297 (Mt)
Thompson, Ephraim 1816 wb-2-129 (Je)
Thompson, Ephraim 1834 wb-10-385 (D)
Thompson, Frederick 1815 wb-4-361 (D)
Thompson, George 1807 wb-1-24# (Ge)
Thompson, George 1841 wb-2-265 (Hr)
Thompson, Gideon 1824 rb-6-55 (Ru)
Thompson, Henry 1828 wb-#79 (Wl)
Thompson, Henry 1846 wb-2-65# (Ge)
Thompson, Henry D. 1835 rb-9-266 (Ru)
Thompson, Henry R. 1848 wb-#156 (Wl)
Thompson, Horace D. 1860 wb-18-242 (D)
Thompson, J. P. 1859 as-c-177 (Ms)
Thompson, Jacob 1857 wb-b-412 (We)
Thompson, James 1792 wb-1-260 (D)
Thompson, James 1811 rb-2-150 (Ru)
Thompson, James 1821 wb-#52 (Mu)
Thompson, James 1845 rb-13-223 (Ru)
Thompson, James 1848 wb-9-67 (Wi)

Thompson, James 1853 wb-a-437 (F)
Thompson, James 1854 wb-#112 (Wl)
Thompson, James 1859 wb-13-85 (Wi)
Thompson, James C. 1849 wb-#169 (Wl)
Thompson, James M. 1849 wb-b-422 (Mu)
Thompson, Jane 1845 rb-j-405 (Mt)
Thompson, Jane 1853 148-1-451 (Ge)
Thompson, Jason 1833 wb-10-258 (D)
Thompson, Jason 1833 wb-A-52 (Ca)
Thompson, Jesse 1839 wb-a-381 (R)
Thompson, Jessee 1838 wb-a-350 (R)
Thompson, Jessee 1859 rb-19-563 (Ru)
Thompson, Jno. L. 1848 wb-4-333 (Hr)
Thompson, John 1793 wb-1-290 (D)
Thompson, John 1797 wb-1-24# (Ge)
Thompson, John 1813 rb-2-230 (Ru)
Thompson, John 1823 wb-#44 (Wl)
Thompson, John 1826 wb-3-0 (Sm)
Thompson, John 1827 rb-6-311 (Ru)
Thompson, John 1831 rb-f-255 (Mt)
Thompson, John 1833 wb-1A-61 (A)
Thompson, John 1835 rb-9-183 (Ru)
Thompson, John 1852 wb-1-209 (Bo)
Thompson, John 1854 rb-17-184 (Ru)
Thompson, John 1859 wb-13-95 (Wi)
Thompson, John B. 1861 wb-#134 (Wl)
Thompson, John C. 1855 wb-g-654 (Hn)
Thompson, John F. 1846 wb-d-241 (Ro)
Thompson, John N. 1844 wb-#152 (Wl)
Thompson, John P. 1860 wb-d-74 (L)
Thompson, John W. 1855 wb-16-564 (D)
Thompson, John W. 1857 wb-f-129 (Mu)
Thompson, Joseph 1816 rb-3-103 (Ru)
Thompson, Joseph 1827 rb-6-310 (Ru)
Thompson, Joseph 1839 wb-2-250 (Sn)
Thompson, Joseph C. 1841 wb-c-7 (G)
Thompson, Lawrence 1801? wb-1-66 (Sn)
Thompson, Lewis 1815 rb-b-250 (Mt)
Thompson, M. 1852 wb-1B-308 (A)
Thompson, Margaret 1850 wb-#174 (Wl)
Thompson, Margaret 1854 wb-#112 (Wl)
Thompson, Mary 1855 wb-15-726 (Rb)
Thompson, Mary 1858 rb-19-508 (Ru)
Thompson, Mary 1860 wb-b-103 (Ms)
Thompson, Meredith 1854 wb-3-260 (W)
Thompson, Moses 1842 wb-#139 (Wl)
Thompson, Nancy 1843 wb-3-725 (Ma)
Thompson, Nancy 1852 wb-h-112 (Hu)
Thompson, Nancy 1854 rb-17-160 (Ru)
Thompson, Nathaniel 1848 wb-b-283 (Mu)
Thompson, Orvell 1830 rb-8-1 (Ru)

Thompson, Peter 1846 wb-a2-508 (Mu)
Thompson, Polly D. 1859 wb-17-605 (D)
Thompson, Rebecca C. 1826 rb-6-239 (Ru)
Thompson, Reuben 1835 wb-2-39* (Ma)
Thompson, Robert 1811 wb-#10 (Wl)
Thompson, Robert 1821 wb-7-499 (D)
Thompson, Robert 1844 rb-12-544 (Ru)
Thompson, Robert 1852 wb-h-84 (Hu)
Thompson, Robert 1853 wb-1-142 (Bo)
Thompson, Robert 1860 wb-k-253 (O)
Thompson, Robert C. 1832 wb-5-210 (Wi)
Thompson, Saml. 1803 wb-2-338 (D)
Thompson, Samuel 1827 wb-#67 (Wl)
Thompson, Samuel 1828 wb-#175 (Mc)
Thompson, Sarah 1846 wb-5-27 (Ma)
Thompson, Sarah Ann 1849 wb-g-111 (St)
Thompson, Sarah G. 1838 rb-10-134 (Ru)
Thompson, Susan C. 1856 rb-18-185 (Ru)
Thompson, Thomas 1845 wb-3-243 (Hr)
Thompson, Thomas 1853 wb-e-116 (G)
Thompson, Thomas T. 1827 wb-a-266 (Wh)
Thompson, Virginia W. 1852 rb-16-236 (Ru)
Thompson, William 1829 wb-#31 (Wa)
Thompson, William 1836 wb-d-226 (Hn)
Thompson, William 1841 wb-a-78 (F)
Thompson, William 1842 mr-2-21 (Be)
Thompson, William 1846 wb-d-9 (G)
Thompson, William 1849 wb-#169 (Wl)
Thompson, William 1851 wb-3-117 (W)
Thompson, William 1852 wb-1-8 (Sh)
Thompson, William L. 1836 rb-9-328 (Ru)
Thompson, William P. 1840 wb-12-95* (D)
Thompson, William W. 1860 wb-1-394 (Fr)
Thompson, William sr. 1837 wb-11-67 (D)
Thompson, Willis 1837 wb-b-198 (G)
Thompson, Wm. 1836 rb-9-224 (Ru)
Thompson, Wm. M. 1855 rb-17-531 (Ru)
Thompson, Z. W. 1835 wb-d-129 (Hn)
Thomson, George 1807 as-1-196 (Ge)
Thomson, George 1849 wb-10-209 (K)
Thomson, William 1827 wb-1-70 (Fr)
Thorgmorton, Elisha 1845 wb-b-116 (We)
Thorlton, John 1804 as-1-74 (Ge)
Thorlton, Robert 1803 as-1-15 (Ge)
Thorn, Augustine L. (S?) 1856 wb-7-0 (Sm)
Thorn, David 1814 wb-a-214 (St)
Thorn, James M. 1841 wb-#136 (Wl)
Thorn, Thomas 1816 wb-3-181 (St)
Thorn, Thomas 1847 rb-14-136 (Ru)
Thorn, William 1856 wb-h-540 (Hu)
Thorn, William 1857 ib-1-474 (Wy)

Thornbrugh, Henry 1804 wb-1-28 (Je)
Thornbrugh, William 1796 wb-1-53 (Je)
Thornburg, Benjamin 1835 wb-3-388 (Je)
Thornton, Burwell 1806 wb-1-191 (Wi)
Thornton, Burwell 1817 wb-2-345 (Wi)
Thornton, George L. 1851 wb-15-2 (D)
Thornton, Harriet 1824 wb-3-279 (St)
Thornton, Henry 1841 wb-#135 (Wl)
Thornton, Isaac 1842 wb-b-445 (Hd)
Thornton, James A. jr. 1852 wb-11-321 (K)
Thornton, James A. sr. 1852 wb-11-253 (K)
Thornton, Josiah 1849 ib-1-48 (Wy)
Thornton, Mary 1861 wb-4-415 (La)
Thornton, Michael 1819 wb-1-0 (Sm)
Thornton, Michael 1831 wb-2-0 (Sm)
Thornton, Orville 1859 rb-p-120 (Mt)
Thornton, Owen 1803 rb-a-173 (Mt)
Thornton, Reuben S. 1826 wb-9-56 (D)
Thornton, Samuel 1813 rb-b-107 (Mt)
Thornton, Samuel 1813 rb-b-149 (Mt)
Thornton, Samuel 1822 rb-d-32 (Mt)
Thornton, Seth 1841 wb-#136 (Wl)
Thornton, Thomas D. 1847 wb-4-59 (Je)
Thornton, Thomas J. 1859 wb-a-98 (Ce)
Thornton, Thomas N. 1847 wb-1-430 (La)
Thornton, Thomas N. 1860 wb-4-256 (La)
Thornton, Uriah 1859 wb-f-270 (G)
Thornton, William P. 1852 ib-1-185 (Wy)
Thornton, William R. 1848 wb-#176 (Mc)
Thornton, Yancy 1814 wb-3-40 (St)
Thornton, Yancy 1814 wb-a-237* (St)
Thornton, robert 1850 wb-a-386 (F)
Thorp, charles 1840 wb-1-191 (Li)
Thorpe, John 1852 wb-15-327 (D)
Thorpe, John 1852 wb-15-395 (D)
Throgmortin, J. S. 1848 wb-g-270 (Hn)
Throgmorton, Julius 1847 wb-g-170 (Hn)
Throgmorton, Richard 1834 wb-c-209 (Hn)
Throgmorton, William 1847 wb-b-249 (We)
Thrower, Henry 1840 wb-A-20 (Ca)
Thruston, William 1847 wb-g-163 (Hn)
Thruston, William 1847 wb-g-210 (Hn)
Thurman, Dickenson 1845 wb-1-469 (Hw)
Thurman, Graves 1854 wb-11-188 (Wi)
Thurman, Joseph 1855 wb-6-101 (Ma)
Thurman, Wiley 1847 rb-14-77 (Ru)
Thurman, Wiley 1860 rb-20-702 (Ru)
Thurmon, Fendel C. 1844 wb-1-104 (Sh)
Thurmond, John 1828 lr (Sn)
Thurmond, John S. 1852 wb-4-297 (Mu)
Thurmond, Mary 1852 wb-f-10 (Mu)

Thurmond, Meredith M. 1853 wb-5-35 (Hr)
Thurmond, O. L. 1858 wb-c-258 (L)
Thurmond, William M. 1859 wb-3-562 (Gr)
Thurston, Benjamin 1846 wb-1-290 (Li)
Thurston, J. B. 1855 wb-g-663 (Hn)
Thurston, Jno. R. 1848 rb-l-181 (Mt)
Thurston, Monroe? N. 1857 rb-o-495 (Mt)
Thweat, Francis 1820 wb-3-197 (Wi)
Thweatt, William 1830 wb-3-0 (Sm)
Thwing, J. David 1827 wb-1-6 (Li)
Thwing, Martha 1841 wb-1-187 (Li)
Tidwell, Aquilla 1841 as-b-18 (Di)
Tidwell, Benjamin 1853 wb-a-268 (Di)
Tidwell, Clark 1844 as-b-221 (Di)
Tidwell, Edward 1846 as-b-334 (Di)
Tidwell, Frances 1837 as-a-361 (Di)
Tidwell, Isiah 1848 wb-a-180 (Di)
Tidwell, J. K. 1846 wb-a2-345 (Mu)
Tidwell, James 1839 wb-a-135 (Di)
Tidwell, James 1850 as-c-55 (Di)
Tidwell, Jane 1853 ib-1-210 (Wy)
Tidwell, John 1861 wb-7-89 (Ma)
Tidwell, John K. 1846 wb-a2-368 (Mu)
Tidwell, Knock 1852 ib-1-190 (Wy)
Tidwell, Levi 1823 as-A-114 (Di)
Tidwell, Mason 1850 ib-1-98 (Wy)
Tidwell, Nott 1853 ib-1-207 (Wy)
Tidwell, Richard 1852 ib-1-190 (Wy)
Tier, Nancy 1859 rb-20-130 (Ru)
Tier, Richard V. 1848 rb-14-318 (Ru)
Tigret, C. J. 1851 wb-d-349 (G)
Tilfair, Hugh 1851 wb-2-89 (Sh)
Tilford, Elizabeth 1835 wb-10-517 (D)
Tilford, W. H. 1851 wb-14-629 (D)
Tiller, James 1857 wb-b-46 (F)
Tillery, John 1835 wb-5-335 (K)
Tillery, John 1847 wb-9-319 (K)
Tillery, Richard M. 1860 wb-13-309 (K)
Tillery, Sampson 1847 wb-9-392 (K)
Tillery, Samuel 1827 wb-a-26 (R)
Tillery, William 1859 wb-3-30 (Me)
Tillett, James 1862 wb-5-504 (Je)
Tilley, John 1809 wb-1-4 (Fr)
Tilley, John 1858 wb-f-158 (Ro)
Tilley, William 1860 wb-f-348 (Ro)
Tillman, Elijah 1844 as-a-77 (Ms)
Tillman, James S. 1849 ib-1-38 (Wy)
Tillman, James T. 1844 wb-a-94 (Ms)
Tillman, John 1836 wb-1-498 (Hr)
Tillman, Martha 1853 as-b-133 (Ms)
Tilly, George 1851 as-c-137 (Di)

Tilly, John 1807 rb-2-32 (Ru)
Tilman, Jacob 1821 rb-5-143 (Ru)
Tilman, John 1839 wb-a-35 (Ms)
Tilman, Shadrach 1855 wb-e-310 (G)
Tilmon, Mary 1852 wb-0-112 (Cf)
Tilmore, Jno. 1842 wb-2-373 (Hr)
Tilmore, Lany 1842 wb-2-373 (Hr)
Timberlake, James 1847 wb-7-0 (Sm)
Timmins, Charles 1859 wb-0-162 (Cf)
Timmins, William 1852 wb-2-34 (Li)
Timmins, mbrose 1858 wb-0-165 (Cf)
Timmons, Ambrose 1847 wb-1-319 (Li)
Timms, Elizabeth 1861 wb-18-445 (D)
Timms, Jabez 1857 wb-17-161 (D)
Tims, John 1857 wb-5-73 (Hr)
Tinch, E. P. 1853 rb-16-537 (Ru)
Tinch, Elizabeth 1853 rb-16-603 (Ru)
Tinch, John R. 1835 rb-9-173 (Ru)
Tindal, Noah B. 1844 wb-a2-108 (Mu)
Tindall, E. (Mrs.) 1849 wb-b-435 (Mu)
Tindall, Elizabeth 1848 wb-b-251 (Mu)
Tindall, Henry 1857 wb-12-428 (Wi)
Tindall, John 1854 wb-16-220 (D)
Tindall, John 1855 wb-16-511 (D)
Tindell, Samuel 1859 wb-13-118* (K)
Tiner, Memory 1833 rb-f-484 (Mt)
Tiner, Noah 1818 rb-b-528 (Mt)
Tiner, Selah 1857 wb-6-394 (Ma)
Tinkle, Daniel 1858 wb-f-192 (G)
Tinkle, George 1827 wb-a-82 (G)
Tinkle, L. R. 1857 wb-f-93 (G)
Tinley, Hugh L. 1860 wb-13-259 (K)
Tinley, William 1819 wb-2-237 (Je)
Tinnen, Lemuel 1835 wb-10-412 (D)
Tinnin, Alexander 1811 wb-1-399 (Rb)
Tinnin, John 1815 rb-b-288 (Mt)
Tinnon, Edward 1791 wb-1-11 (Sn)
Tinsley, Ann 1842 wb-1-82 (Sh)
Tinsley, Colly 1849 wb-d-177 (G)
Tinsley, Jackson 1835 wb-1-415 (Ma)
Tinsley, James G. 1861 wb-1-101 (Dy)
Tinsley, Rachael 1854 wb-e-207 (G)
Tinsley, Richard B. 1832 wb-1-210 (Hr)
Tinsley, Samuel B. 1860 lr (Sn)
Tinsley, Starling 1835 wb-x-272* (Mu)
Tinsley, Vernon 1854 rb-17-66 (Ru)
Tinsley?, Richard 1831 wb-1-201 (Hr)
Tipler, George 1861 wb-5-118 (Hr)
Tippet, Erasmus L. 1822 wb-a-149 (Ro)
Tippit, Anne 1822 wb-#41 (Wl)
Tippitt, Joseph 1821 wb-#40 (Wl)

Tipps, John 1815 wb-A-102 (Li)
Tipton, Abraham 1832 wb-5-116 (K)
Tipton, Abraham 1832 wb-5-46 (K)
Tipton, Barney B. 1860 wb-#130 (Wl)
Tipton, David B. 1841 wb-7-163 (K)
Tipton, Edward 1814 wb-4-291 (D)
Tipton, Isaac 1845 wb-9-30 (K)
Tipton, Jacob 1839 abl-1-136 (T)
Tipton, Jacob B. 1852 wb-11-180 (K)
Tipton, James 1856 wb-#119 (Wl)
Tipton, Johnathan 1843 wb-8-68 (K)
Tipton, Jon 1831 wb-#33 (Wa)
Tipton, Jonathan 1843 wb-#14 (Mo)
Tipton, Jonathan 1859? wb-#28 (Mo)
Tipton, Joshua 1793 wb-1-218 (Je)
Tipton, Joshua 1815 wb-#18 (Wl)
Tipton, Joshua 1827 wb-#65 (Wl)
Tipton, Mashac 1850 wb-1-142 (Bo)
Tipton, Rachael 1824 wb-#54 (Wl)
Tipton, Reese 1827 wb-#73 (Wl)
Tipton, Reuben 1837 wb-6-108 (K)
Tipton, Samuel 1851 wb-1-107 (Ct)
Tipton, William 1848 wb-1-196 (Bo)
Tire, Thomas 1805 rb-a-238 (Mt)
Tisdale, Edward 1817 wb-#24 (Wl)
Tison, Aaron 1854 wb-5-155 (Ma)
Titcomb, S. H. 1861 wb-18-533 (D)
Titsworth, Thomas 1857 wb-3-361 (W)
Tittalson, Mildred 1857 rb-o-525 (Mt)
Titterington, Joseph 1844 rb-j-231 (Mt)
Tittle, Adam 1839 wb-1-271 (W)
Tittle, David 1835 wb-1-79 (W)
Tittle, George 1820 wb-1-0 (Sm)
Titus, Ebenezer 1851 wb-2-109 (Sh)
Titus, James 1855 wb-2-184 (Sh)
Titus, R. E. 1844 wb-1-104 (Sh)
Tod, Emma R. 1859 wb-3e-119 (Sh)
Todd, Aaron 1859 rb-20-118 (Ru)
Todd, Abner S. 1858 ib-1-498 (Ca)
Todd, Benjamin 1854 rb-17-1 (Ru)
Todd, David 1849 ib-1-70 (Ca)
Todd, Diana 1851 wb-11-129 (K)
Todd, Fielding 1857 rb-18-326 (Ru)
Todd, George 1834 wb-1-444 (Ma)
Todd, James 1823 wb-a-195 (Ro)
Todd, Jefferson 1858 ib-1-491 (Ca)
Todd, Jeremiah 1848 rb-14-241 (Ru)
Todd, John 1830 wb-1-53 (Li)
Todd, John B. 1851 wb-2-105 (Sh)
Todd, John N. 1846 wb-13-396 (D)
Todd, Joseph J. 1861 wb-3e-183 (Sh)

Todd, Lemuel 1837 wb-d-307 (Hn)
Todd, Low Sr. 1792 wb-1-13 (Je)
Todd, Nancey 1860 wb-4-404 (La)
Todd, Nancy 1858 wb-4-203 (La)
Todd, Presley N. 1852 wb-2-261 (La)
Todd, Robert 1860 rb-20-563 (Ru)
Todd, Robin 1861 rb-21-24 (Ru)
Todd, Sam 1861 rb-p-581 (Mt)
Todd, Samuel 1836 wb-6-11 (K)
Todd, Thomas 1802 lr (Sn)
Todd, William 1841 wb-2-236 (Hr)
Todd, William 1857 wb-b-400 (We)
Todd, William J. 1837 wb-#119 (Wl)
Toland, David W. 1853 wb-h-101 (Hu)
Toland, J. W. 1853 wb-h-127 (Hu)
Toland, Jonathan 1857 wb-h-710 (Hu)
Tolar, John jr. 1835 rb-g-102 (Mt)
Tolar, Robert 1832 wb-8-233 (Rb)
Tolar, Wm. W. 1846 rb-k-145 (Mt)
Tolbert, James R. 1848 wb-A-51 (Ca)
Tolbert, Thomas 1850 wb-14-505 (D)
Toler, Bryant 1848 wb-13-221 (Rb)
Toler, Isaiah 1853 wb-n-176 (Mt)
Toler, John 1845 rb-j-270 (Mt)
Toler, William 1848 rb-l-48 (Mt)
Tollies, Luke 1840 wb-b-354 (G)
Tollison, James M. 1846 wb-13-46 (Rb)
Tolls, George W. 1860 ib-2-178 (Wy)
Tolly, Lucy 1850 wb-g-399 (Hu)
Tolly, William H. 1844 wb-d-192 (O)
Tom, Charles 1838 wb-y-168 (Mu)
Tom, William 1829 wb-#177 (Mu)
Tom, William 1830 wb-#211 (Mu)
Tombes, William 1829 rb-7-303 (Ru)
Tomblin, James 1822 wb-3-355 (Wi)
Tomblin, Judith 1846 wb-1-394 (La)
Tomlin (Tumblin?), William 1830 wb-#177 (Mc)
Tomlinson, Allen 1861 wb-#134 (Wl)
Tomlinson, Euphamia 1856 as-c-39 (Ms)
Tomlinson, George 1853 as-b-115 (Ms)
Tomlinson, Harriet 1855 ib-h-440 (F)
Tomlinson, Hugh 1817 wb-A-233 (Li)
Tomlinson, Isaac 1830 wb-#210 (Mu)
Tomlinson, Isaac B. 1827 wb-#154 (Mu)
Tomlinson, James 1818 wb-2-363 (Wi)
Tomlinson, Richard 1831 wb-1-279 (Ma)
Tomlinson, Susan 1853 wb-xx-219 (St)
Tomlinson, Thomas 1852 wb-b-322 (We)
Tomlinson, Uriah 1846 wb-f-368 (St)
Tomlinson, W. S. 1855 wb-h-70 (St)
Tomlinson, William 1827 wb-b-144 (St)

Tomlinson, William 1827 wb-b-148 (St)
Tomlinson, William 1848 wb-g-34 (Hu)
Tomlinson, William 1851 wb-g-421 (St)
Tomlinson, William S. 1855 wb-h-114 (St)
Tompkins, Lydia 1816 wb-1-224 (Sn)
Tompson, John 1830? wb-1A-35 (A)
Tompson, Randolph 1818 wb-1-0 (Sm)
Tompson, Robert 1854 wb-b-346 (We)
Tompson, Sarah 1841 abl-1-225 (T)
Tompson, William T. 1838 wb-1-45 (Sh)
Tomson, A. G. 1843 wb-3-85 (Hr)
Toncray, Alexander 1854 wb-12-17 (K)
Toney, W. H. C. 1853 wb-16-100 (D)
Toney, William 1815 wb-#14 (Mu)
Tonkery, Mary 1855 wb-12-152 (K)
Toof, Stephen C. 1855 wb-3e-11 (Sh)
Tool, John 1792 wb-1-2 (K)
Toole, James 1850 wb-1-388 (Li)
Toomy, James 1822 wb-a-170 (Ro)
Toomy, Michael 1818 wb-a-198 (Ro)
Toon, James 1839 wb-7-206 (Wi)
Toon, Lewis 1817 wb-2-322 (Wi)
Toone, Ellison 1836 wb-1-538 (Hr)
Toone, Lewis H. 1861 wb-5-123 (Hr)
Toope, Otto 1841 wb-12-237* (D)
Topp, John 1837 wb-11-24 (D)
Torbett, John 1842 wb-#3 (Mo)
Torbitt, George W. 1852 wb-15-459 (D)
Toser, Nancy 1841 wb-1-72 (Sh)
Tote, James 1841 wb-1-360 (W)
Totewine, Isaac (Revd.) 1821 rb-c-510 (Mt)
Totewine, Isaac 1821 rb-c-453 (Mt)
Tottan, Benjamin 1847 wb-f-127+ (O)
Tounzen, Daniel 1825 wb-b-51 (St)
Tovera, John 1831 wb-1A-41 (A)
Towery, John 1844 wb-d-102 (Hd)
Towland, Robert 1851 wb-15-192 (D)
Towles, Joseph 1848 wb-2-356 (W)
Towles, Oliver 1857 wb-17-335 (D)
Towles, Sarah 1848 wb-2-284 (W)
Townley, A. R. 1845 wb-f-263* (Hn)
Townsen, Daniel 1833 wb-c-45 (Hn)
Townsend, Chamberlain 1828 wb-1-15 (La)
Townsend, Edmund 1853 wb-2-63 (Li)
Townsend, Eli 1837 mr-1-281 (Be)
Townsend, George W. 1825 lr (Sn)
Townsend, Joseph 1822 wb-1-343 (Sn)
Townsend, Joseph 1846 wb-a-140 (Cr)
Townsend, Peter 1858 lr (Sn)
Townsend, Samuel 1858 wb-2-222 (Li)
Townsend, Taylor 1832 wb-5-137 (K)

Townsend, Thomas 1842 wb-e-461 (Hu)
Townsley, George 1840 wb-1-139 (Bo)
Townson(Townsend), Nathaniel 1839
   mr-1-59 (Be)
Towson, Catharine 1844 wb-#143 (Wl)
Traburn, John 1830 rb-f-139 (Mt)
Tracey, Erasmus 1850 wb-2-106 (La)
Tracy, A. J. 1837 wb-#116 (Wl)
Tracy, Albert G. 1840 wb-z-7 (Mu)
Tracy, Evan 1845 wb-#148 (Wl)
Tracy, John 1859 wb-13-219* (K)
Tracy, Mary 1859 wb-#130 (Wl)
Tracy, Thomas 1850 wb-#174 (Wl)
Trail, Basil 1812 wb-1-164 (Sn)
Trail, James 1834 wb-2-48# (Ge)
Trail, James 1849 148-1-281 (Ge)
Trail?, F. G. 1855 wb-g-673 (Hn)
Trainum, Jeremiah 1842 wb-z-385 (Mu)
Tramel, Daniel 1861 39-2-426 (Dk)
Tramel, Nicholas 1784 wb-1-10 (D)
Tramell, Martha 1855 wb-n-494 (Mt)
Tramell, Shadrach 1855 wb-n-628 (Mt)
Tramell, William 1860 rb-p-386 (Mt)
Trammell, Sampson 1812 wb-a-124 (St)
Transon, Wallace A. 1857 wb-6-354 (Ma)
Trantham, John K. 1853 wb-10-464 (Wi)
Trantham, William 1851 wb-a-160 (T)
Traughber, John 1830 wb-7-120 (Rb)
Traughber, Michael 1856 wb-16-276 (Rb)
Traughbor, John 1817 wb-3-49 (Rb)
Travilian, Edward 1848 wb-#169 (Wl)
Travis, Amos 1839 rb-10-446 (Ru)
Travis, Amos F. 1832 rb-9-11 (Ru)
Travis, Benjamin F. 1846 wb-b-178 (We)
Travis, Edward 1835 wb-9-125 (Rb)
Travis, Edward 1846 wb-g-135 (Hn)
Travis, Edy 1852 wb-g-514 (Hn)
Travis, George 1852 wb-g-431 (Hn)
Travis, George 1854 wb-g-583 (Hn)
Travis, Jacob 1846 wb-g-108 (Hn)
Travis, James E. 1858 wb-1-364 (Fr)
Travis, John 1827 rb-e-56 (Mt)
Travis, N. M. 1854 wb-e-219 (G)
Travis, W. 1833 rb-9-92 (Ru)
Travis, William 1861 wb-i-325 (St)
Travis, Wm. 1856 ib-1-399 (Ca)
Trayler, P. G. 1846 wb-4-85 (Hr)
Traylor, Hiram B. 1850 wb-g-365 (Hu)
Traylor, Joel 1859 rb-20-114 (Ru)
Traylor, Joel 1859 rb-20-149 (Ru)
Traylor, Polly 1849 wb-g-158 (Hu)

Traylor, William 1848 wb-g-57 (Hu)
Treadway, Isham 1818 wb-3-3 (Rb)
Treese, William C. 1851 ib-1-217 (Cl)
Trent, Jesse 1837 wb-1-467 (Hw)
Trent, Rodney T. 1845 wb-b-111 (We)
Trent, William H. 1854 ib-h-203 (F)
Trentham, Henry 1837 abl-1-29 (T)
Trentham, Zachariah 1841 wb-b-381 (Hd)
Trew (True?), Thomas 1862 wb-#177 (Mc)
Trew, William 1840 5-2-151 (Cl)
Trezevant, J. L. C. 1845 wb-1-115 (Sh)
Trezevant, James 1841 wb-1-69 (Sh)
Trezevant, Mary B. 1852 wb-2-139 (Sh)
Tribble, Abraham 1829 lr (Sn)
Tribble, Eli 1842 rb-12-252 (Ru)
Tribble, Isaiah 1860 wb-#132 (Wl)
Tribble, Shadrich 1849 wb-0-90 (Cf)
Tribble, Spilsby 1799 wb-2-154 (D)
Trice, Anderson 1843 rb-j-22 (Mt)
Trice, Bingham 1859 rb-p-35 (Mt)
Trice, Edward 1832 rb-f-399 (Mt)
Trice, Edward 1848 rb-l-157 (Mt)
Trice, Edward 1849 rb-l-306 (Mt)
Trice, Edward 1855 wb-#117 (Wl)
Trice, Elizabeth 1836 rb-g-453 (Mt)
Trice, Ellen W. 1860 rb-p-384 (Mt)
Trice, G. B. 1853 wb-m-657 (Mt)
Trice, Harriett 1841 rb-i-94 (Mt)
Trice, Harriett E. 1849 rb-l-296 (Mt)
Trice, Henry 1851 wb-m-189 (Mt)
Trice, J. B. 1856 rb-o-170 (Mt)
Trice, James 1833 rb-f-462 (Mt)
Trice, James 1834 rb-f-568 (Mt)
Trice, James 1834 rb-g-42 (Mt)
Trice, James 1836 wb-1-144 (Bo)
Trice, James 1852 wb-m-563 (Mt)
Trice, John 1808 lr (Sn)
Trice, John 1824 wb-4-183 (Rb)
Trice, John 1831 rb-f-215 (Mt)
Trice, John D. 1852 wb-2-125 (Sh)
Trice, Leigh 1848 rb-l-120 (Mt)
Trice, Lewis 1842 rb-i-225 (Mt)
Trice, Loranah 1844 rb-j-187 (Mt)
Trice, Lorand 1844 rb-j-120 (Mt)
Trice, Mary 1855 wb-n-674 (Mt)
Trice, May 1855 wb-n-606 (Mt)
Trice, Mindy 1857 rb-o-363 (Mt)
Trice, Nace F. 1858 rb-o-583 (Mt)
Trice, Nancy 1844 rb-j-264 (Mt)
Trice, Nancy 1848 rb-l-151 (Mt)
Trice, Nay 1856 rb-o-145 (Mt)

Trice, Nay 1856 rb-o-164 (Mt)
Trice, Sally Ann 1849 rb-l-220 (Mt)
Trice, Sarah 1852 wb-m-503 (Mt)
Trice, Sarah 1854 wb-n-377 (Mt)
Trice, Sarah Ann 1847 rb-k-608 (Mt)
Trice, Shepherd 1840 rb-i-2 (Mt)
Trice, Shepherd 1840 rb-i-25 (Mt)
Trice, Susannah 1844 rb-j-82 (Mt)
Trice, Thomas 1846 rb-k-287 (Mt)
Trice, Thomas A. 1860 rb-p-429 (Mt)
Trice, Thomas Jackson 1861 rb-p-629 (Mt)
Trice, Wilie 1857 rb-o-429 (Mt)
Trice, Willis 1858 rb-o-762 (Mt)
Trice, Zackariah 1848 rb-k-751 (Mt)
Trigg, Alanson 1827 lr (Sn)
Trigg, Alanson 1834 wb-#103 (Wl)
Trigg, Ann 1838 rb-h-77 (Mt)
Trigg, Daniel 1830 wb-#87 (Wl)
Trigg, David (Sr.) 1832 wb-#95 (Wl)
Trigg, George H. 1838 rb-h-78 (Mt)
Trigg, Guy S. 1809 wb-4-60 (D)
Trigg, Henry 1837 wb-2-257 (Ma)
Trigg, James 1850 wb-2-84 (Sh)
Trigg, Lucy 1837 wb-1-38 (Sh)
Trigg, William 1817 wb-1-260 (Sn)
Trigg, William 1825 rb-d-474 (Mt)
Trigg, William 1825 rb-d-477 (Mt)
Trigg, William 1827 wb-1-72 (Fr)
Trigg, William 1836 wb-2-183 (Ma)
Trigg, William 1838 rb-h-111 (Mt)
Trigg, William 1839 lr (Gi)
Trigg, William 1841 rb-i-74 (Mt)
Trigg, William K. 1838 wb-6-267 (K)
Trimble, James 1824 wb-8-368 (D)
Trimble, Joseph 1858 rb-19-271 (Ru)
Trimble, William 1853 wb-1-81 (Jo)
Trimble, William 1860 wb-13-231 (Wi)
Triplett, Daniel 1799 wb-1-166 (Je)
Triplett, Lewis 1838 wb-#177 (Mc)
Trisket?, George 1841 wb-5-109 (Gr)
Trobaugh, Daniel 1847 148-1-206 (Ge)
Trobaugh, Frederick 1842 wb-2-58# (Ge)
Trobaugh, Nicholas 1818 wb-1-24# (Ge)
Trobough, Adam 1837 wb-a-73 (T)
Trobough, Henry 1852 wb-a-167 (T)
Trogden, Abraham 1857 wb-a-263 (V)
Troost, Gerard 1851 wb-15-123 (D)
Trotman, Thomas B. 1855 wb-1-333 (Fr)
Trott, Henry 1856 wb-3-284 (W)
Trott, James 1846 wb-5-454 (Gr)
Trotter, Alexander 1795 wb-#5 (Wa)

Trotter, Elizabeth 1831 rb-f-155 (Mt)
Trotter, Isham 1829 rb-e-406 (Mt)
Trotter, Isham R. 1838 wb-a-33 (F)
Trotter, Isham jr. 1831 rb-f-256 (Mt)
Trotter, Isham sr. 1834 rb-f-579 (Mt)
Trotter, James 1851 wb-11-10 (K)
Trotter, John 1840 rb-h-455 (Mt)
Trotter, Joseph 1794 wb-#5 (Wa)
Trotter, Mary Ann 1859 rb-p-278 (Mt)
Trotter, Robert 1810 rb-a-247 (Mt)
Trotter, Robert 1846 wb-#177 (Mc)
Trotter, W. B. 1852 wb-a-423 (F)
Trotter, William B. 1855 ib-h-487 (F)
Trousdale, Elizabeth 1853 wb-16-89 (D)
Trousdale, James 1816 wb-#21 (Mu)
Trousdale, James 1818 lr (Sn)
Trousdale, John sr. 1838 wb-3-0 (Sm)
Trousdale, William 1820 wb-1-0 (Sm)
Trousdale, William 1832 wb-2-0 (Sm)
Trousdale, William 1846 wb-g-76 (Hn)
Trousdall, William W. 1845 wb-f-272* (Hn)
Trout, Adam 1841 wb-#134 (Wl)
Trout, George 1852 wb-11-172 (K)
Trout, John 1840 wb-#177 (Mc)
Trout, John 1858 wb-f-153 (G)
Troville, Henry 1843 rb-i-507 (Mt)
Truan, Perrin Lonis 1861 wb-13-515 (K)
Truant, John Jaques 1858 wb-12-498 (K)
True, John 1815 wb-3-133 (St)
True, Martin 1845 wb-a2-199 (Mu)
Truet, Sarah Sr. 1821 wb-#38 (Wl)
Truett, Elijah 1858 wb-#126 (Wl)
Truett, Henry Sr. 1820 wb-#35 (Wl)
Truett, John 1859 wb-13-246 (Wi)
Truett, William 1817 wb-1-0 (Sm)
Truette, Elijah 1849 r39-1-147 (Dk)
Trull, Nathan 1817 wb-2-324 (Wi)
Trulove, Thomas 1840 wb-z-79 (Mu)
Truman, Miles 1815 rb-3-108 (Ru)
Trumbo, Ambrose 1811 wb-1-143 (Sn)
Trundell, Wilson L. 1860 wb-13-388* (K)
Trundle, James 1843 wb-1-245 (Bo)
Trusty, Lawson 1849 r39-1-145 (Dk)
Tubb, Daniel L. 1852 wb-h-71 (Hu)
Tubb, Elias 1854 wb-h-318 (Hu)
Tubb, Elizabeth 1834 wb-c-332 (St)
Tubb, George 1836 wb-a-129 (Di)
Tubb, James 1846 wb-2-186 (W)
Tubb, John & Mary 1834 wb-#105 (Wl)
Tubb, John B. 1848 r39-1-71 (Dk)
Tubb, Levey 1857 wb-h-667 (Hu)

Tubb, Lovey 1855 wb-h-424 (Hu)
Tubb, Moses 1855 wb-A-107 (Ca)
Tubb, Nathan 1852 wb-h-71 (Hu)
Tubb, Sallie 1857 wb-h-326 (St)
Tubb, Tyrsa 1848 wb-2-329 (W)
Tubb, William 1832 wb-c-232 (St)
Tubb, William 1833 wb-c-281 (St)
Tubb, William sr. 1837 wb-d-77 (St)
Tubbs, Generous 1854 mr-2-576 (Be)
Tubbs, Sallie 1856 wb-h-284 (St)
Tubbs, Sally Y. 1855 wb-h-93 (St)
Tubs, Aquilla 1820 rb-c-364 (Mt)
Tubs, Equilla 1818 rb-c-56 (Mt)
Tuck, Susannah 1849 wb-1-242 (Bo)
Tucker, Alexander S. 1853 wb-c-33 (L)
Tucker, Allen 1812 wb-a-55 (Ro)
Tucker, Allen C. 1856 wb-12-256 (Wi)
Tucker, Almira 1839 rb-10-463 (Ru)
Tucker, Anderson 1857 wb-17-293 (D)
Tucker, B. L. 1831 wb-#92 (Wl)
Tucker, Benjamin L. 1859 wb-#128 (Wl)
Tucker, Catherine C. 1858 wb-3e-66 (Sh)
Tucker, Claibourne L. 1849 rb-15-36 (Ru)
Tucker, Collins 1826 rb-6-262 (Ru)
Tucker, Curle 1815 rb-b-160 (Mt)
Tucker, Daniel 1817 rb-4-94 (Ru)
Tucker, David 1836 rb-9-290 (Ru)
Tucker, Dicy 1844 wb-#4 (Mo)
Tucker, Edmond 1836 wb-10-556 (D)
Tucker, Elizabeth 1861 wb-k-391 (O)
Tucker, Enoch 1836 wb-1-100 (La)
Tucker, Enoch 1847 wb-1-433 (La)
Tucker, G. W. 1853 wb-3-170 (La)
Tucker, George 1823 wb-#54 (Wl)
Tucker, George 1833 wb-#102 (Wl)
Tucker, George 1834 wb-1-56 (La)
Tucker, George B. 1860 lr (Gi)
Tucker, Green 1833 wb-#103 (Wl)
Tucker, James 1815 rb-3-86 (Ru)
Tucker, James 1842 rb-12-256 (Ru)
Tucker, James D. 1860 rb-20-621 (Ru)
Tucker, Jane K. 1844 rb-12-589 (Ru)
Tucker, Jarrett 1809 wb-#7 (Wl)
Tucker, Jeremiah 1843 wb-z-545 (Mu)
Tucker, John 1802 wb-1-77 (Rb)
Tucker, John 1835 wb-a-119 (Di)
Tucker, John 1853 lr (Sn)
Tucker, John Edmond 1839 wb-11-596 (D)
Tucker, John W. 1862 wb-#137 (Wl)
Tucker, Jonathan 1828 wb-#27 (Wa)
Tucker, Joseph 1828 wb-#27 (Wa)

Tucker, Joseph 1861 lr (Gi)
Tucker, Joshua 1861 rb-21-148 (Ru)
Tucker, Joshua C. 1861 rb-21-129 (Ru)
Tucker, Kinchen 1861 rb-20-802 (Ru)
Tucker, Lavinia 1844 rb-12-489 (Ru)
Tucker, Lee 1822 wb-#46 (Wl)
Tucker, Marilda M. 1855 wb-e-305 (G)
Tucker, Martha 1855 wb-e-294 (G)
Tucker, Mary E. 1846 wb-a-298 (F)
Tucker, N. B. 1860 rb-20-340 (Ru)
Tucker, Priscilla 1831 wb-#100 (Wl)
Tucker, Randal 1852 wb-15-268 (D)
Tucker, Ransum 1856 wb-g-763 (Hn)
Tucker, S. R. 1853 wb-e-125 (G)
Tucker, Saml. 1838 rb-10-118 (Ru)
Tucker, Samuel 1803 wb-1-99 (Rb)
Tucker, Samuel 1849 rb-15-60 (Ru)
Tucker, Sylvania 1842 rb-12-107 (Ru)
Tucker, Thos. J. 1857 wb-f-94 (G)
Tucker, Thos. J. 1861 wb-b-111 (F)
Tucker, William 1810 rb-2-100 (Ru)
Tucker, William 1843 wb-1-468 (Hw)
Tucker, William B. 1860 wb-a-294 (T)
Tucker, William D. 1853 wb-a-428 (F)
Tucker, William T. 1837 lr (Gi)
Tucker, Willis 1819 wb-3-39 (Wi)
Tuckere, Louallen 1839 wb-c-34 (Ro)
Tucknis, Henry 1834 wb-x-289 (Mu)
Tufts, Artemas 1844 lr (Sn)
Tuggle, Harris B. 1853 wb-7-0 (Sm)
Tuggle, John 1823 wb-1-0 (Sm)
Tuggle, John H. 1847 wb-#175 (Wl)
Tuggle, Thomas 1830 wb-2-0 (Sm)
Tuggle, Thomas T. 1853 wb-e-19 (Hy)
Tugwell, John L. 1855 wb-e-39 (Hy)
Tuley, Charles 1832? wb-1-90 (Li)
Tuley, William H. 1861 wb-k-406 (O)
Tull, John R. 1852 as-b-45 (Ms)
Tulloch, Magnes 1834 wb-1-168 (Bo)
Tullock, David 1826 wb-5-308 (Rb)
Tullock, John (Dr.) 1805 wb-#3 (Wl)
Tullock, Thomas 1785 wb-1-59 (Sn)
Tulloss, John R. 1857 wb-a-30 (Ce)
Tulloss, Robert C. 1857 wb-12-323 (Wi)
Tulloss, Rodham 1840 wb-7-305 (Wi)
Tulloss, Rodham 1850 wb-9-341 (Wi)
Tullus, John R. 1858 wb-a-44 (Ce)
Tully, Guilford 1859 rb-p-33 (Mt)
Tumblin (Tomlin?), William 1830 wb-#177 (Mc)
Tumey, Catharine 1860 39-2-383 (Dk)
Tune, D. M. 1860 wb-1-396 (Fr)

Tunnel, Esther 1858 wb-#177 (Mc)
Tunnell, John 1829 wb-1A-5 (A)
Tunnell, John 1833 wb-#177 (Mc)
Tunnell, John C. 1849 wb-1B-112 (A)
Tunnell, Spencer 1847 148-1-197 (Ge)
Tunnell, William 1848 wb-e-80 (Ro)
Tunnell, William 1861 wb-1D-7 (A)
Tunnley, Elizabeth J. 1836 wb-3-417 (Je)
Tunstall, George W. 1861 wb-8-0 (Sm)
Tunstall, John A. B. 1836 wb-9-295 (Rb)
Tunstall, Margaret 1844 wb-7-0 (Sm)
Turberville, Miles 1855 ib-h-278 (F)
Turbeville, Absalom 1815 wb-2-145 (K)
Turbeville, Jefferson 1848 wd-14-225 (D)
Turbeville, Rutha 1817 wb-7-128 (D)
Turbeville, Wilie 1848 wb-14-243 (D)
Turbeville, Wilkins S. 1842 wb-12-310* (D)
Turbeville, William 1836 wb-9-225 (Rb)
Turbyville, James 1853 wb-g-542 (Hn)
Turk, Archibald R. 1837 wb-#178 (Mc)
Turk, Thomas 1832 wb-1-144 (Bo)
Turledge, Mary 1826 wb-#139 (Mu)
Turley, James 1840 wb-12-32 (D)
Turley, James N. 1848 wb-10-24 (K)
Turley, Jennett 1838 wb-11-421 (D)
Turley, Thomas 1834 wb-1-54 (Gr)
Turman, James 1793 wb-1-234 (Je)
Turnbo, George sr. 1852 6-2-114 (Le)
Turnbo, Isham 1857 ib-2-44 (Wy)
Turnbo, James 1826 wb-#159 (Mu)
Turnbow, Casey 1859 ib-2-128 (Wy)
Turner, —— 1833 wb-b-17 (G)
Turner, Admir 1833 wb-b-18 (G)
Turner, Adonine? 1859 wb-f-308 (G)
Turner, Alex 1858 wb-13-37 (K)
Turner, Bailey 1823 lr (Sn)
Turner, Benjamin 1823 wb-1-0 (Sm)
Turner, Benjamin 1836 wb-2-143 (Ma)
Turner, Benjamin 1847 wb-4-197 (Hr)
Turner, Berryman 1806 wb-1-0 (Sm)
Turner, David 1817 wb-A-169 (Li)
Turner, E. B. 1856 rb-18-87 (Ru)
Turner, Edward sr. 1852 wb-7-0 (Sm)
Turner, Eleanor 1833 wb-2-0 (Sm)
Turner, Ezebel 1837 wb-3-0 (Sm)
Turner, Francis 1847 wb-1-236 (Fr)
Turner, Frederick 1829 wb-3-0 (Sm)
Turner, George 1805 wb-3-37 (D)
Turner, George 1824 wb-2-0 (Sm)
Turner, George 1836 wb-1-192 (W)
Turner, H. H. B. 1859 wb-17-1 (Rb)

Turner, Hamilton V. 1861 wb-b-120 (Ms)
Turner, Henry 1842 wb-2-500 (Hy)
Turner, Henry 1846 wb-8-408 (Wi)
Turner, Henry H. 1838 wb-1-439 (Hy)
Turner, Hezekiah 1843 wb-3-0 (Sm)
Turner, Isham 1808 wb-#6 (Wl)
Turner, J. E. 1826 wb-5-339 (Rb)
Turner, Jack E. 1826 wb-5-354 (Rb)
Turner, James 1809 wb-#3 (Mu)
Turner, James 1811 wb-4-158 (D)
Turner, James 1815 wb-3-109 (St)
Turner, James 1825 wb-#63 (Wl)
Turner, James 1825 wb-8-439 (D)
Turner, James 1835 wb-6-72 (Wi)
Turner, James 1840 wb-b-408 (Wh)
Turner, James 1850 wb-d-235 (G)
Turner, James 1853 as-b-111 (Ms)
Turner, James 1856 wb-6-391 (Ma)
Turner, James M. 1854 39-2-4 (Dk)
Turner, James T. 1858 wb-b-430 (We)
Turner, Jesse 1815 wb-2-189 (K)
Turner, Jesse 1836 wb-b-120 (G)
Turner, Jno. 1784? wb-1-25 (D)
Turner, John 1830 wb-4-544 (Wi)
Turner, John 1832 wb-1-15 (Sh)
Turner, John 1835 wb-2-193 (Sn)
Turner, John 1854 wb-3-244 (Gr)
Turner, John 1856 wb-1-339 (Fr)
Turner, John 1858 wb-b-37 (Dk)
Turner, John 1859 6-2-145 (Le)
Turner, John 1861 wb-17-256 (Rb)
Turner, John H. 1834 lr (Sn)
Turner, John J. 1843 wb-8-52 (Wi)
Turner, John T. 1831 wb-c-148 (St)
Turner, John jr. 1855 wb-12-110 (K)
Turner, Joseph 1823 rb-5-327 (Ru)
Turner, Joseph B. 1819 wb-7-315 (D)
Turner, Joseph P. 1840 wb-z-14 (Mu)
Turner, Lemuel T. 1816 wb-4-425 (D)
Turner, Lemuel T. 1816 wb-7-18 (D)
Turner, Levi 1860 wb-f-392 (G)
Turner, Lewis 1849 wb-9-250 (Wi)
Turner, Malinda 1841 lr (Sn)
Turner, Margaret 1853 wb-e-106 (G)
Turner, Martha 1839 wb-11-578 (D)
Turner, Martha H. 1848 wb-a-334 (F)
Turner, Mary M. 1858 39-2-258 (Dk)
Turner, Matthew 1841 wb-a-70 (L)
Turner, Medicus R. 1832 wb-9-618 (D)
Turner, Nancy A. 1851 wb-#176 (Wl)
Turner, Nathan 1840 wb-c-140 (Ro)

Turner, Norflet 1855 wb-g-709 (Hn)
Turner, R. A. 1852 wb-15-236 (D)
Turner, Richard A. 1852 wb-15-219 (D)
Turner, Robert 1796 wb-1-221 (Je)
Turner, Robert 1827 wb-#65 (Wl)
Turner, Semion 1827 wb-b-172 (St)
Turner, Simon 1826 wb-#139 (Mu)
Turner, Simon 1835 wb-1-200 (Hy)
Turner, Spratley 1858 wb-b-52 (Ms)
Turner, Stephen H. 1848 lr (Sn)
Turner, Stephen H. 1861 wb-13-499 (Wi)
Turner, Thomas 1832 wb-9-586 (D)
Turner, W. W. 1854 wb-16-358 (D)
Turner, Washington 1853 wb-#110 (Wl)
Turner, Wealthy S. 1830 wb-7-263 (Rb)
Turner, Wesley 1863 wb-2-373 (Li)
Turner, William 1812 wb-#10 (Wl)
Turner, William 1813 wb-#8 (Mu)
Turner, William 1849 rb-l-240 (Mt)
Turner, William 1854 ib-H-142 (F)
Turner, William 1854 wb-a-327 (Ms)
Turner, William A. 1835 wb-1-92 (W)
Turner, Willis 1836 wb-9-269 (Rb)
Turnery, Peter 1804 wb-1-0 (Sm)
Turney, Catherine 1859 39-2-309 (Dk)
Turney, George 1821 wb-1-0 (Sm)
Turney, Haywood 1856 wb-e-82 (Wh)
Turney, Henry sr. 1843 wb-a-48 (Dk)
Turney, Hopkins L. 1857 wb-1-357 (Fr)
Turney, Joseph 1852 r39-1-249 (Dk)
Turney, Rachael 1861 39-2-454 (Dk)
Turnley, John 1851 wb-A-72 (Ca)
Turpin, Edward 1848 lr (Sn)
Turpin, Elizabeth 1861 wb-f-207 (Mu)
Tussell, John 1833 rb-9-78 (Ru)
Tuten, Wiley 1842 wb-c-277 (Ro)
Tutor, Alexander 1848 wb-b-253 (We)
Tutt, Mary 1855 wb-n-526 (Mt)
Tweedy, Joseph 1813 rb-2-219 (Ru)
Tweedy, Pascal J. 1832 wb-1-104 (Hy)
Twidy, Joseph 1823 rb-5-272 (Ru)
Twigg, John O. 1847 wb-b-225 (We)
Twigg, Timothy 1845 rb-13-417 (Ru)
Twiggs, Jacob 1851 wb-d-293 (G)
Twiggs, Manerva 1852 wb-e-14 (G)
Twitty, L. H. 1856 as-b-230 (Ms)
Twitty, Martin H. 1859 as-c-149 (Ms)
Twitty, William W. 1859 as-c-149 (Ms)
Twitty, Winn sr. 1856 as-b-222 (Ms)
Tyer, Thomas 1821 rb-c-487 (Mt)
Tyler, John D. 1860 rb-p-470 (Mt)

Tyler, Kinhelm T. S. 1834 wb-x-254 (Mu)
Tyler, Richard D. 1858 wb-a-280 (T)
Tyler, Truman 1859 wb-f-171 (Mu)
Tyler, William 1820 wb-#18 (Wa)
Tyler, William B. 1856 rb-o-22 (Mt)
Tylor, Aron 1826 wb-2-528 (Je)
Tylour, Noah 1818 rb-c-34 (Mt)
Tyner, Memory 1833 rb-f-516 (Mt)
Tyner, Sally 1837 wb-1-323 (Hy)
Tyner, William C. 1851 wb-14-621 (D)
Tyns, Edwin 1841 wb-2-300 (Hy)
Tyre, Mary 1823 wb-1-0 (Sm)
Tyre, William 1823 wb-1-0 (Sm)
Tyree, Cyrus 1854 ib-1-288 (Wy)
Tyree, Henry 1852 wb-15-348 (D)
Tyree, Nicholas 1845 r39-1-2 (Dk)
Tyree, Richmond C. 1825 lr (Sn)
Tyree, Thomas W. 1836 wb-d-53 (St)
Tyree, William A. 1829 lr (Sn)
Tyson, Aaron 1857 wb-6-382 (Ma)
Tyson, Calvin 1848 wb-g-277 (Hn)
Tyson, J. B. 1860 wb-7-80 (Ma)
Tyson, Joel S. 1861 wb-h-496 (Hn)
Tyson, John 1837 wb-2-207 (Ma)
Tyson, Sally 1860 rb-p-501 (Mt)
Tyson, Samuel E. 1846 wb-g-152 (Hn)
Tyson, Thomas D. 1848 wb-d-109 (G)
Tyson, Uriah 1850 wb-m-41 (Mt)
Tyson, William 1860 rb-p-351 (Mt)
Tyson, Wright 1851 wb-g-388 (Hn)
Tyus, Benjamin J. 1852 wb-e-6 (Hy)
Tyus, Frederick W. 1857 wb-e-60 (Hy)

- U -

Uhles, Frederick 1848 wb-3-0 (Sm)
Umstead, Richard 1853 wb-e-53 (G)
Underdown, George 1847 wb-#178 (Mc)
Underdown, Thomas A. 1853 wb-#179 (Mc)
Underwood, Alexr. 1800 wb-2-192 (D)
Underwood, Catharine 1858 wb-17-476 (D)
Underwood, Edmund 1836 rb-9-345 (Ru)
Underwood, Edwin 1836 rb-9-359 (Ru)
Underwood, Elijah 1813 wb-2-57 (K)
Underwood, Elisha 1837 wb-#119 (Wl)
Underwood, F. 1854 wb-#113 (Wl)
Underwood, George 1850 wb-14-390 (Rb)
Underwood, Hugh 1856 wb-12-278 (K)
Underwood, James 1847 wb-#179 (Mc)
Underwood, John 1817 rb-4-79 (Ru)
Underwood, John 1858 wb-1-37 (Se)

Underwood, Levi S. 1833 rb-9-74 (Ru)
Underwood, Levi S. 1836 rb-9-125 (Ru)
Underwood, Nathan 1842 wb-#138 (Wl)
Underwood, Perry 1828 wb-#72 (Wl)
Underwood, Susan 1857 wb-1C-345 (A)
Underwood, Thomas 1832 wb-#96 (Wl)
Underwood, William 1847 rb-14-52 (Ru)
Underwood, Willy 1858 as-c-547 (Di)
Upchurch, A. F. 1852 wb-3-117 (W)
Upchurch, Abram? 1857 wb-3-362 (W)
Upchurch, Ambrose F. 1852 r39-1-229 (Dk)
Upchurch, Eli 1855 wb-g-628 (Hn)
Upchurch, J. J. 1858 wb-h-214 (Hn)
Upchurch, John 1854 wb-g-621 (Hn)
Upchurch, Joseph 1850 r39-1-171 (Dk)
Upchurch, Joshua 1844 wb-f-298 (Hn)
Upchurch, William 1847 wb-g-202 (Hn)
Upton, James 1826 wb-3-0 (Sm)
Urey, James 1816 rb-b-329 (Mt)
Urquhart, James 1838 wb-a-35 (F)
Ury, Isaac 1816 rb-b-361 (Mt)
Ury, Nancy 1823 rb-d-160 (Mt)
Uselton, Elenor 1860 wb-00-8 (Cf)
Usher, B. 1854 ib-h-4 (F)
Usher, Thomas sr. 1839 wb-2-47 (Hr)
Usher, W. W. 1848 wb-4-311 (Hr)
Usher, William W. 1848 wb-4-285 (Hr)
Usrey, Samuel 1834 wb-b-150 (Wh)
Usrey, William 1841 wb-c-2 (Wh)
Ussery, Mastin C. 1858 wb-5-83 (Hr)
Ussery, Welcome 1859 wb-5-94 (Hr)
Ussery, William 1853 lr (Gi)
Ussery, William 1859 wb-b-83 (Ms)
Utley, William H. 1818 wb-7-240 (D)

- V -

Vaden, Anna 1860 wb-7-78 (La)
Vaden, Anna 1861 wb-5-78 (La)
Vaden, D. D. 1858 wb-f-175 (G)
Vaden, William 1849 wb-7-0 (Sm)
Valentine, Charles 1853 wb-n-5 (Mt)
Valentine, Charles A. 1847 wb-f-127+ (O)
Valentine, Hardy 1860 wb-h-459 (Hn)
Valentine, S. K. 1856 wb-b-377 (We)
Valient, Martha 1857 wb-j-248 (O)
Valient, Robert C. 1854 wb-i-182 (O)
Van Meter, William A. 1854 wb-12-46 (K)
Van Vleck, C. A. (Rev.) 1846 wb-2-64# (Ge)
VanVector, Benjamin 1823 wb-2-146# (Ge)
Vanatta, Samuel 1858 wb-b-42 (Dk)

Vanatta, Samuel 1859 39-2-291 (Dk)
Vanbebber, Isaac 1858 ib-2-583 (Cl)
Vance, Adam 1846 wb-d-261 (Hd)
Vance, Daniel 1845 wb-#146 (Wl)
Vance, David 1847 wb-13-188 (Rb)
Vance, David 1851 wb-1-264 (Bo)
Vance, David sr. 1831 lr (Sn)
Vance, Elisha Q. 1855 wb-16-577 (D)
Vance, Elizabeth H. 1858 rb-o-674 (Mt)
Vance, James 1846 148-1-179 (Ge)
Vance, James M. 1861 lr (Gi)
Vance, James sr. 1853 wb-5-205 (Je)
Vance, John 1842 wb-4-2 (Je)
Vance, Martin 1860 wb-k-171 (O)
Vance, Mary 1857 wb-5-498 (Je)
Vance, Patrick 1803 wb-1-122 (K)
Vance, Philip 1836 wb-2-213 (Sn)
Vance, Robert 1829 rb-f-5 (Mt)
Vance, Saml. 1819 rb-d-190 (Mt)
Vance, Samuel 1829 rb-f-6 (Mt)
Vance, Samuel 1839 wb-5-3 (Gr)
Vance, Samuel 1858 ib-1-553 (Ca)
Vance, Samuel B. 1830 rb-f-81 (Mt)
Vance, Sarah 1830 wb-1-56 (Li)
Vandavor, Arnold 1827 wb-a-292 (Wh)
Vanderpool, Lewis 1854 wb-#179 (Mc)
Vanderpool, Rebecca 1779 wb-#1 (Wa)
Vanderville, John 1845 wb-13-357 (D)
Vandike, William 1831 rb-8-401 (Ru)
Vandiver, John 1829 wb-b-111 (Wh)
Vandyke, Freeman 1830 wb-3-104 (Je)
Vandyke, John 1845 wb-g-63 (Hn)
Vanerson, Elizabeth 1854 wb-3-171 (W)
Vanhook, Aaron 1824 as-A-38 (Di)
Vanhook, Richard 1823 wb-4-76 (Rb)
Vanhook, Robert 1855 wb-h-431 (Hu)
Vanhook, Victoria 1858 as-c-565 (Di)
Vanhooser, Isaac 1831 wb-1-61 (W)
Vanhoozer, Jackson 1856 wb-#121 (Wl)
Vanhuss, Matthias 1856 wb-2-23 (Ct)
Vanison, Albert G. 1846 wb-7-0 (Sm)
Vanleer, Bernard 1833 wb-10-65 (D)
Vanleer, Hannah 1836 wb-10-544 (D)
Vann, Valentine S. 1855 wb-6-44 (Ma)
Vannatta, Christopher 1815 Wb-2-166 (Wi)
Vannatta, James 1861 wb-b-84 (Dk)
Vannatta, Peter 1826 wb-3-0 (Sm)
Vannatta, William 1847 r39-1-36 (Dk)
Vannoy, Noah 1833 wb-3-257 (Je)
Vannoy, Patrick 1836 wb-3-507 (Je)
Vanover, Hannah 1861 39-2-453 (Dk)

Vanover, Martha 1861 39-2-453 (Dk)
Vanpelt, Benjamin 1817 wb-2-39# (Ge)
Vansandt, Isaiah 1789 wb-2-145# (Ge)
Vantrease, Jacob 1828 wb-#77 (Wl)
Vantrease, Jacob 1850 wb-#173 (Wl)
Vantrease, John 1859 39-2-303 (Dk)
Vantrease, Nicholas 1859 wb-#128 (Wl)
Vantrease, William H. 1856 wb-#121 (Wl)
Vanzandt, Andrew J. 1849 wb-#179 (Mc)
Vanzandt, Jacob 1815 wb-1-27 (Fr)
Vanzandt, John Sr. 1834 wb-#179 (Mc)
Vardell, John 1815 rb-3-104 (Ru)
Varnel, John 1832 wb-#179 (Mc)
Varner, Adam 1844 wb-d-113 (Hd)
Varner, James 1821 wb-1-0 (Sm)
Varner, John R. 1850 wb-3-20 (W)
Varner, Robert 1850 wb-e-254 (Ro)
Varrell, Mary 1831 wb-a-133 (Di)
Vaughan, A. W. 1860 rb-20-640 (Ru)
Vaughan, Allen 1858 wb-1-478 (Hw)
Vaughan, Anderson J. 1844 wb-8-178 (Wi)
Vaughan, Dixon 1849 wb-b-400 (Mu)
Vaughan, Drury 1827 rb-7-101 (Ru)
Vaughan, Drury 1827 rb-7-298 (Ru)
Vaughan, Elisha 1835 rb-9-225 (Ru)
Vaughan, Henry A. 1854 rb-16-714 (Ru)
Vaughan, Henry A. 1854 rb-16-795 (Ru)
Vaughan, James 1840 wb-1-474 (Hw)
Vaughan, James 1860 39-2-357 (Dk)
Vaughan, Joel 1829 wb-7-40 (Rb)
Vaughan, John 1820 wb-1-471 (Hw)
Vaughan, John 1841 wb-z-179 (Mu)
Vaughan, John 1842 wb-1-474 (Hw)
Vaughan, John M. 1835 wb-1-472 (Hw)
Vaughan, John P. 1841 rb-i-201 (Mt)
Vaughan, John S. 1845 rb-13-386 (Ru)
Vaughan, Joshua P. 1829 rb-e-486 (Mt)
Vaughan, Littleton 1849 wb-b-470 (Mu)
Vaughan, Mildred L. 1844 rb-13-42 (Ru)
Vaughan, Milton 1838 wb-#179 (Mc)
Vaughan, Person C. 1854 wb-e-244 (G)
Vaughan, Peter R. 1841 rb-11-206 (Ru)
Vaughan, Peter R. 1854 rb-17-131 (Ru)
Vaughan, Randolph 1858 wb-17-457 (D)
Vaughan, Richard 1850 rb-15-395 (Ru)
Vaughan, Richard B. 1855 rb-17-359 (Ru)
Vaughan, Robert 1848 wb-9-61 (Wi)
Vaughan, Robert C. 1855 wb-11-461 (Wi)
Vaughan, Sarah 1849 rb-15-281 (Ru)
Vaughan, Sarah R. 1849 rb-15-78 (Ru)
Vaughan, Sterling F. 1855 wb-b-10 (F)

Vaughan, Thomas 1855 wb-#180 (Mc)
Vaughan, Thomas J. 1851 wb-#180 (Mc)
Vaughan, W. A. 1860 wb-f-358 (G)
Vaughan, W. C. 1861 rb-p-615 (Mt)
Vaughan, William 1828 rb-7-35 (Ru)
Vaughan, William 1844 rb-12-589 (Ru)
Vaughan, William B. 1845 rb-13-224 (Ru)
Vaughan, William P. 1835 wb-b-68 (G)
Vaughn, Abraham 1832 wb-#114 (Wl)
Vaughn, Benjamin 1839 wb-b-355 (Wh)
Vaughn, David 1824 wb-a-220 (Ro)
Vaughn, David 1838 wb-11-182 (D)
Vaughn, Edmon H. 1842 wb-1-79 (Sh)
Vaughn, J. C. 1848 wb-14-283 (D)
Vaughn, James 1830 wb-#85 (Wl)
Vaughn, James 1831 wb-5-77 (Wi)
Vaughn, James 1836 wb-6-182 (Wi)
Vaughn, James 1858 rb-o-709 (Mt)
Vaughn, James L. 1852 wb-3-38 (La)
Vaughn, John 1848 wb-1-239 (Me)
Vaughn, John Turner 1840 wb-#129 (Wl)
Vaughn, Martha 1835 wb-10-515 (D)
Vaughn, Peter 1831 wb-1-69 (Li)
Vaughn, Richard 1822 wb-#47 (Wl)
Vaughn, Richard D. 1840 wb-7-319 (Wi)
Vaughn, Richard W. 1840 wb-#131 (Wl)
Vaughn, Sarah 1857 wb-17-338 (D)
Vaughn, Thomas 1807 wb-#5 (Wl)
Vaughn, Thomas 1859 wb-#129 (Wl)
Vaughn, Thomas J. 1854 ib-H-132 (F)
Vaughn, W. C. 1858 rb-p-15 (Mt)
Vaughn, W. W. 1859 wb-4-275 (La)
Vaughn, William 1857 wb-4-120 (La)
Vaughn, William L. 1845 wb#18 (Gu)
Vaughn, Williard L. 1847 wb#19 (Gu)
Vaught, Andrew (Sr.) 1853 wb-#24 (Mo)
Vaught, Andrew 1853 wb-#9 (Mo)
Vaught, Elijah 1844 wb-#155 (Wl)
Vaught, Nancy 1853 wb-1-79 (Jo)
Vaught, Simeon 1824 rb-6-56 (Ru)
Vaught, William C. 1839 wb-a-75 (T)
Vaught, Wm. 1841 wb-b-405 (G)
Vaulx, Catherine 1852 wb-15-361 (D)
Vaulx, Daniel 1815 wb-4-389 (D)
Vaulx, Daniel 1816 wb-7-52 (D)
Vaulx, Sarah 1859 wb-e-134 (Hy)
Vawter, W. B. 1860 rb-20-737 (Ru)
Veal, Thomas 1851 wb-14-549 (Rb)
Veale, Agness 1851 wb-15-3 (Rb)
Veasey, Fielding L. 1829 wb-b-78 (Hn)
Veck, Richd. 1829 wb-6-499 (Rb)

Venable, Daniel 1816 rb-b-331 (Mt)
Venable, Daniel 1827 rb-e-76 (Mt)
Venable, James 1860 wb-h-508 (Hn)
Venable, Larkin 1857 wb-h-131 (Hn)
Ventor, John S. 1824 wb-3-347 (St)
Ventress, Eliza 1848 wb-a-340 (F)
Verd, William 1855 39-2-96 (Dk)
Verhain, William 1854 wb-h-12 (St)
Verhine, John W. 1846 wb-f-62 (O)
Verhines, William sr. 1854 wb-xx-394 (St)
Vermillion, Jesse H. 1840 wb-b-416 (Wh)
Vernon, Abraham 1825 wb-1-472 (Hw)
Vernon, Green 1861 wb-13-391 (Wi)
Vernon, Harlen 1850 wb-1-476 (Hw)
Vernon, Harrison 1837 wb-1-8 (Me)
Vernon, J. C. C. 1834 rb-9-118 (Ru)
Vernon, John C. C. 1834 rb-9-129 (Ru)
Vernon, John D. 1848 wb-9-117 (Wi)
Vernon, Nathan 1854 wb-1-476 (Hw)
Vernon, Nehemiah 1815 wb-2-274 (Rb)
Vernon, Obediah 1831 wb-5-2 (Wi)
Vernon, Richard 1840 wb-7-309 (Wi)
Vernon, Robert 1846 wb-8-486 (Wi)
Vernon, Saml. 1786 wb-1-46 (D)
Vernon, Tinsley 1854 rb-16-713 (Ru)
Vernor, Henry 1857 as-c-65 (Ms)
Verser, Nathan 1828 wb-1-89 (Ma)
Vesey, Freeden L. 1837 wb-d-297 (Hn)
Vest, Samuel 1837 wb-a-9 (Ms)
Vestal, Isaac 1855 149-1-1 1/2 (Ge)
Vestal, J. M. 1861 wb-17-252 (Rb)
Vestal, Silas 1833 wb-2-42# (Ge)
Veverret, Lancelot 1827 wb-#67 (Wl)
Viar, William 1855 39-2-123 (Dk)
Viars, Rebecca 1837 wb-b-76 (Hd)
Vicars, James 1845 wb-2-121 (Wi)
Vick, Augustine 1857 39-2-182 (Dk)
Vick, Elizabeth 1853 wb-a-267 (Di)
Vick, Jonas 1840 lr (Gi)
Vick, Richard 1829 wb-6-500 (Rb)
Vick, Robert 1826 wb-9-1 (D)
Vick, Rowland 1823 rb-d-88 (Mt)
Vick, Wilson 1858 rb-o-539 (Mt)
Vickers, John 1843 wb-1-221 (Li)
Vickers, Joseph 1837 wb-1-255 (W)
Vickers, W. J. 1859 wb-i-115 (St)
Vickers, William 1827 wb-1-8 (W)
Vincent, Hungerford 1818 wb-#125 (Mu)
Vincent, Jacob G. 1852 wb-h-Dec (O)
Vincent, James 1854? wb-#25 (Mo)
Vincent, James 1855 wb-6-151 (Ma)

Vincent, John 1853 wb-a-322 (Ms)
Vincent, John 1861 wb-1-101 (Su)
Vincent, John M. 1857 wb-b-402 (We)
Vincent, Julia 1859 wb-17-622 (D)
Vincent, Mary 1853 wb-#24 (Mo)
Vincent, Matilda T. 1857 wb-b-408 (We)
Vincent, Thomas 1843 wb-3-680 (Ma)
Vincent, Thomas W. 1821 wb-#47 (Mu)
Vincent, Thomas W. 1831 wb-#216 (Mu)
Vineyard, David 1816 rb-b-375 (Mt)
Vineyard, Tabler 1843 wb-1-180 (Bo)
Vinson, Addison 1827 wb-1-546 (Ma)
Vinson, Axam 1826 wb-b-93 (St)
Vinson, David 1856 wb-a-273 (Cr)
Vinson, Elizabeth 1835 wb-c-449 (St)
Vinson, Elizabeth 1835 wb-c-463 (St)
Vinson, Henry 1841 rb-12-31 (Ru)
Vinson, Henry 1842 wb-a-104 (Cr)
Vinson, James 1818 lr (Sn)
Vinson, James 1825 wb-b-10 (St)
Vinson, James 1847 wb-f-467 (St)
Vinson, Jane 1833 lr (Sn)
Vinson, John 1806 wb-#4 (Wl)
Vinson, John sr. 1846 wb-5-17 (Ma)
Vinson, Mary B. 1849 wb-g-95 (St)
Vinson, Rachell 1841 rb-12-44 (Ru)
Vinson, Richard 1848 ib-1-10 (Ca)
Vinters, John S. 1815 wb-3-75 (St)
Vinyard, John 1834 wb-1-74 (Gr)
Vinyard, Martin 1854 wb-3-192 (Gr)
Violett, Thomas 1831 wb-#124 (Wl)
Vivrett, Elizabeth 1861 wb-#134 (Wl)
Vivrett, Henry 1853 wb-#180 (Wl)
Vivrett, Micajah 1816 wb-#22 (Wl)
Vivrett, Nancy 1848 wb-#163 (Wl)
Vivrett, William B. 1847 wb-#155 (Wl)
Vivrett, William D. 1839 wb-#125 (Wl)
Vogh, Margaret (Mrs.) 1854 wb-2-171 (Sh)
Volentine, William A. 1856 wb-6-213 (Ma)
Voorhies, Garret L. 1859 wb-f-179 (Mu)
Voorhies, Garrett L. (Dr.) 1823 wb-#56 (Mu)
Voorhies, Peter Imlay 1856 wb-f-101 (Mu)
Voorhies, Peter J. 1856 wb-f-104 (Mu)
Voorhies, Polly J. 1826 wb-#139 (Mu)
Voss, Smith 1848 wb-2-20 (La)
Voss, William 1846 wb-1-386 (La)
Voucher, George 1857 wb-h-328 (St)
Voucher, George W. 1852 wb-xx-82 (St)

- W -

Waddell, John 1828 wb-#27 (Wa)
Waddell, Samuel D. 1829 wb-1-210 (Ma)
Waddle, Elizabeth B. 1830 wb-1-282 (Ma)
Waddle, Jonathan 1836 wb-#34 (Wa)
Waddle, Sparling 1858 149-1-110 (Ge)
Waddy, Granville 1836 wb-d-260 (Hn)
Waddy, Samuel 1841 wb-e-267 (Hn)
Wade, Ann 1845 rb-13-412 (Ru)
Wade, Ann 1858 rb-19-391 (Ru)
Wade, Austin M. 1851 rb-4-279 (Mu)
Wade, Dabney 1817 wb-#34 (Mu)
Wade, Dabney 1827 wb-#157 (Mu)
Wade, Daniel 1848 wb-1B-58 (A)
Wade, Daniel F. 1853 wb-11-30 (Wi)
Wade, Edward 1835 wb-1-388 (Hr)
Wade, Francis 1822 wb-#67 (Mu)
Wade, Francis 1844 wb-13-60 (D)
Wade, Hullory 1855 wb-e-346 (G)
Wade, Isaac 1841 wb-#135 (Wl)
Wade, J. C. 1857 rb-18-612 (Ru)
Wade, James 1845 rb-13-224 (Ru)
Wade, Janadab 1857 wb-1-501 (Hw)
Wade, John 1803 wb-1-126 (Rb)
Wade, John 1842 rb-12-233 (Ru)
Wade, John C. 1856 rb-17-614 (Ru)
Wade, John C. 1860 wb-7-79 (Ma)
Wade, John sr. 1840 rb-10-488 (Ru)
Wade, Louisa 1821 wb-#125 (Mu)
Wade, Mary 1844 rb-12-487 (Ru)
Wade, Mary 1858 rb-19-384 (Ru)
Wade, Mary M. 1860 wb-b-110 (Ms)
Wade, Noah 1840 wb-b-352 (G)
Wade, Plummer H. 1853 wb-a-240 (Dk)
Wade, Robert 1849 wb-#170 (Wl)
Wade, Samuel 1861 wb-k-490 (O)
Wade, Sarah 1841 wb-3-365 (Ma)
Wade, Sarah 1856 rb-17-623 (Ru)
Wade, Seth 1825 wb-a-85 (Hn)
Wade, Simpson H. 1847 wb-9-9 (Wi)
Wade, Susan 1852 wb-e-9 (G)
Wade, Suse 1818? wb-#119 (Mu)
Wade, Thomas 1839 rb-10-430 (Ru)
Wade, Walter 1849 rb-15-140 (Ru)
Wade, Washington H. 1851 mr-2-417 (Be)
Wade, William 1849 rb-15-134 (Ru)
Wade, William A. 1834 wb-3-0 (Sm)
Wade, William M. 1856 39-2-139 (Dk)
Wade, Wilson L. 1857 rb-18-556 (Ru)
Wade, Wilson N. 1858 wb-f-212 (G)

Wade, Wilson N. 1859 wb-f-260 (G)
Wadkins, Osa 1836 wb-a-162 (O)
Wadkins, Samuel 1841 mr-1-338 (Be)
Wadley, Samuel 1854 rb-17-30 (Ru)
Wadsworth, Jason 1807 wb-1-171 (Wi)
Wafford, Jesse 1814 wb-a-219a (St)
Wagers, James 1822 rb-d-81 (Mt)
Waggener, Richard 1858 wb-b-425 (We)
Waggoner, Alfred T. 1853 wb-10-494 (Wi)
Waggoner, Christopher 1849 wb-g-148 (Hu)
Waggoner, Daniel 1833 wb-1-98 (Li)
Waggoner, Daniel 1837 wb-b-69 (Hd)
Waggoner, Daniel D. 1844 wb-e-637 (Hu)
Waggoner, Daniel L. 1842 wb-e-456 (Hu)
Waggoner, George 1815 wb-A-103 (Li)
Waggoner, George 1845 wb-1-255 (Li)
Waggoner, James M. 1853 wb-10-531 (Wi)
Waggoner, John 1808 wb-1-258 (K)
Waggoner, John 1825 wb-4-38 (K)
Waggoner, Martha 1844 wb-d-108 (Hd)
Waggoner, Matthew 1854 wb-16-349 (D)
Waggoner, Rhoda Ann 1851 wb-9-674 (Wi)
Waggoner, Sarah 1855 wb-3-277 (Gr)
Waggoner, Valentine 1853 wb-10-494 (Wi)
Waggoner, William 1849 33-3-144 (Gr)
Waggoner, William 1849 wb-#170 (Wl)
Wagler, John 1814 wb-4-305 (D)
Wagner, Charles Henry 1857 wb-17-262 (D)
Wagner, David sr. 1845 wb-1-11 (Jo)
Wagner, Eliza 1857 wb-1-352 (Fr)
Wagner, Joseph G. 1856 wb-1-108 (Jo)
Wagner, Mathew 1802 wb-1-27 (Ct)
Wagner, McClelland 1857 wb-1-116 (Jo)
Wagner, Susannah 1850 wb-1-54 (Jo)
Wagnon, John P. 1842 wb-1-80 (Sh)
Wagoner, Jacob 1858 wb-17-510 (D)
Wagstaff, John 1838 lr (Gi)
Wagster, John 1854 wb-b*-39 (O)
Waide, James 1842 wb-#180 (Mc)
Wainright, John 1840 wb-2-86 (Hy)
Wainwright, G. T. 1854 ib-H-139 (F)
Wainwright, George T. 1856 ib-h-513 (F)
Wainwright, Sarah T. 1854 ib-h-211 (F)
Wair, George T. 1819 wb-3-4 (Rb)
Wait, George 1858 wb-0-158 (Cf)
Waite, George 1858 wb-3-398 (W)
Wakefield, Abel 1838 wb-1-156 (La)
Wakefield, B. H. 1853 wb-1-324 (Fr)
Wakefield, Joseph 1851 wb-10-96 (Wi)
Wakefield, Thomas 1846 wb-1-227 (Fr)
Wakefield, Thomas 1860 wb-1-404 (Fr)

Wakefield, Thomas E. Jr. 1861 wb-1-405 (Fr)
Walch, John B. 1838 wb-11-468 (D)
Walden, Austin S. 1850 wb-10-487 (K)
Walden, Jno. W. 1860 wb-18-382 (D)
Walden, John E. 1848 rb-14-389 (Ru)
Waldin, Austin L. 1852 wb-11-323 (K)
Waldron, J. W. 1861 wb-18-476 (D)
Waldron, Rebecca 1805 wb-#4 (Wl)
Waldron, Sarah D. 1834 wb-10-287 (D)
Waldron, Thomas A. R. 1851 wb-#50 (Wa)
Waldron, William 1857 wb-17-382 (D)
Waldrop, Dandrige 1854 wb-i-194 (O)
Waldrop, Enoch P. 1858 wb-f-138 (G)
Waldrop, John 1858 wb-f-138 (G)
Waldrop, John 1859 wb-f-304 (G)
Waldrop, Nancy 1856 wb-f-19 (G)
Waldrop, Nancy? 1858 wb-f-179 (G)
Waldrope, D. B. 1852 wb-h-Mar (O)
Waldrope, Mahala 1849 wb-d-178 (G)
Waldrope, Willis A. 1855 wb-e-357 (G)
Waldrum, Joseph 1829 lr (Sn)
Waldrup, James 1841 wb-b-404 (G)
Wale, Martin B. 1850 ib-1-120 (Ca)
Wale, Martin B. 1853 ib-1-265 (Ca)
Walk, Anthony 1817 wb-1-0 (Sm)
Walker, Adam 1852 wb-5-159 (Je)
Walker, Albert B. 1839 wb-6-413 (K)
Walker, Alex 1840 wb-e-3 (St)
Walker, Alexander 1825 wb-b-66 (St)
Walker, Alexander 1840 wb-12-33 (D)
Walker, Alexander 1851 wb-4-151 (Mu)
Walker, Alexander 1855 39-2-86 (Dk)
Walker, Alexander jr. 1842 wb-e-228 (St)
Walker, Andrew J. 1850 rb-15-323 (Ru)
Walker, Andrew W. 1850 wb-1-396 (Li)
Walker, Anson 1861 wb-b-115 (Ms)
Walker, Archibald 1827 wb-a-4 (T)
Walker, Benjamin 1842 as-b-133 (Di)
Walker, Benjamin 1854 wb-3-259 (Gr)
Walker, Buckner 1850 wb-e-209 (Ro)
Walker, Burrel 1852 ib-1-156 (Wy)
Walker, Caswell L. 1861 wb-#18 (Mo)
Walker, Charles 1828 rb-7-28 (Ru)
Walker, Charles 1832 wb-1-37 (La)
Walker, Daby 1836 wb-6-31 (K)
Walker, Daniel 1834 wb-a-260 (R)
Walker, David 1806 wb-#4 (Wl)
Walker, David 1816 mr (Gi)
Walker, David 1847 rb-k-421 (Mt)
Walker, David A. 1855 wb-a-229 (V)
Walker, Davis 1814 wb-a-25 (Wh)

Walker, Delila 1844? wb-#140 (Wl)
Walker, Doritha 1852 wb-d-54 (Wh)
Walker, Edmond E. 1840 wb-#180 (Mc)
Walker, Elihu G. 1836 wb-b-109 (G)
Walker, Elish A. 1837 wb-a-329 (R)
Walker, Elizabeth 1825 wb-4-72 (K)
Walker, Elizabeth 1852 148-1-412 (Ge)
Walker, Elizabeth 1853 wb-e-103 (G)
Walker, Elizabeth 1855 wb-a-288 (Di)
Walker, Elmore 1834 wb-10-348 (D)
Walker, Francis H. 1847 wb-1-494 (Hw)
Walker, Francis M. 1852 wb-h-Nov (O)
Walker, Freeman 1836 wb-6-154 (Wi)
Walker, George 1822 wb-3-382 (K)
Walker, George 1825 wb-a-3 (R)
Walker, George 1838 wb-6-241 (K)
Walker, George W. 1858 wb-7-0 (Sm)
Walker, Giley 1829 wb-6-474 (Rb)
Walker, Griffith 1831 wb-#217 (Mu)
Walker, Hanch 1815 Wb-2-177 (Wi)
Walker, Hardridge 1856 wb-16-126 (Rb)
Walker, Henrietta 1842 wb-c-30 (G)
Walker, Henry 1824 wb-3-699 (Wi)
Walker, Henry 1831 wb-#89 (Wl)
Walker, Henry 1842 wb-#139 (Wl)
Walker, Henry 1854 wb-11-209 (Wi)
Walker, Henry 1854 wb-j-9 (O)
Walker, Henry 1860 wb-b-92 (Ms)
Walker, Henry D. 1846 mr-2-187 (Be)
Walker, Henry F. 1841 wb-b-36 (We)
Walker, Herbert 1829 wb-#82 (Wl)
Walker, Hervey D. 1848 mr-2-286 (Be)
Walker, Hugh 1802 wb-1-89 (K)
Walker, Isaac 1843 as-b-156 (Di)
Walker, Isaac E. 1862 wb#8 (Gu)
Walker, J. G. 1859 gs-1-397 (F)
Walker, Jacob 1850 wb-10-385 (K)
Walker, James 1791 wb-1-25# (Ge)
Walker, James 1794 wb-1-41 (Je)
Walker, James 1802 as-1-1 (Ge)
Walker, James 1815 rb-3-56 (Ru)
Walker, James 1824 wb-4-184 (Rb)
Walker, James 1829 wb-1-34 (Li)
Walker, James 1830 wb-9-377 (D)
Walker, James 1836 5-2-63 (Cl)
Walker, James 1840 wb-z-74 (Mu)
Walker, James 1843 wb-f-178 (Hn)
Walker, James 1853 wb-#180 (Mc)
Walker, James 1854 ib-2-72 (Cl)
Walker, James 1856 wb-g-740 (Hn)
Walker, James 1858 wb-1-221 (Be)

Walker, James 1858 wb-12-506 (K)
Walker, James 1859 wb#7 (Gu)
Walker, James 1860 wb-h-417 (Hn)
Walker, James 1861 wb-h-501 (Hn)
Walker, James D. 1849 wb-#170 (Wl)
Walker, James H. 1836 wb-b-319 (Ro)
Walker, James H. 1848 wb-2-314 (W)
Walker, James M. 1846 wb-c-345 (G)
Walker, James M. 1848 as-b-423 (Di)
Walker, James S. 1823 wb-#212 (Mu)
Walker, James S. 1836 wb-y-203 (Mu)
Walker, Jealsy 1829 wb-7-44 (Rb)
Walker, Jennet 1806 wb-3-98 (D)
Walker, Jennit 1806 wb-3-99 (D)
Walker, Jeremiah 1854 wb-1-27 (Gu)
Walker, Jeremiah 1857 wb-5-500 (Je)
Walker, Jesse 1807 wb-1-331 (Je)
Walker, Job 1854 ib-h-34 (F)
Walker, Joel 1844 wb-8-187 (Wi)
Walker, John 1810 wb-1-313 (K)
Walker, John 1815 rb-3-73 (Ru)
Walker, John 1818 wb-1-484 (Hw)
Walker, John 1818 wb-7-247 (D)
Walker, John 1824 wb-3-721 (Wi)
Walker, John 1827 wb-3-0 (Sm)
Walker, John 1828 wb-1-17 (W)
Walker, John 1839 wb-y-593 (Mu)
Walker, John 1840 rb-h-386 (Mt)
Walker, John 1842 wb-1-500 (W)
Walker, John 1843 wb-8-17 (Wi)
Walker, John 1848 wb-g-108 (Hu)
Walker, John 1850 wb-c-398 (Wh)
Walker, John 1850 wb-c-406 (Wh)
Walker, John 1856 wb-f-30 (Ro)
Walker, John 1857 wb-2-84# (Ge)
Walker, John A. 1861 wb-18-625 (D)
Walker, John B. 1841 wb-1-405 (W)
Walker, John J. (Sr.) 1854 wb#22 (Gu)
Walker, John J. 1838 wb-1-1 (Gu)
Walker, John Jr. 1834 wb-#180 (Mc)
Walker, John P. 1857 wb-f-20 (G)
Walker, John Wesley 1849 wb-2-81 (La)
Walker, John sr. 1796 wb-1-25# (Ge)
Walker, Jonathan 1816 wb-7-10 (D)
Walker, Jonathan T. 1848 ib-1-59 (Cl)
Walker, Joseph 1844 wb-3-450 (Hy)
Walker, Joseph 1847 rb-k-601 (Mt)
Walker, Joseph 1851 ib-1-211 (Cl)
Walker, Joseph W. 1861 wb-18-535 (D)
Walker, Joshua 1849 mr-2-311 (Be)
Walker, Joshua 1859 as-c-160 (Ms)

Walker, Julia A. 1858 wb-c-245 (L)
Walker, Lytle 1840 wb-#127 (Wl)
Walker, Madison 1853 wb-m-632 (Mt)
Walker, Margaret 1841 wb-12-177* (D)
Walker, Martha 1841 rb-11-285 (Ru)
Walker, Mary 1803 as-1-32 (Ge)
Walker, Mary 1835 wb-1-366 (Hr)
Walker, Mary 1853 wb-10-495 (Wi)
Walker, Mary 1854 wb-d-222 (Wh)
Walker, Mary 1855 wb-11-509 (Wi)
Walker, Mathew P. 1851 wb-14-573 (D)
Walker, Matthew 1848 wb-9-487 (K)
Walker, Milner 1849 wb-#172 (Wl)
Walker, Nancy 1836 wb-10-582 (D)
Walker, Nancy 1844 wb-#142 (Wl)
Walker, Nancy 1852 mr-2-445 (Be)
Walker, Nicholas 1835 wb-10-519 (D)
Walker, Noah 1827 wb-4-204 (Wi)
Walker, Noah 1834 wb-#104 (Wl)
Walker, Osborn 1854 wb-d-222 (Wh)
Walker, P. B. 1842 wb-2-398 (Hr)
Walker, P. H. 1855 wb-#26 (Mo)
Walker, Philip 1802 wb-2-231 (D)
Walker, Philip 1826 wb-9-66 (D)
Walker, Pleasant H. 1833 wb-10-159 (D)
Walker, Pleasant H. 1833 wb-10-72 (D)
Walker, Polly 1825 as-b-73 (St)
Walker, Polly 1859 wb-13-194 (K)
Walker, R. B. 1859 wb-a-113 (Ce)
Walker, Rebecca 1843 wb-#140 (Wl)
Walker, Reuben 1846 wb-9-194 (K)
Walker, Robert 1829 wb-a-69 (R)
Walker, Robert 1843 wb-1-256 (La)
Walker, Robert 1846 rb-k-51 (Mt)
Walker, Robert F. 1845 wb-1-364 (La)
Walker, Robert T. 1838 wb-11-219 (D)
Walker, Saml. (Dr.) 1837 wb-1-556 (Hr)
Walker, Samuel 1840 wb-#132 (Wl)
Walker, Samuel 1850 wb-#171 (Wl)
Walker, Samuel B. 1835 wb-1-424 (Hr)
Walker, Samuel R. 1823 wb-a-180 (Ro)
Walker, Sarah 1820 wb-1-0 (Sm)
Walker, Stephen 1857 wb-2-172 (Li)
Walker, Theophilus A. 1833 wb-b-215 (Ro)
Walker, Theophilus J. 1834 wb-b-242 (Ro)
Walker, Thomas 1823 wb-#60 (Mu)
Walker, Thomas 1841 wb-z-173 (Mu)
Walker, Thomas 1850 wb-b-293 (We)
Walker, Thomas 1855 wb-f-60 (Mu)
Walker, Thomas 1856 wb-e-471 (G)
Walker, Thomas 1857 wb-h-442 (St)

Walker, Thomas 1858 wb-a-68 (Ce)
Walker, Thomas G. 1851 wb-4-527 (Mu)
Walker, Tilman P. 1858 wb-j-358 (O)
Walker, W. B. H. 1862? wb-#135 (Wl)
Walker, W. W. 1855 ib-h-392 (F)
Walker, Washington 1813 wb-#19 (Mu)
Walker, West 1822 wb-3-359 (K)
Walker, William (Sr.) 1828 wb-#76 (Wl)
Walker, William 1798 wb-0-24 (K)
Walker, William 1815 wb-4-339 (D)
Walker, William 1829 wb-#86 (Wl)
Walker, William 1835 rb-9-247 (Ru)
Walker, William 1836 mr-1-327 (Be)
Walker, William 1840 abl-1-204 (T)
Walker, William 1841 wb-#43 (Wa)
Walker, William 1841 wb-e-281 (Hn)
Walker, William 1844 wb-#140 (Wl)
Walker, William 1847 wb-9-415 (K)
Walker, William 1857 wb-a-265 (T)
Walker, William C. 1857 wb-12-475 (Wi)
Walker, William H. 1833 rb-9-75 (Ru)
Walker, William S. 1841 wb-#134 (Wl)
Walker, William sr. 1849 mr-2-348 (Be)
Walker, Willson 1847 wb-g-169 (Hn)
Walker, Zach J. 1832 wb-b-188 (Ro)
Walkup, Lewis M. 1857 rb-18-359 (Ru)
Wall, A. J. 1854 as-b-157 (Ms)
Wall, Bird 1831 wb-#93 (Wl)
Wall, Burgess 1848 as-b-437 (Di)
Wall, Catherine 1860 wb-i-220 (St)
Wall, Charles 1815 rb-b-74 (Mt)
Wall, Cordy 1835 wb-c-452 (St)
Wall, David 1854 wb-15-611 (Rb)
Wall, Edmond 1850 wb-9-461 (Wi)
Wall, Elijah 1856 rb-o-222 (Mt)
Wall, F. T. 1861 wb-i-333 (St)
Wall, Guilford 1857 wb-5-497 (Je)
Wall, Henry L. 1853 wb-xx-208 (St)
Wall, Henry L. jr. 1858 wb-i-31 (St)
Wall, J. J. 1839 wb-y-332 (Mu)
Wall, J? K. 1858 gs-1-164 (F)
Wall, James C. 1852 wb-m-445 (Mt)
Wall, James P. 1837 wb-e-36 (Hu)
Wall, John 1830 wb-c-46 (St)
Wall, John 1852 wb-2-122 (Sh)
Wall, John 1854 as-b-172 (Ms)
Wall, John 1855 wb-h-153 (St)
Wall, John 1856 wb-g-723 (Hn)
Wall, John E. 1854 wb-11-266 (Wi)
Wall, John jr. 1855 wb-g-650 (Hn)
Wall, Johnson (Capt.) 1822 rb-d-97 (Mt)

Wall, Johnson 1822 rb-d-59 (Mt)
Wall, Johnson 1831 rb-f-181 (Mt)
Wall, Johnson 1837 rb-h-38 (Mt)
Wall, Joshua J. 1842 wb-z-395 (Mu)
Wall, Martha 1856 wb-0-141 (Cf)
Wall, Nancy 1850 as-c-47 (Di)
Wall, Pierce? 1798 wb-1-44 (Sn)
Wall, William 1827 wb-2-29# (Ge)
Wall, William W. 1835 wb-#109 (Wl)
Wall, William W. 1848 wb-9-180 (Wi)
Wallace, A. A. 1853 wb-1C-1 (A)
Wallace, Abraham 1834 wb-1-155 (Bo)
Wallace, Alfred 1858 as-c-126 (Ms)
Wallace, Amos S. 1841 wb-b-394 (G)
Wallace, B. R. B. 1851 wb-14-582 (D)
Wallace, Barkley M. 1835 wb-5-340 (K)
Wallace, Cyrus A. 1856 wb-6-231 (Ma)
Wallace, David 1841 wb-1A-333 (A)
Wallace, Edward 1834 lw (Ct)
Wallace, Elias 1821 wb-a-159 (Wh)
Wallace, Elizabeth 1845 wb-0-49 (Cf)
Wallace, Elizabeth 1847 148-1-181 (Ge)
Wallace, George W. 1831 wb-c-149 (St)
Wallace, James 1828 wb-3-0 (Sm)
Wallace, Jesse 1825 wb-8-463 (D)
Wallace, Jesse 1844 wb-1-145 (Bo)
Wallace, John 1818 rb-4-125 (Ru)
Wallace, John 1834 rb-9-166 (Ru)
Wallace, John 1839? wb-2-52# (Ge)
Wallace, John 1844 rb-12-576 (Ru)
Wallace, John 1850 148-1-325 (Ge)
Wallace, John sr. 1841 rb-11-212 (Ru)
Wallace, Joseph 1821 lr (Sn)
Wallace, M. E. (Mrs.) 1856 wb-3-335 (W)
Wallace, Mallissa 1856 as-b-223 (Ms)
Wallace, Martha 1831 rb-f-260 (Mt)
Wallace, Mary E. 1857 wb-3-348 (W)
Wallace, Mathew 1839 wb-1-153 (Bo)
Wallace, Matthew 1837 wb-a-6 (Ms)
Wallace, Ruth A. 1858 wb-12-459 (K)
Wallace, Samuel 1855 wb-1-164 (Bo)
Wallace, William (Sr.) 1851 wb-#8 (Mo)
Wallace, William 1799 wb-1-213 (Bo)
Wallace, William 1823 wb-A-354 (Li)
Wallace, William 1825 wb-8-445 (D)
Wallace, William 1825 wb-b-37 (St)
Wallace, William 1842 wb-b-416 (Hd)
Wallace, William 1856 wb-12-227 (K)
Wallace, William S. 1849 wb-c-348 (Wh)
Wallace, _____ 1841 wb-b-382 (Hd)
Wallan, Joseph 1816 rb-4-2 (Ru)

Wallan, William 1839 as-a-9 (Ms)
Wallen, John 1852 ib-2-57 (Cl)
Wallens, Charles W. 1831 wb-1-194 (Hr)
Waller, Alfred 1851 wb-9-658 (Wi)
Waller, Avey 1860 wb-e-319 (Wh)
Waller, Benjamin 1818 rb-4-114 (Ru)
Waller, Benjamin 1847 wb-a-315 (F)
Waller, Benjamin P. 1844 rb-12-499 (Ru)
Waller, Benjamin P. 1844 rb-12-501 (Ru)
Waller, Benjamin P. jr. 1846 rb-13-713 (Ru)
Waller, Joel 1842 wb-12-302* (D)
Waller, John H. 1854 wb-11-404 (Wi)
Waller, Joseph 1850 wb-9-366 (Wi)
Waller, Joseph S. 1842 wb-7-589 (Wi)
Waller, M. M. (Dr.) 1852 wb-a-412 (F)
Waller, Philip 1844 lr (Gi)
Waller, Pleasant 1842 wb-c-69 (Wh)
Waller, Robert 1837 rb-g-553 (Mt)
Waller, Thomas 1846 wb-13-373 (D)
Waller, William 1820 rb-c-282 (Mt)
Waller, William 1821 wb-a-138 (Ro)
Wallers, Fanny 1855 wb-1-495 (Hw)
Wallers, Spencer 1846 wb-g-111 (Hn)
Wallice, Susannah 1826 wb-b-125 (St)
Wallin, Elizabeth 1858 wb-#181 (Mc)
Wallin, Isaac Jr. 1849 wb-#182 (Mc)
Wallin, James B. 1841 5-2-240 (Cl)
Walling, James 1850 wb-c-405 (Wh)
Walling, James 1851 wb-a-153 (V)
Walling, James jr. 1840 wb-b-366 (Wh)
Walling, James sr. 1850 wb-c-376 (Wh)
Walling, Jesse 1841 wb-c-18 (Wh)
Walling, Jessee 1851 wb-a-149 (V)
Walling, John Sr. 1836 wb-#182 (Mc)
Walling, Nancy 1850 wb-c-396 (Wh)
Walling, William 1844 wb-c-159 (Wh)
Wallingford, Isaac 1851 wb-d-356 (G)
Wallis, Biddy 1854 wb-#25 (Mo)
Wallis, George 1818 wb-1-0 (Sm)
Wallis, James 1841 wb-#4 (Mo)
Wallis, John (Capt.) 1817 rb-4-5 (Ru)
Wallis, John 1824 rb-6-18 (Ru)
Wallis, John 1857 ib-2-27 (Wy)
Wallis, Jos. B. 1851 as-b-31 (Ms)
Wallis, Laban jr. 1855 wb-e-21 (Wh)
Wallis, Laban sr. 1860 wb-e-314 (Wh)
Wallis, Mary 1837 wb-b-280 (Wh)
Wallis, Nathan 1860 wb-k-172 (O)
Wallis, Prior 1861 wb-#182 (Mc)
Wallis, Robert 1846 wb-a2-511 (Mu)
Wallis, Stephen 1859 wb-e-313 (Wh)

Wallon, David J. 1845 wb-12-462 (Rb)
Walls, Edmond 1848 wb-A-49 (Ca)
Walls, H. T. 1855 ib-1-356 (Ca)
Walls, James 1845 wb-a-239 (F)
Walls, John 1848 wb-d-148 (G)
Walls, Joshua 1833 wb-1-85 (Li)
Walls, T. H. 1857 ib-1-441 (Ca)
Walls, William 1823 rb-5-261 (Ru)
Walpole, Charles 1851 rb-16-118 (Ru)
Walpole, Francis 1855 wb-c-47 (L)
Walpole, John 1841 wb-a-76 (L)
Walpole, John P. 1828 rb-7-10 (Ru)
Walpole, Thomas 1861 wb-d-93 (L)
Walpole, William S. 1850 wb-b-106 (L)
Walsh, James 1835 wb-#109 (Wl)
Walsh, John 1852 wb-2-125 (Sh)
Walsh, Thomas 1853 wb-2-147 (Sh)
Walten, Timothy 1858 gs-1-86 (F)
Walter, Peter 1809? wb-#23 (Wa)
Walters, C. W. 1837 wb-1-317 (Hr)
Walters, Eli A. 1861 wb-13-398 (Wi)
Walters, Isaac 1842 wb-5-176 (Gr)
Walters, Laban 1854 wb-11-258 (Wi)
Walters, M. 1856 wb-j-141 (O)
Walters, Obadiah 1836 wb-1-120 (Gr)
Walters, Robert 1843 wb-f-164* (Hn)
Walters, Solomon 1833 wb-1-487 (Hw)
Walters, Spencer 1846 wb-g-78 (Hn)
Walters, Tabitha E. 1846 wb-g-124 (Hn)
Walters, W. M. 1844 wb-f-229 (Hn)
Walters, William 1839 wb-e-63 (Hn)
Walters, William 1840 wb-e-134 (Hn)
Walton, A. C. 1834 wb-#104 (Wl)
Walton, A. L. 1846 wb-12-614 (Rb)
Walton, Alexander 1846 wb-12-570 (Rb)
Walton, Ann H. 1855 wb-2-187 (Sh)
Walton, David J. 1846 wb-12-611 (Rb)
Walton, Drury 1810 wb-1-137 (Sn)
Walton, E. L. 1859 rb-p-279 (Mt)
Walton, Edward 1819 rb-c-216 (Mt)
Walton, Edward 1820 rb-c-287 (Mt)
Walton, Edward 1820 rb-c-340 (Mt)
Walton, Elizabeth 1859 wb-16-690 (Rb)
Walton, George A. 1847 wb-a-76 (Dk)
Walton, George L. 1816 wb-2-243 (Wi)
Walton, Isaac 1823 wb-1-0 (Sm)
Walton, Isaac 1840 wb-2-270 (Sn)
Walton, James 1842 wb-11-267 (Rb)
Walton, James 1855 wb-16-92 (Rb)
Walton, John A. 1849 wb-g-60 (O)
Walton, John D. 1860 wb-k-347 (O)

Walton, Josiah 1816 wb-2-203 (Wi)
Walton, Josiah S. 1819 wb-3-35 (Wi)
Walton, L. C. 1861 wb-k-428 (O)
Walton, Langhorn T. 1821 Wb-3-246 (Wi)
Walton, Martin 1844 wb-12-251 (Rb)
Walton, Meridith 1855 wb-16-66 (Rb)
Walton, Milly 1822 wb-#120 (Mu)
Walton, Simon 1852 wb-15-165 (Rb)
Walton, Thomas G. 1826 wb-1-0 (Sm)
Walton, William 1817 rb-b-396 (Mt)
Walton, William 1819 wb-1-0 (Sm)
Walton, William J. 1859 wb-18-106 (D)
Wamack, Daniel 1856 wb-#182 (Mc)
Wamack, Jacob 1847 wb-#182 (Mc)
Wamack, Thomas 1847 wb-#183 (Mc)
Wammack, Richard 1819 wb-#34 (Wl)
Wammack, Richard Sr. 1819 wb-#34 (Wl)
Wammack, William 1843 wb-1-558 (W)
Wamuch, Joseph 1856 wb-2-300 (Me)
Wand, James 1845 wb-13-230 (D)
Ward, A. M. 1852 wb-g-471 (Hn)
Ward, Alexander 1796 wb-1-4 (Je)
Ward, Benjamin 1847 rb-14-176 (Ru)
Ward, Benjamin 1860 rb-20-668 (Ru)
Ward, Best 1858 rb-19-460 (Ru)
Ward, Burrel 1856 rb-18-121 (Ru)
Ward, Catharine 1860 wb-b-442 (We)
Ward, D. C. 1843 wb-3-0 (Sm)
Ward, Daniel 1816 wb-2-266 (K)
Ward, Daniel 1861 wb-18-468 (D)
Ward, Edward 1838 wb-1-40 (Sh)
Ward, Elizabeth 1837 wb-1-32 (Sh)
Ward, Elizabeth 1848 wb-b-171 (Mu)
Ward, Ezekiel 1847 rb-14-134 (Ru)
Ward, Ezekiel jr. 1841 rb-11-284 (Ru)
Ward, George 1832 wb-a-195 (G)
Ward, Hezekiah 1836 wb-x-343 (Mu)
Ward, Howell 1839 wb-b-130 (O)
Ward, J. H. 1859 iv-1-575 (Ca)
Ward, Jame 1823 wb-A-344 (Li)
Ward, James 1837 wb-3-441 (Je)
Ward, Jesse 1853 rb-16-707 (Ru)
Ward, Jessee 1848 ib-1-62 (Cl)
Ward, John (Sr.) 1846 wb-#159 (Wl)
Ward, John 1796 wb-1-6 (Je)
Ward, John 1844 wb-#143 (Wl)
Ward, John 1845 wb-7-0 (Sm)
Ward, John 1848 wb-7-0 (Sm)
Ward, John F. 1834 wb-1-489 (Ma)
Ward, John N. 1856 wb-f-18 (G)
Ward, John T. 1826 wb-#135 (Mu)

Ward, John W. 1860 wb-k-144 (O)
Ward, Joseph P. 1853 wb-2-147 (Sh)
Ward, Josiah 1842 wb-f-109 (Hn)
Ward, Laura 1845 wb-4-289 (Ma)
Ward, Littleton L. 1850 wb-g-270 (O)
Ward, Lucinda Jane 1843 rb-i-518 (Mt)
Ward, Martha 1857 rb-18-633 (Ru)
Ward, Mary 1816 wb-#16 (Mu)
Ward, Mary 1816 wb-#24 (Mu)
Ward, Mary 1842 rb-12-178 (Ru)
Ward, Mary 1852 rb-16-341 (Ru)
Ward, Messer 1826 wb-b-81 (St)
Ward, Nancy 1831 wb-9-564 (D)
Ward, Nichodemus 1848 wb-1-225 (Me)
Ward, Norflett H. 1853 wb-5-137 (Ma)
Ward, Ransom 1826 wb-#62 (Wl)
Ward, Rebecah 1808 wb-3-214 (D)
Ward, Robert 1815 wb-1-0 (Sm)
Ward, Robert 1847 rb-14-198 (Ru)
Ward, Robert S. 1856 wb-1-87 (Be)
Ward, Roland 1859 wb-16-689 (Rb)
Ward, Samuel 1831 wb-5-42 (Wi)
Ward, Sarah 1853 wb-15-530 (D)
Ward, Swain 1840 wb-b-253 (Hd)
Ward, Thomas 1844 wb-4-292 (Ma)
Ward, Thomas N. 1854 rb-17-210 (Ru)
Ward, Thomas S. 1852 rb-16-343 (Ru)
Ward, Thompson 1845 rb-13-65 (Ru)
Ward, W. 1851 wb-2-86 (Me)
Ward, William (Doctor) 1836 rb-9-304 (Ru)
Ward, William 1815 wb-a-62 (Ro)
Ward, William 1835 rb-9-215 (Ru)
Ward, William 1847 rb-14-166 (Ru)
Ward, William 1850 wb-g-311 (Hu)
Ward, William C. 1828 wb-9-170 (D)
Warden, Francis H. 1843 rb-i-553 (Mt)
Warden, James 1832 wb-x-28 (Mu)
Warden, Joseph 1832 wb-#241 (Mu)
Warden, William J. 1859 wb-f-169 (Mu)
Wardlow, William W. 1831 wb-#223 (Mu)
Ware, Dudley 1842 wb-#138 (Wl)
Ware, James D. 1856 wb-e-46 (Hy)
Ware, James R. 1857 wb-h-151 (Hn)
Ware, John 1861 wb-b-70 (Dk)
Ware, Peter D. 1840 wb-y-644 (Mu)
Ware, Robert 1842 wb-1-79 (Sh)
Ware, William 1836 wb-1-460 (Hr)
Waren, Eli 1859 wb-1-9 (Su)
Wares, Jacob 1842 wb-4-5 (Je)
Warfield, James B. 1840 rb-h-420 (Mt)
Warfield, Jane W.? 1838 rb-h-168 (Mt)

Warfield, Laban 1837 rb-g-587 (Mt)
Warfield, Laban 1837 rb-h-61 (Mt)
Warfield, Mathias 1857 wb-f-129 (Mu)
Warfield, Matilda 1847 wb-#154 (Wl)
Warford, John sr. 1847 r39-1-47 (Dk)
Warlick, Philip 1842 wb-3-533 (Ma)
Warmack, Frederick C. 1821 wb-3-297 (K)
Warmack, Rachael 1839 wb-#127 (Wl)
Warmack, Richard 1861 wb-18-420 (D)
Warmack, Thomas 1841 wb-12-219* (D)
Warmack, William 1840 wb-12-39* (D)
Warmath, Thomas 1861 wb-a-307 (T)
Warmick, Henry 1846 wb-c-347 (G)
Warmoth, H. H. 1849 wb-5-74 (Ma)
Warmouth, John 1852 wb-15-325 (D)
Warmuth, Thomas 1853 wb-16-129 (D)
Warmuth, William 1860 wb-18-380 (D)
Warnick, James 1804 wb-#2 (Wl)
Warr, John 1846 wb-4-97 (Hr)
Warren, Archibald 1832 wb-b-91 (Wh)
Warren, B. E. 1858 wb-j-426 (O)
Warren, Benjamin 1846 wb-a2-537 (Mu)
Warren, Benjamin 1859 wb-#129 (Wl)
Warren, Blewford 1828 wb-a-314 (Wh)
Warren, Bluford sr. 1857 wb-e-170 (Wh)
Warren, Charles 1829 wb-#81 (Wl)
Warren, David 1826 wb-1-25 (Hr)
Warren, Drury 1828 rb-7-30 (Ru)
Warren, Drury 1852 wb-10-141 (Wi)
Warren, Edwin 1855 wb-e-308 (G)
Warren, Eliza Jane 1851 wb-#177 (Wl)
Warren, Goodloe 1835 wb-d-120 (Hn)
Warren, Green 1829 wb-#80 (Wl)
Warren, Green B. 1828 wb-#78 (Wl)
Warren, Green B. 1838 wb-#123 (Wl)
Warren, Henry 1844 wb-1-181 (Bo)
Warren, Henry 1846 wb-1-280 (Li)
Warren, Henry 1849 ib-1-90 (Ca)
Warren, Isaiah 1859 wb-16-790 (Rb)
Warren, Jacob 1816 wb-2-336 (Rb)
Warren, Jacob 1853 wb-#13 (Mo)
Warren, Jesse 1840 wb-10-530 (Rb)
Warren, Jesse 1840 wb-10-531 (Rb)
Warren, Joel 1834 wb-1-51 (La)
Warren, John 1813 wb-#38 (Wl)
Warren, John 1816 rb-3-218 (Ru)
Warren, John 1816 rb-3-226 (Ru)
Warren, John 1820 wb-A-286 (Li)
Warren, John 1830 rb-8-78 (Ru)
Warren, John 1837 wb-10-46 (Rb)
Warren, John 1860 wb-e-366 (Wh)

Warren, John Goodloe 1842 wb-e-458 (Hu)
Warren, John H. 1836 wb-a-2 (F)
Warren, John H. 1855 ib-h-394 (F)
Warren, John H. B. E. 1837 rb-9-404 (Ru)
Warren, John J. 1836 rb-9-361 (Ru)
Warren, John J. 1843 wb-e-620 (Hu)
Warren, John Sr. 1860 wb-13-377 (Wi)
Warren, Joseph 1846 wb-4-104 (Hr)
Warren, Martha L. 1844 wb-#157 (Wl)
Warren, Martin 1852 wb-15-198 (Rb)
Warren, Mary 1824 rb-6-1 (Ru)
Warren, Michael 1807 wb-1-174 (Wi)
Warren, Narcissa A. 1853 wb-10-528 (Wi)
Warren, Penney 1832 wb-1-68 (Hy)
Warren, Prucella 1857 wb-7-0 (Sm)
Warren, R. B. 1848 wb-#163 (Wl)
Warren, Robert 1826 wb-1-159 (Bo)
Warren, Robert 1826 wb-1-249 (Bo)
Warren, Robert B. 1840 rb-10-490 (Ru)
Warren, S. J. 1848 rb-k-795 (Mt)
Warren, Sarah 1857 wb-e-170 (Wh)
Warren, Sebrena 1848 wb-f-496 (St)
Warren, Solomon 1848 wb-#167 (Wl)
Warren, Stewart 1857 wb-e-170 (Wh)
Warren, Stewart 1857 wb-e-202 (Wh)
Warren, Thomas 1810 wb-4-92 (D)
Warren, Thomas 1836 wb-#110 (Wl)
Warren, Wesley 1853 wb-g-534 (Hn)
Warren, William 1822 wb-3-362 (Wi)
Warren, William 1837 wb-6-429 (Wi)
Warren, William 1839 wb-b-293 (G)
Warren, William 1842 as-a-57 (Ms)
Warren, William 1852 rb-16-311 (Ru)
Warren, William 1859 wb-f-324 (G)
Warren, William R. 1835 wb-1-122 (Li)
Warrener, Thomas 1820 eb-1-107 (C)
Warrick, Jacob 1808 wb-1-272 (K)
Warrin, Goodlow 1833 wb-1-358 (Ma)
Wash, Caty 1825 rb-d-476 (Mt)
Wash, W. 1859 wb-3e-112 (Sh)
Washbern, Thomas 1846 wb-b-157 (We)
Washburn, Lewis 1815 wb-1-0 (Sm)
Washburn, Reuben 1843 wb-1-229 (Li)
Washburn, Thomas 1846 wb-1-129 (Sh)
Washburn, Willshire 1855 wb-7-0 (Sm)
Washington, Andrew 1835 wb-9-61 (Rb)
Washington, Gilbert J. 1847 wb-14-51 (D)
Washington, Gray 1808 wb-4-18 (D)
Washington, James G. 1838 wb-11-397 (D)
Washington, James G. 1852 wb-15-286 (D)
Washington, Janet 1828 wb-9-155 (D)

Washington, Joseph 1849 wb-14-108 (Rb)
Washington, Margaret 1854 wb-15-600 (Rb)
Washington, Sally 1841 rb-i-202 (Mt)
Washington, Thomas 1818 rb-4-167 (Ru)
Washington, Thomas 1833 rb-9-19 (Ru)
Wassom, Cornelius 1839 wb-#184 (Mc)
Wassom, Jacob L. 1857 wb-1-130 (R)
Wasson, Abel B. 1838 wb-1-180 (La)
Wasson, Abner 1816 wb-#40 (Wl)
Wasson, E. E. 1860 wb-3-65 (Me)
Wasson, Edward 1860 wb-3-64 (Me)
Wasson, Franklin 1856 wb-1-86 (R)
Wasson, James H. 1845 wb-1-372 (La)
Wasson, John 1845 wb-12-333 (Rb)
Wasson, John 1855 wb-3-402 (La)
Wasson, John B. 1847 wb-13-132 (Rb)
Wasson, L. A. 1850 rb-15-363 (Ru)
Wasson, Logan 1856 rb-17-701 (Ru)
Wasson, Logan A. 1855 rb-17-459 (Ru)
Wasson, Logan H. 1850 rb-15-298 (Ru)
Wasson, Robert 1837 rb-9-435 (Ru)
Wasson, Samuel 1825 wb-#142 (Mu)
Wasson, Samuel 1826 wb-#143 (Mu)
Wasson, Samuel M. 1859 wb-4-221 (La)
Wassum, Jacob 1831 wb-a-93 (R)
Waterhouse, Richard G. 1827 wb-a-31 (R)
Waters, Heneneyra 1860 rb-p-446 (Mt)
Waters, James 1848 wb-2-32 (La)
Waters, John 1840 wb-7-224 (Wi)
Waters, M. 1858 wb-j-372 (O)
Waters, Obediah 1828 wb-4-281 (Wi)
Waters, Shelah (Jr.) 1847 wb-#153 (Wl)
Waters, Shelah 1848 wb-#166 (Wl)
Waters, William 1835 wb-#110 (Wl)
Waters, William 1860 wb-1-325 (Be)
Wates, Alexander 1851 wb-15-140 (D)
Watkin, John G. 1837 wb-d-308 (Hn)
Watkins, Archibald 1823 wb-1-0 (Sm)
Watkins, Benj. R. 1854 wb-b-263 (L)
Watkins, Benjamin 1815 rb-b-256 (Mt)
Watkins, Benjamin H. 1812 rb-b-100 (Mt)
Watkins, David 1852 wb-xx-5 (St)
Watkins, Fredrick 1830 rb-8-149 (Ru)
Watkins, H. C. 1837 wb-1-344 (Hy)
Watkins, Henry 1855? wb-2-189 (Sh)
Watkins, Henry 1857 wb-3e-45 (Sh)
Watkins, Henry H. 1841 rb-i-217 (Mt)
Watkins, Henry L. 1846 rb-k-212 (Mt)
Watkins, Henry M. 1837 rb-9-426 (Ru)
Watkins, Henry M. 1837 wb-1-313 (Hy)
Watkins, Ichabod 1836 wb-1-472 (Hr)

Watkins, Isaac 1833 wb-10-196 (D)
Watkins, Jacob 1799 wb-2-160 (D)
Watkins, Jacob 1836 wb-6-208 (Wi)
Watkins, James 1808 rb-a-81 (Mt)
Watkins, James 1842 wb-1-508 (W)
Watkins, James 1845 wb-f-277* (Hn)
Watkins, Jno. K. 1833 wb-c-10 (Hn)
Watkins, John 1814 wb-2-170 (Rb)
Watkins, John 1822 wb-2-373 (Je)
Watkins, John 1823 rb-d-255 (Mt)
Watkins, John 1831 wb-5-92 (K)
Watkins, John 1850 as-c-97 (Di)
Watkins, John 1856 wb-h-486 (Hu)
Watkins, John M. 1859 rb-20-78 (Ru)
Watkins, Joseph R. 1856 rb-o-204 (Mt)
Watkins, Martha 1838 rb-10-229 (Ru)
Watkins, Nancy 1840 wb-7-278 (Wi)
Watkins, Owen L. 1834 wb-5-379 (Wi)
Watkins, Owen T. 1833 wb-5-287 (Wi)
Watkins, Phillip 1852 wb-15-326 (D)
Watkins, Richard 1836 rb-9-289 (Ru)
Watkins, Richard 1837 wb-3-437 (Je)
Watkins, Richard 1847 wb-a-328 (F)
Watkins, Robert H. 1855 lr (Gi)
Watkins, Roxana 1858 rb-19-401 (Ru)
Watkins, Samuel 1857 wb-e-76 (Hy)
Watkins, Samuel P. 1839 wb-y-461 (Mu)
Watkins, Thomas 1828 wb-9-269 (D)
Watkins, Thomas G. 1830 wb-3-78 (Je)
Watkins, Thomas J. 1838 wb-11-459 (D)
Watkins, Thomas J. 1839 wb-11-522 (D)
Watkins, Thomas S. 1841 wb-12-113* (D)
Watkins, Thos. 1841 wb-a-66 (F)
Watkins, Thos. P. 1841 wb-a-62 (F)
Watkins, William 1841 wb-12-122* (D)
Watkins, William E. 1851 wb-15-152 (D)
Watkins, William E. jr. 1848 wb-14-282 (D)
Watkins, Wilson L. 1861 rb-21-12 (Ru)
Waton, Milly 1822 wb-#120 (Mu)
Wats, James 1856 wb-j-101 (O)
Wats, James C. 1852 wb-h-28 (Hu)
Watson, A. L. 1846 wb-13-42 (Rb)
Watson, Allas 1827 rb-e-93 (Mt)
Watson, Atheldred 1848 wb-2-352 (W)
Watson, B. O. 1857 wb-12-434 (Wi)
Watson, C. E. 1855 wb-h-69 (St)
Watson, David 1855 wb-1-34 (Be)
Watson, David 1859 wb-3-534 (Gr)
Watson, David 1859 wb-4-17 (Gr)
Watson, David J. 1845 wb-12-525 (Rb)
Watson, David R. 1851 wb-15-122 (D)

Watson, Elias 1812 wb-a-137 (St)
Watson, George 1830 wb-a-11 (T)
Watson, George 1831 wb-8-9 (Rb)
Watson, George W. 1853 r39-1-275 (Dk)
Watson, George W. 1853 wb-15-445 (Rb)
Watson, Henry 1855 wb#23 (Gu)
Watson, Henry P. 1860 rb-p-335 (Mt)
Watson, James 1843 wb-#135 (Wl)
Watson, James 1845 wb-13-320 (D)
Watson, Jane 1855 wb-12-6 (Wi)
Watson, Jane 1861 lr (Sn)
Watson, John 1814 wb-#15 (Wl)
Watson, John 1841 wb-b-291 (Hd)
Watson, John 1841 wb-b-398 (Hd)
Watson, John 1851 wb-10-120 (Wi)
Watson, John 1851 wb-10-91 (Wi)
Watson, John 1851 wb-d-8 (Wh)
Watson, John 1859 wb-f-177 (Mu)
Watson, John A. 1861 wb-f-407 (G)
Watson, John E. 1852 wb-b-170 (L)
Watson, John J. 1845 wb-8-245 (Wi)
Watson, John sr. 1851 wb-d-1 (Wh)
Watson, Jonathan 1799 wb-#7 (Wa)
Watson, Jonathan R. 1858 wb-17-494 (D)
Watson, Joseph 1841 wb-#137 (Wl)
Watson, Josiah 1833 rb-f-476 (Mt)
Watson, Josiah 1833 wb-10-90 (D)
Watson, L. N. 1859 wb-k-70 (O)
Watson, Lucy 1830 wb-#86 (Wl)
Watson, Margaret 1845 wb-12-423 (Rb)
Watson, Margaret 1858 wb-2-247 (Li)
Watson, Matthew 1831 wb-8-9 (Rb)
Watson, Oran D. 1823 wb-a-25 (Hn)
Watson, Oran D. 1835 wb-d-57 (Hn)
Watson, Peter B. 1845 wb-a2-280 (Mu)
Watson, Peter P. 1845 wb-a2-300 (Mu)
Watson, Robert 1836 wb-1-164 (Gr)
Watson, Robert 1846 wb-c-245 (Wh)
Watson, Samuel 1844 lr (Gi)
Watson, Susan 1845 wb-13-294 (D)
Watson, Thomas 1826 wb-#136 (Mu)
Watson, Thomas T. 1846 wb-f-379 (St)
Watson, W. A. 1855 wb-j-38 (O)
Watson, W. D. 1856 wb-17-70 (D)
Watson, Wilkins 1858 rb-o-600 (Mt)
Watson, Will 1800 wb-#7 (Wa)
Watson, William 1817 rb-b-463 (Mt)
Watson, William 1844 wb-12-228 (Rb)
Watson, William 1847 wb-b-40 (Mu)
Watson, William 1851 wb-#26 (Mo)
Watson, William 1858 wb-#16 (Mo)

Watson, William 1860 wb-17-108 (Rb)
Watson, William 1860 wb-17-140 (Rb)
Watson, William W. 1858 wb-j-386 (O)
Watsworth, Amos 1844 wb-5-335 (Gr)
Watt, J. E. 1855 as-b-194 (Ms)
Watt, James 1805 rb-a-274 (Mt)
Watt, James 1817 rb-b-494 (Mt)
Watt, James N. 1853 wb-5-123 (Ma)
Watt, James N. sr. 1855 wb-6-21 (Ma)
Watt, Joseph 1839 wb-7-3 (K)
Watt, Margaret 1840 wb-7-47 (K)
Wattenbarger, Adam (Sr.) 1823 wb-#21 (Wa)
Wattenbarger, Jacob 1852 wb-2-75# (Ge)
Wattenbarger, John Adam 1859 wb-2-89# (Ge)
Watterford, Maria Jane 1859 wb-13-174 (K)
Watterson, Margaret 1826 wb-1-579 (Hw)
Watterson, Wm. S. 1851 wb-0-99 (Cf)
Watts, Ann M. 1854 ib-h-22 (F)
Watts, James 1813 wb-#10 (Mu)
Watts, Thomas 1837 wb-10-35 (Rb)
Watts, William 1850 wb-14-344 (Rb)
Watts, Wilson 1850 wb-14-344 (Rb)
Watwood, James 1811 rb-b-15 (Mt)
Watwood, W. (Mrs.) 1856 rb-o-143 (Mt)
Watwood, William 1852 wb-m-544 (Mt)
Waugh, Richard 1842 as-b-74 (Di)
Waugh, William P. 1853 wb-1-75 (Jo)
Waurld?, Turene 1853 wb-i-83 (O)
Wayman, Kirtley 1860 wb-3e-128 (Sh)
Waymire, Valentine 1856 wb-3-305 (Gr)
Weakley, Benjamin 1814 rb-b-196 (Mt)
Weakley, Hannah 1814 rb-b-204 (Mt)
Weakley, Isaac 1854 wb-n-363 (Mt)
Weakley, John C. H. 1859 wb-a-97 (Ce)
Weakley, Joshua 1824 rb-d-331 (Mt)
Weakley, Joshua 1836 rb-g-414 (Mt)
Weakley, Margaret 1834 rb-f-543 (Mt)
Weakley, Nimrod 1814 wb-4-290 (D)
Weakley, P. H. 1860 wb-a-174 (Ce)
Weakley, Prudence 1855 wb-n-505 (Mt)
Weakley, Robert 1816 rb-b-347 (Mt)
Weakley, Robert 1838 as-a-419 (Di)
Weakley, Robert 1845 wb-13-267 (D)
Weakley, Robert 1859 wb-17-584 (D)
Weakley, Robert jr. 1816 rb-b-352 (Mt)
Weakley, Samuel 1832 wb-10-39 (D)
Weakley, Samuel 1854 wb-n-339 (Mt)
Weakley, Sarah 1860 wb-a-148 (Ce)
Weakley, Thomas 1831 rb-f-154 (Mt)
Weakley, Thomas 1831 rb-f-156 (Mt)
Weakley, Wm. L. 1828 wb-a-115 (G)

Weakly, John H. 1848 rb-k-799 (Mt)
Weakly, Mary 1847 rb-k-419 (Mt)
Weakly, Robert L. 1858 rb-19-236 (Ru)
Weaks, Andrew 1850 wb-g-381 (Hn)
Weaks, Benjamin 1861 wb-h-498 (Hn)
Weaks, Charles 1832 wb-c-184 (St)
Weaks, Emma H. 1859 wb-i-150 (St)
Weaks, Francis S. 1843 wb-e-239 (St)
Weaks, Henry 1853 wb-xx-166 (St)
Weaks, Hewett 1845 wb-g-12 (Hn)
Weaks, Huet 1844 wb-f-233 (Hn)
Weaks, John F. 1838 wb-d-191 (St)
Weaks, John S. 1861 wb-i-301 (St)
Weaks, Margaret 1860 wb-h-485 (Hn)
Weaks, Mark 1852 wb-xx-131 (St)
Weaks, Mary Jane 1848 wb-f-495 (St)
Wear, James 1845 wb-1-93 (Bo)
Wear, Jonathan 1832 wb-1-159 (Bo)
Wear, Joseph 1809 wb-1-156 (Bo)
Wear, Margaret 1849 wb-1-256 (Bo)
Wear, Margaret S. 1853? wb-#10 (Mo)
Wear, Margret B. 1848 wb-1-226 (Bo)
Wear, Samuel 1802 wb-1-159 (Bo)
Wear, Thomas 1829 wb-1-158 (Bo)
Wearen, John 1803 wb-a-5 (Ro)
Weather, James 1829 wb-#84 (Wl)
Weatherford, Elisha 1806 wb-1-0 (Sm)
Weatherford, Judith 1840 lr (Sn)
Weatherford, Martha 1857 wb-f-121 (G)
Weatherford, Nancy 1831 wb-9-540 (D)
Weatherford, Thomas 1815 wb-3-107 (St)
Weatherly, Abner 1834 rb-9-211 (Ru)
Weatherly, Mary 1836 rb-9-203 (Ru)
Weatherly, William 1846 wb-13-384 (D)
Weatherly, Woodson H. 1861 wb-#184 (Mc)
Weatherred, Francis sr. 1830 lr (Sn)
Weatherred, William 1850 lr (Sn)
Weathers, Bracston? 1848 wb-#184 (Mc)
Weathers, Wilson 1859 wb-#16 (Mo)
Weatherspoon, Winfrey 1853 rb-16-402 (Ru)
Weaver, A. Smith 1852 wb-4-4 (Je)
Weaver, Abraham 1845 wb-5-2 (Ma)
Weaver, Adam S. 1853 wb-5-190 (Je)
Weaver, Arthur 1860 wb-4-383 (La)
Weaver, B. 1851 wb-2-185 (La)
Weaver, Benjamin 1840 wb-2-172 (Hy)
Weaver, Benjamin 1851 wb-2-211 (La)
Weaver, Hannah 1852? wb-1B-315 (A)
Weaver, Isaac 1851 wb-#8 (Mo)
Weaver, Jacob 1839 wb-1A-343 (A)
Weaver, James 1850 wb-g-300 (St)

Weaver, James sr. 1850 wb-g-231 (St)
Weaver, Jane 1849 wb-10-179 (K)
Weaver, Jane M. 1849 wb-10-120 (K)
Weaver, John 1850 wb-#171 (Wl)
Weaver, Joshua 1841 wb-3-339 (Ma)
Weaver, Lucy 1844 wb-a-117 (F)
Weaver, Mark 1862 wb-i-357 (St)
Weaver, Martha 1838 wb-a-34 (Ms)
Weaver, Mary B. 1851 lr (Sn)
Weaver, Miles 1847 as-a-135 (Ms)
Weaver, Nancy 1857 wb-4-126 (La)
Weaver, Nancy 1858 wb-i-17 (St)
Weaver, Perlina Jane 1853 wb-5-178 (Je)
Weaver, Peter 1832 wb-5-157 (K)
Weaver, Philip 1846 wb-5-34 (Ma)
Weaver, Polly 1835 wb-5-354 (K)
Weaver, Robert 1855 wb-12-71 (K)
Weaver, Sarah 1843 wb-3-354 (Hy)
Weaver, Shadrack 1849 wb-a-199 (Ms)
Weaver, Thomas 1812 eb-1-19 (C)
Weaver, William 1833 wb-b-122 (Wh)
Weaver, Wm. 1849? wb-1B-148 (A)
Weaver, _____ (Mrs.) 1852 wb-d-121 (Wh)
Weaver?, Samuel 1851 wb-c-450 (Wh)
Webb, A. J. 1847 wb-d-62 (G)
Webb, Aaron 1855 rb-17-504 (Ru)
Webb, Ann 1854 wb-5-348 (Je)
Webb, Elizabeth 1829 wb-#28 (Wa)
Webb, Elizabeth 1847 rb-14-80 (Ru)
Webb, Francis 1844 wb-f-235 (Hn)
Webb, Francis 1844 wb-g-146 (Hn)
Webb, George 1834 wb-#103 (Wl)
Webb, George 1843 wb-e-251 (St)
Webb, George 1851 wb-1B-253 (A)
Webb, Henry R. 1844 wb-c-137 (G)
Webb, Henry Y. 1836 wb-6-93 (Wi)
Webb, Hiram 1857 wb-1-117 (Pe)
Webb, Hugh 1856 wb-e-460 (G)
Webb, Hugh S. 1831 rb-8-301 (Ru)
Webb, James L. 1860 wb-3e-132 (Sh)
Webb, Jesse 1847 wb-4-21 (Je)
Webb, Jesse sr. 1835 wb-1-101 (W)
Webb, John 1831 wb-1-77 (We)
Webb, John 1836 wb-#113 (Wl)
Webb, John 1838 wb-y-329 (Mu)
Webb, John 1842 wb-12-327* (D)
Webb, John 1848 wb-10-78 (K)
Webb, John 1859 wb-17-626 (D)
Webb, John J. 1822 wb-#40 (Mu)
Webb, Joseph 1816 wb-2-212 (K)
Webb, Joseph 1856 wb-j-235 (O)

Webb, Julias 1834 wb-1-81 (W)
Webb, Kinchen 1836 wb-2-141 (Ma)
Webb, Lewis 1841 wb-1-385 (W)
Webb, Lucy Jane 1850 wb-#160 (Wl)
Webb, Mahala 1857 rb-19-81 (Ru)
Webb, Mary 1850 wb-#175 (Wl)
Webb, Mary 1852 rb-16-343 (Ru)
Webb, Mary 1857 wb-1-173 (Bo)
Webb, Morris 1837 lr (Gi)
Webb, Nancy 1848 wb-b-286 (We)
Webb, Nancy 1851 wb-#178 (Wl)
Webb, R. P. 1854 wb-3-266 (W)
Webb, Richard J. 1823 wb-#52 (Wl)
Webb, Robert 1859 wb-e-112 (Hy)
Webb, Ross 1816 wb-#20 (Wl)
Webb, Rubin 1855 ib-h-411 (F)
Webb, Theoderick 1851 wb-1-496 (Hw)
Webb, Thomas 1838 wb-#121 (Wl)
Webb, William 1826 wb-2-531 (Je)
Webb, William 1827 wb-1-280 (Ma)
Webb, William 1829 wb-1-105 (Ma)
Webb, William 1830 wb-#86 (Wl)
Webb, William 1840 wb-7-249 (Wi)
Webb, William 1846 wb-c-229 (Wh)
Webb, William 1860 wb-f-346 (G)
Webb, William C. 1856 ib-1-383 (Wy)
Webb, William L. 1848 wb-9-160 (Wi)
Webb, William Smith 1836 wb-2-206 (Sn)
Webber, James 1849 wb-1B-87 (A)
Webber, John 1853 wb-15-518 (D)
Webster, Felix G. 1859 wb-f-159 (Mu)
Webster, James 1853 wb-1-496 (Hw)
Webster, Jesse 1847 wb-4-141 (Hr)
Webster, John 1838 wb-2-14 (Hr)
Webster, John G. 1826 wb-#134 (Mu)
Webster, Jonathan 1815 wb-#111 (Mu)
Webster, Jonathan 1842 wb-0-33 (Cf)
Webster, Jonathan 1843 wb-z-494 (Mu)
Webster, Peter 1814 wb-1-0 (Sm)
Webster, Reuben 1790 wb-1-480 (Hw)
Webster, William 1841 wb-e-131 (St)
Webster, William J. 1859 wb-f-160 (Mu)
Webster, Wilson B. 1842 wb-3-636 (Ma)
Weddington, Robert Green 1861 wb-f-404 (G)
Weed, O. 1851 wb-m-249 (Mt)
Weedon, Mary Jane 1849 ib-1-57 (Ca)
Weeks, Samuel 1845 wb-1-220 (Fr)
Weeks, Samuel 1849 wb-1-266 (Fr)
Weeks, Susan Jane 1854 wb-g-546 (Hn)
Weeks, William 1826 wb-b-134 (St)
Weemes, William 1824 wb-#87 (Mu)

Weems, Charles 1824 wb-#145 (Mu)
Weems, James 1819 wb-1-25# (Ge)
Weems, John 1812 wb-2-34# (Ge)
Weems, John 1821? wb-#125 (Mu)
Weems, Nancy 1846 148-1-148 (Ge)
Weems, Thomas B. 1861 149-1-233 (Ge)
Weger, Henry 1818 rb-4-138 (Ru)
Weir, Ann 1842 wb-3-626 (Ma)
Weir, Elias 1857 wb-#184 (Mc)
Weir, James N. 1847 wb-#184 (Mc)
Weir, John 1800 wb-#8 (Wa)
Weir, John 1828 wb-#79 (Wl)
Weir, John 1835 wb-2-8 (Ma)
Weir, Mary (Mrs.) 1849 ib-1-82 (Cl)
Weir, William 1854 wb-15-640 (Rb)
Welbern, Isaac Y. 1860 wb-k-251 (O)
Welbourn, William G. 1856 wb-j-182 (O)
Welbourne, William J. 1854 wb-i-233 (O)
Welburn, Isaac Y. 1861 wb-b*-2 (O)
Welch, Dempsey 1855 wb-6-141 (Ma)
Welch, Elizabeth 1825 wb-1-486 (Hw)
Welch, Elizabeth 1846 rb-13-692 (Ru)
Welch, Francis 1844 wb-f-256* (Hn)
Welch, George 1853 wb-d-146 (Wh)
Welch, Harvy B. 1861 as-c-235 (Ms)
Welch, James 1835 wb-#117 (Wl)
Welch, John 1819 wb-2-252 (Je)
Welch, John 1842 wb-3-640 (Ma)
Welch, John M. 1861 wb-b-461 (We)
Welch, Lafayette 1858 wb-h-534 (St)
Welch, Richard 1861 wb-f-414 (G)
Welch, Thomas 1809 rb-2-82 (Ru)
Welch, Thomas 1833 wb-10-208 (D)
Welch, Thomas 1833 wb-10-227 (D)
Welch, Thomas 1843 rb-12-349 (Ru)
Welch, Thomas A. 1858 wb-4-185 (La)
Welch, Vernal W. 1844 wb-4-276 (Ma)
Welch, William 1855 as-b-179 (Ms)
Welchance, Rosannah 1845 wb-#42 (Wa)
Welcker, George L. 1848 wb-e-104 (Ro)
Welcker, Henry 1839 wb-c-37 (Ro)
Welcker, James M. 1858 wb-13-31 (K)
Welcker, James M. 1858 wb-13-54 (K)
Welcker, John F. 1862 wb-f-449 (Ro)
Welcker, Mary Jane 1855 wb-e-530 (Ro)
Weldon, William B. 1847 wb-g-229 (Hn)
Welker, Jacob 1839 wb-6-477 (K)
Welker, Jacob 1844 rb-j-121 (Mt)
Welker, William L. 1831 wb-#185 (Mc)
Well, David M. 1856 wb-16-249 (Rb)
Weller, Charles 1837 wb-a-59 (T)

Wells, Aaron 1842 wb-1-200 (Li)
Wells, Barna B. 1828 wb-#185 (Mc)
Wells, Betsy 1852 wb-10-386 (Wi)
Wells, David 1844 wb-a2-1 (Mu)
Wells, Elisha 1829 rb-e-425 (Mt)
Wells, George 1838 wb-6-283 (K)
Wells, George 1857 wb-2-90# (Ge)
Wells, Hartwell B. 1848 wb-a-341 (F)
Wells, Hiram 1837 wb-11-124 (D)
Wells, Israel 1850 148-1-305 (Ge)
Wells, James 1835 wb-b-138 (Hd)
Wells, Jesse 1844 wb-8-307 (K)
Wells, Jesse sr. 1844 wb-8-361 (K)
Wells, John 1816 wb-2-209 (Wi)
Wells, John 1840 wb-2-154 (Hy)
Wells, John 1858? ib-2-541 (Cl)
Wells, Lewis 1852 wb-15-199 (Rb)
Wells, Lewis 1852 wb-15-201 (Rb)
Wells, Littleberry N? 1855 wb-a-382 (Ms)
Wells, Martin sr. 1803 rb-a-170 (Mt)
Wells, Nathan 1851 rb-4-181 (Mu)
Wells, Randolph Dulaney 1860 wb-1-504 (Hw)
Wells, Samuel 1851 wb-4-328 (Mu)
Wells, Thomas 1860 wb-f-197 (Mu)
Wells, Thomas P. 1861 wb-#185 (Mc)
Wells, William 1823 wb-8-184 (D)
Wells?, William 1853 wb-a-217 (Cr)
Wellsberger, Hiram 1861 wb-1-104 (Dy)
Wendel, David 1841 rb-11-293 (Ru)
Wendel, David 1844 rb-12-554 (Ru)
Wendel, David D. 1840 rb-11-57 (Ru)
Wendel, William 1844 wb-1-98 (Sh)
Wendel, William 1844 wd-13-23 (D)
Wescott, George 1852 wb-a-177 (T)
Wescott, Patience 1852 wb-a-181 (T)
Wesling, H. H. 1856 wb-17-102 (D)
Wessells, John 1860 wb-18-250 (D)
Wesson, A. R. 1853 mr-2-500 (Be)
Wesson, Wilkins 1855 ib-h-456 (F)
Wesson, William 1849 wb-2-64 (Sh)
West, Allen 1854 wb-#26 (Mo)
West, Anderson 1848 wb-A-46 (Ca)
West, Andrew 1830 lr (Sn)
West, Ann 1837 wb-9-315 (Rb)
West, Asa 1818 rb-4-175 (Ru)
West, Claiborn D. 1861 rb-p-642 (Mt)
West, David R. 1861 149-1-223 (Ge)
West, Edward 1842? wb-#49 (Wa)
West, Elizabeth (Mrs.) 1818 rb-b-514 (Mt)
West, Elizabeth 1817 rb-b-469 (Mt)
West, Elizabeth 1852 as-c-186 (Di)

West, Elizabeth 1852 wb-10-241 (Wi)
West, Elizabeth the elder 1817 rb-b-387 (Mt)
West, Felix 1856 ib-1-462 (Wy)
West, George 1810 rb-a-389 (Mt)
West, George 1826 as-a-166 (Di)
West, George 1837 rb-10-1 (Ru)
West, George 1841 as-b-34 (Di)
West, George 1847 rb-14-107 (Ru)
West, George A. 1821 wb-3-317 (Rb)
West, Isaac 1826 wb-a-11 (R)
West, Isaac 1833 wb-c-302 (St)
West, Isaac 1841 wb-7-412 (Wi)
West, James 1833 wb-b-210 (Ro)
West, James 1834 wb-1-488 (Hw)
West, James 1850 wb-1-405 (Li)
West, James 1851 ib-1-122 (Wy)
West, James H. 1853 wb-xx-285 (St)
West, John 1824? as-A-39 (Di)
West, John 1836 wb-1-196 (W)
West, John 1849 wb-9-275 (Wi)
West, John 1857 ib-1-476 (Wy)
West, John F. 1854 39-2-21 (Dk)
West, John F. 1856 39-2-127 (Dk)
West, John S. 1856 wb-f-114 (Mu)
West, Levi 1830 rb-8-220 (Ru)
West, Marina 1830 wb-7-201 (Rb)
West, Mary 1856 wb-12-271 (Wi)
West, Mary Ann 1847 wb-14-101 (D)
West, Micajah 1805 wb-3-34 (D)
West, Micajah 1805 wb-3-48 (D)
West, Napolian B. 1832 as-a-217 (Di)
West, Rhodes 1853 wb-2-55 (Li)
West, Richard 1848 148-1-238 (Ge)
West, Richard 1861 149-1-215 (Ge)
West, Robert 1826 as-A-121 (Di)
West, Robert 1850 wb-a-230 (Di)
West, Robert J. 1857 as-c-425 (Di)
West, Samuel 1834 wb-1-98 (Gr)
West, Simion 1843 wb-2-370 (Fr)
West, Simpson 1843 wb-1-213 (Fr)
West, Thomas 1848 wb-a-82 (Dk)
West, W. J. 1861 wb-f-496 (Ro)
West, Warren 1838 wb-a-360 (R)
West, Wiley B. 1859 39-2-285 (Dk)
West, Wiley W. 1850 wb-d-272 (G)
West, William B. 1824? as-A-17 (Di)
West, William H. 1836 wb-d-27 (St)
Westbrook, Abraham 1846 wb-4-72 (Hr)
Westbrook, Gray 1861 wb-7-93 (Ma)
Westbrook, Henry J. P. 1856 wb-j-154 (O)
Wester, Daniel 1857 wb-f-119 (Ro)

Wester, Daniel L. 1841 wb-c-195 (Ro)
Wester, Kinchen 1824 wb-3-325 (St)
Westmoreland, Jessee 1811 wb-4-160 (D)
Westmoreland, Reuben 1818 wb-7-274 (D)
Weston, Frederick 1835 wb-c-409 (St)
Weston, Jesse 1815 wb-3-69 (St)
Wetherald, James 1828 wb-9-245 (D)
Wethered, Polly 1855 wb-f-63 (Mu)
Wetherford, Archabald 1851 ib-1-183 (Ca)
Wetherford, Hill 1861 wb-d-94 (L)
Wetherington, Jos. 1841 wb-e-194 (Hn)
Wetherly, Joseph 1816 wb-a-52 (Wh)
Wetter, Henry 1850 wb-2-71 (Sh)
Wetzel, Lewis 1848 wb-14-267 (D)
Wetzell, Elisabeth 1842 wb-1-171 (Bo)
Whalen, Wily M. 1853 wb-5-309 (Je)
Whaley, Elijah 1859 39-2-319 (Dk)
Whaley, John 1835 lw (Ct)
Whaly, Rachel 1850 wb-1-71 (Jo)
Wharry, L. C. 1862 wb-f-437 (G)
Wharton, C. J. 1857 wb-17-251 (D)
Wharton, C. J. F. 1856 wb-17-271 (D)
Wharton, George 1824 wb-8-383 (D)
Wharton, Jesse 1833 wb-10-181 (D)
Wharton, John 1816 wb-4-467 (D)
Wharton, John 1841 wb-3-302 (Ma)
Wharton, Lucinda 1849 wb-14-421 (D)
Wharton, Samuel L. 1833 wb-10-172 (D)
Wharton, William 1816 wb-7-31 (D)
Wheat, Azariah 1852 wb-e-345 (Ro)
Wheat, John 1834 wb-x-176 (Mu)
Wheat, Levi 1849 wb-e-156 (Ro)
Wheatley, Albert G. 1851 wb-m-352 (Mt)
Wheatley, Francis 1859 gs-1-243 (F)
Wheatley, James 1842 rb-i-440 (Mt)
Wheatley, Lawson 1860 wb-3e-141 (Sh)
Wheatley, Levina 1837 wb-1-37 (Sh)
Wheatley, Seth 1858 wb-3e-68 (Sh)
Wheatley, Starling 1845 mr-2-161 (Be)
Wheaton, Calvin 1818 wb-2-399 (Wi)
Wheaton, Daniel 1805 wb-3-16 (D)
Wheaton, Jane 1812 wb-1-322 (Wi)
Wheaton, Jane 1822 wb-3-582 (Wi)
Wheaton, John L. 1834 wb-5-345 (Wi)
Wheaton, Sterling 1823 wb-3-640 (Wi)
Wheeler, Benjamin 1826 eb-1-158 (C)
Wheeler, Benjamin 1842 lr (Gi)
Wheeler, Elijah 1844 wb-b-65 (We)
Wheeler, Henry 1818 rb-4-159 (Ru)
Wheeler, Isaac 1831 wb-2-40# (Ge)
Wheeler, James 1807 as-1-180 (Ge)

Wheeler, Jesse 1835 wb-1-148 (Bo)
Wheeler, John 1827 wb-#70 (Wl)
Wheeler, John 1856 wb-j-150 (O)
Wheeler, Margaret 1839 eb-1-425 (C)
Wheeler, Margarett 1840 eb-1-429 (C)
Wheeler, Nancy 1853 lr (Gi)
Wheeler, Nathan 1816 wb-#20 (Wl)
Wheeler, Peter 1853 wb-1-165 (Bo)
Wheeler, Richard 1813 eb-1-28 (C)
Whelan, James G. 1814 rb-b-193 (Mt)
Whelan, Richard 1836 wb-1A-143 (A)
Wheland, James 1812 rb-b-56 (Mt)
Whelby, Saml. 1847 wb-4-248 (Hr)
Wheless, Elizabeth 1847 wb-b-217 (We)
Wheless, Henry 1846 rb-k-269 (Mt)
Wheless, Joseph 1844 rb-j-217 (Mt)
Wheless, Wesley 1861 wb-18-637 (D)
Wherry, Andrew 1834 wb-1-20 (Sh)
Wherry, Thomas 1858 wb-3e-75 (Sh)
Wherry, William S. 1827 lr (Sn)
Whetsell, Michael 1831 wb-#186 (Mc)
Whippel, William A. 1845 wb-e-157 (O)
Whitaberry, Ephraim 1860 wb-1D-4 (A)
Whitaker, Eli B. 1852 ib-1-166 (Wy)
Whitaker, John 1834 wb-x-235 (Mu)
Whitaker, John 1837 wb-1-142 (Li)
Whitaker, John 1854 wb-d-167 (Wh)
Whitaker, John J. 1853 wb-2-54 (Li)
Whitaker, Johnson 1800 wb-#7 (Wa)
Whitaker, Mark 1842 wb-1-207? (Li)
Whitaker, Nancy 1852 wb-2-29 (Li)
Whitaker, Robert W. 1852 wb-15-443 (D)
White, Abiah 1856 wb-12-115 (Wi)
White, Abner N. 1835 wb-6-48 (Wi)
White, Abram 1839 wb-7-192 (Wi)
White, Abram 1854 wb-2-79# (Ge)
White, Albert 1856 ib-h-481 (F)
White, Alexander 1815 wb-A-93 (Li)
White, Alexander 1817 wb-A-167 (Li)
White, Allen S. 1842 wb-c-28 (G)
White, Ann 1842 wb-1-152 (Bo)
White, Ann E. 1847 wb-9-322 (K)
White, Ann L. 1855 wb-12-112 (K)
White, Apias 1840 wb-a-58 (F)
White, Archibald 1815 wb-1-0 (Sm)
White, Arthur 1820 wb-7-422 (D)
White, Bartholemew 1825 wb-a-6 (Cr)
White, Barton 1843 wb-#186 (Mc)
White, Bembry 1858 wb-e-90 (Hy)
White, Benjamin 1827 wb-4-255 (Wi)
White, Benjamin F. 1841 wb-7-459 (Wi)

White, Beverly W. 1839 wb-11-575 (D)
White, Blumer 1821 rb-5-79 (Ru)
White, Cader 1840 wb-2-142 (Hy)
White, Chapman 1825 wb-3-754 (Wi)
White, Charles 1848 wb-e-86 (Ro)
White, Charles A. C. 1826 wb-4-144 (K)
White, Charles P. 1849 wb-g-169 (Hu)
White, Christian 1811 wb-#12 (Wa)
White, D. J. 1859 wb-4-282 (La)
White, D. O. 1857 wb-4-133 (La)
White, Daniel 1836 wb-#186 (Mc)
White, Daniel J. 1861 wb-5-67 (La)
White, David 1831 wb-1-152 (Bo)
White, David 1855 wb-#55 (Wa)
White, Dolly 1849 wb-10-168 (K)
White, Edward 1837 wb-#120 (Wl)
White, Elias C. 1851 wb-g-526 (Hu)
White, Elisha 1844 mr (Gi)
White, Elisha 1860 wb-#186 (Mc)
White, Elizabeth 1854 wb-i-203 (O)
White, Elizabeth N. E. 1848 wb-g-125 (Hu)
White, Eppy 1857 wb-3e-44 (Sh)
White, Francis 1840 wb-2-265 (Sn)
White, Franklin P. 1844 wb-8-208 (Wi)
White, Frederick 1850 148-1-329 (Ge)
White, George 1833 wb-#100 (Wl)
White, George 1838 wb-1-150 (La)
White, George 1842 wb-#137 (Wl)
White, George 1850 wb-9-356 (Wi)
White, George W. 1844 wb-4-254 (Ma)
White, George W. 1859 wb-f-178 (Mu)
White, Gordon 1835 wb-1-150 (Bo)
White, Green L. 1845 wb-e-168 (O)
White, H. A. M. 1860 wb-13-277 (K)
White, Hannah 1838 wb-3-514 (Je)
White, Henry 1815 Wb-2-136 (Wi)
White, Henry 1820 wb-3-210 (K)
White, Henry 1856 rb-18-236 (Ru)
White, Hiram 1845 wb-e-38 (O)
White, Holland L. 1838 wb-7-17 (Wi)
White, Hugh 1854 wb-12-43 (K)
White, Hugh L. 1861 wb-13-519 (K)
White, Hugh Lawson 1840 wb-7-68 (K)
White, Isaac 1819 wb-#17 (Wa)
White, J. N. 1848 wd-14-186 (D)
White, Jacob 1844 wb-2-70# (Ge)
White, Jacob 1856 wb-16-248 (Rb)
White, James 1821 wb-#119 (Mu)
White, James 1822 wb-3-342 (K)
White, James 1838 wb-a-141 (Di)
White, James 1843 wb-f-190* (Hn)

White, James C. 1842 wb-7-578 (Wi)
White, James C. 1856 ib-h-500 (F)
White, James D. 1838 wb-2-32 (Hr)
White, James M. 1852 wb-a-424 (F)
White, James M. 1861 wb-13-521 (K)
White, Jehu 1793 wb-1-6 (K)
White, Jesse N. 1851 wb-14-591 (D)
White, Jesse W. 1854 wb-n-432 (Mt)
White, Jim 1854 wb-n-415 (Mt)
White, Jno. 1837 wb-1-533 (Hr)
White, John 1796 wb-#6 (Wa)
White, John 1819 lr (Sn)
White, John 1820 rb-c-386 (Mt)
White, John 1820 wb-2-318 (Je)
White, John 1823 wb-#45 (Wl)
White, John 1825 wb-4-39 (Wi)
White, John 1827 rb-e-249 (Mt)
White, John 1829 wb-2-30# (Ge)
White, John 1836 wb-9-228 (Rb)
White, John 1841 wb-b-296 (Hd)
White, John 1846 wb-1-228 (Bo)
White, John 1849 wb-g-101 (O)
White, John 1850 148-1-343 (Ge)
White, John 1852 wb-#111 (Wl)
White, John 1859 wb-f-311 (G)
White, John D. 1849 wb-2-56 (Sh)
White, John sr. 1846 wb-c-240 (Wh)
White, Jonathan 1816 wb-a-76 (Ro)
White, Jonathan 1818 lr (Sn)
White, Jonathan D. 1819 wb-a-127 (Ro)
White, Joseph 1793 wb-0-4 (K)
White, Joseph 1805 as-1-119 (Ge)
White, Joseph 1805 wb-1-26# (Ge)
White, Joseph 1819 wb-2-225 (Je)
White, Joseph 1835 wb-1-490 (Hw)
White, Joseph 1841 wb-1-69 (Sh)
White, Joseph 1841 wb-2-57# (Ge)
White, Joseph 1852 wb-15-375 (D)
White, Joseph 1858 wb-f-216 (G)
White, Joseph M. 1849 wb-d-199 (G)
White, Joshua 1815 wb-4-354 (D)
White, Joshua 1820 wb-7-423 (D)
White, Joshua 1841 wb-a-149 (Di)
White, Judah 1846 wb-b-201 (We)
White, King 1838 wb-2-37 (Hr)
White, King 1842 wb-b-422 (Hd)
White, L. L. 1836 wb-1-464 (Hr)
White, Levi 1848 rb-14-410 (Ru)
White, Levi sr. 1849 rb-14-522 (Ru)
White, Littleberry W. 1860 wb-#130 (Wl)
White, Lucinda 1859 wb-2-298 (Li)

White, Lucy 1816 wb-7-74 (D)
White, Margaret A. 1854 lr (Gi)
White, Mark 1849 lr (Sn)
White, Martha 1846 wb-8-402 (Wi)
White, Martha 1847 rb-k-688 (Mt)
White, Martha M. 1858 wb-12-540 (Wi)
White, Mary 1813 wb-2-54 (K)
White, Mary 1859 rb-20-241 (Ru)
White, Mathew 1847 rb-k-507 (Mt)
White, Miles 1861 wb-13-479 (Wi)
White, Minerva F. 1843 wb-f-147* (Hn)
White, Montgomery 1863 ib-2-586 (Cl)
White, Mordecai 1842 wb-7-548 (Wi)
White, Moses 1819 wb-a-115 (Ro)
White, Moses 1830 wb-5-21 (K)
White, Moses 1830 wb-5-7 (K)
White, Moses 1840 wb-7-114 (K)
White, Moses 1843 wb-d-56 (Ro)
White, Nancy 1845 wb-d-125 (Hd)
White, Nancy 1851 wb-10-3 (Wi)
White, Nancy 1859 wb-f-179 (Mu)
White, Nancy 1860-wb-#132 (Wl)
White, Nathan 1847 lr (Sn)
White, Nathaniel 1834 wb-#186 (Mc)
White, Noah 1860 wb-7-69 (Ma)
White, Owen 1835 wb-8-459 (Rb)
White, Patience 1860 wb-f-386 (G)
White, Philemon 1858 wb-b-429 (We)
White, R. J. 1855 wb-16-455 (D)
White, R. M. 1848 ib-1-20 (Ca)
White, Rachel C. 1842 wb-3-637 (Ma)
White, Reuben 1847 wb-d-354 (Hd)
White, Richard 1840 wb-c-140 (Ro)
White, Richard 1847 148-1-211 (Ge)
White, Richard 1849 wb-5-54 (Je)
White, Richard D. 1828 wb-#74 (Wl)
White, Richard H. 1854 rb-17-322 (Ru)
White, Robert 1826 wb-4-72 (Wi)
White, Robert 1827 wb-1-67 (Ma)
White, Robert 1834 wb-1-539 (Ma)
White, Robert 1839 wb-2-265 (Sn)
White, Robert 1840 wb-7-220 (Wi)
White, Robert 1851 wb-10-3 (Wi)
White, Robert J. 1858 wb-17-436 (D)
White, Ruben 1852 wb-a-248 (Di)
White, S. A. 1860 wb-13-281 (K)
White, Sally 1841 wb-7-485 (Wi)
White, Samuel 1804 wb-1-286 (Je)
White, Samuel 1814 wb-A-51 (Li)
White, Samuel 1816 wb-1-0 (Sm)
White, Samuel 1820 wb-2-324 (Je)

White, Samuel 1854 wb-5-335 (Je)
White, Sarah 1820 wb-7-416 (D)
White, Solomon 1837 wb-1-340 (Hy)
White, Stephen 1846 rb-13-532 (Ru)
White, Stokley N. 1848 rb-14-486 (Ru)
White, Surrell 1843 wb-a-101 (Ms)
White, Susan 1857 mr (Gi)
White, Susan A. 1851 wb-10-151 (Wi)
White, Susanna 1852 wb-xx-80 (St)
White, Thomas 1811 rb-2-146 (Ru)
White, Thomas 1835 wb-2-186 (Sn)
White, Thomas 1837 wb-d-111 (St)
White, Thomas 1849 wb-g-230 (Hu)
White, Thomas 1859 wb-3-306 (Sn)
White, Thomas B. 1855 wb-16-530 (D)
White, Thompson D. 1844 wb-3-449 (Hy)
White, W. A. 1848 wb-g-128 (Hu)
White, W. C. 1846 wb-4-40 (Hr)
White, W. C. 1852 wb-g-570 (Hu)
White, W. S. 1842 rb-i-396 (Mt)
White, Wiley B. 1860 wb-13-364 (Wi)
White, William 1808 rb-a-328 (Mt)
White, William 1820? wb-#118 (Mu)
White, William 1824 lr (Sn)
White, William 1836 wb-1-146 (Bo)
White, William 1836 wb-2-103 (Ma)
White, William 1837 wb-11-27 (D)
White, William 1841 as-a-507 (Di)
White, William 1844 wb-d-266 (O)
White, William 1850 wb-2-146 (La)
White, William 1850 wb-9-431 (Wi)
White, William 1854 wb-15-558 (Rb)
White, William 1858 wb-#187 (Mc)
White, William A. 1848 wb-g-112 (Hu)
White, William C. 1846 wb-4-94 (Hr)
White, William H. 1859 wb-#128 (Wl)
White, William M. 1855 wb-12-173 (K)
White, William S. 1842 rb-i-417 (Mt)
White, William W. 1848 wb-2-28 (La)
White, Willis 1832 wb-10-9 (D)
White, Wilson 1827 wb-4-212 (Wi)
White, Wm. 1852 rb-16-322 (Ru)
White, Wm. W. 1852 rb-16-327 (Ru)
White, Woodson P. 1839 wb-b-355 (Wh)
Whitebery, George 1858 wb-1C-387 (A)
Whitehead, Benjamin 1800 rb-a-126 (Mt)
Whitehead, Benjamin 1815 rb-b-166 (Mt)
Whitehead, Benjamin 1837 rb-g-534 (Mt)
Whitehead, J. C. 1858 wb-16-568 (Rb)
Whitehead, J. O. 1860 wb-17-27 (Rb)
Whitehead, Jacob 1817 wb-A-153 (Li)

Whitehead, James 1841 wb-#136 (Wl)
Whitehead, M. S. (Mrs.) 1837 wb-10-480 (Rb)
Whitehead, Marillo S. 1839 wb-10-3* (Rb)
Whitehead, Martha S. 1840 wb-10-484 (Rb)
Whitehead, Mary 1844 wb-3-202 (Hr)
Whitehead, Robert 1833 wb-8-269 (Rb)
Whitehead, Robt. A. M. S. 1843 wb-12-41 (Rb)
Whitehead, Thomas 1859 wb-k-102 (O)
Whitehead, W. H. 1856 wb-16-293 (Rb)
Whitehead, W. N. 1858 wb-1-251 (Be)
Whitehead, William 1817 wb-A-170 (Li)
Whitehead, William 1836 rb-g-469 (Mt)
Whitehorn, Sally 1842 wb-2-332 (Hr)
Whitehurst, Batson 1823 wb-1-485 (Hw)
Whitelaw, James 1842 wb-3-438 (Hy)
Whitelaw, Patrick H. 1853 wb-e-16 (Hy)
Whiteman, James S. 1854 wb-12-3 (K)
Whitenburg, Joseph 1817 wb-A-236 (Li)
Whiteside, Abraham 1823 wb-#49 (Mu)
Whiteside, Jonathan 1860 wb-k-344 (O)
Whiteside, Margaret 1845 A-468-2 (Le)
Whiteside, R. P. 1857 as-c-75 (Ms)
Whiteside, Richard C. 1852 wb-f-12 (Mu)
Whiteside, Samuel 1850 A-468-137 (Le)
Whiteside, Thomas 1832 wb-9-571 (D)
Whiteside, William 1835 wb-x-297 (Mu)
Whitesides, Abram (Dr.) 1821 wb-#122 (Mu)
Whitesides, Hugh 1840 wb-z-113 (Mu)
Whitesides, Thomas 1851 33-3-364 (Gr)
Whitesides, Thomas 1853 lr (Sn)
Whitesides, William 1822 wb-#96 (Mu)
Whitfield, Ansel 1848 ib-1-10 (Ca)
Whitfield, Bryan 1825 rb-d-471 (Mt)
Whitfield, Bryan 1825 rb-d-478 (Mt)
Whitfield, Bryan 1827 rb-e-197 (Mt)
Whitfield, Henry 1834 wb-2-40 (Ma)
Whitfield, John W. 1848 wb-14-273 (D)
Whitfield, Lewis 1838 rb-h-79 (Mt)
Whitfield, Lewis 1841 rb-i-72 (Mt)
Whitfield, Marrie Susan 1855 wb-n-696 (Mt)
Whitfield, Mary 1859 rb-p-110 (Mt)
Whitfield, Mary E. 1851 wb-m-324 (Mt)
Whitfield, Mathew 1827 rb-7-294 (Ru)
Whitfield, Nathan Bryan 1858 rb-o-710 (Mt)
Whitfield, Needham 1859 rb-p-278 (Mt)
Whitfield, Thomas Ruffin 1837 wb-x-462 (Mu)
Whitfield, W. B. 1856 rb-o-154 (Mt)
Whitfield, Wilkins 1841 wb-7-444 (Wi)
Whitfield, William 1834 wb-1-54 (La)
Whitfield, William 1839 wb-e-51 (Hn)
Whitfield, William B. 1853 wb-n-62 (Mt)

Whitfield, William B. 1853 wb-n-62 (Mt)
Whitfield, William O. 1855 wb-b-1 (F)
Whitford, Lewis 1841 wb-2-216 (Hr)
Whitford, Mary 1851 wb-g-478 (St)
Whitford, Thomas 1844 wb-3-173 (Hr)
Whitford, Willis 1831 wb-c-110 (St)
Whiting, George W. 1834 wb-8-401 (Rb)
Whiting, John 1834 wb-10-286 (D)
Whitledge, Thomas sr. 1816 rb-b-370 (Mt)
Whitley, Joab 1816 wb-4-428 (D)
Whitley, John R. 1855 wb-d-295 (Wh)
Whitley, Mary 1824 wb-3-703 (Wi)
Whitley, Sharp R. 1860 wb-e-359 (Wh)
Whitley, T. A. 1858 wb-12-479 (K)
Whitley, Thomas 1845 wb-13-233 (D)
Whitley, Wiley 1831 wb-2-0 (Sm)
Whitley, Willie 1833 wb-2-0 (Sm)
Whitlidge, Thomas 1810 rb-a-347 (Mt)
Whitlock, Alexander 1826 wb-#22 (Wa)
Whitlock, Ann 1861 wb-b-62 (Dk)
Whitlock, Ann 1861 wb-b-64 (Dk)
Whitlock, George 1852 wb-7-0 (Sm)
Whitlock, Hardin 1850 wb-g-355 (Hn)
Whitlock, J. E. 1856 ib-h-542 (F)
Whitlock, James 1840 wb-5-86 (Gr)
Whitlock, James 1852 wb-3-49 (Gr)
Whitlock, John 1843 wb-#41 (Wa)
Whitlock, John 1849 wb-#48 (Wa)
Whitlock, John 1851 wb-#50 (Wa)
Whitlock, John J. 1851 wb-d-365 (G)
Whitlock, Nancy 1848 wb-#165 (Wl)
Whitlock, Thomas 1848 wb-#157 (Wl)
Whitlock, William 1818 wb-#26 (Wl)
Whitlow, Henderson 1841 wb-b-300 (Hd)
Whitlow, Henry 1840 wb-3-176 (Ma)
Whitly, Lewis 1816 rb-3-84 (Ru)
Whitly, Starling 1843 mr-2-56 (Be)
Whitman, Jacob 1858 ib-C-178 (C)
Whitman, Jacob 1858 iv-C-11 (C)
Whitmill, Drew S. 1819 rb-c-79 (Mt)
Whitmore, Gowen 1817 rb-4-61 (Ru)
Whitnel, Mary 1814 rb-2-288 (Ru)
Whitney, Edward 1850 wb-a-381 (F)
Whitsett, Absalom 1854 wb-a-338 (Ms)
Whitsett, Absolem 1813 wb-A-45 (Li)
Whitsett, James 1843 as-a-74 (Ms)
Whitsett, Jane 1842 wb-12-385* (D)
Whitsett, John O. 1834 rb-f-542 (Mt)
Whitsett, N. P. 1851 33-3-331 (Gr)
Whitsett, Nathan P. 1843 wb-5-278 (Gr)
Whitsett, Reuben E. 1853 wb-16-188 (D)

Whitsett, Ruben 1853 wb-16-111 (D)
Whitside, Martha M. 1841 wb-b-283 (O)
Whitsitt, James 1850 wb-14-509 (D)
Whitsitt, James M. 1840 wb-12-84* (D)
Whitsitt, Joseph W. 1860 wb-18-356 (D)
Whitsley, Joseph 1818 wb-a-114 (Wh)
Whitson, Abraham Sr. 1819 wb-#34 (Wl)
Whitson, Anne 1829 wb-#191 (Mu)
Whitson, Joseph 1795? wb-#22 (Wa)
Whitson, Joseph 1859 wb-e-210 (Wh)
Whitson, Joseph 1859 wb-e-272 (Wh)
Whitson, William 1783 wb-#6 (Wa)
Whitson, William 1806 wb-#1 (Mu)
Whitt, Edward M. 1850 33-3-273 (Gr)
Whittemore, Abraham 1842 wb-12-270* (D)
Whittemore, Clement 1826 wb-8-552 (D)
Whittemore, Clemment 1826 wb-9-18 (D)
Whittemore, John H. 1861 wb-18-455 (D)
Whittemore, Nancy 1828 wb-9-268 (D)
Whittemore, William V. 1861 wb-18-457 (D)
Whitten, George 1856 ib-1-393 (Wy)
Whitten, John 1849 ib-1-30 (Wy)
Whitten, Melton 1859 ib-2-182 (Wy)
Whitten, Stephen 1837 rb-9-441 (Ru)
Whittenberg, Frederick 1804 as-1-79 (Ge)
Whittenberg, John W. 1859 wb-1-159 (R)
Whittenburg, Frederick 1804 wb-1-25# (Ge)
Whittenburg, James 1861 149-1-232 (Ge)
Whittenburge, Henry 1853 wb-1-147 (Bo)
Whittenton, John 1856 wb-e-55 (Hy)
Whittington, Andrew 1846 wb-1-396 (La)
Whitton, James M. 1839 wb-b-303 (G)
Whitwell, Ann 1839 wb-a-136 (Di)
Whitworth, Abraham 1861 wb-4-432 (La)
Whitworth, Edwin 1840 as-a-31 (Ms)
Whitworth, Elizabeth 1848 rb-k-746 (Mt)
Whitworth, James 1829 lr (Sn)
Whitworth, John 1801 wb-1-59 (Sn)
Whitworth, John 1842 rb-i-301 (Mt)
Whitworth, Louiza 1847 rb-k-508 (Mt)
Whitworth, Mary 1851 as-b-42 (Ms)
Whoberry, Elizabeth 1821 rb-5-158 (Ru)
Whorley, George 1844 wb-d-76 (Hd)
Whorton, Rebecca 1836 wb-1-221 (W)
Whoser, Jefferson 1859 wb-#187 (Mc)
Whyte, Phereby S. 1855 wb-16-591 (D)
Whyte, Robert 1845 wb-13-216 (D)
Wiatt, John F. 1825 wb-1-112 (Ma)
Wicker, William A. 1855 wb-j-8 (O)
Wickham, Nathan 1854 wb-n-392 (Mt)
Wickham, Robert H. 1837 wb-a-25 (F)

Widby, Lawson 1856 wb-1-107 (Jo)
Widby, William 1847 wb-1-34 (Jo)
Wieners, Catharine 1860 wb-3e-143 (Sh)
Wier, Cary 1852 wb-#179 (Wl)
Wier, George 1833 wb-#98 (Wl)
Wier, James 1837 wb-#116 (Wl)
Wier, James 1849 ib-1-82 (Cl)
Wier, James J. 1841 wb-#133 (Wl)
Wier, John 1828 wb-#76 (Wl)
Wier, Thomas V. 1853 wb-#109 (Wl)
Wier, William L. 1859 wb-#129 (Wl)
Wigger, Henry 1818 rb-4-151 (Ru)
Wiggin, Cany 1824 as-a-158 (Di)
Wiggin, John P. 1837 wb-2-182 (Fr)
Wiggins, Cary 1824 as-b-96 (Di)
Wiggins, Henry 1798 wb-2-108 (D)
Wiggins, John D. 1838 wb-#187 (Mc)
Wiggins, Mary 1835 wb-b-57 (G)
Wiggins, Michael 1815 wb-1-207 (Bo)
Wiggins, Thomas 1835 wb-b-56 (G)
Wigglesworth, Benjamin 1853 wb-16-134 (D)
Wilbanks, Berryman 1824 wb-a-54 (Hn)
Wilbanks, Spencer 1846 wb-b-143 (We)
Wilborn, Jonathan 1840 wb-b-234 (Hd)
Wilborn, Robert 1832 wb-3-0 (Sm)
Wilbourn, A. 1858 wb-4-16 (La)
Wilbourn, Jasper 1852 wb-2-240 (La)
Wilbourn, Jasper N. 1852 wb-2-241 (La)
Wilbourn, Joshua 1842 wb-a-113 (Cr)
Wilburn, F. G. 1838 wb-7-65 (Wi)
Wilburn, Felix G. 1841 wb-7-392 (Wi)
Wilburn, Nicholas 1836 wb-6-111 (Wi)
Wilcher, Joseph 1818 wb-A-255 (Li)
Wilcox, James T. 1851 wb-2-94 (Sh)
Wilcox, John E. 1839 rb-h-281 (Mt)
Wilcox, Mary 1851 wb-#51 (Wa)
Wilcox, Miles 1852 wb-1-69 (Jo)
Wilcox, Robert J. 1853 wb-f-138 (Mu)
Wilcox, Samuel 1811 rb-a-380 (Mt)
Wilcox, Samuel 1821 rb-c-492 (Mt)
Wilcox, Samuel Ethelbert 1859 rb-p-142 (Mt)
Wilcox, Thomas 1814 wb-4-290 (D)
Wilcox, Thomas 1834 wb-10-375 (D)
Wilcox, Thomas 1857 wb-c-168 (L)
Wilcox, William 1830 wb-1-7 (Sh)
Wilder, Burrell B. 1857 wb-a-306 (Cr)
Wilder, Michael 1848 wb-d-129 (G)
Wilder, Moses 1840 wb-a-11 (Dk)
Wildredge, Edmund 1840 wb-e-348 (Hu)
Wilee, Thurman 1847 rb-14-181 (Ru)
Wilee, William H. 1841 wb-z-218 (Mu)

Wileman, William 1838 wb-1-172 (Fr)
Wiley, Alexander 1849 wb-1-347 (Li)
Wiley, Ann 1847 wb-a-171 (Di)
Wiley, David 1836 wb-a-127 (Di)
Wiley, Henry 1810 wb-1-356 (Je)
Wiley, Henry 1835 wb-1-114 (W)
Wiley, Hugh 1823 wb-#136 (Wl)
Wiley, James 1856 wb-j-94 (O)
Wiley, John 1843 wb-d-84 (Ro)
Wiley, John 1857 wb-f-125 (Mu)
Wiley, John M. 1852 as-c-170 (Di)
Wiley, Jonathan 1830 wb-a-20 (Cr)
Wiley, Joseph 1848 as-b-462 (Di)
Wiley, Josiah K. 1847 as-b-334 (Di)
Wiley, Lydia 1860 wb-4-345 (La)
Wiley, Mary 1841 wb-2-403 (Hy)
Wiley, Polly B. 1856 ib-2-363 (Cl)
Wiley, Robert 1824 wb-#78 (Mu)
Wiley, William 1842 wb-a-151 (Di)
Wiley, Wm. 1860 wb-4-345 (La)
Wilhite, Jeremiah 1852 wb-d-121 (Wh)
Wilhite, Reuben 1853 wb-#24 (Mo)
Wilhite, Reuben 1862 wb-e-417 (Wh)
Wilhite, Samuel 1842 wb-2-57# (Ge)
Wilhite, Solomon 1851 148-1-369 (Ge)
Wilhite, William 1860 149-1-310 (Ge)
Wilhoit, Katharine 1842 wb-2-58# (Ge)
Wilhoit, Solomon 1824 wb-1-25# (Ge)
Wilhoit, William 1856 149-1-46 (Ge)
Wilhoite, Isaac 1857 149-1-70 (Ge)
Wilhoite, John W. 1856 wb-2-90# (Ge)
Wilhoite, William 1850 148-1-341 (Ge)
Wiliamson, Lindy 1840 wb-b-353 (G)
Wilker, Jacob 1844 wb-8-294 (K)
Wilkerson, Coburn 1851 wb-5-19 (Hr)
Wilkerson, George 1816 rb-b-353 (Mt)
Wilkerson, Isaac A. 1857 wb-h-152 (Hn)
Wilkerson, James 1848 wb-4-356 (Hr)
Wilkerson, Jehu 1836 rb-g-305 (Mt)
Wilkerson, John 1835 rb-g-233 (Mt)
Wilkerson, John 1846 as-b-307 (Di)
Wilkerson, Lewis 1858 lr (Gi)
Wilkerson, Meredith 1851 wb-#177 (Wl)
Wilkerson, Prudy 1807 wb-#5 (Wl)
Wilkerson, Richard 1841 wb-10-591 (Rb)
Wilkerson, Richard 1841 wb-10-593 (Rb)
Wilkerson, Sarah 1853 wb-7-0 (Sm)
Wilkerson, Thomas 1856 wb-4-53 (Je)
Wilkerson, William 1843 wb-12-427* (D)
Wilkes, Ann 1848? lr (Sn)
Wilkes, Benjamin 1827 wb-#161 (Mu)

Wilkes, Daniel 1823 wb-#61 (Mu)
Wilkes, Daniel 1824 wb-#72 (Mu)
Wilkes, Daniel 1833 wb-5-320 (Wi)
Wilkes, Daniel 1836 wb-6-183 (Wi)
Wilkes, Jacob 1840 wb-7-8 (K)
Wilkes, James 1830 wb-9-367 (D)
Wilkes, John 1831 wb-#217 (Mu)
Wilkes, Margaret E. 1861 wb-b-114 (Ms)
Wilkes, Mary K. 1847 wb-b-157 (Mu)
Wilkes, Minor 1829 wb-#189 (Mu)
Wilkes, Minor 1854 lr (Gi)
Wilkes, Richard W. 1849 lr (Gi)
Wilkes, Thomas 1810 wb-4-107 (D)
Wilkes, William 1857 wb-6-437 (Ma)
Wilkes, William B. 1831 wb-#230 (Mu)
Wilkins, Alexander 1853 wb-a-265 (Di)
Wilkins, Benjamin 1845 wb-13-248 (D)
Wilkins, Charlotte 1858 wb-1-88 (Dy)
Wilkins, James 1834 wb-b-30 (G)
Wilkins, John 1855 wb-i-249 (O)
Wilkins, John 1862 wb-f-432 (G)
Wilkins, L. John 1847 wb-d-63 (G)
Wilkins, Lewellen 1847 wb-b-220 (We)
Wilkins, Little John 1847 wb-d-47 (G)
Wilkins, Reuben 1840 wb-#188 (Mc)
Wilkins, Robert 1855 ib-h-399 (F)
Wilkins, Robt. 1841 wb-a-61 (F)
Wilkins, Tabitha 1818 lr (Gi)
Wilkins, W. J. 1857 wb-16-356 (Rb)
Wilkins, West 1842 wb-a-94 (T)
Wilkins, William 1806 wb-1-16 (Wi)
Wilkins, William 1819 wb-3-55 (Wi)
Wilkins, William 1861 wb-a-302 (T)
Wilkins, Willis J. 1857 wb-16-368 (Rb)
Wilkins, Wm. E. 1858 gs-1-187 (F)
Wilkinson, Allen 1819 wb-1-0 (Sm)
Wilkinson, Benjamin 1820 wb-7-409 (D)
Wilkinson, Bethunia A. 1859 wb-5-101 (Hr)
Wilkinson, Eleanor 1849 wb#18 (Gu)
Wilkinson, Francis 1847 wb-4-189 (Hr)
Wilkinson, Geo. W. 1847 wb-4-189 (Hr)
Wilkinson, Halena 1848 rb-l-179 (Mt)
Wilkinson, Hubbard S. 1845 rb-13-190 (Ru)
Wilkinson, James 1849 wb-g-315 (Hn)
Wilkinson, Jesse B. 1819 wb-7-314 (D)
Wilkinson, John 1830 wb-1-86 (Fr)
Wilkinson, John 1834 wb-1-355 (Hr)
Wilkinson, Jonathan 1858 wb-17-440 (D)
Wilkinson, Kinchen T. 1817 wb-7-163 (D)
Wilkinson, Mournen 1844 wd-13-25 (D)
Wilkinson, Richard 1860 wb-2-85# (Ge)

Wilkinson, Spotswood 1854 wb-h-37 (St)
Wilkinson, William 1831 wb-5-13 (Wi)
Wilkinson, William 1841 wb-12-102* (D)
Wilkinson, William 1842 wb-c-236 (O)
Wilkinson, William sr. 1829 wb-9-274 (D)
Wilkison, Jessee 1799 wb-2-185 (D)
Wilkison, Mary 1837 wb-9-377 (Rb)
Wilks, Elizabeth 1823 wb-#46 (Mu)
Wilks, J. M. 1844 wb-12-228 (Rb)
Wilks, James M. 1846 wb-13-37 (Rb)
Wilks, Jane 1828 wb-#172 (Mu)
Wilks, Jane 1839 as-a-4 (Ma)
Wilks, John 1853 as-b-126 (Ms)
Wilks, John B. 1822 wb-#121 (Mu)
Wilks, John H. 1855 wb-16-11 (Rb)
Wilks, Josiah 1831 wb-#232 (Mu)
Wilks, Mary 1838 wb-11-335 (D)
Wilks, Minor C. 1825 wb-#132 (Mu)
Wilks, Polly O. 1855 wb-e-295 (G)
Wilks, Richard 1844 wb-12-229 (Rb)
Wilks, Richard S. 1844 wb-12-294 (Rb)
Wilks, Richard sr. 1821 wb-1-336 (Sn)
Wilks, William 1851 rb-15-600 (Ru)
Wilks, William H. 1849 rb-15-117 (Ru)
Will, Jeramiah T. 1839 wb-s-363 (Wh)
Willaford, Delila 1846 wb-c-312 (G)
Willard, Beverly 1821 wb-#40 (Wl)
Willard, Henry 1859 wb-c-308 (L)
Willard, Isabel 1829 wb-#85 (Wl)
Willard, J. W. 1859 wb-c-315 (L)
Willard, James 1827 wb-#70 (Wl)
Willard, Joel 1815 wb-#16 (Wl)
Willburn, William M. 1842 wb-a-91 (F)
Willcockson, George 1799 wb-1-82 (Je)
Willeford, Willis 1847 rb-14-83 (Ru)
Willet, Alexander 1851 148-1-361 (Ge)
Willet, Enoch 1831 wb-b-95 (Ro)
Willet, Zadock 1823 wb-#19 (Wa)
Willett, Elizabeth 1840 wb-c-182 (Ro)
Willett, Elizabeth 1854 wb-e-471 (Ro)
Willett, G. W. 1856 wb-#57 (Wa)
Willett, James W. 1841 wb-c-228 (Ro)
Willett, Joseph 1849 wb-2-44 (Sh)
Willett, Richard 1813 wb-1-336 (Wi)
Willey, John 1835 wb-a-115 (Di)
Willey, Mary 1849 as-b-413 (Di)
Willfle, Christopher 1817 wb-1-483 (Hw)
Willhoit, Isaac 1846 148-1-170 (Ge)
William, Benjamin 1824 rb-d-311 (Mt)
Williams, Abel 1848 wb-e-99 (Ro)
Williams, Abel 1855 wb-15-773 (Rb)

Williams, Able 1817 wb-#25 (Wl)
Williams, Absolum 1812 rb-2-188 (Ru)
Williams, Agnes 1838 wb-#122 (Wl)
Williams, Alexander 1838 wb-6-275 (K)
Williams, Alexander 1852 wb-2-75# (Ge)
Williams, Alexander M. 1847 wb-f-115 (O)
Williams, Alfred 1848 as-a-158 (Ms)
Williams, Allen 1841 wb-b-35 (We)
Williams, Allen 1852 wb-2-74# (Ge)
Williams, Allen 1859 wb-7-36 (Ma)
Williams, Amos 1857 wb-6-369 (Ma)
Williams, Anderson 1815 wb-1-0 (Sm)
Williams, Anderson 1850 wb-b-618 (Mu)
Williams, Anderson 1859 wb-7-53 (Ma)
Williams, Anderson 1861 wb-1-62 (Se)
Williams, Anderson jr. 1860 wb-7-85 (Ma)
Williams, Ann K. 1852 33-3-423 (Gr)
Williams, Anna 1853 wb-2-81 (Li)
Williams, Archelaus 1812 wb-4-188 (D)
Williams, Arthur 1800? wb-1-130 (Je)
Williams, Arthur 1820 wb-3-124 (Rb)
Williams, Arthur 1850 wb-a-384 (F)
Williams, B. 1855 wb-1C-221 (A)
Williams, Basheba 1861 wb-d-107 (L)
Williams, Benjamin 1811 wb-1-144 (Sn)
Williams, Benjamin 1849 wb-2-69# (Ge)
Williams, Benjamin 1857 wb-4-217 (La)
Williams, Benjamin M. 1837 wb-2-18 (Li)
Williams, Bennett 1824 wb-#74 (Mu)
Williams, Berry 1843 wb-e-244 (St)
Williams, Berry P. 1857 wb-12-446 (Wi)
Williams, Briant 1840 wb-b-21 (We)
Williams, Bridges 1855 wb-3-341 (La)
Williams, C. 1836 wb-10-643 (D)
Williams, C. H. 1852 mr-2-431 (Be)
Williams, Charles 1844 wb-a-82 (Ms)
Williams, Charles 1852 mr-2-456 (Be)
Williams, Charles 1853 mr-2-517 (Be)
Williams, Charles 1856 wb-1-84 (Be)
Williams, Charles E. 1854 wb-2-155 (Sh)
Williams, Charles L. 1859 rb-p-251 (Mt)
Williams, Charlott 1861 wb-17-254 (Rb)
Williams, Christopher 1838 wb-11-194 (D)
Williams, Curtis 1789 wb-1-123 (D)
Williams, D. H. 1855 wb-n-700 (Mt)
Williams, D. M. 1815 wb-a-198 (Ro)
Williams, D. R. 1857 wb-h-84 (Hn)
Williams, Daniel 1830 wb-1-139 (Hr)
Williams, Daniel 1834 wb-8-333 (Rb)
Williams, Daniel 1845 as-b-302 (Di)
Williams, Daniel Sr. 1794 wb-1-302 (D)

Williams, David 1809 wb-1-157 (Bo)
Williams, David 1835 rb-9-178 (Ru)
Williams, Diana 1838 wb-6-472 (Wi)
Williams, Dudley 1845 wb-f-258 (St)
Williams, Edmund 1794 wb-1-2 (Ct)
Williams, Edmund 1795 wb-#6 (Wa)
Williams, Edward 1813 wb-1-0 (Sm)
Williams, Edward 1834 eb-1-312 (C)
Williams, Edward 1835 wb-x-249* (Mu)
Williams, Edward 1837 wb-1-316 (Hy)
Williams, Edwin M. 1859 gs-1-510 (F)
Williams, Eli 1859 wb-f-257 (G)
Williams, Elijah 1856 wb-12-70 (Wi)
Williams, Elisha 1815 wb-2-266 (Rb)
Williams, Elisha 1815 wb-2-280 (Rb)
Williams, Elisha 1858 wb-h-450 (St)
Williams, Elisha 1858 wb-h-456 (St)
Williams, Elisha D. 1854 wb-g-586 (Hn)
Williams, Elisha jr. 1849 rb-14-500 (Ru)
Williams, Elisha sr. 1847 wb-f-391 (St)
Williams, Eliza 1858 wb-f-130 (G)
Williams, Elizabeth 1841 148-1-24 (Ge)
Williams, Elizabeth 1842 wb-#146 (Wl)
Williams, Elizabeth 1847 wb-c-267 (Wh)
Williams, Elizabeth 1847 wb-f-469 (St)
Williams, Elizabeth 1850 wb-a-232 (Ms)
Williams, Elizabeth B. 1838 wb-d-231 (St)
Williams, Ellener 1858 wb-e-98 (Hy)
Williams, Ephraim 1835 wb-5-348 (K)
Williams, Ephraim 1835 wb-d-68 (Hn)
Williams, Ephraim C. 1832 wb-5-198 (Wi)
Williams, Ethelburt C. 1854 wb-15-465 (Rb)
Williams, Etheldred 1847 wb-5-494 (Gr)
Williams, Etheldred 1849 wb-14-288 (D)
Williams, Evander M. 1857 wb-17-179 (D)
Williams, Fielding L. 1845 rb-k-4 (Mt)
Williams, Frances 1843 wb-11-456 (Rb)
Williams, Francis 1808 wb-3-195 (D)
Williams, Francis 1844 wb-f-220 (Hn)
Williams, Francis 1861 wb-k-495 (O)
Williams, Francis Marion 1845 wb-f-259 (St)
Williams, Frederick or Andrew 1832
    wb-#188 (Mc)
Williams, Freeman 1847 wb-a-310 (F)
Williams, Garland 1827 wb-6-83 (Rb)
Williams, Geo. 1849 wb-14-215 (Rb)
Williams, Geo. W. 1831 wb-7-432 (Rb)
Williams, George 1841 wb-a-85 (L)
Williams, George 1844 rb-j-102 (Mt)
Williams, George 1846 lw (Ct)
Williams, George 1855 wb-1-497 (Hw)

Williams, George C. 1840 lw (Ct)
Williams, George R. 1858 wb-c-232 (L)
Williams, Gilbert 1854 39-2-44 (Dk)
Williams, Green 1832 wb-x-55 (Mu)
Williams, Green B. 1851 wb-g-397 (Hn)
Williams, Greenberry 1823 wb-#56 (Mu)
Williams, Griffith 1823 wb-4-18 (Rb)
Williams, Hannah 1830 wb-3-124 (Je)
Williams, Hannah 1843 wb-5-254 (Gr)
Williams, Hannah 1848 wb-c-305 (Wh)
Williams, Hardin 1840 wb-z-88 (Mu)
Williams, Hector 1825 lr (Sn)
Williams, Henry 1827 rb-e-172 (Mt)
Williams, Henry 1851 wb-m-320 (Mt)
Williams, Henry 1852 wb-10-370 (Wi)
Williams, Henry C. 1829 wb-3-0 (Sm)
Williams, Henry J. 1853 rb-16-564 (Ru)
Williams, Hester Ann 1853 wb-e-96 (G)
Williams, Hiram 1814 wb-#14 (Wl)
Williams, Howel 1849 wb-#172 (Wl)
Williams, Hugh 1845 148-1-137 (Ge)
Williams, Isaac 1810 wb-1-363 (Rb)
Williams, Isaac 1824 wb-2-427 (Je)
Williams, Isaac 1852 wb-15-260 (D)
Williams, Isaac 1858 wb-a-328 (Cr)
Williams, Isham 1846 wb-12-531 (Rb)
Williams, J. D. 1861 wb-k-391 (O)
Williams, J. J. 1839 wb-b-175 (Hd)
Williams, J. L. 1844 mr-2-96 (Be)
Williams, J. S. 1832 rb-f-327 (Mt)
Williams, Jacob 1819 wb-1-31 (Fr)
Williams, James 1815 eb-1-49 (C)
Williams, James 1820 wb-#35 (Wl)
Williams, James 1831 wb-#188 (Mc)
Williams, James 1832 wb-5-198 (Wi)
Williams, James 1833 wb-#100 (Wl)
Williams, James 1833 wb-1-18 (Sh)
Williams, James 1841 wb-3-466 (Ma)
Williams, James 1847 wb-14-24 (D)
Williams, James 1852 as-b-97 (Ms)
Williams, James 1853 wb-a-205 (T)
Williams, James 1853 wb-n-174 (Mt)
Williams, James 1854 wb-n-211 (Mt)
Williams, James 1860 wb-#132 (Wl)
Williams, James H. 1824 wb-#79 (Mu)
Williams, James P. 1854 wb-#115 (Wl)
Williams, James R. 1846 wb-8-516 (Wi)
Williams, James R. 1847 wb-14-36 (D)
Williams, James T. 1828 wb-b-125 (Hn)
Williams, James W. 1847 wb-8-572 (Wi)
Williams, James W. 1850 wb-b-105 (L)

Williams, James sr. 1850 wb-a-246 (Ms)
Williams, Jane 1811 wb-4-164 (D)
Williams, Jeptha 1837 wb-#117 (Wl)
Williams, Jeremiah 1842 wb-3-489 (Ma)
Williams, Jerry 1858 wb-f-131 (G)
Williams, Jesse 1818 wb-3-39 (Rb)
Williams, Jesse 1836 rb-g-469 (Mt)
Williams, Jesse 1858 wb-16-645 (Rb)
Williams, Jessee 1818 wb-3-105 (Rb)
Williams, Jessee 1836 rb-g-480 (Mt)
Williams, Jessee 1847 wb-d-39 (G)
Williams, Jessee 1855 wb-e-338 (G)
Williams, Jno. P. 1854 wb-n-210 (Mt)
Williams, Joel 1846 wb-9-193 (K)
Williams, John 1803 wb-1-119 (K)
Williams, John 1805 wb-3-15 (D)
Williams, John 1808 wb-1-157 (Bo)
Williams, John 1809 wb-4-29 (D)
Williams, John 1815 rb-3-76 (Ru)
Williams, John 1816 wb-3-148 (St)
Williams, John 1819 wb-7-335 (D)
Williams, John 1823 rb-d-188 (Mt)
Williams, John 1827 wb-6-160 (Rb)
Williams, John 1832 wb-c-212 (St)
Williams, John 1834 wb-1-134 (Hy)
Williams, John 1836 wb-d-158 (Hn)
Williams, John 1837 wb-6-162 (K)
Williams, John 1840 rb-h-381 (Mt)
Williams, John 1843 wb-1-228 (Bo)
Williams, John 1844 wb-d-285 (O)
Williams, John 1846 wb-4-105 (Hr)
Williams, John 1847 wb-5-505 (Gr)
Williams, John 1847 wb-d-81 (G)
Williams, John 1849 33-3-100 (Gr)
Williams, John 1852 as-b-80 (Ms)
Williams, John 1852 wb-11-256 (K)
Williams, John 1853 wb-e-418 (Ro)
Williams, John 1855 wb-5-502 (Je)
Williams, John 1859 39-2-283 (Dk)
Williams, John 1859 wb-13-94 (Wi)
Williams, John 1864 wb-1-502 (Hw)
Williams, John E. 1852 rb-4-279 (Mu)
Williams, John J. 1840 wb-b-236 (Hd)
Williams, John J. P. 1852 rb-16-291 (Ru)
Williams, John Jr. 1820 wb-3-137 (Rb)
Williams, John L. 1852 wb-2-12 (Ct)
Williams, John M. 1847 wb-2-141 (Gr)
Williams, John M. 1854 wb-g-587 (Hn)
Williams, John N. 1838 rb-h-30 (Mt)
Williams, John P. 1847 rb-k-617 (Mt)
Williams, John P. 1853 wb-h-Apr (O)

Williams, John R. 1854 wb-#25 (Mo)
Williams, John Sr. 1847 wb-1-138 (Ct)
Williams, John V. 1836 wb-d-217 (Hn)
Williams, John jr. 1845 wb-e-45 (O)
Williams, John jr. 1848 wb-g-237 (Hn)
Williams, John sr. 1859 wb-17-612 (D)
Williams, Jonathan 1819 wb-7-331 (D)
Williams, Jonathan 1840 wb-7-129 (K)
Williams, Jonathan 1847 33-3-19 (Gr)
Williams, Jordan 1822 wb-#43 (Wl)
Williams, Joseph 1804 wb-1-34 (Je)
Williams, Joseph 1845 wb-e-52 (O)
Williams, Joseph 1853 wb-xx-261 (St)
Williams, Joseph 1860 wb-f-345 (G)
Williams, Joseph John 1861 wb-5-111 (Hr)
Williams, Josiah F. 1852 wb-15-374 (D)
Williams, Kinchen C. 1844 wb-1-340 (La)
Williams, Lawrence 1835 wb-2-19 (Ma)
Williams, Lemmy 1846 wb-f-309 (St)
Williams, Leoner 1850 wb-14-476 (D)
Williams, Lewilling 1839 wb-1-52 (Sh)
Williams, Lewis 1839 wb-a-27 (L)
Williams, Lewis 1844 wb-d-131 (Hd)
Williams, Littleberry 1818 wb-7-229 (D)
Williams, Littleberry 1853 wb-10-548 (Wi)
Williams, Lucy 1847 wb-g-215 (Hn)
Williams, Lucy 1853 wb-15-445 (Rb)
Williams, M. D. L. 1860 wb-a-154 (Ce)
Williams, M. M. 1855 wb-16-35 (Rb)
Williams, Mabina 1838 wb-6-290 (K)
Williams, Malinda 1839 wb-6-397 (K)
Williams, Malinda 1860 wb-f-370 (G)
Williams, Margaret 1824 wb-#77 (Mu)
Williams, Margaret 1849 wb-10-296 (K)
Williams, Margaret 1854 lr (Gi)
Williams, Margaret 1859 wb-18-106 (D)
Williams, Marion 1845 wb-f-257 (St)
Williams, Marrie Ann Elizabeth 1856
    rb-o-37 (Mt)
Williams, Martha 1854 wb-e-230 (G)
Williams, Martha 1857 wb-17-377 (D)
Williams, Martha A. 1851 rb-4-243 (Mu)
Williams, Mary 1818 wb-2-376 (Rb)
Williams, Mary 1828 wb-2-0 (Sm)
Williams, Mary 1841 rb-i-207 (Mt)
Williams, Mary 1847 r39-1-47 (Dk)
Williams, Mary 1850 r39-1-155 (Dk)
Williams, Mary 1852 wb-m-564 (Mt)
Williams, Mary W. 1841 rb-i-221 (Mt)
Williams, Mathew 1820 wb-7-413 (D)
Williams, Mathew 1850 mr-2-376 (Be)

Williams, Mathew 1861 wb-1-376 (Be)
Williams, Mathew J. 1852 wb-15-210 (Rb)
Williams, Mathew J. 1852 wb-15-211 (Rb)
Williams, Mattey 1839 rb-h-333 (Mt)
Williams, Matthew 1797 wb-1-20 (Rb)
Williams, Matthew 1797 wb-1-21 (Rb)
Williams, Meredith 1826 rb-d-530 (Mt)
Williams, Meredith 1834 wb-8-313 (Rb)
Williams, Merser 1831 wb-2-0 (Sm)
Williams, Miles 1827 wb-b-173 (St)
Williams, Miles 1834 wb-c-323 (St)
Williams, Minnie A. E. 1856 rb-o-97 (Mt)
Williams, Morgan 1812 wb-1-0 (Sm)
Williams, Nancy 1838 wb-#188 (Mc)
Williams, Nancy 1855 wb-g-709 (Hn)
Williams, Nancy G. 1854 wb-2-160 (Sh)
Williams, Nathan 1838 wb-d-236* (Hn)
Williams, Nathan 1844 wb-13-73 (D)
Williams, Nathan 1845 wb-2-91 (W)
Williams, Nathan 1859 wb-a-334 (Cr)
Williams, Nathan jr. 1843 wb-f-120* (Hn)
Williams, Nathan sr. 1844 wb-f-210 (Hn)
Williams, Nathaniel 1828 wb-#177 (Mu)
Williams, Nelly 1849 wb-2-45 (La)
Williams, Newton C. 1847 wb-9-390 (K)
Williams, Nimrod 1819 wb-7-323 (D)
Williams, Norris 1843 wb-3-691 (Ma)
Williams, Patience 1848 rb-l-126 (Mt)
Williams, Permenas 1821 wb-#70 (Mu)
Williams, Philimon 1796 wb-2-44 (D)
Williams, Philip 1842 wb-12-385* (D)
Williams, R. 1854 wb-i-207 (O)
Williams, R. J. 1856 wb-16-279 (Rb)
Williams, R. L. 1854 ib-H-194 (F)
Williams, R. N. 1857 wb-17-357 (D)
Williams, R. W. 1861 wb-17-176 (Rb)
Williams, Rachel 1851 r39-1-217 (Dk)
Williams, Richard 1838 wb-1-217 (Bo)
Williams, Richard J. 1856 wb-16-294 (Rb)
Williams, Richard N. 1834 as-a-248 (Di)
Williams, Richmond D. 1854 39-2-1 (Dk)
Williams, Robert 1786 wb-1-479 (Hw)
Williams, Robert 1826 wb-9-67 (D)
Williams, Robert 1841 wb-z-276 (Mu)
Williams, Robert 1846 wb-#150 (Wl)
Williams, Robert M. 1854 as-b-156 (Ms)
Williams, Roger S. 1845 as-a-78 (Ms)
Williams, Ruth 1849 wb-b-434 (Mu)
Williams, Sally 1827 wb-2-0 (Sm)
Williams, Sally 1837 wb-d-122 (St)
Williams, Samuel (Sr.) 1844 wb-#140 (Wl)

Williams, Samuel 1806 rb-2-12 (Ru)
Williams, Samuel 1826 wb-5-315 (Rb)
Williams, Samuel 1834 wb-5-381 (Wi)
Williams, Samuel 1840 abl-1-199 (T)
Williams, Samuel 1840 wb-a-85 (T)
Williams, Samuel 1840 wb-b-194 (Hd)
Williams, Samuel 1841 wb-11-87 (Rb)
Williams, Samuel 1842 wb-11-194 (Rb)
Williams, Samuel 1845 wb-#158 (Wl)
Williams, Samuel 1848 r39-1-73 (Dk)
Williams, Samuel C. 1849 wb-2-50 (Sh)
Williams, Samuel H. 1835 wb-x-329 (Mu)
Williams, Samuel H. 1850 wb-b-597 (Mu)
Williams, Sarah 1838 wb-1-172 (We)
Williams, Sarah 1847 wb-13-178 (Rb)
Williams, Sarah 1854 ib-1-271 (Wy)
Williams, Septimus 1845 rb-j-446 (Mt)
Williams, Sherod 1831 wb-1-99 (Fr)
Williams, Sidda 1849 wb-a-371 (F)
Williams, Silas sr. 1851 ib-1-223 (Cl)
Williams, Simon 1852 wb-15-427 (D)
Williams, Solomon 1838 wb-a-31 (F)
Williams, Solomon 1844 wb-f-274 (Hn)
Williams, Squire 1859 as-c-163 (Ms)
Williams, Susan Ann 1850 wb-g-346 (Hn)
Williams, Temperance 1861 wb-4-433 (La)
Williams, Thomas 1816 wb-7-5 (D)
Williams, Thomas 1825 wb-5-96 (Rb)
Williams, Thomas 1830 wb-b-15 (Wh)
Williams, Thomas 1835 wb-6-21 (Wi)
Williams, Thomas 1836 wb-x-406 (Mu)
Williams, Thomas 1843 wb-12-1 (Rb)
Williams, Thomas 1843 wb-12-42 (Rb)
Williams, Thomas 1844 wb-3-454 (Hy)
Williams, Thomas 1846 wb-4-68 (Hr)
Williams, Thomas 1849 rb-l-206 (Mt)
Williams, Thomas 1854 wb-d-223 (Wh)
Williams, Thomas 1855 ib-h-285 (F)
Williams, Thomas 1859 wb-4-327 (La)
Williams, Thomas 1859 wb-h-334 (Hn)
Williams, Thomas C. 1848 rb-l-153 (Mt)
Williams, Thomas H. 1851 wb-14-413 (Rb)
Williams, Thomas H. 1860 wb-1-99 (Dy)
Williams, Thomas Jefferson 1837 wb-#117 (Wl)
Williams, Thomas L. 1857 wb-12-320 (K)
Williams, Thomas S. 1851 wb-14-579 (D)
Williams, Thomas W. 1849 lr (Gi)
Williams, Tryphena 1851 wb-5-101 (Ma)
Williams, Tully 1820 wb-7-412 (D)
Williams, Vincent 1853 wb-15-326 (Rb)
Williams, Vincent 1853 wb-15-328 (Rb)

Williams, W. A. 1858 wb-a-53 (Ce)
Williams, W. T. 1858 as-c-514 (Di)
Williams, W. W. 1847 wb-a-316 (F)
Williams, W. W. 1852 wb-g-465 (Hn)
Williams, Washington 1845 wb-#149 (Wl)
Williams, Wiley 1839 wb-7-209 (Wi)
Williams, William 1813 rb-b-216 (Mt)
Williams, William 1815 wb-#29 (Mu)
Williams, William 1816 wb-3-191 (St)
Williams, William 1819 wb-2-239 (Je)
Williams, William 1824 wb-3-739 (Wi)
Williams, William 1824 wb-8-307 (D)
Williams, William 1828 wb-b-317 (St)
Williams, William 1838 wb-5-5 (Gr)
Williams, William 1840 wb-a-90 (Ms)
Williams, William 1842 lr (Sn)
Williams, William 1846 wb-c-222 (Wh)
Williams, William 1847 wb-f-447 (St)
Williams, William 1848 ib-1-12 (Wy)
Williams, William 1848 wb-1-341 (Li)
Williams, William 1849 wb-#163 (Wl)
Williams, William 1850 wb-a-91 (Dk)
Williams, William 1851 r39-1-211 (Dk)
Williams, William 1854 wb-12-56 (K)
Williams, William 1854 wb-n-416 (Mt)
Williams, William 1855 wb-2-110 (Li)
Williams, William 1858 wb-12-611 (Wi)
Williams, William 1858 wb-2-87# (Ge)
Williams, William 1858 wb-c-255 (L)
Williams, William B. 1844 wb-#143 (Wl)
Williams, William C. 1843 wb-f-3 (St)
Williams, William C. 1861 wb-17-258 (Rb)
Williams, William F. 1840 wb-5-95 (Gr)
Williams, William F. 1851 wb-3-128 (Gr)
Williams, William G. 1816 wb-#24 (Wl)
Williams, William G. 1856 wb-6-260 (Ma)
Williams, William H. 1824? wb-#85 (Mu)
Williams, William H. 1837 rb-g-490 (Mt)
Williams, William H. 1853 mr-2-492 (Be)
Williams, William H. 1858 wb-i-13 (St)
Williams, William L. 1837 wb-b-71 (Hd)
Williams, William P. 1846 wb-c-281 (G)
Williams, William P. 1852 wb-h-Sep (O)
Williams, William P. 1857 rb-o-344 (Mt)
Williams, William S. 1860 wb-3e-138 (Sh)
Williams, William jr. 1814 rb-b-69 (Mt)
Williams, William sr. 1822 wb-1-0 (Sm)
Williams, William sr. 1838 wb-1-317 (Gr)
Williams, William sr. 1842 as-a-85 (Ms)
Williams, Williamson 1854 wb-#113 (Wl)
Williams, Williamson 1860 wb-i-232 (St)

Williams, Willis 1837 wb-11-77 (D)
Williams, Willis 1840 wb-7-249 (Wi)
Williams, Willis L. 1844 wb-f-238 (Hn)
Williams, Wilson 1850 wb-b-97 (L)
Williams, Wilson 1853 wb-e-61 (G)
Williams, Wilson 1858 wb-17-489 (D)
Williams, Wilson 1858 wb-17-536 (D)
Williams, Wm. 1834 rb-9-165 (Ru)
Williams, Wright 1815 wb-A-79 (Li)
Williams, Wright 1847 wb-d-337 (Hd)
Williams, Zachariah 1847 wb-b-245 (We)
Williams, Zachariah 1847 wb-b-260 (We)
Williamson, Ann 1833 wb-1-124 (Fr)
Williamson, Anthony 1860 wb-7-69 (Ma)
Williamson, Ellen B. 1859 wb-b-78 (F)
Williamson, Frederick 1838 wb-a-40 (F)
Williamson, George sr. 1856 wb-6-296 (Ma)
Williamson, Green 1820 wb-#119 (Mu)
Williamson, Henry C. 1831 wb-5-3 (Wi)
Williamson, James 1834 wb-#104 (Wl)
Williamson, James 1852 wb-10-373 (Wi)
Williamson, James 1857 wb-17-189 (D)
Williamson, James 1857 wb-7-0 (Sm)
Williamson, Jas. 1802 wb-2-256 (D)
Williamson, Jesse 1855 wb-3e-1 (Sh)
Williamson, John 1826 rb-d-545 (Mt)
Williamson, John 1829 wb-#83 (Wl)
Williamson, John 1834 wb-10-289 (D)
Williamson, John A. 1835 wb-2-84 (Ma)
Williamson, John A. 1856 wb-6-255 (Ma)
Williamson, John G. 1831 wb-5-49 (Wi)
Williamson, John S. 1825 rb-d-450 (Mt)
Williamson, John S. 1834 rb-f-572 (Mt)
Williamson, John T. (S?) 1829 rb-e-470 (Mt)
Williamson, Littleton 1835 rb-9-269 (Ru)
Williamson, Martha 1828 wb-4-358 (Wi)
Williamson, Mary 1854 as-b-168 (Ms)
Williamson, Patsey H. 1854 wb-f-47 (Mu)
Williamson, Richard 1852 wb-10-263 (Wi)
Williamson, Robert 1820 wb-3-197 (Wi)
Williamson, Russel M. 1845 wb-a2-182 (Mu)
Williamson, Samuel M. 1847 wb-a-299 (F)
Williamson, Silas 1820? wb-#118 (Mu)
Williamson, Thomas 1816 wb-2-252 (Wi)
Williamson, Thomas 1825 wb-1-50 (Ma)
Williamson, Thomas 1834 wb-#104 (Wl)
Williamson, Thomas 1836 wb-2-46# (Ge)
Williamson, W. L. 1847 wb-a-151 (Cr)
Williamson, William H. 1829 wb-#189 (Mu)
Williard, George 1838 wb-1-2 (Su)
Williard, Z. 1853 ib-h-214 (F)

Willie, J. K. 1848 as-b-444 (Di)
Willie, Mary 1842 wb-3-252 (Hy)
Willie, William 1843 as-b-199 (Di)
Williford, Britain 1829 lr (Gi)
Williford, William 1816 rb-4-4 (Ru)
Williford, Willie 1854 wb-g-605 (Hn)
Williford, Willis 1846 rb-13-742 (Ru)
Williford, Willis 1846 wb-d-21 (G)
Willingham, James 1861 wb-e-156 (Hy)
Willingham, Margery E. 1844 wb-b-79 (We)
Willingham, William 1844 wb-b-85 (We)
Willis, Caleb 1827 lr (Sn)
Willis, Charles T. 1837 abl-1-46 (T)
Willis, Daniel S. 1858 lr (Sn)
Willis, David T. 1848 wb#19 (Gu)
Willis, Davis 1839 as-a-17 (Ms)
Willis, Drucilla 1822 wb-3-360 (Rb)
Willis, Edward 1834 wb-#103 (Wl)
Willis, Elijah 1857 wb-16-380 (Rb)
Willis, Elisha 1828 rb-e-273 (Mt)
Willis, Francis 1799 lr (Sn)
Willis, Francis H. 1834 wb-x-194 (Mu)
Willis, G. W. 1849 wb-14-190 (Rb)
Willis, George 1846 wb-8-494 (Wi)
Willis, Henton 1859 wb-f-309 (G)
Willis, James 1844 wb-#157 (Wl)
Willis, James A. 1837 wb-d-174* (Hn)
Willis, James M. 1841 wb-#135 (Wl)
Willis, John 1828 wb-3-0 (Sm)
Willis, John 1837 wb-3-0 (Sm)
Willis, John M. 1861 wb-i-345 (St)
Willis, John S. 1854 ib-2-295 (Cl)
Willis, Joseph 1843 wb-0-37 (Cf)
Willis, Joseph 1860 wb-a-174 (Ce)
Willis, Judith H. 1858 wb-16-619 (Rb)
Willis, Larkin 1859 wb-1-493 (Hw)
Willis, Martha 1850 wb-a-239 (Ms)
Willis, Mary 1858 wb-16-681 (Rb)
Willis, Meshac 1818 wb-#119 (Mu)
Willis, Nancy B. 1840 wb-z-94 (Mu)
Willis, Nancy L. 1853 lr (Sn)
Willis, Nathaniel 1846 wb-a2-455 (Mu)
Willis, Phinneus 1820 wb-3-114 (Rb)
Willis, Plummer 1819 wb-3-189 (Rb)
Willis, Sallie 1855 rb-o-3 (Mt)
Willis, Samuel 1814 wb-#29 (Mu)
Willis, Sarah 1850 wb#20 (Gu)
Willis, Sarrah E. (Miss) 1856 rb-o-25 (Mt)
Willis, Thomas 1847 as-a-138 (Ms)
Willis, William 1841 wb-#134 (Wl)
Willis, William 1858 wb-#128 (Wl)

Willis, William W. 1830 wb-#221 (Mu)
Willis, Wilson 1845 wb-12-541 (Rb)
Willis, Woodson 1846 5-3-185 (Cl)
Williss, William 1823 wb-a-196 (Ro)
Willitt, Thomas G. 1834 wb-#189 (Mc)
Willouby, Solomon 1850 wb-5-1 (Hr)
Willoughby, Andrew 1833 wb-c-55 (Hn)
Willoughby, Ewing 1855 wb-5-56 (Hr)
Willoughby, Sarah 1831 eb-1-268 (C)
Willoughby, Vinson 1850 wb-4-579* (Hr)
Willoughby, Vinson 1850 wb-4-582 (Hr)
Willoughby, William 1852 wb-2-79# (Ge)
Wills, Benjamin D. 1819 rb-c-203 (Mt)
Wills, Benjn. 1811 wb-1-398 (Rb)
Wills, David 1822 wb-8-126 (D)
Wills, David 1853 wb-11-433 (K)
Wills, George 1798 wb-1-32 (Rb)
Wills, George 1851 rb-15-616 (Ru)
Wills, John L. 1851 wb-m-274 (Mt)
Wills, Lewis 1852 wb-1-102 (Jo)
Wills, Lewis 1855 wb-1-99 (Jo)
Wills, Macy 1860 rb-20-344 (Ru)
Wills, Polly 1840 wb-3-0 (Sm)
Wills, Samuel 1849 wb-b-479 (Mu)
Wills, Thomas 1834 wb-x-175 (Mu)
Wills, Thomas sr. 1821 Wb-3-259 (Wi)
Wills, William 1845 wb-12-372 (Rb)
Willson, Aaron 1808 wb-4-18 (D)
Willson, Abram 1836 wb-3-374 (Je)
Willson, David 1847 5-3-213 (Cl)
Willson, David 1849 ib-1-144 (Cl)
Willson, James 1836 wb-a-310 (R)
Willson, John P. 1843 wb-a-102 (F)
Willson, Minus P. 1852 wb-g-410 (Hn)
Willson, Nancy 1854 rb-17-272 (Ru)
Willson, Nancy 1855 wb-e-263 (G)
Willson, Polly 1825 rb-d-420 (Mt)
Willson, Sarah 1847 wb-g-204 (Hn)
Willson, William 1848 wb-9-449 (K)
Willson, William A. 1828 wb-#168 (Mu)
Willson, William A. 1847 wb-g-205 (Hn)
Willson, William H. 1840 wb-5-115 (Gr)
Willson, William L. 1837 wb-a-63 (T)
Willum, A. 1855 wb-3-302 (La)
Willum, Ananias 1855 wb-3-307 (La)
Willy, Willis 1852 wb-a-241 (Di)
Wilmoth, Durham 1860 39-2-392 (Dk)
Wilmoth, John 1859 39-2-298 (Dk)
Wilsford, James 1850 wb-2-100 (La)
Wilson, A. B. 1850 mr-2-372 (Be)
Wilson, A. L. 1866 wb-#14 (Mo)

Wilson, Abraham 1838 eb-1-394 (C)
Wilson, Alexander 1823 wb-1-147 (Bo)
Wilson, Alexander 1834 wb-x-251 (Mu)
Wilson, Andrew 1827 wb-#72 (Wl)
Wilson, Andrew 1849 wb-14-144 (Rb)
Wilson, Asa 1831 wb-a-115 (R)
Wilson, Benjamin 1856 wb-e-409 (G)
Wilson, Benjamin 1860 wb-1-139 (Jo)
Wilson, Benjamine 1819 rb-c-76 (Mt)
Wilson, Boon 1860 wb-2-300 (Li)
Wilson, Charles 1824 wb-#144 (Mu)
Wilson, Charlotte M. 1853 wb-g-512 (Hn)
Wilson, Claiborn 1842 wb-3-0 (Sm)
Wilson, Cornelius 1824 wb-#86 (Mu)
Wilson, Daniel 1817 wb-2-192 (Je)
Wilson, Daniel 1821 wb-#121 (Mu)
Wilson, David 1803 wb-1-77 (Sn)
Wilson, David 1815 eb-1-45 (C)
Wilson, David 1829 wb-#27 (Wa)
Wilson, David 1839 abl-1-120 (T)
Wilson, David 1852 wb-2-99 (Me)
Wilson, David 1861 wb-a-303 (T)
Wilson, David C. 1854 wb-xx-324 (St)
Wilson, Dorothy T. 1852 wb-m-580 (Mt)
Wilson, Elijah 1847 wb-7-0 (Sm)
Wilson, Elizabeth 1831 wb-#92 (Wl)
Wilson, Elizabeth 1859 wb-18-65 (D)
Wilson, Ephraim 1816 wb-2-38# (Ge)
Wilson, Ewing 1827 wb-#58 (Wl)
Wilson, George 1850 wb-14-481 (D)
Wilson, Green 1853 wb-a-323 (Ms)
Wilson, Green 1855 as-b-180 (Ms)
Wilson, Hamilton 1847 rb-k-602 (Mt)
Wilson, Hartwell 1861 wb-17-256 (Rb)
Wilson, Hartwell 1861 wb-17-269 (Rb)
Wilson, Hartwell B. 1841 wb-c-1 (Wh)
Wilson, Henrietta 1828 wb-4-300 (Wi)
Wilson, Henry 1852 wb-4-382 (Mu)
Wilson, Henry T. 1862 wb-h-557 (Hn)
Wilson, Hiram 1850 as-b-9 (Ms)
Wilson, Hiram 1853 ib-1-316 (Ca)
Wilson, Hiram 1854 wb-a-333 (Ms)
Wilson, Isaac 1861 wb-5-112 (Hr)
Wilson, Isaac B. 1861 wb-13-425 (Wi)
Wilson, Isreal 1855 wb-12-72 (K)
Wilson, J. J. 1854 ib-H-179 (F)
Wilson, J. S. 1853 as-b-125 (Ms)
Wilson, James 1795 wb-1-41 (K)
Wilson, James 1811 wb-4-143 (D)
Wilson, James 1811 wb-4-154 (D)
Wilson, James 1817 rb-4-87 (Ru)

Wilson, James 1819 wb-3-7 (Rb)
Wilson, James 1821 rb-c-542 (Mt)
Wilson, James 1826 wb-4-137 (Wi)
Wilson, James 1830 as-a-202 (Di)
Wilson, James 1831 rb-f-203 (Mt)
Wilson, James 1834 wb-#114 (Wl)
Wilson, James 1836 wb-1-182 (W)
Wilson, James 1840 wb-2-66 (Hy)
Wilson, James 1841 wb-#189 (Mc)
Wilson, James 1846 as-a-84 (Ms)
Wilson, James 1854 wb-#189 (Mc)
Wilson, James 1856 wb-b-23 (F)
Wilson, James 1858 wb-f-139 (G)
Wilson, James 1858 wb-h-480 (St)
Wilson, James 1859 rb-p-296 (Mt)
Wilson, James 1860 wb-k-204 (O)
Wilson, James A. 1861 wb-2-342 (Li)
Wilson, James C. 1818 lr (Sn)
Wilson, James C. 1861 wb-i-332 (St)
Wilson, James H. 1847 rb-14-5 (Ru)
Wilson, James M. 1856 wb-3e-31 (Sh)
Wilson, James R. 1854 ib-h-30 (F)
Wilson, James W. 1851 wb-#175 (Wl)
Wilson, James sr. 1838 wb-6-516 (Wi)
Wilson, Jane 1838 wb-1-45 (Sh)
Wilson, Jane 1853 wb-11-35 (Wi)
Wilson, Jenney (Jane) 1832 wb-a-308 (F)
Wilson, John 1806 lw (Ct)
Wilson, John 1809 ib-1-268 (Ge)
Wilson, John 1814 rb-2-272 (Ru)
Wilson, John 1815 wb-2-37# (Ge)
Wilson, John 1819 rb-c-180 (Mt)
Wilson, John 1821 wb-#190 (Mc)
Wilson, John 1821 wb-7-494 (D)
Wilson, John 1822 wb-3-388 (Rb)
Wilson, John 1827 wb-#155 (Mu)
Wilson, John 1827 wb-4-174 (Wi)
Wilson, John 1833 wb-1-302 (Hr)
Wilson, John 1834 wb-1-120 (Hy)
Wilson, John 1836 lr (Sn)
Wilson, John 1839 wb-a-46 (Ms)
Wilson, John 1846 wb-#150 (Wl)
Wilson, John 1853 wb-11-1 (Wi)
Wilson, John 1854 wb-0-128 (Cf)
Wilson, John 1855 wb-1-95 (Jo)
Wilson, John 1860 wb-i-224 (St)
Wilson, John 1861 wb-f-471 (Ro)
Wilson, John B. 1853 wb-a-425 (F)
Wilson, John C. 1844 wb-4-217 (Ma)
Wilson, John H. 1838 wb-a-3 (Ms)
Wilson, John L. 1851 wb-9-717 (Wi)

Wilson, John M. 1851 wb-2-85 (Sh)
Wilson, John R. 1854 wb-16-429 (D)
Wilson, John R. 1856 wb-#121 (Wl)
Wilson, John S. 1848 wb-9-206 (Wi)
Wilson, John S. 1859 wb-13-301 (Wi)
Wilson, John W. 1845 148-1-104 (Ge)
Wilson, John W. 1858 wb-1-22 (Br)
Wilson, Jonathan 1818 wb-2-203 (Je)
Wilson, Jonathan 1857 lr (Sn)
Wilson, Joseph 1806 wb-#4 (Wl)
Wilson, Joseph 1823 wb-3-650 (Wi)
Wilson, Joseph 1833 lr (Sn)
Wilson, Joseph 1834 wb-1-161 (Bo)
Wilson, Joseph 1844 5-3-5 (Cl)
Wilson, Joseph 1856 wb-e-409 (G)
Wilson, Joseph H. B. 1855 wb-g-628 (Hn)
Wilson, Josiah 1851 wb-a-266 (Ms)
Wilson, Josiah 1857 wb-12-322 (Wi)
Wilson, Josiah P. 1856 wb-b-23 (F)
Wilson, Leander 1851 wb-#190 (Mc)
Wilson, Lewis D. 1848 wb-2-27 (Sh)
Wilson, Littleberry R. 1859 wb-e-212 (Wh)
Wilson, Lucinda 1843 wb-3-659 (Ma)
Wilson, Lucinda C. 1844 wb-4-174 (Ma)
Wilson, Lucy E. 1858 rb-o-585 (Mt)
Wilson, M. P. 1852 wb-g-468 (Hn)
Wilson, M. S. 1860 wb-h-419 (Hn)
Wilson, Margaret 1828 wb-4-321 (Wi)
Wilson, Margaret R. 1860 wb-a-364 (Cr)
Wilson, Margret 1836 wb-a-41 (T)
Wilson, Mariah 1852 as-b-56 (Ms)
Wilson, Mark 1840 wb-7-223 (Wi)
Wilson, Martha 1820 rb-c-329 (Mt)
Wilson, Martha 1821 wb-#37 (Wl)
Wilson, Martha 1838 wb-a-72 (T)
Wilson, Mary 1833 wb-1-95 (Li)
Wilson, Mary 1836 wb-1-147 (Fr)
Wilson, Mary 1851 lr (Sn)
Wilson, Mary Ann 1857 wb-6-419 (Ma)
Wilson, Matthew 1853 wb-e-75 (G)
Wilson, Micheal 1860 wb-f-365 (Ro)
Wilson, Micheal 1861 wb-f-447 (Ro)
Wilson, Minas N. 1850 as-b-32 (Ms)
Wilson, Moses 1852 as-b-95 (Ms)
Wilson, Moses 1853 ib-1-222 (Wy)
Wilson, N. J. 1856 as-b-238 (Ms)
Wilson, Philip 1850 wb-e-212 (Ro)
Wilson, R. P. 1860 wb-17-57 (Rb)
Wilson, R. P. 1861 wb-17-255 (Rb)
Wilson, Rachael 1852 wb-1-76 (Jo)
Wilson, Rebecca 1841 wb-4-32 (Je)

Wilson, Richard 1822 wb-1-0 (Sm)
Wilson, Robert 1819 wb-3-95 (Wi)
Wilson, Robert 1822 wb-1-163 (Bo)
Wilson, Robert 1832 wb-1-89 (Li)
Wilson, Robert 1835 wb-6-79 (Wi)
Wilson, Robert 1840 as-a-25 (Ms)
Wilson, Robert 1841 abl-1-228* (T)
Wilson, Robert 1841 wb-1-197 (Li)
Wilson, Robert 1843 wb-3-12 (Sn)
Wilson, Robert 1844 wb-a2-117 (Mu)
Wilson, Robert 1851 rb-4-265 (Mu)
Wilson, Robert 1860 wb-18-234 (D)
Wilson, Robert A. 1829 wb-3-0 (Sm)
Wilson, Robert B. 1852 wb-h-May (O)
Wilson, Robert W. 1860 wb-7-73 (Ma)
Wilson, Robt. 1840 wb-3-273 (Ma)
Wilson, Saml. 1831 rb-8-192 (Ru)
Wilson, Saml. J. 1836 rb-9-281 (Ru)
Wilson, Saml. S. 1837 rb-10-42 (Ru)
Wilson, Samuel 1812 wb-#50 (Wl)
Wilson, Samuel 1812 wb-1-305 (Wi)
Wilson, Samuel 1812 wb-2-18 (Wi)
Wilson, Samuel 1814 lr (Sn)
Wilson, Samuel 1822 wb-3-309 (Wi)
Wilson, Samuel 1827 lw (Ct)
Wilson, Samuel 1853 wb-#190 (Mc)
Wilson, Samuel 1853 wb-e-73 (G)
Wilson, Samuel 1854 wb-h-56 (St)
Wilson, Samuel 1858 rb-o-565 (Mt)
Wilson, Samuel D. 1855 wb-11-582 (Wi)
Wilson, Samuel J. 1851 wb-10-325 (Wi)
Wilson, Samuel S. 1854 wb-11-134 (Wi)
Wilson, Sandford 1814 rb-b-183 (Mt)
Wilson, Sanford 1814 rb-b-176 (Mt)
Wilson, Sanford 1848 rb-k-803 (Mt)
Wilson, Sarah 1857 wb-#191 (Mc)
Wilson, Tapley 1845 wb-1-22 (Jo)
Wilson, Thomas 1811 wb-4-162 (D)
Wilson, Thomas 1812 wb-4-174 (D)
Wilson, Thomas 1816 wb-A-147 (Li)
Wilson, Thomas 1818 wb-2-377 (Wi)
Wilson, Thomas 1823 wb-a-36 (Hn)
Wilson, Thomas 1825 wb-#55 (Wl)
Wilson, Thomas 1828 wb-4-310 (Wi)
Wilson, Thomas 1839 wb-1A-248 (A)
Wilson, Thomas 1851 wb-1-294 (Fr)
Wilson, Thomas 1852 rb-16-341 (Ru)
Wilson, Thomas 1852 wb-10-385 (Wi)
Wilson, Thomas 1853 wb-16-185 (D)
Wilson, Thomas 1856 wb-b-27 (Ms)
Wilson, Thomas 1860 wb-h-487 (Hn)

Wilson, Thomas B. 1859 wb-2-289 (Li)
Wilson, Thomas D. 1846 wb-f-96 (O)
Wilson, Thomas J. 1860 wb-i-238 (St)
Wilson, Violet M. 1853 as-b-78 (Ms)
Wilson, W. H. 1859 rb-19-567 (Ru)
Wilson, William 1815 wb-1-0 (Sm)
Wilson, William 1825 wb-a-204 (Wh)
Wilson, William 1840 5-2-155 (Cl)
Wilson, William 1840 wb-1-353 (W)
Wilson, William 1852 wb-1-73 (Jo)
Wilson, William 1854 ib-2-138 (Cl)
Wilson, William 1854 ib-h-71 (F)
Wilson, William 1858 wb#5 (Gu)
Wilson, William 1858 wb-a-322* (Cr)
Wilson? William A. 1856? ib-2-282 (Cl)
Wilson, William B. 1851 wb-0-98 (Cf)
Wilson, William C. 1828 wb-a-54 (R)
Wilson, William C. 1841 wb-12-129* (D)
Wilson, William D. 1853 wb-xx-260 (St)
Wilson, William F. 1859 wb-17-622 (D)
Wilson, William H. 1822 wb-#87 (Mu)
Wilson, William H. 1842 abl-1-311 (T)
Wilson, William J. 1853 ib-1-273 (Wy)
Wilson, William L. 1837 abl-1-32 (T)
Wilson, William L. 1849 abl-1-147 (T)
Wilson, William M. 1837 wb-a-183 (O)
Wilson, William P. 1848 wb-d-139 (G)
Wilson, Wm. H. 1859 rb-20-38 (Ru)
Wilson, Z. 1858 wb-h-293 (Hn)
Wilson, Zaccheus 1842 wb-7-588 (Wi)
Wilson, Zaccheus 1856 wb-h-300 (Hn)
Wimberley, Joseph 1858 wb-16-653 (Rb)
Wimberly, George S. 1857 rb-o-448 (Mt)
Wimberly, Henry 1833 wb-c-274 (St)
Wimberly, James 1842 wb-e-206 (St)
Wimberly, Joseph 1812 wb-1-433 (Rb)
Wimberly, Levi 1846 wb-f-374 (St)
Wimberly, Levi 1846 wb-f-381 (St)
Wimberly, Lewis 1817 wb-1-0 (Sm)
Wimberly, Robert H. 1857 rb-o-444 (Mt)
Wimberly, Sarah 1827 wb-5-444 (Rb)
Wimberly, William 1833 wb-c-86 (Hn)
Wimpee, Tyre 1818 wb-2-393 (Wi)
Winborn, Elihu 1843 wb-d-64 (Hd)
Winburne, Alfred W. 1830 wb-1-176 (Hr)
Winbush, Watson 1850 wb-g-346 (Hn)
Wincher, Rebecca Fisher 1855 wb-#191 (Mc)
Winchester, James 1826 lr (Sn)
Winchester, Lucy L. 1861 wb-3e-169 (Sh)
Winchester, M. B. 1857 wb-3e-43 (Sh)
Winchester, Stephen 1815 wb-1-209 (Sn)

Winder, James 1844 wb-#191 (Mc)
Winder, Nat 1851 wb-#191 (Mc)
Windham, Reuben 1795 wb-1-480 (Hw)
Windle, Susannah 1816 wb-4-465 (D)
Windrow, Henry 1826 rb-6-257 (Ru)
Windrow, Henry 1837 rb-9-424 (Ru)
Windrow, Henry L. 1855 wb-c-42 (L)
Windrow, Richard 1806 wb-1-24 (Wi)
Windsor, Jonathan 1837 wb-b-73 (Hd)
Windsor, _____ 1846 wb-d-229 (Hd)
Winegar, Andrew 1810 wb-1-481 (Hw)
Winegar, Andrew 1835 wb-1-489 (Hw)
Wineheart, John 1833 wb-3-271 (Je)
Winfield, Grafton 1859 wb-16-771 (Rb)
Winfield, J. E. 1852 wb-15-216 (Rb)
Winfield, Joel T. 1844 wb-a-223 (F)
Winfield, John G. 1838 wb-11-473 (D)
Winfield, Joseph 1852 wb-15-173 (Rb)
Winfield, Joseph 1856 wb-16-180 (Rb)
Winfield, W. S. 1855 ib-h-414 (F)
Winfield, William 1854 ib-H-180 (F)
Winford, Benjamin 1826 wb-#65 (Wl)
Winford, Sophia 1852 wb-1-302 (Fr)
Winford, William W. 1841 wb-#133 (Wl)
Winfree, Wilson 1827 wb-3-0 (Sm)
Winfrey, John A. 1856 wb-b-25 (F)
Winfrey, John S. 1838 wb-11-190 (D)
Winfrey, John T. 1850 wb-7-0 (Sm)
Wingate, Isaac 1855 wb-1-49 (Dy)
Wingfield, Joseph 1838 wb-y-156 (Mu)
Wingfield, Lucy 1856 wb-f-88 (Mu)
Wingo, Joseph A. 1861 wb-a-380 (Cr)
Wingo, Sarah (Miss) 1836 rb-9-313 (Ru)
Winkle, John 1861 wb-#65 (Wa)
Winkler, Ephraim 1825 wb-1-0 (Sm)
Winkler, Jerry C. 1852 wb-1-293 (Fr)
Winn, Banister 1842 wb-z-338 (Mu)
Winn, Daniel 1846 wb-e-294 (O)
Winn, Henry 1831 wb-8-7 (Rb)
Winn, John 1814 rb-2-298 (Ru)
Winn, John 1828 wb-#75 (Wl)
Winn, Orpha 1837 wb-10-34 (Rb)
Winn, P. P. 1843 wb-z-512 (Mu)
Winn, Peter 1830 wb-7-287 (Rb)
Winn, Philip P. 1843 wb-z-519 (Mu)
Winn, Richard (General) 1819 wb-#119 (Mu)
Winn, Richard 1809 wb-4-46 (D)
Winn, Richard 1816 wb-7-16 (D)
Winn, Richard 1824 wb-#74 (Mu)
Winn, Willis Hunley 1836 wb-a-47 (T)
Winn, Woodson 1852 lr (Sn)

Winnard, William 1855 39-2-84 (Dk)
Winns, William 1817 wb-#39 (Mu)
Winset, Anias 1838 wb-6-464 (Wi)
Winset, John 1814 wb-#13 (Wl)
Winsett, Amos 1836 wb-6-197 (Wi)
Winsett, Robert 1812 wb-1-325 (Wi)
Winsett, Robert 1823 wb-3-649 (Wi)
Winsett, William 1820 wb-3-164 (Wi)
Winslow, Joseph 1828 mr (Gi)
Winslow, Joseph 1834 wb-b-148 (Hd)
Winstead, Charles 1855 wb-h-472 (Hu)
Winstead, Charles sr. 1855 wb-h-430 (Hu)
Winstead, Francis 1842 wb-1-493 (Hw)
Winstead, John 1822 wb-3-585 (Wi)
Winstead, Lucy Ann 1836 wb-6-134 (Wi)
Winstead, Mary 1837 wb-6-377 (Wi)
Winstead, Samuel 1851 wb-10-49 (Wi)
Winstead, William 1831 wb-5-44 (Wi)
Winstead, William 1843 wb-8-121 (Wi)
Winston, Ann 1838 wb-#130 (Wl)
Winston, Anthony 1828 wb-#74 (Wl)
Winston, Candace 1857 wb-b-417 (We)
Winston, David 1848 wb-b-282 (We)
Winston, Dorothea S. 1854 wb-2-168 (Sh)
Winston, Francis 1841 wb-11-205 (Ru)
Winston, J. J. 1849 wb-#169 (Wl)
Winston, Joseph 1844 rb-j-230 (Mt)
Winston, Mary 1841 wb-b-34 (We)
Winston, Nathaniel 1856 rb-17-788 (Ru)
Winston, Peter M. 1847 wb-14-8 (D)
Winston, Samuel W. 1841 wb-#133 (Wl)
Winston, Sarah 1841 wb-#135 (Wl)
Winston, Spilsby C. 1837 wb-2-217 (Sn)
Winston, Thomas 1846 wb-b-193 (We)
Winston, Thos. J. 1844 wb-a-119 (F)
Winston, William L. 1852 wb-a-157 (T)
Winston, William N. 1854 wb-5-152 (Ma)
Winter, Ambrose V. 1830 wb-#87 (Wl)
Winter, Marth 1849 wb-#164 (Wl)
Winter, Robert 1853 wb-15-478 (D)
Winter, Samuel 1833 wb-1-148 (Bo)
Winters, A. V. 1843? wb-#142 (Wl)
Winters, Caleb 1843 wb-11-364 (Rb)
Winters, Elisha 1818 wb-#29 (Wl)
Winters, Emily 1857 wb-16-552 (Rb)
Winters, George 1855 wb-n-495 (Mt)
Winters, Isaac 1860 wb-17-22 (Rb)
Winters, John 1854 wb-#113 (Wl)
Winters, Josiah C. 1854 wb-15-575 (Rb)
Winters, Lewis 1837 wb-d-118 (St)
Winters, Mary H. 1851 wb-14-519 (Rb)

Winters, Moses 1798 wb-1-26 (Rb)
Winters, Sallie 1856 wb-16-275 (Rb)
Winters, ____ 1843 wb-#141 (Wl)
Wintin, James 1849 wb-e-177 (Ro)
Wintin, John 1846 wb-d-232 (Ro)
Winton, George 1839 wb-1A-216 (A)
Winton, James 1834 wb-1-69 (W)
Winton, Stephen 1858 wb-2-420 (Me)
Wirick, John 1860 wb-f-326 (Ro)
Wirt, Henry 1847 wb-a-326 (F)
Wisdom, Elizabeth 1851 wb-d-4 (Wh)
Wisdom, John M. 1858 rb-o-779 (Mt)
Wisdom, Larkin 1846 wb-c-242 (Wh)
Wisdom, Thomas 1818 wb-a-115 (Wh)
Wisdom, William 1842 wb-c-65 (Wh)
Wisdom, William H. 1859 wb-4-214 (La)
Wise, Henry 1846 wb-1-142 (Sh)
Wise, James 1852 wb-2-41 (Li)
Wisecarver, John 1844 wb-2-61# (Ge)
Wisecarver, Samuel 1859 wb-2-101# (Ge)
Wiseman, James 1854 wb-a-218 (T)
Wiseman, Jane 1855 mr-2-645 (Be)
Wiseman, John 1861 wb-1-382 (Be)
Wiseman, John B. 1841 wb-#134 (Wl)
Wiseman, Samuel 1852 mr-2-453 (Be)
Wiseman, Tho. 1847 as-b-376 (Di)
Wiseman, William D. 1848 mr-2-297 (Be)
Wisener, James 1856 wb-12-221 (Wi)
Wisenor, Henry 1826 wb-4-114 (Wi)
Wisenor, Henry 1837 wb-6-359 (Wi)
Wisner, Amanda N. 1849 as-a-186 (Ms)
Wisner, Martin 1802 wb-2-224 (D)
Witcher, Daniel 1815 wb-1-0 (Sm)
Witherington, Joseph 1841 wb-e-205 (Hn)
Witherington, William 1815 wb-2-149 (Wi)
Withers, John 1816 wb-1-244 (Sn)
Withers, Martha 1838 wb-b-249 (G)
Withers, Thomas 1794 lr (Sn)
Witherspoon, Alexander 1826 wb-#64 (Wl)
Witherspoon, Elizabeth A. 1853 wb-f-17 (Mu)
Witherspoon, Enos S. 1850 wb-A-71 (Ca)
Witherspoon, Franklin 1853 ib-1-275 (Wy)
Witherspoon, James 1812 wb-1-207 (Bo)
Witherspoon, John 1841 rb-12-7 (Ru)
Witherspoon, Sarah 1860 wb-f-191 (Mu)
Witherspoon, Wesley 1856 wb-f-87 (Mu)
Witherspoon, Winfrey 1852 rb-16-191 (Ru)
Withington, James 1855 wb-e-390 (G)
Wits, Sary 1859 39-2-305 (Dk)
Witt, Abner 1852 r39-1-237 (Dk)
Witt, Betsy 1812 wb-2-11 (K)

Witt, Caleb 1826 wb-2-562 (Je)
Witt, Charles 1796 wb-1-56 (K)
Witt, Elijah 1806 wb-1-309 (Je)
Witt, George 1815 wb-2-206 (K)
Witt, George 1849 wb-4-74 (Je)
Witt, George C. 1814 wb-A-66 (Li)
Witt, George R. 1849 wb-a-347 (F)
Witt, James 1853 wb-11-340 (K)
Witt, Jeremiah T. 1843 wb-c-115 (Wh)
Witt, John 1825 wb-4-95 (K)
Witt, John 1857 wb-e-106 (Wh)
Witt, John 1857 wb-e-133 (Wh)
Witt, Joseph 1820 wb-2-217 (Je)
Witt, Joseph 1842 wb-1-63 (Me)
Witt, Mills 1833 wb-10-161 (D)
Witt, Nathaniel 1826 wb-#191 (Mc)
Witt, Sally 1837 wb-#191 (Mc)
Witt, Sampson 1858 wb-e-209 (Wh)
Witt, Sampson 1859 wb-e-271 (Wh)
Witten, John 1840 wb-1-36 (Me)
Witten, John W. 1841 wb-1-52 (Me)
Woehrle, Jacob C. 1853 wb-16-87 (D)
Woerhrle, J. C. 1852 wb-15-222 (D)
Wofford, Jesse 1816 wb-3-156 (St)
Wofford, John 1843 wb-f-99 (St)
Wofford, William 1844 wb-f-302 (Hn)
Wofford, William 1858 wb-2-249 (Li)
Wolaver, Philip 1857 149-1-58 (Ge)
Woldridge, Thomas E. 1839 wb-7-215 (Wi)
Wolf, Elizabeth 1857 wb-17-258 (D)
Wolf, George 1815 wb-A-76 (Li)
Wolf, George 1849 wb-10-171 (K)
Wolf, John 1856 wb-#11 (Mo)
Wolf, Leroy 1836 wb-1-209 (W)
Wolf, Levi 1838 wb-1-315 (W)
Wolf, Moses 1851 33-3-348 (Gr)
Wolf, Phillip P. 1837 wb-11-1 (D)
Wolfe, Charles 1819 wb-1-482 (Hw)
Wolfe, Elizabeth 1859 wb-13-182 (Wi)
Wolfe, George Sr. 1839 wb-1-491 (Hw)
Wolfe, Samuel 1848 wb-14-242 (D)
Wolfe, William 1861 wb-13-471 (Wi)
Wolfenbarger, Joseph 1855 wb-3-256 (Gr)
Wolfenbarger, Rebecca 1854 wb-3-207 (Gr)
Wolfenbarger, Tandy 1847 wb-5-489 (Gr)
Wolff, John 1854 wb-#192 (Mc)
Wolff, Mary E. 1842 wb-#192 (Mc)
Wolfinbarger, Peter 1834 wb-5-269 (K)
Wollard, John 1854 wb-#111 (Wl)
Wolsey, Feethias 1835 wb-b-267 (Ro)
Womack, Abner 1856 wb-3-279 (W)

Womack, Richard 1839 wb-#126 (Wl)
Womack, William H. 1831? wb-1-44 (Hy)
Womble, Doctor W. 1842 wb-a-99 (F)
Wommack, Richard 1862 wb-#137 (Wl)
Wommack, Thomas 1862 wb-#135 (Wl)
Wood, Alexander 1858 wb-a-272 (T)
Wood, Allen 1848 wb-9-148 (Wi)
Wood, Ann 1853 rb-16-465 (Ru)
Wood, Archer S. 1852 wb-#178 (Wl)
Wood, B. F. 1858 ib-1-555 (Ca)
Wood, Bartholomew 1827 wb-1-13 (W)
Wood, Charles 1841 wb-a-63 (F)
Wood, Christopher 1827 wb-4-256 (Wi)
Wood, Christopher C. 1860 wb-1-326 (Be)
Wood, Curtis 1847 wb-1-441 (La)
Wood, D. W. 1842 wb-2-400 (Hr)
Wood, Daniel 1805 wb-1-180 (K)
Wood, David F. 1845 wb-#147 (Wl)
Wood, Eleanor 1842 wb-a-95 (L)
Wood, Elijah 1856 wb-1-61 (Be)
Wood, Elizabeth 1852 rb-16-237 (Ru)
Wood, Elizabeth 1858 wb-12-555 (Wi)
Wood, Elizabeth B. 1860 wb-13-265 (Wi)
Wood, Elizabeth W. 1857 wb-f-23 (G)
Wood, Ephraim 1851 wb-10-55 (Wi)
Wood, Euphemia 1853 wb-10-595 (Wi)
Wood, Francis M. 1843 wb-3-178 (Hy)
Wood, George 1842 wb-c-82 (G)
Wood, George 1857 wb-a-248 (V)
Wood, George 1860 rb-20-407 (Ru)
Wood, George W. 1859 rb-20-239 (Ru)
Wood, George sr. 1854 wb-a-146 (V)
Wood, Harrison 1847 wb-1-157 (Me)
Wood, Isum 1839 wb-10-265 (Rb)
Wood, James 1823 wb-1-0 (Sm)
Wood, James 1832 wb-3-198 (Je)
Wood, James 1840 wb-2-147 (Hy)
Wood, James 1842 wb-1-436 (W)
Wood, James 1845 rb-j-393 (Mt)
Wood, James 1845 wb-#149 (Wl)
Wood, James 1853 wb-#108 (Wl)
Wood, James 1853 wb-5-222 (Je)
Wood, James B. 1860 rb-p-446 (Mt)
Wood, Jesse 1835 rb-9-259 (Ru)
Wood, John 1821 Wb-3-264 (Wi)
Wood, John 1827 rb-8-53 (Ru)
Wood, John 1832 wb-3-0 (Sm)
Wood, John 1832 wb-a-157 (R)
Wood, John 1836 wb-2-204 (Sn)
Wood, John 1839 rb-10-301 (Ru)
Wood, John 1839 wb-A-16 (Ca)

Wood, John 1844 wb-1-107 (Sh)
Wood, John 1849 wb-10-152 (K)
Wood, John 1852 as-2-247 (Ge)
Wood, John 1855 ib-h-399 (F)
Wood, John H. 1861 27-lw (Hd)
Wood, John L. 1813 wb-4-210 (D)
Wood, John L. 1823 wb-#59 (Mu)
Wood, John S. 1834 wb-5-434 (Wi)
Wood, John S. 1835 wb-6-85 (Wi)
Wood, John S. 1847 wb-b-212 (We)
Wood, John Scott 1812 wb-4-181 (D)
Wood, Johnson 1835 wb-6-45 (Wi)
Wood, Johnson 1845 wb-8-282 (Wi)
Wood, Jonathan 1793 wb-1-15 (Je)
Wood, Joshua 1780 wb-#6 (Wa)
Wood, Josiah 1846 wb-8-419 (Wi)
Wood, Josiah 1856 wb-#119 (Wl)
Wood, Lott 1827 lr (Sn)
Wood, M. 1845 wb-f-268 (Hn)
Wood, Margaret 1815 wb-4-363 (D)
Wood, Margaret 1815 wb-4-376 (D)
Wood, Mary 1834 rb-9-145 (Ru)
Wood, Mary 1845 rb-j-393 (Mt)
Wood, Mary 1846 wb-g-77 (Hn)
Wood, Miland 1841 rb-i-103 (Mt)
Wood, Miland 1841 rb-i-116 (Mt)
Wood, Mitchel 1849 rb-14-521 (Ru)
Wood, Nancey 1834 wb-a-45 (Cr)
Wood, Nancy 1828 rb-7-336 (Ru)
Wood, Nancy 1844 rb-13-1 (Ru)
Wood, Orren L. 1835 rb-9-261 (Ru)
Wood, Owen L. 1836 rb-9-317 (Ru)
Wood, Peter H. 1854 mr-2-593 (Be)
Wood, R. L. 1844 wb-3-159 (Hr)
Wood, Rebecca 1839 wb-#125 (Wl)
Wood, Reuben 1835 wb-#112 (Wl)
Wood, Richard 1833 wb-#192 (Mc)
Wood, Robert 1836 wb-a-52 (Cr)
Wood, Robert 1843 wb-12-399* (D)
Wood, Robert L. 1842 wb-2-384 (Hr)
Wood, Robert T. 1850 wb-b-98 (L)
Wood, S. M. 1850 wb-4-596 (Hr)
Wood, Samuel 1800 wb-#8 (Wa)
Wood, Sarah 1829 wb-4-382 (Wi)
Wood, Solomon H. 1850 wb-2-20 (Me)
Wood, Solomon O. 1837 wb-1-7 (Me)
Wood, Solomon O. 1851 wb-2-77 (Me)
Wood, Squire 1821 wb-1-0 (Sm)
Wood, Susan 1851 rb-16-121 (Ru)
Wood, Thomas 1826 rb-6-300 (Ru)
Wood, Thomas 1837 wb-#116 (Wl)

Wood, Thomas 1849 wb-2-55 (Sh)
Wood, Thompson 1850 wb-9-410 (Wi)
Wood, W. W. 1853 rb-16-645 (Ru)
Wood, William 1817 rb-4-60 (Ru)
Wood, William 1840 wb-b-4 (We)
Wood, William 1845 wb-f-301 (Hn)
Wood, William 1847 wb-g-3 (Hu)
Wood, William 1849 wb-a-184 (Ms)
Wood, William 1853 rb-16-673 (Ru)
Wood, William 1857 wb-1-116 (Be)
Wood, William M. 1841 wb-2-255 (Hy)
Wood, William W. 1850 wb-9-379 (Wi)
Woodall, C. 1860 wb-17-141 (Rb)
Woodall, David 1832 wb-#192 (Mc)
Woodall, John 1847 wb-#192 (Mc)
Woodall, Mary E. 1847 wb-8-520 (Wi)
Woodall, William 1853 wb-3-187 (Sn)
Woodard, Aaron 1805 wb-1-169 (Je)
Woodard, Arthur 1856 wb-16-251 (Rb)
Woodard, Chesly? 1852 wb-4-572 (Mu)
Woodard, Cordy 1845 wb-f-244 (St)
Woodard, Daniel 1820 wb-7-409 (D)
Woodard, David 1857 wb-16-348 (Rb)
Woodard, Delila 1838 wb-10-144 (Rb)
Woodard, Delila 1839 wb-10-270 (Rb)
Woodard, James 1861 wb-17-262 (Rb)
Woodard, John 1839 wb-10-402 (Rb)
Woodard, Kinchen H. 1855 wb-16-113 (Rb)
Woodard, Kinchen H. 1855 wb-16-253 (Rb)
Woodard, Mary A. 1857 wb-16-373 (Rb)
Woodard, Mary Ann 1857 wb-16-430 (Rb)
Woodard, Noah 1820 wb-3-125 (Rb)
Woodard, Noah 1820 wb-3-55 (Rb)
Woodard, Parson 1837 wb-9-316 (Rb)
Woodard, Ruth 1860 wb-17-61 (Rb)
Woodard, Ruth 1860 wb-17-77 (Rb)
Woodard, Susan 1846 wb-13-82 (Rb)
Woodard, Thomas 1809 wb-4-32 (D)
Woodard, Thomas 1836 wb-9-218 (Rb)
Woodard, Thomas 1861 wb-17-260 (Rb)
Woodard, William 1812 wb-2-36 (Je)
Woodard, William 1853 wb-i-55 (O)
Woodard, William 1856 wb-16-275 (Rb)
Woodcock, Henry 1819 wb-1-0 (Sm)
Woodcock, John 1834 wb-10-306 (D)
Woodcock, Margaret 1861 wb-19-1 (D)
Woodcock, Thomas 1821 wb-#41 (Wl)
Woodcock, William 1816 wb-1-0 (Sm)
Woodfin, William 1812 wb-4-193 (D)
Woodford, Thomas 1859 wb-i-116 (St)
Woodlee, David 1836 wb-1-150 (W)

Woodlee, Jacob 1850 wb-3-77 (W)
Woodlee, Jefferson 1835 wb-1-124 (W)
Woodlee, John 1835 wb-1-97 (W)
Woodlee, John 1848 wb-2-358 (W)
Woodlee, Reuben 1840 wb-1-314 (W)
Woodley, Elijah 1858 wb-3-418 (W)
Woodloe, Abner 1848 wb-2-257 (W)
Woodloe, Jacob sr. 1850 wb-3-58 (W)
Woodmore, James 1848 wb-7-0 (Sm)
Woodmore, James W. 1839 rb-h-334 (Mt)
Woodred, George 1834 wb-#105 (Wl)
Woodrow, Susannah 1812 wb-#12 (Wa)
Woodruff, Mathew 1853 wb-15-238 (Rb)
Woodruff, Mathew 1853 wb-15-239 (Rb)
Woodrum, Jacob 1842 wb-#137 (Wl)
Woods, Alexander 1840 wb-e-156 (Hn)
Woods, Allen N. 1837 wb-a-14 (Ms)
Woods, Andrew 1810 wb-1-8 (Fr)
Woods, Archibald 1859 gs-1-216 (F)
Woods, David 1854 wb-16-311 (D)
Woods, David W. 1840 wb-2-168 (Hr)
Woods, Enos 1806 wb-1-216 (K)
Woods, Francis H. 1849 wb-a-195 (Ms)
Woods, G. W. W. 1851 wb-2-40 (Me)
Woods, Hannah 1835 wb-1-143 (Fr)
Woods, J. B. 1860 rb-p-472 (Mt)
Woods, James 1847 wb-1-242 (Fr)
Woods, James 1854 as-b-174 (Ms)
Woods, James H. 1859 wb-#192 (Mc)
Woods, John 1815 rb-3-8 (Ru)
Woods, John 1815 wb-1-26 (Fr)
Woods, John 1837 wb-1-145 (Bo)
Woods, Joseph 1860 wb-18-168 (D)
Woods, Levi S. 1857 wb-a-315 (Cr)
Woods, Lish 1859 rb-19-568 (Ru)
Woods, Martha Jane 1857 wb-12-419 (K)
Woods, Michael 1858 wb-2-87# (Ge)
Woods, Nancy 1844 rb-13-38 (Ru)
Woods, Peter M. 1854 mr-2-598 (Be)
Woods, Peter M. 1855 mr-2-608 (Be)
Woods, Polly 1845 wb-f-267 (Hn)
Woods, Richard 1805 wb-1-25# (Ge)
Woods, Richard M. 1845 wb-2-63# (Ge)
Woods, Samuel M. 1849 wb-4-495 (Hr)
Woods, Sarah 1819 wb-1-26# (Ge)
Woods, Syssily N. 1858 rb-19-427 (Ru)
Woods, Thomas C. 1846 rb-13-541 (Ru)
Woods, William 1831 wb-a-26 (Cr)
Woods, William 1832 wb-a-129 (R)
Woods, William 1840 wb-1-187 (Fr)
Woods, William J. 1851 wb-2-93 (Sh)

Woodside, William 1851 wb-2-165 (La)

Woodsides, B. E. 1858 39-2-264 (Dk)

Woodsides, William B. 1856 39-2-167 (Dk)

Woodsides, William B. E. 1856 39-2-192 (Dk)

Woodson, Cuffy 1836 wb-x-376 (Mu)

Woodson, E. H. 1857 wb-a-30 (Ce)

Woodson, Elizabeth 1857 wb-a-18 (Ce)

Woodson, Elizabeth H. 1858 wb-a-36 (Ce)

Woodson, Green 1844 wb-c-194 (G)

Woodson, James P. 1862 wb-f-433 (G)

Woodson, John 1813 wb-1-0 (Sm)

Woodson, John K. 1858 wb-16-564 (Rb)

Woodson, John L. 1857 wb-3e-50 (Sh)

Woodson, Joseph 1855 wb-n-658 (Mt)

Woodson, Joseph J. 1860 wb-a-166 (Ce)

Woodson, Peter 1847 wb-13-149 (Rb)

Woodson, Peter 1859 wb-16-707 (Rb)

Woodson, Richard V. 1835 wb-d-52 (Hn)

Woodson, Thomas 1836 wb-b-84 (G)

Woodson, Thomas J. 1836 wb-10-537 (D)

Woodson, Tucker 1846 wb-7-0 (Sm)

Woodward, Abraham 1817 wb-2-184 (Je)

Woodward, Baker 1833 wb-#101 (Wl)

Woodward, Caroline M. 1841 wb-12-134* (D)

Woodward, Dorcas 1841 as-a-39 (Ms)

Woodward, Edmond 1851 wb-15-146 (D)

Woodward, Edward 1848 wb-14-258 (D)

Woodward, George P. 1851 wb-14-587 (D)

Woodward, Hezekiah 1835 wb-2-23 (Ma)

Woodward, Jesse 1856 wb-a-295 (Di)

Woodward, John 1827 wb-a-17 (R)

Woodward, John 1853 wb-16-181 (D)

Woodward, Judith 1853 wb-16-174 (D)

Woodward, Micajah 1808 wb-4-6 (D)

Woodward, Moses C. 1861 wb-2-345 (Li)

Woodward, Richard 1840 wb-10-541 (Rb)

Woodward, Richard 1841 wb-10-589 (Rb)

Woodward, Thos. 1809 wb-4-48 (D)

Woodward, William 1814 wb-#14 (Wl)

Woodward, William 1843 wb-a-110 (Ms)

Woody, Archibald 1839 wb-y-471 (Mu)

Woody, John 1842 wb-c-302 (Ro)

Woody, Samuel 1855 wb-f-80 (Mu)

Woody, William 1817 wb-A-154 (Li)

Woolard, John 1843 wb-c-117 (G)

Woolard, Thomas W. 1831 rb-8-221 (Ru)

Woolard, Wherry? 1858 wb-f-213 (G)

Wooldrage, Martha 1830 wb-#84 (Wl)

Wooldridge, Egbert 1858 wb-3e-79 (Sh)

Wooldridge, John 1844 wb-a2-65 (Mu)

Wooldridge, John H. 1844 wb-a2-84 (Mu)

Wooldridge, Josiah 1825 wb-4-6 (Wi)

Wooldridge, Marcellus C. 1858 wb-#28 (Mo)

Wooldridge, William 1817 wb-#29 (Wl)

Wooldridge, William F. 1825 wb-4-31 (Wi)

Woolen, Edward 1832 wb-#98 (Wl)

Woolen, Joshua 1860 wb-#131 (Wl)

Woolen, Moses 1859 wb-#130 (Wl)

Woolfolk, Austin 1847 wb-5-64 (Ma)

Woolfork, Joseph 1831 rb-f-227 (Mt)

Woollard, Simeon 1841 wb-#134 (Wl)

Woolsey, Elizabeth 1840 wb-c-172 (Ro)

Woolsey, John 1819 wb-1-24# (Ge)

Woolsey, John 1840 wb-c-174 (Ro)

Woolsey, John B. 1843 wb-d-78 (Ro)

Woolsey, R. D. 1856 wb-3e-24 (Sh)

Woolsey, Richard D. 1854 wb-2-151 (Sh)

Woolsey, Sarah 1857 wb-2-85# (Ge)

Woolsey, Thomas 1797 wb-1-26# (Ge)

Woolsey, William 1846 wb-2-64# (Ge)

Woolsey, William 1858 149-1-108 (Ge)

Woolsey, Zephaniah 1801 wb-1-24# (Ge)

Woolsey, Zephaniah 1844 wb-d-127 (Ro)

Woolsey, Zepheniah 1807 as-1-187 (Ge)

Woosley, Peter 1818 wb-#69 (Mu)

Wooten, Arthur F. 1860 wb-a-297 (T)

Wooten, Benjamin 1859 wb-8-39 (Sm)

Wooten, H. D. 1860 rb-20-642 (Ru)

Wooten, H. D. P. 1860 rb-20-678 (Ru)

Wooten, James S. 1852 wb-5-49 (Je)

Wooten, James W. 1854 rb-17-185 (Ru)

Wooten, William 1814 wb-1-0 (Sm)

Wooton, John 1817 wb-#25 (Wl)

Wooton, S. O. 1860 wb-3-94 (La)

Wootten, Mary 1825 rb-d-426 (Mt)

Wootten, Polly 1825 rb-d-419 (Mt)

Word, Best 1859 rb-19-602 (Ru)

Word, James 1839 wb-#128 (Wl)

Word, John 1821 wb-#39 (Wl)

Word, John H. 1847 wb-#155 (Wl)

Word, Martin R. 1826 wb-4-100 (Wi)

Word, Mary 1855 rb-17-494 (Ru)

Word, Messer 1831 wb-c-119 (St)

Word, Nancy 1854 wb-11-256 (Wi)

Word, Nancy 1854 wb-11-320 (Wi)

Word, Nichodemus 1851 wb-2-62 (Me)

Word, Rhoda 1830 wb-c-40 (St)

Word, Samuel 1831 wb-5-78 (Wi)

Word, Seth 1845 rb-j-350 (Mt)

Word, Simeon 1842 wb-e-202 (St)

Word, Thomas 1840 wb-b-359 (G)

Worden, John 1842 wb-e-229 (St)

Worden, M. B. 1861 wb-i-275 (St)
Work, Andrew 1850 wb-a-202 (Di)
Work, J. A. 1861 wb-a-229 (Ce)
Work, John 1835 rb-9-216 (Ru)
Work, John 1845 rb-13-147 (Ru)
Work, John 1858 as-c-571 (Di)
Work, Martha 1855 wb-16-510 (D)
Work, Robert 1853 as-c-243 (Di)
Work, Samuel 1851 wb-14-574 (D)
Work, William M. 1849 wb-e-133 (Ro)
Worke, Ann 1849 rb-15-107 (Ru)
Workman, Allen R. 1847 wb-b-231 (We)
Workman, Richard 1845 wb-b-125 (We)
Workman?, Alfred 1846 wb-c-297 (G)
Works, Aaron 1846 wb-2-338 (W)
World, Tarene 1857 wb-j-264 (O)
Worldly, Sarah 1827 wb-2-608 (Je)
Worley, Eliza 1841 wb-2-308 (Hr)
Worley, Finch 1853 wb-d-148 (Wh)
Worley, George 1840 wb-b-379 (Hd)
Worley, John 1847 wb-d-297 (Hd)
Worley, John sr. 1815 wb-a-34 (Wh)
Worley, William 1830 wb-1-51 (W)
Wormeley, Mary H. 1858 wb-3e-73 (Sh)
Wormley, John C. 1847 wb-b-16 (Mu)
Worphis, James 1858 wb-h-266 (Hn)
Worrell, Thomas 1838 rb-h-125 (Mt)
Worrell, Thomas 1839 rb-h-222 (Mt)
Worrell, W. B. 1855 ib-h-400 (F)
Worrick, Herod 1852 wb-h-85 (Hu)
Worseley, W. W. 1852 wb-g-704 (Hn)
Worsham, Allison 1809 wb-1-149 (Bo)
Worsham, Sarah 1854 wb-g-604 (Hn)
Worsham, Thomas 1849 wb-14-145 (Rb)
Wortham, Benjamin H. 1847 wb-b-171 (Mu)
Wortham, Charles 1849 wb-d-167 (G)
Wortham, James Faucete 1859 wb-e-114 (Hy)
Wortham, Lewis L. 1842 wb-z-329 (Mu)
Wortham, Mary 1839 wb-b-280 (G)
Wortham, Mary H. 1861 wb-f-215 (Mu)
Wortham, Robert S. 1847 wb-1-143 (Sh)
Wortham, Samuel H. 1839 wb-y-443 (Mu)
Wortham, William 1839 wb-y-399 (Mu)
Worthington, Ann 1849 rb-l-358 (Mt)
Worthington, Joseph 1840 wb-1A-286 (A)
Worthington, Peter 1856 wb-h-485 (Hu)
Worthington, Susanah 1850? wb-1B-193 (A)
Worthington, William 1818 wb-2-368 (Wi)
Worthington, William 1827? wb-1A-11 (A)
Wrather, Asa 1843 rb-12-312 (Ru)
Wrather, Baker 1856 rb-18-118 (Ru)

Wrather, Liza 1844 wb-#145 (Wl)
Wray, Alcey 1835 wb-#107 (Wl)
Wray, Ealy 1835 wb-#111 (Wl)
Wray, John 1833 wb-#99 (Wl)
Wray, John 1856 mr (Gi)
Wray, John 1860 wb-b-91 (F)
Wray, John B. 1855 wb-b-8 (F)
Wray, Joseph 1819 rb-c-136 (Mt)
Wray, Luke 1814 wb-#15 (Wl)
Wray, Moses P. 1848 wb-b-257 (We)
Wray, Moses P. 1848 wb-b-267 (We)
Wray, Nathan 1806 rb-a-443 (Mt)
Wray, Thomas 1829 wb-#80 (Wl)
Wray, Thomas 1840 rb-10-567 (Ru)
Wray, Thomas 1854 wb-#113 (Wl)
Wray, Thomas J. 1840 rb-10-490 (Ru)
Wray, William 1843 wb-12-465* (D)
Wray, William 1853 wb-16-123 (D)
Wray, William 1862 wb-#135 (Wl)
Wren, Cicero A. 1850 wb-9-437 (Wi)
Wren, George 1830 wb-#213 (Mu)
Wren, Thomas 1855 wb-f-54 (Mu)
Wren, William 1826 wb-#143 (Mu)
Wrenn, David 1840 wb-3-205 (Ma)
Wrenn, David J. 1841 wb-3-400 (Ma)
Wrenn, Elizabeth 1843 wb-3-721 (Ma)
Wrenn, George 1853 wb-f-16 (Mu)
Wrenn, William 1836 wb-2-208 (Ma)
Wrenn, William 1854 wb-e-153 (G)
Wright, Agness 1860 wb-a-285 (T)
Wright, Alexander 1852 wb-a-161 (T)
Wright, Archibald 1816 wb-1-0 (Sm)
Wright, Benjamin 1858 wb-3e-65 (Sh)
Wright, Byrd 1816 wb-#24 (Wl)
Wright, C. M. 1853 wb-h-Mar (O)
Wright, Catharine 1852 wb-5-24 (Je)
Wright, Charles 1826 wb-9-61 (D)
Wright, Charles 1846 wb-13-367 (D)
Wright, Charles 1854 wb-#115 (Wl)
Wright, Charlotte 1851 wb-#179 (Wl)
Wright, Cleher? M. 1853 wb-i-98 (O)
Wright, David 1856 wb-7-0 (Sm)
Wright, Elizabeth 1824 wb-1-0 (Sm)
Wright, Elizabeth 1847 wb-e-32 (Ro)
Wright, Fielding 1847 wb-13-63 (Rb)
Wright, Frances 1856 wb-3e-21 (Sh)
Wright, Francis (Sr.) 1814 wb-#37 (Mu)
Wright, Francis 1808 rb-2-35 (Ru)
Wright, Francis 1813? wb-#7 (Mu)
Wright, Francis 1824 wb-8-385 (D)
Wright, Francis 1843 wb-z-442 (Mu)

Wyatt, Richard 1860 wb-2-321 (Li)
Wyatt, Robert 1850 wb-g-254 (St)
Wyatt, Sarah 1859 wb-#193 (Mc)
Wyatt, Sarrah 1856 rb-o-40 (Mt)
Wyatt, Spencer 1853 wb-15-574 (D)
Wyatt, Thomas 1824 wb-3-320 (St)
Wyatt, Thomas 1853 wb-xx-221 (St)
Wyatt, Thomas 1855 rb-o-1 (Mt)
Wyatt, Thomas S. 1841 wb-7-468 (Wi)
Wyatt, William 1852 wb-#193 (Mc)
Wyatt, William S. 1846 wb-c-280 (G)
Wyatt, Z. 1847 wb-g-283 (Hn)
Wyatt, Zacariah 1847 wb-g-164 (Hn)
Wyatt, Zachariah 1853 mr-2-504 (Be)
Wygull, Delila 1859 wb-1-308 (Be)
Wyke, Senior? 1820 wb-#119 (Mu)
Wykel, Marshel W. 1860 wb-2-91# (Ge)
Wykel, William 1855 wb-2-82# (Ge)
Wykle, Marshall L. 1861 149-1-239 (Ge)
Wylie, James 1853 wb-i-86 (O)
Wyllie, Mary V. 1847 lr (Sn)
Wyllie, Phileman W. 1836 wb-2-202 (Sn)
Wyly, James 1847 wb-1-240 (Bo)
Wyly, James 1857 wb-1-140 (Be)
Wyly, Robert 1809 ib-1-266 (Ge)
Wynn, Henry 1835 wb-c-407 (St)
Wynn, Henry H. 1835 wb-c-418 (St)
Wynn, Jane 1835 wb-8-457 (Rb)
Wynn, Peter 1818 wb-1-273 (Sn)
Wynn, Peter D. 1859 wb-3e-108 (Sh)
Wynn, Rebecca 1826 wb-#69 (Wl)
Wynn, Samuel 1835 wb-d-100 (Hn)
Wynn, Thomas 1824 wb-3-316 (St)
Wynn, Thomas 1827 wb-b-214 (St)
Wynn, Thomas R. 1856 wb-2-150 (Li)
Wynn, W. G. 1857 wb-h-309 (St)
Wynn, Winnifred 1846 wb-f-360 (St)
Wynne, Albert H. 1851 wb-14-563 (D)
Wynne, Bowling D. 1844 wb-#145 (Wl)
Wynne, Devereaux 1820 wb-#35 (Wl)
Wynne, Elizabeth C. 1860 wb-#132 (Wl)
Wynne, George 1845 rb-j-406 (Mt)
Wynne, J. W. 1858 wb-#127 (Wl)
Wynne, John K. 1840 wb-#153 (Wl)
Wynne, John L. 1829 wb-#83 (Wl)
Wynne, Manerva M. 1832 wb-#98 (Wl)
Wynne, Robert 1802 wb-#1 (Wl)
Wynne, William 1832 wb-#138 (Wl)
Wynne, William 1845 wb-#158 (Wl)
Wynns, Angeline 1860 wb-i-174 (St)
Wynns, Bird 1848 rb-14-485 (Ru)

Wynns, Gabriel 1849 wb-g-149 (St)
Wynns, H. M. 1857 wb-h-348 (St)
Wynns, Henry 1854 wb-xx-344 (St)
Wynns, Henry M. 1857 wb-h-391 (St)
Wynns, Mary C. 1838 wb-d-283 (St)
Wynns, William G. 1845 wb-f-253 (St)
Wyrick, Martin 1850 33-3-304 (Gr)
Wyrick, Phillip 1848 33-3-44 (Gr)
Wyrick, William 1846 wb-5-465 (Gr)

- Y -

Yaden, Joseph 1844 wb-5-301 (Gr)
Yancey, Robert 1858 gs-1-200 (F)
Yancy, A. S. 1856 ib-h-544 (F)
Yancy, Joel C. 1851 wb-a-407 (F)
Yancy, Joel L. 1854 ib-H-122 (F)
Yancy, Nelly B. 1842 wb-8-12 (K)
Yancy, William 1810 rb-b-142 (Mt)
Yandell, Elizabeth 1840 rb-10-608 (Ru)
Yandell, Elizabeth 1840 rb-10-625 (Ru)
Yandell, James 1852 wb-#110 (Wl)
Yandell, William 1830 rb-8-46 (Ru)
Yandell, Willson 1828 rb-7-284 (Ru)
Yandell, Wilson (Dr.) 1830 rb-8-11 (Ru)
Yarberough, James 1815 wb-#11 (Mu)
Yarborough, James 1856 wb-g-737 (Hn)
Yarborough, Jesse 1815 wb-#19 (Mu)
Yarborough, Mary R. 1861 as-c-239 (Ms)
Yarborough, William 1826 wb-4-74 (Wi)
Yarbrough, Archibald 1854 wb-5-155 (Ma)
Yarbrough, Britton 1815 lr (Gi)
Yarbrough, David 1841 lr (Gi)
Yarbrough, Elizabeth R. 1859 wb-7-52 (Ma)
Yarbrough, George 1847 rb-k-323 (Mt)
Yarbrough, Henry 1843 wb-a-105 (T)
Yarbrough, James 1861 wb-18-606 (D)
Yarbrough, John 1855 wb-n-571 (Mt)
Yarbrough, Joseph J. 1832 wb-1-65 (Hy)
Yarbrough, Mary (Mrs) 1858 rb-o-577 (Mt)
Yarbrough, Mary 1860 rb-p-458 (Mt)
Yarbrough, Milly 1850 wb-2-103 (La)
Yarbrough, Moses 1840 rb-i-22 (Mt)
Yarbrough, Nancie 1858 rb-o-540 (Mt)
Yarbrough, Richard 1857 wb-12-361 (Wi)
Yarbrough, Richard S. 1837 wb-6-356 (Wi)
Yarbrough, Richard S. 1853 wb-10-552 (Wi)
Yarbrough, Sampson 1856 as-b-204 (Ms)
Yarbrough, Samuel 1832 wb-c-189 (St)
Yarbrough, William H. 1859 wb-3e-124 (Sh)
Yardley, Benjamin 1856 rb-18-237 (Ru)

Yardley, John W. 1855 rb-17-530 (Ru)
Yardley, Thomas 1849 rb-15-203 (Ru)
Yarnel, Daniel 1820 wb-3-140 (K)
Yarnell, Joseph 1826 wb-4-164 (K)
Yarnell, Stephen 1824 wb-#48 (Wl)
Yarrell, Mary 1838 as-a-440 (Di)
Yates, Belfield C. 1859 rb-p-18 (Mt)
Yates, Chesley 1850 wb-d-262 (G)
Yates, Daniel 1814 wb-#22 (Mu)
Yates, Daniel 1814 wb-#40 (Mu)
Yates, J. B. 1832 wb-#95 (Wl)
Yates, James 1816 wb-2-299 (Rb)
Yates, James 1857 as-c-429 (Di)
Yates, James G. 1845 rb-j-430 (Mt)
Yates, James sr. 1844 wb-12-210 (Rb)
Yates, Jessee 1840 wb-b-347 (G)
Yates, John B. 1846 wb-#152 (Wl)
Yates, Lydia 1853 wb-15-229 (Rb)
Yates, Rebecca 1844 wb-12-247 (Rb)
Yates, Reuben 1854 wb-3-191 (Gr)
Yates, Riley 1836 wb-1-498 (Hr)
Yates, Thomas 1834 wb-8-396 (Rb)
Yates, Thomas 1853 wb-d-112 (Wh)
Yates, Thomas 1853 wb-d-149 (Wh)
Yates, Thomas P. 1846 wb-4-72 (Hr)
Yates, William 1845 wb-12-435 (Rb)
Yates, Willie B. 1848 rb-k-745 (Mt)
Yeager, Daniel 1834 wb-#30 (Wa)
Yeager, Ruben 1823 wb-A-329 (Li)
Yeager, Solomon 1851 wb-d-50 (Wh)
Yeager, Solomon sr. 1853 wb-d-198 (Wh)
Yeakley, Henry 1826 wb-1-26# (Ge)
Yeakley, Isaiah 1843 148-1-65 (Ge)
Yearby, William 1815 rb-3-54 (Ru)
Yeargan, Bartlett 1852 wb-10-203 (Wi)
Yearout, Abraham 1845 wb-9-31 (K)
Yearout, William 1840 wb-3-295 (Ma)
Yearwood, Frederick 1821 rb-5-139 (Ru)
Yearwood, James 1853 rb-16-710 (Ru)
Yearwood, James P. 1854 rb-16-726 (Ru)
Yearwood, John 1822 rb-5-204 (Ru)
Yearwood, John 1847 rb-14-6 (Ru)
Yearwood, John 1847 rb-14-66 (Ru)
Yearwood, William 1823 rb-6-27 (Ru)
Yearwood, William M. 1849 wb-#193 (Mc)
Yeary, Wm. H. 1837 5-2-6 (Cl)
Yeates, Benjamin 1816 wb-2-37# (Ge)
Yeates, Freeman 1849 wb-g-261 (Hu)
Yeates, Izma 1848 wb-g-104 (Hu)
Yeates, Reddick 1852 wb-h-73 (Hu)
Yeates, Reddick sr. 1852 wb-h-72 (Hu)

Yeates, Thomas 1855 wb-d-288 (Wh)
Yeatman, Thomas 1834 wb-10-277 (D)
Yell, James 1839 wb-0-11 (Cf)
Yellowby, William G. 1840 wb-12-77* (D)
Yerger, Michael 1844 wb-#139 (Wl)
Yoakam, Valentine 1829 wb-b-38 (Ro)
Yoakley, Benjamin L. 1848 wb-1-138 (Su)
Yoakum, Isaac 1857? ib-2-390 (Cl)
Yoast, Andrew J. 1848 wb-9-442 (K)
Yocum, George 1815 wb-A-105 (Li)
Yoes, John 1823 rb-5-328 (Ru)
Yong, Elisha 1856 wb-g-731 (Hn)
Yong, Hugh 1837 wb-d-123* (Hn)
Yong, Isaac 1853 wb-A-88 (Ca)
York, Aaron 1815 wb-2-189 (K)
York, Abraham 1815 wb-2-143 (K)
York, Henry 1847 wb-1B-30 (A)
York, Henry 1849 wb-1B-106 (A)
York, James 1839 wb-3-105 (Ma)
York, James 1841 wb-7-448 (Wi)
York, Matilda 1846 wb-8-483 (Wi)
York, Silas R. 1836 wb-1-176 (W)
Yost, Francis 1834 wb-5-313 (K)
Yost, James C. 1861 wb-f-415 (Ro)
Yost, Peter 1825 wb-4-89 (K)
Young, A. B. 1847 wb-13-184 (Rb)
Young, A. D. 1860 wb-17-42 (Rb)
Young, A. H. 1860 wb-A-160 (Ca)
Young, Abraham 1835 wb-9-117 (Rb)
Young, Abraham B. 1847 wb-13-168 (Rb)
Young, Albert 1855 wb-3-234 (Gr)
Young, Alexander 1808 wb-#6 (Wl)
Young, Alexander 1838 wb-1-191 (Fr)
Young, Alexander A. 1843 wb-#139 (Wl)
Young, Alfonzo 1825 wb-2-0 (Sm)
Young, Alfred D. 1860 wb-17-52 (Rb)
Young, Allen H. 1823 wb-#65 (Mu)
Young, Ann O. (Martin) 1839 rb-h-272 (Mt)
Young, Archabald M. 1839 wb-b-291 (G)
Young, B. F. 1857 wb-16-378 (Rb)
Young, Bannister 1814 wb-#29 (Wl)
Young, Charles 1796 wb-#24 (Wa)
Young, Charles 1846 wb-#150 (Wl)
Young, Daniel 1820 wb-7-421 (D)
Young, Daniel 1860 wb-18-231 (D)
Young, Daniel 1860 wb-18-232 (D)
Young, David 1858 wb-f-178 (G)
Young, Demetrius 1831 wb-#90 (Wl)
Young, Dorrell 1823 rb-d-211 (Mt)
Young, Elenor 1826 wb-8-535 (D)
Young, Elizabeth (Mrs.) 1858 wb-#28 (Mo)

Young, Elizabeth 1819 wb-3-13 (Wi)
Young, Emanuel 1832 wb-1-12 (Sh)
Young, Esau 1852 wb-4-561 (Mu)
Young, Esther 1853 wb-#38 (Wa)
Young, Evan 1851 wb-4-285 (Mu)
Young, F. J. 1842 wb-12-325* (D)
Young, G. L. 1859 wb-16-810 (Rb)
Young, G. M. 1856 ib-h-534 (F)
Young, Gilbert 1836 wb-#111 (Wl)
Young, Harriet 1838 wb-11-112 (D)
Young, Henry 1810 lr (Sn)
Young, Henry 1831 wb-1-64 (W)
Young, Henry 1847 wb-A-48 (Ca)
Young, Hugh 1836 wb-e-278 (Hn)
Young, Isham 1836 wb-b-327 (Ro)
Young, J. F. 1860 wb-17-64 (Rb)
Young, J. M. 1847 wb-b-186 (Mu)
Young, Jacob F. 1858 wb-16-679 (Rb)
Young, Jacob F. 1860 wb-17-143 (Rb)
Young, Jacob F. 1860 wb-17-302 (Rb)
Young, James 1835 wb-5-381 (K)
Young, James 1836 wb-b-216 (Wh)
Young, James 1852 wb-f-13 (Mu)
Young, James B. 1843 wb-8-123 (Wi)
Young, James P. 1834 wb-#31 (Wa)
Young, Jeremiah 1854 ib-2-77 (Cl)
Young, John 1796? wb-#24 (Wa)
Young, John 1820 wb-3-176 (Rb)
Young, John 1834 wb-1-508 (Hw)
Young, John 1836 wb-1-213 (Hy)
Young, John 1838 lr (Gi)
Young, John 1853 wb-h-152 (Hn)
Young, John 1856 wb-2-302 (Me)
Young, John 1856 wb-e-99 (Wh)
Young, John C. 1831 wb-5-98 (K)
Young, John S. 1860 wb-18-347 (D)
Young, John W. 1853 wb-e-50 (G)
Young, John sr. 1853 wb-2-331 (Me)
Young, Joseph 1822 wb-#19 (Wa)
Young, Joseph 1828 wb-2-90 (Sn)
Young, Margaret 1853 wb-1-510 (Hw)
Young, Margaret 1857 wb-16-371 (Rb)
Young, Mark 1861 wb-18-446 (D)
Young, Mark sr. 1859 wb-17-616 (D)
Young, Mary 1810 wb-#11 (Wa)
Young, Mary 1841 wb-e-308 (Hn)
Young, Mary 1857 wb-17-306 (D)
Young, Matthew 1836 wb-a-63 (O)
Young, Merlin 1841 wb-3-468 (Ma)
Young, Milton 1834 wb-3-0 (Sm)
Young, Nancy 1858 wb-16-634 (Rb)

Young, Nancy O. 1839 rb-h-220 (Mt)
Young, Nathaniel 1846 wb-a2-459 (Mu)
Young, Peter 1823 wb-#58 (Mu)
Young, Peter 1824 wb-#69 (Mu)
Young, Phebe 1810 wb-#11 (Wa)
Young, Rachael S. 1859 wb-3e-103 (Sh)
Young, Robert 1792 wb-#4 (Wa)
Young, Robert 1804 wb-1-506 (Hw)
Young, Robert 1806 wb-#10 (Wa)
Young, Robert 1836 wb-a-39 (T)
Young, Robert R. 1855 wb-#11 (Mo)
Young, S. 1854 ib-H-116 (F)
Young, Samuel 1855 ib-h-273 (F)
Young, Stephen 1838 wb-#122 (Wl)
Young, Thomas 1813 wb-A-31 (Li)
Young, Thomas 1824 wb-1-59 (Fr)
Young, Thomas L. 1843 lr (Gi)
Young, Thomas W. 1841 lr (Gi)
Young, Uriah 1852 wb-15-168 (Rb)
Young, W. 1854 wb-1C-118 (A)
Young, Wiley B. 1854 wb-#194 (Mc)
Young, Wilkins 1827 wb-#26 (Wa)
Young, William 1815 wb-A-89 (Li)
Young, William 1838 wb-d-243* (Hn)
Young, William 1847 wb-b-233 (We)
Young, William C. 1848 wb-g-94 (Hu)
Young, William M. 1841 abl-1-166 (T)
Young, William P. 1838 wb-1-449 (Hy)
Young, William W. 1855 wb-b-368 (We)
Young, Willis 1840 wb-1-185 (Fr)
Young, Wily 1858 wb-1C-426 (A)
Youngblood, A. G. 1830 wb-#220 (Mu)
Youngblood, Jonathan 1852 wb-3-140 (W)
Youree, Alexander 1811 lr (Sn)
Youree, David 1834 rb-9-146 (Ru)
Youree, Francis 1853 rb-16-617 (Ru)
Youree, Francis A. 1853 rb-16-403 (Ru)
Youree, James 1845 rb-13-389 (Ru)
Youree, James sr. 1835 rb-9-208 (Ru)
Youree, Joseph 1840 rb-10-478 (Ru)
Youree, Susan 1858 rb-19-209 (Ru)
Youree, Susannah 1857 rb-19-125 (Ru)
Youree, William P. 1817 lr (Sn)
Yous, John 1821 rb-5-161 (Ru)
Yow, John 1845 wb-g-40 (Hn)
Yowell, Joel 1855 wb-a-386 (Ms)

- Z -

Zachary, Allen 1858 rb-19-355 (Ru)
Zachary, Benjamin 1858 wb-12-610 (Wi)

Zachary, Crawford 1836 wb-10-597 (D)
Zachary, G. G. 1852 wb-15-270 (D)
Zachary, Gilbert 1841 wb-7-276 (K)
Zachary, Griffin G. 1853 wb-16-122 (D)
Zachary, Josiah 1858 rb-19-354 (Ru)
Zachary, Malkigah 1858 rb-19-354 (Ru)
Zachary, Mary 1857 wb-7-0 (Sm)
Zachary, Susan 1855 wb-12-90 (K)
Zachary, William 1832 wb-5-46 (K)
Zachary, William 1859 wb-13-50 (Wi)
Zachary, William C. 1836 wb-6-91 (Wi)
Zachery, Allen 1846 wb-#151 (Wl)
Zachery, Joshua 1830 rb-8-413 (Ru)
Zachry, Elizabeth 1840 rb-10-581 (Ru)
Zachry, Nathan 1818 wb-1-0 (Sm)
Zachry, Sarah B. 1840 rb-10-477 (Ru)
Zackery, Cynthia 1844 wb-#144 (Wl)
Zackery, H. L. 1842 wb-#138 (Wl)
Zackery, Mary 1859 wb-13-94 (Wi)
Zackery, Stokes 1836 wb-#114 (Wl)
Zackry, Granville 1856 ib-h-547 (F)
Zech, Jacob 1843 wb-11-322 (Rb)
Zech, John 1842 wb-11-193 (Rb)
Zeigler, William 1846 wb-1-140 (Me)
Zeigler, William 1848 wb-1-161 (Me)
Zellars, George 1844 wb-d-250 (O)
Zellars, John 1835 wb-a-31 (O)
Zellars, Mary J. 1844 wb-d-235 (O)
Zellers, Thomas 1840 wb-b-218 (O)
Zetty, Christian (Sr.) 1841 wb-#35 (Wa)
Zetty, Christian 1847 wb-#46 (Wa)
Ziegler, Jacob 1837 wb-#194 (Mc)
Zimmerman, Joseph 1861 wb-#194 (Mc)
Zollicoffer, G. D. 1855 wb-16-455 (D)
Zollicoffer, John I. 1839 wb-z-22 (Mu)
Zollicoffer, John J. 1840 wb-z-227 (Mu)

BIBLIOGRAPHY

Books

Boyer, Reba Bayless, *Monroe County, Tennessee Records 1820-1870, Vol. 2*, Athens, TN, 1970

_____, *Wills and Estate Records of McMinn County, Tennessee 1820-1870*, Athens, TN, 1964

Burgner, Goldene Fillers, *Greene County, Tennessee Wills 1783-1890*, Greeneville, TN, 1981

_____, *Washington County, Tennessee Wills 1777-1872*, Easley, SC, 1983

Garrett, Jill Knight, *Dickson County Handbook*, Easley, SC, 1984

_____ and Marise Parrish Lightfoot, *Maury County, Tennessee Will Books A, B, C-1, D and E, 1807-1832*, Columbia, TN, 1984

Key, F. C., Sue W. Maggart and Jane C. Turner, *Smith County, Tennessee Wills 1803-1896*, Carthage, TN, 1985

Marsh, Helen C. and Timothy R., *Wills & Inventories of Lincoln County, Tennessee 1810-1921*, Shelbyville, TN, 1989

Parker, Clara M., *Giles County Will Abstracts 1814-1900*, Pulaski, TN, 1988

Partlow, Thomas E., *Wilson County, Tennessee Miscellaneous Records 1800-1875*, Lebanon, TN, 1982

_____, *Wilson County, Tennessee Wills, Books 1-13 (1802-50)*, Lebanon, TN, 1981

Sherrill, Charles A., *Grundy County, Tennessee Wills & Estates 1844-1900*, Chattanooga, TN, 1986

Sistler, Byron and Barbara, *Davidson County, TN Wills & Administrations to 1861: An Index*, Nashville, 1989

_____, *Williamson County, TN Wills & Administrations, 1800-1861: An Index*, Nashville, 1989

Wilson, Shirley, *Sumner County, Tennessee Will Abstracts 1788-1882*, Hendersonville, TN, 1987

Works Progress Administration (WPA), *Shelby County Will Books 1C, 2D and 3E, 1830-1862 (3 volumes)*, Nashville, 1937-41

CPSIA information can be obtained at www.ICGtesting.com
Printed in the USA
BVOW010319150213

313134BV00002B/153/P